American Literature

BY THE COMMITTEE ON AFFILIATION OF THE CATHOLIC UNIVERSITY OF AMERICA FOR THE REVISION OF ENGLISH CURRICULA

ROY J. DEFERRARI, Ph.D., LL.D.
Secretary General, The Catholic University of America

SISTER MARY THERESA BRENTANO, O.S.B., Ph.D.
Professor of English, Mount St. Scholastica College

BROTHER EDWARD P. SHEEKEY, F.S.C., A.M.
West Catholic High School, Philadelphia, Pa.

NIHIL OBSTAT:

Arthur J. Scanlan, s.t.d., *Censor Librorum*

IMPRIMATUR:

+ Francis J. Spellman, *Archbishop*
NEW YORK, N. Y.

Feast of the Assumption, 1944

PUBLISHED IN 1944

ACKNOWLEDGMENTS

Grateful acknowledgment is made to the following publishers and individuals for permission to reprint material in copyright.

AMERICA: "Te Deum at Matins" by Sister Mary St. Virginia, B.V.M.; "Our Lady of the Weather" by Alfred Barrett, S.J.; "Riddles" by Sister Maris Stella.

AMERICAN FOLK LORE SOCIETY: "Los Pastores—A Shepherd Play of the Nativity" translated by M. R. Cole.

D. APPLETON-CENTURY COMPANY, INC.: "Thanatopsis," "To a Waterfowl," "The Yellow Violet," and "Hymn of the City" by William Cullen Bryant.

THE BOBBS MERRILL COMPANY: "When the Frost Is on the Punkin" from *Neighborly Poems* by James Whitcomb Riley, copyright 1891, 1919.

BOOK CLUB OF CALIFORNIA: "America for Christendom" from *A Letter to Gabriel Sanchez* by Christopher Columbus, translated by Donald B. Clark.

ALBERT & CHARLES BONI, INC.: "The Mucker Pose" from *Our Business Civilization* by James Truslow Adams.

BRANDT & BRANDT: "Bridewater's Half Dollar" from *Mr. White, the Red Barn, Hell and Bridewater*, published by Doubleday, Doran & Company, Inc., copyright 1935 by Booth Tarkington; "The Bishop's Beggar" by Stephen Vincent Benét, copyright 1942 by the Curtis Publishing Company; "We Made This Thing, This Dream" from *Listen to the People* by Stephen Vincent Benét, copyright 1941 by author.

BRUCE HUMPHRIES, INC.: "The Spy" by Sister Mariella, O.S.B.

BURROWS BROTHERS COMPANY: "The Martyrdom of St. René Goupil" from *The Jesuit Relations* by St. Isaac Jogues, S.J., translated by Reuben Gold Thwaites; "Never to Put on Gala Dress" from *The Jesuit Relations* by Claude Chauchetiere, S.J., translated by Reuben Gold Thwaites.

CHAPMAN & GRIMES, INC.: "The V-a-s-e" from *The V-a-s-e and Other Bric-a-Brac* by James Jeffrey Roche.

COMMONWEAL: "Lily of Light" by Edward F. Garesché, S.J.; "The Husking Contest" by Albert Eisele; "Hard Boiled Parish" by Stephen V. Feeley.

COWARD-McCANN, INC.: *Our Town* by Thornton Wilder, copyright 1938 by Coward-McCann, Inc. No part of this play may be printed in any form whatever without permission in writing from the publishers. Inquiries about any performance whatsoever should be made to the author's agent, Harold Freedman, 101 Park Ave., N.Y.C.

DODD, MEAD & COMPANY, INC.: "A Vagabond Song" from *Songs from Vagabondia* by Bliss Carman; "The Sea Gypsy" by Richard Hovey; "Marquette on the Shores of the Mississippi" by John Jerome Rooney; "At Candle-lightin' Time" by Paul Laurence Dunbar.

DOUBLEDAY, DORAN & COMPANY, INC.: "I Hear America Singing," "When I Heard the Learn'd Astronomer," "Aboard at a Ship's Helm," and "A Noiseless, Patient Spider" from *Leaves of Grass* by Walt Whitman, copyright 1924 by Doubleday, Doran & Company, Inc.; "A Municipal Report" by William Sydney Porter (O. Henry); "Experience" and "I Shall Not Be Afraid" by Aline Kilmer; "The Prayer of a Soldier in France" by Joyce Kilmer; "The Great Nickel Adventure" from *The Circus and Other Essays* by Joyce Kilmer, copyright 1921 by Doubleday, Doran & Company, Inc.; "Those Two Boys" by Franklin P. Adams.

E. P. DUTTON & COMPANY, INC.: "Adrift on the Pacific" by James C. Whittaker; "Quivira" and "Daniel Boone" from *I Sing the Pioneer*, by Arthur Guiterman.

EMPORIA GAZETTE (KANSAS): "Mary White" by William Allen White.

SAMUEL FRENCH: *The Joyous Season* by Philip Barry. All rights reserved. Copyright 1934, by Philip Barry. Caution: Professionals and amateurs are hereby warned that *The Joyous Season* being fully protected under the copyright laws of the United States of America, the British Empire, including the Dominion of Canada, and all other countries of the Copyright Union, is subject to a royalty. All rights including professional, amateur, motion pictures, recitation, public reading, radio broadcasting and the rights of translations into foreign languages are strictly reserved. In its present form this play is dedicated to the reading public only. All inquiries regarding the play should be addressed to Samuel French, at 25 West 45 St., New York, N.Y., or 811 West 7 St., Los Angeles, California, or, if in Canada, to Samuel French (Canada) Ltd., at 480 University Ave., Toronto, Ontario.

HARCOURT, BRACE & COMPANY, INC.: "Mia Carlotta" from *Selected Poems of Thomas Augustine Daly*, "The Easter Story" from *Collected Edition of Heywood Broun*; "The Hangman at Home" by Carl Sandburg; "O Light Invisible, We Praise Thee" from *The Rock* by T. S. Eliot.

HARPER & BROTHERS: "The Celebrated Jumping Frog of Calaveras County" and "A Daring Deed" from *Life on the Mississippi* by Samuel Langhorne Clemens (Mark Twain); "Pontificate of Leo XIII" from *Generation of Materialism* by Carlton J. H. Hayes ; "Under the Lion's Paw" by Hamlin Garland.

HENRY HOLT & COMPANY, INC.: "Mending Wall," "The Death of the Hired Man," "The Road Not Taken," "Birches," "Stopping by Woods on a Snowy Evening" and "The Runaway" from *The Collected Poems of Robert Frost*; "Chicago," and "Lost" from *Smoke and Steel* by Carl Sandburg; "On Kitchens and Cloisters" from *The Golden Ass and Other Essays* by Mary Ellen Chase.

HOUGHTON MIFFLIN & COMPANY: "The Great Carbuncle" by Nathaniel Hawthorne; "Self-Reliance," "Concord Hymn," "The Humblebee," "The Rhodora," and "Forebearance" by Ralph Waldo Emerson; "Hymn to the Night" by Henry Wadsworth Longfellow; "The Vision of Sir Launfal," "To the Dandelion," and "The Courtin'" from *Biglow Papers* by James Russell Lowell; "Telling the Bees," "Maud Muller," and "Centennial Hymn" by John Greenleaf Whittier; "The Fool's Prayer" by Edward Rowland Sill; "Jim Bludso of the Prairie Belle" by John Hay; "Tennessee's Partner" by Bret Harte; "The Wild Ride" from *Happy Ending*, "The Vigil at Arms" from *A Roadside Harp*, and "Borderlands" from *Happy Ending* by Louise Imogen Guiney; "Prayer to the Virgin of Chartres" by Henry Adams; "The Mission of Humor" from *Americans and Others* by Agnes Repplier; "Night Clouds" and "A Lady" from *Sword Blades and Poppy Seeds* by Amy Lowell; "To Be an American" from *American Letter* by Archibald MacLeish.

P. J. KENEDY & SONS: "Fool's Martyrdom" from *Lyric Poems* by William Thomas Walsh.

ALFRED A. KNOPF, INC.: "The Sculptor's Funeral" by Willa Cather.

J. B. LIPPINCOTT COMPANY: "On Unanswering Letters" from *Mince Pie* by Christopher Morley; "Charity" from *Poems* by Theodore Maynard.

LITTLE BROWN & COMPANY: "I Taste A Liquor Never Brewed," "I Never Saw a Moor," "He Ate and Drank the Precious Words," "Much Madness Is Divinest Sense," "It Dropped So Low in My Regard," "To Make a Prairie," and "Success is Counted Sweetest" from *The Poems of Emily Dickinson*, edited by Martha Dickinson Bianchi and Alfred Leete Hampson.

LIVERIGHT PUBLISHING CORPORATION: "Heat" from *Collected Poems of Hilda Doolittle*.

LONGMANS, GREEN & COMPANY, INC.: "Hidden" by Daniel Sargent.

LOUISIANA STATE UNIVERSITY PRESS: "Education for Freedom" by Robert Hutchins.

THE MACMILLAN COMPANY: "Abraham Lincoln Walks at Midnight" and "Franciscan Aspiration" by Vachel Lindsay; "Arcturus in Autumn," "The Net," and "Let It Be Forgotten" by Sara Teasdale; "Silence" from *Songs and Satires* by Edgar Lee Masters; "Lucinda Matlock" and "Ann Rutledge" from *Spoon River Anthology* by Edgar Lee Masters; "The Secret Heart" by Robert P. Tristram Coffin; "A Question of Lovers" by Sister Madeleva; "A Watch in the Night" by Helen C. White; "The City That Never Was" from *The High Romance* by Michael Williams; "Song for a Listener" by Leonard Feeney, S.J.; "In Avila" from *Drink from the Rock* by Sister M. Thérèse, Sor. D.S.

A. C. McCLURG & CO.: "The Religious Element in Education" by John Lancaster Spalding.

THE MONASTINE PRESS: "To Fear" from Crags by Clifford Laube; "The Uninvited" from *The Lantern Burns* by Jessica Powers.

UNIVERSITY OF NEW MEXICO: "How Polca Arrived in Search of Her Husband" from *History of New Mexico* by Gaspar Perez de Villagrá, translated by Gilberto Espinosa.

THE NEW YORKER: "A Little Rain" by Brendan Gill, copyright.

ROCKLAND EDITIONS: "Meditation Six" from *Poetical Works of Edward Taylor*.

CHARLES SCRIBNER'S SONS: "Richard Cory" and "Miniver Cheevy" by Edwin Arlington Robinson.

SPIRIT MAGAZINE: "To a Baffled Idealist" by Joseph G. E. Hopkins; "Southwestern Night" by Fray Angelico Chavez; "Photograph" by James J. Galvin, C.SS.R.

SHEED & WARD. INC.: "The Quest" from *Dark Symphony* by Elizabeth Adams; "Mary and the Modern Ideal" by Walter Farrell, O.P.

Express personal permission has been given by the following holders of copyright material:

Fray Angelico Chavez, Mrs. Finley Peter Dunne, Lucien Harris, Joseph G. E. Hopkins, Blanche Mary Kelly, Dr. Francis Litz, John G. Magee, Virgil Markham, Edgar Lee Masters, Juanita Miller, Agnes Repplier, Mrs. John J. Shea, Wilbur Daniel Steele, Sister Maris Stella, William Allen White, Constance Garland Williams, Mary Fabyan Windeatt.

Introduction

THE social tumult that has reached a climax in our time has powerfully illustrated the truth that a man's ideas influence his course of conduct. A person acts as he thinks. One of the most important tasks of the educator, then, is to train the student to think rightly on all matters that pertain to complete living. The Catholic teacher of literature seeks to show the value of the philosophy of life that underlies the writings that are being studied. The masterpieces of powerful and sincere writers offer much that uplifts and ennobles. Properly selected, the works of these authors not only arouse an awareness of beauty and enthusiasm for great literature but aid the student to enlarge his outlook on life. Yet in a world that is being rapidly dechristianized, the teacher must frequently point out error and inadequacy by contrasting false and incomplete modes of thought with sound views and principles. *American Profile* offers an anthology and a history of American literature which interprets the writings of our authors in the light of fundamental truths. The task of modifying and supplementing a course of study, which the individual Catholic teacher heretofore endeavored to accomplish, has now been facilitated by a text, which, by its selection of material, notes, comments, and explanations, presents an American and Christian view of life. Until the student is given adequate help which trains him to discern and evaluate, he runs the risk of being confused by his reading. Once given the principles by which he may ascertain the value of what he reads, he will be equipped with criteria by which he may make sound judgments in his further reading.

In *American Profile* the ordinary course of study in American literature has been enlarged and completed by the addition of a number of selections by Catholic writers and a history written from a Catholic point of view. The Spanish and French missionaries who came with the first explorers molded a way of life dedicated to the reign of Christ on our continent. The scope of their activities is not usually known or realized. From their efforts came the beginnings of a Catholic literature that was medieval in its motivation of all activity for the glory of God. Such was the birth of the written word on our soil. With the advent of the Maryland colonists an articulate Catholic voice was heard again. A resurgence of Catholic literary effort came during the national period when the descendants of colonial Catholics united with immigrant voices and literary-minded converts to assert the American right to religious freedom threatened at that time by the Native-American movement. An understanding of the achievement of Catholic letters in the United States is impossible without a knowledge of the victories won over prejudice in the first half of the nineteenth century. Catholic authors then refuted the charge that Catholicism is incompatible with the American way of life. Since this sturdy groundwork was laid in the national period, there has been a continuously-advancing structure of Catholic literature in America. While there exists today a new vigor in Catholic letters, particularly in the fields of poetry and biography, this advancement appears less a renaissance or revival than a natural development from the earlier growth of Catholic literature.

In most instances the compilation of a high-school textbook does not call for new exploration into fields of scholarly research. Since the history of the first two hundred fifty years of Catholic literary activity in the colonial period had not been written and since an account of Catholic letters in the national period had not been adequately constructed, it was necessary for these two fields to be investigated before this text could be written. In the interest of brevity large portions of the material uncovered by this research had to be omitted. Because these earlier Catholic authors were overlooked or ignored at the time of their writing, it is almost impossible today to evaluate their contributions rightly. These writings can no longer be seen against the literary modes of their own day nor viewed in the light of the audience for whom they were intended. A survey of this material is significant, however, in order to show the forces that have been instrumental in laying the groundwork of Catholic literature and to reveal likewise the influences which from the beginning have retarded the development of Catholic letters in America. An understanding of these impediments is particularly significant because the same forces which hampered the expression of Catholic thought in the past continue to hamper it today. Neither in the present nor in the past has there been a body of Catholic writing commensurate with the numerical strength of Catholicism and the splendor of its revealed truth largely because there has not been a ready and eager Catholic audience.

It is in the near future that American Catholics can look for a full flowering of their literature. The time is favorable both in the receptiveness of the public and in the preparation of Catholic authors. The breakdown of false liberalism and the need of a solution for bewildering problems have caused the American people to seek spiritual values. On the other hand, Catholic writers, having laid the foundation of their culture and asserted their right to be articulate, have now reached the point where they are prepared to voice the truths which will bring completeness to the American way of life. In an age of realism they stand with the greatest truths of reality. It will be the task of the Catholic student of this generation not only to read the message of the early American Catholics but to prepare himself to enunciate Catholic ideals for his countrymen.

To Reverend Mother Lucy Dooley, O.S.B., President of Mount St. Scholastica College, the staff of *The Catholic High School Literature Series* offer their sincere gratitude for her continuous generosity. They wish likewise to thank the Superiors of other religious communities whose co-operation aided in the production of this volume. To Reverend John W. Simons they extend their appreciation for his valued help and criticism. The contributions of Sister Muriel Tarr, C.S.A., Sister Mary St. Clement, B.V.M., Sister Mary Agatha, B.V.M., Sister Mary Rosalia, B.V.M., and Sister Mary Evangela, B.V.M., are gratefully acknowledged. The editors wish likewise to thank Reverend Francis Borgia Steck, O.F.M., and Joseph J. Reilly for their kind assistance.

Sister Mary Theresa Brentano, O.S.B

Table of Contents

COLONIAL OUTLINES—1492-1775

REVOLUTIONARY DESIGNS—1775-1800

NATIONAL PATTERNS—1800-1865

FRONTIER SKETCHES—1865-1890

REALISTIC VIEWS—1870-1914

CHANGING PERSPECTIVES—1914-1944

TABLE OF CONTENTS

Indians Playing Lacrosse

Colonial Outlines, 1492-1775

LITERATURE OF SPANISH EXPLORATION AND COLONIZATION

The first sketch of America's profile was made in bare outlines when explorers described the vast continent that defied them to chart its boundaries. Men groped along coastlines in search of friendly harbors, plunged into forests to emerge upon unknown plains, and crossed barren land to marvel at sudden beauty. Fear and wonder mingled, for danger lurked in this new country. Yet beyond hazard and fatigue gleamed the reward of this giant continent: wealth, freedom, souls for Christ.

Columbus states an American ideal

The explorers who marveled at America's bounty were gallant soldiers. Spain, militantly Catholic, emerged from a victory over the Mohammedans in a mood for another gigantic task. When half a world suddenly fell to her care, she immediately glimpsed the glory of making her newly-found savages not only children of civilization but also children of Christ. Columbus himself penned the first written dedication of America to the service of God and humanity. Although he was still confused about his geography, the jubilant admiral felt that his discovery would influence the destiny of nations. "And let us, too, be elated," he wrote, "for the exaltation of our Faith and for the augmentation of things temporal, of which not only Spain but all Christendom will be the future partaker." The role of America in world events was thus fittingly inaugurated. Columbus, an Italian in the service of a Spanish monarch, voiced an American ideal which later writers would elaborate.

The relation develops as a literary type

In displaying her wealth, raw America challenged her civilized invaders to match her riches with their strength. Never until Spain stumbled upon a new continent and an unknown race had she such need to combine military valor and Christian virtue. The true *conquistador,* the warrior who could christianize as well as conquer, needed endurance for superhuman marches, shrewdness against savage cunning, valor leashed to forbearance, and above all personal integrity, lest scandal mar the Indian's dawning concept of the term *Christian.* Not all the explorers combined the ingenuity of Ulysses with the fervor of St. Paul. But true or false to their duties as Christian knights, they performed deeds which were matters of tremendous consequence. The soldiers were keenly aware that they were makers of history, and frequently they assumed the role of historians as well. First-hand information was invaluable to the sovereign directly aiding the expedition, to those who had invested money in the venture, and to future settlers. The account or report of travelers became an accepted literary type known as the *relation.* It was at once both spot news and history. The writer in many instances had no particular literary training, nor did he concern himself with this inadequacy. He had taken part in momentous events; the facts that he could relate were sufficient justification for his writing.

The relations of the first explorers are the earliest written accounts which describe the present territory of the United States. Penned first by Spanish, later by English and French travelers and settlers, these writings can only in a restricted sense be classified as American literature. They merit consideration, however, because they reveal what the white man did, thought, and felt amid the untouched splendor of our country; how Amcrica developed as a nation; what traditions she embraces; what are the roots of her culture. In the following pages only those Spanish and French writings will be discussed which treat of the present territory of the United States or affect the beginnings of literature in our country. The large body of Mexican, South American, and Canadian literature of the colonial period which does not bear upon the early backgrounds of the United States is not here presented.

The explorations of the Spanish in our country were a continuation of Spain's policy of conquest and civilization which followed the discovery of America. Wishing to hold as much territory as possible in the New World, Spain sent repeated expeditions for colonization. The rich territory of Mexico and Central America first attracted the settlers. Gradually when this territory was claimed by the first explorers, adventurers hoped to discover equally advantageous sections in the North, over which they could rule. This desire explains the fact that the expeditions were more likely to come from the regions south of our border already settled by Spain, rather than from Spain itself.

THE FIRST RELATIONS

The sweeping plains of our country were first described by a man who trudged across half the continent. A series of disasters combined to start Álvar Núñez Cabeza de Vaca (1490-1559?) on an eight-year journey that began on the Florida peninsula and took him westward to the Gulf of California. De Vaca came with Pánfilo de Narvaez in 1528, expecting to be high-sheriff and treasurer of the settlement which Narvaez would govern. His *Relation* is the record of the tragedies that ultimately reduced Narvaez' expedition of six hundred men to four wandering outcasts. Shipwreck, Indian hostility, exposure, starvation — each in the course of time took its toll of the Spanish troops. After numerous disasters in Florida, Cabeza de Vaca with a handful of survivors was shipwrecked and washed ashore near the present site of Galveston, Texas. Too ill to escape when his companions fled from Indian captivity, he remained among starving masters. He kept alive on roots, berries, and the scrapings from hides, but so barely alive as to arouse even the pity of the savage. Finally, gaining the respect and confidence of the natives, he was able to pass among the tribes as a trader. From time to time vague rumors of his fellow Spaniards reached him. On several occasions Cabeza de Vaca succeeded in meeting three of his original party and with them made plans for escape. In 1534 the four survivors fled from the Indians in an attempt to reach civilization. After experiencing many hardships while crossing Texas, the men proceeded in a southwesterly direction and at last reached the Gulf of California, where they were welcomed by fellow Spaniards.

De Vaca describes the plains

The man who had heard only Indian languages for eight years found it difficult to marshal his ideas into written form. De Vaca's *Relation,* published in Spain in 1542, betrays a confusion of names and places. This vagueness resulted from his inability to localize a long trip on which he had had no maps at his disposal. In an exhausted physical condition, he had forgotten many things. He naturally related in greatest detail those events imprinted by suffering or by their unusual circumstances. De Vaca's narrative brings the reader to the endless stretch of American prairie, where the wanderer had observed the buffaloes as queer "hunchback cows." His story is the story of a man whom faith consoled in peril and who won against the rigors of an untamed continent.

Romance enters the American chronicle

Of the four chroniclers describing De Soto's long wanderings, the most valuable is the *Relation* of the unknown Portuguese soldier designated as The Gentleman of Elvas. This author recounts the spectacular rovings of De Soto in a manner calculated to create interest in the expedition. He interrupts his account of the general's marches to insert the romance of an Indian princess into the literature of American exploration. Long before Captain John Smith wrote of Pocahontas, the chroniclers among De Soto's troops heard from Juan Ortiz' own lips the startling story of an Indian girl's intervention to save a white man's life.

Like Cabeza de Vaca, Juan Ortiz was a survivor of the Narvaez enterprise. He had been captured by the Indian chief, Hirrhiqua, and condemned to slow torture over a burning fire. When Hirrhiqua's daughter — whose name is unfortunately not recorded — interceded for him, Ortiz was allowed to live as a slave. Given the task of guarding the cemetery at night, he incurred the wrath of the chief when a wolf carried off the body of a newly-buried child. In spite of the fact that Ortiz killed the wolf and recaptured the small corpse, he was condemned to death. Once more the princess intervened, this time secretly sending Ortiz to her fiancè, Mucoso, with the request that the Indian brave protect the European from her father.

Here tragedy enters the story of the Indian lovers. Mucoso fulfilled the trust of his promised bride but only at the cost of losing her. The enraged Hirrhiqua, upon discovering that his plan was thwarted, refused to allow his daughter to marry her loyal lover. Ortiz remained under the protection of Mucoso for eleven years. One day he heard of the arrival of De Soto's army and with the permission of Mucoso went out to meet the soldiers. When the Spaniards saw the tattered slave, they thought he was a dangerous savage and would have killed him.

Ortiz invoked the name of the Blessed Virgin, whereby the Spaniards recognized him as a European. De Soto eagerly welcomed Ortiz, for he saw in the outcast's knowledge of geography and savage tongues invaluable aid for his own marches. Filled with gratitude for this new guide and interpreter, the great general thanked Mucoso for his charity toward the captured European and promised him the friendship of Christian warriors.

Priest records his exploration

New Mexico and Arizona enter into the literature of exploration with the *Relation* of the intrepid Franciscan priest, Fray Marcos de Niza. Rumors of Indians who dwelt in seven golden cities in the North caused the viceroy of Mexico to send Fray Marcos on a tour of exploration. On the friar's return, his reports were interpreted optimistically, and Coronado set out on his famous expedition. You may read of the termination of this journey in Arthur Guiterman's poem, "Quivira," presented in the final section of this text.

THE EARLIEST CENTER OF CULTURE IN NORTH AMERICA

While Spanish chroniclers were recording their explorations of lands within the present limits of the United States, their countrymen in colonies south of our borders were not idle. Particularly in Mexico and Cuba the first settlements were rapidly becoming centers of civilization and culture that were to influence the earliest intellectual development of our country.

Black Legend *has influenced historians*

The story of Spain's settlement of the Americas has been so distorted by many historians that the biased accounts have received the term *Black Legend*. It must be remembered that England was not only a powerful commercial rival but also a political and religious enemy of Spain. As a result of deeply-rooted prejudice arising from this fact, historians until recently have presented Spain as a grasping monarchy that took the wealth of the New World and cruelly exploited the Indian.

A true estimate of Spain's conquest of the two Americas can be gained only by considering the benevolent policy of the Spanish crown towards the Indian, which lasted at least up to 1700. It must likewise take into account the zealous work of the Spanish missionaries, and the co-operation of Spanish laymen who looked upon this immigration to the New World not only as a means of increasing their own welfare but an opportunity for aiding in the spread of Christianity. Many laymen, it is true, had no such praiseworthy motives. In an attempt to establish mutual aid between the settler and the Indian, the Spanish government had established the *encomienda*. This was an economic system in which a Spanish landlord undertook to supervise the labor of a group of natives, to teach them the ways of civilization, and to provide them with an opportunity for instruction in the Catholic Faith. Too frequently the Spaniard exacted labor of the savage without fulfilling his corresponding duties of training and christianizing his charges.

The missionary raised such a powerful protest against this abuse of Indian labor that the *encomiendas* were eventually abolished. Foremost in this early crusade for social justice was the powerful voice of the Dominican writer, Bartolomé de las Casas. The soldier, too, brought problems to the missionary. Useful as the military forces had been in penetrating the wilderness and protecting the padre, the presence of armed men invariably aroused fear and suspicion among the Indians. Frequently soldiers attracted to the life of adventurous conquest were restless men, glad to be free from the restraints of civilization. Furthermore, the great distance of the new land from the protection of the Spanish government gave reckless men opportunity for selfishness and cruelty. Missionaries who had been laboring in Mexico, Central America, and parts of South America were deciding that the best means of converting the savages was to go quietly among them and win their complete confidence.

Spain's gift is Catholic culture

In legislating against unruly adventurers and the abuses of Indian labor, the Spanish government sought to give the Indians the same protections it offered to other Spanish subjects. To the Spanish crown, the term conquest meant not only winning victories of military strength but also improving the conquered people. Spain gave to the two Americas a Catholicity untouched by the Protestant Revolt, which had brought heavy losses to the Faith in northern European countries. She gave them likewise a culture that adapted itself to native needs. Spain wished to own the New World, but to own it only as a Catholic country could hope to hold another land: by establishing peaceable, intelligent colonies of Christian people.

Las Casas wrote stirring appeals for the Indians.

In this goal the missionary was the chief factor. The first settlements had been laboratory centers of experiment in which the padres had developed the methods of teaching, at the same time, the truths of the Gospel, the principles of hygiene, the fundamentals of agriculture, and the basic elements of literature and art. The establishment of schools for the higher education of native boys was in accord with Spain's desire for the improvement of the Indian. Santa Cruz College, planned exclusively for the Indians, was established in Mexico City in 1536, one hundred years before the founding of Harvard College. The curriculum included religion and ethics, reading, writing, Latin grammar, rhetoric, medicine, philosophy, music, and drama. The University of Mexico was opened in 1553. From these institutions were to come men prepared for leadership. Trained in languages and in the studies which today correspond to the social and physical sciences, many of these students later proved helpful assistants to missionaries in the territory of the United States.

Literature of instruction is prepared

Significant also for the early missionary labors in our country was the establishment in Mexico of the printing press and the rapid development of a literature especially designed for the instruction of the Indian. Probably the first book printed in America was the *Spiritual Ladder*, a translation by the Dominican Juan de Estada of the Latin original of St. John Climacus. The book was chosen because of its appeal to young novices in religious houses, many of whom would labor as missionaries in our country. Appearing about 1535, the treatise antedated by more than a hundred years the Puritan publication of the *Bay Psalm Book* (1640), usually considered the first book printed in America. The heroic age of Mexican literature, extending from 1522 to 1572, produced catechisms and spiritual treatises, grammars and dictionaries in native Indian tongues, texts in law, philosophy, science, and theology, together with studies on the origin and social aspects of the human race. The "good neighbor policy" may be said to begin with the missionaries in Mexico and Cuba who trained young priests, gave them the fruits of their experiences, published textbooks, and finally led the way to the Florida coast.

Fray Cancer plans to use verse to win Florida Indians

An early missionary who came to Florida unprotected by soldiers intended to use literature as a means for gaining entrance to the savage mind. During his missionary work in Central America, Fray Luis Cancer, a Dominican, had already shown the superiority of the arts over the sword. The fierceness of the Tuzulutlán mountain tribes had caused their region to be known as the Land of War. Fray Cancer devised a plan of gaining entrance to their country through the medium of song. He quickly mastered the tribal language and skillfully put into verse the whole story of man's fall and redemption. Combining his narrative with a simple melody in the style of music familiar among the natives, he secured bells and tribal musical instruments for accompaniment. After carefully training a quartet of Christian Indian peddlers, he sent them into the Land of War. The fierce savages were fascinated by the absorbing story of Christ and demanded repeated performances. Pelted with questions, the Christian natives replied that they would bring peace-loving men who wished only to lead their Indian brothers to the Kind Father Who had figured so largely in the Gospel narrative. The savages welcomed Fray Cancer, whose work was so successful that the name of the country was soon changed to Land of True Peace.

Until 1670 Florida extended from the Chesapeake Bay to Texas. The Indians of this region had resisted colonization as determinedly, if not as fiercely, as the Indians of Tuzulutlán. While Fray Cancer was visiting Spain in 1547, he petitioned the court to allow him to use his methods of catechizing for gaining entrance into Florida. The Crown favorably received the missionary's plans and gave him royal permission for the enterprise. With his ready faculty for composing Gospel verse in Indian dialects, he sailed into Tampa Bay in 1549. With him were three Dominicans and an Indian interpreter. Fray Cancer never had an opportunity to translate his poems of good tidings into the language of the Florida Indians. The pilot of his ship, disobeying the orders of both the Crown and the priest, entered a harbor where, because of previous contacts with white men, the Indians were already hostile. Pretending friendliness, the savages welcomed two of Fray Cancer's companions, Brother Fuentes and Fray Tolosa, only to bring them inland and kill them. A Spaniard from De Soto's expedition, whom the Indians had enslaved, fled to Fray Cancer's ship bearing the news of the Dominicans' death. Despite the protest of his companions, Fray Cancer went ashore two days later, hoping to convince the Indians of his friendliness. At his appearance the savages emerged with arrows and clubs and swiftly martyred the priest, who had knelt down to commend his soul to God. One of the last acts he performed before leaving the ship was to record in his diary the martyrdom of his two companions.

WRITINGS OF EARLY SPANISH SETTLERS

In reading the relations of intrepid explorers, we see the American scene as a background for daring and fantastic deeds. Not until permanent settlements were made, however, could American culture and American literature develop. With the decisive action of Pedro Menéndez, St. Augustine, the first city in the United States, was founded in 1565. As far back as 1526, when the colonizing expedition of Lucas Vásquez de Ayllón had landed from Haiti, the Holy Sacrifice of the Mass had been offered in the land which is now our country. The celebrant was no other than Father Montesinos, the Dominican friar who, by his ardent defense of the Indians of Haiti, became one of the first advocates of the oppressed in the New World. The priests who accompanied succeeding expeditions had also offered the Holy Sacrifice at various places during their travels. The founding of St. Augustine, however, marked the permanent inauguration of Catholic ceremonies in our country and the establishment of the Catholic Church as the oldest religious organization in the United States. An heroic era in missionary labors followed, in which can be traced a continuous thread of literary activity. The first work which figured prominently in this era was written in the rhythmical patterns of verse.

Before considering this verse, it will be helpful to take a backward glance at the oral poetry of the Indian. Previous to his contact with explorers and missionaries, the North American Indian had developed his own primitive types of artistic expression. It is difficult to draw general conclusions concerning the advancement of his culture because the many tribes ranged from fierce savagery to relatively advanced types of living. Customs and ceremonies vary greatly according to locality. We can only conjecture what this oral literature was from the records of white men and from the oral literary tradition which still exists among Indians now living. Scholars today are preserving what remains of Indian song and folklore by making phonograph recordings of the singing of the oldest tribal members. From this late harvesting of primitive material it is possible to find certain features common to Indian literature as a whole.

Indian's song is linked with his belief

The most ancient type of Indian song appears to have been produced from a kind of poetic inspiration, such as a poet today might feel after long meditation. The Indian, however, did not look upon himself as the author. After he had retired to a secluded spot for several days, reflecting and praying to the spirits he worshiped, he believed that he had a dream or a trance in which a spirit appeared to him singing a song. Ever afterwards in time of need that song was effective in procuring the assistance of the spirit. The urgent necessities of the Indian were food, health, and success in battle. Accordingly, he awaited the inspiration of the

spirits particularly powerful in securing these benefits. The warrior believed he received his song from a bird or animal of great speed and cunning. The medicine man thought that he heard his song from a spirit-bird possessing vigor and health. Special spirits were invoked in certain localities. The tribesmen of the plains begged success in the buffalo hunts. The Pueblo Indians of the thirsting Southwest cherished songs which they believed were helpful in bringing rain. The Chippewas of the northern woods sang to obtain an abundance of maple sugar. Evil men possessed songs believed to induce evil rather than good. The song which the Indian believed to be inspired could be repeated only by the owner. When he gave that right to another — even to his own son — he exacted a payment of arrows or rich ornaments. Women seldom received an inspired or dream song. A second type of poetry, social songs having no magical power, appears to be a later development of Indian literature. These songs, sung only for entertainment, show less unity of idea and rhythm than the spirit poetry.

Indian songs usually have few words, but these few are very meaningful or powerful in evoking an image. In some tribes a few phrases will convey the idea or picture; the remainder of the song will consist of meaningless sounds, which are nevertheless significant to the Indian because of their emotional value. Many Indian songs contain no words at all. They are made up wholly of sounds which can be voiced only by an Indian throat. Among the North American tribes poetry is inseparable from music. The melody is frequently accompanied by the gourd, drum, flute, or wooden whistle. To music and words the Indian often adds bodily movement. This movement may be either that of the dance or the rhythmic activity of work.

DOMINGO AGUSTÍN BÁEZ

For centuries the tones of Indian song had floated from wigwam to wigwam and echoed from forest to cliff. In its accents had sounded the soft timbre of the woman's grinding song, the shrill cry of the warrior, the weird invocation of the medicine man. A Jesuit Brother, Domingo Agustín Báez (1538-1569?), was the first man within the territory of the United States to capture Indian speech within the bonds of the written word. In composing rhythmic versions of Christian doctrine, he disciplined native speech to music and dignified it by making it serve as a messenger of the Gospel. Previously travelers, such as Fray Cancer, had made notes or diary entries while upon our soil or within our harbors. Brother Báez is probably the first author to complete a work while living within the boundaries of our country.

Teaching by verses that can easily be memorized has always been a favorite device wherever books have not been readily available. The couplets of the Roman poet Cato were chanted throughout medieval Europe. They served as a means of fixing the rules of Latin grammar and the maxims of moral conduct in the mind of the all too easily distracted schoolboy. Before the Indian could be taught to read and write and before printed texts could be secured from Spain and Mexico, the truths of faith were framed for easy recall within the form of verse. The Indian had preserved his ritual in song. He considered his spirit-song a prayer of invocation. In discouraging the songs of magic and superstition and substituting songs of faith, the missionary satisfied the native's love for rhythmical expression.

Love of song, chief characteristic

Brother Báez's love for song is the distinguishing characteristic of his missionary activity. He was stationed at Salamanca, Spain, when his superior, St. Francis Borgia, finally granted his frequent requests that he be allowed to go to the American missions. While awaiting transportation in the Spanish harbor, Brother Báez catechized the crowds by singing. On the voyage he led the sailors in chanting hymns. When the party arrived in Florida, the versatile Brother was left at St. Augustine to complete preparations for the mission and to instruct the Indians while the priests went on to Havana to found a school. On their return in a few months they discovered that Brother Báez had not only mastered the Timucua dialects but had made rapid progress in the compilation of a rhythmical catechism and grammar which the priests later used as texts. On being sent to a mission on St. Catherine's Island, off the coast of Guale (Georgia), Brother Báez again impressed his superiors with his rare talent with words. He instructed the other brothers and priests in the Indian tongue and speedily produced his second rhythmical catechism and grammar, this time in the Yamasee dialect. Realizing the great aid his talent would be in a mission where thousands of Indians awaited instruction, his superiors planned to send him

to the mainland. But only one more song of Brother Báez is recorded. This was the melody he uttered with his dying breath, when stricken with smallpox after a year on the mission, he sang of the victorious canticle which will be the chant of those who walk weeping upon the earth.

The death of the talented Brother at a time when language difficulties were a major drawback in the teaching of the Gospel was a blow to the Jesuits in Florida. Brother Báez's manuscripts appear to have been lost in an attempt of his companions to carry the Gospel into hitherto unpenetrated regions. It is conjectured that his papers were taken by Father Segura when with five companions he went to establish a mission at Ajácan on the Chesapeake. Betrayed by an Indian convert who relapsed into his pagan customs, the Jesuits were cruelly martyred. Only the altar boy, Alonzo, was left to tell that the Jesuit martyrs — with their missionary crosses — are buried not far from the present capital of the United States. Although Brother Báez's manuscripts are probably permanently lost, it is possible that the graves of the five martyrs will yet be discovered as a precious shrine for American Catholics.

FRAY ALONSO DE ESCOBEDA

Despite the priority of Brother Báez's works among early American writings, his name has remained almost unknown. Similarly, the first historical poem which describes our country has lain unpublished for more than three centuries. This is the lengthy work entitled *La Florida* by the Franciscan Fray Alonso de Escobeda. Fray Escobeda was the poet-historian of the heroic age of missionary endeavor in Florida. In his case a missionary's zeal was supplemented by a poet's sensitivity. Fray Escobeda's own experiences had called for heroic courage and endurance. On his way to the New World he had been captured by pirates, detained in Havana, and had come to a dangerous and barren country shortly after Sir Francis Drake and his English pirates had devastated Florida settlements, even to their orchards. He was keenly aware that a paganism entrenched by sorcery was matching forces with Christian morality at the outposts of civilization. When the martyrdom of five of his Franciscan confreres occurred in an Indian uprising in Georgia, Fray Escobeda witnessed the resentment of the natives towards a faith that would take from them their degrading pleasures.

Fray Escobeda's historical poem, *La Florida,* was written towards the end of the sixteenth century or the beginning of the seventeenth. Despite its value as a document of the early Spanish settlement, it remains in manuscript form in the National Library at Madrid. The manuscript comprises four hundred forty-nine pages written in *octava real*, a popular stanzaic form. In a reliable historical account of an heroic Spanish enterprise, Escobeda describes the labors and martyrdom of his confreres in Florida and records his own stirring experiences. He shows a dramatic sense when elaborating various incidents in which Christian endeavor triumphs over pagan resistance. The author's piety and Christian hope mingle with gratitude for God's help in perilous events. Observations on the primitive Florida landscape occur frequently throughout the poem. Escobeda's facility with meter and rhyme give his lines simplicity, grace, and fluency of expression. He aims at an exact narration of historical fact rather than an imaginative presentation. Occasionally, however, apt figurative language lifts his material into the sphere of imaginative expression.

GASPAR PÉREZ DE VILLAGRÁ

When in 1598 Juan de Oñate led four hundred persons into New Mexico, he had in his company Gaspar Pérez de Villagrá (1555c.-1620). This gallant officer related the conquests of the expedition in a narrative poem called *The History of New Mexico*. Oñate had hoped to pass peacefully into New Mexico, but the massacre of some of his men convinced him that the Indians must be punished or the whole party would be lost. After killing the group of Spaniards, the Indians had withdrawn to the fortress of Ácoma, a sky city on a rock four hundred fifty feet high. In an attempt to storm the Ácoma, twelve Spaniards quietly scaled the rock until they reached one of its outlying pinnacles. At night other Spaniards dragged logs up the butte on which the twelve were perilously stationed, and at daybreak, casting one of the logs across the abyss to the main rock, they began to cross this improvised bridge. Only a few Spaniards had gained the main cliff when one of the men caught his foot in the rope and accidentally pulled the log after him. With the handful of Spaniards on the main rock cut off from their comrades, the entire party was in jeopardy. At this crisis Villagrá, with the agility

of a schoolboy, leaped across the gulf and thrust the log back for his companions to grasp. His decisive action enabled the Spanish army to cross the rude bridge and successfully storm the Indian city.

Although Villagrá's *History* minimizes his achievement in the daring encounter, contemporary writers record the importance of his services to the expedition. His chronicle, which is important as an historical document rather than as poetry, was published in Spanish in 1610. The author's knowledge of literature gives a classical flavor to his composition, and his consciousness of the historian's mission caused him to supply exact dates of events, names of missionaries, soldiers, and officers, and details of perilous adventures. In using verse form in his *History,* Villagrá follows the Spanish writers of his time who celebrate in poetry the achievements of the army.

CHRISTIAN CULTURE OF THE SOUTH AND WEST

With permanent settlements established in Florida and New Mexico, mission posts were built, as time went on, to fill the intervening gaps between Florida and Arizona. The written word helped to stabilize the Christian culture which was gradually supplanting paganism in the southern and southwestern parts of the United States. The intensity of the missionary's application to linguistic studies equaled his courage in penetrating the wilderness. First, the padre had to persuade the savages to teach him their language. Always untrained, sometimes reluctant to communicate with a pale-faced stranger, these natives were poor teachers even when furnishing vocabulary for the simple objects of daily life.

Despite the difficulties which attended the Indian's first lessons in reading and writing, the natives were soon able to send letters to each other, sometimes within two months of the missionary's first instruction. The writings of Fray Francisco Pareja for the Timucua missions of Florida indicate the scope of the Indians' reading. In addition to a dictionary and grammar in the Timucua and Spanish languages, the Franciscan priest produced books of Christian doctrine and spiritual reading. His *Confessionario*, written in Timucua and in Spanish and published in Mexico in 1613, was designed to help the Indians prepare for confession and to aid the confessor in counseling the Indian penitent. The examination of conscience lists numerous superstitious practices which the Indian had to unlearn at the same time that he strove to acquaint himself with the Gospel and to practice Christian virtue.

The relations and letters of missionaries during this heroic era are too numerous to be listed. In the communications which the priests sent to their religious or civil superiors, the writers frequently expressed the need for more missionaries to labor among the Indians. Often a letter will give an enlightening picture of the missionary's zeal and his ingenuity in using art and the liturgy to quicken the Indians' fervor. Many of the most significant of these documents are still practically unknown, many are unpublished, many are lost; yet one cannot overlook this literature of missionary activity without disregarding the first strata of Christian culture in the United States.

LOS PASTORES

One of the few authentic pieces of folk drama in the United States developed in connection with the labors of the early Franciscans. This is the play *The Shepherds (Los Pastores)*, said to be more than three hundred years old. It is still annually performed by Spanish-speaking people in our southwestern states. Facts concerning the origin of the play are uncertain. Critics agree, however, that it is one of the religious plays which the Franciscan missionaries are known to have brought from Spain or Mexico and adapted to the understanding of Indian groups. As the play was handed down by oral tradition from one generation to another, it developed the qualities of genuine folk literature. Indeed, until recent years no manuscript or printed version of *The Shepherds* existed, a fact which accounts for the different versions among the various groups which give the play.

The Shepherds tells the beautiful story of the men who journeyed to Bethlehem after an angel had announced to them the birth of the Saviour. The introduction into the cast of an Indian wearing feathers and gala dress is one of the ways in which the play was adapted to the native tribes. The play is in line with the medieval tradition of sacred drama known as the mystery and miracle plays. When brought to this country, *The Shepherds* proved valuable in teaching the Christmas story to the Indians. The interest of the natives was keenly aroused, since they themselves were taught to fill the roles. Composed for outdoor staging, the drama is still performed by Spanish-speaking peoples in the back yard of a humble home or in a vacant lot. Public performances have been given in some cities in recent years since historians have reawakened interest in the play. The ordinary troupe of *The Shepherds*, however — and there are many in existence — performs several evenings a week or perhaps night after night during the Christmas season. According to an ancient tradition of the play, the cast stages its performance each night in a different place. In some quarters a lantern is hung outside the door of a home as a sign of welcome to the Christ Child and consequently an indication that the players of *The Shepherds* are invited there. The same audience follows the performers each night, never failing to find new inspiration and devotion in the divine story.

LITERATURE OF ENGLISH EXPLORATION

The nations which colonized America transplanted the civilization of Western Europe to the fresh soil of the New World. American culture, therefore, was influenced by the modes of thought that prevailed among European colonizers. When the Protestant Revolt swept across Europe in the sixteenth century, it separated whole nations from the Catholic Church, the great source of unity in medieval times among people of different nationalities and languages. Of the nations colonizing the New World, the Spanish, Portuguese, and French brought with them a Catholic culture. They held likewise a policy of colonization which reflected the Catholic teachings that had never been exterminated in these nations. If individuals in these colonies disregarded just principles in dealing with the savages, these men were acting directly contrary to the teaching of the Church.

The influence of Protestantism began to affect America when England, Holland, and Sweden established colonies along the eastern seaboard. These nations had been delayed in making settlements because of their engagement with European affairs. When they were finally able to turn their attention to the New World, large areas in North and South America were already under Catholic control. These Protestant nations, therefore, insisted on making their colonies strongholds for their own beliefs in order to prevent Catholic domination in America.

The English-speaking Protestants of the colonial period held, or were influenced by, various religious views. These beliefs may be classified with reference to the amount of dogma and ritual which they retained from the Catholic Church. There were first the Anglicans or members of the Established Church of England. In separating from the Catholic Church, this sect had denied papal supremacy, and had later rejected other doctrinal points. It had retained, however, a number of Catholic dogmas and much of the Catholic ritual. Causing dissension among the Anglicans was a group known as the Puritans. These dissatisfied Church members received their name because they believed that the Anglican Church should be purified from the "contaminations" which remained from Rome. Since the Puritans were influenced by Calvin (1509-1564), they likewise differed from the other Anglicans on the question of interpretation of the Scriptures and other matters of doctrine. The Anglican Church, which had recently insisted on freedom from papal authority, now refused to allow freedom to those who disagreed with its doctrines.

Upon this refusal the Puritans divided into two groups. Some broke completely from the Anglican Church and became known as Separatists or Dissenters. Others, while not openly breaking with the Established Church, eventually so modified their doctrines and practice that they became a religious body separate from the Anglican Church and intolerant of its teaching. A third group went even farther than the Puritans in rejecting Catholic dogma. These men refused to accept any supernatural revelation and became the freethinkers of the so-called Age of Enlightenment, a movement which was to gather force as the eighteenth century progressed.

English describe American shores

For half a century before England made permanent settlements in the New World, her travelers and explorers had sailed along American shores and in some cases had resided for a short time on the coast. Narratives of eyewitnesses remain to tell of brief pauses in Florida and California and to describe the several ill-fated attempts to colonize Virginia during the late sixteenth century. When preparations for another expedition were begun, the whole of England was excited at the prospect of finally establishing a successful American colony. London businessmen discussed the possible gains of those holding

From John Lawson's "A New Voyage in Carolina,"
London, 1709

stock in the Virginia Company, a commercial organization which was providing money for the expedition. Public prayers were offered for the success of the venture in the Established Church of England, for the voyagers were largely Anglican. In an ode which captured the high hope for this perilous trip, the English poet Michael Drayton went so far as to envision the successful poets that might write in the New World.

CAPTAIN JOHN SMITH

The man who inaugurated English writing on American shores was Captain John Smith (1580-1631). His exploits previous to his associations with the Virginia Company were so romantic that he seems to have stepped out of the pages of the *Arabian Nights*. Leaving home at sixteen, he started on his travels in Europe, Asia, and Africa. When fighting with the Austrians against the Turks, he was captured and sold as a slave. He escaped by beating out the brains of his cruel master and dressing in his clothes. When he returned to England, he entered wholeheartedly into the plans of the Virginia

Company. On the voyage his vehement personality brought him into conflict with some of his companions, and his enemies succeeded in having him imprisoned on ship. Upon landing, the captain made known the orders of the Virginia Company concerning those who were to be entrusted with leadership. As Smith's name was among them, he obtained freedom and became active in the direction of the colony. He undertook to learn the language of the Indians, hazarded his life to procure corn from the savages, and won the respect of a number of the colonists for his intrepid courage. Many of the Virginia settlers were gentlemen adventurers, reluctant to do manual work. During the months of starvation that followed the landing, Smith held the colony together with his iron will and his famous order that only those who labored should eat. A burn from gunpowder made it necessary for him to return to England at the same time that reinforcements and a newly-appointed leader arrived at Jamestown.

In the intervals of his adventurous life Smith composed a vivid account of the colony for English stockholders of the Virginia Company. This work, *A True Relation* (1608), was the first English book written in America. A more extensive narrative of the Jamestown enterprise and of Smith's own exciting life in America later appeared in *The General History of Virginia* (1624). Smith has been accused of enlarging upon his facts to obtain dramatic effect and to present himself as the hero of the story. The tale of his rescue by Pocahontas has been questioned by historians, who note that he did not include it in his *True Relation* but in his later work, *The General History.* It is nevertheless possible that the incident was based on fact, since in *The True Relation* Smith acknowledges that he omits a number of events. While some of Smith's facts may be distorted and his account filled with a rough, blustering conceit, he writes in a bold, racy style. Smith's later work, *A Description of New England* (1616), is a sincere attempt to acquaint Englishmen with the opportunities of America.

The second group of English settlers to arrive in America belonged to that division of Puritans known as Separatists or Dissenters. Fearing that religious freedom would result in political freedom, James I made desperate attempts to force the Dissenters to conform to the Anglican faith. A number of Separatists living at Scrooby, England, in 1608 had been so persecuted that they decided to leave their native country in order to obtain religious freedom. The little group migrated to Holland, where they spent twelve years working at trades in Dutch cities. During this time they yearned for the soil which they had tilled in England and sought to preserve their English mode of life amid foreign surroundings. The virgin territory of America brightened before them as a land where they could preserve their nationality and freely practice their religion. In 1620, one hundred and two Pilgrims embarked for the New World on the *Mayflower* and settled at Plymouth, Massachusetts.

WILLIAM BRADFORD

Among the sternly disciplined Pilgrim fathers was William Bradford (1588-1657), who with calmness and fortitude guided the Plymouth colony during the first desolate winters in New England. In the quiet rustic beauty of Austerfield, England, young William Bradford spent his boyhood. An orphan from infancy and the victim of a long illness before he was twelve, he acquired the habit of studying the Bible and developed his spiritual life through long meditation. In William Brewster, at whose home in Scrooby a group of earnest worshipers met regularly, the boy found a father who shared his religious convictions. Against the wishes of his relatives Bradford joined the Separatist Church as a charter member and at seventeen emigrated with his associates to Amsterdam. In Holland he was one of the leaders who persistently advocated the migration of the Pilgrims to America. After arriving at the New England coast, Bradford with a group of leaders went ashore to explore the territory before the entire company should disembark. When he returned to the ship after this brief absence, he discovered that his wife had fallen overboard and drowned. Tragedy and disease took their toll of the Pilgrims during that first winter; and when Governor Carver died, the settlers elected Bradford his successor. Bradford met the problems of the colony with foresight and generosity. When famine threatened the group, he determined the allotment of rations to each individual to prevent unfair division of the food supply. After a plague, he took into his own home many of the children left destitute. As governor of Plymouth for more than thirty years Bradford led his struggling people to prosperity.

Bradford's *History of Plymouth Plantation* records the ideals, sufferings, and progress of the first group of Puritans in America. The chronicle follows the Pilgrims from the time they founded their Separatist Church to the year 1647, when the Plymouth colony had completed its first twenty-seven years. Bradford had seen American history unfold and had played a part in its making. Filled with the same religious zeal that had inspired his people to leave their native land, he recounts in dignified and rhythmical language the hazardous experiences of the Pilgrims while seeking freedom of worship. In the passages in which he affirms the faith of the Puritans despite the hardships of the wilderness, his prose approaches Biblical eloquence. Though there are monotonous stretches in the history, the work is rich in human interest. Occasionally the governor's dry humor relieves his gravity. As historian, Bradford had a strict regard for truth and a clear instructive style. As a Puritan he interprets the Puritan mind, which sees the hand of God in every occurrence.

THE MASSACHUSETTS BAY COMPANY

In contrast to the humble beginnings of the Pilgrims at Plymouth, another group of Puritans who sought refuge in America was large in number, well-educated, and wealthy. They were, accordingly, to be influential in setting the pattern for New England culture. Headed by John Winthrop (1588-1649), whom they elected governor, these colonists sailed for America under the charter of the Massachusetts Bay Company. On their arrival in 1630 they settled in Salem but later moved to Boston. The Puritan ideas which the Massachusetts Bay Colony upheld have had a profound influence on the Protestant civilization of America. Many of the principles governing the Puritan way of life found expression in the journal of John Winthrop, which because of its extensive scope was published under the title *The History of New England*. Although dull from a literary point of view, Winthrop's *History* contributes valuable information concerning the Puritan philosophy of the New Englanders.

Puritan theology has grim teachings

Both groups of Puritans were influenced by the Calvinistic doctrine that God is an Absolute Sovereign, Who, by a mere whim, elects certain souls to salvation while He allows the rest of mankind to suffer eternal punishment. Man is totally depraved and has no free will which he can exercise to incline God's favor towards him. Everything that occurs is regarded as a "special providence" of this Absolute Sovereign. According to Puritan belief, grace is a mechanical force which sends "the elect" to heaven entirely without their co-operation. They, as well as the sinners, are completely helpless. The saints are kept on the path of righteousness without any activity of their own wills. The sinners can only look forward to the dire wrath of God.

Since Calvinism denies free will, the Puritan was constantly haunted by the question: Was he among the few to be saved? Although his minister cautioned him that he could never be absolutely sure that he was among the elect, certain signs gave hopeful indications. One of the important tests was a person's ability to admit his absolute depravity, to acknowledge God's sovereignty, and to conform himself to the will of a Deity Who could send him to hell. Another means by which the Puritan might obtain reassurance was by patiently comparing his conduct with the pattern of holiness outlined in the Scriptures. He scrutinized his conduct to see whether it followed righteous modes of activity; he encouraged himself by comparing his inner assurance of salvation with that of his minister and godly friends. To sin or to become indifferent concerning his salvation was practically to acknowledge that he was among the damned. The Puritan's constant introspection explains his urge to record his inner experiences in diaries and other personal narratives.

The world of the Puritans, while not wholly melancholy, had its grim aspects. In denying that God is just and merciful, the Puritans made God less than God. In denying free will to human beings, they made man less than man. Even the motive of doing good for God's honor and the salvation of one's soul was swept away. The Puritans performed righteous acts merely to *convince* themselves that they were among the elect. For the nervous, the dyspeptic, the scrupulous, the pessimistic, religion was torture.

Puritans retain some Catholic teachings

The Puritan religion, if carried to its logical conclusions, would have needed no ministers; it implied that it was useless to listen to a sermon. The trouble with Puritanism was that neither the congregation nor the minister could be logical. The woodsman who

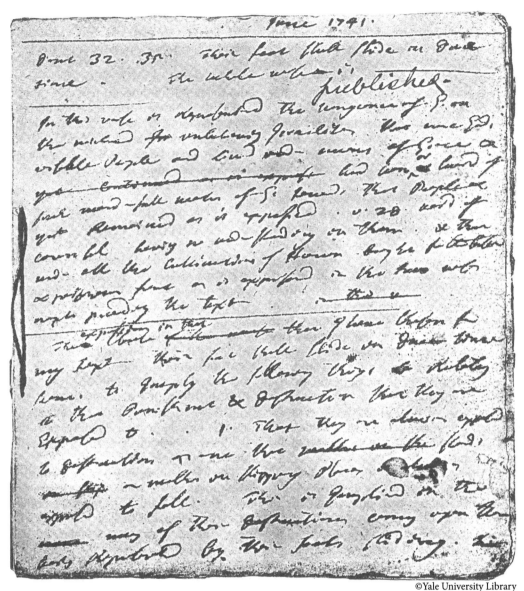

The First of Jonathan Edwards' Notes for His Sermon, Sinners in the Hands of an Angry God

was making a home in the wilderness knew by reason and experience that he was free to labor or to sit idly at home. It was necessary, therefore, to concede that man has freedom in natural activity. Even in supernatural matters, Puritan theology admitted that man possesses some freedom. It taught that the elect were free only to do good and that the wicked were free only to do evil. Further than this the logical minister should not have gone. Yet Puritan literature reveals sermon after sermon in which preachers admonish sinners to be converted from their sins as if they believed that man had a free will to repent. The reason for this inconsistency was

that the Protestant Revolt had broken only partially from Catholic teaching. Catholic truths were still an unacknowledged ingredient in the great bulk of religious beliefs.

Two other considerations help to explain the inconsistency between Puritan doctrine and Puritan practice. It would seem that the denial of free will would lead to fatalism or moral indifference. This, however, was not the case. By its hostility to monasticism, Puritanism destroyed the contemplative ideal and substituted the standard of practical moral duty. Secondly, Calvin borrowed from Luther the doctrine that man is justified by faith and not by works. Since works were without merit and, accordingly, without divine approval or disapproval, the Puritans had only success as the measure of their progress. As a result, worldly prosperity became the standard by which the New Englander estimated his achievement.

Puritanism, it is true, threw a black pall over Christian teaching by distorting Christian truth. It retained, however, many of the teachings of revelation and emphasized the supernatural end of man. By doing so, it helped to mold our national thought along Christian lines. It was important for America that these early English colonists believed in God, in the divinity of Christ, in prayer, sin, hell, and heaven. From these beliefs came their respect for moral law, their adherence to duty, their regard for family ties, and their practice of seeking enjoyment in the innocent pleasures of home life. From these, also, came their sincere religious strivings. Puritan beliefs had a profound effect upon Puritan culture. Education was developed to train ministers as religious and political leaders and to enable laymen to read the Bible. Religious discussion supplied impetus for writers and publishers. Boston, the most influential cultural center of the English colonies, was also the point from which religious thought radiated. Consequently, the cultural tradition stemming from English Puritanism, rather than from French or Spanish Catholicism or even from English Anglicanism, has been the most influential in the final shaping of the American profile.

THE ENGLISH CATHOLIC TRADITION: TOLERATION

Four years after Winthrop's colony was organized exclusively for Puritans, another group of Englishmen founded a colony offering religious freedom to all. In establishing a settlement on the principle of religious toleration, the English Catholics who migrated to Maryland made their first contribution to American thought. In 1634 was begun an experiment which no other English colony of the period attempted to undertake: Catholics and Protestants living side by side in strict equality, each man at liberty to worship according to the dictates of his conscience.

The Maryland colony was the realization of an ideal in the mind of Sir George Calvert, the first Lord Baltimore. A convert to Catholicism but still a favorite of the king, Calvert resigned as secretary of state and undertook to alleviate the sufferings of his persecuted fellow-Catholics by founding a haven in America. He intended, moreover, to offer refuge not only to Catholics but to the members of any persecuted sect. The severity of the climate caused the failure of Lord Baltimore's first attempt to establish such a settlement in Newfoundland. In 1632, while he was negotiating for a royal grant in a more suitable location, Lord Baltimore died. His son, Cecil Calvert, continued the plans inaugurated by his father. The Jesuits whom Cecil Calvert sought to interest in the plan saw in the new colony both a refuge for religious freedom and an opportunity for founding Indian missions in the New World. They gladly gave their counsel and helped to raise money for the project. When the *Ark* and the *Dove* sailed in 1634, two Jesuit priests, Andrew White and John Altham, as well as two Lay Brothers, were aboard.

Father White records Maryland settlement

Andrew White (1579-1656) had received Holy Orders in France in 1605 and had returned to England at a time when a priest could celebrate Mass and minister to Catholics only at the risk of his life. With a soldier's daring, Father White secretly performed his priestly duties until the increased persecution which followed the Gunpowder Plot. He was then sent into exile and threatened with death should he return. Despite the sentence passed upon him, he came back to England and labored there for several years. At the request of Cecil Calvert, Father White's superiors permitted him to join the expedition to the New World. Calvert also requested Father White to write a description of the colony for English Catholics. This document, *A Brief Relation of the Voyage Unto Maryland*, records the journey of the colonists and the early events in the settlement. During the ten years that he labored in Maryland, Father White acted as pastor to the colonists and established extensive missions among the Indians. Having learned their language, he wrote a catechism for the savages and prepared an Indian grammar and dictionary. When the colony was plundered by a group of lawless Englishmen, Father White was captured and taken in chains to England. There he was brought to

A

RELATION

OF

MARYLAND;

Together,

With ⎰ A Map of the Countrey,
The Conditions of Plantation,
His Majesties Charter to the
Lord *Baltemore*, translated
into English.

These Bookes are to bee had, at Master *William Peasley* Esq; his house, on the back-side of *Drury-Lane*, neere the *Cock-pit* Playhouse; or in his absence, at Master *Iohn Morgans* house in high *Holbourne*, over against the *Dolphin*,
London.

September the 8. *Anno Dom.* 1635.

©New York Public Library

trial because of English laws forbidding the presence of priests. As he had been forced to enter the country, he was acquitted of the charges against him, but was exiled to the Low Countries. Since his advanced age prevented his return to his New World mission, Father White eventually made his way back to England under an assumed name. There he died at seventy-seven, worn out by his heroic struggles for the Church.

ROGER WILLIAMS

Two years after the founding of Maryland, another move for religious toleration was made on our shores. Roger Williams (c.1604?-1683), a minister in Salem, Massachusetts, discovered that although the Puritans had come to America to secure religious freedom, they were unwilling to extend it to others. Banished from Massachusetts because he disagreed with Puritan beliefs and methods of church government, Williams founded the first Rhode Island settlement at Providence in 1636. Here he attempted to put into practice his ideas on democratic government and his theory that the Church should be separated from the state. Among Roger

Williams' many controversial writings, *The Bloody Tenet of Persecution* (1644) best sums up his opinions. This pamphlet was one of the works which grew out of a famous series of arguments between Williams and John Cotton. Cumbersome and ponderous in style, Williams' writings are difficult for the modern reader to follow. In his abusive tract against the Quakers in later years, Williams failed to continue the policy of religious toleration he had so ardently championed.

PURITAN POETRY

The Puritans' emphasis on doctrine and morals influenced their attitude towards the arts. As a whole, the Puritans have been accused of condemning any kind of enjoyment, particularly pleasure which results from beauty. It is true that fiction was sternly prohibited and drama disliked. Many of the educated Puritans, however—especially the ministers who had been influenced by the culture of the Renaissance—looked with favor upon literature and welcomed it to their remote backwoods settlements. Poetry and music were considered worthy handmaids of religion. Primarily the Puritans valued the poetry of the Psalms. They accordingly translated David's superb utterances into the crabbed rhyme and metrics of the *Bay Psalm Book,* printed in 1640.

Anne Bradstreet sees poetry as an art

It was a woman, Anne Bradstreet (c.1612-1672), who was first interested in writing poetry not for its usefulness but for its own sake. Before coming to America with her husband when she was eighteen, Anne Bradstreet had known the refinements of a comfortable English home. While spinning or matching pieces for quilts in New England, her thoughts often contrasted her youthful training with the bare life of the American wilderness. With a view of preserving something of her cultural inheritance for her eight children, she phrased clever epigrams from her religious meditations and composed poems in her leisure. Some caustic neighbors considered that she might do well to give her time to her housework rather than to versemaking. Although no critical housewife could charge Mrs. Bradstreet with the neglect of her duties, her relatives reported that she shortened her night's rest in order to write her lengthy poems. As a result of the restricted reading of the Puritan, Anne

Bradstreet used as her models minor writers rather than the great poets. She was a somewhat ambitious writer and composed verses about the seasons of the year, and about scientific and historical matters. Her important work, however, was a handful of brief lyrics, inspired by her faith, her love of her husband and her children. When she celebrates the simple joys of domestic life, she speaks naturally and with fervor. She is, however, unfortunately not able to sustain the lyric strength of her best lines.

Wigglesworth versifies Puritan theology

The author of the first "best seller" among American poets was Michael Wigglesworth (1631-1705), the minister of the Congregational Church at Maiden, Massachusetts. In *The Day of Doom* (1662) Wigglesworth pictured in swinging ballad measure the horrors of Judgment Day as represented by Puritan theology. Throughout two hundred and twenty-four stanzas the narrative vividly and realistically portrays the anger of the Deity and the torture of the damned. Wigglesworth's grotesque and tinkling rhymes betray a certain glee in forecasting the inevitable doom of mankind. Children who committed the poem to memory spelled out the words in fear and awe. Adults read it with a certain fascinated terror. The work has value today as an historical document which sounds the keynote of the morbid aspects of Puritan theology.

EDWARD TAYLOR

The most genuine poet of the thirteen colonies was unknown to the public during his life. Because he was too modest to publish his work and forbade his heirs to print his poetry, Edward Taylor's poems reposed in the Yale Library for nearly two centuries. They were first published in book form in 1939. Existing records give only the bare outlines of Taylor's life. Believing that liberty of conscience could not be enjoyed in his native England, he came to Boston as a youth in his early twenties. His ambition to become a minister took him to Harvard, where he found a roommate in genial Samuel Sewall. When the church members of Westfield, Massachusetts, petitioned Harvard for a minister in 1671, the college offered the post to Taylor. For fifty-eight years he labored as minister and physician in the frontier town.

At his death in 1729 Taylor left a four-hundred-page manuscript containing nearly three hundred poems. To the stanch qualities of a Puritan, he brought mystical exaltation and intense devotion to Christ. His poems were the love songs of his soul to God, in which he expresses his sense of unworthiness and his wistful yearning for spiritual joy. He wrote about common things and drew his metaphors from common objects. Gardening, spinning, sewing, baking, carpentry—all these tasks of the daily routine take on life and color, sound and fragrance through his imaginative treatment. By developing only one figure at a time, he achieved unity of effect and so escaped the weakness of some of his English contemporaries who strewed their poems with metaphors. Not entirely free from the faults of those he imitated, Taylor had the tendency to run to excess in elaborating his ideas.

Although Edward Taylor was a typical Puritan in his scrutiny of the heart and mind, he differs from the ordinary Puritan in his attitude towards the Eucharist. The Puritans believed that the Lord's Supper, as they called the Blessed Sacrament, held only the real spiritual presence but not the physical presence of Christ. In contrast to the rare mention of the Lord's Supper among Puritan writers, Taylor showed an overwhelming devotion to Christ in the Eucharist.

THE PURITAN THEOCRACY

In founding New England, the Puritans believed that they were directed by Providence to establish for the first time the ideal community of the kingdom of God among men. They believed that they were the chosen people of God and that He had established with them a covenant which prevented them from falling into error. People living under this covenant were the saints who had been called or elected to salvation. Only the elect had the right to vote. In this community the ministers who interpreted the word of God were more than mere pastors. Their learning and piety marked them as men to whom God's will was known to an extraordinary degree. God controlled the community, it was thought, through these special spokesmen. They were, consequently, empowered to act as leaders and guides in political as well as religious matters. The rule of God through the ministers was known as a *theocracy*. The strength of theocratic government lay in its ministers, who for a time were able to keep the settlements in their original fervor.

Mather Dynasty rules

Nowhere is the theocracy better illustrated than in the Mather Dynasty, a line of great preachers in the Mather family who for three generations dominated the thinking of Boston. Richard Mather (1596-1669), pastor at Dorchester, Massachusetts, issued a number of controversial works. It was his part in compiling *The Bay Psalm Book*, however, that has given him a place in literary history. In the person of his son, Increase Mather (1639-1723), the dynasty grew in might. Increase wrote more than one hundred fifty works, dealing with history, religion, politics, and science. Forced out of the presidency of Harvard in 1701, he reluctantly saw his power diminish. The new royal charter for Massachusetts in 1691 weakened the theocracy, since it made ownership of property rather than church membership a condition for voting. When Cotton Mather (1663-1728), the son of Increase, succeeded his father as pastor of the old North Church in Boston, he bolstered with unmatched energy and zeal the declining cause of Puritanism. Although his personality was marred by vanity and smugness, he succeeded in molding the thought of his parishioners. Perhaps the sign over his study which warned visitors "Be short" accounts for his gigantic literary production of more than four hundred and fifty writings. To show the greatness of the original theocracy to a generation whose faith was dwindling, Cotton Mather wrote *Magnalia Christi Americana* (1702), a history of the Puritan church in America. Cluttered with allusions and quotations, the book moves ponderously. While sincere in his attempt to be accurate, Mather was too passionately devoted to Puritanism to treat it objectively. By sheer force of leadership he upheld the theocracy at a time that its very foundations were being shaken.

The last of the dynasty, Samuel Mather (1706-1785) shines as a lesser light in comparison with his ancestors. Although carrying on the traditions of the family in his ministry and his authorship, he had none of the intellectual power or influence of his forebears.

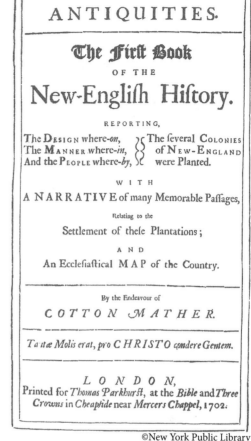

©New York Public Library
Title Page of the Only Surviving Work of Cotton Mather — Widely Used as a Source Book

THE DECLINE OF PURITANISM

The great natural resources of the new country and the Puritans' own thrifty habits brought material success to the New Englanders. They regarded their increased prosperity as a sign of God's favor. As the sterner aspects of Puritanism faded, cleverness in economic matters increased. This eagerness to obtain wealth was in harmony with the general mood of the eighteenth century, which was distinguished for its practicality and worldly wisdom.

What the successful Puritan businessman thought, felt, said, and did is nowhere better told than in the diary of Samuel Sewall. Massachusetts was little more than forty years old when, as a boy of nine, Sewall came to Boston with his parents. By the time he reached manhood and had received two degrees from Harvard, the colony had grown so prosperous that he gave up the idea of entering the ministry and became a merchant. Of all the judges in the Salem witchcraft trials, he was the only one who confessed publicly that he had condemned innocent persons to death. Five years after the trials he stood in the old South Church while a clergyman read his public confession of guilt and error. Though he was austere in the practice of the Puritan religion, he enjoyed throughout his long life the comforts and good cheer which his wealth and position afforded.

Sewall exemplifies turn to worldly interests

In interest and historical value the *Diary of Samuel Sewall* ranks with the well-known works of the English diarists, John Evelyn and Samuel Pepys. Over a period of fifty-five years Sewall was faithful in writing down the happenings of his everyday life, no matter how insignificant or embarrassing they might be. His diary quite unconsciously reveals the ebbing strength of the old Puritan tradition. The shrewd merchant manifests none of the driving religious force of the days of John Winthrop and Roger Williams. Instead, his Puritanism is clearly tempered by worldly interests. His *Diary* shows him bustling about town on some errand of mercy or fraternal correction or hurrying to keep an official appointment. At the same time that he exhibits

© Massachusetts Historical Society

Page from the Diary *of Samuel Sewall*

sincere solicitude for his spiritual welfare and that of his children, he reveals a practical concern about daily happenings, prominent people, and financial success. In describing the weddings and funerals he attended, he gives interesting sidelights on the dress of the company and the food and drinks provided for the guests. In short, Sewall's *Diary* is the honest revelation of a devout Puritan who was gradually turning to a more secular view of life.

Rustic life amuses Madam Knight

The first writer to smile condescendingly at the primitive condition of the American backwoods was Sarah Kemble Knight (1666-1727). A resident of Boston, Massachusetts, Madam Knight during the winter of 1704-1705 undertook a business trip, unaccompanied, from her home to New York. Setting out on horseback, she followed much the same shore line route along which trains now daily rush. Her diary, which has been published as *Private Journal of a Journey from Boston to New York*, gives revealing comments on the life of the frontier and the crude mode of colonial travel.

Colonists insist on free press

The publication of the *Boston News-Letter* in 1704 marks the beginning of the American newspaper. Issued at first as a handwritten newssheet, it was the forerunner of ten other newspapers that sprang up in the colonies before the Revolution. More significant than the appearance of these newspapers, however, was the precedent established for freedom of the press in the trial of a New York journalist, John Peter Zenger. Arrested and brought to court in 1735 for having printed criticism of the governor of New York, Zenger was defended by an able Philadelphia lawer, Andrew Hamilton, who successfully pleaded the case in favor of freedom of the press.

JONATHAN EDWARDS

The last great Puritan, Jonathan Edwards (1703-1758), possessed a brilliant philosophic mind. Equipped with great intellectual powers he was able for a time to retard New England's drift away from Puritanism by his controversial writings.

Edwards combined intellectual discipline and religious fervor with originality and depth of thought. From the age of seven or eight Jonathan held prayer meetings for his playmates, in which he acted as leader of the services. At ten he wrote a tract refuting a companion's statement that the soul is material. Two years later he composed his well-known essay on the habits of the spider. In it the twelve-year-old writer not only presented the fruits of long hours of philosophic speculation in the fields but also revealed logical habits of thought and scientific methods of observation. Before thirteen, Jonathan was studying at Yale, and by the time he was nineteen he was a minister—the colleague of his grandfather at the Congregational church at Northampton, Massachusetts. Assuming the pastorate at the death of his grandfather, Edwards set aside the more liberal policies of his predecessor and insisted that full membership in the church be allowed only to the elect.

Despite a frail constitution Jonathan Edwards adhered to a program of seventy resolutions, which included rising at four and spending thirteen hours in study and writing. Edwards was among the few Puritans who stressed the teaching that the beauty of nature urges man to love the Creator. When, however, Edwards' parishioners began to favor the doctrine of free will, he considered them heretical. Hastening to defend the original Calvinistic view of his forefathers, he returned to the methods of teaching love of God through the fear of damnation. His preaching about Judgment Day was so vivid that his listeners expected the awful scene to be unfolded before them even while he was delivering the sermon. Edwards discarded his ministerial rigidity in his home life, and to his wife and eleven children he showed a kind and loving nature.

Great Awakening precedes decline

The doctrines and sermons of Edwards, together with the emotional preaching of the traveling English evangelist, George Whitefield, occasioned a religious movement known as the Great Awakening. For more than a decade (c.1740-1750) the Great Awakening produced a religious hysteria that spread from Maine to Georgia. Other evangelists adopted the methods of Edwards and Whitefield. The number of fits, faintings, and outcries during a sermon became the measure of a preacher's success. The audience looked upon the manifestation of violent emotion as a sign of the bestowal of God's grace. More than a few frightened listeners, despairing of salvation, committed suicide.

The Great Awakening was Puritanism's last stand. Although it temporarily revived Calvinistic teachings, it ended in a decline from which Puritanism never recovered. Resentful of Jonathan Edwards' extreme measures, a rebellious group of his parishioners secured his dismissal in 1750. Practically an exile, he went to Stockbridge, Massachusetts, as a missionary to the Housatonic River Indians. In the quiet of his new surroundings Edwards continued to write and study. In 1758 he was called to the presidency of New Jersey College (now Princeton University), but the honor came too late. Within three months after assuming his new office, he died the victim of smallpox.

Last great Puritan is mystic

In a number of his youthful writings and in a fragment of prose entitled "Nature," Edwards exhibits a sensitive love of beauty. In such sermons as *Sinners in the Hands of an Angry God* (1741), however, he bends his mastery of human emotion to the immediate purpose of conversion through fear. His most profound work, a treatise on *The Freedom of the Will* (1754), leads to the conclusion that man's nature is wholly depraved but that by God's grace some are saved. In his lifelong service to the dogmas of Puritanism, Jonathan Edwards sacrificed a great literary career. A poet and a mystic at heart, he suppressed his literary inclinations and lent his calm, relentless logic and his powerful imagination to theological arguments.

CULTURAL BEGINNINGS IN PHILADELPHIA

Just as Father White had reported the news of religious freedom to encourage English Catholics to come to Maryland, so William Penn (1644-1718) wrote to attract colonists to his Quaker settlement. The Quakers were a religious group which had carried to the farthest degree the Protestant doctrine of private interpretation of scriptures. They believed that Christ gave an inner light directly to their souls, and they rejected churches, creeds, the sacraments, and religious rites. Opposed first by the Established Church in England and later by the Massachusetts Puritans, the Quakers settled in Pennsylvania in 1682. In the first years of the colony Penn issued simple treatises which stated his insistence on democratic government, religious freedom, and just treatment of the Indians.

During the colonial period were laid the foundations for the literary and cultural leadership which Philadelphia was to assume during the eighteenth and early nineteenth centuries. The magazine literature of the United States saw its beginning in the city of brotherly love with the publication of the *American Magazine* in 1741. The Quakers, like the Puritans, regarded playgoing with abhorrence. As conditions grew more settled, however, some stirrings of dramatic interest were made throughout the colonies. Theaters were built in Charleston, Williamsburg, Boston, New York, and Philadelphia—where the Walnut Street Theatre has good claim to be regarded as the oldest surviving playhouse in the country. In 1759 a Philadelphia poet, Thomas Godfrey (1736-1763), wrote a blank verse tragedy entitled *The Prince of Parthia*, which was the first American drama to be presented on the professional stage.

LATER DEVELOPMENTS IN VIRGINIA

During the years when pioneers were pouring into Puritan, Catholic, and Quaker colonies, culture in the first Virginia settlements was advancing. In the century since John Smith and his men faced the cruel and dangerous wilderness, the colonists had developed their resources and raised their standard of living. They now aspired to the refinements of the English country gentleman. Particularly in the older settlements along the coast line, stately homes had been built to replace the first crude shelters. Servants, slaves, abundant food, and gracious manners made possible a hospitality that grew to be a tradition. This landed aristocracy did not, however, live in the idleness and ease that fiction writers have sometimes pictured. They worked unceasingly to make their land productive and their surroundings beautiful and even elegant. Often they were forced to take over the tasks of dishonest overseers or incompetent servants.

Byrd's writings reveal Virginia aristocrat

William Byrd (1674-1744), an ancestor of Admiral Richard E. Byrd, represents the aristocratic life of the Virginia landowners of his day. An education in the best English schools developed in Byrd an interest in literature, science, and law. It gave him also a gallant manner that made him an asset both in the drawing room and places of assembly. During his years on the continent he lived in distinguished society and acquired a cosmopolitan attitude towards life. He returned to America a broad-minded young aristocrat, interested in the pursuit of learning and in the improvement of the colony. His position as an intelligent young man of the ruling class led him to serve the state in numerous public offices. In the direction of the great family estate at Westover, Virginia, he found a stimulus to his ingenuity. Here he accumulated a library of four thousand volumes (perhaps the finest private collection in the colonies) and imported contemporary English books and periodicals. He improved the family mansion at Westover until it was one of the most handsome showplaces of the time; he increased his landholdings from several thousand to one hundred seventy-nine thousand acres and had the city of Richmond laid out on property belonging to him.

As an enjoyable means of expression and of entertaining his family and friends, William Byrd composed a number of journals and histories which reveal his rare wit, keen powers of observation, and zest for life. After directing a party which surveyed the disputed Virginia-North Carolina boundary line in 1728, Byrd wrote his *History of the Dividing Line*.

LATER DEVELOPMENTS IN MARYLAND

While Maryland colonists, with their Virginia neighbors, had made material and social progress, the Catholic leaders had not been able to continue their original policy. Unlike the Puritans, the original Maryland pioneers had not made church membership a requirement for citizenship. Anglicans and Puritans rapidly pushed into the hospitable territory and eventually usurped leadership. Catholic influence soon suffered a sharp decline. Clever insinuations led William III to suspect the loyalty of his Catholic subjects in Maryland. In 1691 the king revoked the original charter. The land was taken over by the English crown, and the Anglican Church became the established religion. Catholics were now outlaws in their own haven. From this date until the Revolution, laws against Catholics in America began to thicken the statute books. Catholics lost their civil rights. At one time or another, their priests were forbidden to exercise their sacred faculties; parents were prohibited from securing Catholic education for their

Westover, the Ancestral Home of the Byrd Family

children, either in the colonies or abroad; Catholic teachers were subject to imprisonment; Catholics were doubly taxed. Nowhere in the colonies was a Catholic permitted to hold public office, since he would have been forced to subscribe to the English Test Oath, an act which was equivalent to a denial of his Faith.

The severity with which these laws were enforced depended upon the prejudice of the local governing group. To have professed the Catholic religion in New England or in the southern colonies would have been considered treason; a priest entering these British provinces endangered his life. In Maryland the old Catholic families were frequently rich and influential enough to cause the neighboring Protestants to wink at their practice of religion. The new immigrants, the poor, the wage earner, and the indentured servant bore the brunt of displeasure. Gradually the law forbidding Catholic worship was modified to allow Mass in private homes in Maryland. Religious activity centered around a few colonial manors to which were annexed chapels, known as *mass houses*. In William Penn's colony alone was public worship by Catholics permitted. The few priests in the colonies resided in Maryland and in

Pennsylvania, and from these points went to administer the sacraments secretly to Catholics in Delaware, New Jersey, New York, and Virginia.

Priest leads Catholic poets

It was one of these priestly journeys in 1750 that was the occasion of probably the first poem by an English Catholic in America. The missionary route of Reverend John Lewis, S.J. (1721-1788) took him over a large section of Maryland. Having come from Europe a year before, where he had studied at the college of the English Jesuits at St. Omer in French Flanders, the young priest took up residence at Bohemia, Maryland. Here the Jesuits conducted Bohemia Manor, the celebrated preparatory school of colonial times, which unlike most Catholic schools was not moved from place to place or discontinued entirely. From this center Father Lewis visited Annapolis, White Marsh, Elkridge, Christine, St. Inigoes, and Newtown. A trip from Patapsco is made memorable by his poem entitled *The Rev. Father Lewis— His Journey from Patapsco to Annapolis, April 4, 1750*. In the pioneer stretches of Maryland, where a dozen priests cared for some sixteen thousand Catholics, the priest's reflections during his journey might well have been troubled. But they were not. Like Chaucer Father Lewis rode horseback on top of an April world, and his lines record the freshness of earth and sky. His verse form is the heroic couplet of the classical school of Dryden and Pope. His description, however, has the calmness and repose with which his English contemporaries, the early romantic poets, were depicting rural scenes. Details in the poem reveal its American setting.

His power to suggest an image and the fluency of his verse indicate that if Father Lewis had been given the leisure to write, he could have won a place among the poets of his day. This poem, however, obviously produced for his own amusement, is the only surviving example of Father Lewis' poetic power. Manuscripts of his sermons which have been preserved give evidence of his kindness and persuasive zeal. Father Lewis did eventually assume the care of the sixteen thousand Catholics in Maryland— as well as the seven thousand in Pennsylvania—when in 1768 he became superior of the Jesuit missions in the two colonies. Remaining in that office until the suppression of the Jesuit Society in 1773, he discharged his duties so zealously that during the Revolution he was named Vicar-General of all the American missions.

Penal laws prohibit Catholic literature

The penal laws made the development of Catholic literature impossible in the English colonies. The printing of Catholic books was prohibited. Many who could not afford to import books from Europe made handwritten copies of the missal and portions of the Bible. Parents not rich enough to defy the law were forced to send their children to Protestant teachers or have them grow up with little schooling. Catholics were tolerated in Protestant communities only because their labor was needed. Whenever Catholics gained the slightest influence, their Protestant neighbors immediately became alarmed. They showed their displeasure by enforcing the penal laws more strictly or by threatening to do so. Under these circumstances there could be no Catholic reading public. Despite the dark years of persecution, the contribution of Maryland Catholics is noteworthy. In promoting the policy of religious toleration and refusing to establish a state religion, the original colonists had established a precedent which was later continued by the national government.

LITERATURE OF FRENCH EXPLORATION

While English colonization was implanting civilization along the Atlantic seaboard, the early Spanish settlements in the South continued to develop. During these same years of the seventeenth century the French were entering the territory of the United States through their gateway in the North and were laying the foundations of a Catholic culture in the northern states and down the Mississippi Valley. The writings of Champlain show that the founder of Quebec also knew our eastern shores and upper New York state. The Frenchmen proved to be the supreme river-farers of the New World. Their theory of exploration held that the finding of a river gave the discoverers a right to all the territory drained by its tributaries. In view of this belief Frenchmen claimed for their sovereign the vast lands between Quebec and New Orleans. Throughout the Great Lakes region and down the Mississippi, they built a chain of crude military posts. Beside these fortifications the French priests erected the missions. It was chiefly through the writings of French explorers and missionaries, then, that the world first came to know this interior region of the future United States.

Jesuit Relations *depict interior America*

The largest published body of this material is the *Jesuit Relations*, a series of accounts covering the labors of the Jesuits in New France from 1611 to 1716. Since New France during this period comprised one extensive colony, the *Relations* record events which took place in the Canadian provinces, as well as in the present territory of the United States. Much of the material for these books was gathered from the journals which each Jesuit yearly submitted to his superior in Montreal or Quebec. From the journals, letters, records of exploration, and from oral accounts of visiting Jesuits, the superior annually composed a narrative covering the most important events of the year. In assembling the material to be sent to the Jesuit Provincial in France and published there, the Canadian superior sometimes followed the exact words of the original writer but more often combined and summarized accounts.

The *Jesuit Relations* present history written at the very time of its happening—history which had as its authors adventurous men trained in letters, science, and psychology. The missionary, writing in a squalid camp amid the distractions of savage war whoops or the noisy strife of fur traders, recorded the folklore, mythology, and details of Indian life that have served the modern scholar in his study of Indian races. The narratives picture life in the forest: the long canoe journeys on hunting and fishing expeditions, the baptism of dying infants —even when the child's death would be attributed superstitiously to the Blackrobe—the ferocious jealousy of medicine men, which ended in outbursts of cruelty under the guise of religious ceremony. The style of these narratives is simple and direct, with but casual mention of the trials that made the missionary's life a continued martyrdom.

EARLY DESCRIPTIONS OF THE MISSISSIPPI

A mighty river shrouded with mystery and romance is the source of a vivid body of colonial literature written first in the language of the French explorers and centuries later translated into English. The Spanish had called these waters the River of the Holy Spirit; they had buried De Soto in its depths. To the Indians of the North it was the Mitchi Sipi (Great Water). White men spoke of the riches to which this waterway might lead if, by cutting a path westward across the continent, it provided an outlet to the Orient. But more than a hundred years passed after De Soto had crossed the great river before French explorers in 1673 determined the point at which the Mississippi empties.

The *Jesuit Relations* preserve a narrative of disputed authorship which describes the expedition in 1673 of Louis Joliet[1] (1645-1700) and Père Jacques Marquette (1637-1675). By following the Mississippi until they reached the Arkansas River, the explorer and priest proved that the Great Water is a highway dividing our country in two. They established the fact that the Mississippi empties into the Gulf of Mexico and does not flow westward into the Pacific. The *Relation* of the expedition is an interesting narrative, at times stirring and beautiful. The chronicle shows Joliet and Marquette passing the site of cities that were yet to be and observing,

along the Mississippi, landmarks which remain today. It suggests likewise the joy and peace that entered the Indian cabins where Père Marquette paused to teach the Word of God.

The great enterprise begun by Joliet and Père Marquette was further advanced by the prince of explorers, Robert Cavelier, sieur de La Salle (1643-1687). With the daring plan of securing the whole Mississippi Valley for France, La Salle in 1682 sailed to the mouth of the Mississippi, where he took possession of all the territory drained by its waters. With this magnificent feat he claimed for France a realm greater than all France itself.

La Salle's explorations yield material for histories

Eyewitnesses of the three great expeditions made by La Salle have left accounts in which they describe the waterway between Quebec and New Orleans in its primitive condition; these historians show us La Salle and his men building their crude forts along the Illinois and St. Joseph Rivers, or crossing the trackless forests of Illinois, Indiana, Ohio, and Pennsylvania. The pages of these journals and histories record the martyrdom of the aged Franciscan priest, Gabriel de la Ribourde, who, when he retired to pray in the Illinois country,[2] was attacked by Indians; they tell of the disorder, ill will, and mutiny which pursued La Salle on his final expedition until his death by treachery.

Among the companions and historians of La Salle, Louis Hennepin (1640?-1701?), a priest who took part only in the first voyage, is most widely known. After his return to France in 1681, Père Hennepin wrote an account of La Salle's first attempt to reach the Mississippi, entitled *Description of Louisiana* (1683). The book also records the priest's independent explorations, on one of which he discovered the Falls of St. Anthony in Minnesota. Hennepin's later works in which he falsely claims for himself discoveries made by La Salle, have discredited his reputation as a historian.

Illinois language cast in written form

Records left by the early missionaries of New France show that the French priests, like their Spanish co-workers, saw the possibilities of using the written word as

---

[1] The explorer usually spelled his name Jolliet.

[2] The present states of Ohio, Wisconsin, and parts of Minnesota, Michigan and Illinois.

Missionaries were aflame with one great aim:
to preach the Gospel and convert souls to Christ.

a means of converting the Indians. Jacques Gravier, S.J., who came to the Jesuit mission in the Illinois country in 1689, mastered the language of the tribe and compiled a grammar in the Illinois tongue. A fellow Jesuit, Jean de Boullanger, during his stay in New France between 1703 and 1729, composed a grammar, a dictionary, and a catechism in the same language.

The vast forests which once stretched across the states of Wisconsin, Michigan, Iowa, Illinois, and Minnesota were first described by Frenchmen. Pierre Esprit Radisson (1620?-1710) and a companion were apparently the first white men in Minnesota and the first explorers of northern Wisconsin and Lake Superior. Falling into disfavor with the French, Radisson composed an account of his travels in English in the hope of establishing trade relations with Englishmen. His *Voyages*, with its clumsy sentences and amusing errors, has been classed as a literary curiosity. It nevertheless contains valuable information on the American wilderness. Nicolas Perrot (1644-1718), who lived among or visited the tribes inhabiting Michigan, Wisconsin, Illinois, Iowa, and Minnesota, wrote three books, only one of which remains today. This work, the *Memoir on the Manners, Customs, and Religion of the North American Indians*,

gives an excellent treatment of native customs in regard to hunting, marriages, funerals, games, and religious beliefs among the tribes of the northern states.

Lahonton praises savage state

A colorful work on the American scene that may be praised for its literary merits as well as for its historical value came from the pen of a dashing young French marine, Louis-Armand, the Baron of Lahonton (1666-1716). While serving France on military expeditions along the upper Great Lakes, the Miami River, Mackinac, and the neighboring regions, the Baron learned much of life in the wigwam and of the Indian character. A decided cynic with a passion for justice, Lahonton had long brooded over the ills of civilization. He finally came to believe that he had found a solution for social evils in the simplicity of the savage state. As a result he made his *Voyages to North America* (1703) a biting satire on European civilization, wherein he proposed the American wilderness as a state free from the restrictions of hampering laws and offered Indian life as the ideal of development according to nature. Besides this idealistic but obviously false interpretation of the North American Indian, the Baron furnished his readers with an eloquent picture of the frontier, which shows his classical background, caustic wit, and narrative ability. Although admitting the good accomplished by religion and crediting the Jesuit missionaries for their zeal, Lahonton scoffed at religion in general and anticipated the freethinking of French philosophers of the eighteenth century. For some years his entire work was discredited because of his false claim to the discovery of a river in the far West.

LATER SPANISH MISSIONS AND OTHER CULTURAL BEGINNINGS

As the French rapidly expanded their claims and settlements in the interior, Englishmen began to fear that the British might be confined to a narrow strip along the Atlantic coast. Between 1680 and 1763, Spain, France, and England clashed in a series of intercolonial wars. As a result, France lost to England almost all her North American possessions;

Spain received New Orleans and the lands west of the Mississippi, and gave up Florida to England. Five years after the Frenchmen in America became British subjects, the Spaniards entered the present state of California from the south, and Franciscan missionaries a year later opened the first of the famous chain of Spanish missions in California.

Serra's Diary *records expedition*

The pioneer of this great missionary project which brought Spanish culture to the far West was the priest, Junípero Serra (1713-1784). At sixteen Serra had entered the Franciscan Order. Although he longed to work among pagan peoples, his brilliant intellect led to his appointment at Lullian University. There, after some years teaching, he and his friend, Francisco Palou, received permission to go to the New World missions. After his arrival in America, Fray Junípero Serra labored nearly twenty years in Mexico before he began his great life work in the United States. When an expedition headed into California in 1769, Fray Junípero was invited to lead the Franciscans and to be president of the mission which would be established in the new territory. Serra's *Diary*, which records the expedition, shows how eagerly he met the Indians in the upper country and won them to Christianity. During the fifteen years that followed, nine missions dotted the coast line to mark the scenes of his labors. He converted some six thousand Indians to the Faith, taught the Indian women how to sew gaily-colored clothes for their children, and showed the men how to till the land. The missions which he founded became centers where the natives learned reading and writing in Spanish and in native dialects. They likewise learned shoemaking, carpentry, dyeing, weaving, adobe-making, painting, singing, and music. The beloved Franciscan, who had made the phrase *Love God* the familiar greeting of the land, died in 1784 at the mission of Carmel which he had founded.

Palou relates California history

Paraphrasing the words of an earlier Franciscan, Fray Francisco Palou wrote in his biography of Serra: "If this sacred Province had known how to grow a whole grove of such juniper trees, not a single heathen would now remain in all that wild realm of paganism." Palou, who was himself a giant in his missionary labors, became known to posterity as an historian. Within the walls of San Francisco de Asis, which he founded, and at Mission Carmel and Mission Dolores, he composed his historical accounts. Conscious that the missionaries were making history among barbarians, he wished to leave a record of these early cultural beginnings in California. Scholars have long made use of his material as a valuable source of early information on the state.

In his *Life of Father Junípero Serra* (1787), Palou not only tells much of what is known about the venerable priest but also relates the Spanish occupation of California. He based his biography upon his other great chronicle of the Franciscan enterprise, entitled in a four-volume English translation, *Historical Memoirs of California*. The *Memoirs*, the first general history covering the founding of California, are vibrant with human interest. In addition to his writing, Fray Francisco Palou supervised the building and development of the San Francisco Mission. Upon Serra's death he succeeded to the presidency of the California missions. In 1785 Palou's work ended in California, for his superiors recalled him to Mexico to become guardian of the missionary college of San Fernando.

Other Europeans write in America

Spaniards, Englishmen, and Frenchmen were not the only writers through whom Europeans saw the vast new lands across the Atlantic. As immigrants from other countries poured into the New World, they sent reports to the homeland that voiced brave hopes for the America of the future. Among these reports are accounts of the Dutch who settled in New York, of the Swedes who established a colony in Delaware, and of the Germans who founded Germantown, Pennsylvania. Interest in books and reading material was so strong in German settlements in Pennsylvania that it led to the publication of German books and newspapers during the colonial period.

America for Christendom

(From a letter to Gabriel Sanchez)
Christopher Columbus
Translated by Donald B. Clark

Christopher Columbus was not only the famed discoverer of America; he was also the first writer to publish an account of his findings in the Western Hemisphere. The following excerpt from a letter of the admiral reveals something of the exaltation of a man who could take possession of a new world in the name of Christ. It shows also his prophetic vision that this continent was to be a land of destiny.

Now that the undertaking with regard to the new provinces has proved successful, I know you will be pleased. Let me set down for you what was done and what discovered in this journey of ours. It was thirty-three days after leaving Cadiz[1] that we reached the Indian Seas. There I found a number of islands, thickly populated, and took possession of them for our Most Illustrious King, meeting with no opposition and advancing to the occupation with proclamations and banners flying. To the first one we touched—which the Indians called Guanahani—I gave the name of the Holy Saviour, for it was by His aid that we came to this and to the others afterward. All of them I renamed; one I called Saint Mary of the Conception; one, Fernandina; another, Ysabella; still another, Juana;[2] and so on.

Arriving at the last mentioned of these, I sailed a short way toward the west along the coast. But I found no end, so great was its length, and I thought it must not be an island but the continent and country of Cathay[3] itself. As far as I could see, there were neither cities nor towns along the shore line, only a few villages and farms. I did not succeed in speaking with the inhabitants, for they no sooner laid eyes on us than they ran away. I sailed on, thinking that I would find some metropolis or large estate.

Finally I decided not to await results in that direction; nothing new was presenting itself, and the route was taking us northward, just the thing I was seeking to avoid. My intention was to go south, for it was winter on land, and the winds rose against us. I returned to a harbor I had kept in mind and dispatched two of our men inland to ascertain whether there was a king in that country and to look for cities. They proceeded for three days and found innumerable peoples and habitations. But these were small and without organized government. So they returned.

In the meanwhile I gathered from some Indians I had seized that the country was in fact an island. Then hugging the shore, I sailed east for three hundred and twenty-two miles to the extreme end of the land. From there I saw another island, still further to the east, fifty-four miles from Juana, and immediately named it Hispania.[4] Crossing to it, I continued, as at Juana, along the northern side towards the east for five hundred and sixty-four miles. . . .

When I sent two or three of my men to some of the villages to talk with the inhabitants, it often happened that the Indians would advance in a compact mass, only to flee helter-skelter, father pushing son and son treading on father, when they saw our men coming close. And this was not because any one of them had been injured or harmed; for to all of those I approached and with whom I was able to converse, I gave what I had, cloth and many other things, though they made no return. It is their very nature to be fearsome and timid. On the other hand when they understand they are safe, they lose all fear and are simple-hearted, confiding, and most liberal with all they possess. What they have they do not refuse to those that ask. They even encouraged us to demand of them. With deep love they prefer others to themselves; they give much for little and bear with small or no return. I myself prohibited my men from trading them odds and ends of little or negligible value, such as shards[5] of small dishes and plates, or bits of glass, and nails and shoe latchets. The Indians, however, seemed to think they possessed the most exquisite jewels in the world if they were able to get hold of these trifles.

---

[1] *Cadiz.* The Latin translator of the letter evidently confused Cadiz with Palos, the place from which Columbus sailed.

[2] *Juana,* Cuba. The identity of the other islands is uncertain.

[3] *Cathay,* China.

[4] *Hispania,* Haiti.

[5] *shards,* fragments.

One of the sailors got as much gold for a shoe latchet as there is in three *castellanos*,[6] and much else for other things of little price, particularly for new silver *blancas*.[7] For some gold coins they would give whatever the seller wanted: one and a half or two ounces of gold, or thirty or forty pounds of cotton, which they already knew. Even pieces of bows, jars, pitchers, bottles, they would buy with cotton and gold, as if they knew no better than animals. I stopped this because it was an unjust proceeding. I made many beautiful and acceptable presents, taking no return for these; for I wanted to conciliate the natives, to make them worshipers of Christ and fill them with love for our King, our Queen, and all the people of Spain. I also wished them to take real interest in gathering and giving to us those things in which they are affluent and which we greatly lack.

They nourish no form of idolatry but believe profoundly that all strength and power, all good things are in heaven and that I, my ships, and my sailors, had descended thence. After they had once lost their fear, I was everywhere received with this attitude. And they are neither sluggish nor barbarous but have a fine and perspicacious[8] intelligence. Those who navigate that sea give no mean account of their trips. But they have never seen clothing on human beings, nor ships such as ours. As soon as I reached these regions, I forcibly seized some Indians from the first island, so they could learn from us and also give us information about what they knew of these parts. Everything went according to our wishes; it was not long before we understood each other, first by gesture and sign, then by words; and this was of great advantage to us. These men are returning with me, still believing I have descended from heaven, though they have been with us a long time and are with us now. They were the first to proclaim this wherever we landed, repeating to the others in loud voices, "Come, come, and you shall see the men from heaven." So women and men, children and adults, youths and graybeards forgot the fear they had felt such a short time before and pressed to see us; a great crowd filled the road, some bringing food, some drink, but all affected by the greatest love and an almost unbelievable goodwill. All of these islands have many skiffs of solid wood. Though narrow and more swift, they are like our rowing galleys in length and shape and are propelled only by oars. Some of them are large, some small, and some of medium size. Many of the larger boats are rowed from eighteen cross banks.[9] These they use in navigating from one to another of the innumerable islands; they are the vehicles of their trade and commerce. I saw some of these skiffs or rowing galleys that had seventy or eighty oars men. In all the islands there is among the inhabitants no difference of appearance, custom, or language; they all understand each other. This is extremely favorable to what is, I believe, the urgent wish of our Serene Majesties, the conversion of these people to the holy Christian faith, to which, as far as I could observe, they are accessible and inclined. . . .

Truly, all this is deeply remarkable; but it surpasses our merit; it is due to the holy Christian faith and the religious piety of our rulers. What the human intellect itself could not achieve, that was granted to the human by the divine. For God hears His servants, even in impossible things, when they cherish His commands. And this is the case with us, for we have attained what no mortal strength has hitherto sufficed for. If anyone has written or spoken of these islands, it was in vagueness and conjecture; none claimed to have seen them; so they seemed almost mythical. Therefore let the King and the Queen, the rulers, and their fortunate territories, and all the other countries of Christendom give thanks to Jesus Christ, our Saviour and Lord, Who has graced us with such a victory and such possessions. Let processions be celebrated and the sacred solemnities be gone through. Let the holy sanctuaries be hung with garlands for the festival, that Christ may exult on earth as He exults in heaven when He foresees that the souls of so many peoples, lost hitherto, will be saved. And let us, too, be elated, for the exaltation of our Faith and for the augmentation of things temporal, of which not only Spain but all Christendom will be the future partaker. This brief account I send to you of what has happened. Farewell.

CHRISTOPHER COLUMBUS
Admiral of the Ocean Fleet
March 14, 1493

---

[6] *castellanos*, old Spanish coins bearing the Castilian arms.

[7] *blancas*, coins, originally of silver.

[8] *perspicacious* (pûr-spĭ-kā´shus), clear-sighted.

[9] *cross banks*, benches for the rowers.

VIEWING THE AUTHOR'S IDEAS

1. What principle of justice does Columbus state concerning the treatment of the Indian?

2. How did Columbus strive to win the Indians to Christianity?

3. To what earlier explorers and writers does Columbus allude?

4. Why did Columbus suggest giving thanks to God?

EVALUATING HIS MANNER OF EXPRESSION

What points of orderly arrangement indicate that the narrative was carefully constructed? Give instances of concise description.

How Polca Arrived in Search of Her Husband

(From *History of New Mexico)*
Gaspar Pérez de Villagrá
Translated by Gilberto Espinosa

In his expedition to New Mexico Juan de Oñate appointed a company under Villagrá to find a passage to the Rio Grande. During an attack on a band of Indians, the Spanish explorers seized several natives as prisoners. They later released all of these except Milco and Mompil, whom they retained as guides in their search for the river. In the selection from Villagrá's History of New Mexico *Spanish chivalry bows admiringly before the natural grace and loveliness of an Indian woman. Polca's love for her husband, Milco, serves as her passport in and out of the conqueror's tent. Her fidelity to Milco and her deep grief at his desertion so stirs the Spanish writer that he pauses at the beginning of this canto to comment upon love as the great motivating force in human activity. Villagrá paints in warm colors the figure of a lovely Indian madonna against the background of the New Mexican mesas.*

THERE was never a worthy or noble deed wrought which did not owe its success to love. Love is the principal force that guides and shapes our destinies. Without love there can be no peace or pleasure in this life. Where there is love, there we will find joy and happiness. With love all difficulties are surmounted and overcome. It is the crucible[1] in which all the finer qualities of man are brought out.

The truth of the above is shown by an incident which is worthy of being related here. I was in conversation with Mompil, inquiring about the details of the map he had drawn, when we saw a comely Indian woman approaching in the distance. Now she would walk; now she would run. It was very evident from her actions that she was in great distress. In her arms she carried a beautiful babe who nursed at his mother's breast, happy in his innocent way and unaware of the troubles of his afflicted mother. From her shoulders hung a bag in which she carried two hares and a rabbit.

The sergeant, noting her noble appearance and the grace with which she bore herself, ordered that she be allowed to enter the camp unmolested, for she was a woman whose beauty and grace merited every consideration and respect. Beauty, although it is but a temporary gift which soon fades away and disappears like the flowers, nevertheless, because of its very nature merits honor and respect.

She entered the camp greatly agitated, as we later learned, by the flame of love and devotion which filled her breast. Like a faithful hound which has become lost and which finally meets the hunter, crouches before him, wagging its tail and licking his hands, trying to show its devotion and its pleasure at being with him again, so this woman approached Milco and embraced him long and tenderly. Then noting that he and Mompil were seated on the ground, she quickly gathered an armful of weeds and made a cushion for each of them. She then took a cloth from her bag and wiped their brows.

The savage then turned toward us and smilingly attempted to hide her grief and terror and told us that Milco was her husband and the father of the babe at her

---

[1] *crucible*, a vessel used for melting metals and other chemical substances; hence any severe test or trial.

breast. She offered to remain with us as our slave if we would but free her husband, begging us that for the sake of the tender infant we do him no harm. Her sincere and pitiful pleadings proved the deep and tender love she bore her husband. Her looks as much as said, "Take me, body and soul, and do with me what you will; inflict upon me any punishment that you choose, but let my husband go free."

Like another Triaria, wife of Vitellius,[2] who, putting aside her female attire, armed herself and went forth to battle by her husband's side and sought the place of danger that her husband might not be harmed, this savage offered herself that her husband might go safe. In her sad countenance we read the willingness to undergo a hundred thousand deaths if only her husband might remain unharmed.

No noble heart could withstand such an appeal. The noble sergeant assured her with kind words that no harm was to be done her husband and that he would be freed. At these words Polca laughed with joy and thanked the sergeant again and again.

Polca then set about preparing a meal for the two savages. After they had satisfied their wants, she and Milco talked together for a long time. She then told us that they had agreed that she was to remain in his stead while Milco went for two companions. We agreed and he departed, leaving his precious jewel with us.

Milco, like a wild horse which, having been confined in a stall, for the first time breaks the walls of his prison and rushes off, left at topmost speed and did not pause until he had reached the summit of a hill some distance away: Here he turned and shouted to Polca and Mompil, argued with them awhile, and then turned and disappeared.

Polca turned to us, sobbing as though her heart would break and informed us that her husband had shamefully abandoned her, for he had said that he was not going to come back. This conduct was as base as that of the cruel Theseus who abandoned the noble Ariadne[3] to the cruel and savage monster from which she herself had saved him.

Such is the lack of appreciation and ungratefulness of a brutal heart. The more benefits he receives, the more ingratitude he returns. How few there are who really know how to appreciate true love, and how many are those who are only too ready to return evil for good.

Not only among savage and uncultured people is this failing prevalent, but even among those who consider themselves more exalted; among nobles as well as plebeians, among rich as well as poor, among married and single men, yes, even between father and son, we mortals are the same.

One can never tell what evil deceit, treason, and falsity are hidden in the hearts of our fellow men. This evil trait has been the cause of betrayals, sufferings, crimes, and even war. Outside of Satan himself, who of all men created by God could better illustrate the truth of these facts than this wretched savage? How easily he betrayed his simple, ignorant spouse, for it is easy to deceive one who loves well!

O human love! What misery you bring to men! How traitorously you repay those who blindly place their trust in you!

Not even a dumb brute would have betrayed his mate as this ignoble savage did.

Polca would not be consoled. With tears streaming down her face, she kept looking toward the setting sun, the direction in which Milco had disappeared.

We now made camp for the night. The sentries were all assigned to their posts, and we lay down to rest our tired bodies that we might set forth on the morrow in search of the mighty river.[4]

In the dead of the night, when everyone was sound asleep, Polca awoke, and noticing that Mompil was gone, gave a loud cry which awoke us all. When we understood what she was telling us, and we realized that our only means of finding our way out of these savage regions had gone, we were struck dumb; our blood froze. Bitterly we reproached ourselves for not taking better precautions, and we reproached the sentinels for their carelessness, consoling ourselves by blaming them. Polca stood by terrified, trembling with fear, like a prisoner awaiting execution.

In the morning we met to consider what we should do. The sergeant, realizing that no good could come from bewailing our situation and that sad looks would not remedy anything, spoke as follows:

---

[2] *Vitellius*, Lucius Vitellius, brother of Aulus Vitellius, who was Emperor of Rome.

[3] *cruel Theseus . . . noble Ariadne*. The Athenian hero Theseus determined to free his city from the yearly tribute of seven youths and seven maidens to the Minotaur, a monster kept in the Labyrinth of Minos, King of Crete. Theseus went to Crete as one of the doomed youths, and with the help of Ariadne he was able to kill the monster. He took Ariadne away with him and abandoned her at the island of Naxos, not, as Villagrá says, to the cruel monster from which she had saved him.

[4] *mighty river*, the Rio Grande.

"My comrades, let us not forget that God Who is our unfailing guide will not forget those who follow in His footsteps. There are many paths through life; some lead through pleasant woods and grassy meadows. Leave these easy journeys for those who are of faint heart. There are other pathways which lead through desert plains and rough and stony regions, where only the brave and strong can journey. Let no one be discouraged, come what will. Who knows but that our Lord is merely putting us to the test to see if we are true and noble men, worthy of greater things? Let us put our faith in Him and continue with strength and courage. This captive here is but a half league's journey from her people. Let us give her the freedom for which she longs."

We all approved the sergeant's words; and so, clothing the captive and making her many gifts, we told her she could go. She hardly realized this could be true, and trembling with emotion thanked us all, embracing each man in his turn. Four times she set forth, and each time she returned to thank us again. For the fifth time she returned, and taking her babe from her breast, she handed him to the sergeant as much as to say, "This is all I have to offer you; take him."

The sergeant fondled the infant and tenderly kissed him, then returning him to the mother, told her to be on her way. So leaving us, she set out in the direction her husband had departed.

VIEWING THE AUTHOR'S IDEAS

1. How did Polca show at the beginning of her visit that she merited respect? What aspects of Indian civilization are revealed by the kind attentions she showed to her husband?

2. Contrast the emotions shown by Milco and Polca. What do you think of Milco's action in allowing his wife to remain in his place?

3. What indications does the sergeant give that he was a brave warrior and a Christian gentleman? What chivalrous attitudes does the writer reveal?

4. In the eighteenth century the philosopher Rousseau taught that civilization degrades mankind and that the savage state presents man in the condition of natural goodness. From Villagrá's narrative would you argue for or against Rousseau's theory? Which group of men showed more respect for womanhood; more appreciation for generous affection? How would the discipline of Christianity and civilization have affected the tender womanly qualities of Polca?

EVALUATING HIS MANNER OF EXPRESSION

1. Which of the author's similes and metaphors seem to have been borrowed from his reading? Which figures may he have taken from his own experience as a warrior and adventurer?

2. Do the author's comments seem to hamper or enhance his narrative? Which remarks indicate wide experience and conviction?

3. The *History of New Mexico,* you will remember, is here given in prose translation. What poetic qualities can you observe in the contents of Villagrá's history? List qualities that you consider desirable in a historian. Do you believe that Villagrá is entitled to greater recognition as a poet than as a writer of history? Prove your answer. What is the value of Villagrá's history today?

The Shepherds

(A Play of the Nativity)

The Shepherds, *possibly the oldest surviving drama in America, is usually staged with a minimum of detail. At one end of the rectangular stage, Bethlehem is represented by a manger or a table covered with white, on which are placed statues of the Infant Jesus, of Mary, and Joseph. In some versions a living character, usually a young girl attired in white, plays the part of the Blessed Mother. At the opposite end of the stage is "Hell Mouth," often indicated by a black oilcloth curtain. Hell Mouth serves as an entrance and exit for Lucifer. A dozen shepherds occupy the center space of the* stage. Just as Bethlehem represents heaven and spiritual good, so Hell Mouth stands for evil and sin. The shepherds symbolize mankind, and the central part of the stage on which they appear, is intended to signify earth.

Though reverent and inspirational, the play permits the introduction of a comic element. In presenting humor side by side with devotional subject matter, The Shepherds *follows the medieval sacred dramas in which it is rooted. Throughout the play speeches are interspersed with songs. Tinkling bells serve as the only musical accompaniment. In the last scene shepherds gather round the crib and by pulling streamers attached to the manger, they rock the Infant to sleep while they sing a tender cradle song.*

Of the seventeen characters represented in this version of The Shepherds, *the following selection presents only eight. They include Lucifer, the archangel Michael, and the shepherds Cucharón, Meliso, Toringo, Bartolo, Parrado, and Bato. As the selection begins, Lucifer has determined to find out what these men know about the coming of Christ. He is thwarted, however, by the replies of Cucharón.*

(LUCIFER *enters*)

LUCIFER (aside): Grouped on these hills the
    shepherds lie
Sleeping. I summon all my craft
To steal their souls. All Hell assist!

(To SHEPHERDS)

Shepherds, be not afraid of me.
I am a man, no savage beast,
And all I ask is shelter, food,
And fire — a stranger's right . . .

(To CUCHARÓN)

Whence com'st thou, shepherd?

CUCHARÓN: From the camp,
Good sir.

LUCIFER: I ask thy country, fool.

CUCHARÓN: My cousin's dead, God rest his soul!

LUCIFER: Knave, how darest thou jest with me?

CUCHARÓN: Nay, I spake true. Now let me pass.

LUCIFER: Later, mayhap, if so I choose. . . .
(aside) This simpleton may serve my turn,
Reveal what heaven hides from me;
For oft God grants these innocents
Grace to perceive His high designs.

(*to* CUCHARÓN)

Look, thou, shepherd, answer truly,
And naught of harm shall come to thee;
But palter[1] with me, and thy flesh,
To quiv'ring morsels torn, shall bleed
A warning to the world!

CUCHARÓN: This is
A fearful threat! Ah! how my teeth
Do chatter! God grant some good end!

LUCIFER: Say, then, hast heard the gossips tell
Of the Messiah's birth, or that
He soon shall come?

CUCHARÓN: O sir, kind sir,

[1] *palter*, trifle.

Matías is my cousin, sir!
Two years ago, by accident
He slew a man, was banished for't,
But some days since they pardoned him.
Had he come home with lightning speed,
He might be here — or near at least.

LUCIFER: Matías, fool! I said not so!
Again, good shepherd, answer me.
The true Messiah's born, or no?

CUCHARÓN: There is no True Matías! I
By the same token now recall
I saw him circumcised and stood
For him at baptism. Him we named
"Matías" plain, no hint of "True."
'Twas for his father, Matthew, sir,
First cousin to my father, and
Akin to my old Grandpa, who
Married his cousin german. See,
Good sir, these Mats descend each one
From old Mathusalem; and he
They say was grandson of Matán.
Matthew who killed his ma-in-law
Descended, by my uncle's side
From Aaron. I believe, kind sir,
My grandfather must be the True
Mathías!

LUCIFER: Cease thy chatter, fool!
Must flames burn the truth from thee?

CUCHARÓN: What flames!
Ah, no, kind sir, I recollect
Here in this very village I
Knew one Matias, smith by trade.
An *honest* man, still I'll not swear
He is the *True* Matias.

LUCIFER: Now
By the fierce fire that tortures me,
Thy heart I'll tear from out thy breast!
Slave! . . . Thy family pedigree
Thou dar'st recite, while I consume
In helpless rage!

(*Seizes* CUCHARÓN)

CUCHARÓN: O God! I burn!

LUCIFER: That name affronts me!

CUCHARÓN: In God's name!
I burn!

LUCIFER: At that name's power
I loose my hold; but saving it
I should have swallowed thee in flames . . .
(To aid the shepherds to reach Bethlehem unharmed, the archangel Michael appears. In a dramatic battle Lucifer is banished to Hell Mouth.)

ANGEL: What! Lucifer, thou lingerest still?

Begone! and let these shepherds haste
To see the Word made human flesh.
Arise, thou loathsome beast, plunge down
The yawning chasm, where damning sin
Will prove itself thy sharpest pain.
Gird up thy loins, since from the earth
Thy Maker exiles thee for aye,
While man receives through sovereign grace
The gift of love which conquers sin.

LUCIFER: A crater, belching poisonous fire,
I fain would bury rescued man
Beneath the lava of my hate!
Hopeless with thee my further strife;
Man must I tempt, and should I fail,
Eternal enemies we rest,
And all will follow in God's plan
When I, engulfed, embitter Hell.

ANGEL: To thy abode, Demon! Depart,
Iniquitous phantom, I command!
Plunge in the abyss, well-earned thy pain!

LUCIFER: How, Michael, thou pursuest me still!
Then know me wrathful foe to all,—
Aspic,[2] gad-fly, raging lion,
Thunderbolt charged with deadly fire!
For man has sorely wounded me.
I sigh and groan and weep with rage,
Calling for surcease[3]—since to speak
One's sorrow dulls its sharpest pang.
Now all will follow in God's plan
When I, engulfed, embitter Hell.

(SATAN *vanishes*)

(Having been delivered from the wiles of Satan, the shepherds approach Bethlehem. Each shepherd sings a song and recites a prayer as he offers his simple gifts to the Christ Child. Excerpts from only a few of the speeches are here given.)

Song

Above the shouting multitude
   As I lay thinking dreamily
I heard a voice from out the wood,
   Chanting, chanting joyfully:
"Ye shepherds, sleeping night away
   In mountain pasture wild,
Seek Bethlehem, make no delay,
   Adore the Holy Child."

Prayer

Here see the Saviour of the world,
Low lying on the stable straw,
He, Who to save mankind from sin,
Was born of Mary, Anna's child,

The gracious, prophet-promised maid,
Saint Joseph's blessed, spotless wife.
My heart beats high to see His face! . . .

MELISO: Mighty Princess, heavenly Queen,
Mother! Vouchsafe to pardon me,
A foolish shepherd and thy slave.
No costly gift I bring thy Child,
But be thou pleased to share with Him
My rustic offering of a cheese.
Heaven's peace be on Thee, Holy Rose,
Toringo comes to kiss Thy feet.

(Singing)

TORINGO: *Now at last I'm able*
   By fortune's kind behaviour,
To bring a pretty cradle
   And rock the Infant Saviour. . . .

(Spoken)

Peace be on Thee, Thou Holy Rose,
Cucharón comes to kiss Thy feet.

CUCHARÓN: *Dancing and singing*
   Like bird on a tree
Joyfully bringing
   Tamales to Thee.

Prayer

At Thy feet with grateful heart,
This shepherd boy in perfect love
Adores Thy great Nativity,
I sorrow that I may not bring
Rich gifts as merits Thy great love.
I offer these poor cakes, and gaze
Unworthy on Thy splendor. Now
Farewell, farewell, Thou Holy Rose,
Bartolo comes to kiss Thy feet. . . .

BARTOLO: I bring Thee milk, and honey wild,
Poor gifts! O would that wealth were mine
To offer! Now for song and dance.
I must arrange the serenade,
So pardon, all, for any faults
You may have noted in my part.

PARRADO: Right, Bartolo, while Mary sleeps
And Joseph rests, with joyful tone,—
But softly not to wake the Child,
Rather to soothe His slumber light,—
Chant Him a tender lullaby.

Song

Hush-a-bye, my little Son,
   Hush-a-bye, my heart of gold;
Softly slumber, little One,
   Night is dark and wind blows cold.
Now Thou sleep'st, little treasure,
   Gracious, tender, heavenly-wise;
Beauty finds in Thee her measure,

---

[2] *aspic*, a venomous asp.

[3] *surcease*, an end.

Though Thou com'st in humble guise . . . .

PARRADO: The hour has come. Without delay
We must depart. Dear Mary, thou,
And Joseph, too, thy servants bless.
Humbly kneeling, see this shepherd,
Waiting joyfully the blessing.
Friends, raise your voices one and all
To say farewell.

VIEWING THE AUTHOR'S IDEAS

1. In what way does Lucifer show his cleverness?

2. Point out instances in which the shepherds appear to be more like Spaniards than like the shepherds of Judea at the time of Our Lord's birth.

3. How does the selection illustrate the simplicity of spirit characteristic of those who carry on the tradition of *The Shepherds*?

I Would Rather Live Here Than Anywhere Else

(From *A Description of New England*)
Captain John Smith

A Description of New England was quite as much an advertisement as the colorful "touraides" written today to encourage travel by air and trail. But Smith was a seer as well as a salesman. His adventurous rovings had enabled him to speak authoritatively of colonial opportunities, and he voices his argument in the challenging tone that heralds the spirit of American enterprise.

. . . WHO can but approve this a most excellent place, both for health and fertility? And of all the four parts of the world that I have yet seen not inhabited, could I have but means to transport a colony, I would rather live here than anywhere else; and if it did not maintain itself, were we but once indifferently well-fitted, let us starve. . . .

And here are no hard landlords to rack us with high rents, or extorted fines to consume us; no tedious pleas in law to consume us with their many years' disputations for justice; no multitudes to occasion such impediments to good orders, as in popular states. So freely hath God and his Majesty bestowed those blessings on them that will attempt to obtain them, as here every man may be master and owner of his own labor and land, or the greatest part in a small time. If he have nothing but his hands, he may set up this trade and by industry quickly grow rich, spending but half that time well which in England we abuse in idleness, worse, or as ill. . . .

Who can desire more content that hath small means or but only his merit to advance his fortune than to tread and plant that ground he hath purchased by the hazard of his life? If he have but the taste of virtue and magnanimity, what to such a mind can be more pleasant than planting and building a foundation for his posterity, got from the rude earth by God's blessing and his own industry, without prejudice to any; or more agreeable to God than to seek to convert those poor savages to know Christ and humanity, whose labors with discretion will triply requite the charge and pains? What so truly suits with honor and honesty as the discovering things unknown, erecting towns, peopling countries, informing the ignorant, reforming things unjust, teaching virtue; and gain to our native mother country a kingdom to attend her; find employment for those that are idle because they know not what to do; so far from wronging any, as to cause posterity to remember thee, and remembering thee, ever honor that remembrance with praise? . . .

And lest any should think the toil might be insupportable, though these things may be had by labor and diligence, I assure myself there are [those] who delight extremely in vain pleasure that take much more pains in England to enjoy it than I should do here [in New England] to gain wealth sufficient. And yet I think they should not have half such sweet content, for our pleasure here is still gains; in England, charges and loss. Here nature and liberty afford us that freely which in England we want, or it costeth us dearly. What pleasure can be more than (being tired with any occasion ashore, in planting vines, fruits, or herbs, in contriving their own grounds to the pleasure of their own minds, their fields, gardens, orchards, buildings, ships, and other works, etc.) to recreate themselves before their own doors, in their own boats upon the sea, where man, woman, and child, with a small hook and line by angling may take divers sorts of excellent fish at their pleasures? And is it not pretty sport to pull up two pence, six pence, and twelve pence as fast as you can haul and veer[1] a line? . . . And what sport doth yield a more pleasing content and less hurt or charge than angling with a hook and crossing the sweet air from isle to isle over the silent streams of a calm sea? Wherein the most curious may find pleasure, profit, and content. . . .

And what have ever been the works of the greatest princes of the earth but planting of countries and civilizing barbarous and inhuman nations to civility and humanity, whose eternal actions fill our histories? Lastly, the Portuguese and Spaniards, whose everliving actions [are] before our eyes, will testify with them our idleness and ingratitude to all posterities; and the neglect of our duties in our piety and religion we owe

[1] *haul and veer*, draw in and let out.

our God, our King, and country; and want of charity to these poor savages, whose country we challenge, use, and possess; except we be but made to use and mar what our forefathers made, or but only tell what they did, or esteem ourselves too good to take the like pains. Was it virtue in them to provide that [which] doth maintain us, and baseness for us to do the like for others? Surely, no.

Then seeing we are not born for ourselves, but each to help other, and our abilities are much alike at the hour of our birth and the minute of our death; seeing our good deeds or our bad, by faith in Christ's merits, is all we have to carry our souls to heaven or hell; seeing honor is our lives' ambition and our ambition after death to have an honorable memory of our life; and seeing by no means we would be abated of the dignities and glories of our predecessors, let us imitate their virtues to be worthily their successors.

VIEWING THE AUTHOR'S IDEAS

Smith appeals to at least seven motives which stimulate men to activity: desire for property, the pleasure of leisure, desire for honor, desire to benefit others, patriotic fervor, initiative, and religious zeal. List these seven headings and classify each of his arguments under one of these motives. Under which headings do you find the greatest number of motives?

EVALUATING HIS MANNER OF EXPRESSION

How does parallel structure help Smith to attain clarity despite his long sentences?

Pocahontas, the King's Dearest Daughter

(From *The General History of Virginia*)

Captain John Smith

Whether or not we believe that Pocahontas saved the life of John Smith, we can at least welcome the lovely Indian maiden who stands at the threshold of our literary history. She is one of our authentic folk heroines. Carl Sandburg speaks of her as "lovely as a poplar, sweet as a red haw in November or as a papaw in May." Vachel Lindsay sees her as a symbol of the American spirit. This unadorned account by Captain John Smith opens with his capture by the Indians while he had been seeking food in the wilderness.

THEIR order in conducting him was thus: Drawing themselves all in file, the King in the midst had all their pieces and swords borne before him. Captain Smith was led after him by three great savages, holding him fast by each arm, and on each side went six in file with their arrows nocked.[1] . . . Smith they conducted to a long house, where thirty or forty tall fellows did guard him; and ere long more bread and venison was

[1] *nocked*, fitted to the bowstring ready for shooting.

brought him than would have served twenty men. I think his stomach at that time was not very good. What he left they put in baskets and tied over his head. About midnight they set the meat again before him; all this time not one of them would eat a bite with him, till the next morning they brought him as much more. And then did they eat all the old and reserved the new as they had done the other, which made him think they would fat him to eat him. Yet in this desperate estate, to defend him from the cold, one Moacassater brought him his gown in requital of some beads and toys Smith had given him at his first arrival in Virginia. . . .

At last they brought him to Meronocomoco[2] where was Powhatan, their Emperor. Here more than two hundred of those grim courtiers stood wondering at him as he had been a monster, till Powhatan and his train had put themselves in their greatest braveries.[3] Before a fire, upon a seat like a bedstead, he sat covered with a great robe made of raccoon skins, and all the tails hanging by. On either hand did sit a young wench of sixteen or eighteen years, and along on each side the house, two rows of men, and behind them as many women, with all their heads and shoulders painted red; many of their heads bedecked with the white down of birds, but every one with something, and a great chain of white beads about their necks.

At his entrance before the King all the people gave a great shout. The Queen of Appomattox was appointed to bring him water to wash his hands, and another brought him a bunch of feathers, instead of a towel, to dry them. Having feasted him after their best barbarous manner they could, a long consultation was held; but the conclusion was, two great stones were brought before Powhatan. Then as many as could, laid hands on him, dragged him to them, and thereon laid his head. And being ready with their clubs to beat out his brains, Pocahontas, the King's dearest daughter, when no entreaty could prevail, got his head in her arms and laid her own upon his to save him from death; whereat the Emperor was contented he should live to make him hatchets, and her bells, beads, and copper; for they thought him as well of all occupations[4] as themselves. For the King himself will make his own robes, shoes, bows, arrows, pots; plant, hunt, or do anything so well as the rest.

> They say he bore a pleasant show,
> But sure his heart was sad.
> For who can pleasant be, and rest,
> That lives in fear and dread;
> And having life suspected, doth
> It still suspected lead.

Two days after, Powhatan, having disguised himself in the fearfullest manner he could, caused Captain Smith to be brought forth to a great house in the woods and there upon a mat by the fire to be left alone. Not long after, from behind a mat that divided the house, was made the most doleful noise he ever heard. Then Powhatan, more like a devil than a man, with some two hundred more as black as himself, came unto him and told him now they were friends, and presently he should go to Jamestown, to send him two great guns and a grindstone; for which he would give him the country of Capahowosick and forever esteem him as his son Nantaquoud.

So to Jamestown with twelve guides Powhatan sent him.

VIEWING THE AUTHOR'S IDEAS

1. The Indians frequently fed their prisoners well in order that they might be stronger under torture. What made Smith suspicious of his captors' generosity with food?

2. Among the Indians, women were sometimes permitted to claim a captive for adoption in the tribe. In the case of Captain John Smith, how did Pocahontas exercise this privilege?

3. How would you interpret Pocahontas' action in the final scene?

EVALUATING HIS MANNER OF EXPRESSION

1. As a storyteller Smith had the gift of making his tale picturesque and vivid. Point to several concrete details which add interest to the narrative.

2. What motives may have caused Smith to write this account in the third person? How does this method contribute objectivity and detachment to the narrative?

---

[2] *Meronocomoco*, Powhatan's capital on the York River, twelve miles from Jamestown.
[3] *braveries*, showy robes and ornaments.

[4] *as well . . . occupations*, as skilled in all crafts.

Amongst Godly and Sober Men

(From *A History of Plymouth Plantation*)
William Bradford

The first written expression of the democratic idea in America was drawn up not on the soil of our country but on the waters washing her coast. A stormy sea had brought the Mayflower *to the New England shore, far north of Virginia where the Pilgrims had expected to land. As this region was outside the jurisdiction of the Virginia Company of London, the documents of authorization which the Pilgrims held from that company could not be enforced. For a time it appeared that the new settlers would land without the protection of a governing body. Already unruly members among the group boasted that they would obey no authority. At this critical period the leaders of the company asserted the right of a majority to make and administer laws for the common good. Forty-one persons signed the Mayflower Compact upon which the government of the colony was to be based.*

In order to reimburse the financial company which had sponsored their voyage to America, the Pilgrims had signed an agreement to hold all goods and profits in a common stock for a period of seven years. After the third winter the colonists were facing starvation. Bradford here describes the relief effected by a return to a system which recognized the rights of private property.

THE BEGINNINGS OF AMERICAN DEMOCRACY
(1620)

I SHALL a little return back and begin with a combination[1] made by them before they came ashore, being the first foundation of their government in this place; occasioned partly by the discontented and mutinous speeches that some of the strangers amongst them had let fall from them in the ship (that when they came ashore, they would use their own liberty; for none had power to command them, the patent[2] they had being for Virginia and not for New England, which belonged to another government with which the Virginia Company had nothing to do), and partly that such an act by them done (this their condition considered) might be as firm as any patent and in some respects more sure.

[1] *combination*, agreement.
[2] *patent*, document conferring rights and privileges.

The form was as followeth:

In the name of God, amen. We whose names are underwritten, the loyal subjects of our dread sovereign lord, King James, by the grace of God, of Great Britain, France, and Ireland, King, Defender of the Faith, etc., having undertaken for the glory of God and advancement of the Christian faith, and honor of our king and country, a voyage to plant the first colony in the northern parts of Virginia, do by these presents solemnly and mutually in the presence of God and one of another, covenant and combine ourselves together into a civil body politic for our better ordering and preservation and furtherance of the ends aforesaid; and by virtue hereof to enact, constitute, and frame such just and equal laws, ordinances, acts, constitutions, and offices, from time to time, as shall be thought most meet and convenient for the general good of the colony, unto which we promise all due submission and obedience. In witness whereof, we have hereunder subscribed our names at Cape Cod, the eleventh of November, in the year of the reign of our sovereign lord, King James of England, France, and Ireland, the eighteenth, and of Scotland, the fifty-fourth. Anno Domini 1620.

TRIALS OF THE FIRST WINTER (1620)

After this they chose, or rather confirmed, Mr. John Carver, a man godly and well-approved amongst them, their governor for that year. And after they had provided a place for their goods, or common store (which were long in unloading for want of boats, foulness of winter weather, and sickness of divers), and begun some small cottages for their habitation as time would admit, they met and consulted of laws and orders, both for their civil and military government, as the necessity of their condition did require, still adding thereunto as urgent occasion in several times, and as cases did require.

In these hard and difficult beginnings, they found some discontents and murmurings arise amongst some, and mutinous speeches and carriages in other, but they were soon quelled and overcome by the wisdom, patience, and just and equal carriage of things by the Governor and better part, which clave faithfully together in the main. But that which was most sad and lamentable was that in two or three months' time half of their company died, especially in January and February, being the depth of winter and wanting houses and other comforts; being infected with the scurvy and other diseases which this long voyage and their inaccommodate condition had brought upon them; so as there died sometimes two or three of a day in the foresaid time; that of one hundred and odd persons, scarce fifty remained. And of these in the time of most distress, there was but six or seven sound persons, who (to their great commendations be it spoken) spared no pains, night nor day, but with abundance of toil and hazard of their own health, fetched them wood, made them fires, dressed them meat, made their beds, washed their loathsome clothes, clothed and unclothed them; in a word did all the homely and necessary offices for them which dainty and queasy stomachs cannot endure to hear named, and all this willingly and cheerfully without any grudging in the least, showing herein their true love unto their friends and brethren — a rare example and worthy to be remembered. Two of these seven were Mr. William Brewster, their Reverend Elder, and Myles Standish[3], their captain and military commander, unto whom myself and many others were much beholden in our low and sick condition. And yet the Lord so upheld these persons, as in this general calamity they were not at all infected either with sickness or lameness. And what I said of these, I may say of many others who died in this general visitation, and others yet living; that whilst they had health, yea, or any strength continuing, they were not wanting to any that had need of them. And I doubt not but their recompense is with the Lord. . . .

THE FAILURE OF AN EXPERIMENT IN COMMON OWNERSHIP (1623)

All this while no supply was heard of, neither knew they when they might expect any. So they began to think how they might raise as much corn as they could and obtain a better crop than they had done, that they might not still thus languish in misery. At length, after much debate of things, the Governor, with the advice of the chiefest among them, gave way that they should set corn every man for his own particular, and in that regard trust to themselves; in all other things to go on in the general way as before. And so assigned to every family a parcel of land, according to the proportion of their number for that end — only for present use, but made no division for inheritance — and ranged all boys and youth under some family. This had very good success; for it made all hands very industrious, so as much more corn was planted than otherwise would have been by any means the Governor or any other could use; and saved him a great deal of trouble and gave far better content. The women now went willingly into the field and took their little ones with them to set corn, which before would allege weakness and inability; whom to have compelled would have been thought great tyranny and oppression.

The experience that was had in this common course and condition, tried sundry years and that amongst godly and sober men, may well evince the vanity of that conceit of Plato[4] and other ancients, applauded by some of later times: that the taking away of property and bringing in community into a commonwealth would make them happy and flourishing; as if they were wiser than God. For this community, so far as it was, was found to breed much confusion and discontent, and retard much employment that would have been to their benefit and comfort. For the young men that were most able and fit for labor and service did repine that they should spend their time and strength to work for other men's wives and children without any recompense. The strong, or man of parts, had no more division of victuals and clothes than he that was weak and not able to do a quarter the other could. This was thought injustice. The aged and graver men, to be ranked and equalized in labors and victuals, clothes, etc., with the meaner and younger sort, thought it some indignity and disrespect unto them. And for men's wives to be commanded to do service for other men, as dressing their meat, washing their clothes, etc., they deemed it a kind of slavery; neither could many husbands well brook it. Upon the point, all being to have alike and all to do alike, they thought themselves in the like condition and one

---

[3] *Myles Standish*, a soldier of fortune whom the Pilgrims hired to accompany them on their voyage. He claimed descent from the noble Catholic family, Standish of Standish. His indifference to the religion of the Pilgrims led many to suspect that he was a Catholic. He is the hero of Longfellow's *Courtship of Miles Standish*.

[4] *that conceit of Plato*. Plato, a Greek philosopher who lived four hundred years before Christ, believed that private ownership of property is the cause of all the troubles of mankind. In his opinion, the ideal state would be composed of virtuous people holding all things in common. He realized, however, that for ordinary men individual ownership of property is best.

as good as another; and so, if it did not cut of those relations that God hath set amongst men, yet it did at least much diminish and take of the mutual respects that should be preserved among them. And would have been worse if they had been men of another condition. Let none object this is men's corruption and nothing to the course itself. I answer, seeing all men have this corruption in them, God in His wisdom saw another course fitter for them.

VIEWING THE AUTHOR'S IDEAS

1. Why might a compact drawn up by the colonists be as "firm as any patent"?

2. What democratic principles stated in the *Mayflower Compact* are incorporated into our laws and constitutions today?

3. In what way was the charity of the colonists during sickness typical of the American spirit of neighborliness? In what ways were the circumstances unusual?

4. What new signs of interest were immediately manifested when the responsibility of the individual ownership was given to the colonists?

5. What reaction to a "classless society" had been given by young men of the settlement; by the strong; by the old; by married people? What final argument does Bradford use to condemn the "conceit of Plato"?

EVALUATING HIS MANNER OF EXPRESSION

Bradford's prose is simple, dignified, and adapted to his purpose. Show how each of the three incidents here recorded is expressed in language suitable to the subject matter presented.

A Trophy to Christ

(From *A Brief Relation of the Voyage unto Maryland*)
Andrew White, S.J.

On account of the Penal Laws, Cecil Calvert had commissioned the Maryland colonists to "cause all acts of the Roman Catholic religion to be done as privately as may be . . ." The free atmosphere of the New World, however, invited the open practice of religion, and the Maryland Catholics celebrated their arrival with fitting public ceremonies. Evidently because of Calvert's prohibition, Father White's English version limits the description of these ceremonies to the words "And here we offered." In the Latin account sent to his superiors, the priest describes the Mass in some detail. In the portion of the Relation *presented here, a translation of the description of the Mass which appears in the Latin version has been substituted for the abbreviated English account.*

. . . AT our first coming we found (as we were told) all in arms; the King of Piscatoway had drawn together five hundred bowmen, great fires were made all over the country, and the bigness of our ship made the natives report we came in a canoe as big as an island, with so many men as trees were in a wood, with great terror unto them all. Thus we sailed some twenty leagues up the river to Heron Island, so called for the infinite swarms of herons thereon. This we called

St. Clement's[1]; here we first came ashore. Here by the overturning of a shallop[2] [in] which we had almost lost our maids which we brought along, the linen they went to wash was much of it lost, which is no small matter in these parts. The ground is here, as in many places, covered with pokeberries (a little wild walnut, hard of shell, but with a sweet kernel), with acorns, black walnut, cedar, sassafras, vines, salad herbs, and such like. It is not above four hundred acres, and therefore too little to seat upon[3] for us. Therefore they have designed it for a fort to command the river, meaning to raise another on the mainland against it and so to keep the river from foreign trade, here being the narrowest of the river.

On the day of the Annunciation of the Most Holy Virgin Mary in the year 1634, we celebrated the Mass for the first time on this island. This had never been done before in this part of the world.[4] After we had completed the Sacrifice, we took upon our shoulders a great cross,

[1] *St. Clement's*, now Blackiston's Island.
[2] *shallop*, a light, open boat.
[3] *seat upon*, make a settlement.
[4] *This . . . part of the world.* Father White apparently overlooked the fact that Mass was offered at the Spanish settlement of Ayllon in 1526 and at the Mission of Axacan on the shores of the Chesapeake in 1570.

which we had hewn out of a tree, and advancing in order to the appointed place, with the assistance of the Governor[5] and his associates and the other Catholics, we erected a trophy to Christ the Saviour, humbly reciting on our bended knees the litanies of the Sacred Cross, with great emotion.

Here our Governor was advised not to settle himself till he spoke with the Emperor of Piscatoway and told him the cause of his coming (to wit) to teach them a divine doctrine, whereby to lead them to heaven and to enrich with such ornaments of civil life[6] as our own country abounded withal, not doubting but this Emperor being satisfied, the other kings would be more peaceable. With this intention he took our pinnace[7] and went therein higher up the river. In their way they found still all the Indians fled from their houses; till coming to Potomac town, he found there the king thereof, a child governed by Archihoe, his uncle. Here by an interpreter they had some speech with Archihoe, a grave and considerate man, and showed his errors[8] in part unto him, which he seemed to acknowledge, bidding them all very welcome. They could proceed but little with him in matters of religion, their interpreter being a Protestant of Virginia, but promised shortly to return to him, some one or other; which he desired they would and promised they should have the best entertainment they could make them; and his men should hunt and fish for them, and he and they would divide whatsoever they got, being — as they all generally be — of a very loving and kind nature.

From here they went to Piscatoway, the seat of the Emperor, where five hundred bowmen came to meet them at the water side. Here the Emperor, less fearing than the rest, came privately aboard, where he found kind usage; and perceiving we came with good meaning toward them, gave leave to us to set down[9] where we pleased. . . .

Whilst our Governor was abroad, the Indians began to lose fear and come to our court of guard[10] and sometimes aboard our ship, wondering where the tree should grow, out of which so great a canoe should be hewn, supposing it to be all of one piece as their canoes use

to be. They trembled to hear our ordnance,[11] thinking them fearfuller than any thunder they had ever heard.

The Governor being returned from Piscatoway, by Fleet's directions[12] we came some nine or ten leagues lower in the river Potomac to a lesser river on the north side of it as big as Thames, which we call St. George's. This river makes two excellent bays, wherein might harbor three hundred sail of one thousand ton apiece, with very great safety: the one called St. George's Bay; the other, more inward, St. Mary's. On the one side of this river lives the King of Yoacomicoe; on the other our plantation is seated about half a mile from the water, and our town we call St. Mary's.

To avoid all occasion of dislike and color of wrong, we bought the space of thirty miles of ground of them for axes, hoes, cloth, and hatchets — which we call Augusta Carolina. It made them more willing to entertain us, for that they had wars with the Susquehannas, who come sometimes upon them and waste and spoil them and their country. For thus they hope by our means to be safe, God disposing things thus for those which were to come to bring the light of His holy law to these distressed, poor infidels; so that they do indeed like us better for coming so well provided, assuring themselves of greater safety by living by us. Is not this miraculous that a nation, a few days before in general arms against us and our enterprise, should like lambs yield themselves, glad of our company, giving us houses, land, and livings for a trifle? *Digitus Dei est hic*,[13] and some great good is meant toward this people.

VIEWING THE AUTHOR'S IDEAS

1. What disturbances had the news of the approaching colonists made among the Indians? What mishap occurred? Why was it particularly disastrous?

2. Describe the formal ceremonies by which Maryland was dedicated.

3. What reason did the English Catholics advance to the Indians to justify their arrival?

4. From the plans for exchange made between the Maryland settlers and the Indians, which group of people would receive greater profit?

5. What happenings caused the author to conclude "the finger of God is here"?

[5] *Governor*, Leonard Calvert, brother of Cecil Calvert, Lord Baltimore.

[6] *ornaments of civil life*, refinements of civilization.

[7] *pinnace*, a light vessel, navigated by oars and sails.

[8] *errors*, false beliefs of his pagan religion.

[9] *to set down*, to establish a colony.

[10] *court of guard* [obsolete], corps of guards.

[11] *ordnance*, heavy firearms; cannon.

[12] *by Fleet's directions*. Captain Henry Fleet of Virginia, who had lived with the Indians and knew their language, was engaged to act as guide and interpreter in purchasing a site for the settlement.

[13] *Digitus Dei est hic*, the finger of God is here.

The Martyrdom of St. René Goupil

(From *The Jesuit Relations*)
St. Isaac Jogues, S.J.
Translated by Reuben Gold Thwaites

One of the most moving narratives in the Jesuit Relations *is this account of a saint by a saint and a martyr by a martyr. Father Isaac Jogues, fellow captive and sufferer with René Goupil, received his crown later than his companion and so lived to record this testimony of his young friend's heroism. His chronicle pictures René as a man of desires who brought to the wilderness his gaiety, tenderness, and ardor, and who wrested from its torturous trail the incomparable exchange of his religious profession and martyrdom.*

RENÉ Goupil was a native of Anjou,[1] who in the bloom of his youth urgently requested to be received into our novitiate at Paris, where he remained some months with much edification. His bodily indispositions having taken from him the happiness of consecrating himself to God in holy religion, for which he had a strong desire, he journeyed when his health improved to New France in order to serve the Society there, since he had not had the blessing of giving himself to it in old France. And in order to do nothing in his own right, although he was fully master of his own actions, he totally submitted himself to the guidance of the Superior of the mission,[2] who employed him two whole years in the meanest offices about the house, in which he acquitted himself with great humility and charity. He was also given the care of nursing the sick and the wounded at the hospital,[3] which he did with much skill — for he understood surgery well — as with affection and love, continually seeing our Lord in their persons. He left so sweet an odor of his goodness and his other virtues in that place that his memory is still blessed there.

When we came down from the Hurons[4] in July, 1642, we asked Reverend Father Vimont to let us take him with us because the Hurons had great need of a surgeon. He granted our request.

I cannot express the joy which this good young man felt when the Superior told him that he might make ready for the journey. Nevertheless, he well knew the great dangers that await one upon the river; he knew how the Iroquois[5] were enraged against the French. Yet that could not prevent him, at the least sign of the will of him to whom he had voluntarily committed all his concerns, from setting forth for Three Rivers.[6]

We departed thence on the first of August, the day after the feast of Our Blessed Father.[7] On the second, we encountered the enemies, who, separated into two bands, were awaiting us with the advantage which a great number of chosen men fighting on land can have over a small and promiscuous band who are upon the water in scattered canoes of bark.

Nearly all the Hurons had fled into the woods, and as they had left us, we were seized. On this occasion his virtue was very manifest; for, as soon as he saw himself captured, he said to me: "O my Father, God be blessed; He has permitted it, He has willed it — His holy will be done. I love it, I desire it, I cherish it, I embrace it with all the strength of my heart." Meantime, while the enemies pursued the fugitives, I heard his confession and gave him absolution, not knowing what might befall us after our capture. The enemies, having returned from their hunt, fell upon us like mad dogs, with sharp teeth, tearing out our nails and crushing our fingers, which he endured with much patience and courage.

His presence of mind in so grievous a mishap appeared especially in this, that he aided me (notwithstanding the pain of his wounds) as well as he could in the instruction of the captive Hurons who were not Christians. While I was instructing them separately and as they came,

---

[1] *Anjou*, a former province of France.

[2] *Superior of the mission*, Father Vimont, Superior of the Jesuit mission at Quebec.

[3] *hospital*, Hotel Dieu at Quebec.

[4] *came down . . . Hurons*. An expedition headed by Father Jogues had come down to Quebec from the Huron mission of St. Mary on Lake Huron. It was now returning to the mission.

[5] *Iroquois*, (Ĭr´ŏ-kwoi) the confederacy of tribes known as the Five Nations, who lived in northern New York.

[6] *Three Rivers*, a fortified French settlement eighty-four miles from Quebec.

[7] *Our Blessed Father*, St. Ignatius Loyola, founder of the Jesuits.

he called my attention to the fact that a poor old man named Ondouterraon, was among those whom they would probably kill on the spot, their custom being always to sacrifice some one in the heat of their fury. I instructed this man at leisure, while the enemies were attending to the distribution of the plunder from twelve canoes, some of which were laden with necessaries for our Fathers among the Hurons. The booty being divided, they killed this poor old man almost at the same moment in which I had just given him a new birth through the salutary water of holy baptism. We still had this consolation during the journey that we made in going to the enemies' country,[8] that we were together; on this journey I was witness to many virtues.

Upon the road he [René] was always occupied with God. His words and the discourses that he held were all expressive of submission to the commands of the Divine Providence and showed a willing acceptance of the death which God was sending him. He gave himself to Him as a sacrifice to be reduced to ashes by the fires of the Iroquois, which that good Father's hand would kindle. He sought the means to please Him in all things and everywhere. One day he said to me (it was soon after our capture, while we were still on the way): "My Father, God has always given me a great desire to consecrate myself to His holy service by the vows of religion in His holy Society; my sins have rendered me unworthy of this grace until this hour. I nevertheless hope that our Lord will be pleased with the offering which I wish now to make Him, by taking, in the best manner that I can, the vows of the Society in the presence of my God and before you." This being granted to him, he uttered the vows with much devotion.

Covered with wounds as he was, he dressed those of other persons — the enemies who had received some blow in the fight, as well as the prisoners themselves. He opened a vein for a sick Iroquois; and all that with as much charity as if he had done it to persons very friendly.

His humility and the obedience which he rendered to those who had captured him confounded me. Two Iroquois who conveyed us both in their canoe told me that I must take a paddle and use it; I would do nothing of the kind, being proud even in death. They addressed him in the same way some time afterward, and immediately

he began to paddle; and when the barbarians tried to drive me by his example to do the like, he, having perceived it, asked my pardon. I sometimes suggested to him along the way the idea of escaping, since the liberty they gave us furnished him sufficient opportunity for this; but as for myself, I could not leave the French and twenty-four or twenty-five Huron captives. He would never do so, committing himself in everything to the will of our Lord, who inspired him with no thought of doing what I proposed.

On the lake[9] we met two hundred Iroquois, who came to Richelieu[10] while the French were beginning to build the fort; these loaded us with blows, covered us with blood, and made us experience the rage of those who are possessed by the demon. All the outrages and these cruelties he endured with great patience and charity toward those who ill-treated him.

On approaching the first village,[11] where we were treated so cruelly, he showed a most uncommon patience and gentleness. Having fallen under the shower of blows from clubs and iron rods with which they attacked us and being unable to rise again, he was brought — as it were, half dead — upon the scaffold where we already were, in the middle of the village; but he was in so pitiful a condition that he would have inspired compassion in cruelty itself. He was all bruised with blows, and in his face one distinguished nothing but the whites of his eyes; but he was so much the more beautiful in the sight of the angels as he was disfigured and similar to Him of Whom it is said: *Vidimus cum quasi leprosum, etc.; non erat ei species neque decer.*[12]

Hardly had he taken a little breath, as well as we, when they came to give him three blows on his shoulders with a heavy club, as they had done to us before. When they had cut off my thumb, as I was the most conspicuous, they turned to him and cut his right thumb at the first joint, while he continually uttered during this torment, "Jesus, Mary, Joseph." During six days, in which we were exposed to all those who wished to do us some harm, he showed an admirable gentleness; he had his whole breast burned by the coals and hot cinders which

8 *the enemies' country*, the country of the Iroquois in northern New York.

9 *the lake*, Lake Champlain.

10 *Richelieu*, a fort on the St. Lawrence at the mouth of the Richelieu River.

11 *the first village*, Ossernenon, now the town of Auriesville, near Albany, where St. René Goupil suffered martyrdom in 1642.

12 *vidimus . . . neque decer.* "We saw Him as a leper, etc."; "there was no beauty nor comeliness in Him." Isa. 53:2.

the young lads threw upon our bodies at night, when we were bound flat on the earth. Nature furnished more skill to me than to him for avoiding a part of these pains.

After they had given us life, at the very time when a little before they had warned us to prepare for being burned, he fell sick, suffering great inconveniences in every respect and especially in regard to the food, to which he was not accustomed. In that, one might say most truly, *Non cibus utilis aegro*.[13] I could not relieve him, for I was also very sick and had none of my fingers sound or entire.

But this urges me to come to his death, at which nothing was wanting to make him a martyr.

After we had been in the country six weeks (as confusion arose in the councils of the Iroquois, some of whom were quite willing that we should be taken back), we lost the hope, which I did not consider very great, of again seeing Three Rivers that year. We accordingly consoled one another in the divine arrangement of things; and we were preparing for everything that it might ordain for us. He did not quite realize the danger in which we were (I saw it better than he), and this often led me to tell him that we should hold ourselves in readiness. One day, then, as in the grief of our souls we had gone forth from the village in order to pray more suitably and with less disturbance, two young men came after us to tell us that we must return home. I had some presentiment of what was to happen and said to him: "My dearest brother, let us commend ourselves to Our Lord and to our good Mother, the Blessed Virgin; these people have some evil design, as I think." We had offered ourselves to Our Lord shortly before with much devotion, beseeching Him to receive our lives and our blood and to unite them with His life and His blood for the salvation of these poor peoples. We accordingly returned toward the village, reciting our rosary, of which we had already said four decades. When we stopped near the gate of the village to see what they might say to us, one of these two Iroquois draws a hatchet, which he held concealed under a blanket, and deals a blow with it on the head of René, who was before him. He falls motionless, his face to the ground, pronouncing the holy name of Jesus (often we admonished each other that this holy name should end both our voices and our

lives). At the blow I turn round and see a hatchet all bloody; I kneel down to receive the blow which was to unite me with my dear companion; but, as they hesitate, I rise again and run to the dying man, who was quite near. They dealt him two other blows with the hatchet on the head and dispatched him, but not until I had first given him absolution, which I had been wont to give him every two days since our captivity; and this was a day on which he had already confessed.

It was the twenty-ninth of September, the feast of St. Michael, when this angel in innocence and this martyr of Jesus Christ gave his life for Him who had given him His. . . . I give him this title not only because he was killed by the enemies of God and of His Church and in the exercise of an ardent charity toward his neighbor, placing himself in evident peril for the love of God, but especially because he was killed on account of prayer, and notably for the sake of the holy Cross.

He was in a cabin where he nearly always said the prayers, which little pleased a superstitious old man who was there. One day, seeing a little child of three or four years in the cabin, with an excess of devotion and of love for the Cross and with a simplicity which we who are more prudent than he according to the flesh would not have shown, he took off his cap, put it on this child's head, and made a great sign of the cross upon its body. The old man seeing that, commanded a young man of his cabin, who was about to leave for the war, to kill him — which order he executed, as we have said.

Even the child's mother, on a journey in which I happened to be with her, told me that it was because of this sign of the cross that he had been killed. And the old man who had given the command that he should be slain, one day when they called me to his cabin to eat, when I had previously made the sign of the cross, said to me: "That is what we hate; that is why we killed thy companion, and why they will kill thee. Our neighbors, the Europeans,[14] do not do so."

VIEWING THE AUTHOR'S IDEAS

1. What natural traits of character fitted René Goupil for the religious life? What signs of zeal had he shown when in old France; when allowed to accompany Father Jogues; when captured?

---

[13] *non cibus utilis aegro.* Food is not useful to the sick.

[14] *Our neighbors, the Europeans,* the Dutch of New Amsterdam and the Puritans of New England.

2. Under what circumstances did René pronounce his vows? What immediate preparation did he have for making them; for his death?

3. Explain René's motive in accepting the oar. How did he react when his acceptance caused Father Jogues to be urged to row? What specific sufferings of René does Father Jogues mention? How does the priest minimize his own trials? Why can you infer that Jogues shared all of Goupil's tortures?

4. What proof does Father Jogues give that "nothing was wanting to make Goupil a martyr"? Why was the chief's anger especially aimed at Goupil? Explain the words "Our neighbors, the Europeans, do not do so."

5. Contrast the characters of Goupil and Jogues. How was each particularly fitted for his work in the conversion of the Indians? What qualities in the life of the two martyrs aided them to persevere despite torture?

EVALUATING HIS MANNER OF EXPRESSION

Would you judge that Father Jogues employed the method of understatement or of complete presentation when describing the torture inflicted by the savages? What is the value of this method of treatment from the artistic point of view; from its significancy as a revelation of his own character?

Never to Put On Gala Dress

(From *The Jesuit Relations*)
Claude Chauchetière, S.J.
Translated by Reuben Gold Thwaites

The smoke that curled upward from the savage Mohawk village of Ossernenon in 1656 drifted over the present site of Auriesville, New York. In this valley, textile from lake-fed rivers, Kateri Tekakwitha was born. Her mother was an Algonquin Christian, who after her capture by the Mohawks married into the tribe. Who knows what gifts this mother's heart may not have petitioned from Heaven as she traced the sign of the cross on the little girl's forehead? Yet at four years of age, Kateri was left alone with pagan relatives, pock-marked and with impaired eyesight as a result of the smallpox that had taken her parents. Even before the arrival of the blackrobes brought baptism in 1675, she lived the life of a Christian virgin, resisting the forcible attempts of her relatives to have her marry. In order to walk uninterruptedly her way of pain and purity, Kateri escaped to the Indian Mission of St. Francis Xavier at Kanawake, Canada, where she spent the last three years of her life. This account, written two years after her death, describes the mortifications of the Indian women inspired by Kateri's example.

DURING the past two years their fervor has greatly augmented since God has removed from this world one of these devout savage women who live like nuns. She died with the reputation of sanctity. We cease not to say Masses to thank God for the graces that we believe we receive every day through her intercession. Journeys are continually made to her tomb; and the savages, following her example, have become better Christians than they were. We daily see wonders worked through her intercession. Her name was Kateri Tekakwitha. During her lifetime she made an agreement with a friend to make each other suffer, because she was too weak to do so by herself owing to her continual illness. She had begged her companion to do her the charity of severely chastising her with blows from a whip. This they did for a year without anyone knowing it, and for that purpose they withdrew every Sunday into a cabin in the middle of the cemetery; and there taking in their hands willow shoots, they mingled prayers with penance. Finally, when one of the two saw that her companion had fallen sick at the end of the year, she was pressed by scruples to reveal the matter and to ask whether she had not sinned in what she had done.

At that time people here used only willow shoots or thorns, which here are very long; but since they have heard of the disciplines, of iron girdles, and of similar instruments of penance, the use of these daily becomes more general. And as the men have found that the women use them, they will not let themselves be outdone and ask us to permit them to use these every day, but we will not allow it.

The women to the number of eight or ten began the practice; and the wife of the *dogique*[1] — that is to say, of him who leads the singing and says the prayers — is among the number. She it is who in her husband's absence also causes the prayers to be said aloud and leads the singing; and in this capacity she assembles the devout women of whom we have spoken who call themselves *Sisters.* They tell one another their faults and deliberate together upon what must be done for the relief of the poor in the village, whose number is so great that there are almost as many poor as there are savages.

The sort of monastery that they maintain here has its rules. They have promised God never to put on their gala dress (for savage women have some taste and take pride in adorning themselves with porcelain beads, with vermilion, which they apply to their cheeks, and with earrings and bracelets). They assist one another in the fields; they meet together to incite one another to virtue; and one of them has been received as a nun in the hospital of Montreal. . . .

There are aged women, veterans in the Faith, who instruct the others, as missionaries would do; and God thereby supplies the want of these which we experience. There are many women who have shared their fields, thus, as it were, taking the bread from their own mouths to give it to the newcomers, who are not yet in a position to do anything for them in return, in order to win them to God. When there are widows and sick persons, the captains make their families work for the love of God at building cabins for those who have none. Some live in the woods in the same state of innocence as do those in the village; and they return with consciences as pure as when they went away. And I may state without exaggeration that when they return, we do not find in many of them matter for absolution; and yet they are sufficiently enlightened to accuse themselves of the least imperfections — such as slight distractions during their prayers, petty acts of impatience, some instance of forgetfulness, and things which, in their case, are often virtues. Modesty is natural to them. When they

[1] *dogique*, leader.

pray or sing in the church, they do so with so much devotion that all the French settlers here who see them are impressed by it and say that they are more devout than we allege. I was forgetting to tell you that, when they are in the woods, they have the Sundays and feast days marked by small lines to the number of seven, one for each day of the week. We mark crosses upon the lines that indicate the feast days and the Sundays, and they observe these very exactly.

VIEWING THE AUTHOR'S IDEAS

1. In your opinion which of the writer's statements give the greatest proof of Kateri Tekakwitha's holiness? Discuss the reason why Kateri preferred greater suffering than that caused by her continual illness.

2. Contrast the Indians' attitude toward women in Villagrá's tale with the desire of these Christian men to imitate the mortification of their tribeswomen. How do you account for the difference? In what way is the influence exerted by the Christian Indian women in keeping with the theory that womankind sets the moral standard in every group?

3. List the two types of activities among the women, noting on one side those good works which were done primarily for their own perfection, and on the other side those which first of all benefited others.

4. Read from the *Acts of the Apostles* 4:32-35, the passage which describes the manner in which the first Christians shared with one another. What actions of the Indians were in accord with this line of conduct? What social consciousness does this show?

5. What picture of common prayer among the Indians is given? What other liturgical acts of the Catholic religion did the Indians practice?

6. Point out sentences which reveal that the religious spirit of the Indian converts edified the author.

7. What did the writer mean when he wrote: "Modesty is natural to them"?

EVALUATING HIS MANNER OF EXPRESSION

Father Chauchetière is one of Kateri Tekakwitha's first biographers. Show how he manifests a detached spirit when he writes. Why would this be desirable in repeating incidents in the life of a saint?

Meditation Six

Edward Taylor

Men rarely look at money for the purpose of stirring their fancy. Yet a bright round coin with its authorized impress offers a challenge to the imagination. Christ used a coin in teaching the distinction between the homage to be given to God and to Caesar. His words lingered in the mind of Edward Taylor, who associated them with the statement from Genesis, "And God created man in His own image." In developing the idea of this creation as the work of a coinmaker, Taylor made use of the strained or elaborate type of comparison known as a conceit. When developed at great length, a conceit gives a poem decided unity. This same development may, however, overemphasize the intellectual element in the poem, thus causing the comparison to seem extravagant or artificial.

Canticles II:1: I am . . . the lily of the valleys.

AM I Thy gold or purse, Lord, for Thy wealth,
  Whether in mine or mint refined for Thee?
I'm counted so, but count me o'er Thyself
  Lest gold-washed[1] face and brass in heart I be.
    I fear my touchstone[2] touches[3] when I try
    Me and my counted gold too overly.

Am I new-minted by Thy stamp indeed?
  Mine eyes are dim; I cannot clearly see.
Be Thou my spectacles that I may read
  Thine image and inscription stamped on me.
    If Thy bright image do upon me stand,
    I am a golden angel[4] in Thy hand.

Lord, make my soul Thy plate: Thine image bright
  Within the circle of the same enfoil.[5]
And on its brims in golden letters write
  Thy superscription in an holy style.
    Then I shall be Thy money, Thou my hoard;[6]
    Let me Thy angel be, be Thou my Lord.

VIEWING THE AUTHOR'S IDEAS

1. According to Puritan theology, when would a soul be God's gold?

2. How would it be "in mine or mint refined" and "new-minted"?

3. What fear of Taylor shows the Puritan's self-scrutiny in regard to his election?

4. Explain the play on words in "golden angel." Under what circumstances does the poet consider the soul is really God's coin?

5. Quote any lines in which the poet seems to ask God's help in achieving salvation.

EVALUATING HIS MANNER OF EXPRESSION

1. Enumerate the features of the coin which Taylor uses to develop his comparison.

2. Discuss the effectiveness of the rhetorical devices of question; repetition; direct address.

3. Quote passages that show the poet's warm religious feeling.

4. Explain the use of the words *counted* and *count* in the third line of the first stanza.

5. How does the fifth line in the last stanza show a strong contrast?

6. Explain the contrast and pun found in the last line.

[1] *gold-washed*, gold-plated.

[2] *touchstone*, a stone used to test the purity of gold or silver.

[3] *touches*, marks made by rubbing gold or silver on a touchstone to test the purity of the metal.

[4] *angel*, an English gold coin bearing the figure of St. Michael the Archangel slaying the dragon. It was issued during the years between 1470 and 1634.

[5] *enfoil*, adorn or engrave.

[6] *hoard*, treasure.

Address of Thanks

The Chiefs of the Timucua Indians
Translated by Albert S. Gatschet

Cautiously picking their way through the intricacies of formal speech, five Timucua chiefs here present an eloquent comment on the persuasive power of Catholic leadership.

To Our King Our Lord:

Always we have been your subjects, but now with more reason and with whole heart are we your subjects, and intend to speak in this way.

Some white governors you have sent us, but like Don Diego[1] we have seen none; former white governors stay here, but like him we have not seen any. Therefore we invoke [upon you] the grace of God; he has succored us, the chiefs and poor subjects, with clothing, and for this cause we show our gratitude. Those white governors who came [here], had they all been like the present one, we would be better Christians, and there would be many more Christians in existence. For our benefit he has worked a great deal, and in person has visited all settlements of Christians and unbelievers, has helped us with advice, and having during all his trouble never neglected to attend Holy Mass, we hence call him a saint; all the priests who assist us, he told us to honor and reverence, as he has done himself before our eyes. We therefore pray you to let the governor stay many years with us, for he works for our weal, advising us to hear Mass and listen to the teachings of the priests. Therefore, we supplicate that God bestow His graces upon this white governor, our adviser. We all pray God

he may give life [to him], and thus we constantly pray and wish.

We all present have thus spoken at San Mateo, the twentieth and eighth day of the year [16]88. Don Francisco was speaker,[2] and he Francisco Martinez. Don Pedro, chief of San Pedro. Don Diego, chief of Machaua. Ventura, chief of Asile. Gregorio, chief of San Juan.

VIEWING THE AUTHORS' IDEAS

1. Why did the Indians say "now with more reason and with whole heart are we your subjects"?
2. What qualities of Christian leadership had Don Diego shown? Which of these seemed to make the greatest impression on the Indians?
3. Which statement of the letter is most significant concerning the question of the white man's conduct and the conversion of the Indian?
4. What qualities do the signers of the letter reveal?
5. How does the letter reveal that the Indians have been well-trained in the Catholic religion?
6. What influence of the missionaries can be found in the names of the chiefs?

EVALUATING THEIR MANNER OF EXPRESSION

1. What unusual sentence structure indicates that the Indian manner of expression differs from the English idiom?
2. Discuss the line of reasoning that the chiefs use in this letter. Do they offer sufficient evidence for their conclusions?

---

[1] *Don Diego*, Diego Quiroba y Losado. Spanish Governor of Florida.

[2] *speaker*, the chairman of the group, who spoke the words of the letter to the scribe.

A Puritan's Diary

Samuel Sewall

Samuel Sewall is scarcely a romantic lover. He is too greatly concerned with the cost of almonds and books, too much interested in the disposition of his intended wife's property. But neither does he pay court to an enamored young belle. Irresistible and self-assured, Madam Winthrop encourages

Sewall, only to reveal her desire for a coach, her disgust for his bald head, and her interest in a share of his wealth. The reader is accordingly not surprised when she eventually allows the parlor fire to die out and neglects to put on a clean frock for his visits. Perhaps one would be expecting too much to look for romance in the second courtship of a Puritan. Remarriage after the death of one's mate was a common occurrence in colonial times, when hardship or epidemic frequently carried away a husband or a wife. Indeed, a common act of neighborliness consisted in helping a lone widow or widower to choose a new mate.

JANUARY 13, 1677. Giving my chickens meat, it came to my mind that I gave them nothing save Indian corn and water, and yet they ate it and thrived very well; and that that food was necessary for them, how mean soever, which much affected me and convinced what need I stood in of spiritual food and that I should not nauseate[1] daily duties of prayer, etc.

January 13, 1696. . . . When I came in past seven at night, my wife met me in the entry and told me Betty[2] had surprised them. I was surprised with the abruptness of the relation. It seems Betty Sewall had given some signs of dejection and sorrow; but a little after dinner she burst out into an amazing cry, which caused all the family to cry too. Her mother asked the reason; she gave none. At last she said she was afraid she should go to hell, her sins were not pardoned. She was first wounded by my reading a sermon of Mr. Norton's[3] about the fifth of January. Text, John 7:34, "Ye shall seek Me and shall not find me." And those words in the sermon, John 8:21, "Ye shall seek me and shall die in your sins," ran in her mind and terrified her greatly. And staying at home, January 12, she read out of Mr. Cotton Mather, "Why hath Satan filled thy heart?" which increased her fear. Her mother asked her whether she prayed. She answered yes, but feared her prayers were not heard because her sins not pardoned. Mr. Willard,[4] though sent for timelier, yet not being told of the message, . . . he came not till after I came home. He discoursed with Betty, who could not give a distinct account but was confused, as his phrase was, and as had experienced in himself. Mr. Willard prayed excellently. The Lord bring light and comfort out of this dark and dreadful cloud and grant that Christ's being formed in my dear child may be the issue of these painful pangs.

October 15 [1717]. My wife got some relapse by a new cold and grew very bad. Sent for Mr. Oakes,[5] and he sat up with me all night.

[October] 16. The distemper increases; yet my wife speaks to me to go to bed.

[October] 17. Thursday, I asked my wife whether 'twere best for me to go to Lecture;[6] she said, "I can't tell"; so I stayed at home. Put up a note.[7] It being my son's lecture and I absent, 'twas taken much notice of.[8] Major General Winthrop and his lady visited us. I thank her that she would visit my poor wife.

Friday, October 18. My wife grows worse and exceedingly restless. Prayed God to look upon her. Asked not after my going to bed. Had the advice of Mr. Williams and Dr. Cutler.[9]

Seventh Day, October 19. Called Dr. C. Mather to pray, which he did excellently in the dining room, having suggested good thoughts to my wife before he went down. After Mr. Wadsworth[10] prayed in the chamber when 'twas supposed that my wife took little notice. About a quarter of an hour past four, my dear wife expired in the afternoon, whereby the chamber was filled with a flood of tears. God is teaching me a new lesson; to live a widower's life. Lord help me to learn; and be a sun and shield to me, now so much of my comfort and defense are taken away.

March 14 [1718]. Deacon Marion comes to me, sits with me a great while in the evening. After a great deal of discourse about his courtship, he told [me] the Olivers said they wished I would court their aunt.[11] I said little, but said 'twas not five months since I buried my dear wife. Had said before 'twas hard to know whether best to marry again or no; whom to marry. Gave him a book of the Berlin Jewish converts.[12]

October 1 [1720]. Saturday. I dine at Mr. Stoddard's; from thence I went to Madam Winthrop's just at three.

---

[1] *nauseate,* feel distaste for.

[2] *Betty,* Sewall's fifteen-year-old daughter.

[3] *a sermon of Mr. Norton's.* John Norton was a Puritan minister who wrote numerous sermons and theological works.

[4] *Mr. Willard,* pastor of Old South Church, Boston.

[5] *Mr. Oakes,* Doctor Thomas Oakes, a Boston physician.

[6] *Lecture,* the Thursday church services.

[7] *put up a note,* sent a note to the pastor asking the prayers of the congregation.

[8] *my son's lecture . . . much notice of.* Absence from church services caused inquiry to be made. Sewall's failure to be present was especially remarked on the occasion as his son Joseph gave the lecture.

[9] *Mr. Williams and Dr. Cutler,* Boston physicians.

[10] *Mr. Wadsworth,* a Puritan minister and writer.

[11] *aunt,* Madam Winthrop.

[12] *Berlin Jewish converts,* a work by Cotton Mather, entitled *Faith Encouraged. A Strange Impression from Heaven on the Minds of Some Jewish Children at the City of Berlin* (1718).

Spoke to her, saying my loving wife had died so soon and suddenly, 'twas hardly convenient for me to think of marrying again; however, I came to this resolution, that I would not make my court to any person without first consulting with her. Had a pleasant discourse about seven single persons sitting in the foreseat[13] September twenty-ninth; viz, Madam Rebecca Dudley, Katherine Winthrop, Bridget Usher, Deliverance Legg, Rebecca Lloyd, Lydia Colman, Elizabeth Bellingham. She propounded one and another for me, but none would do; said Mrs. Lloyd was about her age.

October 12. . . . Mrs. Anne Cotton came to door ('twas before eight), said Madam Winthrop was within, directed me into the little room, where she was full of work behind a stand. Mrs. Cotton came in and stood. Madam Winthrop pointed to her to set me a chair. Madam Winthrop's countenance was much changed from what 'twas on Monday; looked dark and lowering. At last the work (black stuff or silk) was taken away; I got my chair in place, had some converse, but very cold and indifferent to what 'twas before. Asked her to acquit me of rudeness if I drew off her glove. Inquiring the reason, I told her 'twas great odds between handling a dead goat and a living lady. Got it off. I told her I had one petition to ask of her — that was that she would take off the negative[14] she laid on me the third of October. She readily answered she could not and enlarged upon it; she told me of it so soon as she could; could not leave her house, children, neighbors, business. I told her she might do some good to help and support me. Mentioning Mrs. Gookin (Nath.), the Widow Weld was spoken of; said I had visited Mrs. Denison.[15] I told her "Yes!" Afterward I said if after a first and second vagary[16] she would accept of me returning, her victorious kindness and good will would be very obliging. She thanked me for my book (Mr. Mayhew's sermon) but said not a word of the letter.[17] When she insisted on the negative, I prayed there might be no more thunder and lightning;[18] I should not sleep all night. I gave her Dr. Preston, *The Church's Marriage and the Church's Carriage*, which cost me six shillings at the sale. The door was standing open; Mr. Airs came in, hung up his hat, and sat down. After awhile, Madam Winthrop moving, he went out. John Eyre looked in; I said, "How do ye?" or "Your servant, Mr. Eyre," but heard no word from him. Sarah filled a glass of wine; she drank to me, I to her; she sent Juno home with me with a good lantern. I gave her six pence and bid her thank her mistress. In some of our discourse, I told her I had rather go to the Stone House[19] adjoining to her than come to her against her mind. Told her the reason why I came every other night lest I should drink too deep draughts of pleasure. . . .

October 19. Midweek. Visited Madam Winthrop. Sarah told me she was at Mr. Walley's; would not come home till late. I gave her Hannah three oranges with her duty, not knowing whether I should find her or no. Was ready to go home; but said if I knew she was there, I would go thither. Sarah seemed to speak with pretty good courage she would be there. I went and found her there with Mr. Walley and his wife in the little room below. At seven o'clock I mentioned going home; at eight I put on my coat and quickly waited on her home. She found occasion to speak loud to the servant, as if she had a mind to be known. Was courteous to me, but took occasion to speak pretty earnestly about my keeping a coach. I said 'twould cost one hundred pounds per annum; she said 'twould cost me but forty.

October 20 . . . At council, Colonel Townsend spake to me of my hood; should get a wig. I said 'twas my chief ornament; I wore it for sake of the day. Brother Odlin, and Sam, Mary, and Jane Hirst dine with us. Promised to wait on the Governor[20] about seven. Madam Winthrop not being at Lecture, I went thither first; found her very serene with her daughter Noyes, Mrs. Dering, and the Widow Shipreeve, sitting at a little table, she in her armed chair. She drank to me, and I to Mrs. Noyes. After a while prayed the favor to speak with her. She took one of the candles and went into the best room, closed the shutters, sat down upon the couch. She told me Madam Usher had been there and said the coach must be set on wheels, and not by rusting. She spake something of my needing a wig. Asked me what

---

[13] *foreseat*, a seat near the pulpit in which prominent members of the congregation sat.

[14] *negative*, Madam Winthrop had refused to marry him on October 3. He had begged her to give the matter further consideration.

[15] *Mrs. Gookin . . . Widow Weld . . . Mrs. Denison*, widows to whom Sewall might pay his court.

[16] *vagary*. Sewall here means discontinuing his courtship of Madam Winthrop to make his suit to other widows.

[17] *thanked me . . . the letter*. Sewall had written to Madam Winthrop on October 11 and sent her one of the sermons of Experience Mayhew, a famous Puritan missionary to the Indians.

[18] *thunder and lightning*, Sewall was extremely afraid of thunder and lightning.

[19] *Stone House*, a tavern.

[20] *the Governor*, Governor Dudley of Massachusetts.

her sister said to me. I told her she said if her sister were for it, she would not hinder it. But I told her she did not say she would be glad to have me for her brother. Said, "I shall keep you in the cold"; and asked her if she would be within tomorrow night, for we had had but a running feat. She said she could not tell whether she should or no. I took leave. As we were drinking at the Governor's, he said in England the ladies minded little more than that they might have money and coaches to ride in. I said, "And New England brooks its name."[21] At which Mr. Dudley smiled. Governor said they were not quite so bad here.

October 21. Friday. My son, the minister, came to me P.M. by appointment, and we pray for one another in the old chamber, more especially respecting my courtship. About six o'clock I go to Madam Winthrop's. Sarah told me her mistress was gone out, but did not tell me whither she went. She presently ordered me a fire; so I went in, having Dr. Sibbes' *Bowels*[22] with me to read. I read the two first sermons; still nobody came in. At last, about nine o'clock Mr. John Eyre[23] came in; I took opportunity to say to him, as I had done to Mrs. Noyes[24] before, that I hoped my visiting his mother would not be disagreeable to him; he answered me with much respect. When 'twas after nine o'clock, he of himself said he would go and call her; she was but at one of his brothers'; awhile after, I heard Madam Winthrop's voice inquiring something about John. After a good while and clapping the garden door twice or thrice, she came in. I mentioned something of the lateness; she bantered and said I was later. She received me courteously. I asked when our proceedings[25] should be made public; she said they were like to be no more public than they were already. Offered no wine that I remember. I rose up at eleven o'clock to come away, saying I would put on my coat. She offered not to help me. I prayed her that Juno might light me home; she opened the shutter and said 'twas pretty light abroad; Juno was weary and gone to bed. So I came home by starlight as well as I could. At my first coming in, I gave Sarah five shillings. I writ Mr. Eyre his name in his book with the date October 21,

1720. It cost me eight shillings. *Jehovah-jireh!*[26] Madam told me she had visited M. Mico, Wendell, and William Clark of the South [Church].

November 2. Midweek. Went again and found Mrs. Allen there, who went quickly out. Gave her about one half pound of sugar almonds; cost three shillings per pound. Carried them on Monday. She seemed pleased with them, asked what they cost. Spake of giving her a hundred pounds per annum if I died before her. Asked her what sum she would give me if she should die first. Said I would give her time to consider of it. She said she had heard as if I had given all to my children by deeds of gift. I told her 'twas a mistake. Point Judith[27] was mine, etc. That in England, I owned, my father's desire was that it should go to my eldest son; 'twas twenty pounds per annum; she thought 'twas forty. I think when I seemed to excuse pressing this, she seemed to think 'twas best to speak of it; a long winter was coming on. Gave me a glass or two of canary.[28]

November 4. Friday. Went again about seven o'clock; found Mr. John Walley and his wife; sat discoursing pleasantly. I showed them Isaac Moses's [an Indian] writing. Madam W. served comfits[29] to us. After a while a table was spread, and supper was set. I urged Mr. Walley to crave a blessing; but he put it upon me. About nine they went away. I asked Madam what fashioned necklace I should present her with; she said, "None at all." I asked her whereabout we left off last time, mentioned what I offered to give her, asked her what she would give me; she said she could not change her condition. . . . She charged me with saying that she must put away Juno[30] if she came to me; I utterly denied it, it never came in my heart; yet she insisted upon it, saying it came in upon discourse about the Indian woman that obtained her freedom this court. About ten I said I would not disturb the good orders of her house and came away, she not seeming pleased with my coming away. Spake to her about David Jefferies; had not seen him.

Monday. November 7. My son prayed in the old chamber. Our time had been taken up by Son and Daughter Cooper's visit, so that I read only the 130th and 143rd Psalm. 'Twas on the account of my courtship.

[21] *brooks its name*, carries its name well.

[22] *Dr. Sibbes' Bowels*, a book by Richard Sibbes, entitled *Bowels Opened: or a Discovery of the Union Betwixt Christ and His Church*.

[23] *Mr. John Eyre*, Madam Winthrop's son by her first marriage.

[24] *Mrs. Noyes*, Madam Winthrop's daughter.

[25] *proceedings*, engagement.

[26] *Jehovah-jireh!* the Lord will provide.

[27] *Point Judith*, Sewall's land at Narragansett Bay.

[28] *canary*, a sweet wine made on the Canary Islands.

[29] *comfits*, candied or dried fruits.

[30] *put away Juno*. Juno was a slave, and Sewall was opposed to slavery.

I went to Madam Winthrop; found her rocking little Katee in the cradle. I excused my coming so late (near eight). She set me an armed chair and cushion; and so the cradle was between her armed chair and mine. Gave her the remnant of my almonds; she did not eat of them as before but laid them away; I said I came to inquire whether she had altered her mind since Friday or remained of the same mind still. She said, "Thereabouts." I told her I loved her, and was so fond as to think that she loved me. She said she had a great respect for me. I told her I had made her an offer without asking any advice; she had so many to advise with that 'twas a hindrance. The fire was come to one short brand besides the block, which brand was set up in end; at last it fell to pieces, and no recruit was made. She gave me a glass of wine. I think I repeated again that I would go home and bewail my rashness in making more haste than good speed. I would endeavor to contain myself and not go on to solicit her to do that which she could not consent to. Took leave of her. As came down the steps she bid me have a care. Treated me courteously. Told her she had entered the fourth year of her widowhood. I had given her the *News-Letter* before. I did not bid her draw off her glove as sometimes I had done. Her dress was not so clean as sometimes it had been. *Jehovah-jireh!*

Midweek. November 9. Dine at Brother Stoddard's; were so kind as to inquire of me if they should invite Madam Winthrop; I answered, "No."

VIEWING THE AUTHOR'S IDEAS

1. How does this selection reflect Puritan manners and modes of thought; the place of religion in Puritan life? What Puritan belief does Betty's story illustrate?

2. What evidence of changing standards of living are reflected in the attitudes of Madam Winthrop?

3. Trace the course of Sewall's courtship of Madam Winthrop.

4. What were the chief causes of contention between Sewall and Madam Winthrop? Do you think she would have accepted him if he had yielded to all her demands?

EVALUATING HIS MANNER OF EXPRESSION

1. Cite instances of unconscious humor, frank realism, and unwitting self-portraiture which make Sewall's *Diary* a classic.

2. Madam Winthrop stands out clearly in Sewall's story of his courtship. By what means does the author show her various characteristics? Give specific illustrations.

3. Get a copy of Pepys' *Diary* and compare it with Sewall's in terseness, humor, and self-revelation.

A Visit to Colonel Spotswood

(From *A Progress to the Mines*)

William Byrd

In the fall of 1732 William Byrd journeyed from his own beautiful Westover plantation on the James River to visit Colonel Spotswood's mines, located on a forty-five-thousand-acre estate bordering the Rappahannock. In his Progress to the Mines *Colonel Byrd preserved for his descendants a day-by-day account of his four-day visit. The Westover Manuscripts, the bound volume containing this piece, lay unpublished for more than a hundred years. It is valued today not only for its sprightly, witty style, but also because it pictures the genial, cosmopolitan Virginia plantation life of the early eighteenth century.*

[S]EPTEMBER] 27 [1732] . . . I came into the main country road that leads from Fredericksburg to Germanna, which last place I reached in ten miles more. This famous town consists of Colonel Spotswood's enchanted castle on one side of the street and a baker's dozen of ruinous tenements on the other, where so many German families had dwelt some years ago, but are now removed ten miles higher in the fork of Rappahannock to land of their own. There had also been a chapel about a bowshot[1] from the Colonel's house, at the end of an avenue of cherry trees, but some pious people had lately burnt it down with intent to get another nearer to their own homes. Here I arrived about three o'clock and found only Mrs. Spotswood at home, who received

---

[1] *bowshot*, the distance an arrow travels when shot from a bow.

her old acquaintance with many a gracious smile. I was carried into a room elegantly set off with pier glasses,[2] the largest of which came soon after to an odd misfortune. Amongst other favorite animals that cheered this lady's solitude, a brace[3] of tame deer ran familiarly about the house, and one of them came to stare at me as a stranger. But unluckily spying his own figure in the glass, he made a spring over the tea table that stood under it and shattered the glass to pieces; and falling back upon the tea table, made a terrible fracas[4] among the china. This exploit was so sudden and accompanied with such a noise that it surprised me and perfectly frightened Mrs. Spotswood. But 'twas worth all the damage to show the moderation and good humor with which she bore this disaster. In the evening the noble Colonel came home from his mines, who saluted me very civilly, and Mrs. Spotswood's sister, Miss Theky, who had been to meet him *en cavalier*,[5] was so kind as to bid me welcome. We talked over a legend[6] of old stories, supped about nine, and then prattled with the ladies till 'twas time for a traveler to retire. In the meantime I observed my old friend to be very uxorious[7] and exceedingly fond of his children. This was so opposite to the maxims he used to preach up before he was married that I could not forbear rubbing up the memory of them. But he gave a very good-natured turn to his change of sentiments by alleging that whoever brings a poor gentle woman into so solitary a place, from all her friends and acquaintance, would be ungrateful not to use her and all that belongs to her with all possible tenderness.

28. We all kept snug in our several apartments till nine except Miss Theky, who was the housewife of the family. At that hour we met over a pot of coffee, which was not quite strong enough to give us the palsy. After breakfast the Colonel and I left the ladies to their domestic affairs and took a turn in the garden, which has nothing beautiful but three terrace walks that fall in slopes one below another. I let him understand that besides the pleasure of paying him a visit I came to be instructed by so great a master in the mystery of making of iron, wherein he had led the way and was the Tubal-cain[8] of Virginia. He corrected me a little there by assuring me he was not only the first in this country but the first in North America who had erected a regular furnace.[9] That they ran altogether upon bloomeries[10] in New England and Pennsylvania till his example had made them attempt greater works. But in this last colony they have so few ships to carry their iron to Great Britain that they must be content to make it only for their own use and must be obliged to manufacture it when they have done. That he hoped he had done the country very great service by setting so good an example. That the four furnaces now at work in Virginia circulated a great sum of money for provisions and all other necessities in the adjacent counties. . . .

Our conversation on this subject continued till dinner, which was both elegant and plentiful. The afternoon was devoted to the ladies, who showed me one of their most beautiful walks. They conducted me through a shady lane to the landing and by the way made me drink some very fine water that issued from a marble fountain and ran incessantly. Just behind it was a covered bench where Miss Theky often sat and bewailed her virginity.[11] Then we proceeded to the river, which is the south branch of Rappahannock, about fifty yards wide and so rapid that the ferryboat is drawn over by a chain, and therefore called the Rapidan. At night we drank prosperity to all the Colonel's projects in a bowl of rack punch[12] and then retired to our devotions.

29. Having employed about two hours in retirement, I sallied out at the first summons to breakfast, where our conversation with the ladies, like whip sillabub,[13] was very pretty but has nothing in it. This it seems was Miss Theky's birthday, upon which I made her my compliments and wished she might live twice as long a married woman as she had lived a maid. I did not presume to pry into the secret of her age, nor was she forward to disclose it for this humble reason, lest I should think her wisdom fell short of her years.

---

[2] *pier glasses*, large high mirrors, generally occupying the wall space between windows.

[3] *brace*, a pair.

[4] *fracas*, uproar.

[5] *en cavalier*, on horseback.

[6] *legend*, The word is here confused with *legion*, a great number.

[7] *uxorious*, unusually fond of, or submissive to, one's wife.

[8] *Tubal-cain*, a Biblical character to whom the invention of the art of forging metals is ascribed.

[9] *regular furnace*, a blast furnace in which iron ore is refined in a single process.

[10] *bloomeries*, primitive forges for making wrought-iron blocks from the ore. In comparison with the blast furnace method, the bloomery process is crude.

[11] *virginity*, spinsterhood.

[12] *rack punch*, a drink made with wine.

[13] *whip sillabub*, sweetened cream, flavored with wine and beaten to a froth.

. . . We had a Michaelmas goose[14] for dinner, of Miss Theky's own raising, who was now good-natured enough to forget the jeopardy of her dog.[15] In the afternoon we walked in a meadow by the riverside, which winds in the form of a horseshoe about Germanna, making it a peninsula containing about four hundred acres. Rappahannock forks about fourteen miles below this place, the northern branch being the larger, and consequently must be the river that bounds my Lord Fairfax's grant of the Northern Neck.[16]

30. The sun rose clear this morning, and so did I and finished all my little affairs by breakfast. It was then resolved to wait on[17] the ladies on horseback, since the bright sun, the fine air, and the wholesome exercise all invited us to it. We forded the river a little above the ferry and rode six miles up the Neck to a fine level piece of rich land, where we found about twenty plants of ginseng[18] with the scarlet berries growing on the top of the middle stalk. The root of this is of wonderful virtue in many cases, particularly to raise the spirits and promote perspiration, which makes it a specific[19] in colds and coughs. The Colonel complimented me with all we found in return for my telling him the virtues of it. We were all pleased to find so much of this king of plants so near the Colonel's habitation and growing, too, upon his own land; but were, however, surprised to find it upon level ground, after we had been told it grew only upon the north side of stony mountains. I carried home this treasure with as much joy as if every root had been a graft of the tree of life and washed and dried it carefully. This airing made us as hungry as so many hawks, so that between appetite and a very good

dinner 'twas difficult to eat like a philosopher.[20] In the afternoon the ladies walked me about amongst all their little animals with which they amuse themselves and furnish the table; the worst of it is, they are so tender-hearted they shed a silent tear every time any of them are killed.

VIEWING THE AUTHOR'S IDEAS

1. Point out details in the Spotswood home which show wealth and comfort; a chivalrous respect for women; courtesy and hospitality; love of outdoor life; harmonious family relationships; religious practices. Select passages which illustrate Byrd's good humor; his optimism; his business enterprise.

2. What trends in American economic life are revealed in Byrd's description of Germanna; in Colonel Spotswood's account of his mining business? State some of the results of these trends today. What services did Colonel Spotswood render to his country by developing the mining industry?

EVALUATING HIS MANNER OF EXPRESSION

1. What is Byrd's attitude toward Miss Theky; Mrs. Spotswood; the Colonel?

2. Read one of the essays of Joseph Addison depicting the manners of eighteenth century society. Note any resemblances between the English and the American writer. Cite witty comments of Byrd which show the Addisonian touch.

3. Attractive qualities of travel literature are interesting observations upon people, vivid impressions of scenes, amusing anecdotes, humorous comments upon manners and customs. Show how these qualities are exemplified in Byrd's account of his visit to Colonel Spotswood. Write a journal of a trip you have recently made. In your account try to include all the admirable features of Byrd's journal.

4. Byrd's journal gives a picture of the country gentleman of Virginia in colonial days. Compare Byrd's account of Southern colonial life with the picture of New England as revealed by Samuel Sewall. Which of the two diarists has the greater literary charm?

---

[14] *Michaelmas (mĭk'-el-măs) goose.* According to a popular tradition Queen Elizabeth established the custom of eating a goose on the feast of St. Michael, September 29, in commemoration of the destruction of the Spanish Armada.

[15] *jeopardy of her dog.* The Colonel had that morning threatened to kill Miss Theky's dog for a trifling misdemeanor.

[16] *Lord Fairfax . . . Northern Neck.* Lord Fairfax owned about six million acres of land in the Northern Neck, the section of Virginia between the Potomac and the Rappahannock.

[17] *wait on*, accompany.

[18] *ginseng*, a medicinal plant.

[19] *specific*, remedy.

[20] *like a philosopher*, with moderation.

Journey from Patapsco to Annapolis, April 4, 1750

John Lewis, S.J.

At Georgetown University lies the yellowed manuscript of what is probably the first Catholic poem written in the thirteen colonies. The following lines are taken from Father Lewis' description of his journey. Patapsco, his starting point, is a settlement south of Baltimore in Anne Arundel county.

HERE various flowers grace the teeming plains
Adorned by Nature's hand with beauteous stains.
First-born of Spring, the bloodroot there appears,
Whose golden root a silver blossom rears.
In spreading tufts see there the crowfoot blue,   5
On whose green leaves still shines a globous[1] dew;
Behold the cinquefoil with its dazzling dye
Of flaming yellow, wounds the tender eye;
But there, inclosed, the grassy wheat is seen
To heal the aching sight with cheerful green.   10
   Safe in yon cottage dwells the monarch swain,
His subject flocks, close-grazing, hide the plain . . .
His sons robust his daily labor share
Patient of toil, companions of his care.
And all their toils with sweet success are crown'd.   15
In graceful ranks their trees adorn the ground.
The peach, the plum, the apple tree here are found-
Delicious fruits — which from their kernels rise,
So fruitful is the soil, so mild the skies.
The lowly quince yon sloping hill o'ershades,   20
Here lofty cherry trees erect their heads;
Low at whose sandy base the river glides,
Slow-rolling near their height his languid tides.
Shade above shade the trees in rising ranks
Clothe with eternal green his sleepy banks . . .   25
   The sun near setting now arrays his head
In milder beams and lengthens ev'ry shade.
The rising clouds usurping on the day
A bright variety of dyes display;
About the wide horizon swift then fly   30
And chase a change of colors round the sky.
And now I view but half the flaming sphere,
Now one faint glimmer shoots along the air,
And all his golden glories disappear.

---

[1] *globous,* shaped like a sphere.

VIEWING THE AUTHOR'S IDEAS

1. What native plants and trees does the poet observe on his journey?

2. What use does he make of details to suggest an atmosphere of peace and beauty?

3. How is sunset pictured in the poem?

Sinners in the Hands of an Angry God

Application [of the Text]
Jonathan Edwards

"Sinners in the Hands of an Angry God," the best known of Puritan sermons, was developed to convince the hearers that they were dangling over the pit of hell. It is not surprising that in the course of its delivery the members of the congregation grasped at the church pillars to keep from falling or hysterically cried aloud. Yet the preacher was the spiritually-sensitive Jonathan Edwards, who could teach the love of God and could pause in ecstatic awe over the Creator's beauty revealed in nature. The fumes of brimstone perceptible in these paragraphs from the sermon can be explained as the results of Puritan logic. Having denied God's justice in allowing all men free will to work out their salvation, the Puritan preacher could only picture God as an angry Deity about to vent His wrath on those unfortunate mortals whom He had not called to election.

THE use may be of awakening to unconverted persons in this congregation. This that you have heard is the case of every one of you that are out of Christ. That world of misery, that lake of burning brimstone, is extended abroad under you. There is the dreadful pit of the glowing flames of the wrath of God; there is hell's wide gaping mouth open; and you have nothing to stand upon nor anything to take hold of; there is nothing between you and hell but the air; 'tis only the power and mere pleasure of God that holds you up.

You probably are not sensible of this; you find you are kept out of hell but do not see the hand of God in it; but look at other things, as the good state of your bodily constitution, your care of your own life, and the means you use for your own preservation. But indeed these things are nothing; if God should withdraw His hand, they would avail no more to keep you from falling than the thin air to hold up a person that is suspended in it.

Your wickedness makes you as it were heavy as lead and to tend downwards with great weight and pressure towards hell; and if God should let you go, you would immediately sink and swiftly descend and plunge into the bottomless gulf; and your healthy constitution, and your own care and prudence, and best contrivance, and all your righteousness, would have no more influence to uphold you and keep you out of hell than a spider's web would have to stop a falling rock. Were it not that so is the sovereign pleasure of God, the earth would not bear you one moment, for you are a burden to it; the creation groans with you; the creature is made subject to the bondage of your corruption, not willingly; the sun does not willingly shine on you to give you light to serve sin and Satan; the earth does not willingly yield her increase to satisfy your lusts, nor is it willingly a stage for your wickedness to be acted upon; the air does not willingly serve you for breath to maintain the flame of life in your vitals, while you spend your life in the service of God's enemies. God's creatures are good and were made for men to serve God with, and do not willingly subserve to any other purpose, and groan when they are abused to purposes so directly contrary to their nature and end. And the world would spew you out were it not for the sovereign hand of Him who hath subjected it in hope. There are the black clouds of God's wrath now hanging directly over your heads, full of the dreadful storm and big with thunder; and were it not for the restraining hand of God, it would immediately burst forth upon you. The sovereign pleasure of God for the present stays His rough wind; otherwise it would come with fury, and your destruction would come like a whirlwind, and you would be like the chaff of the summer threshing floor.

The wrath of God is like great waters that are dammed for the present; they increase more and more and rise higher and higher, till an outlet is given; and the longer the stream is stopped, the more rapid and mighty is its course when once it is let loose. 'Tis true that judgment against your evil works has not been executed hitherto; the floods of God's vengeance have been withheld; but your guilt in the meantime is constantly increasing, and you are every day treasuring up more wrath; the waters are continually rising and waxing more and more mighty; and there is nothing but the mere pleasure of God that holds the waters back, that are unwilling to be stopped and press hard to go forward. If God should only withdraw His hand from the floodgate, it would immediately fly open, and the fiery floods of the fierceness and wrath of God would rush forth with inconceivable fury and would come upon you with omnipotent power; and if your strength were ten thousand times greater than it is, yea, ten thousand times greater than the strength of the stoutest, sturdiest devil in hell, it would be nothing to withstand or endure it.

The bow of God's wrath is bent, and the arrow made ready on the string; and justice bends the arrow at your heart and strains the bow; and it is nothing but the mere pleasure of God, and that of an angry God without any promise or obligation at all, that keeps the arrow one moment from being made drunk with your blood.

Thus are all you that never passed under a great change of heart by the mighty power of the Spirit of God upon your souls; all that were never born again, and made new creatures, and raised from being dead in sin to a state of new, and before altogether unexperienced, light and life (however you may have reformed your life in many things, and may have had religious affections, and may keep up a form of religion in your families and closets and in the house of God, and may be strict in it) you are thus in the hands of an angry God; 'tis nothing but His mere pleasure that keeps you from being this moment swallowed up in everlasting destruction.

However unconvinced you may now be of the truth of what you hear, by and by you will be fully convinced of it. Those that are gone from being in the like circumstances with you see it was so with them; for destruction came suddenly upon most of them when they expected nothing of it and while they were saying, *peace and safety.* Now they see that those things that they depended on for peace and safety were nothing but thin air and empty shadows.

The God that holds you over the pit of hell, much as one holds a spider or some loathsome insect over the fire, abhors you and is dreadfully provoked; His wrath towards you burns like fire; He looks upon you as worthy of nothing else but to be cast into the fire; He is of purer eyes than to bear to have you in His sight; you are ten thousand times so abominable in His eyes as the most hateful venomous serpent is in ours. You have offended Him infinitely more than ever a stubborn rebel did his prince; and yet 'tis nothing but His hand that holds you from falling into the fire every moment. 'Tis to be ascribed to nothing else that you did not go to hell the last night; that you were suffered to awake again in this world after you closed your eyes to sleep. And there is no other reason to be given why you have not dropped into hell since you arose in the morning, but that God's hand has held you up. There is no other reason to be given why you have not dropped into hell since you have sat here in the House of God, provoking His pure eyes by your sinful, wicked manner of attending His solemn worship; yea, there is nothing else that is to be given as a reason why you do not this very moment drop down into hell.

O Sinner! Consider the fearful danger you are in. It is a great furnace of wrath, a wide and bottomless pit, full of the fire of wrath, that you are held over in the hand of that God Whose wrath is provoked and incensed as much against you as against many of the damned in hell. You hang by a slender thread with the flames of divine wrath flashing about it and ready every moment to singe it and burn it asunder; and you have no interest in any Mediator and nothing to lay hold of to save yourself, nothing to keep off the flames of wrath, nothing of your own, nothing that you have ever done, nothing that you can do, to induce God to spare you one moment.

VIEWING THE AUTHOR'S IDEAS

1. What would the term "out of Christ" mean in the Puritan system of theology?

2. Select the statements throughout the sermon intended to make the members of the congregation aware that they are on the brink of hell.

3. Edwards distinguishes between two kinds of men. Who are those who "pass under a great change of heart"? Describe the state of those who "may keep up a form of religion."

4. If you were to prepare a sermon on hell, how would your arguments differ from Edwards on the question of (a) the attitude of God toward the sinner (b) the ability of the sinner to obtain pardon (c) the torments of hell itself.

EVALUATING HIS MANNER OF EXPRESSION

1. Under stress of emotion an author may attribute to inanimate nature the feelings or traits of human beings. This imaginative usage has been termed the *pathetic fallacy.* In what instances has Jonathan Edwards attributed to nature the feelings of mankind? Compare his statement "the sun does not willingly shine on you . . ." with the words of Christ in *Matt.* 5:44-45.

2. Although Jonathan Edwards' style is plain and direct, it gains force from its imagery, orderliness, and cadenced sentences. Point out effective images in the sermon; examples of logical development of thought; sentences having a rhythmical flow of language.

A Missioner's Diary

Fray Junípero Serra

Here is a week's diary of the Apostle of California. Fray Junípero Serra's days were curiously alike. His "gentiles," the inquisitive and simple-hearted Indians, had stolen his heart as they had stolen his spectacles and would have liked to take his habit. There were urgent reasons in 1769 for establishing missions and fortified settlements in California. In Alaska, Russia showed a curious interest in the Pacific Coast. The Franciscans, having taken over the Jesuit missions in Lower California, were eager to extend their apostolic labors northward. Charles III of Spain ordered Don Joseph de Galvez, Visitador-General of New Spain, to send soldiers and missionaries into Upper California "to establish the Catholic Faith, to extend the Spanish dominion, and to check ambitious schemes of a foreign nation." Four expeditions set out for San Diego from Lower California early in 1769, two by sea and two by land. Don Fernando de Rivera, Captain of the Presidio, commanded the first land division with Fray Juan Crespi and Fray Fernando Parron as accompanying missionaries. Fray Junípero Serra went with the second expedition, commanded by Don Gaspar de Portola, Governor of California. In his Diary *Fray Junípero tells of the journey which began at Mission Loreto on March 28, 1769, and ended July 1 at San Diego. Over steep hills and sandy ravines, through regions smiling with trees and flowers, the party struggled in the direction of the coast, always hoping to see the Pacific from the top of the next hill. By June 24, feast of St. John the Baptist, the travelers had reached the rough land leading to San Diego, where the ocean was often in sight. The* Diary *continues the story from this point.*

ON THE Twenty-Fourth, Feast of the Holy Precursor, San Juan,[1] after Mass a market was set up, the soldiers and gentiles[2] trading little white handkerchiefs, which the latter greatly crave, for various strings of fresh fish in which they well showed themselves not to be a bit fools, because if the handkerchief was small, also the fish were less that they gave for it, without haggling or disputes doing any good. And if the cloth were a half larger, they corresponded to it with a double quantity of their fish. We took leave of such good people and set out following our road, that today was of four hours and a half, in the direction of the north, leaving the sea behind us at the setting out. We walked along a very rocky arroyo,[3] and then we undertook to climb a very steep and rocky hill. After about an hour of walking, the sea showed itself to us again. It looked near but was quite far if we tried to get near it. We crossed a very leafy arroyo of sycamores and oaks, but without water. At last, over various rises and hills we came to a very large valley with fine pastures and trees at its ends, with its good arroyo and pool of good water; a site, as it appears, for another very good mission, that we call San Juan Bautista. We slept under a very corpulent oak, and here we lacked the privilege of California of exemption from fleas, because we were covered with them and some ticks. We had an abundance of gentiles, as well along the road as after our arrival; those from near-by places on the road came to us, no less pleasant than those passed. By asking them, among other things, if they wished that I should remain with them there, they told me, "Yes." It gave me great grief to see these gentiles, so many souls and

---

[1] *San Juan,* St. John the Baptist.

[2] *gentiles,* unconverted Indians.

[3] *arroyo,* a small, often dry, channel carved by water.

so domestic,[4] and to have to leave them. It was a great affliction to me.

On the twenty-fifth after Mass and the other things that offered, we set out ahead and along a very different road, the most of it in sight of the sea. At the end of three hours and a half that the day's journey lasted today, we came to explore the valley where we stopped. But the descent to it was most long and very steep. It seemed more like sliding than walking, and all the earth so movable that it seemed dust, in which the beasts stuck. But at last we finished it, and we halted in the bottom of a luxuriant plain that already appears like a mission formed, not only on account of the arrangement of the place but also on account of the many huts of the gentiles that are scattered over it. The land has great verdure, much water, many trees; and from a very large pool that is in the middle of the place, proceeds an estuary[5] that goes to empty into the sea, which is in sight through an opening that the hills make in front, although at sight it appears that its shore would be two leagues distant.

Many pieces of land are full of rushes and tules,[6] and among the willows are many grape vines. On the north side a *cañada*[7] issues that afterwards divides into various arms according to the variable disposition of the hills, and it is all thick with trees, large and leafy. To all it seemed an excellent site for a mission, better than any of the preceding. I called it San Juan Capistrano. Along the road we saw jack rabbits, cottontails, and herds of antelope. But greater was the number of poor sheep wandering in such great numbers of gentiles of both sexes and of all ages, that not only do not flee from us like others at the beginning, but stick to us, as well along the road as at the stopping place, as if all their lives they had known us and treated with us; so there is no heart for leaving them thus. I invited them all to San Diego. May God fetch them to us there or bring them ministers who shall guide them to heaven in their own land, as it is, and as He has conceded it to them, so good and gladsome.

On the twenty-sixth we continued ahead, and the first thing was to climb a most high hill. Afterwards, very long mesas[8] followed for us, of such height that we seemed to have under our feet all the most high hills that on all sides offered themselves to our sight. Now hills, slopes, and barrancas[9] offered, and at the end of five hours that the day's journey today lasted, we saw that we had to descend to a depth so great and so precipitous that it gave one the horrors to look at it. Everyone dismounted, and half walking and half dragging, falling and getting up, we descended to the valley not less luxuriant than the preceding site. It is near the sea, where the coast is wild, although somewhat further above; but on the shore it makes a kind of bay, where the waves break gently.

We called it San Francisco Solano, with the confidence that under the patronage of the holy Apostle of the Spanish Indies such a multitude of gentile Indians as have come together here to us will be reduced to the bosom of the Church. Although we have seen so many, we had not seen so many together until here. And of their affability I cannot find a worthy description. Besides innumerable men, a great number of women and children sat in a circle around me, and one wished that I should take one of the children in my arms awhile. It was a nursing child, and thus I held it with good wishes to baptize it, until I returned it. I make the sign of the cross on all of them, and I make them say, "Jesus, Maria." I give them what I can. I caress them as best I may; and thus we are passing on, as now there is no way of doing better work.

That which may be feared from these poor things and cause suspicion and oblige one to go among them with some caution is the great desire or mania which they manifest for anything of cloth or any little trifle that they imagine conduces to their adornment. Food they care little for, because they are stuffed and accordingly are fat; the Señor Governor[10] would like most of them for grenadiers[11] on account of their lofty stature. But for any little cloths of colors, or for any cloth, they are capable of becoming beside themselves, as the phrase is, and overrun everything. When I give them anything to eat, they usually tell me with very clear signs that they do not want food, but to give them my habit, and they catch me by the sleeve. If I had conceded it to all who have proposed this to me, there would be quite a big enough community of gentile friars. That which I wish I

---

[4] *domestic,* gentle.

[5] *estuary,* the mouth of a river where the tide meets the river current.

[6] *tules,* large bulrushes, which grow abundantly in California.

[7] *cañada,* a canyon.

[8] *mesas,* flat-topped hills with steeply sloping sides.

[9] *barrancas,* ravines with steep sides.

[10] *Señor Governor,* Governor Portola.

[11] *grenadiers,* soldiers of special regiments.

could fix well in their hearts is the *induimini Dominum Jesum Christum*.[12] May that Most Providential Father that dresses the birds with feathers, the hills with grass, etc., concede it to them. Amen. I note here, on account of what was seen on the day's journey following, that if this place seems too costly to cultivate on account of what has been expressed, at less than a league's distance, following the coast, another green valley offers that also ends at the sea with a gentle coast, along whose center a great estuary is seen running down to near the sea close to the water. In case that close to the sea is salt, it is most credible it would not be if its water were held above; whence it appears that it could irrigate all the plain, which is also very pleasant and without that thicket of brush like the preceding. And granted that two missions will not be put in the distance of a league, both places can be used for one; and choose for the settlement that which most pleases.

On the twenty-seventh we set out early in the morning, already notified by our sergeant that the day's journey was long. All the gentility[13] was present at our setting out, and men and women went following us along the road. The journey was all along the seacoast, the land all level but full of ravines or barrancas of pure earth that the water had formed running down to the sea from the hills; and it was for me one of the most molestful day's journeys that we have had. It lasted six hours and something over. Along said road, aside from the place that I have mentioned with its estuary, we saw the land to be thick with good mescales,[14] that now for a long time we had not seen. But I feel that these gentiles think little of them on account of the abundance of fish and other foods . . . Women and children gathered about us, till the number became such that I did not count them. Their affability declined to familiarity, for if in sign of affection we put our hands on their heads or shoulders, they did the same to us; and if they saw us seated, there they sat close to us, and always with the mania that we should give them everything they saw, without stopping at little things. They begged my habit from me; from the Governor his leather jacket, waistcoat, breeches, and all he had on; and thus to the rest. They even bothered me enough to give them my spectacles. And because

for one whose actions, it seemed to me, signified that I lend them to him, I took them off and God knows what it cost me to recover them again because he fled with them. At last, after a thousand difficulties, I recovered them after they had been in the hands of the women who hankered for them.

On the twenty-eighth we were detained for a rest for the beasts, and that day in the middle of the morning they advised us that they saw many people on horseback coming; and in a short while the said sergeant[15] arrived with ten soldiers more (of those of the first division of the expedition that by order of the Señor Captain Rivera came from the post of San Diego to meet the Señor Governor and his suite) with fresh beasts and letters that from the two padres, Fray Juan Crespi and Fray Fernando Parron, came to me; this news livening all desires for our arrival.

On the twenty-ninth, early in the morning, the Governor with his servant and eight soldiers advanced ahead of us to arrive the same day at the fort of San Diego, and thus it was. I said Mass, and those who remained heard it, and plenty of gentiles saw it with much attention. In the afternoon the day's journey of two hours and a half was made with guides from San Diego.

On the thirtieth we set out in the morning, and the first thing was to cross a barranca and surmount the opposite hill; and after a little of climbings and descents a most long track was discovered to us of coast plain that we had to follow, keeping all the hills to the right. And along the coast was all this day's journey that lasted four hours and a half; but there were so many barrancas that we had to pass (without being able to elude nor go around the head of even one since their direction was from the mountains) that although I passed all of them praying and trying to do acts of conformity,[16] etc., my heart came to be compressed much, seeing in each one the danger; and that at times on coming out of one, it was soon to cross another, without rest. But like things of this world they came to an end, and at a little more than three hours walking we arrived at a rancheria[17] very populous with gentiles . . . That we might arrive better rested at San Diego the day following, we passed on

---

12 *induimini . . . Christum*, "put ye on the Lord Jesus Christ," *Rom*, 13:14.

13 *gentility*, the Indians.

14 *mescales*, cacti.

15 *said sergeant*, Jose Ortega, sergeant of the first land division.

16 *acts of conformity*, short prayers of resignation to God's will.

17 *rancheria*, a collection of rude Indian huts.

ahead with the intention of arriving at another ranchería, distant some leagues, where there was sufficient water, although very inferior in quantity and quality to that which we left.

The way was level; the guides knew by the wind where the fort was. We took a straight cut, leaving on the right hand the traveled road. And in little more than an hour we found fine pasture land and a beautiful brook of good water. Here we stopped at a place which neither the sergeant, who had traveled the road for the third time, and others for the fifth, had seen. I say the fifth, because soldiers had gone twice from San Diego for mescales to medicate the sick.

VIEWING THE AUTHOR'S IDEAS

1. How did Serra gain the affection of the Indians? What conviction inspired his attitude toward them?

2. Cite passages in Fray Junípero's diary which show that he was mindful of Christ's commission to missionaries.

3. What missionary activities are carried on in the Church today? What inspiration could Confraternity workers find in the diary of Fray Junípero?

4. Make a list of the traits of Indian character observed by Fray Junípero. Compare the Indians described in this selection with those you have met in previous selections.

5. State comments in the diary which indicate that Fray Junípero recognized the importance of social and economic improvement in the work of evangelization. Is a recognition of this fact important in missionary work today?

EVALUATING HIS MANNER OF EXPRESSION

1. How does the diary of Fray Junípero differ from those of Samuel Sewall and William Byrd? What features do the three accounts have in common?

2. Cite passages to show Fray Junípero's keen power of observation; his choice of interesting and effective details; his sense of humor.

3. What details in diction and structure reveal that this diary was translated from a foreign language?

4. From the diary select six Spanish words that are now included in our language.

QUESTIONS FOR REVIEW

Copy the numbers 1 to 15 in your notebook. Next to each number print the letter of the word or phrase that correctly completes the sentence.

1. In his *Relation* Cabeza de Vaca (a) predicts that America will be an outstanding country (b) tells the story of a man whom faith consoled in peril and who won against the rigors of an untamed continent (c) praises Spain and the Spanish explorers.

2. Helpful in the early missionary labors were (a) the disciplined soldiery and the friendly Indians (b) the rapid development of a literature designed for the instruction of the Indian (c) the success of the *encomienda* system and the wealth of the Spaniards.

3. Previous to his contact with explorer and missionary, the North American Indian (a) had developed his own primitive type of artistic expression (b) had no literature, oral or written (c) had been so occupied with gaining a livelihood that he had no time for creating song or folklore.

4. A Jesuit Brother, Domingo Agustín Báez, was probably the first man (a) to compose Indian poetry (b) to produce an historical poem on Florida (c) to write a book while residing in the present territory of the United States.

5. *La Florida* by Fray Alonso de Escobeda (a) commemorates the founding of St. Augustine (b) is a rhymed catechism for the Indians of Florida (c) is the first poem which describes our country.

6. Villagrá's *History of New Mexico* (a) celebrates in prose the first coming of the Spaniards to New Mexico (b) narrates in verse the conquest of New Mexico by the Spaniards (c) relates the search for the Seven Golden Cities of Cibola.

7. The writings of the early missionaries in the United States (a) helped stabilize Christian culture in the southern and southwestern parts of our country (b) did not reflect the life and times of the missionary and his people (c) were a factor in the development of lyric poetry.

8. John Smith (a) provided the Virginia settlers with amusing fictional narratives for leisure reading (b) encouraged Englishmen to migrate by pointing out opportunities in America (c) reflected in his writings his desire to exploit the Indians.

9. Bradford's writing interprets the Puritan mind which (a) saw the hand of God in every occurrence (b) stressed man's intellectual powers rather than his spiritual (c) emphasized this life without regard for the next.

10. Winthrop's *History of New England* (a) attracts many readers because of its startling statements (b) presents clear pictures of Puritan toleration and forbearance (c) contributes valuable information on the Puritan philosophy of the New Englanders.

11. The urge of the Puritans to record their inner experiences in diaries and other personal narratives may be traced to (a) the habit of introspection which caused them to seek evidence of their election to salvation (b) the emphasis on artistic writing in Puritan education (c) love of exhibiting themselves in flattering circumstances.

12. By retaining many truths of revelation and emphasizing the supernatural end of man, Puritanism (a) eventually led America back to Catholicism (b) helped mold American thought along Christian lines (e) left an impress of deep religious feeling on all our subsequent writers.

13. Education was encouraged by the Puritans (a) to enable members of this sect to go into other colonies as missionaries (b) to train ministers as religious and political leaders and to enable laymen to read the Bible (c) to teach citizens to participate in democratic government.

14. The cultural tradition that has been most influential in the final shaping of the American profile has been that which stems from (a) English Anglicanism (b) Spanish Catholicism (c) English Puritanism.

15. Sewall's *Diary* (a) is the honest revelation of the devout Puritan who was gradually turning to a more secular view of life (b) shows the Puritan in an uncomplimentary manner (c) reflects the passionate desire of the common man for absolute freedom.

Copy the numbers 1 to 8 in your notebook. Next to each number print the capital letter T *if the statement is true or the capital letter* F *if the statement is false.*

1. The relation was a journal that was at once both spot news and history.

2. The French soldier who explored and conquered in the New World was called a *conquistador*.

3. Las Casas was the most outstanding figure among the champions for the rights of the Indian.

4. The "good neighbor policy" may be said to begin with the missionaries in Cuba and Mexico who trained young priests, gave them the fruits of their experience, and finally led the way to the Florida coast.

5. Biased accounts of French colonization in the New World have been termed *Black Legend*.

6. Probably the first book printed in the New World is *The Spiritual Ladder*.

7. Indian literature begins with the coming of the white man to America.

8. The first poem which describes our country has lain unpublished for more than three centuries.

Copy the numbers 1 to 5 in your notebook. Next to each number write the word or words which correctly complete the sentence.

1. An authentic piece of folk literature is the religious play.....

2. The first English book written in America is John Smith's . . . . .

3. Bradford's. . . . . records the ideals, sufferings, and progress of the first group of Puritans in America.

4. Puritan doctrines were influenced by the heretical teachings of. . . . .

5. The idea of creating poetry for its own sake and not for its usefulness was brought to Puritan literature in America by. . . . .

QUESTIONS FOR WRITTEN OR ORAL DISCUSSION

1. How did Columbus forecast the role of America in world events?

2. What theme later treated by John Smith is developed in the *Relation* of the Gentleman of Elvas?

3. What significance had the Great Awakening in the history of Puritanism?

4. What factors militated against the success of the *encomienda* system?

5. How did Spain contribute to the culture of America?

6. What was Fray Cancer's method of converting the savage?

7. Which nations brought Catholic culture to America; which brought Protestant culture?

8. State the main Puritan doctrines.

9. Why could not the doctrines of Puritanism be carried to their logical conclusion?

10. Explain how worldly prosperity became the standard by which the New Englander estimated his progress.

11. Name some of the Catholic teachings which still prevailed in the belief of the early Puritans.

12. In what manner does Wigglesworth's *Day of Doom* portray the awesome Day of Judgment?

13. What part did Jonathan Edwards have in the history of Puritanism?

14. Of what significance are the *Jesuit Relations*?

SUGGESTIONS FOR READING

Austin, Jane G., *Standish of Standish* (Houghton, New York). Love and romance entered even into the grim, stern life of the Puritans in Massachusetts. Jane Austin gives a prose version of Longfellow's *Courtship of Miles Standish* which pictures the rivalry of Standish and John Alden for Priscilla.

Berger, John A. *Franciscan Missions of California* (Putnam, New York). An attractive make-up and an abundance of pictures aids in the portrayal of the fascinating history of missionary activity in California. Indians and Franciscans are flashed upon the screen as they build the twenty-one great missions in the state.

Boyd, Thomas, *Shadow of the Long Knives* (Scribner, New York). Charity McDermott stands forth as a splendid example of the courageous pioneer woman. Border warfare and continual threat from Indians made life uncertain.

Cather, Willa, *Shadows on the Rock* (Knopf, New York). This story breathes the hardy and courageous spirit of the French in settling Quebec. There is little dramatic action, but events are charmingly related.

Catherwood, Mary Hartwell, *The Romance of Dollard* (Appleton, New York). This novel depicts the heroism of young officer Dollard and his men, who prevent the capture of Montreal. *Lady of Fort St. John* (Houghton, Mifflin), by the same author, is an enjoyable novel of early French life in Canada.

Earle, Alice Morse, *Home Life in Colonial Days* (Macmillan, New York). The author endeavors to reproduce colonial days by describing the social life and customs of the times.

Farnum, Mabel, *Seven Golden Cities* (Bruce, Milwaukee). A modern writer presents the character of Fray Marcos de Niza in all his strength.

Hawthorne, Hildegarde, *California Missions* (Appleton, New York). Nathaniel Hawthorne's granddaughter gives a beautiful, sympathetic, and intelligent picture of the heroic missionary endeavor in California. Dramatic stories and charming illustrations make the book fascinating.

Holland, Robert E., S.J., *The Song of Tekakwitha* (Fordham Univ. Press, New York). Father Holland calls Tekakwitha "the real heroine of our American forest." For this reason he employs the same meter that Longfellow used for his immortal story of the Indian hero, "The Song of Hiawatha." Colored illustrations add to the appeal of this romance of sanctity.

Johnston, Mary, *To Have and To Hold* (Grosset, New York). Color, love, and adventure harmonize in this vigorous tale of the early days of Virginia.

Kenny, Michael, S.J., *The Romance of the Floridas* (Bruce, Milwaukee). This is a popular and fascinating account of early Dominican, Jesuit, and Franciscan missionary endeavors in the Southwest. A supplementary sketch treats present-day missionary activity in that section of the country.

Lummis, Charles F., *The Spanish Pioneers* (McClurg, Chicago). The non-Catholic author endeavors to give honor to whom honor is due. He presents an authentic and interesting picture of one of the most romantic and gallant phases of American history.

McDowell, Franklin Davey, *Champlain Road* (Bruce, Milwaukee). Champlain explored the St. Lawrence River and founded Quebec. This story of Indian life and missionary endeavor in Canada helps to complete the picture found in Talbot's *Saint Among Savages.*

Parker, Gilbert, *The Seats of the Mighty* (Appleton, New York). The seats of the mighty, France and England in America, had been tottering for years. The triumph of Wolfe over Montcalm on the heights of Quebec enthroned England in the New World. Parker in his novel recounts the campaigns, sieges, and diplomacies which led to the conquest of Quebec.

Phelan, Thomas Patrick, *Catholics in Colonial Days* (Kenedy, New York). Opposition proves the strength of ideals. Catholics in the English colonies remained loyal to God and to American ideals in spite of difficulties. This is a good source book for an understanding of our Catholic origin and history.

Pratt, Edwin John, "*Brébeuf and His Brethren,*" (Basilian Press). A non-Catholic Canadian poet has written an inspiring poem about the North American martyrs.

Pyle, Howard, *Jack Ballister's Fortunes* (Appleton, New York). Through the adventures of Jack Ballister, a young English gentleman who was kidnapped in England and carried to Virginia, the traffic of kidnapping to supply labor for rich planters is exposed. Ballister falls into the hands of Blackbeard, a notorious pirate.

Repplier, Agnes, *Père Marquette* (Doubleday, New York). In her best style the author gives the story of the intrepid French Jesuit missionary.

Repplier, Agnes, *Junipero Serra* (Doubleday, New York). This biography furnishes a charming account of the pioneer missionary to the Far West. *The Spirit of Serra* by Rev. Thomas F. Cullen (Franciscan Mission Press) also treats the apostle of California.

Steck, Francis Borgia, O.F.M., *Education in Spanish North America During the Sixteenth Century* (National Catholic Welfare Conference, Washington, D.C.). An historian here relates the unique achievement of the religious orders who educated young men and women in colonial Spanish America. Another valuable discussion of educational developments in early America may be found in Father Steck's "The First College in America: Santa Cruz de Tlatelolco," in *The Catholic Educational Review* (Washington, D.C.), XXXIV (1936), 449-462, 603-617.

Talbot, Francis X., S.J., *Saint Among Savages* (Harper, New York). Father Talbot gives a vivid, powerful account of St. Isaac Jogues, the Jesuit martyr.

Wynne, John Joseph, S.J., *Jesuit Martyrs of North America* (Martyrs Shrine, Auriesville, New York). The relics of eight martyrs, canonized in our own day, are enshrined in Auriesville. Father Wynne recounts the heroic deeds of such men as Brébeuf, Goupil, and Jogues.

Revolutionary Designs, 1775-1800

ORIGINS OF THE REVOLUTION

From earliest times the colonists had unconsciously been etching a design sharply distinctive among human activities: the American way of life. Outwardly eighteenth-century existence in our land did not differ greatly from that of Europeans. In both continents picturesque women in hooped petticoats and brocaded satins sparkled in drawing rooms among gentlemen in broadcloth and velvet. Housewives carded wool in summer and dipped candles in fall. Yet as the century progressed, the American colonists on the eastern seaboard showed that they were not merely English subjects, that they had their own way of thinking and living.

Already in colonial times the American scene was a patchwork of nationalities. English, Scotch, Irish, French, German, Swedes — all brought their own customs and the rich flavor of their homeland traditions. Despite their prejudices and frequent quarrels, the colonists were making significant discoveries. At first the men of each colony had been inclined to look upon their territory as an independent settlement. But soon they came to realize that their little section of the country had interests and problems in common with its neighbors. On basic principles of colonial policy, the settlers were inclined to agree with each other against England. Particularly the large number of immigrants not of English extraction tended to criticize the policy of Britain when it interfered with their individual rights. As a result of America's geographic isolation, the children of British immigrants felt that their native land had an identity separate from that of England. Gradually the admixture of various peoples and philosophies made the colonists aware that they had developed a new nation. "Here," wrote Crèvecœur at the opening of the Revolution, "individuals are melted into a new race of men."

Americans are independent thinkers

England, too, came to understand that the colonists were different — even contrary people. The most striking way in which the Americans had emphasized their difference was in their manner of doing their own thinking and insisting on managing their own affairs. During the first hundred years of her colonization of America, England had been busily engaged in European wars. She could, accordingly, give little time to her new possessions and little attention to the complaints of her colonial governors. These complaints had been alike. The merchant, the farmer, the trapper, the plantation owner — each had been loyal enough as a subject of the English crown. He had obeyed His Majesty's laws, which had compelled him to send his raw materials to England and to accept her manufactured products. He had even acquiesced to sending his goods in English merchant ships. But one thing he would not do: he would not let an outsider dictate the policies of his own local government.

The colonists did not at first realize that their democratic way of life would call for separation from England. It was the action of a group of blundering English ministers which forced the Americans to define the principles for which they stood. The immediate cause for the Revolution was unjust taxation. After her long, expensive wars Britain felt that the colonies should share in paying the costs. In 1765 Parliament passed the Stamp Act to raise revenues for this purpose. The colonists resisted so vehemently that England repealed the act the next year. Determined to assert its power, Parliament in 1767 again laid duties on tea, glass, and other articles imported into America and sent soldiers to enforce the new act. Although the Boston Massacre (1770) brought the repeal of all duties except the tax on tea, the resentment of the colonists did not decrease. Rather, it reached a climax in the Boston Tea Party of December, 1773. Shortly afterwards, the British closed Boston Harbor until restitution would be made to the East India Company. When the news of these events spread from colony to colony, Americans came to a great realization: they valued their American privileges so highly that they were ready to die to preserve the liberties which were an essential part of life in their new country. In declaring war, the leaders of the Revolution were not radicals who sought to overthrow law and order; they were men who fought to save their rightful liberties and the democratic way of life that had grown up in the wilderness. Revolutionary literature gave expression to the ideals for which the colonists fought.

Declaration echoes St. Thomas

Foremost among these democratic principles was the recognition of the dignity of the human personality. The Revolutionary Fathers did not set out to construct a new political theory. They were practical men with a problem. Faced with difficulty, they sought justification for their beliefs in current religious and philosophical teachings. As has already been stated, Protestantism rejected only some of the traditional Christian beliefs. Among the teachings that remained was the doctrine of St. Thomas Aquinas concerning the origin of civil authority. This great philosopher taught that man, as a creature of God, possesses certain natural rights. He can, consequently, delegate his authority to a ruler who, by governing for the common good, will preserve these rights. Civil authority, then, although coming from God, is a natural law and resides in the community itself. Men are accordingly free to establish any form of just government they desire. The leaders of the Revolution did not receive this doctrine from St. Thomas directly. Jefferson and possibly Madison were aware of the teaching of Suarez and Bellarmine, Jesuit writers who explained and developed the political and social doctrine of the Scholastic philosophers. Others among the Founding Fathers read these teachings thinned out and watered down in writings of such philosophers as Locke who were influenced by medieval thought. The significant thing is that they *did* receive and restate the principles and give their countrymen an opportunity to put them into practice. They thus protected Americans from the short-lived freedoms resulting from the belief that civil authority comes from man and can be taken away by man.

Revolution needs Catholic support

By a strange turn of events the position of Catholics was suddenly altered with the outbreak of revolution. Fifteen years before, the practice of the Catholic religion had still been fraught with danger. As late as 1760 bigoted leaders had proposed to confiscate all the lands of Catholics in Maryland. One of the conditions of the peace of 1763 was that Catholics would be allowed to practice their religion in the lands ceded to England by France. The Quebec Act of 1774 safeguarded religious toleration to Catholics in Canada and in the former French possessions west of the Alleghenies. As a result of this decree, the American stronghold of Protestantism was hemmed in by Catholic Canada on the north, by Catholic Frenchmen on the west, and by the Catholic Spaniards of Florida on the south. The Puritans were strongly opposed to this concession to religious freedom. Their indignation no doubt hastened the rebellion against the mother country.

Faced with the might of England, however, the colonists were jolted into a compromise. Alone against the British, they could not hope to succeed in winning their rights. They needed Catholic support. They wanted the help of France. They sought the friendship of Canada. They considered the sympathy of the French population in the West essential to victory. It was important that they have the cooperation of colonial Maryland, whose aid depended somewhat on the attitude of her leading citizens, especially Charles Carroll of Carrollton. France answered the cry for help with both men and money. A commission was sent to win Canada as a colonial ally. The Canadians, however, had not yet forgotten American opposition to the Quebec Act and were not to be won. In the West, the French were willing to favor the colonial cause. With victory so largely dependent on Catholic aid, it was obviously beneficial for Protestant sects to lay aside their hatred of the despised religion and to welcome the men who were willing to join wholeheartedly in the fight for freedom. Catholics, recently harried and without power, were now respected in the colonies for their influence. The war, for a time at least, had rescued them from oppression.

THE AGE OF REASON IN AMERICA

In the Revolutionary period the colonists were occupied with the problem of becoming a free nation. In addition to the urgency of their own needs, they were interested in the general course of world events and influenced by ideas that reached them from the European continent. Both in Europe and America, people of the eighteenth century were giving less attention to supernatural aims and more to material prosperity. Various reform measures within the Protestant churches attempted to check religious indifference. We have already observed the efforts of Jonathan Edwards in the Great Awakening. In the last third of the eighteenth century, Methodism was brought from England to America. Begun as an attempt to enkindle fervor in the Anglican churches, this sect later gave rise to numerous separate denominations. The Methodist preachers had a wide appeal among American audiences, since they softened the teaching of Calvin by admitting that free will made repentance possible. The manner in which revivals or camp meetings were conducted appealed greatly to the emotions. When during the services an individual believed that he had received the assurance of pardon, he gave public testimony of the interior communication he had been given.

Despite these reform movements, the practical and worldly-wise view of life that prevailed in the eighteenth century continued to modify American thought. As a result of beliefs popular in Europe at this time, the colonists were beginning to question the truths of revelation. The prevailing philosophers in France, Germany, and England were teaching that reason should be the sole source of truth and that men should accept only what reason tells them. These thinkers were accordingly known as *rationalists*. Various social and philosophic forces contributed to the development of rationalism. We shall briefly discuss two of these causes. First, belief in divinely-revealed truths was declining. The early American Protestant — Puritan, Methodist, or Anglican — had looked with reverence upon his religious beliefs as a body of truths made known by God. Within its doctrine, however, Protestantism carried the seed of its own destruction. In the revolt of the sixteenth century, Luther had made the Bible the sole source of truth, had substituted it for the living voice of the Church, and had allowed each man to interpret Biblical teaching. This private judgment resulted in contradictory doctrines, confusion, and dissension. People realized that one truth cannot contradict another truth. They accordingly felt it necessary to re-examine Christian teachings as explained by the various Protestant sects.

Secondly, recent advances in scientific knowledge had given men great confidence in their intellectual powers. From 1530 to 1700 sensational progress had been made in the sciences of astronomy and mathematics,

physics, and biology. When private interpretation split Protestantism into dissenting sects, some men wished to reject revelation and to depend wholly upon the facts and methods of science. The period 1700 to 1765 is often called *The Age of Reason*. In the special sense in which the rationalists used the term, *reason* meant the process of applying the results of scientific investigation and laboratory experiment to the whole sphere of man's activity. They hoped to explain and define God by purely natural means. The movement which wished to shape man's ideas regarding conduct, society, and government according to this particular type of reasoning is known as the *Enlightenment*. In France a group of authors, later called the *Encyclopedists,* produced a large body of writing influenced by the teachings of rationalism. The best known of these writers was Voltaire.

As rationalistic thought developed in England, it assumed certain beliefs which became known as *scientific deism*. Although the deists differed in many of their doctrines, they largely agreed in rejecting religious authority and substituting the conclusions of their own minds. Since their reason told them that the universe must have a Creator, they admitted the existence of God. They admitted also the design, order, and beauty which the Creator revealed in His handiwork. Without revelation, however, they found their knowledge of God very meager, and they spoke of Him as a faraway, indifferent First Cause, a kind of absentee Creator, with no interest in His creatures. He had in the beginning, they believed, wound up the universe as a person might wind a gigantic toy. He had then allowed it to spin on according to the unchangeable laws which He had established; He would not suspend natural laws to work a miracle.

Deism influences American thought

In contrast to the pessimism of the Puritans, who had considered man wholly depraved, deism led to an easy optimism which has characterized much later American thinking. The deists believed that man has his origins in the same mechanistic laws that control the material world. Overlooking the fact of original sin, they considered that man is naturally good and capable of unlimited improvement. They looked forward to a time when, as events unfolded according to their mechanical scheme, man would eventually arrive at a state of perfection. Although a reaction against Puritanism and opposed to its teaching, deism strengthened two Puritan ideas. Like Puritanism, it offered a mechanical view of life. The Calvinists saw grace as a force which carries man to heaven without his choice or co-operation. The deists viewed the universe as a mechanical world in which the unfolding of natural laws would bring ultimate satisfaction. Both systems of thought regarded material prosperity and success as important goals of man's achievement.

Deism was not a substitute of one kind of spirituality for another. Rather it was a movement against the spiritual in favor of a worldly view of life. In the deist creed there is no undivided Trinity, no redeeming Christ, no sacraments as channels of grace, no promise of heaven, no certain knowledge of man's destiny, no way of achieving it. It is impossible for the human heart to love the indifferent First Cause that the deist has pictured. Neither can man exercise supernatural charity towards his fellows. In place of charity the deist substitutes *humanitarianism,* the consideration of man for the sake of man. In his morality, the deist likewise passes from the supernatural to the natural plane. He exercises natural virtues, such as industry because it pays, or decency and good fellowship because he desires social approval. Having no supernatural aims or helps, man is forced to occupy himself wholly with material activities and satisfactions. To get the greatest enjoyment from natural pleasure, the deist recommends that men use reasonable restraint. Experience, however, shows that man tends to use natural pleasure to excess. Even the pagan philosophers admit that over-indulgence brings pain. Deism, though urging moral virtue in theory, tends in practice to end in license and sensuality.

BENJAMIN FRANKLIN

Better, perhaps, than anyone else in America, Benjamin Franklin (1706-1790) illustrates the various aspects of rationalistic thought and activity. He went further than most of his countrymen and practically broke with Christianity. In doing so, he threw the force of his tremendous prestige on the side of rationalistic tendencies in America. He was a powerful influence, therefore, in the movement which was bringing American thought from the plane of revealed religion into the purely natural realm. Later in his life, Franklin seems to have reverted to some of the Christian beliefs he had held as a boy.

The tenth son of a candlemaker in Boston, Franklin received no classroom instruction after he was taken into his father's shop at the age of ten. The discontented boy threatened to run away until his father finally compromised by apprenticing him to his half brother, James, who was a printer. In the printing shop Benjamin was happy because he had access to a source of education — books he could read while taking his lunch, books he could study by candlelight far into the night. When his relations with his half brother became strained, the spirited young Franklin stuffed his extra clothes into his pockets and went to Philadelphia. The story of his walking down the street munching a roll of bread while his future wife looked on with amusement is a familiar tale. With characteristic shrewdness and industry, he soon gained prominence in Philadelphia as author and publisher.

Promotes humanitarian views

Intellectually curious, Franklin made himself familiar not only with the beliefs of the Puritan thinkers but with the ideas of eighteenth-century philosophers. Accepting the main tenets of deism, he pictured a Supreme Being Who was so aloof that He showed no interest in His creatures. Although Franklin himself questioned the divinity of Christ, he stated that he would not deny this belief to those whom it aided in achieving virtuous conduct. Holding that man is essentially good, he sought to make him master of his environment through scientific inventions. Franklin made benevolent use of his discoveries by refusing to take out patents which would have restricted their use. Bifocal glasses, stoves, and lightning rods are only a few of the inventions by which he sought to serve his fellow men. In his desire to improve living conditions, he organized fire and police departments in Philadelphia and obtained funds for a city hospital. To raise cultural standards, he organized a circulating library, established an academy which later became the University of Pennsylvania, and founded the American Philosophical Society.

Although his motives were, by his own statements, natural rather than supernatural, Franklin never lost the benevolent aspirations given him in his boyhood by Cotton Mather's *Essays to Do Good.* Throughout his life, certain overtones of Puritanism are discernible in Franklin's thinking. In contrast to the violent anti-clericalism of some of the rationalists, Franklin's attitudes were never bitter. He was a kind of benevolent non-believer. He wanted no troublesome doctrines; he preferred to have all men submerge their individual differences and agree in philosophic tranquility. He placed special emphasis on material progress, material success. He was a powerful voice in persuading man to live by purely natural motives, to seek entirely worldly ends, to take satisfaction in merely practical achievement. His was always the middle way. Excess and self-indulgence led to disaster; consequently, he advocated the enjoyment of pleasure within the dictates of prudence. With his genius, his vitality, his personality, one regrets that such a great American pursued no quest of the spirit, never penetrated into the mysteries of life. Franklin was literally the apostle of common sense—a common sense directed to natural goals.

In addition to his great achievements in science, Franklin became the most important writer of Revolutionary times. He published the second monthly magazine issued in America, the *Pennsylvania Gazette*, which is considered the forerunner of *The Saturday Evening Post. Poor Richard's Almanack*, which he issued annually for a quarter of a century (1733-1758), was not only a calendar containing all sorts of odd information but a literary miscellany filled with maxims and witticisms gathered from observation and reading.

Autobiography *is American classic*

Overshadowing Franklin's other literary works is the *Autobiography*, written with the practical purpose of leaving for his descendants a record of his successful career. In the literature of personal memoirs the *Autobiography* is a masterpiece. Written in a style as direct as Franklin himself, it relates the forceful story of the author's life up to the year 1757, when he entered public service for the colonies. The *Autobiography* is the first literary classic produced by an American. During his old age in Paris, Franklin wrote his delightful *Bagatelles* (1779?-1784) or trifles, a collection of graceful

© New York Public Library

Title Page of a 1794 Edition of Franklin's Works

letters and light essays composed for the amusement of his French friends. A host of pamphlets and discourses testify to Franklin's sincere interest in controversy. In the thirteen thousand documents which comprise one collection of his unpublished works, he touches upon every philosophic and political theory in which eighteenth-century thinkers were interested.

Franklin was already seventy-two years old when the colonies declared their independence, yet he worked with great energy to win victory for the American cause. The diplomat of the Revolution, he persuaded France to make an alliance with the colonies, and to send the French fleet and supplies. Later Franklin helped make the treaty of peace with England. When he signed the Constitution in 1787, he placed his approval upon the plan of government which has made America a great nation. This was his last major service to his country, as he died in 1790.

MICHEL-GUILLAUME ST. JEAN DE CRÈVECŒUR

Next to Franklin, Michel-Guillaume St. Jean de Crèvecœur (1735-1813) wrote the most literary prose of the period. The baptismal certificate of Crèvecœur shows that he was born of a noble Catholic family of Caen, France. His desire to come to the New World was realized in 1754, when he sailed to Canada to fight under Montcalm. After the fall of Quebec he drifted into the colonies and took out naturalization papers in New York. In 1769 he married a non-Catholic and settled down to a quiet life on a farm in Orange County. Like other immigrants of that time he gradually gave up the practice of his religion. It is doubtful whether he ever regained his faith, although he later became one of the trustees of the first Catholic Church in New York.

When the Revolution broke out, Crèvecœur wished to remain neutral, although his sympathy was with the Tories. Suspected by the English of giving information to the patriots, he was thrown into prison and was finally sent to France. Here he took part in the gay court life and made the acquaintance of Benjamin Franklin. His *Letters from an American Farmer* (1782) made him famous throughout Europe. In 1783 he returned to New York as French consul to find that his wife had died in an Indian raid, his farmhouse had been burned to the ground, and his children were living with charitable strangers in Boston. As consul Crèvecœur labored ceaselessly to promote friendly relations between France and America. He returned to his own country in 1790 and died in 1813.

Crèvecœur pictured America as a haven for the weary and oppressed people of Europe. Here was perfectly realized his romantic dream of simple life in unspoiled surroundings. His pages glow with enthusiasm for rural life and with admiration of the American landscape.

PATRICK HENRY

Typical of those who felt that the colonists would have to fight to maintain their liberties was Patrick Henry (1736-1799). The great orator and statesman grew up on a small plantation in what was then the backwoods of Virginia. He studied at a country school until he was ten, when his father taught him Latin and Greek. Failure as a merchant and farmer led him to the study of law. Soon he was elected to the Virginia House of Burgesses, where his famous resolutions against the Stamp Act sent his name ringing through the colonies. Though Patrick Henry could dress well when the occasion demanded, he often wore simple old clothes to win the confidence of the common people. The tall, rawboned Virginian gained no particular attention at the First Continental Congress until he began his stirring call for unity. As governor of his state during three years of the war, he supplied Washington's army with food, clothing, and ammunition. When peace came, Henry declined all public offices in the new government, preferring to end his days on his estate in the Blue Ridge Mountains. His last speech was a fervent appeal for union: "Stand by the government. United we stand, divided we fall. Let us not split into factions, which must destroy that union." He died in 1799, the same year as Washington.

THE WAR FOR INDEPENDENCE

The struggle for independence which began with the battles of Lexington and Concord lasted for eight years. The Second Continental Congress, which assembled in May, 1775, appointed George Washington commander in chief of the American army. On July 6, the Congress adopted a Declaration of the Causes and Necessity of Taking up Arms. The patriots well knew the seriousness of the step they had taken. Defeat would mean the loss of their lives and fortunes. They understood, moreover, that the colonies by themselves could not withstand the power of England. The assistance, or at least the neutrality, of Canada was necessary. Accordingly, in February, 1776, Congress sent Benjamin Franklin, Samuel Chase, and Charles Carroll of Carrollton to promote the American cause and to bring Canada into the union as the fourteenth colony. The Commission failed to achieve its object because the Canadians were satisfied with the concessions of the Quebec Act by which England had assured them of political and religious liberty. They did not wish to risk losing either by joining the English colonists.

On June 7, 1776, Richard Henry Lee introduced in Congress his famous resolution in which he affirmed "That these United Colonies are, and of right ought to be, free and independent states . . ." Congress in quick

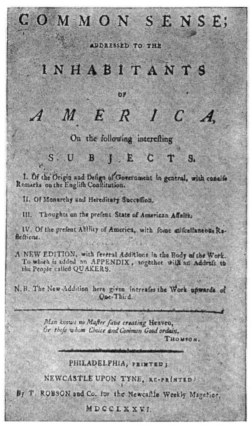

Paine's Common Sense *pointed the way to the impending break of the colonists from England.*

order appointed Thomas Jefferson, Benjamin Franklin, John Adams, Roger Sherman, and Robert Livingston to draft the Declaration of Independence, which was adopted July 4, 1776. This declaration was confirmed by final victory over the English armies in 1781.

The literature of the Revolution was largely political in content and purpose. The people had to be convinced of the justice of their cause and all the world had to be told the reasons for the Declaration of Independence. Pamphlets and broadsides in prose and verse were produced quickly and distributed widely. Ballads, letters, and essays appearing in periodicals united the colonies in the common cause. Written by men who were scholars and thinkers, many of the political essays of the Revolution live today as classics in their field. The greater part of the writing, however, was not literature and died with the occasion that inspired it.

In the gloomiest days, Thomas Paine (1737-1809), an Englishman by birth, wrote stirring pamphlets in which he counseled the colonists to sever their connection with England. Paine was a passionate lover of political and economic freedom. He was at the scene of action during the American Revolution and again at the time of the French Revolution. His pamphlet, *Common Sense* (1776), stirred the colonists to complete separation from England and anticipated the Declaration of Independence. More than one hundred thousand copies of the essay were sold in three months. In December of 1776 he wrote the first number of *The Crisis*, a series of sixteen pamphlets beginning with the stirring call to arms: "These are the times that try men's souls." Paine's works are written in a style that is eloquent and forceful. His pages ring with stirring appeals to his readers and with bold arguments. A scientific deist, he rejected Christianity because he thought that it was an obstacle to democratic progress. Because of his attacks on the Christian religion in *The Age of Reason* (1794-95), and his defense of the French Revolution in *The Rights of Man* (1791-92), he lost the esteem of many Americans.

THOMAS JEFFERSON

Thomas Jefferson (1743-1826) was well prepared by training and experience to write the Declaration of Independence. The son of a hardy pioneer who ardently believed in American liberties, Jefferson grew to manhood on a broad-acred plantation in western Virginia. At a country school he made friends with the sons of backwoodsmen in their buckskin trousers, rough hunting shirts, and coonskin caps. He admired the small farmers and tobacco growers, the hunters and trappers of the western frontier — hardworking, honest men, and progressive democrats. At the College of William and Mary, Jefferson developed his literary talents and acquired a classical education. While he was studying law, he read Sydney, Locke, and Filmer, authors from whom he learned indirectly the theories of government expounded by St. Thomas, Cardinal Bellarmine, and other great writers of the Church. Jefferson was always happiest at Monticello, the beautiful hilltop mansion which he built on his Virginia plantation. Although his home life was that of an aristocrat, he championed the cause of the common people.

As a member of the Continental Congress and as governor of Virginia, Jefferson played an active role in the cause of freedom. Entrusted with the composition of the Declaration of Independence, he labored for two weeks to give it that power and dignity which make it one of the greatest political documents of the world. The Declaration reflects the high ideals and the profound principles of government upon which the American nation is founded.

For several years after the war Jefferson served as minister to France. In 1785 he wrote the Virginia Statute of Religious Freedom, which guaranteed that no man in that state should be deprived of civil rights or persecuted on account of his religion. As first Secretary of State in the new government, he led the Anti-Federalists, the party opposed to a strong central government. In 1800 he was elected the third president of the United States. At the close of his eight years in office he could rejoice that peace, democracy, and simplicity had characterized his administration. He had tried to reduce the expenses of government and to avoid war. He had doubled the size of the United States by the purchase of Louisiana. After the presidency he devoted much of his time to the University of Virginia, which he had founded. It was a singular coincidence that Jefferson and John Adams both died on the fiftieth anniversary of the Declaration of Independence, July 4, 1826.

FRANCIS HOPKINSON

By his comic ballads and witty essays, Francis Hopkinson (1737-1791) lightened some of the darkest moments of the Revolution. Even his personal appearance amused people. John Adams wrote to his wife in 1776: "He is one of your pretty, little curious men. His head is not bigger than a large apple . . . I have not met with anything in natural history more amusing and entertaining than his personal appearance—yet he is genteel and well-bred and very social." From the day Hopkinson enrolled in the Philadelphia Academy as a boy of sixteen, Benjamin Franklin took a fatherly interest in his career. The youth had already attracted attention as a writer of verse and light periodical essays when the Revolution enlisted his literary talents. His initial satire in the service of the patriots was a clever

"The Battle of the Kegs"

ridicule of king and Parliament called *A Pretty Story* (1774). When Burgoyne tried to frighten the colonies by a fiery proclamation, Hopkinson wrote his *Answer* (1777), which made the Americans laugh in spite of their fears. His *Camp Ballad* was a marching song for the soldiers. When Americans were discouraged, his comic ballad, "The Battle of the Kegs" (1778), spread cheer from Georgia to Maine. Though not the greatest of Hopkinson's works, it is the one by which he is best remembered. Only a few years before his death he loyally defended the new Constitution in a clever allegory called *The New Roof.* Hopkinson's sprightly satires were a diversion from his more serious tasks. He acted as chairman of the Navy Committee in the Continental Congress and was a signer of the Declaration of Independence. It was he who designed the first American flag. For ten years he was judge of admiralty for the State of Pennsylvania. After the war Hopkinson became America's first composer and wrote both lyrics and songs. His *Seven Songs for the Harpsichord and Forte-Piano* (1788) was the first book of music published by an American.

PHILIP FRENEAU

The history of the Revolution can be read in the songs, rollicking ballads, and savage lampoons of the young poet Philip Freneau (1752-1832). The hurried verse in which he commemorated events that were still news won for him the title of poet of the Revolution. It was not in these hurried verses, however, but in his graceful nature lyrics and ballads of the sea that the true poet was to emerge.

When men first talked of revolution, Freneau was yet a dreamy boy, wandering in the woods or watching the ocean from a high hill. His father, a cultured French immigrant, engaged the best tutors for his son and sent the boy to Princeton. With his classmates — Aaron Burr, James Madison, and Richard Henry Lee — Freneau berated British tyranny and wrote crude satires against the Tories. In collaboration with the future novelist Hugh Henry Brackenridge, he wrote a commencement ode depicting the future glory of an America which would extend from the Atlantic to the Pacific. Freneau taught for several years, resigned his position, and at the outbreak of the war joined in the conflict by hurling satires against the enemy. Late in 1775 he sailed to the West Indies, where the strange beauty of these tropic islands inspired his romantic poems, "The House of Night," and "The Beauties of Santa Cruz." During the progress of the Revolution he was taken from a privateer which he had outfitted and was confined to a British prison ship. On this floating jail, he saw his companions die one by one from starvation and ill-treatment. Freneau himself was long at the point of death before he managed to escape. Patriots who read his condemnation of the enemy in "The British Prison Ship" took new courage. Two of his best Revolutionary poems, "Eutaw Springs" and "The Victory of Captain Paul Jones," fanned the flames of patriotism.

The war over, Freneau became editor of *Freeman's Journal* in Philadelphia and contributed some of his most permanent poetry to this newspaper. From 1784 to 1790 he sailed in command of a merchant vessel, voyaging as far as the Canary Islands.

He recorded his adventures in naval ballads that echo the roaring waves and tempestuous winds of the Atlantic main. Returning to Philadelphia in 1791, he again fought for liberty as editor of the Jeffersonian *National Gazette.* His vigorous attacks on Hamilton caused Washington to dub him "that rascal Freneau." During his last years Freneau's poetic powers declined. He met death as a result of exposure in a snowstorm in which he had lost his way.

Freneau was definitely in advance of his time. He dreamed of a poetic career in the days when America

Philip Freneau, Father of American Poetry

was yet unconcerned over the artistic achievements of her citizens. Realizing that his country's immediate need was for writing that would appeal to the practical-minded, he reluctantly set aside his exalted ideals of literature and began writing fiery patriotic verse. His controversial work in journalism after the war also followed the dictates of necessity rather than art. Again he chose to be a champion of the common man.

At the rare times when Freneau was free to write as he wished, he showed himself a pioneer of romantic art. He spurned the artificiality and conventional forms then in vogue among contemporary English poets. Instead of generalizing on nature as the majority of the American poets before him had done, he depicted the life of the American forest, field, and stream. Most of the early American poets had taken their imagery from the English countryside; Freneau found beauty in the common things within his own sight. He was the first of our writers to give a poetic treatment of the American Indian; his sea ballads added the atmosphere of the ocean to our literature. The title of Father of American poetry belongs to him because he led later poets to find inspiration in the American landscape.

THE EMERGENCE OF THE NEW NATION

The surrender of Cornwallis at Yorktown in 1781 ended the Revolution, even though the peace treaty was not signed until 1783. Because of the weakness in the Articles of Confederation, it appeared that the democracy won by the war was doomed to failure. "What a triumph for the advocates of despotism to find that we are incapable of governing ourselves and that systems founded on the basis of equal liberty are merely ideal and fallacious!" wrote Washington in the anguish of his soul.

The colonists saw that reorganization was necessary to save the new nation, and a group of leaders met in Philadelphia, May 25, 1787, to draft a constitution for the United States. Some of the delegates favored a strong federal government with a president and senators elected for life. They feared that a mob spirit would rule if the people and the states were given too much power; they dreaded lest there would soon be thirteen small warring countries instead of one united nation. Others, wishing to avoid a monarchy or a dictatorship, insisted that the people rightfully have a major part in the government. All were willing to discuss and agree for the welfare of their country.

As the Constitution was first written, many farsighted men, including Jefferson, opposed its adoption. As a consequence, the first Congress completed the Constitution by adding the first ten amendments known as the Bill of Rights. These amendments guarantee to Americans those inalienable natural rights which the colonists had fought to preserve. Under the wise laws of our Constitution, the United States has become the greatest representative democracy the world has ever known.

Violent and bitter dissension between parties marked the early years of the Federal government. The Anti-Federalists, championed by Jefferson, and the Federalists, led by Hamilton, took sides against each other and waged a spirited political war.

ALEXANDER HAMILTON

A bitter fight for the ratification of the Constitution followed its publication in 1787. National leaders wrote hundreds of pamphlets and political essays. More literary than most of the writing which advocated adoption of the Constitution were the essays that comprise *The Federalist* (1787-1788), the joint work of Hamilton, Madison, and Jay. Alexander Hamilton (1757-1804) planned the series and wrote most of the eighty-five articles, which first appeared in the New York *Independent Journal.*

Alexander Hamilton began life as a poor boy in the West Indies. Left an orphan at eleven, he early faced the responsibilities of a man. He was a gay, high-spirited lad, however, and found life in a Santa Cruz countinghouse a dull existence. Casting about for some relief from his humdrum activity, he longed for the approaching war. He did not know that his pen rather than his sword was to bring release. His description of a hurricane published in a local newspaper was so vivid that his admiring relatives sent him to New York to finish his education. He was only fifteen when he landed in the United States. Ready for King's College (the forerunner of Columbia University) after one year in grammar school, Hamilton determined to finish his course in the shortest possible time. Dawn frequently found him studying or writing. After two years he was forced to leave college because of unsettled political conditions.

In July 1774, the seventeen-year-old youth dashed to a public platform and urged Americans to resist British tyranny. From this date until his death, Hamilton's mind and heart were bent upon making America a great, independent nation. As a soldier he was cited for bravery in action. Had not Washington called him to his staff as military secretary, he might be known today as one of America's great generals. He has been called the scholar of the Revolution. He wrote Washington's famous dispatches and later helped him to phrase his *Farewell Address.*

After the war Hamilton envisioned a great, united America, while many contemplated only thirteen separate states loosely held together by the weak Articles of Confederation. Hamilton loved liberty, but he believed it would be best safeguarded under the rule of a chosen body of citizens. Favoring a limited monarchy, he felt the Constitution framed in 1787 gave too much power to the people. But as a defender of strong centralized government he overcame his personal feelings and fought for its ratification. The papers which comprise *The Federalist* are a masterly defense of the Constitution.

© New York Public Library

The Federalist *advocated the adoption of the Constitution.*

At every crisis he wrote stirring appeals that contributed to order, union, and progress. He preferred to see his rival, Thomas Jefferson, at the head of the nation rather than Aaron Burr, a member of his own party but a selfish politician. His fight to save his country at this time led to the duel with Burr, in which he lost his life in 1804.

JOHN CARROLL

Political independence from England heralded freedom of religion for America. With the coming of peace, missionaries in the United States realized that the new nation could no longer remain subject to an English bishop. At a meeting of six deputies of the American clergy in 1783, the priests petitioned Rome that Reverend John Lewis be formally appointed Superior of the Church in the United States with power of administering Confirmation. In view of the priest's advanced age, however, the Vatican named a younger man, Reverend John Carroll (1735-1815) as Prefect Apostolic of the United States in 1784. Five years later when Rome came to realize that an independent republic should have its own hierarchy, he was raised to the bishopric. America's first great churchman was a farsighted, courageous priest capable of dealing with the problems of his turbulent times. A patriotic and religious spirit mark his writings which forcibly state the Catholic position.

By inheritance and experience John Carroll was singularly equipped to guide Catholic America. He was a descendant of the valiant group of Maryland Catholics who for generations had cherished their religion despite the penal laws. Often denied civic and social rights and many times witness to the defection of their fellow Catholics, these men maintained the Faith. Having risked their lives and their fortunes for American freedom, the Carrolls could appreciate the political and religious liberties that came with the Revolution. From this stalwart family of Catholic leaders came the Father of the American hierarchy. As a boy of twelve or thirteen, John Carroll had gone abroad to St. Omer's after his studies at Bohemia Manor. At the conclusion of his liberal education, John Carroll entered the Society of Jesus in France. During the period of his preparation for the priesthood the Jesuits were expelled from France (1762), and with other members of the Society, John was forced to flee to Belgium. Ordained in 1769, he was shortly afterwards sent by his superiors on an extensive trip through Europe as traveling tutor to the son of an English peer. Broadened through education and travels that acquainted him with the peoples of many countries, strengthened by the hardships of the Jesuit expulsion, John Carroll accepted the blow of the suppression of the Jesuit Society in 1773. Alert to the signs of a gathering storm in America, he felt that he should return home, and in June, 1774, he came back to his mother's estate in Maryland. In addition to saying Mass for his relatives and the Catholics of the vicinity, he acted as a missionary to those people who could have no parish. At times he traveled as far as seventy-five miles on a sick call. In 1776 he was asked to accompany the commission to Canada, since it was hoped that the presence of a

John Carroll, Archbishop of Baltimore

priest in the party might advance the American cause with Catholic Canadians. Out of the mission grew the strong friendship between John Carroll and Benjamin Franklin, a member of the commission.

Appointed Prefect Apostolic, John Carroll resided in Baltimore, where he charmed both Catholics and Protestants by his eloquence. He engaged in municipal affairs and especially in establishing schools. He was president of a charity school, trustee of St. John's College, Annapolis, head of the Library Company, Baltimore, and founder of the institution that is now Georgetown University. The phrases pertaining to freedom of religion in the Constitution owe their existence, at least in part, to the priest's representation to Congress.

When Baltimore was declared an archdiocese in 1808, Bishop Carroll was made the first archbishop. During the quarter century that he directed the affairs of the Church in the United States, John Carroll saw the increase of the clergy from thirty priests to a hierarchy of five bishops and more than a hundred priests. The laity had grown from about twenty thousand to five times that number.

The controversial writings, pastoral treatises, and letters of Archbishop Carroll possess clarity, force, and dignity. In refutation of the attack of an ex-Jesuit on the Church in America, he wrote *An Address to the Roman Catholics of the United States in America* (1784), the first book written by a Catholic and published in this country. Among his many other writings, *A Discourse*

on General Washington (1800), delivered on a day of national mourning for the first president, is an eloquent tribute to the Father of his country.

Catholic autobiography excites interest

The first autobiographical account of an American convert was written in 1784 by Reverend John Thayer (1758-1815), a scholarly priest who had turned from the Puritan ministry to Catholicism. The fact that a Boston Puritan had returned to convert his fellow Bostonians after his baptism and ordination in Rome was enough to arouse widespread interest in the little book. Although courageous and ardent in his zeal, Reverend John Thayer was hampered in his ministry by the fact that he never lost the stern, unbending attitudes of his early Puritan life.

GEORGE WASHINGTON

Of all the men who shaped the destinies of America in the Revolutionary period, George Washington (1732-1799) was undoubtedly the greatest. Twice he came forward to lead his country through a serious crisis—first as commander of the patriot forces and secondly as president of the new nation. For eight years the Continental Army followed him through hardship and defeat to final victory and independence. He enjoyed only a few years of peace at Mount Vernon when again he was called to guide the Republic through its first eight unsteady years.

Prepared by natural gifts and education for leadership of men, Washington began to manifest his abilities when he was only sixteen years old. Lord Fairfax was so favorably impressed with the tall, serious young surveyor of Mount Vernon that he sent him to survey his vast tracts of land on the western frontier. On the long, hard journeys through the wilderness, Washington gained a reputation for manly courage and self-reliance. His evident proficiency led to his appointment at twenty-two as a colonel in the French and Indian War. After this war he wrote to his half brother Lawrence that, when two horses were shot from under him and four bullets went through his coat, he had been saved only by "the all-powerful dispensation of Providence."

For sixteen years Washington served Virginia as a member of the House of Burgesses. When the colonies were rallying to the support of Massachusetts in 1774, he declared in a meeting of the assembly: "I will raise one thousand men, subsist them at my own expense, and march myself at their head for the relief of Boston." During the Revolution he was commander in chief of the American forces. After the victory of Yorktown the people regarded him so highly that he might have ruled the new nation as king; yet he gave up his commission and returned to Mount Vernon as a private citizen. He presided at the Constitutional Convention in 1787 and was afterwards unanimously elected first president of the new republic. When his second term was drawing to a close, Washington published his *Farewell Address* (1796). Three years later America mourned his death.

The letters and documents of Washington form an important part of American political writing. His *Diaries*, in which he carefully noted the occurrences of almost every day throughout a long period of his life, have great historical value. His *Farewell Address* has been called one of the few great discourses on government.

CHARLES CARROLL

No one person except perhaps Washington himself gave more of his time and money to the American cause than Charles Carroll of Carrollton (1737-1832). Led by a desire for religious, as well as civil, liberty, he promoted the Revolution from its beginning. At the First Continental Congress in 1774 he insisted on American independence; his faithful championship of Washington at one time helped save the commander in chief from being removed from office upon the instigation of General Conway; he aided in securing the French alliance and attempted to win Canadian help by serving on the Commission to Canada; he was the first man to affix his signature to the Declaration of Independence, the only Roman Catholic to sign. Later as Senator from Maryland and chairman of the committee which drafted the First Amendment to the Constitution, he was largely responsible for the phrase: "Congress shall make no laws respecting an establishment of religion or prohibiting free exercise thereof." With these words he made a gift of the Maryland tradition to the people of the United States.

Charles Carroll of Carrollton was singularly devoted to the cause of his new nation and the welfare of his fellow Catholics.

At eleven Charles Carroll had crossed the Atlantic to continue his studies at St. Omer's and at the Temple in London. After completing his education abroad, he insisted on returning home. Though barred from the practice of law for which he was well prepared, he nevertheless became an influential leader in Maryland. As early as 1763 Charles Carroll had shown himself in advance of the thought of his contemporaries when he wrote: "America is a growing country; in time it will and must be independent." Familiar with Catholic treatises on government, he saw in the Declaration a document based on Christian principles. With the outbreak of war he threw himself enthusiastically into the struggle for freedom. After the peace Carroll served four years as Senator from Maryland. In 1797, having freed thirty of his own slaves at one time, he introduced into the Maryland state legislature a bill for the abolition of slavery.

Though primarily a statesman, Carroll deserves a place among the political writers of the period. He wrote hundreds of letters which echo the history of the time. His *Journal During His Visit to Canada in 1776* is a vivid commentary on methods of travel and life in the colonies at the beginning of the war. No more masterly defense of colonial rights exists than his *Letters of the*

First Citizen, published in the *Maryland Gazette* from February to July, 1773. In the clear though laborious style of the eighteenth century, the letters show a classical background, knowledge of law, depth of thought, and careful research in the problems of government.

MATHEW CAREY

One of the most vigorous and prolific writers of the time was the fiery Irish Catholic immigrant, Mathew Carey (1760-1839). At nineteen he was forced to leave Ireland and to seek refuge in France because of the turmoil caused by his pamphlet, "The Urgent Necessity of an Immediate Repeal of the Whole Penal Code against Roman Catholics." In the suburbs of Paris he worked in the printing shop of Benjamin Franklin. Returning to Ireland after his pamphlet had been forgotten, Carey published a journal of his own but was imprisoned when he again protested against English tyranny. This confinement permitted him to reflect that the republic across the Atlantic would be the place to find liberty.

Disguised in woman's clothes Carey escaped. Arriving in Philadelphia in 1784, he was able to establish the *Pennsylvania Herald* through Lafayette's gift of four hundred dollars. Within a few years Carey's journalistic endeavors made him a force in America. In 1786 he published the first American literary magazine, *The American Museum*. This monthly periodical stimulated the growth of magazines that have mushroomed in America during the past century and a half.

As an energetic publisher, Carey contributed to the cultivation of America's literary taste in its formative years. The first edition of the Douay Bible in the United States came from his press in 1790. For over a period of thirty-five years he supplied the public with textbooks, law commentaries, novels, encyclopedias, histories, and dictionaries. Many of these books he edited himself.

While maintaining a flourishing book business, Carey continually sought to improve the conditions of laborers and the poor. His *Miscellaneous Essays* (1830) contain a forceful defense of the unfortunate and underprivileged. In politics Carey was not a narrow partisan. When sectional and party feeling threatened to disrupt the union in 1814, he condemned the faults of both Federalists and Anti-Federalists in his *Olive Branch* (1814). This work, together with his *Vindiciae*

Hibernicae (1823), a spirited defense of Irish Catholics, are considered his best books. In addition to being an essayist, editor, and publisher, Mathew Carey was something of a poet. His verse includes an ode to Benjamin Franklin and several satires.

THE BEGINNINGS OF JOURNALISM AND IMAGINATIVE LITERATURE

The outlook of the literary artist on the eve of the Revolution was not optimistic. Only a very limited class of persons saw the value of literature as a fine art. Writers could not yet earn a living with the pen, and the country was soon to enter into a war which demanded a practical patriotic literature to serve the needs of the moment. Despite these adverse circumstances, young men in the colleges, who at an earlier period would have been absorbed in theology, were beginning to show a literary consciousness. A Yale graduate, John Trumbull, was instrumental in adding the study of modern literature and composition to the college curriculum. Noah Webster was already advocating literary and cultural independence from England; but partly because of the importation of European books, American writers followed European models even when they developed American themes. English writers such as Alexander Pope set the fashion for verse, satire, patriotic epic, and the use of the heroic couplet in American writings.

Newspapers serve American cause

During the Revolutionary War the newspaper began its growth as an instrument shaping public opinion. Exerting little influence at the beginning of the conflict, the newssheet gradually assumed more importance as the tension between the colonies and the mother country increased. It was soon passed from hand to hand and read aloud in the taverns and at the docks. Its contents were repeated, discussed, at times memorized. By the time peace had come, these newspapers had risen to new prestige and were regarded as a necessity in the home.

The printers of the Revolution, who usually served also as publishers or editors, were pioneers of the press. No obstacle could check their activities. Under bombardment from the British, they stole out of the occupied cities, taking their heavy wooden presses with them to nearby points, from which they encouraged the patriots with a constant stream of editorial comment.

During the occupation of Boston, the office of the *Gazette* was moved up the river to Watertown during the night. Another Boston journal, the *Massachusetts Spy*, was taken to Worcester. At the occupation of New York three papers, the *Journal*, the *Gazette and Weekly Mercury*, and the *Packet*, escaped the British by swift flight to distant points. The *Pennsylvania Gazette* and the *Pennsylvania Packet* found refuge in other cities during the British possession of Philadelphia. In Newport, Rhode Island, the patriotic printer buried the press and type of the *Mercury* only to exhume them after the British had left the city.

The patriot editors showed a keen perception in identifying as history the most significant events of the time. Often they were hindered by primitive methods of communication that brought news to them weeks after it had occurred. When the scarcity of paper threatened the continuance of their journals, these men issued a rallying call for old linen and cotton clothing that could be converted into paper. Washington himself came to the rescue of a printer near Morristown by giving him old tent cloth belonging to the Continental Army. The poorly-inked sheets which the old wooden presses of the Revolution turned out seem inferior by comparison with those produced by a modern letter duplicator; yet these papers were the invaluable means by which the people were prepared for independence and war and informed of the principles for which patriots were willing to fight. In these newspapers were clarified fundamental American ideals.

THE HARTFORD WITS

The first glimmerings of a national consciousness that was to flourish in the next century manifested itself in poems singing the glory of America and her future destiny. A number of Yale poets, known as the Hartford Wits, became the leaders of a group which followed neo-classical writers. Like the English neo-classicists they made the literature of ancient Greece and Rome their models and by allusion and quotation frequently displayed their knowledge of the ancient classics. In their works the neo-classicists exhibited restrained imagination and laid emphasis on style and form. Among the Americans who followed this tradition, Timothy Dwight, Joel Barlow, and John Trumbull were outstanding. Passages of true poetry in their work indicate what they might have accomplished had not the war diverted them from the pursuit of artistic writing. Each of them produced some artistic writing and another group of works that should be designated as political. Before the war John Trumbull (1750-1831) had written *The Progress of Dullness* (1772-73), a brilliant satire on education. During the Revolution his outstanding contribution was *McFingal* (1782), a political skit satirizing the Tories. Chief among the Hartford Wits, Timothy Dwight (1752-1817) is best remembered for his *Greenfield Hill* (1794), a poetic account of the history of America and a picture of her future glory; for *The Conquest of Canaan* (1785), a religious epic; and for *The Triumph of Infidelity* (1788), a satire on European deism. Another writer of this group, Joel Barlow (1754-1812), was ambitious to write the great epic of America. But his attempt at this enterprise, *The Columbiad* (1807), is less known than his brief poem, "Hasty Pudding" (1796), written in praise of the New England dish of boiled Indian meal. Other poets in this group include David Humphreys, Lemuel Hopkins, Theodore Dwight, and Richard Alsop.

THE FIRST AMERICAN NOVEL

Because Puritan disapproval of fiction persisted in America, the novel was tardy in developing. For many years *The Power of Sympathy* (1789) was considered the first American novel. Later research has uncovered the *Adventures of Alonso: Containing Some Striking Anecdotes of the Present Prime Minister of Portugal*, published in England in 1775 "by a native of Maryland, some years resident in Lisbon." Evidence points to Thomas Atwood Digges (1741?-1821?), a member of an old Catholic family of Warburton, Maryland, as the author of this romantic novel. Digges had lived abroad in Lisbon, Passy, and London. An intimate friend of Washington, Jefferson, and Madison, he actively supported the

American cause during the Revolutionary War, even while residing on foreign soil. The book, which condemns despotic government, relates the adventures of the young Portuguese Alonso. The flippant tone of the writer occasionally betrays the prevalent anticlerical attitude of the eighteenth century.

The American appetite for fiction, long restrained, developed rapidly during the last decade of the eighteenth century. In order that their stories might escape censure, writers eagerly contrived plots that would point to an obvious moral. Ornate, sentimental, and effusive, these tales cautiously followed European models.

By insisting upon native subject matter and background, Charles Brockden Brown (1771-1810) contributed to the development of the American novel. In *Wieland* (1798), Brown borrowed the machinery of the Gothic romance, a popular type of English fiction which increased suspense by introducing sensational events and supernatural horrors. The ventriloquist villain, the adventurous sleepwalker, spontaneous combustion in the human body—all these gruesome elements of subject matter made possible the first financial successes in fiction. Although Brown's novels show excessive sentiment and a lack of narrative skill, he brought a certain independence and strength to American fiction. In finding a place for the American wilderness and the native Indian in the pages of our novels, he anticipated by more than twenty years the contribution of James Fenimore Cooper.

DRAMA DURING THE REVOLUTION

Although drama had up to this time received little attention as a literary form, the few significant plays that were written reflect the patriotism of the times. In 1787 *The Contrast*, a comedy by Royall Tyler (1757-1826), was produced in New York. It is a truly American play, perhaps the first that may be so called. The scene is laid in this country; the characters are Americans; and the play treats of the American spirit and way of life. It offers likewise the first presentation of the typical Yankee, lean, dry, naive, and shrewd.

The war for independence, it is true, arrested literary development, for literature was called into the service of political writing. Nevertheless, the Revolution, in permanently uniting the thirteen colonies, pointed the way towards a national culture.

The Surrender at Yorktown

Training for Writing

(From *The Autobiography*)
Benjamin Franklin

Believing that his posterity might be interested in the story of his life, Franklin began his Autobiography *one summer in England in the form of a letter to his son. The account of his rise in the world is one of the earliest American success stories. Step by step he records his progress towards the things he desired, frankly revealing both his faults and virtues. This personal narrative is not only the first book of real literary value written by an American but also one of the world's masterpieces of autobiographical writing. The following excerpt shows the systematic way by which Franklin achieved the clear, simple style for which he is noted.*

FROM a child I was fond of reading, and all the little money that came into my hands was ever laid out in books. Pleased with the *Pilgrim's Progress*,[1] my first collection was of John Bunyan's works in separate little volumes. I afterwards sold them to enable me to buy R. Burton's *Historical Collections*;[2] they were small chapmen's books and cheap, forty or fifty in all. My father's little library consisted chiefly of books in polemic divinity,[3] most of which I read, and have since often regretted that at a time when I had such a thirst for knowledge, more proper books had not fallen in my way, since it was now resolved I should not be a clergyman. *Plutarch's Lives*[4] there was, in which I read abundantly, and I still think that time spent to great advantage. There was also a book of Defoe's called *Essay on Projects*[5] and another of Dr. Mather's called *Essays to do Good*,[6] which perhaps gave me a turn of thinking that had an influence on some of the principal future events of my life.

This bookish inclination at length determined my father to make me a printer, though he had already one son (James) of that profession. In 1717 my brother James returned from England with a press and letters[7] to set up his business in Boston. I liked it much better than that of my father but still had a hankering for the sea. To prevent the apprehended effect of such an inclination, my father was impatient to have me bound to my brother. I stood out some time but at last was persuaded and signed the indentures[8] when I was yet but twelve years old. I was to serve as an apprentice till I was twenty-one years of age, only I was to be allowed a journeyman's[9] wages during the last year. In a little time I made great proficiency in the business and became a useful hand to my brother. I now had access to better books. An acquaintance with the apprentices of booksellers enabled me sometimes to borrow a small one, which I was careful to return soon and clean. Often I sat in my room reading the greater part of the night when the book was borrowed in the evening and had to be returned early in the morning, lest it should be missed or wanted.

And after some time an ingenious tradesman, Mr. Matthew Adams, who had a pretty collection of books and who frequented our printing house, took notice of me, invited me to come to his library, and very kindly lent me such books as I chose to read. I now took a fancy to poetry and made some little pieces; my brother, thinking it might turn to account, encouraged me and put me on composing occasional ballads. One was called "The Lighthouse Tragedy" and contained an account of the drowning of Captain Worthilake[10] with his two daughters; the other was a sailor's song on the taking of Teach[11] (or Blackbeard) the pirate. They were wretched stuff in the Grub Street[12] ballad style; and when they were printed, he sent me about the town

---

[1] *Pilgrim's Progress*, a famous allegory by the seventeenth-century English writer John Bunyan.

[2] *R. Burton's Historical Collections*, books written by Nathaniel Crouch under the pen name of R. Burton. Books sold by wandering peddlers called chapmen were referred to as chapmen's books.

[3] *polemic divinity*, religious controversy.

[4] *Plutarch's Lives*, biographies of famous Greeks and Romans by the Greek writer Plutarch, who lived in the first century a.d.

[5] *Defoe's . . . Projects*, essays on social and economic problems by Daniel Defoe, author of Robinson Crusoe.

[6] *Dr. Mather . . . Do Good*, Cotton Mather's *Bonifacius. An Essay upon the Good That Is To Be Devised and Designed by Those Who Desire to Answer the Great End of Life and Do Good While They Live.*

[7] *letters*, type.

[8] *indentures*, contracts by which an apprentice is bound to the master.

[9] *journeyman*, a worker who has learned a trade.

[10] *Captain Worthilake*. In November, 1718, George Worthilake, Boston Lighthouse keeper, was drowned with his wife and daughter (not two daughters, as Franklin states).

[11] *Teach*, Edward Teach, an English pirate, who was killed off the coast of North Carolina in November, 1718.

[12] *Grub Street*, a street in London where needy authors lived. The term came to be applied to dull writing of any kind.

to sell them. The first sold wonderfully, the event being recent, having made a great noise. This flattered my vanity; but my father discouraged me by ridiculing my performances and telling me versemakers were generally beggars. So I escaped being a poet, most probably a very bad one; but as prose writing has been of great use to me in the course of my life and was a principal means of my advancement, I shall tell you how, in such a situation, I acquired what little ability I have in that way.

There was another bookish lad in the town, John Collins by name, with whom I was intimately acquainted. We sometimes disputed, and very fond we were of argument and very desirous of confuting one another, which disputatious turn, by the way, is apt to become a very bad habit, making people often extremely disagreeable in company by the contradiction that is necessary to bring it into practice; and thence, besides souring and spoiling the conversation, is productive of disgusts and perhaps enmities where you have occasion for friendship. I had caught it by reading my father's books of dispute about religion. Persons of good sense, I have since observed, seldom fall into it, except lawyers, university men, and men of all sorts that have been bred at Edinburgh.[13]

A question was once, somehow or other, started between Collins and me of the propriety of educating the female sex in learning and their abilities for study. He was of the opinion that it was improper and that they were naturally unequal to it. I took the contrary side, perhaps a little for dispute's sake. He was naturally more eloquent, had a ready plenty of words, and sometimes, as I thought, bore me down more by his fluency than by the strength of his reasons. As we parted without settling the point and were not to see one another again for some time, I sat down to put my arguments in writing, which I copied fair and sent to him. He answered and I replied. Three or four letters of a side had passed when my father happened to find my papers and read them. Without entering into the discussion, he took occasion to talk to me about the manner of my writing; observed that, though I had the advantage of my antagonist in correct spelling and pointing[14] (which I owed to the printing house), I fell far short in elegance of expression, in method and perspicuity, of which he convinced me by

several instances. I saw the justice of his remarks and thence grew more attentive to the manner in writing and determined to endeavor at improvement.

About this time I met with an odd volume of *The Spectator*.[15] It was the third. I had never before seen any of them. I bought it, read it over and over, and was much delighted with it. I thought the writing excellent and wished if possible to imitate it. With this view I took some of the papers and, making short hints of the sentiment in each sentence, laid them by a few days; and then without looking at the book tried to complete the papers again by expressing each hinted sentiment at length and as fully as it had been expressed before in any suitable words that should come to hand. Then I compared my *Spectator* with the original, discovered some of my faults, and corrected them. But I found I wanted a stock of words or a readiness in recollecting and using them, which I thought I should have acquired before that time if I had gone on making verses; since the continual occasion for words of the same import but of different length to suit the measure or of different sound for the rhyme, would have laid me under a constant necessity of searching for variety and also have tended to fix that variety in my mind and make me master of it. Therefore I took some of the tales and turned them into verse; and after a time when I had pretty well forgotten the prose turned them back again. I also sometimes jumbled my collections of hints into confusion and after some weeks endeavored to reduce them into the best order before I began to form the full sentence and complete the paper. This was to teach me method in the arrangement of thoughts. By comparing my work afterwards with the original, I discovered many faults and amended them; but I sometimes had the pleasure of fancying that in certain particulars of small import I had been lucky enough to improve the method or the language, and this encouraged me to think I might possibly in time come to be a tolerable English writer, of which I was extremely ambitious. My time for these exercises and for reading was at night after work or before it began in the morning, or on Sundays when I contrived to be in the printing house alone . . .

My brother had, in 1720 or 1721, begun to print a newspaper. It was the second that appeared in America

---

13 *Edinburgh*, the University of Edinburgh in Scotland.
14 *pointing*, punctuation.

15 *The Spectator*, a daily journal containing light essays, written and published by Joseph Addison and Richard Steele in London during the eighteenth century.

and was called *The New England Courant*.[16] The only one before it was the *Boston News-Letter*. I remember his being dissuaded by some of his friends from the undertaking as not likely to succeed, one newspaper being in their judgment enough for America. At this time (1771) there are not less than five-and-twenty. He went on, however, with the undertaking; and after having worked in composing the types and printing off the sheets, I was employed to carry the papers through the streets to the customers.

He had some ingenious men among his friends who amused themselves by writing little pieces for this paper, which gained it credit and made it more in demand; and these gentlemen often visited us. Hearing their conversations and their account of the approbation their papers were received with, I was excited to try my hand among them; but being still a boy and suspecting that my brother would object to printing anything of mine in his paper if he knew it to be mine, I contrived to disguise my hand; and writing an anonymous paper,[17] I put it in at night under the door of the printing house. It was found in the morning and communicated to his writing friends when they called in as usual. They read it,

[16] *second . . . New England Courant. The New England Courant* was the fourth newspaper that appeared in America. It is not surprising that Franklin's memory for details failed him after fifty years. He was doubtless thinking of the fact that his brother was the printer of *The Boston Gazette*, the second newspaper in America.

[17] *an anonymous paper*, the first of the Dogood papers, which were published in the *Courant* from April to October, 1722, when Franklin was only sixteen years old. He wrote these essays under the assumed name of Silence Dogood, supposed to be the widow of a parson.

commented on it in my hearing, and I had the exquisite pleasure of finding it met with their approbation and that, in their different guesses at the author, none were named but men of some character among us for learning and ingenuity. I suppose now that I was rather lucky in my judges and that perhaps they were not really so very good ones as I then esteemed them.

VIEWING THE AUTHOR'S IDEAS

1. Show how Franklin heeded his own maxim, "Opportunity knocks but once." How does this selection confirm the statement that Franklin was a self-made man?

2. Compare and contrast the types of books read by modern youth with those read by Franklin.

3. How does the subject of Franklin's debate with Collins reflect the attitude of the eighteenth century? Suggest other topics which they might have debated.

4. What did Franklin hope to derive from his attempt to write poetry?

5. How does this selection reveal Franklin's shrewd Yankee thrift; his self-complacency; his practical views of life; his interest in conduct and manners?

EVALUATING HIS MANNER OF EXPRESSION

1. Franklin wrote in a plain, businesslike style, devoid of ornament or affectation. Show that this statement is true of the selection.

2. Find examples of Franklin's humor.

To Madame Helvétius

Benjamin Franklin

Liberty and the simple life were popular topics when Franklin arrived in France as the emissary of the thirteen American colonies. His fur cap and spectacles, his long, straight hair and plain brown coat caused a sensation among the powdered heads of Paris. Peasants, nobility, and royalty hailed him as a simple philosopher destined to restore the golden age. Above all, his wit and droll humor charmed the French ladies, and their beauty and gaiety captivated him. Not far away from Passy, where he took up his residence, lived Madame Helvétius, a beautiful widow of sixty, surrounded by her two daughters, her birds, and her chickens. Franklin, whose wife had died a few years previously, became a close friend of Madame Helvétius, and he eventually invited the Frenchwoman to marry him. Even after he wrote this delightful bagatelle, Madame Helvétius remained firm in her decision not to remarry.

MORTIFIED at the barbarous resolution pronounced by you so positively yesterday evening, that you would remain single the rest of your life as a compliment due to the memory of your husband, I retired to my chamber. Throwing myself upon my bed, I dreamt that I was dead and was transported to the Elysian Fields.[1]

I was asked whether I wished to see any persons in particular; to which I replied that I wished to see the philosophers.

"There are two who live here at hand in this garden; they are good neighbors and very friendly towards one another."[2]

"Who are they?"

"Socrates[3] and Helvétius."[4]

"I esteem them both highly; but let me see Helvétius first, because I understand a little French but not a word of Greek."

I was conducted to him; he received me with much courtesy, having known me, he said, by character some time past. He asked me a thousand questions relative to the war,[5] the present state of religion, of liberty, of the government in France.

"You do not inquire, then," said I, "after your dear friend, Madame Helvétius; yet she loves you exceedingly; I was in her company not more than an hour ago."

"Ah," said he, "you make me recur to my past happiness, which ought to be forgotten in order to be more happy here. For many years I could think of nothing but her, though at length I am consoled. I have taken another wife, the most like her that I could find; she is not indeed altogether so handsome, but she has a great fund of wit and good sense, and her whole study is to please me. She is at this moment gone to fetch the best nectar and ambrosia[6] to regale me; stay here awhile and you will see her."

"I perceive," said I, "that your former friend is more faithful to you than you are to her; she has had several good offers but has refused them all. I will confess to you that I loved her extremely; but she was cruel to me and rejected me peremptorily for your sake."

"I pity you sincerely," said he, "for she is an excellent woman, handsome and amiable. But do not the Abbé de la R. and the Abbé M.[7] visit her?"

"Certainly they do; not one of your friends has dropped her acquaintance."

"If you had gained the Abbé M. with a bribe of good coffee and cream, perhaps you would have succeeded; for he is as deep a reasoner as Duns Scotus[8] or St. Thomas;[9] he arranges and methodizes his arguments in such a manner that they are almost irresistible. Or if by a fine edition of some old classic, you had gained the Abbé de la R. to speak *against* you, that would have been still better; as I always observed that when he recommended anything to her, she had a great inclination to do directly the contrary."

As he finished these words, the new Madame Helvétius entered with the nectar, and I recognized her immediately as my former American friend, Mrs. Franklin! I reclaimed her but she answered me coldly:

"I was a good wife to you for forty-nine years and four months, nearly half a century; let that content you. I have formed a new connection here, which will last to eternity."

Indignant at this refusal of my Eurydice,[10] I immediately resolved to quit those ungrateful shades[11] and return to this good world again to behold the sun and you! Here I am; let us *avenge ourselves!*

VIEWING THE AUTHOR'S IDEAS

1. What aspect of Franklin's nature are revealed in this letter that are not found in the selection from *The Autobiography*?

2. How did Franklin try to convince Madame Helvétius that in the next world her husband was no longer concerned about her? How does Helvétius evaluate his former wife?

3. In view of the fact that Socrates' wife, Xanthippe, had been quarrelsome and peevish, what advice might the Greek philosopher have offered?

EVALUATING HIS MANNER OF EXPRESSION

1. Why does Franklin present the story of his sojourn in the Elysian Fields in the form of a dream?

2. The narrative elements in this letter foreshadow the development of the short story. Discuss the effective way in which the first paragraph presents the situation and the characters; the way in which the author suggests the

---

[1] *Elysian Fields*, in Greek mythology the dwelling place of the happy souls after death.

[2] The dialogue has been paragraphed by the editors.

[3] *Socrates*, a Greek philosopher.

[4] *Helvétius*, Claude Adrien Helvétius, a French philosopher and the husband of Madame Helvétius.

[5] *war*, The American Revolution.

[6] *nectar and ambrosia*, in Greek and Roman mythology the food and drink of the gods.

[7] *Abbé de la R. and Abbé M.*, Abbé de la Roche and Abbé Morellet, friends of Franklin.

[8] *Duns Scotus*, a scholastic philosopher called the *Subtle Doctor*, who died in 1308.

[9] *St. Thomas*, the greatest of the scholastic philosophers, who was called the *Angelic Doctor*.

[10] *Eurydice (ū-rĭd'ĭ-sē)*. The poet Orpheus so loved his wife, Eurydice, that when she died he sought her in the abode of the dead. There he charmed Pluto with his music and thus obtained permission for his wife to return with him to earth on condition that she would not look back.

[11] *shades*, souls after their separation from the body.

antecedent action; and the steps by which he leads to a climax in the disclosure of the new wife's identity. What clashes of character are presented in the letter?

3. Explain the following expressions: (a) "nectar and ambrosia to regale me" (b) "ungrateful shades" (c) "the refusal of my Eurydice."

4. How is this letter imaginative; whimsical; subtle?

5. Make a list of allusions to religion; to classical lore; to Greek history; to French society.

What Is an American?

(From *Letters from an American Farmer*)
Michel-Guillaume St. Jean de Crèvecœur[1]

One of the most widely-read books of the eighteenth century was Crèvecœur's Letters from an American Farmer. *Rousseau and the romanticists had stimulated an interest in the idyllic aspects of rural life. The physiocrats stressed the powers of nature as a source of public wealth and national prosperity. Here was a book written by a real farmer in America, a newly emancipated nation about which everyone was talking, a land where industry was unfettered and the common man led a comfortable life in an environment unspoiled by the conventions of older civilizations. In the following selection the author idealizes the simple ways of the American farmer and forecasts the new American type that was to emerge from the mixture of races then pouring into this country.*

I WISH I could be acquainted with the feelings and thoughts which must agitate the heart and present themselves to the mind of an enlightened Englishman when he first lands on this continent. He must greatly rejoice that he lived at a time to see this fair country discovered and settled; he must necessarily feel a share of national pride when he views the chain of settlements which embellishes these extended shores. When he says to himself, this is the work of my countrymen, who, when convulsed by factions, afflicted by a variety of miseries and wants, restless and impatient, took refuge here. They brought along with them their national genius, to which they principally owe what liberty they enjoy and what substance they possess. Here he sees the industry of his native country displayed in a new manner and traces in their works the embryos of all the arts, sciences, and ingenuity which flourish in Europe. Here he beholds fair cities, substantial villages, extensive fields, an immense country filled with decent houses, good roads, orchards, meadows, and bridges, where an hundred years ago all was wild, woody, and uncultivated! What a train of pleasing ideas this fair spectacle must suggest; it is a prospect which must inspire a good citizen with the most heartfelt pleasure. The difficulty consists in the manner of viewing so extensive a scene. He is arrived on a new continent; a modern society offers itself to his contemplation, different from what he had hitherto seen. It is not composed, as in Europe, of great lords who possess everything and of a herd of people who have nothing. Here are no aristocratical families, no courts, no kings, no bishops, no ecclesiastical dominion, no invisible power giving to a few a very visible one; no great manufacturers employing thousands, no great refinements of luxury. The rich and the poor are not so far removed from each other as they are in Europe. Some few towns excepted, we are all tillers of the earth, from Nova Scotia to West Florida. We are a people of cultivators, scattered over an immense territory, communicating with each other by means of good roads and navigable rivers, united by the silken bands of mild government, all respecting the laws without dreading their power, because they are equitable. We are all animated with the spirit of an industry which is unfettered and unrestrained, because each person works for himself. If he travels through our rural districts, he views not the hostile castle and the haughty mansion, contrasted with the clay-built hut and miserable cabin, where cattle and men help to keep each other warm and dwell in meanness, smoke, and indigence. A pleasing uniformity of decent competence appears throughout

---

[1] *Crèvecœur (krĕv-kúr´).*

our habitations. The meanest of our log houses is a dry and comfortable habitation. Lawyer or merchant are the fairest titles our towns afford; that of a farmer is the only appellation of the rural inhabitants of our country. It must take some time ere he can reconcile himself to our dictionary, which is but short in words of dignity and names of honor. There on a Sunday he sees a congregation of respectable farmers and their wives, all clad in neat homespun, well mounted or riding in their own humble wagons. There is not among them an esquire, saving the unlettered magistrate. There he sees a parson as simple as his flock, a farmer who does not riot on the labor of others. We have no princes for whom we toil, starve, and bleed: we are the most perfect society now existing in the world. Here man is free as he ought to be; nor is this pleasing equality so transitory as many others are. Many ages will not see the shores of our great lakes replenished with inland nations, nor the unknown bounds of North America entirely peopled. Who can tell how far it extends? Who can tell the millions of men whom it will feed and contain? For no European foot has as yet traveled half the extent of this mighty continent!

The next wish of this traveler will be to know whence came all these people. They are a mixture of English, Scotch, Irish, French, Dutch, Germans, and Swedes. From this promiscuous breed, that race now called Americans have arisen. The eastern provinces[2] must indeed be excepted, as being the unmixed descendants of Englishmen. I have heard many wish that they had been more intermixed also: for my part, I am no wisher and think it much better as it has happened. They exhibit a most conspicuous figure in this great and variegated picture; they too enter for a great share in the pleasing perspective displayed in these thirteen provinces. I know it is fashionable to reflect on[3] them, but I respect them for what they have done; for the accuracy and wisdom with which they have settled their territory; for the decency of their manners; for their early love of letters; their ancient college, the first in this hemisphere;[4] for their industry, which to me who am but a farmer, is the criterion of everything. There never was a people, situated as they are, who with so

ungrateful a soil have done more in so short a time. Do you think that the monarchical ingredients which are more prevalent in other governments have purged them from all foul stains? Their histories assert the contrary.

In this great American asylum the poor of Europe have by some means met together, and in consequence of various causes; to what purpose should they ask one another what countrymen they are? Alas, two thirds of them had no country. Can a wretch who wanders about, who works and starves, whose life is a continual scene of sore affliction or pinching penury—can that man call England or any other kingdom his country? A country that had no bread for him, whose fields procured him no harvest, who met with nothing but the frowns of the rich, the severity of the laws, with jails and punishments; who owned not a single foot of the extensive surface of this planet? No! urged by a variety of motives, here they came. Everything has tended to regenerate them: new laws, a new mode of living, a new social system; here they are become men; in Europe they were as so many useless plants, wanting vegetative mold and refreshing showers; they withered and were mowed down by want, hunger, and war; but now by the power of transplantation, like all other plants, they have taken root and flourished! Formerly they were not numbered in any civil lists of their country, except in those of the poor; here they rank as citizens. By what invisible power has this surprising metamorphosis[5] been performed? By that of the laws and that of their industry. The laws, the indulgent laws, protect them as they arrive, stamping on them the symbol of adoption; they receive ample rewards for their labors; these accumulated rewards procure them lands; those lands confer on them the title of freemen, and to that title every benefit is affixed which men can possible require. This is the great operation daily performed by our laws. From whence proceed these laws? From our government. Whence the government? It is derived from the original genius and strong desire of the people, ratified and confirmed by the crown. This is the great chain which links us all; this is the picture which every province exhibits, Nova Scotia excepted. There the crown has done all; either there were no people who had genius, or it was not much attended to; the consequence is, that the province is very thinly inhabited indeed; the power of the crown in conjunction with the mosquitoes

[2] *eastern provinces*, the New England States.

[3] *reflect on*, censure.

[4] *ancient college . . . hemisphere*. The author here refers to Harvard College, founded in 1636. The first college in the western hemisphere was the College of Santa Cruz, Mexico, founded in 1536.

[5] *metamorphosis*, change.

has prevented men from settling there. Yet some parts of it flourished once, and it contained a mild, harmless set of people. But for the fault of a few leaders, the whole were banished.[6] The greatest political error the crown ever committed in America was to cut off men from a country which wanted nothing but men!

What attachment can a poor European emigrant have for a country where he had nothing? The knowledge of the language, the love of a few kindred as poor as himself were the only cords that tied him; his country is now that which gives him land, bread, protection, and consequence. *Ubi panis, ibi patria*,[7] is the motto of all emigrants. What then is the American, this new man? He is either an European or the descendant of an European; hence that strange mixture of blood, which you will find in no other country. I could point out to you a family whose grandfather was an Englishman, whose wife was Dutch, whose son married a French woman, and whose present four sons have now four wives of different nations. *He* is an American, who, leaving behind him all his ancient prejudices and manners, receives new ones from the new mode of life he has embraced, the new government he obeys, and the new rank he holds. He becomes an American by being received in the broad lap of our great *Alma Mater*.[8] Here individuals of all nations are melted into a new race of men, whose labors and posterity will one day cause great changes in the world. Americans are the western pilgrims, who are carrying along with them that great mass of arts, sciences, vigor, and industry which began long since in the east; they will finish the great circle. The Americans were once scattered all over Europe; here they are incorporated into one of the finest systems of population which has ever appeared, and which will hereafter become distinct by the power of the different climates they inhabit. The American ought therefore to love this country much better than that wherein either he or his forefathers were born. Here the rewards of his industry follow with equal steps the progress of his labor; his labor is founded on the basis of nature, *self-interest*; can it want a stronger allurement? Wives and children, who before in-vain demanded of him a morsel of bread, now, fat and frolicsome, gladly help their father to clear

those fields whence exuberant crops are to arise to feed and to clothe them all; without any part being claimed, either by a despotic prince, a rich abbot, or a mighty lord. Here religion demands but little of him; a small voluntary salary to the minister, and gratitude to God; can he refuse these? The American is a new man, who acts upon new principles; he must therefore entertain new ideas and form new opinions. From involuntary idleness, servile dependence, penury, and useless labor, he has passed to toils of a very different nature, rewarded by ample subsistence.—This is an American. . . .

VIEWING THE AUTHOR'S IDEAS

1. Discuss this selection from the standpoint of a foreigner's attitude toward America as "the promised land." What are some of the problems confronting the immigrant today?

2. What statement suggests the phrase "melting pot"? What is the meaning of this phrase? List the characteristics of "this new man," the American, described by Crèvecœur. According to Crèvecœur, why should the immigrant love America more than the land of his birth? How does the author show the dignity and importance of agriculture?

3. Point out the advantages of country life and the importance of the farmer in the economic life of a nation. How has farming in America changed since Crèvecœur's time?

4. In what words does the author praise the individualism of pioneer American life? What evils in modern America have resulted from an excess of individualism?

5. What attitude towards religion is manifested in this essay? What statements show that Crèvecœur was affected by the anticlerical attitude current in France during his time?

EVALUATING HIS MANNER OF EXPRESSION

1. Show whether the author's point of view is objective or subjective.

2. Find illustrations of the following romantic traits in this essay: a) the sentimental idealization of rural life in America b) the exaltation of individual freedom c) the mood of aspiration and enthusiasm.

3. Crèvecœur's prose is highly emotional, imaginative, and at times oratorical. Cite examples of his use of vivid figures of speech, picturesque imagery; repetition, exclamation; question, negation; contrast and climax.

4. Comment on the variety of sentence structure exemplified in this essay. Point out errors of syntax. Can you account for these?

---

[6] *the fault . . . banished.* The author here alludes to the banishment of the Acadians in 1755 and their dispersal throughout the British colonies.

[7] *Ubi panis, ibi patria*, where a man's bread is, there is his country.

[8] *Alma Mater*, fostering mother

Speech in the Virginia Convention

Patrick Henry

With this impassioned call to arms, Virginia's allegiance to the Revolutionary cause became a certainty. On the morning of March 23, 1775, spectators crowded the aisles and packed the open windows as the delegates to the Virginia Revolutionary Convention assembled at old St. John's Church in Richmond. The resolution of Patrick Henry that Virginia "be immediately put into a posture of defense" met with opposition from some wealthy plantation owners. Convinced that no compromise could be made with the unreasonable policies of George III, Henry rose and delivered his famous appeal for armed resistance. Washington and Jefferson were among those who saw his white face and the unearthly gleam in his eyes and heard the mighty vibrations of his voice. Colonel Edward Carrington, perched in an east window, was so affected by the plea that he jumped to the floor, crying out, "Let me be buried on this spot!" His tomb now marks this place. Patrick Henry's speeches form an important part of Revolutionary literature.

No exact copies of Patrick Henry's speeches have come down to us. This oration is preserved in William Wirt's life of the famous statesman. Wirt's copy of the speech is based upon reliable reports from two of Patrick Henry's listeners.

No man, Mr. President, thinks more highly than I do of the patriotism as well as abilities of the very worthy gentlemen who have just addressed the House. But different men often see the same subjects in different lights; and therefore I hope it will not be thought disrespectful to those gentlemen if, entertaining as I do opinions of a character very opposite to theirs, I should speak forth my sentiments freely and without reserve. This is no time for ceremony. The question before the House is one of awful moment to this country. For my own part, I consider it as nothing less than a question of freedom or slavery. And in proportion to the magnitude of the subject ought to be the freedom of the debate. It is only in this way that we can hope to arrive at truth and fulfill the great responsibility which we hold to God and our country. Should I keep back my opinions at such a time through fear of giving offense, I should consider myself as guilty of treason towards my country and of an act of disloyalty toward the majesty of Heaven, which I revere above all earthly kings.

Mr. President, it is natural to man to indulge in the illusions of hope. We are apt to shut our eyes against a painful truth and listen to the song of that siren[1] till she transforms us into beasts. Is this the part of wise men engaged in a great and arduous struggle for liberty? Are we disposed to be of the number of those who, having eyes, see not, and having ears, hear not the things which so nearly concern their temporal salvation? For my part, whatever anguish of spirit it may cost, I am willing to know the whole truth, to know the worst, and to provide for it.

I have but one lamp by which my feet are guided; and that is the lamp of experience. I know of no way of judging of the future but by the past. And judging by the past, I wish to know what there has been in the conduct of the British ministry for the last ten years to justify those hopes with which gentlemen have been pleased to solace themselves and the House? Is it that insidious smile with which our petition has been lately received?[2] Trust it not, sir; it will prove a snare to your feet. Suffer not yourselves to be betrayed with a kiss. Ask yourselves how this gracious reception of our petition comports with those warlike preparations which cover our waters and darken our land. Are fleets and armies necessary to a work of love and reconciliation? Have we shown ourselves so unwilling to be reconciled that force must be called in to win back our love? Let us not deceive ourselves, sir. These are the implements of war and subjugation, the last arguments to which kings resort.

I ask gentlemen, sir, what means this martial array,[3] if its purpose be not to force us to submission? Can gentlemen assign any other possible motive for it? Has Great Britain any enemy in this quarter of the world to call for all this accumulation of navies and armies? No, sir, she has none. They are meant for us; they can be meant for no other. They are sent over to bind and rivet

---

[1] *siren*, a pagan divinity who lured mariners to destruction by her songs. Henry here confuses the sirens with Circe, who transformed men into beasts.

[2] *insidious smile . . . received.* Henry here refers to the rumors from London that the oppressive acts of the British government were about to be repealed.

[3] *martial array*, British forces stationed at Boston.

upon us those chains which the British ministry have been so long forging. And what have we to oppose to them? Shall we try argument? Sir, we have been trying that for the last ten years. Have we anything new to offer upon the subject? Nothing. We have held the subject up in every light of which it is capable; but it has been all in vain. Shall we resort to entreaty and humble supplication? What terms shall we find which have not been already exhausted? Let us not, I beseech you, sir, deceive ourselves longer. Sir, we have done everything that could be done to avert the storm which is now coming on. We have petitioned, we have remonstrated, we have supplicated, we have prostrated ourselves before the throne and have implored its interposition to arrest the tyrannical hands of the ministry and parliament. Our petitions have been slighted; our remonstrances have produced additional violence and insult; our supplications have been disregarded; and we have been spurned with contempt from the foot of the throne. In vain after these things may we indulge the fond hope of peace and reconciliation. There is no longer any room for hope. If we wish to be free, if we mean to preserve inviolate those inestimable privileges for which we have been so long contending, if we mean not basely to abandon the noble struggle in which we have been so long engaged and which we have pledged ourselves never to abandon until the glorious object of our contest shall be obtained, we must fight!—I repeat it, sir, we must fight!! An appeal to arms and to the God of Hosts is all that is left us!

They tell us, sir, that we are weak, unable to cope with so formidable an adversary. But when shall we be stronger? Will it be the next week or the next year? Will it be when we are totally disarmed and when a British guard shall be stationed in every house? Shall we gather strength by irresolution and inaction? Shall we acquire the means of effectual resistance by lying supinely on our backs and hugging the delusive phantom of hope until our enemies shall have bound us hand and foot? Sir, we are not weak if we make a proper use of those means which the God of nature hath placed in our power. Three millions of people armed in the holy cause of liberty and in such a country as that which we possess are invincible by any force which our enemy can send against us. Besides, sir, we shall not fight our battles alone. There is a just God Who presides over the destinies of nations and Who will

raise up friends to fight our battles for us. The battle, sir, is not to the strong alone; it is to the vigilant, the active, the brave. Besides, sir, we have no election. If we were base enough to desire it, it is now too late to retire from the contest. There is no retreat but in submission and slavery! Our chains are forged. Their clanking may be heard on the plains of Boston![4] The war is inevitable—and let it come! I repeat it, sir, let it come!

It is in vain, sir, to extenuate the matter. Gentlemen may cry, peace, peace—but there is no peace. The war is actually begun! The next gale that sweeps from the north will bring to our ears the clash of resounding arms! Our brethren are already in the field! Why stand we here idle? What is it that gentlemen wish? What would they have? Is life so dear, or peace so sweet as to be purchased at the price of chains and slavery? Forbid it, Almighty God! I know not what course others may take; but as for me, give me liberty or give me death!

VIEWING THE AUTHOR'S IDEAS

1. Sketch briefly the political situation in March, 1775, which called for this speech. What specific acts of British oppression led to the Revolutionary War? Which of these does Henry emphasize?

2. Why were the American colonies justified in fighting to preserve their liberties? Is there any indication in the speech that Patrick Henry thought of separation from England at this time?

3. Why did the colonists have such an ardent love of liberty? What evidences can you give that Americans today still cherish their liberties and free institutions?

4. Show how the following prophetic statements in Patrick Henry's speech were later fulfilled: (a) "There is a just God Who presides over the destinies of nations and Who will raise up friends to fight our battles for us." (b) "The next gale that sweeps from the north will bring to our ears the clash of resounding arms."

EVALUATING HIS MANNER OF EXPRESSION

1. A critic has said of Patrick Henry's speech: "It is a bit of melody as from an old fife at Lexington; it is simple; it is strong; it compacts in a few Saxon words the whole story of the Revolutionary struggle." Find specific examples of the following: (a) ringing, musical phrases (b) repetition, figures of speech, rhetorical questions, and climax (c) concise and vivid statements of the progress of the struggle with England.

---

[4] *their clanking . . . Boston.* The British army under General Gage was ready to crush the spirit of rebellion in Boston. On April 19, less than a month after Patrick Henry's speech, the first shot was fired at Lexington.

2. Which passages reveal Henry's leadership and sense of responsibility; his love of God and country?

3. The language of the Bible has had a deep influence upon English literary style. What echoes of Holy Scripture do you find in Henry's speech? Discuss the emotional values of these allusions.

4. Compare Patrick Henry's speech with some modern radio addresses delivered at a time of national crisis.

5. The concluding part of a speech is known as the *peroration.* Read aloud the paragraphs which form the conclusion of Patrick Henry's speech. What makes this peroration unforgettable?

The Declaration of Independence

Thomas Jefferson

Our heritage of American freedom is embodied in this powerful document of the Revolution. At the hazard of their lives a small band of patriots signed this formal declaration of separation from Great Britain in July, 1776, a year after the Revolutionary War had begun. In formulating this stirring document, Thomas Jefferson gives expression to the American mind, which holds that man has certain natural rights. The Declaration is the first national manifesto to set forth fundamental Christian principles of civil government. It affirms the equality of men in the sight of God, the dignity and worth of the human personality, and the right of a people to establish a just rule. The dignity of form and grandeur of language with which Jefferson states these human rights make the document a great contribution to our literary as well as our intellectual history.

WHEN in the course of human events it becomes necessary for one people to dissolve the political bands which have connected them with another, and to assume among the powers of the earth the separate and equal station to which the laws of nature and of nature's God entitle them, a decent respect to the opinions of mankind requires that they should declare the causes which impel them to the separation.

We hold these truths to be self-evident: That all men are created equal; that they are endowed by their Creator with certain inalienable[1] rights; that among these are life, liberty, and the pursuit of happiness. That to secure these rights, governments are instituted among men, deriving their just powers from the consent of the governed. That whenever any form of government becomes destructive of these ends, it is the right of the people to alter or abolish it and to institute new government, laying its foundation on such principles and organizing its powers in such form as to them shall seem most likely to effect their safety and happiness. Prudence, indeed, will dictate that governments long established should not be changed for light and transient causes; and accordingly all experience hath shown that mankind are more disposed to suffer while evils are sufferable than to right themselves by abolishing the forms to which they are accustomed. But when a long train of abuses and usurpations,[2] pursuing invariably the same object, evinces a design to reduce them under absolute despotism, it is their right, it is their duty to throw off such government and to provide new guards for their future security. Such has been the patient sufferance of these colonies; and such is now the necessity which constrains them to alter their former systems of government. The history of the present King of Great Britain is a history of repeated injuries and usurpations, all having in direct object the establishment of an absolute tyranny over these states. To prove this, let facts be submitted to a candid world.

1. He has refused his assent to laws the most wholesome and necessary for the public good.

2. He has forbidden his governors to pass laws of immediate and pressing importance unless suspended in their operations till his assent should be obtained; and, when so suspended, he has utterly neglected to attend to them.

3. He has refused to pass other laws for the accommodation of large districts of people, unless those people would relinquish the right of representation in the Legislature — a right inestimable to them, and formidable to tyrants only.

---

[1] *inalienable*, incapable of being transferred.

[2] *usurpations*, illegal seizures.

4. He has called together legislative bodies at places unusual, uncomfortable, and distant from the repository of their public records, for the sole purpose of fatiguing them into compliance with his measures.

5. He has dissolved representative houses repeatedly, for opposing, with manly firmness, his invasions on the rights of the people.

6. He has refused, for a long time after such dissolutions, to cause others to be elected, whereby the legislative powers, incapable of annihilation, have returned to the people at large for their exercise; the State remaining, in the meantime, exposed to all the dangers of invasions from without, and convulsions within.

7. He has endeavored to prevent the population of these States; for that purpose obstructing the laws for the naturalization of foreigners; refusing to pass others to encourage their migration hither, and raising the conditions of new appropriations of lands.

8. He has obstructed the administration of justice, by refusing his assent to laws for establishing judiciary powers.

9. He has made judges dependent on his will alone for the tenure of their offices, and the amount and payment of their salaries.

10. He has erected a multitude of new offices, and sent hither swarms of officers to harass our people and eat out their substance.

11. He has kept among us in times of peace, standing armies, without the consent of our Legislatures.

12. He has affected to render the military independent of, and superior to, the civil power.

13. He has combined with others to subject us to a jurisdiction foreign to our constitutions, and unacknowledged by our laws; giving his assent to their acts of pretended legislation:

14. For quartering large bodies of armed troops among us;

15. For protecting them, by a mock trial, from punishment for any murders which they should commit on the inhabitants of these States;

16. For cutting off our trade with all parts of the world;

17. For imposing taxes on us without our consent;

18. For depriving us, in many cases, of the benefits of trial by jury;

19. For transporting us beyond seas, to be tried for pretended offences;

20. For abolishing the free system of English laws in a neighboring province, establishing therein an arbitrary government, and enlarging its boundaries, so as to render it at once an example and fit instrument for introducing the same absolute rule into these colonies;

21. For taking away our charters, abolishing our most valuable laws, and altering, fundamentally, the forms of our governments;

22. For suspending our own Legislatures, and declaring themselves invested with power to legislate for us in all cases whatsoever.

23. He has abdicated government here, by declaring us out of his protection, and waging war against us.

24. He has plundered our seas, ravaged our coasts, burned our towns, and destroyed the lives of our people.

25. He is at this time transporting large armies of foreign mercenaries to complete the works of death, desolation, and tyranny, already begun with circumstances of cruelty and perfidy scarcely paralleled in the most barbarous ages, and totally unworthy the head of a civilized nation.

26. He has constrained our fellow-citizens, taken captive on the high seas, to bear arms against their country, to become the executioners of their friends and brethren, or to fall themselves by their hands.

27. He has excited domestic insurrection among us, and has endeavored to bring on the inhabitants of our frontiers the merciless Indian savages, whose known rule of warfare is an undistinguished destruction of all ages, sexes, and conditions.

In every stage of these oppressions we have petitioned for redress in the most humble terms. Our repeated petitions have been answered only by repeated injuries. A prince whose character is thus marked by every act which may define a tyrant is unfit to be the ruler of a free people.

Nor have we been wanting in attentions to our British brethren. We have warned them from time to time of attempts by their legislature to extend an unwarrantable jurisdiction over us. We have reminded them of the circumstances of our emigration and settlement here. We have appealed to their native justice and magnanimity, and we have conjured them by the ties of our common kindred to disavow these usurpations which would inevitably interrupt our connection and correspondence. They too have been deaf to the voice of justice and of consanguinity. We must, therefore, acquiesce in the necessity which denounces our separation and hold them, as we hold the rest of mankind, enemies in war, in peace friends.

We, therefore, the representatives of the United States of America, in General Congress assembled, appealing to the Supreme Judge of the world for the rectitude of our intentions, do, in the name and by the authority of the good people of these colonies, solemnly publish and declare: that these united colonies are, and of right ought to be, free and independent states; that they are absolved from all allegiance to the British crown, and that all political connection between them and the State of Great Britain is, and ought to be, totally dissolved; and that as free and independent states, they have full power to levy war, conclude peace, contract alliances, establish commerce, and to do all other acts and things which independent states may of right do.

And for the support of this declaration, with a firm reliance on the protection of Divine Providence, we mutually pledge to each other our lives, our fortunes, and our sacred honor.

VIEWING THE AUTHOR'S IDEAS

1. In what words does the *Declaration of Independence* affirm the sovereignty of God and the dignity of the human personality?

2. A comparison of the *Declaration of Independence* and excerpts from the writings of two Catholic scholars, St. Thomas Aquinas (1225?-1274?) and St. Robert Bellarmine (1542-1621), show a striking similarity of phrasing. Find clauses in the *Declaration* which express the following principles:

a) Bellarmine: "All men are equal, not in wisdom or grace, but in the essence and nature of mankind"; "It depends on the consent of the multitude to constitute over itself a king, consul, or other magistrate."

b) St. Thomas: "To ordain anything for the common good belongs either to the whole people or to someone who is the vice-regent of the whole people."

EVALUATING HIS MANNER OF EXPRESSION

1. Show that Jefferson has achieved "the tone and spirit called for by the occasion" of the *Declaration of Independence*.

2. Point out logical reasoning of the *Declaration* in its (a) presentation of political doctrine (b) statement of grievances (c) declaration of freedom.

The Battle of the Kegs

Francis Hopkinson

A poet of today would scarcely find humor in the frightful destruction of modern submarine warfare. Yet one of the first attempts to use torpedoes against enemy ships inspired this mirthful Revolutionary ballad. The idea of employing undersea boats and floating mines in naval warfare was an early example of American inventive genius. In 1775 David Bushnell constructed his famous "turtle," a tortoise-shaped submarine with a torpedo timed to explode after the submarine had withdrawn a safe distance from the battleship. Two attempts to sink British vessels failed because it was impossible to obtain skilled operators. Bushnell then charged a large number of kegs with gunpowder and sent them floating down the Delaware at ebb tide against the English fleet in Philadelphia harbor. One of these torpedoes, as Bushnell called them, actually blew up a small boat; but ice delayed the remainder and prevented further destruction.

British seamen were filled with consternation and fired upon all floating objects in the harbor. Popular ridicule caused the inventor to abandon a scheme that under proper conditions might have proved disastrous to British shipping. Bushnell had, however, succeeded in making English naval officers fearful of "Yankee tricks." Hopkinson published a prose satire of the event and followed it with this humorous ballad. Historians estimate that the poem did as much to cheer the patriots at a critical period as the winning of a considerable battle.

GALLANTS, attend and hear a friend
   Trill forth harmonious ditty;
Strange things I'll tell which late befell
   In Philadelphia city.

'Twas early day, as poets say,   5
   Just when the sun was rising,
A soldier stood on a log of wood
   And saw a thing surprising.

As in amaze he stood to gaze,
   The truth can't be denied, sir,   10
He spied a score of kegs or more
   Come floating down the tide, sir.

A sailor, too, in jerkin[1] blue,
   This strange appearance viewing,
First damned his eyes in great surprise,   15
   Then said, "Some mischiefs brewing:

"These kegs, I'm told, the rebels hold,
   Packed up like pickled herring;
And they're come down to attack the town
   In this new way of ferrying."   20

The soldier flew, the sailor too,
   And scared almost to death, sir,
Wore out their shoes to spread the news
   And ran till out of breath, sir.

Now up and down throughout the town   25
   Most frantic scenes were acted;
And some ran here and others there,
   Like men almost distracted.

Some "Fire!" cried, which some denied,
   But said the earth had quaked;   30
And girls and boys, with hideous noise,
   Ran through the streets half naked.

Sir William,[2] he, snug as a flea, . . .
   Awaked by such a clatter,
He rubs his eyes and boldly cries,   35
   "For God's sake, what's the matter?"

At his bedside he then espied
   Sir Erskine[3] at command, sir;
Upon one foot he had one boot
   And t'other in his hand, sir.   40

"Arise, arise!" Sir Erskine cries;
   "The rebels, more's the pity,
Without a boat are all afloat
   And ranged before the city.

"The motley crew, in vessels new,   45
   With Satan for their guide, sir,
Packed up in bags or wooden kegs,
   Come driving down the tide, sir.

Therefore prepare for bloody war;
   These kegs must all be routed,   50
Or surely we despised shall be,
   And British courage doubted."

The royal band now ready stand,
   All ranged in dread array, sir,
With stomachs stout, to see it out   55
   And make a bloody day, sir.

The cannons roar from shore to shore,
   The small arms make a rattle;
Since wars began, I'm sure no man
   Ere saw so strange a battle.   60

The rebel dales, the rebel vales,
   With rebel trees surrounded,
The distant woods, the hills and floods,
   With rebel echoes sounded.

The fish below swam to and fro,   65
   Attacked from every quarter;
"Why sure," thought they, "the devil's to pay
   'Mongst folks above the water."

The kegs, 'tis said, though strongly made
   Of rebel staves and hoops, sir,   70
Could not oppose their powerful foes,
   The conquering British troops, sir.

From morn till night these men of might
   Displayed amazing courage,
And when the sun was fairly down,   75
   Retired to sup their porridge.

[1] *jerkin*, a jacket or short coat.
[2] *Sir William*, the British general, Sir William Howe, then stationed at Philadelphia.
[3] *Sir Erskine*, Sir William Erskine, quartermaster of the British troops.

An hundred men with each a pen,
   Or more, upon my word, sir,
It is most true would be too few
   Their valor to record, sir.   80

Such feats did they perform that day
   Against those wicked kegs, sir,
That years to come, if they get home,
   They'll make their boasts and brags, sir.

VIEWING THE AUTHOR'S IDEAS

1. What aspects of the incident does the author exaggerate in order to heighten the comic effect? What details does he use to show the panic of the British?

2. In what light does Hopkinson portray the British soldiers? How does he show the inefficiency of their officers?

3. Show that Hopkinson's satire is devoid of bitterness toward the enemy. Why is goodnatured ridicule more effective than bitter invective?

4. Why was this ballad especially significant in affecting the morale of the Revolutionary soldiers?

EVALUATING HIS MANNER OF EXPRESSION

1. A later development of the medieval folk ballad was the *broadside*, a ballad printed on one side of the sheet and intended to be sung and sold on the street or market place. When the subject matter of a broadside chronicled a contemporary event, the poem served one of the functions of a newspaper. The broadside usually swings along with a vigorous measure, and the content is sometimes marred by coarse or vulgar intrusions. In "The Battle of the Kegs," pick out specific resemblances to the broadside or to the medieval ballad.

2. Discuss the effectiveness of the dialogue. Show how the speeches of the different characters contribute to the progress of the story and the vividness of the action.

3. *Irony* is a manner of expression in which the meaning intended is the opposite of that expressed; *hyperbole* is extravagant exaggeration; *anticlimax* is a series in which the last element is less important than those which precede. Find examples of irony, hyperbole, and anticlimax in this poem.

4. *Mock-heroic* is the term applied to a grave or exalted treatment of a ridiculous subject. Point out examples of mock-heroic treatment in "The Ballad of the Kegs."

Representative Democracy

(From *The Federalist*)
Alexander Hamilton

The establishment of a just and enduring form of government was the aim of the builders of the American republic. How best to safeguard the new nation from the dangers inherent in popular rule and at the same time preserve their hard-won liberties were questions that agitated all patriotic citizens. It is no wonder, therefore, that the stormiest battle of American political history was waged over the Constitution. In The Federalist, *from which the following selection is taken, Alexander Hamilton valiantly championed the adoption of the Constitution. Though this particular essay has sometimes been attributed to James Madison, the weight of evidence points to Hamilton as its author.*

THE aim of every political constitution is, or ought to be, first to obtain for rulers men who possess most wisdom to discern and most virtue to pursue the common good of the society; and in the next place, to take the most effectual precautions for keeping them virtuous whilst they continue to hold their public trust. The elective mode of obtaining rulers is the characteristic policy of republican government. The means relied on in this form of government for preventing their degeneracy are numerous and various. The most effectual one is such a limitation of the term of appointments as will maintain a proper responsibility to the people.

Let me now ask what circumstance there is in the constitution of the House of Representatives that violates the principles of republican government or favors the elevation of the few on the ruins of the many? Let me ask whether every circumstance is not, on the contrary, strictly conformable to these principles and scrupulously impartial to the rights and pretensions[1] of every class and description of citizens?

---

[1] *pretensions*, claims to honor because of merit.

Who are to be the electors of the federal representatives? Not the rich, more than the poor; not the learned, more than the ignorant; not the haughty heirs of distinguished names, more than the humble sons of obscurity and unpropitious fortune. The electors are to be the great body of the people of the United States. They are to be the same who exercise the right in every State of electing the corresponding branch of the legislature of the State.

Who are to be the objects of popular choice? Every citizen whose merit may recommend him to the esteem and confidence of his country. No qualification of wealth, of birth, of religious faith, or of civil profession is permitted to fetter the judgment or disappoint the inclination of the people.

If we consider the situation of the men on whom the free suffrages[2] of their fellow citizens may confer the representative trust, we shall find it involving every security which can be devised or desired for their fidelity to their constituents.[3]

In the first place, as they will have been distinguished by the preference of their fellow citizens, we are to presume that in general they will be somewhat distinguished also by those qualities which entitle them to it and which promise a sincere and scrupulous regard to the nature of their engagements.

In the second place, they will enter into the public service under circumstances which cannot fail to produce a temporary affection at least to their constituents. There is in every breast a sensibility to marks of honor, of favor, of esteem, and of confidence which, apart from all considerations of interest, is some pledge for grateful and benevolent returns. Ingratitude is a common topic of declamation against human nature; and it must be confessed that instances of it are but too frequent and flagrant, both in public and in private life. But the universal and extreme indignation which it inspires is itself a proof of the energy and prevalence of the contrary sentiment.

In the third place, those ties which bind the representative to his constituents are strengthened by motives of a more selfish nature. His pride and vanity attach him to a form of government which favors his pretensions and gives him a share in its honors and distinctions. Whatever hopes or projects might be entertained by a few aspiring characters, it must

generally happen that a great proportion of the men deriving their advancement from their influence with the people would have more to hope from a preservation of the favor than from innovations in the government subversive of the authority of the people.

All these securities, however, would be found very insufficient without the restraint of frequent elections. Hence, in the fourth place, the House of Representatives is so constituted as to support in the members an habitual recollection of their dependence on the people. Before the sentiments impressed on their minds by the mode of their elevation can be effaced by the exercise of power, they will be compelled to anticipate the moment when their power is to cease; when their exercise of it is to be reviewed; and when they must descend to the level from which they were raised, there forever to remain unless a faithful discharge of their trust shall have established their title to a renewal of it.

I will add, as a fifth circumstance in the situation of the House of Representatives restraining them from oppressive measures, that they can make no law which will not have its full operation on themselves and their friends as well as on the great mass of the society. This has always been deemed one of the strongest bonds by which human policy can connect the rulers and the people together. It creates between them that communion of interests and sympathy of sentiments of which few governments have furnished examples, but without which every government degenerates into tyranny. If it be asked what is to restrain the House of Representatives from making legal discriminations in favor of themselves and a particular class of society, I answer: the genius[4] of the whole system; the nature of just and constitutional laws; and above all, the vigilant and manly spirit which actuates the people of America — a spirit which nourishes freedom and in return is nourished by it.

If this spirit shall ever be so far debased as to tolerate a law not obligatory on the legislature as well as on the people, the people will be prepared to tolerate anything but liberty.

Such will be the relation between the House of Representatives and their constituents. Duty, gratitude, interest, ambition itself are the chords by which they will be bound to fidelity and sympathy with the great mass of the people. It is possible that these may all be insufficient

---

[2] *free suffrages*, votes.

[3] *constituents*, residents of a Congressional district.

[4] *genius*, inherent nature.

to control the caprice and wickedness of man. But are they not all that government will admit and that human prudence can devise? Are they not the genuine and the characteristic means by which republican government provides for the liberty and happiness of the people? Are they not the identical means on which every State government in the Union relies for the attainment of these important ends?

VIEWING THE AUTHOR'S IDEAS

1. In your own words state the qualifications which Hamilton believes desirable in candidates for public office.

2. What democratic principles are manifested in the method of electing members to the House of Representatives?

3. In what five ways does the American system of government endeavor to safeguard the fidelity of representatives to their constituents?

4. What obligations of the voter are implied in Hamilton's mention of "the vigilant and manly spirit which actuates the people of America"?

5. What is a pure democracy?

EVALUATING HIS MANNER OF EXPRESSION

1. *The Federalist* has been called one of the "world's greatest politico-literary masterpieces." What characteristics of style make it an effective discussion of governmental principles?

2. Show that the author appeals to the intellect rather than to the emotions.

3. Clarity and force are attained by *balance,* that is, the use of the same structure in the parts of a compound sentence. This sentence structure becomes *antithesis* when strongly contrasted ideas or phrases are balanced against each other. Find a striking example of antithesis in the selection. Point out examples of balance.

An Address of the Catholics of the United States to George Washington

John Carroll

During the colonial period Catholics suffered more from persecution than any other religious group. It was natural, therefore, that they should rally to the Revolutionary cause and support the Constitution, which guaranteed their rights of civil and religious liberty. When Washington was elected president of the new republic, American Catholics united with other denominations in pledging their loyalty to the government. The following address has been attributed to Bishop Carroll, who signed it in behalf of the clergy. Outstanding Catholic laymen who affixed their signatures to the document were Charles Carroll of Carrollton, Daniel Carroll, Dominick Lynch, and Thomas Fitzsimons. Of these men Daniel Carroll and Thomas Fitzsimons were members of the Constitutional Convention.

WE have been long impatient to testify our joy and unbounded confidence on your being called by a unanimous vote to the first station of a country in which that unanimity[1] could not have been obtained without the previous merit of unexampled services, of eminent wisdom, and unblemished virtue. Our

congratulations have not reach ed you sooner because our scattered situation prevented our communication and the collecting of those sentiments which warmed every breath. But the delay has furnished us with the opportunity, not merely of presaging[2] the happiness to be expected under your administration, but of bearing testimony to that which we experience already.

It is your peculiar talent in war and in peace to afford security to those who commit their protection into your hands. In war you shield them from the ravages of armed hostility; in peace you establish public tranquillity by the justice and moderation not less than by the vigor of your government. By example as well as by vigilance you extend the influence of laws on the manners of our fellow citizens. You encourage respect for religion and inculcate by words and actions that principle on which the welfare of nations so much depends: that a Superintending Providence governs the events of the works and watches over the conduct of men. Your exalted maxims and unwearied attention

---

[1] *unanimity* (ū-nă-nĭm´ĭ-tĭ), state of being unanimous or of one mind.

[2] *presaging,* foreshadowing.

to the moral and physical improvement of our country have produced already the happiest effects. Under your administration America is animated with zeal for the attainment and encouragement of useful literature. She improves her agriculture, extends her commerce, acquires with foreign nations a dignity unknown to her before. From these events, in which none can feel a warmer interest than ourselves, we derive additional pleasure by recollecting that you, Sir, have been the principal instrument to effect so rapid a change in our political situation.

This prospect of national prosperity is peculiarly pleasing to us on another account; because, whilst our country preserves her freedom and independence, we shall have a well-founded title to claim from her justice the equal rights of citizenship as the price of our blood spilt under your eyes and of our common exertions for her defense under your auspicious conduct — rights rendered more dear to us by the remembrance of former hardships. When we pray for the preservation of them where they have been granted and expect the full extension of them from the justice of those States which still restrict them — when we solicit the protection of Heaven over our common country, we neither omit nor can omit recommending your preservation to the singular care of Divine Providence; because we conceive that no human means are so available to promote the welfare of the United States as the prolongation of your health and life, in which are included the energy of your example, the wisdom of your counsels, and the persuasive eloquence of your virtues.

VIEWING THE AUTHOR'S IDEAS

1. List the "unexampled services" which had merited for Washington his unanimous election as first president of the United States.

2. Enumerate the characteristics of good government mentioned in this address. How are they embodied in our Constitution? Contrast our principles of democratic government with those of foreign countries ruled by dictators.

3. What hardships did Catholics suffer because of their Faith during the colonial period? Since the Revolution, what hostile movements against the Church have been restrained by constitutional freedom of religion?

4. Write a brief account of the condition of the Church in the United States at the time this address was written.

To the Catholics of the United States

George Washington

The graciousness of the great is apparent in Washington's reply to the address of American Catholics. His words give gallant recognition of the contribution of the Church to the new republic. They likewise lucidly state the right to freedom of worship. The importance of Washington's reply as a document of religious liberty was seen not only in America. In England, where the letter appeared in newspapers, it was hailed as the harbinger of religious freedom for oppressed peoples in all parts of the world.

Gentlemen,

While I now receive with much satisfaction your congratulations on my being called by a unanimous vote to the first station in my country, I cannot but duly notice your politeness in offering an apology for the unavoidable delay. As that delay has given you an opportunity of realizing instead of anticipating the benefits of the general government, you will do me the justice to believe that your testimony of the increase of the public prosperity enhances the pleasure which I should otherwise have experienced from your affectionate address.

I feel that my conduct in war and in peace has met with more general approbation than could have reasonably been expected; and I find myself disposed to consider that fortunate circumstance, in a great degree, resulting from the able support and extraordinary candor of my fellow citizens of all denominations.

The prospect of national prosperity now before us is truly animating and ought to excite the exertions of all good men to establish and secure the happiness of their country in the permanent duration of its freedom and independence. America, under the smiles of Divine Providence, the protection of a good government, and the cultivation of manners, morals, and piety, cannot fail of attaining an uncommon degree of eminence in literature, commerce, agriculture, improvements at home, and respectability abroad.

As mankind becomes more liberal, they will be more apt to allow that all those who conduct themselves worthy members of the community are equally entitled to the protection of civil government. I hope ever to see America among the foremost nations in examples of justice and liberality. And I presume that your fellow citizens will not forget the patriotic part which you took in the accomplishment of their Revolution and the establishment of their government — or the important assistance which they received from a nation in which the Roman Catholic faith is professed.

I thank you, Gentlemen, for your kind concern for me. While my life and health shall continue, in whatever situation I may be, it shall be my constant endeavor to justify the favorable sentiments which you are pleased to express of my conduct. And may the members of your Society in America, animated alone by the pure spirit of Christianity and still conducting themselves as the faithful subjects of our free Government, enjoy every temporal and spiritual felicity.

VIEWING THE AUTHOR'S IDEAS

1. What condition for the permanence of American democracy are mentioned in the third paragraph of Washington's reply? Are all these conditions equally regarded today? Discuss.

2. Which passages show Washington's love of religious and political liberty? How can you account for the President's unbiased attitude at a time when religious prejudice was strong?

3. Give a brief account of Washington's friendship with Lafayette and with other prominent Catholics of the period. What important assistance did France render to America during the Revolutionary War?

4. Make a list of outstanding Catholics who gave their lives or services to the Revolutionary cause. Mention important contributions made by each.

EVALUATING HIS MANNER OF EXPRESSION

Washington once said that he wished his sentiments to "be handed to the public in an honest, unaffected, simple garb." In what ways does this letter achieve his ideal?

Farewell Address

George Washington

The wisdom and compelling style of Washington's parting address make it a classic of American political literature. It has influenced the views of statesmen and students of political history for nearly one hundred fifty years and deserves a place in the education of every American. Washington's love and concern for the growing young nation are evident in his vital words concerning the importance of a strong central government and the dangers of party strife and entangling foreign relationships. The address was published in the American Daily Advertiser *of Philadelphia towards the close of Washington's second term. Although it is known that Washington had asked the help of Alexander Hamilton, and previously of James Madison, in preparing the address, he did not release his farewell message for publication until he had revised it carefully and made it conform to his exact sentiments.*

FRIENDS and Fellow Citizens — The period for a new election of a citizen to administer the executive government of the United States being not far distant, and the time actually arrived when your thoughts must be employed in designating the person who is to be clothed with that important trust, it appears to me proper, especially as it may conduce to a more distinct expression of the public voice, that I should now apprise you of the resolution I have formed to decline being considered among the number of those out of whom a choice is to be made. . . .

A solicitude for your welfare, which cannot end but with my life, and the apprehension of danger, natural to that solicitude, urge me on an occasion like the present to offer to your solemn contemplation and to recommend to your frequent review some sentiments which are the result of much reflection, of no inconsiderable observation, and which appear to me all important to the permanency of your felicity as a people. These will be offered to you with the more freedom, as you can only see in them the disinterested warnings of a parting friend, who can possibly have no personal motive to bias his counsel. Nor can I forget, as an encouragement to it, your indulgent reception of my sentiments on a former and not dissimilar occasion.[1]

Interwoven as is the love of liberty with every ligament of your hearts, no recommendation of mine is necessary to fortify or confirm the attachment.

The unity of government which constitutes you one people is also now dear to you. It is justly so, for it is a main pillar in the edifice of your real independence, the support of your tranquillity at home, your peace abroad, of your safety, of your prosperity, of that very liberty which you so highly prize. But as it is easy to foresee that from different causes and from different quarters much pains will be taken, many artifices employed, to weaken in your minds the conviction of this truth; as this is the point in your political fortress against which the batteries of internal and external enemies will be most constantly and actively (though often covertly and insidiously) directed, it is of infinite moment that you should properly estimate the immense value of your national union to your collective and individual happiness; that you should cherish a cordial, habitual, and immovable attachment to it; accustoming yourselves to think and speak of it as of the palladium[2] of your political safety and prosperity; watching for its preservation with jealous anxiety; discountenancing whatever may suggest even a suspicion that it can in any event be abandoned; and indignantly frowning upon the first dawning of every attempt to alienate any portion of our country from the rest, or to enfeeble the sacred ties which now link together the various parts . . .

In contemplating the causes which may disturb our Union, it occurs as matter of serious concern that any ground should have been furnished for characterizing parties by geographical discriminations, Northern and Southern, Atlantic and Western; whence designing men may endeavor to excite a belief that there is a real difference of local interests and views. One of the expedients of party to acquire influence within particular districts is to misrepresent the opinions and aims of other districts. You cannot shield yourselves too much against the jealousies and heartburnings which spring from these misrepresentations; they tend to render alien to each other those who ought to be bound together by fraternal affection. . . .

To the efficacy and permanency of your Union a government for the whole is indispensable. No alliances, however strict, between the parts can be an adequate substitute; they must inevitably experience the infractions and interruptions which all alliances in all times have experienced. Sensible of this momentous truth, you have improved upon your first essay[3] by the adoption of a Constitution of Government better calculated than your former for an intimate Union and for the efficacious management of your common concerns. This government, the offspring of your own choice, uninfluenced and unawed, adopted upon full investigation and mature deliberation, completely free of its principles, in the distribution of its powers, uniting security with energy, and containing within itself a provision for its own amendment, has a just claim to your confidence and your support. Respect for its authority, compliance with its laws, acquiescence in its measures are duties enjoined by the fundamental maxims of true liberty. The basis of our political systems is the right of the people to make and to alter their constitutions of government. But the constitution which at any time exists, till changed by an explicit and authentic act of the whole people, is sacredly obligatory upon all. The very idea of the power and the right of the people to establish government presupposes the duty of every individual to obey the established government.

All obstructions to the execution of the laws, all combinations and associations, under whatever plausible character, with the real design to direct, control, counteract, or awe the regular deliberation and action of the constituted authorities are destructive of this fundamental principle and of fatal tendency. They serve to organize faction, to give it an artificial and extraordinary force, to put in the place of the delegated will of the nation the will of a party, often a small but artful and enterprising minority of the community;

---

[1] *not dissimilar occasion*, the occasion of his farewell address to Congress on resigning his commission as commander in chief of the American army.

[2] *palladium*, a safeguard.

[3] *first essay*, the *Articles of Confederation*.

and, according to the alternate triumphs of different parties, to make the public administration the mirror of the ill-concerted and incongruous projects of faction rather than the organ of consistent and wholesome plans digested by common counsels and modified by mutual interests.

However combinations or associations of the above description may now and then answer popular ends, they are likely in the course of time and things to become potent engines, by which cunning, ambitious, and unprincipled men will be enabled to subvert the power of the people and to usurp for themselves the reins of government, destroying afterwards the very engines which have lifted them to unjust dominion.

Towards the preservation of your government and the permanency of your present happy state, it is requisite, not only that you steadily discountenance irregular oppositions to its acknowledged authority, but also that you resist with care the spirit of innovation[4] upon its principles, however specious the pretexts. One method of assault may be to effect in the forms of the constitution alterations which will impair the energy of the system and thus to undermine what cannot be directly overthrown. In all the changes to which you may be invited, remember that time and habit are at least as necessary to fix the true character of governments as of other human institutions; that experience is the surest standard by which to test the real tendency of the existing constitution of a country; that facility in changes, upon the credit of mere hypothesis[5] and opinion, exposes to perpetual change, from the endless variety of hypothesis and opinion; and remember especially that for the efficient management of your common interests in a country so extensive as ours, a government of as much vigor as is consistent with the perfect security of liberty is indispensable. Liberty itself will find in such a government, with powers properly distributed and adjusted, its surest guardian. It is, indeed, little else than a name, where the government is too feeble to withstand the enterprises of faction, to confine each member of the society within the limits prescribed by the laws, and to maintain all in the secure and tranquil enjoyment of the rights of person and property.

I have already intimated to you the danger of parties in the state, with particular reference to the founding of them on geographical discriminations. Let me now take a more comprehensive view and warn you in the most solemn manner against the baneful effects of the spirit of party, generally.

This spirit, unfortunately, is inseparable from our nature, having its root in the strongest passions of the human mind. It exists under different shapes in all governments, more or less stifled, controlled, or repressed; but in those of the popular form, it is seen in its greatest rankness and is truly their worst enemy.

The alternate domination of one faction over another, sharpened by the spirit of revenge, natural to party dissension, which in different ages and countries has perpetuated the most horrid enormities, is itself a frightful despotism. But this leads at length to a more formal and permanent despotism. The disorders and miseries which result gradually incline the minds of men to seek security and repose in the absolute power of an individual; and sooner or later the chief of some prevailing faction, more able or more fortunate than his competitors, turns this disposition to the purposes of his own elevation, on the ruins of public liberty.

Of all the dispositions and habits which lead to political prosperity, religion and morality are indispensable supports. In vain would that man claim the tribute of patriotism who should labor to subvert these great pillars of human happiness, these firmest props of the duties of men and citizens. The mere politician, equally with the pious man, ought to respect and cherish them. A volume could not trace all their connections with private and public felicity. Let it be simply asked: Where is the security for property, for reputation, for life, if the sense of religious obligation desert the oaths which are the instruments of investigation in courts of justice? And let us with caution indulge the supposition that morality can be maintained without religion. Whatever may be conceded to the influence of refined education on minds of peculiar structure, reason and experience both forbid us to expect that national morality can prevail in exclusion of religious principle.

It is substantially true that virtue or morality is a necessary spring of popular government. The rule, indeed, extends with more or less force to every species of free government. Who that is a sincere friend to it can

---

[4] *spirit of innovation*, spirit of change.

[5] *hypothesis*, supposition.

look with indifference upon the attempts to shake the foundation of the fabric?

Promote then, as an object of primary importance institutions for the general diffusion of knowledge. In proportion as the structure of a government gives force to public opinion, it is essential that public opinion should be enlightened. . . .

Observe good faith and justice toward all nations; cultivate peace and harmony with all. Religion and morality enjoin this conduct; and can it be that good policy does not equally enjoin it? It will be worthy of a free, enlightened, and at no distant period, a great nation, to give to mankind the magnanimous and too novel example of a people always guided by an exalted justice and benevolence. Who can doubt that, in the course of time and things, the fruits of such a plan would richly repay any temporary advantages which might be lost by a steady adherence to it? Can it be that Providence has not connected the permanent felicity of a nation with its virtue? The experiment, at least, is recommended by every sentiment which ennobles human nature. Alas! is it rendered impossible by its vices? . . .

The great rule of conduct for us in regard to foreign nations is, in extending our commercial relations, to have with them as little political connection as possible. So far as we have already formed engagements, let them be fulfilled with perfect good faith. Here let us stop.

Europe has a set of primary interests which to us have none, or a very remote, relation. Hence she must be engaged in frequent controversies, the causes of which are essentially foreign to our concerns. Hence, therefore, it must be unwise in us to implicate ourselves by artificial ties in the ordinary vicissitudes of her politics, or the ordinary combinations and collisions of her friendships or enmities.

Our detached and distant situation invites and enables us to pursue a different course. If we remain one people under an efficient government, the period is not far off when we may defy material injury from external annoyance; when we may take such an attitude as will cause the neutrality we may at any time resolve upon to be scrupulously respected; when belligerent nations, under the impossibility of making acquisitions upon us, will not lightly hazard the giving us provocation; when we may choose peace or war, as our interest guided by justice, shall counsel. . . .

In offering to you, my countrymen, these counsels of an old and affectionate friend, I dare not hope they will make the strong and lasting impression I could wish; that they will control the usual current of the passions or prevent our nation from running the course which has hitherto marked the destiny of nations. But, if I may even flatter myself that they may be productive of some partial benefit, some occasional good; that they may now and then recur to moderate the fury of the party spirit, to warn against the mischiefs of foreign intrigue, to guard against the imposture of pretended patriotism; this hope will be a full recompense for the solicitude for your welfare, by which they have been dictated. . . .

Though, in reviewing the incidents of my administration, I am unconscious of intentional error, I am nevertheless too sensible of my defects not to think it probable that I may have committed many errors. Whatever they may be, I fervently beseech the Almighty to avert or mitigate the evils to which they may tend. I shall also carry with me the hope that my country will never cease to view them with indulgence; and that, after forty-five years of my life dedicated to its service with an upright zeal, the faults of incompetent abilities will be consigned to oblivion, as myself must soon be to the mansions of rest.

Relying on its kindness in this as in other things, and actuated by that fervent love towards it which is so natural to a man who views in it the native soil of himself and his progenitors for several generations, I anticipate with pleasing expectation that retreat in which I promise myself to realize without alloy the sweet enjoyment of partaking, in the midst of my fellow citizens, the benign influence of good laws under a free government, the ever favorite object of my heart and the happy reward, as I trust, of our mutual cares, labors, and dangers.

VIEWING THE AUTHOR'S IDEAS

1. What were Washington's motives for his "disinterested warnings"? In the eyes of the President what is the importance of the union in the American system of government? How can Americans guard against any threat to national unity?

2. What democratic characteristics does Washington attribute to the Constitution? State the obligation which is imposed upon the people by their right to establish their own government. What is the underlying purpose of combinations and associations which oppose the execution of the law? If such factions attain power, what may they eventually do?

3. Did Washington advocate that there should be no amendments to the Constitution in the future? Discuss. How may the miseries and disorders of party factions eventually lead to despotism?

4. By what arguments does Washington show that religion and morality are supports to private and public welfare? Summarize the President's foreign policy as expressed in this selection. How are Americans now regarding the principle of isolationism?

5. What attitude had Washington towards the errors of his administration? What enjoyments did he anticipate for his years of retirement?

EVALUATING HIS MANNER OF EXPRESSION

1. Select and memorize what you consider the best passages from the viewpoint of content and style.

2. The diction in the *Farewell Address* is dignified, stately, and at times highly ornate. Which passages best exemplify these qualities?

Dangers Threatening the Republic

Charles Carroll

The leading Catholic American of his time, Charles Carroll of Carrollton knew the problems of American government through twenty-five years in public office. His service to his country had caused him to be considered for the presidency in 1792, when Washington was contemplating retirement. To James McHenry, Secretary of War in Adams' administration, Carroll confided his anxiety in 1800 over the impending defeat of the Federalist party and the Jeffersonian policy of championing the cause of the French Revolution. In this letter, one of the most forcible of the hundreds he wrote, he shows that the nation must be defended from false philosophies, which undermine peace and security and lead to the downfall of free government.

Annapolis, 4th Nov., 1800

Dear Sir,

If our country should continue to be the sport of parties, if the mass of the people should be exasperated and roused to pillage the more wealthy, social order will be subverted, anarchy will follow, succeded by despotism. These changes have, in that order of succession, taken place in France; yet the men, so far as I am informed, who style themselves Republicans[1] very generally wish success to France. In other words, the friends of *freedom here* are the friends of Bonaparte,[2] who has established by a military force the most despotic government in Europe. How are we to reconcile this contradiction of their *avowed* principles? . . .

If the people of this country were united, it would have nothing to fear from foreign powers; but unhappily this is not the case. Many of the opposers of the present administration,[3] I suspect, want change of the Federal Constitution. If that should be altered or weakened so as to be rendered a dead letter,[4] it will not answer the purposes of its formation and will expire from mere inanity.[5] Other confederacies will start up and the scene of the Grecian states,[6] after an interval of more than two thousand years, will be renewed on this continent; and some British or Bonaparte will melt the whole of them into one mass of despotism.

These events will be hastened by the pretended philosophy of France.[7] Divine revelation has been scoffed at by the philosophers of the present day, the immortality of the soul treated as the dreams of fools or the invention of knaves, and death has been declared

---

[1] *Republicans*, the followers of Jefferson, who believed in popular rule in opposition to the Federalists, who believed in a strong central government.

[2] *Bonaparte*. In 1799 Napoleon Bonaparte overthrew the government established by the French Revolution and made himself virtually absolute as First Consul.

[3] *the present administration*, the Federalist administration of John Adams, which was opposed by the Republicans.

[4] *dead letter*, a law that has lost its force or authority.

[5] *inanity*, uselessness.

[6] *the scene of the Grecian states*. Disunion among the Greek states enabled the Macedonians under Philip and his son, Alexander the Great, to gain political control of Greece. Though the Greeks tried to form other confederacies, they never succeeded in throwing off the Macedonian yoke and were finally conquered by Rome in 197, B.C.

[7] *pretended philosophy of France*. Carroll here refers to such eighteenth-century French philosophers as Diderot, Voltaire, and Rousseau, who attacked religion and the teachings of Christianity.

by public authority an eternal sleep. These opinions are gaining ground among us and silently sapping the foundations of a religion, the encouragement of the good, the terror of evildoers, and the consolation of the poor, the miserable, and the distressed. Remove the hope and dread of future rewards and punishments, the most powerful restraint on wicked actions, and the strongest inducement to virtuous ones is done away. Virtue may be said is its own reward. I believe it to be so and even in this life the only source of happiness; and this intimate and necessary connection between virtue and happiness here and between vice and misery is to my mind one of the surest pledges of happiness or misery in a future state of existence. But how few practice virtue for its own reward! Some of happy disposition and temperament, calm reflecting men exempt in a great degree from the turbulence of passions, may be virtuous for virtue's sake. Small, however, is the number who are guided by reason alone and who can always subject their passions to its dictates. He who can thus act may be said to be virtuous; but reason is often enlisted on the side of the passions, or at best, when most wanted, is weakest — hence the necessity of a superior motive for acting virtuously. Now, what motive can be stronger than the belief founded on revelation that a virtuous life will be rewarded by a happy immortality? Without morals a republic cannot subsist any length of time. They, therefore, who are decrying the Christian religion, whose morality is so sublime and pure, which denounces against the wicked, eternal misery and insures to the good eternal happiness, are undermining the solid foundation of morals, the best security for the duration of free governments.

If there be force in this reasoning, what judgment ought we to form of our pretended Republicans, who admire and applaud the proceedings of revolutionary France?

These declaimers in favor of freedom and equality act in such a questionable shape[8] that I cannot help suspecting their sincerity.

[8] *shape*, manner.

This is a long preaching letter and I fear a tedious and dull one; but you wished to know my sentiments about the present parties and impending fate of our country, and I could not give them without developing the reasoning of my opinion. You see that I almost despair of the commonwealth. The end of every legitimate government is the security of life, liberty, and property; if this country is to be revolutionized none of these will be secured. . . .

Although your remaining rather a spectator of, than an actor in, the passing scenes is founded on a proper motive, yet you will find it impossible to retain a neutral character nor do I think it fit you should. We ought all, each in our several spheres, to endeavor to set the public mind right and to administer antidotes to the poison that is widely spreading through the country. . . .

VIEWING THE AUTHOR'S IDEAS

1. According to Carroll, what is the usual course of radical revolution? How did the American Revolution differ from the French Revolution?

2. How were the Republicans of this period inconsistent in their support of the French Revolution?

3. What did Carroll foresee as a result of disunion and a desire to alter the Constitution? How have wise statesmen since Carroll's time regarded the authority of the Constitution? What tendency to disregard constitutional authority may be noticed among political leaders today?

4. How did Carroll prove that false philosophies lead to the downfall of free government? What erroneous philosophies threaten the security of America today?

5. In what passage does Carroll emphasize the responsibility of individual citizens for good government? How can each citizen contribute to the preservation of free government?

EVALUATING HIS MANNER OF EXPRESSION

1. Point out passages written in colloquial style. What characteristics of style are found in the more formal parts of the letter?

2. What statements reveal Carroll's knowledge of law and Christian philosophy?

The Indian Burying Ground

Philip Freneau

Freneau was the first American poet to see romance in the Indian. Here he dwells imaginatively on the Indian custom of burying the dead in a sitting posture, surrounded by bows, arrows, and bright ornaments.

IN SPITE of all the learned have said,
   I still, my old opinion keep;
The posture that we give the dead
   Points out the soul's eternal sleep.

Not so the ancients of these lands —   5
   The Indian, when from life released,
Again is seated with his friends,
   And shares again the joyous feast.

His imaged birds and painted bowl,
   And venison for a journey dressed,   10
Bespeak the nature of the soul,
   Activity, that knows no rest.

His bow, for action ready bent,
   And arrows with a head of stone
Can only mean that life is spent,   15
   And not the old ideas gone.

Thou, stranger, that shalt come this way,
   No fraud upon the dead commit —
Observe the swelling turf and say
   They do not lie, but here they sit.   20

Here still a lofty rock remains,
   On which the curious eye may trace
(Now wasted, half, by wearing rains)
   The fancies of a ruder race.

Here still an aged elm aspires,   25
   Beneath whose far-projecting shade
(And which the shepherd still admires)
   The children of the forest played!

There oft a restless Indian queen
   (Pale Shebah[1] with her braided hair)   30
And many a barbarous form is seen
   To chide the man that lingers there.

By midnight moons, o'er moistening dews,
   In habit for the chase arrayed,
The hunter still the deer pursues,   35
   The hunter and the deer, a shade!

And long shall timorous fancy see
   The painted chief and pointed spear,
And Reason's self shall bow the knee
   To shadows and delusions here.   40

VIEWING THE AUTHOR'S IDEAS

1. What attitude towards death does the poet reveal in lines 3-4? Why does the Church show such reverence and respect for the dead in her burial rites?

2. Is there any evidence that Freneau believes the Indian superior to the white man? Discuss the reasons for your answer.

3. What aspects of Indian life does the poet emphasize?

EVALUATING HIS MANNER OF EXPRESSION

1. How does Freneau create the mood of pensive melancholy? What romantic attitude towards the past is found in this poem?

2. An allusion may evoke the atmosphere or feelings associated with some character, story, or event of the past. Discuss the effectiveness of the allusion in line 30.

3. The poetic merit of "The Indian Burying Ground" is uneven. In your opinion, which are the best lines; which the least artistic?

[1] *Shebah.* The Queen of Shebah came from the South to see Solomon and to test his wisdom.

The Wild Honeysuckle

Philip Freneau

This portrayal of the frail beauty of the honeysuckle shows the power of American wild life to inspire Freneau. The poem has been called our first genuine nature lyric. Instead of generalizing about nature, Freneau drew attention to a specific object.

FAIR flower, that dost so comely grow,
   Hid in this silent, dull retreat,
Untouched thy honeyed blossoms blow,
Unseen thy little branches greet;
     No roving foot shall crush thee here,   5
     No busy hand provoke a tear.

By Nature's self in white arrayed,
She bade thee shun the vulgar eye,
And planted here the guardian shade,
And sent soft waters murmuring by;   10
     Thus quietly thy summer goes,
     Thy days declining to repose.

Smit with those charms that must decay,
I grieve to see your future doom;
They died—nor were those flowers more gay,   15
The flowers that did in Eden bloom;
     Unpitying frosts, and Autumn's power
     Shall leave no vestige of this flower.

From morning suns and evening dews
At first thy little being came;   20
If nothing once, you nothing lose,
For when you die you are the same;
     The space between is but an hour,
     The frail duration of a flower.

VIEWING THE AUTHOR'S IDEAS

1. How do the first two stanzas reflect the ideal of peace and seclusion? In what way do they suggest the hidden life?

2. How does the thought of death affect the poet? Contrast Freneau's attitude with that expressed by St. Paul in *Phil.* 1:21 and *Phil.* 1:23.

3. From Freneau's lines what difference can you see between the life of a flower and the life of man?

4. Why is the allusion to the flowers of the Garden of Eden effective?

EVALUATING HIS MANNER OF EXPRESSION

1. What is the mood of this poem?

2. This poem is an *apostrophe,* that is, a figure of speech in which the writer addresses a person or thing, an abstract idea or imaginary object. Discuss the effectiveness of this device.

3. Find a line containing *onomatopoeia,* or the use of words whose sound suggests the sense.

Report on Female Wages

(From *Miscellaneous Essays*)
Mathew Carey

As materialism with its attendant evils developed in America, Mathew Carey raised his voice against social and economic wrong. Injustices of all kinds aroused his indignation and led him to write hurried protests, often published at his own expense. Urged by the spirit of Christian charity, he took an active part in numerous organizations for civic betterment and the relief of human misery. For years his private charities included gifts of food and clothing to hundreds of poor persons. As chairman of a committee appointed to investigate conditions among women workers in Philadelphia, he wrote the report from which the following selection is taken. It was later presented in his Miscellaneous Essays, *a volume which best illustrates his manifold interests and activities.*

THE Subscribers, a committee appointed by the town meeting of the citizens of the city and county of Philadelphia on the twenty-first of last month "to ascertain whether those who are able and willing to work can in general procure employment; what is the effect upon the comfort, happiness, and morals of the females who depend on their work for support; of the low rate of wages paid to that class of society; to what extent the sufferings of the poor are attributable to those low wages; and what is the effect of benevolent or assistance societies on the industry of the laboring poor," — beg leave to report: . . .

That they are convinced from a careful examination of the subject that the wages paid to seamstresses who work in their own apartments, to spoolers,[1] to spinners, to folders of printed books, and in many cases to those who take in washing, are utterly inadequate to their support, even if fully employed, particularly if they have children unable to aid them in their industry, as is often the case; whereas the work is so precarious that they are often unemployed, sometimes for a whole week together, and very frequently one or two days in each week. In many cases no small portion of their time is spent in seeking and waiting for work, and in taking it home when done.

That in the different branches above specified, industrious and expert women, unencumbered with families and with steady employment, cannot average more than a dollar and a quarter per week; that their room rent is generally fifty cents, sometimes sixty-two and a half; and fuel probably costs about a quarter of a dollar per week on an average through the year. Thus in the case of constant unceasing employment (a case that rarely occurs) there remains but about half a dollar per week, or twenty-six per annum, for meat, drink, and clothing; and supposing only eight weeks in the year unemployed through sickness, want of work, or attention to children (and this is but a moderate calculation), the amount for food and clothing would be reduced to the most miserable pittance of sixteen dollars per annum! Can we wonder at the harrowing misery and distress that prevail among this class under such a deplorable state of things?

That, it is a most lamentable fact that among the women thus "ground to the earth" by such inadequate wages are to be found numbers of widows with small children, who, by the untimely deaths of their husbands and those reverses of fortune to which human affairs

are liable, have been gradually reduced from a state of comfort and affluence to penury and thrown upon the world with no other dependence than their needles to support themselves and their offspring.

That although it is freely admitted that great distress and poverty arise from habits of dissipation and intemperance of husbands and their shameful neglect to make that provision for their wives and children which they are bound to do by the laws of God and man (and which, it is to be deeply regretted, the laws do not duly enforce), yet we feel satisfied that those deplorable and pernicious habits do not produce half the wretchedness to which meritorious females are subjected in this city, of which the greater portion arises from the other source which we have stated, and which places before this class the alternatives of begging, applying to the overseers of the poor, stealing, or starving.

That the scenes of distress and suffering which we have witnessed in our various visits to the dwellings of women who depend on their labor for support, resulting from inadequate wages, are of the most afflicting kind and can scarcely be believed but by those by whom they have been beheld. We have found cases of women whose husbands have been for weeks disabled by accidents or by sickness produced from working on canals,[2] surrounded by pestiferous miasmata,[3] who have had to support their husbands and three or four children by spooling at twenty cents per hundred skeins, by spinning at as low a rate of compensation, by washing and rough drying at twenty or twenty-five cents per dozen, or by making shirts and pantaloons at twelve and a half cents each.

That it is a great error to suppose, as is too frequently supposed, that every person in this community, able and willing to work, can procure employment; as there are many persons of both sexes, more particularly females, who are at all times partially and frequently wholly unemployed, although anxious to procure employment. There is almost always a great deficiency of employment for females, which is the chief reason why their wages are so disproportioned to those of males.

That there are few errors more pernicious, more destitute of foundation than the idea which has of late years been industriously propagated: that the benevolent societies of this city produce idleness and

---

[1] *spoolers*, workers who wind yarn on spools.

[2] *working on canals*. During this period the Erie Canal and many other canals were being built to connect the East with the rapidly-developing West.

[3] *miasmata* (mī-ăz′mâ-tâ), noxious inhalations from swamps or from decaying matter.

dissipation by inducing the poor to depend on them instead of depending on industry. The whole of the annual subscriptions for last year to seven of the most prominent of these societies, embracing, it is believed, nearly all of any importance, was only $1069; and the whole of their disbursements, only $3740, a sum which obviously could not materially affect the industry of the many thousands, male and female, who have to work for their living. And it is of the last importance in the consideration of this question to take notice that most part of these disbursements was for work done by aged women and for food and clothing furnished to super-annuated men and women and destitute children. . . .

That the funds of those societies are managed with great prudence and circumspection, as the ladies humanely visit the poor in their habitation, ascertain the extent of their sufferings as well as the nature of their claims for relief, and afford such aid as the cases respectively may require and as their very limited means warrant. We think it but justice to declare that we cannot conceive of any mode in which the same amount of money could do more effectual good; and we believe that the beneficence of the managers adds luster to the character of the city. They are admirably calculated to be almoners to the wealthy, who are unable to seek out proper objects of charity and are constantly liable to gross imposition. . . .

For evils of the magnitude and inveteracy of those under which the women suffer who depend on their labor for support, it is difficult to devise a remedy. A complete remedy is perhaps impracticable. They may, however, and we hope will, be mitigated. The mitigation must wholly depend on the humanity and the sense of justice of those by whom they are employed, who, for the honor of human nature it is to be supposed, have not been aware of the fact that the wages they have been paying were inadequate to the purchase of food, raiment, and lodging; and who, now that the real state of the case is made manifest, will probably, as they certainly ought to, increase those wages. Although the great and increasing competition in trade renders it necessary to use rigid economy in the expense of producing articles for market, it can never palliate, far less justify, the oppression of the ill-fated people engaged in the production, by whose labors large fortunes are made and their employers enabled to live in ease and opulence.

It is peculiarly incumbent on those wealthy ladies who employ seamstresses or washerwomen and who ought to feel sympathy for the sufferings of their sex to give them such wages as will not only yield them a present support, but enable them to make provision for times of sickness or scarcity of employment. It is painful to state, but regard for truth obliges us to state, that in this respect sufficient attention is not generally paid to the sacred rule of "doing unto others as we would have others do unto us." A moderate degree of attention to this rule would annihilate a great portion of the distress of hundreds of suffering females.

One important means of mitigating the distress of this class would be to increase as far as possible the diversity of female employments by which that competition which has produced the pernicious reduction of wages would be diminished.

The Committee hope they will be pardoned for touching on a subject analogous to the object of their appointment although not embraced in its terms. It is to recommend to the most serious consideration of the benevolent of their fellow citizens the establishment of "a society for bettering the condition of the poor" by encouraging habits of order, regularity, and cleanliness in their persons and apartments; by instructing them in the most economical modes of cooking their food; by inducing them to send their children to school and, when arrived at a proper age, to bind them apprentices to useful trades, and to lodge the little surplus of their earnings, when they have any surplus, in the saving fund; by enabling them to purchase fuel and other necessaries at reasonable rates; in a word, by inculcating on them those principles and that kind of conduct which are calculated to elevate them in their own estimation and in that of society at large. Societies of this description have produced the most salutary effects on the comfort and morals of the poor in various parts of Great Britain.

And while the Committee press on the humane and wealthy part of the community the propriety of aiding in a greater degree than heretofore (by their own exertions and through the various benevolent societies that exist among us, and whose funds are at present greatly reduced) to alleviate the distresses of the numerous widows and orphans and the really deserving poor and helpless of every description, they would likewise suggest to housekeepers and heads of families the propriety of seeking out and employing in the situation of domestics in their several families destitute females, who, by the frowns of fortune, have been reduced to distress. Hundreds of this description are to be found within the precincts of the city and liberties,[4] who, if properly encouraged, would be grateful for means of employment thus afforded them and who might profit by the precept and example set before them in the houses of respectable citizens. Perhaps there are few ties in common life more binding than those that are found to exist between a benevolent master and mistress and a faithful female servant who has grown up under their own eyes and under their care and protection and that of their descendants.

VIEWING THE AUTHOR'S IDEAS

1. What four questions did the committee propose to answer in this survey? Summarize briefly the findings of the committee on each of these four heads.

2. List Carey's recommendations for remedying the conditions revealed by the survey. Distinguish between destitution and voluntary poverty. What is your attitude

towards the layman's renunciation of luxuries for spiritual motives?

3. Name the advantages of organized charity mentioned by Carey. List some of the most important forms of organized charity sponsored by the Church today. What does Christian charity towards the poor require of the individual?

4. Cite passages in which Carey emphasizes the moral obligation of paying just wages. What was his attitude toward competition in industry? Mention some social and economic problems in America today which are the result of competition.

EVALUATING HIS MANNER OF EXPRESSION

1. A report of an investigation or a survey should present an authentic and impartial statement of aims, findings, and recommendations. Show whether Carey's report fulfills these requirements.

2. What indications of rapid and unrevised writing can you find in the report? Cite instances of Carey's clear, vigorous, and often eloquent style.

3. How does Carey's style compare with that of Hamilton and Jefferson?

---

[4] *within the precincts . . . and liberties*, within the limits and jurisdiction of the city.

QUESTIONS FOR REVIEW

Copy the numbers 1 to 15 in your notebook. Next to each number print the letter marking the word or phrase which correctly completes the sentence.

1. The deist believed that (a) man is naturally good and capable of continuous improvement (b) each man receives sufficient grace to be saved (c) man is totally depraved.

2. The chief point of similarity among the deists was an attitude of mind which led them (a) to investigate the Church founded by Christ (b) to reject authority and substitute the conclusions of their own reason (c) to study Scholastic philosophy.

3. Benjamin Franklin was influential in (a) strengthening Puritanism in America (b) bringing American beliefs from a supernatural to a natural plane (c) spreading Anglican doctrines.

4. As a writer Jefferson is best known for composing (a) the Virginia Statute of Religious Freedom (b) the Declaration of Independence (c) a history of Virginia.

5. A famous comic ballad of Revolutionary times is (a) "The Battle of the Kegs" (b) "The Indian Burying Ground" (c) "Greenfield Hill."

6. The title "Poet of the Revolution" has been given to (a) Mathew Carey (b) Francis Hopkinson (c) Philip Freneau.

7. Washington's most famous piece of writing is his (a) *Diaries* (b) *Farewell Address* (c) *Letters and Papers*.

8. The first convert to write his autobiography was (a) Crèvecœur (b) John Thayer (c) Mathew Carey.

9. During the Revolution the newspaper in America (a) began to shape public opinion (b) had to cease publication (c) was without influence.

10. Neo-classicism in America was marked by (a) flights of fancy and irregular verse forms (b) individuality in style and subject matter (c) restrained imagination and emphasis on style and form.

11. The novel was slow in developing in America because (a) Puritan disapproval of fiction persisted (b) the native American scene was incapable of inspiring writers (c) American writers confined their efforts to poetry.

12. Charles Brockden Brown contributed to the development of the American novel by (a) insisting upon native subject matter and background (b) refusing to borrow the machinery of the Gothic romance (c) using European subject matter.

13. Evidence points to the fact that the first novel by an American was written by (a) Thomas Atwood Digges (b) Charles Brockden Brown (c) Charles Carroll.

14. *The Contrast* by Royall Tyler (a) brought to the stage the character of the typical Yankee (b) was a patriotic drama composed to encourage the colonists (c) was a tragedy centering around a famous spy.

15. Franklin's most famous work is his (a) *Bagatelles* (b) *Autobiography* (c) *Poor Richard's Almanack*.

Copy the numbers 1 to 15 in your notebook. Next to each number print the capital letter T *if the statement is true, or the capital letter* F *if the statement is false.*

1. Thomas Paine wrote stirring pamphlets in which he counseled the colonists to remain loyal to Great Britain.

2. Mathew Carey was an American-born writer who agreed with whichever political party was in power.

3. The literature of the Revolution contains few writings of a political and controversial nature.

4. Crèvecœur is remembered as an early Revolutionary poet.

5. Archbishop Carroll's achievements for the Church and his fellow citizens made him a respected figure in the early days of the republic.

6. Patrick Henry's only public speech was the famous call for unity at the First Continental Congress.

7. Francis Hopkinson is notable as an early writer who led later poets to find inspiration in the American landscape.

8. The Revolutionary Fathers who read Locke received indirectly the teachings of St. Thomas concerning the origin of human authority.

9. The majority of the papers in *The Federalist* were written by Hamilton.

10. The Revolutionary period was an era of great literary productivity in America.

11. The deists denied revelation and miracles.

12. A practical and worldly-wise view of life prevailed in America during the eighteenth century.

13. Recognition of the dignity of the human personality is one of the principles for which the Revolutionary Fathers fought.

14. A movement which aimed to shape man's ideas according to rationalistic beliefs was known as the Enlightenment.

15. The writings of Charles Carroll of Carrollton were chiefly books on travel.

QUESTIONS FOR WRITTEN OR ORAL DISCUSSION

1. Name some of the factors which caused Americans to develop their own way of living and thinking.

2. How did the Revolution affect the position of Catholics in the colonies?

3. Point out the errors of the beliefs of the deists.

4. Briefly state the literary contribution of Benjamin Franklin.

5. Discuss the influence of the newspaper during the Revolution.

SUGGESTIONS FOR READING

Atherton, Gertrude, *The Conquerors* (Macmillan, New York). The story built around Alexander Hamilton, "the conqueror," is an interesting and authentic account of his career. Such historical characters as Washington, Lafayette, Adams, Madison, and Burr are introduced.

Bacheller, Irving, *In the Days of Poor Richard* (Bobbs-Merrill, Indianapolis). The courage of the Yankees often surprised the British. This is a story of Indians, warfare, love, and politics.

Bacheller, Irving, *The Master of Chaos* (Bobbs-Merrill, Indianapolis). George Washington as commander in chief of the American forces brought courage to the colonists and system to the war effort. Battles of the war are reviewed.

Barrett, James Francis, *The Loyalist* (Kenedy, New York). Love, intrigue, and adventure enter into this Catholic account of the Revolution.

Dyer, Walter A., *Sons of Liberty* (Holt, New York). Paul Revere, John Adams, James Otis, and other sons of liberty come to life in this story. They enact the Boston Tea Party, Paul's famous ride, and the Battle of Bunker Hill.

Eaton, Jeannette, *Leader of Destiny: George Washington* (Harcourt, New York). In this book by a noted biographer, George Washington stands forth as the charming gentleman, the zealous patriot, the man of principle and action.

Ford, Paul Leicester, *Janice Meredith* (Grosset, New York). The desperate battles and the major events of the Revolutionary War are exceedingly real. The coquettish heroine and the patriotic hero are straight from the land of romance. George Washington and Alexander Hamilton play an important part in the story.

Johnston, Mary, *Lewis Rand* (Houghton, New York). The scene of the story is Virginia just after the ratification of the Constitution. Jefferson and Hamilton are the chief historical characters.

Lisitzky, Gene, *Thomas Jefferson* (Viking Press, New York). The great lover of freedom, Thomas Jefferson, comes to life again in the pages of this excellent biography.

Mitchell, Silas Weir, *Hugh Wynne* (Burt, New York). The action centers around the imaginary character of a free Quaker, Hugh Wynne, who, contrary to the religious belief of his sect, fights for the Revolutionary cause.

Nicolay, Helen, *Boys' Life of George Washington* (Appleton, New York). The author has given a dependable, readable, entertaining life.

Roberts, Kenneth, *Arundel* (Doubleday, New York). Steven Nason of Arundel took an active part in Benedict Arnold's secret expedition against Quebec. Good pictures of forests, Indians, and pioneer life are sketched in this story.

Roberts, Kenneth, *Oliver Wiswell* (Doubleday, New York). The author presents the Revolution from the point of view of a Tory. The story is full of suspense, adventure, and realistic scenes of battle.

Sabatini, Rafael, *The Carolinian* (Houghton, New York). The course of true love never did run smooth. Because of his loyalty to the cause of the colonists, Harry Latimer is forced to break his engagement to the daughter of a Tory. The lovers struggle against the background of the Revolution.

Sargent, Daniel, *Our Land and Our Lady* (Longmans, New York). For an interesting account of the first bishop in America, read the story of John Carroll on pages 143-167.

Thompson, D. P., *The Green Mountain Boys* (Grosset, New York). Ethan Allan and his "Green Mountain Boys" of Vermont captured Fort Ticonderoga "in the name of Great Jehovah and the Continental Congress."

Trevor, Frederick, *On the Trail of Washington* (Appleton, New York). This book, written in a simple, honest style, gives a complete picture of Washington the man.

George Washington's Inaugural at Independence Hall, 1793

Authors of the United States, mid-nineteenth century, reading from left to right: first row, seated, Miss Sedgwick, Mrs. Sigourney, Mrs. Southworth, Longfellow, Bryant, Halleck, Irving, R. H. Dana, Margaret Fuller, Channing, Mrs. Stowe, Mrs. Kirkland, Whittier. Second row, standing, Kennedy, Holmes, Willis, Mitchell, Morris, Poe, Tuckerman, Hawthorne, Simms, P. Pendleton Cooke, Hoffman, Cooper, Prescott. Bancroft, Parke, Godwin, Motley, Beecher, Curtis, Emerson, Lowell, Bokar, Bayard Taylor, Saxe. Left staircase, Mrs. Mowatt Ritchie, Prentice, Alice Gary, G. W. Kendall. Right staircase, Cozzens, Gallagher, Stoddard, Mrs. Amelia Welby.

National Patterns, 1800-1865

EARLY NATIONAL LITERATURE, 1800-1835

The years 1800-1835 mark the epoch of America's buoyant youth. Enthusiasm and optimism increased as men contemplated their country as a nation of destiny — a nation wherein the democratic ideal would reach full development.

American aspirations were no idle dreams, as the country's expansion and material prosperity soon testified. The Louisiana Purchase in 1803 and the purchase of Florida in 1819 more than doubled the area of the new nation. The Erie Canal pointed the way westward for eager pioneers and made New York City a great port. As factories appeared along the rivers of New England and the Middle Atlantic states, the North assumed industrial leadership. The widespread use of the cotton gin increased the wealth of the South. In the new territory to the West steamboats were beginning to navigate the rivers. Towns on these waterways rapidly became flourishing trade centers. In 1830 a steam locomotive capable of the astounding speed of thirteen miles an hour puffed its way along the wooden rails of the Baltimore and Ohio line.

Goal: cultural independence

Alert to progress in every line, people turned their attention to the arts. The American scene and the American ideal furnished impetus to poets, painters, and architects, stirring them to give form to America's cultural patterns. In this brisk atmosphere literature as a fine art developed. But the expression of American life in literary productions was not achieved without groping efforts. For the most part, writers still had only European models and European forms of expression. Some critics, biased in favor of European authors, gave less than justice to the writings of their countrymen. Others, wishing to applaud everything that was American, paid more attention to the origin of a work than to its intrinsic merit. Discerning readers patiently waited until the noble store of American ideals and traditions should receive adequate treatment. The advent of a national literature worthy of the name was hastened by scornful comments of British reviewers and travelers. When the English wit Sydney Smith asked, "Who reads an American book?" he roused among Americans a strong determination to produce an able native literature. Such writers as Bryant, Irving, and Cooper were soon contributing works that won the admiration of Europe. Portraying our native life against native backgrounds, these authors showed that America was capable of cultural as well as political independence.

ROMANTICISM

A study of the national period of our literature is necessarily a study of romanticism as it appeared in America. As an historical movement, romanticism reached America from Europe, where it had begun as a reaction against the rationalism of the early eighteenth century. At this time, you will remember, rationalistic philosophers had reduced religion to a cold, bare admission that the world has a Creator. They had likewise limited the natural exercise of man's mental faculties. A person was expected to use his brain. His heart and spiritual aspirations were not to intrude into society. Men gradually rebelled against the artificial life that had restricted the full development of their individual powers. The system of thought they proceeded to construct took its ideas from a great many sources. Although reacting against rationalism, they preferred the rationalistic doctrine that human nature is naturally good to the Puritan belief that man is depraved. Consequently, prominent among their teachings, was the optimistic belief that man, like everything else in nature, can reach perfection by falling in line with the natural laws of the universe. The individual, consequently, was to be given unlimited freedom to develop his powers.

Romanticism has many characteristics

In his writings, the romanticist gave full play to his emotions, recorded his desires, analyzed his feelings, and pondered on his destiny. This portrayal of the author's own mental state is a romantic characteristic known as *subjectivity*. The writers likewise depicted the emotions of others. They gave expression to the love, tenderness, mirth, pride, despair, mystery, and terror of other men and thus tried to prove that they had rediscovered the heart of mankind.

The romanticist also removed the literary bonds which restricted his imagination. He was weary of the careful art forms that resulted in simplicity, beauty, and symmetry. To loveliness he wished to add the elements of strangeness and mystery. He wished to arouse awe and wonder. His words, consequently, suggest rather than define. His style is impressionistic; his decoration sometimes exaggerated; his beauty likely to be picturesque and fantastic. At times his work may even be grotesque.

Romantic tendencies frequently lead to excesses that bring man far from his spiritual aims. Despite this fact, the romanticist strongly asserts the need of his spiritual nature. The note of aspiration in his writing is strong. Frequently he cannot state the precise object of his longing, yet he perseveres in his vague search. Often his yearnings take him out of his age, give him a sense of nearness to the infinite, and urge him to portray his ideal even inadequately by allegory or symbol. When the romanticist believes it is possible to achieve his quest, he is optimistic. When hope eludes him, he experiences deep melancholy.

Dissatisfied with his present surroundings, the romanticist frequently turns to the past and to remote places, where distance softens the sharp edge of reality and makes life appear closer to his ideal. Ancient and medieval Europe, the Orient, the South Seas — all yield plot and atmosphere for legends, popular ballads, historical romances. Nature likewise beckons the romanticist as a source of delight, inspiration, moral teaching, and healing. The common man is often praised because he is considered to be closer to nature and less repressed by an artificial standard of society.

American romanticism has its own aspects

American romanticism, while influenced by the European movement, had its distinctive characteristics. The American had already achieved political liberty. If his individualistic spirit urged him to make money, he could go West and develop the immense natural resources of the frontier. Romanticism in this country, consequently, generally lacked that aggressive and dissatisfied spirit which in the European movement led to the French Revolution. The emphasis on morality which remained from colonial America strengthened the inherent idealistic note. American romanticism was colored by our national optimism, by our closeness to rural life and to the frontier. In returning to the past, American writers found inspiring subject matter in intrepid colonists, Revolutionary heroes, and buckskin-clad frontiersmen.

It should not be thought that romanticism had no influence in America before 1800. The doctrines of the American Revolution had emphasized the essential worth of the individual and the equality of all men. American democracy provided a way of life in which the common man found opportunity to achieve success. Philip Freneau had begun to praise the natural beauties of the American scene in his poetry and to point out the figure of the American Indian as potential material for American literature. That Freneau was not aloof from the allurement of mysterious beauty is shown by his use of the luxuriant settings of the West Indies. In transplanting the Gothic romance to American soil, Charles Brockden Brown had substituted tomahawks for pistols and the dark mystery of the American forest for the dim passages of feudal manors.

Since the expression of romanticism in American literature varied according to the locality from which the literature came, a sectional division provides a convenient framework for study. The Middle Atlantic states, with their rapid commercial growth and increased prosperity, provided one locality for American writers of the national period. The South, with its cultivated plantations and rugged frontier lands, provided another. New England, the home of transcendentalism and of the genteel writers, furnished America of the national period with a philosophy and standards for evaluating both life and literature.

WASHINGTON IRVING

When his contemporaries made the acquaintance of Washington Irving (1783-1859), they saw in the man the same genial nature, gentle humor, and sentiment that they had admired in Irving the writer. The youngest of eleven children of a British family settled in New York, Washington Irving was a delicate child but

Washington Irving

quick and keen beyond his years. He was a typical boy who loved hunting and fishing and rambling over the countryside. But he enjoyed, too, browsing for hours in his father's library, where he found a particular delight in the humorous, satirical style of Joseph Addison and Oliver Goldsmith. When Irving was threatened with consumption in 1804, his brothers sent him to Europe, where he remained for two years. He returned to America in good health, with many tales and a store of useful information for future writing. Admitted to the bar in 1806, he made little effort to practice the profession in which his family hoped to see him succeed. The death of his fiancée in 1809 caused him deep sorrow, and he never married. After participating in the War of 1812, Irving went to London and remained in Europe for seventeen years. With the failure of the family hardware business, he was left without funds and for the first time turned to writing as a means of earning a livelihood. Under this necessity he produced some of his most vigorous work. His *Sketch Book* and *Bracebridge Hall* gave him a literary reputation in England at a time when most Englishmen still regarded Americans as savages wearing feathers in their hair.

Irving uses native materials

Irving's literary career began in 1807 with the publication of the *Salmagundi Papers*. In these essays Irving, together with his brother William and with

James Kirke Paulding, indulged in good-natured criticism of American social and literary manners, showing himself a master of the ludicrous. In 1809, Irving began his Knickerbocker hoax. As advance publicity he used a clever piece of foolery which led the public to believe they were being offered a learned and scholarly document in *Knickerbocker's History of New York*. The book, limited to a treatment of the early Dutch colonial period, proved to be a comical, mock-heroic account dedicated facetiously, to the New York Historical Society.

The Sketch Book (1819-20), *Bracebridge Hall* (1822), and *Tales of a Traveler* (1824) reveal Irving's deepening interest in early history and his ability to write leisurely, entertaining narrative. But Irving did not confine himself to the American scene. Squire Bracebridge is the romantic ideal of the country squire of Merrie England. The tales and sketches in these volumes are of uneven merit, however, and indicate that Irving stood in need of new materials.

He wins European recognition

These new materials lay at hand in Spain, where Irving went as a member of the American legation in 1826. He lived in the romantic castle-fortress of the Alhambra at Granada and steeped himself in the legends of Spain and Arabia. *The Alhambra* (1832) reflects the magic splendor of the romantic setting in tales of exquisite loveliness.

Irving returned to America in 1832, an author possessed of an international reputation and the friendship of men like Sir Walter Scott and Lord Byron. Irving continued to be a prolific writer, but his later works are labored accounts of travel, adventure, and biography that seldom rise to the level of artistic writings. Irving's last years were spent at Sunnyside, his home near Tarrytown on the Hudson. He died in 1859, not long after he had completed the last chapter of his five-volume life of George Washington.

Prose tales and essays containing genuine characters had been written before Irving's time. In the tales of this writer, however, the two types are united in a conscious effort to produce something new. To the narrative Irving added a distinctive atmosphere, setting, humor, a unified tone, finished style, and human appeal to give us a new type — the American short story. Later writers were to show that Irving's long prefaces and descriptions

©New York Public Library
An Illustration for Rip Van Winkle
Used in an Early Edition

of his own feelings have no proper place in this literary form, but Irving wrote forty-eight narrative pieces which are essentially short stories.

Washington Irving had been at his best in the world of romanticized history. He brought to life from the bare bones of early colonial history characters filled with vigorous life and hearty, even grotesque humor, creating through them a world of legend and giving to America a tradition that has become a part of the national heritage. Corpulent Wouter Van Twiller has become a symbol of the conviviality and stolidness of the Dutch of early New York. Awkward Ichabod and lazy Rip Van Winkle have proved by their own experience that the New World, too, has its goblins, ghosts, and enchantments. Diedrich Knickerbocker, the Dutch historian created by Washington Irving, will live forever in American legendary lore. Washington Irving, seeker of a tradition, achieved the distinction of becoming the maker of one as well.

JAMES FENIMORE COOPER

Carl Van Doren points out in his work on the American novel that the subject matter of American romance centers around the Revolution, the Settlement, and the Frontier. To Cooper belongs the distinction of having employed each of these successfully in his fiction. Moreover, like Irving, he created characters that have become immortal in American literature. By merging reality with the idealized concept of the "noble savage," Cooper established the literary tradition of the American Indian.

James Fenimore Cooper (1789-1851) was born at Burlington, New Jersey, but spent much of his life in and around Copperstown on Lake Otsego, about sixty miles from Albany. Fascinated by the sea, he served for five years in the United States Navy. After his marriage he settled down to the life of a country gentleman. His wife was instrumental in plunging him into a literary career. One evening as they were reading together a sentimental English novel, he became disgusted and exclaimed that he could write a better story. His wife challenged him to produce the book. Although his first effort was unsuccessful, it stimulated his interest in fiction writing. The failure of *Precaution*, a conventional novel on English society, spurred him on to greater endeavor.

Cooper sees romance in history

Searching about for subject matter more appealing to his American readers, he decided upon a patriotic theme centering around the Revolution. The result was *The Spy* (1821), the first romance of the American Revolution and the first important American novel. While the outline of the story was not original, its breathtaking action proved popular with readers and Harvey Birch, the self-sacrificing spy in the service of Washington, was the first of Cooper's immortal characters. *The Spy* was favorably received and encouraged Cooper to write more stories on American themes having an American background.

Settlement and frontier life furnished Cooper inspiration for a series of novels which have come to be known as the Leather-Stocking tales. These stories record the adventurous life of the rugged pioneer Natty Bumppo. They were not written in chronological sequence, but the reader may obtain the succession of events in the hero's life by reading the books in the following order: *The Deerslayer* (1841), *The Last of the Mohicans* (1826), *The Pathfinder* (1840), *The Pioneers* (1823), and *The Prairie* (1827). In his westward migration Leather-Stocking, who appears under various names, symbolizes the pioneer spirit of the American nation. His heroic Indian friends, Chingachgook and Uncas, lend an epic quality to the narrative.

Turning to the sea for subject matter, Cooper determined to use his sailor's knowledge to write a better

A Scene from Cooper's The Last of the Mohicans

novel than *The Pirate* by Sir Walter Scott. In *The Pilot* (1824) Cooper again achieved success. John Paul Jones is the pilot in the novel, and Long Tom Coffin, the old sailor, is the Leather-Stocking of the sea.

Leather-Stocking has enduring fame

Although the novels of Cooper are weak in construction and full of impossible situations, the newness of their subject matter and their appeal made him one of the most popular American authors of the nineteenth century. Like many romantic writers, Cooper idealized his characters. His heroes and heroines are a little unbelievable at times. Cooper would have us believe that the honesty, integrity, and manly courage of his characters come from their contacts with nature, unhampered as they are by social conventions. He was decidedly weak in his portrayal of women characters. They are largely sentimental types of women devoid of personality. Although Cooper wrote more than thirty volumes, he is best remembered for *The Spy*, the Leather-Stocking tales, and *The Pilot*. These three form a link of what might well be considered a national prose epic. They comprise a literary record of the nation's birth and expansion.

WILLIAM CULLEN BRYANT

The picture of William Cullen Bryant (1794-1878) that lingers in most minds is that of a dignified poet going in and out of a newspaper office in New York. Yet there was a time when in the long winter evenings a small boy had in imagination fought the wars of the

Bryant Home

Greeks and Trojans in the attic of his Berkshire home in western Massachusetts, thus bringing the classics to life again in his own New England. A richly packed library occupied his time when he was not working on the farm. His greatest interest lay, however, in the woods and streams close to his home. The boy was soon scratching verses which were at first almost too stiff to move, so heavily were they draped in the elaborate diction of the eighteenth-century poets. At seventeen he wrote "Thanatopsis" and hastily hid it in his desk, where it lay for six years. It is the great Puritan dirge, and although intended to be optimistic, has in it a note of pagan pessimism. The references to nature are lovely, but the thought of the poem does not go beyond the sepulchre to the glorious awakening of another life. The poem reveals Bryant's youthful uncertainty about traditional Calvinism.

Faced with the necessity of earning a living, Bryant resolutely turned to the study of law and was admitted to the bar at the age of twenty-one. But his heart was in his poetry and he kept adding manuscript to the pile of hidden masterpieces in his desk. His father found them, sent them to a publisher, and as soon as the poems reached the public, Bryant's literary reputation was secure. For nine years the young poet practiced law and only in his leisure followed the urge to write. By the time he launched into a journalistic career in New York at thirty-one, he was famous as a poet.

Poet describes American nature

Poetry, however, was only one of Bryant's interests. Hard-working, cultured, conservative, he was the right man to become a focal point through which the best traditions of the old world could radiate quietly out into the new. As editor of the New York *Evening Post* he took an active and influential part in shaping American political life. Never losing his love for his native New England countryside, he nevertheless found time to enjoy European travel. The inhibitions of his earlier Puritanism gradually dropped away, leaving his mind broadly alert yet never radical. He retained a sane and happy sense of God's presence, not only in nature, but also in the "voices and footfalls of the numberless throngs" of city-dwellers. His countrymen saw in his patriarchal figure the great American poet. His voice lent dignity, stability, and cultural expression to the American scene.

Romantic and Puritan strain mingle

Bryant's was the first poetry to treat of the American scene in a manner to satisfy critics both at home and abroad. He could write poetry well because he felt keenly concerning the need it could supply. Since Bryant held that a poem must be essentially moral and that its subject matter should come from nature, his own poetry presented nature moralized. Bryant was a romanticist with a Puritan background. While his romantic nature responded enthusiastically to the charms of nature, his Puritan training restrained his emotions by the force of serious reflection. It was this strain of seriousness that led Bryant to see the world of beautiful nature as the common tomb of man or to see beyond the lonely flight of a waterfowl, God, the guide of all His creatures.

Bryant deserves to be remembered not only as a poet and journalist but as a scholar. His translations of the *Iliad* (1870) and the *Odyssey* (1871-1872) are still among the best poetic versions of Homer's immortal epics. Much of Bryant's critical work on such writers as Irving, Cooper, and Halleck is to be found in his *Letters of a Traveler* (1850) and in his *Orations and Addresses* (1859).

EARLY CATHOLIC LITERATURE OF THE NATIONAL PERIOD

The literature of the national period reveals America in search of a spiritual ideal. With the breakdown of Puritanism and the dissatisfaction with rationalism, many people began to re-examine their religious positions. In this era of spiritual turmoil, the Catholic

Church might have exercised great influence among non-Catholics. Longfellow, Hawthorne, and Lowell had frequently written passages that were almost Catholic in their conception. Whittier showed admiration for Catholic heroes and ideals. Unfortunately, when men were acknowledging a spiritual need, new barriers of prejudice appeared to obscure the Church as a source of truth. The entire pattern of Catholic literature in the national period was designed as a result of the opposition to the Church which manifested itself at this time.

The early years of the nineteenth century were an energetic period of Catholic literary activity. Catholic literature was young, it is true. It showed the exuberance, idealism, self-confidence, and immaturity of youth. This vigor showed itself in the manly defense of Catholicity; in the fervent dedication to Catholic letters of the talent of noted converts; in the militant action of a press that was emerging in various sections of the country. At this time Catholics recognized the need for a literature to express their ideals.

Maryland, the cradle of American Catholic literature in the English tongue, was the scene of the most prominent literary activity in the first three decades of the nineteenth century. At Baltimore, where Catholics held important positions and where Archbishop Carroll was the most noted citizen until his death in 1815, a group of writers found an encouraging audience. Here the Catholic bishops held their First Provincial Council in 1829. Here in 1846 they petitioned that the Immaculate Conception be named Patroness of the United States. In the vicinity were several Catholic colleges. Close to the Maryland center of Catholic activity were Washington and Philadelphia, cities which also played their part in the development of Catholic literature.

In the forties New York vied with Maryland for leadership in Catholic letters, partly because prominent writers from Maryland and the New England states went to New York at that time. In New England, too, a number of literary men were united in their belief in the future of Catholic letters. The scattered Catholic population of the South allowed little exchange of literary interests. It is significant to note, however, that even in these isolated sections, the diaries of authors contain records of comfort and encouragement resulting from friendly meetings between Catholic writers.

TWO PIONEER AUTHORS

At Emmitsburg, Maryland, Elizabeth Seton (1774-1821) found a haven for the first parochial schools. The writings of this sainted widow who became a religious foundress have been edited by an archbishop who was her grandson, Most Reverend Robert Seton, D.D. The two volumes are entitled *The Memoir, Letters, and Journal of Elizabeth Seton, Convert to the Catholic Faith and Sister of Charity*. As charming in her memoir as in the manner of her sanctity, Mother Seton is worthy to stand at the head of a long line of Catholic women authors, both secular and religious. Her work aptly expresses her distinctive personality, her womanly tenderness, and her spiritual depth.

One of the earliest Catholic writers in the nineteenth century made his influence felt in the field of secular letters. By constantly exhorting his countrymen to be American in their writings, Robert Walsh (1784-1859) became a noted figure in the movement for cultural independence. He has been called generalissimo of the "Paper War," a verbal combat in which British writers attacked the citizens, institutions, and social standards of America. Walsh's *Appeal from the Judgment of Great Britain Respecting the United States* (1819), which exposed the misrepresentations of American life by Englishmen, was one of the most widely read books of the day. Occasionally Walsh, like other Americans, showed more enthusiasm than discernment in acclaiming national greatness. At Philadelphia Walsh founded in 1811 the first quarterly magazine in the United States, the *American Review of History and Politics*. His two volumes of essays, *Didactics* (1836), contain selections from his newspaper and magazine writings.

NATIVE-AMERICAN MOVEMENT

On the battleground of public opinion during the national period was to be refought and rewon the conflict in defense of the fundamental right of religious freedom. This right as asserted by the Federal Constitution was not by any means universally accepted in theory, still less in practice. Many of the states retained provisions against Catholics beyond the first half of the century. Under the Constitution the right to regulate religious affairs, to determine qualifications for citizenship, and to decide the question of a state church remained in the power of the state.

Many currents flowed into the great waves of anti-Catholic prejudice which broke between 1829 and 1856. With the influx of Catholic immigrants after 1812, Protestants began to fear that their leadership might be usurped. As Irish families climbed out of steerage with no wealth but their faith, smouldering prejudices were re-enkindled. From one hundred twenty Catholics in Boston in 1790, the number had increased to 40,000 by 1845.

The objections against Catholics on racial, social, political, and economic grounds took the form of a protest known as the Native-American movement. Preachers and writers attracted large audiences before whom they denounced the practices and doctrines of the Church. By misrepresenting the spiritual authority of the Pope, they devised their chief argument: Catholics could not be good citizens because they served a foreign power. In a receptive mood, many Protestants welcomed papers, magazines, and books which misrepresented the priesthood and conventual life. People who believed these attacks gathered to burn churches and convents. The revival of the Native-American movement in 1852 led to the founding of a political party which aimed to exclude Catholics from public office. Because its members answered, "I don't know," when questioned concerning the program of the organization, the society was soon referred to as the Know-Nothing party. Mobs, riots, and attacks on Church property were resumed. After the defeat of the party in the presidential election of 1856, the influence of Know-Nothingism rapidly declined.

Religious liberty threatened

Today the uprisings of Native-Americanism appear as the activities of an ill-informed and ill-advised group. At the time of its power, however, the movement constituted a menace to religious freedom. Its purpose was to deny citizenship to Catholics and ultimately to exterminate the Church in America. One means to obtain this end was to reduce the immigrant to social slavery by lengthening his period of probation for citizenship to twenty-five years. When actual bills for such measures were introduced into the legislature of some states, Catholics saw that what they needed — and needed at once — was a literature that would clearly define the position of the Church.

THE RISE OF CATHOLIC JOURNALISM

The rapid development of Catholic journalism in the national period was the answer to the imperative need of the Church for defense. For a long time priests had been looking towards the press as a means of uniting their widely scattered flocks. In Detroit as early as 1806, one of Bishop Carroll's clergymen, Reverend Gabriel Richard, had introduced a spoken newspaper after the manner of the ancient town crier. In the summer of 1809, without the aid of railway express, Father Richard succeeded in having a printing press brought from Baltimore. With this machine the priest's publisher produced Michigan's first newspaper, the *Michigan Essay or Impartial Observer*. Unfortunately Father Richard's parishioners were not able to support the paper, and the priest could not offer a second issue.

It was not until John England, Bishop of Charleston, South Carolina, marshaled his splendid intellectual force for the founding of the *United States Catholic Miscellany* in 1822 that Catholic journalism could boast of its first truly Catholic newspaper. In 1829 the bishops who met at Baltimore for the First Provincial Council recommended the establishment and support of the Catholic press. As a result of their decision, the *Metropolitan*, the first Catholic magazine in the United States, was established the next year. The development of Catholic journalism from 1822 to 1833 saw the rise of a number of Catholic newspapers which acted as spearheads in the offensive against error and prejudice. In almost every center where Catholic literature developed, there first appeared a newspaper which strengthened Catholic morale, combatted bigotry against the Church, and started Catholic writers on a career of authorship. In most instances, likewise, a noted clergyman or bishop was the energizing force behind the paper, either through his editorial contribution or his encouragement and guidance of journalistic activity. During the vital period between 1829-1833, Catholic papers were begun in Boston, New York, Cincinnati, St. Louis, Philadelphia, Washington, and Hartford, Connecticut.

THE WRITERS OF APOLOGETICS

The persistent attack on Catholic teaching acted as a literary stimulus to the leaders of the Catholic Church. Many of the dioceses at this time were in a period of formation. Bishops were hard pressed with the administrative duties of building churches, schools, and orphanages. Visitation and confirmation tours took them in many cases over large areas. They catechized the faithful in the basement of churches and aided pastors by taking ten-hour shifts in the confessional. Intermingled with such arduous duties was the task of refuting current attacks by setting forth Catholic belief in a logical and systematic manner. The thick volumes of controversial works on the shelves of Catholic libraries today testify to the energy of the stalwart members of the American hierarchy. Centuries before them the Fathers of the Church had developed Catholic teachings and refuted heretics. In line with these apologetic writings, the American bishops proceeded to prove that Catholicism could adapt itself to the New World and its institutions, that the Church is the friend of democracy and the advocate of patriotism. The controversy frequently took the form of a series of newspaper articles in which the Catholic writer answered the arguments of his opponent. Out of the spirited defense of the Church there developed in the American hierarchy a tradition of noble controversial writers. During the national period the names of John England, John Hughes, Martin Spalding, John Purcell, Francis Patrick Kenrick, and his brother, Peter Richard Kenrick, are remembered as carrying out this high apologetic task.

One of the able prelates who brought Celtic courage, intellectual resourcefulness, decisive action, and undeniable eloquence to his public defense of the Church was John Hughes (1797-1864), archbishop of New York. As a young man of twenty, Hughes had appeared at Mount St. Mary's Seminary, Emmitsburg, asking to work in the garden in recompense for his education — an education with which he served the Church in America by guiding Catholics in New York through the stormy years of the Native-American movement. Archbishop Hughes never faltered before an opponent; indeed he seemed at his best when meeting his adversaries in public debate. Today his logical and convincing arguments on questions concerning church property, Catholic education, and numerous other subjects may be found in his *Sermons, Letters, Lectures,* and *Speeches.*

Most Rev. John Hughes, Archbishop of New York

THE DEVELOPMENT OF CATHOLIC POETRY

When we speak of a tradition, we understand a settled, cohesive, and continuous pattern of life. We think of a people who have lived in a distinct region for a long period, whose race memory is long, and whose interest, aspirations, beliefs, and customs are a common heritage. It is in this sense that we speak of a Puritan tradition in New England or of a Cavalier tradition in the South. We cannot speak of a Catholic literary tradition in America except in a modified sense, for we are, for the most part, too close to immigrant origins, and our cultural stability is too recent. And if this is true of tradition in the larger sense, it is even more true of a poetic tradition, for a tradition in poetry, as a rule, arises only after a community has been safely and solidly established.

In contrast to the isolated voices of John Lewis, S.J. and Mathew Carey before 1800, the larger number of minor Catholic authors in the national period indicates that Catholics had become articulate as a group. In this era came that impetus for creative work which results from a receptive audience, a medium of publication, and sufficient contact among authors to make possible an interchange of ideas. The writers of this time constantly stress love of God and of country. Interwoven with these themes are loyalty to the cause of liberty under law, hunger for justice, distrust of materialism, a readiness to defend the Faith, and devotion to the Blessed Virgin Mary. From these roots have sprung a flowering of poetry that is today one of the most significant contributions of American Catholic literature.

Poem is Bishop's welcome

An instance of poetic activity on the frontier is the welcome by Reverend Stephen Badin (1768-1853) to the first bishop of Kentucky, Benedict Joseph Flaget. Coming by flatboat in 1811 to a diocese of log cabins, Bishop Flaget was met at Bardstown by his people, who had prepared an altar between four saplings. There was no cathedral for a solemn procession after Bishop Flaget had disembarked and donned his episcopal robes; but to commemorate the event, there was a sonorous Latin poem, which Father Badin, the priest of the saddle, had composed in welcome. Father Badin — incidentally the first priest ordained within the limits of the original thirteen states — later wrote several doctrinal and controversial works.

Harney has lyric gift

In the day when American authors faced the ridicule of English critics, John Milton Harney (1789-1825), a young physician in Kentucky, wrote a charming poetic fairy tale which he entitled *Crystalina* (1816). He issued the work under the signature "by an American" and in a challenging preface asked for a just evaluation of an American's workmanship. The graceful tale, which presents the folklore of the Scottish Highlanders, exhibits the poet's unusual skill and sensitiveness.

After his wife's death and his own serious illness, Doctor Harney entered the Catholic Church. Upon the physician's death were found the manuscripts of a number of genuine lyrics, one of which, "Echo and the Lover," has been frequently reprinted.

Pise encourages poets

In the cultured personality of Charles Constantine Pise (1802-1866), Catholic letters found their first versatile author. The Maryland priest, whose graciousness led to his appointment as chaplain of the United States Senate, was a poet, essayist, novelist, historian, controversialist, and editor. Father Pise inaugurated the first definite program for the promotion of Catholic poetry in America. As joint editor of the *Catholic Expositor* in New York, he featured in the periodical each year the works of an outstanding Catholic American poet. He likewise gave generous space to other writers of Catholic poetry. In 1833 appeared a volume of Father Pise's poetry, *The Pleasures of Religion and Other Poems*. His blank-verse version of "The Acts of the Apostles" best illustrates perhaps his chaste style.

Shea treats Irish legends

Among the Catholic poets whom Father Pise encouraged was an Irish immigrant, John Augustus Shea (1802-1845). A talented journalist who had issued a volume of poetry before coming to America, Shea quickly advanced in editorial positions at Philadelphia, Washington, and New York. His *Adolph and Other Poems* (1831) is one of the first books of Catholic poetry published in America. Two other volumes of his poems appeared in America during Shea's lifetime, and after his death his son published a partial collection of his work. Shea's longer narratives based on Irish legend have the spontaneous melody of genuine inspiration. In occasional lyric passages he exhibits economy of phrase and imaginative vigor. Associated with Father Pise and John Augustus Shea was Charles James Cannon, a writer of short stories and drama, whose large body of lyric poetry shows his facile expression.

Wouter Van Twiller

(From Diedrich Knickerbocker's *History of New York*)
Washington Irving

The aristocratic descendants of the early Dutch settlers of New York did not relish a literary hoax by Washington Irving. The joke was artfully contrived. First press notices heralded a forthcoming treatise entitled A History of New York from the Beginning of the World to the End of the Dutch Dynasty. *They announced that a pompous study was about to be printed under circumstances that were themselves sensational. The historian, one Diedrich Knickerbocker, was reported to have failed to pay his rent, and his landlord had seized the manuscript for publication. The Dutch aristocracy eagerly opened the two volumes only to find their ancestors amusingly caricatured. The ire of the leading citizens descended upon Diedrich Knickerbocker, who was soon identified as Washington Irving. Eventually the chagrin was forgotten. Americans as a whole remember, however, that Irving invested an obscure era of New York's past with imaginative and whimsical charm and that he recorded the city traditions in comic form, linking the community together in the fellowship of a hearty laugh.*

The renowned Wouter (or Walter) Van Twiller was descended from a long line of Dutch burgomasters, who had successively dozed away their lives and grown fat upon the bench of magistracy in Rotterdam; and who had comported themselves with such singular wisdom and propriety that they were never either heard or talked of — which, next to being universally applauded, should be the object of ambition of all magistrates and rulers. There are two opposite ways by which some men make a figure in the world: one, by talking faster than they think, and the other, by holding their tongues and not thinking at all. By the first, many a smatterer acquires the reputation of a man of quick parts; by the other, many a dunderpate, like the owl, the stupidest of birds, comes to be considered the very type of wisdom. This, by the way, is a casual remark, which I would not for the universe have it thought I apply to Governor Van Twiller. It is true he was a man shut up within himself like an oyster and rarely spoke except in monosyllables, but then it was allowed he seldom said a foolish thing.

So invincible was his gravity that he was never known to laugh or even to smile through the whole course of a long and prosperous life. Nay, if a joke were uttered in his presence that set light-minded hearers in a roar, it was observed to throw him into a state of perplexity. Sometimes he would deign to inquire into the matter; and when, after much explanation, the joke was made as plain as a pikestaff, he would continue to smoke his pipe in silence and, at length, knocking out the ashes, would exclaim, "Well! I see nothing in all that to laugh about."

With all his reflective habits he never made up his mind on a subject. His adherents accounted for this by the astonishing magnitude of his ideas. He conceived every subject on so grand a scale that he had not room in his head to turn it over and examine both sides of it. Certain it is, that, if any matter were propounded to him on which ordinary mortals would rashly determine at first glance, he would put on a vague, mysterious look, shake his capacious head, smoke some time in profound silence, and at length observe that "he had his doubts about the matter"; which gained him the reputation of a man slow of belief and not easily imposed upon. What is more, it gained him a lasting name; for to this habit of the mind has been attributed his surname of Twiller, which is said to be a corruption of the original Twijfler, or in plain English, *Doubter.*

The person of this illustrious old gentleman was formed and proportioned as though it had been molded by the hands of some cunning Dutch statuary as a model of majesty and lordly grandeur. He was exactly five feet, six inches in height, and six feet, five inches in circumference. His head was a perfect sphere and of such stupendous dimensions that Dame Nature, with all her sex's ingenuity, would have been puzzled to construct a neck capable of supporting it; wherefore she wisely declined the attempt and settled it firmly on the top of his backbone, just between the shoulders. His body was oblong and particularly capacious at bottom; which was wisely ordered by Providence, seeing that he was a man of sedentary habits and very averse to the idle labor of walking. His legs were short but sturdy in proportion to the weight they had to sustain; so that when erect he had not a little the appearance of a beer barrel on skids. His face, that infallible index of the mind, presented a vast expanse, unfurrowed by any of those lines and angles which disfigure the human countenance with what is termed expression. Two small gray eyes twinkled feebly in the midst, like two stars of lesser magnitude in a hazy firmament; and his full-fed cheeks, which seemed to have taken toll of everything that went into his mouth, were curiously mottled and streaked with dusky red, like a Spitzenberg apple.

His habits were as regular as his person. He daily took his four stated meals, appropriating exactly an hour to each; he smoked and doubted eight hours, and he slept the remaining twelve of the four-and-twenty. Such was the renowned Wouter Van Twiller—a true philosopher, for his mind was either elevated above, or tranquilly settled below, the cares and perplexities of this world. He had lived in it for years without feeling the least curiosity to know whether the sun revolved round it, or it round the sun; and he had watched for at least half a century the smoke curling from his pipe to the ceiling without once troubling his head with any of those numerous theories by which a philosopher would have perplexed his brain in accounting for its rising above the surrounding atmosphere.

In his council he presided with great state and solemnity. He sat in a huge chair of solid oak, hewn in the celebrated forest of the Hague, fabricated by an experienced timmerman[1] of Amsterdam, and curiously carved about the arms and feet into exact imitations of gigantic eagle's claws. Instead of a scepter, he swayed a long Turkish pipe, wrought with jasmine and amber, which had been presented to a stadtholder[2] of Holland at the conclusion of a treaty with one of the petty Barbary powers.[3] In this stately chair would he sit, and this magnificent pipe would he smoke, shaking his right knee with a constant motion and fixing his eye for hours together upon a little print of Amsterdam, which

hung in a black frame against the opposite wall of the council chamber. Nay, it has ever been said that when any deliberation of extraordinary length and intricacy was on the carpet, the renowned Wouter would shut his eyes for full two hours at a time that he might not be disturbed by external objects; and at such times the internal commotion of his mind was evinced by certain regular guttural sounds, which his admirers declared were merely the noise of conflict made by his contending doubts and opinions.

It is with infinite difficulty I have been enabled to collect these biographical anecdotes of the great man under consideration. The facts respecting him were so scattered and vague, and divers of them so questionable in point of authenticity that I have had to give up the search after many and decline the admission of still more which would have tended to heighten the coloring of his portrait.

I have been the more anxious to delineate fully the person and habits of Wouter Van Twiller, from the consideration that he was not only the first, but also the best governor[4] that ever presided over this ancient and respectable province; and so tranquil and benevolent was his reign that I do not find throughout the whole of it a single instance of any offender being brought to punishment—a most indubitable sign of a merciful governor and a case unparalleled, excepting in the reign of the illustrious King Log,[5] from whom it is hinted the renowned Van Twiller was a lineal descendant.

The very outset of the career of this excellent magistrate was distinguished by an example of legal acumen that gave flattering presage of a wise and equitable administration. The morning after he had been installed in office, and at the moment that he was making his breakfast from a prodigious earthen dish filled with milk and Indian pudding, he was interrupted by the appearance of Wandle Schoonhoven, a very important old burgher of New Amsterdam, who complained bitterly of one Barent Bleecker, inasmuch as he refused to come to a settlement of accounts, seeing that there was

---

[1] timmerman, a cabinetmaker.

[2] stadtholder, chief executive officer of the United Provinces of the Netherlands.

[3] Barbary powers, countries on the north coast of Africa.

[4] first, . . . governor, Wouter Van Twiller was actually the fifth governor of New Amsterdam. When Irving wrote his history, however, only one predecessor was known to historians.

[5] King Log. When the frogs in one of Aesop's Fables asked Jupiter for a king, he gave them a log of wood, which satisfied them until they discovered the deception.

a heavy balance in favor of the said Wandle. Governor Van Twiller, as I have already observed, was a man of few words; he was likewise a mortal enemy to multiplying writings—or being disturbed at his breakfast. Having listened attentively to the statement of Wandle Schoonhoven, giving an occasional grunt as he shoveled a spoonful of Indian pudding into his mouth—either as a sign that he relished the dish or comprehended the story—he called unto him his constable, and pulling out of his breeches pocket a huge jack knife, dispatched it after the defendant as a summons, accompanied by his tobacco box as a warrant.

This summary process was as effectual in those simple days as was the seal ring of the great Haroun-al-Raschid[6] among the true believers. The two parties being confronted before him, each produced a book of accounts written in a language and character that would have puzzled any but a High-Dutch commentator or a learned decipherer of Egyptian obelisks.[7] The sage Wouter took them one after the other, and having poised them in his hands and attentively counted over the number of leaves, fell straightway into a very great doubt and smoked for half an hour without saying a word; at length, laying his finger beside his nose and shutting his eyes for a moment, with the air of a man who has just caught a subtle idea by the tail, he slowly took his pipe from his mouth, puffed forth a column of tobacco-smoke, and with marvelous gravity and solemnity pronounced that, having carefully counted over the leaves and weighed the books, it was found that one was just as thick and as heavy as the other: therefore, it was the final opinion of the court that the accounts were equally balanced: therefore, Wandle should give Barent a receipt, and Barent should give Wandle a receipt, and the constable should pay the costs.

This decision, being straightway made known, diffused general joy throughout New Amsterdam, for the people immediately perceived that they had a very wise and equitable magistrate to rule over them. But its happiest effect was that not another lawsuit took place throughout the whole of his administration; and the office of constable fell into such decay that there was not one of those losel scouts[8] known in the province for many years. I am the more particular in dwelling on this transaction, not only because I deem it one of the most sage and righteous judgments on record and well worthy the attention of modern magistrates, but because it was a miraculous event in the history of the renowned Wouter—being the only time he was ever known to come to a decision in the whole course of his life.

VIEWING THE AUTHOR'S IDEAS

1. According to Irving, how do great men gain public notice? For what was Wouter Van Twiller noted? By what means did he gain this reputation? How did he budget his time?

2. What policy of government did Van Twiller follow? Would this policy succeed under actual conditions?

3. Why would Irving's amusing caricature of Van Twiller irritate the descendants of the old Dutch families?

4. Show that the targets of Irving's good-natured satire are indolence, stupidity, pedantry, and political inefficiency.

EVALUATING HIS MANNER OF EXPRESSION

1. Discuss the methods of characterization used by Irving in this selection.

2. Point out passages in which mock seriousness is mingled with a show of historical accuracy. How does this device contribute to the humorous effect?

3. Which of the following phrases best describe Irving's humor: cynical and disparaging, boisterous and crude; "an ounce of truth buried in a bushel of absurdity"; burlesque and capricious; gently ironic and good-natured.

4. An interest in the picturesque past of our nation was a characteristic of American romanticism. How does Irving give to the early history of New Amsterdam something of the charm and romance of the legendary past of Europe?

5. Read Book III of Knickerbocker's *A History of New York* to learn how Wouter Van Twiller finally came to slumber with his fathers after slumbering so often with his contemporaries.

---

[6] *Haroun-al-Raschid,* a caliph of Baghdad in the eighth century.

[7] *Egyptian obelisks,* tapering, four-sided pillars covered with hieroglyphic writing.

[8] *losel scouts,* worthless officers.

The Author's Account of Himself

(From *The Sketch Book*)
Washington Irving

"I am of this mind with Homer, that as the snaile that crept out of her shel was turned eftsoons into a toad, and thereby was forced to make a stoole to sit on; so the traveller that stragleth from his owne country is in a short time transformed into so monstrous a shape, that he is faine to alter his mansion with his manners, and to live where he can, not where he would."

Lyly's *Euphues*

Thackeray called Washington Irving "the first ambassador whom the New World of Letters sent to the Old." At that time America needed an ambassador of Irving's refinement and wit, for many Europeans were inclined to regard contemptuously the civilization of the New World. "I was looked upon," wrote Irving, "as something new and strange in literature, a kind of demi-savage with a feather in his hand instead of in his head." Conscious of Europe's storied past and sensitive to our own lack of national folklore, Irving set about creating some American traditions. He invented the Knickerbocker legend of early New York and gave us such picturesque characters as Ichabod Crane and Rip Van Winkle. The Sketch Book, containing the first distinctively literary essays in America, won for Irving the respect of numerous European critics. This opening essay from his work reveals both Irving's loyalty to America and his recognition of European culture.

I WAS always fond of visiting new scenes and observing strange characters and manners. Even when a mere child I began my travels and made many tours of discovery into foreign parts and unknown regions of my native city, to the frequent alarm of my parents and the emolument of the town crier. As I grew into boyhood, I extended the range of my observations. My holiday afternoons were spent in rambles about the surrounding country. I made myself familiar with all its places famous in history or fable. I knew every spot where a murder or robbery had been committed or a ghost seen. I visited the neighboring villages and added greatly to my stock of knowledge by noting their habits and customs and conversing with their sages and great men. I even journeyed one long summer's day to the summit of the most distant hill, whence I stretched my eye over many a mile of *terra incognita*[1] and was astonished to find how vast a globe I inhabited.

This rambling propensity strengthened with my years. Books of voyages and travels became my passion, and in devouring their contents, I neglected the regular exercises of the school. How wistfully would I wander about the pierheads in fine weather and watch the parting ships bound to distant climes—with what longing eyes would I gaze after their lessening sails and waft myself in imagination to the ends of the earth!

Further reading and thinking, though they brought this vague inclination into more reasonable bounds, only served to make it more decided. I visited various parts of my own country; and had I been merely a lover of fine scenery, I should have felt little desire to seek elsewhere its gratification; for on no country have the charms of nature been more prodigally lavished. Her mighty lakes, like oceans of liquid silver; her mountains, with their bright aerial tints; her valleys, teeming with wild fertility; her tremendous cataracts, thundering in their solitudes; her boundless plains, waving with spontaneous verdure; her broad, deep rivers, rolling in solemn silence to the ocean; her trackless forests, where vegetation puts forth all its magnificence; her skies kindling with the magic of summer clouds and glorious sunshine—no, never need an American look beyond his own country for the sublime and beautiful of natural scenery.

But Europe held forth the charms of storied and poetical association. There were to be seen the masterpieces of art, the refinements of highly-cultivated society, the quaint peculiarities of ancient and local custom. My native country was full of youthful promise; Europe was rich in the accumulated treasures of age. Her very ruins told the history of times gone by, and every moldering stone was a chronicle. I longed to wander over the scenes of renowned achievement, to tread, as it were, in the footsteps of antiquity, to loiter about the ruined castle,

[1] *terra incognita*, unexplored country.

to meditate on the falling tower—to escape, in short, from the commonplace realities of the present and lose myself among the shadowy grandeurs of the past.

I had, beside all this, an earnest desire to see the great men of the earth. We have, it is true, our great men in America; not a city but has an ample share of them. I have mingled among them in my time and been almost withered by the shade into which they cast me; for there is nothing so baleful[2] to a small man as the shade of a great one, particularly the great man of a city. But I was anxious to see the great men of Europe; for I had read in the works of various philosophers that all animals degenerated in America, and man among the number. A great man of Europe, thought I, must therefore be as superior to a great man of America as a peak of the Alps to a highland of the Hudson; and in this idea I was confirmed by observing the comparative importance and swelling magnitude of many English travelers among us, who, I was assured, were very little people in their own country. I will visit this land of wonders, thought I, and see the gigantic race from which I am degenerated.

It has been either my good or evil lot to have my roving passion gratified. I have wandered through different countries and witnessed many of the shifting scenes of life. I cannot say that I have studied them with the eye of a philosopher but rather with the sauntering gaze with which humble lovers of the picturesque stroll from the window of one print shop to another, caught sometimes by the delineations of beauty, sometimes by the distortions of caricature, and sometimes by the loveliness of landscape. As it is the fashion for modern tourists to travel pencil in hand and bring home their portfolios filled with sketches, I am disposed to get up a few for the entertainment of my friends. When, however I look over the hints and memorandums I have taken down for the purpose, my heart almost fails me at finding how my idle humor has led me aside from the great objects studied by every regular traveler who would make a book. I fear I shall give equal disappointment with an unlucky landscape painter who had traveled on the continent but, following the bent of his vagrant inclination, had sketched in nooks and corners and by-places. His sketchbook was accordingly crowned with cottages and landscapes and obscure ruins; but he had neglected to paint St. Peter's or the Coliseum, the cascade of Terni[3] or the bay of Naples, and had not a single glacier or volcano in his whole collection.

VIEWING THE AUTHOR'S IDEAS

1. How did Irving's boyhood rambles arouse a romantic interest in the legendary past of America; in strange, faraway places? What influence had books in further stimulating this interest? Which selections in *The Sketch Book* grew out of these experiences?

2. In what passages does the attitude of English travelers in America provoke Irving's irony and satire?

3. Where does Irving show the romantic trait of interest in the wild aspects of natural scenery? Where does he show the romantic attitude toward Europe's medieval past?

4. In what way has American scenery changed since Irving's day? What modern invention frequently replaces the portfolio drawings of earlier tourists?

5. Show how the contents of Irving's notebook reveal the author's interest in romanticized history rather than in scholarly historical work.

EVALUATING HIS MANNER OF EXPRESSION

1. How does the introductory quotation explain Irving's reasons for turning to European themes? How is his purpose expressed in the last paragraph of the essay?

2. Point out examples of the genial and elusive humor for which Irving was noted.

3. Account for the effectiveness of the paragraphs in which the author describes the glories of America and the storied charms of Europe.

4. The romanticist had a sentimental interest in the humble and obscure; the classicist preferred the formal and imposing. How does Irving contrast these two attitudes in the last sentence?

5. To what extent does Irving succeed in escaping from the "commonplace realities" in his work?

6. What qualities of Irving's style do you recognize in this selection?

---

2 *baleful*, painful.

3 *Terni*, a town in northern Italy.

Thanatopsis[1]

William Cullen Bryant

When Bryant's father submitted "Thanatopsis" to the North American Review, the editor objected that no one this side of the Atlantic could have written the poem, much less a boy of seventeen.

As a meditation on death the work is a clear but incomplete view. The young writer did, however, compose a great nature poem. He describes the majesty of earth as the tomb of past generations and suggests the universality of the grave. In the ability to answer the summons unfalteringly lies the dignity of death. The author omits, however, any discussion of the supernatural aspects of life and eternity.

To him who in the love of Nature holds
 Communion with her visible forms, she speaks
A various language; for his gayer hours
She has a voice of gladness and a smile
And eloquence of beauty, and she glides   5
Into his darker musings with a mild
And healing sympathy that steals away
Their sharpness ere he is aware. When thoughts
Of the last bitter hour come like a blight
Over thy spirit, and sad images   10
Of the stern agony, and shroud, and pall,
And breathless darkness, and the narrow house,
Make thee to shudder and grow sick at heart;—
Go forth, under the open sky, and list
To Nature's teachings, while from all around—   15
Earth and her waters and the depths of air—
Comes a still voice.—Yet a few days, and thee
The all-beholding sun shall see no more
In all his course; nor yet in the cold ground
Where thy pale form was laid with many tears,   20
Nor in the embrace of ocean, shall exist
Thy image. Earth, that nourished thee, shall claim
Thy growth, to be resolved to earth again,
And, lost each human trace, surrendering up
Thine individual being, shalt thou go   25
To mix forever with the elements,
To be a brother to the insensible rock
And to the sluggish clod, which the rude swain
Turns with his share[2] and treads upon. The oak
Shall send his roots abroad and pierce thy mold. 30

Yet not to thine eternal resting place
Shalt thou retire alone, nor couldst thou wish
Couch more magnificent. Thou shalt lie down
With patriarchs of the infant world—with kings,
The powerful of the earth—the wise, the good,   35
Fair forms, and hoary seers of ages past,
All in one mighty sepulcher. The hills,
Rock-ribbed and ancient as the sun—the vales
Stretching in pensive quietness between;
The venerable woods—rivers that move   40
In majesty and the complaining brooks
That make the meadows green; and, poured round all,
Old Ocean's gray and melancholy waste—
Are but the solemn decorations all
Of the great tomb of man. The golden sun,   45
The planets, all the infinite host of heaven,
Are shining on the sad abodes of death
Through the still lapse of ages. All that tread
The globe are but a handful to the tribes
That slumber in its bosom.—Take the wings   50
Of morning, pierce the Barcan wilderness[3]
Or lose thyself in the continuous woods
Where rolls the Oregon,[4] and hears no sound
Save his own dashings—yet the dead are there;
And millions in those solitudes, since first   55
The flight of years began, have laid them down
In their last sleep—the dead reign there alone.
So shalt thou rest, and what if thou withdraw
In silence from the living, and no friend
Take note of thy departure? All that breathe   60
Will share thy destiny. The gay will laugh
When thou art gone, the solemn brood of care
Plod on, and each one as before will chase
His favorite phantom; yet all these shall leave
Their mirth and their employments and shall come 65

---

[1] *Thanatopsis*, a word formed from two Greek words, meaning "a view of death."

[2] *share*, ploughshare.

[3] *Barcan wilderness*, the desert region of North Africa. The poet here refers to the unsettled lands of the West.

[4] *Oregon*, the Columbia River in Oregon.

And make their bed with thee. As the long train
Of ages glides away, the sons of men,
The youth in life's green spring, and he who goes
In the full strength of years, matron and maid,
The speechless babe, and the gray-headed man—   70
Shall one by one be gathered to thy side
By those who in their turn shall follow them.

So live, that when thy summons comes to join
The innumerable caravan which moves
To that mysterious realm where each shall take   75
His chamber in the silent halls of death,
Thou go not, like the quarry slave at night,
Scourged to his dungeon, but, sustained and soothed
By an unfaltering trust, approach thy grave,
Like one who wraps the drapery of his couch   80
About him, and lies down to pleasant dreams.

VIEWING THE AUTHOR'S IDEAS

1. A summary of the main ideas in "Thanatopsis" may be obtained by studying the poem in seven divisions. State the thought expressed in each of the following sections: 1-8; 9-17; 18-30; 31-48; 49-57; 58-72; 73-81.

2. What central idea in the liturgy of Ash Wednesday is suggested in lines 17-30? Read *Genesis* 3:19 for an expression of this truth. Comment on the accuracy of Bryant's description

of life as "each one chasing his favorite phantom." Do you know anyone who, like Masefield, asks after life only "a quiet sleep and a sweet dream"?

3. How would you expand Bryant's "So live . . ."? State any additions or changes you would make in the content of this poem to make it a complete view rather than a partial view of death.

4. Report on the last moments of Benedict, Juliana Falconieri, and others who had especially peaceful deaths. Who is the patron of a happy death? Does the Church have a votive Mass in petition for a happy death?

5. Bryant has been called a combination of the Puritan and the romanticist. What expressions reveal Puritan austerity and deep but restrained emotion? How does Bryant show the romanticist's response to nature; his interest in the past?

EVALUATING HIS MANNER OF EXPRESSION

1. Discuss whether powerful thought or majestic expression contributes most to the excellence of Bryant's poem.

2. The opening lines and the conclusion were written ten years after the first draft of the poem. Why do critics say that the conclusion keeps the poem from being completely pagan?

3. More than a hundred years after the poem was written, "Thanatopsis" ranked third in a newspaper poll to determine America's favorite poem. How can you account for its enduring fame? Note other poems written in this period which are still universal favorites.

To a Waterfowl

William Cullen Bryant

One spring evening as young Bryant trudged towards Plainsfield, Massachusetts, the problem of choosing between the careers of law and journalism weighed upon him. He looked up to discover a symbol of his own life in the flight of a lone bird, separated from its companions yet certain of its way. In the lyric which he wrote on reaching his destination, Bryant gives impassioned expression to his faith in God's guidance of human affairs.

WHITHER, midst falling dew,
    While glow the heavens with the
       last steps of day,
Far, through their rosy depths, dost thou pursue
    Thy solitary way?

Vainly the fowler's eye   5
Might mark thy distant flight to do thee wrong,
As, darkly painted on the crimson sky,
    Thy figure floats along.

Seek'st thou the plashy brink
Of weedy lake, or marge of river wide,   10
Or where the rocking billows rise and sink
    On the chafed ocean side?

There is a Power whose care
Teaches thy way along that pathless coast—
The desert and illimitable air—   15
    Lone wandering, but not lost.

All day thy wings have fanned
At that far height the cold, thin atmosphere,
Yet stoop not, weary, to the welcome land,
    Though the dark night is near,   20

And soon that toil shall end;
Soon shalt thou find a summer home and rest
And scream among thy fellows; reeds shall bend
    Soon, o'er thy sheltered nest.

Thou'rt gone, the abyss of heaven   25
Hath swallowed up thy form; yet on my heart
Deeply has sunk the lesson thou hast given
    And shall not soon depart.

He who, from zone to zone,
Guides through the boundless sky
                thy certain flight,   30
In the long way that I must tread alone,
    Will lead my steps aright.

VIEWING THE AUTHOR'S IDEAS

1. What colorful phrases and images in the first two stanzas create the atmosphere of early twilight?

2. How does the poet describe the bird's destination and habits?

3. In the fourth and last stanzas how is the bird's flight related to the poet's problems?

EVALUATING HIS MANNER OF EXPRESSION

1. What colors predominate in the poem? How do the scenes and atmosphere furnish a background for the emotions expressed?

2. Observe the alliteration in the fourth and sixth stanzas. Find lines in which the rhythm seems suited to the bird's flight. By what means has the poet imitated the movement of the reeds in lines 23-24?

The Yellow Violet

William Cullen Bryant

In a spirit akin to that of the English Wordsworth, America's first great nature poet gives us a sensitive study of a flower. The moral note on which he ends his lyric seems to grow quite naturally out of his reflections.

WHEN beechen buds begin to swell,
    And woods the bluebird's warble know,
The yellow violet's modest bell
    Peeps from the last year's leaves below.

Ere russet fields their green resume,   5
    Sweet flower, I love, in forest bare,
To meet thee when thy faint perfume
    Alone is in the virgin air.

Of all her train, the hands of Spring
    First plant thee in the watery mold,   10
And I have seen thee blossoming
    Beside the snowbank's edges cold.

The parent sun who bade thee view
    Pale skies, and chilling moisture sip
Has bathed thee in his own bright hue   15
    And streaked with jet thy glowing lip.

Yet slight thy form, and low thy seat,
    And earthward bent thy gentle eye,
Unapt the passing view to meet
    When loftier flowers are flaunting nigh.   20

Oft, in the sunless April day
    Thy early smile has stayed my walk;
But midst the gorgeous blooms of May
    I passed thee on thy humble stalk.

So they who climb to wealth forget   25
    The friends in darker fortunes tried.
I copied them—but I regret
    That I should ape the ways of pride.

And when again the genial hour
　　Awakes the painted tribes[1] of light,   30
I'll not o'erlook the modest flower
　　That made the woods of April bright.

VIEWING THE AUTHOR'S IDEAS

1. In what places and at what times of the year has Bryant
found the yellow violet? Describe its color and fragrance.

2. What observations on the actions of human beings

[1] *painted tribes*, an eighteenth century conventional expression meaning flowers.

does the poet draw from his neglect of the flower? Why is
ingratitude a despised trait?

3. How does this poem illustrate Bryant's ever-recurring
theme of nature's power to heal?

EVALUATING HIS MANNER OF EXPRESSION

1. What detailed observations show that Bryant is conscious,
not only of the yellow violet, but of nature's many-sided life?

2. Find instances of alliteration. Explain the meaning of "the
hands of Spring"; "violet's modest bell"; "russet fields"; "thy
glowing lip"; "painted tribes"; "parent sun."

Hymn of the City

William Cullen Bryant

*In his early poetry Bryant found tranquillity when
contemplating nature in solitude. Later his active
editorial experiences in New York City led him to listen
for God's voice in the murmur of the throng and to find
His Spirit at work in the restless surging through city
streets.*

Nᴏᴛ in the solitude
　　Alone may man commune with Heaven,
　　　　or see
　　Only in savage wood
And sunny vale the present Deity;
　　Or only hear His voice   5
Where the winds whisper and the waves rejoice.

　　Even here do I behold
Thy steps, Almighty!—here, amidst the crowd
　　Through the great city rolled
With everlasting murmur deep and loud,   10
　　Choking the ways that wind
'Mongst the proud piles, the work of human kind.

　　Thy golden sunshine comes
From the round heaven and on their dwellings lies
　　And lights their inner homes;   15
For them Thou fill'st with air the unbounded skies

　　And givest them the stores
Of ocean and the harvests of its shores.

　　Thy Spirit is around,
Quickening the restless mass that sweeps along;   20
　　And this eternal sound—
Voices and footfalls of the numberless throng—
　　Like the resounding sea
Or like the rainy tempest, speaks of Thee.

　　And when the hours of rest   25
Come, like a calm upon the mid-sea brine,
　　Hushing its billowy breast—
The quiet of that moment too is thine;
　　It breathes of Him who keeps
The vast and helpless city while it sleeps.

VIEWING THE AUTHOR'S IDEAS

1. In what aspects of nature had Bryant first sought God?
What broader view had he now attained? What contrast is
implied in the second stanza?

2. What gifts of God does the poet find in the city? What
sounds in metropolitan life speak of the Creator? To what
sounds in nature are these overtones compared? What part of
the day is like the ocean calm? How does that moment also
suggest God's presence?

3. By what means are men "quickened by the Spirit"? Report on the growth of study clubs as a means of furthering awareness of spiritual things.

How does this lyric exemplify the truth that the poet looks upon the same scene as the ordinary person but sees more?

The Echo and the Lover

John Milton Harney

In this poem Echo is an elusive nymph, who always manages to have the last word. By a clever twist, her response offers a tantalizing answer to an impatient lover, who seeks information concerning the subtle ways of winning his beloved.

Lover: Echo! mysterious nymph, declare
Of what you're made, and what you are—
Echo: "Air!"

Lover: 'Mid airy cliffs, and places high,
Sweet Echo! listening, love, you lie—
Echo: "You lie!"

Lover: You but resuscitate dead sounds—
Hark! how my voice revives, resounds!
Echo: "Zounds!"

Lover: I'll question you before I go—
Come, answer me more apropos!
Echo: "Poh! poh!"

Lover: Tell me, fair nymph, if e'er you saw
So sweet a girl as Phoebe Shaw!
Echo: "Pshaw!"

Lover: Say, what will win that frisking coney
Into the toils of matrimony!
Echo: "Money!"

Lover: Has Phoebe not a heavenly brow?
Is it not white as pearl — as snow?
Echo: ". . .No!"

Lover: Her eyes! Was ever such a pair?
Are the stars brighter than they are?
Echo: "They are!"

Lover: Echo, you lie, but you can't deceive me;
Her eyes eclipse the stars, believe me—
Echo: "Leave me!"

Lover: But come, you saucy, pert romancer,
Who is as fair as Phoebe? Answer.
Echo: "Ann, sir!"

What is the theme of the poem? Point out the use of word play in the lyric.

The American Flag

Charles Constantine Pise

In the nineteenth century the allegiance of a Catholic to his Church was frequently misunderstood. Prejudiced and misinformed citizens harbored the idea that the Catholic's submission to papal teachings in matters of faith and morals interfered with fidelity to his country.

The shadow which this unjust attitude cast on Catholics in public life is reflected in Father Pise's lyric. An ardent patriot and at one time a chaplain of the United States Senate, the priest reaffirmed his love of God and country in a poem that spoke for thousands of American Catholics.

They say I do not love thee,
 Flag of my native land,
Whose meteor folds above me
 To the free breeze expand,
Thy broad stripes proudly streaming, 5
And thy stars so brightly gleaming.

They say I would forsake thee,
 Should some dark crisis lower;
That, recreant, I should make thee
 Crouch to some foreign power; 10
Seduced by license ample,
On thee, blest flag, to trample!

They say that bolts of thunder
 Cast in the forge of Rome[1]
May rise and bring thee under, 15
 Flag of my native home,
And with one blow dissever
My heart from thee forever.

False are the words they utter,
 Ungenerous their brand; 20
And rash the oaths they mutter,
 Flag of my native land;
Whilst still in hope above me
Thou wavest—and I love thee!

God is my love's first duty, 25
 To whose eternal Name
Be praise for all thy beauty,
 Thy grandeur and thy fame;
But ever have I reckoned
Thine, native flag, my second. 30

Woe to the foe or stranger
 Whose sacrilegious hand
Would touch thee or endanger,
 Flag of my native land!
Though some would fain discard thee, 35
Mine should be raised to guard thee.

Then wave, thou first of banners,
 And in thy gentle shade,
Beliefs, opinions, manners,
 Promiscuously be laid; 40
And there all discord ended,
Our hearts and souls be blended.

Stream on, stream on before us,
 Thou labarum[2] of light,
While in our generous chorus 45
 Our vows to thee we plight;
Unfaithful to thee—never!
My native land forever!

VIEWING THE AUTHOR'S IDEAS

1. Who are the persons referred to in the first line as "they"? Does intolerance or lack of correct information more often cause the Church to be misunderstood? Discuss.

2. What prejudiced idea that crops up in America from time to time is mentioned in the second and third stanzas? What type of interest does the Pope have in the problems of nations?

3. To whom does the poet say we owe first allegiance? Does this fact in any way interfere with patriotism? How does the Catholic religion in itself foster love of country? What is done in Catholic schools to further patriotic efforts?

4. Why is patriotism based on religion more enduring than loyalty founded on sentiment? Contrast attitudes towards country in a democracy with those held in a totalitarian state.

5. What promise does the poet make to defend the flag? Is this attitude typical of a good Catholic? In what sense can patriotism unite all classes and all religions?

EVALUATING HIS MANNER OF EXPRESSION

1. What is the historical value of the poem?

2. List the various emotions here portrayed. In what lines do you get the most intense feeling? What is the emotional value of the refrain?

---

[1] *Rome,* the Catholic Church.

[2] *labarum,* the standard adopted by Constantine after his conversion to Christianity. It bore a monogram of the first two letters (XP) of the name of Christ in the Greek form.

A Westerly View of the Colleges in Cambridge, New England, by Paul Revere

THE NEW ENGLAND RENAISSANCE

With the acquisition between 1845 and 1848 of Texas, Oregon, California, and the Southwest, America extended her broad arms from the Atlantic to the Pacific. Amid this expansion the democratic ideal grew apace. Upon the inauguration of the frontiersman Andrew Jackson, the people seemed at last to have come into their own. From a Europe of famines and unsuccessful revolutions streamed immigrants to swell the national population. Along the waterways and across the prairies settlers trekked westward in search of new wealth.

The astounding growth of the new nation was to reveal both virtues and vices in American life. Advancing industry brought the evils of child labor, sweatshops, and monopolies; prejudices of various kinds took deep root; in many instances pioneer individualism degenerated into greed and materialism; scientific development over-emphasized the importance of sense experience; material gains were frequently accompanied by a spiritual loss.

In this world of growth and change New England maintained its cultural dominance with difficulty. Already the theocratic structure of Puritan society had begun to totter; before the end of the century that structure, once so formidable and imposing, was to lie in ruins. The downfall of Puritan society is to be accounted for by its own inherent weakness. It had proposed a way of life so at variance with normal human instincts and so in opposition to the dictates of reason that the threat of rebellion was always present. From the beginning there had been an impassable breach between Puritan doctrine and Puritan practice. And now, from the sons and grandsons of Puritan divines, was to come the attack on the doctrine itself.

The intellectual effort involved in the attack on Puritanism was responsible for the cultural reawakening of New England. First there came those who claimed that reason was the only sure guide in religious matters, and they rejected Christianity outright. Then came the Universalists, who modified Puritan thought radically when they claimed that God's grace would eventually save all men, and blithely dispensed with the necessity of hell. The Unitarians went a step further and denied the reality of sin and redemption. They thought that man was quite capable of reaching perfection through his own unaided efforts. Not needing a redeemer, they dismissed the Second Person of the Trinity; not needing grace, they dismissed the Third Person of the Trinity. It is for this reason that they were called Unitarians.

Christian beliefs decline

The religious movement which touched literature most closely, however, was transcendentalism. It is an offshoot of Unitarianism and differs from it by its refusal to accept the distinction between God and creatures. The goodness of man soon became the divinity of man; all creation, men and things, were but aspects of the Divine Mind. This merging of God and His creation into a single reality is called *pantheism*, which derives from a Greek word meaning "everything (is) God." From the point of view of logic, it would seem that if everything is God, there is no God, for there is no Superior Being to whom we owe allegiance. Logically, then, the tendency of pantheism is in the direction of atheism, or the frank denial of God. A confused religious idealism prevented the transcendentalists from taking this logical step. In this they were peculiarly consistent, for they affected a contempt for logic as a means of approaching truth.

It must not be thought that these onslaughts against Puritan thought were wholly successful. Indeed, so ingrained was the Puritan habit of life that its traces are still perceptible in American folkways. The significant point about these attacks is that they prepared the way for a disbelief in Protestant Christianity among a group of people who had been its most ardent supporters. Others were to follow their example.

New England leads again

It was between the years 1835 to 1860 that the New England States recovered the intellectual leadership lost to them since the days of Jonathan Edwards. In contrast to the sudden booms and uncertain wealth of the western pioneers, the New Englanders had enjoyed a long and seasoned prosperity. They now had the leisure to pursue their cultural aspirations. The renewal of creative energy in this region has been called the New England Renaissance.

It must not be thought, however, that this intellectual reawakening was a full-fledged New England product. It was the eruption in American life of German Romanticism, a movement in rebellion against the rationalism and materialism which had dominated eighteenth-century thought. Cultural traffic between New England and Germany was brisk, and most Harvard professors made dutiful pilgrimage to the German universities. While transcendentalism, from the purely religious side, must be viewed as a modification of Unitarianism, in its broader aspects it must be seen as the New England contribution to an almost world-wide philosophic revolution. Transcendentalism is both less original and less provincial than is usually thought.

The first to give impetus to American transcendentalism was the Unitarian minister, William Ellery Channing. Like other Unitarians, Channing rejected the Calvinistic doctrine that man is totally depraved in favor of the doctrine that man is naturally good and capable of unlimited perfection. By teaching the doctrine of unlimited natural progress for man and society, he prepared the way for a further rejection of religious doctrine.

Among the Unitarians was a young minister, Ralph Waldo Emerson, who felt the necessity of going beyond Channing in his departure from traditional religion. He resigned his ministry and, with a group of other liberal thinkers, formed the Transcendental Club. Though these men differed greatly among themselves and could agree on no single system of thought, all were nevertheless largely influenced by German ideas as they drifted down to them directly or through interpreters and men of letters.

Intuition is new guide

The most immediate force behind their thought, and especially Emerson's, was the English poet Coleridge, whose *Aids to Reflection* had been brought out in 1829 by President Marsh of the University of Vermont. Behind Coleridge's thought lay the gigantic shadow of Schelling, the cloudy German idealist. The main tenets of transcendental thought seem to be the following: (1) sense knowledge is unreliable; (2) all reality is, in the long run, spiritual; (3) the only apt instrument for getting in touch with the world outside of one's self is the mind; (4) by the mind, however, they do not understand the reasoning process, which is also unreliable, but a special faculty which puts them *immediately* in touch with truth without any other aid or contact; (5) all reality is one, which, when capitalized, (One) is frequently called God or the Oversoul; (6) there is no distinction between God, men, and things, for they are all participants of the One. The term *transcendentalism* was later to be given to any systems of beliefs which stressed inspiration or intuition, as a method of arriving at truth.

Emphasis is on spirit

From a practical viewpoint, American transcendentalism was an attempt to restore spiritual values through a certain contempt for material reality. It escaped from being a thing of cloudland only through Yankee practicality and Puritan moral earnestness. Through reliance on the Oversoul, the transcendentalists hoped to reshape the life around them and thereby to manufacture a better world. Intensely serious, they felt the responsibility to fit themselves for their reforming task by withdrawing from the world from time to time to receive messages from the Oversoul. Social experiments

Brook Farm, a Haven for Transcendentalists

were entered upon with enthusiasm. At Brook Farm George Ripley encouraged transcendentalists to live a common life in the interests of plain living and high thinking. Bronson Alcott, at Fruitlands, added the further incentive of self-denial. And, solitary and aloof, Henry David Thoreau went his own individualistic way and withdrew to his hut near Walden Pond "to confront the essential facts of life."

Ralph Waldo Emerson

Behind all the high thinking and plain living, behind all the variations of social experiment, and behind all the robust literary activity of the transcendentalist brethren, was the prophetic figure of Ralph Waldo Emerson. For two generations Emerson inspired the American mind.

RALPH WALDO EMERSON

In the August of 1837, in an oration called *The American Scholar* before the Phi Beta Kappa Society at Cambridge, Emerson spoke words that were strangely moving: "The scholar is that man who must take up into himself all the ability of the time, all the contributions of the past, all the hopes of the future. He must be a university of knowledges. . . . The world is nothing, the man is all; in yourself is the law of all nature; in yourself slumbers the whole of Reason; it is for you to know all; it is for you to dare all." He then went on to tell his hearers that Americans had listened too long "to the courtly muses of Europe," and he concluded with the following prophecy: "We will walk on our own feet; we will work with our own hands; we will speak with our own minds." This is the Emerson who excited Thoreau and Whitman; it is the Emerson who, whatever his contradictions and inconsistencies, called for a native literature in America.

Born in historic Concord twenty-seven years after the signing of the Declaration of Independence, Ralph Waldo Emerson (1803-1882) had a heritage of seven generations of ministers and scholars. Young Emerson was a dreamer and often in church was given to pondering the meaning of common words, such as *black* and *white,* until he reached a point in his mental musings where one word meant the same as another. At five or six years Emerson began the study of Latin, the Bible, and the English classics. He found mathematics perplexing; all his life he avoided the subject. An element that contributed much to the sharpening of the boy's mind and the development of his individuality was the influence of his aunt, Mary Moody Emerson, a woman who was a strange complex of Puritan and liberal tendencies. Coming under her influence when he was eight years old, Emerson was moved to ambitious thought and diligent study. She encouraged him to avoid the ordinary boyish pastimes and strove to acquaint his active mind with the chief thought of the day. She it was who put him on the path of his philosophic views of nature.

At the Boston Latin School Emerson's reading of Wordsworth, Coleridge, and Shelley intensified his love of nature. At Harvard the young boy, barely in his teens, occupied his time with poetry, Greek, Latin, history, philosophy. He faithfully recorded his intellectual adventures in the pages of his *Journal.* He did not care for debate and found the logical method of arriving at truth an annoying waste of time. He preferred to ponder and read, but he accepted only those views which confirmed ideas which he had already formed. He regarded the mind as a world complete in itself, the source of all truth, a radiation of the Divine Intelligence.

Emerson urges self-reliance

After teaching two years at a girls' school, Emerson decided on a lifework. Many considerations, among them the desire for renown, solitude, and an assured income, made him choose the ministry. In 1825 he entered the divinity school at Cambridge. Here he had to come to grips with the terms of his religious beliefs and to make decisions concerning them. He concluded that one's consciousness is more trustworthy than evidence or experience; that logic and reason do not lead to truth; that the only secure knowledge is that gained through intuition, the unfailing "inner light."

After several years in the ministry, Emerson resigned his position. He had found that his views no longer were in conformity with those of his church. Shortly after his resignation Emerson sailed for Europe to visit Wordsworth, Coleridge, and Carlyle. He wished to compare his own philosophic views with those of the writers whose works he had read. A conversation with Carlyle convinced Emerson that he was right in his own beliefs, and he was happy to learn that others shared his pantheistic views. He returned to America resolved to set forth his thoughts for the benefit of his fellow Americans. He wished to convert New England, to make a ministry of the new gospel, and to deliver to all Americans the tablets of his commandments, "Judge for yourself," "Obey yourself," "Reverence thyself," "Cultivate self-reliance."

Maxims are inconsistent

We have seen the main ideas of Emerson's philosophy in the discussion of transcendentalism. In lectures and essays he spoke and wrote with the assurance of prophecy. It is impossible to reduce his thought to a logical sequence, but it must be remembered that contradictions did not bother Emerson, for opposition of ideas was the very stuff of his method. Whitman merely echoes the master when he writes:

"Do I contradict myself?

Very well then I contradict myself . . ."

When carried to its logical conclusion, Emerson's philosophy denies, among other things, God as a Person distinct from His creation, the essential differences between objects, the testimony of the senses, the reliability of reason, and the existence of moral evil. His audience was flattered by his references to their godlike possibilities, the sanctity of inner urges, a future bursting with grandiose achievement, the Messianic role of America as the leader of the nations. It is Emerson's optimism, his buoyancy, his prophetic sense of conviction which triumphed; the intricate philosophic system which was meant to support these moods has been ignored.

Emerson's essays are practically revisions of his lectures. In composing them, he leafed through his journals or lyceum lectures, picking out sentences that seemed to apply to his topic. His writings are really sermons inlaid with the errors of his philosophic system. Emerson firmly believed that literature was a branch of religion; the minister in him was never completely defrocked. Emerson's prose style is involved and incoherent, but the most boring of paragraphs is likely to be illuminated with an epigram of startling power and precision. Highly stimulating, such epigrams find their way time and time again into the speeches and writings of other men. Emerson is one of the most quoted writers in world literature. His chief prose writings are *Nature* (1837), *Essays* (1841), *Essays, Second Series* (1844), *Representative Men* (1850), and *English Traits* (1856).

For the most part Emerson's verse serves the same teaching function as his prose. It is the vehicle for the expression of his favorite ideas. There is a remarkable resemblance between his quatrains and those of Emily Dickinson. Epigrammatic and concise, they reveal a freshness of imagery altogether without parallel in more highly advertised poets of his day.

The Sage of Concord lived on to assist at the obsequies of several who had been his youthful disciples. His declining years, however, were marked with an almost complete failure of memory. Death made its quiet entry in 1882, when Emerson was in his seventy-ninth year. Of his inspirational force and influence there can be no doubt. If, after the intervention of two world wars, his thought appears to be superficial, it is largely because, as a modern English poet has expressed it, he lacked "the Vision of Evil." To probe the vision of evil was the task of Hawthorne and Melville. Emerson is remembered today as a representative figure of the culture of his times.

HENRY DAVID THOREAU

While Emerson looked upon nature's beauty from the open windows of his study, Henry David Thoreau (1817-1862) was cutting logs to build a hut at Walden Pond. In the midst of nature he intended to lead a life of simplicity, free from material concerns; there he could be

Henry David Thoreau

alone with his soul, view society from a serene distance, commune with nature, and delight in its obedience to the absolute laws which govern all existence.

Unlike many of his literary contemporaries, Thoreau did not come from a wealthy or distinguished family. His father was a pencilmaker. Although young Thoreau had earned his degree from Harvard in 1833, he refused formal graduation because he was unwilling to pay a fee for his diploma. Always intent on securing his rights as an individual, he argued that he possessed an education. What need had he of a diploma to show the world? For two years Thoreau lived with the Emersons. He likewise spent some time with the family of Orestes Brownson. At one time he joined his father in the manufacture of pencils. When he had succeeded in making the perfect pencil, however, he considered that he would waste his time if he remained longer in this trade. He preferred to work as a carpenter or gardener only a few weeks each year, just long enough to obtain money for the bare necessities of life. The rest of his time he read, wrote, or enjoyed nature. During the two years and two months which he spent at Walden Pond, near Concord, he reduced life to its simplest terms.

Thoreau deplored a growing economic system in which men gave the best years of their life to produce objects which he considered trinkets. He believed that civilization creates artificial needs, that luxuries become necessities, that men hurry forward in a feverish existence until they lose all purpose in life. He was convinced that formalism had bogged down the institutions of church and state into a mire from which no beauty could come forth. Thoreau dispensed with a great many comforts men usually consider necessary and separated himself from society and religious organizations. In doing so he hoped to show men that they were enslaved by the conventions of society, by the faulty operation of government, and by a religion which could no longer nourish their spiritual life.

Is critic of social institutions

As a critic of social institutions, Thoreau was so filled with a realization of existing evils that he was unable to see any good in the institutions themselves. Instead of trying to improve men's organizations for working together in harmony, he abandoned these institutions because of their faults. In disdaining society, he failed to take into account the social nature of man, which makes association with his fellows necessary for the majority of individuals. Self-improvement was Thoreau's highest aim. For a time he looked upon the abolition of slavery as a great cause. When John Brown was hanged, Thoreau lost all trust in human nature. In his religious views he was equally nearsighted. Seeing flaws in Calvinism, he condemned all religion and looked for no supernatural aid in his search for truth. Walden itself was an unsuccessful experiment, for nature could not give Thoreau the Final Good which he sought.

In his voluminous diaries which constitute fourteen books, Thoreau left a record of his life, his observations of nature, and his general outlook on life. Most important among his works are his essays "Walking" and "Civil Disobedience" and the books, *A Week on the Concord and Merrimack Rivers* (1849) and *Walden* (1854). In passages of lovely, often lucid prose he conveys to his readers his great delight in nature, his high faith in the undeveloped powers of the human spirit, and his scorn for a materialistic age.

Nathaniel Hawthorne

NATHANIEL HAWTHORNE

Until he was fifty, Nathaniel Hawthorne (1804-1864) never went farther from his native New England than Niagara Falls. "New England," he once said, "is quite as large a lump of earth as my heart can readily take in." Hawthorne had been born and reared at Salem, Massachusetts, at a time when the town was noted for the retired, secluded lives of its inhabitants. The gloomy Hawthorne home was filled with memories of sterner days. The author came of stock that had lived in New England since 1630 and numbered among his ancestors one of the judges in the Salem witchcraft trials. When Hawthorne was four, his father died, and thereafter his mother lived almost exclusively to herself, taking her meals alone. Hawthorne and his sisters likewise kept to their own rooms. Even in the Maine lake country, where young Hawthorne spent part of his boyhood, he seems to have had no companions but grew more surely into the habit of solitude. Books were his closest friends, and he lived an inner life of intense thought that left an indelible mark on all his writings.

After four years at Bowdoin College, where he made a lifelong friend in the future president, Franklin Pierce, and was a classmate of Longfellow, Hawthorne returned home to dwell apart from society for twelve years. The laborious hours he spent at writing were on the whole a period of preparation, for he burned much more than he published. In 1837 with the publication of *Twice-Told Tales* and the beginning of his interest in Sophia Peabody, his future wife, he emerged from seclusion. In order to earn enough money to enable him to marry, he took a position for a time at the Boston Customhouse.

A year spent at Brook Farm, Massachusetts, Ripley's transcendentalist community, convinced him that it was not as he had hoped, the place where he and Sophia could find happiness. After his marriage Hawthorne for several years made an attempt to earn his living by his pen. Financial conditions forced him to return to more remunerative work, but during a period of unemployment he completed *The Scarlet Letter*, which at last made him famous. In 1853 President Pierce sent him to Liverpool as American consul, and after resigning from the position three years later he traveled in Europe and lived in Italy and England. Upon his return home in 1860 Hawthorne's health broke, and he died four years later, leaving two romances unfinished.

Sin and its effects, theme of novels

Instead of using the story merely for the purpose of entertainment as Irving had done, or solely to achieve an intense emotional effect, Hawthorne made it an artistic means of conveying a profound moral lesson. Where Irving had told an unhurried, rambling tale, Hawthorne depicted a single dramatic situation. Although an artist in technique, he was not, like Poe, concerned with art alone. To the story he brought his deep insight into human nature and his ability to analyze character.

Hawthorne wrote short tales dealing with the history of New England, with moral truths, and with observations of life itself; he also produced longer *romances*, as he preferred to call his novels. Among his best-known tales are "The Gray Champion," "The Birthmark," "Rappaccini's Daughter," "Ethan Brand," and "The Ambitious Guest." His tales are collected under the titles: *Twice-Told Tales* (1837), *Twice-Told Tales: Second Series* (1842), *Mosses from an Old Manse* (1846), and *The Snow Image* (1851).

In his longer tales Hawthorne displays the same high craftsmanship and concern with spiritual reality which characterizes his stories. He continued to call his long tales romances, pointing out that the novel portrays the ordinary course of events in man's life while his romances presented truth under unusual and sometimes idealized circumstances.

The most popular of Hawthorne's romances are his masterpiece, *The Scarlet Letter* (1850), *The House of Seven*

Herman Melville

Gables (1851), and *The Marble Faun* (1860). In each of these narratives the dominant interest is the revelation of the effect of sin upon human character. Hawthorne is at his best in presenting the human soul gripped in a moral crisis. In beautiful prose that borrows something of the rhythm of solemn music, he conveys a sense of the profound mystery of life touched with tragedy. He is a moralist, it is true, but he is primarily an artist.

HERMAN MELVILLE

In 1846 people in New York who knew Herman Melville (1819-1891) would point him out to their friends as "the man who had lived with the cannibals." Melville's childhood had been spent in the comfort and ease of a pleasant New York home. Bankruptcy and the death of his father, however, left the family almost destitute, and the boy was forced to leave school and work hard at many uncongenial occupations. At seventeen he shipped as cabin boy on a sailboat bound for Liverpool. The urge of the sea entered his soul and eventually sent him around the world. On a later voyage in the equatorial Pacific, Melville and a companion escaped from a brutal sea captain, were held prisoners by the friendly cannibal Typees, and after breaking away from their captors, wandered among the Pacific Islands with further escapades. On his return home after nearly four years' absence Melville wrote his adventures in books that for a time made him famous. When he turned to a more serious type of work, however, and published his masterpiece, *Moby Dick,* the book was not favorably received.

Melville's readers were not prepared for the dark colors he spread upon his canvas. His popularity waned until at last he was forced to earn his living by working at the New York Customhouse. Although he continued to produce poetry and shorter novels up to the time of his death, his books found no favor with his contemporaries.

Adventures on board a whaling vessel, among cannibals in the South Sea Islands, and on a frigate in the United States Navy provided Herman Melville with subject matter and with a philosophy of life out of which to fashion literature of lasting merit. Equipped by nature with an extraordinary gift of storytelling, Melville possessed a love for fine literary craftsmanship. He should have met with success had he not been tossed about by the chaos of unrest he sensed in the world at large and within his own soul as well.

Moby Dick, *a great sea story*

Melville had learned through bitter personal experience that all things do not, as the transcendentalists would have had one believe, resolve themselves in good. Evil was not merely seeming reality; evil was a tremendous force in the world of nature and in the heart of man. Beneath the serenity of a sunlit sea, swam Moby Dick, a menace to the well-being of whaling men. Underneath the apparent calm of a human soul, surged inclinations and motives that could bring untold suffering into the lives of men. Melville had experienced the latent cruelty of nature and of man at first hand. He traced it to its source in original sin and, realizing its inevitability, allowed it to drive him to a cynical bitterness.

Melville explores the nature of evil

In 1851 appeared Melville's masterpiece, *Moby Dick,* the saga of stalwart men who went down to the sea a-whaling. No better tale of whales and whaling has ever been written. *Moby Dick,* however, is more than a tale of adventure; it is an exploration into the nature of ever-present evil as well. Captain Ahab, fanatical in his zeal to come to grips with the evil latent behind the whiteness of the monstrous white whale, himself becomes evil in his frenzy. Casting aside all reliance on any beneficent power, Ahab becomes the victim of his own intellectual pride and blasphemes his Creator. The symbolism in the book is as important as the breathless action and the detailed accounts of the whaler's life.

It was not until his centenary in 1919 that Melville gained recognition. The pessimistic postwar world could understand his use of shadow because it had experienced the force of the powers of evil. Today Melville holds his rightful place as an excellent prose stylist and as a masterful writer of the sea. *Moby Dick* is America's most skillful allegory on the problem of evil.

HENRY WADSWORTH LONGFELLOW

While searching for spiritual reality, New England writers took care lest anything in material reality offend their readers. Conscious of America's cultural inadequacy, they sought to polish the manners and the writings of their time. Eager to establish an intellectual and social tradition in America, men like Holmes deplored the self-made man. In contrast they admired the man who had tumbled about in a well-stocked library as a boy and had grown up to inherit family portraits and valuable plates. Lowell and Longfellow by study, by translation, and by teaching brought to America the literary culture, not only of England, but also of all Europe. In doing so, they added foreign influences to native movements. The distinguished writers of New England belonged to a level of society which Oliver Wendell Holmes humorously called the *Brahmins.* The word was taken from the name of the priestly caste among the Hindus. The term has survived in literary history to indicate the aristocratic and cultural characteristics which these writers exhibit.

Henry Wadsworth Longfellow opened a broad and quiet mind to the sunshine of many lands and times; his poetry reflected the gentler moods of the romantic movement, while its storms passed him by. The most invigorating forces at work in his poetry came to him through history and through foreign languages. History was all about him. Indians, Pilgrim Fathers, colonial heroes still walked abroad in his imagination. How could they help it when he lived in the Craigie House, where

© B. F. Williamson

Longfellow's Sketch of the Famous
"Spreading Chestnut Tree"

Washington had lived before him? As for languages, his professorships at Bowdoin and at Harvard gave him leisurely travels in Europe and an easy familiarity with a half dozen literatures.

So it happened that as Longfellow grew older, his fame spread over two continents. Kings sent him gifts in recognition of his learning; workmen clasped his hand in the street to thank him for writing "A Psalm of Life"; men of letters spent the evenings at his Dante Club, where he read his verse aloud. He had something to say to all and could say it with unfailing charm.

Longfellow's verses are musical and his expression is lucid. His appeal to the heart and to moral sentiment gives his poetry an old-fashioned flavor today. But his careless imagery offends discriminating readers. Yet Longfellow remains the favorite singer of the common man. "A Psalm of Life," "Excelsior," and "The Builders" have carried moral inspiration to many. "The Children's Hour," "The Village Blacksmith," and "The Day Is Done" have provided pleasant oases in the desert of grade-school readers for too long to be lightly passed over. His best lyrics are the sonnets in the series "Divina Commedia," which he wrote while he was translating Dante's *Divine Comedy*.

Longfellow worked in dramatic poetry also, planning a trilogy to be called *Christus: A Mystery*. This poetic drama was to portray the spirit of Christianity as it had appeared in the primitive church, during the Middle Ages, and in Puritan New England. The best section is *The Golden Legend* (1851), which treats of the Middle Ages.

Narrative poems display mastery

It was in the realm of narrative poetry, however, that Longfellow produced his best work. Using the literary ballad and the metrical romance, he exhibited a swift, direct narrative power that has never lost its charm. "The Skeleton in Armor," "The Wreck of the Hesperus," and "Paul Revere's Ride" are familiar examples of his shorter narrative poems. *Evangeline* (1847), *The Song of Hiawatha* (1855), and *The Courtship of Miles Standish* (1858) use material out of American history in the creation of national idylls. From these evolve characters that have become a part of the country's literary heritage. Longfellow also gave to American literature the legends of many European lands. He was, in the finest sense of the word, a translator, having rendered into English a thick volume of *Poets and Poetry of Europe*.

Longfellow was the first American Protestant author to seek inspiration in Catholic life and tradition. However, he readily places tales sympathetic to Catholicism beside stories with hostile implications. The luster of the Ages of Faith glowed warmly to his romantic vision, but the Church with her uncompromising doctrines appeared an enemy of the intellectual freedom he advocated. Overlooking the fact that love of God rests on faith, he dreamed of a universal religion which would merge all dogmas and emphasize only practical charity.

Those who are willing to scour the vast storehouse of Longfellow's output of verse will undoubtedly come upon lyrics of fresh and lasting beauty. More than most poets, however, Longfellow needs to be re-edited and reassessed. In the meantime he remains for most readers of poetry "the fallen prince of popularity." The triumphs which cannot be taken from him are his creative vigor, his mastery of metrical forms, and his extraordinary gift of verse translation.

JAMES RUSSELL LOWELL

Not far from Craigie House, Longfellow's home in Cambridge, stands Elmwood, where another poet and scholar of the same period lived. After graduation from Harvard, James Russell Lowell (1819-1891) practiced law. Finding himself unsuited for this profession, he devoted his time to writing. In 1844 he married Maria

A Scene from "The Courtin'," a Poem by James Russell Lowell

White, herself a talented author, and the two devoted their youthful energies to the cause of abolition and various other reforms. Eventually Lowell became a Harvard professor, first editor of the *Atlantic Monthly*, minister to England and Spain, fireside critic of all things human, and general man of letters whose thoughts, caustic, humorous, meditative and always influential, reached the world largely through essays. In the midst of all these duties he also found time to write poetry.

His poetic range is wide and his expression flexible. A deep regard for the stateliness of poetry caused Lowell to use the ode form more than most American poets. The carved and ample stanzas of an ode bestowed a title of nobility on the common dandelion. Yet he knew better than to strain a simple theme. When it came to "The Courtin'," he chose dialect, wit, and a rough-and-tumble meter to carry the warmth of Huldy's kitchen and to tell of what happened there.

As a poet Lowell never reached the heights. Although he warned others against the dangers of didacticism and believed that pleasure was the legitimate end of poetry, he also held that the poet's duty was to elevate the mind of man. As a result, his own verse is filled with empty rhetoric and treats old themes in a verse style that has

little to recommend it beyond occasional descriptive beauty. The truth is that Lowell had a poor ear for the more delicate musical qualities of verse. Even the popular "Vision of Sir Launfal" is imitative of Tennyson; and its nobility of theme is not sufficient to redeem it from being a merely average performance.

Scholar and critic

Lowell was among the last of the Brahmins and shared their virtues and shortcomings. Essentially conservative, he nevertheless kept his feet firmly on the earth, was fond of social intercourse, and could boast of a solid learning. A vigorous critic, he wanted a native American literature, although his regional prejudice made him distrustful of southern writers. *A Fable for Critics*, written in a jogging, unpretentious meter, presents a panorama of American writers as they appeared in the middle of the century to a sensitive and well-read man of letters. The *Biglow Papers*, first written out of his hatred of the imperialism of the Mexican War, is a grotesque but diverting mixture of homely satire, moral aphorisms, Yankee dialect, and literary criticism.

By his contemporaries Lowell was recognized as the most representative man of letters in America. While

James Russell Lowell

not achieving mastery in prose or verse, he lived a full and cultured life and generously used his pen in the service of important social and political issues. Lowell filled many posts in his lifetime, acting in the capacity of poet, editor, lecturer, professor, critic, diplomat, reformer, and gentleman-scholar. Next to Longfellow, no one did more than he to introduce into America the riches of European culture. His chief value lies in the fact that he demonstrated in his own life the value of a cultured heritage.

OLIVER WENDELL HOLMES

Something of the eighteenth-century spirit of urbanity seems to have been infused into Oliver Wendell Holmes (1809-1894), who himself admits that he was trained in the school of Alexander Pope.

Oliver Wendell Holmes was born in Cambridge, Massachusetts. After his graduation from Harvard he studied law for a brief period and then decided to become a physician. He began his ten years of private practice with the pun: "The smallest fevers gratefully received." When he was appointed professor of anatomy in the Harvard medical school, he was given the sleepy hour from one to two for his lecture, because he could be counted on to keep his students awake. One of his pupils wrote: "He enters and is greeted with a mighty shout and stamps of applause. Then silence and there

begins a charming hour of description, analysis, simple anecdote, harmless pun which clothes the dry bones with poetic imagery, and enlivens a hard, fatiguing day with humor." What Holmes did for his students for an hour, he did for the world at large throughout a long life. While retaining his position as a lecturer of anatomy, he established a literary reputation, first by his witty poetry, later with his prose.

That poetry made no pretensions. Its language was the language of conversation with the minimum of poetic device; it was made to sing by simple, swift-moving, clean-cut rhythms. If some of the tales it told tended to be trite, a masculine movement of the lines checked sentiment from becoming sentimental. Sacred themes, as in "A Mother's Secret," were handled with a reverence that was better than grandeur. Holmes moralized without apology, described nature in conventional but sincere phrases, grew indignant when necessary, and most of all he laughed. The laughter was of the kind that is shared by a friend at no one else's expense.

Oliver Wendell Holmes

Essays reveal Brahmin ideals

Holmes was nearly fifty when the familiar, conversational essays known as *The Autocrat of the Breakfast-Table* began to appear in the *Atlantic Monthly*. The autocrat, of course, is Holmes himself, and his conversations reveal his complacent acceptance of the ideals of the Brahmins as those of the best way of American life. Since the essays proved popular, Holmes continued them in *The Professor at the Breakfast-Table* (1859), *The Poet at the Breakfast-Table* (1872), and *Over the Teacups* (1891). It fell to Holmes's lot to be the last leaf on the tree of the New England school of writers. He lived to commemorate Lowell and to write Whittier's obituary. When he closed his own eyes, it was upon a New England that had changed greatly from the one in which he was born.

Holmes is important in the history of American literature because of his skill in writing *vers de société*, light, fanciful, humorous verse, and because of his mastery of the conversational essay. "The Last Leaf," "My Aunt," and "Dorothy Q." are among the best of his light verse. The versatile physician would not have been so widely loved, however, had he been merely funny. Americans looked to him for more than humor. Once at least, in "The Chambered Nautilus," he gave expression to the deep music of thought, calm and resonant, like the sound of the sea and the silence of heaven. Though threatened to be outranked in fame by his son, the illustrious Chief Justice, his own place in the hearts of reading Americans is secure.

JOHN GREENLEAF WHITTIER

Whittier (1807-1892) once wrote to an editor, "I cannot be sufficiently thankful to the Divine Providence that so early called my attention to the great interests of humanity, saving me from a selfish pursuit of literary reputation." The man who wrote these words wore the closefitting coat of a Quaker, carried his tall body with the rangy ease of a worker in the outdoors, and had the fiery dark eyes of a reformer. On his Massachusetts farm he had once been his own "Barefoot Boy" obliged to steal an education from random books. The books were of two kinds, the works of English poets and histories of colonial times. They helped to make a patriotic poet of him, while teaching enough to launch him on an active journalistic career.

Poet uses simple meters

Of all our poets he is, perhaps, the one who most needs selection. Foreign touches acquired from his reading sound out of place in his verse, and his literary allusions are unconvincing; his vocabulary is spare; his versification flows too easily to escape monotony. His words and rhythms were at their best when used on the

©New York Public Library
Page from a Very Early Edition

simplest of American themes: a tale of Barbara Frietchie, "to show that one heart was loyal yet"; a picture of home firelight when the family is snowbound; an outdoor reverie of "the might have been" in "Maud Muller"; or deep sorrow, guessed though unexpressed, in "the sundown's blaze on her windowpane" when a loved one has gone. When he brings humor and pathos side by side, the humor gets the upper hand, as in "The Reading Demon."

In verse as simple and, at times, as prosaic as New England life itself, Whittier pursued his favorite themes, abolition of slavery and description of life on a New England farm. In his career as journalist he had to face the question of slavery versus human rights, and all his powers were roused to serve the cause of the Abolitionists. His poetic gifts followed him into his reform work, while at the same time they kept a part of his mind aloof in a world of the imagination. Between 1837 and 1860 Whittier produced ten volumes of verse, much of it dealing with the slavery question.

New England, favorite theme

Whittier's best poetry is descriptive of rural New England of the pre-Civil War period. "The Barefoot Boy," "Snow-bound," and his nature poems reveal the restraint of feeling, the concrete diction, and the objective imagery that are the properties of excellent poetry. If one removes from Whittier's verse the moral tags which have no appeal for present-day readers, he will discover in the simplicity of Whittier's poetic expression an affinity to Robert Frost or to Edna St. Vincent Millay. "Skipper Ireson's Ride," "Telling the Bees," and on a lower degree of excellence, "Maud Muller" reveal Whittier's ability as a narrative poet.

Orestes Augustus Brownson

LATER CATHOLIC LITERATURE OF THE NATIONAL PERIOD

ORESTES BROWNSON

Into the confusion of nineteenth-century thought came the massive warrior Orestes Brownson (1803-1876). As a child reading Jonathan Edwards, little Orestes had been trained for battle. Breathlessly he had watched the dragon-like powers of sin and error pull men to the trap door of hell. As a man — an "intellectual desperado," according to his own description — he set out to find truth. In his impulsiveness he went far in the wrong direction. He fought the giants of falsehood barehanded all the way back. His popularity when he reached his goal was that of a victor in a land he had devastated.

Born into an old family at Stockbridge, Vermont, Brownson was left fatherless at an early age. For six years his mother struggled to keep the five children together. Poverty finally forced her to send Orestes to live with an elderly couple in the neighboring village of Royalton. When he was fourteen years old, he left Royalton to rejoin his family, who had moved to Ballston, New York. In the academy of this town, he received his only formal schooling.

Brownson reflects nineteenth century thought

Brownson's long sojourn after truth led him to refute — or embrace and then refute — practically every religious and economic theory that appeared in the first half of the nineteenth century. As an agitator for the improvement of the working classes, he endorsed extravagant theories of socialism. In contact with glib deists, he held fleeting doubts concerning the existence of God. For a while he considered the theories of transcendentalism. He was, in turn, a Presbyterian, a Universalist minister, and a Unitarian minister.

All this time Brownson was nearing the truth by exploding one false system after another. His writings betrayed the step he must inevitably take. Finally a Protestant editor refused an article, declaring it was "as Catholic as Rome itself." Men who had felt the smiting blows of this intellectual pugilist were willing that he should fight elsewhere. A contemporary remarked, "He'll wreck whatever he anchors to; and I hope it is the Roman Church." In May, 1844, the tall figure of Brownson stood at Bishop Fenwick's door in Boston and asked to see His Lordship. Brownson's long search for truth was over; he was received into the Catholic Church, October 20, 1844,

Quarterly Review *exposes error*

For the next thirty years Brownson devoted his energies to the defense of the Church and the promotion of Catholic culture. This he did largely through the publication of his books and through *Brownson's Quarterly Review*, a periodical that was an outgrowth of a magazine he had founded while in contact with New

England intellectual and literary leaders. Brownson's published works include much controversial and philosophic material; *Charles Elwood* (1840), a novel; and *The American Republic: Its Constitution, Tendencies, and Destiny* (1866), a masterly analysis of American government. His autobiography, *The Convert* (1854), shows his reasons for joining the Church and defending it thereafter. Brownson's writings have been published in twenty volumes, and his uncollected works would fill another twenty-five.

Brownson valued the free expression of his opinion so highly that he was willing to print a whole magazine to provide an open platform for his views. The public always knew what he was thinking. His particular genius was his ability to find the weak spot in the thought of those about him. When he saw his contemporaries blowing bubbles of impractical reforms, he bruised their feelings by demanding that some concrete values result from their impractical dreams. The Transcendental Club pronounced him "unbearable" and ceased to invite him to their meetings. He made them fumble to unholster weak arguments; he demanded authority for their statements; he even pointed out brilliant rebuttals they *might* have used. Brownson's contacts even after his conversion were not always pleasant. As a layman and a convert writing on philosophical subjects, as a prominent figure without much formal education, as an original thinker with a Protestant background, and as a domineering and rugged personality, he often disagreed with his associates in Catholic circles.

The most frequent charge made against Brownson was that he was inconsistent. Before his conversion he opened himself to this criticism by defending many causes which closer investigation later led him to oppose. On the whole, however, his search for truth follows a logical sequence from the time he gave up Calvinism to the period of his entrance into the Catholic Church. He always remained impulsive. Even among his best friends his changes of mood seem sometimes to have brought changes of mind. In his first attempts to help others to see the truths of Catholicism, he used logical thrusts that ripped open their arguments. Realizing that this method defeated but did not convince his opponents, he later sought to win Protestants by showing the ways in which Catholicism offered what they desired. In using this more psychological manner of approach, Brownson made the mistake of expressing too liberal views. He later came to realize his errors and reaffirmed his loyalty to the Church. Brownson's temperament and the circumstances of his life caused him to remain always a somewhat lonely figure, zealous in his aspirations, gruff in his reactions, capable of warm affections which rarely manifested themselves.

Brownson attracts non-Catholic readers

Brownson's roaring voice and powerful physique were matched by a gigantic intellect. It was his greatness of stature that made him accept the Church as the only authority higher than his own mental powers. For that Church he sacrificed opportunities for wealth and popularity and devoted thirty-two years to tireless labor. Out of the pursuit of his lifelong quest for truth came a great contribution to American letters: the spectacle of the diverse currents of nineteenth-century thought as reflected, one after another, within the mind of a single individual. In the field of literary criticism he sought to elevate the standards of Catholic authors by showing them that their greatest inspiration for writing comes from their Faith. At its best his own style is vigorous, concrete, and pungent; at its worst it is assertive and unpolished, but always clear and forceful. To the Catholic journals appearing in different parts of the country, Brownson added his *Review*, which appealed to a certain group of intellectual Protestants and gained favorable recognition for the Catholic press outside the members of its own faith. Entering the Church from the ranks of those inimical to her, he saw both the safeguards which the Church brings to democracy and likewise the opportunity of the Church to adapt itself to American life and customs. In the history of Catholic literature Brownson's great philosophic mind towers above that of any other layman.

ISAAC HECKER

Brownson shared his hopes for a vigorous Catholic literature in America with a friend and fellow convert,

Isaac Hecker, Founder of the Paulists

Isaac Hecker (1819-1888). Born in New York of German parents, Hecker felt throughout his childhood that God desired him to do some special work. Family finances compelled the child to leave school at ten. He first secured a position as errand boy for a Methodist newspaper. Later he became an apprentice to his two elder brothers, who were bakers. When Brownson lectured in New York in 1841, Hecker found in him a sympathetic friend. He confided to Brownson his dissatisfaction with Methodism, his desire for an education, and his reluctance to continue in the baker's trade. Brownson encouraged the young man to try the Brook Farm association. While at Brook Farm, where everyone participated in some manual labor, Hecker acted as community baker and attended the classes which were part of the program for self-improvement. Sojourners at the farm were impressed with the singular refinement and sincerity of the young man in a white baker's cap, whom they saw in the kitchen. Despite the fact that Brook Farm gave Hecker an opportunity for the education he so desired, the youth left in disappointment for another experiment: Bronson Alcott's community at Fruitlands. Again failing to find the ideal conditions he had expected, Hecker returned after a few weeks to his family. His friendship with Brownson matured during the next several years and resulted in the mutual aid of these two ardent seekers for truth. Hecker entered the Church in 1844, a few months before Brownson.

Attracted to a missionary vocation, Hecker went to Belgium to make his novitiate in the Congregation of the Most Holy Redeemer. After his ordination he returned to New York, where, with a number of other American Redemptorists, he engaged in fruitful missionary work among non-Catholic and Catholic immigrants. His experience with his countrymen caused him to believe that Americans were fair-minded and would cast aside their bigotry and hatred when they learned the true nature of Catholic beliefs. In order that Father Hecker and several companions might make the apostolate of non-Catholics their chief work in America, the Pope released the little group from their vows as Redemptorists. They then founded the Missionary Priests of St. Paul the Apostle, more familiarly known as the Paulists. As superior of the new congregation, Father Hecker devoted the remainder of his life to the spread of the Faith in America.

Catholic World *established*

In addition to the labor of missionary activity, Father Hecker understood the necessity of forming the public mind through journals and magazines. Accordingly in 1865 he founded the *Catholic World*. It was the only Catholic magazine in the country at the time of its foundation, since the *Metropolitan* had ceased publication and *Brownson's Review* was temporarily suspended. The periodical presented many aspects of American culture; it offered articles on religion, philosophy, literature, the arts and sciences, as well as a refutation of modern errors. It aimed to present Catholicism accurately, forcibly, and artistically. Its files for the first thirty years are perhaps the best record of the progress made by Catholic letters during those decades. Father Hecker continued his apostolate of the pen, writing three works on apologetics, founding the Paulist Press, and establishing a Catholic magazine for youth. Shortly after Father Hecker died in 1888, Cardinal Newman wrote: "I have ever felt that there was this sort of unity in our lives — that we had both begun a work of the same kind, he in America and I in England."

THE INFLUENCE OF THE OXFORD MOVEMENT IN AMERICA

The temper of the nineteenth century in America was one of religious inquiry. In keeping with this spirit, a group of American Anglicans followed with great interest a movement headed by John Henry Newman that arose in the English Episcopalian (or Anglican) Church in 1833. The purpose of Newman and his companions was to quicken the fervor of Anglicans by proving that the Anglican Church was in a line of direct descent from the Church of the Apostles. Because the leaders of this movement were often associated with the University of Oxford, it came to be known as the Oxford Movement. Newman's research resulted in his conviction that the Catholic Church is the true Church. Although the influence of Newman's writings showed itself in various parts of America, the General Protestant Episcopal Seminary in New York was the center of interest in the Oxford Movement. The desire to re-establish Catholic life and practices was so intense in Anglican circles that several attempts were made in America to restore the monastic system. Like Newman, a number of American Episcopalian ministers, seminarians, and laymen examined the origins of the Anglican Church and became convinced that they must embrace Catholicism. As a result of their decision, the ranks of Catholic authors were enlarged by a number of writers of great culture, education, virtue, and zeal. From the Episcopal Church of New York came the later Catholic authors James McMaster, John D. Bryant, Clarence E. Walworth, and Jedidiah V. Huntington. From Baltimore came Augustine Hewit. In the South the Oxford Movement led to the Church Levi Silliman Ives, the only Anglican bishop to be converted, and one of his clergymen, Donald MacLeod. Other writers, less directly influenced by the Oxford Movement, also entered the Church during this period.

JAMES McMASTER

The particular delight of James McMaster (1820-1886) was to expose error. At the General Protestant Episcopal Seminary in New York he was a frank spokesman among the students who were turning to Catholicism. His questions invariably touched the most vulnerable points of Anglican doctrine; his defense of his views had a way of placing his professors in the most uncomfortable position possible. On entering the Church in 1845, he was eager for the priesthood and with Isaac Hecker embarked for Europe to enter the novitiate of the Redemptorists in Belgium. The kind discernment of his superiors aided him to realize that his opinionated and argumentative disposition was not suited to the religious life. Acting on the advice of the men whom he greatly revered, he returned to America to defend the Church by his writing. In 1848 he bought *Freeman's Journal* from Archbishop Hughes. From that date until his death the weekly was a forcible organ for the expression of his energetic ideas, personal prejudices, and deeply humble faith. Of the many causes for which he battled, none benefited more than the parochial school system. Aghast at the fact that public schools made no provision for religious teaching, McMaster promoted the organization of the Catholic school system. The sting of his zealous condemnation of indifferentism was so sharp that even the most apathetic feared to come under his censorship.

Some Catholic voices of New England

Because of their interest in transcendentalism, Brownson and Hecker are usually associated with New England. Actually Brownson's career as a writer was divided between New York and Boston. Hecker's and McMaster's literary activities took place largely in New York. New England, however, had its own group of writers in the national period. The *Jesuit or Catholic Sentinel,* founded by Bishop Fenwick, had opened the way for authorship. This organ changed owners and names several times in its early years and emerged as the *Boston Pilot* in 1829. The venerable *Pilot* has become a household word in its service to the Catholic cause. During the nineteenth century the paper had among its editors many figures renowned in the history of Catholic literature.

CHARLES BULLARD FAIRBANKS

From the New England writers who gathered at Worcester, Massachusetts, came Charles Bullard Fairbanks (1827-1859), a convert who passed from Unitarianism to Episcopalianism and thence to

Catholicism. The young man wrote a group of fifteen travel sketches and thirteen essays in a philosophical vein, which he published under the title *"Aguecheek,"* an allusion to a Shakespearean character in *Twelfth Night.* The book was republished in 1912 as *My Unknown Chum.* The depth and simplicity of Fairbanks, his ease of phrase and delightful humor, account for the wide popularity of this first successful Catholic writer of informal essays.

LATER CATHOLIC POETS

JEDIDIAH V. HUNTINGTON

Having rooted itself in soil at first inhospitable, Catholic poetry was now to be enriched by the spirit of a distinguished convert, Jedidiah Huntington. Born in New York of Episcopalian parents, Huntington was ordained minister at twenty-six and became rector of the Episcopal Church at Middlebury, Vermont. As tireless in his search for truth as he was keen in poetic perception, he resigned his rectorship in order to investigate his religious doubts. After years of uncertainty the full light of the Faith overswept him during a visit to Rome. Together with his wife he was received into the Church in 1849. Huntington's volume, *Poems*, published in 1843 shows that he was even then close to the Church. He drew inspiration from the Divine Office, which he read regularly in the Benedictine breviary. His translations from the hymns of the liturgy have the spirit and fervor of the original. In a number of poems Huntington gives an elevated treatment of the sanctified love of marriage.

JOHN DELEVAU BRYANT

In 1839 John Delevau Bryant (1811-1877), the son of a Philadelphia Episcopal rector, entered the General Theological Seminary of the Protestant Episcopal Church in New York. At the end of Bryant's first year at the seminary his friends considered he was seriously stricken with "Roman fever," as interest in the Catholic Church was then called by Anglicans. They hoped that his proposed trip to Rome would cure him, but to their disappointment he returned from his travels in 1842 and became a Catholic. Bryant entered upon the career of physician after his conversion but in addition to engaging in professional work, wrote fiction and poetry as well as a doctrinal treatise on the Immaculate Conception.

Doctor Bryant wrote the most ambitious work yet attempted by an American Catholic poet, an epic in twelve books entitled *The Redemption* and published in 1859. In presenting the exalted theme of God made man, the author drew his material from the Bible and Catholic teaching. The work is particularly Catholic in its presentation of the Immaculate Conception as the key to the Redemption. Not satisfied with his first version, Bryant continued to improve the poem throughout his lifetime and at his death left a completely-revised edition which he hoped would be republished. It was thoughtlessly destroyed when his library passed into the hands of strangers after his death.

Miles is representative poet

George Henry Miles (1824-1871) was a poet and dramatist of distinction. Born at Baltimore, he was educated at Mount St. Mary's, Emmitsburg, where he became a convert. Although he entered the legal profession, he found his talents better suited to literary work and began contributing poetry, sketches, and novels in serial form to Catholic periodicals. Two volumes of his poetry were published during his lifetime. The best collection of his poems, *Said the Rose and Other Lyrics*, appeared after his death. The masculine force of his work is balanced by his disciplined and sensitive spirituality.

Randall composes battle cry

James Ryder Randall (1839-1908), journalist and poet, was born in Baltimore. After some years of traveling in South America and the West Indies, he taught in Louisiana and later turned to journalism. His "Maryland, My Maryland" became the battle cry of his native state. It was not until 1908, the year of Randall's death at Augusta, Georgia, that the first collection of

James Ryder Randall

his verse was published under the title *Maryland, My Maryland, and Other Poems*. Many of his poems give eloquent testimony to his stanch Catholic character.

McGee's poems show Celtic strain

Linked with the Boston writers is Thomas D'Arcy McGee (1825-1868), an Irish immigrant who began his literary career with the *Boston Pilot*. His tempestuous activity in the cause of Irish freedom is of less importance to us than his collected *Poems* (1868). McGee's poetry bears the impress of a great heart, impassioned with a love for Ireland and for liberty. The poems are Celtic in their bardic quality, with a hint of sadness behind the harping and a prayer of pity above the pitch of battle.

THE RISE OF CATHOLIC FICTION

Catholic fiction rose in the national period as a result of a twofold need: the urgency of providing attractive literature for Catholics and the necessity of answering written and spoken calumnies against the Faith. The first need was undoubtedly the greater. Previous to this period the offerings of Catholic booksellers had consisted mainly of doctrinal treatises or books of devotion. Many of these works were by English authors or were translations from European writers. In contrast to this heavier type of reading material, secular literature was presenting the strongly imaginative appeal of the novel. The market was overcrowded with romantic novels, some of them immoral or insidiously hostile to Catholicity.

In answering charges against the Church, the Catholic writer of fiction had an apostolic aim. He knew that many Americans who were believing subtle and pernicious slanders would not read doctrinal literature to ascertain Catholic truth. Yet it was possible that these people would peruse a book of fiction if it should fall into their hands. Through fiction, then, misinformed citizens could obtain a true picture of the Church.

Early novels emphasize moral teachings

With such high aims, it would appear that the Catholic writer would have been joyously welcomed by readers and critics. Such was not the case. Puritan hostility to fiction had permeated even to Catholic circles; the prevalence of immoral novels caused all fictional writing to be viewed with suspicion. The first novels were harshly criticized. As late as 1853 an article appeared in the *Metropolitan* "Are We to Have Fiction?" which indicated that the question was not yet settled in Catholic minds.

While the more conservative among the Catholic reading public were being accustomed to the novel, Catholic fiction writers proceeded with caution. They called attention to the instructive value of their narrative; they stressed moral aims. In their own fervor they frequently interrupted their stories to present long theological discussions. Judged by present-day tastes the style is often stilted and artificial; the plots have a tendency to run to melodrama; the characters are often wholly virtuous or completely villainous. Despite these inadequacies the early Catholic novelists performed a decided service. Their works were suited to the tastes of readers of that day. For their audience they refined manners and elevated Catholic ideals, appealed to dreams and aspirations of youth, and made virtue attractive. From a literary point of view, their novels were equal in merit and sometimes superior to popular fiction of the time. The didactic purpose of our early fiction writers and their technique of combining a moral with a story unfortunately left its impress on the later Catholic fiction of the nineteenth century and on some works of the twentieth.

Although fiction attributed to a Catholic author appeared as early as 1775, the novel of a truly Catholic tone began with the farsighted and versatile priest, Charles Constantine Pise (1801-1866). With his own wide culture and literary background, Father Pise realized the need of developing popular types of Catholic reading. A man of action, he sought to further this aim by producing a number of novels. With the immediate purpose of offering a refutation of a vicious anti-Catholic novel entitled *Father Clement*, the priest presented *Father Rowland* (1829). The first Catholic novel sold for thirty-seven and a half cents and did not even print the author's name on the title page. The book is little more than an exposition of doctrine through the use of dialogue, characterization, and local color. In the ideal priest around whom the story centers, readers saw a reflection of Archbishop Carroll. Father Pise's second novel, *The Indian Cottage* (1829) defended the divinity of Christ against Unitarian doctrine. These books were a great innovation. Many who did not appreciate Father Pise's broad aims criticized the new venture so fiercely that the priest was forced to postpone for some time further contributions to fiction.

Boyce uses novel to defend Irish

In Worcester, Massachusetts, John Boyce (1810-1864), a secular priest and an Irish immigrant writing under the name of Paul Peppergrass, was first to use the novel in defense of the oppressed immigrant. *Shandy M'Guire* (1848), his first and best-known novel, treats the struggle between Catholics and Protestants in the North of Ireland. The tale combines humor and pathos and exhibits true Irish fire and drama. It is skillful and authentic in characterization, in dialect, and in its portrayal of Irish peasant life. In later novels Father

Boyce continued his aim of making the Irish immigrant aware of his invaluable heritage and creating respect for Catholicity in the public mind.

Bryant adds love interest

Another writer who helped to broaden the scope of Catholic fiction during the national period was the poet John Delevau Bryant. His best known novel is *Pauline Seward* (1847), which went through more than ten editions. To the main theme of the heroine's attempt to find the true faith, the author adds the interest of a love story. Long expositions of Catholic belief delay the development of the plot, and the conversation of the characters is often stilted.

Huntington insists on literary standards

Jedidiah Vincent Huntington was the first writer to realize that if Catholic fiction was to be a literary product it must cast off its obvious moral and didactic trappings and emerge as a thing of beauty, which by its own radiance would reflect the Catholic ideal. Huntington's first efforts at fiction did not please his Catholic audience. The reading of French novels had somewhat blunted his sensibilities and as a consequence he presented material which many readers found distasteful or suggestive. Sincere in his desire to write without giving offense, Huntington finally achieved *Rosemary, or Life and Death* (1860). The book was enthusiastically received and was probably the most widely read Catholic novel of the period. A weird, exciting tale, it held readers absorbed as they followed the heroine in her supposed death, resuscitation, and subsequent happy marriage. In his literary workmanship Huntington excelled the Catholic novelists who preceded him. He presented material dramatically, was artistic in description, and careful in diction.

Women enter fiction field

Catholic women, too, realized the need for Catholic fiction. The convert writer Anna Hanson Dorsey (1815-1896) produced nearly twenty novels and long tales. *Tangled Paths* (1879) and *Palms* (1887) are usually considered her best works. Her novels, short stories, and

B. F. Williamson

Anna Hanson Dorsey

juvenile fiction are not merely pietistic tales but give a convincing picture of the joys and satisfactions to be found in the Catholic way of life. Despite the weakness of her plots and sketchy characterization, Mrs. Dorsey deserves a place in the history of Catholic fiction. She blazed the trail for Catholic women writers and showed the rich

B. F. Williamson

Mary Anne Sadlier

possibilities of fiction built upon Catholic principles.

The works of Mary Anne Madden Sadlier (1820-1903), the most prolific Catholic writer of the period, provided moral and spiritual elevation to the immigrant during the trying years of his adjustment to American life. *The Blakes and the Flanigans* (1855) is typical of the author's novels which deal with the moral, social, and economic problems of the immigrant. Swift-moving action, interesting characterization, and emotional appeal make Mrs. Sadlier's works entertaining reading despite their didactic purpose. Like many of her fellow-craftsmen, this Irish-American writer gives her characters an artificial and unnatural piety. Her works are valuable today as sociological documents picturing the status of the immigrant before he was absorbed into American life.

THE CATHOLIC SHORT STORY

The brevity of the short story and the fact that it treats intensively significant moments in the lives of individuals make it a suitable medium for conveying Catholic principles. The development of the secular literary magazine was in some measure responsible for the popularity of the short story. The beginnings of the Catholic short story may be traced in such early Catholic periodicals as the *United States Catholic Miscellany* (1822), the *Metropolitan or Catholic Monthly* (1830), and the *Catholic Expositor* (1841). The various steps in the development of the short story, of the leisurely romantic tale, of the mildly realistic story with dialect and local color, and of the crisp modern impressionistic or problem story—all have their parallels in the history of the Catholic short story.

A survey of early Catholic magazines reveals that the first Catholic short stories met with much the same opposition that was shown to fiction in general at this time in the United States. The distrust of fiction may partially explain the number of anonymous short narratives, as well as the fashion of giving such subtitles as "a true story," "founded on fact," "a domestic tale of real life." Just as some of the early tales of Irving and Hawthorne were drawn from European sources, so were the early Catholic short stories. Many of them were translations or adaptations of narratives from Catholic Germany, France, and Ireland.

Prior to 1865 the names of three Catholics stand out as pioneers in the development of the short story. Two of these writers, Charles James Cannon and Anna Hanson Dorsey were definitely Catholic in outlook. Perhaps it is just one of the ironies of life that Fitz-James O'Brien, an Irishman by birth, who with his spiritual heritage, his imaginative powers, and popularity as a writer could have promoted the Catholic short story, should have contributed so little in a positive way towards its development.

Patriotic and religious motives fanned into action the poetic and imaginative gifts of Charles James Cannon (1800-1860). Throughout his life Cannon was expressly proud of his Irish ancestry, his Catholic faith, and his American birth. He spent his days as a clerk and his evenings in writing. In 1835 he published *Facts, Feelings, and Fancies*, a collection of poems and tales. The stories are largely sentimental, melodramatic and tinged with the extravagances of the Gothic school of fiction. A second volume of short tales, *Ravellings from the Web of Life* (1855), reveals maturity, apostolic design, and has in it the lilt and witchery of romance. *Ravellings from the Web of Life* comprises six tales told by members of a family and their friends. The scope of the stories reveals a number of life situations and each narrator tells a story which might well have come within his own experience. While the tales show observation and descriptive power on the part of the author and reveal a kindliness and a sympathetic understanding of the human heart, they are often marred by didacticism.

FITZ-JAMES O'BRIEN

Because of his fondness for the weird and uncanny and his use of morbid, mysterious, pseudoscientific stories, Fitz-James O'Brien (1828-1862) has been called the "Celtic Poe." O'Brien, however, has a lighter, more vivacious touch than Poe, and his stories lack the witchery, the magic, the high spiritual note found in Celtic literature.

O'Brien came from Ireland. He arrived in New York in 1852 with letters of introduction to influential people. Soon he won his way into social and literary circles. He achieved almost immediate success as a free-lance writer and for a period of ten years contributed to such magazines as *Harpers* and the *Atlantic Monthly*.

O'Brien's instantaneous success and popularity were due as much to his dynamic personality as to his electrifying powers of imagination. He became the leader of a group of young journalists, actors, poets, and artists who, because of their irregularity of living, were styled Bohemians. The outbreak of the Civil War put an end to O'Brien's undisciplined life. He enlisted in the New York National Guard and died as a result of a severe wound. His last words were somewhat prophetic. Speaking to his literary executors, he said, "After I'm dead I may turn out to be a bigger man than while living."

Two of O'Brien's best stories are "The Diamond Lens" and "What Was It?" Like his other narratives, they illustrate the author's creative power and ease in writing. O'Brien could tell a good story; he was clever, spirited, and versatile. He lacked, however, the patience to develop his talents and the discipline of mental and imaginative power so necessary in producing a work of art. The influences of Hawthorne and Poe are evident in his stories. But whereas Poe was the artist, Hawthorne the moralist, O'Brien is neither artist nor moralist. Nearly all his stories have an unsatisfactory ending; in some of them there is a vague attempt to represent a moral element. He does succeed in giving a sense of actuality to his tales of magic, wonder, or morbid mental states. By means of his unconventional subject matter, his freshness of approach, and brilliancy of style, he put verve and virility into the short story. But he is Catholic only in name and often offends by his want of taste and lack of moral perceptions.

Self-Reliance

Ralph Waldo Emerson

Have faith in yourself; do not bury the talents entrusted to you; be not conformed to the ways of the world — this is Emerson's message of self-reliance, a noble message and worth heeding. It can be a tonic for the indolent and timid and a revelation to the unthinking follower of convention. The proud, selfish man, on the other hand, may find in these counsels excuse for discarding the wisdom of the past and denying all authority. Curiously enough, Emerson realized that this extreme doctrine of self-reliance was not a safe one for all men to follow. Reflecting once upon man's capacity for evil, he wrote in his Journal, *"What a hell we should make of the world if we could do what we would."*

I READ the other day some verses written by an eminent painter[1] which were original and not conventional. The soul always hears an admonition in such lines, let the subject be what it may. The sentiment they instill is of more value than any thought they may contain. To believe your own thought, to believe that what is true for you in your private heart is true for all men — that is genius. Speak your latent conviction, and it shall be the universal sense; for the inmost in due time becomes the outmost, and our first thought is rendered back to us by the trumpets of the Last Judgment. Familiar as the voice of the mind is to each, the highest merit we ascribe to Moses, Plato, and Milton is that they set at naught books and traditions[2] and spoke not what men, but what *they* thought. A man should learn to detect and watch that gleam of light which flashes across his mind from within, more than the luster of the firmament of bards and sages. Yet he dismisses without notice his thought because it is his. In every work of genius we recognize our own rejected thoughts; they come back to us with a certain alienated majesty. Great works of art have no more affecting lesson for us than this. They teach us to abide by our spontaneous impression with good-humored inflexibility then most when the whole cry of voices is on the other side. Else tomorrow a stranger will say with masterly good sense precisely what we have thought and felt all the time, and we shall be forced to take with shame our own opinion from another.

There is a time in every man's education when he arrives at the conviction that envy is ignorance; that imitation is suicide; that he must take himself for better, for worse as his portion; that though the wide universe is full of good, no kernel of nourishing corn can come to him but through his toil bestowed on that plot of ground which is given to him to till. The power which resides in him is new in nature, and none but he knows what that is which he can do, nor does he know until he has tried. Not for nothing one face, one character, one fact, makes much impression on him, and another none. This sculpture in the memory is not without pre-established harmony. The eye was placed where one ray should fall, that it might testify of that particular ray. We but half express ourselves and are ashamed of that divine idea which each of us represents. It may be safely trusted as proportionate and of good issues, so it be faithfully imparted, but God will not have His work made manifest by cowards. A man is relieved and gay when he has put his heart into his work and done his best; but what he has said or done otherwise shall give him no peace. It is a deliverance which does not deliver. In the attempt his genius deserts him; no muse befriends; no invention, no hope.

Trust thyself; every heart vibrates to that iron string. Accept the place the Divine Providence has found for you, the society of your contemporaries, the connection of events. Great men have always done so and confided themselves childlike to the genius of their age, betraying their perception that the absolutely trustworthy was seated at their heart, working through their hands, predominating in all their being. And we are now men and must accept in the highest mind the same transcendent destiny; and not minors and invalids in a protected corner, not cowards fleeing before a revolution, but guides, redeemers, and benefactors, obeying the Almighty effort and advancing on Chaos and the Dark.
. . .

Society everywhere is in conspiracy against the manhood of every one of its members. Society is a joint-stock company, in which the members agree, for the better securing of his bread to each shareholder,

---

[1] *verses . . . eminent painter.* It is not known to whom Emerson referred. Some have suggested William Blake. Michelangelo and Washington Allston were also painters who wrote verse.

[2] *traditions*, customs and beliefs handed down from the past.

to surrender the liberty and culture of the eater. The virtue in most request is conformity. Self-reliance is its aversion. It loves not realities and creators but names and customs.

Whoso would be a man must be a nonconformist.[3] He who would gather immortal palms must not be hindered by the name of goodness but must explore if it be goodness. Nothing is at last sacred but the integrity of your own mind. Absolve you to yourself,[4] and you shall have the suffrage of the world. . . .

I am ashamed to think how easily we capitulate[5] to badges and names, to large societies and dead institutions. Every decent and well-spoken individual affects and sways me more than is right. I ought to go upright and vital and speak the rude truth in all ways. If malice and vanity wear the coat of philanthropy, shall that pass? If an angry bigot assumes this bountiful cause of Abolition and comes to me with his last news from Barbados,[6] why should I not say to him, "Go love thy infant; love thy wood chopper; be good-natured and modest; have that grace; and never varnish your hard, uncharitable ambition with this incredible tenderness for black folk a thousand miles off. Thy love afar is spite at home." Rough and graceless would be such greeting, but truth is handsomer than the affectation of love. Your goodness must have some edge to it — else it is none. The doctrine of hatred must be preached, as the counteraction of the doctrine of love, when that pules and whines. I shun father and mother and wife and brother when my genius calls me. I would write on the lintels[7] of the doorpost, *Whim*. I hope it is somewhat better than whim at last, but we cannot spend the day in explanation. Expect me not to show cause why I seek or why I exclude company. Then again, do not tell me, as a good man did today, of my obligation to put all poor men in good situations. Are they my poor? I tell thee, thou foolish philanthropist, that I grudge the dollar, the dime, the cent I give to such men as do not belong to me and to whom I do not belong. There is a class of persons to whom by all spiritual affinity I am bought and sold; for them I will go to prison if need be; but

your miscellaneous popular charities; the education at college of fools; the building of meeting houses to the vain end to which many now stand; alms to sots, and the thousandfold Relief Societies; — though I confess with shame I sometime succumb and give the dollar, it is a wicked dollar, which by and by I shall have the manhood to withhold. . . .

What I must do is all that concerns me, not what the people think. This rule, equally arduous in actual and in intellectual life, may serve for the whole distinction between greatness and meanness. It is the harder because you will always find those who think they know what is your duty better than you know it. It is easy in the world to live after the world's opinion; it is easy in solitude to live after our own; but the great man is he who in the midst of the crowd keeps with perfect sweetness the independence of solitude. . . .

For nonconformity the world whips you with its displeasure. And therefore a man must know how to estimate a sour face. The bystanders look askance on him in the public street or in the friend's parlor. If this aversation[8] had its origin in contempt and resistance like his own, he might well go home with a sad countenance; but the sour faces of the multitude, like their sweet faces, have no deep cause but are put on and off as the wind blows and a newspaper directs. Yet is the discontent of the multitude more formidable than that of the senate and the college. It is easy enough for a firm man who knows the world to brook the rage of the cultivated classes. Their rage is decorous and prudent, for they are timid, as being very vulnerable themselves. But when to their feminine rage the indignation of the people is added, when the ignorant and the poor are aroused, when the unintelligent brute force that lies at the bottom of society is made to growl and mow,[9] it needs the habit of magnanimity and religion to treat it godlike as a trifle of no concernment. . . .

Society never advances. It recedes as fast on one side as it gains on the other. It undergoes continual changes; it is barbarous, it is civilized, it is christianized, it is rich, it is scientific; but this change is not amelioration. For every thing that is given some thing is taken. Society acquires new arts and loses old instincts. What a contrast between the well-clad, reading, writing, thinking American with

---

[3] *nonconformist*, one who refuses to conform to established customs and ideas.

[4] *absolve you to yourself*, free yourself from the obligation of thinking for yourself; in other words, conform to the opinions of others.

[5] *capitulate*, surrender.

[6] *Barbados*, an island in the West Indies where during Emerson's time the natives were in slavery.

[7] *lintels*, horizontal beams above doors or windows.

[8] *aversation*, aversion.

[9] *mow*, mock or make grimaces.

a watch, a pencil, and a bill of exchange in his pocket, and the naked New Zealander, whose property is a club, a spear, a mat, and an undivided twentieth of a shed to sleep under! But compare the health of the two men, and you shall see that the white man has lost his aboriginal strength. If the traveler tell us truly, strike the savage with a broad-ax, and in a day or two the flesh shall unite and heal as if you struck the blow into soft pitch, and the same blow shall send the white man to his grave.

The civilized man has built a coach, but has lost the use of his feet. He is supported on crutches but lacks so much support of muscle. He has a fine Geneva watch,[10] but he fails of the skill to tell the hour by the sun. A Greenwich nautical almanac[11] he has; and so being sure of the information when he wants it, the man in the street does not know a star in the sky. The solstice he does not observe; the equinox he knows as little; and the whole bright calendar of the year is without a dial in his mind. His notebooks impair his memory; his libraries overload his wit; the insurance office increases the number of accidents; and it may be a question whether machinery does not encumber; whether we have not lost by refinement some energy, by a Christianity entrenched in establishments and forms some vigor of wild virtue. For every Stoic was a Stoic; but in Christendom where is the Christian?

VIEWING THE AUTHOR'S IDEAS

1. What does Emerson mean when he says, "A man should learn to detect and watch the gleam of light which flashes across his mind from within, more than the luster of the firmament of bards and sages"? Show the error of the transcendentalist, who follows this inner "gleam of light" as the only guide. Why are the impulses of even noble men conflicting? What would happen to society as a whole if each man's own convictions were the only standard of conduct?

2. Discuss the importance of inspiration for the writer or inventor. To what extent do men of genius "set at nought books and tradition"? To what extent do they rely upon them?

3. Give instances when imitation is "suicide." When is it praiseworthy and necessary? In what words does Emerson urge us to develop our God-given talents and to fulfill our destiny in life?

4. What does Emerson mean when he says, "Whoso would be a man must be a nonconformist"? When, in your life, has adherence to principle demanded courage to be different? Give examples of conformity to public opinion; to the dictates of society; to the maxims of the world. What would Emerson think of modern propaganda and mob thinking?

5. Emerson says that he begrudges the cent given to the poor in conformity to public opinion. What other unsocial attitudes would he prefer to take rather than conform to convention? What effect would the increased social consciousness prevalent today have upon the appeal and influence of his attitudes?

6. Emerson believes that for every gain there is some loss. List his illustrations which show that this principle of compensation may be applied to the progress of society.

7. Discuss Emerson's doctrine of self-reliance in the light of the following statement from Pope Pius XI's encyclical *Reconstruction of the Social Order:* "Man endowed with social nature is placed here on earth in order that he may spend his life in society and under an authority ordained by God, that he may develop and evolve to the full all his faculties to the praise and glory of his Creator."

EVALUATING HIS MANNER OF EXPRESSION

1. Few writers have excelled Emerson in the construction of brilliant epigrams. Select ten maxims from this essay.

2. Emerson's omission of transitional words and phrases makes it difficult to follow his thought. List five sentences in this essay which do not depend for their meaning upon a previous sentence.

3. Point out examples of striking metaphor; clever definition; effective use of rhetorical question and exclamation.

4. Expand the following pithy statements:
God will not have His work made manifest by cowards.
It [half-hearted effort] is a deliverance which does not deliver.
Absolve you to yourself, and you shall have the suffrage of the world.
I am ashamed to think how easily we capitulate to badges and names.
Thy love afar is spite at home.
For nonconformity the world whips you with its displeasure.

5. Can you detect passages which show a weakness in logic? Emerson was fond of making general statements without giving a sufficient number of particular instances to warrant the generalization. How many of these can you find?

6. Point out and discuss some of the half-truths Emerson enunciates.

7. Aristotle, one of the greatest of the Greek critics, said that every literary work should have a beginning, a middle, and an end. Has Emerson observed this recommendation in his essay "Self-Reliance"?

---

[10] *Geneva watch*, a watch with a Geneva stop to prevent overwinding.

[11] *Greenwich nautical almanac*, an almanac for navigators based upon Greenwich, or standard time.

Concord Hymn

Ralph Waldo Emerson

The initial shot of the American Revolution was fired at Concord, April 19, 1775, the day after Paul Revere's ride. It was fitting that Emerson, the "Concord sage," should write the hymn sung at the completion of the Battle Monument, July 4, 1837. Thirty-eight years later a statue, The Minuteman, *was erected at the end of the Concord Bridge opposite the first memorial. On this occasion Emerson's hymn was again sung and the first stanza inscribed at the base of the statue.*

By the rude bridge that arched the flood,
  Their flag to April's breeze unfurled,
Here once the embattled farmers stood
  And fired the shot heard round the world.

The foe long since in silence slept;   5
  Alike the conqueror silent sleeps;
And Time the ruined bridge has swept
  Down the dark stream which seaward creeps.

On this green bank, by this soft stream,
  We set today a votive stone,
That memory may their deed redeem,   10
  When, like our sires, our sons are gone.

Spirit, that made those heroes dare
  To die and leave their children free,
Bid Time and Nature gently spare   15
  The shaft we raise to them and thee.

VIEWING THE AUTHOR'S IDEAS

1. Explain the statement that the first shot of the American Revolution was "heard round the world." Discuss the ways in which it still re-echoes today. To what extent has the pattern of American democracy been copied elsewhere?

2. What sacred and enduring possessions bind together succeeding generations of Americans?

3. How does the current United States army compare with the embattled farmers in training, remuneration, and prestige?

4. Arrange a display of photographs showing famous national monuments. What memorials are in your locality?

EVALUATING HIS MANNER OF EXPRESSION

Account for the increasing solemnity of each stanza. Comment on the last line as a worthy climax. Select four examples of inversion and discuss the compression achieved by their use. What words in the first stanza are poetic and noteworthy? Why?

The Humblebee

Ralph Waldo Emerson

The reader with a sensitive ear will find the burly, dozing humblebee in these lines, steering his zigzag course amid the colors and perfumes of a drowsy summer day. He will catch, too, strains of Emerson's philosophy as the poet observes the bee "sipping only what is sweet."

Burly, dozing humblebee,[1]
  Where thou art is clime for me.
Let them sail for Porto Rique
Far-off heats through seas to seek;
I will follow thee alone,   5

Thou animated torrid zone!
Zigzag steerer, desert cheerer,
Let me chase thy waving lines;
Keep me nearer, me thy hearer,
Singing over shrubs and vines.   10

Insect lover of the sun,
Joy of thy dominion!
Sailor of the atmosphere;
Swimmer through the waves of air;
Voyager of light and noon;   15

[1] *humblebee,* bumblebee.

Epicurean[2] of June;
Wait, I prithee, till I come
Within earshot of thy hum—
All without is martyrdom.

When the south wind, in May days,   20
With a net of shining haze
Silvers the horizon wall,
And with softness touching all,
Tints the human countenance
With the color of romance,   25
And infusing subtle heats,
Turns the sod to violets,
Thou, in sunny solitudes,
Rover of the underwoods,
The green silence dost displace   30
With thy mellow, breezy bass.

Hot midsummer's petted crone,
Sweet to me thy drowsy tone
Tells of countless sunny hours,
Long days, and solid banks of flowers;   35
Of gulfs of sweetness without bound
In Indian wildernesses found;
Of Syrian peace, immortal leisure,
Firmest cheer, and birdlike pleasure.

Aught unsavory or unclean   40
Hath my insect never seen;
But violets and bilberry bells,
Maple sap and daffodels,
Grass with green flag half-mast high,
Succory[3] to match the sky,   45
Columbine with horn of honey,
Scented fern and agrimony,[4]
Clover, catchfly, adder's tongue,
And brier roses, dwelt among;
All beside was unknown waste,   50
All was picture as he passed.

Wiser far than human seer,
Yellow-breeched philosopher!
Seeing only what is fair,
Sipping only what is sweet,   55

Thou dost mock at fate and care,
Leave the chaff and take the wheat.
When the fierce northwestern blast
Cools sea and land so far and fast,
Thou already slumberest deep;   60
Woe and want thou canst outsleep;
Want and woe, which torture us,
Thy sleep makes ridiculous.

VIEWING THE AUTHOR'S IDEAS

1. What habits of the bee has the poet observed in the first stanza? How does he associate the insect with the tropics?

2. What lines show that the hum of the bee holds a peculiar fascination for the poet? What aspects of nature in May are mentioned? In lines 20-27, how does Emerson capture the essence of early summer? Select the line of this stanza which you consider most picturesque.

3. By what details does the poet reproduce the drowsiness of midsummer in lines 32-39?

4. Name some places where the bee finds nectar. What is the wisdom of the "yellow-breeched philosopher"? Why does the poet consider him wiser than human beings? What similarity is there between Emerson's bee and the lilies of the field in *Matt.* 6:28-29?

5. What attitude towards evil does Emerson advocate? Is his plan always workable? Discuss its strong and weak points. What is the attitude of the Church towards the presence of evil in the world? How are we guided to "only what is fair" in the choice of books, magazines, and movies?

EVALUATING HIS MANNER OF EXPRESSION

1. The effective use of onomatopoeia is one of the merits of this poem. Which words indicate the buzzing of the bee; which its humming?

2. List the metaphors which apply to the bee. Explain those which have reference to the sea. Choose the three metaphors you consider most vivid and show what comparison each contains.

3. A liberty taken with the rules of spelling and grammar for a poetic purpose is known as poetic *license*. For what metrical purpose does the writer use the spelling "Porto Rique" and "daffodel"?

4. Which appealed to Emerson most: the bee itself, its environment, or its message? In your opinion, what contributes most to the merit of the poem: onomatopoeia, the lengthy litany of apt names, the vivid descriptions of nature, the moral?

---

[2] *Epicurean*, a follower of Epicurus, a Greek philosopher who taught that pleasure is the chief good in life.

[3] *succory*, a plant cultivated for its roots and used as a salad; also called chicory.

[4] *agrimony*, a plant of the rose family, having yellow flowers and bristly fruits.

The Rhodora

Ralph Waldo Emerson

ON BEING ASKED, WHENCE IS THE FLOWER?

Hungry for beauty, men sometimes ask why God causes loveliness to bloom in obscure places. In this poem Emerson undertakes to answer the question. You may not consider his reply a clear-cut, crystal truth. Can you add anything to his argument that "Beauty is its own excuse for being"?

IN May, when seawinds pierced our solitudes,
I found the fresh Rhodora[1] in the woods,
Spreading its leafless blooms in a damp nook
To please the desert and the sluggish brook.
The purple[2] petals, fallen in the pool,   5
Made the black water with their beauty gay;
Here might the redbird come his plumes to cool
And court the flower that cheapens his array.

Rhodora! if the sages ask thee why
This charm is wasted on the earth and sky,   10
Tell them, dear, that if eyes were made for seeing,
Then Beauty is its own excuse for being:
Why thou wert there, O rival of the rose!

I never thought to ask, I never knew;
But in my simple ignorance suppose   15
The selfsame Power that brought me there brought you.

[1] *rhodora*, a New England shrub with delicate pink flowers.
[2] *purple*, formerly a color approaching crimson; also, brilliant or showy.

VIEWING THE AUTHOR'S IDEAS

Creation is a manifestation of God's beauty, goodness, power, and other attributes designed to increase His extrinsic glory. How do flowers give glory to God? In line with this reasoning, how would you explain that beauty unseen by men is not wasted? Are these conclusions a more adequate answer to the problem than the argument Emerson presents?

EVALUATING HIS MANNER OF EXPRESSION

1. What colors and scenes does the poet use to provide an effective background for the rhodora? How does he use contrast to heighten the beauty of the flower?

2. Is the particular merit of the poem in its beautiful description or in its challenge to thought? Discuss.

3. Discuss the artistic touch in the comparison of the flower and the redbird. Point out the whimsicality in the comparison.

4. Discuss the final line of the poem for its transcendental implications.

Forbearance

Ralph Waldo Emerson

In this poem Emerson discusses the kinds of self-control he desires in a friend. Sincere appreciation of noble deeds is one of the important elements of friendship. But how to express it? Some persons are so effusive that they cause embarrassment; others are so silent that they appear unappreciative. Do you think that Emerson presents an adequate solution?

HAST thou named all the birds without a gun?
Loved the wood rose and left it on its stalk?
At rich men's tables eaten bread and pulse?[1]
Unarmed, faced danger with a heart of trust?
And loved so well a high behavior

[1] *pulse*, a porridge made of meal or such vegetables as peas or beans.

In man or maid that thou from speech refrained,
Nobility more nobly to repay?
O, be my friend and teach me to be thine!

VIEWING THE AUTHOR'S IDEAS

1. Name the five different types of self-control which the poet recommends.

2. Report on present-day trends in the study of wild life. Is forbearance apparent?

3. Discuss the value of Emerson's idea concerning the silent appreciation of noble action. Do you think more people suffer from too much appreciation or from too great neglect? To what abuses in conversation is Emerson evidently objecting?

Where I Lived and What I Lived For

(From *Walden*)
Henry David Thoreau

From 1845 to 1847 Thoreau lived in a secluded cabin which he had built for himself on the shore of Walden Pond near Concord. He had been accustomed to spending so many of his days there that making the woods his permanent residence merely meant remaining at the hut for the night. It was not the self-denial of the hermits that led Thoreau into the wilderness. He wanted to enjoy the pleasures of freedom and ease, to read and to write, and to find the divine in nature. With the hermit's ascetic disregard for material things, he wore old clothes, lived on vegetables and berries, and supplied his corporal needs on an annual expenditure of less than nine dollars. By working at odd jobs one day a week he could earn enough to live the other six. Thoreau's eccentric individualism is not desirable for imitation, but his detachment and simplicity have a refreshing message.

WHEN first I took up my abode in the woods, that is, began to spend my nights as well as days there, which by accident was on Independence Day, or the Fourth of July, 1845, my house was not finished for winter but was merely a defense against the rain, without plastering or chimney, the walls being of rough, weather-stained boards, with wide chinks, which made it cool at night. The upright white hewn studs and freshly planed door and window casings gave it a clean and airy look, especially in the morning, when its timbers were saturated with dew, so that I fancied that by noon some sweet gum would exude from them. To my imagination it retained throughout the day more or less of this auroral[1] character, reminding me of a certain house on a mountain which I had visited a year before. This was an airy and unplastered cabin, fit to entertain a traveling god and where a goddess might trail her garments. The winds which passed over my dwelling were such as sweep over the ridges of mountains, bearing the broken strains, or celestial parts only, of terrestrial music. The morning wind forever blows, the poem of creation is uninterrupted; but few are the ears that hear it. Olympus[2] is but the outside of the earth everywhere. The only house I had been the owner of before, if

I except a boat, was a tent, which I used occasionally when making excursions in the summer, and this is still rolled up in my garret; but the boat, after passing from hand to hand, has gone down the stream of time. With this more substantial shelter about me I had made some progress toward settling in the world. This frame, so slightly clad, was a sort of crystallization around me and reacted on the builder. It was suggestive somewhat as a picture in outlines. I did not need to go outdoors to take the air, for the atmosphere within had lost none of its freshness. It was not so much within doors as behind a door where I sat even in the rainiest weather. The Harivansa[3] says, "An abode without birds is like a meat without seasoning." Such was not my abode, for I found myself suddenly neighbor to the birds, not by having imprisoned one but having caged myself near them. I was not only nearer to some of those which commonly frequent the garden and the orchard, but to those wilder and more thrilling songsters of the forest which never, or rarely, serenade a villager — the wood thrush, the veery, the scarlet tanager, the field sparrow, the whippoorwill, and many others.

I was seated by the shore of a small pond about a mile and a half south of the village of Concord and somewhat higher than it, in the midst of an extensive wood between that town and Lincoln, and about two miles south of that our only field known to fame, Concord Battleground; but I was so low in the woods that the opposite shore half a mile off, like the rest covered with wood, was my most distant horizon. For the first week whenever I looked out on the pond, it impressed me like a tarn high up on the side of a mountain, its bottom far above the surface of other lakes; and as the sun rose, I saw it throwing off its nightly clothing of mist, and here and there by degrees its soft ripples or its smooth reflecting surface was revealed, while the mists, like ghosts, were stealthily withdrawing in every direction into the woods as at the breaking up of some nocturnal conventicle. The very dew seemed to hang upon the trees later into the day than usual, as on the sides of mountains.

---

[1] *auroral*, pertaining to the dawn.
[2] *Olympus*, a mountain on which the gods of ancient Greece were thought to dwell.
[3] *Harivansa*, a poem written in Sanskrit, the language of ancient India.

This small lake was of most value as a neighbor in the intervals of a gentle rainstorm in August, when, both air and water being perfectly still but the sky overcast, midafternoon had all the serenity of evening; and the wood thrush sang around and was heard from shore to shore. A lake like this is never smoother than at such a time; and the clear portion of the air above it being shallow and darkened by clouds, the water, full of light and reflections, becomes a lower heaven itself so much the more important. From a hilltop near by, where the wood had been recently cut off, there was a pleasing vista southward across the pond through a wide indentation in the hills which form the shore there, where their opposite sides sloping toward each other suggested a stream flowing out in that direction through a wooded valley, but stream there was none. That way I looked between and over the near green hills to some distant and higher ones in the horizon, tinged with blue. Indeed, by standing on tiptoe I could catch a glimpse of some of the peaks of the still bluer and more distant mountain ranges in the northwest, those true-blue coins from heaven's own mint, and also of some portion of the village. But in other directions, even from this point, I could not see over or beyond the woods which surrounded me. It is well to have some water in your neighborhood to give buoyancy to and float the earth. One value even of the smallest well is that when you look into it you see that earth is not continent but insular. This is as important as that it keeps butter cool. When I looked across the pond from this peak toward the Sudbury meadows, which in time of flood I distinguished elevated perhaps by a mirage in their seething valley, like a coin in a basin, all the earth beyond the pond appeared like a thin crust insulated and floated even by this small sheet of intervening water; and I was reminded that this on which I dwelt was but *dry land*. . . .

I went to the woods because I wished to live deliberately, to front only the essential facts of life and see if I could not learn what it had to teach, and not, when I came to die, discover that I had not lived. I did not wish to live what was not life, living is so dear; nor did I wish to practice resignation, unless it was quite necessary. I wanted to live deep and suck out all the marrow of life, to live so sturdily and Spartanlike[4] as to put to rout all that was not life, to cut a broad swath and shave close, to drive life in a corner and reduce it to its lowest terms; and, if it proved to be mean, why then to get the whole and genuine meanness of it and publish its meanness to the world; or if it were sublime, to know it by experience and be able to give a true account of it in my next excursion. . . .

Still we live meanly, like ants; though the fable tells us that we were long ago changed into men; like pygmies we fight with cranes; it is error upon error and clout upon clout, and our best virtue has for its occasion a superfluous and evitable wretchedness. Our life is frittered away by detail. An honest man has hardly need to count more than his ten fingers, or in extreme cases he may add his ten toes and lump the rest. Simplicity, simplicity, simplicity! I say, let your affairs be as two or three, and not a hundred or a thousand; instead of a million count half a dozen, and keep your accounts on your thumbnail. In the midst of this chopping sea of civilized life such as the clouds and storms and quicksands and thousand and one items to be allowed for, that a man has to live, if he would not founder and go to the bottom and not make his port at all, by dead reckoning, and he must be a great calculator indeed who succeeds. Simplify, simplify. Instead of three meals a day, if it be necessary eat but one; instead of a hundred dishes, five; and reduce other things in proportion. Our life is like a German Confederacy made up of petty states, with its boundary forever fluctuating, so that even a German cannot tell you how it is bounded at any moment. The nation itself, with all its so-called internal improvements, which by the way are all external and superficial, is just such an unwieldy and overgrown establishment, cluttered with furniture and tripped up by its own traps, ruined by luxury and heedless expense, by want of calculation and a worthy aim, as the million households in the land; and the only cure for it, as for them, is in a rigid economy, a stern and more than Spartan simplicity of life and elevation of purpose. It lives too fast. Men think that it is essential that the *Nation* have commerce and export ice and talk through a telegraph and ride thirty miles an hour, without a doubt, whether *they* do or not; but whether we should live like baboons or like men is a little uncertain.

Shams and delusions are esteemed for soundest truth, while reality is fabulous. If men would steadily observe realities only, and not allow themselves to be

---

[4] *Spartanlike*, like the people of ancient Sparta, noted for their frugality and self-discipline.

deluded, life, to compare it with such things as we know, would be like a fairy tale, and the Arabian Nights entertainment. If we respected only what is inevitable and has a right to be, music and poetry would resound along the streets. When we are unhurried and wise, we perceive that only great and worthy things have any permanent and absolute existence—that petty fears and petty pleasures are but the shadow of the reality. This is always exhilarating and sublime. By closing the eyes, and slumbering, and consenting to be deceived by shows, men established and confirmed their daily life of routine and habit everywhere, which still is built on purely illusory foundations.

VIEWING THE AUTHOR'S IDEAS

1. What is implied in Thoreau's statement that he began to spend his nights as well as his days in the woods? List the aspects of nature and of life in the woods that appealed most to Thoreau.

2. In what passages does the author admit his pleasure in ownership? Contrast his way of securing the companionship of birds with that usually adopted by city dwellers. What attitudes are illustrated in Thoreau's statement that wells serve other important purposes besides keeping butter cool?

3. Cite the author's reasons for going to live alone in the woods. How did his motives differ from those of the hermits who lived in the desert? Compare Thoreau's attitude with that expressed in the *Imitation of Christ*: "As often as I went among men I returned less a man."

4. What essential and valuable experiences did Thoreau miss in his life of solitude? What sublime and mean aspects of life would one face in living in the woods?

5. In what words does Thoreau express his scorn of civilized life; of the American idea of national power and progress? What recommendations does he make for the simplification of life? Mention some ways by which modern life might be simplified.

EVALUATING HIS MANNER OF EXPRESSION

1. Explain the classical allusions in
a) "Fit to entertain a traveling god and where a goddess might trail her garments."
b) "Olympus is but the outside of earth everywhere."
c) "To live so sturdily and Spartanlike."
2. How does this selection illustrate the romantic attitude toward nature? How does it betray romantic individualism?
3. Point out passages that are vividly picturesque or poetic in style. Find forceful epigrammatic sentences and striking metaphors. Explain the meaning of the following passages:
a) "Winds . . . bearing the broken strains, or celestial parts only, of terrestrial music."
b) "The morning wind blows forever, the poem of creation is uninterrupted."
c) "Whether we should live like baboons or like men is a little uncertain."

The Great Carbuncle

Nathaniel Hawthorne

Hawthorne had frequently heard the Indian legend that far up in the White Mountains gleamed a brilliant red gem known as the Great Carbuncle. In this story, he uses the jewel as a symbol of the happiness sought by men. Each of the searchers sees the treasure as a means of achieving his own desires. In pursuing this end, all work in a spirit of pride, forgetting the common brotherhood which should unite them. Only two young people view the Great Carbuncle without tragedy, and even they decide that the jewel can bring them no good. After finding the awe-inspiring stone, they resolve to return to the joys of simple life.

It is obvious that the Great Carbuncle does not represent the search of the Christian for happiness. If such were the case, Matthew and Hannah certainly would have claimed their treasure. The jewel is really a symbol of some fruitless and blighting desire which intensifies man's selfish tendencies. Hawthorne had seen many people aspiring to the objective of transcendental mysticism, union with the Oversoul of the Universe. Confident that evil can be remedied only by the eradication of sin from the hearts of men, Hawthorne had no sympathy with those who considered man divine and capable of reaching God by his own unaided powers.

AT nightfall once in the olden time, on the rugged side of one of the Crystal Hills, a party of adventurers were refreshing themselves after a toilsome and fruitless quest for the Great Carbuncle. They had come thither, not as friends or partners in the enterprise, but each, save one youthful pair, impelled by his own selfish and solitary longing for this wondrous gem. Their feeling of brotherhood, however, was strong enough to induce them to contribute a mutual aid in building a rude hut of branches and kindling a great fire of shattered pines that had drifted down the headlong current of the Ammonoosuc[1], on the lower bank of which they were to pass the night. There was but one of their number, perhaps, who had become so esstranged from natural sympathies by the absorbing spell of the pursuit as to acknowledge no satisfaction at the sight of human faces in the remote and solitary region whither they had ascended. A vast extent of wilderness lay between them and the nearest settlement, while scant a mile above their heads was that black verge where the hills throw off their shaggy mantle of forest trees and either robe themselves in clouds or tower naked into the sky. The roar of the Ammonoosuc would have been too awful for endurance if only a solitary man had listened while the mountain stream talked with the wind.

The adventurers, therefore, exchanged hospitable greetings and welcomed one another to the hut, where each man was the host and all were the guests of the whole company. They spread their individual supplies of food on the flat surface of a rock and partook of a general repast, at the close of which a sentiment of good fellowship was perceptible among the party, though repressed by the idea that the renewed search for the Great Carbuncle must make them strangers again in the morning. Seven men and one young woman, they warmed themselves together at the fire, which extended its bright wall along the whole front of their wigwam. As they observed the various and contrasted figures that made up the assemblage, each man looking like a caricature of himself in the unsteady light that flickered over him, they came mutually to the conclusion that an odder society had never met in city or wilderness, on mountain or plain.

[1] *the Ammonoosuc*, a river in New Hampshire.

The eldest of the group — a tall, lean, weather-beaten man some sixty years of age — was clad in the skins of wild animals, whose fashion of dress he did well to imitate since the deer, the wolf, and the bear had long been his most intimate companions. He was one of those ill-fated mortals such as the Indians told of, whom in their early youth the Great Carbuncle smote with a peculiar madness and became the passionate dream of their existence. All who visited that region knew him as "the Seeker" and by no other name. As none could remember when he first took up the search, there went a fable in the valley of the Saco that for his inordinate lust after the Great Carbuncle he had been condemned to wander along the mountains till the end of time, still with the same feverish hopes at sunrise, the same despair at eve. Near this miserable Seeker sat a little elderly personage wearing a high-crowned hat shaped somewhat like a crucible. He was from beyond the sea — a Doctor Cacaphodel, who had wilted and dried himself into a mummy by continually stooping over charcoal furnaces and inhaling unwholesome fumes during his researches in chemistry and alchemy. It was told of him — whether truly or not — that at the commencement of his studies he had drained his body of all its richest blood and wasted it, with other inestimable ingredients, in an unsuccessful experiment, and had never been a well man since. Another of the adventurers was Master Ichabod Pigsnort, a weighty merchant and selectman of Boston and an elder of the famous Mr. Norton's church. His enemies had a ridiculous story that Master Pigsnort was accustomed to spend a whole hour after prayer time every morning and evening in wallowing naked among an immense quantity of pine-tree shillings, which were the earliest silver coinage of Massachusetts. The fourth whom we shall notice had no name that his companions knew of and was chiefly distinguished by a sneer that always contorted his thin visage and by a prodigious pair of spectacles which were supposed to deform and discolor the whole face of nature to this gentleman's perception. The fifth adventurer likewise lacked a name, which was the greater pity as he appeared to be a poet. He was a bright-eyed man but woefully pined away, which was no more than natural if, as some people affirmed, his ordinary diet was fog, morning mist, and a slice of the densest cloud within his reach, sauced with moonshine whenever he could get it. Certain it is that the poetry which flowed from him had a smack of all these dainties. The sixth of the party was a young man of haughty mien who sat somewhat apart from the rest, wearing his plumed hat loftily among his elders, while the fire glittered on the rich embroidery of his dress and gleamed intensely on the jeweled pommel of his sword. This was the Lord de Vere, who when at home was said to spend much of his time in the burial vault of his dead progenitors rummaging their moldy coffins in search of all the earthly pride and vainglory that was hidden among bones and dust; so that, besides his own share, he had the collected haughtiness of his whole line of ancestry.

Lastly, there was a handsome youth in rustic garb and by his side a blooming little person in whom a delicate shade of maiden reserve was just melting into the rich glow of a young wife's affection. Her name was Hannah, and her husband's Matthew — two homely names, yet well enough adapted to the simple pair who seemed strangely out of place among the whimsical fraternity whose wits had been set agog by the Great Carbuncle.

Beneath the shelter of one hut, in the bright blaze of the same fire, sat this varied group of adventurers, all so intent upon a single object that of whatever else they began to speak their closing words were sure to be illuminated with the Great Carbuncle. Several related the circumstances that brought them thither. One had listened to a traveler's tale of this marvelous stone in his own distant country and had immediately been seized with such a thirst for beholding it as could only be quenched in its intensest luster. Another, so long ago as when the famous Captain Smith visited these coasts, had seen it blazing far at sea and had felt no rest in all the intervening years till now that he took up the search. A third, being encamped on a hunting expedition full forty miles south of the White Mountains,[2] awoke at midnight and beheld the Great Carbuncle gleaming like a meteor so that the shadows of the trees fell backward from it. They spoke of the innumerable attempts which had been made to reach the spot and of the singular fatality which had hitherto withheld success from all adventurers, though it might seem so easy to follow to its source a light that overpowered the moon and almost matched the sun. It was observable that each smiled scornfully at the madness of every other in anticipating better fortune than the past, yet nourished a scarcely hidden conviction that he would himself be the favored one.

As if to allay their too sanguine hopes, they recurred to the Indian traditions that a spirit kept watch about the gem and bewildered those who sought it either by removing it from peak to peak of the higher hills or by calling up a mist from the enchanted lake over which it hung. But these tales were deemed unworthy of credit, all professing to believe that the search had been baffled by want of sagacity or perseverance in the adventurers, or such other causes as might naturally obstruct the passage to any given point among the intricacies of forest, valley, and mountain.

In a pause of the conversation the wearer of the prodigious spectacles looked round upon the party, making each individual in turn the object of the sneer which invariably dwelt upon his countenance.

"So, fellow pilgrims," said he "here we are, seven wise men and one fair damsel who doubtless is as wise as any graybeard of the company. Here we are, I say, all bound on the same goodly enterprise. Methinks, now, it were not amiss that each of us declare what he proposes to do with the Great Carbuncle provided he have the good hap[3] to clutch it. What says our friend in the bearskin? How mean you, good sir, to enjoy the prize which you have been seeking, the Lord knows how long, among the Crystal Hills?"

"How enjoy it!" exclaimed the aged Seeker bitterly. "I hope for no enjoyment from it; that folly has passed long ago. I keep up the search for this accursed stone because the vain ambition of my youth has become a fate upon me in old age. The pursuit alone is my strength, the energy of my soul, the warmth of my blood, and the pith and marrow of my bones! Were I to turn back upon it, I should fall down dead on the hither side of the Notch, which is the gateway of this mountain region. Yet not to have my wasted lifetime back again would I give up my hopes of the Great Carbuncle. Having found it, I shall bear it to a certain cavern that I wot[4] of, and there, grasping it in my arms, lie down and die and keep it buried with me forever."

[2] *White Mountains*, a mountain range in northern New Hampshire.

[3] *good hap*, good fortune.

[4] *wot*, know.

"O wretch regardless of the interests of science," cried Doctor Cacaphodel with philosophic indignation, "thou art not worthy to behold even from afar off the luster of this most precious gem that ever was concocted in the laboratory of Nature. Mine is the sole purpose for which a wise man may desire the possession of the Great Carbuncle. Immediately on obtaining it — for I have a presentiment, good people, that the prize is reserved to crown my scientific reputation — I shall return to Europe and employ my remaining years in reducing it to its first elements. A portion of the stone will I grind to impalpable powder, other parts shall be dissolved in acids, or whatever solvents will act upon so admirable a composition, and the remainder I design to melt in the crucible or set on fire with the blowpipe. By these various methods I shall gain an accurate analysis, and finally bestow the result of my labors upon the words in a folio volume."

"Excellent!" quoth the man with the spectacles. "Nor need you hesitate, learned sir, on account of the necessary destruction of the gem, since the perusal of your folio may teach every mother's son of us to concoct a Great Carbuncle of his own."

"But verily," said Master Ichabod Pigsnort, "for mine own part I object to the making of these counterfeits, as being calculated to reduce the marketable value of the true gem. I tell ye frankly, sirs, I have an interest in keeping up the price. Here have I quitted my regular traffic,[5] leaving my warehouse in the care of my clerks and putting my credit to great hazard, and furthermore have put myself in peril of death or captivity by the accursed heathen savages, and all this without daring to ask the prayers of the congregation, because the quest for the Great Carbuncle is deemed little better than a traffic with the evil one. Now, think ye that I would have done this grievous wrong to my soul, body, reputation, and estate without a reasonable chance of profit?"

"Not I, pious Master Pigsnort," said the man with the spectacles. "I never laid such a great folly to thy charge."

"Truly, I hope not," said the merchant. "Now, as touching this Great Carbuncle, I am free to own that I have never had a glimpse of it, but be it only the hundredth part so bright as people tell, it will surely outvalue the Great Mogul's best diamond,[6] which he holds at an incalculable sum; wherefore I am minded to put the Great Carbuncle on shipboard and voyage with it to England, France, Spain, Italy, or into heathendom if Providence should send me thither, and, in a word, dispose of the gem to the best bidder among the potentates of the earth, that he may place it among his crown jewels. If any of ye have a wiser plan, let him expound it."

"That have I, thou sordid man!" exclaimed the poet. "Dost thou desire nothing brighter than gold, that thou wouldst transmute all this ethereal luster into such dross as thou wallowest in already? For myself, hiding the jewel under my cloak, I shall hie me back to my attic chamber in one of the darksome alleys of London. There night and day will I gaze upon it. My soul shall drink its radiance; it shall be diffused throughout my intellectual powers and gleam brightly in every line of poesy that I indite. Thus long ages after I am gone the splendor of the Great Carbuncle will blaze around my name."

"Well said, Master Poet!" cried he of the spectacles. "Hide it under thy cloak, sayest thou? Why, it will gleam through the holes and make thee look like a jack-o'-lantern!"

"To think," ejaculated the Lord de Vere, rather to himself than his companions, the best of whom he held utterly unworthy of his intercourse — "to think that a fellow in a tattered cloak should talk of conveying the Great Carbuncle to a garret in Grub Street! Have not I resolved within myself that the whole earth contains no fitter ornament for the great hall of my ancestral castle? There shall it flame for ages, making a noonday of midnight, glittering on the suits of armor, the banners, and the escutcheons that hang around the wall, and keeping bright the memory of heroes. Wherefore have all other adventurers sought the prize in vain but that I might win it and make it a symbol of the glories of our lofty line. And never on the diadem of the White Mountains did the Great Carbuncle hold a place half so honored as is reserved for it in the hall of the de Veres!"

"It is a noble thought," said the Cynic, with an obsequious sneer. "Yet might I presume to say so, the gem would make a rare sepulchral lamp and would

---

[5] *traffic*, business.

[6] *Great Mogul's best diamond*, a diamond weighing 787 carats, which belonged to the Great Mogul, or ruler of the Mongolian empire.

display the glories of your Lordship's progenitors more truly in the ancestral vault than in the castle hall."

"Nay, forsooth," observed Matthew, the young rustic, who sat hand in hand with his bride, "the gentleman has bethought himself of a profitable use for this bright stone. Hannah here and I are seeking it for a like purpose."

"How, fellow?" exclaimed his Lordship in surprise. "What castle hall hast thou to hang it in?"

"No castle," replied Matthew, "but as neat a cottage as any within sight of the Crystal Hills. Ye must know, friends, that Hannah and I, being wedded the last week, have taken up the search of the Great Carbuncle because we shall need its light in the long winter evenings, and it will be such a pretty thing to show the neighbors when they visit us! It will shine through the house so that we may pick up a pin in any corner and will set all the windows a-glowing as if there were a great fire of pine knots in the chimney. And then how pleasant, when we awake in the night, to be able to see one another's faces!"

There was a general smile among the adventurers at the simplicity of the young couple's project in regard to this wondrous and invaluable stone with which the greatest monarch on earth might have been proud to adorn his palace. Especially the man with spectacles who had sneered at all the company in turn now twisted his visage into such an expression of ill-natured mirth that Matthew asked him, rather peevishly, what he himself meant to do with the Great Carbuncle.

"The Great Carbuncle!" answered the Cynic with ineffable scorn. "Why you blockhead, there is no such thing *in rerum natura*.[7] I have come three thousand miles and am resolved to set my foot on every peak of these mountains and poke my head into every chasm for the sole purpose of demonstrating to the satisfaction of any man one whit less an ass than thyself that the Great Carbuncle is all a humbug."

Vain and foolish were the motives that had brought most of the adventurers to the Crystal Hills, but none so vain, so foolish, and so impious too, as that of the scoffer with the prodigious spectacles. He was one of those wretched and evil men whose yearnings are downward to the darkness instead of heavenward and who, could

they but extinguish the lights which God hath kindled for us, would count the midnight gloom their chiefest glory.

As the Cynic spoke, several of the party were startled by a gleam of red splendor that showed the huge shapes of the surrounding mountains and the rock-bestrewn bed of the turbulent river with an illumination unlike that of their fire on the trunks and black boughs of the forest trees. They listened for the roll of thunder but heard nothing and were glad that the tempest came not near them. The stars — those dial points of heaven — now warned the adventurers to close their eyes on the blazing logs and open them in dreams to the glow of the Great Carbuncle.

The young married couple had taken their lodgings in the farthest corner of the wigwam and were separated from the rest of the party by a curtain of curiously woven twigs such as might have hung in deep festoons around the bridal bower of Eve. The modest little wife had wrought this piece of tapestry while the other guests were talking. She and her husband fell asleep with hands tenderly clasped and awoke from visions of unearthly radiance to meet the more blessed light of one another's eyes. They awoke at the same instant and with one happy smile beaming over their two faces which grew brighter with their consciousness of the reality of life and love. But no sooner did she recollect where they were than the bride peered through the interstices of the leafy curtain and saw that the outer room of the hut was deserted.

"Up, dear Matthew!" cried she, in haste. "The strange folk are all gone. Up this very minute, or we shall lose the Great Carbuncle!"

In truth, so little did these poor young people deserve the mighty prize which had lured them thither that they had slept peacefully all night and till the summits of the hills were glittering with sunshine, while the other adventurers had tossed their limbs in feverish wakefulness or dreamed of climbing precipices and set off to realize their dreams with the earliest peep of dawn. But Matthew and Hannah after their calm rest were as light as two young deer and merely stopped to say their prayers and wash themselves in a cold pool of the Ammonoosuc, and then to taste a morsel of food ere they turned their faces to the mountain side. It was a

7 *in rerum natura*, in the nature of things.

sweet emblem of conjugal affection as they toiled up the difficult ascent, gathering strength from the mutual aid which they afforded.

After several little accidents, such as a torn robe, a lost shoe, and the entanglement of Hannah's hair in a bough, they reached the upper verge of the forest and were now to pursue a more adventurous course. The innumerable trunks and heavy foliage of the trees had hitherto shut in their thoughts, which now shrank affrighted from the region of wind and cloud and naked rocks and desolate sunshine that rose immeasurably above them. They gazed back at the obscure wilderness which they had traversed and longed to be buried again in its depths rather than trust themselves to so vast and visible a solitude.

"Shall we go on?" said Matthew, throwing his arm around Hannah's waist both to protect her and to comfort his heart by drawing her close to it.

But the little bride, simple as she was, had a woman's love of jewels and could not forego the hope of possessing the very brightest in the world in spite of the perils with which it must be won.

"Let us climb a little higher," whispered she, yet tremulously, as she turned her face upward to the lonely sky.

"Come, then," said Matthew, mustering his manly courage and drawing her along with him; for she became timid again the moment that he grew bold.

And upward, accordingly, went the pilgrims of the Great Carbuncle, now treading upon the tops and thickly interwoven branches of dwarf pines which by the growth of centuries, though mossy with age, had barely reached three feet in altitude. Next they came to masses and fragments of naked rock heaped confusedly together like a cairn[8] reared by giants in memory of a giant chief. In this bleak realm of upper air nothing breathed, nothing grew; there was no life but what was concentered in their two hearts; they had climbed so high that Nature herself seemed no longer to keep them company. She lingered beneath them within the verge of the forest trees and sent a farewell glance after her children as they strayed where her own green footprints had never been. But soon they were to be hidden from her eye. Densely and dark the mists began

to gather below, casting black spots of shadow on the vast landscape and sailing heavily to one center as if the loftiest mountain peak had summoned a council of its kindred clouds. Finally the vapors welded themselves, as it were, into a mass, presenting the appearance of a pavement over which the wanderers might have trodden, but where they would vainly have sought an avenue of the blessed earth which they had lost. And the lovers yearned to behold that green earth again — more intensely, alas! than beneath a clouded sky they had ever desired a glimpse of heaven. They even felt it a relief to their desolation when the mists, creeping gradually up the mountain, concealed its lonely peak and thus annihilated — at least for them — the whole region of visible space. But they drew closer together with a fond and melancholy gaze, dreading lest the universal cloud should snatch them from each other's sight. Still, perhaps, they would have been resolute to climb as far and as high between earth and heaven as they could find foothold if Hannah's strength had not begun to fail, and with that her courage also. Her breath grew short. She refused to burden her husband with her weight, but often tottered against his side and recovered herself each time by a feebler effort. At last she sank down on one of the rocky steps of the acclivity.

"We are lost, dear Matthew," said she mournfully; "we shall never find our way to the earth again. And oh, how happy we might have been in our cottage!"

"Dear heart, we will yet be happy there," answered Matthew. "Look! In this direction the sunshine penetrates the dismal mist; by its aid I can direct our course to the passage of the Notch. Let us go back, love, and dream no more of the Great Carbuncle."

"The sun cannot be yonder," said Hannah with despondence. "By this time it must be noon; if there could ever be any sunshine here, it would come from above our heads."

"But look!" repeated Matthew in a somewhat altered tone. "It is brightening every moment. If not sunshine, what can it be?"

Nor could the young bride any longer deny that a radiance was breaking through the mist and changing its dim hue to a dusky red, which continually grew more vivid as if brilliant particles were interfused with the gloom. Now, also, the cloud began to roll away from

[8] *cairn*, a heap of stones for a memorial.

the mountain, while as it heavily withdrew, one object after another started out of its impenetrable obscurity into sight with precisely the effect of a new creation before the indistinctness of the old chaos had been completely swallowed up. As the process went on, they saw the gleaming of water close at their feet and found themselves on the very border of a mountain lake, deep, bright, clear, and calmly beautiful, spreading from brim to brim of a basin that had been scooped out of the solid rock. A ray of glory flashed across its surface. The pilgrims looked whence it should proceed but closed their eyes, with a thrill of awful admiration, to exclude the fervid splendor that glowed from the brow of a cliff impending over the enchanted lake.

For the simple pair had now reached that lake of mystery and had found the long-sought shrine of the Great Carbuncle.

They threw their arms around each other and trembled at their own success; for as the legends of this wondrous gem rushed thick upon their memory, they felt themselves marked out by fate, and the consciousness was fearful. Often from childhood upward they had seen it shining like a distant star, and now that star was throwing its intensest luster on their hearts. They seemed changed to one another's eyes in the red brilliancy that flamed upon their cheeks, while it lent the same fire to the lake, the rocks, and sky, and to the mists which had rolled back before its power. But with their next glance they beheld an object that drew their attention even from the mighty stone. At the base of the cliff, directly beneath the Great Carbuncle, appeared the figure of a man with his arms extended in the act of climbing and his face turned upward as if to drink the full gush of splendor. But he stirred not, no more than if changed to marble.

"It is the Seeker," whispered Hannah, convulsively grasping her husband's arm. "Matthew, he is dead."

"The joy of success has killed him," replied Matthew, trembling violently. "Or perhaps the very light of the Great Carbuncle was death."

"The Great Carbuncle!" cried a peevish voice behind them. "The Great Humbug! If you have found it, prithee point it out to me."

They turned their heads, and there was the Cynic with his prodigious spectacles set carefully on his nose, staring now at the lake, now at the rocks, now at the distant masses of vapor, now right at the Great Carbuncle itself, yet seemingly as unconscious of its light as if all the scattered clouds were condensed about his person. Though its radiance actually threw the shadow of the unbeliever at his own feet as he turned his back upon the glorious jewel, he would not be convinced that there was the least glimmer there.

"Where is your Great Humbug?" he repeated. "I challenge you to make me see it."

"There!" said Matthew, incensed at such perverse blindness and turning the Cynic round toward the illuminated cliff. "Take off those abominable spectacles, and you cannot help seeing it."

Now these colored spectacles probably darkened the Cynic's sight in at least as great a degree as the smoked glasses through which people gaze at an eclipse. With resolute bravado, however, he snatched them from his nose and fixed a bold stare full upon the ruddy blaze of the Great Carbuncle. But scarcely had he encountered it when with a deep, shuddering groan he dropped his head and pressed both hands across his miserable eyes. Thenceforth there was in very truth no light of the Great Carbuncle, nor any other light on earth, nor light of heaven itself, for the poor Cynic. So long accustomed to view all objects through a medium that deprived them of every glimpse of brightness, a single flash of so glorious a phenomenon, striking upon his naked vision, had blinded him forever.

"Matthew," said Hannah, clinging to him, "let us go hence."

Matthew saw that she was faint, and kneeling down, supported her in his arms while he threw some of the thrillingly cold water of the enchanted lake upon her face and bosom. It revived her but could not renovate her courage.

"Yes, dearest," cried Matthew, pressing her tremulous form to his breast, "we will go hence and return to our humble cottage. The blessed sunshine and the quiet moonlight shall come through our window. We will kindle the cheerful glow of our hearth at eventide and be happy in its light. But never again will we desire more light than all the world may share with us."

"No," said his bride, "for how could we live by day or sleep by night in this awful blaze of the Great Carbuncle?"

Out of the hollow of their hands they drank each a draft from the lake, which presented them its waters uncontaminated by an earthly lip. Then, lending their guidance to the blinded Cynic, who uttered not a word and even stifled his groans in his own most wretched heart, they began to descend the mountain. Yet as they left the shore, till then untrodden, of the spirit's lake, they threw a farewell glance toward the cliff and beheld the vapors gathering in dense volumes, through which the gem burned duskily.

As touching the other pilgrims of the Great Carbuncle, the legend goes on to tell that the worshipful Master Ichabod Pigsnort soon gave up the quest as a desperate speculation and wisely resolved to betake himself again to his warehouse near the town dock in Boston. But as he passed through the Notch of the mountains, a war party of Indians captured our unlucky merchant and carried him to Montreal, there holding him in bondage till by the payment of a heavy ransom he had woefully subtracted from his hoard of pine-tree shillings. By his long absence, moreover, his affairs had become so disordered that for the rest of his life, instead of wallowing in silver, he had seldom a sixpence-worth of copper. Doctor Cacaphodel, the alchemist, returned to his laboratory with a prodigious fragment of granite, which he ground to powder, dissolved in acids, melted in the crucible, and burned with the blowpipe and published the result of his experiments in one of the heaviest folios of the day. And for all these purposes the gem itself could not have answered better than the granite. The poet, by a somewhat similar mistake, made prize of a great piece of ice which he found in a sunless chasm of the mountains and swore that it corresponded in all points with his idea of the Great Carbuncle. The critics said that, if his poetry lacked the splendor of the gem, it retained all the coldness of the ice. The Lord de Vere went back to his ancestral hall, where he contented himself with a wax-lighted chandelier and filled in due course of time another coffin in the ancestral vault. As the funeral torches gleamed within that dark receptacle, there was no need of the Great Carbuncle to show the vanity of earthly pomp.

The Cynic, having cast aside his spectacles, wandered about the world a miserable object and was punished with an agonizing desire of light for the willful blindness of his former life. The whole night long he would lift his splendor-blasted orbs to the moon and stars; he turned his face eastward at sunrise as duly as a Persian idolater; he made a pilgrimage to Rome to witness the magnificent illumination of St. Peter's Church and finally perished in the Great Fire of London,[9] into the midst of which he had thrust himself with the desperate idea of catching one feeble ray from the blaze that was kindling earth and heaven.

Matthew and his bride spent many peaceful years and were fond of telling the legend of the Great Carbuncle. The tale, however, towards the close of their lengthened lives did not meet with the full credence that had been accorded to it by those who remembered the ancient luster of the gem. For it is affirmed that from the hour when two mortals had shown themselves so simply wise as to reject a jewel which would have dimmed all earthly things, its splendor waned. When other pilgrims reached the cliff, they found only an opaque stone with particles of mica glittering on its surface. There is also a tradition that as the youthful pair departed, the gem was loosened from the forehead of the cliff and fell into the enchanted lake, and that at noontide the Seeker's form may still be seen to bend over its quenchless gleam.

Some few believe that this inestimable stone is blazing as of old and say that they have caught its radiance like a flash of summer lightning far down the valley of the Saco. And be it owned that many a mile from the Crystal Hills I saw a wondrous light around their summits and was lured by the faith of poesy to be the latest pilgrim of the Great Carbuncle.

VIEWING THE AUTHOR'S IDEAS

1. What human traits and aspirations are represented in the characters of this story? How do they exemplify certain types of American characters today? What vain and selfish motives impelled the characters in their search for the Great Carbuncle?

2. Hawthorne once wrote, "All that isolates damns; all that associates saves." How had the quest of the Great Carbuncle alienated all the characters from their fellow men? What are some of the forms that the isolating sin of pride takes?

3. Why does the author describe the ascent of the young couple rather than the journey of one of the other characters? How were Matthew and Hannah tempted to give up the quest? How were they disillusioned at the end?

---

[9] *Great Fire of London*, the fire of September, 1666, which destroyed the greater part of London.

4. Hawthorne condemned the transcendentalists for identifying nature and man's soul with their concept of divinity called the Oversoul. In the light of this condemnation, comment on the passage beginning, "In this bleak realm of upper air nothing breathed . . ." Who first saw the Great Carbuncle? Why were Hannah and Matthew the only ones to receive enlightenment from the vision of the Great Carbuncle?

5. This story presents only erroneous methods of seeking happiness. How would you rewrite or continue the allegory in order to furnish more positive guidance for obtaining joy?

EVALUATING HIS MANNER OF EXPRESSION

1. Of the three elements, plot, setting, and character, which is most important in this story? When does one first become deeply interested in the action? How does Hawthorne's moral purpose give unity to the story?

2. Show that all the characters in this story are mere types or symbols of some human trait. How are they in accord with the author's allegorical purpose?

3. What legendary material of America does the story contain? Show that the narrative illustrates Hawthorne's frequent discussion of sin and evil in the human heart.

The Chase—Third Day

(From *Moby Dick*)
Herman Melville

Moby Dick *is a story of thrilling adventures on the whaling ship* Pequod. *More than this, Ahab's vindictive quest of the white whale symbolizes the awful conflict between good and evil in this world.*

The narrative preceding the climax of the third day's chase recounts Captain Ahab's vow to kill the great whale. Having lost a leg in an encounter with the mysterious monster known to mariners as Moby Dick, *the Captain becomes a bitter monomaniac, obsessed with the single purpose of vengeance against his hated foe. He sails from Nantucket in the* Pequod, *at the head of a mongrel crew of castaways, renegades, and cannibals. To the one who would first sight the white whale, he promises a gold doubloon nailed to the mainmast.*

The cruise is not without the usual exciting adventures of sighting, pursuing, and capturing ordinary whales, but the spirit-spout of Moby Dick, directing its snow-white fountain to the sky, constantly reminds the crew of the malicious object of their wild pursuit. Then one morning a cry comes from the mainmast, "There she blows! There she blows! A hump like a snow hill! It is Moby Dick." Ahab is first to sight the monster and claims for himself the gold doubloon. The boats

are lowered and the chase begins. The first day Ahab barely escapes death; the second, he loses his ivory leg. On the third day, the chase ends in the following dramatic story of Ahab's losing fight.

THE morning of the third day dawned fair and fresh, and once more the solitary nightman at the fore masthead was relieved by crowds of the daylight lookouts, who dotted every mast and almost every spar.

"D'ye see him?" cried Ahab; but the whale was not yet in sight.

"In his infallible wake, though; but follow that wake, that's all. Helm there; steady, as thou goest and hast been going. What a lovely day again! Were it a new-made world and made for a summer house to the angels and this morning the first of its throwing open to them, a fairer day could not dawn upon that world. Here's food for thought had Ahab time to think, but Ahab never thinks; he only feels, feels, feels; *that's* tingling enough for mortal man! To think's audacity. God only has that right and privilege. Thinking is or ought to be a coolness and a calmness; and our poor hearts throb, and our poor brains beat too much for that. And yet I've sometimes thought my brain was very calm — frozen calm, this old skull cracks so, like a glass in which the contents turn to ice and shiver it. And still this hair is growing now; this moment growing, and heat must breed it; but no, it's like that sort of common grass that will grow anywhere between the earthy clefts of Greenland ice or in Vesuvius lava. How the wild winds blow it; they whip it about me as the torn shreds of split sails lash the tossed ship they cling to. A vile wind that has no doubt blown ere this through prison corridors and cells and wards of hospitals and ventilated them and now comes blowing hither as innocent as fleeces. Out upon it! — it's tainted. Were I the wind, I'd blow no more on such a wicked, miserable world. I'd crawl somewhere to a cave and slink there. And yet, 'tis a noble and heroic thing, the wind! Who ever conquered it? In every fight it has the last and bitterest blow. Run tilting at it, and you but run through it. Ha! a coward wind that strikes stark-naked men but will not stand to receive a single blow. Even Ahab is a braver thing — a nobler thing than *that*. Would now the wind but had a body; but all the things that most exasperate and outrage mortal man, all these things are bodiless but only bodiless as objects, not as agents. There's a most special, a most cunning, oh, a most malicious difference! And yet I say again and swear it now that there's something all glorious and gracious in the wind. These warm trade winds, at least, that in the clear heavens blow straight on in strong and steadfast, vigorous mildness and veer not from their mark, however the baser currents of the sea may turn and tack and mightiest Mississippis of the land shift and swerve about, uncertain where to go at last. And by the eternal poles, these same trades that so directly blow my good ship on; these trades, or something like them — something so unchangeable and full as strong, blow my keeled soul along! To it! Aloft there! What d'ye see?"

"Nothing, sir."

"Nothing! and noon at hand! The doubloon[1] goes a-begging! See the sun! Aye, aye, it must be so. I've oversailed him. How, got the start? Aye, he's chasing *me* now; not I, *him* — that's bad; I might have known it, too.

Fool! the lines — the harpoons he's towing. Aye, aye. I have run him by last night. About! about! Come down, all of ye, but the regular lookouts! Man the braces!"[2]

Steering as she had done, the wind had been somewhat on the *Pequod's* quarter, so that now being pointed in the reverse direction, the braced ship sailed hard upon the breeze as she rechurned the cream in her own white wake.

"Against the wind he now steers for the open jaw," murmured Starbuck to himself, as he coiled the new-hauled main brace upon the rail. "God keep us, but already my bones feel damp within me and from the inside wet my flesh. I misdoubt me that I disobey my God in obeying him!"

"Stand by to sway me up!" cried Ahab, advancing to the hempen basket. "We should meet him soon."

"Aye, aye, sir," and straightway Starbuck did Ahab's bidding, and once more Ahab swung on high.

A whole hour now passed; gold-beaten out to ages. Time itself now held long breaths with keen suspense. But at last, some three points off the weather bow, Ahab descried the spout[3] again, and instantly from the three mastheads three shrieks went up as if the tongues of fire had voiced it.

"Forehead to forehead I meet thee this third time, Moby Dick! On deck there! — brace sharper up; crowd her into the wind's eye. He's too far off to lower yet, Mr. Starbuck. The sails shake! Stand over that helmsman with a topmaul![4] So, so; he travels fast, and I must down. But let me have one more good round look aloft here at the sea; there's time for that. An old, old sight, and yet somehow so young; aye, and not changed a wink since I first saw it, a boy, from the sandhills of Nantucket! The same! — the same! — the same to Noah as to me. There's a soft shower to leeward.[5] Such lovely leewardings! They must lead somewhere — to something else than common land, more palmy than the palms. Leeward! the White Whale goes that way; look to windward, then; the better if the bitterer quarter. But good-by, good-by, old masthead! What's this? — green? Aye, tiny mosses in these warped cracks. No such green weather stains on

---

[1] *doubloon*, a Spanish gold coin worth about sixteen dollars.

[2] *braces*, ropes for swinging the yards, or sail supports, into place.

[3] *spout*, a column of water which the whale blows upward as he rises to the surface to expel the old air and take in the new.

[4] *topmaul*, a heavy hammer.

[5] *leeward*, side opposite to the direction from which the wind blows.

Ahab's head! There's the difference now between man's old age and matter's. But aye, old mast, we both grow old together; sound in our hulls though, are we not, my ship? Aye, minus a leg, that's all. By heaven! this dead wood has the better of my live flesh every way. I can't compare with it; and I've known some ships made of dead trees outlast the lives of men made of the most vital stuff of vital fathers. What's that he said? He should still go before me, my pilot; and yet to be seen again?[6] But where? Shall I have eyes at the bottom of the sea, supposing I descend those endless stairs? And all night I've been sailing from him, wherever he did sink to. Aye, aye, like many more thou told'st direful truth as touching thyself, O Parsee;[7] but, Ahab, there thy shot fell short. Good-by, masthead — keep a good eye upon the whale the while I'm gone. We'll talk tomorrow, nay tonight, when the White Whale lies down there, tied by head and tail."

He gave the word; and still gazing round him, was steadily lowered through the cloven blue air to the deck.

In due time the boats were lowered; but as standing in his shallop's stern, Ahab just hovered upon the point of the descent, he waved to the mate, who held one of the tackle ropes on deck, and bade him pause.

"Starbuck!"

"Sir?"

"For the third time my soul's ship starts upon this voyage, Starbuck."

"Aye, sir, thou wilt have it so."

"Some ships sail from their ports and ever afterward are missing, Starbuck!"

"Truth, sir; saddest truth."

"Some men die at ebb tide; some at low water; some at the full of the flood. And I feel now like a billow that's all one crested comb, Starbuck. I am old—shake hands with me, man."

Their hands met; their eyes fastened; Starbuck's tears the glue.

"Oh, my captain, my captain! — noble heart — go not — go not! See, it's a brave man that weeps; how great the agony of the persuasion then!"

"Lower away!" cried Ahab, tossing the mate's arm from him. "Stand by, the crew!"

In an instant the boat was pulling round close under the stern.

"The sharks! the sharks!" cried a voice from the low cabin window there; "O master, my master, come back!"

But Ahab heard nothing; for his own voice was high-lifted then; and the boat leaped on.

Yet the voice spake true; for scarce had he pushed from the ship when numbers of sharks, seemingly rising from out the dark waters beneath the hull, maliciously snapped at the blades of the oars every time they dipped in the water and in this way accompanied the boat with their bites. It is a thing not uncommonly happening to the whaleboats in those swarming seas, the sharks at times apparently following them in the same prescient way that vultures hover over the banners of marching regiments in the east. But these were the first sharks that had been observed by the *Pequod* since the White Whale had been first descried; and whether it was that Ahab's crew were all such tiger-yellow barbarians and therefore their flesh more musky to the senses of the sharks — a matter sometimes well known to affect them — however it was, they seemed to follow that one boat without molesting the others.

"Heart of wrought steel!" murmured Starbuck, gazing over the side and following with his eyes the receding boat, "canst thou yet ring boldly to that sight, lowering thy keel among ravening sharks and followed by them, open-mouthed, to the chase; and this the critical third day?—For when three days flow together in one continuous intense pursuit, be sure the first is the morning, the second the noon, and the third the evening and the end of that thing — be that end what it may. Oh! my God! what is this that shoots through me and leaves me so deadly calm, yet expectant — fixed at the top of a shudder? Future things swim before me, as in empty outlines and skeletons; all the past is somehow grown dim. Mary, girl! thou fadest in pale glories behind me; boy![8] I seem to see but thy eyes grown wondrous blue. Strangest problems of life seem clearing; but clouds sweep between. Is my journey's end coming? My legs feel faint like his who has footed it all day. Feel thy heart — beats it yet? Stir thyself, Starbuck! — stave

---

[6] *before me . . . seen again.* The Parsee, or fire worshiper, had foretold that Ahab would not die until three things had been fulfilled: 1) that the Parsee would go before him and yet be seen again; 2) that hemp only could kill him; 3) that he would see two hearses on the sea, one not made with mortal hands and the other made of wood grown in America. From this prophecy Ahab concluded that he was immortal and that he would be victorious in his fight with Moby Dick.

[7] *direful truth . . . O Parsee.* The Parsee was missing after the encounter with the whale on the previous day.

[8] *Mary, girl! . . . boy!* Starbuck here alludes to his wife and child in Nantucket.

it off — move, move! speak aloud! Masthead there! See ye my boy's hand on the hill? — crazed — aloft there! — keep thy keenest eye upon the boats — mark well the whale! Ho! again! — drive off that hawk! see! he pecks, he tears the vane" — pointing to the red flag flying at the main-truck[9] — "Ha! he soars away with it! Where's the old man now? See'st thou that sight, oh Ahab? — shudder, shudder!"

The boats had not gone very far when by a signal from the mastheads — a downward-pointed arm — Ahab knew that the whale had sounded;[10] but intending to be near him at the next rising, he held on his way a little sideways from the vessel, the becharmed crew maintaining the profoundest silence as the head-beat waves hammered and hammered against the opposing bow.

"Drive, drive in your nails, O ye waves! To their uttermost heads drive them in! Ye but strike a thing without a lid; and no coffin and no hearse can be mine —and hemp only can kill me![11] Ha! Ha!"

Suddenly the waters around them slowly swelled in broad circles, then quickly upheaved as if sideways sliding from a submerged berg of ice swiftly rising to the surface. A low rumbling sound was heard; a subterraneous hum; and then all held their breaths as bedraggled with trailing ropes and harpoons and lances, a vast form shot lengthwise but obliquely[12] from the sea. Shrouded in a thin drooping veil of mist, it hovered for a moment in the rainbowed air, and then fell swamping back into the deep. Crushed thirty feet upward, the waters flashed for an instant like heaps of fountains, then brokenly sank in a shower of flakes, leaving the circling surface creamed like new milk round the marble trunk of the whale.

"Give way!" cried Ahab to the oarsmen, and the boats darted forward to the attack; but maddened by yesterday's fresh irons that corroded in him, Moby Dick seemed combinedly possessed by all the angels that fell from heaven. The wide tiers of welded tendons overspreading his broad white forehead beneath the transparent skin looked knitted together, as head on

he came churning his tail among the boats and once more flailed them apart, spilling out the irons and lances from the two mates' boats and dashing in one side of the upper part of their bows but leaving Ahab's almost without a scar.

While Daggoo and Queequeg[13] were stopping the strained planks, and as the whale, swimming out from them, turned and showed one entire flank as he shot by them again, at that moment a quick cry went up. Lashed round and round to the fish's back, piniond in the turns upon turns in which during the past night the whale had reeled the involutions of the lines around him, the half-torn body of the Parsee was seen, his sable raiment frayed to shreds, his distended eyes turned full upon old Ahab.

The harpoon dropped from his hand.

"Befooled, befooled!" — drawing in a long lean breath — "Aye, Parsee! I see thee again. Aye, and thou goest before; and *this,* this then is the hearse that thou didst promise.[14] But I hold thee to the last letter of thy word. Where is the second hearse? Away, mates, to the ship! Those boats are useless now; repair them if ye can in time, and return to me; if not, Ahab is enough to die. Down, men! The first thing that but offers to jump from this boat I stand in, that thing I harpoon. Ye are not other men, but my arms and my legs; and so obey me. Where's the whale? Gone down again?"

But he looked too nigh the boat; for as if bent upon escaping with the corpse he bore and as if the particular place of the last encounter had been but a stage in his leeward voyage, Moby Dick was now again steadily swimming forward, and had almost passed the ship, which thus far had been sailing in the contrary direction to him, though for the present her headway had been stopped. He seemed swimming with his utmost velocity and now only intent upon pursuing his own straight path in the sea.

"Oh! Ahab," cried Starbuck, "not too late is it even now the third day, to desist. See! Moby Dick seeks thee not. It is thou, thou, that madly seekest him!"

Setting sail to the rising wind, the lonely boat was swiftly impelled to leeward by both oars and canvas. And at last when Ahab was sliding by the vessel so

---

[9] *main-truck,* a wooden cap at the head of the mainmast for reeving the flag.

[10] *sounded,* submerged.

[11] *hemp , . . kill me,* an allusion to the prophecy of the Parsee.

[12] *obliquely,* in a slanting manner.

[13] *Daggoo and Queequeg,* harpooners.

[14] *hearse . . . promise.* The whale thus became the first hearse of the prophecy, one not made by human hands.

near as plainly to distinguish Starbuck's face as he leaned over the rail, he hailed him to turn the vessel about and follow him, not too swiftly, at a judicious interval. Glancing upward, he saw Tashtego, Queequeg, and Daggoo eagerly mounting to the three mastheads, while the oarsmen were rocking in the two staved boats which had just been hoisted to the side and were busily at work in repairing them. One after the other through the portholes as he sped, he also caught flying glimpses of Stubb and Flask[15] busying themselves on deck among bundles of new irons and lances. As he saw all this, as he heard the hammers in the broken boats, far other hammers seemed driving a nail into his heart. But he rallied. And now marking that the vane or flag was gone from the main masthead, he shouted to Tashtego,[16] who had just gained that perch, to descend again for another flag and a hammer and nails, and so nail it to the mast.

Whether fagged by the three days' running chase and the resistance to his swimming in the knotted hamper he bore, or whether it was some latent deceitfulness and malice in him — whichever was true, the White Whale's way now began to abate, as it seemed from the boat so rapidly nearing him once more; though indeed the whale's last start had not been so long a one as before. And still as Ahab glided over the waves, the unpitying sharks accompanied him and so pertinaciously stuck to the boat and so continually bit at the plying oars that the blades became jagged and crunched and left small splinters in the sea at almost every dip.

"Heed them not! Those teeth but give new rowlocks to your oars. Pull on! 'Tis the better rest, the shark's jaw than the yielding water."

"But at every bite, sir, the thin blades grow smaller and smaller!"

"They will last long enough! Pull on! But who can tell," he muttered, "whether these sharks swim to feast on the whale or on Ahab? But pull on! Aye, all alive, now — we near him. The helm! take the helm! let me pass," — and so saying, two of the oarsmen helped him forward to the bows of the still flying boat.

At length as the craft was cast to one side and ran ranging along with the White Whale's flank, he seemed strangely oblivious of its advance — as the whale sometimes will — and Ahab was fairly within the smoky mountain mist which, thrown off from the whale's spout, curled round his great, Monadnock[17] hump. He was even thus close to him; when, with body arched back and both arms lengthwise high-lifted to the poise, he darted his fierce iron and his far fiercer curse into the hated whale. As both steel and curse sank to the socket as if sucked into a morass, Moby Dick sideways writhed, spasmodically rolled his nigh flank against the bow, and without staving a hole in it so suddenly canted the boat over that had it not been for the elevated part of the gunwale to which he then clung, Ahab would once more have been tossed into the sea. As it was, three of the oarsmen, who foreknew not the precise instant of the dart and were therefore unprepared for its effects — these were flung out, but so fell that in an instant two of them clutched the gunwale again and rising to its level on a combing wave, hurled themselves bodily inboard again, the third man helplessly dropping astern but still afloat and swimming.

Almost simultaneously, with a mighty volition of ungraduated, instantaneous swiftness, the White Whale darted through the weltering sea. But when Ahab cried out to the steersman to take new turns with the line and hold it so, and commanded the crew to turn round on their seats and tow the boat up to the mark, the moment the treacherous line felt that double strain and tug, it snapped in the empty air!

"What breaks in me? Some sinew cracks! — 'tis whole again; oars! oars! Burst in upon him!"

Hearing the tremendous rush of the sea-crashing boat, the whale wheeled round to present his blank forehead at bay; but in that evolution, catching sight of the nearing black hull of the ship, seemingly seeing in it the source of all his persecutions, bethinking it — it may be — a larger and nobler foe, of a sudden he bore down upon its advancing prow, smiting his jaws amid fiery showers of foam.

Ahab staggered; his hand smote his forehead. "I grow blind; hands, stretch out before me that I may yet grope my way. Is't night?"

"The whale! The ship!" cried the cringing oarsmen.

"Oars! oars! Slope downwards to thy depths, O sea, that ere it be forever too late, Ahab may slide this last, last time upon his mark! I see, the ship! the ship! Dash on, my men! Will ye not save my ship?"

---

[15] *Stubb and Flask*, second mates.

[16] *Tashtego*, an Indian harpooner.

[17] *Monadnock*, a mountain in New Hampshire.

But as the oarsmen violently forced their boat through the sledge-hammering seas, the before whale-smitten bow ends of two planks burst through, and in an instant almost the temporarily disabled boat lay nearly level with the waves, its half-wading, splashing crew trying hard to stop the gap and bale out the pouring water.

Meantime, for that one beholding instant Tashtego's masthead hammer remained suspended in his hand; and the red flag, half-wrapping him as with a plaid, then streamed itself straight out from him as his own forward-flowing heart, while Starbuck and Stubb, standing upon the bowsprit beneath, caught sight of the down-coming monster just as soon as he.

"The whale, the whale! Up helm, up helm! O all ye sweet powers of air, now hug me close! Let not Starbuck die, if die he must, in a woman's fainting fit. Up helm, I say. Ye fools, the jaw! the jaw! Is this the end of all my bursting prayers, all my lifelong fidelities? O, Ahab, Ahab, lo, thy work. Steady! helmsman, steady. Nay, nay! Up helm again! He turns to meet us! Oh, his unappeasable brow drives on towards one whose duty tells him he cannot depart. My God, stand by me now!

"Stand not by me but stand under me, whoever you are that will now help Stubb; for Stubb, too, sticks here. I grin at thee, thou grinning whale! Who ever helped Stubb or kept Stubb awake but Stubb's own unwinking eye? And now poor Stubb goes to bed upon a mattress that is all too soft. Would it were stuffed with brushwood! I grin at thee, thou grinning whale! Look ye, sun, moon, and stars! I call ye assassins of as good a fellow as ever spouted up his ghost. For all that, I would yet ring glasses with ye, would ye but hand the cup! Oh, oh, oh, oh! thou grinning whale, but there'll be plenty of gulping soon! Why fly ye not, O Ahab? For me, off shoes and jacket to it; let Stubb die in his drawers! A most moldy and over-salted death, though; — cherries! cherries! cherries! O Flask, for one red cherry ere we die!"

"Cherries? I only wish that we were where they grow. O Stubb, I hope my poor mother's drawn my part-pay ere this; if not, few coppers will come to her now, for the voyage is up."

From the ship's bows nearly all the seamen now hung inactive; hammers, bits of plank, lances, and harpoons mechanically retained in their hands just as they had darted from their various employments; all their enchanted eyes intent upon the whale, which from side to side strangely vibrating his predestinating head, sent a broad band of over-spreading semicircular foam before him as he rushed. Retribution, swift vengeance, eternal malice were in his whole aspect, and spite of all that mortal man could do, the solid white buttress of his forehead smote the ship's starboard bow, till men and timbers reeled. Some fell flat upon their faces. Like dislodged trucks the heads of the harpooners aloft shook on their bull-like necks. Through the breach they heard the waters pour as mountain torrents down a flume.[18]

"The ship! The hearse! — the second hearse!" cried Ahab from the boat; "its wood could only be American!"[19]

Diving beneath the settling ship, the whale ran quivering along its keel; but turning under water, swiftly shot to the surface again, far off the other bow but within a few wards of Ahab's boat, where for a time he lay quiescent.

"I turn my body from the sun. What ho, Tashtego! let me hear thy hammer. O ye three unsurrendered spires of mine; thou uncracked keel and only god-bullied hull; thou firm deck and haughty helm and pole-pointed prow — death-glorious ship! must ye then perish, and without me? Am I cut off from the last fond pride of meanest ship-wrecked captains? O lonely death on lonely life! Oh, now I feel my topmost greatness lies in my topmost grief. Ho, ho! from all your furthest bounds pour ye now in, ye bold billows of my whole foregone life, and top this one piled comber[20] of my death! Towards thee I roll, thou all-destroying but unconquering whale; to the last I grapple with thee; from hell's heart I stab at thee; for hate's sake I spit my last breath at thee. Sink all coffins and all hearses to one common pool! And since neither can be mine, let me then tow to pieces while still chasing thee, though tied to thee, thou damned whale! *Thus,* I give up the spear!"

The harpoon was darted; the stricken whale flew forward; with igniting velocity the line ran through the groove; ran foul. Ahab stopped to clear it; he did clear it; but the flying turn caught him round the neck, and voicelessly as Turkish mutes bowstring their victim, he was shot out of the boat ere the crew knew he was gone. Next instant the heavy eye splice in the rope's final end

---

[18] *flume,* a pipe.

[19] *its wood . . . American.* The *Pequod* thus became the second hearse foretold by the Parsee.

[20] *comber,* a long curling wave.

flew out of the stark-empty tub,[21] knocked down an oarsman, and smiting the sea, disappeared in its depths.

For an instant the tranced boat's crew stood still, then turned. "The ship? Great God, where is the ship?" Soon they through dim, bewildering mediums saw her sidelong fading phantom as in the gaseous fata morgana,[22] only the uppermost masts out of water, while fixed by infatuation or fidelity or fate to their once lofty perches, the pagan harpooners still maintained their sinking lookouts on the sea. And now concentric circles seized the lone boat itself and all its crew and each floating oar and every lancepole, and spinning animate and inanimate all round and round in one vortex, carried the smallest chip of the *Pequod* out of sight.

But as the last whelmings intermixingly poured themselves over the sunken head of the Indian at the mainmast, leaving a few inches of the erect spar yet visible together with long streaming yards of the flag, which calmly undulated with ironical coincidings over the destroying billows they almost touched — at that instant, a red arm and a hammer hovered backwardly uplifted in the open air in the act of nailing the flag faster and yet faster to the subsiding spar. A skyhawk that tauntingly had followed the main-truck downwards from its natural home among the stars, pecking at the flag and incommoding Tashtego there — this bird now chanced to intercept its broad fluttering wing between the hammer and the wood; and simultaneously feeling that ethereal thrill, the submerged savage beneath in his death gasp kept his hammer frozen there; and so the bird of heaven, with unearthly shrieks and his imperial beak thrust upward and his whole captive form folded in the flag of Ahab, went down with his ship, which like Satan would not sink to hell till she had dragged a living part of heaven along with her and helmeted herself with it.

Now small fowls flew screaming over the yet yawning gulf; a sullen white surf beat against its steep sides; then all collapsed, and the great shroud of the sea rolled on as it rolled five thousand years ago.

EPILOGUE

"And I only am escaped
alone to tell Thee."

Job

The drama's done. Why then here does anyone step forth? — Because one did survive the wreck.[23]

It so chanced that after the Parsee's disappearance I was he whom the Fates ordained to take the place of Ahab's bowsman when that bowsman assumed the vacant post; the same who, when on the last day the three men were tossed from out of the rocking boat, was dropped astern. So floating on the margin of the ensuing scene and in full sight of it when the half-spent suction of the sunk ship reached me, I was then, but slowly, drawn towards the closing vortex. When I reached it, it had subsided to a creamy pool. Round and round then, and ever contracting towards the buttonlike black bubble at the axis of that slowly wheeling circle, like another Ixion[24] I did revolve. Till gaining that vital center, the black bubble upward burst; and now liberated by reason of its cunning spring and owing to its great buoyancy, rising with great force, the coffin life buoy shot lengthwise from the sea, fell over, and floated by my side. Buoyed up by that coffin for almost one whole day and night, I floated on a soft and dirgelike main. The unharming sharks, they glided by as if with padlocks on their mouths; the savage sea hawks sailed with sheathed beaks. On the second day, a sail drew near, nearer, and picked me up at last. It was the devious-cruising "Rachel" that, in her retracing search after her missing children, only found another orphan.

VIEWING THE AUTHOR'S IDEAS

1. Show how fact and fiction are mingled in this selection. What information does the author give concerning life on a whaling vessel and the method of capturing whales?

2. From the earliest times men have pondered over the problem of evil. Some, unable to reconcile God's wisdom and goodness with the many physical and moral imperfections in the world, have been led to despair and loss of faith. In what spirit does Ahab ponder upon this problem in his first long soliloquy? What explanation do reason and faith give for "all the things that most exasperate and outrage mortal man"?

---

[21] *eye splice . . . tub.* The harpoon rope with an eye splice or loop in the end of it was coiled in a tub from which it was let out when the whale was pierced and tried to get away. Usually the sailors fastened the rope to the boat as soon as possible and let the whale tow it until he was tired out. In this instance Ahab did not succeed in fastening the rope, and as it whirred out of the tub, it caught him around the neck, thus causing his death "by hemp" as foretold by the Parsee.

[22] *fata morgana,* a deceptive optical phenomenon caused by ascending waves of heated air.

[23] *one . . . wreck.* Ishmael, the narrator of the story, was the only survivor.

[24] *Ixion,* a king in Greek mythology who for his punishment in the underworld was bound to a revolving wheel.

3. What two statements of Ahab show that his quest is meant to be a symbol of the voyage of the human soul? Find statements which show that Moby Dick symbolizes demonic evil. In his treatment of the characters of Ahab and his renegade crew, how does the author show that even the worst of men have some good qualities?

4. Account for the tragic outcome of Ahab's conflict with the forces of evil embodied in *Moby Dick*. Cite passages which show that he sensed approaching tragedy. How do the other characters express their premonition of the impending doom?

EVALUATING HIS MANNER OF EXPRESSION

1. The story of the third day's chase has all the elements of drama. What changes would be necessary to make it a powerful one-act play?

2. The influence of Shakespeare is seen in the long soliloquies found in the highly dramatic dialogue. Compare the soliloquies of Ahab with the following speeches in the plays of Shakespeare beginning:

Oh, that this too, too solid flesh would melt . . .
  Hamlet, Act II, Scene 1
To be or not to be—that is the question . . .
  Hamlet, Act II, Scene 1
How all occasions do inform against me . . .
  Hamlet, Act IV, Scene 5
Blow, winds, and crack your cheeks! rage! blow!
  King Lear, Act III, Scene 2
Thou think'st 'tis much that this contention's storm
  . . . *King Lear,* Act III, Scene 4
Is it a dagger which I see before me . . .
  Macbeth, Act II, Scene 1.

Hymn to the Night

Henry Wadsworth Longfellow

Even in the period of sorrow following the death of his young wife, Longfellow seems to have escaped harsh reality. Simply, mildly, and with aspirations toward the spiritual, he reveals the healing power of night's beauty.

I HEARD the trailing garments of the Night
  Sweep through her marble halls!
I saw her sable skirts all fringed with light
  From the celestial walls!

I felt her presence by its spell of might   5
  Stoop o'er me from above;
The calm, majestic presence of the Night,
  As of the one I love.

I heard the sounds of sorrow and delight,
  The manifold, soft chimes,   10
That fill the haunted chambers of the Night,
  Like some old poet's rhymes.

From the cool cisterns of the midnight air
  My spirit drank repose;
The fountain of perpetual peace flows there —   15
  From those deep cisterns flows.

O holy Night! from thee I learn to bear
  What man has borne before!
Thou layest thy finger on the lips of Care,
  And they complain no more.   20

Peace! Peace! Orestes-like[1] I breathe this prayer!
  Descend with broad-winged flight,
The welcome, the thrice-prayed for, the most fair,
  The best-beloved Night!

VIEWING THE AUTHOR'S IDEAS

1. How does the poet use sight and hearing in describing Night in the first stanza? How does the second stanza continue the personification? To whom is the presence of Night likened?

2. Why is *haunted* an effective word to describe the "chambers of the Night"? What sounds are blended in the manifold soft chimes?

3. From what sources does the poet's spirit drink repose? How are these cisterns further described? What does the poet learn from Night? How is she a gentle teacher?

---

[1] *Orestes-like*, like Orestes, a character in Greek mythology who prayed to the goddess Athena for peace from the avenging Furies.

4. How could a person seeking relief from sorrow be called *Orestes-like?* In this last petition how is night likened to a bird?

1. Show that the old poet's rhymes of line 12 would be the lines of a romantic poet.

2. To how many things does the poet compare night? Do you think the poem gains or loses by these various comparisons?

Serenade

(From *The Spanish Student*)
Henry Wadsworth Longfellow

This simple love song, familiar to many in the musical setting of Berthold Tours, is contained in Longfellow's poetic drama, The Spanish Student. *The atmosphere of nocturnal beauty and the suggestion of dreaminess show Longfellow's tendency to use idyllic settings.*

STARS of the summer night!
Far in yon azure deeps
Hide, hide your golden light!
   She sleeps!
My lady sleeps!   5
   Sleeps!

Moon of the summer night!
   Far down yon western steeps
Sink, sink in silver light!
   She sleeps!   10
My lady sleeps!
   Sleeps!

Wind of the summer night!
   Where yonder woodbine creeps,

Fold, fold thy pinions light!   15
   She sleeps!
My lady sleeps!
   Sleeps!

Dreams of the summer night!
   Tell her, her lover keeps   20
Watch! while in slumbers light
   She sleeps!
My lady sleeps!
   Sleeps!

Explain the reason for the fanciful command which the poet gives in each stanza.

1. What words give a romantic atmosphere to the night? How do the sounds in the refrain suggest the hush of night and the quiet of sleep?

2. How is the poem typical of Longfellow's gentleness and tenderness in the expression of emotion?

The Arsenal[1] at Springfield

Henry Wadsworth Longfellow

The idea for this poem came during a visit which Longfellow and his wife made at the Springfield arsenal. Looking upon the cylindrical lines of guns stacked one upon another, Mrs. Longfellow noted the similarity to organ pipes. His imagination fired, the poet wrote these stanzas which rise and fall with the melody of deep organ tones. In the first seven stanzas the sound increases to a mighty crescendo, culminating with the thunder of modern warfare. The discords then quietly resolve into sweet harmony until the voice of Christ says, "Peace!"

---

[1] *arsenal,* an establishment for the storage of arms.

THIS is the Arsenal. From floor to ceiling,
  Like a huge organ, rise the burnished arms;
But from their silent pipes[2] no anthem pealing
  Startles the villages with strange alarms.

Ah! what a sound will rise, how wild and dreary,   5
  When the death angel touches those swift keys!
What loud lament and dismal Miserere[3]
  Will mingle with their awful symphonies!

I hear even now the infinite, fierce chorus,
  The cries of agony, the endless groan,   10
Which, through the ages that have gone before us,
  In long reverberations[4] reach our own.

On helm[5] and harness[6] rings the Saxon hammer,[7]
  Through Cimbric forest[8] roars the Norseman's song,
And loud, amid the universal clamor,   15
  O'er distant deserts sounds the Tartar gong.[9]

I hear the Florentine, who from his palace
  Wheels out his battle bell[10] with dreadful din,
And Aztec priests upon their teocallis[11]
  Beat the wild war drums made of serpent's skin;   20

The tumult of each sacked and burning village;
  The shout that every prayer for mercy drowns;
The soldiers' revels in the midst of pillage;
  The wail of famine in beleaguered towns;

The bursting shell, the gateway wrenched asunder,   25
  The rattling musketry, the clashing blade;
And ever and anon, in tones of thunder,
  The diapason[12] of the cannonade.

Is it, O man, with such discordant noises,
  With such accursèd instruments as these,
Thou drownest Nature's sweet and kindly voices   31
  And jarrest the celestial harmonies?

Were half the power that fills the world with terror,
  Were half the wealth bestowed on camps and courts
Given to redeem the human mind from error,   35
  There were no need of arsenals or forts:

The warrior's name would be a name abhorréd!
  And every nation that should lift again
Its hand against a brother, on its forehead
  Would wear forevermore the curse of Cain!   40

Down the dark future, through long generations,
  The echoing sounds grow fainter and then cease;
And like a bell, with solemn, sweet vibrations,
  I hear once more the voice of Christ say, "Peace!"

Peace! and no longer from its brazen portals   45
  The blast of War's great organ shakes the skies!
But beautiful as songs of the immortals,
  The holy melodies of love arise.

VIEWING THE AUTHOR'S IDEAS

1. Explain the poet's simile. How do the two kinds of pipes differ? What music is made upon the swift keys? Who is the organist? Who are the choir?

2. What music do the pipes bring to the poet? Describe the noise accompanying Saxon warfare. How did the Norsemen approach battle? What called the Tartar to war? With what summons did the Florentines and Aztecs begin the fight?

3. List the sounds which accompany the use of weapons and firearms. What new sounds have been added by the introduction of mechanized warfare? What major wars have taken place since Longfellow published this poem?

4. Explain the author's idea in lines 33-36. What means would you suggest "to redeem the human mind from error"? On what must lasting peace be based?

5. What qualities does the poet attribute to the voice of Christ? What songs follow His words?

EVALUATING HIS MANNER OF EXPRESSION

1. How does the poet secure the effect of increasing volume in sound as he builds towards the climax of the poem in line 28? Why is it fitting that this climax shall occur at the discharge of the cannon? In what lines does the sound of the words help to intensify the emotional effect? Contrast the melody of the last two lines of the poem with the passages describing the sounds of conflict.

2. Longfellow avoids realism even when writing of the horrors of war. How does he make his description of battle more picturesque than realistic? What expressions contribute to the imagery; to the emotion?

---

[2] *silent pipes*, the highly-burnished gun barrels.

[3] *Miserere*, a penitential psalm beginning, "Have mercy upon me, O Lord."

[4] *reverberations*, echoes.

[5] *helm*, helmet.

[6] *harness*, armor.

[7] *Saxon hammer*, the battle club of the Saxons.

[8] *Cimbric forest*, the forests of the Cimbri, an ancient German tribe.

[9] *Tartar gong*, battle gong of the Tartars, tribes inhabiting parts of Russia and Siberia.

[10] *Florentine . . . battle bell.* The warriors of Florence beat upon the martinella or battle bell, when they went into conflict.

[11] *teocallis* (tē-ô-kăl'-ĭz), Aztec or Mexican pyramids surmounted by temples.

[12] *diapason* (dī'á-pā'-zŭn), the entire range of tones.

The Skeleton in Armor

Henry Wadsworth Longfellow

In this stirring ballad Longfellow has made America a refuge for a bold Viking and his stolen bride. The skeleton in armor and the lofty tower are not fictional, although the legend the poet weaves from these materials is entirely his own creation. A skeleton clad in ancient armor had actually been dug up in Fall River, Massachusetts, two years before Longfellow wrote the narrative. At Newport, Rhode Island, stood an old round tower said to have been built by tenth-century Norse explorers.

"SPEAK! speak! thou fearful guest!
   Who, with thy hollow breast
Still in rude armor drest,
   Comest to daunt me!
Wrapt not in Eastern balms,[1]   5
But with thy fleshless palms
Stretched, as if by asking alms,
   Why dost thou haunt me?"

Then, from those cavernous eyes
Pale flashes seemed to rise   10
As when the Northern skies
   Gleam in December;[2]
And like the water's flow
Under December snow,
Came a dull voice of woe   15
   From the heart's chamber.

"I was a Viking[3] old!
My deeds, though manifold,
No Skald[4] in song has told,
   No saga[5] taught thee!   20
Take heed, that in thy verse
Thou dost the tale rehearse,
Else dread a dead man's curse;
   For this I sought thee.

"Far in the Northern Land,   25
By the wild Baltic's strand,

I, with my childish hand,
   Tamed the gerfalcon;[6]
And with my skates fast-bound,
Skimmed the half-frozen Sound,   30
That the poor whimpering hound
   Trembled to walk on.

"Oft to his frozen lair
Tracked I the grizzly bear,
While from my path the hare   35
   Fled like a shadow;
Oft through the forest dark
Followed the werewolf's[7] bark
Until the soaring lark
   Sang from the meadow.   40

"But when I older grew,
Joining a corsair's[8] crew,
O'er the dark sea I flew
   With the marauders.
Wild was the life we led;   45
Many the souls that sped,
Many the hearts that bled
   By our stern orders.

"Many a wassail bout[9]
Wore the long Winter out;   50
Often our midnight shout
   Set the cocks crowing
As we the Berserk's[10] tale
Measured in cups of ale,
Draining the oaken pail,   55
   Filled to o'erflowing.

"Once as I told in glee
Tales of the stormy sea,
Soft eyes did gaze on me,
   Burning yet tender;   60
And as the white stars shine
On the dark Norway pine,

---

[1] *Eastern balms*, spices used by the Egyptians in embalming the dead.

[2] *Northern skies . . . December*, an allusion to the aurora borealis or northern lights.

[3] *Viking*, a Norse pirate. The Vikings plundered the coast of Europe from the eighth to the tenth century.

[4] *Skald*, an ancient Scandinavian bard.

[5] *saga*, a Scandinavian story of heroic deeds.

[6] *gerfalcon*, a species of hawk used in hunting fowl.

[7] *werewolf*, a person having the power to change himself into a wolf.

[8] *corsair*, a pirate.

[9] *wassail bout*, a drinking contest.

[10] *Berserk*, a Norse warrior who fought with the frenzied fury of a wild animal.

On that dark heart of mine
  Fell their soft splendor.

"I wooed the blue-eyed maid,   65
Yielding, yet half afraid,
And in the forest's shade
  Our vows were plighted.
Under its loosened vest
Fluttered her little breast,   70
Like birds within their nest
  By the hawk frighted.

"Bright in her father's hall
Shields gleamed upon the wall,
Loud sang the minstrels all,   75
  Chanting his glory;
When of old Hildebrand
I asked his daughter's hand,
Mute did the minstrels stand
  To hear my story.   80

"While the brown ale he quaffed,
Loud then the champion laughed,
And as the wind-gusts waft
  The sea foam brightly,
So the loud laugh of scorn,   85
Out of those lips unshorn,
From the deep drinking horn
  Blew the foam lightly.

"She was a Prince's child,
I but a Viking wild,   90
And though she blushed and smiled,
  I was discarded!
Should not the dove so white
Follow the sea mew's[11] flight,
Why did they leave that night   95
  Her nest unguarded?

"Scarce had I put to sea,
Bearing the maid with me,
Fairest of all was she
  Among the Norsemen!   100
When on the white seastrand,
Waving his armèd hand,
Saw we old Hildebrand
  With twenty horsemen.

"Then launched they to the blast,   105
Bent like a reed each mast,
Yet we were gaining fast,
  When the wind failed us;
And with a sudden flaw
Came round the gusty Skaw,[12]   110
So that our foe we saw
  Laugh as he hailed us.

"And as to catch the gale
Round veered the flapping sail,
'Death!' was the helmsman's hail,   115
  'Death without quarter!'
Midships with iron keel
Struck we her ribs of steel;
Down her black hulk did reel
  Through the black water!   120

"As with his wings aslant
Sails the fierce cormorant,[13]
Seeking some rocky haunt,
  With his prey laden,
So toward the open main,   125
Beating to sea again,
Through the wild hurricane
  Bore I the maiden.

"Three weeks we westward bore,
And when the storm was o'er,   130
Cloudlike we saw the shore
  Stretching to leeward;
There for my lady's bower
Built I the lofty tower,
Which, to this very hour,   135
  Stands looking seaward.

"There lived we many years;
Time dried the maiden's tears;
She had forgot her fears,
  She was a mother;   140
Death closed her mild blue eyes,
Under that tower she lies;
Ne'er shall the sun arise
  On such another!

"Still grew my bosom then,   145
Still as a stagnant fen!

---

[11] *sea mew*, a sea gull.

[12] *Skaw*, Cape Skagen on the coast of Denmark.
[13] *cormorant*, a sea raven given to gluttony.

Hateful to me were men,
  The sunlight hateful!
In the vast forest here,
Clad in my warlike gear,   150
Fell I upon my spear,
  Oh, death was grateful!

"Thus, seamed with many scars,
Bursting these prison bars,
Up to its native stars   155
  My soul ascended!
There from the flowing bowl
Deep drinks the warrior's soul,
Skoal![14] to the Northland! skoal!"
Thus the tale ended.   160

VIEWING THE AUTHOR'S IDEAS

1. How does the poem explain the presence of the skeleton on the New England coast? What other explanations might be made? Give a brief account of early Norse explorations in America.

2. What does the poem reveal concerning the life and customs of the Norseman? Describe the scene in Hildebrand's hall.

3. How does the poet show the strength and courage of the Vikings; their lawlessness; their disregard for human life;

[14] *skoal*, a Scandinavian salutation when drinking a toast.

their love of the sea; their respect for women?

4. How was the bride finally reconciled to her lonely life in the New World? What lines show her sorrow at the tragic death of her father and at the separation from her native land? Find lines which seem to indicate that the Viking later regretted his rash action.

5. In your opinion why did the Viking prefer suicide to a return to his native land? What details are barely suggested in lines 95-96; 119-120? Compare the Norseman's view of death with that expressed in "The Indian Burying Ground."

EVALUATING HIS MANNER OF EXPRESSION

1. Give the time and setting of the story. What lines show that the poem is Longfellow's own invention and not based upon an old Norse legend?

2. Where is dialogue employed in the ballad? How does this poem differ from the old English ballads in the use of conversational elements? In what way does the rhythm contribute to the rapid movement of the story? Find examples of picturesque imagery.

3. From the suggestions given in the poem, describe the personal appearance of the chief characters. What elemental human emotions are depicted in the actions of these characters?

4. Show how the following ballad conventions are used: curses; bequests; story told by the dead returned to life; abduction of a beautiful maiden; preternatural beings.

5. Compare the ballad with Sir Walter Scott's "Lochinvar."

Divina Commedia

Henry Wadsworth Longfellow

After his second wife's death Longfellow sought distraction from his grief by occupying himself with a translation of Dante's Divine Comedy. *To precede and follow each of the three major divisions, the* Inferno, Purgatorio, *and* Paradiso, *the poet wrote six sonnets. In the first sonnet he compares the* Divine Comedy *to a cathedral which he enters to kneel in prayer and retreat from the world. The sixth sonnet is an apostrophe to Dante showing the great Italian's place in history. This series of poems represents Longfellow's finest work.*

SONNET 1

OFT have I seen at some cathedral door
  A laborer, pausing in the dust and heat,
Lay down his burden, and with reverent feet
Enter and cross himself, and on the floor
Kneel to repeat his paternoster[1] o'er;   5
Far off the noises of the world retreat;
The loud vociferations[2] of the street

[1] *paternoster*, the Our Father.
[2] *vociferations*, outcries.

Become an undistinguishable roar.
So, as I enter here from day to day
And leave my burden at this minster gate,[3]   10
Kneeling in prayer and not ashamed to pray,
The tumult of the time disconsolate[4]
To inarticulate murmurs dies away,
While the eternal ages watch and wait.

SONNET VI

O star of morning and of liberty![5]
O bringer of the light, whose splendor shines
Above the darkness of the Apennines,[6]
Forerunner of the day that is to be!
The voices of the city and the sea,   75
The voices of the mountains and the pines,
Repeat thy song, till the familiar lines
Are footpaths for the thought of Italy!
Thy flame is blown abroad from all the heights,
Through all the nations, and a sound is heard   80
As of a mighty wind, and men devout,
Strangers of Rome, and the new proselytes,[7]
In their own language hear the wondrous word,
And many are amazed and many doubt.

[3] *minster gate*, cathedral door.
[4] *the time disconsolate*, the Civil War.
[5] *O star . . . liberty*, Dante, the prophet of Italian freedom.
[6] *Apennines*, an Italian mountain range.
[7] *proselytes*, new converts.

VIEWING THE AUTHOR'S IDEAS

SONNET I

1. What makes the scene described more typical of Europe than of the United States? How is the interior of the cathedral contrasted with the outside world?

2. What burden did Longfellow wish to forget by finding a haven in literature? How did conditions in America at this time increase his sadness?

SONNET VI

1. What great tribute does the poet pay to Dante in the first two lines? How might Dante be said to be "a bringer of light"? In what way was he "forerunner of the day that is to be"?

2. Which lines show that the *Divine Comedy* became known throughout the world; was translated into many languages; had great power wherever it was read? What different effects did it have on its readers?

EVALUATING HIS MANNER OF EXPRESSION

1. These poems are examples of the Petrarchan or Italian sonnet, also called the regular sonnet. How does the octave, or first eight lines, give a situation in each poem? How does each sestet, or final six lines, present an application?

2. The rhyme scheme of the octave in an Italian sonnet runs *abba, abba*. In the sestet more freedom of arrangement is allowed. Give the rhyme scheme of the sestet in each of these sonnets.

The Warning

Henry Wadsworth Longfellow

In a day when open attacks upon slavery were unpopular, Longfellow saw grave injustice in the position of the American Negro. To him the Biblical story of Samson symbolized the history of the oppressed race. With unusual sternness he warns that unless the Negro is awarded his full rights, punishment and destruction will descend upon the people who have caused his suffering.

The sentiments expressed in this poem might well serve as warning today, when the racial question is among our most serious problems.

BEWARE! The Israelite of old who tore
The lion in his path[1]—when, poor and blind,
He saw the blessed light of heaven no more,
   Shorn of his noble strength and forced to grind

[1] *Israelite . . . lion in his path.* On a journey in his youth, Samson had been given strength to kill a lion which came towards him, raging and roaring. As judge of the Israelites he had been unconquered by the Philistines until he confided to Dalila that his strength lay in his unshorn hair. After Dalila had caused his hair to be cut, the Philistines captured and blinded Samson and humiliatingly bound him to the pillars of the house in which they were feasting. Having prayed that he might avenge the enemies of God, Samson shook the pillars of the edifice, pulling down the house and destroying himself and a great multitude of Philistines.

In prison, and at last led forth to be   5
A pander[2] to Philistine revelry —

Upon the pillars of the temple laid
  His desperate hands, and in its overthrow
Destroyed himself and with him those who made
  A cruel mockery of his sightless woe;   10
The poor blind slave, the scoff and jest of all,
Expired, and thousands perished in the fall!

There is a poor blind Samson in this land,
  Shorn of his strength and bound in bonds of steel,
Who may in some grim revel raise his hand   15
  And shake the pillars of this commonweal,
Till the vast temple of our liberties
A shapeless mass of wreck and rubbish lies.

[2] *pander,* a minister to the passions of others.

1. To what incident in Samson's youth do the first two lines refer? What great suffering came to him later in life? How did he bring death to himself and destruction upon the Philistines who had mocked him?

2. Whom did Longfellow consider the American Samson? In what way was the modern Samson "shorn of his strength and bound in bonds of steel"?

3. How was Longfellow's prediction fulfilled in the Civil War? In what manner may the nation be further punished for injustice to a minority group?

4. Longfellow has sometimes been criticized for failing to evaluate the social changes of his times. In your opinion, how does this poem help to soften the charge?

EVALUATING HIS MANNER OF EXPRESSION

The third stanza of the poem is an extended metaphor. By reference to the early stanzas show the various comparisons which the poet makes.

Hiawatha's Departure

(From *The Song of Hiawatha*)
Henry Wadsworth Longfellow

In The Song of Hiawatha *Longfellow wove together various Indian traditions to form a narrative poem "as sweet and wholesome as maize." The author based his idealization of Indian life upon numerous legends drawn chiefly from the works of Henry Rowe Schoolcraft. Combining an Iroquois national hero with a mythical figure of the Algonquins, Longfellow constructed the superhuman character of Hiawatha. Like the Algonquin spirit, Manabozho, Hiawatha was born of the West Wind. His mother was the daughter of the fair Nokomis, who had fallen from the moon. Like the Iroquois hero, the noble Hiawatha conquered the evil enemies of his people and taught them the arts of peace. At last the time came for him to return to the "regions of the home wind," the Land of the Hereafter. As he prepared for his departure, he joyfully welcomed the Black Robe who brought the light of Christianity to the Indians. The closing scene of the poem is a paraphrase of the account in* The Jesuit Relations *of Father Marquette's visit to the Algonquins in 1673.*

BY THE shore of Gitche Gumee,[1]
  By the shining Big-Sea Water,
At the doorway of his wigwam,
In the pleasant summer morning,
Hiawatha stood and waited.   5
  All the air was full of freshness,
All the earth was bright and joyous,
And before him, through the sunshine,
Westward toward the neighboring forest
Passed in golden swarms the Ahmo,   10
Passed the bees, the honey makers,
Burning, singing in the sunshine.
  Bright above him shone the heavens,
Level spread the lake before him,
From its bosom leaped the sturgeon,   15
Sparkling, flashing in the sunshine;
On its margin the great forest
Stood reflected in the water;

[1] *Gitche Gumee,* the Algonquin name for Lake Superior, meaning great water.

Every treetop had its shadow,
Motionless beneath the water.   20
  From the brow of Hiawatha
Gone was every trace of sorrow,
As the fog from off the water,
As the mist from off the meadow.
With a smile of joy and triumph,   25
With a look of exultation,
As of one who in a vision
Sees what is to be, but is not,
Stood and waited Hiawatha.
  Toward the sun his hands were lifted,   30
Both the palms spread out against it,
And between the parted fingers
Fell the sunshine on his features,
Flecked with light his naked shoulders,
As it falls and flecks an oak tree   35
Through the rifted leaves and branches.
  O'er the water floating, flying,
Something in the hazy distance,
Something in the mists of morning,
Loomed and lifted from the water,   40
Now seemed floating, now seemed flying,
Coming nearer, nearer, nearer.
  Was it Shingebis, the diver?
Or the pelican, the Shada?
Or the heron, the Shuh-shuh-gah?   45
Or the white goose, Waw-be-wawa,
With the water dripping, flashing,
From its glossy neck and feathers?
  It was neither goose nor diver,
Neither pelican nor heron,   50
O'er the water floating, flying,
Through the shining mist of morning,
But a birch canoe with paddles,
Rising, sinking on the water,
Dripping, flashing in the sunshine,   55
And within it came a people
From the distant land of Wabun,[2]
From the farthest realms of morning,
Came the Black Robe chief, the Prophet,
He the Priest of Prayer, the Paleface,   60
With his guides and his companions.
  And the noble Hiawatha
With his hands aloft extended,

Held aloft in sign of welcome,
Waited, full of exultation,   65
Till the birch canoe with paddles
Grated on the shining pebbles,
Stranded on the sandy margin,
Till the Black Robe chief, the Paleface,
With the cross upon his bosom,   70
Landed on the sandy margin.
  Then the joyous Hiawatha
Cried aloud and spake in this wise:
"Beautiful is the sun, O strangers,
When you come so far to see us!   75
All our town in peace awaits you,
All our doors stand open for you;
You shall enter all our wigwams,
For the heart's right hand we give you.
  "Never bloomed the earth so gayly,   80
Never shone the sun so brightly,
As today they shine and blossom
When you come so far to see us!
Never was our lake so tranquil,
Nor so free from rocks and sand bars;   85
For your birch canoe in passing
Has removed both rock and sand bar!
  "Never before had our tobacco
Such a sweet and pleasant flavor,
Never the broad leaves of our cornfields   90
Were so beautiful to look on
As they seem to us this morning
When you come so far to see us!"
  And the Black Robe chief made answer,
Stammered in this speech a little,   95
Speaking words yet unfamiliar:
"Peace be with you, Hiawatha,
Peace of prayer and peace of pardon,
Peace of Christ and joy of Mary!"
  Then the generous Hiawatha   100
Led the strangers to his wigwam,
Seated them on skins of bison,
Seated them on skins of ermine,
And the careful old Nokomis[3]
Brought them food in bowls of basswood,
Water brought in birchen dippers,   106
And the calumet, the peace pipe,

---

[2] *Wabun*, the East Wind.

[3] *Nokomis*, a grandmother; the mother of Winonah and the grandmother of Hiawatha.

Filled and lighted for their smoking.
  All the old men of the village,
All the warriors of the nation,   110
All the Jossakeeds, the prophets,
The magicians, the Wabenos.
And the medicine men, the Medas,
Came to bid the strangers welcome;
"It is well," they said, "O brothers,   115
That you come so far to see us!"
  In a circle round the doorway,
With their pipes they sat in silence,
Waiting to behold the strangers,
Waiting to receive their message;   120
Till the Black Robe chief, the Paleface,
From the wigwam came to greet them,
Stammering in his speech a little,
Speaking words yet unfamiliar;
"It is well," they said, "O brother,   125
That you come so far to see us!"
  Then the Black Robe chief, the prophet,
Told his message to the people,
Told the purport of his mission,
Told them of the Virgin Mary,   130
And her blessed Son, the Saviour,
How in distant lands and ages
He had lived on earth as we do;
How He fasted, prayed, and labored;
How the Jews, the tribe accursed,   135
Mocked Him, scourged Him, crucified Him;
How He rose from where they laid Him;
Walked again with His disciples
And ascended into heaven.
  And the chiefs made answer saying: 140
"We have listened to your message,
We have heard your words of wisdom,
We will think on what you tell us.
It is well for us, O brothers,
That you come so far to see us!"   145
  Then they rose up and departed
Each one homeward to his wigwam,
To the young men and the women
Told the story of the strangers
Whom the Master of Life had sent them   150
From the shining land of Wabun.
  Heavy with the heat and silence

Grew the afternoon of summer;
With a drowsy sound the forest
Whispered round the sultry wigwam;   155
With a sound of sleep the water
Rippled on the beach below it;
From the cornfields shrill and ceaseless
Sang the grasshopper, Pah-Puk-keena;
And the guests of Hiawatha,   160
Weary with the heat of Summer,
Slumbered in the sultry wigwam.
  Slowly o'er the simmering landscape
Fell the evening's dusk and coolness,
And the long and level sunbeams   165
Shot their spears into the forest,
Breaking through its shields of shadow.
Rushed into each secret ambush,
Searched each thicket, dingle, hollow;
Still the guests of Hiawatha   170
Slumbered in the silent wigwam.
  From his place rose Hiawatha,
Bade farewell to old Nokomis,
Spake in whispers, spake in this wise,
Did not wake the guests that slumbered: 175
"I am going, O Nokomis,
On a long and distant journey,
To the portals of the Sunset,
To the regions of the home wind,
Of the northwest wind, Keewaydin.   180
But these guests I leave behind me,
In your watch and ward I leave them;
See that never harm comes near them,
See that never fear molests them,
Never danger nor suspicion,   185
Never want of food or shelter,
In the lodge of Hiawatha!"
  Forth into the village went he,
Bade farewell to all the warriors,
Bade farewell to all the young men, 190
Spake persuading, spake in this wise:
"I am going, O my people,
On a long and distant journey;
Many moons and many winters
Will have come and will have vanished, 195
Ere I come again to see you.
But my guests I leave behind me;

Listen to their words of wisdom,
Listen to the truth they tell you,
For the Master of Life has sent them   200
From the land of light and morning!"
On the shore stood Hiawatha,
Turned and waved his hand at parting;
On the clear and luminous water
Launched his birch canoe for sailing;   205
From the pebbles of the margin
Shoved it forth into the water;
Whispered to it, "Westward! westward!"
And with speed it darted forward.

   And the evening sun descending   210
Set the clouds on fire with redness,
Burned the broad sky, like a prairie,
Left upon the level water
One long track and trail of splendor
Down whose stream as down a river,   215
Westward, westward Hiawatha
Sailed into the fiery sunset,
Sailed into the purple vapors,
Sailed into the dusk of evening.

   And the people from the margin   220
Watched him floating, rising, sinking,
Till the birch canoe seemed lifted
High into that sea of splendor.
Till it sank into the vapors
Like the new moon slowly, slowly   225
Sinking in the purple distance.

   And they said, "Farewell forever!"
Said "Farewell, O Hiawatha!"
And the forests, dark and lonely,
Moved through all their depths of darkness,   230
Sighed, "Farewell, O Hiawatha!"
And the waves upon the margin
Rising, rippling on the pebbles,
Sobbed, "Farewell, O Hiawatha!"
And the heron, the Shuh-shuh-gah,   235
From her haunts among the fen lands
Screamed, "Farewell, O Hiawatha!"

   Thus departed Hiawatha,
Hiawatha, the Beloved,
In the glory of the sunset,   240
In the purple mists of evening,
To the regions of the home wind,
Of the northwest wind, Keewaydin,

To the Islands of the Blessed,
To the Kingdom of Ponemah,   245
To the Land of the Hereafter!

VIEWING THE AUTHOR'S IDEAS

1. What aspects of Indian life are highly idealized in this selection? Compare Longfellow's portrayal of the Indian with that of Father Jogues and Fray Junípero Serra. What Indian beliefs and customs are mentioned in this poem?

2. According to the Jesuit narrative the Indians received the missionaries with marks of honor and courtesy. How does Longfellow account for the friendly reception of the Black Robe chief and his companions? In what way does the incident reflect the missionaries' desire to convert the Indians?

3. Contrast the exultation in the opening section with the wistful sadness of the closing lines. What attitude towards death is reflected in the poem? How may Hiawatha's departure be considered as a poetic interpretation of the Indians' withdrawal at the coming of the white man?

4. Compare the poet's account of the visit of the Black Robe chief with the following prose abstracts from *The Jesuit Relations:*

(a) At the door of the cabin in which we were to be received was an old man who awaited us in a rather surprising attitude, which constitutes part of the ceremonial that they observe when they receive strangers. This man stood erect . . . with his hands extended and lifted toward the sun as if he wished to protect himself from its rays, which nevertheless shone upon his face through his fingers. When we came near him, he paid us this compliment: "How beautiful the sun is, O Frenchman, when thou comest to visit us! All our village awaits thee, and thou shall enter all our cabins in peace." Having said this, he made us enter his own, in which were a crowd of people; they devoured us with their eyes but nevertheless observed profound silence. . . .

(b) When I had finished my speech, the Captain arose, and resting his hand upon the head of a little slave whom he wished to give us, he spoke thus: "I thank thee, Black Gown, and thee, O Frenchman" — addressing himself to Monsieur Jolliet — "for having taken so much trouble to come to visit us. Never has the earth been so beautiful or the sun so bright as today. Never has our river been so calm or so clear of rocks which your canoes have removed in passing; never has our tobacco tasted so good or our corn appeared so fine as we now see them. . . ."

EVALUATING HIS MANNER OF EXPRESSION

1. What is the setting of this narrative? How does the poet create the atmosphere of the primitive forest?

2. How does the selection exemplify the sentimental attitude toward the Indian as a vanished race? Show that it also reflects a romantic view of nature and the simple life.

3. In this poem Longfellow uses the monotonous rhythm and the frequent repetitions and parallels of the old Finnish folk epic, the *Kalevala*. Why is this primitive form especially effective in *Hiawatha*? An example of the poet's use of parallel structure is found in lines 54-55, where in each case two participles are followed by a prepositional phrase. Find other examples.

4. What effect is produced by the poet's use of Indian names for the elements of nature and the creatures of the woods? List the most picturesque passages; point out the most musical lines. Find examples of onomatopoeia and figures of speech.

5. Read "The Passing of Arthur" in Tennyson's *Idylls of the King* and note its similarity in character and incident to "Hiawatha's Departure."

Old Ironsides

Oliver Wendell Holmes

When the gallant frigate Constitution *was condemned to dismantling in 1830, Holmes wrote a poem which saved the ship and enshrined it as a national relic. The vessel had seen service in the war against Mediterranean pirates, had participated in a naval victory over the British in 1812, and had earned the nickname "Old Ironsides" for her valiant endurance. The public opinion aroused by Holmes caused the* Constitution *to be rebuilt in 1833. When the rotting timbers demanded further renovation in 1928, the frigate was restored to its original form.*

AYE, TEAR her tattered ensign down!
   Long has it waved on high,
And many an eye has danced to see
   That banner in the sky;
Beneath it rung the battle shout,   5
   And burst the cannon's roar —
The meteor of the ocean air
   Shall sweep the clouds no more!

Her decks, once red with heroes' blood,
   Where knelt the vanquished foe,   10
When winds were hurrying o'er the flood,
   And waves were white below,
No more shall feel the victor's tread
   Or know the conquered knee —
The harpies[1] of the shore shall pluck   15
   The eagle of the sea!

Oh, better that her shattered hulk
   Should sink beneath the wave;
Her thunders shook the mighty deep,
   And there should be her grave;   20
Nail to the mast her holy flag,
   Set every threadbare sail,
And give her to the god of storms,
   The lightning and the gale!

VIEWING THE AUTHOR'S IDEAS

1. What events connected with the glorious past of the ship does Holmes use to stir sentiment? To what emotions does he appeal in recalling this history?

2. What fate does he prefer for the frigate rather than dismantling?

3. Is the attitude towards ships and planes of World War II comparable to Holmes's feeling toward the *Constitution?* Bring to class clippings which record notable war records for vessels and airplanes.

EVALUATING HIS MANNER OF EXPRESSION

1. Explain the metaphor in lines 7-8. Who are the "harpies of the shore"?

2. How does the poet end the last stanza?

---

[1] *harpies*, mythical creatures with the head of a woman and the body of a vulture sent by Juno to plunder the table of Phineas; hence, any rapacious person, or plunderer.

The Last Leaf

Oliver Wendell Holmes

This poem is a fusion of humor and pathos, inspired by the lonely figure of Major Thomas Melville, grandfather of the author of Moby Dick. *In his cocked hat and breeches of the Revolutionary era, the old veteran appeared to his fellow citizens as a walking museum piece. The major was said to have been among those who cast the tea overboard at Boston Harbor.*

I saw him once before
As he passed by the door,
   And again
The pavement stones resound
As he totters o'er the ground   5
   With his cane.

They say that in his prime,
Ere the pruning knife of Time
   Cut him down,
Not a better man was found   10
By the crier on his round
   Through the town.

But now he walks the streets,
And he looks at all he meets.
   Sad and wan;   15
And he shakes his feeble head,
That it seems as if he said,
   "They are gone."

The mossy marbles rest
On the lips that he has pressed   20
   In their bloom;
And the names he loved to hear
Have been carved for many a year
   On the tomb.

My grandmamma has said —   25
Poor old lady, she is dead
   Long ago —
That he had a Roman nose,
And his cheek was like a rose
   In the snow.   30

But now his nose is thin,
And it rests upon his chin
   Like a staff,

And a crook is in his back,
And a melancholy crack   35
   In his laugh.

I know it is a sin
For me to sit and grin
   At him here;
But the old three-cornered hat   40
And the breeches and all that
   Are so queer!

And if I should live to be
The last leaf upon the tree
   In the spring,   45
Let them smile, as I do now,
At the old forsaken bough
   Where I cling.

VIEWING THE AUTHOR'S IDEAS

1. Holmes was twenty-two when he published this poem. What lines show the attitude of youth towards age?

2. What fact of the old man's youth does the poet mention? Name the visible signs of old age in the veteran. Describe his costume.

3. At eighty-five Holmes wrote that he had lived to be an illustration of his own poem. What permission had he given the younger generation? How does the last stanza illustrate the cycle of man's life and the succession of generations?

4. The term *old* can be either a stigma or a compliment. Which is it in the following fields: religion, transportation, music, architecture, medicine, courtesy, speech, sanitation, painting, politics? Draw a conclusion as to which types of things grow old and which kinds are perennially young.

EVALUATING HIS MANNER OF EXPRESSION

1. Explain the metaphor of "the last leaf." How does the figure of "the pruning knife of time" apply?

2. Lincoln was said to have expressed a special admiration for the stanza beginning "The mossy marbles rest . . ." In your opinion what makes this stanza among the best Holmes has written?

3. Does humor or pathos predominate? Is the last stanza necessary in order to justify Holmes's humorous outlook on age?

4. What does "forsaken bough" mean in line 47?

My Aunt

Oliver Wendell Holmes

Here again Holmes gives a light touch to his wit when commenting on people and manners. The subject of his humor is a typical maiden aunt of the early nineteenth century. The New England spinster, bred in a finishing school, given little useful learning, and unsuited to earn her own living, did not hold an enviable position in society. The maiden in these verses calls forth Holmes's gayest raillery because she clings to the styles of her girlhood long after youth has passed.

My aunt! My dear unmarried aunt!
   Long years have o'er her flown;
Yet still she strains the aching clasp
   That binds her virgin zone;
I know it hurts her — though she looks   5
   As cheerful as she can;
Her waist is ampler than her life,
   For life is but a span.[1]

My aunt! my poor deluded aunt!
   Her hair is almost gray;   10
Why will she train that winter curl
   In such a springlike way?
How can she lay her glasses down
   And say she reads as well,
When through a double convex lens   15
   She just makes out to spell?

Her father — grandpapa! forgive
   This erring lip its smiles —
Vowed she should make the finest girl
   Within a hundred miles;   20
He sent her to a stylish school;
   'Twas in her thirteenth June;
And with her as the rules required,
   "Two towels and a spoon."

They braced my aunt against a board   25
   To make her straight and tall;
They laced her up, they starved her down
   To make her light and small;

They pinched her feet, they singed her hair,
   They screwed it up with pins —   30
Oh, never mortal suffered more
   In penance for her sins.

So, when my precious aunt was done,
   My grandsire brought her back
(By daylight, lest some rabid youth   35
   Might follow on the track);
"Ah!" said my grandsire, as he shook
   Some powder in his pan,[2]
"What could this lovely creature do
   Against a desperate man!"   40

Alas! nor chariot, nor barouche,[3]
   Nor bandit cavalcade,
Tore from the trembling father's arms
   His all-accomplished maid.
For her how happy had it been!   45
   And Heaven had spared to me
To see one sad, ungathered rose
   On my ancestral tree.

VIEWING THE AUTHOR'S IDEAS

1. What specific actions of his aunt does Holmes find humorous? Is the attempt to conceal age usually successful?

2. What was the function of the finishing school of the last century? What has replaced this institution today?

3. Explain the following expressions: winter curl; springlike way; double convex lens; powder in his pan; bandit cavalcade; ungathered rose; ancestral tree.

EVALUATING HIS MANNER OF EXPRESSION

1. Which of the following devices are employed to produce humor: puns, exaggeration, mock seriousness, understatement, satire? Quote passages to support your opinion.

2. Do you find any pathos in this poem? If so, in what lines?

---

[1] *Her waist . . . span,* a word play on span, in which the meaning "a distance between the end of the thumb and the end of the little finger extended" is used in place of the meaning "a limited space of time."

[2] *pan,* the hollow place for powder in the lock of an old gun.

[3] *barouche,* (bȧ-rōōsh') a four-wheeled carriage.

The Chambered Nautilus

Oliver Wendell Holmes

Holmes often rowed his small skiff out into Boston harbor before sunrise. Around him were strange ships, bringing thoughts of the tropical seas where dwells the little shellfish called the pearly nautilus. The name of this mollusk is derived from the Greek word meaning sailor. Ancient writers erroneously supposed that its membranous tentacles served as sails. Each year the nautilus builds a new and larger chamber in its spiral home. Closing up the old room with a dividing wall, it dwells successively in its enlarging compartments until it attains full growth. In the life history of the chambered nautilus Holmes sees a parallel to spiritual development.

THIS is the ship of pearl, which, poets feign,
  Sails the unshadowed main —
  The venturous bark that flings
On the sweet summer wind its purpled wings
In gulfs enchanted, where the siren sings,   5
  And coral reefs lie bare,
Where the cold sea-maids[1] rise to sun their streaming
    hair.

Its webs of living gauze no more unfurl;
  Wrecked is the ship of pearl!
  And every chambered cell   10
Where its dim dreaming life was wont to dwell,
As the frail tenant shaped his growing shell,
  Before thee lies revealed —
Its irised ceiling[2] rent, its sunless crypt unsealed!

Year after year beheld the silent toil   15
  That spread his lustrous coil;
  Still, as the spiral grew,
He left the past year's dwelling for the new,
Stole with soft step its shining archway through,
  Built up its idle door,   20
Stretched in his last-found home and knew the old no
    more.

Thanks for the heavenly message brought by thee,
  Child of the wandering sea,
  Cast from her lap, forlorn!
From thy dead lips a clearer note is born   25
Than ever Triton[3] blew from wreathèd horn!
  While on mine ear it rings,
Through the deep caves of thought I hear a voice that
    sings: —

Build thee more stately mansions, O my soul,
  As the swift seasons roll!   30
  Leave thy low-vaulted past!
Let each new temple, nobler than the last,
Shut thee from heaven with a dome more vast,
  Till thou at length art free,
Leaving thine outgrown shell by life's unresting sea!   35

[1] *sea-maids*, mermaids, half woman and half fish according to mythology.
[2] *irised ceiling*. The pearly lining of the shell is colored like the iris or rainbow.

VIEWING THE AUTHOR'S IDEAS

1. To what old belief concerning the nautilus does the poet refer in the opening lines? How does the second line express the fact that the sun's rays fall directly on tropical waters? What colorful details and classical allusions create the enchanting atmosphere of the South Seas?

2. Name the aspects of delicate beauty which the poet sees in the wrecked shell. What line suggests a resemblance of the spiral home to a beautiful cathedral?

3. What elements in spiritual growth are similar to the silent toil of the nautilus? How does the shellfish illustrate the beauty of humble labor?

4. How does the message of the nautilus come to the poet? Express this message.

5. Mention some specific ways by which one may build "more stately mansions" for the soul by development of mental and spiritual powers. Compare the last stanza with *John* 14:2-3.

EVALUATING HIS MANNER OF EXPRESSION

1. Contrast the mood of the first stanza with that of the second. What is the mood of the last stanza? Note the effect achieved in lines 29-35 by the recurrence of the long *o* sound.

[3] *Triton*, in Greek mythology, a sea god who at the command of Neptune raised or calmed the waves by a blast on a conch shell. The passage in which this allusion occurs is an echo of the last line of Wordsworth's sonnet "The World Is Too Much With Us." : "Or hear old Triton blow his wreathèd horn."

2. What device in lines four and five contributes to the music of the poem? Find similar examples in other lines.

3. In *sails* and *main* in the second line the poet uses assonance. Select three other examples in the poem.

4. Show what the poet achieved by the following expressions: "Frail tenant," "irised ceiling," "stole with soft step," "child of the wandering sea," "deep caves of thought."

5. What is the apostrophe in the last stanza? Why does the poet use this figure?

On Conversation

(From *The Autocrat of the Breakfast Table*)
Oliver Wendell Holmes

Lowell accepted the editorship of the Atlantic Monthly *on condition that Holmes would become a regular contributor. As each publication date approached, the genial Doctor submitted the easy, informal essays which were later collected in* The Autocrat of the Breakfast Table. *Soon all America was reading the amusing discourse of the Autocrat as eagerly as the fictitious boarders listened to it at the Boston boardinghouse. Gathered round the breakfast table are the reserved New England types Holmes had learned to know so well on his lecture tours and in his wide medical practice. The Autocrat, a writer and wit, holds absolute sway in the conversation except when some member of the group responds with a characteristic gesture or ventures some timid question or remark.*

THE Atlantic obeys the moon, and its LUNIVERSARY[1] has come round again. I have gathered up some hasty notes of my remarks made since the last high tides, which I respectfully submit. Please to remember this is talk; just as easy and just as formal as I choose to make it.

I never saw an author in my life — saving perhaps one — that did not purr as audibly as a full-grown domestic cat *(Felis Catus, Linn.)*[2] on having his fur smoothed in the right way by a skillful hand.

But let me give you a caution. Be very careful how you tell an author he is droll. Ten to one he will hate you; and if he does, be sure he can do you a mischief and very probably will. Say you cried over his romance or his verses, and he will love you and send you a copy. You can laugh over that as much as you like — in private.

Wonder why authors and actors are ashamed of being funny? Why, there are obvious reasons and deep philosophical ones. The clown knows very well that the women are not in love with him but with Hamlet, the fellow in the black cloak and plumed hat. Passion never laughs. The wit knows that his place is at the tail of a procession.

If you want the deep underlying reason, I must take more time to tell it. There is a perfect consciousness in every form of wit — using that term in its general sense — that its essence consists in a partial and incomplete view of whatever it touches. It throws a single ray, separated from the rest — red, yellow, blue, or any intermediate shade — upon an object; never white light; that is the province of wisdom. We get beautiful effects from wit — all the prismatic colors — but never the object as it is in fair daylight. A pun, which is a kind of wit, is a different and much shallower trick in mental optics throwing the shadows of two objects so that one overlies the other. Poetry uses the rainbow tints for special effects but always keeps its essential objects in the purest white light of truth. Will you allow me to pursue this subject a little further?

[They didn't allow me at that time, for somebody happened to scrape the floor with his chair just then; which accidental sound, as all must have noticed, has the instantaneous effect that the cutting of the yellow hair by Iris had upon infelix Dido.[3] It broke the charm, and that breakfast was over.]

---

[1] *Luniversary,* a word coined by Holmes from *luna,* moon, and *vertere,* to turn.

[2] *(Felis catus, Linn.),* the scientific nomenclature of cat according to Linnaeus, an eighteenth-century biologist.

[3] *infelix Dido,* unhappy Dido. According to ancient mythology, Proserpina, the goddess of the dead, released the spirit from the body by cutting a lock from the hair of the dying person. Dido was released by Iris, the messenger of the gods.

— Don't flatter yourselves that friendship authorizes you to say disagreeable things to your intimates. On the contrary, the nearer you come into relation with a person, the more necessary do tact and courtesy become. Except in cases of necessity, which are rare, leave your friend to learn unpleasant truths from his enemies; they are ready enough to tell them. . . .

But remember that talking is one of the fine arts — the noblest, the most important, and the most difficult — and that its fluent harmonies may be spoiled by the intrusion of a single harsh note. Therefore conversation which is suggestive rather than argumentative, which lets out the most of each talker's results of thought, is commonly the pleasantest and the most profitable. It is not easy at the best for two persons talking together to make the most of each other's thoughts, there are so many of them.

[The company looked as if they wanted an explanation.]

When John and Thomas, for instance, are talking together, it is natural enough that among the six there should be more or less confusion and apprehension.

[Our landlady turned pale — no doubt she thought there was a screw loose in my intellects — and that involved the probable loss of a boarder. A severe-looking person, who wears a Spanish cloak and a sad cheek fluted by the passions of the melodrama, whom I understand to be the professional ruffian of the neighboring theater, alluded with a certain lifting of the brow, drawing down the corners of the mouth, and somewhat rasping *voce di petto,*[4] to Falstaff's nine men in buckram.[5] Everybody looked up. I believe the old gentleman opposite was afraid I should seize the carving knife; at any rate he slid it to one side, as it were carelessly.]

I think, I said, I can make it plain to Benjamin Franklin[6] here that there are at least six personalities distinctly to be recognized as taking part in that dialogue between John and Thomas.

Three Johns
1. The real John; known only to his Maker.
2. John's ideal John, never the real one, and often very unlike him.
3. Thomas's ideal John, never the real John, nor John's John, but often very unlike either.

Three Thomases
1. The real Thomas.
2. Thomas's ideal Thomas.
3. John's ideal Thomas.

Only one of the three Johns is taxed; only one can be weighed on a platform balance; but the other two are just as important in the conversation. Let us suppose the real John to be old, dull, and ill-looking. But as the Higher Powers have not conferred on men the gift of seeing themselves in the true light, John very possibly conceives himself to be youthful, witty, and fascinating, and talks from the point of view of this ideal. Thomas, again, believes him to be an artful rogue, we will say; therefore, he *is,* so far as Thomas's attitude in the conversation is concerned, an artful rogue, though really simple and stupid. The same conditions apply to the three Thomases. It follows that until a man can be found who knows himself as his Maker knows him, or who sees himself as others see him, there must be at least six persons engaged in every dialogue between two. Of these, the least important, philosophically speaking, is the one that we have called the real person. No wonder two disputants often get angry, when there are six of them talking and listening all at the same time.

[A very unphilosophical application of the above remarks was made by a young fellow answering to the name of John, who sits near me at table. A certain basket of peaches, a rare vegetable little known to boardinghouses, was on its way to me via this unlettered Johannes.[7] He appropriated the three that remained in the basket, remarking that there was just one apiece for him. I convinced him that his practical inference was hasty and illogical, but in the meantime he had eaten the peaches.]

---

[4] *voce di petto,* (vō' chä dē pĕt tō) deep chest tone.

[5] *Falstaff's . . . buckram.* In Shakespeare's *Henry IV* Falstaff flees when attacked by robbers. In his humorous account of the adventure, he gradually increases the number he encountered from two to nine, and from nine to eleven.

[6] *Benjamin Franklin,* the landlady's youngest son.

[7] *via . . . Johannes,* by way of this uneducated John.

VIEWING THE AUTHOR'S IDEAS

1. What topics does the Autocrat discuss? Cite evidences of Holmes's knowledge of science, literature, and languages. What incident shows that his discussion was above the comprehension of the group at the breakfast table?

2. What qualities does Holmes consider most important in conversation? Why is tact and courtesy necessary between friends? When are friendly admonitions necessary?

3. How do the boarders react to the statement that six personalities are involved in every conversation between two persons? What does the Autocrat's explanation reveal concerning Holmes's ability as a teacher at the Harvard medical school?

4. How does the author show that the real person is least important in most conversations? How do our feelings and prejudices color our estimates of the worth and character of other people? How does self-love influence our estimate of our own personality?

5. What application of the Autocrat's remarks did the young fellow called John make? How do you think the Autocrat convinced him that his action was hasty and illogical?

EVALUATING HIS MANNER OF EXPRESSION

1. What excuse does Holmes offer to the readers of the *Atlantic Monthly* for his informal style? How does he show his appreciation of the enthusiastic reaction to his "droll" remarks? What were the advantages of putting his essays in the form of imaginary talk at a breakfast table?

2. The subtitle of *The Autocrat of the Breakfast Table* is "Every man his own Boswell." It was suggested by Boswell's *Life of Johnson,* which is almost entirely a record of Doctor Johnson's conversation. In what sense is Holmes "his own Boswell"?

3. What distinction does the Autocrat make between wit and poetry? Show that his definition of a pun applies to the following examples given in the first essay of this series:

   a) Roe replied by asking, when charity was like a top. . . . Roe then said, "When it begins to hum."
   b) Lord Bacon playfully declared himself a descendant of 'Og, the King of Bashan.

4. Mention instances of clever delineation of character by speech and action.

5. By consulting the dictionary, find whether the word *luniversary,* coined by Holmes, has been sanctioned by usage.

The Vision of Sir Launfal

James Russell Lowell

The quest of the Holy Grail has long provided writers with a symbol of the pursuit of high ideals. Lowell uses the legend to express the truth that opportunities for unselfish service are always present. Vowing to find the Holy Grail, the proud Sir Launfal retires to sleep on the eve of his departure. In a dream he spends his entire life in the fruitless search for the sacred treasure. Out of his suffering and humiliations comes the ability to see Christ in the poor. Old and broken, he returns to his castle, where he gives a drink to a leper at the gate. Before Sir Launfal awakes, the leper assumes the glorified figure of Christ; and in the wooden cup which the knight had offered the outcast, he sees the Holy Grail.

According to medieval legend, the Holy Grail or chalice used by Christ at the Last Supper was brought to England by Joseph of Arimathea. Guarded for many generations, it was an object of devout pilgrimage. When one of the keepers broke his promise to be chaste in thought, word, and deed, the sacred cup disappeared. The finding of the Grail became a lifelong quest for Arthur's noble knights. As Sir Galahad had merited the vision by his purity of

heart, Sir Launfal was rewarded for his Christlike charity and sympathy.

PRELUDE TO PART FIRST

OVER his keys the musing organist,
   Beginning doubtfully and far away,
First lets his fingers wander as they list,
   And builds a bridge from Dreamland for his lay.
Then, as the touch of his loved instrument   5
   Gives hope and fervor, nearer draws his theme,
First guessed by faint, auroral flushes sent
   Along the wavering vista of his dream.

Not only around our infancy
   Doth Heaven with all its splendors lie;[1]   10
Daily, with souls that cringe and plot,
   We Sinais climb[2] and know it not.

---

[1] *Not only . . . splendors lie,* an echo of Wordsworth's "Ode on the Intimations of Immortality," line 67.

[2] *Sinais climb.* Moses ascended Mount Sinai to talk with God.

Over our manhood bend the skies;
  Against our fallen and traitor lives
The great winds utter prophecies;   15
  With our faint hearts the mountain strives;
Its arms outstretched, the druid wood[3]
  Waits with its benedicite;[4]
And to our age's drowsy blood
  Still shouts the inspiring sea.   20
Earth gets its price for what earth gives us:
  The beggar is taxed for a corner to die in,
The priest hath his fee who comes and shrives us.
  We bargain for the graves we lie in;
At the devil's booth are all things sold,   25
Each ounce of dross costs its ounce of gold;
  For a cap and bells[5] our lives we pay,
Bubbles we buy with a whole soul's tasking.
  'Tis Heaven alone that is given away,
  'Tis only God may be had for the asking;   30
No price is set on the lavish summer;
June may be had by the poorest comer.

And what is so rare as a day in June?
  Then, if ever, come perfect days;
Then heaven tries earth if it be in tune,   35
  And over it softly her warm ear lays;
Whether we look, or whether we listen,
We hear life murmur or see it glisten;
Every clod feels a stir of might,
  An instinct within it that reaches and towers,   40
And, groping blindly above it for light,
  Climbs to a soul in grass and flowers.
The flush of life may well be seen
  Thrilling back over hills and valleys;
The cowslip startles in meadows green,   45
  The buttercup catches the sun in its chalice,
And there's never a leaf or a blade too mean
  To be some happy creature's palace;
The little bird sits at his door in the sun,
  Atilt like a blossom among the leaves,   50
And lets his illumined being o'errun
  With the deluge of summer it receives;
His mate feels the eggs beneath her wings,
And the heart in her dumb breast flutters and sings;

He sings to the wide world, and she to her nest —   55
In the nice ear of Nature which song is the best?

Now is the high tide of the year,
  And whatever of life hath ebbed away
Comes flooding back with a ripply cheer
  Into every bare inlet and creek and bay.   60
Now the heart is so full that a drop overfills it;
We are happy now because God wills it.
No matter how barren the past may have been,
'Tis enough for us now that the leaves are green.
We sit in the warm shade and feel right well   65
How the sap creeps up and the blossoms swell;
We may shut our eyes, but we cannot help knowing
That skies are clear and grass is growing.
The breeze comes whispering in our ear
That dandelions are blossoming near,   70
  That maize has sprouted, that streams are flowing,
That the river is bluer than the sky,
That the robin is plastering his house hard by;
And if the breeze kept the good news back,
For other couriers we should not lack;   75
  We could guess it all by yon heifer's lowing—
And hark! how clear bold chanticleer,
Warmed with the new wine of the year,
  Tells all in his lusty crowing!

Joy comes, grief goes, we know not how;   80
Everything is happy now,
  Everything is upward striving.
'Tis as easy now for the heart to be true
As for grass to be green or skies to be blue—
  'Tis the natural way of living.   85
Who knows whither the clouds have fled?
  In the unscarred heaven they leave no wake;
And the eyes forget the tears they have shed,
  The heart forgets its sorrow and ache;
The soul partakes the season's youth,   90
  And the sulphurous rifts of passion and woe
Lie deep 'neath a silence pure and smooth,
  Like burnt-out craters healed with snow.
What wonder if Sir Launfal now
Remembered the keeping of his vow?   95

---

[3] *druid wood*. The oak was sacred to the druids, or ancient Celtic priests.

[4] *benedicite*, blessing, from the Latin imperative "bless ye."

[5] *cap and bells*. In the Middle Ages the court jester or fool wore a pointed cap and bells.

PART FIRST

I

"My golden spurs now bring to me,
  And bring to me my richest mail,
For tomorrow I go over land and sea
  In search of the Holy Grail.
Shall never a bed for me be spread,   100
Nor shall a pillow be under my head,
Till I begin my vow to keep.
Here on the rushes will I sleep,
And perchance there may come a vision true
Ere day create the world anew."   105
    Slowly Sir Launfal's eyes grew dim;
    Slumber fell like a cloud on him,
And into his soul the vision flew.

II

The crows flapped over by twos and threes;
In the pool drowsed the cattle up to their knees;   110
  The little birds sang as if it were
  The one day of summer in all the year;
And the very leaves seemed to sing on the trees.
The castle alone in the landscape lay
Like an outpost of winter, dull and gray;   115
'Twas the proudest hall in the North Countree,
And never its gates might opened be
Save to lord or lady of high degree.
Summer besieged it on every side,
But the churlish stone her assaults defied;   120
She could not scale the chilly wall,
Though around it for leagues her pavilions tall
Stretched left and right
Over the hills and out of sight.
  Green and broad was every tent,   125
  And out of each a murmur went
Till the breeze fell off at night.

III

The drawbridge dropped with a surly clang,
And through the dark arch a charger sprang,
Bearing Sir Launfal, the maiden[6] knight,   130
In his gilded mail, that flamed so bright
It seemed the dark castle had gathered all
Those shafts the fierce sun had shot over its wall

[6] *maiden*, untried.

In his siege of three hundred summers long,
And, binding them all in one blazing sheaf,   135
  Had cast them forth; so, young and strong,
And lightsome as a locust leaf,
Sir Launfal flashed forth in his unscarred mail
To seek in all climes for the Holy Grail.

IV

It was morning on hill and stream and tree,   140
  And morning in the young knight's heart;
Only the castle moodily
Rebuffed the gifts of the sunshine free
  And gloomed by itself apart;
The season brimmed all other things up   145
Full as the rain fills the pitcher plant's cup.

V

As Sir Launfal made morn through the darksome gate,
  He was 'ware of a leper, crouched by the same.
Who begged with his hand and moaned as he sate;
  And a loathing over Sir Launfal came.   150
The sunshine went out of his soul with a thrill,
  The flesh 'neath his armor 'gan shrink and crawl,
And midway its leap his heart stood still
  Like a frozen waterfall;
For this man, so foul and bent of stature,   155
Rasped harshly against his dainty nature,
And seemed the one blot on the summer morn —
So he tossed him a piece of gold in scorn.

VI

The leper raised not the gold from the dust:
"Better to me the poor man's crust,   160
Better the blessing of the poor,
Though I turn me empty from his door;
That is no true alms which the hand can hold;
He gives nothing but worthless gold
  Who gives from a sense of duty;   165
But he who gives but a slender mite,
And gives to that which is out of sight,
  That thread of the all-sustaining Beauty
Which runs through all and doth all unite —
The hand cannot clasp the whole of his alms,   170
The heart outstretches its eager palms,
For a god goes with it and makes it store
To the soul that was starving in darkness before."

PRELUDE TO PART SECOND

Down swept the chill wind from the mountain peak,
From the snow five thousand summers old; 175
On open wold⁷ and hilltop bleak
   It had gathered all the cold,
And whirled it like sleet on the wanderer's cheek.
It carried a shiver everywhere
From the unleafed boughs and pastures bare; 180
The little brook heard it and built a roof
'Neath which he could house him, winter-proof;
All night by the white stars' frosty gleams
He groined his arches and matched his beams;
Slender and clear were his crystal spars 185
As the lashes of light that trim the stars;
He sculptured every summer delight
In the halls and chambers out of sight;
Sometimes his tinkling waters slipped
Down through a frost-leaved forest crypt, 190
Long, sparkling aisles of steel-stemmed trees
Bending to counterfeit a breeze;
Sometimes the roof no fretwork knew
But silvery mosses that downward grew;
Sometimes it was carved in sharp relief 195
With quaint arabesques of ice-fern leaf;
Sometimes it was simply smooth and clear
For the gladness of heaven to shine through, and here
He had caught the nodding bulrush tops
And hung them thickly with diamond-drops, 200
That crystaled the beams of moon and sun,
And made a star of every one.
No mortal builder's most rare device
Could match this winter palace of ice;
'Twas as if every image that mirrored lay 205
   In his depths serene through the summer day,
Each fleeting shadow of earth and sky,
   Lest the happy model should be lost,
Had been mimicked in fairy masonry
   By the elfin builders of the frost. 210

Within the hall are song and laughter;
   The cheeks of Christmas grow red and jolly;
And sprouting is every corbel⁸ and rafter
   With lightsome green of ivy and holly.
Through the deep gulf of the chimney wide 215

Wallows the Yule log's roaring tide;
The broad flame pennons droop and flap
   And belly and tug as a flag in the wind;
Like a locust shrills the imprisoned sap,
   Hunted to death in its galleries blind 220
And swift little troops of silent sparks,
Now pausing, now scattering away as in fear,
Go threading the soot forest's tangled darks
   Like herds of startled deer.
But the wind without was eager and sharp; 225
Of Sir Launfal's gray hair it makes a harp,
   And rattles and wrings
     The icy strings,
   Singing, in dreary monotone,
   A Christmas carol of its own, 230
Whose burden still, as he might guess,
   Was "Shelterless, shelterless, shelterless!"
The voice of the seneschal⁹ flared like a torch
As he shouted the wanderer away from the porch,
And he sat in the gateway and saw all night 235
   The great hall fire, so cheery and bold,
   Through the window slits of the castle old,
Build out its piers of ruddy light
   Against the drift of the cold. 239

PART SECOND

I

There was never a leaf on bush or tree,
The bare boughs rattled shudderingly;
The river was dumb and could not speak,
   For the weaver Winter its shroud had spun;
A single crow on the treetop bleak
   From his shining feathers shed off the cold sun; 245
Again it was morning, but shrunk and cold,
As if her veins were sapless and old,
And she rose up decrepitly
For a last dim look at earth and sea.

II

Sir Launfal turned from his own hard gate, 250
For another heir in his earldom sate;
An old, bent man, worn out and frail,
He came back from seeking the Holy Grail.
Little he recked of his earldom's loss;
No more on his surcoat was blazoned the cross; 255

---

⁷ *wold*, an upland plain.
⁸ *corbel*, projection or bracket.

⁹ *seneschal*, the head steward of a castle.

But deep in his soul the sign he wore,
The badge of the suffering and the poor.

III

Sir Launfal's raiment thin and spare
Was idle mail 'gainst the barbèd air,
For it was just at the Christmas time.   260
So he mused, as he sat, of a sunnier clime,
And sought for a shelter from cold and snow
In the light and warmth of long ago;
He sees the snakelike caravan crawl
O'er the edge of the desert, black and small,   265
Then nearer and nearer, till, one by one,
He can count the camels in the sun,
As over the red-hot sands they pass
To where, in its slender necklace of grass,
The little spring laughed and leaped in the shade,   270
And with its own self like an infant played,
And waved its signal of palms.

IV

"For Christ's sweet sake, I beg an alms" —
The happy camels may reach the spring,
But Sir Launfal sees naught save the gruesome
      thing,   275
The leper, lank as the rain-blanched bone,
That cowers beside him, a thing as lone
And white as the ice isles of Northern seas,
In the desolate horror of his disease.

V

And Sir Launfal said, "I behold in thee   280
An image of Him who died on the tree.
Thou also hast had thy crown of thorns;
Thou also hast had the world's buffets and scorns;
And to thy life were not denied
The wounds in the hands and feet and side.   285
Mild Mary's Son, acknowledge me;
Behold, through him, I give to Thee!"

VI

Then the soul of the leper stood up in his eyes
   And looked at Sir Launfal, and straightway he
Remembered in what a haughtier guise   290
   He had flung an alms to leprosie,
When he girt his young life up in gilded mail

And set forth in search of the Holy Grail.
The heart within him was ashes and dust;
He parted in twain his single crust,   295
He broke the ice on the streamlet's brink,
And gave the leper to eat and drink;
'Twas a moldy crust of coarse, brown bread,
   'Twas water out of a wooden bowl —
Yet with fine wheaten bread was the leper fed,   300
   And 'twas red wine he drank with his thirsty soul.

VII

As Sir Launfal mused with a downcast face,
A light shone round about the place;
The leper no longer crouched at his side,
But stood before him glorified,   305
Shining and tall and fair and straight
As the pillar that stood by the Beautiful Gate[10] —
Himself the Gate whereby men can
Enter the temple of God in Man.

VIII

His words were shed softer than leaves
      from the pine,   310
And they fell on Sir Launfal as snows on the brine,
That mingle their softness and quiet in one
With the shaggy unrest they float down upon;
And the voice that was calmer than silence said,
"Lo, it is I, be not afraid!   315
In many climes, without avail,
Thou has spent thy life for the Holy Grail;
Behold, it is here—this cup which thou
Didst fill at the streamlet for Me but now;
This crust is My body broken for thee;   320
This water His blood that died on the tree;
The Holy Supper is kept, indeed,
In whatso we share with another's need;
Not what we give, but what we share —
For the gift without the giver is bare;   325
Who gives himself with his alms feeds three —
Himself, his hungering neighbor, and Me."

IX

Sir Launfal awoke as from a swound;[11]
"The Grail in my castle here is found!

---

[10] *Beautiful Gate*, the gate of the temple of Solomon mentioned in *Acts* 2:3.
[11] *swound*, swoon.

Hang my idle armor up on the wall; 330
Let it be the spider's banquet hall.
He must be fenced with stronger mail
Who would seek and find the Holy Grail."

X

The castle gate stands open now,
   And the wanderer is welcome to the hall 335
As the hangbird[12] is to the elm tree bough.
   No longer scowl the turrets tall;
The summer's long siege at last is o'er.
When the first poor outcast went in at the door,
She entered with him in disguise, 340
And mastered the fortress by surprise.
There is no spot she loves so well on ground;
She lingers and smiles there the whole year round.
The meanest serf on Sir Launfal's land
Has hall and bower at his command; 345
And there's no poor man in the North Countree
But is lord of the earldom as much as he.

VIEWING THE AUTHOR'S IDEAS

1. How do the opening lines suggest that the story of Sir Launfal is drawn entirely from the poet's imagination? From what "Dreamland" did he "build a bridge" for his poem? Where does the dream of Sir Launfal begin?

2. How is Lowell's message to those absorbed in material things expressed in lines 9-95? Compare lines 27-30 with *Matt.* 6:20-34. List the perfections of June that cannot be bought.

3. How did Sir Launfal prepare for his quest of the Holy Grail? What incident shows the hardness of his heart? Contrast his scorn of the leper with the attitude of Father Damien and Brother Dutton; with Christ's treatment of lepers as revealed in *Matt.* 8:2-3 and 10:8 and in *Luke* 17:12-14. Compare the leper's rebuke with *Luke* 21:2-4. Explain lines 166-169.

4. Compare Sir Launfal's return to his castle with his departure. How does the author indicate his age and the hardships he has undergone? What is the meaning of lines 256-257? Explain the significance of Sir Launfal's musings on the Holy Land.

5. What change of attitude toward his fellowmen does the knight's greeting of the leper reveal? How do his words show the Christian attitude towards trials and suffering?

6. In what form did the Holy Grail appear to Sir Launfal? Note the first hint of the Divine Presence. Compare lines 308-309 with *John* 10:9. Of what incidents in the Gospel does our Lord's appearance to Sir Launfal remind you? Compare Sir Launfal's vision with that of Sir Galahad. What did Sir Launfal learn from his dream? Contrast life in the castle at the opening of the story with that at the end. Explain lines 339-340.

EVALUATING HIS MANNER OF EXPRESSION

1. Why did Lowell choose the Middle Ages as the setting for his story? List details that contribute most to the medieval atmosphere.

2. The poet uses nature as a background for human emotions. How does June serve as a background for Sir Launfal's mood at departure? Why is winter a fitting season for his return?

3. By what means does the author construct the fairy masonry of the ice palace? Note the imagery in the following passages: lines 49-52; 129-138; 147; 195-196; 199-202; 217-224; 244-249; 266-272.

4. Comment on the onomatopoeia in lines 109, 128, 227-228, 241, 310-314. Find variations from the prevailing anapaestic meter and four stress lines. How do they indicate a change of mood?

5. Point out examples of simile in lines 310-315.

6. Explain "Let it be the spider's banquet hall." Discuss the imagery in the sentence.

7. In the last stanza, how does the poet refer to *Charity*? What specific words stand for *charity*?

---

[12] *hangbird,* the oriole or any bird that builds a hanging nest.

To the Dandelion

James Russell Lowell

The wealth of all priceless things shines through this poem — the harmless riches of children exultant in their discovery of beauty, the colorful pageant of meadow and woodland, the rich reminiscence of childhood pleasures, and finally a gleam of the reflected glory of Heaven in each human heart. This is the gold of the neglected dandelion, the "dear common flower that grow'st beside the way."

DEAR common flower, that grow'st beside the way,
Fringing the dusty road with harmless gold,
   First pledge of blithesome May,
Which children pluck and full of pride uphold,
   Highhearted buccaneers,[1] o'erjoyed that they   5
An Eldorado in the grass have found,
    Which not the rich earth's ample round
   May match in wealth, thou art more dear to me
   Than all the prouder summer blooms may be.

Gold such as thine ne'er drew the Spanish prow   10
Through the primeval hush of Indian seas,
   Nor wrinkled the lean brow
Of age to rob the lover's heart of ease;
   'Tis the Spring's largess,[2] which she scatters now
To rich and poor alike with lavish hand,   15
    Though most hearts never understand
   To take it at God's value but pass by
   The offered wealth with unrewarded eye.

Thou art mine tropics and mine Italy;
To look at thee unlocks a warmer clime;   20
   The eyes thou givest me
Are in the heart and heed not space or time;
   Not in mid June the golden-cuirassed[3] bee
Feels a more summerlike warm ravishment
    In the white lily's breezy tent,   25
   His fragrant Sybaris,[4] than I, when first
   From the dark green thy yellow circles burst.

Then think I of deep shadows on the grass,
Of meadows where in sun the cattle graze,
   Where, as the breezes pass,   30
The gleaming rushes lean a thousand ways;
   Of leaves that slumber in a cloudy mass
Or whiten in the wind; of waters blue
    That from the distance sparkle through
   Some woodland gap; and of a sky above,   35
   Where one white cloud like a stray lamb doth move.

My childhood's earliest thoughts are linked with thee;
The sight of thee calls back the robin's song,
   Who from the dark old tree
Beside the door sang clearly all day long;   40
   And I, secure in childish piety,
Listened as if I heard an angel sing
    With news from heaven, which he could bring
   Fresh every day to my untainted ears
   When birds and flowers and I were happy peers.   45

How like a prodigal doth nature seem
When thou, for all thy gold, so common art!
   Thou teachest me to deem
More sacredly of every human heart,
   Since each reflects in joy its scanty gleam   50
Of Heaven and could some wondrous secret show—
    Did we but pay the love we owe
   And with a child's undoubting wisdom look
   On all these living pages of God's book.

VIEWING THE AUTHOR'S IDEAS

1. How does Lowell develop the idea that the dandelion is the gold of childhood? Why does he consider the flower to have matchless wealth?

2. Explain the historical allusion in lines 10-11. How could gold "wrinkle the lean brow of age"? How many people take the flower at "God's value"?

3. What associations with foreign places does the dandelion give the poet? Why would a poet desire to be in these two places? To what is his joy at the appearance of the flower compared?

---

[1] *buccaneers*, pirates.
[2] *largess*, bounty.
[3] *golden-cuirassed*, wearing golden armor.
[4] *Sybaris*, a city in Italy noted for its luxury; hence, luxurious abode.

4. Describe the idyllic summer scene Lowell mentions. How does he reveal his childhood enjoyment of nature? How did he then regard birds and flowers?

5. In what way can the dandelion teach the sanctity of the human heart? Explain the way in which each man reflects a gleam of Heaven. According to the poet, under what conditions can a person see this reflection? Would Lowell's interpretation of this reflection differ from that of a person who believed in the Mystical Body?

EVALUATING HIS MANNER OF EXPRESSION

1. Lowell's use of classical and historical allusions reveals his learning. With how many countries and places does he associate our common flower?

2. This poem has been called one of America's genuine nature lyrics. How has an object of nature stirred the poet's imagination; his memory; his emotions; how has it influenced his attitude towards God and man?

3. Select one line that gives a vivid picture of action. What metaphor does the poet apply to the children?

4. What is the figure of speech in each of the following: "the Spanish prow," "the Spring's largess," "his fragrant Sybaris"?

The Courtin'

(From *The Biglow Papers*)
James Russell Lowell

In order to voice his protest against the Mexican War, Lowell created the New England farm hand, Hosea Biglow, supposedly the author of the satiric verses in Yankee dialect called The Biglow Papers. *When the First Series of the* Papers *was going to press, Lowell received word from the printer that there was a blank page to be filled. He sat down and at once improvised an extract from a ballad purported to be written by Mr. Biglow. The printer used only enough of it to fill the gap. In answer to many demands for a conclusion of the ballad, Lowell expanded the poem and made it into a connected narrative which he placed in the second series of* The Biglow Papers. *"The Courtin'" is one of the earliest artistic American poems in dialect. The text presented here is that of the later and expanded version.*

GOD makes sech nights, all white an still
 Fur 'z you can look or listen,
Moonshine an' snow on field an' hill,
 All silence an' all glisten.

Zekle crep' up quite unbeknown   5
 An' peeked in thru' the winder,
An' there sot Huldy all alone,
 'ith no one nigh to hender.

A fireplace filled the room's one side
 With half a cord o' wood in—   10

There warn't no stoves (tell comfort died)
 To bake ye to a puddin'.

The wa'nut logs shot sparkles out
 Towards the pootiest, bless her,
An' leetle flames danced all about   15
 The chiny on the dresser.

Agin the chimbley crooknecks[1] hung,
 An' in amongst 'em rusted
The ole queen's arm[2] thet gran'ther Young
 Fetched back f'om Concord busted.   20

The very room coz she was in
 Seemed warm f'om floor to ceilin',
An' she looked full ez rosy agin
 Ez the apples she was peelin'.

'Twas kin' o' kingdom-come to look   25
 On sech a blessed cretur;
A dogrose blushin' to a brook
 Ain't modester nor sweeter.

He was six foot o' man, A 1,
 Clear grit an' human natur';   30

---

[1] *crooknecks*, squashes.
[2] *queen's arm*, a musket.

None could n't quicker pitch a ton,
   Nor dror a furrer straighter.

He'd sparked[3] it with full twenty gals,
   Hed squired[4] 'em, danced 'em, druv 'em,
Fust this one an' then thet, by spells —   35
   All is, he could n't love 'em.

But long o' her his veins 'ould run
   All crinkly like curled maple,
The side she breshed felt full o' sun
   Ez a south slope in Ap'il.   40

She thought no v'ice hed sech a swing
   Ez hisn in the choir;
My! when he made Ole Hunderd[5] ring,
   She *knowed* the Lord was nigher.

An' she'd blush scarlit, right in prayer,   45
   When her new meetin' bunnet
Felt somehow thru' its crown a pair
   O' blue eyes sot upun it.

Thet night, I tell ye, she looked some!
   She seemed to 've gut a new soul,   50
For she felt sartin-sure he'd come,
   Down to her very shoe sole.

She heered a foot an' knowed it, tu,
   A-raspin' on the scraper —
All ways to once her feelin's flew   55
   Like sparks in burnt-up paper.

He kin' o' l'itered on the mat,
   Some doubtfle o' the sekle;
His heart kep' goin' pitypat,
   But hern went pity Zekle.   60

An' yit she gin her cheer a jerk
   Ez though she wished him furder,
An' on her apples kep' to work,
   Parin' away like murder.

"You want to see my Pa, I s'pose?"   65
   "Wal . . . no . . . I come designin' — "
"To see my Ma? She's sprinklin' clo'es
   Agin tomorrer's i'nin'."

To say why gals acts so or so,
   Or don't, 'ould be presumin';   70
Mebby to mean *yes* an' say *no*
   Comes nateral to women.

He stood a spell on one foot fust
   Then stood a spell on t' other,
An' on which one he felt the wust   75
   He could n't ha' told ye nuther.

Says he, "I'd better call agin";
   Says she, "Think likely, *Mister*":
Thet last word pricked him like a pin,
   An' . . . Wal, he up an' kist her.   80

When Ma bimeby upon 'em slips,
   Huldy sot pale ez ashes,
All kin' o' smily roun' the lips
   An' teary roun' the lashes.

For she was jes' the quiet kind   85
   Whose naturs never vary,
Like streams that keep a summer mind
   Snowhid in Jenooary.

The blood clost roun' her heart felt glued
   Too tight for all expressin',   90
Tell mother see how metters stood
   An' gin 'em both her blessin'.

Then her red come back like the tide
   Down to the Bay o' Fundy,[6]
An' all I know is they was cried[7]   95
   In meetin' come nex' Sunday.

VIEWING THE AUTHOR'S IDEAS

1. Describe the effect of the moonlight. What preference does the speaker show for certain pioneer comforts? What details furnish the atmosphere of serene and cozy home life?

2. List Zekle's characteristics. What was Huldy's opinion of him?

3. Describe Huldy's mood and appearance before Zekle's entrance. How did she receive him? What effect did Zekle's courtship have?

4. Pick out lines which pay tribute to Huldy's personality, character, and simple beauty.

5. How does Huldy show herself to be a good psychologist?

---

[3] *sparked*, courted.
[4] *squired*, escorted.
[5] *Ole Hunderd*, Psalm 100.

[6] *Bay o' Fundy*, a bay separating Nova Scotia from New Brunswick, where the tide sometimes rises over seventy feet.
[7] *they was cried*. The marriage banns were published.

EVALUATING HIS MANNER OF EXPRESSION

1. How does the use of dialect aid the poem? If the verses had been expressed in perfect English, what stanzas would have lost a certain charm? How can a selection in dialect, containing grammatical errors, be literature?

2. What constitutes the humor of the poem?

3. Show that the first four lines contain poetic touches. Decide on other scattered lines that are poetic.

4. Select three similes and discuss their aid to the imagery. Are the similes in keeping with New England rural life?

Telling the Bees

John Greenleaf Whittier

More learned poets have often been at a loss to discover American folklore, but Whittier found it almost at his doorstep. As a basis for this poem he used a folk superstition brought to America from England. The poet explains that "On the death of a member of the family, the bees were at once informed of the event, and their hives dressed in mourning. This ceremonial was supposed to be necessary to prevent the swarms from leaving their hives and seeking a new home." Although Whittier is the poet of the heart and not of the intellect, he shows a fine restraint of emotion in relating the incident of the poem.

HERE is the place; right over the hill
   Runs the path I took;
You can see the gap in the old wall still
   And the steppingstones in the shallow brook.

There is the house, with the gate red-barred,   5
   And the poplars tall;
And the barn's brown length, and the cattle yard,
   And the white horns tossing above the wall.

There are the beehives ranged in the sun;
   And down by the brink   10
Of the brook are her poor flowers, weed-o'errun,
   Pansy and daffodil, rose and pink.

A year has gone, as the tortoise goes,
   Heavy and slow;
And the same rose blows, and the same sun glows,   15
   And the same brook sings of a year ago.

There's the same sweet clover smell in the breeze;
   And the June sun warm
Tangles his wings of fire in the trees,
   Setting as then over Fernside farm.   20

I mind me how with a lover's care
   From my Sunday coat
I brushed off the burs and smoothed my hair
   And cooled at the brookside my brow and throat.

Since we parted, a month had passed,   25
   To love, a year;
Down through the beeches I looked at last
   On the little red gate and the well sweep near.

I can see it all now — the slantwise rain
   Of light through the leaves,   30
The sundown's blaze on her window-pane,
   The bloom of her roses under the eaves.

Just the same as a month before —
   The house and the trees,
The barn's brown gable, the vine by the door —   35
   Nothing changed but the hives of bees.

Before them, under the garden wall,
   Forward and back,
Went drearily singing the chore girl small,
   Draping each hive with a shred of black.   40

Trembling, I listened; the summer sun
   Had the chill of snow,
For I knew she was telling the bees of one
   Gone on the journey we all must go!

Then I said to myself, "My Mary weeps   45
   For the dead today;
Haply her blind old grandsire sleeps
   The fret and the pain of his age away."

But her dog whined low; on the doorway sill,

With his cane to his chin,
The old man sat; and the chore girl still
  Sung to the bees stealing out and in.   50

And the song she was singing ever since
  In my ear sounds on:
"Stay at home, pretty bees, fly not hence!
  Mistress Mary is dead and gone!"   56

VIEWING THE AUTHOR'S IDEAS

1. The opening description of a New England farm of Whittier's day is like a Grant Wood painting, but done with a kindlier touch. The scene is thought to be Whittier's boyhood home. If you were painting the landscape, what would you put in the foreground; the middle space; the background? What color scheme does Whittier suggest?

2. Where does the narrative of the poem begin? What did the returning lover learn from the chore girl?

EVALUATING HIS MANNER OF EXPRESSION

1. "Telling the Bees" is an idyl, that is, a description of rustic or pastoral scenes which are picturesque in their simplicity. How does the poet make use of the commonplace to produce a romantic picture?

2. Some of Whittier's best poetry is told as a reminiscence. How long ago had the events of the poem occurred? In what mood did the lover return to the scene? How does Whittier guard against sentimentality in telling the story?

Maud Muller

John Greenleaf Whittier

Poet of the New England countryside, Whittier here uses an incident in a rustic setting as the basis for one of his most popular romantic poems. "The poem," wrote Whittier, "had no real foundation in fact, though a hint of it may have been found in recalling an incident, trivial in itself, of a journey on the picturesque Maine seaboard with my sister some years before it was written. We had stopped to rest our tired horse under the shade of an apple tree and refresh him with water from a little brook which rippled through the stone wall across the road. A very beautiful young girl in scantest summer attire was at work in the hayfield; and as we talked with her, we noticed that she strove to hide her bare feet by raking the hay over them, blushing as she did so through the tan of her cheek and neck."

MAUD Muller on a summer's day
Raked the meadow sweet with hay.

Beneath her torn hat glowed the wealth
Of simple beauty and rustic health.

Singing, she wrought, and her merry glee   5
The mockbird echoed from his tree.

But when she glanced to the far-off town,
White from its hillslope looking down,

The sweet song died, and a vague unrest
And a nameless longing filled her breast—   10

A wish that she hardly dared to own
For something better than she had known.

The Judge rode slowly down the lane,
Smoothing his horse's chestnut mane.

He drew his bridle in the shade   15
Of the apple trees, to greet the maid,

And asked a draught from the spring that flowed
Through the meadow across the road.

She stooped where the cool spring bubbled up
And filled for him her small tin cup,   20

And blushed as she gave it, looking down
On her feet so bare and her tattered gown.

"Thanks!" said the Judge; "a sweeter draught
From a fairer hand was never quaffed."

He spoke of the grass and flowers and trees,   25
Of the singing birds and the humming bees;

Then talked of the haying and wondered whether
The cloud in the west would bring foul weather.

And Maud forgot her brier-torn gown
And her graceful ankles, bare and brown;   30

And listened, while a pleased surprise
Looked from her long-lashed hazel eyes.

At last, like one who for delay
Seeks a vain excuse, he rode away.

Maud Muller looked and sighed: "Ah me! 35
That I the Judge's bride might be!

"He would dress me up in silks so fine
And praise and toast me at his wine.

"My father should wear a broadcloth coat;
My brother should sail a painted boat. 40

"I'd dress my mother so grand and gay,
And the baby should have a new toy each day.

"And I'd feed the hungry and clothe the poor,
And all should bless me who left our door."

The Judge looked back as he climbed the hill 45
And saw Maud Muller standing still.

"A form more fair, a race more sweet,
Ne'er hath it been my lot to meet.

"And her modest answer and graceful air
Show her wise and good as she is fair. 50

"Would she were mine, and I today,
Like her, a harvester of hay;

"No doubtful balance of rights and wrongs,
Nor weary lawyers with endless tongues,

"But low of cattle and song of birds, 55
And health and quiet and loving words."

But he thought of his sisters, proud and cold,
And his mother, vain of her rank and gold.

So, closing his heart, the Judge rode on,
And Maud was left in the field alone. 60

But the lawyers smiled that afternoon
When he hummed in court an old love tune;

And the young girl mused beside the well
Till the rain on the unraked clover fell.

He wedded a wife of richest dower, 65
Who lived for fashion, as he for power.

Yet oft in his marble hearth's bright glow
He watched a picture come and go;

And sweet Maud Muller's hazel eyes
Looked out in their innocent surprise. 70

Oft, when the wine in his glass was red,
He longed for the wayside well instead;

And closed his eyes on his garnished rooms
To dream of meadows and clover blooms.

And the proud man sighed with a secret pain, 75
"Ah, that I were free again!

"Free as when I rode that day
Where the barefoot maiden raked her hay."

She wedded a man, unlearned and poor,
And many children played round her door. 80

But care and sorrow and childbirth pain
Left their traces on heart and brain.

And oft, when the summer sun shone hot
On the new-mown hay in the meadow lot,

And she heard the little spring brook fall 85
Over the roadside through the wall,

In the shade of the apple tree again
She saw a rider draw his rein;

And, gazing down with timid grace,
She felt his pleased eyes read her face. 90

Sometimes her narrow kitchen walls
Stretched away into stately halls;

The weary wheel to a spinet[1] turned,
The tallow candle an astral[2] burned,

And for him who sat by the chimney lug,[3]
Dozing and grumbling o'er pipe and mug, 96

A manly form at her side she saw,
And joy was duty and love was law.

Then she took up her burden of life again,
Saying only, "It might have been." 100

Alas for maiden, alas for Judge,
For rich repiner and household drudge!

God pity them both! and pity us all
Who vainly the dreams of youth recall.

For of all sad words of tongue or pen, 105
The saddest are these: "It might have been!"

Ah, well! for us all some sweet hope lies
Deeply buried from human eyes;

And in the hereafter angels may
Roll the stone from its grave away! 110

[1] *spinet*, a small harpsichord.

[2] *astral*, a lamp with a circular wick so constructed that the light comes uninterruptedly from the reservoir containing the oil.

[3] *chimney lug*, a pole on which the kettle is hung over the fire; hence, the fireside.

1. Discuss the amount of happiness in Maud Muller's life before the appearance of the judge. What thoughts did the coming of the judge arouse in the girl's mind? What reasons have you for concluding that Maud idealized the judge in thinking of him after he had gone?

2. Name characteristics of Maud which would have made her a good wife. What would have been the effect of the wide difference in upbringing and environment had the two married? Would they have been as happy as each believed when viewing the situation from afar? Discuss.

3. What character traits caused the judge to put aside thoughts of Maud Muller? Find lines which reveal other flaws in the judge's character; lines which show desirable qualities. Judging from these observations, do you think he would have been an ideal husband?

4. Describe the man whom Maud eventually married. Is your sympathy more with Maud or with the judge? Why?

1. Show that Whittier is faithful in presenting the unrest, labor, joys, and sorrows of poverty in rural life. Does he present a realistic treatment of sordid detail or does he touch unpleasant aspects lightly, as a romanticist?

2. Which two lines of the poem are frequently quoted?

Centennial Hymn

John Greenleaf Whittier

In 1876 the Centennial Exposition held in Philadelphia celebrated the first hundred years of American independence. For the occasion Whittier wrote the "Centennial Hymn," which was set to music by John G. Paine. Long years of reading the Bible had given the poet strains of the Hebraic spirit. Like some prophet of the New World he solemnly rededicates the nation to peace and justice.

OUR fathers' God! from out Whose hand
    The centuries fall like grains of sand,
We meet today, united, free,
And loyal to our land and Thee,
To thank Thee for the era done,   5
And trust Thee for the opening one.

Here, where of old, by Thy design,
The fathers spake that word of Thine
Whose echo is the glad refrain
Of rended bolt and falling chain,   10
To grace our festal time, from all
The zones of earth our guests we call.

For art and labor met in truce,
For beauty made the bride of use,
We thank Thee; but withal we crave   15

The austere virtues strong to save,
The honor proof to place or gold,
The manhood never bought nor sold!

Oh make Thou us, through centuries long,
In peace secure, in justice strong;   20
Around our gift of freedom draw
The safeguards of Thy righteous law;
And, cast in some diviner mold,
Let the new cycle[1] shame the old!

Be with us while the New World greets   25
The Old World thronging all its streets,
Unveiling all its triumphs won
By art or toil beneath the sun;
And unto common good ordain
This rival ship of hand and brain.   30

Thou, Who hast here in concord furled
The war flag of a gathered world,
Beneath our Western skies fulfill
The Orient mission of good-will,
And, freighted with love's Golden Fleece,   35
Send back its Argonauts of peace.

[1] *cycle,* century.

VIEWING THE AUTHOR'S IDEAS

VIEWING THE AUTHOR'S IDEAS

1. What is the keynote of the poem as expressed in the first stanza? Name some achievements of our first century of national life.

2. To what word of the founding fathers does Whittier refer? In what documents was it expressed? How could it be called "that word of Thine"? Explain the clause beginning "Whose echo is the glad refrain."

3. In what American achievements do art and labor meet? When is honor "proof to place or gold"? What comment refers to the bribing of statesmen?

4. According to Whittier, what will be the great safeguard to American freedom? What further petitions does he make for our country? Is the new cycle surpassing the first?

EVALUATING HIS MANNER OF EXPRESSION

1. Why is the figure of speech in the first two lines effective?
2. What attitudes reflect the austerity of Whittier's beliefs? How is the tone of solemnity secured?

The Convert

OR LEAVES FROM MY EXPERIENCE

Orestes A. Brownson

Brownson had been a Catholic thirteen years when he wrote the story of his life and conversion in The Convert, *from which this selection is taken. He had tried Calvinism, transcendentalism, and radical socialism and had found them wanting. Like Cardinal Newman and other great converts he discovered a solution to the problem of human destiny in Catholic teaching and discipline.*

The man trained for Catholic action today is somewhat surprised to discover the defensive attitude of the Catholic in Brownson's time. The poor and uneducated immigrants, fleeing from religious persecution in their own countries, were not prepared to assume positions of leadership among the laity. In a society where narrow prejudice abounded, they could do little more than defend their own position.

I HAVE now completed the sketch I proposed to give of my intellectual struggles, failures, and successes from my earliest childhood till my reception by the Bishop of Boston into the communion of the Catholic Church. I have not written to vindicate my ante-Catholic life or to apologize for my conversion. I have aimed to record facts, principles, and reasonings, trials and struggles which have a value independent of the fact that they relate to my personal history. Yet even as the personal history of an earnest soul, working its way under the grace of God from darkness to light, from the lowest abyss of unbelief to a firm, unwavering, and not a blind faith in the old religion so generally rejected and decried by my countrymen, I think my story not wholly worthless or altogether uninstructive — especially when taken in connection with the glimpses it incidentally affords of American thought and life during the greater portion of the earlier half of the present century. Whether what I have written proves me to have been intellectually weak, vacillating, constantly changing, all things by turns, and nothing long, or tolerably firm, consistent and persevering in my search after truth; whether it shows that my seeking admission into the Church for the reasons and in the way and manner I did was a sudden caprice, an act of folly, perhaps of despair, or that it was an act of deliberation, wise, judicious, and for a sufficient reason, my readers are free to judge for themselves.

This much only will I add, that, whether I am believed or not, I can truly say that during the nearly thirteen years of Catholic experience I have found not the slightest reason to regret the step I took. I have had much to try me and enough to shake me, if shaken I could be; but I have not had even the slightest temptation to doubt or the slightest inclination to undo what I have done; and have every day found new and stronger reasons to thank Almighty God for His great mercy in bringing me to the knowledge of His Church and permitting me to enter and live in her communion. I know all that can be said in disparagement of Catholics. I am well versed (perhaps no man more so) in Catholic scandals, but I have not been deceived; I have found all that was promised me, all I looked for. I have found the Church all that her ministers represented her, all my imagination painted her, and infinitely more than I had conceived it possible for her to be. My experience as a Catholic, so far as the Church, her doctrines, her morals, discipline, her influences are concerned, has been a continued succession of agreeable surprises.

I do not pretend that I have found the Catholic population perfect or that I have found in them or in myself no shortcomings, nothing to be censured or regretted; yet I have found that population superior to what I expected, more intellectual, more cultivated, more moral, more active, living, and energetic. Undoubtedly, our Catholic population, made up in great part of the humbler classes of the Catholic populations of the Old World, for three hundred years subjected to the bigotry, intolerance, persecutions, and oppressions of Protestant or quasi-Protestant[1] governments, have traits of character, habits, and manners which the outside non-Catholic American finds unattractive and even repulsive. Certainly in our cities and large towns may be found, I am sorry to say, a comparatively numerous population, nominally Catholic, who are no credit to their religion, to the land of their birth, or to that of their adoption. No Catholic will deny that the children of these are to a great extent shamefully neglected and suffered to grow up without the simplest elementary moral and religious instruction and to become recruits to our vicious population, our rowdies, and our criminals. This is certainly to be deplored but can easily be explained without prejudice to the Church by adverting to the condition to which these individuals were reduced before coming here; to their disappointments and discouragements in a strange land; to their exposure to new and unlooked-for temptations; to the fact that they were by no means the best of Catholics even in their native countries; to their poverty, destitution, ignorance, insufficient culture, and a certain natural shiftlessness and recklessness, and to our great lack of schools, churches, and priests. The proportion, too, that these bear to our whole Catholic population is far less than

is commonly supposed; and they are not so habitually depraved as they appear, for they seldom or never consult appearances and have little skill in concealing their vices. As low and degraded as they are, they never are so low or so vicious as the corresponding class of Protestants in Protestant nations. A Protestant vicious class is always worse than it appears; a Catholic vicious population is less bad. In the worst there is always some germ that with proper care may be nursed into life, that may blossom and bear fruit. In our narrow lanes, blind courts, damp cellars, and unventilated garrets where our people swarm as bees; in the midst of filth and the most squalid wretchedness, the fumes of intemperance and the shouts and imprecations[2] of blasphemy; in what by the outside world would be regarded as the very dens of vice and crime and infamy, we often find individuals who, it may well be presumed, have retained their baptismal innocence, real *Fleurs de Marie,*[3] who remain pure and unsullied and who, in their humble sphere, exhibit brilliant examples of the most heroic Christian virtues.

The majority of our Catholic population is made up of the unlettered peasantry, small mechanics, servant girls, and common laborers from various European countries; and however worthy in themselves or useful to the country to which they have migrated, cannot in a worldly and social point of view, at least, be taken as a fair average of the Catholic population in their native lands. The Catholic nobility, gentry, easy classes, and the better specimens of the professional men have not migrated with them. Two or three millions of the lower, less prosperous, and less cultivated, and sometimes less virtuous class of the European Catholic populations have in a comparatively brief period been cast upon our shores, with little or no provision made for their intellectual, moral, or religious wants. Yet if we look at this population as it is, and is every year becoming, we cannot but be struck with its marvelous energy and progress. The mental activity of Catholics, all things considered, is far more remarkable than that of our non-Catholic countrymen; and in proportion to their numbers and means they contribute far more than any other class of American citizens to the purposes of

---

[1] *quasi-Protestant* (kwä–sĭ), Protestant in a certain degree.

[2] *imprecations,* curses.

[3] *Fleurs de Marie,* Flowers of Mary.

education, both common and liberal; for they receive little or nothing from the public treasury and in addition to supporting numerous schools of their own, they contribute their quota to the support of those of the state.

I do not pretend that the Catholic population of this country are a highly literary people or that they are in any adequate sense an intellectually cultivated people. How could they be, when the great mass of them have had to earn their very means of subsistence, and have had as much as they could do to provide for the first wants of religion and of themselves and families? Yet there is a respectable Catholic-American literature springing up among us, and Catholics have their representatives among the first scholars and scientific men in the land. In metaphysics,[4] in moral and intellectual philosophy, they take already the lead; in natural history and the physical sciences they are not far behind; and let once the barrier between them and the non-Catholic public be broken down, and they will soon take the first position in general and polite literature. As yet our own literary public, owing to the causes I have mentioned, I admit is not large enough to give adequate encouragement to authors; and the general public makes it a point not to recognize our literary labors. But this will not last, for it is against the interest and the genius of liberal scholarship, and Catholic authors will soon find a public adequate to their wants. Non-Catholics do themselves great wrong in acting on the principle that no good can come out of Nazareth; for we have already in what we ourselves write, in what we reprint from our brethren in the British Empire, and in what we translate from French, German, Spanish, and Italian Catholics, a literature far richer and more important, even under a literary and scientific point of view, than they suspect.

I have known long and well the Protestant clergy of the United States, and I am by no means disposed to underrate their native abilities or their learning and science; and, although I think the present generation of ministers falls far below its predecessors, I esteem highly the contributions they have made and are making to the literature and science of our common country. But our Catholic clergy, below in many respects what for various reasons they should be, can compare more than favorably with them (except those among them whose mother tongue was foreign from ours) in the correct and classical use of the English language. They surpass them as a body in logical training, in theological science, and in the accuracy, and not unfrequently in the variety and extent, of their erudition. Indeed, I have found among Catholics a higher tone of thought, morals, manners, and society, than I have ever found, with fair opportunities, among my non-Catholic countrymen; and taking the Catholic population of the country, even as it actually is, under all its disadvantages, there is nothing in it that need make the most cultivated and refined man of letters or of society blush to avow himself a Catholic.

Certainly, I have found cause to complain of Catholics at home and abroad, not indeed as falling below non-Catholic populations but as falling below their own Catholic standard. I find among them, not indeed as universal — far from it — but as too prevalent, habits of thought and modes of action, a lack of manly courage, energy, and directness, which seem to me as unwise as they are offensive to the better class of English and American minds. In matters not of faith there is less unanimity and less liberality, less courtesy and less forbearance in regard to allowable differences of opinion than might be expected. But I have recollected that I am not myself infallible and may complain where I should not. Many things may seem to me wrong only because I am not accustomed to them. Something must be set down to peculiarity of national temperament and development; and even what cannot be justified or excused on either ground can in all cases be traced to causes unconnected with religion. The habits and peculiarities which I find it most difficult to like are evidently due to the fact that the Catholics of this country have migrated for the most part from foreign Catholic populations that have either been oppressed by non-Catholic governments directing their policy to crush and extinguish Catholicity, or by political despotisms which sprang up in Europe after the disastrous Protestant revolt in the sixteenth century, and which recognized in the common people no rights and allowed them no equality with the ruling class. Under the despotic governments of some Catholic countries and the bigotry and intolerance of Protestant states, they could hardly fail to acquire habits not in accordance with the habits of those who have never

---

[4] *metaphysics*, a division of philosophy which treats of the science of being.

been persecuted and have never been forced, in order to live, to study to evade tyrannical laws or the caprices of despotism. Men who are subjected to tyranny, who have to deal with tyrants, and who feel that power is against them and that they can never carry their points by main force, naturally study diplomacy and supply by art what they lack in strength. This art may degenerate into craft. That it occasionally does so with individuals here and elsewhere, it were useless to deny; but the cause is not in the Church or anything she teaches or approves. In fact, many things which Englishmen and Americans complain of in Catholics and the populations of southern Europe have been inherited from the craft and refinement of the old Greco-Roman[5] civilization and transmitted from generation to generation in spite of the Church.

As yet our Catholic population, whether foreign-born or native-born, hardly dare feel themselves freemen in this land of freedom. They have so long been an oppressed people that their freedom here seems hardly real. They have never become reconciled to the old Puritan Commonwealth of England, and they retain with their Catholicity too many reminiscences of the passions and politics of the Bourbons[6] and the Stuarts.[7] They are very generally attached to the republican institutions of the country — no class of our citizens more so — and would defend them at the sacrifice of their lives; but their interior life has not as yet been molded into entire harmony with them; and they have a tendency, in seeking to follow out American democracy, to run into extreme radicalism, or, when seeking to preserve law and order, to run into extreme conservatism.[8] They do not always hit the exact medium. But this need not surprise us, for no one can hit that medium unless his interior life and habits have been formed to it. Non-Catholic foreigners are less able than Catholic foreigners to do it, if we except the English, who have been trained under a system in many respects analogous to our own; and no small portion of our own countrymen, to the manner born,[9] make even more fatal mistakes than are made by any portion of our Catholic population — chiefly,

however, because they adopt a European instead of an American interpretation of our political and social order. Other things being equal, Catholic foreigners far more readily adjust themselves to our institutions than any other class of foreigners; and among Catholics it must be observed that they succeed best who best understand and best practice their religion. They who are least truly American and yield most to the demagogues[10] are those who have very little of Catholicity except the accident of being born of Catholic parents, who had them baptized in infancy. Those are they who bring reproach on the whole body.

That the struggles in Europe have an influence on Catholic thought in this country is very true and, sometimes an unfavorable influence, cannot be denied. A portion of our foreign-born Catholics, subjected at home to the restraints imposed by despotism, feel on coming here that they are loosed from all restraints, and forgetting the obedience they owe to their pastors, to the prelates whom the Holy Ghost has placed over them, become insubordinate and live more as Protestants than as Catholics; another portion, deeply alarmed at the revolutionary spirit and the evils that it has produced in the Old World, distrust the independence and personal dignity the American always preserves in the presence of authority and are half disposed to look upon every American as a rebel at heart, if not an unbeliever. They do not precisely understand the American disposition that bows to the law but never to persons, and is always careful to distinguish between the man and the office; and they are disposed to look upon it as incompatible with the true principle of obedience demanded by the Gospel. But I think these and their conservative brethren in Europe mistake the real American character. There is not in Christendom a more loyal or a more law-abiding people than the genuine people of the United States. I think European Catholics of the conservative party have unfounded suspicion of our loyalty, for I think it a higher and truer loyalty than that which they seem to inculcate. I have wholly mistaken the spirit of the Church, if an enlightened obedience, an obedience that knows wherefore it obeys and is yielded from principle, from conviction, from free will, and from a sense of

---

[5] *Greco-Roman civilization*, the ancient civilization of Greece and Rome.

[6] *Bourbons*, the kings of the family of Bourbon in France.

[7] *Stuarts*, kings of England belonging to the Stuart family of Scotland.

[8] *conservatism*, opposition to change.

[9] *to the manner born*, having lifelong acquaintance with given customs and conditions.

[10] *demagogues*, political leaders who strive to gain influence by arousing the passions or prejudices of the people.

obligation, is not more grateful to her maternal heart than the blind, unreasoning, and cringing submission of those who are strangers to freedom. Servile fear does not rank very high with Catholic theologians; and the Church seeks to govern men, as well as freedmen, as Almighty God governs them; that is, in accordance with the nature with which He has created them, as beings endowed with reason and free will. God adapts his government to our rational and voluntary faculties and governs us without violence to either, and by really satisfying both. The Church does the same and resorts to coercive measures only to repress disorders in the public body. Hence our ecclesiastical rulers are called shepherds, not lords, and shepherds of their Master's flock, not of their own; and are to feed, tend, protect the flock, and take care of its increase for Him with sole reference to His will and His honor and glory. We must love and reverence them for His sake, for the great trust He has confided to them, not for their own sakes as if they owned the flock and governed it in their own name and right for their own pleasure and profit. This idea of power, whether in church or state, as a delegated power or trust, is inseparable from the American mind; and hence the American feels always in its presence his native equality as a man and asserts, even in the most perfect and entire submission, his own personal independence and dignity, knowing that he bows only to the law or to the will of a common Master. His submission he yields, because he knows that it is due, but without servility or pusillanimity.[11]

But though I entertain these views of what have been for a long time the policy of so-called Catholic governments and, so to speak, the politics of European Catholics, I find in them nothing that reflects on the truth or efficiency of the Church; for she has no responsibility in the matter, since, as I have said, she governs men and discharges her mission with a scrupulous regard to the free will of individuals and the autonomy of states. She proffers to all every assistance necessary for the attainment of the most heroic sanctity, but she forces no man to accept that assistance. In her view men owe all they have and are to God, but they are neither slaves nor machines.

In speaking of Catholic nations and comparing them with the Catholic standard, I find, I confess, much to regret, to deplore, and even to blame; but in comparing them with non-Catholic nations, the case is quite different, and I cannot concede that the Catholic population of any country is inferior to any Protestant population, even in those very qualities in respect to which Catholics are usually supposed to be the most deficient. In no Catholic population will you find the flunkyism which Carlyle so unmercifully ridicules in the middling classes of Great Britain; or that respect to mere wealth, that worship of the moneybag, or that base servility to the mob or to public opinion, so common and so ruinous to public and private virtue in the United States. I do not claim any very high merit for our Catholic press; it lacks, with some exceptions, dignity, grasp of thought, and breadth of view, and seems intended for an unlettered community; but it has an earnestness, a sincerity, a freedom, an independence which will be looked for in vain in our non-Catholic press, whether religious or secular. The Catholic population of this country, too, taken as a body, have a personal freedom, an independence, a self-respect, a conscientiousness, a love of truth, and a devotion to principle, not to be found in any other class of American citizens. Their moral tone as well as their moral standard is higher, and they act more uniformly under a sense of deep responsibility to God and to their country. Owing to various circumstances as well as national peculiarities, a certain number of them fall easily under the influence of demagogues; but as a body they are far less demagogical and far less under the influence of demagogues than are non-Catholic Americans. He who knows both classes equally well will not pretend to the contrary. The Catholics of this country, by no means a fair average of the Catholic population of old Catholic countries, do as to the great majority act from honest principle, from sincere and earnest conviction, and are prepared to die sooner than in any grave matters swerve from what they regard as truth and justice. They have the principle and the firmness to stand by what they believe true and just, in good report and evil report, whether the world be with them or against them. They can also be convinced by arguments addressed to their reason and moved by appeals to conscience, to the fear of God, and the love of justice. The non-Catholic has

---

[11] *pusillanimity* (pū-sĭ-là-nĭm'-ĭ-tĭ), cowardliness.

no conception of the treasure the Union possesses in these two or three million Catholics, humble in their outward circumstances as the majority of them are. I have never shown any disposition to palliate[12] or disguise their faults; but, knowing them and my non-Catholic countrymen as I do, I am willing to risk the assertion that with all their faults and shortcomings they are the salt of the American community and the really conservative element in the American population.

I have found valid after thirteen years of experience none of those objections to entering the Catholic communion which I enumerated in a previous chapter, and which made me for a time hesitate to follow the convictions of my own understanding. To err is human; and I do not pretend that I have found Catholics in matters of human prudence, in what belongs to them and not to the Church, all that I could wish. I have found much that I do not like, much that I do not believe reasonable or prudent; but it is all easily explained without any reflection on the truth or efficiency of the Church, or the general wisdom and prudence of her prelates and clergy. Undoubtedly our Catholic population, made up in most part of emigrants from every nation of Europe with every variety of national temper, character, taste, habit, and usage, not yet molded save in religion into one homogeneous[13] body, may present features more or less repulsive to the American wedded to his own peculiar nationality and but recently converted to the Catholic faith; but the very readiness with which these heterogeneous[14] elements amalgamate and the rapidity with which the Catholic body assumes a common character — falls into the current of American life, and takes in all not adverse to religion the tone and features of the country — proves the force of Catholicity and its vast importance in forming a true and noble national character and in generating and sustaining a true, generous, and lofty patriotism. In a few years they will be the Americans of the Americans and on them will rest the performance of the glorious work of sustaining American civilization and realizing the hopes of the founders of our great and growing republic.

Such are the views, feelings, convictions, and hopes of the Convert. But he would be unjust to himself and to his religion if he did not say that not for these reasons, or any like them, is he a Catholic. He loves this country, loves her institutions, he loves her freedom; but he is a Catholic because he believes the Catholic Church the church of God; because he believes her the medium through which God dispenses His grace to man, and through which alone we can hope for heaven. He is a Catholic, because he would believe, love, possess, and obey the truth; because he would know and do God's will; because he would escape hell and gain heaven. Considerations drawn from this world are of minor importance, for man's home is not here, his bliss is not here, his reward is not here; he is made for God, for endless beatitude with Him hereafter; and let him turn as he will, his supreme good as well as duty lies in seeking "the kingdom of God and His justice." That the Church serves the cause of patriotism; that if embraced it is sure to give us a high-toned and chivalric[15] national character; that it enlists conscience in the support of our free institutions and the preservation of our republican freedom as the established order of the country, is a good reason why the American people should not oppose her, and why they should wish her growth and prosperity in our country; but the real reason why we should become Catholics and remain such, is because she is the new creation, regenerated humanity; and without communion with her, we can never see God as He is, or become united to Him as our supreme good in the supernatural order.

VIEWING THE AUTHOR'S IDEAS

1. Why did Brownson enter the Church? Compare his ideas and experiences with those recorded in the biographies you may have read of such famous converts as Newman, Stoddard, Chesterton, Moody, or Noyes. How does Brownson show that the faults of Catholics are not a reflection upon the truths of Catholic doctrine?

2. What attitude of American Catholic immigrants resulted partly from religious and political persecution in the countries from which they came? How does Brownson account for the fact that these immigrants were not representative of the Church in their native lands?

3. What was the effect upon Catholic immigrants of the lack of well-organized parishes; religious schools; priests who

---

[12] *palliate*, to cover with excuses.

[13] *homogeneous* (hō-mō-jē'-nē-ŭs), of the same kind.

[14] *heterogeneous* (hĕt-ĕr-ŏ-jē'-nē-ŭs), having unlike qualities.

[15] *chivalric*, possessing the qualities of the ideal knight in the age of chivalry.

understood their language and traditions? What are Catholic Action groups doing for the foreign-born in our large cities today?

4. What claim does Brownson make for the contribution of Catholics in the United States to education; to literature; to other branches of knowledge? What advances have Catholics made in these fields since Brownson's time?

5. How does the author show that the Church serves the cause of Americanism by emphasis upon the dignity of man and the sacredness of human rights, and by the encouragement of enlightened obedience to the authority of the state as the delegated power of God?

6. To what extent is this prediction of Brownson concerning American Catholics being fulfilled today: "In a few years they will be the Americans of the Americans and upon them will rest the glorious work of sustaining American civilization and realizing the hopes of the founders of our great and growing republic"?

EVALUATING HIS MANNER OF EXPRESSION

1. How does this selection illustrate Brownson's manner of heaping together truths on both sides of a question in order to build up a convincing answer?

2. Discuss the sincerity and picturesqueness of the passage in which Brownson shows that saints can be made in the midst of poverty and vice.

3. Show that this selection presents a dignified and forthright treatment of a controversial subject. Point out instances when Brownson might have been tempted to resort to flippancy and sarcasm.

4. Explain: "reminiscences of the passions and politics of the Bourbons and the Stuarts"; "tendency in seeking to follow out American democracy to run into extreme radicalism"; "yield most to demagogues"; "base servility to the mob or public opinion"; "they are the salt of the American community"; "a high-toned and chivalric national character."

San Sisto

George Henry Miles

In creating this dramatic monologue which interprets an artist's masterpiece, George Henry Miles places himself in the company of Robert Browning and Edwin Arlington Robinson. The speaker is possibly a devoted old guide in the Dresden Gallery, anxious to interpret for visitors Raphael's priceless Sistine Madonna. This picture had been painted for the church of San Sisto at Piacenza, Italy, at the request of the Benedictine monks who desired a processional standard portraying the Virgin and Child, Saint Sixtus, and Saint

Barbara. Lest anyone fail to note the rapt look on the faces of Mother and Child, the speaker explains that, although the figures appear to be facing the spectator, they are in reality high in the bright clouds of the heavens, where the Beatific Vision falls directly within their range of sight. The curtain that had separated them from the celestial scene has been withdrawn, and Virgin and Infant are "face to face with the Unveiled Omnipotence."

THREE hundred years the world has looked at it
    Unwearied — it at Heaven; and here it hangs
In Dresden, making it a Holy City.
It is an old acquaintance; you have met
Copies by thousands — Morghens[1] here and there —   5
But all the sunlight withered. Prints, at best,
Are but the master's shadow — as you see.
I call that face the holiest revelation
God ever made to genius. How or why,
When, or for whom 'twas painted, wherefore ask?   10

[1] *Morghens*, engravings by Rafaello Morghen.

Enough to know, 'tis Raphael, and to feel
His Fornarina[2] was not with him, when
Spurning the slow cartoon,[3] he flashed that face,
That Virgin Mother's half-transfigured face,
On canvas. Yes, they say, 'twas meant to head   15
Some virginal procession; to that banner
Heaven's inmost gates might open, one would think.
But let the picture tell its story — take
Your stand in this far corner. Falls the light
As you would have it? That Saint Barbara[4] —   20
Observe her inclination and the finger
Of Sixtus[5] — both are pointing — *where?* Now look
Below — those grand boy angels; watch their eyes
Fastened — *on whom?* — What, not yet catch my meaning? . . .
Step closer — half a step — no nearer. Mark   25
The Babe's fixed glance of calm equality.
Observe that wondering, rapt, dilated gaze,
The Mother's superhuman joy and fear,
That hushed — that startled adoration! Watch
Those circled cherubs swarming into light,   30
Wreathing their splendid arch, their golden ring,
Around the unveiled vision. Look above
At the *drawn curtain!* — Ah, we do not see
God's self, but *they* do; they are face to face
With the unveiled *Omnipotent!* —   35

[2] *Fornarina*, a model for Raphael, real or fictitious, about whom there has been much controversy.

[3] *cartoon*, a design or study to be copied.

[4] *St. Barbara*, martyr of the early Christian era whose exact dates are unknown.

[5] *Sixtus*, Saint Sixtus II, who was elected Pope in 257 and was martyred in 258, A.D.

VIEWING THE AUTHOR'S IDEAS

1. In a picture of the Sistine Madonna, note each of the speaker's explanations. Discuss any points wherein you disagree with his interpretation. Do St. Sixtus and St. Barbara appear to be directing their attention to the people on earth for whom they intercede or are they contemplating the Beatific Vision?

2. What indications does the speaker give of his knowledge of art; of his ability to communicate his appreciation to spectators; of his sensitive spiritual perceptions?

3. Arrange an exhibit of madonnas. Give reasons why you agree or disagree with the statement that the Sistine face is the "holiest revelation God ever made to genius."

4. In what age did Raphael live? Name other artists who made their art the handmaid of theology. What is the relation of modern art to religion? Do you see more in a painting when you know "how or why, when, or for whom 'twas painted"?

5. If possible, plan a class visit to an art gallery. Compare prints and their originals to prove the poet's words that "prints, at best, are but the master's shadow." Make a hobby of collecting miniature madonnas.

EVALUATING HIS MANNER OF EXPRESSION

1. In a dramatic monologue only one person speaks but his words are addressed to another character or other characters whose presence in the scene the reader is expected to remember. In "San Sisto," to what comments of an unseen auditor or auditors does the speaker reply? By what other means does the author make us aware that the speaker has an audience?

The House Where Poe Wrote "The Raven"

LITERATURE OF THE SOUTH

EDGAR ALLAN POE

Edgar Allan Poe (1809-1849), one of the few American poets with a great international reputation and influence, had a singularly unfortunate career. He was born in Boston in 1809, the son of itinerant actors. Orphaned at the age of three, he was taken into the home of John Allan, wealthy tobacco exporter of Richmond, Virginia. Though treated in all respects as a son, Poe was never formally adopted by his foster parents. From 1815 to 1820 he lived in England, attending academies in London and Stoke Newington. On his return to Richmond he continued his studies and at length entered the University of Virginia.

From this point on, Poe's life becomes a complicated series of brilliant half-starts and thwarted conclusions. Although he was endowed with a vigorous and restless mind, Poe was always to be the victim of his own nervous instability, an instability which manifested itself in an almost continued state of melancholy and occasional excesses in drink. Few literary men have had loftier ideals than Poe; few men have been more haunted by their inability to achieve them. Discharged from the University for disciplinary reasons, Poe went home only to enter upon a series of quarrels with his foster parents. He ran away to Boston, later entered the United States Army under an assumed name, had himself honorably discharged after a little more than a year's service, managed to secure an appointment to West Point, where, after a brief interval, he was once more to come under the disapproval of the authorities. In 1831 he was dismissed from the Military Academy.

All this while Poe's pen had not been idle. He had managed to publish some of his poems, and in the very year of his dismissal from West Point he gave his publisher some new compositions for a second edition of his *Poems.* Among these new compositions were the now famous lyrics "To Helen," "Israfel," and "The City in the Sea." In 1833 Poe won a prize of one hundred dollars for his story "Ms. Found in a Bottle" and soon afterwards began his long but uncertain career in journalism. From 1835 until his death fourteen years later, Poe wrote for, and sometimes edited, some of the leading national magazines.

In 1836 he married a cousin, Virginia Clemm. Very frail in health and many years his junior, she idolized her husband. Poe, in turn, reverenced her and treated her with the greatest delicacy. Poe could boast of one other very close human tie, that with his aunt, Mrs. Maria Clemm. It was she who loyally protected Poe against the effects of his own disordered life. Despite her efforts, however, and Poe's own good intentions, poverty and uncertainty were to harass them always. The truth is that Poe, although remarkably gifted, was almost totally undependable. In 1847 his wife died. Two years later, in a year which saw some of his best works produced, Poe himself was to die.

Poe makes manifold contributions

From the literary viewpoint Poe's life was far from being a failure. He has won fame as a critic, poet, short-story writer, and journalist. He was the first American poet to examine the tools of his trade with scientific exactness; he is among the pioneers in his interest in what goes on in the mind of a writer in the act of creating great literature; he has claim to be considered the inventor of the detective story and of the story which concentrates on atmosphere rather than on plot; he was the great opponent of the "didactic" in literature, that attitude which insists that the chief purpose of literature is to instruct and edify.

If Poe's fame is high in his own country, it is extravagantly high abroad, and especially in France. It would be hard to prove that Poe has really influenced any American poet; yet, he is the father of a whole movement in French poetry. There are many causes for the French admiration of Poe. The French admire

logic, and Poe in his tales of ratiocination is a master logician; the French are much more concerned with critical theory than most American writers, and Poe fulfills the French expectation of what a critical theorist should be. Besides this, Poe's lyrics, sometimes so thin and mechanical to our ears, seem unusually musical when translated into French. Finally, Poe had the good fortune to be championed by a man even greater than he, Charles Baudelaire. This remarkable French poet became Poe's self-appointed European advertiser.

Poe's achievement is considerable, but his gifts were not without their limitations. As a critic he is interesting but hardly profound. He is inclined to examine the effects of poetry on the reader and then to define poetry in terms of its effects. Poetry is judged by its "excitement" value. For Poe, the short lyric is the only kind of poem; he considered a long poem "a contradiction in terms." Both in his verse and in his short stories Poe shows an unhealthy interest in death, disease, melancholy, and beauty in process of decay. For all his skill in maneuvering a story to its conclusion, Poe definitely shows the defects of one who writes according to a formula.

But Poe's genius is robust enough to withstand criticism. In the brief span of forty years he wrote some of the finest criticism of his day, and the magazines with which he was associated rose in quality and circulation through his efforts. He was a careful craftsman, and he brought a skill of execution to his tales which is all the more phenomenal when viewed in the light of the standards of his day. Indeed, it may be said that Poe's greatest single achievement is that he has made it impossible for succeeding authors to write off their literary deficiencies in the name of "inspiration." For Poe was undeniably correct in insisting that writers must be skilled and responsible craftsmen and that they must keep inspiration under rational control. Finally, Poe has left us a few lyric poems which have a strange and haunting beauty.

The short story is defined

Because Poe's method of writing short stories has been so influential, a brief analysis of that method will not

Edgar Allan Poe

but terror has meaning only where there is character and a moral context. Poe's concentration on atmosphere to the neglect of character development is not wholly a virtue. It betrayed him into writing tales of sensation for the sake of sensation. In spite of the elaborate care which he expended on his tales, Poe must be accused of fostering the public taste for "thrillers."

HENRY TIMROD

Henry Timrod (1828-1867), born in Charleston, South Carolina, devoted his poetic gifts to the cause of the South and won the title "Laureate of the Confederacy" for the strength and beauty of his martial poems. In a series of spirited odes, Timrod favored the secession of the states and envisioned a new southern nation. One of his best-known poems, "The Cotton Boll," shows the glorious possibilities of the South for economic and cultural advancement. The poet even dares to hope that through the cultivation and sale of cotton the South may be instrumental in alleviating suffering and bringing about world peace. The outbreak of war had a tremendous effect upon the life and talent of young Timrod. Physically unfit for active duty in the Confederate Army, he served as a correspondent for the *Charleston Mercury*. Previous to the war, he had enjoyed a local reputation for his sentimental verse and had belonged to a brilliant group of literary men. The war matured Timrod's talent, motivated his verse, and turned his "sentimental prettiness" into poetry of strength and beauty. His war poems have an athletic strength which is surprising in contrast to his earlier verse dealing with love and nature. At the time of his death at the age of thirty-nine, Timrod had become a poet of promise. To call him, because of his love of beauty and musical language, "the Keats of the South" implies too much praise. His verse, however, has a sweetness, a simplicity, a charm which marks the true poet. Like Keats he was a victim of misfortune and tuberculosis. Despite war and unfavorable circumstances, his poetry displays no littleness. Timrod was always the gentle, peace-loving, courtly gentleman.

be out of place. Poe claimed that he wrote his stories from the end to the beginning, rather than from the beginning to the end. He meant that he first decided the effect he wished to create, the final impression he wished to leave with the reader. Poe's classic definition of the short story first appeared in a review of Hawthorne's *Twice-Told Tales*.

"Having conceived, with deliberate care, a certain unique or single *effect* to be wrought out, he (the writer) then invents such incidents — he then combines such events as may best aid him in establishing this preconceived effect. If his very initial sentence tend not to the outbringing of this effect, then he has failed in his first step. In the whole composition there should be no word written, of which the tendency, direct or indirect, is not to the one pre-established design . . . "

Poe, then, was not concerned chiefly with character or incident, but with mood or atmosphere. In his own case the effect usually concentrated upon is horror, but modern writers have broadened the short story to include a greater variety of effect. Poe's introductory paragraphs are exceptionally skillful. He captures the mood and atmosphere at once and with a remarkable thrift of words.

Perhaps the great defect of Poe's stories is that they are mostly limited to the creation of one effect, that of horror. Moreover, it is usually a meaningless horror, horror for its own sake. There is terror in life, it is true;

PAUL HAMILTON HAYNE

Paul Hamilton Hayne (1830-1886), classmate and friend of Timrod, was a member of the aristocracy of Charleston. As a young man he had the courage to renounce flattering prospects in the field of law and politics and to choose letters as a profession. His success was immediate. He held important editorial positions and published three volumes of poetry which won the approval of Bryant and the poets of New England. The Civil War, with its devastating effects, ruined him physically and financially and for a time blighted his literary hopes. From the wreckage of the war he went to Copse Hill, near Augusta, Georgia. In the pine country he strove to regain his health and to support his family with his poetry. For twenty years he worked and struggled bravely against ill health and poverty. Hayne was always devoted to his art and faithful to his early promise: "By my literary craft I will win my bread and water, by my pen will I live or starve." Hayne has not the spontaneity of a great lyric poet. His verse, however, is always finished, musical, and romantic in spirit. His mood is that of the plantation owner, looking back with regret to the time before the war. A note of tragedy sounds in many of his patriotic lyrics. His description of the pines in Georgia is singularly beautiful. In every poem a few strong touches lift the more mediocre lines into delicate patterns. Hayne, like many a minor poet, was too imitative to sing decisively in his own key. His voice, however, rings out clear and true when he sings of the beauty, the peace, the "divine stillness" of the tall pines of Georgia.

CATHOLIC WRITERS OF THE SOUTH

JOHN ENGLAND

We have already met the name of Bishop John England (1786-1842) in the general discussion of Catholic controversialists and journalists. To gain some idea of this great prelate's contribution to Catholic letters

Most Rev. John England, Bishop of Charleston

of the South, it is necessary to see Bishop England at work organizing his diocese, which comprised the two Carolinas and Georgia. As he walked barefoot through the streets of Charleston, South Carolina, in his first struggling days, he was not concerned with his abject poverty. He was devising a means of establishing a bond of communication among his flock, many of whom were so isolated that a priest could visit them only once a year. Although without adequate financial support or conspicuous sympathy for his progressive ideas, Bishop England founded the *United States Catholic Miscellany* in 1822. As the only Catholic paper between Maine and Florida and the Atlantic and the Pacific, it was often directly assailed by the enemies of the Church.

Under pressure of necessity, Bishop England became the greatest apologist of the Church in America. When at times the Bishop's pen scored against the enemies of the Church with unusual vigor, his youngest sister, Johanna England, modified the severity of her brother's remarks without diluting his wisdom. This frail young woman, who had crossed the Atlantic and sacrificed her fortune to establish a Catholic newspaper in the poorest diocese in the United States, was our first Catholic woman journalist and editor.

The *Miscellany* contains practically all the writings of John England. After the Bishop's death, his works were assembled from the columns of the paper and published in collected form. In their most recent edition, they are classified as essays, addresses, history, controversy, occasional letters, and doctrinal writing. Bishop England achieved dignity of style and expression, even when composing in haste. He treated many themes with learning and distinction, ease and naturalness. He is, in turn, edifying, charming, fervent, and vigorous. In his controversies a seeker after religious truth will find an answer to every one of the objections commonly brought against the Catholic Church.

O'Hara writes great elegy

Theodore O'Hara (1820-1867), conspicuous as poet, editor, and lawyer of Kentucky, saw service both in the War with Mexico and the Civil War. In his solemnly beautiful poem, "The Bivouac of the Dead" (1847), he commemorated Kentuckians who fell in the battle of Buena Vista. Stanzas from this martial elegy have been carved on monuments in our national cemeteries.

ADRIAN ROUQUETTE

Among the writers of the South, the Abbé Adrian Emmanuel Rouquette (1813-1887), an ardent romanticist and native son of New Orleans, wrote poetry in both French and English. From boyhood his love of solitude and the wilderness was so great that he often fled from civilization to live among the Choctaw Indians of Louisiana. After his ordination in 1846, Rouquette gained renown as a preacher in New Orleans. His greatest satisfaction came, however, when he was given permission to go among the Choctaws as missionary. Although he was more at home in the French language, the inspirational force of the woodland drove the Abbé to compose in English the slender volume entitled *Wild Flowers* (1848). Among flowers he praises the wild lily and the passion flower, and in the spiritual realm he extols the beauty of virginal chastity. His poetry has simplicity, grace, and at times severe economy in diction. His love for Indian life and the state of virginity led him

to compose a series of poems in praise of Catherine Tekakwitha.

TWO SOUTHERN CONVERTS

From his diocese in North Carolina the Episcopal bishop Levi Silliman Ives (1797-1867) followed the Oxford Movement in England. Bishop Ives and one of his young ministers, Cornelius Donald MacLeod (1821-1865), became so interested in reviving the practices of the Catholic Church that they heard one another's confession. At great cost Bishop Ives made his decision to enter the Church and went to Rome to be received as a convert. *The Trials of a Mind in its Progress to Catholicism* (1854) gives the record of his soul's struggle.

MacLeod's investigations, too, led him to the Church, and he made his profession of faith, taking the name Xavier. He eventually became a priest and was killed by a night train while on his way to administer the Last Sacraments. Like Huntington's work, MacLeod's two novels represent an advance in style over the fiction of the previous decades. The conversion story in *Pynnhurst* (1852) is said to be autobiographical. As a novelist MacLeod made use of emotional appeals but had little dramatic action in his work. His description is sometimes excellent, and his sense of humor is evident. He also wrote *Our Lady of Litanies,* a volume of poems, and published a history of devotion to the Blessed Virgin in the United States which begins with the era of the Spanish explorers.

A VOICE FROM THE WESTERN FRONTIER

Although the literary activity of the national period was concentrated in the East, America as a whole faced westward during this era. When Pierre Jean de Smet, S. J. (1801-1873) published in 1843 his first account of the missions he was founding in the Northwest, readers of the letters and travel sketches turned the pages eagerly. With freshness and charm, the missionary records in his voluminous writings the joy of bringing the savages to Christ. Two of Father de Smet's principal works, *Letters* and *Sketches* (1843) and *Oregon Missions* (1847), have been reprinted in the twentieth century because of their valuable information on early western travel and the Indian tribes of the Rocky Mountain region.

THE CIVIL CONFLICT

ABRAHAM LINCOLN

The achievements of Abraham Lincoln (1809-1865) belong for the most part to the realm of history. But his idealism, sincerity, simplicity, strength of intellect, and deep human sympathies were responsible for his great actions and also for his moving prose. In word and deed he became the wielder of a nation's destiny during the trying years of the Civil War. The romantic story of his rise from a log cabin to the White House is too well known to bear repetition.

Two youthful habits helped to make Lincoln's later success as a statesman and as a writer: the reading and evaluating of good books and the ability to think a problem to its logical conclusion. *Robinson Crusoe, Pilgrim's Progress,* Aesop's *Fables,* Weems's *Life of Washington,* and the Bible were sources of inspiration to him. The Bible had a tremendous influence not only upon his personal life but upon the spirit and the style of his prose. In the case of Lincoln one may truly say: "The style is the man." His speeches and letters are simple, genuine, logical, and moving in their appeal. Unlike the trained orators of his day who employed a florid, rhetorical style, Lincoln uses plain, pithy language charged with emotion. The rhythm, the sound, the lofty idealism of his best prose sink into the mind and stir the finer feelings of the heart. His collected works fill twelve volumes. Lincoln was at his best when he sympathetically voiced the fears and aspirations of a nation tested by war. Both "The Gettysburg Address" and the "Second Inaugural Address," because of their directness, precision, and emotional appeal, are masterpieces of American oratory.

The losses on both sides had been so great in the decisive battle of Gettysburg, July, 1863, that part of the battlefield was dedicated as a cemetery. Edward Everett, the famous orator of the day, delivered an eloquent two-hour speech. President Lincoln was then called upon for a "few remarks." In three classic paragraphs he defines democracy and reminds his listeners that our charter of freedom under God has been won at a great sacrifice. His "Second Inaugural Address," delivered towards the close of the Civil War, expresses Lincoln's deep faith and confidence in God and his humble acceptance of the war as just retribution for the wrongs of a nation. The often-quoted passage beginning "With malice towards none; with charity towards all" revealed the magnanimity of the man and suggested a policy for both North and South which would bring about a peace founded on justice and charity.

ABRAM J. RYAN

From Abram J. Ryan (1839-1886), a Catholic chaplain in the Southern army, came "The Conquered Banner." This famous tribute to the fallen flag of the Confederacy was written shortly after the surrender of Lee in April, 1865. The poem is eloquent, impassioned, yet unembittered in its contemplation of high loyalty brought to hopeless defeat. Abram Ryan was born of Irish parentage in Norfolk, Virginia. Shortly after his ordination the guns of Fort Sumter mobilized North and South into armed action. The priest enlisted in the Confederate forces and served until the close of the conflict. After the war he engaged in parish work and journalistic activity in New Orleans and Augusta, Georgia. Three loves dominated Father Ryan's life and poetry: love of Ireland, love of the South, and love of religion. His religious poetry reveals a deeply spiritual tone and a serene happiness in the fulfillment of his priestly duties. A note of wistful sadness and noble restraint characterizes much of his work.

THE DRAMA

From 1800 until the Civil War there was much theatrical activity in America, but no really great plays were produced. Theaters were built all over the country, draughty, uncomfortable, ill-designed structures. Historical themes and action revolving around the Indian and the frontiersman were the favorite offerings. Many of the Indian plays contrasted the courage and loyalty of the "noble savage" with the duplicity of the white man. Typical of the Indian plays is John Augustus Stone's *Metamora,* produced in 1829. The play has as its central character Sèbastian Râle, the French Jesuit missionary who labored for thirty-seven years among the Abnaki Indians of Maine.

Actors star in heroic plays

The drama of this time made little attempt to reproduce situations of actual life. Most of the plays were either long tragedies in blank verse or sentimental comedies. The tragedies often used European subject matter and belong to the class of drama called the heroic play. One character, through his long speeches and emotional display, dominates the scene in the heroic play. Such drama, although entirely lacking in balance, furnished good roles for the actor. Many plays of the period were expressly written for the great tragic actor, Edwin Forrest. *The Gladiator* (1831) by Robert Montgomery Bird and a version of *Francesca da Rimini* (1855) by George Henry Boker are among the best romantic plays produced.

In contrast to the romantic tragedies were the amusing farces, melodramas, and satirical comedies. Distinctive among the social comedies was *Fashion* (1845) by Anna Cora Mowatt Ritchie. This comedy is a clever satire on contemporary life, showing how the typical Yankee outwits his more sophisticated countryman. It is a tribute to the excellence of the play that it was successfully revived some years ago. Two other plays which made their initial appearance during this period have retained their popularity. Otis Skinner made his final appearance in *Uncle Tom's Cabin.* Joseph Jefferson successfully played in *Rip Van Winkle* for many years.

A novel feature of the theatrical activity of the period was the appearance of the showboat. Companies of actors sailed up and down the Mississippi, mooring

A Showboat

at various landings and giving performances for the crowds who came on board to see them. Edna Ferber's novel *Show Boat* (1926) reawakened interest in these floating theaters.

Two Catholic Dramatists

In connection with early nineteenth century drama two Catholic playwrights, Charles James Cannon and George Henry Miles, deserve mention. Cannon's best known play and the only one ever staged is his *Oath of Office* (1850). In addition he wrote half a dozen other romantic tragedies in verse. *The Oath of Office* was dedicated to Franklin Pierce and has as its theme fidelity to public duty. An accumulation of scenes of horror, unrelieved by lighter touches, detracts from the dramatic qualities of Cannon's plays. Occasionally passages of real poetic worth occur in his dramas.

George Henry Miles enjoyed a national reputation for his poetic dramas. His tragedies and comedies were successfully staged in New York, Boston, and Philadelphia. When Miles was twenty-four, his *Mohammed* (1850) won the $1000 prize offered by Edwin Forrest. His *DeSoto* (1852) is an heroic drama based on the conquest and death of the Spanish explorer and discoverer. His *Senor Valiente* and *Mary's Birthday,* comedies based on American life, were popular stage productions.

To Helen

Edgar Allan Poe

Poe was so impressed by the classic beauty of Mrs. Jane Stith Stanard, mother of a school friend whose home he shared one holiday, that he wrote these lines in her honor. He uses the name Helen rather than Jane, both for its greater melodic qualities and its association with Helen of Troy, the ideal of feminine charm. The woman addressed in this poem has a twofold symbolism: she is the embodiment of loveliness, particularly the classic beauty of Greece and Rome; she represents the poet's own creative aspiration, which her qualities have reawakened and stimulated. The lyric is a revelation of a poet's soul responding to the call of beauty. Although Mrs. Stanard died when Poe was only fifteen, he wrote that she remained in his memory as "an angel to my forlorn and darkened nature."

HELEN, thy beauty is to me
  Like those Nicéan[1] barks of yore,
That gently o'er a perfumed sea
  The weary, wayworn wanderer bore
  To his own native shore.   5

On desperate seas long wont to roam,
  Thy hyacinth hair,[2] thy classic face,
Thy Naiad[3] airs have brought me home
  To the glory that was Greece
  And the grandeur that was Rome.   10

Lo! in yon brilliant window niche
  How statuelike I see thee stand,
The agate lamp within thy hand!
  Ah, Psyche,[4] from the regions which
  Are Holy Land!   15

[1] *Nicéan barks*, probably an allusion to the fleet built by Alexander the Great at Nicaea in India to convey his army homeward through the Red Sea. There are also several other explanations of the expression.

[2] *hyacinth hair*, hair clustering around the head in curls like the petals of a hyacinth.

[3] *Naiad*, in Greek mythology, a water nymph who presided over streams.

[4] *Psyche*, in Greek mythology, a beautiful maiden beloved of Cupid. Having angered him one evening by letting a drop of burning oil fall from her lamp upon his shoulder, she was condemned to exile. The lovers were later reunited upon Mount Olympus, the home of the gods.

VIEWING THE AUTHOR'S IDEAS

1. By what means does the poet explain that Helen led him to return to his earlier inspirations? What lines describe his spiritual wanderings? In your opinion what type of person would exert such an influence?

2. Poe was studying Greek and Latin authors when he met Mrs. Stanard. Why did he associate her with classic culture?

3. In what way is the third stanza similar to a picture? What are the classic qualities in this scene?

4. How does the use of the name *Psyche* reveal that the poet's love was on an ideal plane? What do the words "Holy Land" imply?

5. Write a short essay contrasting the inspirational power of Helen of Troy with that of Mary of Nazareth.

EVALUATING HIS MANNER OF EXPRESSION

1. The cultural contribution of Greece was in such arts as drama and sculpture; the influence of Rome was rather in law and conquest. What adjectives does Poe use to contrast the two civilizations?

2. To a great extent, the artistry of this poem consists in beautiful musical effects. One means of achieving harmony is the poet's frequent use of the liquid consonants, *n, l,* and *r.* Point out melodious words and phrases; note instances of alliteration.

3. Some critics think the line "weary, wayworn wanderer" may refer to Odysseus, one of the great heroes of the Trojan War. Do you consider the phrase apt? Does the repetition of long vowels in the line seem to add anything to its effectiveness? Point out other instances of prolonged vowel sounds.

Israfel

Edgar Allan Poe

And the angel Israfel, whose heartstrings are a lute and who has the sweetest voice of all God's creatures.

— Koran[1]

In praising the Mohammedan angel of music, Poe reveals his ecstasy in his own gift of song. Although attributed to the Koran, the words in the description of the angel, "whose heartstrings are a lute," are not from that source. Wishing to say that great poetry comes from the heart, Poe uses the song of an angelic spirit to exemplify his doctrine.

In heaven a spirit doth dwell
"Whose heartstrings are a lute";
None sing so wildly well
As the angel Israfel,
And the giddy stars (so legends tell),   5
Ceasing their hymns, attend the spell
  Of his voice, all mute.

Tottering above
  In her highest noon,
  The enamored moon   10
Blushes with love.
  While, to listen, the red levin[2]
  (With the rapid Pleiads,[3] even, which were seven)
Pauses in heaven.

And they say (the starry choir   15
  And the other listening things)
That Israfeli's fire
Is owing to that lyre
  By which he sits and sings—
The trembling living wire   20
  Of those unusual strings.

But the skies that angel trod,
  Where deep thoughts are a duty,

Where Love's a grown-up god,[4]
  Where the Houri[5] glances are   25
Imbued with all the beauty
  Which we worship in a star.

Therefore, thou art not wrong,
  Israfeli, who despisest
An unimpassioned song;   30
To thee the laurels belong,
  Best bard, because the wisest!
Merrily live, and long!

The ecstasies above
  With thy burning measure suit—   35
  Thy grief, thy joy, thy hate, thy love,
  With the fervor of thy lute—
Well may the stars be mute!

Yes, heaven is thine; but this
  Is a world of sweets and sours;   40
  Our flowers are merely—flowers,
And the shadow of thy perfect bliss
  Is the sunshine of ours.

If I could dwell
Where Israfel   45
  Hath dwelt, and he where I,
He might not sing so wildly well
  A mortal melody,
While a bolder note than this might swell
  From my lyre within the sky.   50

VIEWING THE AUTHOR'S IDEAS

1. Explain the main idea of the poem. Why did Israfel sing so wildly well? What part of Poe's poetic creed is expressed in the fifth stanza?

---

[1] Poe's note is inaccurate. The words are not taken from the Koran. The information that the angel Israfel "has the sweetest voice of all God's creatures" may have been derived from George Sale's *Preliminary Discourse on the Koran.*

[2] *levin,* lightning.

[3] *Pleiads,* a cluster of seven stars, six of which are visible to the eye. According to mythology, Jupiter changed the seven daughters of Atlas and Pleione into this constellation. The seventh star is known as the "lost Pleiad."

[4] *Love's a grown-up god.* Cupid, the Roman god of love, was represented as a winged boy with bow and arrow.

[5] *Houri,* a beautiful maiden of the Mohammedan paradise.

2. Is Poe correct in ascribing so much importance to the poet's environment? Name poets whose misfortune furnished material for some of their best poetry.

3. Why does the poet envy Israfel? Discuss the suitability of Poe's comparison in lines 43-44. How does his comment differ from St. Paul's remark in I *Corinthians* 2:9?

4. From the *Apocalypse* 7:12 report on one heavenly song. What song is daily chanted on earth as the official praise of the Church?

5. State the challenge of the last stanza. What does it show concerning Poe's belief in his own gifts?

EVALUATING HIS MANNER OF EXPRESSION

1. In these stanzas as in others Poe is the master of poetic technique. Find examples of his use of assonance, alliteration, and liquid consonants.

2. Show whether the variety in stanza form adds to, or detracts from, the poem. Discuss the author's use of rhyme.

The Raven

Edgar Allan Poe

Anyone making a careful study of "The Raven" comes upon two seemingly contradictory elements. On the one hand is a poem in which romantic beauty and weird melody meet in a lament for a lovely woman. On the other is Poe's explanation in his "Philosophy of Composition" of the way in which he composed the poem. In coldly calculating remarks he conveys the impression that the masterpiece resulted from a series of logical and mathematical operations. The reader is inclined either to discount Poe's entire explanation as a hoax or to consider his poetry repellent and mechanical. Neither is necessarily the case. Poe knew the means by which melodic and impressive effects could be obtained. The knowledge of these means did not exclude the workings of his genius. Every one of the ideas he describes may have come to him, though not perhaps during the writing of a single poem.

In beginning the poem, Poe tells us, he was primarily concerned with achieving a single emotional effect. Believing beauty to be the most universal of effects, he considers that the highest manifestation of beauty involves sadness. The death of a beautiful woman is in consequence the most poetical theme, and the lips of a bereaved lover are best suited for such a topic. He states that he chose the word nevermore *for the refrain because it combines the long* o *with an* r *to produce a sonorous and melancholy tone. As a pretext for the repetition of the word he chose the raven because it is a nonreasoning creature capable of uttering words.*

In an abstract sense the Lenore of the poem represents womanly beauty, which had always had such power to inspire and attract Poe. More concretely she was probably his wife, Virginia, who was fatally ill when the poem was written.

ONCE upon a midnight dreary, while I pondered, weak and weary,
Over many a quaint and curious volume of forgotten lore—
While I nodded, nearly napping, suddenly there came a tapping,
As of someone gently rapping, rapping at my chamber door.
" 'Tis some visitor," I muttered, "tapping at my chamber door—   5
    Only this and nothing more."

Ah, distinctly I remember it was in the bleak December;
And each separate dying ember wrought its ghost upon the floor.
Eagerly I wished the morrow; vainly I had sought to borrow
From my books surcease of sorrow—sorrow for the lost Lenore,   10
For the rare and radiant maiden whom the angels named Lenore—
    Nameless *here* for evermore.

And the silken sad uncertain rustling of each purple curtain
Thrilled me—filled me with fantastic terrors never felt before;
So that now, to still the beating of my heart, I stood repeating,   15
" 'Tis some visitor entreating entrance at my chamber door,
Some late visitor entreating entrance at my chamber door;—
    This it is and nothing more."

Presently my soul grew stronger; hesitating then no longer,
"Sir," said I, "or Madam, truly your forgiveness I implore;   20
But the fact is I was napping, and so gently you came rapping,
And so faintly you came tapping, tapping at my chamber door;—
That I scarce was sure I heard you"—here I opened wide the door;—
    Darkness there and nothing more.

Deep into that darkness peering, long I stood there wondering, fearing,   25
Doubting, dreaming dreams no mortal ever dared to dream before;
But the silence was unbroken, and the stillness gave no token,
And the only word there spoken was the whispered word, "Lenore?"
This I whispered, and an echo murmured back the word, "Lenore!"
    Merely this and nothing more.   30

Back into the chamber turning, all my soul within me burning,
Soon again I heard a tapping somewhat louder than before.
"Surely," said I, "surely that is something at my window lattice;
Let me see, then, what thereat is, and this mystery explore—
Let my heart be still a moment and this mystery explore;—   35
    'Tis the wind and nothing more."

Open here I flung the shutter, when, with many a flirt and flutter,
In there stepped a stately Raven of the saintly days of yore.
Not the least obeisance made he; not a minute stopped or stayed he;
But, with mien of lord or lady, perched above my chamber door,   40
Perched upon a bust of Pallas[1] just above my chamber door—
    Perched, and sat, and nothing more.

Then this ebony bird beguiling my sad fancy into smiling
By the grave and stern decorum of the countenance it wore,
"Though thy crest be shorn and shaven, thou," I said, "are sure no craven,   45
Ghastly grim and ancient Raven wandering from the nightly shore—
Tell me what thy lordly name is on the night's Plutonian[2] shore!"
    Quoth the Raven, "Nevermore."

Much I marveled this ungainly fowl to hear discourse so plainly,
Though its answer little meaning—little relevancy bore;   50
For we cannot help agreeing that no living human being

[1] *Pallas*, the Greek goddess of wisdom. Poe said that he used the bust of Pallas to suggest the scholarship of the lover.
[2] *Plutonian*, infernal, from Pluto, the god of the lower world.

Ever yet was blessed with seeing bird above his chamber door,
Bird or beast upon the sculptured bust above his chamber door,
   With such name as "Nevermore."

But the Raven, sitting lonely on the placid bust, spoke only   55
That one word, as if his soul in that one word he did outpour.
Nothing further then he uttered, not a feather then he fluttered,
Till I scarcely more than muttered, "Other friends have flown before;
On the morrow *he* will leave me, as my hopes have flown before."
   Then the bird said, "Nevermore."   60

Startled at the stillness broken by reply so aptly spoken,
"Doubtless," said I, "what it utters is its only stock and store,
Caught from some unhappy master whom unmerciful disaster
Followed fast and followed faster till his songs one burden bore—
Till the dirges of his hope that melancholy burden bore   65
   Of 'Never—nevermore.'"

But the Raven still beguiling all my fancy into smiling,
Straight I wheeled a cushioned seat in front of the bird and bust and door;
Then, upon the velvet sinking, I betook myself to linking
Fancy unto fancy, thinking what this ominous bird of yore—   70
What this grim, ungainly, ghastly, gaunt, and ominous bird of yore
   Meant in croaking "Nevermore."

This I sat engaged in guessing, but no syllable expressing
To the fowl whose fiery eyes now burned into my bosom's core;
This and more I sat divining, with my head at ease reclining   75
On the cushion's velvet lining that the lamplight gloated o'er,
But whose velvet violet lining with the lamplight gloating o'er
   She shall press, ah, nevermore!

Then, methought, the air grew denser, perfumed from an unseen censer
Swung by seraphim whose footfalls tinkled on the tufted floor.   80
"Wretch," I cried, "thy God hath lent thee—by these angels he hath sent thee
Respite—respite and nepenthe[3] from thy memories of Lenore!
Quaff, oh quaff this kind nepenthe, and forget this lost Lenore!"
   Quoth the Raven, "Nevermore."

"Prophet!" said I, "thing of evil! prophet still, if bird or devil!   85
Whether tempter sent, or whether tempest tossed thee here ashore,
Desolate yet all undaunted, on this desert land enchanted—
On this home by horror haunted—tell me truly, I implore,
Is there—*is* there balm in Gilead?[4]—tell me—tell me, I implore!"
   Quoth the Raven, "Nevermore."   90

[3] *nepenthe*, a drug used by the ancients to banish sorrow.
[4] *balm in Gilead*, an allusion to *Jeremias* 8:22, meaning hope of relief.

"Prophet!" said I, "thing of evil—prophet still, if bird or devil!
By that heaven that bends above us, by that God we both adore,
Tell this soul with sorrow laden if, within the distant Aidenn,[5]
It shall clasp a sainted maiden whom the angels name Lenore—
Clasp a rare and radiant maiden whom the angels name Lenore!"   95
    Quoth the Raven, "Nevermore."

"Be that word our sign of parting, bird or fiend!" I shrieked, upstarting;
"Get thee back into the tempest and the Night's Plutonian shore!
Leave no black plume as a token of that lie thy soul hath spoken!
Leave my loneliness unbroken!—quit the bust above my door!   100
Take thy beak from out my heart, and take thy form from off my door!"
    Quoth the Raven, "Nevermore."

And the Raven, never flitting, still is sitting, *still* is sitting
On the pallid bust of Pallas just above my chamber door;
And his eyes have all the seeming of a demon's that is dreaming,   105
And the lamplight o'er him streaming throws his shadow on the floor;
And my soul from out that shadow that lies floating on the floor
    Shall be lifted—nevermore!

[5] *Aidenn*, Poe's spelling of Aden, the Mohammedan paradise.

VIEWING THE AUTHOR'S IDEAS

1. At what hour does the action of the poem take place? Account for Poe's choice of this time. How do we know the speaker is something of a student? What is often the effect of sounds one hears when drowsing? How does the time of year contribute to the atmosphere of the poem?

2. Why had the lover buried himself in his books on that particular night? Describe the study. Consult lines 69, 76-77 for further details. List the luxuries which the room held.

3. What explanations does the student try to find for the tapping he hears? What word broke the silence as he peered into the darkness? Describe the mien and bearing of the bird which entered the room. How does the solemn behavior of the raven suggest that it brings a mournful message? What explanation did the lover try to find for the bird's repetition of the word *nevermore?* What penetrating power did the raven's eyes possess?

4. The conversation between the man and the bird in lines 81-102 shows the lover's mounting despair. Whom is the poet addressing in lines 81-83? Why does he desire forgetfulness? When his request is denied him, what does he next ask the bird? What hope for the future does he beg the raven to prophesy? Which of these lines might be interpreted to mean that the raven gave the lover no hope of immortality? Which lines show the bird to be irremovable?

5. The poem definitely ends on a note of despair. How does the bird's permanent presence deny the lover any hope of peace or happiness? How does the lover express the depths to which his spirit has descended?

EVALUATING HIS MANNER OF EXPRESSION

1. To which has the poet given more attention in this poem: sincerely expressing heartfelt grief or achieving the effect of gloom and despair? Give reasons for your answer.

2. Because of Poe's technical skill in this poem he has been called a "metrical gymnast" and a "jingle man." Explain the meaning of this criticism and cite any justification you can see for the charge.

3. Comment on the onomatopoeia in line 13. Find internal rhymes, that is, rhymes within a line, in any stanza of the poem.

4. Why do you suppose that this poem was often Poe's choice for public reading?

Eldorado

Edgar Allan Poe

In the days of the Spanish conquest a legend existed that a king named Eldorado or "the gilded one" ruled over a South American city of fabulous wealth. Filled with a thirst for riches, Spanish adventurers set out to find the city; but always the natives, fearing the Spanish, told them that Eldorado was a little farther on. The word came to mean any place of wealth or abundance. The gold rush of 1849 stirred Poe's imagination as a new Eldorado. To him the search for gold was a symbol of the pursuit of the ideal, a quest which is never quite attained.

GAILY bedight,[1]
  A gallant knight,
In sunshine and in shadow,
  Had journeyed long,
  Singing a song,   5
In search of Eldorado.

  But he grew old—
  This knight so bold—
And o'er his heart a shadow
  Fell as he found   10
  No spot of ground
That looked like Eldorado.

  And as his strength
  Failed him at length,
He met a pilgrim shadow;   15
  "Shadow," said he,
  "Where can it be—
This land of Eldorado?"

"Over the Mountains
  Of the Moon,   20
Down the Valley of the Shadow,
  Ride, boldly ride,"
  The shade replied,
"If you seek for Eldorado!"

---

[1] *bedight*, dressed.

VIEWING THE AUTHOR'S IDEAS

1. In what mood does the knight set out on his quest? Give your opinion whether he is an idealist or a realist and your reason for so judging. How is he typical of any enthusiastic young person beginning his lifework?

2. What change came over the knight as the years went by? In what way does he reveal discouragement in the question he addresses to the pilgrim shadow? State the various ways in which people react when they find it almost impossible to achieve lofty aims. Do more people cease to strive for an ideal because they have attained it or because they have abandoned it?

3. What interpretation would you give the phrase "Over the Mountains of the Moon"? Explain the significance of the words "Down the Valley of the Shadow." What traits of character does one need in order to reach Eldorado?

EVALUATING HIS MANNER OF EXPRESSION

1. How has the poet prevented the shadow—Eldorado rhyme from becoming monotonous?

2. In what lines does Poe achieve a hint of pathos?

3. Poe frequently chose words capable of increasing the emotional effect desired in the poem. What words or phrases in "Eldorado" may have been selected for this reason? How is the rhythm of the poem suited to the various moods expressed or the imagery presented?

Annabel Lee

Edgar Allan Poe

"Annabel Lee" is one of Poe's most haunting lyrics. One would have to look long for a more faultless expression of tender devotion. Melodious and natural, it sings of a love which lasts beyond death. The majority of critics are of the opinion that the poem, possibly the last which Poe wrote, refers to the death of his young wife, Virginia.

IT was many and many a year ago,
  In a kingdom by the sea,
That a maiden there lived whom you may know
  By the name of Annabel Lee;
And this maiden she lived with no other thought   5
  Than to love, and be loved by me.

She was a child and I was a child,
  In this kingdom by the sea;
But we loved with a love that was more than love —
  I and my Annabel Lee —   10
With a love that the winged seraphs of heaven
  Coveted her and me.

And this was the reason that, long ago,
  In the kingdom by the sea,
A wind blew out of a cloud by night   15
  Chilling my Annabel Lee;
So that her highborn kinsmen[1] came
  And bore her away from me,
To shut her up in a sepulcher
  In this kingdom by the sea.   20

The angels, not half so happy in heaven,
  Went envying her and me;
Yes! that was the reason (as all men know,
  In this kingdom by the sea)
That the wind came out of the cloud chilling   25
  And killing my Annabel Lee.

But our love it was stronger by far than the love
  Of those who were older than we —
  Of many far wiser than we;

And neither the angels in heaven above,   30
  Nor the demons down under the sea,
Can ever dissever my soul from the soul
  Of the beautiful Annabel Lee: —

For the moon never beams, without bringing me
    dreams
  Of the beautiful Annabel Lee;   35
And the stars never rise, but I see the bright eyes
  Of the beautiful Annabel Lee;
And so, all the nighttide, I lie down by the side
Of my darling, my darling, my life and my bride,
  In her sepulcher there by the sea —   40
  In her tomb by the side of the sea.

VIEWING THE AUTHOR'S IDEAS

1. Although this poem is a lyric, it is narrative in form. What story does it tell? How does Poe make use of the fact that his wife, Virginia, was not yet fourteen at the time of her marriage?

2. What is the message of the poet concerning the power of love?

3. A sweetheart of Poe's youth, Elmira Shelton, once claimed that this poem was written to her. Her family had broken up her youthful romance with the poet, although she again considered marriage with him shortly before his death. If you were to accept her word concerning the inspiration of the poem, how would it change your interpretation of the lyric?

EVALUATING HIS MANNER OF EXPRESSION

1. Distinguish between *refrain,* or the re-echoing of an entire line, and repetition, the recurrence of parts of a line. Find instances of *repetition* in "Annabel Lee."

2. What imaginative reason is given for the death of Annabel Lee?

3. Describe the effect conveyed by the use of the word *chilling.* Why is it especially appropriate in the seaside setting of the poem? Find words which seem to be used merely because of their melodious sound.

[1] *highborn kinsmen,* the angels.

The Masque of the Red Death

Edgar Allan Poe

This story is a fantasy of brilliance comparable to the dramatic performance popular in the sixteenth century known as the masque. *In these productions color and symbol were united with dancing and dumb show to create a dramatic impression. The narrative elements in Poe's tale are meager — merely a land in which Death stalks abroad and a group of people determined to evade it. Poe's artfulness consists in his use of the entire color scale to convey the impression of this worldly group of revelers. Their rooms of unearthly beauty wind inevitably to the final black chamber wherein the ebony clock strikes out sinister warnings. The efforts of the revelers to forget death cause them to mask as mocking merrymakers, fantastic and grotesque. Into this revelry comes the figure of the Red Death himself. The story is rich in allegorical significance, but having conveyed this powerful effect of the terror of Death and suggested the folly of those who mask against it, Poe gives not one word to the symbolic meaning of his tale.*

THE "Red Death" had long devastated the country. No pestilence had ever been so fatal or so hideous. Blood was its avatar[1] and its seal—the redness and the horror of blood. There were sharp pains and sudden dizziness and then profuse bleeding at the pores, with dissolution. The scarlet stains upon the body and especially upon the face of the victim were the pest ban which shut him out from the aid and from the sympathy of his fellowmen. And the whole seizure, progress, and termination of the disease were the incidents of half an hour.

But the Prince Prospero was happy and dauntless and sagacious. When his dominions were half depopulated, he summoned to his presence a thousand hale and light-hearted friends from among the knights and dames of his court and with these retired to the deep seclusion of one of his castellated abbeys. This was an extensive and magnificent structure, the creation of the Prince's own eccentric yet august taste. A strong and lofty wall girdled it in. This wall had gates of iron. The courtiers, having entered, brought furnaces and massy hammers and welded the bolts. They resolved to leave means neither of ingress or egress to the sudden impulses of despair or of frenzy from within. The abbey was amply provisioned. With such precautions the courtiers might bid defiance to contagion. The external world could take care of itself. In the meantime it was folly to grieve or to think. The Prince had provided all the appliances of pleasure. There were buffoons, there were *improvisatori*,[2] there were ballet dancers, there were musicians, there was Beauty, there was wine. All these and security were within. Without was the "Red Death."

It was toward the close of the fifth or sixth month of his seclusion and while the pestilence raged most furiously abroad that the Prince Prospero entertained his thousand friends at a masked ball of the most unusual magnificence.

It was a voluptuous scene, that masquerade. But first let me tell of the rooms in which it was held. There were seven — an imperial suite. In many palaces, however, such suites form a long and straight vista, while the folding doors slide back nearly to the walls on either hand, so that the view of the whole extent is scarcely impeded. Here the case was very different, as might have been expected from the Prince's love of the bizarre. The apartments were so irregularly disposed that the vision embraced but little more than one at a time. There was a sharp turn at every twenty or thirty yards and at each turn a novel effect. To the right and left, in the middle of each wall, a tall and narrow Gothic window looked out upon a closed corridor which pursued the windings of the suite. These windows were of stained glass whose color varied in accordance with the prevailing hue of the decorations of the chamber into which it opened. That at the eastern extremity was hung, for example, in blue — and vividly blue were its windows. The second chamber was purple in its ornaments and tapestries, and here the panes were purple. The third was green throughout, and so were the casements. The fourth was furnished and lighted with orange, the fifth with white, the sixth with violet. The seventh apartment was closely shrouded in black velvet tapestries that hung all over the ceiling and down the walls, falling in heavy folds upon a carpet of the same material and hue. But

---

[1] *avatar*, embodiment.

[2] *improvisatori*, impromptu inventors of music or poetry.

in this chamber only, the color of the windows failed to correspond with the decorations. The panes here were scarlet — a deep blood-color. Now in no one of the seven apartments was there any lamp or candelabrum amid the profusion of golden ornaments that lay scattered to and fro or depended from the roof. There was no light of any kind emanating from lamp or candle within the suite of chambers. But in the corridors that followed the suite, there stood opposite to each window a heavy tripod, bearing a brazier of fire that projected its rays through the tinted glass and so glaringly illumined the room. And thus were produced a multitude of gaudy and fantastic appearances. But in the western or black chamber the effect of the firelight that streamed upon the dark hangings through the blood-tinted panes was ghastly in the extreme, and produced so wild a look upon the countenances of those who entered that there were few of the company bold enough to set foot within its precincts at all.

It was in this apartment, also, that there stood against the western wall a gigantic clock of ebony. Its pendulum swung to and fro with a dull, heavy monotonous clang; and when the minute hand made the circuit of the face, and the hour was to be stricken, there came from the brazen lungs of the clock a sound which was clear and loud and deep and exceedingly musical, but of so peculiar a note and emphasis that at each lapse of an hour the musicians of the orchestra were constrained to pause momentarily in their performance to hearken to the sound; and thus the waltzers perforce ceased their evolutions; and there was a brief disconcert of the whole gay company; and while the chimes of the clock yet rang, it was observed that the giddiest grew pale, and the more aged and sedate passed their hands over their brows as if in confused reverie or meditation. But when the echoes had fully ceased, a light laughter at once pervaded the assembly; the musicians looked at each other and smiled as if at their own nervousness and folly and made whispering vows, each to the other, that the next chiming of the clock should produce in them no similar emotion; and then after the lapse of sixty minutes (which embrace three thousand and six hundred seconds of the Time that flies), there came yet another chiming of the clock, and then were the same disconcert and tremulousness and meditation as before.

But in spite of these things it was a gay and magnificent revel. The tastes of the Prince were peculiar. He had a fine eye for colors and effects. He disregarded the decora[3] of mere fashion. His plans were bold and fiery, and his conceptions glowed with barbaric luster. There are some who would have thought him mad. His followers felt that he was not. It was necessary to hear and see and touch him to be *sure* that he was not.

He had directed in great part the movable embellishments of the seven chambers upon occasion of this great fête;[4] and it was his own guiding taste which had given character to the masqueraders. Be sure they were grotesque. There were much glare and glitter and piquancy and phantasm — much of what has been since seen in Hernani.[5] There were arabesque[6] figures with unsuited limbs and appointments. There were delirious fancies such as the madman fashions. There was much of the beautiful, much of the wanton, much of the bizarre, something of the terrible, and not a little of that which might have excited disgust. To and fro in the seven chambers there stalked, in fact, a multitude of dreams. And these — the dreams — writhed in and about, taking hue from the rooms and causing the wild music of the orchestra to seem as the echo of their steps. And anon there strikes the ebony clock which stands in the hall of the velvet. And then for a moment all is still, and all is silent save the voice of the clock. The dreams are stiff-frozen as they stand. But the echoes of the chime die away — they have endured but an instant — and a light, half-subdued laughter floats after them as they depart. And now again the music swells, and the dreams live and writhe to and fro more merrily than ever, taking hue from the many tinted windows through which stream the rays from the tripods. But to the chamber which lies most westwardly of the seven there are now none of the maskers who venture; for the night is waning away; and there flows a ruddier light through the blood-colored panes; and the blackness of the sable drapery appalls; and to him whose foot falls upon the sable carpet, there comes from the near clock of ebony a muffled peal more solemnly emphatic than any which reaches *their* ears who indulge in the more remote gaieties of the other apartments.

3 *decora* (plural of decorum), standards.

4 *fête*, entertainment.

5 *Hernani*, a tragedy by Victor Hugo.

6 *arabesque*, exhibiting a style of ornament with an intricate pattern of interlacing lines.

But these other apartments were densely crowded, and in them beat feverishly the heart of life. And the revel went whirling on, until at length there commenced the sounding of midnight upon the clock. And then the music ceased, as I have told; and the evolutions of the waltzers were quieted; and there was an uneasy cessation of all things as before. But now there were twelve strokes to be sounded by the bell of the clock; and thus it happened, perhaps, that more of thought crept, with more of time, into the meditations of the thoughtful among those who reveled. And thus too it happened, perhaps, that before the last echoes of the last chime had utterly sunk into silence, there were many individuals in the crowd who had found leisure to become aware of the presence of a masked figure which had arrested the attention of no single individual before. And the rumor of this new presence having spread itself whisperingly around, there arose at length from the whole company a buzz or murmur, expressive of disapprobation and surprise — then, finally, of terror, of horror, and of disgust.

In an assembly of phantasms such as I have painted, it may well be supposed that no ordinary appearance could have excited such sensation. In truth the masquerade license of the night was nearly unlimited; but the figure in question had out-Heroded Herod[7] and gone beyond the bounds of even the Prince's indefinite decorum. There are chords in the hearts of the most reckless which cannot be touched without emotion. Even with the utterly lost, to whom life and death are equally jests, there are matters of which no jests can be made. The whole company, indeed, seemed now deeply to feel that in the costume and bearing of the stranger neither wit nor propriety existed. The figure was tall and gaunt and shrouded from head to foot in the habiliments of the grave. The mask which concealed the visage was made so nearly to resemble the countenance of a stiffened corpse that the closest scrutiny must have had difficulty in detecting the cheat. And yet all this might have been endured, if not approved, by the mad revelers around. But the mummer had gone so far as to assume the type of the Red Death. His vesture was dabbled in *blood* — and his broad brow, with all the features of the face, was besprinkled with the scarlet horror.

7 *out-Heroded Herod*, outdid in violence; from an allusion in *Hamlet*, Act III, Scene ii, to the blustering role of Herod in the mystery play.

When the eyes of Prince Prospero fell upon this spectral image (which with a slow and solemn movement, as if more fully to sustain its role, stalked to and fro among the waltzers), he was seen to be convulsed in the first moment with a strong shudder either of terror or distaste; but in the next, his brow reddened with rage.

"Who dares?" he demanded hoarsely of the courtiers who stood near him — "who dares insult us with this blasphemous mockery? Seize him and unmask him — that we may know whom we have to hang at sunrise from the battlements!"

It was in the eastern or blue chamber in which stood the Prince Prospero as he uttered these words. They rang throughout the seven rooms loudly and clearly — for the Prince was a bold and robust man, and the music had become hushed at the waving of his hand.

It was in the blue room where stood the Prince with a group of pale courtiers by his side. At first as he spoke, there was a slight rushing movement of this group in the direction of the intruder, who at the moment was also near at hand, and now with deliberate and stately step made closer approach to the speaker. But from a certain nameless awe with which the mad assumption of the mummer had inspired the whole party, there were found none who put forth hand to seize him; so that, unimpeded, he passed within a yard of the Prince's person; and while the vast assembly, as if with one impulse, shrank from the centers of the rooms to the walls, he made his way uninterruptedly but with the same solemn and measured step which had distinguished him from the first, through the blue chamber to the purple — through the purple to the green — through the green to the orange — through this again to the white — and even thence to the violet, ere a decided movement had been made to arrest him. It was then, however, that the Prince Prospero, maddening with rage and the shame of his own momentary cowardice, rushed hurriedly through the six chambers, while none followed him on account of a deadly terror that had seized upon all. He bore aloft a drawn dagger and had approached in rapid impetuosity to within three or four feet of the retreating figure, when the latter, having attained the extremity of the velvet apartment, turned suddenly and confronted his pursuer. There was a sharp cry — and the dagger dropped gleaming upon the sable carpet, upon which instantly afterwards fell prostrate in death the Prince

Prospero. Then, summoning the wild courage of despair, a throng of the revelers at once threw themselves into the black apartment and, seizing the mummer, whose tall figure stood erect and motionless within the shadow of the ebony clock, gasped in unutterable horror at finding the grave cerements[8] and corpselike mask, which they handled with so violent a rudeness, untenanted by any tangible form.

And now was acknowledged the presence of the Red Death. He had come like a thief in the night. And one by one dropped the revelers in the blood-bedewed halls of their revel and died, each in the despairing posture of his fall. And the life of the ebony clock went out with that of the last of the gay. And the flames of the tripods expired. And Darkness and Decay and the Red Death held illimitable dominion over all.

VIEWING THE AUTHOR'S IDEAS

1. By what means did Prince Prospero and his companions think to escape the pestilence? How would they have acted if they had been impelled by motives of unselfishness and pity for the sufferings of others?

[8] *cerements*, grave clothes.

2. What parallel might be drawn between the masqueraders and people who live only for this life? How does the story illustrate the saying that death comes like a thief in the night?

3. How does Poe contrast the security within the abbey with the miseries of the plague-stricken world outside? What reminders of the "Red Death" cast their shadow upon the revels of the Prince and his companions?

4. How does the action of Prince Prospero reflect the attitude of those who are indifferent in remedying social and moral evils which threaten Christian civilization?

EVALUATING HIS MANNER OF EXPRESSION

1. Show how Poe uses plot, character, and setting to intensify the single emotional effect of grotesque terror.

2. How does the initial sentence contribute to this effect? Trace the heightening of the mood of terror to the climax in the closing paragraph when "the Red Death held illimitable dominion over all."

3. Show how Poe uses the symbolism of color in this story to create the impression of terror. How does he use contrast to heighten the intensity of the mood of terror and impending tragedy? What is the effect of the striking of the ebony clock?

4. Cite passages to illustrate the following romantic elements: medieval background; mysterious atmosphere; morbid melancholy; preternatural visitants (beyond the natural).

Ode

Henry Timrod

Sung at the Occasion of Decorating the Graves of the Confederate Dead, at Magnolia Cemetery, Charleston, S. C., 1867

Timrod's poignant but restrained grief is transformed into poetic beauty as he pays tribute to the fallen Confederate soldiers.

SLEEP sweetly in your humble graves,
  Sleep, martyrs of a fallen cause;
Though yet no marble column craves
  The pilgrim here to pause.

In seeds of laurel in the earth   5
  The blossom of your fame is blown,
And somewhere, waiting for its birth,
  The shaft is in the stone!

Meanwhile, behalf the tardy years
  Which keep in trust your storied tombs,
Behold! your sisters bring their tears   11
  And these memorial blooms.

Small tributes! but your shades will smile
  More proudly on these wreaths today
Than when some cannon-molded pile[1]   15
  Shall overlook this bay.

[1] *cannon-molded pile*. Melted cannons are frequently used to make monuments for soldiers.

Stoop, angels, hither from the skies!
   There is no holier spot of ground
Than where defeated valor lies,
   By mourning beauty crowned!   20

VIEWING THE AUTHOR'S IDEAS

1. What questions had divided the North and the South in the Civil War? The Union victory had settled the supremacy of federal over state government. How does this poem show that the outcome of the war had not changed the emotions and personal loyalties of the Southern people?

2. Explain the prophetic words beginning "In seeds of laurel . . ."

3. Since the poem was written, a granite shaft supporting the bronze figure of a color-bearer has been erected at Magnolia Cemetery. In which lines did the poet predict that such a memorial would be raised? What tributes more precious than monuments had Timrod observed?

EVALUATING HIS MANNER OF EXPRESSION

1. What emotions aroused by the Civil War stimulated Timrod? Discuss whether the effect of war on literature is harmful or advantageous.

2. Cite instances of restrained emotion. What attitudes of the poet indicate the tranquillity of his sorrow; loyalty to a lost cause?

Aspects of the Pines

Paul Hamilton Hayne

His Carolina home and his magnificent library burned, Paul Hamilton Hayne retired after the Civil War to the pine barrens of Georgia. Here, while he managed to earn a meager living with his pen, he observed the beauty of warm blue skies, the lyrical song of birds, and the stateliness of tall pines. He knew the trees so intimately that he was alert to every delicate change they underwent from dawn to starlight.

TALL, somber, grim, against the morning sky
   They rise, scarce touched by melancholy airs,
Which stir the fadeless foliage dreamfully,
   As if from realms of mystical despairs.

Tall, somber, grim, they stand with dusky gleams   5
   Brightening to gold within the woodland's core,
Beneath the gracious noontide's tranquil beams —
   But the weird winds of morning sigh no more.

A stillness, strange, divine, ineffable,
   Broods round and o'er them in the wind's
      surcease,   10
And on each tinted copse and shimmering dell
   Rests the mute rapture of deep-hearted peace.

Last, sunset comes — the solemn joy and might
   Borne from the west when cloudless day declines —

Low, flutelike breezes sweep the waves of light,   15
   And, lifting dark green tresses of the pines

Till every lock is luminous — gently float,
   Fraught with hale odors up the heavens afar,
To faint when twilight on her virginal throat
   Wears for a gem the tremulous vesper star.   20

VIEWING THE AUTHOR'S IDEAS

1. What adjectives describe the pines at morning? How does the melancholy atmosphere affect them?

2. When does sunlight finally penetrate the heart of the woods? Quote the lines which suggest the density of the green-needled trees.

3. What part of day brings peace? How does sunlight affect the grove during these hours?

4. Explain how every lock of the pine is made luminous. How is twilight seen as a beautiful woman?

EVALUATING HIS MANNER OF EXPRESSION

1. Notice throughout the poem the interplay between the winds and the pines. In two columns outline the different sound effects and the time of day at which each occurs. In the third column list the corresponding changes of light.

2. Contrast Paul Hamilton Hayne and William Cullen Bryant in respect to the moral note in their poetry.

Maryland, My Maryland

James Ryder Randall

When James Ryder Randall was in New Orleans shortly after the outbreak of the Civil War, he read of a skirmish which occurred when Northern troops passed through his native Baltimore. That night he could not dismiss the newspaper account from his mind. "About midnight," he wrote later, "I rose, lit a candle, and went to my desk. Some powerful spirit appeared to possess me and almost involuntarily I proceeded to write the song of 'My Maryland.' I remember that the idea appeared to take shape first as music in my brain — some wild air that I cannot now recall. The whole poem was dashed off rapidly when once begun. It was not composed in cold blood, but under what might be called a conflagration of the senses, if not an aspiration of the intellect."

THE despot's heel[1] is on thy shore,
    Maryland!
His torch is at thy temple door,
    Maryland!
Avenge the patriotic gore   5
That flecked[2] the streets of Baltimore
And be the battle queen of yore,
    Maryland, my Maryland!

Hark to an excited son's appeal,
    Maryland!   10
My mother State, to thee I kneel,
    Maryland!
For life and death, for woe and weal,
Thy peerless chivalry reveal,
And gird thy beauteous limbs with steel,   15
    Maryland, my Maryland!

Thou wilt not cower in the dust,
    Maryland!
Thy beaming sword shall never rust,
    Maryland!   20
Remember Carroll's sacred trust,[3]
Remember Howard's warlike thrust,[4]

And all thy slumberers with the just,
    Maryland, my Maryland!

Come! 'tis the red dawn of day,   25
    Maryland!
Come with thy panoplied array,
    Maryland!
With Ringgold's spirit for the fray,
With Watson's blood at Monterey,   30
With fearless Lowe and dashing May,[5]
    Maryland, my Maryland!

Come! for thy shield is bright and strong,
    Maryland!
Come! for thy dalliance does thee wrong,   35
    Maryland!
Come to thine own heroic throng
That stalks with liberty along,
And chant thy dauntless slogan song,
    Maryland, my Maryland!   40

Dear Mother! burst the tyrant's chain,
    Maryland!
Virginia should not call in vain,
    Maryland!
She meets her sisters on the plain —   45
"Sic semper!"[6] 'tis the proud refrain
That baffles minions back again,
    Maryland, my Maryland!

I see the blush upon thy cheek,
    Maryland!   50
But thou wast ever bravely meek,
    Maryland!
But lo! there surges forth a shriek
From hill to hill, from creek to creek
Potomac calls to Chesapeake,[7]   55
    Maryland, my Maryland!

---

[1] *The despot's heel*, domination of the North.

[2] *flecked*, streaked.

[3] *Carroll's sacred trust*, the precedent of patriotism established by Charles Carroll of Carrollton.

[4] *Howard's warlike thrust*. John Eager Howard was a famous revolutionary soldier from Maryland.

[5] *Ringgold's spirit . . . dashing May*, a reference to four Maryland soldiers in the War with Mexico.

[6] *Sic semper* [*tyrannis*], "thus ever to tyrants"; motto of Virginia.

[7] *Potomac . . . Chesapeake*, i.e., Virginia calls to Maryland.

Thou wilt not yield the Vandal[8] toll,
    Maryland!
Thou wilt not crook to his control,
    Maryland!   60
Better the fire upon thee roll,
Better the blade, the shot, the bowl,
Than crucifixion of the soul,
    Maryland, my Maryland!

I hear the distant thunder hum,   65
    Maryland!
The Old Line's bugle,[9] fife, and drum,
    Maryland!
She is not dead, nor deaf, nor dumb —
Huzza! she spurns the Northern scum!   70
She breathes! she burns! she'll come! she'll come!
    Maryland, my Maryland!

[8] *vandal*, a wanton destroyer; here, the North.
[9] *Old Line's bugle.* Maryland is called the Old Line State because its northern boundary coincides with the Mason and Dixon Line separating the North and South.

VIEWING THE AUTHOR'S IDEAS

1. What critical situation is revealed in the opening stanza? How does the second line indicate reverence? State the poet's message to Maryland.

2. How does Randall further develop his attitude of reverence? To what Southern ideal does he appeal? Quote the line in which he asks the state to arm. What traditions of the past give him confidence in the present crisis?

3. In what lines does Randall stress the obligation of immediate action? Why does Maryland have a duty to join Virginia and other Southern states?

4. Why is it necessary for Maryland to lay aside her meekness? Under what conditions does the poet believe that war is not only justified but necessary to save honor?

5. What attitude toward the Southern cause is shown in the eighth stanza? Read aloud the words in which Randall reaffirms his ardent confidence in his native state.

EVALUATING HIS MANNER OF EXPRESSION

Point out the emotions and qualities of style which make this poem a stirring song.

The Conquered Banner

Abram Ryan

A broken South mourned its dead and viewed its destruction at the close of the great civil conflict. As chaplain of a Confederate regiment, Father Ryan knew the weariness and broken heart with which men returned to their homes. In this poem, written at a single sitting, he expresses the dejection of the Southerners by showing the sorrow with which they laid aside the flag which had symbolized their cause.

FURL that banner, for 'tis weary;
    Round its staff 'tis drooping dreary;
    Furl it, fold it — it is best;
For there's not a man to wave it,
And there's not a sword to save it,   5
And there's not one left to lave it
In the blood which heroes gave it,
And its foes now scorn and brave it;
    Furl it, hide it — let it rest!

Take that banner down! 'tis tattered;   10
Broken is its staff and shattered;

And the valiant hosts are scattered
    Over whom it floated high.
Oh, 'tis hard for us to fold it,
Hard to think there's none to hold it,   15
Hard that those that once unrolled it
    Now must furl it with a sigh!

Furl that banner — furl it sadly!
Once ten thousands hailed it gladly,
And ten thousands wildly, madly,   20
    Swore it should forever wave;
Swore that foeman's sword should never
Hearts like theirs entwined dissever,
Till that flag should float forever
    O'er their freedom or their grave!   25

Furl it! for the hands that grasped it,
And the hearts that fondly clasped it,
    Cold and dead are lying low;
And that banner — it is trailing,

While around it sounds the wailing   30
    Of its people in their woe.

For, though conquered, they adore it,
Love the cold, dead hands that bore it,
Weep for those who fell before it,
Pardon those who trailed and tore it;   35
And oh, wildly they deplore it,
    Now to furl and fold it so!

Furl that banner! True, 'tis gory,
Yet 'tis wreathed around with glory,
And 'twill live in song and story,   40
    Though its folds are in the dust!
For its fame on brightest pages,
Penned by poets and by sages,
Shall go sounding down the ages —
    Furl its folds though now we must.   45

Furl that banner, softly, slowly!
Treat it gently — it is holy,
    For it droops above the dead.
Touch it not — unfold it never;
Let it droop there, furled forever,   50
    For its people's hopes are fled!

VIEWING THE AUTHOR'S IDEAS

1. Why was it necessary that the banner should be furled? How does this poem show the attitudes with which the South met defeat?

2. What was the hope of Southerners as they hailed the Confederate flag at the opening of the conflict? How does the poet express grief for those fallen in battle?

3. Which lines give evidence of a Christian attitude towards enemies?

4. What characteristics do you associate with the people of the South? In what way does "The Conquered Banner" convey the Southern spirit?

EVALUATING HIS MANNER OF EXPRESSION

1. Compare the mood of Father Ryan's poem to that of Timrod's "Ode." Which line of "The Conquered Banner" carries the greatest pathos?

2. What is the rhyme scheme of the poem? What variations are found in the stanzas?

3. This poem has proved the author's prophecy that the flag of the Confederacy will "live in song and story." Name other poems and stories which commemorate the Confederate cause.

The Gettysburg Address

Abraham Lincoln

This address delivered at the dedication of the Gettysburg Battlefield as a national cemetery, November 19, 1863, has been called the epitaph of the Civil War. A noble eulogy of the brave dead, it has become the rallying cry by which Americans of each succeeding generation have reaffirmed their allegiance to the principles of human freedom.

FOURSCORE and seven years ago our fathers brought forth on this continent a new nation, conceived in liberty and dedicated to the proposition that all men are created equal.

Now we are engaged in a great civil war, testing whether that nation, or any nation so conceived and so dedicated, can long endure. We are met on a great battlefield of that war. We have come to dedicate a portion of that field as a final resting place for those who here gave their lives that that nation might live. It is altogether fitting and proper that we should do this.

But in a larger sense we cannot dedicate, we cannot consecrate, we cannot hallow this ground. The brave men, living and dead, who struggled here, have consecrated it far above our poor power to add or detract. The world will little note nor long remember what we say here, but it can never forget what they did here. It is for us, the living, rather to be dedicated here to the unfinished work which they who fought here have thus far so nobly advanced. It is rather for us to be here dedicated to the great task remaining before us — that from these honored dead we take increased devotion to that cause for which they gave the last full measure of devotion; that we here highly resolve that these dead shall not have died in vain; that this nation, under God, shall have a new birth of freedom; and that government of the people, by the people, for the people, shall not perish from the earth.

VIEWING THE AUTHOR'S IDEAS

1. What was the occasion of the *Gettysburg Address?* Aside from honoring the soldier dead, what purpose animated the speaker?

2. To what important event in our national history does Lincoln allude in the opening sentence? How does he relate the struggle for the preservation of the Union with our struggle for independence? What bearing does Washington's *Farewell Address* have upon the Civil War?

3. In what sense was the Civil War "dedicated to the proposition that all men are created equal"? Show that those Southerners who were fighting for State rights were also fighting for "government of the people, by the people, for the people."

4. Read Carl Sandburg's account of this address in *Abraham Lincoln: The War Years.*

5. How does Lincoln show that he realized the need of calm in the face of the tragedy of the Civil War?

EVALUATING HIS MANNER OF EXPRESSION

1. This address has been called a prose poem. List the poetic qualities upon which this estimate was made.

2. Account for the effectiveness of the concluding sentence, in structure, in its relation to the address as a whole, and as a summary of American democracy. The selection has a special appeal today when democratic ideals are being challenged.

Second Inaugural Address

March 4, 1865

Abraham Lincoln

The main idea in Lincoln's mind as he prepared this speech was not the victory that was almost assured. His thoughts turned rather to a plan for an honorable peace which would reunite the war-torn sections of the country, severed by four years of civil conflict. By charity and good will he wished to cement the Union which had been preserved through his wise guidance. His words show that he does not cast the whole blame upon the defeated. He considers the war a divine retribution due to both North and South for the wrong of slavery.

FELLOW COUNTRYMEN: At this second appearing to take the oath of the presidential office, there is less occasion for an extended address than there was at the first. Then a statement somewhat in detail of a course to be pursued seemed fitting and proper. Now at the expiration of four years, during which public declarations have been constantly called forth on every point and phase of the great contest which still absorbs the attention and engrosses the energies of the nation, little that is new could be presented. The progress of our arms, upon which all else chiefly depends, is as well known to the public as to myself; and it is, I trust, reasonably satisfactory and encouraging to all. With high hope for the future, no prediction in regard to it is ventured.

On the occasion corresponding to this four years ago, all thoughts were anxiously directed to an impending civil war. All dreaded it, all sought to avert it. While the inaugural address was being delivered from this place, devoted altogether to saving the Union without war, insurgent agents were in the city seeking to destroy it without war — seeking to dissolve the Union and divide effects by negotiation. Both parties deprecated war; but one of them would make war rather than let the nation survive, and the other would accept war rather than let it perish. And the war came.

One-eighth of the whole population were colored slaves, not distributed generally over the Union but localized in the southern part of it. These slaves constituted a peculiar and powerful interest. All knew that this interest was, somehow, the cause of the war. To strengthen, perpetuate, and extend this interest was the object for which the insurgents would rend the Union, even by war; while the government claimed no right to do more than to restrict the territorial enlargement of it.

Neither party expected for the war the magnitude or the duration which it has already attained. Neither anticipated that the cause of the conflict might cease with, or even before, the conflict itself should cease. Each looked for an easier triumph and a result less fundamental and astounding. Both read the same Bible and pray to the same God, and each invokes His aid against the other. It may seem strange that any men should dare to ask a just God's assistance in wringing their bread from the sweat of other men's faces; but let us judge not, that we be not judged. The prayers of both could not be answered — that of neither has been answered fully.

The Almighty has His own purposes. "Woe unto the world because of offenses! for it must needs be that offenses come; but woe to that man by whom the offense cometh."[1] If we shall suppose that American slavery is one of those offenses which in the providence of God must needs come, but which, having continued through His appointed time, He now wills to remove, and that He gives to both North and South this terrible war as the woe due to those by whom the offense came, shall we discern therein any departure from those divine attributes which the believers in a living God always ascribe to Him? Fondly do we hope — fervently do we pray — that this mighty scourge of war may speedily pass away. Yet if God wills that it continue until all the wealth piled by the bondmen's two hundred and fifty years of unrequited toil shall be sunk and until every drop of blood drawn with the lash shall be paid by another drawn with the sword, as was said three thousand years ago, so still it must be said, "The judgments of the Lord are true and righteous altogether."[2]

With malice toward none; with charity for all; with firmness in the right, as God gives us to see the right, let us strive on to finish the work we are in; to bind up the nation's wounds; to care for him who shall have borne the battle, and for his widow and his orphan — to do all which may achieve and cherish a just and lasting peace among ourselves and with all nations.

VIEWING THE AUTHOR'S IDEAS

1. What contrast existed between conditions at the time of Lincoln's first and second inaugural address? How soon after the second address did the Civil War end? Explain the statement beginning "Neither anticipated . . ."

2. What view of slavery did Lincoln express in this address? What was the view of those who opposed abolition? To what extent before the war did the federal government claim the right to restrict slavery? In what sense might it be said that the modern capitalist is guilty of "wringing his bread from the sweat of other men's faces"?

3. According to Lincoln, what was the chief cause of the Civil War? How did the South justify its struggle for the extension and continuation of slavery? In what sense were the prayers of neither side fully answered?

4. What explanation of God's purposes in permitting the Civil War does Lincoln offer? In what way might this explanation be applied to World War II? How would Lincoln answer those who find it hard to reconcile God's Providence with the existence of temporal evils?

5. What do Lincoln's concluding words reveal of the reconstruction policy he had planned for the South? In what spirit was the reconstruction actually carried out?

EVALUATING HIS MANNER OF EXPRESSION

1. What is the mood of this address? Show the relation between Lincoln's deep feeling and his qualities of poetic expression.

2. In addition to the direct quotations from the Bible, list Scriptural allusions. What is the emotional effect of these passages?

3. Find examples of the effective use of balanced sentence structure.

4. What qualities make the last paragraph a memorable conclusion for the address?

---

[1] *Woe . . . cometh*, King James version: *Matt.* 18:7.

[2] *The Judgments . . . altogether*, King James version: *Ps.* 19:9.

QUESTIONS FOR REVIEW

In your notebook copy the numbers from 1 to 10. After selecting the correct choice, write the complete statement.

1. The first writers to portray American life against native backgrounds were (A) Emerson, Thoreau, and Poe (B) Bryant, Cooper, and Irving (C) Hawthorne, Harte, Lowell (D) Holmes, Adams, Franklin.

2. The Gothic romance was transplanted to American soil by (A) Philip Freneau (B) James Fenimore Cooper (C) Nathaniel Hawthorne (D) Charles Brockden Brown.

3. Romantic influences were manifested in America before 1800 in the writings of (A) Franklin and Washington (B) Emerson and Thoreau (C) Brown and Freneau (D) Cooper and Lowell.

4. The first important American novel was (A) *The Sketch Book* (B) *The Spy* (C) *Precaution* (D) *Tales of a Traveler.*

5. The literary tradition of the American Indian was established by (A) Irving (B) Freneau (C) Bryant (D) Cooper.

6. In his own migration westward, Leather-Stocking symbolizes (A) the crudity of the early American (B) the restlessness of the American people (C) the strength of the natural man (D) the pioneering spirit of the American nation.

7. The most famous poem by William Cullen Bryant is (A) "The Indian Burying Ground" (B) "To a Waterfowl" (C) "Thanatopsis" (D) "Snowbound."

8. The first Catholic magazine in the United States, established in 1830 was (A) the *Michigan Essay* (B) the *United States Catholic Miscellany* (C) the *Metropolitan* (D) the *American Review of History and Politics.*

9. Hawthorne's masterpiece is (A) *The Marble Faun* (B) *The House of the Seven Gables* (C) *The Snow Image* (D) *The Scarlet Letter.*

10. In his stories Poe was chiefly concerned with (A) character and incident (B) plot and dialogue (C) surprise endings and significant detail (D) mood and atmosphere.

Read each statement carefully. Then write in your notebook only those statements that are TRUE.

1. The national period of our literature was a period of romanticism.

2. Romanticism in Europe began as a reaction against the rationalism of the early eighteenth century.

3. Rationalism limited the exercise of man's mental faculties.

4. The romanticist frequently turns to the past and to remote places to discover material for his writings.

5. Nature attracts the romantic writer as a source of delight, inspiration, moral teaching, and healing.

6. The common man is often praised in romantic writing because he is considered to be closer to nature and less repressed by an artificial standard of society.

7. Romanticism in America was colored by our national optimism, by our closeness to rural life and to the frontier.

8. Intrepid colonists, Revolutionary heroes, and buckskin-clad frontiersmen furnished material for the romantic writers of the national period.

9. The South furnished America of the national period with a philosophy and standard for evaluating both life and literature.

10. In 1795 Washington Irving turned to writing as a means of earning a livelihood.

11. *The Sketch Book* and *Bracebridge Hall* won for Irving a literary reputation in England.

12. Irving's writings reveal his interest in native materials.

13. The narratives of Irving are improved by long prefaces and descriptions of the author's own feelings.

14. Through his romanticized history, Washington Irving has created a world of legend and has contributed toward a tradition that is part of the national heritage.

15. When Cooper came to write about the sea, his work was a failure.

16. Although the novels of Cooper are weak in construction and full of impossible situations, their novelty of subject matter and dramatic force makes them popular.

17. In his portrayal of women characters Cooper is at his best.

18. "Thanatopsis" contains a pessimistic note, revealing its author's youthful uncertainty about traditional Calvinism.

19. Believing that God's presence could be readily perceived in the country, Bryant never came to realize that God is in the cities also.

20. The entire pattern of Catholic literature in the national period was designed as a defense for the Faith.

21. Catholic journalism had its beginnings in the early part of the nineteenth century.

22. Catholic poets in the early days of our country stressed the themes of love of God and country.

23. Reverend Charles Constantine Pise inaugurated the first definite program for the promotion of Catholic poetry in America.

24. Transcendentalism, as a philosophy and a body of religious beliefs, originated in New England.

25. Emerson contributed to American culture by calling for a native literature.

26. Emerson is one of the most quoted writers in world literature because his writings contain stimulating epigrams.

27. Irving told a story for entertainment; Hawthorne made it an artistic means of conveying a profound moral lesson.

28. *Moby Dick* is a tale of adventure and an exploration into the nature of ever-present evil.

29. Longfellow was a master of narrative poetry.

30. James Russell Lowell was a better scholar and critic than poet.

In your notebook copy each of the following statements, writing in the correct word or words that complete the sentence.

1. The portrayal of an author's own mental state is a romantic characteristic known as _____ .

2. Strangeness, mystery, picturesque beauty, and power of suggestion are elements found in the _____ writers.

3. The earliest American writer to win international reputation and renown was _____ .

4. The first poet to treat of the American scene in a manner to satisfy critics at home and abroad was _____ .

5. Writing done in defense of a cause is called _____ .

6. A settled, cohesive, and continuous pattern of life is suggested by the word _____ .

7. The earliest versatile Catholic author in our literature was _____ .

8. One of the first Catholics possessed of the gift of lyricism was _____ .

9. The false doctrine that confuses man and the Divine, merging God and His Creation into a simple reality, is known as _____ .

10. A system of beliefs which ignores logic and stresses inspiration or intuition as a method of arriving at truth is called _____ .

QUESTIONS FOR DISCUSSION

1. Explain the cause of the downfall of Puritan society.

2. What elements caused the rapid growth and expansion of our nation in the first half of the nineteenth century?

3. Show the absurdity in the beliefs of *pantheism*. What is its ultimate end?

4. Itemize and discuss the main tenets of transcendental thought.

5. Why is Emerson's philosophy considered inadequate and erroneous?

6. What was Thoreau's purpose in living at Walden Pond?

7. What two ideas of Thoreau do you consider acceptable?

8. Explain why Poe had greater influence in France than in America.

9. Show how the influence of the Oxford Movement was reflected in America.

10. Discuss the rise of Catholic fiction in the national period of our literature.

SUGGESTIONS FOR READING

Burton, Katherine, *In No Strange Land* (Longmans, New York). Mrs. Burton sketches the lives of converts who were affected in some way by the American tradition of culture and democracy.

Burton, Katherine, *Sorrow Built a Bridge* (Longmans, New York). The book has an appropriate title. The loss of father, mother, sister, baby, husband purified Rose Hawthorne Lathrop, the daughter of Nathaniel Hawthorne, and enabled her to do great things for God. She consecrated her life to the cancerous poor of New York and, as Mother Alphonsa, founded hospitals to carry on her work.

Burton, Katherine, *Celestial Homespun* (Longmans, New York). This is one of the latest of Mrs. Burton's fictional biographies and is concerned chiefly with the life of Isaac Hecker, convert and founder of the Paulists.

Churchill, Winston, *The Crisis* (Grosset, New York). The crisis is the war between the states. Lincoln, Sherman, and Grant, as well as a proud southern belle, figure in this historical romance. The magnanimity of Lincoln is dramatically portrayed.

Churchill, Winston, *The Crossing* (Grosset, New York). Sturdy pioneers paved the way for settlers and farmers. *The Crossing* describes the exploits of George Rogers Clark and the acquisition of Kentucky, Indiana, Illinois, and Louisiana.

Drinkwater, John, *Abraham Lincoln* (Houghton, New York). An Englishman has written a powerful play depicting the closing years of Lincoln's life.

Fox, John, Jr., *The Little Shepherd of Kingdom Come* (Grosset, New York). The setting for the story is the charming bluegrass country. The people of Kentucky were divided in their views on slavery; brother often took up arms against brother. The hero fought in the Union Army under Grant.

Hawthorne, Hildegarde, *Youth's Captain* (Longmans, New York). This book gives not only an intimate and interesting account of the life of Ralph Waldo Emerson but also furnishes a splendid background for an understanding of the Transcendentalists and the experimenters at Brook Farm and Fruitlands.

Johnston, Mary, *The Long Roll* (Houghton, New York). This is a long tale of the Civil War which stresses the heroism of the Confederates.

Maynard, Theodore, *Orestes Brownson, Yankee, Radical, Catholic* (Macmillan, New York). Orestes Brownson's conversion to the Catholic Church caused a sensation in his day. The philosophic struggles cited make the book difficult. It is recommended to the superior student.

Meigs, Cornelia, *Invincible Louisa* (Little, Brown, Boston). Louisa May Alcott, the author of *Little Women* and other charming stories of child life in New England, lives again in this popular biography by Miss Meigs, herself a specialist in delightful stories for children.

Morrow, Honore Willsie, *The Great Captain* (Morrow, New York). This volume contains: *Forever Free*, showing the heroic way in which Lincoln met opposition, failure, and plots in the discharge of his executive duties; *The Last Full Measure* pictures Lincoln's great trust in mankind and his unwillingness to have body guards; a conspiracy against his life is formed long before the fatal shot. *With Malice Towards None* relates the experiences of the armies during the last two years of the Civil War. Lincoln shows his magnanimity to the conquered.

Nicolay, Helen, *Boys' Life of Lincoln* (Appleton-Century, New York). Helen Nicolay specializes in writing easy, entertaining, and slightly idealized biographies of famous Americans. Similar biographies by the same author are those of George Washington, Thomas Jefferson, Alexander Hamilton, Ulysses S. Grant, and Andrew Jackson.

Page, Elizabeth, *The Tree of Liberty* (Farrar & Rinehart, New York). The democratic spirit of which we boast today was born of conflict and tears. We get a glimpse of this struggle and how the conflict between the aristocratic notions of Hamilton and the democratic ideals of Jefferson affected the Howards of Virginia.

Perry, Bliss, *The Heart of Emerson's Essays* (Houghton, New York). This book contains selections from Emerson's complete works. It is valuable in so far as Emerson's thought is considered the core of Transcendentalism in America.

Repplier, Agnes, *Mère Marie of the Ursulines* (Garden City Pub. Co., New York). Women, too, have a courageous spirit of adventure as Miss Repplier shows in her biography of the young French widow who became the foundress of the Ursulines in Canada.

Shepherd, Odell, *Pedlar's Progress: the Life of Bronson Alcott* (Little, Brown, Boston). The title fits the book. In the days of his young manhood, Bronson Alcott peddled wares; in his maturity he peddled ideas. Carlyle speaking of him said he is "like a venerable Don Quixote, whom nobody can laugh at without loving." Alcott had unique notions on education, farming, and cooperatives.

Andrews, Mary Raymond Shipman, *The Perfect Tribute* (Scribner, New York, 1906). Lincoln felt that his Gettysburg speech had been a failure. That same evening he was by chance called upon to draw up a will for a dying soldier. The Southern soldier praised the speech and died resting his hand in that of the great Lincoln.

Stowe, Harriet Beecher, *Uncle Tom's Cabin* (Houghton, New York). It is a propaganda novel having historic interest. The author hoped to arouse public sentiment against slavery, and, therefore, exaggerated many incidents. The novel helped to promote the Abolition movement.

Washington, Booker T., *Up from Slavery* (Houghton, New York). This is an honest, fascinating, inspirational story of the author's life. Booker T. Washington, a Negro, rose from slavery to international fame and became the intellectual emancipator of his people.

Whalen, Doran, *Granite for God's House* (Sheed & Ward, New York). This biography of Orestes Brownson, thinker, convert, philosopher, and journalist, will challenge the ambitious student. He will enjoy, too, acquaintance with Ripley, Hawthorne, and Dana.

Brooks, Van Wyck, *The Flowering of New England* (Dutton, New York). This work merited the 1936 Pulitzer Prize in literary history. It is a splendid source book for what has been called the golden age of American literature. The author gives intimate sketches of the important literary men of the period.

Young, Stark, *So Red the Rose* (Scribner, New York). The Civil War is seen from the point of view of the Southerner. A charming picture of life on a great plantation of the Old South.

IN SEARCH OF ELDORADO

Pioneers on horseback and covered wagons made their way west.

Frontier Sketches, 1865-1890

When the battle smoke cleared away after the Civil War, a new America stood revealed. This was a country to which the westward movement brought a consciousness of widely-different regions within its own boundaries, — a country that was beginning to compute the vast wealth of its natural resources and was looking to science and invention for a means of getting the greatest profit from land and industry. Old ways wcrc changing. Modern America was coming into being. The literature of the 1870s and 1880s reflects the shifting social, cultural, and economic standards of the nation. Since the migration to the West was the dominant phase of American life for three decades after the war, the most significant pictures of this period were the frontier sketches.

The frontier had always been a distinctive feature of American life. When men failed to find their fortunes in settled areas, they looked to the West as a land of promise. After the Civil War a mighty procession passed westward to settle the land between the Kansas-Nebraska tier of states and California. The discovery of gold in the Sierras and of silver in the Rockies set in motion the great exodus. The Homestead Act of 1862 gave impetus to the rush for land.

The hazards of migration and the sturdiness of frontier life provided both tone and subject matter for the literature of the West. Pioneers on horseback or in covered wagons faced choking heat, lurking disease, and hostile Indians. Many sought to escape these perils by following long sea routes. They sailed around South America or traveled across Nicaragua or the Isthmus of Panama to take ship again for San Francisco. The travelers by sea exchanged the trials of the prairie for tropical diseases, poor food, and the treachery of unscrupulous sea captains. Unmarked roadside graves and burials at sea in the dark of the night accounted for more than half the people who started on that great migration. Only the strong reached the goal, men and women whose endurance and will power equaled their spirit of high adventure.

Humor develops on the frontier

The frontier folk found that humor helped them to endure the hardships of their mode of life. Humor was not new in American literature — Irving, Lowell, and Holmes had already made distinctive contributions. But the new school of humor arising along the frontier was more original. These Western humorists were distinctively American humorists. Among the writers of this bluff, hearty humor were "John Phoenix" (George Horatio Derby), "Artemus Ward" (Charles Farrar Browne), "Petroleum V. Nasby" (David Ross Locke), "Josh Billings" (Henry Wheeler Shaw), and finally the master, "Mark Twain" (Samuel Langhorne Clemens).

Folklore grows out of American life

The rapid settlement of the frontier brought adventurous men to isolated sections where reading material was almost unknown. From the entertainment which men in these remote regions improvised for themselves came a significant body of folk literature. The cowboy had his songs of the range; the lumberjack, his tall tales; the mountaineer, his yarns; the Negro, his folk songs. Certain traits are common to the whole body of folk song. It is usually anonymous in authorship; it is largely in verse form; its themes and melodies are often adapted from various sources; the same song exists in many different versions.

Cowboy songs are of particular significance in the study of American literature because in them the spirit of the West still lives in all its vastness, hospitality, and sentiment. These ballads recall the era when cattle rangers drove their herds hundreds of miles up the trail from Texas to some shipping point in Kansas, led young steers from Arizona to graze in Montana, or fought off Indians. Thrown upon their own resources for amusement, the ranchers gathered by the light of campfires at night and told in song their longings and exciting experiences. Later, alone with the herd, they found that singing broke the monotony of the drive. The slow, mournful tunes were soothing to the cattle; more than once they speeded the laggard or prevented a stampede.

The largest body of American folk songs came from the Negro. His stories about animals reveal a sense of humor; his work-chants give rhythm to the labor of a group; his "blues" have been widely imitated. Best among the creative expressions of the Negro are the spirituals. These songs are the cry of an oppressed race for spiritual help, the utterance of a people to whom singing brings relief. Although the melodies show some contact with African and European music and with the hymns of American revival meetings, they are such a distinctive combination as to constitute a special cultural contribution. Worded in simple, often childish language, these songs have the appeal of a deeply emotional utterance. They are marked by strong rhythms and usually contain a refrain. Through these folk songs one can better understand the outlook of the American Negro.

Fiction of local color arises

From the West also came impetus towards a literary movement known as the writing of *local color*. Fiction or verse of the local-color school emphasized the special features of a locality as well as the customs, dress, dialect, and modes of life of the inhabitants. Local color was not entirely new in the period following the Civil War. Lowell had anticipated it in the dialect of the *Biglow Papers,* and Whittier had sung the charms of the New England landscape in his nature poems. But it was the California stories of Bret Harte that brought a gust of freshness across the country and gave a deep breath to the critics of the Atlantic seaboard, almost suffocating from the stifling atmosphere of a prolonged romanticism. The power of the western scene to capture the imagination of readers throughout the country gave a suggestion to other short-story writers in America. Perhaps their own localities might be as advantageously developed. Soon authors were portraying in their fiction the scenery, people, customs, and dialects of many sections of the country. The new literature included narratives from the timberlands of Minnesota, from the Mississippi region, from the gold camps of Nevada and California, from the bayou country and the cotton fields of the South, as well as from New England and the middle border. The local-color writers paved the way for the novelists of the realistic school. They also aided in the development of the American short story. The emphasis on local peculiarities was something new in literature, and it stands as an especially American contribution to the literature of the world.

WALT WHITMAN

Almost from the beginning of our national history American men of letters had been hoping for the arrival of a poet who would be great and at the same time distinctively American. This longed-for poet would be the laureate of democracy and he would owe little or nothing to foreign models or influences. Many people have thought, and many still think, that this hope was at last realized in Walt Whitman (1819-1892).

Walt Whitman was born on a farm near Huntington, Long Island, of parents who were of a mingled English, Welsh, and Dutch ancestry. When he was four years old, the family moved to Brooklyn, then but a sprawling village. His education was haphazard, for Whitman was an inattentive and lazy scholar. At the age of eleven or twelve, his formal schooling was over. He was always, however, to be a great reader, but he read much rather than well, and the laziness which made him a poor reader of textbooks made him a poor reader of other books. Whitman was never to be a penetrating critic.

Until the time he was thirty, Whitman made his living chiefly through working on newspapers in and around Brooklyn and in New Orleans. A visit to Chicago and St. Louis brought him into contact with the frontier. It was chiefly through his work on the newspapers that Whitman acquired his large awareness of social and political issues as well as his acquaintance with the national, as opposed to the merely local, scene. He was ever to be an ardent patriot and he firmly believed that America was better than any other country in the world.

Whitman undertakes to be American prophet

Whitman's family had been Quakers, and although he himself was to form a kind of religion quite his own, the Quaker influence never entirely left him. In his poetry, for example, he always followed the Quaker custom of referring to the days of the week as First Day, Second Day, and so on. In his earlier years Whitman was moral even to the point of narrowness. He condemned prize fights and the use of coffee, tea, and tobacco. Somewhere between 1847 and 1855, however, Whitman underwent a great emotional and spiritual crisis. When it was over, he was an entirely different personality. He was the completely "natural"

Walt Whitman

man, impatient of law and restraint, immensely in love with his own body, certain of his godlike stature, and convinced of his mission as the prophet of the American way of life. It was from this new Whitman that was to proceed the strange and disturbing book, *Leaves of Grass.*

In the transformation of Whitman many forces had been at work, but among the more powerful of these forces were the writings of Emerson. In later life the poet was not always willing to admit the influence of the sage of Concord, but the following confession is unmistakable: "I was simmering, simmering, simmering; Emerson brought me to a boil." Emerson, too, was certain of the divinity of the average man; he had looked upon America as the laboratory of all future greatness; he had been impatient of law and restraint, and in essays like "Self-Reliance" he had urged his readers to obey their "inner voices" rather than custom, reason, or external revelation. Whitman was the alarming fulfillment of the Emersonian dream.

From the time of the publication of the first edition of *Leaves of Grass* in 1855, the external events of Whitman's life assume little importance; it is his book which matters. It is true, however, that the incidents of the Civil War somewhat modified his exuberant optimism, that in later life he became increasingly aware of spiritual values, and that, although ever cherishing the democratic dream, he grew more and more critical of what he considered the corruption and stupidities of federal and local government. Perhaps his most important single experience between 1855 and his death at Camden, New Jersey, in 1892 was his brief career as volunteer nurse during the Civil War. Here, in the army hospitals of the national capital, his genuine humanitarian sympathies received worthy and devoted exercise.

Leaves of Grass

Whitman set the type for the first edition of *Leaves of Grass* with his own hands and sent gift copies to important men of letters. It is said that Whittier threw his copy into the fire, but Emerson read his and gave it generous praise. Whitman, much to Emerson's later embarrassment, exploited these words of praise by reprinting them the next year in a second edition of his poems. What was the nature of the poetry which excited such contradictory reactions?

Whitman sees a world in which the fellowship of man is the only religion; he sees democratic America leading the way toward this world utopia; he urges each man to fulfill the godhead within himself by obedience to impulse and opposition to law; he calls for great leaders and offers himself as the model to be followed; he has no time for creeds or churches; he has no belief in sin, either original or actual; he believes that Christ was divine, but no more so than himself; he sees the world forever progressing toward the ideal through the impetus of love; he is optimistic as only one who denies evil can be; he is egotistic as only one who is convinced of his divinity can be.

It is clear to the Catholic that Whitman is a false prophet. The two aspects of his message which seem closest to Christian thought — love of neighbor and a deep regard for a form of government which champions the dignity and liberty of man — are grounded on beliefs totally at variance with Christian Revelation. According to Whitman's belief, we are expected to love our neighbor because he shares in our divinity; we are expected to uphold democracy because it guarantees unlimited personal freedom. Neither reason nor experience supports these assumptions, and Revelation flatly rejects them. Whitman has

enthusiasm and sincerity, and these virtues have won him many admirers. When, however, his message is put to the severe test of reason, it proves altogether disappointing. The voice within was not that of a god but a ventriloquist. On the other hand, if we look at his gospel in the light of the New England Puritan inheritance, we can easily understand its appeal. But if man is not totally depraved, neither is he a god; if it is inhuman to repress all natural instincts, it is bestial to allow them free rein.

New technique reflects poet's freedom

If Whitman was daring in what he said, he was more daring still in his manner of saying it. In *Leaves of Grass* he deliberately set out to write his poetry in a new way, a way which would be adequate for his message and suitable to his role as prophet. He substituted large, loose rhythms for the regular metrical line. He found precedent for this in the broad cadences of his King James version of the Bible, where the lines are more rhythmic than those of normal prose and less rhythmic than those of normal poetry. He claims to have derived his notion of rhythm from listening to the irregular cadences of the sea. He may also have been influenced by the melodic line of the operatic arias of which he was so fond.

Whitman, in his search for originality, used other devices. Of these his favorites were parallel structure and repetition. Often a dozen lines of a poem will begin with the same word or phrase; his frequent enumerations of things and men tend to monotony. Whitman's strong point is his imagery, particularly when it is based on sensation of touch or vision.

It seems that Whitman's confidence in his method was greater than results have justified, for he was sure that this method would forever outlaw from serious verse the older metrical technique. This has by no means been the case. On the other hand, it is evident that his flexible rhythms have encouraged a greater freedom of emotional expression. Later poets have profited by Whitman's example. The great weakness of free verse is in its tendency toward that formlessness which is the negation of art. Whether or not Whitman is able to survive that tendency the reader must decide. Many who have rejected the prophet have accepted the poet.

JOHN HAY

John Hay (1838-1905), a Midwestern writer, is best known as a diplomat and scholar. He was born in Indiana but soon moved to Illinois. He was a friend of Abraham Lincoln, whom he followed to the White House in the capacity of secretary. In collaboration with John Nicolay, Hay published in 1890 a monumental biography of Lincoln in ten volumes.

Hay's most important contribution to American literature was his *Pike County Ballads* (1871). Like Bret Harte, he was a pioneer in writing dialect verse, imitating the language of the backwoods people. Following Harte's method of approach, Hay capitalized upon the candor, self-reliance, emotions, heroism, and trickery of the unlettered people of Pike County, Illinois. "Jim Bludso" and "Little Breeches" are among the most appealing of Hay's ballads. According to Bayard Taylor, "A Pike in the California dialect is a native of Missouri, Arkansas, northern Texas, or southern Illinois. The first immigrants that came over the plains were men from Pike County, Missouri, and the phrase, 'Pike County Man,' . . . was abbreviated into 'A Pike.'"

JOAQUIN MILLER

One poet of the frontier, Joaquin Miller (1841-1913), actually lived the romantic, adventurous life he describes. Although he left a mass of biographical material, it is difficult to separate fact from fiction, because of his habit of romanticizing. Miller was always something of a poseur, craved admiration, and was jealous of his reputation as poet of the frontier. "My cradle," he says, "was a covered wagon, pointed west. I was born in a covered wagon, I am told, at about the time it crossed the line dividing Indiana from Ohio." The truth of the matter is that he was born in Liberty, Indiana, of Quaker parents and was named Cincinnatus Heine. He later assumed the name of Joaquin, taking it from a Mexican bandit who had befriended him.

At the age of eleven, Nat, as he was called, accompanied his parents to Oregon in search of gold. The journey was an extremely difficult one, beset with drought, cholera, and hardships of all kinds. The trip made an impression upon the imaginative boy. Tired of farm life in Oregon and goaded on by his restless

Joaquin Miller

spirit of adventure, Miller ran away from home and went to California. After three adventurous years spent in mining camps and in contact with the Indians, he returned home. Settling down in Oregon, he attended college and established a business. In a few years he had made a fortune transporting silver over the mountains. Soon the life of a businessman, even in those exciting days of forest fires, buffalo stampedes, bandits, and horse thieves, became tiresome. Miller next took up the study of law and eventually drifted into newspaper work.

Miller's thrilling experiences in the Rocky Mountain district, coupled with his taste for writing, which had been whetted through his newspaper work, decided his future course of action. At his own expense he published two volumes of books, *Specimens* (1868) and *Joaquin et al* (1869). The second volume was dedicated "to the bards of San Francisco." Miller popularized the idea that he was the only poet who had been born, and who had lived, on the frontier.

In his eagerness for new scenes and more adventure, Miller went to Europe and visited Scotland and England. While in London, he submitted some of his verses to editors who refused to publish them. He brought out a private printing of *Pacific Poems* (1870), which created a mild sensation. *Songs of the Sierras* (1871) met with an outburst of approval. Almost overnight Miller became a literary lion. He discovered early that Englishmen expected an American from the western part of the United States to be wild and uncouth, so he went about London in chaps and sombrero. The last years of his life were passed in Oakland, California. He established a home called "Heights," built on a barren cliff overlooking sea and mountains. In his old age he came to look upon himself as a veteran spokesman of America.

For all his posing and romantic exaggeration, Miller is sincere when he writes about the West. He does not possess the humor of Mark Twain and Bret Harte, nor is he interested in the many details suggestive of local color. Rather, Miller is at his best describing in swinging, hearty rhythm the great stretches of land in the Rocky Mountain ranges. Prairies, mountains, and the sea made up his world, and he peopled it with adventurous men and women, who were not always true to life. Miller once said, "The world is one great poem, because it is very grand, very good, and very beautiful."

THE GENTEEL TRADITION

Literature in New England suffered a decline in the generation that followed Emerson, Thoreau, Lowell, Holmes, and Longfellow. Many of the most energetic young people from the traditional old stock had joined the westward migration. Already the immigrants walked boldly on Boston Common. The aristocratic Bostonians might still control the wealth, but the newcomers had the vote. Despite New England's struggle and protest, her ascendancy was being superseded by the overwhelming force of new frontiers.

The new currents flowing into our national life and letters were ignored or scorned by the group of cultivated young writers who remained to uphold the standards of the old aristocracy. Blinded to the significance of new literary developments, they had no respect for the frontier because it had no tradition. They considered the humor and unpolished dialects of the West a corruption of language and taste. Rejecting this fresh and vital material, they limited their writing to outworn topics and conventional forms. To them literature was merely refined and pleasing expression,

marked above all by good breeding and cultivated taste. The standard which they sought desperately to uphold despite changing times has been called the "genteel tradition." Through the pages of the *Atlantic Monthly*, their chief medium of expression, these writers endeavored to bolster New England's waning strength in American letters. In poetry Thomas Bailey Aldrich perhaps best exemplifies the genteel tradition. Bayard Taylor and Edward Rowland Sill, though they wandered far from the East, also belong to this group of authors.

EDWARD ROWLAND SILL

Among the writers of the genteel tradition is Edward Rowland Sill (1841-1887). Born in Connecticut and a graduate of Yale, he was forced because of frail health to live in the West. For eight years he was a professor of literature at the University of California. His whole life was one of conflict. Not only was his eastern culture challenged by western crudeness, but the growing skepticism of the age caused him religious doubts. Yearning of soul, and a groping for a solution to the problems of life, constitute the subject matter of his poems. Although a minor writer because of his narrow range of subject matter and his lack of originality, Sill is remembered for two poems, "The Fool's Prayer" and "Opportunity."

BENJAMIN DIONYSIUS HILL

Benjamin Dionysius Hill (Father Edmund of the Heart of Mary) (1842-1916) was the son of an Anglican clergyman. The young man prepared for a medical career but later entered the Anglican ministry. As a young minister he felt himself drawn to the Catholic Church while reading the literature of the Oxford Movement. The study of the Church led to Hill's conversion. In 1868 he entered the Society of St. Paul in New York and was ordained in 1871. In the Society his immediate superior was Father Fidelis of the Cross (James Kent Stone), the convert author of *Awakening and What Followed*. When Father Fidelis sought entrance into the order of Passionist priests, Father Edmund followed him. Later he accompanied Father Fidelis on a mission to South America. The poet-priest died in England in 1916.

The sensitive, gentle nature of Father Edmund sought to express in poetry the wonders he had discovered in Catholic doctrine. He wrote a host of poems especially designed to inspire in Catholic priests and laymen a chivalrous devotion to the Queen of Queens. *Mariae Corolla (A Wreath for Mary)* contains much of his poetry to Mary. Another volume of *Poems* (1876) shows his special devotion to the Passion of Christ; other lyrics in the same volume pay tribute to the friends whom his winning nature readily attracted. Father Edmund brought an artistic technique to devotional subjects, and a vein of mysticism runs through his poems.

DANIEL HUDSON, C.S.C.

A link between the transcendental culture of New England and Catholic literary developments in the Middle West may be found in Daniel Hudson, C.S.C. (1849-1934), the directive spirit of the *Ave Maria* in its formative years. This Catholic periodical had been founded in 1865, a short time after Father Hecker issued the first number of the *Catholic World*. Under Father Hudson's editorship, the *Ave Maria* became as literary and artistic as it was devotionally sound and inspiring. Daniel Hudson was born in Nahant, near Boston. The young boy's deep piety was fostered by his mother, who went four miles to church each Sunday with her children in order to attend Mass. The boy's father was a sincere Methodist. Daniel's instinct for truth, beauty, and literary artistry was stimulated by his contacts with Hawthorne, Lowell, Longfellow, and Emerson at a bookshop and in the publishing house where the lad worked. Courses in the classics, philosophy, and theology at the Jesuit College of the Holy Cross and at the University of Notre Dame fitted Hudson to become an outstanding editor. Soon after his ordination, the priest was given charge of the *Ave Maria*, and for fifty-five years he charted its course. Father Hudson was not only discriminating in his literary taste and judgment but had the ability to recognize, encourage, and develop talent in others. Many a successful Catholic writer of fiction and poetry owes a debt of gratitude to this priest and editor.

Sidney Lanier

SIDNEY LANIER

In striking contrast to Walt Whitman, with his "barbaric yawp" and pagan freshness, is the spiritual idealism of Sidney Lanier. In many ways Lanier was a remarkable individual. Possessing an intensely religious spirit, unusual talent, and indomitable courage, he was one of the first Southerners to meet the challenge of the changed conditions following the Civil War.

Sidney Lanier was born in Macon, Georgia, February 3, 1842. As a young boy he showed remarkable musical talent and became in time a skilled flutist. His father discouraged any thought of a musical career for his son. Lanier attended Oglethorpe College in Georgia and later became a tutor there. The outbreak of the Civil War upset his plans of going to Europe to work for a doctor's degree.

For Lanier the war was a call to duty. He enlisted and fought with unquestioning idealism. Although he was in no major battles, he was taken prisoner during the last year of the war, while on blockade service. During several months confinement in the "hell-hole" of Point Lookout Prison, the flute which he had smuggled in was a great comfort to him. Here he cultivated the friendship of a fellow prisoner, John Bannister Tabb, a poet and kindred spirit.

Novel gives realistic war picture

Released after the war, Lanier returned to his home to find his mother in a dying condition, the family impoverished, and the morale of the South at a low ebb. Although he himself was in a weakened condition, having become the victim of tuberculosis, he proved a brave fighter, a stanch American, and a man of great courage. The next several years were spent in hard work as a clerk, teacher, and a student of law. During odd moments he wrote prose and poetry. His first novel, *Tiger Lilies*, appeared in 1867. In his realistic presentation of war material, Lanier anticipated Stephen Crane.

Lanier married Mary Day, a girl from Georgia, and continued for some time his arduous tasks. In a few years it was necessary for him to seek a more healthful climate. In 1872 he went to Texas and while there he met an old German bandmaster, who became enthusiastic over Lanier's skill with the flute. This encouragement awakened Lanier's old ambition to become a professional musician. He went north and happily secured the position of first flutist in the Peabody Orchestra of Baltimore.

The search for a means of livelihood was over. The cultural life of Baltimore and Lanier's association with Peabody Institute and Johns Hopkins University stimulated his literary and scholarly ambition. In 1877 he was invited to give a course of lectures on English literature at Johns Hopkins. The years spent in Baltimore, although replete with scholarly and intellectual compensation, were full of suffering. Talent, inspiration, and opportunity were his, yet his physical strength could not support the demands of genius. In the midst of exacting rehearsals, musical engagements, and scholarly lectures, Lanier wrote the poetry by which he is best known today. Much of Lanier's work is in fragments. It was written hurriedly and without revision. Several years of this feverish activity were fast consuming the little hold he had upon life. In 1881 he went to the mountains of North Carolina, where he soon died.

Musical poetry has spiritual note

Besides *Tiger Lilies,* Lanier wrote other prose works, including *The Boy's King Arthur* (1880) and *The Science of English Verse* (1880). Primarily a poet, Lanier was well qualified to give his own theory on the art of versification. He maintained that poetry and music are "blood brothers," since both appeal to the ear and to what he calls the universal sense of rhythm. It was his conviction that the sound of words independent of their meaning have the power to create a mood. He endeavored to put his theory into practice and produced what have been called *symphonic poems.* Skilled in the use of rhythm, rhyme, colorful vowels, and liquid consonants, Lanier was a master of technique and has produced some of the most musical works in our literature. He was a genuine poet, as well as a verse technician. His poems contain such themes as love, hope, beauty, trust in God, and patriotism. He is vehement in his condemnation of a materialism which crushes spiritual values. "Corn" and "The Symphony," both treating social themes, are more than imaginative poems of verbal beauty; they are powerful protests against the crushing effects of materialism, which is killing Christian chivalry and beauty. According to Lanier, "Only love, sole musicmaster, blest, can dispel the oppression, bitterness, and hatred in the world."

JAMES JEFFREY ROCHE

One of the Irish poets who served a period of editorship on the *Boston Pilot* was James Jeffrey Roche. (1847-1908). Roche first came from his native land to Prince Edward Island, Canada, and in 1866 arrived in Boston. His three volumes of poems show him to be a capable writer of serious poetry as well as satirical verse. His adopted country sent him as United States consul to Genoa, and later to Berne, Switzerland, where he died in 1908.

JAMES WHITCOMB RILEY

James Whitcomb Riley (1849-1916), the "Hoosier poet," born in Greenfield, Indiana, has a prominent place among the poets of dialect and local color. He wrote two kinds of verse: sentimental and humorous. He had the gift of appealing to some deep-seated love or common experience which conjured up for his readers a host of memories. The titles of many of his poems include the word "old," and his themes often suggest happy days of long ago. His first volume of verse, *The Old Swimmin' Hole and 'Leven More Poems* (1883), with its quaint humor, homespun philosophy, and bold pathos, was widely popular. Some of Riley's best humorous verse is to be found in his eccentric character sketches and in his verses for children. "The Raggedy Man," "Doc Siffers," "Little Orphant Annie," and "Old Aunt Mary" are universal favorites. *Afterwhiles* (1887), *Rhymes of Children* (1890), and *Poems Here at Home* (1893) were read by thousands.

Much of Riley's success as a writer of "folk poetry" was achieved through his skillful use of dialect. He attempted to catch the twang of homely speech, a twang which gives a savor to what otherwise might have been too much a matter of rhymed sentiment. His fondness for dialect causes him to employ it upon occasions when there is no reason for its use. Riley at times shows a skill and fluency in handling rhythm and was, perhaps, potentially a greater poet than his works show.

EUGENE FIELD

Eugene Field (1850-1895), like Riley, was primarily a journalist. He collected his newspaper verse and in 1889 published his first volume, *A Little Book of Western Verse*. About half a dozen additional volumes of poetry followed in quick succession. Field always looked upon himself as a Westerner, and took pride in his native city, St. Louis.

While the verse of Field has something of the pathos and humor of Riley, it is more universal in its appeal and shows a greater delicacy of touch. All of Riley's poems bear the stamp of local color and are intimately associated with some phase of rural home life. Field draws his material and technique from many lands, even imitating the odes of Horace. His best poems are those relating to child life. Although many of them are a trifle sentimental, they have a musical and fairy-like charm. "Little Boy Blue" and "Dutch Lullaby" have been set to music and appeal to older people as well as to children.

John Bannister Tabb

JOHN BANNISTER TABB

John Bannister Tabb (1845-1909) spent his childhood on the extensive plantation of his parents near Richmond, Virginia, where he had a little slave boy to carry out his commands. The luxury of his early surroundings was in strange contrast to the squalid Maryland prison camp where he was held a captive during the Civil War. Serving as a blockade runner for the Confederate Navy though he was only a boy in his teens, Tabb had sailed to many foreign ports before the capture of his ship. After the war he determined to enter the Episcopal ministry. His contacts with Alfred Curtis, a young Episcopalian rector who favored many Catholic beliefs and practices, led him to make a closer investigation of the claims of the Anglican Church. Together the two men faced the same questions that had confronted Newman. Neither came to a decision at this time, but in 1872 Tabb entered the Catholic Church a few months before Curtis, later Bishop of Wilmington, made his profession of faith in England. Tabb was ordained to the secular priesthood in 1884 after his studies at St. Charles College, Ellicott City, Maryland. Here he spent the remainder of his life as a teacher of English. His sharp wit and ability to illustrate a point by means of cartoons enlivened the classroom. Father Tabb taught rhetoric from his own textbook, characteristically entitled *Bone Rules or Skeleton of English Grammar* and dedicated to "My pupils, active and passive, perfect and imperfect, past, present, and future (in whatever mood they may be.)" In his last years the priest's blindness forced him to resign from teaching.

Father Tabb introduced a new kind of nature poetry into American literature. To understand his method and his contribution, one should remember that he excelled in handling the short stanza, especially the quatrain or stanza of four lines. He drew many of his themes from common objects in life — lakes, hills, stars, trees, rain, silk, human eyes, cats, shadows, musical instruments. To these themes he gave a penetrating and highly original interpretation. His method was to connect the natural object of which he was writing to some scriptural incident or doctrinal teaching. This union was achieved by means of the metaphor. In the instance of one quatrain, the poet chose the music of Lanier's flute as his subject. The flute is here symbolic of the encouragement that a man's words may give his friend. The poet writes:

> When palsied at the pool of thought
>   The Poet's words were found,
> Thy voice the healing Angel brought
>   To touch them into sound.

In these lines the writer has taken the metaphor of the angel's stirring the waters from an incident related in the Gospel of St. John. The result is a natural idea interpreted in religious language. At times Father Tabb used the opposite of this procedure. In these latter poems he uses the natural object to illustrate a scriptural lesson or a point of Catholic doctrine. In "The Immaculate Conception" we have such a poem. Here metaphors taken from nature interpret the sinlessness of Mary's nature. The poem reads:

> A dewdrop of the darkness born
>   Wherein no shadow lies;
> The blossom of a barren thorn
>   Whereof no petal dies;

> A rainbow beauty, passion free,
>   Wherewith was veiled eternity.

As a variation of these two types, the poet sometimes uses one Biblical passage to interpret another. In other poems blending the themes of nature and religion, the Scriptural or doctrinal material is replaced by illustrations from the liturgy, the sacraments, the devotions of the Church, legends of the saints, or ethical points.

Father Tabb's method would have been ineffective had his metaphors been forced. But in his hands this poetic device has a spontaneous quality which carries an idea gracefully into its spiritual meaning. With him brevity is a keynote. The omission of a single word would detract from the essence of the poem. While only a few of the priest's poems are strictly religious verse, his treatment of his subject matter makes him a religious poet.

Not all of Father Tabb's poetry falls under these three variations of his distinctive method. The writer of more than a thousand poems, he likewise employs the more usual verse forms and methods of treatment. Since much of his best work, however, packs a thought into a single image or symbol, he has been called "poet of the single metaphor." In addition to his rare gift of crystallizing great wisdom within the compass of a few lines, his style is chaste and incisive. Numerous volumes of the priest's poems were published during his lifetime, and several collections have appeared since his death.

EMILY DICKINSON

Emily Dickinson (1830-1886) is unique among the poets of this period. She lived a secluded life at Amherst, Massachusetts, was reticent about her personal affairs, and scorned publicity. Her poetry, however, reveals the full life of one who lives by the spirit. Her timeless themes — life, love, suffering, and eternity — make her a poet for all ages.

During her lifetime Emily Dickinson wrote more than a thousand brief lyrics, which she tucked away in her desk. Only a few poems were published while she was living — none of them with her permission.

Emily Dickinson

Occasionally she showed some of her work to her sister-in-law, "her sister Sue," who shared her confidence, and to other close friends. Her manuscripts yielded material for six volumes of poetry which have been published since the poet's death. Unknown in life, Emily Dickinson has attained a reputation outranking that of any other woman poet in the English language.

Emily Dickinson's lyrics reflect the treasured experiences of a rich inner life. In the sharpness of her imagery and in the daring originality of her metaphors she anticipated the aims of the imagist poets of the twentieth century. Her poems are brief but profound, powerful yet delicate in expression. Packed with emotion, they appeal to readers as a reflection of universal experience. Because their concise and brilliant style is suited to twentieth-century tastes, the popularity of Emily Dickinson's poetry continues to grow.

EDWIN MARKHAM

Edwin Markham (1852-1940) was born in Oregon, spent a number of years in California, but afterwards moved to the East. His poems are more aloof from his surroundings and more universal in their appeal than those of many Western writers. He found himself famous after the publication of his forceful poem, "The Man with the Hoe," inspired by a painting of Millet.

The poem appeared in practically every newspaper in the country. This encouraging success directed Markham's activities into literary channels. He moved to the East and spent the next twenty-five years of his life writing and reading his own verse. All of his poems show an intense sense of beauty and an equally intense desire for social justice. He had a profound interest in the common man, typified by Lincoln, to whom he paid eloquent tribute in his poem, "Lincoln, the Man of the People." Markham will live in American literature through these two poems.

RICHARD MALCOLM JOHNSTON

That a truly great man is capable of rising above narrow bigotry, petty jealousies, and blighting human respect is manifest in the life and works of Richard Malcolm Johnston (1822-1898). Born in Hancock County, Georgia, Johnston grew up in an atmosphere of culture and refinement, slightly tinged with religious prejudice. The first four years of his school life were spent in the "old field school," where discipline was very severe. "The Goosepond School" (1857), Johnston's first story, and many other tales are built upon incidents and characters drawn from these early years. For fifteen years Johnston alternated between the practice of law and teaching. The Civil War marked a turning point in his life. Since his ideas about secession were not in harmony with those of the people of Athens, he resigned his position at the University of Georgia and opened a school at Sparta, Georgia. The ruined condition of the South and heavy financial losses caused Johnston to move with his family to Baltimore after the war. Here he conducted a boarding school for boys. Forty of his former pupils followed him to the new school, but when he entered the Catholic Church in 1877, he lost the Georgia patronage.

While in Georgia, Johnston had submitted stories to Southern magazines. He collected this fiction and published *Georgia Sketches by an Old Man* (1864). The stories received little recognition outside the state. In Baltimore he continued to write and was encouraged and helped by the friendly criticism of Sidney Lanier. A second volume of stories, *Dukesborough Tales* (1871), appeared under the pen name of Philemon Perch. In 1893 Johnston retired from teaching and devoted himself to writing tales about his beloved Georgia. He contributed to the leading magazines of the country and published several more volumes of short fiction. In addition to the books already named, some of the author's best-known collections are: *Mr. Absolom Billingslea and Other Georgia Folk* (1888), *Mr. Fortner's Martial Claims and Other Stories* (1892), and *Old Times in Middle Georgia* (1897). Johnston's stories are significant in the development of realism. In his use of dialect and local color, he antedated Bret Harte and George Washington Cable. His stories are told with simplicity and directness and reveal the customs, manners, social distinctions, feuds, and religious controversies found in Middle Georgia during the early nineteenth century. In Johnston's stories, plot is always subordinate to character. In portraying the foibles of human nature, he affords fun and mingles human and moral philosophy.

BRET HARTE

Bret Harte's father was a sensitive lover of books who knew five languages but who was unable to eke out a living as a traveling teacher. The cultural heritage which he gave to his son, Francis Brett (1836-1902), fostered the boy's interest in literature. This taste was to be a compensation for the frail lad's inability to engage in sports. As a boy Francis wished to become a writer. His father's early death, however, forced the boy to be self-supporting at sixteen. Hoping to improve the family fortunes, his mother left New York for California and later sent for Frank and his sister. On their arrival the young people were disappointed in their new surroundings and disheartened by the news of their mother's remarriage. Harte's yearning for adventure caused him to try many odd jobs in the West, one of which was mining. In this occupation his frailty overcame his ambition. Evenings he spent reading and writing. Experience on small journals, additional leisure for creative work, and the helpful criticism of his associates led to the improvement of his literary style. In 1868 he was made first editor of the *Overland Monthly*, the western counterpart of the *Atlantic Monthly*.

Noticing the lack of literary material on California in an issue he was preparing, he wrote "The Luck of Roaring Camp," a short story of life in a western mining town, and printed it under the signature Bret Harte. "The Luck of Roaring Camp" was Bret Harte's luck also. With the publication of this story his reputation was made. Three years later, after he had written such stories as "The Outcasts of Poker Flat" and "Tennessee's Partner," he was offered ten thousand dollars a year by the *Atlantic Monthly* to produce stories of California life. Since his seventeen years in the West had been only an exile, he gladly accepted the dazzling offer and the opportunity to return to the cultured East.

Bret Harte had a great love of literary tradition and would have had little interest in continuing to use western subject matter had not the public insisted on more of the mining-camp stories which had made him famous. He was now too far removed from the West to feel its influence, and his work steadily weakened. For a time, as American consul to Germany and to Scotland, he was able to live in the cultural atmosphere of Europe, for which he had great reverence. In his last years, finding a more ready market for his work in English journals, he lived on meager funds in London in order to support his family in New York. The stories of this period are imperfect copies of his early California tales.

Again and again Harte used the same formula. He never wrote quite the whole truth. Selecting characters who were notoriously bad, he introduced some heroic act into their lives with the result that the reader came to regard such characters as ideal. This method makes use of *moral contrast*. Harte's stories of the Spanish friars who had figured in California history are among the most consciously artistic of his writings. His first claim to literary fame comes from the impetus he gave to the local-color movement. By 1880, every important region of America had a writer to introduce it to other sections of the country, as Bret Harte had brought the atmosphere of the California mining camp to the East.

SAMUEL LANGHORNE CLEMENS (MARK TWAIN)

Samuel Langhorne Clemens, more widely known as "Mark Twain," lived an intense life, experiencing three major phases of nineteenth-century activity:

Mark Twain

the settling of the midwestern frontier, the era of the steamboat on the Mississippi, and the gold rush to the Rocky Mountains. He was born in Florida, Missouri, in 1835. Shortly after his birth the Clemens family moved to Hannibal, then a small, back-country town in Missouri, where slavery existed side by side with a vigorous western democracy and the rough lawlessness of the frontier. He always thought that he had experienced an unusual boyhood and never tired of stressing the influence the Mississippi had upon his life. The steamship's coming to Hannibal every day made him desire to see the world. When his father died, the boy gladly left school and was apprenticed to a local printer at the age of twelve. After learning the trade, he traveled as a journeyman printer to St. Louis, New York, Philadelphia, and Keokuk, Iowa. This journey, lasting several months, enabled him to see the more civilized sections of the United States before going West. At the age of twenty-two, Clemens realized his youthful ambition of becoming a steamship pilot on the Mississippi. In the 1850s the steamship had much the same allurement that the airplane has today. Samuel became a skilled pilot. He liked the work and always maintained that it had great educational value for him. It gave him an opportunity to study all classes and types of humanity.

The outbreak of the Civil War in 1861 closed the river traffic. Clemens tried to enlist in the Confederate Cavalry, but the Union soldiers disbanded his troop, and

he was forced to flee to escape capture. He roamed over the West, spending his time in mining camps and in newspaper offices, being employed for a short period on the Virginia City *Enterprise* in Nevada. To this paper he contributed humorous sketches under the pseudonym of "Mark Twain," a term used by Mississippi river-men to signify a sounding depth of two fathoms (twelve feet). In 1864, Twain became involved in a duel and was forced to leave Nevada. He went to San Francisco, where he came under the influence of Bret Harte, who at that time had acquired skill in creating stories of local color. Harte encouraged Twain to write sketches portraying life in San Francisco.

Frontier humor brings popularity

In 1867 Twain published his first collection of narratives, *The Celebrated Jumping Frog of Calaveras County and Other Sketches*. The distinct humor of the stories and their freshness won popularity for their author and attracted to him the attention of critics who were looking for new material. The editor of the *Alta Californian*, a well-known western periodical, commissioned Twain to go to Europe and Palestine and write accounts of his trip. The letters which he sent back were published as *The Innocents Abroad* (1869). Despite the coarseness, bigotry, wanton ignorance, and lack of appreciation of spiritual values manifested in his book, it had a tremendous sale because of Twain's appeal as a narrator.

The trip to Europe, moreover, brought personal romance into the life of Mark Twain. Charles Langdon, his friend and companion on the trip, had with him a picture of his sister. From the picture Twain fell in love with the young lady and in 1870 married Olivia Langdon of Elmira, New York. At the time of his marriage, Twain was editor of the *Brooklyn Express* and was determined to lead the life of a literary man. Crude and uneducated, he profited from the help which his wife gave him in preparing his books. Susy Clemens, in her youthful biography of her father, says: "Ever since papa and mama were married, papa has written his books and then taken them to mama in manuscript, and she has expergated." During the next fifteen years Mark Twain produced the books by which he will be long remembered. *Roughing It* (1872) presents with much gusto and vividness the rough-and-tumble life of the western plains. By 1875, *Old Times on the Mississippi* was ready for publication. This was later included in a more extended work, *Life on the Mississippi* (1893), picturing the romantic days of the old steamboat traffic. The work is largely autobiographical. Thrilling and amusing incidents are told from the viewpoint of an animated cub pilot. *The Adventures of Tom Sawyer* (1876) and *The Adventures of Huckleberry Finn* (1884) are among Mark Twain's finest pieces of regional writing. In them the sleepy little village of his boyhood and the entire Mississippi Valley come to life. In immortalizing these passing phases of American life, Twain has contributed to history as well as to literature.

Tom Sawyer was an innovation in fiction dealing with boys. Up to the time of Twain, stories for boys had been didactic; the heroes were often insipid types, not real boys. Tom Sawyer is a representative American boy, the incarnation of universal boyhood. From a literary point of view, *Huckleberry Finn* is by far the better work. The story is consistently told and keeps within the psychological bounds of the chief actors.

Satirical and pessimistic works

Mark Twain's later work is satirical and pessimistic. He had always looked upon himself as a philosopher, and as time went on, he began to take himself seriously as a social historian. *A Connecticut Yankee in King Arthur's Court* (1889) is a satire on medieval chivalry. Twain labored over his *Personal Recollections of Joan of Arc* (1896) and intended it to be an intelligent and sympathetic appreciation of the Maid of Orleans. Some of the Eastern journals, however, reviewed the book as a burlesque. After suffering financial losses and after the deaths of his wife and daughter, Twain became more and more critical of contemporary writers and Christian traditions. With all his irreverence and blasphemy, Mark Twain was not an atheist but a deist wrestling with the problem of evil. Without faith in a personal God directing the destinies of men and capable of bringing good out of evil, Mark Twain could find no explanation for the cruelty and injustice in the world. He came at times to look upon man as an animal in conflict with other animals, or as a mechanical being incapable of moral judgments. The cynicism and despondency of his

later years is revealed in his "bible," an essay entitled "What is Man?" A hopeless victim of generalization and totally lacking the power of anything like subtle distinctions, Twain condemned mankind for the shortcomings of men and even identified God with Satan in *The Mysterious Stranger.*

Mark Twain won his reputation as a humorist. His humor, however, is the broad, coarse comedy of the frontier. Most of the great comic writers of the world have related their humor to character in dramatic situations. Twain's fun consists in crude, bold, sometimes picturesque aphorisms having in them a grain of truth. Whether or not this humor endures, he has a secure place in American literature as a writer of local color who immortalized the frontier life of the Middle West.

GEORGE WASHINGTON CABLE

The old French quarter of New Orleans furnished George Washington Cable (1844-1925) with a highly picturesque and romantic locale for his stories. Its winding streets, old-world gardens, latticed windows, iron-grilled balconies, and lovely Creole ladies set his sensitive imagination to work at tales of dreamy romance. Nor did Cable confine himself to the city itself. The entire bayou country entered his writings. The marshes, the swamps, and the inhabitants of the Louisiana back country with their quaint dialect and their fierce pride even amid material and cultural poverty — all these picturesque elements lend to his works a charm redolent of semi-tropical nature and of old-world civilization.

Stories depict Creole

Cable's Creoles were the descendants of the early French settlers of New Orleans. The term *Creole* is used to refer to those families of French or Spanish ancestry in Louisiana who retain the language and customs of their forefathers. A retiring people, they have little interest in the outside world as long as nothing disturbs their little havens on the Mississippi and along the great bayous. They are Catholics, loyal to the Church and to its customs. In the lives of the Creoles who live so deeply within themselves, Cable found romance and gallantry, courage and loyalty.

A native of the flower-laden city of New Orleans, George Washington Cable was reared in a home of culture. When the boy was fifteen, his father died after having failed in business. George went to work in a custom warehouse, later clerked for a merchant, and during the Civil War enlisted in the Confederate Army. Biographers have remarked that he could no more keep from studying than from breathing. Riding off to war with the Mississippi Cavalry, he smuggled into his soldier's kit a few books of classics and higher mathematics, which he thoroughly enjoyed during the more quiet moments of the campaign. A paroled prisoner after the conflict, he was brought back to New Orleans, where he worked at bookkeeping and contributed to the *Daily Picayune.* In 1871 his newspaper employer asked him to do some historical sketches on local charities. While ransacking the city archives and yellowed files of newspapers, Cable found not only the desired information but abundant ideas for stories of Old New Orleans. These stories, which first appeared in *Scribners* and *Appleton's,* were later collected in a single volume, *Old Creole Days* (1879). In 1880 Cable published his first novel, *The Grandissimes,* which presents one of the most noted pictures of the Negro in American literature.

Emphasis is on character

Cable had a brilliant and polished style. He drenched his stories with local color and used settings that could have been found nowhere else in the world. His emphasis was always upon character rather than plot. Yet he failed to understand the Catholicity of the people he was describing. In so doing, he omitted an element which was essential for an accurate presentation. After the unfavorable reception of his novel, *The Silent South* (1885), a work that defended the Southern Negro, Cable moved to Massachusetts. He devoted his time to writing literary criticism and lecture tours, but the period of his best creative work was over. The languorous charm native to New Orleans could not survive in a colder climate.

IRWIN RUSSELL

Irwin Russell (1853-1879) was among the first of the Southern writers to introduce the Negro into literature.

Potentially a true artist, he died before he could develop his talent. Russell was born in Mississippi and later spent some time in St. Louis. At sixteen he entered the Catholic Church. By a special act of the legislature of Mississippi, he was admitted to the bar at nineteen.

While reading some folk verse in an issue of *Scribners Magazine,* Russell first realized the possibilities of the Negro dialect and his own facility in imitating the Negro's manner of speech. He had frequently played on the banjo while the Negro cook sang her religious hymns and at the end of her songs had improvised humorous pieces for her delight. As a result of this realization of his gifts, Russell began to submit light verse to various periodicals. Possessing a sympathetic understanding of the Negro race, he turned in time to the creation of serious poetry. In "Christmas Night in the Quarters," he gave a comprehensive view of Negro life. Because of its scope, this dialect poem of the pre-war South has been called a little epic. Hoping to further his career as a poet, Russell went to New York, but failing health forced him to return South.

Irwin Russell's poems were not collected until nine years after his death. The slender volume represents authentic Mississippi Negro dialect and displays an honest understanding of the Negro. Bold and striking pictures of plantation life reveal the Negro's loyalty and affection for his master, his humor and homespun philosophy, his superstitions, his religious aspirations, and poetic temperament. Other writers of dialect verse acknowledged their indebtedness to Russell for his authentic representation of the Negro character.

JOEL CHANDLER HARRIS

The mother of Joel Chandler Harris (1848-1908) belonged to a wealthy, aristocratic Georgia family, that disowned her when she married a man who was her social inferior. Deserted by her husband, Mrs. Harris brought up her son in a little cottage at the rear of a plantation and supported herself and the child by sewing and menial work. She carried on much of Joel's education by reading good fiction aloud to him. During his mother's busy hours, Joel was free to roam the plantation, making friends with horses, dogs, rabbits, pickaninnies, and the old Negroes who had grown too feeble to work in the cotton fields. In order to lighten his

Joel Chandler Harris

entire Negro race, especially at that moment when the old order of life among the Negroes was passing into the new. In Uncle Remus may be seen the childlike simplicity of the race, the shrewdness, the quaint humor, the pathos, the common sense, the swift repartee, and withal a great depth of character. Br'er Rabbit is the Negro himself, surrounded on all sides by brutality and superior force but in the end triumphant by means of his superior cunning. Harris also wrote novels and sketches, but it is for the Br'er Rabbit stories that he is best remembered. These tales have appeared in a number of collections among which are: *Uncle Remus: His Songs and Sayings* (1880), *Nights with Uncle Remus* (1883), *Told by Uncle Remus* (1905), and *Uncle Remus and the Little Boy* (1910). The stories have been translated into more than twenty-five languages.

Harris wrote the stories in a simple, natural form yet in a careful literary style. These tales show the poetic side of the Negro. His work has unusual literary significance, since in addition to producing stories of authentic local color and dialect, he utilized the materials of Negro folklore. Harris had married a beautiful French-Canadian girl, and he and his wife reared their large family in the Catholic Faith. The author often spoke of the inspiration his wife and children had given him in matters of religion. As a result, the shy man who had been a Protestant all his life had a request to make when death drew near. He wished to become a Catholic. Shortly after his baptism he died.

mother's financial burden, Joel became an apprentice at thirteen to Joseph Addison Turner, a wealthy planter of Turnwold, Georgia, who owned and published the *Countryman*. The print shop was an open cabin in the woods of Turner's plantation. Joel lived with the Turner family and had free access to his employer's library of a thousand volumes. The cultured Southern gentleman supervised the boy's reading and writing with the results that may be seen in the work Harris later produced. One hundred slaves lived happily on the plantation, and from them Harris learned something about each phase of a bondsman's life. He listened particularly to the songs in the slave quarters and to the tales of the old Negroes. Before the Civil War put an abrupt end to this period of his life, Harris had acquired a vast store of knowledge from this little world in the deep South.

KATE O'FLAHERTY CHOPIN

After 1888 the quality of the local-color story declined. Many writers who had not the genius for the art were attracted to the field because of the popularity of short fiction. Stories of local color were still in demand, but they were of a decidedly inferior type to the fiction of George Washington Cable and Bret Harte. One writer, Kate O'Flaherty Chopin (1851-1904), by reason of her natural ability and art, wrote distinguished short stories picturing the Creoles and the Acadians in Louisiana. Kate Chopin stands out today as a master in technique, portraying realistically and emotionally the exterior and interior life of an emotional and sincere people.

Uncle Remus tells animal stories

After the war Harris worked on several southern newspapers and was editor of the *Atlanta Constitution* for twenty years. It was to fill the columns of this paper that he began writing his animal stories in Negro dialect. The tales were not original but were recast from folk stories he had heard from plantation Negroes. In creating the character of Uncle Remus, the narrator of these tales, he drew from his reminiscences of old Negroes he had known. Uncle Remus represents the

Born in St. Louis, Kate O'Flaherty was the daughter of prosperous parents who belonged to the aristocracy of the city. After her graduation from the Convent of the Sacred Heart, Kate was for two years one of the belles of St. Louis. At nineteen she married Oscar Chopin of New Orleans, who held a prominent position in the cotton industry. Kate Chopin avoided as much as possible the formal Creole society of New Orleans, preferring association with genuine people to the shams and conventions of an artificial social life. In 1821 the Chopins and their four children moved to Cloutiersville, a remote little French village in Louisiana, not far from Natchitoches, the oldest town in the state. Here Kate Chopin entered wholeheartedly into the joys and sorrows of the simple, pious folk. After the sudden death of her husband, she returned to St. Louis and at the suggestion of friends began writing stories about the people whom she had known and loved in Louisiana. Her reputation and power as a writer of fiction grew steadily until she published a realistic novel which shocked the sensibilities of her readers. The unfavorable reception of this work dampened her creative spirit. For a time, too, she gave up the practice of her religious duties. She returned to the Church some time before her death.

As a short-story writer Kate Chopin has an assured place in the history of American fiction. Her stories are more than sketches in local color picturing the swamps and bayous of central Louisiana. She understands the heart of the Creoles and 'Cajuns. She strikes a universal note in her emotional and dramatic presentation of love, hate, and fear. In *Bayou Folk* (1894) she gives a graceful, deft, sympathetic, and truthful picture of all classes of Creoles. *A Night in Acadie* (1897) is more elevated in spirit, revealing the intellectual and spiritual forces which motivated the lives and prompted the self-sacrifice and devotedness of the Acadians of Louisiana. Kate Chopin was always a Catholic at heart and never more so than in her beautiful and truthful portrayal of the simple folk of Natchitoches Parish. In her clear conception of character, restrained intensity, and skillful handling of plot, she has a place in the first ranks of American short-story writers.

JOHN LANCASTER SPALDING

"If the saints knew how to make themselves amiable, they could conquer the world," wrote Bishop John Lancaster Spalding (1840-1916). The wide range of Spalding's influence is proof of his own lovableness and refinement. The same graciousness which marked the bearing of the noted clergyman characterized the essays in which he blends sound principles of education with exact Christian ideals. Bishop Spalding's social graces followed naturally from a family which traced its ancestry to Edward III of England and from the private schooling which his cultured mother gave him in their Kentucky home until he was twelve. After the young man's study abroad and his ordination in Louvain in 1863, his theological gifts were soon recognized. He resigned prominent ecclesiastical posts, however, to organize the first Negro parish in Louisville, Kentucky. During the years which followed his consecration as Bishop of Peoria, Illinois, in 1877, John Lancaster Spalding's interest in social problems led to constant activity on behalf of the immigrant and the laborer.

Probably Spalding's greatest effort as an educator began at the Second Plenary Council at Baltimore, in 1866 when he urged the establishment of a center of Catholic culture — "a home of both ancient wisdom and modern learning." The dream continued through the years, as he wrote and spoke for it. It reached a degree of realization when, as speaker at the laying of the cornerstone of the Catholic University in 1888, he acknowledged Mary Gwendolen Caldwell's generous gift of $300,000, a sum which he had been instrumental in procuring. Despite his influence in the foundation of the Catholic University, he declined the honor of being its first rector. A paralytic stroke in 1908 caused him to resign his bishopric. He was then made a titular archbishop.

As an essayist John Lancaster Spalding writes with rhetorical elegance and uniform excellence. The titles of his dozen books — *Education and the Higher Life, Means and Ends of Education, Thoughts and Theories of Life and Education*, for example — indicate his insistence on the importance of true ideals. His numerous essays on education clarify the position of the Church, the family, and the state in relationship to the instruction and training of the child.

© Brown Brothers

John Gilmary Shea

JOHN GILMARY SHEA

John Dawson Shea (1824-1892), the son of an Irish immigrant, was a shy, studious boy with great interest in books, birds, and flowers. As a young man he learned Spanish while working in the countinghouse of a Spanish merchant in New York. In 1848 young Shea entered the Society of Jesus but after four years' preparation for religious life decided that it was his vocation to serve the Church as a layman. As a Jesuit novice he exchanged his middle name for Gilmary, or Mary's servant, which he retained throughout his life.

John Gilmary Shea became the leading historian of the Catholic Church in America, and his contribution in the field remains indispensable today. The scattered materials of American Catholic history were practically untouched when he entered the field. No effort had been made to preserve and organize the original documents of Catholic history in our country — the priceless letters, diaries, and other manuscripts relating to Catholic beginnings. Shea had not only the historian's accuracy and impartiality but a positive genius for ferreting out original sources. Scarcely a fact concerning American Catholicism that had been discovered up to his time remained unknown to him. By means of his indefatigable research and voluminous writings, Shea actually saved our Catholic past from oblivion. At the same time, he made Catholic America conscious of its history and prepared for the scholarly research of such writers as Peter Guilday in the twentieth century. To his regret, much that he wished to do could not be completed in his lifetime. Since his Catholic historical writings in no way provided for the support of his family, he was constantly constrained to translate foreign works, compile textbooks, write popular works, and serve as the anonymous editor of secular magazines. Even these various enterprises left him so near to poverty that at times only his pride kept him from calling on friends for financial aid.

During his busy lifetime Shea produced or edited approximately one hundred works. Of his own original writings, which grew out of the vast information he had amassed, the greatest is his *History of the Catholic Church* (1886-1892) in four volumes. No historian can ever write of the early years of the Church in America without consulting these volumes; no later work has ever replaced them. In his concern for accuracy, Shea made no attempt to achieve dramatic effect, but the story he unfolded has in itself an epic strength.

SARAH ORNE JEWETT

When Sarah Orne Jewett (1849-1909) realized that sophisticated summer boarders were laughing at her beloved Maine village folk, she determined to write of her fellow New Englanders so that all the world might know the worth of their lives of magnificent simplicity and granite-like integrity. In her short stories, among the best American local-color fiction has to offer, Miss Jewett portrayed the people she had known intimately from her childhood. Her father had been a physician, and she had been his constant companion on his professional calls. Her tales treat of the sufferings that make up the common lot of humankind — poverty, loneliness, old age — and they often reveal the fierce struggle caused by family pride and the individual's effort to preserve personal independence. Gently, tenderly, even pathetically, she tells stories of brave souls who endure in a region from which the vigor of youth has slipped away. Although Miss Jewett did not close her eyes to the bleakness and drabness of their existence, she wrote of them in such a way that her readers might open their eyes to the splendors of sacrifice and renunciation that form an integral part of their everyday life.

Sarah Orne Jewett's stories first appeared in the *Atlantic Monthly* but were later collected into volumes. *Deephaven* (1877), *A White Heron and Other Stories* (1886), and *The Country of the Pointed Firs* (1896) contain the best of her work.

MARY E. WILKINS FREEMAN

Mary E. Wilkins Freeman (1852-1930) was born in a small Massachusetts town and grew to know intimately the village and farm life of New England, where lingered a decayed Puritanism. When her father died after many years of invalidism, the young woman learned the meaning of hardship and privation. She had done some creative work for her own amusement in earlier years, but now she set about to earn a living by her writing. Her work slowly gained recognition.

Mary E. Wilkins was not content to present only the external aspects of the eastern Massachusetts region. She laid bare the somber soul of New England as well. Her stories grew out of sharp insight into the lives of the men and women around her. She looked deeply and unflinchingly into the world she knew and with objective analysis pointed out the blighting, narrowing effects of the rigid Puritan system. In her stories of embittered spinsters and deserted wives, she painted realistic pictures of joyless existence. The heroism of her characters was impressive but no more gracious than the granite hills of New England.

Like Sarah Orne Jewett, Mary E. Wilkins Freeman did her best work in the short story form. *A Humble Romance* (1887), *A New England Nun* (1891), and *Pembroke* (1894) are volumes which contain her best stories. After her marriage in 1902, Mrs. Freeman left New England and lived in Metuchen, New Jersey.

CHARLES WARREN STODDARD

Charles Warren Stoddard (1843-1909), an adventurer and romanticist, fell under the influence of Robert Louis Stevenson and Bret Harte, whom he met in San Francisco. Stevenson gave Stoddard an interest in the South Seas, and Harte directed his literary ambitions into the channel of local color. Trips to Hawaii and Tahiti inspired his warm-colored sketches of tropical life in the Pacific. His *South Sea Idylls* (1873), picturesque stories carefully written and manifesting sympathy towards the people of the distant land, have become an American classic.

Although Stoddard was born in Rochester, New York, his family moved to California during the gold rush of 1849. Stoddard attended the University of California and became foreign correspondent for a San Francisco paper. His position gave him opportunity for travel in Europe and in the Pacific. In 1867 Stoddard became a Catholic and from that time forward threw the force of his energetic spirit into promoting the cause of the Church. For several years he taught at the University of Notre Dame and later at the Catholic University of America.

Stoddard achieved distinction in various literary fields: the essay, biography, travel, and fiction. His works appeared in the best secular and Catholic periodicals of the country. William Dean Howells includes Stoddard's "A Prodigal in Tahiti" in his anthology of representative short stories. Joe Lahaina, the youth doomed to the leper colony of Molokai, makes an indelible impression on the reader. Stoddard's *Lepers of Molokai* called attention to the heroic work of Father Damien and prompted Robert Louis Stevenson's defense of the self-sacrificing missionary.

FRANCIS MARION CRAWFORD

Both the life and works of Francis Marion Crawford (1854-1909) reveal a man who was a citizen of the world. The son of an American sculptor living in Italy, the boy spent his first twelve years amid the luxurious and cultured surroundings of a Roman estate. He studied under private tutors and traveled extensively on the Continent before he was sent to school in Concord, New Hampshire, at thirteen. Crawford received his higher education at universities in England, Germany, and Italy. In order to complete the study of Sanskrit, begun at Rome, he went in 1879 to India, where he became a newspaper correspondent. Although Rome had long before made him a Catholic at heart, he entered the Church while in India. Returning to the United States, he published his first novel in 1882 and thereafter produced one or two books a year during the remainder of his life. After his marriage in 1885, he resided at his estate in Sorrento, Italy, leaving only to travel.

Crawford brought a rich fund of experience and a many-sided personality to the creation of his forty-five romantic novels. The pageantry of far lands and strange people parades across the pages of his writings. Nowhere can the reader more easily learn to know his international neighbors than in Crawford's works, which furnish an American view of the nationalities of the civilized world. The novels of Roman setting are Crawford's best. His Catholicity enables him to understand the Latin temperament and the religious views of Italians and Spaniards better than any other writer in the English language. Sympathy and conviction mark his portrayal of Roman society in the *Saracinesca* series, which follows a modern family of the nobility through several generations. In his theory of the novel Crawford held that a work of fiction is a little "pocket theater" with no other purpose than to entertain. On the stage of his novels he placed, against picturesque backgrounds, vivid characters whose dialogue sparkles. His story never fails in rapid movement. Tense dramatic situations, such as feuds, murder, jealousy, violent temptation, duels, and blackmail maintain suspense to the end. In presenting both the good and evil in life, Crawford held high moral standards. He does not portray sin as excusable or ultimately desirable but shows its consequences and the power of grace in the renunciation of evil. His novels are notable for upholding the sanctity of marriage and the ideal of womanhood.

MARY AGNES TINCKER

Mary Agnes Tincker (1831-1907), a convert, born in Ellsworth, Maine, won distinction for two of her novels, *The House of Yorke* and *Grapes and Thorns*. Her best short stories, set against a New England background, picture the reaction of the somber provincial Puritan to the joyous ideals of Catholicism. *Autumn Leaves* (1898) is a representative volume.

FRANCES CHRISTINE TIERNAN

Frances Christine Tiernan (1846-1920), who wrote fiction under the pen name, Christian Reid, was a romanticist by nature. A daughter of the old South, she was the first Catholic novelist of North Carolina. After her reception into the Church she turned to the apostolate of exemplifying Catholic teachings in fiction. The background of her writing reflects not only her native environment but also her travels in the West Indies, France, and Italy. During a period of nearly fifty years, Christian Reid turned out more than forty novels, numerous short stories, poems, and several dramas. The more important of her novels fall into two classes: novels of character, such as *A Heart of Steel* (1883), and melodramatic tales in which plot dominates, as in *The Man of the Family* (1896). Christian Reid's early short stories are artificial. The characters are mere types, and the plots are exaggerated. Her stories of Mexican life, however, show a marked improvement in the treatment of dramatic situations and character. In them lovely descriptions of the southern lands blend with spiritual beauty. Throughout her works Christian Reid sought to promote Catholic ideals by writing of men and women as they should be, rather than as they are.

Whoopee Ti Yi Yo, Git Along Little Dogies

Among our native American songs none are more picturesque than the cowboy ballads. These songs tell of the long treks of drovers and herds from the ranges to the cattle markets. They reflect the cowboy's loneliness, his longing for home, and his love for the open spaces.

As I walked out one morning for pleasure,
I spied a cowpuncher[1] all riding alone;
His hat was throwed back and his spurs was a-jingling,
As he approached me a-singin' this song.

    Whoopee ti yi yo, git along little dogies,[2]
    It's your misfortune, and none of my own,
    Whoopee ti yi yo, git along little dogies,
    For you know Wyoming will be your new home.

Early in the spring we round up the dogies,
Mark and brand and bob off their tails;
Round up our horses, load up the chuck wagon,[3]
Then throw the dogies upon the trail.

It's whooping and yelling and driving the dogies;
Oh, how I wish you would go on;
It's whooping and punching and go on little dogies,
For you know Wyoming will be your new home.

Some boys goes up the trail for pleasure,
But that's where you get it most awfully wrong;
For you haven't any idea the trouble they give us
While we go driving them all along.

When the night comes on and we hold them on the
    bedground,
These little dogies that roll on so slow;
Roll up the herd and cut out the strays,[4]
And roll the little dogies that never rolled before.

Your mother she was raised way down in Texas,
Where the jimson weed and sandburs grow;
Now we'll fill you up on prickly pear[5] and cholla[6]
Till you are ready for the trail to Idaho.

Oh you'll be soup for Uncle Sam's Injuns;
"It's beef, heap beef," I hear them cry.
Git along, git along, git along little dogies,
You're going to be beef steers by and by.

VIEWING THE AUTHOR'S IDEAS

1. What hardships of cowboy life are depicted in the poem? How does it reflect the attitude of the herders toward their rough life?
2. What destinations of the dogies are mentioned in this poem?
3. How is the Texas range depicted in the seventh stanza? Is the picture exaggerated?
4. What reference to the Indian reservations is made in lines 29-30?

EVALUATING HIS MANNER OF EXPRESSION

What characteristics of the cowboy's speech are exemplified in the ballad?

---

[1] *cowpuncher*, a cowboy.
[2] *dogies*, yearling calves.
[3] *chuck wagon*, a wagon with provisions and a stove, used on ranches.

[4] *strays*, animals that have left their own herd or enclosure.
[5] *prickly pear*, a species of cactus with pear-shaped leaves.
[6] *cholla*, cactus.

A Home on the Range

This ballad reveals the cowboy's love of the breezy expanses and the freedom of the ranges.

Oh, give me a home where the buffalo roam,
Where the deer and the antelope play,
Where seldom is heard a discouraging word
And the skies are not cloudy all day.

Home, home on the range,
Where the deer and the antelope play;
Where seldom is heard a discouraging word
And the skies are not cloudy all day.

Where the air is so pure, the zephyrs so free,
The breezes so balmy and light,

That I would not exchange my home on the range
For all of the cities so bright.

The red man was pressed from this part of the West,
He's likely no more to return
To the banks of Red River where seldom if ever
Their flickering campfires burn.

How often at night when the heavens are bright
With the light from the glittering stars,
Have I stood here amazed and asked as I gazed
If their glory exceeds that of ours.

Oh, I love these wild flowers in this dear land of ours,
The curlew I love to hear scream,
And I love the white rocks and the antelope flocks
That graze on the mountaintops green.

Oh, give me a land where the bright diamond sand
Flows leisurely down the stream;
Where the graceful white swan goes gliding along
Like a maid in a heavenly dream.

Then I would not exchange my home on the range,
Where the deer and the antelope play;
Where seldom is heard a discouraging word
And the skies are not cloudy all day.

Home, home on the range,
Where the deer and the antelope play;
Where seldom is heard a discouraging word
And the skies are not cloudy all day.

VIEWING THE AUTHOR'S IDEAS

1. Make a list of all the aspects of the cattle range which appeal to this cowboy. How does his attitude differ from that of the singer in "Whoopee Ti Yi Yo, Git Along Little Dogies"?
2. To what period does the ballad singer refer in the fourth stanza?

EVALUATING HIS MANNER OF EXPRESSION

1. How can you account for the popularity of "Home on the Range"?
2. Find lines that show the cowboy's love of beauty.
3. What is the effect of the internal rhyme?

Swing Low, Sweet Chariot

The Negro has given to the spiritual a distinctive folk quality. Melody more than words voices the religious aspirations of the race. This spiritual expresses the Negro's longing for the happiness of heaven.

I looked over Jordan and what did I see,
　Comin' for to carry me home?
A band of angels comin' afteh me,
　Comin' for to carry me home.

Chorus

Swing low, sweet chariot,
　Comin' for to carry me home;
Swing low, sweet chariot,
　Comin' for to carry me home.

If you git there befo' I do,
　Comin' for to carry me home,

Just tell 'em I'm a comin' too,
　Comin' for to carry me home.

Chorus

Swing low, sweet chariot,
　Comin' for to carry me home;
Swing low, sweet chariot,
　Comin' for to carry me home.

Chorus

I ain't been to heb'n, but I been tol',
　Comin' for to carry me home,
De streets in heb'n am paved wid gol',
　Comin' for to carry me home.

Swing low, sweet chariot,
　Comin' for to carry me home;
Swing low, sweet chariot,
　Comin' for to carry me home.

I'm sometimes up and sometimes down,
 Comin' for to carry me home;
But still my soul am hebenly-boun',
 Comin' for to carry me home.

Chorus

Swing low, sweet chariot,
 Comin' for to carry me home;
Swing low, sweet chariot,
 Comin' for to carry me home.

VIEWING THE AUTHOR'S IDEAS

1. What attitude toward death is expressed in the song? Upon what Biblical quotation is the conception of heaven based? Why should this view of paradise have appealed to the Negro?

2. How does this spiritual reflect the Negro's longing for a better life? Discuss the implications in the first line of the last stanza.

EVALUATING HIS MANNER OF EXPRESSION

1. What part does repetition play in the song? Indicate the rhyme scheme.

2. In what respects does the song resemble the folk ballad?

Goin' to Walk All Ovah God's Heb'n

Simple ideas and homely expressions give this spiritual the impromptu quality of the early Negro folk hymn. Piece by piece the singer puts on his heavenly robes until he is completely garbed for the angelic choir.

I got a robe, you got a robe,
 All God's chillun got a robe;
When I git to heb'n goin' to put on my robe,
 Goin' to shout all ovah God's heb'n.
 Heb'n, heb'n, ev'rybody talk about heb'n
  ain't goin' dere, 5
 Heb'n, heb'n, goin' to shout all ovah God's heb'n.

I got-a shoes, you got-a shoes,
 All God's chillun got-a shoes;
When I git to heb'n goin' to put on my shoes,
 Goin' to walk all ovah God's heb'n. 10
 Heb'n, heb'n, ev'rybody talk about heb'n
  ain't goin' dere,
 Heb'n, heb'n, goin' to walk all ovah God's heb'n.

I got-a wings, you got-a wings
 All God's chillun got-a wings;
When I git to heb'n goin' to put on my wings, 15
 Goin' to fly all ovah God's heb'n.
 Heb'n, heb'n, ev'rybody talk about heb'n
  ain't goin' dere,
 Heb'n, heb'n, goin' to fly all ovah God's heb'n.

I got-a crown, you got-a crown
 All God's chillun got-a crown; 20
When I git to heb'n goin' to put on my crown,
 Goin' to walk all ovah God's heb'n.
 Heb'n, heb'n, ev'rybody talk about heb'n
  ain't goin' dere,
 Heb'n, heb'n, goin' to walk all ovah God's heb'n.

I got-a harp, you got-a harp, 25
 All God's chillun got-a harp;
When I git to heb'n goin' to play on my harp,
 Goin' to play all ovah God's heb'n.
 Heb'n, heb'n, ev'rybody talk about heb'n
  ain't goin' dere,
 Heb'n, heb'n, goin' to play all ovah God's heb'n. 30

VIEWING THE AUTHOR'S IDEAS

1. What kind of heaven does the singer picture? How do these desires suggest the deprivations of the Negro in this world?

2. Which lines indicate that the Negro expects to be free from the restrictions of race and color in heaven. How does the song reveal his assurance of salvation?

3. In what way does this spiritual reveal the childlike simplicity and directness of the Negro?

EVALUATING HIS MANNER OF EXPRESSION

1. Show that the spiritual is built almost entirely upon repetition and refrain.

2. In your opinion are the details of the hymn arranged in order of climax?
3. Why would the melody be of special importance in this spiritual?

Go Down, Moses

As the Negro sang this plaintive hymn, he saw in Israel's bondage a symbol of his own slavery.

When Israel was in Egypt's land,
  Let my people go;
Oppressed so hard dey could not stand,
  Let my people go.

Chorus

Go down, Moses,
  'Way down in Egypt land,
Tell ole Pharaoh,
  Let my people go.

Thus spoke the Lord, bold Moses said,
  Let my people go;
If not, I'll smite your first-born dead,
  Let my people go.

Chorus

Go down, Moses,
  'Way down in Egypt land,

Tell ole Pharaoh,
  Let my people go.

No more shall dey in bondage toil,
  Let my people go;
Let dem come out wid Egypt's spoil,
  Let my people go.

Chorus

Go down, Moses,
  'Way down in Egypt land,
Tell ole Pharaoh,
  Let my people go.

VIEWING THE AUTHOR'S IDEAS

1. How does the song reflect the hardships of slavery?
2. Tell the story of Moses upon which the spiritual is based.

EVALUATING HIS MANNER OF EXPRESSION

What is the effect of the refrain? Point out instances of the lack of coherence in the song.

I Hear America Singing

Walt Whitman

It is good to sing at one's work. The swing of a song drives out fatigue and makes the heaviest task go forward. America — the land of opportunity, the land of industry — sends up a song from forge and forest. The poet hears the chorus through which, like an accompaniment, throbs the rhythm of work itself.

I HEAR America singing, the varied carols I hear,
Those of mechanics, each one singing his as it
  should be, blithe and strong,

The carpenter singing his as he measures his plank or
  beam,
The mason singing his as he makes ready for work or
  leaves off work,
The boatman singing what belongs to him in his boat,
  the deck hand singing on the steamboat deck,   5
The shoemaker singing as he sits on his bench, the
  hatter singing as he stands,
The woodcutter's song, the plowboy's on his way in
  the morning, or at noon intermission or at sundown,

The delicious singing of the mother, or of the young
   wife at work, or of the girl sewing or washing,
Each singing what belongs to him or her and to none
   else,
The day what belongs to the day — at night the party
   of young fellows, robust, friendly,   10
Singing with open mouths their strong melodious
   songs.

VIEWING THE AUTHOR'S IDEAS

1. Aspiring to sing of the average American citizen, Whitman was one of the first writers to see industry as a fitting subject for poetry. In what way does the poem show his broad contacts with life?

2. How do the singers in Whitman's poem express the spirit of democracy? Which classes of people has the poet omitted from his pageant of American life? What may have been the reason for this omission?

3. Discuss Whitman's concept of the dignity of labor.

EVALUATING HIS MANNER OF EXPRESSION

1. In place of the conventional metrical patterns, Whitman uses the phrase as a unit of rhythm. Point out several phrases each of which constitutes such a unit.

2. Find instances in which the use of parallel structure emphasizes the repetition of the idea. What key words have been repeated?

When I Heard the Learn'd Astronomer

Walt Whitman

Having had only a meager schooling himself and having learned much through broad experience, Whitman retained a certain distrust for formal learning. So strong was his feeling for nature that he seemed to resent any attempts at mathematical conclusions concerning its phenomena.

WHEN I heard the learn'd astronomer,
   When the proofs, the figures, were ranged in
      columns before me,
When I was shown the charts and diagrams, to add,
      divide, and measure them,
When I, sitting, heard the astronomer where he
      lectured with much applause in the lecture
      room,
How soon, unaccountable, I became tired and sick,
Till rising and gliding out, I wander'd off by myself
In the mystical moist night air, and from time to time
Looked up in perfect silence at the stars.

VIEWING THE AUTHOR'S IDEAS

1. What facts indicate that the lecture was actually a good one? What was the poet's attitude towards the scientist? Why was this reaction unaccountable?

2. Had the astronomer known the poet's evaluation of the lecture, what might have been his estimate of Whitman? What is the basic difference between the viewpoint of the scientist and the poet?

3. What could the poet learn by looking up in silence at the stars? What knowledge would he be unable to obtain by his own meditation? Mention the merits of learning by experience; of learning from books and other men.

4. How do some of the best modern lectures in planetaria and observatories combine the scientist's exactitude and the poet's awareness of beauty?

EVALUATING HIS MANNER OF EXPRESSION

1. What unpoetic words and phrases have been used to describe the lecture? Contrast this language with the beauty of expression in the last three lines. What deliberate effects have been achieved by the transition from scientific to poetic terms?

2. How do the lines of the poem vary in length? Show that they have been divided according to the beginning and ending of a thought. How many sentences does the poem contain?

Aboard at a Ship's Helm

Walt Whitman

As a background for his analogy Whitman dramatically pictures a critical incident in a young helmsman's voyage. Then briefly suggesting the likeness of the ship's course to the journey of the soul, the poet breaks off with abruptness that indicates the awesome thoughts evoked by his comparison.

ABOARD at a ship's helm,
A young steersman steering with care.

Through fog on a seacoast dolefully ringing,
An ocean bell[1] — O a warning bell, rock'd by the waves.
O you give good notice indeed, you bell by the sea reefs ringing,   5
Ringing, ringing, to warn the ship from its wreck-place.

For as on the alert, O steersman, you mind the loud admonition,
The bows turn, the freighted ship tacking speeds away under her gray sails,

The beautiful and noble ship with all her precious wealth speeds away gayly and safe.

But O the ship, the immortal ship! O ship aboard the ship!   10
Ship of the body, ship of the soul, voyaging, voyaging, voyaging.

[1] *ocean bell*, a buoy with a bell which is rung by the action of the waves to warn ships of shoals and rocks.

VIEWING THE AUTHOR'S IDEAS

1. In what danger does the young helmsman find his ship? What is an ocean bell? How does the poet portray the tense moment when the ship turns from the dangerous rocks?

2. What is meant by "the ship aboard the ship"? In the voyage of the soul what represents the "wreck-place"; the "warning bell"; the "precious wealth" of the ship?

EVALUATING HIS MANNER OF EXPRESSION

1. Part of Whitman's realism consists in an attempt to reproduce the free, flowing, patterns in nature. The rise and fall of his cadences may be compared to larger and lesser waves lapping against the shore. Read aloud phrases in which you see the similarity of his rhythm to the surge of the ocean waters.

A Noiseless, Patient Spider

Walt Whitman

Although Whitman here reveals the reflective quality of his poetry, he shows his limitations as a philosopher. Like the spider spinning its filament, he too would fling a gossamer thread as a bridge to his final destiny. To him life is a joyous, stupendous force, but he is obviously uncertain about its direction.

A NOISELESS, patient spider,
I mark'd where on a little promontory it stood isolated,
Marked how to explore the vacant vast surrounding,

It launched forth filament,[1] filament, filament, out of itself,
Ever unreeling them, ever tirelessly speeding them.   5

And you, O my soul, where you stand,
Surrounded, detached, in measureless oceans of space,
Ceaselessly musing, venturing, throwing, seeking the spheres to connect them,
Till the bridge you will need be formed, till the ductile[2] anchor hold,

[1] *filament*, thread.
[2] *ductile*, capable of being drawn out into a thread or wire.

Till the gossamer[3] thread you fling catch somewhere,
     O my soul.   10

VIEWING THE AUTHOR'S IDEAS

1. What action of the spider did the poet contemplate? What comparison did he make with the soul of man?

2. In what sense is the soul of man surrounded in "measureless oceans of space"? How is it at the same time detached? What two spheres does man's soul seek to connect?

3. Quote the words which indicate the poet's uncertainty of his final destination. How do reason and Divine Revelation

[3] *gossamer*, light and flimsy.

disprove Whitman's suggestion that each man must find his own solution to the problem of human destiny? What "bridge" has God actually given man?

EVALUATING HIS MANNER OF EXPRESSION

1. Within a sentence Whitman achieves rhythm by varying short with long phrases. Show the variety of phrase length within one of the sentences. Find parallels in the poem.

2. Which of these poetic elements can you find in the four poems by Whitman: rhythm, rhyme, metrical foot, alliteration, repetition, assonance, onomatopoeia, regular length of line?

Jim Bludso

(Of the Prairie Belle)

John Hay

In the days when steamboats thronged the Mississippi, Oliver Fairchild, engineer of the steamboat Fashion, *heroically saved the ship's crew in the manner described in this ballad. The poet calls the hero Jim Bludso and chooses the name* Prairie Belle *as a picturesque title for the ship. The ballad depicts the dialect and the rough manner of the Pikes, so called because of their residence in the two Pike Counties, one in Missouri and the other in Illinois. These river-faring men became the chief figures in the local-color literature of the upper Mississippi valley. This poem is one of the six* Pike County Ballads *in which Hay recreated the characters and scenes of his boyhood.*

WALL, no! I can't tell whar he lives,
     Because he don't live, you see;
Leastways, he's got out of the habit
     Of livin' like you and me.
Whar have you been for the last three year   5
     That you haven't heard folks tell
How Jimmy Bludso passed in his checks,
     The night of the *Prairie Belle?*

He weren't no saint — them engineers
     Is all pretty much alike—   10
One wife in Natchez-under-the-Hill[1]
     And another here in Pike.

[1] *Natchez-under-the-Hill*, Natchez, Mississippi, a river town famous in steamboat days.

A keerless man in his talk was Jim,
     And an awkward man in a row,
But he never flunked, and he never lied —   15
     I reckon he never knowed how.

And this was all the religion he had—
     To treat his engine well;
Never be passed on the river;
     To mind the pilot's bell;   20
And if ever the *Prairie Belle* took fire—
     A thousand times he swore,
He'd hold her nozzle agin the bank
     Till the last soul got ashore.

All boats has their day on the Mississip,   25
     And her day come at last —
The *Movastar* was a better boat,
     But the *Belle* she *wouldn't* be passed.
And so she come tarin' along that night —
     The oldest craft on the line —   30
With a Negro squat on her safety valve
     And her furnace crammed, rosin and pine.

The fire bust out as she clared the bar
     And burnt a hole in the night,
And quick as flash she turned, and made   35
     For that wilier bank on the right.

There was running and cursing, but Jim yelled out
  Over all the infernal roar,
"I'll hold her nozzle agin the bank
  Till the last galoot's[2] ashore."   40

Through the hot, black breath of the burnin' boat
  Jim Bludso's voice was heard,
And they all had trust in his cussedness
  And knowed he would keep his word.
And sure's you're born, they all got off   45
  Afore the smokestacks fell —
And Bludso's ghost went up alone
  In the smoke of the *Prairie Belle*.

He weren't no saint — but at jedgment
  I'd run my chances with Jim,   50
'Longside of some pious gentlemen
  That wouldn't shook hands with him.
He seen his duty, a dead sure thing —
  And went for it thar and then:
And Christ ain't a goin' to be too hard   55
  On a man that died for men.

[2] *galoot* [slang], an uncouth, awkward fellow.

VIEWING THE AUTHOR'S IDEAS

1. To whom does the narrator tell the story? How does he reveal the fact that Jim Bludso is dead? What lines indicate that the loss of the *Prairie Belle* was a favorite topic of conversation?

2. What good qualities did Jim's rough nature conceal? How did devotion to duty make his work similar to a religion?

3. What details prepare the reader for the losing race with the *Movastar*? How does Jim's previous resolution to save the crew excuse his rashness? Why did the Negro sit on the safety valve?

4. How does the vivid description of the burning boat heighten the impression of Jim's heroism? Why is no credit given to the pilot for helping to save the crew?

5. Upon what does the speaker base his assurance of Jim's salvation? Compare his statements in the last stanza with *John* 15:13 and I *Peter* 4:8.

EVALUATING HIS MANNER OF EXPRESSION

1. What is the setting of the incident? Compare the dialect with that in Lowell's "The Courtin'." How does "Jim Bludso" resemble other ballads you have read?

2. Explain the homely metaphors in lines 7 and 24. What mental pictures are suggested by the vivid imagery in lines 34 and 41?

Kit Carson's Ride

Joaquin Miller

Against the broad, free background of the Texas prairies, the author projects this spirited tale. Although the incident cannot be verified as authentic, it is daring enough to have occurred in the life of the famous scout and Indian fighter, Kit Carson. A stirring example of the local-color poetry of the West, the ballad helped win for its author the title of the "Oregon Byron." The poet uses a setting that was familiar to him as pony-express messenger and frontiersman.

ROOM! room to turn round in, to breathe and be
    free,
To grow to be a giant, to sail as at sea
With the speed of the wind on a steed with his mane
To the wind, without pathway or route or a rein.

Room! room to be free where the white border'd sea   5
Blows a kiss to a brother as boundless as he;
Where the buffalo come like a cloud on the plain,
Pouring on like the tide of a storm-driven main,
And the lodge of the hunter to friend or to foe
Offers rest; and unquestion'd you come or you go.   10
My plains of America! Seas of wild lands!
From a land in the seas in a raiment of foam,
That has reached to a stranger the welcome of home,[1]
I turn to you, lean to you, lift you my hands.

  Run? Run? See this flank, sir, and I do love
        him so!   15

[1] *From a land . . . welcome of home.* Miller's writing had met with an enthusiastic reception in England, where the poet was living at the time he wrote this ballad.

But he's blind, badger blind.[2] Whoa, Pache,[3] boy
     whoa,
No, you wouldn't believe it to look at his eyes,
But he's blind, badger blind, and it happen'd this wise:

"We lay in the grass and the sunburnt clover
That spread on the ground like a great brown cover   20
Northward and southward, and west and away
To the Brazos,[4] where our lodges lay,
One broad and unbroken level of brown.
We were waiting the curtains of night to come down
To cover us trio and conceal our flight   25
With my brown bride, won from an Indian town
That lay in the rear the full ride of a night.

"We lounged in the grass — her eyes were in mine,
And her hands on my knee, and her hair was as wine
In its wealth and its flood, pouring on and all over   30
Her bosom wine red, and press'd never by one.
Her touch was as warm as the tinge of the clover
Burnt brown as it reach'd to the kiss of the sun.
Her words they were low as the lute-throated dove
And as laden with love as the heart when it beats   35
In its hot, eager answer to earliest love,
Or the bee hurried home by its burthen of sweets.

"We lay low in the grass on the broad plain levels,
Old Revels[5] and I, and my stolen brown bride;
'Forty full miles if a foot, and the devils   40
Of red Comanches[6] are hot on the track
When once they strike it. Let the sun go down
Soon, very soon,' muttered bearded old Revels
As he peer'd at the sun, lying low on his back,
Holding fast to his lasso. Then he jerk'd
     at his steed   45
And he sprang to his feet, and glanced swiftly around,
And then dropp'd as if shot, with an ear to the
     ground;
Then again to his feet, and to me, to my bride,
While his eyes were like flame, his face like a shroud,
His form like a king, and his beard like a cloud,   50

And his voice loud and shrill, as both trumpet and
     reed —
'Pull, pull in your lassoes, and bridle to steed,
And speed you if ever for life you would speed.
Aye, ride for your lives, for your lives you must ride!
For the plain is aflame, the prairie on fire,   55
And the feet of wild horses hard flying before
I heard like a sea breaking high on the shore,
While the buffalo come like a surge of the sea,
Driven far by the flame, driving fast on the three
As a hurricane comes, crushing palms in his ire.'   60

"We drew in the lassoes, seized the saddle and rein,
Threw them on, cinched them on, cinched them over
     again,
And again drew the girth; and spring we to horse,
With head to Brazos, with a sound in the air
Like the surge of a sea, with a flash in the eye,   65
From that red wall of flame reaching up to the sky —
A red wall of flame and a black rolling sea
Rushing fast upon us, as the wind sweeping free
And afar from the desert blown hollow and hoarse.

"Not a word, not a wail from a lip was let fall,   70
We broke not a whisper, we breathed not a prayer.
There was work to be done, there was death in the air,
And the chance was as one to a thousand for all.

"Twenty miles! . . . thirty miles . . . a dim distant
     speck . . .
Then a long reaching line and the Brazos in sight!   75
And I rose in my seat with a shout of delight.
I stood in my stirrup, and looked to my right —
But Revels was gone; I glanced by my shoulder
And saw his horse stagger; I saw his head drooping
Hard down on his breast and his naked breast
     stooping   80
Low down to the mane, as so swifter and bolder
Ran reaching out for us the red-footed fire.
He rode neck to neck with a buffalo bull
That made the earth shake where he came in his
     course,
The monarch of millions, with shaggy mane full   85
Of smoke and of dust, and it shook with desire
Of battle, with rage and with bellowings hoarse.
His keen, crooked horns, through the storm of his
     mane,

---

[2] *badger blind*, an allusion to the phrase "as blind as a badger." The fact that the burrowing animal sees well at night but only with difficulty during the day has given rise to this expression.

[3] *Pache*. The name of the horse was probably derived from Apache, a warlike tribe of Southwest Indians.

[4] *Brazos*, a river in Texas.

[5] *Old Revels*, a friend and fellow scout of Kit Carson.

[6] *Comanches*, fierce Indians.

Like black lances lifted and lifted again;
And I looked but this once, for the fire licked
    through,   90
And Revels was gone, as we rode two and two.

  "I look'd to my left then — and nose, neck, and
    shoulder
Sank slowly, sank surely, till back to my thighs,
And up through the black blowing veil of her hair
Did beam full in mine her two marvelous eyes,   95
With a longing and love yet a look of despair
And of pity for me, as she felt the smoke fold her,
And flames leaping far for her glorious hair.
Her sinking horse falter'd, plunged, fell and was gone
As I reached through the flame and I bore her
    still on.   100
On! into the Brazos, she, Pache, and I —
Poor, burnt, blinded Pache. I love him . . .
That's why."

VIEWING THE AUTHOR'S IDEAS

1. How does the lyric introduction reflect the spirit of the West? What lines show the westerner's hospitality; the similarity between the sea and western plains of America? How had England given Miller "the welcome of home"?

What lines show his admiration of England and his homesickness for America?

2. The poem takes the form of a monologue. Who is the speaker? What question does he answer? Is the poem a story of Kit Carson; of an Indian bride; or of the horse Pache? Why did the story not begin with the flight from the camp of the Comanches?

3. How far had the fleeing trio come when the story opens? Why did they ride only at night? What made Revels so anxious for the sun to go down? How did he discover the approaching fire?

4. How does the poet indicate the rapid rate at which the fire traveled? What details heighten the suspense? How does the author achieve his purpose of describing "a prairie fire on the plains, driving buffalo and all other life before it into a river"?

EVALUATING HIS MANNER OF EXPRESSION

1. Find on a map of Texas the place where this incident occurred.

2. Joaquin Miller once wrote, "To me a poem is a picture." How does he subordinate action to description in this poem?

3. Show by comparison with Browning's "How They Brought the Good News from Ghent to Aix" that "Kit Carson's Ride" is imitative in form but original in subject matter. What romantic note adds interest to the ride in the latter poem? How does the rhythm suggest the galloping of the horses?

Columbus

Joaquin Miller

In the indomitable courage of Columbus, Joaquin Miller saw the same spirit that animated the hardy pioneers who unfurled the starlit flag on the shores of the Pacific.

BEHIND him lay the gray Azores,[1]
  Behind the Gates of Hercules;[2]
Before him not the ghost of shores;
  Before him only shoreless seas.
The good mate said: "Now must we pray,   5
  For lo! the very stars are gone.

Brave Adm'r'l, speak, what shall I say?"
  "Why, say: 'Sail on! sail on! and on!'"

"My men grow mutinous day by day;
  My men grow ghastly wan and weak."   10
The stout mate thought of home; a spray
  Of salt wave washed his swarthy cheek.
"What shall I say, brave Adm'r'l, say,
  If we sight nought but seas at dawn?"
"Why, you shall say at break of day: 15
  'Sail on! sail on! sail on! and on!'"

---

[1] *Azores,* an island group in the Atlantic.

[2] *Gates of Hercules,* the Strait of Gibraltar. According to Greek mythology, Hercules tore asunder the two rocky headlands, where the Atlantic meets the Mediterranean.

They sailed and sailed, as winds might blow,
    Until at last the blanched mate said:
"Why, now not even God would know
    Should I and all my men fall dead.   20
These very winds forget their way,
    For God from these dread seas is gone.
Now speak, brave Adm'r'l, speak and say —"
    He said: "Sail on! sail on! and on!"

They sailed. They sailed. Then spake the mate: 25
    "This mad sea shows his teeth tonight.
He curls his lip, he lies in wait
    With lifted teeth as if to bite!
Brave Adm'r'l, say but one good word:
    What shall we do when hope is gone?"   30
The words leapt like a leaping sword:
    "Sail on! sail on! sail on! and on!"

Then, pale and worn, he kept his deck,
    And peered through darkness. Ah, that night
Of all dark nights! And then a speck —   35
    A light! A light! At last a light!
It grew, a starlit flag unfurled!
    It grew to be Time's burst of dawn.

He gained a world; he gave that world
    Its grandest lesson: "On! sail on."   40

VIEWING THE AUTHOR'S IDEAS

1. How is the vast loneliness of mid-ocean suggested in the first four lines? Why does the author begin his narrative at this point? How does he show the weariness and length of the voyage?

2. What spirit animated the mate? How does the author show the courage of Columbus? What contrasting types of character are here illustrated?

3. In view of the motives which Columbus expressed in his letter to Sanchez, what part did faith play in the Admiral's determination? What attitude is expressed in line 31? Why did Columbus remain on deck peering through the darkness on the last night of the voyage?

4. Which lines indicate the Admiral's wonder; his triumph; his gratitude at the discovery of land? Explain the line "It grew, a starlit flag unfurled."

EVALUATING HIS MANNER OF EXPRESSION

Discuss the poet's use of repetition; refrain; dialogue.

The Fool's Prayer

Edward Rowland Sill

Because the jester of medieval times could cloak his thoughts with humor and mock seriousness, he was, in a sense, the only man at court free to speak frankly. When the king in this poem calls for a mock prayer, the fool unexpectedly offers an earnest petition which reveals the follies of the nobles.

THE royal feast was done; the king
    Sought some new sport to banish care,
And to his jester cried: "Sir Fool,
    Kneel down, and make for us a prayer!"

The jester doffed his cap and bells   5
    And stood the mocking court before;
They could not see the bitter smile
    Behind the painted grin he wore.

He bowed his head and bent his knee
    Upon the monarch's silken stool;   10
His pleading voice arose: "O Lord,
    Be merciful to me, a fool!

"No pity, Lord, could change the heart
    From red with wrong to white as wool;
The rod must heal the sin: but Lord,   15
    Be merciful to me, a fool!

" 'Tis not by guilt the onward sweep
    Of truth and right, O Lord, we stay;
'Tis by our follies that so long
    We hold the earth from heaven away.   20

"These clumsy feet, still in the mire,
   Go crushing blossoms without end;
These hard, well-meaning hands we thrust
   Among the heartstrings of a friend.

"The ill-timed truth we might have kept —   25
   Who knows how sharp it pierced and stung?
The word we had not sense to say —
   Who knows how grandly it had rung!

"Our faults no tenderness should ask,
   The chastening stripes must cleanse them all;   30
But for our blunders — oh, in shame
   Before the eyes of Heaven we fall.

"Earth bears no balsam for mistakes;
   Men crown the knave and scourge the tool
That did his will; but Thou, O Lord,   35
   Be merciful to me, a fool!"

The room was hushed; in silence rose
   The king, and sought his gardens cool,
And walked apart, and murmured low,
   "Be merciful to me, a fool!"

VIEWING THE AUTHOR'S IDEAS

1. What lines reveal the jester's attitude towards the court? How does his prayer rebuke the king for his request?

2. According to the poet what is necessary to change the heart from "red with wrong to white as wool"? To what do "the rod" and "the chastening stripes" refer?

3. What follies do "clumsy feet" and "hard, well-meaning hands" commit? Express in your own words the meaning of the seventh stanza.

4. How does history show that "Men crown the knave and scourge the tool that did his will"? What censure of the king is contained in these words? Explain the line "Earth bears no balsam for mistakes."

5. What impression did the fool's prayer make upon the court? What reflections may the king have made as he walked in the garden?

EVALUATING HIS MANNER OF EXPRESSION

1. A single incident is here developed into a brief, dramatic story. What is the opening situation; the climax; the closing scene?

2. Does the fool paint a self-portrait in his prayer, or does he identify himself with those who err foolishly? Does the king belong to any particular period, or is he typical of all times?

To St. Mary Magdalen

Benjamin Dionysius Hill
(Father Edmund of the Heart of Mary, C. P.)

Artists and poets can give the penitent Mary Magdalen no greater crown than the golden aureola of her hair, with which she wiped the feet of Christ.

'MID the white spouses of the Sacred Heart,
   After its Queen, the nearest, dearest thou:
Yet the aureola[1] around thy brow
Is not the virgins' — thine a throne apart.
Nor yet, my Saint, does faith-illumined art   5
   Thy hand with palm of martyrdom endow;

And when thy hair is all it will allow
Of glory to thy head, we do not start.
O more than virgin in thy penitent love!
   And more than martyr in thy passionate woe!   10
   Who knelt not with thee on the gory sod,
How should they now sit throned with thee above?
Or where the crown our worship could bestow
   Like that long gold which wiped the feet of God?

VIEWING THE AUTHOR'S IDEAS

1. What place in heaven does the poet assign to St. Mary Magdalen? What scenes of the Gospel narrative are suggested in line 9; lines 10-11; line 14?

---

[1] *aureola*, in fine art, the halo around the head of a sacred personage; in theology, a celestial crown added to the bliss of heaven to distinguish virgins, martyrs, and Doctors of the Church.

2. Find examples of the "faith-illumined art" in which the saint appears. Compare the ways in which she is portrayed in the various pictures.

Compare the rhyme scheme of this sonnet with that of Longfellow's sonnets from the "Divina Commedia." What question is raised in the first eight lines? How is it answered in the sestet?

A Ballad of Trees and the Master

Sidney Lanier

Lanier's great love for the forest led him to visualize the part which the woodland played at Gethsemane and Calvary. In this unusual but reverent treatment the poet sees the trees as angels ministering to Christ in the Garden of Olives and supporting Him upon the Cross.

INTO the woods my Master went,
Clean forspent,[1] forspent.
Into the woods my Master came,
Forspent with love and shame.
But the olives they were not blind to Him,   5
The little gray leaves were kind to Him:
The thorn tree had a mind to Him
When into the woods He came.

Out of the woods my Master went,
And He was all content.   10
Out of the woods my Master came,
Content with death and shame.
When Death and Shame would woo Him last,
From under the trees they drew Him last:

'Twas on a tree they slew Him — last   15
When out of the woods He came.

[1] *forspent*, utterly exhausted.

1. Why was Our Lord "forspent" when He entered Gethsemane? How were the trees a reproach to the disciples and His enemies?

2. What does the poem reveal concerning Lanier's attitude towards his own suffering? How does it show the author's faith in Christ?

1. The language of the poem is as simple as that of the Gospel narrative. How is the absence of descriptive detail in keeping with the mood of the poem?

2. Restraint in depicting tragedy is one of the qualities of art. How does the second stanza exemplify this quality? What is the effect of the closing lines?

3. How does the rhyme link the two divisions of the poem? What is the effect of the triple rhyme near the end of each stanza?

Tampa Robins

Sidney Lanier

In this lyric Lanier captures the gay laughter, buoyant spirits, and bright movements of the robin as the bird threads the mazes of his orange-tree sky.

THE robin laughed in the orange tree:
"Ho, windy North, a fig for thee;
While breasts are red and wings are bold

And green trees wave us globes of gold,
     Time's scythe shall reap but bliss for me —   5
     Sunlight, song, and the orange tree.

"Burn, golden globes in leafy sky,
My orange planets: crimson I
Will shine and shoot among the spheres

(Blithe meteor that no mortal fears)   10
  And thrid[1] the heavenly orange tree
  With orbits bright of minstrelsy.

"If that I hate wild winter's spite —
The gibbet trees, the world in white,
The sky but gray wind over a grave —   15
Why should I ache, the season's slave?
  I'll sing from the top of the orange tree:
  Gramercy,[2] winter's tyranny.

"I'll south with the sun and keep my clime;
My wing is king of the summer time;   20
My breast to the sun his torch shall hold;
And I'll call down through the green and gold:
  Time, take thy scythe, reap bliss for me,
  Bestir thee under the orange tree."

[1] *thrid*, thread.
[2] *gramercy*, an archaic exclamation, expressing thanks, surprise, or sudden emotion.

VIEWING THE AUTHOR'S IDEAS

1. By what striking details does the poet create the warm, colorful atmosphere of the South? In what words and phrases does he depict the movements of the robin; his color; his song?

2. Trace the comparison of the robin to a meteor flashing among the orange planets.

3. In the third stanza, how does the poet suggest the cruelty of the Northern winter? In what words does the robin bid a defiant farewell to winter's tyranny?

EVALUATING HIS MANNER OF EXPRESSION

1. What vowel sounds are repeated with melodious effect in lines 5-6; in line 14? Find examples in which rhyme, alliteration, and assonance contribute to the harmony of sound.

2. Discuss the poet's use of contrast. List the most striking metaphors.

The Marshes of Glynn

Sidney Lanier

The orchestral harmonies of this ode convey the beauty of dim live oaks and the luxuriant sea marshes of Georgia. Written only a few years before death ended Lanier's struggle against disease and poverty, the poem is an exultant song of trust in Divine Providence. Variety of rhythm and harmony of tone make this poem a symphony in words. The ode is one of six "Hymns to the Marshes" which Lanier proposed to write.

GLOOMS of the live oaks, beautiful-braided and
      woven
With intricate shades of the vines that myriad-cloven
  Clamber the forks of the multiform boughs —
      Emerald twilights —
      Virginal shy lights   5
Wrought of the leaves to allure to the whisper of vows,
When lovers pace timidly down through the green
      colonnades
Of the dim sweet woods, of the dear dark woods,
  Of the heavenly woods and glades,
That run to the radiant marginal sand beach
      within   10
  The wide sea marshes of Glynn —

Beautiful glooms, soft dusks in the noonday fire —
Wildwood privacies, closets of lone desire,
Chamber from chamber parted with wavering arras[1]
      of leaves —
Cells for the passionate pleasure of prayer to the soul
      that grieves,   15
Pure with a sense of the passing of saints through the
      wood,
Cool for the dutiful weighing of ill with good —
O braided dusks of the oak and woven shades of the
      vine,
While the riotous noonday sun of the June day long
      did shine,
Ye held me fast in your heart and I held you fast in
      mine;   20
But now when the noon is no more, and riot is rest,
And the sun is await at the ponderous gate of the
      West,
And the slant yellow beam down the wood aisle doth
      seem

[1] *arras*, a rich fabric with inwoven figures or scenes.

Like a lane into heaven that leads from a dream —
Aye, now, when my soul all day hath drunken the soul
      of the oak,   25
And my heart is at ease from men, and the wearisome
      sound of the stroke
  Of the scythe of time and the trowel[2] of trade is low,
   And belief overmasters doubt, and I know that I
      know,
    And my spirit is grown to a lordly great compass
      within,
That the length and the breadth and the sweep of the
      marshes of Glynn   30
Will work me no fear like the fear they have wrought
      me of yore
When length was fatigue, and when breadth was but
      bitterness sore,
And when terror and shrinking and dreary unnamable
      pain
Drew over me out of the merciless miles of the plain —

Oh, now, unafraid, I am fain to face   35
    The vast sweet visage of space!
To the edge of the wood I am drawn, I am drawn,
Where the gray beach glimmering runs, as a belt of
      the dawn,
    For a mete[3] and a mark
      To the forest dark —   40
    So:
Affable live oak, leaning low —
Thus — with your favor — soft, with a reverent hand,
(Not lightly touching your person, Lord of the land!)
Bending your beauty aside, with a step I stand   45
On the firm-packed sand,
      Free
By a world of marsh that borders a world of sea.
Sinuous southward and sinuous northward the
      shimmering band
  Of the sand beach fastens the fringe of the marsh to
      the folds of the land.   50
Inward and outward to northward and southward the
      beach lines linger and curl
As a silver-wrought garment that clings to and follows
      the firm sweet limbs of a girl.

[2] *trowel*, a tool used by bricklayers and plasterers to smooth or shape plastic material.
[3] *mete*, boundary.

Vanishing, swerving, evermore curving again into
      sight,
Softly the sand beach wavers away to a dim gray
      looping of light.
And what if behind me to westward the wall of the
      woods stands high?   55
The world lies east: how ample, the marsh and the sea
      and the sky!
A league and a league of marsh grass, waist-high broad
      in the blade,
Green, and all of a height, and unflecked with a light
      or a shade,
Stretch leisurely off, in a pleasant plain,
To the terminal blue of the main.   60

Oh, what is abroad in the marsh and the terminal sea?
    Somehow my soul seems suddenly free
From the weighing of fate and the sad discussion of
      sin,
By the length and the breadth and the sweep of the
      marshes of Glynn.

Ye marshes, how candid and simple and nothing-
      witholding and free   65
Ye publish yourselves to the sky and offer yourselves to
      the sea!
Tolerant plains, that suffer the sea and the rains and
      the sun,
Ye spread and span like the catholic man who hath
      mightily won
God out of knowledge and good out of infinite pain
And sight out of blindness and purity out of
      a stain.   70

As the marsh hen secretly builds on the watery sod,
Behold I will build me a nest on the greatness of God;
I will fly in the greatness of God as the marsh hen flies
In the freedom that fills all the space 'twixt the marsh
      and the skies;
By so many roots as the marsh grass sends
      in the sod,   75
I will heartily lay me ahold on the greatness of God.
Oh, like to the greatness of God is the greatness
      within
The range of the marshes, the liberal marshes of
      Glynn.

And the sea lends large, as the marsh; lo, out of his
      plenty the sea
Pours fast; full soon the time of the flood tide
        must be.   80
Look how the grace of the sea doth go
About and about through the intricate channels that
      flow
        Here and there,
          Everywhere,
Till his waters have flooded the uttermost creeks and
      the low-lying lanes,   85
And the marsh is meshed with a million veins,
That like as with rosy and silvery essences flow
In the rose-and-silver evening glow.
        Farewell, my lord Sun!
The creeks overflow; a thousand rivulets run   90
'Twixt the roots of the sod; the blades of the marsh
      grass stir;
Passeth a hurrying sound of wings that westward
      whirr;
Passeth, and all is still; and the currents cease to run;
And the sea and the marsh are one.
How still the plains of the waters be!   95
The tide is in his ecstasy.
The tide is at his highest height;
        And it is night.
And now from the Vast of the Lord will the waters of
      sleep
Roll in on the souls of men,   100
But who will reveal to our waking ken
The forms that swim and the shapes that creep
      Under the waters of sleep?
And I would I could know what swimmeth below
      when the tide comes in
On the length and the breadth of the marvelous
      marshes of Glynn.   105

VIEWING THE AUTHOR'S IDEAS

1. Lines 1-40 give the poet's impression of a day spent in the deep live-oak woods that slope down to the marshes of Glynn. The Southern live oak is an evergreen tree, growing to immense size, with wide-spreading gnarled and twisted branches. Spanish moss hangs like gray curtains from the trees. In the opening lines how does the poet describe the shadows cast by the trees? What further details complete the picture of the cool woodland? How does the poet describe the quiet approach of evening; the soothing effect of the woods? Upon what aspects of modern life does he comment in lines 26-28?

2. Lines 41-78 describe how the poet leaves the woods and, standing on the shimmering sand beach, views the grassy marshes stretching away to the blue sea. What line gives his first impression of the marshes? How does he describe the marsh grass? What is implied in lines 68-70? What aspects of the marshes inspire Lanier's hymn of trust in God in lines 71-78?

3. In lines 79-105 the poet views the tide rising until the marsh and sea are one, and night falls over the scene. What pictures of the gradually rising tide does the author present? How does he indicate the moment of the sun's setting? What sounds break the stillness? How does he indicate the solemn moment when the tide becomes full? What thoughts does the rising tide suggest? Explain lines 101-103.

EVALUATING HIS MANNER OF EXPRESSION

1. An *ode* is a poem elevated in thought and tone. It is generally written in complex stanza forms with lines of varying length. Count the number of lines in each stanza. Note the varying length of lines in any one stanza.

2. In *The Science of English Verse* Lanier states that orchestral effects in poetry may be achieved by "the deft marshaling of consonants and vowels" against "the infantry tramp of rhythm." What pattern of end rhyme is used most frequently in this poem? Find variations from this pattern. List examples of internal rhyme; of feminine rhyme. Point out lines in which alliteration and assonance are most pronounced.

3. Find variations from the anapaestic rhythm in the poem. The length of lines ranges from dimeter in line 39 to hexameter in line 26. Quote lines that vary from these patterns.

4. What lines do you consider most picturesque? List all the expressions used to describe the woodland glades. What romantic attitude toward nature is illustrated in line 20 and in lines 41-43? Select three examples of apostrophe.

5. What meter is used in the poem?

The V-a-s-e

James Jeffrey Roche

Universality of style makes it difficult to determine the locality of people. In speech, however, section differs from section, as this little poem shows. As you read, be sure to note the sound of the rhyme, for in the rhyme scheme lies the key to the various pronunciations of the word vase.

FROM the madding[1] crowd they stand apart,
   The maidens four and the work of art;

And none might tell from sight alone
In which had culture ripest grown —

The Gotham[2] Million fair to see,   5
The Philadelphia Pedigree,

The Boston mind of azure hue,
Or the soulful soul from Kalamazoo —

For all loved art in a seemly way,
With an earnest soul and a capital A.   10

Long they worshiped; but no one broke
The sacred stillness, until up spoke

The Western one from the nameless place
Who blushing said: "What a lovely vase!"

Over three faces a sad smile flew,   15
And they edged away from Kalamazoo.

But Gotham's haughty soul was stirred
To crush the stranger with one small word.

Deftly hiding reproof in praise,
She cries: " 'Tis, indeed, a lovely vaze!"   20

But brief her unworthy triumph when
The lofty one from the home of Penn,

With the consciousness of two grandpapas,
Exclaims: "It is quite a lovely vahs!"

And glances round with an anxious thrill   25
Awaiting the word of Beacon Hill.[3]

But the Boston maid smiles courteously
And gently murmurs: "Oh, pardon me!

"I did not catch your remark, because
I was so entranced with that charming vaws!"   30

VIEWING THE AUTHOR'S IDEAS

1. From what places were the four young women? What was their attitude towards art? Select the line that shows the beauty of the vase held them spellbound.

2. What resulted when the first girl broke the stillness? How did the girl from New York reprove her? Show that the girl from Philadelphia was direct. What qualities did the Boston girl show? How did she reveal them?

3. Look up the pronunciation of vase in a dictionary; decide which girl's pronunciation was correct.

EVALUATING HIS MANNER OF EXPRESSION

1. Name two things that the poet satirizes.

2. For which maid does the poet seem to show preference? Prove your answer by referring to specific words and phrases.

3. A characteristic of each of the girls indicates the locality from which she comes. State the section of the country suggested by the following descriptive phrases: (a) stressing distinguished ancestry; (b) emphasizing intellectual activity; (c) having pretentions to wisdom; (d) expressing deep feeling.

---

[1] *madding*, wild; furious.

[2] *Gotham*, a popular name given to New York City by Irving because the inhabitants were such wiseacres.

[3] *Beacon Hill*, a section of Boston which represents wealth and culture.

When the Frost Is on the Punkin

James Whitcomb Riley

In his homely Hoosier dialect, an Indiana farmer expresses the sense of well-being which autumn brings. He enjoys the sight of his ample harvest and finds time to rest after the work and heat of the summer. Riley's verse abounds in pictures of the simple, wholehearted people of the Indiana farmlands.

WHEN the frost is on the punkin and the fodder's in the shock,
 And you hear the kyouck and gobble of the struttin' turkey cock,
And the clackin' of the guineys, and the cluckin' of the hens,
And the rooster's hallylooer as he tiptoes on the fence;
Oh, it's then's the time a feller is a-feelin' at his best,   5
With the risin' sun to greet him from a night of peaceful rest,
As he leaves the house, bareheaded, and goes out to feed the stock,
When the frost is on the punkin and the fodder's in the shock.

They's something kindo' hartylike about the atmusfere
When the heat of summer's over and the coolin' fall is here —   10
Of course we miss the flowers, and the blossums on the trees,
And the mumble of the hummin'birds and buzzin' of the bees
But the air's so appetizin'; and the landscape through the haze
Of a crisp and sunny morning of the airly autumn days
Is a pictur' that no painter has the colorin' to mock —   15
When the frost is on the punkin and the fodder's in the shock.

The husky, rusty russel of the tossels of the corn,
And the raspin' of the tangled leaves, as golden as the morn;
The stubble' in the furries[1] — kindo' lonesomelike, but still
A-preachin' sermuns to us of the barns they growed to fill;   20
The strawstack in the medder, and the reaper in the shed;
The hosses in theyr stalls below — the clover overhead!
Oh, it sets my hart a-clickin' like the tickin' of a clock,
When the frost is on the punkin and the fodder's in the shock!

Then your apples all is gethered, and the ones a feller keeps   25
Is poured around the cellar floor in red and yeller heaps;
And your cider makin's over, and your wimmern folks is through
With their mince and apple butter, and theyr souse[2] and sausage, too!

I don't know how to tell it — but ef sich a thing could be
As the Angels wantin' boardin', and they'd call around on *me* —   30
I'd want to 'commodate 'em — all the whole indurin' flock —
When the frost is on the punkin and the fodder's in the shock!

---

[1] *furries*, furrows.
[2] *souse*, pickled pigs' feet or other food steeped in vinegar.

VIEWING THE AUTHOR'S IDEAS

1. How does the poet suggest that autumn is the most pleasant time of year for the farmer? List details which show that the year's work is over. How is the plentiful harvest indicated? What attitude of the farmer is expressed in lines 19-20 and 29-31?

2. How would the farmer's observations in spring and summer differ from those of autumn? What do you believe would be the farmer's impressions during spring and summer?

3. What activities of farm women does the poet mention in lines 27-28? How do they differ from those of women in cities?

4. Compare the farmer's day in autumn with that of the factory worker; of a business executive. What solutions for some of the problems of city life are suggested by the poem?

5. Why are some farmers in America not so happy and prosperous as the one in this poem? Suggest remedies for some of the unsatisfactory conditions of farm life.

EVALUATING HIS MANNER OF EXPRESSION

1. What is the mood of the poem? How does the refrain emphasize the coolness and leisure of the autumn days? What is the effect of the swinging rhythm; of the Hoosier dialect?

2. List the words and phrases which depict the sounds of the farmyard and fields; the colors of autumn; the zest of cool days.

3. Account for the popularity of this poem.

Little Boy Blue

Eugene Field

Most of Eugene Field's verse was written for his newspaper column in the Chicago Daily News. *This touching elegy on the death of a child has attained great popularity.*

THE little toy dog is covered with dust,
  But sturdy and stanch he stands;
The little toy soldier is red with rust,
  And his musket molds in his hands.
Time was when the little toy dog was new,   5
  And the soldier was passing fair;
And that was the time when our Little Boy Blue
  Kissed them and put them there.

"Now don't you go till I come," he said,
  "And don't you make any noise!"   10
So, toddling off to his trundle bed,
  He dreamt of the pretty toys;
And, as he was dreaming, an angel song
  Awakened our Little Boy Blue —

Oh! the years are many, the years are long,   15
  But the little toy friends are true!

Aye, faithful to Little Boy Blue they stand,
  Each in the same old place,
Awaiting the touch of a little hand,
  The smile of a little face;   20
And they wonder, as waiting the long years through
  In the dust of that little chair,
What has become of our Little Boy Blue,
  Since he kissed them and put them there.

VIEWING THE AUTHOR'S IDEAS

1. What memories of the little boy do the toys recall? How does the verse show the parents' devotion and grief?

2. What beautiful thought is expressed in lines 13-14?

EVALUATING HIS MANNER OF EXPRESSION

1. What is an elegy? Which lines express the deepest pathos?

2. Account for the poem's wide appeal.

Overflow

John Bannister Tabb

This poem conveys the sustained rapture and intensity of the thrush's song. Recurrence of rhyme and variation in the length of the lines suggest the soaring quality of the bird's melody.

Hush!
With sudden gush
As from a fountain, sings in yonder bush
The Hermit Thrush.

Hark!   5
Did ever Lark
With swifter scintillations fling the spark
That fires the dark?

Again,
Like April rain   10
Of mist and sunshine mingled, moves the strain
O'er hill and plain.

Strong
As love, O Song,
In flame or torrent sweep through Life along,   15
O'er grief and wrong.

VIEWING THE AUTHOR'S IDEAS

1. What experience does this poem recapture for the poet?

2. Why does the poet compare the song of the thrush with that of the lark?

3. In what way is the song of the lark like April rain; like love?

EVALUATING HIS MANNER OF EXPRESSION

1. Repeat aloud the rhymes in each of the four stanzas. In what way does the variation of sound effects suggest the ascending notes of the thrush's song?

2. Which lines are alliterative? What is the effect of varying the length of the lines? Select three similes.

The Peak

John Bannister Tabb

A friendship, a treasured experience, an ideal — any of these may be the snowcapped peak of which the poet speaks.

As on some solitary height
Abides, in summer's fierce despite,
Snow blossom that no sun can blight,
 No frost can kill;

So, in my soul — all else below
To change succumbing — stands aglow
One wreath of immemorial snow,
 Unscattered still.

VIEWING THE AUTHOR'S IDEAS

1. What is the subject of the verb *abides?*
2. Explain the meaning of *despite.*
3. What two things are compared in this poem?
4. Why is the wreath in the poet's soul still unscattered?

EVALUATING HIS MANNER OF EXPRESSION

What is the rhyme scheme? How do the short lines contribute to the effectiveness of the poem?

Christic and the Pagan

John Bannister Tabb

Through nature worship and symbolic rites the pagan sought union with divinity. In this poem Christ assures the seeker that He is the End of his search.

I HAD no god but these,
  The sacerdotal trees,
And they uplifted me.
  "I hung upon a tree."

The sun and moon I saw,   5
  With reverential awe
Subdues me day and night,
  "I am the perfect Light."

Within a lifeless stone —
  All other gods unknown,   10
I sought divinity.
  "The Cornerstone am I."

For sacrificial feast
  I slaughtered man and beast
Each recompense to gain.   15
  "So I, a Lamb, was slain.

Yea; such My hungering grace
  That wherever My face
Is hidden, none may grope
  Beyond eternal Hope."   20

VIEWING THE AUTHOR'S IDEAS

1. What pagan beliefs and practices are mentioned in this poem? How does Christ fulfill the pagan's desire for knowledge and worship of God?
2. Explain the meaning of the last stanza.

EVALUATING HIS MANNER OF EXPRESSION

1. Explain the metaphor in the second line.
2. Find three Biblical allusions in the answers of our Saviour.

Quatrains

John Bannister Tabb

Father Tabb's power to condense vast thoughts into a short space gives force to his poetry. These quatrains exemplify his speed, strength, and intensity.

Father Damien

O GOD, the cleanest offering
  Of tainted earth below,
Unblushing to Thy feet we bring —
  "A leper white as snow!"

A Phonograph

Hark! What his fellow warblers heard
  And uttered in the light,
Their phonograph, the mockingbird,
  Repeats to them at night.

Deep unto Deep

Where limpid waters lie between
There only heaven to heaven is seen;
Where flows the tide of mutual tears,
There only heart to heart appears.

The Dandelion

With locks of gold today,
Tomorrow silver gray,
Then blossom-bald. Behold,
O Man, thy fortune told!

The Assumption

Nor Bethlehem nor Nazareth,
    Apart from Mary's care;
Nor Heaven itself a home for Him
    Were not His mother there!

Helplessness

In patience as in labor must thou be
    A follower of Me,
Whose hands and feet, when most I wrought for thee,
    Were nailed unto a tree.

VIEWING THE AUTHOR'S IDEAS

Father Damien
    Explain this tribute to the leper priest.
The Phonograph
    1. Suggest other titles for this poem.
    2. Why is the mockingbird like a phonograph?

Deep unto Deep
    1. What things are compared in these four lines?
    2. Explain the meaning of the third line.
The Dandelion
    What characteristic of man does the poet stress?
The Assumption
    1. According to the poet, why was Mary taken up into Heaven? Discuss the clever use of the word *home* in the third line.
    2. How does the poem suggest Mary's place in the Church?
Helplessness
    1. Explain the meaning of the word *patience.*
    2. When did Christ do His greatest work for man?

EVALUATING HIS MANNER OF EXPRESSION

1. What gives these quatrains their gemlike brilliance? Select three metaphors. In which quatrains does the poet employ a conceit?

2. Compare these quatrains with the brief lyrics of Emily Dickinson. What qualities of Father Tabb's short poems do you like?

I Taste a Liquor Never Brewed

Emily Dickinson

In playful imagery the poet here expresses her exhilaration over the splendor of Nature.

I TASTE a liquor never brewed,
    From tankards scooped in pearl;
Not all the vats upon the Rhine
    Yield such an alcohol!

Inebriate of air am I,   5
    And debauchee of dew,
Reeling, through endless summer days,
    From inns of molten blue.

When landlords turn the drunken bee
    Out of the foxglove's door,   10
When butterflies renounce their drams,
    I shall but drink the more!

Till seraphs swing their snowy hats,
    And saints to windows run,
To see the little tippler   15
    Leaning against the sun!

VIEWING THE AUTHOR'S IDEAS

1. What is the liquor that stimulates the poet?
2. Who is the "little tippler"?

EVALUATING HER MANNER OF EXPRESSION

In what respects is the imagery whimsical? Which words are unusual? Explain the metaphors in lines 2, 8, and 9-10.

I Never Saw a Moor

Emily Dickinson

To Emily Dickinson belief in the Unseen is as easy to accept as the loveliness of distant places on which she has not gazed.

I NEVER saw a moor,
  I never saw the sea;
Yet know I how the heather looks,
  And what a wave must be.

I never spoke with God,
  Nor visited in heaven;
Yet certain am I of the spot
  As if the chart were given.

VIEWING THE AUTHOR'S IDEAS

1. What gives the poet such insight as is here expressed? How much information about the world do we daily accept on human faith?
2. Does the poem embody a thought or represent an event? Explain.

EVALUATING HER MANNER OF EXPRESSION

1. How is the second stanza an application of the first?
2. Does simplicity of form add to, or detract from, the poem?

He Ate and Drank the Precious Words

Emily Dickinson

Here the poet shows how a book can bring a message to the heart, freeing the spirit from its narrow boundaries.

HE ate and drank the precious words,
  His spirit grew robust;
He knew no more that he was poor,
Nor that his frame was dust.
He danced along the dingy days,
And this bequest of wings
Was but a book. What liberty
A loosened spirit brings!

VIEWING THE AUTHOR'S IDEAS

1. To what does this poem refer?
2. How can reading make one free in spirit?
3. What other benefits come with reading?

EVALUATING HER MANNER OF EXPRESSION

1. Explain the unusual figure of speech in this poem. Is line 6 consistent with the rest of the imagery?
2. Select a line that is especially alliterative.

Much Madness Is Divinest Sense

Emily Dickinson

Possessed of keen penetration, the poet is often able to see sanity in eccentric actions, and folly in meaningless customs.

MUCH madness is divinest sense
  To a discerning eye;
Much sense the starkest madness.
'Tis the majority

In this, as all, prevails.
Assent, and you are sane;
Demur — you're straightway dangerous
And handled with a chain.

VIEWING THE AUTHOR'S IDEAS

Should one always be out of step with others? How is one to decide?

It Dropped So Low in My Regard

Emily Dickinson

The poet compares her disillusionment about a friendship or a cherished idea to the shattering of a piece of china.

IT DROPPED so low in my regard
I heard it hit the ground,
And go to pieces on the stones
  At bottom of my mind;

Yet blamed the fate that fractured, less
  Than I reviled myself
For entertaining plated wares
  Upon my silver shelf.

VIEWING THE AUTHOR'S IDEAS

1. What was the "it" that dropped so far in the poet's regard?
2. Whom does the poet blame for her unpleasant experience?

EVALUATING HER MANNER OF EXPRESSION

1. In the first stanza to what does the poet compare the thing shattered? Explain the figure in the last two lines. Is the metaphor mixed?
2. What does the lyric reveal about the poet's own character and personality?
3. Suggest a one-word title for the poem.

To Make a Prairie

Emily Dickinson

This recipe will be successful if, like Emily Dickinson, you have a poet's mind.

TO MAKE a prairie it takes a clover and one bee —
  One clover, and a bee,
And reverie.
The reverie alone will do
If bees are few.

VIEWING THE AUTHOR'S IDEAS

1. What is the thought in this poem? What is meant by reverie?
2. List the things that a clover and a bee might suggest to the imagination.

EVALUATING HER MANNER OF EXPRESSION

Does the poem gain or lose by its brevity? Compare the treatment of the bee with that in Emerson's "The Humblebee." Discuss the poet's use of repetition and rhyme.

Success Is Counted Sweetest

Emily Dickinson

This lyric may suggest to you a new measuring stick for the joys of success.

SUCCESS is counted sweetest
By those who ne'er succeed.
To comprehend a nectar
Requires the sorest need.

Not one of all the purple host   5
Who took the flag today,
Can tell the definition,
So plain, of victory,
As he defeated, dying,
On whose forbidden ear   10
The distant strains of triumph
Break, agonizing clear.

VIEWING THE AUTHOR'S IDEAS

Do you agree with the first statement in the poem? Defend your answer. What examples does the poet give to prove her surprising statement? What is the meaning of *forbidden* in line 10?

EVALUATING HER MANNER OF EXPRESSION

1. Does thought or feeling predominate in this poem?
2. In what line does the poet fail to use an expected rhyme?

Lincoln, the Man of the People

Edwin Markham

Markham's love of social justice is reflected in this tribute to the man who wrote the "declaration of independence" for American Negroes. The poem was ranked above all other poetic tributes to Lincoln when it was chosen to be read at the dedication of the Lincoln Memorial in 1922.

When the Norn Mother[1] saw the Whirlwind Hour[2]
Greatening and darkening as it hurried on,
She left the Heaven of Heroes and came down
To make a man to meet the mortal need.
She took the tried clay of the common road —   5
Clay warm yet with the genial heat of earth,
Dashed through it all a strain of prophecy,
Tempered the heap with thrill of human tears,
Then mixed a laughter with the serious stuff.
Into the shape she breathed a flame to light   10
That tender, tragic, ever-changing face;
And laid on him a sense of Mystic Powers,
Moving — all hushed — behind the mortal veil.
Here was a man to hold against the world,
A man to match the mountains and the sea.   15
The color of the ground was in him, the red earth,
The smack and tang of elemental things;
The rectitude and patience of the cliff,
The good will of the rain that loves all leaves,
The friendly welcome of the wayside well,   20
The courage of the bird that dares the sea,
The gladness of the wind that shakes the corn,
The pity of the snow that hides all scars,
The secrecy of streams that make their way

Under the mountain to the rifted rock,   25
The tolerance and equity of light
That gives as freely to the shrinking flower
As to the great oak flaring to the wind —
To the grave's low hill as to the Matterhorn[3]
That shoulders out the sky. Sprung from the West,   30
He drank the valorous youth of a new world.
The strength of virgin forests braced his mind,

The hush of spacious prairies stilled his soul,
His words were oaks in acorns; and his thoughts
Were roots that firmly gripped the granite truth.   35

Up from log cabin to the Capitol,
One fire was on his spirit, one resolve —
To send the keen ax to the root of wrong,
Clearing a free way for the feet of God,
The eyes of conscience testing every stroke,   40
To make his deed the measure of a man.
He built the rail pile as he built the State,
Pouring his rugged strength through every blow;
The grip that swung the ax in Illinois
Was on the pen that set a people free.   45

So came the Captain with the mighty heart;
And when the judgment thunders split the house,
Wrenching the rafters from their ancient rest,
He held the ridgepole up, and spiked again
The rafters of the home. He held his place —   50
Held the long purpose like a growing tree —
Held on through blame and faltered not at praise —
Towering in calm roughhewn sublimity.

[1] *Norn Mother*, in Scandinavian folklore, a mighty being who ruled over the fates of men.

[2] *Whirlwind Hour*, the approaching Civil War.

[3] *Matterhorn*, a famous peak in the Alps between Italy and Switzerland.

And when he fell in whirlwind, he went down
As when a lordly cedar, green with boughs,   55
Goes down with a great shout upon the hills,
And leaves a lonesome place against the sky.

VIEWING THE AUTHOR'S IDEAS

1. What mortal need of his country did Lincoln meet? On what occasion in our history did another great man meet a similar crisis?

2. What characteristics of Lincoln are shown in lines 6-9? Which line describes the face of Lincoln? What is implied in lines 14-15? List all the qualities of Lincoln suggested in the second stanza.

3. What wrong did Lincoln resolve to right? Which lines allude to his rise from obscurity to eminence? Quote the passage from the *Declaration of Independence* which was Lincoln's principle in "setting a people free."

4. What is implied in the expression "When the judgment thunders split the house"? Compare this statement with the fifth paragraph of Lincoln's *Second Inaugural Address.* Explain lines 49-50 of the poem.

5. What lines describe the death of Lincoln? Why will Lincoln's name always be revered by the people?

EVALUATING HIS MANNER OF EXPRESSION

1. Discuss the fitness of the poet's use of blank verse.

2. Which lines contain vivid imagery? Why is the Homeric simile in lines 54-57 effective?

3. How does the poem show the author's intense desire for social justice?

Tennessee's Partner

Bret Harte

Bret Harte's portrayal of life in the western mining camps extended the frontiers of the American short story. This vivid narrative depicts the recklessness and lawlessness which followed the gold rush. Isolation from home ties, from the aids of religion and the restraints of law resulted in a feverish chaotic society, which Harte was quick to recognize as a rich source of literary material. Here, as in many of his stories, he develops his principal characters through the use of moral contrast. He places debased persons in critical situations which call forth an unexpected display of good qualities or heroism. Although the story is plainly an attempt at realism, it portrays the evasion of truth and reality which is sometimes a characteristic of the romantic mind.

I DO NOT think that we ever knew his real name. Our ignorance of it certainly never gave us any social inconvenience, for at Sandy Bar in 1854 most men were christened anew. Sometimes these appellatives were derived from some distinctiveness of dress, as in the case of "Dungaree Jack"; or from some peculiarity of habit, as shown in "Saleratus[1] Bill," so called from an undue proportion of that chemical in his daily bread; or from some unlucky slip, as exhibited in "The Iron Pirate," a mild, inoffensive man, who earned that baleful title by his unfortunate mispronunciation of the term "iron pyrites."[2] Perhaps this may have been the beginning of a rude heraldry; but I am constrained to think that it was because a man's real name in that day rested solely upon his own unsupported statement. "Call yourself Clifford, do you?" said Boston, addressing a timid newcomer with infinite scorn; "hell is full of such Cliffords!" He then introduced the unfortunate man, whose name happened to be really Clifford, as "Jaybird Charley"—an unhallowed inspiration of the moment that clung to him ever after.

But to return to Tennessee's Partner, whom we never knew by any other than this relative title. That he had ever existed as a separate and distinct individuality we only learned later. It seems that in 1853 he left Poker Flat to go to San Francisco, ostensibly to procure a wife. He never got any farther than Stockton. At that place he was attracted by a young person who waited upon the table at the hotel where he took his meals. One morning he said something to her which caused her to smile not unkindly, to somewhat coquettishly

---

[1] *saleratus,* baking soda.

[2] *iron pyrites,* a common mineral, pale brass-yellow in color; fool's gold.

break a plate of toast over his upturned, serious, simple face, and to retreat to the kitchen. He followed her and emerged a few moments later, covered with more toast and victory. That day week they were married by a justice of the peace and returned to Poker Flat. I am aware that something more might be made of this episode, but I prefer to tell it as it was current at Sandy Bar — in the gulches and bar-rooms — where all sentiment was modified by a strong sense of humor.

Of their married felicity but little is known, perhaps for the reason that Tennessee, then living with his partner, one day took occasion to say something to the bride on his own account, at which, it is said, she smiled not unkindly and chastely retreated — this time as far as Marysville, where Tennessee followed her, and where they went to housekeeping without the aid of a justice of the peace. Tennessee's Partner took the loss of his wife simply and seriously, as was his fashion. But to everybody's surprise, when Tennessee one day returned from Marysville without his partner's wife—she having smiled and retreated with somebody else—Tennessee's Partner was the first man to shake his hand and greet him with affection. The boys who had gathered in the canyon to see the shooting were naturally indignant. Their indignation might have found vent in sarcasm but for a certain look in Tennessee's Partner's eye that indicated a lack of humorous appreciation. In fact, he was a grave man with a steady application to practical detail which was unpleasant in a difficulty.

Meanwhile a popular feeling against Tennessee had grown up on the Bar. He was known to be a gambler; he was suspected to be a thief. In these suspicions Tennessee's Partner was equally compromised; his continued intimacy with Tennessee after the affair above quoted could only be accounted for on the hypothesis of a copartnership of crime. At last Tennessee's guilt became flagrant. One day he overtook a stranger on his way to Red Dog. The stranger afterward related that Tennessee beguiled the time with interesting anecdote and reminiscence but illogically concluded the interview in the following words: "And now, young man, I'll trouble you for your knife, your pistols, and your money. You see your weepings may get you into trouble at Red Dog, and your money's temptation to the evilly disposed. I think you said your address was San Francisco. I shall endeavor to call." It may be stated

here that Tennessee had a fine flow of humor, which no business preoccupation could wholly subdue.

This exploit was his last. Red Dog and Sandy Bar made common cause against the highwayman. Tennessee was hunted in very much the same fashion as his prototype, the grizzly. As the toils closed around him, he made a desperate rush through the Bar, emptying his revolver at the crowd before the Arcade Saloon, and so on up Grizzly Canyon; but at its farther extremity he was stopped by a small man on a gray horse. The men looked at each other a moment in silence. Both were fearless, both self-possessed and independent, and both types of a civilization that in the seventeenth century would have been called heroic, but in the nineteenth simply "reckless."

"What have you got there? — I call," said Tennessee quietly.

"Two bowers and an ace," said the stranger as quietly, showing two revolvers and a bowie knife.

"That takes me," returned Tennessee; and, with this gambler's epigram, he threw away his useless pistol and rode back with his captor.

It was a warm night. The cool breeze which usually sprang up with the going down of the sun behind the chaparral[3]-crested mountain was that evening withheld from Sandy Bar. The little canyon was stifling with heated resinous odors, and the decaying driftwood on the Bar sent forth faint, sickening exhalations. The feverishness of day and its fierce passions still filled the camp. Lights moved restlessly along the bank of the river, striking no answering reflection from its tawny current. Against the blackness of the pines the windows of the old loft above the express office stood out staringly bright; and through their curtainless panes the loungers below could see the forms of those who were even then deciding the fate of Tennessee. And above all this, etched on the dark firmament, rose the Sierra, remote and passionless, crowned with remoter passionless stars.

The trial of Tennessee was conducted as fairly as was consistent with a judge and jury who felt themselves to some extent obliged to justify in their verdict the previous irregularities of arrest and indictment. The law of Sandy Bar was implacable but not vengeful. The excitement and personal feeling of the chase were over;

---

[3] *chaparral,* an impenetrable thicket of thorny shrubs or dwarf trees.

with Tennessee safe in their hands, they were ready to listen patiently to any defense, which they were already satisfied was insufficient. There being no doubt in their own minds, they were willing to give the prisoner the benefit of any that might exist. Secure in the hypothesis that he ought to be hanged on general principles, they indulged him with more latitude of defense than his reckless hardihood seemed to ask. The judge appeared to be more anxious than the prisoner, who, otherwise unconcerned, evidently took a grim pleasure in the responsibility he had created. "I don't take any hand in this yer game," had been his invariable but good-humored reply to all questions. The judge — who was also his captor — for a moment vaguely regretted that he had not shot him "on sight" that morning but presently dismissed his human weakness as unworthy of the judicial mind. Nevertheless, when there was a tap at the door, and it was said that Tennessee's Partner was there on behalf of the prisoner, he was admitted at once without question. Perhaps the younger members of the jury, to whom the proceedings were becoming irksomely thoughtful, hailed him as a relief.

For he was not, certainly, an imposing figure. Short and stout, with a square face sunburned into a preternatural redness, clad in a loose duck "jumper" and trousers streaked and splashed with red soil, his aspect under any circumstances would have been quaint and was now even ridiculous. As he stooped to deposit at his feet a heavy carpetbag he was carrying, it became obvious from partially developed legends and inscriptions that the material with which his trousers had been patched had been originally intended for a less ambitious covering. Yet he advanced with great gravity, and after shaking the hand of each person in the room with labored cordiality, he wiped his serious, perplexed face on a red bandana handkerchief a shade lighter than his complexion, laid his powerful hand upon the table to steady himself, and thus addressed the Judge:

"I was passin' by," he began by way of apology, "and I thought I'd just step in and see how things was gettin' on with Tennessee thar — my pardner. It's such a hot night. I disremember any sich weather before on the Bar."

He paused a moment, but nobody volunteering any other meteorological[4] recollection, he again had

recourse to his pocket handkerchief and for some moments mopped his face diligently.

"Have you anything to say on behalf of the prisoner?" said the Judge finally.

"Thet's it," said Tennessee's Partner in a tone of relief. "I come yar as Tennessee's pardner — knowing him nigh on four year, off and on, wet and dry, in luck and out o' luck. His ways ain't allers my ways, but thar ain't any p'ints in that young man, thar ain't any liveliness as he's been up to, as I don't know. And you sez to me, sez you — confidential-like and between man and man — sez you, 'Do you know anything in his behalf?' and I sez to you, sez I — confidential-like, as between man and man —'what should a man know of his pardner?'"

"Is this all you have to say?" asked the Judge impatiently, feeling, perhaps that a dangerous sympathy of humor was beginning to humanize the court.

"Thet's so," continued Tennessee's Partner. "It ain't for me to say anything agin' him. And now, what's the case? Here's Tennessee wants money, wants it bad, and don't like to ask it of an old pardner. Well, what does Tennessee do? He lays for a stranger, and he fetches that stranger; and you lays for *him*, and you fetches *him*; and the honors is easy. And I put it to you, bein' a fa'r-minded man, and to you, gentlemen all, as fa'r-minded men, ef this isn't so."

"Prisoner," said the Judge, interrupting, "have you any question to ask this man."

"No! no!" continued Tennessee's Partner hastily. "I play this yer hand alone. To come down to bed rock, it's just like this: Tennessee, thar, has played it pretty rough and expensive-like on a stranger and on this yer camp. And now what's the fair thing? Some would say more, some would say less. Here's seventeen hundred dollars in coarse gold and a watch — it's about all my pile — and call it square!" And before a hand could be raised to prevent him, he had emptied the contents of the carpetbag upon the table.

For a moment his life was in jeopardy. One or two men sprang to their feet, several hands groped for hidden weapons, and a suggestion to "throw him from the window" was only overridden by a gesture from the Judge. Tennessee laughed. And apparently oblivious of the excitement, Tennessee's Partner improved the opportunity to mop his face again with his handkerchief.

---

[4] *meteorological*, pertaining to the weather.

When order was restored, and the man was made to understand, by the use of forcible figures and rhetoric, that Tennessee's offense could not be condoned by money, his face took a more serious and sanguinary hue, and those who were nearest to him noticed that his rough hand trembled slightly on the table. He hesitated a moment as he slowly returned the gold to the carpetbag, as if he had not yet entirely caught the elevated sense of justice which swayed the tribunal and was perplexed with the belief that he had not offered enough. Then he turned to the Judge, and saying, "This yer is a lone hand, played alone, and without my pardner," he bowed to the jury and was about to withdraw when the Judge called him back:

"If you have anything to say to Tennessee, you had better say it now."

For the first time that evening the eyes of the prisoner and his strange advocate met. Tennessee smiled, showed his white teeth, and saying, "Euchred,[5] old man!" held out his hand. Tennessee's Partner took it in his own, and saying, "I just dropped in as I was passin' to see how things was gettin' on," let the hand passively fall; and adding that "it was a warm night," again mopped his face with his handkerchief and without another word withdrew.

The two men never again met each other alive. For the unparalleled insult of a bribe offered to Judge Lynch — who, whether bigoted, weak, or narrow, was at least incorruptible — firmly fixed in the mind of that mythical personage any wavering determination of Tennessee's fate; and at the break of day he was marched, closely guarded, to meet it at the top of Marley's Hill.

How he met it, how cool he was, how he refused to say anything, how perfect were the arrangements of the committee, were all duly reported, with the addition of a warning moral and example to all future evildoers, in the *Red Dog Clarion,* by its editor, who was present, and to whose vigorous English I cheerfully refer the reader. But the beauty of that midsummer morning, the blessed amity of earth and air and sky, the awakened life of the free woods and hills, the joyous renewal and promise of Nature, and above all the infinite serenity that thrilled through each was not reported, as not being a part of the social lesson. And yet, when the weak and foolish deed was done, and a life, with its possibilities and responsibilities, had passed out of the misshapen thing that dangled between earth and sky, the birds sang, the flowers bloomed, the sun shone as cheerily as before; and possibly the *Red Dog Clarion* was right.

Tennessee's Partner was not in the group that surrounded the ominous tree. But as they turned to disperse, attention was drawn to the singular appearance of a motionless donkey cart halted at the side of the road. As they approached, they at once recognized the venerable "Jenny" and the two-wheeled cart as the property of Tennessee's Partner, used by him in carrying dirt from his claim; and a few paces distant the owner of the equipage himself, sitting under a buckeye tree, wiping the perspiration from his glowing face. In answer to an inquiry, he said he had come for the body of the "diseased," "if it was all the same to the committee." He didn't wish to "hurry anything"; he could "wait." He was not working that day; and when the gentlemen were done with the "diseased," he would take him. "Ef thar is any present," he added in his simple, serious way, "as would care to jine in the fun'l, they kin come." Perhaps it was from a sense of humor, which I have already intimated was a feature of Sandy Bar — perhaps it was from something even better than that, but two thirds of the loungers accepted the invitation at once.

It was noon when the body of Tennessee was delivered into the hands of his partner. As the cart drew up to the fatal tree, we noticed that it contained a rough oblong box — apparently made from a section of sluicing[6]— and half filled with bark and the tassels of pine. The cart was further decorated with slips of willow and made fragrant with buckeye blossoms. When the body was deposited in the box, Tennessee's Partner drew over it a piece of tarred canvas, and gravely mounting the narrow seat in front, with his feet upon the shafts, urged the little donkey forward. The equipage moved slowly on at that decorous pace which was habitual with Jenny even under less solemn circumstances. The men — half curiously, half jestingly, but all good-humoredly — strolled along beside the cart, some in advance, some a little in the rear of the homely catafalque.[7] But whether

---

[5] *euchred,* defeated in the game of euchre. As a slang expression the word implies defeat in any scheme.

[6] *section of sluicing.* The sluice is a long trough in which gold-bearing gravel is washed. A sluice box, or single section, is usually about twelve feet long.

[7] *catafalque,* a temporary structure used for the public exhibition of the remains in the funerals of eminent persons.

from the narrowing of the road or some present sense of decorum, as the cart passed on, the company fell to the rear in couples, keeping step and otherwise assuming the external show of a formal procession. Jack Folinsbee, who had at the outset played a funeral march in dumb show upon an imaginary trombone, desisted from a lack of sympathy and appreciation — not having, perhaps, your true humorist's capacity to be content with the enjoyment of his own fun.

The way led through Grizzly Canyon, by this time clothed in funeral drapery and shadows. The redwoods, burying their moccasined feet in the red soil, stood in Indian file along the track, trailing an uncouth benediction from their bending boughs upon the passing bier. A hare, surprised into helpless inactivity, sat upright and pulsating in the ferns by the roadside as the cortège went by. Squirrels hastened to gain a secure outlook from higher boughs; and the bluejays, spreading their wings, fluttered before them like outriders, until the outskirts of Sandy Bar were reached, and the solitary cabin of Tennessee's Partner.

Viewed under more favorable circumstances, it would not have been a cheerful place. The unpicturesque site, the rude and unlovely outlines, the unsavory details, which distinguish the nest-building of the California miner, were all here with the dreariness of decay superadded. A few paces from the cabin there was a rough inclosure, which in the brief days of Tennessee's Partner's matrimonial felicity had been used as a garden but was now overgrown with fern. As we approached it, we were surprised to find that what we had taken for a recent attempt at cultivation was the broken soil about an open grave.

The cart was halted before the inclosure, and rejecting the offers of assistance with the same air of simple self-reliance he had displayed throughout, Tennessee's Partner lifted the rough coffin on his back and deposited it unaided within the shallow grave. He then nailed down the board which served as a lid, and mounting a little mound of earth beside it, took off his hat and slowly mopped his face with his handkerchief. This the crowd felt was a preliminary to speech, and they disposed themselves variously on stumps and boulders and sat expectant.

"When a man," began Tennessee's Partner, slowly, "has been running free all day, what's the natural thing for him to do? Why, to come home. And if he ain't in a condition to go home, what can his best friend do? Why, bring him home. And here's Tennessee has been running free, and we brings him home from his wandering." He paused and picked up a fragment of quartz, rubbed it thoughtfully on his sleeve, and went on: "It ain't the first time that I've packed him on my back, as you see'd me now. It ain't the first time that I brought him to this yer cabin when he couldn't help himself; it ain't the first time that I and Jinny have waited for him on yon hill and picked him up and so fetched him home, when he couldn't speak and didn't know me. And now that it's the last time, why" — he paused and rubbed the quartz gently on his sleeve — "you see it's sort of rough on his pardner. And now, gentlemen," he added abruptly, picking up his long-handled shovel, "the fun'l's over; and my thanks, and Tennessee's thanks, to you for your trouble."

Resisting any proffers of assistance, he began to fill in the grave, turning his back upon the crowd, that after a few moments' hesitation gradually withdrew. As they crossed the little ridge that hid Sandy Bar from view, some, looking back, thought they could see Tennessee's Partner, his work done, sitting upon the grave, his shovel between his knees and his face buried in his red bandana handkerchief. But it was argued by others that you couldn't tell his face from his handkerchief at that distance, and this point remained undecided.

In the reaction that followed the feverish excitement of that day, Tennessee's Partner was not forgotten. A secret investigation had cleared him of any complicity in Tennessee's guilt and left only a suspicion of his general sanity. Sandy Bar made a point of calling on him and proffering various uncouth but well-meant kindnesses. But from that day his rude health and great strength seemed visibly to decline; and when the rainy season fairly set in, and the tiny grass blades were beginning to peep from the rocky mound above Tennessee's grave, he took to his bed.

One night, when the pines beside the cabin were swaying in the storm and trailing their slender fingers over the roof, and the roar and rush of the swollen river were heard below, Tennessee's Partner lifted his head from the pillow, saying, "It is time to go to Tennessee; I must put Jinny to the cart;" and would have risen from his bed but for the restraint of his attendant.

Struggling, he still pursued his singular fancy: "There, now, steady, Jinny — steady, old girl. How dark it is! Look out for the ruts — and look out for him, too, old gal. Sometimes, you know, when he's blind drunk, he drops right in the trail. Keep on straight up to the pine on the top of the hill. Thar! I told you so! — thar he is — coming this way, too — all by himself, sober, and his face a-shining. Tennessee! Pardner!"

And so they met.

VIEWING THE AUTHOR'S IDEAS

1. Describe the setting of the story. What information does the author give about the previous life of the main characters? How does he account for the peculiar names by which Tennessee and his partner were known? What explanation did the people of Sandy Bar offer for the unusual friendship between the two men?

2. How does the story reflect the lawlessness of Western mining camps in 1854? Why were the arrest, indictment, and trial of Tennessee "irregular"? What attitude towards the law and towards Tennessee's offense did the partner express before the court? How did the court interpret the partner's attempt to "condone" his friend's offense with money? Note the irony in the phrases "elevated sense of justice" and "unparalleled insult of a bribe."

3. How does the author's sentimental treatment of the death and burial of the outlaw obscure Tennessee's guilt and responsibility for his crime? What attitude towards capital punishment is reflected in the comments on the execution? Why is punishment for crime necessary?

4. What good qualities does Tennessee's Partner manifest in his loyalty to his friend? What event in the association of the two men would normally have caused a break in the friendship? Point out humorous oddities and incongruities of character and appearance which help to account for the partner's unusual attachment.

5. Why is the death of Tennessee's Partner a fitting conclusion? How does the closing scene indicate that Tennessee's tragic death was never absent from his partner's mind?

EVALUATING HIS MANNER OF EXPRESSION

1. How does the use of local color help to secure unity of effect? What period of time does the story cover? What part of the story contains the climax?

2. List details which create the picturesque background of the mining camp. Discuss your reasons for judging that the principals in the story are real characters or merely caricatures.

3. Show the effective way in which the author uses nature as a background for the trial, death, and funeral of Tennessee.

4. Humor in the story results chiefly from the author's use of irony and understatement. How does humorous understatement prevent the funeral scene from being sentimental?

The Celebrated Jumping Frog of Calaveras County

Samuel Langhorne Clemens (Mark Twain)

"The Celebrated Jumping Frog" offers an example of the way in which an author's genius turned an unvarnished story into a masterpiece of American humor. Samuel Clemens, better known as Mark Twain, heard this tale during his brief mining experience in California. It was a rainy afternoon and Twain and his mining partner took shelter in a tavern. The narrator was an old man who pretended to see nothing humorous in the tale and droned it off monotonously. Twain was amused, and during the next several days he mimicked him to his partner: "I don't see no p'ints about this pan o' dirt that's any better'n any other pan o' dirt." When Twain wrote his version of the story, he became famous almost overnight. Having no idea that he had achieved a masterpiece of humor, *he was at first inclined to be irritated that the New York critics had chosen for approval a "villainous backwoods sketch."*

IN COMPLIANCE with the request of a friend of mine who wrote me from the East, I called on good-natured, garrulous old Simon Wheeler and inquired after my friend's friend, *Leonidas* W. Smiley, as requested to do; and I hereunto append the result. I have a lurking suspicion that *Leonidas* W. Smiley is a myth; that my friend never knew such a personage; and that he only conjectured that, if I asked old Wheeler about him, it would remind him of his infamous *Jim*

Smiley, and he would go to work and bore me to death with some infernal reminiscence of his as long and tedious as it should be useless to me. If that was the design, it certainly succeeded.

I found Simon Wheeler dozing comfortably by the barroom stove of the old, dilapidated tavern in the ancient mining camp of Angel's, and I noticed that he was fat and bald-headed, and had an expression of winning gentleness and simplicity upon his tranquil countenance. He roused up and gave me good day. I told him a friend of mine had commissioned me to make some inquiries about a cherished companion of his boyhood named *Leonidas* W. Smiley—*Rev. Leonidas* W. Smiley—a young minister of the Gospel, who he had heard was at one time a resident of Angel's Camp. I added that, if Mr. Wheeler could tell me anything about this Rev. Leonidas W. Smiley, I would feel under many obligations to him.

Simon Wheeler backed me into a corner and blockaded me there with his chair, and then sat me down and reeled off the monotonous narrative which follows this paragraph. He never smiled, he never frowned, he never changed his voice from the gentle-flowing key to which he tuned the initial sentence, he never betrayed the slightest suspicion of enthusiasm; but all through the interminable narrative there ran a vein of impressive earnestness and sincerity, which showed me plainly that, so far from his imagining that there was anything ridiculous or funny about his story, he regarded it as a really important matter and admired its two heroes as men of transcendent genius in finesse.[1] To me, the spectacle of a man drifting serenely along through such a queer yarn without ever smiling, was exquisitely absurd. As I said before, I asked him to tell me what he knew of Rev. Leonidas W. Smiley, and he replied as follows. I let him go on in his own way, and never interrupted him once:

There was a feller here once by the name of Jim Smiley, in the winter of '49—or maybe it was the spring of '50—I don't recollect exactly, somehow, though what makes me think it was one or the other is because I remember the big flume[2] wasn't finished when he first came to the camp; but anyway, he was the curiousest man about always betting on anything that turned up you ever see, if he could get anybody to bet on the other side; and if he couldn't, he'd change sides. Any way what suited the other man would suit him—any way just so's he got a bet, *he* was satisfied. But still he was lucky, uncommon lucky; he most always come out winner. He was always ready and laying for a chance; there couldn't be no solitary thing mentioned but that feller'd offer to bet on it, and take any side you please, as I was just telling you. If there was a horse race, you'd find him flush or you'd find him busted at the end of it; if there was a dog fight, he'd bet on it; if there was a cat fight, he'd bet on it; if there was a chicken fight, he'd bet on it; why, if there was two birds setting on a fence, he would bet you which one would fly first; or if there was a camp meeting, he would be there reg'lar, to bet on Parson Walker, which he judged to be the best exhorter about here, and so he was, too, and a good man. If he even seen a straddle-bug start to go anywheres, he would bet you how long it would take him to get to wherever he was going to, and if you took him up, he would foller that straddle-bug to Mexico but what he would find out where he was bound for and how long he was on the road. Lots of the boys here has seen that Smiley, and can tell you about him. Why, it never made no difference to *him*—he would bet on *any*thing—the dangdest feller. Parson Walker's wife laid very sick once, for a good while, and it seemed as if they warn't going to save her; but one morning he come in, and Smiley asked how she was, and he said she was considerable better—thank the Lord for his inf'nit mercy—and coming on so smart that, with the blessing of Prov'dence, she'd get well yet; and Smiley, before he thought, says, "Well, I'll risk two-and-a-half that she don't, any way."

Thish-yer Smiley had a mare—the boys called her the fifteen-minute nag, but that was only in fun, you know, because, of course, she was faster than that—and he used to win money on that horse, for all she was so slow and always had the asthma, or the distemper, or the consumption, or something of that kind. They used to give her two or three hundred yards start and then pass her under way; but always at the fag-end of the race she'd get excited and desperate-like, and come cavorting and straddling up, and scattering her legs around limber, sometimes in the air and sometimes out to one side amongst the fences, and kicking up m-o-r-e

---

[1] *finesse*, cunning.
[2] *flume*, an inclined channel for conveying logs down a mountain side.

dust, and raising m-o-r-e racket with her coughing and sneezing and blowing her nose — and always fetch up at the stand just about a neck ahead, as near as you could cipher it down.

And he had a little small bull pup, that to look at him you'd think he wan't worth a cent, but to set around and look ornery and lay for a chance to steal something. But as soon as money was up on him, he was a different dog; his underjaw'd begin to stick out like the fo'castle of a steamboat, and his teeth would uncover, and shine savage like the furnaces. And a dog might tackle him, and bullyrag him, and bite him, and throw him over his shoulder two or three times, and Andrew Jackson—which was the name of the pup—Andrew Jackson would never let on but what he was satisfied and hadn't expected nothing else—and the bets being doubled and doubled on the other side all the time till the money was all up; and then all of a sudden he would grab that other dog jest by the j'int of his hind leg and freeze to it—not chaw, you understand, but only jest grip and hang on till they throwed up the sponge,[3] if it was a year. Smiley always come out winner on that pup, till he harnessed a dog once that didn't have no hind legs, because they'd been sawed off by a circular saw, and when the thing had gone along far enough, and the money was all up, and he come to make a snatch for his pet holt, he saw in a minute how he'd been imposed on, and how the other dog had been in the door, so to speak, and he 'peared surprised, and then he looked sorter discouraged-like, and didn't try no more to win the fight, and so he got shucked out bad. He gave Smiley a look as much as to say his heart was broke, and it was his fault for putting up a dog that hadn't no hind legs for him to take holt of, which was his main dependence in a fight, and then he limped off a piece and laid down and died. It was a good pup, was that Andrew Jackson, and would have made a name for hisself if he'd lived, for the stuff was in him, and he had genius — I know it, because he hadn't had no opportunities to speak of, and it don't stand to reason that a dog could make such a fight as he could under them circumstances, if he hadn't no talent. It always makes me feel sorry when I think of that last fight of his'n, and the way it turned out.

Well, thish-yer Smiley had rat terriers, and chicken cocks, and tom cats, and all them kind of things, till you couldn't rest, and you couldn't fetch nothing for him to bet on but he'd match you. He ketched a frog one day, and took him home, and said he cal'klated to edercate him; and so he never done nothing for three months but set in his back yard and learn that frog to jump. And you bet he *did* learn him, too. He'd give him a little punch behind, and the next minute you'd see that frog whirling in the air like a doughnut—see him turn one summerset, or maybe a couple, if he got a good start, and come down flat-footed and all right, like a cat. He got him up so in the matter of catching flies and kept him in practice so constant that he'd nail a fly every time as far as he could see him. Smiley said all a frog wanted was edercation, and he could do most anything—and I believe him. Why, I've seen him set Dan'l Webster down here on this floor—Dan'l Webster was the name of the frog—and sing out, "Flies, Dan'l, Flies!" and quicker'n you could wink, he'd spring straight up, and snake a fly off'n the counter there, and flop down on the floor again as solid as a gob of mud, and fall to scratching the side of his head with his hind foot as indifferent as if he hadn't no idea he'd been doin' any more'n any frog might do. You never see a frog as modest and straightfor'ard as he was, for all he was so gifted. And when it come to fair and square jumping on a dead level, he could get over more ground at one straddle than any animal of his breed you ever see. Jumping on a dead level was his strong suit, you understand; and when it come to that, Smiley would ante up[4] money on him as long as he had a red.[5] Smiley was monstrous proud of that frog, and well he might be, for fellers that hed traveled and been everywheres, all said he laid over any frog that ever *they* see.

Well, Smiley kept the beast in a little lattice box, and he used to fetch him down town sometimes and lay for a bet. One day a feller—a stranger in the camp, he was—come across him with his box and says:

"What might it be that you've got in the box?"

And Smiley says, sorter indifferent like, "It might be a parrot, or it might be a canary, maybe, but it ain't—it's only just a frog."

And the feller took it and looked at it careful, and turned it round this way and that, and says, "H'm—so 'tis. Well, what's he good for?"

[3] *throwed up the sponge*, a slang expression used by boxers, meaning gave up.

[4] *ante up*, stake.

[5] *red*, a copper cent; so called because of its reddish color.

"Well," Smiley says, easy and careless. "He's good enough for one thing, I should judge—he can outjump any frog in Calaveras[6] county."

The feller took the box again, and took another long, particular look, and give it back to Smiley, and says, very deliberate, "Well, I don't see no p'ints about that frog that's any better'n any other frog."

"Maybe you don't," Smiley says. "Maybe you understand frogs, and maybe you don't understand 'em; maybe you've had experience, and maybe you an't only a amuture, as it were. Anyways, I've got my opinion, and I'll risk forty dollars that he can outjump any frog in Calaveras county."

And the feller studied a minute, and then says, kinder sad like, "Well, I'm only a stranger here, and I ain't got no frog; but if I had a frog, I'd bet you."

And then Smiley says, "That's all right—that's all right—if you'll hold my box a minute, I'll go and get you a frog." And so the feller took the box and put up his forty dollars along with Smiley's and set down to wait.

So he set there a good while thinking and thinking to hisself, and then he got the frog out and pried his mouth open and took a teaspoon and filled him full of quail shot—filled him pretty near up to his chin—and set him on the floor. Smiley he went to the swamp and slopped around in the mud for a long time, and finally he ketched a frog, and fetched him in, and give him to this feller, and says:

"Now, if you're ready, set him alongside of Dan'l, with his forepaws just even with Dan'l, and I'll give the word." Then he says, "One-two-three-jump!" and him and the feller touched up the frogs from behind, and the new frog hopped off, but Dan'l gave a heave and hysted up his shoulders—so—like a Frenchman, but it wan't no use—he couldn't budge; he was planted as solid as an anvil, and he couldn't no more stir than if he was anchored out. Smiley was a good deal surprised, and he was disgusted too; but he didn't have no idea what the matter was, of course.

The feller took the money and started away; and when he was going out at the door, he sorter jerked his thumb over his shoulders—this way—at Dan'l and says again, very deliberate, "Well, I don't see no p'ints about that frog that's better'n any other frog."

Smiley he stood scratching his head and looking down at Dan'l a long time, and at last he says, "I do wonder what in the nation that frog throwed off for—I wonder if there an't something the matter with him—he 'pears to look mighty baggy, somehow." And he ketched Dan'l by the nap of the neck and lifted him up and says, "Why, blame my cats, if he don't weigh five pound!" and turned him upside down, and he belched out a double handful of shot. And then he see how it was, and he was the maddest man—he set the frog down and took out after that feller, but he never ketched him. And—

Here Simon Wheeler heard his name called from the front yard, and got up to see what was wanted. And turning to me as he moved away, he said, "Just set where you are, stranger, and rest easy—I ain't going to be gone a second."

But, by your leave, I did not think that a continuation of the history of the enterprising vagabond *Jim* Smiley would be likely to afford me much information concerning the *Rev. Leonidas* W. Smiley, and so I started away.

At the door I met the sociable Wheeler returning, and he buttonholed me and recommenced:

"Well, thish-yer Smiley had a yaller one-eyed cow that didn't have no tail, only jest a short stump like a bannanner, and—"

"Oh, hang Smiley and his afflicted cow!" I muttered, good-naturedly, and bidding the old gentleman good day, I departed.

VIEWING THE AUTHOR'S IDEAS

1. Explain why Mark Twain thought L. W. Smiley was a myth.

2. What allusions to the gold rush fix the time of the story? In what respects were Wheeler and Smiley typical of the people of the mining camps? What do the names of the pup and the frog suggest? Find references to Mark Twain's experiences on the Mississippi.

3. How did Smiley prepare his listener for the yarn about the frog? What is the purpose of the story about the pup?

4. What parts of the story are probable? Which details are intentionally exaggerated?

5. Why does the author not remain to hear another yarn?

---

[6] *Calaveras County*, a county in the California mining district.

EVALUATING HIS MANNER OF EXPRESSION

1. What device does Mark Twain use to introduce the story?

2. What is the setting of the tale? How did Mark Twain become acquainted with life in a mining camp? List local-color details that add interest to the story.

3. Compare the dialect in this story with that in "Tennessee's Partner." How does Mark Twain's treatment of camp life differ from that of Bret Harte?

4. Point out examples of exaggerated expressions.

5. Upon what three elements does the humor in this story depend? How does the portrayal of Wheeler and Smiley show Mark Twain's power of characterization?

A Daring Deed

(From *Life on the Mississippi*)

Samuel Langhorne Clemens

(Mark Twain)

This exciting incident is told from the viewpoint of a cub pilot who was just learning the intricacies of guiding a vessel. The event occurred in the days when steamboating on the Mississippi was in its heyday. A short time before, the author had arranged to have Horace Bixby, a famous helmsman, teach him navigation. Mark Twain finally received his license and became a regular pilot.

WHEN I returned to the pilot house, St. Louis was gone and I was lost. Here was a piece of river which was all down in my book, but I could make neither head nor tail of it; you understand, it was turned around. I had seen it when coming upstream, but I had never faced about to see how it looked when it was behind me. My heart broke again, for it was plain that I had got to learn this troublesome river *both* ways.

The pilot house was full of pilots, going down to "look at the river." What is called the "upper river" (the two hundred miles between St. Louis and Cairo, where the Ohio comes in) was low; and the Mississippi changes its channel so constantly that the pilots used to always find it necessary to run down to Cairo to take a fresh look, when their boats were to lie in port for a week; that is, when the water was at a low stage. A deal of this "looking at the river" was done by poor fellows who seldom had a berth[1] and whose only hope of getting one lay in their being always freshly posted and therefore ready to drop into the shoes of some reputable pilot for a single trip, on account of such pilot's sudden illness or some other necessity. And a good many of them constantly ran up and down inspecting the river, not because they ever really hoped to get a berth, but because (they being guests of the boat) it was cheaper to "look at the river" than stay ashore and pay board. In time these fellows grew dainty in their tastes and only infested boats that had an established reputation for setting good tables. All visiting pilots were useful, for they were always ready and willing, winter or summer, night or day, to go out in the yawl and help buoy the channel[2] or assist the boat's pilots in any way they could. They were likewise welcomed because all pilots are tireless talkers when gathered together; and as they talk only about the river, they are always understood and are always interesting. Your true pilot cares nothing about anything on earth but the river, and his pride in his occupation surpasses the pride of kings.

We had a fine company of these river inspectors along this trip. There were eight or ten, and there was abundance of room for them in our great pilot house. Two or three of them wore polished silk hats, elaborate shirt fronts, diamond breastpins, kid gloves, and patent-leather boots. They were choice in their English and bore themselves with a dignity proper to men of solid means and prodigious reputation as pilots. The others were more or less loosely clad and wore upon their heads tall felt cones that were suggestive of the days of the Commonwealth.[3]

---

[1] *berth*, appointment as regular pilot.

[2] *buoy the channel*, place the buoy in the river channel to indicate its shoals.

[3] *Commonwealth*, the Puritan commonwealth of England from 1649 to 1660. The Puritans wore tall pointed hats.

I was a cipher in this august company and felt subdued, not to say torpid. I was not even of sufficient consequence to assist at the wheel when it was necessary to put the tiller hard down in a hurry; the guest that stood nearest did that when occasion required — and this was pretty much all the time because of the crookedness of the channel and the scant water. I stood in a corner, and the talk I listened to took the hope all out of me. One visitor said to another:

"Jim, how did you run Plum Point, coming up?"

"It was in the night, there, and I ran it the way one of the boys on the *Diana* told me; started out about fifty yards above the woodpile on the false point and held on the cabin under Plum Point till I raised the reef — quarter less twain[4] — then straightened up for the middle bar till I got well abreast the old one-limbed cottonwood in the bend, then got my stern on the cottonwood and head on the low place above the point and came through a-booming — nine and a half."

"Pretty square crossing, ain't it?"

"Yes, but the upper bar's working down fast."

Another pilot spoke up and said:

"I had better water than that and ran it lower down; started out from the false point — mark twain — raised the second reef abreast the big snag in the bend and had quarter less twain."

One of the gorgeous ones remarked:

"I don't want to find fault with your leadsmen, but that's a good deal of water for Plum Point, it seems to me."

There was an approving nod all around as this quiet snub dropped on the boaster and settled him. And so they went on talk-talk-talking. Meantime, the thing that was running in my mind was, "Now, if my ears hear aright, I have not only to get the names of all the towns and islands and bends and so on by heart; but I must even get up a warm personal acquaintanceship with every old snag and one-limbed cotton-wood and obscure woodpile that ornaments the banks of this river for twelve hundred miles; and more than that, I must actually know where these things are in the dark, unless these guests are gifted with eyes that can pierce through two miles of solid blackness. I wish the piloting business was in Jericho and I had never thought of it."

At dusk Mr. Bixby tapped the big bell three times (the signal to land), and the captain emerged from the drawing room in the forward end of the texas[5] and looked up inquiringly. Mr. Bixby said:

"We will lay up here all night, captain."

"Very well, sir."

That was all. The boat came to shore and was tied up for the night. It seemed to me a fine thing that the pilot could do as he pleased, without asking so grand a captain's permission. I took my supper and went immediately to bed, discouraged by my day's observations and experiences. My late voyage's notebooking was but a confusion of meaningless names. It had tangled me all up in a knot every time I had looked at it in the daytime. I now hoped for respite in sleep; but no, it reveled all through my head till sunrise again, a frantic and tireless nightmare.

Next morning I felt pretty rusty and low-spirited. We went booming along, taking a good many chances, for we were anxious to "get out of the river" (as getting out to Cairo was called) before night should overtake us. But Mr. Bixby's partner, the other pilot, presently grounded the boat, and we lost so much time getting her off that it was plain the darkness would overtake us a good long way above the mouth. This was a great misfortune, especially to certain of our visiting pilots whose boats would have to wait for their return no matter how long that might be. It sobered the pilot-house talk a good deal. Coming upstream, pilots did not mind low water or any kind of darkness; nothing stopped them but fog. But downstream work different; a boat was too nearly helpless with a stiff current pushing behind her; so it was not customary to run downstream at night in low water.

There seemed to be one small hope, however; if we could get through the intricate and dangerous Hat Island crossing before night, we could venture the rest, for we would have plainer sailing and better water. But it would be insanity to attempt Hat Island at night. So there was a deal of looking at watches all the rest of the day and a constant ciphering upon the speed we were making. Hat Island was the eternal subject; sometimes

[4] *quarter less twain.* The pilot made his way through dangerous channels with the aid of soundings taken by the leadsmen, one on the left and one on the right of the prow. Terms used when measuring the depth of the water were: "Mark three," indicating three fathoms, or eighteen feet; "quarter less three," two and three quarter fathoms, or sixteen and one half feet; "half twain," two and a half fathoms, or fifteen feet; "mark twain," two fathoms, or twelve feet.

[5] *texas*, a structure on the hurricane deck containing the officers' quarters. Staterooms were named after states; and as the officers' rooms were largest, they received the name of the largest state in the Union.

hope was high; and sometimes we were delayed in a bad crossing and down it went again. For hours all hands lay under the burden of this suppressed excitement; it was even communicated to me, and I got to feeling so solicitous about Hat Island and under such an awful pressure of responsibility that I wished I might have had five minutes on shore to draw a good, full, relieving breath and start all over again. We were standing no regular watches. Each of our pilots ran such portions of the river as he had run when coming upstream because of his greater familiarity with it, but both remained in the pilot house constantly.

An hour before sunset Mr. Bixby took the wheel, and Mr. W. stepped aside. For the next thirty minutes every man held his watch in his hand and was restless, silent, and uneasy. At last somebody said with a doomful sigh:

"Well, yonder's Hat Island — and we can't make it."

All the watches closed with a snap; everybody sighed and muttered something about its being "too bad, too bad — ah, if we could *only* have got here half an hour sooner!" and the place was thick with the atmosphere of disappointment. Some started to go out but loitered, hearing no bell tap to land. The sun dipped behind the horizon; the boat went on. Inquiring looks passed from one guest to another; and one who had his hand on the doorknob and had turned it, waited, then presently took away his hand and let the knob turn back again. We bore steadily down the bend. More looks were exchanged and nods of surprised admiration — but no words. Insensibly the men drew together behind Mr. Bixby, as the sky darkened and one or two dim stars came out. The dead silence and sense of waiting became oppressive. Mr. Bixby pulled the cord, and two deep, mellow notes from the big bell floated off on the night. Then a pause, and one more note was struck. The watchman's voice followed from the hurricane deck:

"Labboard lead, there! Stabboard[6] lead!"

The cries of the leadsmen began to rise out of the distance and were gruffly repeated by the word passers on the hurricane deck.

"M-a-r-k three! M-a-r-k three! Quarter-less-three! Half twain! M-a-r-k twain! Quarter-less—"

Mr. Bixby pulled two bell ropes and was answered by faint jinglings far below in the engine room, and our speed slackened. The steam began to whistle through the gauge cocks. The cries of the leadsmen went on — and it is a weird sound, always, in the night. Every pilot in the lot was watching now with fixed eyes and talking under his breath. Nobody was calm and easy but Mr. Bixby. He would put his wheel down and stand on a spoke, and as the steamer swung into her (to me) utterly invisible marks — for we seemed to be in the midst of a wide and gloomy sea — he would meet and fasten her there. Out of the murmur of half-audible talk one caught a coherent sentence now and then — such as:

"There; she's over the first reef all right!"

After a pause another subdued voice: "Her stern's coming down just *exactly* right, by *George!*"

"Now she's in the marks; over she goes!" Somebody else muttered: "Oh, it was done beautiful — *beautiful!*" Now the engines were stopped altogether, and we drifted with the current. Not that I could see the boat drift, for I could not, the stars being all gone by this time. This drifting was the dismalest work; it held one's heart still. Presently I discovered a blacker gloom than that which surrounded us. It was the head of the island. We were closing right down upon it. We entered its deeper shadow, and so imminent seemed the peril that I was likely to suffocate; and I had the strongest impulse to do *something,* anything, to save the vessel. But still Mr. Bixby stood by his wheel, silent, intent as a cat; and all the pilots stood shoulder to shoulder at his back.

"She'll not make it!" somebody whispered.

The water grew shoaler and shoaler, by the leadman's cries, till it was down to: "Eight-and-a-half! E-i-g-h-t feet! E-i-g-h-t feet! Seven-and —"

Mr. Bixby said warningly through his speaking tube to the engineer:

"Stand by, now!"

"Aye, aye, sir!"

"Seven-and-a-half! Seven feet! *Six*-and —"

We touched bottom! Instantly Mr. Bixby set a lot of bells ringing, shouted through the tube, "*Now,* let her have it — every ounce you've got!" then to his partner, "Put her hard down! snatch her! snatch her!" The boat rasped and ground her way through the sand, hung upon the apex of disaster a single tremendous instant, and then over she went! And such a shout as went up at Mr. Bixby's back never loosened the roof of a pilot house before!

---

[6] *Labboard . . . Stabboard,* larboard, or left, and starboard, or right. This was a call to the leadsmen to sound on both sides of the ship.

There was no more trouble after that. Mr. Bixby was a hero that night; and it was some little time, too, before his exploit ceased to be talked about by rivermen.

Fully to realize the marvelous precision required in laying the great steamer in her marks in that murky waste of water, one should know that not only must she pick her intricate way through snags and blind reefs and then shave the head of the island so closely as to brush the overhanging foliage with her stern, but at one place she must pass almost within arm's reach of a sunken and invisible wreck that would snatch the hull timbers from under her if she should strike it, and destroy a quarter of a million dollars' worth of steamboat and cargo in five minutes and maybe a hundred and fifty human lives into the bargain.

The last remark I heard that night was a compliment to Mr. Bixby uttered in soliloquy and with unction by one of our guests. He said:

"By the Shadow of Death, but he's a lightning pilot!"

VIEWING THE AUTHOR'S IDEAS

1. Find the statement which expresses the pilots' pride in their occupation. What interesting information does the author give concerning the visiting pilots? Why was the upper river especially difficult to navigate?

2. What was the position of the cub pilot? Describe Twain's feelings on this trip. About what topics did the pilots usually talk?

3. What incident showed Mr. Bixby's importance? Why was it necessary to pass Hat Island before night? What delayed the boat?

4. How did Mr. Bixby meet the challenge of piloting the boat through the dangerous stretch of the river? What is the moment of greatest suspense?

5. What did the beginner learn about piloting on this trip?

EVALUATING HIS MANNER OF EXPRESSION

1. Why is this narrative especially interesting? Select the most vivid passages.

2. What traits of the lightning pilot are depicted in the character of Mr. Bixby?

Jean-ah Poquelin

George Washington Cable

One of the best examples of the Southern story of local color, "Jean-ah Poquelin" depicts the old French Quarter of New Orleans in the era following the Louisiana Purchase. The narrative forcefully portrays the conflict between the vanishing Creole civilization and the new American regime. Although Cable's work suffers from his inability to understand the loyalty of the Creoles to their Catholic traditions, no other writer has succeeded so well in portraying the lives of these descendants of the early French and Spanish settlers of Louisiana.

I

IN THE first decade of the present century,[1] when the newly established American government was the most hateful thing in Louisiana — when the Creoles were still kicking at such vile innovations as the trial by jury, American dances, anti-smuggling laws, and the printing of the Governor's proclamation in English— when the Anglo-American flood[2] that was presently to burst in a crevasse of immigration upon the delta had thus far been felt only as slippery seepage which made the Creole tremble for his footing — there stood, a short distance above what is now Canal Street and considerably back from the line of villas which fringed the river bank on Tchoupitoulas Road, an old colonial plantation house half in ruin.

It stood aloof from civilization, the tracts that had once been its indigo fields given over to their first noxious wildness and grown up into one of the horridest marshes within a circuit of fifty miles.

The house was of heavy cypress, lifted up on pillars, grim, solid, and spiritless, its massive build a strong reminder of days still earlier when every man had been his own peace officer and the insurrection of the blacks a daily contingency. Its dark, weather-beaten roof and sides were hoisted up above the jungly plain in a distracted way, like a gigantic ammunition wagon stuck in the mud and abandoned by some retreating army. Around it was a dense growth of low water willows,

[1] *present century*, 1800-1900.
[2] *Anglo-American flood*, Americans of English descent.

with half a hundred sorts of thorny or fetid bushes, savage strangers alike to the "language of flowers" and to the botanist's Greek. They were hung with countless strands of discolored and prickly smilax, and the impassable mud below bristled with chevaux-de-frise[3] of the dwarf palmetto. Two lone forest trees, dead cypresses, stood in the center of the marsh, dotted with roosting vultures. The shallow strips of water were hid by myriads of aquatic plants, under whose coarse and spiritless flowers, could one have seen it, was a harbor of reptiles, great and small, to make one shudder to the end of his days.

The house was on a slightly raised spot, the levee of a draining canal. The waters of this canal did not run; they crawled and were full of big, ravening fish and alligators that held it against all comers.

Such was the home of old Jean Marie Poquelin, once an opulent indigo planter standing high in the esteem of his small, proud circle of exclusively male acquaintances in the old city; now a hermit, alike shunned by and shunning all who had ever known him. "The last of his line," said the gossips. His father lies under the floor of the St. Louis Cathedral, with the wife of his youth on one side and the wife of his old age on the other. Old Jean visits the spot daily. His half brother — alas! there was a mystery; no one knew what had become of the gentle, young half brother, more than thirty years his junior, whom once he seemed so fondly to love, but who, seven years ago, had disappeared suddenly, once for all, and left no clue of his fate.

They had seemed to live so happily in each other's love. No father, mother, wife to either, no kindred upon earth. The elder, a bold, frank, impetuous, chivalric adventurer; the younger a gentle, studious, book-loving recluse; they lived upon the ancestral estate like mated birds, one always on the wing, the other always in the nest.

There was no trait in Jean Marie Poquelin, said the old gossips, for which he was so well known among his few friends as his apparent fondness for his "little brother." "Jacques said this," and "Jacques was good," or "wise," or "just," or "far-sighted," as the nature of the case required; and "he should ask Jacques as soon as he got home," since Jacques was never elsewhere to be seen.

It was between the roving character of the one brother and the bookishness of the other that the estate fell into decay. Jean Marie, generous gentleman, gambled the slaves away one by one, until none was left, man or woman, but one old African mute.

The indigo fields and the vats of Louisiana had been gradually abandoned as unremunerative. Certain enterprising men had substituted the culture of sugar; but while the recluse was too apathetic to take so active a course, the other saw larger, and at that time, equally respectable profits, first in smuggling and later in the African slave trade. What harm could he see in it? The whole people said it was vitally necessary, and to minister to a vital public necessity — good enough, certainly, and so he laid up many a doubloon that made him none the worse in the public regard.

One day old Jean Marie was about to start upon a voyage that was to be longer, much longer, than any he had yet made. Jacques had begged him hard for many days not to go, but he laughed him off and finally said, kissing him:

Adieu 'tit frère.[4]

"No," said Jacques, "I shall go with you."

They left the old hulk of a house in the sole care of the African mute and went away to the Guinea coast together.

II

Two years after, old Poquelin came home without his vessel. He must have arrived at his house by night. No one saw him come. No one saw "his little brother"; rumor whispered that he, too, had returned, but he had never been seen again.

A dark suspicion fell upon the old slave trader. No matter that the few kept the many reminded of the tenderness that had ever marked his bearing to the missing man. The many shook their heads. "You know he has a quick and fearful temper"; and "why does he cover his loss with mystery?" "Grief would out with the truth."

"But," said the charitable few, "look in his face; see that expression of true humanity." The many did look in his face, and, as he looked in theirs, he read the silent question: "Where is thy brother Abel?" The few were silenced, his former friends died off, and the name of

---

[3] *cheveaux-de-frise*, barriers made by the matted roots of the palmetto.

[4] *Adieu 'tit frère*, good-by, little brother.

Jean Marie Poquelin became a symbol of witchery, devilish crime, and hideous nursery fictions.

The man and his house were alike shunned. The snipe and duck hunters forsook the marsh, and the woodcutters abandoned the canal. Sometimes the hardier boys who ventured out there snake-shooting heard a slow thumping of oarlocks on the canal. They would look at each other for a moment, half in consternation, half in glee, then rush from their sport in wanton haste to assail with their jibes the unoffending, withered old man who in rusty attire sat in the stern of a skiff, rowed homeward by his white-headed African mute.

"O Jean-ah Poquelin! O Jean-ah! Jean-ah Poquelin!"

It was not necessary to utter more than that. No hint of wickedness, deformity, or any physical or moral demerit; merely the name and tone of mockery: "Oh, Jean-ah Poquelin!" and while they tumbled one over another in their needless haste to fly, he would rise carefully from his seat, while the aged mute, with downcast face, went on rowing, and rolling up his brown fist and extending it toward the urchins, would pour forth such an unholy broadside of French imprecation and invective as would all but craze them with delight.

Among both blacks and whites the house was the object of a thousand superstitions. Every midnight, they affirmed, the *feu follet*[5] came out of the marsh and ran in and out of the rooms, flashing from window to window. The story of some lads, whose words in ordinary statements were worthless, was generally credited, that the night they camped in the woods rather than pass the place after dark, they saw about sunset every window blood-red, and on each of the four chimneys an owl sitting, which turned his head three times round and moaned and laughed with a human voice. There was a bottomless well, everybody professed to know, beneath the sill of the big front door under the rotten veranda; whoever set his foot upon that threshold disappeared forever in the depth below.

What wonder the marsh grew as wild as Africa! Take all the Faubourg Ste. Marie[6] and half the ancient city, you would not find one graceless daredevil reckless enough to pass within a hundred yards of the house after nightfall.

The alien races pouring into old New Orleans began to find the few streets named for the Bourbon princes too strait for them. The wheel of fortune, beginning to whirl, threw them off beyond the ancient corporation lines and sowed civilization and even trade upon the lands of the Graviers and Girods. Fields became roads, roads streets. Everywhere the leveler[7] was peering through his glass, rodsmen were whacking their way through willow brakers and rose hedges, and the sweating Irishmen tossed the blue clay up with their long-handled shovels.

"Ha! that is all very well," quoth Jean-Baptistes, feeling the reproach of an enterprise that asked neither co-operation nor advice of them, "but wait till they come yonder to Jean Poquelin's marsh; ha! ha! ha!" The supposed predicament so delighted them that they put on a mock terror and whirled about in an assumed stampede, then caught their clasped hands between their knees in excess of mirth and laughed until the tears ran; for whether the street-makers mired in the marsh or contrived to cut through old "Jean-ah's" property, either event would be joyful. Meantime a line of tiny rods, with bits of white paper in their split tops, gradually extended its way straight through the haunted ground and across the canal diagonally.

"We shall fill that ditch," said the men in mud boots, and brushed close along the chained and padlocked gate of the haunted mansion. Ah, Jean-ah Poquelin, those were not Creole boys, to be stampeded with a little hard swearing.

He went to the Governor. That official scanned the odd figure with no slight interest. Jean Poquelin was of short, broad frame, with a bronzed leonine face. His brow was ample and deeply furrowed. His eye, large and black, was bold and open like that of a war horse, and his jaws shut together with the firmness of iron. He was dressed in a suit of Attakapas[8] cottonade, and his shirt, unbuttoned and thrown back from the throat and bosom sailor wise, showed a herculean breast, hard and grizzled. There was no fierceness or defiance in his look, no harsh ungentleness, no symptom of his unlawful life or violent temper; but rather a peaceful and peaceable fearlessness. Across the whole face, not marked in one or another feature but as it were laid softly upon the

[5] *feu follet*, the will-o'-the-wisp, a light that appears over marshy grounds at night, caused by the combustion of marsh gas.
[6] *Faubourg Ste. Marie*, the suburb of Ste. Marie.
[7] *leveler*, surveyor.
[8] *Attakapas*, Indian tribe of Louisiana.

countenance like an almost imperceptible veil, was the imprint of some great grief. A careless eye might easily overlook it; but, once seen, there it hung — faint but unmistakable.

The Governor bowed.

"*Parlez-vous francais?*"[9] asked the figure.

"I would rather talk English, if you can do so," said the Governor.

"My name, Jean Poquelin."

"How can I serve you, Mr. Poquelin?"

"My 'ouse is yond'; *dans le marais là-bas.*"[10]

The Governor bowed.

"Dat *marais* billong to me."

"Yes, sir."

"To me; Jean Poquelin; I hown 'im meself."

"Well, sir?"

"He don't billong to you; I get him from me father."

"That is perfectly true, Mr. Poquelin, as far as I am aware."

"You want to make strit pass yond'?"

"I do not know, sir; it is quite probable; but the city will indemnify you for any loss you may suffer — you will get paid, you understand."

"Strit can't pass dare."

"You will have to see the municipal authorities about that, Mr. Poquelin."

A bitter smile came upon the old man's face:

"*Pardon, Monsieur*, you is not *le Gouverneur?*"

"Yes."

"*Mais*,[11] yes. Your har *le Gouverneur* — yes. Veh-well, I come to you. I tell you strit *can't pass* at me 'ouse."

"But you will have to see — "

"I come to you. You is *le Gouverneur*. I know not the new laws. I ham a Fr-r-rench-a-man! Fr-r-rench-a-man have something *aller au contraire*[12] — he come at his *Gouverneur*. I come to you. If me had not been bought from me king like *bossals*[13] in the hold time, de king gof — France would-a-show *Monsieur le Gouverneur* to take care his men to make strit in right places. *Mais*, I know; we billong to *Monsieur le President*. I want you do somesin for me, eh?"

"What is it?" asked the patient Governor.

"I want you tell *Monsieur le President* strit — can't — pass — at me — 'ouse."

"Have a chair, Mr. Poquelin"; but the old man did not stir. The Governor took a quill and wrote a line to a city official, introducing Mr. Poquelin and asking for him every possible courtesy. He handed it to him, instructing him where to present it.

"Mr. Poquelin," he said with a conciliatory smile, "tell me, is it your house that our Creole citizens tell such odd stories about?"

The old man glared sternly upon the speaker and with immovable features said:

"You don't see me trade some Guinea Negro?"

"Oh, no."

"You don't see me make some smugglin'?"

"No, sir; not at all."

"But, I am Jean Marie Poquelin. I mine me hown bizniss. Dat all right? *Adieu.*"

He put his hat on and withdrew. By and by he stood, letter in hand, before the person to whom it was addressed.

This person employed an interpreter.

"He says," said the interpreter to the officer, "he come to make you the fair warning how you muz not make the street pas' at his 'ouse."

The officer remarked that "such impudence was refreshing"; but the experienced interpreter translated freely.

"He says: 'Why don't want?'" said the interpreter.

The old slave trader answered at some length.

"He says," said the interpreter, again turning to the officer, "the marass is a too unhealth' for peopl' to live."

"But we expect to drain his old marsh; it's not going to be a marsh."

"*Il dit*[14] — " The interpreter explained in French.

The old man answered tersely.

"He says the canal is private property," said the interpreter.

"Oh! *that* old ditch; that's to be filled up. Tell the old man we're going to fix him up nicely."

Translation being duly made, the man in power was amused to see a thundercloud gathering on the old man's face.

"Tell him," he added, "by the time we finish, there'll not be a ghost left in his shanty."

The interpreter began to translate, but —

"*J'comprends,*[15] *j'comprends,*" said the old man, with an impatient gesture, and burst forth, pouring curses upon the United States, the President, the Territory of Orleans, Congress, the Governor and all his subordinates, striding out of the apartment as he cursed, while the object of his maledictions roared with merriment and rammed the floor with his foot.

"Why, it will make his old place worth ten dollars to one," said the official to the interpreter.

"'Tis not for de worse of de property," said the interpreter.

"I should guess not," said the other, whittling his chair — "seems to me as if some of these old Creoles would liever live in a crawfish hole than to have a neighbor."

"You know what make old Jean Poquelin ack like that? I will tell you. You know —"

The interpreter was rolling a cigarette and paused to light his tinder; then, as the smoke poured in a thick double stream from his nostrils, he said in a solemn whisper:

"He is a witch."

"Ho, ho, ho!" laughed the other.

"You don't believe it? What do you want to bet?" cried the interpreter, jerking himself half up and thrusting out one arm while he bared it of his coatsleeve with the hand of the other. "What you want to bet?"

"How do you know?" asked the official.

"Das what I goin' to tell you. You know, one evening I was shooting some *grosbec*.[16] I killed three; but I had trouble to find them, it was becoming so dark. When I have them, I start' to come home; then I got to pas' at Jean Poquelin's house."

"Ho, ho, ho!" laughed the other, throwing his leg over the arm of the chair.

"Wait," said the interpreter. "I come along slow, not making some noises; still, still — "

"And scared," said the smiling one.

"*Mais*, wait. I get all pas' the 'ouse. 'Ah!' I say; 'all right!' Then I see two thing' before! Hah! I get as cold and humide, and shake like a leaf. You think it was nothing? There I see, so plain as can be (though it was making nearly dark) I see Jean-Marie-Po-que-lin walkin' right in front, and right there beside of him

was something like a man — but not a man — white like paint! — I dropp' on the grass from scared — they pass'; so sure as I live, 'twas the ghos' of Jacques Poquelin, his brother!"

"Pooh!" said the listener.

"I'll put my han' in the fire," said the interpreter.

"But did you never think," asked the other, "that that might be Jack Poquelin, as you call him, alive and well, and for some cause hid away by his brother?"

"But there har' no cause!" said the other, and the entrance of third parties changed the subject.

III

Some months passed and the street was opened. A canal was first dug through the marsh, the small one which passed so close to Jean Poquelin's house was filled, and the street, or rather a sunny road, just touched the corner of the old mansion's dooryard. The morass ran dry. Its venomous denizens slipped away through the bulrushes, the cattle roaming freely upon its hardened surface trampled the superabundant undergrowth. The bellowing frogs croaked to westward. Lilies and the flower-de-luce sprang up in the place of reeds; smilax and poison oak gave way to the purple-plumed ironweed and pink spiderwort; the bindweeds ran everywhere blooming as they ran, and on one of the dead cypresses a giant creeper hung its green burden of foliage and lifted its scarlet trumpets. Sparrows and redbirds flitted through the bushes, and dewberries grew ripe beneath. Over all these came a sweet, dry smell of salubrity which the place had not known since the sediments of the Mississippi first lifted it from the sea.

But its owner did not build. Over the willow brakes and down the vista of the open street, bright new houses, some singly, some by ranks, were prying in on the old man's privacy. They even settled down toward his southern side. First a woodcutter's hut or two, and all at once the faubourg had flanked and half surrounded him and his dried-up marsh.

Ah! then the common people began to hate him. "The old tyrant!" "You don't mean an old *tyrant*?" "Well, then, why don't he build when the public need demands it? What does he live in that un-neighborly way for?" "The old pirate!" "The old kidnapper!" How easily even the most ultra-Louisianians put on the imported virtues of the North when they could be brought to bear against the hermit. "There he goes, with the boys after him!

---

[15] *J'comprends*, I understand.

[16] *grosbec*, the grosbeak, a bird of the finch family.

Ah! ha! ha! Jean-ah Poquelin! Ah! Jean-ah! Aha! aha! Jean-ah Marie! Jean-ah Poquelin! The old villain!" How merrily the swarming Américains echo the spirit of persecution! "The old fraud," they say — "pretends to live in a haunted house, does he? We'll tar and feather him some day. Guess we can fix him."

He cannot be rowed home along the old canal now; he walks. He has broken sadly of late, and the street urchins are ever at his heels. It is like the days when they cried: "Go up, thou baldhead," and the old man now and then turns and delivers ineffectual curses.

To the Creoles — to the incoming lower class of superstitious Germans, Irish, Sicilians, and others — he became an omen and embodiment of public and private ill fortune. Upon him all the vagaries of their superstitions gathered and grew. If a house caught fire, it was imputed to his machinations. Did a woman go off in a fit, he had bewitched her. Did a child stray off for an hour, the mother shivered with the apprehension that Jean Poquelin had offered him to strange gods. The house was the subject of every bad boy's invention who loved to contrive ghostly lies. "As long as that house stands, we shall have bad luck. Do you not see our peas and beans dying, our cabbages and lettuce going to seed, and our gardens turning to dust, while every day you can see it raining in the woods? The rain will never pass old Poquelin's house. He keeps a fetish.[17] He has conquered the whole Faubourg Ste. Marie. And why, the old wretch? Simply because our playful and innocent children call after him as he passes."

A "Building and Improvement Company," which had not yet got its charter, "but was going to," and which had not, indeed, any tangible capital yet, but "was going to have some," joined the "Jean-ah Poquelin" war. The haunted property would be such a capital site for a market house! They sent a deputation to the old mansion to ask its occupant to sell. The deputation never got beyond the chained gate and a very barren interview with the African mute. The President of the Board was then empowered (for he had studied French in Pennsylvania and was considered qualified) to call and persuade M. Poquelin to subscribe to the company's stock; but —

"Fact is, gentlemen," he said at the next meeting, "it would take us at least twelve months to make Mr.

Pokaleen understand the original features of our system, and he wouldn't subscribe when we'd done; besides, the only way to see him is to stop him on the street."

There was a great laugh from the Board; they couldn't help it. "Better meet a bear robbed of her whelps," said one.

"You're mistaken as to that," said the President. "I did meet him and stopped him and found him quite polite. But I could get no satisfaction from him; the fellow wouldn't talk in French, and when I spoke in English, he hoisted his old shoulders up and gave the same answer to everything I said."

"And that was — ?" asked one or two, impatient of the pause.

"That it 'don't worse w'ile.'"

One of the Board said: "Mr. President, this market house project, as I take it, is not altogether a selfish one; the community is to be benefited by it. We may feel that we are working in the public interest (the Board smiled knowingly), if we employ all possible means to oust this old nuisance from among us. You may know that at the time the street was cut through, this old Poquelann did all he could to prevent it. It was owing to a certain connection which I had with that affair that I heard a ghost story (smiles, followed by a sudden dignified check) — ghost story, which, of course, I am not going to relate, but I *may* say that my profound conviction, arising from a prolonged study of that story, is that this old villain, John Poquelann, has his brother locked up in that old house. Now, if this is so, and we can fix it on him, I merely *suggest* that we can make the matter highly useful. I don't know," he added, beginning to sit down, "but that is an action we owe to the community — hem!"

"How do you propose to handle the subject?" asked the President.

"I was thinking," said the speaker, "that, as a Board of Directors, it would be unadvisable for us to authorize any action involving trespass; but if you, for instance, Mr. President, should, as it were, for mere curiosity, *request* some one, as, for instance, our excellent Secretary, simply as a personal favor to look into the matter — this is merely a suggestion."

The Secretary smiled sufficiently to be understood that, while he certainly did not consider such preposterous service a part of his duties as secretary,

---

[17] *fetish*, charm.

he might, notwithstanding, accede to the President's request; and the Board adjourned.

Little White, as the Secretary was called, was a mild, kindhearted little man, who, nevertheless, had no fear of anything, unless it was the fear of being unkind.

"I tell you frankly," he privately said to the President, "I go into this purely for reasons of my own."

The next day a little after nightfall one might have descried this little man slipping along the rear fence of the Poquelin place, preparatory to vaulting over into the rank, grass-grown yard and bearing himself altogether more after the manner of a collector of rare chickens than according to the usage of secretaries.

The picture presented to his eye was not calculated to enliven his mind. The old mansion stood out against the western sky, black and silent. One long, lurid pencil stroke along a sky of slate was all that was left of daylight. No sign of life was apparent; no light at any window, unless it might have been on the side of the house hidden from view. No owls were on the chimneys; no dogs were in the yard.

He entered the place and ventured up behind a small cabin which stood apart from the house. Through one of its many crannies he easily detected the African mute crouched before a flickering pine knot, his head on his knees, fast asleep.

He concluded to enter the mansion and, with that view, stood and scanned it. The broad rear steps of the veranda would not serve him; he might meet someone midway. He was measuring with his eyes the proportions of one of the pillars which supported it and estimating the practicability of climbing it, when he heard a footstep. Someone had dragged a chair out toward the railing, then seemed to change his mind and began to pace the veranda, his footfalls resounding on the dry boards with singular loudness. Little White drew a step backward, got the figure between himself and the sky, and at once recognized the short, broad-shouldered form of old Jean Poquelin.

He sat down upon a billet of wood and, to escape the stings of a whining cloud of mosquitoes, shrouded his face and neck in his handkerchief, leaving his eyes uncovered.

He had sat there but a moment when he noticed a strange, sickening odor, faint, as if coming from a distance, but loathsome and horrid.

Whence could it come? Not from the cabin; not from the marsh, for it was as dry as powder. It was not in the air; it seemed to come from the ground.

Rising up, he noticed, for the first time, a few steps before him a narrow footpath leading toward the house. He glanced down it — ha! right there was someone coming — ghostly white!

Quick as thought and as noiselessly, he lay down at full length against the cabin. It was bold strategy, and yet, there was no denying it, Little White felt that he was frightened. "It is not a ghost," he said to himself. "I *know* it cannot be a ghost"; but the perspiration burst out at every pore, and the air seemed to thicken with heat. "It is a living man," he said in his thoughts. "I hear his footstep, and I hear old Poquelin's footsteps, too, separately, over on the veranda. I am not discovered; the thing has passed; there is that odor again; what a smell of death! Is it coming back? Yes. It stops at the door of the cabin. Is it peering in at the sleeping mute? It moves away. It is in the path again. Now it is gone." He shuddered. "Now, if I dare venture, the mystery is solved." He rose cautiously, close against the cabin, and peered along the path.

The figure of a man, a presence if not a body — but whether clad in some white stuff or naked, the darkness would not allow him to determine — had turned and now with a seeming painful gait moved slowly from him. "Great Heaven! Can it be that the dead do walk?" He withdrew again the hands which had gone to his eyes. The dreadful object passed between two pillars and under the house. He listened. There was a faint sound as of feet upon a staircase; then all was still except the measured tread of Jean Poquelin walking on the veranda and the heavy respirations of the mute slumbering in the cabin.

The little Secretary was about to retreat; but as he looked once more toward the haunted house, a dim light appeared in the crack of a closed window, and presently old Jean Poquelin came dragging his chair and sat down close against the shining cranny. He spoke in a low, tender tone in the French tongue, making some inquiry. An answer came from within. Was it the voice of a human? So unnatural was it — so hollow, so discordant, so unearthly — that the stealthy listener shuddered again from head to foot; and when something stirred in some bushes near by — though it may have been nothing more than a rat — and came scuttling through the grass, the little Secretary actually turned and fled. As he left the enclosure, he moved with bolder leisure through the bushes; yet now and then he spoke aloud: "Oh, oh! I see, I understand!" and shut his eyes in his hands.

IV

How strange that henceforth Little White was the champion of Jean Poquelin! In season and out of season — wherever a word was uttered against him — the Secretary, with a quiet, aggressive force that instantly arrested gossip, demanded upon what authority the statement or conjecture was made; but as he did not condescend to explain his own remarkable attitude, it was not long before the disrelish and suspicion that followed Jean Poquelin so many years fell also upon him.

It was only the next evening but one after his adventure that he made himself a source of sullen amazement to one hundred and fifty boys by ordering them to desist from their wanton hallooing. Old Jean Poquelin, standing and shaking his cane, rolling out his long-drawn maledictions, paused and stared, then gave the Secretary a courteous bow and started on. The boys, save one, from pure astonishment, ceased; but a ruffianly little Irish lad, more daring than any had yet been, threw a big hurtling clod that struck old Poquelin between the shoulders and burst like a shell. The enraged old man wheeled with uplifted staff to give chase to scampering vagabond; and — he may have tripped, or he may not, but he fell full length. Little White hastened to help him up, but he waved him off with a fierce imprecation and staggering to his feet, resumed his way homeward. His lips were reddened with blood.

Little White was on his way to the meeting of the Board. He would have given all he dared spend to have stayed away; for he felt both too fierce and too tremulous to brook the criticisms that were likely to be made.

"I can't help it, gentlemen; I can't help to make a case against the old man, and I'm not going to."

"We did not expect this disappointment, Mr. White."

"I can't help that, sir. No, sir; you had better not appoint any more investigations. Somebody'll investigate himself into trouble. No, sir; it isn't a threat, it is only my advice; but I warn you that whoever takes the task in hand will rue it to his dying day — which may be hastened too."

The President expressed himself "surprised."

"I don't care a rush," answered Little White, wildly and foolishly, "I don't care a rush if you are, sir. No, my nerves are not disordered; my head's as clear as a bell. No, I'm *not* excited."

A director remarked that the Secretary looked as though he had waked from a nightmare.

"Well, sir, if you want to know the fact, I have; and if you choose to cultivate old Poquelin's society, you can have one too."

"White," called a facetious member, but White did not notice. "White," he called again.

"What?" demanded White, with a scowl.

"Did you see a ghost?"

"Yes, sir; I did," cried White, hitting the table and handing the President a paper which brought the Board to other business.

The story got among the gossips that somebody (they were afraid to say Little White) had been to the Poquelin mansion by night and beheld something appalling. The rumor was but a shadow of the truth, magnified and distorted as is the manner of shadows. He had seen skeletons walking and had barely escaped the clutches of one by making the sign of the cross.

Some madcap boys, with an appetite for the horrible, plucked up courage to venture through the dried marsh by the cattle path and come before the house at a spectral hour when the air was full of bats. Something which they but half saw — half a sight was enough — sent them tearing back through the willow brakes and acacia bushes to their homes, where they fairly dropped down and cried:

"Was it white?" "No — yes — nearly so — we can't tell — but we saw it." And one could hardly doubt, to look at their ashen faces, that they had, whatever it was.

"If that old rascal lived in the country we come from," said certain Américains, "he'd have been tarred and feathered before now, wouldn't he, Sanders?"

"Well, now, he just would."

"And we'd have him rid on a rail, wouldn't we?"

"That's what I allow."

"Tell you what you *could* do." They were talking to some rollicking Creoles who had assumed an absolute necessity for doing *something*. "What is it you call this thing where an old man marries a young girl, and you come out with horns and —"

"Charivari?"[18] asked the Creoles.

"Yes, that's it. Why don't you shivaree him?" Felicitous suggestion.

Little White, with his wife beside him, was sitting on their doorstep on the sidewalk as Creole custom had taught them, looking toward the sunset. They had moved into the lately opened street. The view was not attractive on the score of beauty. The houses were small and scattered, and across the flat commons, spite of the lofty tangle of weeds and bushes and spite of the thickets of acacia, they needs must see the dismal old Poquelin mansion, tilted awry and shutting out the declining sun. The moon, white and slender, was hanging the tip of its horn over one of the chimneys.

"And you say," said the Secretary, "the old black man has been going by here alone? Patty, suppose old Poquelin should be concocting some mischief; he don't lack provocation; the way that clod hit him the other day was enough to have killed him. Why, Patty, he dropped as quick as *that!* No wonder you haven't seen him. I wonder if they haven't heard something about him up at the drugstore. Suppose I go and see."

"Do," said his wife.

She sat alone for half an hour, watching that sudden going out of the day peculiar to the latitude.

"That moon is ghost enough for one house," she said as her husband returned. "It has gone right down the chimney."

"Patty," said Little White, "the drug clerk says the boys are going to shivaree old Poquelin tonight. I'm going to try to stop it."

"Why, White," said his wife, "you'd better not. You'll get hurt."

"No, I'll not."

"Yes, you will."

"I'm going to sit out here until they come along. They're compelled to pass right by here."

"Why, White, it may be midnight before they start; you're not going to sit out here till then."

"Yes, I am."

"Well, you're very foolish," said Mrs. White in an undertone, looking anxious and tapping one of the steps with her foot.

They sat a very long time talking over little family matters.

"What's that?" at last said Mrs. White.

"That's the nine o'clock gun," said White; and they relapsed into a long-sustained, drowsy silence.

"Patty, you'd better go in and go to bed," said he at last.

"I'm not sleepy."

"Well, you're very foolish," quietly remarked Little White; and again silence fell upon them.

"Patty, suppose I walk out to the old house and see if I can find out anything."

"Suppose," said she, "you don't do any such — listen!"

Down the street arose a great hubbub. Dogs and boys were howling and barking; men were laughing, shouting, groaning, and blowing horns, whooping, and clanking cowbells, whinnying, and howling, and rattling pots and pans.

"They are coming this way," said Little White. "You had better go in the house, Patty."

"So had you."

"No, I'm going to see if I can't stop them."

"Why, White!"

"I'll be back in a minute," said White and went toward the noise.

In a few moments the little Secretary met the mob. The pen hesitates on the word, for there is a respectable difference, measurable only on the scale of the half century, between a mob and a charivari. Little White lifted his ineffectual voice. He faced the head of the disorderly column and cast himself about as if he were made of wood and moved by the jerk of a string. He rushed to one who seemed from the size and clatter of his tin pan to be a leader. *"Stop these fellows, Bienvenu, stop them just a minute till I tell them something."* Bienvenu turned and brandished his instruments of discord in an imploring way to the crowd. They slackened their pace; two or three hushed their horns and joined the prayer of Little White and Bienvenu for silence. The throng halted. The hush was delicious.

"Bienvenu," said Little White, "don't shivaree old Poquelin tonight; he's—"

---

[18] *charivari*, (shä-rê-vä´re) mock serenade of discordant noises, made with kettles, tin horns, etc. The English dialect form is a corruption of charivari, *shivaree*.

"My fwang," said the swaying Bienvenu, "who tail you I goin' to chahivahi somebody, eh? You sink beckause I make a little playfool wiz zis tin pan zat I am *dhonk?*"

"Oh, no, Bienvenu, old fellow, you're all right. I was afraid you might not know that old Poquelin was sick, you know, but you're not going there, are you?"

"My fwang, I vay soy to tail you zat you ah dhonk as de dev'. I am *shem* of you. I ham ze servan' of ze *publique. Zese citoyens* goin' to wickwest Jean Poquelin to give to the Ursuline two hondred fifty dolla'—"

"*Hé quoi!*" cried a listener. "*Cinq cent piastres, oui!*"[19]

"*Oui!*" said Bienvenu, "and if he wiffuse, we make him some lit' *musique;* ta-ra ta!" He hoisted a merry hand and foot, then frowning, added: "Old Poquelin got no bizniz dhink s'much w'isky."

"But, gentlemen," said Little White, around whom a circle had gathered, "the old man is very sick."

"My faith!" cried a tiny Creole, "we did not make him to be sick. W'en we have say we going make *le charivari,* do you want that we hall tell a lie? My faith! 'sfools!"

"But you can shivaree somebody else," said desperate Little White.

"*Oui!*" cried Bienvenu, "et *chahivahi* Jean-ah Poquelin to mo'w!"

"Let us go to Madame Schneider!" cried two or three, and amid huzzas and confused cries, among which was heard a stentorian Celtic call for drinks, the crowd again began to move.

"*Cent piastres pour l'hôpital de charité!*"[20]

"Hurrah!"

"One hongred dolla' for Charity hospital!"

"Hurrah!"

"Wang!" went a tin pan, the crowd yelled, and Pandemonium gaped again. They were off at a right angle.

Nodding, Mrs. White looked at the mantel clock.

"Well, if it isn't way after midnight."

The hideous noise down street was passing beyond earshot. She raised a sash and listened. For a moment there was silence. Someone came to the door.

"Is that you, White?"

"Yes." He entered. "I succeeded, Patty."

"Did you?" said Patty joyfully.

"Yes. They've gone down to shivaree the old Dutchwoman who married her stepdaughter's sweetheart. They say she has got to pay a hundred dollars to the hospital before they stop."

V

The couple retired, and Mrs. White slumbered. She was awakened by her husband snapping the lid of his watch.

"What time?" she asked.

"Half past three. Patty, I haven't slept a wink. Those fellows are out yet. Don't you hear them?"

"Why, White they're coming this way!"

"I know they are," said White, sliding out of bed and drawing on his clothes, "and they're coming fast. You'd better go away from that window, Patty. My! what a clatter."

"Here they are," said Mrs. White, but her husband was gone. Two or three hundred men and boys passed the place at a rapid walk straight down the broad, new street toward the hated house of ghosts. The din was terrific. She saw Little White at the head of the rabble brandishing his arms and trying in vain to make himself heard; but they only shook their heads, laughing and hooting the louder, and so passed, bearing him on before them.

Swiftly they pass out from among the houses, away from the dim oil lamps of the street, out into the broad, starlit commons, and enter the willow jungles of the haunted ground. Some hearts fail, and their owners lag behind and turn back, suddenly remembering how near morning it is. But the most part push on, tearing the air with their clamor.

Down ahead of them in the long, thick-darkened way there is — singularly enough — a faint, dancing light. It must be very near the old house; it is. It has stopped now. It is a lantern and is under a well-known sapling which has grown up on the wayside since the canal was filled. Now it swings mysteriously to and fro. A goodly number of the more ghost-fearing give up the sport; but a full hundred move onward at a run, doubling their devilish howling and banging.

Yes; it is a lantern, and there are two persons under the tree. The crowd draws near — drops into a walk; one of the two is the old African mute; he lifts the lantern up so that it shines on the other; the crowd recoils; there

[19] *Hé quoi! . . . cinq cent piastres, oui!* Oh, what! . . . five hundred dollars, yes!

[20] *Cent piastres pour l'hôpital de charité!* One hundred dollars for the charity hospital!

is a hush of all clangor, and all at once with a cry of mingled fright and horror from every throat the whole throng rushes back, dropping everything, sweeping past Little White and hurrying on, never stopping until the jungle is left behind; and then to find that not one in ten has seen the cause of the stampede, and not one of the tenth is certain what it was.

There is one huge fellow among them who looks capable of any villainy. He finds something to mount on and in the Creole patois[21] calls a general halt. Bienvenu sinks down and, vainly trying to recline gracefully, resigns the leadership. The herd gather round the speaker; he assures them they have been outraged. Their right peaceably to traverse the public streets has been trampled upon. Shall such encroachments be endured? It is now daybreak. Let them go now by the open light of day and force a free passage of the public highway!

A scattering consent was the response, and the crowd, thinned now and drowsy, straggled quietly down toward the old house. Some drifted ahead, others sauntered behind, but everyone, as he again neared the tree, came to a standstill. Little White sat upon a bank of turf on the opposite side of the way looking very stern and sad. To each newcomer he put the same question:

"Did you come here to go to old Poquelin's?"

"Yes."

"He's dead." And if the shocked hearer started away he would say: "Don't go away."

"Why not?"

"I want you to go to the funeral presently."

If some Louisianian, too loyal to dear France or Spain to understand English, looked bewildered, someone would interpret for him; and presently they went. Little White led the van, the crowd trooping after him down the middle of the way. The gate, that had never been seen before unchained, was open. Stern Little White stopped a short distance from it; the rabble stopped behind him. Something was moving out from under the veranda. The many whisperers stretched upward to see. The African mute came very slowly toward the gate, leading by a cord in the nose a small brown bull, which was harnessed to a rude cart. On the flat body of the cart, under a black cloth, were seen the outlines of a long box.

"Hat's off, gentlemen," said Little White as the box came in view, and the crowd silently uncovered.

"Gentlemen," said Little White, "here come the last remains of Jean Marie Poquelin, a better man, I'm afraid, with all his sins — yes, a better — a kinder man to his blood — a man of more self-forgetful goodness — than all of you put together will ever dare to be."

There was a profound hush as the vehicle came creaking through the gate; but when it turned away from them toward the forest, those in front started suddenly. There was a backward rush, then all stood still again, staring one way; for there, behind the bier, with eyes cast down and labored step, walked the living remains — all that was left — of little Jacques Poquelin, the long-hidden brother — a leper as white as snow.

Dumb with horror, the cringing crowd gazed upon the walking death. They watched, in silent awe, the slow *cortège* creep down the long straight road and lessen on the view, until by and by it stopped where a wild, unfrequented path branched off into the undergrowth toward the rear of the ancient city.

"They are going to the *Terre aux Lepreux*,"[22] said one of the crowd. The rest watched them in silence.

The little bull was set free; the mute, with strength of an ape, lifted the long box to his shoulder. For a moment more the mute and the leper stood in sight while the former adjusted his burden; then, without one backward glance upon the unkind human world, turning their faces toward the ridge in the depths of the swamp known as the Leper's Land, they stepped into the jungle, disappeared, and were never seen again.

VIEWING THE AUTHOR'S IDEAS

1. What historical event paved the way for the arrival of English-speaking people in Louisiana? What civilizing forces were at work before the coming of United States citizens? At what points in American Profile have you already met the influence of the French and Spanish cultures?

2. What traits of Poquelin are revealed by his sacrifice? How does his sense of values differ from those of the people around him? Which modes of thinking represent the best attitudes in American life; which the least desirable? List details which show how tenaciously the Creoles adhered to their language and customs.

3. How did Jean-ah Poquelin's kindness to his brother entail risks for others? Was he justified in his actions? In taking care of the sick, what consideration should be given to the well members of the family and the neighbors?

4. How did Jean-ah Poquelin's desire to keep his brother

---

[21] *patois*, dialect.

[22] *Terre aux Lepreux*, Land of the Lepers.

with him contrast with the attitude of those who advocate putting an end to the lives of aged? What is meant by euthanasia? What is your attitude toward it?

EVALUATING HIS MANNER OF EXPRESSION

1. What was Cable's attitude toward the Creoles? How does the author's neglect of religious influence in Creole life affect the story?

2. How does the author create the atmosphere of a decaying civilization? List local color details. What aspects of early Louisiana life are suggested? Discuss the author's use of dialect.

3. At what point in the story is the mystery surrounding Jean-ah Poquelin and his brother first mentioned? Trace the gradual heightening of suspense until the mystery is finally solved. How does White's change of attitude prepare us for the conclusion?

4. Discuss the tragic aspects of the story. Does pathos arise as much from the affliction of the brother as from the total misunderstanding of Jean-ah Poquelin's actions?

The Wonderful Tar Baby Story

(From *Uncle Remus: His Songs and His Sayings*)
Joel Chandler Harris

Joel Chandler Harris has preserved some of the most interesting folklore of the Southern Negro. The animal stories of Uncle Remus have their counterpart in fables current among the Indians of both North and South America and among various African tribes. In the genial white-haired Negro and the eager little boy, Harris gives a glimpse of the plantation life he knew so intimately.

In the story preceding the narratives presented here, Br'er Fox had invited Br'er Rabbit to dinner intending to make a meal of him. Br'er Fox had everything in readiness to kill a chicken for the occasion. Br'er Rabbit, seeing through the plot, offered to get some calamus root to season the chicken. Thus he outwitted Br'er Fox and escaped.

"DIDN'T the fox *never* catch the rabbit, Uncle Remus?" asked the little boy[1] the next evening.

"He come mighty nigh it, honey, sho's you born — Br'er Fox did. One day atter Br'er Rabbit fool 'im wid dat calamus root, Br'er Fox went ter wuk en got 'im some tar, en mix it wid some turkentime, en fix up a contrapshun wat he call a Tar Baby, en he tuck dish yer Tar Baby en he sot 'er in de big road, en den he lay off in de bushes fer to see wat de news wuz gwineter be. En he didn't hatter wait long, nudder, kaze bimeby here come Br'er Rabbit pacin' down de road — lippity-clippity, clippity-lippity — des ez sassy ez a jay bird. Br'er Fox,

he lay low. Br'er Rabbit come prancin' 'long twel he spy de Tar Baby, en den he fotch up on his behime legs like he wuz 'stonished. De Tar Baby, she sot dar, she did, en Br'er Fox, he lay low.

" 'Mawnin'!' sez Br'er Rabbit, sezee — 'nice wedder dis mawnin',' sezee.

"Tar Baby ain't sayin' nothin', en Br'er Fox, he lay low.

" 'How duz yo' sym'tums seem ter segashuate?'[2] sez Br'er Rabbit, sezee.

"Br'er Fox, he wink his eye slow, en lay low, en de Tar Baby, she ain't sayin' nothin'.

" 'How you come on, den? Is you deaf?' sez Br'er Rabbit, sezee. 'Kaze if you is, I kin holler louder,' sezee.

"Tar Baby stay still, en Br'er Fox he lay low.

" 'Youer stuck up, dat's w'at you is,' says Br'er Rabbit, sezee, 'en I'm gwineter kyore you, dat's w'at I'm a gwineter do,' sezee.

"Br'er Fox, he sorter chuckle in his stummuck, he did, but Tar Baby ain't sayin' nothin'.

" 'I'm gwineter larn you how ter talk ter 'spectubble fokes ef hit's de las' ack,' sez Br'er Rabbit, sezee. 'Ef you don't take off dat hat en tell me howdy, I'm gwineter bus' you wide open,' sezee.

"Tar Baby stay still, en Br'er Fox, he lay low.

"Br'er Rabbit keep on axin' 'im, en de Tar Baby, she

---

[1] *the little boy*, son of the plantation owner.

[2] *How . . . segashuate?* The word sagaciate [slang] means *to fare* or *thrive*.

keep on sayin' nothin', 'twel present'y Br'er Rabbit draw back wid his fis', he did, en blip he tuck 'er side er de head. His fis' stuck, en he can't pull loose. De tar hilt 'im. But Tar Baby, she stay still, en Br'er Fox, he lay low.

" 'Ef you don't lemme loose, I'll knock you agin,' sez Br'er Rabbit, sezee, en wid dat he fotch 'er a wipe wid de udder han', en dat stuck. Tar Baby, she ain't sayin' nothin', en Br'er Fox, he lay low.

" 'Tu'n me loose, fo' I kick de natal stuffin' outen you,' sez Br'er Rabbit, sezee, but de Tar Baby, she ain't sayin' nothin'. She des hilt on, en den Br'er Rabbit lose de use er his feet in de same way. Br'er Fox, he lay low. Den Br'er Rabbit squall out dat ef de Tar Baby don't tu'n 'im loose he butt 'er cranksided. En den he butted, en his head got stuck. Den Br'er Fox, he sa'ntered fort', lookin' des ez innercent ez one er yo' mammy's mockin' birds.

" 'Howdy, Br'er Rabbit,' sez Br'er Fox, sezee. 'You look sorter stuck up dis mawnin',' sezee, en den he rolled on de groun', en laughed en laughed twel he couldn't laugh no mo'. 'I speck you'll take dinner wid me dis time, Br'er Rabbit. I done laid in some calamus root, en I ain't gwineter take no skuse,' sez Br'er Fox, sezee."

Here Uncle Remus paused and drew a two-pound yam[3] out of the ashes.

"Did the fox eat the rabbit?" asked the little boy to whom the story had been told.

"Dat's all de fur de tale goes," replied the old man. "He mout, en den agin he moutent. Some say Jedge B'ar come 'long en loosed 'im — some say he didn't. I hear Mis' Sally[4] callin'. You better run 'long."

HOW MR. RABBIT WAS TOO SHARP FOR MR. FOX

"Uncle Remus," said the little boy one evening, when he had found the old man with little or nothing to do, "did the fox kill and eat the rabbit when he caught him with the Tar Baby?"

"Law, honey, ain't I tell you 'bout dat?" replied the old darky, chuckling slyly. "I 'clar ter grashus I ought er tole you dat, but old man Nod[5] wuz ridin' on my eyelids 'twel a leetle mo'n I'd a dis'member'd my own name, en den on to dat here come yo' mamy hollerin' atter you.

"W'at I tell you w'en I fus' begin? I tole you Br'er Rabbit wuz a monstus soon[6] creetur; leas'ways dat's w'at I laid out fer ter tell you. Well, den, honey, don't you go en make no udder calkalashuns, kaze in dem days Br'er Rabbit en his fambly wuz at de head er de gang w'en enny racket wuz on han', en dar dey stayed. 'Fo' you begins fer ter wipe yo' eyes 'bout Br'er Rabbit, you wait en see whar'bouts Br'er Rabbit gwineter fetch up at. But dat's needer yer ner dar.

"W'en Br'er Fox fine Br'er Rabbit mixed up wid de Tar Baby, he feel mighty good, en he roll on de groun' en laff. Bimeby he up'n say, sezee:

" 'Well, I speck I got you dis time, Br'er Rabbit,' sezee; 'maybe I ain't, but I speck I is. You been runnin' roun' here sassin' atter me a mighty long time, but I speck you done come ter de en' er de row. You bin cuttin' up yo' capers en bouncin' 'roun' in dis neighberhood ontwel you come ter b'leeve yo'se'f de boss er de whole gang. En den youer allers some'rs whar you got no bizness,' sez Br'er Fox, sezee. 'Who ax you fer ter come en strike up a 'quaintance wid dish yer Tar Baby? En who stuck you up dar whar you iz? Nobody in de roun' worril. You des tuck en jam yo'se'f on dat Tar Baby widout waitin' fer enny invite,' sez Br'er Fox, sezee, 'en dar you is en dar you'll stay twel I fixes up a breshpile and fires her up, kaze I'm gwineter bobbycue you dis day, sho,' sez Br'er Fox, sezee.

"Den Br'er Rabbit talk mighty 'umble.

" 'I don't keer w'at you do wid me, Br'er Fox,' sezee, 'so you don't fling me in dat brier patch. Roas' me, Br'er Fox,' sezee, 'but don't fling me in dat brier patch,' sezee.

" 'Hit's so much trouble fer ter kindle a fier,' sez Br'er Fox, sezee, 'dat I speck I'll hatter hang you,' sezee.

" 'Hang me des ez high as you please, Br'er Fox,' sez Br'er Rabbit, sezee, 'but do fer de Lord's sake don't fling me in dat brier patch,' sezee.

" 'I ain't got no string,' sez Br'er Fox, sezee, 'en now I speck I'll hatter drown you,' sezee.

" 'Drown me des ez deep ez you please, Br'er Fox,' sez Br'er Rabbit, sezee, 'but do don't fling me in dat brier patch,' sezee.

" 'Dey ain't no water nigh,' sez Br'er Fox, sezee, 'en now I speck I'll hatter skin you,' sezee.

---

[3] *yam,* a variety of sweet potato.

[4] *Mis' Sally,* mother of the little boy and mistress of the plantation.

[5] *old man Nod,* old man of the Land of Nod, a figurative expression meaning the state of sleep.

[6] *soon,* clever.

" 'Skin me, Br'er Fox,' sez Br'er Rabbit, sezee, 'snatch out my eyeballs, t'ar out my years by de roots, en cut off my legs,' sezee, 'but do please, Br'er Fox, don't fling me in dat brier patch,' sezee.

"Co'se Br'er Fox wanter hurt Br'er Rabbit bad ez he kin, so he cotch 'im by de behime legs en slung 'im right in de middle er de brier patch. Dar wuz a considerbul flutter whar Br'er Rabbit struck de bushes, en Br'er Fox sorter hang 'roun' fer ter see w'at wuz gwineter happen. Bimeby he hear somebody call 'im, en way up de hill he see Br'er Rabbit settin' cross-legged on a chinkapin log koamin' de pitch outen his har wid a chip, Den Br'er Fox know dat he bin swop off mighty bad. Br'er Rabbit wuz bleedzed fer ter fling back some er his sass, en he holler out:

" 'Bred en bawn in a brier patch, Br'er Fox — bred en bawn in a brier patch!' en wid dat he skip out des ez lively as a cricket in de embers."

VIEWING THE AUTHOR'S IDEAS

1. How is suspense created at the beginning of the first story? What hints of the outcome does Uncle Remus give? How does the conclusion of the first story arouse interest in the next?

2. What passage shows Uncle Remus' knowledge of the natural habits of the rabbit? What human characteristics does the old Negro attribute to Br'er Rabbit and Br'er Fox? How do these stories show the Negro's imagination and homely wisdom?

3. What double meaning is contained in Br'er Fox's greeting, "You look sorter stuck up dis mawnin'"? When had Br'er Rabbit used the same expression? Of what mischief does Br'er Fox accuse Br'er Rabbit?

4. The fox is noted for its slyness. How is this characteristic exemplified in Br'er Fox's attempts to catch Br'er Rabbit?

5. How is the rabbit's natural simplicity shown in Br'er Rabbit's encounter with the Tar Baby? In Negro fables the weak rabbit always evades his stronger enemies by his cunning. How is this fact exemplified in the way Br'er Rabbit outwitted Br'er Fox?

EVALUATING HIS MANNER OF EXPRESSION

1. Show that these stories have the simplicity and directness of folk tales.

2. What does dialect contribute to the stories?

3. Select passages which show Uncle Remus' quaint humor; his common sense; his ready wit.

Regret

Kate Chopin

Restraint, compression, and artistry are displayed in this charming story. It is rich in local color, revealing life in a rural French parish of Louisiana. At the same time it is universal in theme. That Kate Chopin, herself a mother, understood the joys of motherhood, is evident from this narrative.

MAMZELLE Aurélie possessed a good strong figure, ruddy cheeks, hair that was changing from brown to gray, and a determined eye. She wore a man's hat about the farm, and an old blue army overcoat when it was cold, and sometimes topboots.

Mamzelle Aurélie had never thought of marrying. She had never been in love. At the age of twenty she had received a proposal, which she had promptly declined, and at the age of fifty she had not yet lived to regret it.

So she was quite alone in the world, except for her dog Ponto, and the Negroes who lived in her cabins and worked her crops, and the fowls, a few cows, a couple of mules, her gun (with which she shot chicken-hawks), and her religion.

One morning Mamzelle Aurélie stood upon her gallery, contemplating, with arms akimbo, a small band of very small children who, to all intents and purposes, might have fallen from the clouds, so unexpected and bewildering was their coming, and so unwelcome. They were the children of her nearest neighbor, Odile, who was not such a near neighbor, after all.

The young woman had appeared but five minutes before, accompanied by these four children. In her arms she carried little Elodie; she dragged Ti Nomme by an unwilling hand; while Marcéline and Marcélette followed with irresolute steps.

Her face was red and disfigured from tears and excitement. She had been summoned to a neighboring parish[1] by the dangerous illness of her mother; her husband was away in Texas—it seemed to her a million miles away; and Valsin was waiting with the mule-cart to drive her to the station.

"It's no question, Mamzelle Aurélie; you jus' got to keep those youngsters fo' me tell I come back. Dieu sait,[2] I would n' botha you with 'em if it was any otha way to do! Make 'em mine you, Mamzelle Aurélie; don' spare 'em. Me, there, I'm half crazy between the chil'ren, an' Léon not home, an' maybe not even to fine po' maman alive encore!"[3]—a harrowing possibility which drove Odile to take a final hasty and convulsive leave of her disconsolate family.

She left them crowded into the narrow strip of shade on the porch of the long, low house; the white sunlight was beating in on the white old boards; some chickens were scratching in the grass at the foot of the steps, and one had boldly mounted, and was stepping heavily, solemnly, and aimlessly across the gallery. There was a pleasant odor of pinks in the air, and the sound of Negroes' laughter was coming across the flowering cotton-field.

Mamzelle Aurélie stood contemplating the children. She looked with a critical eye upon Marcéline, who had been left staggering beneath the weight of the chubby Elodie. She surveyed with the same calculating air Marcélette mingling her silent tears with the audible grief and rebellion of Ti Nomme. During those few contemplative moments she was collecting herself, determining upon a line of action which should be identical with a line of duty. She began by feeding them.

If Mamzelle Aurélie's responsibilities might have begun and ended there, they could easily have been dismissed; for her larder was amply provided against an emergency of this nature. But little children are not little pigs; they require and demand attentions which were wholly unexpected by Mamzelle Aurélie, and which she was ill prepared to give.

She was, indeed, very inept in her management of Odile's children during the first few days. How could she know that Marcélette always wept when spoken to in a loud and commanding tone of voice? It was a peculiarity of Marcélette's. She became acquainted with Ti Nomme's passion for flowers only when he had plucked all the choicest gardenias and pinks for the apparent purpose of critically studying their botanical construction.

"'Tain't enough to tell 'im, Mamzelle Aurélie," Marcéline instructed her; "you got to tie 'im in a chair. It's w'at maman all time do w'en he's bad: she tie 'im in a chair." The chair in which Mamzelle Aurélie tied Ti Nomme was roomy and comfortable, and he seized the opportunity to take a nap in it, the afternoon being warm.

At night, when she ordered them one and all to bed as she would have shooed the chickens into the hen house, they stayed uncomprehending before her. What about the little white nightgowns that had to be taken from the pillowslip in which they were brought over, and shaken by some strong hand till they snapped like ox-whips? What about the tub of water which had to be brought and set in the middle of the floor, in which the little tired, dusty, sunbrowned feet had every one to be washed sweet and clean? And it made Marcéline and Marcélette laugh merrily—the idea that Mamzelle Aurélie should for a moment have believed that Ti Nomme could fall asleep without being told the story of *Croque-mitaine*[4] or *Loup-garou,*[5] or both; or that Elodie could fall asleep without being rocked and sung to.

"I tell you, Aunt Ruby," Mamzelle Aurélie informed her cook in confidence; "me, I'd rather manage a dozen plantation' than fo' chil'ren. It's terrassent![6] Bonté![7] Don't talk to me about chil'ren!"

"'Tain't ispected sich as you would know airy thing 'bout 'em, Mamzelle Aurélie. I see dat plainly yistiddy w'en I spy dat li'le chile playin' wid yo' baskit o' keys. You don' know dat makes chillun grow up hard-headed, to play wid keys? Des like it make 'em teeth hard to look in a lookin'-glass. Them's the things you got to know in the raisin' an' manigement o' chillun."

[1] *parish*, a civil division in Louisiana, corresponding to a county in other states.
[2] *Dieu sait*, God knows.
[3] *encore*, still.
[4] *Croque-mitaine*, the bugbear or the imaginary monster, sometimes mentioned to frighten children.
[5] *Loup-garou*, the man turned into a wolf.
[6] *terrassent*, terrifying.
[7] *Bonté*, good.

Mamzelle Aurélie certainly did not pretend or aspire to such subtle and far-reaching knowledge on the subject as Aunt Ruby possessed, who had "raised five an' bared (buried) six" in her day. She was glad enough to learn a few little mother-tricks to serve the moment's need.

Ti Nomme's sticky fingers compelled her to unearth white aprons that she had not worn for years, and she had to accustom herself to his moist kisses—the expressions of an affectionate and exuberant nature. She got down her sewing basket, which she seldom used, from the top shelf of the armoire,[8] and placed it within the ready and easy reach which torn slips and buttonless waists demanded. It took her some days to become accustomed to the laughing, the crying, the chattering that echoed through the house and around it all day long. And it was not the first or the second night that she could sleep comfortably with little Elodie's hot, plump body pressed close against her, and the little one's warm breath beating her cheek like the fanning of a bird's wing.

But at the end of two weeks Mamzelle Aurélie had grown quite used to these things, and she no longer complained.

It was also at the end of two weeks that Mamzelle Aurélie, one evening, looking away toward the crib where the cattle were being fed, saw Valsin's blue cart turning the bend of the road. Odile sat beside the mulatto, upright and alert. As they drew near, the young woman's beaming face indicated that her homecoming was a happy one.

But this coming, unannounced and unexpected, threw Mamzelle Aurélie into a flutter that was almost agitation. The children had to be gathered. Where was Ti Nomme? Yonder in the shed, putting an edge on his knife at the grindstone. And Marcéline and Marcélette? Cutting and fashioning doll-rags in the corner of the gallery. As for Elodie, she was safe enough in Mamzelle Aurélie's arms; and she had screamed with delight at sight of the familiar blue cart which was bringing her mother back to her.

[8] *armoire*, cupboard.

The excitement was all over, and they were gone. How still it was when they were gone! Mamzelle Aurélie stood upon the gallery, looking and listening. She could no longer see the cart; the red sunset and the blue-gray twilight had together flung a purple mist across the fields and road that hid it from her view. She could no longer hear the wheezing and creaking of its wheels. But she could still faintly hear the shrill, glad voices of the children.

She turned into the house. There was much work awaiting her, for the children had left a sad disorder behind them; but she did not at once set about the task of righting it. Mamzelle Aurélie seated herself beside the table. She gave one slow glance through the room, into which the evening shadows were creeping and deepening around her solitary figure. She let her head fall down upon her bended arm, and began to cry. Oh, but she cried! Not softly, as women often do. She cried like a man, with sobs that seemed to tear her very soul. She did not notice Ponto licking her hand.

VIEWING THE AUTHOR'S IDEAS

1. What details given in the first two paragraphs help to characterize Mamzelle Aurélie?

2. How does the author suggest that Mamzelle Aurélie's life was rather empty? How did she try to compensate for her lack of human interest? Do you think that she was sympathetic and warmhearted by nature?

3. What details show that the writer had an intimate understanding of the needs of childhood? Which seemed more important to her: the physical, emotional, or spiritual?

4. Are there any evidences that a spirit of true charity animated the lives of the French Catholics of Louisiana?

5. Discuss the appropriateness of the title.

EVALUATING HER MANNER OF EXPRESSION

1. Compare the first and the last paragraphs. Notice the details and the effect of the emotional restraint the author employs. Has Mamzelle's character essentially changed at the close of the story?

2. Point out instances of local color in the description of the landscape and in dialogue.

3. Kate Chopin shows care in her choice of words, particularly in her use of verbs and adjectives. Find some apt expressions.

The Religious Element in Education

John Lancaster Spalding

On numerous occasions Bishop Spalding reiterated that Catholic schools have been established to enable children to grow up in an atmosphere wherein learning blends with piety. His reasons for this view are set forth in the following essay from Means and Ends of Education.

APART from all theories and systems of belief and thought, public opinion in America sets strongly against the denominational school.

The question of education is considered from a practical rather than from a theoretical point of view, and public sentiment on the subject may be embodied in the following words: The civilized world now recognizes the necessity of popular education. In a government of the people, such as this is, intelligence should be universal. In such a government, to be ignorant is not merely to be weak; it is also to be dangerous to the common welfare, for the ignorant are not only the victims of circumstances; they are the instruments which unscrupulous and designing men make use of to taint the source of political authority and to thwart the will of the people. To protect itself, the State is forced to establish schools and to see that all acquire at least the rudiments of letters. This is so plain a case that argument becomes ridiculous. They who doubt the good of knowledge are not to be reasoned with; and in America not to see that it is necessary, is to know nothing of our political, commercial, and social life. But the American State can give only a secular education, for it is separate from the church; and its citizens profess such various and even conflicting beliefs that in establishing a school system, it is compelled to eliminate the question of religion. Church and State are separate institutions, and their functions are different and distinct. The church seeks to turn men from sin that they may become pleasing to God and save their souls; the State takes no cognizance of sin but strives to prevent crime and to secure to all its citizens the enjoyment of life, liberty, and property. Americans are a Christian people. Religious zeal impelled their ancestors to the New World; and when schools were first established here, they were established by the churches, and religious instruction formed an important part of the education they gave. This was natural, and it was desirable even in primitive times when each colony had its own creed and worship, when society was simple and the State as yet was imperfectly organized. Here, as in the Old World, the school was the daughter of the church, and she has doubtless rendered invaluable service to civilization by fostering a love for knowledge among barbarous races and in struggling communities. But the task of maintaining a school system such as the requirements of a great and progressive nation demand is beyond her strength. This is so at least when the church is split into jealous and warring sects.

To introduce the spirit of sectarianism into the classroom would destroy the harmony and goodwill among citizens, which it is one of the aims of the common school to cherish. There is, besides, no reason why this should be done, since the family and the church give all the religious instruction which children are capable of receiving.

This, it seems to me, is a fair presentation of the views and ideas which go to the making of current American opinion on the question of religious instruction in State schools; and current opinion, when the subject matter is not susceptible of physical demonstration, cannot be turned suddenly in an opposite direction. . . .

The Catholic view of the school question is as clearly defined as it is well known. It rests upon the general ground that man is created for a supernatural end and that the Church is the divinely appointed agency to help him to attain his supreme destiny. If education is a training for completeness of life, its primary element is the religious, for complete life is life with God. Hence we may not assume an attitude toward the child, whether in the home, in the church, or in the school, which might imply that life apart from God could be anything else than broken and fragmentary. A complete man is not one whose mind only is active and enlightened; but he is a complete man who is alive in all his faculties. The truly human is found not in knowledge alone but also in faith, in hope, in love, in pure-mindedness, in reverence, in the sense of beauty, in devoutness, in the thrill of awe, which Goethe says is the highest thing in man. If the teacher is forbidden to touch upon religion, the source of these noble virtues and ideal moods is sealed. His work and influence become mechanical, and he will form but commonplace and vulgar men. And if an educational system is established on this narrow and material basis, the result will be deterioration of the national type and the loss of the finer qualities which make men many-sided and interesting, which are the safeguards of personal purity and of unselfish conduct.

Religion is the vital element in character, and to treat it as though it were but an incidental phase of man's life is to blunder in a matter of the highest and most serious import. Man is born to act, and thought is valuable mainly as a guide to action. Now the chief inspiration to action, and above all to right action, is found in faith, hope, and love — the virtues of religion, and not in knowledge, the virtue of the intellect. Knowledge, indeed, is effectual only when it is loved, believed in, and held to be a ground for hope. Man does not live on bread alone; and if he is brought up to look to material things as to the chief good, his higher faculties will be stunted. If to do rightly rather than to think keenly is man's chief business here on earth, then the virtues of religion are more important than those of the intellect; for to think is to be unresolved, whereas to believe is to be impelled in the direction of one's faith. In epochs of doubt, things fall to decay; in epochs of faith the powers that make for full and vigorous life hold sway. The education which forms character is indispensable; that which trains the mind is desirable. The essential element in human life is conduct; and conduct springs from what we believe, cling to, love, and yearn for, vastly more than from what we know. The decadence and ruin of individuals and of societies come from lack of virtue, not from lack of knowledge. "The hard and valuable part of education," says Locke,[1] "is virtue; this is the solid and substantial good which the teacher should never cease to inculcate till the young man places his strength, his glory, and his pleasure in it." We may of course distinguish between morality and religion, between ethics and theology. As a matter of fact,

however, moral laws have everywhere reposed upon the basis of religion, and their sanction has been sought in the principles of faith. As an immoral religion is false, so, if there is no God, a moral law is meaningless.

Theorists may be able to construct a system of ethics upon a foundation of materialism; but their mechanical and utilitarian[2] doctrines have not the power to exalt the imagination or to confirm the will. Their educational value is feeble. Here in America we have already passed the stage of social development in which we might hold out to the young, as an ideal, the hope of becoming President of the Republic or the possessor of millions of money. We know what sorry men presidents and millionaires may be. We cannot look upon our country simply as a wide racecourse with well-filled purses hanging at the goal for the prize winners. We clearly perceive that a man's possessions are not himself and that he is or ought to be more than anything which can belong to him. Ideals of excellence, therefore, must be substituted for those of success. Opinion governs the world, but ideals draw souls and stimulate to noble action. The more we transform with the aid of machinery the world of matter, the more necessary does it become that we make plain to all that man's true home is the world of thought and love, of hope and aspiration. The ideals of utilitarianism and secularism[3] are unsatisfactory. They make no appeal to the infinite in man, to that in him which makes pursuit better than possession and which, could he believe there is no absolute truth, love, and beauty, would lead him to despair. Today, as of old, the soul is born of God and for God and finds no peace unless it rest in Him. . . .

To exclude religion is to exclude the spirit of reverence, of gentleness and obedience, of modesty and purity; it is to exclude the spirit by which the barbarians have been civilized, by which woman has been uplifted and ennobled and the child made sacred. From many sides the demand is made that the State schools exercise a greater moral influence, that they be made efficient in forming character as well as in training the mind. It is recognized that knowing how to read and write does not insure good behavior. Since the State assumes the office of teacher, there is a disposition among parents to

[1] *Locke*, an English philosopher of the seventeenth century.

[2] *utilitarian*, merely useful.

[3] *secularism*, a view of life that excludes religion.

make the school responsible for their children's morals as well as for their minds, and thus the influence of the home is weakened. Whatever the causes may be, there seems to be a tendency both in private and in public life to lower ethical standards. The moral influence of the secular school is necessarily feeble, since our ideas of right and wrong are so interfused with the principles of Christianity that to ignore our religious convictions is practically to put aside the question of conscience. If the State may take no cognizance of sin, neither may its school do so. But in morals, sin is the vital matter; crime is but its legal aspect. Men begin as sinners before they end as criminals.

The atmosphere of religion is the natural medium for the development of character. If we appeal to the sense of duty, we assume belief in God and in the freedom of the will; if we strive to awaken enthusiasm for the human brotherhood, we imply a divine fatherhood. Accordingly, as we accept or reject the doctrines of religion, the sphere of moral action, the nature of the distinction between right and wrong, and the motives of conduct all change. In the purely secular school only secular morality may be taught; and whatever our opinion of this system of ethics may otherwise be, it is manifestly deficient in the power which appeals to the heart and the conscience. The child lives in a world which imagination creates, where faith, hope, and love beckon to realms of beauty and delight. The spiritual and moral truths which are to become the very life breath of his soul he apprehends mystically, not logically. Heaven lies about him; he lives in wonderland and feels the thrill of awe as naturally as he looks with wide-open eyes. Do not seek to persuade him by telling him that honesty is the best policy, that poverty overtakes the drunkard, that lechery breeds disease, that to act for the common welfare is the surest way to get what is good for one's self; for such teaching will not only leave him unimpressed, but it will seem to him profane and almost immoral. He wants to feel that he is the child of God, of the infinitely good and all-wonderful; that in his father, divine wisdom and strength are revealed; in his mother, divine tenderness and love. He so believes and trusts in God that it is our fault if he knows that men can be base. In nothing does the godlike character of Christ show forth more beautifully than in His reverence for children. Shall we profess to believe in Him and yet forbid His name to be spoken in the houses where we seek to train the little ones whom He loved? Shall we shut out Him whose example has done more to humanize, ennoble, and uplift the race of man than all the teachings of the philosophers and all disquisitions of the moralists? If the thinkers, from Plato to Aristotle to Kant and Pestalozzi, who have dealt with the problems of education have held that virtue is its chief aim and end, shall we thrust from the school the one ideal character who for nearly nineteen hundred years has been the chief inspiration to righteousness and heroism? . . .

We all, and especially the young, are influenced by example more than by precepts and maxims; and it is unjust and unreasonable to exclude from the schoolroom the living presence of the noblest and best men and women, of those whose words and deeds have created our Christian civilization. In the example of their lives we have truth and justice, goodness and greatness in concrete form; and the young who are brought into contact with these centers of influence will be filled with admiration and enthusiasm; they will be made gentle and reverent, and they will learn to realize the ever-fresh charm and force of personal purity. Teachers who have no moral criteria, no ideals, no counsels of perfection, no devotion to God and godlike men cannot educate, if the proper meaning of education is the complete unfolding of all man's powers.

The school, of course, is but one of the many agencies by which education is given. We are under the influence of our whole environment, — physical, moral, and intellectual; political, social, and religious; and if, in all this, aught were different, we ourselves should be other. The family is a school, and the church is a school; and current American opinion assigns to them the business of moral and religious education. But this implies that conduct and character are of secondary importance; it supposes that the child may be made subject to opposite influences at home and in the school, and not thereby have his finer sense of reverence, truth, and goodness deadened. The subduing of the lower nature, of the outward to the inner man, is a thing so arduous that reason, religion, and law combined often fail to accomplish it. If one should propose to do away with schools altogether and to leave education to the family and the Church, he would be justly considered ridiculous; because the carelessness of parents and the inability of the ministry of the Church would involve the prevalence of illiteracy. Now, to leave moral and religious education to the family and the churches involves for similar reasons the prevalence of indifference, sin, and crime. If illiteracy is a menace to free institutions, vice and irreligion are a greater menace. The corrupt are always bad citizens; the ignorant are not necessarily so. Parents who would not have their children taught to read and write, were there no free schools, will as a rule neglect their religious and moral education. In giving religious instruction to the young, the churches are plainly at a disadvantage; for they have the child but an hour or two in seven days, and they get into their Sunday classes only the children of the more devout.

If the chief end of education is virtue; if conduct is three-fourths of life; if character is indispensable, while knowledge is only useful, — then it follows that religion — which, more than any other vital influence, has power to create virtue, to inspire conduct, and to mold character — should enter into all the processes of education. Our school system, then, does not rest upon a philosophic view of life and education. We have done what it was easiest to do, not what it was best to do; and in this, as in other instances, churchmen have been willing to sacrifice the interests of the nation to the whims of a narrow and jealous temper. The denominational system of popular education is the right system. The secular system is the wrong system. The practical difficulties to be overcome that religious instruction may be given in the schools are relatively unimportant and would be set aside if the people were thoroughly persuaded of its necessity. . . .

No system, however, can give assurance that the school is good. To determine this, we must know the spirit which lives in it. The intellectual, moral, and religious atmosphere which the child breathes there, is of far more importance, from an educational point of view, than any doctrines he may learn by rote, than any acts of worship he may perform.

The teacher makes the school; and when high, pure, devout, and enlightened men and women educate,

the conditions favorable to mental and moral growth will be found, provided a false system does not compel them to assume a part and play a role, while the true self — the faith, hope, and love whereby they live — is condemned to inaction. The deeper tendency of the present age is not, I think, to exclude religion from any vital process but rather to widen the content of the idea of religion until it embrace the whole life of man. The worship of God is not now the worship of infinite wisdom, holiness, and justice alone, but is also the worship of the humane, the beautiful, and the industriously active. Whether we work for knowledge or freedom, or purity or strength, or beauty or health, or aught else that is friendly to completeness of life, we work with God and for God. In the school, as in whatever other place in the boundless universe a man may find himself, he finds himself with God, in Him moves, lives, and has his being.

VIEWING THE AUTHOR'S IDEAS

1. How do people regard popular education? What reasons do they have for this view? Why do not secular schools give religious instruction? State three reasons why all schools should provide this benefit.

2. What is the Catholic view on education and schools? How does the writer show that development of soul is more important than development of mind? What advantages come with the spirit of religion?

3. How does the influence of religious teaching help the community? Explain the difference between ethics and morals; between crime and sin.

4. In what way is Christ's attitude towards children a guidepost for those who instruct the young? How does Bishop Spalding argue for virtuous teachers? Besides the school, what other forces help to educate the pupil?

5. Sketch briefly Spalding's argument for the maintenance of the parochial school. What form of popular education does he consider most useful in a democracy? State his discussion. How does he regard the teacher and his calling?

EVALUATING HIS MANNER OF EXPRESSION

1. In introducing the discussion, how does Bishop Spalding show fairness?

2. List the reasons given to prove that "education is training for completeness of life."

QUESTIONS FOR REVIEW

In your notebook copy the numbers from 1 to 5. After selecting the correct choice, write the complete statement.

1. The California stories that first cheered the critics of the East were written by (A) John Hay (B) Joaquin Miller (C) Walt Whitman (D) Bret Harte.

2. Walt Whitman's determination to be the great American poet may be traced in part to his reading of (A) Lowell (B) Holmes (C) Emerson (D) Whittier.

3. *The Pike County Ballads* were written by (A) John Hay (B) Bret Harte (C) Joaquin Miller (D) Walt Whitman.

4. Joaquin Miller's reputation as a poet was established by his (A) *Pacific Poems* (B) *Specimens* (C) *Songs of the Sierras* (D) *Joaquin et al.*

5. From a literary point of view, Mark Twain's best book is (A) *Tom Sawyer* (B) *Huckleberry Finn* (C) *Roughing It* (D) *Personal Recollections of Joan of Arc.*

Read each statement carefully. Then write in your notebook only those statements that are TRUE.

1. The hazards of migration and the sturdiness of frontier life provided both tone and subject matter for the literature of the West.

2. Humor helped the frontier folk to endure the hardships of their way of life.

3. Early humor in America and that which was developed on the frontier were basically the same.

4. Artemus Ward, Josh Billings, and Mark Twain were frontier humorists.

5. In cowboy songs the spirit of the West still lives in all its vastness, hospitality, and sentiment.

6. The largest body of American folk songs came from the cowboy.

7. Spirituals represent the cry of an oppressed race for spiritual help, the utterance of a people to whom singing brings relief.

8. Local color was a new literary phenomenon, showing itself for the first time after 1870.

9. The local-color writers paved the way for the novelists of the realistic school and aided in the development of the American short story.

10. Emphasis on local peculiarities, a new direction in literature after the Civil War, stands as an American contribution to the literature of the world.

11. In poetry Whitman's strength is his imagery, particularly when it is based on sensation of touch or vision.

12. The weakness of free verse is its tendency toward that formlessness which is the negation of art.

13. Joaquin Miller lived a romantic adventurous life in the West.

14. Miller is at his best in describing in swinging, hearty rhythm the great stretches of land in the Rocky Mountain ranges.

15. Sidney Lanier has produced some of the most musical works in American literature.

16. Much of James Whitcomb Riley's success as a writer was achieved through his skillful use of dialect.

17. Father Tabb's poetry excels in crystallizing great wisdom within the compass of a few lines.

18. Bret Harte's first claim to literary honor comes from the impetus he gave to the local-color movement.

19. The humor of Mark Twain is not in the tradition of the great comic writers of the world.

20. Joel Chandler Harris' "Uncle Remus" stories show the poetic side of the Negro.

QUESTIONS FOR DISCUSSION

1. How did the migration to the West after the Civil War affect the literature of America?

2. Discuss the beginnings of folk literature in the Western section of America.

3. What traits are common to the whole body of folk song?

4. Compare the songs of the cowboy with the spirituals of the Negro.

5. How was the writing known as local color given impetus by life in the West?

6. Point out the errors in Whitman's theories and in his message in *Leaves of Grass.*

7. How did New England writers regard the exuberance of the writers of the frontier?

8. Contrast Whitman and Lanier as lyricists and philosophers.

9. Show that Mark Twain's theories on life and God are erroneous.

10. Discuss the humor of Mark Twain.

SUGGESTIONS FOR READING

Aldrich, Bess Streeter, *A Lantern in Her Hand* (Appleton-Century, New York). Hardships, drought, grasshopper invasions, hot winds did not daunt Abbie Deal in her endeavor to establish a home in early Nebraska. Mrs. Aldrich draws a quiet, forceful picture of pioneer life.

Aldrich, Bess Streeter, *Spring Comes on Forever* (Appleton-Century, New York). This story of pioneer days in Nebraska centers around two German-American families. The novel is written in the simple and easy style which makes Mrs. Aldrich's books a delight. *Song of the Years* by the same author depicts happy family life in the pioneer days of Iowa. Jeremiah Martin with his wife and nine children courageously face difficulties and subdue obstacles in their effort to build a home in the wilderness.

Cable, George Washington, *Old Creole Days* (Scribner, New York). Mystery, romance, and love blend in these stories of life in old Catholic Louisiana.

Cicognani, Amleto Giovanni, *Sanctity in America* (St. Anthony Guild Press, Paterson, New Jersey). This collected biography of saintly Americans by the Apostolic Delegate to America might well be included in frontier sketches. Among those intrepid souls who did pioneer work for Christ in America were St. Frances Xavier Cabrini and St. Rose Philippine Duchesne.

Code, Rev. Joseph B., *The Veil Is Lifted* (Bruce, Milwaukee). Great souls in their unselfishness build for the future. This book gives fascinating sketches of the Mother Foundresses of American Religious Orders.

Donovan, Josephine, *Black Soil* (Stratford, Boston). This novel pictures the Irish struggling against the odds of pioneer life in Iowa. There is human interest in the story of Tom and Nell Connor trying to build a comfortable home in the wilderness. German, Dutch, and Austrian settlers show a spirit of co-operation.

Eggleston, Edward, *The Hoosier Schoolmaster* (Scribner, New York). The novel is a perennial favorite because its roots are deep in human nature and in American life. The story recounts the experiences of a young teacher in backwoods Indiana.

Heagney, Harold Jerome, *The Blockade Runner: A Tale of Adventure Aboard* the Robert E. Lee (Longmans, New York). This is a fascinating tale about the Civil War. John Bannister Tabb and Sidney Lanier feature in the story.

Hough, Emerson, *The Covered Wagon* (Grosset, New York). Rivalry for the love of Molly Wingate adds interest to this historical novel, recounting the hardships of a group of immigrants to Oregon in search of gold.

Jackson, Helen Hunt, *Ramona* (Little, Brown, Boston). This is a powerful, picturesque, sympathetic picture of Spanish and Indian life in California. It reveals the white man's injustice to the Indian. Ramona and her Indian husband are cruelly driven from their homes by avaricious hordes of Americans. Ramona displays remarkable loyalty and courage.

Lane, Rose Wilder, *Let the Hurricane Roar* (Longmans, New York). Youth is by nature courageous and craves adventure. A newly-married couple face the perils of pioneer life in Dakota in the 1870s. The story is told with a reserve which makes the love, sacrifice, and fidelity to duty seem real.

Lovelace, Maud H., *Early Candlelight* (Grosset, New York). The author recounts the coming of the pioneers to Minnesota. Graphic details reveal the life, the pleasures, and the hardships of the settlers. The Mississippi was an important means of travel in those days.

Page, Thomas Nelson, *In Ole Virginia* (Scribner, New York). Page has been called the "apologist for the Old South." His stories glorify southern aristocratic life. Page did for Virginia what Bret Harte had done for San Francisco, and George Washington Cable for New Orleans—he popularized that section of the country.

Roberts, Elizabeth Madox, *The Great Meadow* (Viking Press). To hew homes out of the wilderness, to live in constant fear of lurking Indians called for physical courage. A variation of the theme of Tennyson's *Enoch Arden* adds to the interest of the book.

Roosevelt, Theodore, *The Strenuous Life* (Appleton-Century, New York). There is vitality and inspiration in this collection of essays which appeal to normal boys. "The American Boy" is a general favorite.

Wister, Owen, *The Virginian* (Grosset, New York). A rough-riding cowboy, through his chivalry and daring, wins the love of a pretty school teacher from Vermont. Wyoming, with its mountains, pure air, roaming buffalo and wild antelope was once the cowboy's paradise.

White, Stewart Edward, *The Long Rifle* (Double-day, New York). Daniel Boone wins the long rifle at a shooting match in Pennsylvania. A courageous young friend of Boone's inherits it and carries it to explore the Rocky Mountains. Active and thrilling incidents are found in this novel of pioneer life.

Harvesters Resting — A Realistic Painting by Thomas Eakins

Realistic Views, 1870-1914

The free winds from the western frontier did not sweep across America unimpeded. They were challenged by the clouds rising in ever greater density from increasing numbers of factory smokestacks. In the wake of westward expansion followed another profound change in American life: the domination of the machine. New mechanical inventions speeded industrial operations. Transcontinental railroads revolutionized marketing by causing factories to be built in areas where raw materials were produced. Boys and girls left the farms to work in crowded industrial centers. Beside them labored a new influx of immigrants who could find employment only under a system of mass production. Many of these immigrants kept to themselves in overcrowded quarters and were Americanized slowly. With politics the servant of the capitalist, the interests of the poor were sacrificed to the will of the mighty.

As Americans watched the industrial development of their nation, they saw certain citizens using their freedom to deprive other citizens of essential rights.

Capitalists had formed huge monopolies for the purpose of destroying smaller competitors and obtaining unjust gains on manufactured products. Speed, consolidation, and concentration became the prime objectives of industry. America had increased her wealth enormously during the years of industrial expansion. These riches, however, were concentrated in the hands of the few. The poverty of the lower classes was becoming a national problem. Government officials were being bribed to grant political favors. The machine threatened to defeat man, whose genius had brought it into being. The individual lost footing and was swept headlong into the millrace of new urban industrialized America. By 1900, the American industrial revolution had been effected. Against the evils of industrialism came the strong voice of American protest. Reform measures resulted and in them certain restrictions were imposed on business enterprise. Laws were adopted to safeguard public welfare. Americans were learning how vigilantly their beloved democracy had to be safeguarded. And yet the struggle between individual greed and public interest continues today.

In contrast to the first period of optimistic expansion, the farmers of the Middle West became bitter towards the end of the 1880s. At its best, pioneer living demanded strong hearts and hands. Cold, poor homes, strenuous labor, grasshoppers, crop failures, debts for tools, and overproduction soon made the farmer suspicious of his share of the national inheritance. Many were beaten by hardship. Railroad companies which had received millions of acres free from the government charged high rates for transporting grain. Frequently the railroad made more on the produce of the land than did the farmer. Out of the helpless struggle to keep mortgaged lands came defiant and rebellious voices.

The materialistic aims of the industrial age were accompanied by a sharp decline in American culture. The westward expansion had tended to level class distinctions. The handiwork of the craftsman had been displaced by the uniform products of the machine. Men whose rough individualism had enabled them to amass fortunes were now plagued by their wives and daughters to spend it elegantly. With haste a restless age set about to express its individuality. The unity and harmony of early American art, which had derived from European traditions, was banished. In its stead came extravagant and ornamental patterns in architecture, interior decoration, and dress. In buildings appeared such oddities as the brownstone front, spiderweb verandas, and gingerbread fretwork. It was the era in which women built framework within their skirts and padded their hairdress. Men were fastidious in handlebar mustaches, false shirt fronts, celluloid collars, and diamond-studded tiepins. The East that furnished factory supplies to the expanding West drew in the largest share of the exploited new wealth. The new economic vigor on the Atlantic seacoast brought into being social climbers who threatened the exclusive circles that had ruled Boston and New York. Frequently men of older cultural standards found the age so barren that they voluntarily exiled themselves in European countries.

In the realm of thought, also, far-reaching changes were in progress. Science, the chief instrument in bringing about the industrial revolution, caused an intellectual upheaval as well. Man used science to increase his physical comforts in a way very different from that by which he applied scientific knowledge to his views about life. New discoveries were not adopted in the physical world until they had been tested and proved. The engineer calculated the strength of the steel before he constructed his bridge. The electrician computed the exact circuit of the coils in the pulsing dynamo. Men did not exercise the same caution in applying recent discoveries to the study of the human personality. They made the mistake of thinking that physical laws could be transferred to the spiritual realm. From the hypotheses of science they proceeded to furnish an explanation of the origin of man's acts. The fact that an individual has a free will imposes upon him moral obligations. Yet many writers conveniently cast aside these responsibilities by denying their spiritual nature and looking upon themselves as powerless atoms subject only to physical laws.

With all the perversity of man-made systems of thought, the new view of life was lacking in the joy it promised. The creed that annihilated good and evil swept away also the hope of reward for the manifold sufferings of life, which still persisted, despite the advances of science. Materialistic writers offered little consolation when they assured the common man that fate was not malignant but merely indifferent. Where there had once existed the common belief in a benign Providence, there now seemed to be only the vast dumbness of the physical universe. In it man was a particle of imprisoned energy arising to momentary awareness in the continuous changes about him. In their spiritual uncertainty and economic struggle, people became pessimistic. Writers no longer hid the problems of life behind the veil of romantic loveliness. They tore aside all veils with ruthless hands and began to write realistically.

THE DIFFERENCE BETWEEN ROMANTIC, REALISTIC, AND NATURALISTIC ART

Before viewing the nature of realism, you may find it helpful to consider briefly why the artist is impelled to create and why others enjoy his production. Man is constantly facing the query "What is life, anyhow?" A humorist has suggested that this common question be expressed as the briefest poem in the English language:

Why
I?

In man's experience, his reason, his study of science and history, and particularly in his religion, he finds the answer to this question. But he does not wish only to see things reasonably. He wishes to *make* a representation of his thoughts in a reasonable manner. In addition to his work of gaining food and a livelihood, he seeks to satisfy his creative impulse. He tries to represent by his own handiwork the meaning of his existence. In art, then, as in a framework, he sets off his interpretation of some aspect of his life. If he is a competent artist, he has glimpsed some of the glory and some of the tragedy of human endeavor. If his picture of life is correct, he is able to show how the shadow of man's weakness darkens his spirit. In beholding this spectacle, the onlooker finds his emotions purified and ennobled. The artist's aim is not to teach people how to live; it is to make them *want* to live. From this enlightening view of some aspect of life, the ordinary man returns refreshed to his humdrum tasks.

Only the artist who has adequate vision — and skill corresponding to his insight — can produce a work that will enlighten and inspire his fellow men. The discernment and emotion of the competent artist make him not only powerfully aware of beauty of form, color, and sound but also conscious that he has some part in the earth about him, that he breathes its air and is nourished by its plenty. In poetry, for example, the very rise and fall of the author's language indicate his surge of emotion as he gives voice to his reaction to life. The true artist meditates upon the relationship of all objects to himself and seeks to express the larger relationship of all things within the universe. He is not content until he has shown that all things have a purpose, that everything has its place in some large design. He aims at a complete view, although it is not necessary that he portray life in its entirety. He may treat of a minor detail — such as a flower or a stone. In his picture even the simplest flower will have a meaning because life has a meaning.

Particularly does the great artist seek to show the way by which his personality will come to its measure of completeness. Lastly, he wishes to portray the path by which he may pass to the enjoyment of complete happiness. It is at this point that the artist must have faith if he would span the bridge between time and eternity. It is faith that will show grace and free will as the means by which man may be successful in his moral conflict and so fulfill his destiny.

In your study of literature it is of the greatest importance that you learn to appraise the interpretation of the artist and measure it according to your standards of truth. The lives of the authors you have read in this book, the progression of ideas from century to century, have been presented primarily to help you to become a competent thinker and critic in the reading you will do. It is as important to be able to know what is wrong in a book you are reading as to remember what is right. The purpose of your literary study, then, is to enable you to enjoy and appraise the works of others and to aid you to worthy self-expression when you turn to creative endeavor.

It is readily apparent that the artist's attitude towards life powerfully influences the treatment of his subject matter. A writer may look upon life 1) with a tendency to idealize and so sees more than is objectively present, 2) viewing things fairly accurately, 3) with a pessimistic outlook, seeing less than actually exists. Or he may combine one of these attitudes with another, according to his purpose or his mood when writing.

If he tends to see an ideal situation rather than a real one, he is said to treat life in a romantic way. As you will observe by looking back over the authors of the national period, the romantic artist offers an illuminating view of life to the extent that his power to depict the relationships within reality is well directed or ill directed. With men whose faith does not provide them with a stabilizing sense of direction, the romantic temper tends to run to excesses. Emerson extolled the individual until man became a deity in his own opinion. In a lesser error of enthusiasm, the eighteenth-century romanticists had praised the uncivilized Indian until they viewed him as the "noble savage." If, however, the romantic tendency to exalt is directed to an object worthy of praise, an inspirational view of life will result. Even the difficulties which weak human nature must surmount are seen as a glorious and stimulating challenge. Man is made to reach spiritual heights. Romanticism is the mood for spiritual aspiration. When a romanticist like Gerard Manley Hopkins exclaims, "The world is charged with the grandeur of God!" he has seized upon a theme which cannot be overstated.

The futile dreams or emotional excesses of many romantic writers frequently bring the reaction of stern realism. The word *realistic* has been associated frequently with disagreeable or incomplete views of life. It may be well, then, to consider what kind of writer the true realist actually is. He is a man who looks life in the face, viewing both the good and the bad in their true proportion. He is prepared to accept a certain amount of pain. He expects some joy but not so much that he can be easily disappointed. Above all, he wants to see things happen. Like that of the romanticist, the illuminating power of the realistic writer depends upon the fund of truth to which he brings his piercing eyes and his dynamic energy. A writer cannot, in the exact sense of the term, write realistically about a family living in a tenement house unless he knows the truth about that family. He has to know the details of their squalor, poverty, and deprivation. But he also has to be able to see their struggle in terms of its power to contribute to their ultimate happiness. Consequently, a writer cannot tell the whole truth about a tenement-house family without seeing their existence in the light of Creation, the Fall, the Incarnation, and the Redemption. The family fits into a realistic picture of life only in an acceptance of the power of grace, of Christ Who spans the difference between human and divine reality, and of the Trinity, Who is all Actuality, all Being.

It is obvious that the Catholic attitude towards realism is in harmony with the Catholic expression of romanticism. The most adequate view of life combines the practicality of Christian endeavor with the exaltation of Christian faith. So likewise the most satisfactory kind of art combines Christian idealism and realism. The art of the Middle Ages was essentially a combination of these two methods of treatment. The spires of Gothic cathedrals pointed heavenwards, but the grinning demons of the waterspouts reminded the churchgoer that he was still of earth. The greatest romantic theme of the Middle Ages — the story of the quest for the Holy Grail — pictures man's search after God. In the symbolism of the Cup is expressed the great reality of God's union with man in the Holy Eucharist. Dante, who aspires to lead his reader even to the ecstatic

The Chess Players *by Thomas Eakins —*
An Instance of Realism in Art

joy of the Beatific Vision, likewise realistically pictures demons with pitchforks casting back sinners into the burning mire.

In proportion as a writer drifts away from a recognition of the major realities of God and man's search for Him, his picture of life will be incomplete. The majority of modern writers who pride themselves on their realistic attitude for the most part have not come to the complete vision in which they see the actualities of the material world united with those of the spiritual. Many modern realists, although confused concerning their belief in spiritual realities, do not deny the existence of these realities or refuse to recognize moral law. They are concerned primarily with an exact and impartial picture of ordinary people and monotonous incidents — insisting that people and incidents are usually ordinary and monotonous. This type of writer is like the scientist in his observation of minute details and like the historian in his insistence on accuracy. He keeps notebook records of the thoughts and feelings of his characters. He records few adventures and creates fewer heroes. He deals with mechanics, farmers, miners, politicians, and stenographers. Whereas the romanticist usually concludes his book with a wedding, the realist opens his work with the nuptials and spends the remaining chapters describing the way in which the couple evade bill collectors, attend funerals, eat their meals, tolerate the misbehavior of their children, and repeat the small talk of their neighbors. Usually the realist manages to get his central character into some major difficulty. Often he does not state how the conflict ends because he does not know. Despite the fact that the honest modern realist paints truth as he knows it, his vision is frequently incomplete.

So far we have considered both romanticism and realism and the ways in which the artist's belief about life influences his use of these methods. The third type of approach, the distorted or pessimistic treatment, is a corruption of the realistic view. Writers of this school depict man as the helpless pawn of physical or economic forces over which he has no control. Since these authors look upon man as merely another animal of the physical or natural world, this type of writing is called *naturalism*. Naturalists fall into two main divisions, both of which deny that man has a free will. The first group, influenced by Darwin, holds that the individual is controlled by inner drives and instincts. He follows these desires, impulses, and habits much as a moth is impelled towards a light. The second group, reflecting the ideas of Karl Marx, looks upon man as a victim of an economic system which determines almost all his actions. They see him as a creature so tricked by fate and baffled by circumstances that they consider him incapable of moral obligations.

Since naturalists deny free will and man's power of self-discipline, they do not write novels about men who have conquered through manly effort or attained culture and refinement through education and self-improvement. Instead they show marked preferences for sordid scenes and abnormal personalities. The characters they depict are frequently men of strong passions and dwarfed intellects, neurotics, or men who have fallen from an earlier ideal. The naturalistic writer uses the microscope and the dissecting knife of the laboratory, and too often the case history of the psychiatrist. He then presents the sufferings of diseased minds and bodies and the horrors that degrade society as a picture of the whole of life.

Naturalistic philosophy sweeps away the glamour of fiction in the same way it shatters the wonder of life. In story, as in fact, man is fascinating to his fellow beings because he *can* achieve heroism against tremendous odds. Even when overcome by brute force, he is, by virtue of his will and intellect, superior to the unconscious elements of the universe which may take his life. It is the recognition of human dignity that has furnished the novelist with his store of absorbing plots.

If such moral issues as loyalty, honesty, and chastity were not at stake, there would be no reason why a reader would follow the action of a fictional hero with continued eagerness. Man could not applaud another man's conduct if both were mere bundles of blind impulses. A robot has a difficult time rivaling an actual man — even in fiction.

Realism and naturalism entrenched themselves slowly in American literature. Realism came first. It was foreshadowed by the work of the local-color school, with writers' faithful representations of local scenery and dialect. Side by side with this vogue of writing appeared the mildly realistic novels of such writers as Henry James and William Dean Howells. It is not always possible to distinguish a writer of this early period as being either a strictly realistic or romantic author, since the two trends were frequently interwoven. After 1890 many writers struck out boldly in a more pronounced realistic pace. The changing social order not only affected the subject matter of the novelists but their spirit in treating it. Looking upon America, they resented the evils of the machine age: the domination of capitalism, the political corruption, the poverty of the lower-class city dweller, the plight of the farmer. The criticism of social evils was voiced in the novel of humanitarian protest. Narratives which treat some sociological phase of American life have since that time been an important element in our fiction. Almost simultaneously with the humanitarian fiction rose the problem novel, which deals frankly with some ethical question.

Realism had come to stay. In its final stage, the grimness of the more pronounced realists degenerated into naturalism. In contemporary fiction, realism and naturalism are often combined in one story. It must be remembered, moreover, that the realism of the twentieth century does not exclude romanticism. Finally, and not infrequently, a writer incorporates all three elements of realism, naturalism, and romanticism into a single work.

HENRY JAMES

Mark Twain's contempt for literary models and sentimental fiction led to a careless freedom and a realistic approach. Henry James and William Dean

Howells, more conscious artists, focused attention on the novel as a literary form and helped to stem the boisterous realism of Twain and, at least for a time, the sordid realism of the naturalistic school. Both James and Howells agreed that the novel should become more intellectual; that character, rather than incident, should dominate; that ordinary individuals in ordinary circumstances could be made more significant matter for fiction.

Henry James, Jr., was born in New York City, April 15, 1843. His father was a man of cultivated taste, a writer, a clergyman, and a philosopher. James's grandfather was among the first millionaires in this country. He had come from Ireland with practically no education, yet he amassed a fortune through his shrewdness. Reared in an atmosphere of wealth and leisure, educated by private tutors and accustomed to trips to Europe, Henry James, Jr. became a somewhat snobbish young man, scorning American culture. He felt however, that if he wished to live in this country, he should have some profession, at least nominally. He attended Harvard Law School and while there began to write critical articles and fiction. He became interested in the French short-story writers and used them as models for fiction. His success came slowly, only after painstaking study of his art. For ten years he worked as an apprentice, polishing his form. Then, about 1872, he resolved to become a professional man of letters, to give up his residence in this country, always to work leisurely, and to be satisfied only with his best work.

Henry James went to England to practice the art of living as well as the art of fiction. He felt that America was too noisy, too business-minded, too money-mad to afford leisure for the complete living so necessary for truly artistic writing. His narrow sympathies, his contacts only with aristocrats and intellectuals — many of them foreigners — prevented him from catching the real spirit of the American people. Although he wrote for an American audience and pictured Americans against a foreign background, his stories and novels were never popular in the United States. He frequently chose an inferior American and contrasted that character with a highly cultured Englishman or Frenchman. In this way he gave Europeans a false impression of the social and cultural life in our country. Many of his stories are concerned with some aspect of the expatriate. In 1915

Henry James

he renounced his American citizenship and became a British subject. He died in 1916.

Henry James created what he called the novel of international manners, and was a pioneer in the psychological novel so popular at the present time. In his analysis of mental processes, he was influenced by his brother, William, the well-known psychologist and professor at Harvard. Although Henry James wrote a dozen full-length novels and about as many shorter stories, a few titles will serve to suggest his realistic handling of material and his interest in psychological reactions.

In *Daisy Miller* (1879), a novelette, James shows the misunderstanding to which a frank, fun-loving, flirtatious American girl is subjected when her actions are evaluated according to the terms of old-world social conventions. *The Portrait of a Lady* (1881) is a masterpiece among the works of James. It is readable and entertaining and has much more action than *Daisy Miller*. In it is portrayed the tragedy that entered the life of a generous, high-spirited young lady who had taken up living abroad, and who had married a fortune-seeker. *The Ambassadors* (1903), James's favorite work, is a splendid example of his use of psychological realism. Lambert Strether has been sent to Europe by Chad Newsome's mother to save Chad from the pernicious Parisian influence and to bring him back to Wollett,

Massachusetts, and to the life of a manufacturer. But his mission was not successful because he himself became convinced of the intellectual and cultural superiority of Europe.

While Henry James analyzes well the thoughts of his characters, he rarely gives a glimpse into their hearts. His range of sympathies and interests is narrow. But within those bounds, he achieves success. Most of his stories are lacking in spontaneity; they are too carefully planned and studied. Because of the lack of action in the novels and the degree of sophistication in many of them, the works of Henry James will never be widely read. He does, however, occupy an important place in the history of American fiction. Through his presentation of psychological material, his skillful analysis of character, and his mastery of technique, Henry James raised the tone of the American novel and exerted a tremendous influence upon succeeding writers.

WILLIAM DEAN HOWELLS

William Dean Howells, unlike Henry James, was born in a somewhat crude household in Martins Ferry, Ohio, in 1837. He came from a family which fostered American traditions and had imbibed all that was good in the American way of life. Howells' father, a printer, encouraged his children to read by supplying a library containing many of the world's classics. Although Howells had little formal education, he supplemented it by his reading and experience in the print shop, where he had learned to set type before he was tall enough to reach the type cases. Through study he broadened his vision and gradually gained confidence in his ability to criticize and write. His one desire was to become associated with the intellectual life of Boston.

In 1860 in collaboration with J. J. Piatt, Howells published a volume entitled *Poems of Two Friends.* Through his work in the journalistic field, he was gradually building up a reputation for himself. He was called upon to write a campaign biography for Abraham Lincoln. From this work, came an appointment to the consulship in Venice. This position left him with considerable leisure time, which he spent in self-cultivation and intellectual growth. He learned Italian and French and read many literary works in the original

foreign tongues. He also took time to write poetry and travel sketches. When he returned to the United States in 1866, he was offered the position of assistant editor of the *Atlantic Monthly.* Howells was fond of editorial work; his own apprenticeship helped him to criticize others and to encourage aspiring young writers. From 1886 to 1891 he was on the staff of *Harper's Magazine,* conducting a department called "The Editor's Easy Chair." Much of his formal criticism appeared in this column. Through his work on magazines, Howells had an opportunity to direct the course of American literature into the channels of new realism. Carl Van Doren, an able American critic, believes that the influence of William Dean Howells as editor and critic was so important as to make of the man himself "almost a literary movement."

From 1866 until the time of his death in 1920, Howells grew in creative power. He had a more far-reaching influence upon the development of the novel than did Henry James. Both by word and by example Howells attempted to use the realistic technique in every field of literature, poetry, novel, and drama. His two best-known novels are *A Modern Instance* (1882) and *The Rise of Silas Lapham* (1885). The former, which treats the divorce question, is an early example of the problem novel. The latter introduces the character of the self-made businessman to American literature. In a sympathetic and objective manner, the story portrays the conflict between newly-rich families and cultivated Brahmin society. In both novels Howells attempts to show the significance of common things in the lives of ordinary individuals. He places emphasis on human nature and genially satirizes some of the foibles and social conventions of the day. The occasional tragic note in his work may be traced, perhaps, to his reading of Russian novels.

While most of Howells' novels treat of major human problems, his plays are usually light in subject matter and in method of treatment. Many of them are farces concerned with amusing situations that touch only the surface of life. A small amount of action is supplemented by a skillful use of brilliant dialogue. Howells never looked upon himself as a dramatist but took delight in poking fun at human nature, especially in sophisticated society.

William Dean Howells

Howells' strongest work is in the novel, where his realism is at its best. He succeeded in presenting a truthful picture of American life. Although regarded as somewhat of an innovator in his own day, Howells condemned the brutal and morbid treatment offered by the naturalistic school of fiction.

JOHN BOYLE O'REILLY

An influential figure in the development of Catholic literature in America was John Boyle O'Reilly (1844-1890). The literary and editorial skill of this Irish immigrant quickly brought the respect and admiration of Boston. O'Reilly used his influence and his magnetic personality to further the cause of Catholic culture. A native of Ireland, he was charged with complicity in the Fenian rebellion and sentenced to penal servitude in Australia. Amid the brutality of prison life he found solace in the *Imitation of Christ* and composed poetry which he scratched with a nail on the wall of his cell. In the hope of breaking his proud spirit, his jailers showed him the black-bordered envelope which brought the news of his mother's death and then kept the letter from him for six months. Eventually he escaped to America and became editor and joint owner of the *Boston Pilot.* Under his direction the paper, already national in circulation, became a Catholic voice which made

a deep impression on readers of all denominations. The editor's breadth of view, sympathy, and spirit of comradeship made a link between Irish Catholics and Protestant New Englanders. O'Reilly received many honors, among them an invitation to compose and read the ode at the dedication of a national monument to the Pilgrim Fathers. In addition to his journalistic work, O'Reilly wrote both fiction and poetry. His novel, *Moondyne Joe* (1875), which draws upon his experiences in Australia, treats the adventures of an Irish prisoner in a penal colony. The lyrics of his four volumes of poetry have a permanent freshness and loveliness. In addition to the songs of his native Ireland, he extols the ideal of democracy, which was doubly dear to him because of the tyranny which he had undergone.

LOUISE IMOGEN GUINEY

As editor of the *Pilot,* John Boyle O'Reilly saw promise in the fresh, spontaneous poems which a young Boston girl was submitting under several pen names. The girl was Louise Imogen Guiney (1861-1920), the first great Catholic woman poet of America and one of the great women poets in the English language. She was a thoroughly modern woman in her many-sided personality and her strong initiative. She gloried in the military tradition of her ancestors, particularly of her father, who led his regiment to battle more than thirty times in the Civil War. When she made her first visit to Elmhurst Academy at Providence, Rhode Island, at eleven years of age, she carried with her a toy gun and marbles. This equipment was intended to express her somewhat militant skepticism of the regime of convent schools. During her six years with the Religious of the Sacred Heart at Elmhurst, however, she exchanged her early doubts for enthusiastic convictions. It was during these years that she began to see that the most splendid victories are inner triumphs.

Four years after her graduation Louise Guiney published her first collection of poems. The death of her father had made it necessary for her to earn her living, and she confidently took a position as postmistress at Auburndale, Massachusetts. The members of the town were still violently anti-Catholic. In a belligerent outburst against the appointment, the citizens united in a general boycott of the local post office. Louise valiantly stayed in her position. There is reason to believe that her mother's opposition to a young suitor further added to the girl's tortured spirit at this time.

In 1895 Louise took up residence in England, not to escape from her trials but to gain the perspective to rise above them. The unpleasant happenings at Auburndale had left her without bitterness. They merely enabled her to develop the moral attitude that pervades her work. It is significant that her best poems were written about this time. There were other reasons for her residence abroad. The struggle against poverty was less keen in England, and the young writer's literary hunger was both stimulated and satisfied by her friendship with Katharine Tynan, Lionel Johnson, the Meynells, and many other authors. Her first stay abroad was short; but in 1901, after her mother's death, she left the United States to live permanently in England. For the next nineteen years she resided near Oxford University, returning to her native land only for two brief visits.

To an exceptional degree Louise Imogen Guiney lived the Christian ideal which her poetry celebrates. She combined a zest for living with a clear-cut pattern for sanctity. The poet who saw nature as the handiwork of God was a lover of the outdoor world, of boating, swimming, and fencing. With her great St. Bernard dogs by her side, she strode with free movement over the outdoor world as across a great playground. She saw life as a colorful tournament in which the true knight was ready to die in fulfilling his vow. Defeat he might encounter often, but always he could be confident of the ultimate victory of the spirit.

Under the symbolism of medieval chivalry the poet sang of self-control, self-sacrifice, and fidelity. She lived under rigid self-discipline. Her gaiety and charm drew many friends and admirers to her cottage. Yet she set herself to her chosen duty and refused the distractions of popular acclaim. Her poetry sings of a spiritual goal as the quest of knight errantry. It voices the joy of abandonment to God, of absolute surrender, of spiritual detachment. This high spirituality had its practical counterpart in a score of parish activities. The poet assisted poor missions, attended to details of processions, composed hymns, catalogued parish libraries, and organized Catholic lecture clubs. Her dynamic charity stimulated the co-operation of others.

After Louise Guiney had published four volumes of poetry, she collected her most representative poems under the title *Happy Ending* (1909). Her work is consistently powerful in its deep spirituality, superb imagery, spirited expression, and finished workmanship. "The Wild Ride" and "A Carol" are two poems in contrasting moods which may be taken as typical, showing at once her lyrical energy and exquisite purity of tone.

In her scholarly research Louise Imogen Guiney generously gave her energies to a neglected group of the past: the English poets of the seventeenth century who refused to conform to the Established Church. For seven years she examined old manuscripts and books for the writings of those who put Catholic truths into poetry at a time when the penal laws forbade the writing or publishing of Catholic literature. Her search yielded the poems of some seventy authors. Since this volume was not completed at the time she died, the manuscript was not published until 1939, when it appeared as *Recusant Poets*. Among the distinctive treatises of Louise Imogen Guiney's study of obscure heroes is a life of Saint Edmund Campion. As a literary critic she stands in the first rank. In her numerous studies, particularly of seventeenth-century authors, she is fearless, just, appreciative, temperate, and almost always correct in her judgments. In addition to her power of discerning literary excellence, she shows a rare ability to judge works in their relation to ethical standards.

Louise Imogen Guiney produced one volume of short stories, *Lovers' St. Ruth's and Three Other Tales* (1895). Although the stories are inferior to her poetry, they show an individuality, quaintness, and charm.

In *Patrins* (1897), which contains the most mature of her essays, the author exhibits her tranquil manner, power of penetration, and wide learning. The essays, like her poems, assert the philosophy of peace in self-denial and of dependence upon God.

The same gracious tone that characterizes Louise Imogen Guiney's essays also pervades her letters, of which she had written more than three thousand by 1911.

RICHARD HOVEY

Richard Hovey (1864-1900) wrote poems of the out-of-doors. He was a restless spirit who never utilized to the full his poetic talents. Born in a little town in Illinois, the son of a college professor, he had many educational opportunities. He attended Dartmouth College and later studied art and theology. He drifted into journalism and attempted acting and playwrighting. He was attracted to the Belgian dramatist, Maeterlinck, and translated some of his plays. The French symbolists, too, fascinated him. After his marriage he attempted to lead the life of a man of letters, and for a time he taught at Barnard College. At his death he left a number of unfinished works.

His poems represent two classes of works: his vagabondia verse and his more serious poems on the Arthurian legends. The volumes of *Songs from Vagabondia* (1896) and *More Songs from Vagabondia* (1901), written in collaboration with Bliss Carman, represent his best poetic effort. These two poets in their vigorous lyrics of outdoor life raised "a protest against the warped convention-bound lives of the materialistic, money-making Americans of their day." The freshness of diction and free movement of the lines are an integral part of these open-road poems.

BLISS CARMAN

Bliss Carman (1861-1929) was a Canadian by birth, who made pure sound and color into rich symbols for his thought. He did great service to American letters as an editor and collector, and in his vagabond way, beat a picturesque trail between New Brunswick and New York. The carefree, gypsy-like attitude of Hovey and Carman was a protest not only against social conventions but against the more restrained conservative verse of their day.

MAURICE FRANCIS EGAN

By his voluminous writings, his scholarly attainments, and his leadership in Catholic letters, Maurice Francis Egan (1852-1924) won recognition at the turn of the century. Born in Philadelphia, he attended La Salle College in his native city and received his university training at Georgetown. As a young journalist, he became associated with the valiant, but then aging, lion of Catholic editors, James McMaster of *Freeman's*

Journal. In 1888 Egan went to Notre Dame as professor of English Literature and later he held a similar position at the Catholic University of America. Appointed United States minister to Denmark, he served with eminent ability in that post for ten years. His last years were crowned with literary and diplomatic honors.

Maurice Francis Egan produced some forty volumes of literary criticism, essays, fiction, biography, and poetry. He had the tolerance, the sense of humor, the broad interests, and the power of self-criticism that become the critic. His literary theory was sound. Literature, he believed, need never contain a forced moral, yet it cannot ignore the divine origin of the soul nor the operation of the moral law. In his informal essays Egan discussed a wide range of modern topics. Written in a witty, gay style, these essays convey truth with a light touch. Sixteen of Egan's works may be classed as fiction. His *Life Around Us* (1906), a collection of tales, touches many aspects of Catholic life. In *The Wiles of Sexton Maginnis,* a series of witty sketches centering around a parish sexton, Egan introduced a new figure into Catholic fiction. The author particularly enjoyed the writing of stories for boys, whose innocent pranks, gigantic hopes and fears he thoroughly understood. His non-fiction prose includes a character study of St. Francis and *Recollections of a Happy Life* (1924), the writer's own memoirs. In poetry, Egan is chiefly remembered for a few melodious and thought-provoking sonnets which show his mastery of form. The optimism of Christianity fills his lines. His poetic style is quiet, elevated, and restrained, yet full of warmth and glowing spirituality.

CHARLES J. O'MALLEY

Charles J. O'Malley (1857-1910) devoted the greater part of his professional career to editing Catholic newspapers and magazines in Cincinnati, Louisville, Pittsburgh, Syracuse, and Chicago. As an editor he encouraged youthful talent and spent his own leisure in creative work. Besides his two volumes of poems, *Autumn Leaves* (1879) and *Building of the Moon* (1894), he wrote a biography of Leo XIII.

JOHN JEROME ROONEY

Many of the poems of John Jerome Rooney (1866-1934) were written on the margin of a newspaper as he braced himself against the sway of the trolley or "elevated" taking him to work. Poetry was a diversion for this lawyer and journalist, who turned out vigorous, flowing verse as a means of championing a cause or commemorating an important event. After receiving his B.A. degree from Mount St. Mary's College, Emmitsburg, Rooney took a position as reporter on the Philadelphia *Record,* where he covered developments in labor. He later studied law, wrote special articles on legal questions for New York newspapers, and served as a member of the New York State Board of Claims.

WILLIAM VAUGHN MOODY

William Vaughn Moody (1869-1910) was one of the best and most scholarly poets of his time. A native of Indiana, he taught English at Harvard and at the University of Chicago. He was never a popular writer but had a select and appreciative group of admirers. Edwin Arlington Robinson, an outstanding poet of the twentieth century, acknowledges his indebtedness to Moody. Deeply versed in the tradition of the past, Moody sought to fuse the past with the present. He took seriously what he considered the duty of the poet: to become the spokesman of his day. Moody was decidedly an intellectual and philosophical poet, whose appeal is chiefly to scholars.

Moody realistically calls attention to the social evils of his day, but fails to offer an adequate solution. In "Gloucester Moors," he uses the figure of a ship to picture humanity as the victim of social injustice. "The Brute" presents a vision of modern machinery enslaving men. "An Ode in Time of Hesitation" and "On a Soldier Fallen in the Philippines" are protests against imperialism. "The Quarry" is an allegorical poem condemning the European nations that desired to divide China among themselves.

HENRY ADAMS

Though living in the late nineteenth century, Henry Adams (1838-1918) stood apart from the turmoil of his age as one viewing a parade. He followed no literary trend of his times. With the eyes of the critic, he viewed the vast pageantry of human life from ancient to modern times, seeking to find the meaning of life in its progression. Repelled by the materialistic and acquisitive spirit of his own time, he found in the Middle Ages the harmony and unity of life for which he sought. In his search for truth, his reason drew him to Catholicism. He was, however, a man torn by doubt, and an ingrained pessimism kept him from accepting the truths of the Faith.

In his own person Henry Adams embodied the highest cultural advantages that Boston could offer. He was a lover of the arts, a haunter of philosophies, a companion of statesmen, a teacher of history, an editor, and a writer. As historian of his own country, he produced authoritative works in the polished style of a master. Despite the many fields into which he drifted, Adams never felt at home in a civilization which he felt was corrupt. He plunged into the study of philosophy and wandered in foreign lands. At the cathedrals of Mont St. Michel and Chartres in France he found the closest approach to inner peace he had ever known. The contemplation of the civilization which had produced this architecture led him to understand the unity of spirit of medieval life. Here at last he saw an age in which manifold activity tended to a single goal: the glorification of God. In *Mont St. Michel and Chartres* (1913) Adams wrote a singularly beautiful book on the art and architecture of the Middle Ages. He interprets the whole era in the light of devotion to the Virgin Mary. Although his limited knowledge of Catholicism did not enable him to explain aright the entire doctrine of Mary's relationship to the Trinity, he grasped the teaching of Our Lady's intercessory power.

To becloud this clear vision came the doubts which resulted from Adams' reading of materialistic philosophers. The author's thinking turned about two focal points. From the past beckoned revealed religion, represented by the statue of Our Lady in the Cathedral of Chartres. From modern philosophy, on the other hand, he had glimpsed the idea of man's being attracted, like an atom, without any will of his own, towards the Central Force of the universe. As a symbol of this mechanistic force dominating all life,

Henry Adams

he used the recent invention of the dynamo. He did not know from which of these two beliefs the salvation of America was to come. So he wrote his single poem, the magnificent *Prayer to the Virgin of Chartres*. It is a poem of spare and towering grandeur; its clean-cut lines are ardent with the passion of a lifetime. In it he gives tongue to the conflict that tore him. While he did not dare to answer his own question, the answer is there, implicitly. His prayer to the dynamo is not a prayer at all but a defiant challenge to the terror and uncertainty of the machine. His prayer to Our Lady is a prayer indeed. In her — and he speaks with no question in his voice — are "The strength, the knowledge, and the thought of God."

As a sequel to his medieval study the author wrote *The Education of Henry Adams* (1918). This autobiography is as indicative of his skepticism of modern civilization as Mont St. Michel had been of his trust in the Middle Ages. In its study of his own failure to find a worthy purpose in life, the book becomes a criticism of the age. It is an unflinching analysis of modern education, which he regards as a garment draped on a mannikin. The author is frank in self-criticism as well as in his charges against modern America. The autobiography reveals his attempt to study society in the light of all existing information and his inability to see an ordered plan in the long history of humanity. Henry Adams' passionate desire to understand the world and to find

ultimate truth was not attained. Apparently he was no nearer his goal at the end of his struggle than at the beginning.

THOMAS AUGUSTINE DALY

The flavorful dialect of Thomas Augustine Daly's immigrant poems has made them scrapbook items and recitation pieces from coast to coast. Not so generally known is the fact that their author has written serious lyrics of stirring and sustained beauty which celebrate the emotions of home life.

T. A. Daly (1871-) has been in newspaper work since he interrupted his college course to enter journalism. He has been associated with various Philadelphia papers. His numerous dialect poems helped to bring to American citizens a consciousness of their obligation to contribute to the Americanization of the immigrant. In the hearts of these foreigners he found a poem — sometimes a gay song, again a cry of sorrow — but always a note which showed their kinship as men with the people of their new country. T. A. Daly's ability to tell a story, sketch a character, portray genuine emotion, and to sustain suspense make his dialect poems skillful and sensitive interpretations of immigrant life. Many poems from his six volumes were reissued in his *Selected Poems* in 1936.

PAUL LAURENCE DUNBAR

Not long after the Civil War, Paul Laurence Dunbar (1872-1906), grew up in Ohio. The son of two Kentucky slaves, he was educated in the public schools of Dayton. After selling his first book of poems, Dunbar continued to publish poetry until he reached international fame. *Oak and Ivy* (1893) and *Majors and Minors* (1895) were written while he was an elevator operator, and even when success reached him, he preferred a quiet life among books to starting any kind of social revolution. He felt that he could best prepare for the social betterment of his race by showing that the Negro had something to contribute to culture. Dunbar wrote for poetry's sake, not for any cause, and would not have written in his dialect had it not been popular with the public. Many of his poems are in straightforward English, but in spite of himself dialect released the poet's best powers. The affection, the pathos, the whimsy of Negro family life, and the lilt of Negro music are best heard in his native verses. Dunbar served as an assistant at the Library of Congress and in 1898 married an author, Alice Ruth Moore. A rigorous program of writing and lecturing broke the poet's health, and he died in Dayton in 1906.

WILLIAM SYDNEY PORTER (O. HENRY)

William Sydney Porter (1862-1910) was born in Greensboro, North Carolina. He had little formal education. The best part of his training was gained through his employment in a drugstore. Even before the days of the popular drugstore lunch counter, strollers, loafers, and occasionally good storytellers met for entertainment in the village store. O. Henry soon became interested in studying the types of character who frequented the drugstore, and read in odd moments the magazines and newspapers at his disposal. Porter was always an ambitious man. When he was twenty-one he went to try his fortune on the Texas frontier. His friends had advised a change of climate as he seemed to be developing lung trouble. For two years O. Henry led the life of a cowboy and under the blue skies of Texas read the *Arabian Nights* and delved into Shakespeare, Dickens, and Tennyson. He then moved to Austin, married in 1887, and spent the next ten years of his life as a clerk, bookkeeper, and teller in a bank. In the meantime he was writing short sketches and sending them to the Detroit *Free Press*. In 1894 he left the bank and devoted himself to newspaper work. He gained experience on the small-town paper, founded a humorous weekly that failed, and finally moved to Houston. There he studied the big daily newspapers and had hopes of achieving success as a journalist.

Porter's dreams were shattered when he was called to face a charge of embezzlement. He was held responsible for the eleven-hundred-dollar shortage in the bank where he had formerly worked. Although innocent of the theft, evidence was against him. He might have been acquitted had he not been seized with sudden fear when he was about to be tried. He ran off to Central America but returned in 1898, when he heard that his wife was ill. While in the United States he was apprehended and sentenced to the federal prison in Columbus, Ohio.

O. Henry

The writing of stories from his prison cell in order to buy Christmas presents for his little daughter launched Porter on his literary career. During his long hours as night clerk in the prison pharmacy he mastered the art of short fiction writing. From the dead walls of the prison came stories vibrant with life. By the end of his prison term in 1901, O. Henry, as he signed his work, was well known to the public. It is significant that he named one of his best collections *The Four Million*. He never wrote for the social group called "the Four Hundred," but for the masses in whose uneventful lives he saw love, pathos, and little acts of heroism.

After his release from prison Porter went to Pittsburgh and then to New York, where he spent the rest of his life writing almost continuously. By 1903 four editors demanding stories sought him. Generous and ambitious by nature, he agreed to do more work than he could actually accomplish. There were times when he hid from the messenger boy demanding copy. O. Henry was a prolific writer. His varied and unusual experiences, his love of humanity, and his insight into character furnished material and power for volumes of stories. His best fiction, however, was written during the last few years of his life. When he died in 1910 at the peak of fortune and fame, the public was clamoring for more stories.

Although the work of O. Henry is very uneven, a number of his best stories will remain a permanent part of our literature. He was a social historian, a commentator on life, an explorer of great cities. In his search for characters, he studied the lives of the persons who interested him. This is probably why his stories, although romantic in plot, have such a realistic appeal. O. Henry often idealized the characters and the personalities he admired. However rough or crude his men and women may be, they are morally good. In the lives of his characters he often shows the conflict between their ideal and their real selves. O. Henry was a master in plot construction and narrative power. He has been unsurpassed in the technique of handling the surprise ending. His characters are always clear cut, colorfully and forcefully presented. His humorous style at once captivates the interest of the reader. Crudeness and excessive slang somewhat detract from the perennial enjoyment of his stories. A glossary is already needed to understand some of his fiction. His best stories, however, are devoid of slang and make a universal appeal.

[HANNIBAL] HAMLIN GARLAND

[Hannibal] Hamlin Garland (1860-1940) used the technique of realism in writing of farm life in the Middle West. Like the naturalistic writers he endeavored to interpret contemporary life without offering a solution to many of its problems. Garland was born in Wisconsin and spent his youth in the rural districts of Iowa, Wisconsin, and Dakota. He had himself suffered from the poverty, sordidness, and squalor which he later portrayed in his short stories. The fires of resentment which had smoldered in his heart as a child at length burned through the very pages of his writings. Embittered by the deprivations of his family and discouraged by a futile struggle against economic forces, Garland manifested his reaction in harshly realistic representations of rural life.

So sternly depressing were Garland's early stories that at first the more dignified magazines refused to publish them. In 1891 he published a volume of stories, *Main-Travelled Roads*. William Dean Howells read the stories and sensed the strong current of propaganda present in them. In a friendly spirit, Howells warned Garland not to permit his earnest humanitarian spirit to detract from the art of his fiction. Many of Garland's earlier stories are, however, lacking in artistic balance and are nothing else but propaganda against the life he is describing. He does, despite the bitterness in his heart, succeed in idealizing the men and women he had known on the middle border.

The later work of Hamlin Garland is far more genial than his earlier stories. The natural tendency to idealize the past may be somewhat responsible for his change in attitude. His success as a writer may have induced him to forget the bitterness of his early days. In some of his later stories he actually became the defender of life on the soil. He uses the material of his earlier stories, but he is in the first place a literary artist and an idealist. Although he spent the last years of his life lecturing in the East and in writing, he never forgot the call of the open country. In 1917, he wrote *A Son of the Middle Border,* an autobiographical work. This was followed in 1921 by *A Daughter of the Middle Border,* which is a tribute to his mother and those stanch women who struggled for existence on the Middle West frontier. *Back Trailers to the Middle Border* (1928) describes the experiences of Easterners who have made their homes in the Middle West. All of Garland's stories relating to rural life have an historical as well as a literary importance. Garland holds a significant place in the history of American literature for his stern realism, which gave the deathblow to the restrained realism of Howells and his school.

STEPHEN CRANE

Stephen Crane (1871-1900) was the first writer of naturalistic fiction in America. His life was short but full of activity, his career brief but lasting in its influence. His detached, objective presentation of scenes and characters tends to intensify the irony and passion which give such poignancy to his novels.

Stephen Crane was born in Newark, New Jersey, of an old American family, proud of its military traditions. One of his ancestors had signed the Declaration of Independence, relatives on both sides of his family had been soldiers. Crane's father was a Methodist minister.

Stephen, a delicate, undisciplined child, rebelled at the monotony of school life. He did, however, attend Lafayette College and Syracuse University, where he succeeded in becoming captain of the baseball team. His interest in writing led him to leave school without graduating and to engage in newspaper work. As a young reporter in New York he had showed himself resourceful and skilled in reporting sensational details. His work in the slum districts of New York brought him into contact with the more sordid phases of city life. He attempted to use this material in a realistic novel. Because of the lack of taste and the unwholesome attitude towards life it showed, no publisher would print it.

In search of more appealing material on which to display his naturalistic technique, Crane decided upon the subject of war. Drawing upon his athletic experience of college days, he recalled that contestants often entered the field with fear in their hearts. At the first clash of teams, however, all fear disappeared. Crane wondered if a similar cowering apprehension, followed by exhilaration of spirits, took place in the hearts of soldiers. Although Crane at the time of writing the novel had not yet experienced war, he read books describing the world's great battles and consulted veterans of the Civil War. The result was a powerful, realistic story, *The Red Badge of Courage* (1895). Crane was the first American writer to present in detailed fashion the thoughts and feelings of a soldier before, during, and after a battle. It is a tribute to the imaginative power of Crane that after experiencing in the Cuban War situations similar to those described in his novel, he declared that he would not change a word of it. Crane not only strips war of all its glamour, making it a horrible reality, but he deprives his hero of noble motives. Henry Fleming was at heart a coward, who feared the criticism of his fellow men as much as he feared death. His bravery under fire is not prompted by an unselfish devotion to a cause but by an instinct for self-preservation. Crane wrote other novels besides *The Red Badge of Courage,* and in most of them he pictures the inner struggles of man. He acknowledges that there is in man a continual conflict between passion and the moral law. Only too frequently, however, by means of specious reasoning, his characters try to excuse their moral weaknesses. Herein consists much of the pathetic irony of Crane.

Because of the popularity of *The Red Badge of Courage,* Crane was in great demand as a war correspondent. Tense living in the battle zones of the world injured his health. Crane was as much of an innovator in poetry as in prose. The title of one of his collections, *War Is Kind* (1899), suggests the irony of his verse. There is a boldness, a fierce restraint about his short pungent poems that make him unique among the poets of his time. In his disregard of rhythm, rhyme, conventional stanza, and in the newness of his subject matter, he has been called a pioneer in the "New Poetry Movement." Crane is neither a great novelist nor a good poet, but he is original and daring in his writing. As a stylist he has many faults, but it is in his philosophy of pessimism that he reveals his greatest weakness. Despair and cynicism are frequent notes in his writings. The school of naturalistic fiction began in America with the novels of Stephen Crane.

BENJAMIN FRANKLIN NORRIS

Benjamin Franklin Norris (1870-1902), a friend and contemporary of Stephen Crane, was born in Chicago. When Norris was fourteen years of age, his father retired and moved with his family to San Francisco. Norris desired to become a painter and spent some time studying art in Paris. Here he came under the influence of Émile Zola, one of the chief promoters of the naturalistic school of French writers. Norris then turned his attention from the study of painting to that of fiction. He returned to the United States, attended the University of California, studied for a year at Harvard, and then began an apprenticeship as a newspaper reporter. Like Crane, he became a foreign correspondent and served in Cuba, reporting for *McClure's Magazine.*

Norris early planned to write a realistic trilogy of novels which would represent some aspect of our national life. He chose the economic problem of raising and selling wheat. Fortunes had been made and lost and scandals had arisen over the growth and sale of this staple product. Norris planned the trilogy to include the production, distribution, and consumption of wheat. Only two novels, *The Octopus* (1901), describing the growing of wheat and the conflict between the farmers and the railroad, and *The Pit* (1903), treating the distribution of grain and the exchange market, were completed. The third volume, *The Wolf,* which would have told the story of how American wheat relieved European famine, was only outlined. Norris died before completing the trilogy.

All of Norris's novels are studies in social and economic problems. Like many other writers of the naturalistic school, Norris presents an incomplete, distorted picture of life. He totally overlooks man's supernatural nature and his ability to rise superior to his environment. His works are devoid of idealism, feeling, and sentiment. His gripping, vigorous style is often lacking in restraint and artistic finish. Stephen Crane and Frank Norris were the chief exponents of the naturalistic school in America. They carried the realism of Howells and his problem novel to the extreme of brutal naturalism.

JACK LONDON

Boisterous, brawny, bronze-skinned Jack London (1876-1916) delighted an urban population with romantic tales glorifying primitive impulses and extolling the superman. He made a fortune on his adventurous stories describing rugged life in the Northwest.

London cleverly gave the reading public the diet it demanded. The last quarter of the nineteenth century was the era of Theodore Roosevelt and the "strenuous life" program; it was a time of vigorous social criticism. London capitalized on his own experiences, building out of them romantic stories, realistic in appearance. His heroes are giants and supermen in unusual circumstances. Yet he can quicken the pulse, inspire wonder or fear through his description of yawning canyons, leaping cataracts, howling wolves, and baying dogs.

Jack London was born in San Francisco and spent most of his early life there. The fact that his father was a policeman did not hinder him from taking part in the rough-and-tumble life of a Western town. Poverty forced London to leave school. He joined a gang of ruffians who styled themselves "Oyster Pirates" and who were troublemakers around the piers of San Francisco. At eighteen he broke away from this reckless

Jack London

life with its demoralizing surroundings and went on a sealing voyage in the Pacific. An attack of scurvy forced his return home, but as soon as he recovered he started on a trapping tour throughout the United States. He was arrested for vagrancy in Niagara Falls and served a thirty-day term in jail. His sympathies for the outcast led him to embrace Socialism.

Realizing, as he says in his autobiography, that he was "down in the cellar of society," he decided to better his condition through education. He threw all the force of his titanic energy into the task of preparing himself for college. Although he had no previous high-school training, he was able within a few months to pass the entrance examination of the University of California. The daily routine of college classes was too dull for him. In 1898 he joined the gold rush to the Klondike region, where he found, not a fortune, but material for the vigorous fiction he began to publish two years later. One of his most representative novels, *The Call of the Wild* (1903), has its setting in Alaska. London is at his best in describing scenes of savage beauty in the frozen North. He has the facility to combine stirring accounts of adventure with sensitive descriptions of nature.

London's stories, often autobiographical, frequently become problem novels. *The Sea Wolf* (1904) and *Martin Eden* (1909) are social studies.

In practically all of his stories he pictures men struggling against gigantic odds, which call into play the brutal forces of their nature. According to Jack London, man is little more than an animal in conflict with other animals and with the brutal forces of nature. Some critics have remarked that his men are like animals and his animals like men. His supermen have no consciences. Unlike Bret Harte, who always upheld law and moral order, Jack London knows only the law of physical force. He does, however, possess the storyteller's gift of lively imagination, narrative force, and vivid characterization. He was a potential artist whose commercial interests did not permit artistic development. Although he presents a false attitude towards life and his best works are marked by crudeness and vulgarity, he had a remarkable influence upon the development of the naturalistic novel.

AGNES REPPLIER

For more than fifty years Agnes Repplier (1858-) has been writing essays, and for a great many of those years she has been regarded, without challenge, as dean of American essayists. Her historical and biographical work also shows her to be a writer of wide and mature range and of distinctive style. Agnes Repplier's childhood seems not to have foreshadowed literary fame. She did not learn to read until she was ten years old, but her remarkable memory absorbed poetry "by the yard" as her mother recited it to her. Agnes spent her school days under the Religious of the Sacred Heart at Eden Hall, Torresdale, Pennsylvania. She has depicted her boarding-school life in the book, *In Our Convent Days* (1905). Later she attended a finishing school in her native Philadelphia. She was educated, too, in her father's drawing room, where she met the spirits of Jane Austen, Shakespeare, Lamb, and Froissart.

Agnes Repplier began her writing career in the field of the short story. Advised by Father Hecker that she might do better work in the essay form, she followed his suggestion and in time became the most distinguished American essayist. Five universities — Pennsylvania, Yale, Columbia, Princeton, and Marquette — have

Agnes Repplier

honored her with the degree Doctor of Literature. Her essays, more than two hundred of which have appeared since 1888, show unmistakably the gift of observation. Whether she is reflecting on men or books or only on her favorite cat, she sees in a swift glance not only the whole but all its detailed aspects. *The Fireside Sphinx* (1901), which someone has called a "tabby" anthology, is full of wise thoughts, though she pretends to be writing merely to the memory of her cat, Agrippina. *To Think of Tea* (1932), observations on famous English tea-drinkers, caused an English don to admit, "We have no essayist like her in England." Her *Eight Decades* (1937), published when she was eighty, is remarkable for its vigor of thought and crisp wit.

In her comments upon modern trends Agnes Repplier shows herself an essayist of independent thought. The philosophy of life which she infuses into her writing is based on the idea that "life is a grave affair with which we are charged and which we must conduct and terminate with honor." Frequently she uses wit and irony to destroy false assumptions. With her keen insight and wide background she is often able to present a truth with learning gleaned from the past. Her appraisals are singularly free from emotion or sentiment. They remain of value because they are governed by reason and tolerance, detachment and restraint.

Biographies by Agnes Repplier have been characterized as history written by an artist. Her work in this field includes lives of *Père Marquette* (1929) and *Junípero Serra* (1933). Her *Mère Marie of the Ursulines* (1931) portrays a woman of true heroism who carried the contemplative life and the ideal of education for God to the snowy, sun-bright rocks of Quebec.

An analysis of any one of her essays or biographies reveals the habit of exact word choice, a sensitivity to sound which matches the word to the sense, an ability to manage sentences surely, and a discreet use of figures of speech.

WILLIAM ALLEN WHITE

William Allen White (1868-1944) was one of the most brilliant journalists of the Midwest. A stanch believer in the democratic spirit of small-town, middle-class society, he was identified all his life with Emporia, Kansas. Through his literary editorials voicing strong patriotism and American idealism, he became known throughout the country.

The son of a pioneer school teacher and a country doctor, White attended Emporia College for one year, and finally completed his education at the University of Kansas. He worked for a time on newspapers in Kansas City and in 1893 bought the *Emporia Gazette*. In 1917 he was an observer for the American Red Cross in France and was sent as a delegate to the Russian conference in 1919.

William Allen White's love of social justice and his fear of the devastating effects of industrialism led him to write problem novels. *At the Court of Boyville* (1899) is a glorification of the small town where democratic ideals flourish. *A Certain Rich Man* (1909) is a study in contrasts between industrial and rural America. *In the Heart of a Fool* (1918) reveals the gradual disintegration of a small town and the decline of civic and moral virtues under the pressure of industrialism. William Allen White did not consider himself a fiction writer. His stories, however, are rich in idealism and are in striking contrast to those of Sinclair Lewis, who uses a similar background.

FINLEY PETER DUNNE

The criticism of the Machine Age was not always somber and foreboding. Occasionally the powerful weapon of derisive laughter was used against the folly of the era. One such writer who looked out from the vantage point of his Catholic principles was a Chicago journalist, Finley Peter Dunne (1867-1936). Dunne created as his mouthpiece Mr. Dooley, an Irish saloonkeeper, who delivered keen wit and wisdom in a rich brogue. Mr. Dooley voiced his satire on the social and political scene without ever becoming involved in party differences. He often courageously championed prominent persons who were misunderstood.

The opinions of Mr. Dooley first achieved national popularity as a syndicated newspaper column. Between 1898 and 1911 nine Mr. Dooley books made permanent the practical, homespun philosophy of the humorous commentator. Selections from these books have been published anew as *Mr. Dooley at His Best* (1938). Dunne was at various times editor of the *Chicago Journal*, *Collier's*, and *American Magazine*. He has left in his work a supremely readable record of what the middle-class citizen thought concerning contemporary issues.

DRAMA

Although the Civil War marks a point of change in the history of the American stage, the conflict was not immediately followed by any very significant developments in drama itself. Theatrical technique was improved, but it was not until the end of the century that any creative drama was produced. Before 1870 many of the plays were scissors-and-paste editions of older plays, many of them of foreign origin. After the Civil War, varied forces combined to give a new impetus to acting. The industrial revolution caused a number of people to congregate in commercial centers. Playgoing superseded dancing, card-playing, and horse racing as forms of entertainment. New and better copyright laws protected the playwright. The rise of capitalism encouraged the establishment of large playhouses. The numerous local play companies, existing throughout the country before the war, now gave way to the Broadway

"The Girl of the Golden West": When this play was presented, it was considered the last word in realism on the stage.

commercial theater. Among the theatrical managers of the day were Dion Boucicault and Augustin Daly.

Dion Boucicault (1820-1890) was an Irishman by birth. Before coming to America, he had written and produced plays both in London and in Paris. Many of Boucicault's early plays in this country were stage adaptations of popular novels. His greatest contribution, however, to the American theater was his interpretation of the Irish character. Only too frequently American plays treating of Irish life had followed English models in their burlesque and sentimental treatment of the Irish. Boucicault was a friend of Joseph Jefferson and wrote the stage version of *Rip Van Winkle* (1865), which Jefferson played for many years. Boucicault adopted or improvised more than one hundred thirty plays, none of them having literary value. He is remembered today as a writer of stirring melodramas.

A more constructive and far-reaching influence as stage manager and playwright was Augustin Daly (1838-1899). His moral and artistic standards were

higher than those of Boucicault. By insisting upon personal decorum among his actors and by raising their salaries, he elevated the status of the actor in this country.

Augustin Daly was born in Norfolk, Virginia. After the death of his father, a sea captain, the family moved to New York. Augustin became interested in journalism and was theater critic for five New York newspapers at the same time. He finally became a playwright and stage manager. Daly's dramatic sense did not lead him to scorn the appeal of the melodramatic. One of his first plays, *Under the Gaslight* (1867), is realistic and melodramatic. His adherence to Catholic standards of morality is seen to advantage in *Divorce* (1871). About the time that divorce was being made legal in the United States, there were a number of plays written on the subject. Most of these plays spoke of the marriage bond in a light and humorous vein. Daly's play pictured selfishness as the prime cause of divorce.

After 1870 there was a growing interest in realism and in social drama. Important changes likewise took place in the theater itself. Realism, too, inspired a new point of view towards historical material. Plays about the Civil War continued to be written and acted. Representative of these war plays were *Held by the Enemy* (1886) and *Secret Service* (1895) by William Gillette, and *Shenandoah* (1888) by Bronson Howard. But Howard, "the dean of American drama," was primarily interested in the problems of social adjustment in a democratic country. *The Henrietta,* produced in 1887 and often revived, treats of big business and speculation in a mine.

Important changes came about in the theater itself. Steele MacKaye (1842-1894), actor and author, was instrumental in bringing about improvements in lighting and scene construction. He likewise promoted the idea of a national American art theater. He believed in studying the aesthetics of acting and insisted that the players be thoroughly trained to give more realistic interpretations. Stage realism and local color further developed during the 1890s and early years of the twentieth century. A tendency toward a serious study of contemporary problems likewise became more manifest.

James A. Herne (1839-1901) standardized the character of the Yankee in his shrewd and lifelike portrayal in *Shore Acres* (1892). Clyde Fitch, one of the most talented playwrights of his day, introduced into the drama such historical characters as *Nathan Hale* (1898) and *Barbara Frietchie* (1899). His sparkling and witty comedies of contemporary New York, such as *The Girl with the Green Eyes* (1902), were highly entertaining. Augustus Thomas (1857-1934) and David Belasco (1859-1931) popularized the drama of local color. Thomas presented sectional studies in his *Alabama* (1891) and *Arizona* (1899). Belasco was outstanding both as an author and producer. His *Girl of the Golden West* (1905) has been made into an opera, and his *Return of Peter Grimm* (1911), written for the actor David Warfield, is still presented, particularly on the amateur stage. As a producer Belasco emphasized details of stage realism.

William Vaughn Moody, mentioned earlier, although but casually associated with the theater, produced some of the best and most serious dramas of the period. He was particularly interested in the poetic drama and planned a trilogy which was to treat of the meaning and mystery of life and the destiny of the human race. *The Masque of Judgment* (1900) and *The Fire Bringer* (1904) were classical in form. The third play of the trilogy, *The Death of Eve,* was never completed. *The Faith Healer* (1909) was idealistic in nature and pointed to religion as the universal healer of the ills of mankind. *The Great Divide* (1909), the most popular of Moody's plays, was, at the time of its writing, welcomed as the great American play. It had a popular run on Broadway. In it Moody endeavored to present the conflict in temperament and ideals between people living on the Eastern seaboard and those of the interior.

The Catholic drama, like the secular drama of the period, pointed the way to a fuller development in the twentieth century. John Talbot Smith, because of his interest in the parish theater, might be considered a pioneer in the various Catholic theater activities of our day. He founded the Catholic Actors' Guild. Father Smith, like Percy MacKaye, realized the need of more serious and artistic plays. Both men felt that the theater should not merely entertain but should present ideas and guide the public taste. Percy MacKaye thought that this change from melodramatic and cheap vaudeville productions to more elevating and artistic plays could be effected through amateur groups such as the Little Theater. Father Smith encouraged the Parish Theater to stimulate Catholic and American ideals. His book, *The Parish Theater* (1901), was written at a time when he was the leading Catholic spokesman on the drama in America.

CONDÉ BENOIST PALLEN

Condé Benoist Pallen (1858-1929) was one of the outstanding scholars of his day. His classical background, thorough training, and broad knowledge of Thomistic philosophy made him an authoritative interpreter of Catholic life and literature. He was born in St. Louis, educated at St. Louis University and at Georgetown. After spending two years studying in Rome, he was appointed editor of *Church Progress,* the official weekly paper for the archdiocese of St. Louis.

For ten years he was professor of philosophy at St. Louis University. Throughout his life he was much in demand as a lecturer on literary and philosophic subjects. Some of these lectures were later collected and published as *Philosophy of Literature* (1897) and *Epochs of Literature* (1898). *The Meaning of the Idylls of the King* (1904) was a spiritual interpretation of Tennyson's masterpiece.

For more than twenty years Conde Pallen was associated with John J. Wynne, S.J., on the mammoth task of publishing *The Catholic Encyclopedia*. Pallen was advisory editor of *The New International Encyclopedia* and the *Encyclopedia Americana*. He possessed the scholar's passion for truth and was the champion of Catholic philosophy and ideals.

HENRY HARLAND

Henry Harland (1861-1905), a convert who wrote fiction, left several brilliant novels and numerous short stories of masterly technique. His work communicates to the reader his sense of humor, his appreciation of beauty, and his belief in the romance of living.

In his youth Harland had studied theology at Harvard, but feeling dissatisfied with his course, he left the United States to spend a year in Italy. There he mingled in exclusive artistic circles. He came home convinced of the truth of Catholicism but postponed his entrance into the Church. After his marriage Harland lived in New York and fitted his literary career into office work by writing each morning between the hours of four and eight. His early fiction, written under the name of Sidney Luska, is inferior.

After 1887 Harland spent practically the remainder of his life abroad, living at various times in Paris, London, and Italy. His three volumes of short stories belong to the early years of his European residence. As editor of the *Yellow Book*, a famous literary quarterly published in London, Harland had close contact with the "art for art's sake" group of writers then flourishing in England. In their endeavor to record beauty and emotion, many of these authors made their work a mere presentation of passion and sensation. Harland's own stories represent the happier phases of the aesthetic movement. They capture and present fleeting emotions

and transitory moods. The religious note and the cosmopolitan atmosphere of *Mademoiselle Miss* (1893), *Grey Roses* (1895), and *Comedy and Errors* (1898) are perhaps due to the author's travels in Europe and in America. From Maupassant Harland had effectively learned concentration and the repression of unnecessary details.

In 1897 both Harland and his wife were received into the Church. With his conversion the author entered into the period of his finest creative work, which includes three gaily philosophic novels and one unfinished book. *The Cardinal's Snuff Box* (1898), *The Lady Paramount* (1902), and *My Friend Prospero* (1904) are sparkling in style, artistic in technique. Under Harland's whimsy and mirth lies the core of eternal truth. Before his early death he had proved himself master of the comic vein which skillfully conveys a deep message.

JOHN TALBOT SMITH

John Talbot Smith (1855-1923), priest, educator, and journalist, wrote sympathetic novels and short stories of the people in northern New York among whom he labored. Most of his fiction has for its setting the little mountainous towns along the Canadian border. His work reveals two distinct groups of people: the French Canadians and their Irish neighbors. Father Smith was born at Saratoga, New York, and received his early education from the Christian Brothers in Albany. After completing his theological studies he served as pastor in missions along Lake Champlain and later edited the *Catholic Review* in New York City. The priest's intense interest in the social aspects of Catholic life led him to blaze the trail in various pioneer activities. Besides the Actors' Guild he founded a Catholic Writers' Guild and served as president of the Catholic Summer School in New York.

The writing of fiction was for Father Smith a diversion from more strenuous activities. His work is less didactic than that of most Catholic writers of the time, and he shows the ability to develop plot and create lifelike characters. His best novel is *Saranac: A Story of Lake Champlain*. His most outstanding short stories, collected in *His Honor the Mayor and Other Stories*

(1891), show careful planning and artistic presentation. Among the priest's other works are juvenile fiction and a life of Brother Azarias, F.S.C., a noted literary critic and essayist.

FRANCIS JAMES FINN, S.J.

In Catholic fiction Tom Playfair and Percy Wynn take their places beside Tom Sawyer and Huck Finn as memorable characters. Francis James Finn, S.J.

(1859- 1928), who popularized the boarding-school life of a small town in Kansas, wrote numerous stories on boy life. All his narratives have the idealism that appeals to youth. Daniel A. Lord, S.J., who attributes his vocation to Father Finn, remarks: "From these boys of fiction … I came to believe in the manliness of piety." Father Finn's stories have been popular not only in America but also abroad, where they have been translated into at least six foreign languages. Braille editions have been made in the United States and England.

Spinning by Firelight *(1894), by Henry Ossawa Tanner — Another Example of Realistic Art*

The Wild Ride

Louise Imogen Guiney

The Knights of the Grail in this poem are the valiant souls who ride joyously in a spiritual quest.

I HEAR in my heart, I hear in its ominous pulses,
All day, on the road, the hoofs of invisible horses,
All night, from their stalls, the importunate pawing
    and neighing.

Let cowards and laggards fall back! but alert to the
    saddle,
Weatherworn and abreast, go men of our galloping
    legion,   5
With a stirrup cup[1] each to the lily of women that
    loves him.

The trail is through dolor and dread, over
    crags and morasses;
There are shapes by the way, there are things that
    appall or entice us:
What odds? We are Knights of the Grail; we are
    vowed to the riding.

Thought's self is a vanishing wing, and joy
    is a cobweb,   10
And friendship a flower in the dust, and glory a
    sunbeam;
Not here is our prize, nor, alas! after these our
    pursuing.

A dipping of plumes, a tear, a shake of the bridle,
A passing salute to this world and her pitiful beauty:
We hurry with never a word in the track
    of our fathers.   15

(I hear in my heart, I hear in its ominous pulses
All day, on the road, the hoofs of invisible horses,
All night, from their stalls, the importunate pawing
    and neighing.)

We spur to a land of no name, outracing
    the stormwind;
We leap to the infinite dark like sparks
    from the anvil.   20
Thou leadest, O God! All's well with Thy troopers that
    follow.

[1] *stirrup cup*, a cup of wine which a rider drinks at the moment of departure; a farewell cup.

VIEWING THE AUTHOR'S IDEAS

1. In this poem what does the quest of the Grail symbolize? How does the poet suggest the eagerness of the Knights to be off? What words show the bravery and chivalry of the riders?

2. Quote the lines which describe the road over which the Knights must travel. What is their attitude towards the difficulties of their journey? Mention some of the things which may "appall and entice" those who seek a high spiritual good.

3. How do the Knights regard self; joy; friendship; glory? In what spirit do they sacrifice worldly pleasures? To whom does the poet refer in the phrase "the track of our fathers"?

4. By what striking imagery in the last stanza does the poet suggest the high goal of the riders and the insistence of their pursuit? What thought gives assurance to these troopers of God? Compare St. Paul, *I Cor.* 13:12.

EVALUATING HER MANNER OF EXPRESSION

1. Why is the anapaestic rhythm suitable to this poem? What is the effect of closing the lines on a weak stress?

2. Point out examples of alliteration; of onomatopoeia.

3. Discuss the effectiveness of the symbolism in the fourth stanza. Explain the figurative language in lines 19-20.

The Vigil at Arms

Louise Imogen Guiney

Chivalry again provides Louise Imogen Guiney with poetic symbolism. After keeping the vigil at arms, the knight goes forth to battle with high resolve, knowing that even in apparent failure he may be victorious.

KEEP holy watch with silence, prayer, and fasting
Till morning break, and every bugle play;
Unto the One aware from everlasting
Dear are the winners: thou art more than they.

Forth from this peace on manhood's way thou goest,
Flushed with resolve and radiant in mail;
Blessing supreme for men unborn thou sowest,
O knight elect! O soul ordained to fail!

VIEWING THE AUTHOR'S IDEAS

1. To whom are the words of the poem addressed? Of what is the knight a symbol?

2. How does the knight keep the vigil at arms? In what spirit does he go forth into battle?

3. Who is the "One aware from everlasting"? When is apparent failure a success in His eyes?

EVALUATING HER MANNER OF EXPRESSION

1. How does the mood of this poem differ from that of "The Wild Ride"? Does thought or feeling predominate?

2. Compare the poem with Emily Dickinson's "Success Is Counted Sweetest." Which do you like better?

3. What is the rhyme scheme? Why are the feminine rhymes effective? Select lines in which assonance and alliteration increase the melody.

Borderlands

Louise Imogen Guiney

Natural loveliness brings the poet so close to God that she calls this description of an April evening "Borderlands."

THROUGH all the evening,
   All the virginal long evening,
Down the blossomed aisle of April, it is dread[1] to walk
      alone;
For there the intangible is nigh, the lost is
      ever-during;[2]
And who would suffer again beneath a too divine
      alluring,[3]
Keen as the ancient drift of sleep on dying faces
      blown?
Yet in the valley,
At a turn of the orchard alley,

When a wild aroma touched me in the moist and
      moveless air,
Like breath indeed from out Thee, or as airy vesture[4]
      round Thee,
Then was it I went faintly, for fear I had nearly found
      Thee.
O Hidden, O Perfect, O Desired! O first and final
      Fair![5]

VIEWING THE AUTHOR'S IDEAS

1. Why did the poet fear to walk alone in the blossomed aisle of the orchard?

2. What did the wild aroma suggest to the poet? How is nature the vesture of God? What attitude toward God is expressed in the last two lines?

[1] *dread*, awe-inspiring.

[2] *ever-during*, everlasting.

[3] *alluring*, attraction.

[4] *vesture*, garment.

[5] *Fair*, Divine Beauty.

A Vagabond Song

Bliss Carman

To one in whom the spirit of wanderlust is strong, October beckons with her gay attire and her crisp, clear call.

THERE is something in the autumn that is native
    to my blood —
Touch of manner, hint of mood;
And my heart is like a rhyme,
With the yellow and the purple and the crimson
    keeping time.

The scarlet of the maples can shake me like a cry   5
Of bugles going by.
And my lonely spirit thrills
To see the frosty asters like a smoke upon the hills.

There is something in October sets the gypsy blood
    astir;
We must rise and follow her,   10
When from every hill of fame
She calls and calls each vagabond by name.

VIEWING THE AUTHOR'S IDEAS

1. Does autumn affect all people as it does the poet? Give reasons. Under what circumstances have you experienced this mood?

2. What details of autumn move the poet?

3. Poems have been written about all the seasons of the year. Which season seems to have influenced most poets?

EVALUATING HIS MANNER OF EXPRESSION

1. To which senses do the following expressions appeal: (a) keeping time; (b) bugles going by; (c) gypsy blood astir? What characteristics of a vagabond do these three expressions suggest?

2. How does the rhythm of the poem help to establish the mood?

The Sea Gypsy

Richard Hovey

The ocean sunset sets water and sails afire and enkindles the poet's longing for adventure and romance.

I AM fevered with the sunset,
  I am fretful with the bay,
For the wander thirst is on me
And my soul is in Cathay.[1]

There's a schooner in the offing,   5
With her topsails shot with fire,
And my heart is gone aboard her
For the Islands of Desire.

I must forth again tomorrow!
With the sunset I must be   10
Hull down on the trail of rapture
In the wonder of the sea.

VIEWING THE AUTHOR'S IDEAS

1. What are the causes that urge the poet to travel?

2. Explain the title of the poem. Besides gypsy, what other names are given to people who like to wander? Show the difference in meaning between these names.

EVALUATING HIS MANNER OF EXPRESSION

1. Find words in the poem which describe the fire of the sunset and its effect on the objects it enkindles.

2. From each stanza select the phrase that is the most suggestive of adventure.

3. Contrast this poem with Carman's "A Vagabond Song." Which poem reveals a stronger desire to travel? Discuss.

[1] *Cathay*, China.

Vigil of the Immaculate Conception

Maurice Francis Egan

In the white beauty of the December night the poet sees a symbol of the Immaculate Conception.

A SWORD of silver cuts the fields asunder —
A silver sword tonight, a lake in June —
And plains of snow reflect the maples under
The silver arrows of a wintry moon.

The trees are white with moonlight and with
ice-pearls;   5
The trees are white, like ghosts we see in dreams;
The air is still; there are no moaning wind-whirls;
And one sees silence in the quivering beams.

December night, December night, how glowing
Thy frozen rains upon our warm hearts lie;   10
Our God upon this vigil is bestowing
A thousand graces from the silver sky.

O moon, O symbol of Our Lady's whiteness;
O snow, O symbol of Our Lady's heart;
O night, chaste night, bejeweled with argent
brightness,   15
How sweet, how bright, how loving, kind thou art!

O miracle; tomorrow and tomorrow,
In tender reverence shall no praise abate;
For from all seasons shall we new jewels borrow
To deck the Mother born immaculate.   20

VIEWING THE AUTHOR'S IDEAS

1. To what is the moonlight compared in the first stanza?

2. What phrases suggest the stillness of the winter night? What jewels are chosen to adorn Our Lady?

3. Suggest other feasts of Our Lady and the corresponding jewels a poet's mind might contrive.

EVALUATING HIS MANNER OF EXPRESSION

1. What is the mood of the poem?

2. Which lines best depict the winter night? What relation between the Immaculate Conception and the bright vigil is expressed in the fourth stanza?

3. When a poet shifts his point of view, he compels the reader to turn with him. What shift occurs in this poem? Does it mar or improve the total effect?

The Poet's Harvesting

Charles J. O'Malley

Have you ever wondered from what source a poet derives his material? A reading of this poem will show that nothing in life and nature is lost to the inspired observer.

I GATHER my poems out of the heart of the clover,
Out of the wayside weeds, out of the meadows
about me —
In gleams from the dewdrop's soul, from wings of
birds shaken downward,
Poems the night rain brings, shot through the beeches
incessant;

Poems the grasshopper sings, beating his noonday
labor;   5
The gossamer web is a rhythm, blown from the valley
of Quiet —
A rondeau[1] that turns on itself, folded in shimmering
garments;
And, when the whirling flakes are tangled, at dusk, in
the thickets,

[1] *rondeau*, fixed lyrical form of thirteen lines and only two rhymes.

The voice of Song outcries in the bleat of lambs on
    the hillside.

"All things sing to me — cry: laughter, or tears, or
    music.   10
The storm hath its rhythmical beat; the day its
    musical cadence:

Ever an ebb or a flow — a flame, or a mournful
    nightfall,
A rivulet, bearded with moss, to me is Theocritus[2]
    singing;
A violet, bursting in spring, thrills me with exquisite
    music;
A child's voice, heard in the dusk, shakes me with
    infinite pathos,   15
The flash of the daybreak's sword, the march of the
    midnight planets,

2 *Theocritus* (thē-ŏk'rĭ-tŭs), A Greek pastoral poet.

The sweep of the mighty winds, the shout of the
    prophet-voiced thunder,
Restlessly throb in my soul, and shape themselves into
    measure."

VIEWING THE AUTHOR'S IDEAS

1. Where does the poet gather his poems? What things sing to him?

2. From what sources in nature does the poet draw his imagery; his rhythms; his musical tones; his moods and emotional effects?

3. In what does the poet find inspiration for a rondeau; for pastoral poetry? In line 14 what sound does the author hear?

EVALUATING HIS MANNER OF EXPRESSION

1. What is the meaning of the title? Compare the first two lines with Emily Dickinson's "To Make a Prairie." Note the accumulation of detail in this poem.

2. Find three examples of personification.

Marquette on the Shores of the Mississippi

John Jerome Rooney

In this lyric the poet visualizes the priest-explorer on the great river and among the tribes that lined its banks.

HERE in the midnight of the solemn wood,
  He heard a roar as of a mighty wind,
The onward rush of waters unconfined
Trampling in legions through the solitude.
Then lo! before him swept the conquering flood,   5
  Free as the freedom of the truth-strong mind
  Which hills of Doubt could neither hide nor bind,
Which all in vain the valley mounds withstood!
With glowing eye he saw the prancing tide
  With yellow mane rush onward through
    the night   10

Into the vastness he had never trod;
Nor dreamt of conquest of that kingdom wide
  As down the flood his spirit took its flight
  Seeking the long-lost children of his God.

VIEWING THE AUTHOR'S IDEAS

1. Indicate words or phrases in the poem that may be interpreted to mean the following: (a) the darkness of paganism; (b) the true faith; (c) the large numbers of Indians.

2. What scene is described in the first eight lines?

3. Explain the thought of the poem.

Prayer to the Virgin of Chartres[1]

Henry Adams

Henry Adams continually sought a satisfactory explanation of man's origin and destiny. Longing for the peace of a sure faith, he found his spirit elevated as he contemplated the figures of Virgin and Child at the great French cathedral. In his prayer to the Virgin the poet identifies himself with successive generations living during the ages of faith and later separating themselves from the Church at the time of the Protestant Revolt.

Gracious Lady: —
Simple as when I asked your aid before;
Humble as when I prayed for grace in vain
Seven hundred years ago; weak, weary, sore
In heart and hope, I ask your help again.

You, who remember all, remember me;   5
An English scholar of a Norman name,
I was a thousand who then crossed the sea
To wrangle in the Paris schools for fame.[2]
When your Byzantine portal[3] was still young,
I prayed there with my master Abélard;[4]   10
When Ave Maris Stella was first sung,
I helped to sing it here with Saint Bernard.[5]

When Blanche set up your gorgeous Rose of France,[6]
I stood among the servants of the Queen;
And when Saint Louis made his penitence,[7]
I followed barefoot where the King had been.   16

For centuries I brought you all my cares
And vexed you with the murmurs of a child;
You heard the tedious burden of my prayers;

You could not grant them, but at least you smiled.   20

If then I left you, it was not my crime,
Or if a crime, it was not mine alone,
All children wander with the truant Time.
Pardon me too! You pardoned once your Son!

For He said to you: "Wist ye not that I   25
Must be about my Father's business?" So,
Seeking His Father, He pursued His way
Straight to the Cross towards which we all must go.

So I too wandered off among the host
That racked the earth to find the Father's clue.   30
I did not find the Father, but I lost
What now I value more, the mother — you![8]

I thought the fault was yours that foiled my search;
I turned and broke your image on its throne,
Cast down my idol and resumed my march
To claim the Father's empire for my own.   36

Crossing the hostile sea, our greedy band
Saw rising hills and forests in the blue;
Our Father's kingdom in the promised land!
We seized it and dethroned the Father too.   40
And now we are the Father, with our brood,
Ruling the Infinite, not Three but One;
We made our world and saw that it was good;
Ourselves we worship, and we have no Son.

Yet we have gods, for even our strong nerve   45
Falters before the Energy we own.
Which shall be master? Which of us shall serve?
Which wears the fetters? Which shall bear the crown?

Brave though we be, we dread to face the Sphinx
Or answer the old riddle[9] she still asks.   50
Strong as we are, our reckless courage shrinks
To look beyond the piecework of our tasks.

---

[1] *Chartres*, the Cathedral at Chartres, France, consecrated in 1260 — one of the finest Gothic cathedrals in the world. The stained glass windows represent in magnificent symbolism the glorification of the Blessed Virgin.

[2] *To wrangle . . . fame.* In the twelfth century scholars from all parts of the world flocked to the University of Paris to take part in the contests of scholastic philosophy.

[3] *Byzantine portal*, the entrance to the cathedral, which is in the architectural style of the Byzantine Empire.

[4] *Abélard*, a French scholastic philosopher and teacher, whose learning drew students from all countries.

[5] *Ave Maris Stella . . . Saint Bernard*. The famous hymn, "Ave Maris Stella" (Hail, Star of Ocean), has often been ascribed to Saint Bernard. It was known, however, as early as the ninth century.

[6] *When Blanche . . . France.* Blanche of Castile, the mother of St. Louis, gave many of the windows of the cathedral, including the famous rose window.

[7] *St. Louis . . . penitence.* St. Louis spent long hours in prayer, fasting, and penance. He made a pilgrimage to Chartres, traveling a distance of seven leagues on foot.

[8] *the mother—you!* The poet regrets that, in leaving the Church, Protestants did not find the Father but also lost the Blessed Virgin, who would have led them to God.

[9] *Sphinx . . . old riddle.* The famous Sphinx at Thebes destroyed all passers-by who failed to answer its riddle: "What walks on four legs in the morning, on two at noon, and on three in the evening?" The answer is man, who crawls when a baby, walks on two feet in his prime, and is supported by a cane in his old age.

But when we must, we pray as in the past
Before the Cross on which your Son was nailed.
Listen, dear lady! You shall hear the last   55
Of the strange prayers Humanity has wailed.

VIEWING THE AUTHOR'S IDEAS

1. In what spirit does the poet appeal to Our Lady? How long ago had a similar prayer been offered to Mary? Why had Englishmen journeyed to France at that time?

2. In lines 9-20 how does the poet describe the devotion to Our Lady during the thirteenth century? What lines show the childlike faith of the Middle Ages?

3. What claim to Our Lady's pardon does the poet make for those who left her? Who are the people that "racked the earth to find the Father's clue"? What regret does the poet express in lines 31-32? How do lines 33-36 refer to the Protestant attitude towards the Blessed Virgin?

4. What reference to the Puritans' settlement in America is made in lines 37-40? In what words does the poet express the denial of God in modern times? What are the gods of modern materialism?

5. What problems does the agnostic fear to face? Why will Our Lady hear the last strange prayer of Humanity?

EVALUATING HIS MANNER OF EXPRESSION

Discuss the effectiveness of the quiet rhythm and the conversational tone.

Mia Carlotta

Thomas Augustine Daly

Daly's ear for Italian-American dialect is quick and true. Here with subtle humor he depicts the lively emotion of a gallant suitor, confident of his sweetheart's loyalty.

GIUSEPPE, da barber, ees greata for "mash,"[1]
He gotta da bigga, da blacka mustache,
Good clo'es an' good styla an' playnta good cash.
W'enevra Giuseppe ees walk on da street,
Da peopla dey talka, "How nobby! how neat!   5
How softa da handa, how smalla da feet."

He leefta hees hat, an' he shaka hees curls,
An' smila weeth teetha so shiny like pearls;
Oh, manny da heart of da seely young girls
    He gotta.
    Yes, playnta he gotta —   10
      But notta
      Carlotta!

Giuseppe, da barber, he maka da eye,
An' lika da steam engine puffa an' sigh,
For catcha Carlotta w'en she ees go by.   15

Carlotta she walka weeth nose in da air,
An' look through Giuseppe weeth faraway stare,

As eef she no see dere ees som'body dere.

Giuseppe, da barber, he gotta da cash,
He gotta da clo'es an' da bigga mustache,   20
He gotta da seely young girls for da "mash,"
    But notta —
    You bat my life, notta —
      Carlotta.
      I gotta!   25

VIEWING THE AUTHOR'S IDEAS

1. What characteristics does the speaker reveal? How does he show his sense of superiority? What is amusing in his attitude?

2. From suggestions in the poem describe Carlotta.

3. Does this poem throw any light on human nature; on practical matters?

EVALUATING HIS MANNER OF EXPRESSION

1. To get the full flavor of dialect poems, one must read them aloud. After practicing, read this poem to a group.

2. How does the dialect contribute to the humor of the poem; to the rhythmic effect; to the rhyme scheme?

3. In which lines do you detect (a) scorn; (b) satire; (c) self-satisfaction?

[1] *"mash,"* flirtation.

At Candle-Lightin' Time

Paul Laurence Dunbar

Within this graceful lyric in Negro dialect Paul Laurence Dunbar gives an appealing picture of family joy in a cabin home.

When I come in f'om de co'n-fiel' aftah
  wo'kin' ha'd all day,
It's amazin' nice to fin' my suppah all erpon de way;
An' it's nice to smell de coffee bubblin' ovah in de pot,
An' it's fine to see de meat a-sizzlin' teasin'-lak an' hot.

But when suppah-time is ovah, an' de t'ings is cleahed
  away
Den de happy hours dat foller are de sweetes' of de
  day.
When my co'ncob pipe is sta'ted, an' de smoke is
  drawin' prime,
My ole 'ooman says, "I reckon, Ike, it's candle-lightin'
  time."

Den de chillun snuggle up to me, an' all commence to
  call,
"Oh, say, Daddy, now it's time to mek de shadders on
  de wall."
So I puts my han's togethah, — evah daddy knows de
  way, —
An' de chillun snuggle closer roun' ez I
  begin to say: —

"Fus thing, hyeah come Mistah Rabbit; don' you see
  him wo'k his eahs?
Huh, uh! dis mus' be a donkey, — look, how
  innercent he 'pears!

Dah's de ole black swan a-swimmin' — ain't she got a'
  awful neck?
Who's dis feller dat's a-comin'? Why, dat's ole dog
  Tray, I 'spec'!"

Dat'de way I run on, tryin' fu' to please 'em all I can;
Den I hollahs, "Now be keerful — dis hyeah las' 's de
  buga man!"
An' dey runs an' hides dey faces; dey ain't skeered —
  dey's lettin' on:
But de play ain't raaly ovah twell dat buga man is
  gone.

So I jes' teks up my banjo, an' I play a little chune,
An' you see dem haids come peepin' out to listen
  mighty soon.
Den my wife says, "Sich a pappy fu' to give you sich a
  fright!
Jes' you go to baid, an' leave him; say yo' prayers an'
  say good night."

VIEWING THE AUTHOR'S IDEAS

1. What aspects of Negro life does Dunbar stress in this poem?

2. Select passages which show the Negro's love of home; love of children; contentment; religion.

3. Compare the Negro in this poem with Uncle Remus.

EVALUATING HIS MANNER OF EXPRESSION

1. What is the mood of this poem? How does it resemble that of Riley's "When the Frost is on the Punkin"?

2. What is the effect of the slow rhythm and long lines?

Under the Lion's Paw

Hamlin Garland

This story is typical of Hamlin Garland's photographic sketches of his boyhood experiences on an Iowa farm. Returning to his midwestern home after a number of years in Boston, he was sharply reminded of the social and economic evils that had resulted from uncontrolled land speculation. Aroused by the misery and hardships which the prairie farmers had suffered, he wrote this grimly realistic story.

IT was the last of autumn and first day of winter coming together. All day long the plowmen on their prairie farms had moved to and fro in their wide level fields through the falling snow, which melted as it fell, wetting them to the skin — all day, notwithstanding the frequent squalls of snow, the dripping, desolate clouds, and the muck of the furrows, black and tenacious as tar.

Under their dripping harness the horses swung to and fro silently with that marvelous uncomplaining patience which marks the horse. All day the wild geese, honking wildly as they sprawled sidewise down the wind, seemed to be fleeing from an enemy behind; and with neck outthrust and wings extended, sailed down the wind, soon lost to sight.

Yet the plowman behind his plow, though the snow lay on his ragged greatcoat and the cold, clinging mud rose on his heavy boots, fettering him like gyves, whistled in the very beard of the gale. As day passed, the snow, ceasing to melt, lay along the plowed land and lodged in the depth of the stubble, till on each slow round the last furrow stood out black and shining as jet between the plowed land and the gray stubble.

When night began to fall, and the geese, flying low, began to alight invisibly in the near cornfield, Stephen Council was still at work "finishing a land." He rode on his sulky plow[1] when going with the wind, but walked when facing it. Sitting bent and cold but cheery under his slouch hat, he talked encouragingly to his four-in-hand.[2]

"Come round there, boys! — Round agin! We got t' finish this land. Come in there, Dan! *Stiddy,* Kate, — stiddy! None o' y'r tantrums, Kittie. It's purty tuff, but got a be did. *Tchk! tchk!* Step along, Pete! Don't let Kate git y'r singletree[3] on the wheel. *Once* more!"

They seemed to know what he meant and that this was the last round, for they worked with greater vigor than before.

"Once more, boys, an' then, sez I, oats an' a nice warm stall, an' sleep f'r all."

By the time the last furrow was turned on the land, it was too dark to see the house, and the snow was changing to rain again. The tired and hungry man could see the light from the kitchen shining through the leafless hedge, and he lifted a great shout, "Supper f'r a half a dozen!"

It was nearly eight o'clock by the time he had finished his chores and started for supper. He was picking his way carefully through the mud, when the tall form of a man loomed up before him with a premonitory cough.

"Waddy ye want?" was the rather startled question of the farmer.

"Well, ye see," began the stranger in a deprecating tone, "we'd like t' git in f'r the night. We've tried every house f'r the last two miles, but they hadn't any room f'r us. My wife's jest about sick, 'n' the children are cold and hungry — "

"Oh, y' want 'o stay all night, eh?"

"Yes, sir, it 'ud be a great accom — "

"Waal, I dont make it a practice t' turn anybuddy way hungry, not on sech nights as this. Drive right in. We ain't got much, but sech as it is — "

But the stranger had disappeared. And soon his steaming, weary team, with drooping heads and swinging singletrees, moved past the well to the block beside the path. Council stood at the side of the schooner[4] and helped the children out — two little half-sleeping children — and then a small woman with a babe in her arms.

"There ye go!" he shouted jovially to the children. "*Now* we're all right! Run right along to the house there an' tell Mam' Council you wants sumpthin' t' eat. Right this way, Mis' — keep right off t' the right there. I'll go an' git a lantern. Come," he said to the dazed and silent group at his side.

"Mother," he shouted, as he neared the fragrant and warmly-lighted kitchen, "here are some wayfarers an' folks who need sumpthin' t' eat an' a place t' snooze." He ended by pushing them all in.

Mrs. Council, a large, jolly, rather coarse-looking woman, took the children in her arms. "Come right in, you little rabbits. 'Most asleep, hey? Now here's a drink o' milk f'r each o' ye. I'll have s'm tea in a minute. Take off y'r things and set up t' the fire."

While she set the children to drinking milk, Council got out his lantern and went out to the barn to help the stranger about his team, where his loud, hearty voice could be heard as it came and went between the haymow and the stalls.

---

[1] *sulky plow,* a plow having wheels and a seat for the driver.

[2] *four-in-hand,* a four-horse team.

[3] *singletree,* a bar to which the traces of a harnessed horse are fixed.

[4] *schooner,* a prairie schooner or large covered wagon used by emigrants in crossing the prairies.

The woman came to light as a small, timid, and discouraged-looking woman, but still pretty in a thin and sorrowful way.

"Land sakes! An' you've traveled all the way from Clear Lake t'day in this mud! Waal! waal! No wonder you're all tired out. Don't wait f'r the men, Mis' — " She hesitated, waiting for the name.

"Haskins."

"Mis' Haskins, set right up to the table an' take a good swig o' tea whilst I make y' s'm toast. It's green tea, an' it's good. I tell Council as I git older I don't seem to enjoy young hyson n'r gunpowder.[5] I want the reel green tea jest as it comes off'n the vines. Seems t' have more heart in it, some way. Don't s'pose it has. Council says it's all in m' eye."

Going on in this easy way, she soon had the children filled with bread and milk and the woman thoroughly at home, eating some toast and sweet-melon pickles and sipping the tea.

"See the little rats!" she laughed at the children. "They're full as they can stick now, and they want to go to bed. Now, don't git up, Mis' Haskins; set right where you are an' let me look after 'em. I know all about young ones, though I'm all alone now. Jane went an' married last fall. But, as I tell Council, it's lucky we keep our health. Set right there, Mis' Haskins; I won't have you stir a finger."

It was an unmeasured pleasure to sit there in the warm, homely kitchen, the jovial chatter of the housewife driving out and holding at bay the growl of the impotent, cheated wind.

The little woman's eyes filled with tears, which fell down upon the sleeping baby in her arms. The world was not so desolate and cold and hopeless, after all.

"Now I hope Council won't stop out there and talk politics all night. He's the greatest man to talk politics an' read the *Tribune* — How old is it?"

She broke off and peered down at the face of the babe.

"Two months 'n' five days," said the mother, with a mother's exactness.

"Ye don't say! I want 'o know! The dear little pudzy-wudzy!" she went on, stirring it up in the neighborhood of the ribs with her fat forefinger.

"Pooty tough on 'oo to go gallivant'n' 'cross lots this way — "

"Yes, that's so; a man can't lift a mountain," said Council, entering the door. "Mother, this is Mr. Haskins, from Kansas. He's been eat up 'n' drove out by grasshoppers."

"Glad t' see yeh! — Pa, empty that washbasin 'n' give him a chance t' wash."

Haskins was a tall man, with a thin, gloomy face. His hair was a reddish brown like his coat and seemed equally faded by the wind and sun; and his sallow face, though hard and set, was pathetic somehow. You would have felt that he had suffered much by the line of his mouth showing under his thin, yellow mustache.

"Hain't Ike got home yet, Sairy?"

"Hain't seen 'im."

"W-a-a-l, set right up, Mr. Haskins; wade right into what we've got; 'tain't much but we manage to live on it — she gits fat on it," laughed Council, pointing his thumb at his wife.

After supper, while the women put the children to bed, Haskins and Council talked on, seated near the huge cooking stove, the steam rising from their wet clothing. In the Western fashion Council told as much of his own life as he drew from his guest. He asked but few questions, but by and by the story of Haskins' struggles and defeat came out. The story was a terrible one; but he told it quietly, seated with his elbows on his knees, gazing most of the time at the hearth.

"I didn't like the looks of the country, anyhow," Haskins said, partly rising and glancing at his wife. "I was ust 't' northern Ingyannie, where we have lots o' timber 'n' lots o' rain, 'n' I didn't like the looks o' that dry prairie. What galled me the worst was goin' s' far away acrosst so much fine land layin' all through here vacant."

"And the 'hoppers eat ye four years, hand runnin', did they?"

"Eat! They wiped us out. They chawed everything that was green. They jest set around waitin' f'r us to die t' eat us, too. My God! I ust t' dream of 'em sittin' 'round on the bedpost, six feet long, workin' their jaws. They eet the fork handles. They got worse 'n' worse till they jest rolled on one another, piled up like snow in winter. Well, it ain't no use. If I was t' talk all winter, I couldn't tell nawthin'. But all the while I couldn't help thinkin' of all that land back here that nobuddy was usin' that I ought 'o had 'stead o' bein' out there in that cussed country."

[5] *young hyson n'r gunpowder*, brands of tea.

"Waal, why didn't ye stop an' settle here?" asked Ike, who had come in and was eating his supper.

"For the simple reason that you fellers wanted ten 'r fifteen dollars an acre fer the bare land, and I had no money fer that kind o' thing."

"Yes, I do my own work," Mrs. Council was heard to say in the pause which followed. "I'm a gettin' purty heavy t' be on m' laigs all day, but we can't afford t' hire, so I keep rackin' around somehow, like a foundered horse. S' lame — I tell Council he can't tell how lame I am, f'r I'm jest as lame in one laig as t' other." And the good soul laughed at the joke on herself as she took a handful of flour and dusted the biscuit board to keep the dough from sticking.

"Well, I hain't *never* been very strong," said Mrs. Haskins. "Our folks was Canadians an' small-boned, and then since my last child I hain't got up again fairly. I don't like t' complain. Tim has about all he can bear now — but they was days this week when I jest wanted to lay right down an' die."

"Waal, now, I'll tell ye," said Council from his side of the stove, silencing everybody with his good-natured roar, "I'd go down and see Butler, *anyway,* if I was you. I guess he'd let you have his place purty cheap; the farm's all run down. He's ben anxious t' let t' somebuddy next year. It 'ud be a good chance fer you. Anyhow, you go to bed and sleep like a babe. I've got some plowin' t' do, anyhow, an' we'll see if somethin' can't be done about your case. Ike, you go out an' see if the horses is all right, an' I'll show the folks t' bed."

When the tired husband and wife were lying under the generous quilts of the spare bed, Haskins listened a moment to the wind in the eaves and then said, with a slow and solemn tone:

"There are people in this world who are good enough t' be angels, an' only haff t' die to *be* angels."

II

Jim Butler was one of those men called in the West "land poor." Early in the history of Rock River he had come into the town and started in the grocery business in a small way, occupying a small building in a mean part of the town. At this period of his life he earned all he got and was up early and late, sorting beans, working over butter, and carting his goods to and from the station. But a change came over him at the end of

the second year when he sold a lot of land for four times what he paid for it. From that time forward he believed in land speculation as the surest way of getting rich. Every cent he could save or spare from his trade, he put into land at forced sale or mortgages on land, which were "just as good as the wheat," he was accustomed to say.

Farm after farm fell into his hands, until he was recognized as one of the leading landowners of the county. His mortgages were scattered all over Cedar County; and as they slowly but surely fell in, he sought usually to retain the former owner as tenant.

He was not ready to foreclose; indeed, he had the name of being one of the easiest men in the town. He let the debtor off again and again, extending the time whenever possible.

"I don't want y'r land," he said. "All I'm after is the int'rest on my money — that's all. Now, if y' want 'o stay on the farm, why, I'll give y' a good chance. I can't have the land lyin' vacant." And in many cases the owner remained as tenant.

In the meantime he had sold his store; he couldn't spend time in it; he was mainly occupied now with sitting around town on rainy days smoking and "gassin' with the boys," or in riding to and from his farms. In fishing time he fished a good deal. Doc Grimes, Ben Ashley, and Cal Cheatham were his cronies on these fishing excursions or hunting trips in the time of chickens or partridges. In winter they went to northern Wisconsin to shoot deer.

In spite of all these signs of easy life, Butler persisted in saying he "hadn't money to pay taxes on his land" and was careful to convey the impression that he was poor in spite of his twenty farms. At one time he was said to be worth fifty thousand dollars, but land had been a little slow of sale of late, so that he was not worth so much.

A fine farm, known as the Higley place, had fallen into his hands in the usual way the previous year, and he had not been able to find a tenant for it. Poor Higley, after working himself nearly to death on it in the attempt to lift the mortgage, had gone off to Dakota, leaving the farm and his curse to Butler.

This was the farm which Council advised Haskins to apply for, and the next day Council hitched up his team and drove down town to see Butler.

"You jest let *me* do the talking" he said. "We'll find him wearin' out his pants on some salt barrel somew'ers; and if he thought you *wanted* a place, he'd sock it to you hot and heavy. You jest keep quiet; I'll fix 'im."

Butler was seated in Ben Ashley's store telling fish yarns when Council sauntered in casually.

"Hello, But; lyin' agin, hey?"

"Hello, Steve! how goes it?"

"Oh, so-so. Too dang much rain these days. I thought it was goin' t' freeze up f'h good last night. Tight squeak if I get m' plowin' done. How's farmin' with you these days?"

"Bad. Plowin' ain't half done."

"It 'ud be a religious idee f'r you t' go out an' take a hand y'rself."

"I don't half to," said Butler with a wink.

"Got anybody on the Higley place?"

"No. Know of anybody?"

"Wall, no; not eggsackly. I've got a relation back t' Michigan who's ben hot an' cold on the idee o' comin' West f'r some time. *Might* come if he could get a good layout. What do you talk on the farm?"

"Well, I d' know. I'll rent it on shares or I'll rent in money rent."

"Waal, how much money, say?"

"Well, say ten per cent on the price — two-fifty."

"Waal, that ain't bad. Wait on 'im till 'e thrashes?"

Haskins listened eagerly to his important question, but Council was coolly eating a dried apple which he had speared out of a barrel with his knife. Butler studied him carefully.

"Well, knocks me out of twenty-five dollars interest."

"My relation 'll need all he's got t' git his crops in," said Council in the safe, indifferent way.

"Well, all right; *say* wait," concluded Butler.

"All right; this is the man. Haskins, this is Mr. Butler — no relation to Ben — the hardest-working man in Cedar County."

On the way home Haskins said: "I ain't much better off. I'd like that farm; it's a good farm, but it's all run down, an' so'm I. I could make a good farm of it if I had half a show. But I can't stock it n'r seed it."

"Waal, now, don't you worry," roared Council in his ear. "We'll pull y' through somehow till next harvest. He's agreed t' hire it plowed, an' you can earn a hundred dollars plowin', an' y' c'n git the seed o' me an' pay me back when y' can."

Haskins was silent with emotion, but at last he said, "I ain't got nothin' t' live on."

"Now, don't you worry 'bout that. You jest make your headquarters at ol' Steve Council's. Mother'll take a pile o' comfort in havin' y'r wife an' children 'round. Y' see, Jane's married off lately, an' Ike's away a good 'eal; so we'll be darn glad t' have y' stop with us this winter. Nex' spring we'll see if y' can't git a start agin." And he chirruped to the team, which sprang forward with the rumbling, clattering wagon.

"Say, looky here, Council, you can't do this. I never saw — " shouted Haskins in his neighbor's ear.

Council moved about uneasily in his seat and stopped his stammering gratitude by saying: "Hold on, now; don't make such a fuss over a little thing. When I see a man down, an' things all on top of 'm, I jest like t' kick 'em off an' help 'm up. That's the kind of religion I got, an' it's about the *only* kind."

They rode the rest of the way home in silence. And when the red light of the lamp shone out into the darkness of the cold and windy night, and he thought of this refuge for his children and wife, Haskins could have put his arm around the neck of his burly companion and squeezed him like a lover. But he contented himself with saying, "Steve Council, you'll git y'r pay f'r this some day."

"Don't want any pay. My religion ain't run on such business principles."

The wind was growing colder, and the ground was covered with a white frost as they turned into the gate of the Council farm, and the children came rushing out, shouting, "Papa's come!" They hardly looked like the same children who had sat at the table the night before. Their torpidity, under the influence of sunshine and Mother Council, had given way to a sort of spasmodic cheerfulness, as insects in winter revive when laid on the hearth.

III

Haskins worked like a fiend, and his wife, like the heroic woman that she was, bore also uncomplainingly the most terrible burdens. They rose early and toiled without intermission till the darkness fell on the plain, then tumbled into bed, every bone and muscle aching with fatigue, to rise with the sun next morning to the same round of the same ferocity of labor.

The eldest boy drove a team all through the spring, plowing and seeding, milked the cows, and did chores innumerable, in most ways taking the place of a man.

An infinitely pathetic but common figure this boy on the American farm, where there is no law against child labor. To see him in his coarse clothing, his huge boots, and his ragged cap, as he staggered with a pail of water from the well or trudged in the cold and cheerless dawn out into the frosty field behind his team, gave the city-bred visitor a sharp pang of sympathetic pain. Yet Haskins loved his boy and would have saved him from this if he could, but he could not.

By June, the first year, the result of such Herculean toil began to show on the farm. The yard was cleaned up and sown to grass, the garden plowed and planted, and the house mended.

Council had given them four of his cows.

"Take 'em an' run 'em on shares. I don't want 'o milk s' many. Ike's away s' much now, Sat'd'ys an' Sundays, I can't stand the bother anyhow."

Other men, seeing the confidence of Council in the newcomer, had sold him tools on time; and as he was really an able farmer, he soon had round him many evidences of his care and thrift. At the advice of Council he had taken the farm for three years, with the privilege of re-renting or buying at the end of the term.

"It's a good bargain, an' y' want 'o nail it," said Council. "If you have any kind ov a crop, you c'n pay y'er debts an' keep seed an' bread."

The new hope which now sprang up in the heart of Haskins and his wife grew great almost as a pain by the time the wide field of wheat began to wave and swirl in the wind of July. Day after day he would snatch a few moments after supper to go and look at it.

"Have ye seen the wheat t'day, Nettie?" he asked one night as he rose from supper.

"No, Tim, I ain't had time."

"Well, take time now. Let's go look at it."

She threw an old hat on her head — Tommy's hat — and, looking almost pretty in her thin, sad way, went out with her husband to the hedge.

"Ain't it grand, Nettie? Just look at it."

It was grand. Level, russet here and there, heavy-headed, wide as a lake, and full of multitudinous whispers and gleams of wealth, it stretched away before the gazers like the fabled field of the cloth of gold.

"Oh, I think — I *hope* we'll have a good crop, Tim; and oh, how good the people have been to us!"

"Yes; I don't know where we'd be t'day if it hadn't been f'r Council and his wife."

"They're the best people in the world," said the little woman, with a great sob of gratitude.

"We'll be in the field on Monday, sure," said Haskins, gripping the rail on the fence as if already at the work of the harvest.

The harvest came, bounteous, glorious; but the winds came and blew it into tangles, and the rain matted it here and there close to the ground, increasing the work of gathering it threefold.

Oh, how they toiled in those glorious days! Clothing dripping with sweat, arms aching, filled with briers, fingers raw and bleeding, backs broken with the weight of heavy bundles, Haskins and his man toiled on. Tommy drove the harvester, while his father and a hired man bound on the machine. In this way they cut ten acres every day; and almost every night after supper, when the hand went to bed, Haskins returned to the field, shocking the bound grain in the light of the moon. Many a night he worked till his anxious wife came out at ten o'clock to call him in to rest and lunch.

At the same time she cooked for the men, took care of the children, washed and ironed, milked the cows at night, made the butter, and sometimes fed the horses and watered them while her husband kept at the shocking.

No slave in the Roman galleys could have toiled so frightfully and lived, for this man thought himself a free man and that he was working for his wife and babes.

When he sank into his bed with a deep groan of relief, too tired to change his grimy, dripping clothing, he felt that he was getting nearer and nearer to a home of his own and pushing the wolf of want a little farther from his door.

There is no despair so deep as the despair of a homeless man or woman. To roam the roads of the country or the streets of the city, to feel there is no rood of ground on which the feet can rest, to halt weary and hungry outside lighted windows and hear laughter and song within — these are the hungers and rebellions that drive men to crime and women to shame.

It was the memory of this homelessness and the fear of its coming again that spurred Timothy Haskins and Nettie, his wife, to such ferocious labor during that first year.

IV

" 'M, yes; 'm, yes; first-rate," said Butler, as his eye took in the neat garden, the pigpen, and the well-filled barnyard. "You're gitt'n' quite a stock around yeh. Done well, eh?"

Haskins was showing Butler around the place. He had not seen it for a year, having spent the year in Washington and Boston with Ashley, his brother-in-law, who had been elected to Congress.

"Yes, I've laid out a good deal of money durin' the last three years. I've paid out three hundred dollars f'r fencin'."

"Um — h'm! I see. I see," said Butler while Haskins went on:

"The kitchen there cost two hundred; the barn ain't cost much in money, but I've put a lot o' time on it. I've dug a new well, and I –"

"Yes, yes, I see. You've done well. Stock worth a thousand dollars," said Butler, picking his teeth with a straw.

"About that," said Haskins modestly. "We begin to feel 's if we was gett'n' a home f'r ourselves, but we've worked hard. I tell you we begin to feel it, Mr. Butler, and we're goin' t' begin to ease up purty soon. We've been kind o' plannin' a trip back t' *her* folks after the fall plowin's done."

"*Eggs*-actly!" said Butler, who was evidently thinking of something else. "I suppose you've kind o' calc'lated on stayin' here three years more?"

"Well, yes. Fact is, I think I c'n buy the farm this fall if you'll give me a reasonable show."

"Um — m! What do you call a reasonable show?"

"Well, say a quarter down and three years' time."

Butler looked at the huge stacks of wheat which filled the yard, over which the chickens were fluttering and crawling, catching grasshoppers, and out of which the crickets were singing innumerably. He smiled in a peculiar way as he said, "Oh, I won't be hard on yeh. But what did you expect to pay f'r the place?"

"Why, about what you offered it for before, two thousand five hundred; or *possibly* three thousand dollars," he added quickly as he saw the owner shake his head.

"This farm is worth five thousand and five hundred dollars," said Butler in a careless and decided voice.

"*What!*" almost shrieked the astounded Haskins. "What's that? Five thousand? Why, that's double what you offered it for three years ago."

"Of course, and it's worth it. It was all run down then; now it's in good shape. You've laid out fifteen hundred dollars in improvements according to your own story."

"But *you* had nothin' t' do about that. It's my work an' my money."

"You bet it was; but it's my land."

"But what's to pay me for all my — "

"Ain't you had the use of 'em?" replied Butler, smiling calmly into his face.

Haskins was like a man struck on the head with a sandbag; he couldn't think; he stammered as he tried to say: "But — I never'd git the use — You'd rob me! More'n that: you agreed — you promised that I could buy or rent at the end of three years at — "

"That's all right. But I didn't say I'd let you carry off the improvements nor that I'd go on renting the farm at two-fifty. The land is doubled in value, it don't matter how; it don't enter into the question; an' now you can pay me five hundred dollars a year rent, or take it on your own terms at fifty-five hundred, or — git out."

He was turning away when Haskins, the sweat pouring from his face, fronted him, saying again:

"But *you've* done nothing to make it so. You hain't added a cent. I put it all there myself, expectin' to buy. I worked an' sweat to improve it. I was workin' for myself an' babes — "

"Well, why didn't you buy when I offered to sell? What y' kickin' about?"

"I'm kickin' about payin' you twice f'r my own things — my own fences, my own kitchen, my own garden."

Butler laughed. "You're too green to eat, young feller. *Your* improvements! The law will sing another tune."

"But I trusted your word."

"Never trust anybody, my friend. Besides, I didn't promise not to do this thing. Why, man, don't look at me like that. Don't take me for a thief. It's the law. The reg'lar thing. Everybody does it."

"I don't care if they do. It's stealin' jest the same. You take three thousand dollars of my money — the work o' my hands and my wife's." He broke down at this point. He was not a strong man mentally. He could face hardship, ceaseless toil, but he could not face the cold and sneering face of Butler.

"But I don't take it," said Butler coolly. "All you've got to do is to go on jest as you've been a-doin', or give me a thousand dollars down and a mortgage at ten per cent on the rest."

Haskins sat down blindly on a bundle of oats near by and with staring eyes and drooping head went over the situation. He was under the lion's paw. He felt a horrible numbness in his heart and limbs. He was hid in a mist, and there was no path out.

Butler walked about, looking at the huge stacks of grain and pulling now and again a few handfuls out, shelling the heads in his hands and blowing the chaff away. He hummed a little tune as he did so. He had an accommodating air of waiting.

Haskins was in the midst of the terrible toil of the last year. He was walking again in the rain and the mud behind his plow; he felt the dust and dirt of the threshing. The ferocious husking time, with its cutting wind and biting, clinging snows, lay hard upon him. Then he thought of his wife, how she had cheerfully cooked and baked without holiday and without rest.

"Well, what do you think of it?" inquired the cool, mocking, insinuating voice of Butler.

"I think you're a thief and a liar!" shouted Haskins, leaping up. "A blackhearted houn'!" Butler's smile maddened him; with a sudden leap he caught a fork in his hands and whirled it in the air. "You'll never rob another man, damn ye!" he grated through his teeth, a look of pitiless ferocity in his accusing eyes.

Butler shrank and quivered, expecting the blow; stood, held hypnotized by the eyes of the man he had a moment before despised — a man transformed into an avenging demon. But in the deadly hush between the lift of the weapon and its fall there came a gush of faint, childish laughter; and then across the range of his vision, far away and dim, he saw the sun-bright head of his baby girl, as, with the pretty, tottering run of a two-year-old, she moved across the grass of the dooryard. His hands relaxed; the fork fell to the ground; his head lowered.

"Make out y'r deed an' mor'gage, an' git of'n my land, an' don't ye never cross my line again; if y' do, I'll kill ye."

Butler backed away from the man in wild haste and, climbing into his buggy with trembling limbs, drove off down the road, leaving Haskins seated dumbly on the sunny piles of sheaves, his head sunk into his hands.

VIEWING THE AUTHOR'S IDEAS

1. Are people usually as charitable and generous as the Councils; as selfish and cowardly as Butler; as industrious as Haskins? Discuss.

2. What sort of religion did Council profess? What views did he have on religion? Show the fallacy in his statement. Did Council have an understanding of what religion involves?

3. Was Butler correct in his retort that "The law will sing another tune"? What economic evils does this story depict? What comment is made on child labor?

4. What influences contributed to the family-centered life depicted in this story?

5. To which of the following influences would you ascribe the misery depicted in the story: (a) environment (b) labor conditions (c) the perversity of human nature? Explain.

EVALUATING HIS MANNER OF EXPRESSION

1. Show the contrast at the opening of the story between the character of Council and the dullness of the day. Does Council maintain this character throughout? Select details from the first four paragraphs showing that Council was a man of action.

2. Notice the vividness of such descriptions as "wild geese, honking wildly as they sprawled sidewise down the wind." Select three similar passages.

3. Where is the climax in the story? How does the author lead up to the climax? What does he achieve by the gradual movement?

4. Discuss the conclusion of the story. Is it satisfactory? Compare the mood at the end with that at the beginning.

5. To what special emotions does the author appeal? At what point is the feeling most intense? What general effect has Garland's story?

6. Point out faithful descriptions of Midwestern scenery.

7. Show several instances in which the author uses realism.

8. What is the meaning of the title of the story? What emotion does the narrative arouse?

The Mission of Humor

Agnes Repplier

A genial and kindly observer of American life, Agnes Repplier shows to what extent humorists have not yet fulfilled their mission. In a style that is pleasantly satirical, she reveals typical deficiencies in American wit.

AMERICAN humor is the pride of American hearts. It is held to be our splendid national characteristic, which we flaunt in the faces of other nations, conceiving them to have been less favored by Providence. Just as the most effective way to disparage an author or an acquaintance — and we have often occasion to disparage both — is to say that he lacks a sense of humor, so the most effective criticism we can pass upon a nation is to deny it this valuable quality. American critics have written the most charming things about the keenness of American speech, the breadth and insight of American drollery, the electric current in American veins; and we, reading these pleasant felicitations, are wont to thank God with greater fervor than the occasion demands that we are more merry and wise than our neighbors. Brander Matthews, for example, has told us that there are newspaper writers in New York who have cultivated a wit "not unlike Voltaire's." He mistrusts this wit because he finds it "corroding and disintegrating," but he makes the comparison with that casual assurance which is a feature of American criticism.

Indeed, our delight in our own humor has tempted us to overrate both its literary value and its corrective qualities. We are never so apt to lose our sense of proportion as when we consider those beloved writers whom we hold to be humorists because they have made us laugh. It may be conceded that, as a people, we have an abiding and somewhat disquieting sense of fun. We are nimble of speech; we are more prone to levity than to seriousness; we are able to recognize a vital truth when it is presented to us under the familiar aspect of a jest; and we habitually allow ourselves certain forms of exaggeration, accepting, perhaps unconsciously, Hazlitt's verdict: "Lying is a species of wit, and shows spirit and invention." It is true also that no adequate provision is made in this country for the defective but valuable class without humor, which in England is exceedingly well cared for. American letters, American journalism, and American speech are so colored by pleasantries, so accentuated by ridicule that the silent and stodgy men, who are apt to represent a nation's real strength, hardly know where to turn for a little saving dullness. A deep vein of irony runs through every grade of society, making it possible for us to laugh at our own bitter discomfiture and to scoff with startling distinctness at the evils which we passively permit. Just as the French monarchy under Louis the Fourteenth was wittily defined as despotism tempered by epigram, so the United States has been described as a free republic fettered by jokes; and the taunt conveys a half-truth which it is worth our while to consider. . . .

Perhaps we laugh too readily. Perhaps we are sometimes amused when we ought to be angry. Perhaps we jest when it is our plain duty to reform. Here lies the danger of our national light-mindedness — for it is seldom lightheartedness; we are no whit more lighthearted than our neighbors. A carping English critic has declared that American humor consists in speaking of hideous things with levity; and while so harsh a charge is necessarily unjust, it makes clear one abiding difference between the nations. An Englishman never laughs — except offically in *Punch*[1] — over any form of political degradation. He is not in the least amused by jobbery, by bad service, by broken pledges. The seamy side of civilized life is not to him a subject for sympathetic mirth. He can pity the stupidity which does not perceive that it is cheated and betrayed; but penetration allied to indifference awakens his wondering contempt. "If you think it amusing to be imposed on," an Englishwoman once said to me, "you need never be at a loss for a joke."

In good truth we know what a man is like by the things he finds laughable; we gauge both his understanding and his culture by his sense of the becoming and of

---

[1] *Punch*, a famous English humorous and satirical weekly.

the absurd. If the capacity for laughter be one of the things which separate men from brutes, the quality of laughter draws a sharp dividing line between the trained intelligence and the vacant mind. The humor of a race interprets the character of a race; and the mental condition of which laughter is the expression is something which it behooves the student of human nature and the student of national traits to understand very clearly.

Now our American humor is, on the whole, good-tempered and decent. It is scandalously irreverent (reverence is a quality which seems to have been left out of our composition); but it has neither the pitilessness of the Latin nor the grossness of the Teuton jest. As Gilbert said of Sir Beerbohm Tree's[2] *Hamlet,* it is funny without being coarse. We have at our best the art of being amusing in an agreeable, almost an amiable, fashion; but then we have also the rare good fortune to be very easily amused. Think of the current jokes provided for our entertainment week by week and day by day. Think of the comic supplement of our Sunday newspapers, designed for the refreshment of the feeble-minded and calculated to blight the spirits of any ordinarily intelligent household. Think of the debilitated jests and stories which a time-honored custom inserts at the back of some of our magazines. It seems to be the custom of happy American parents to report to editors the infantile prattle of their engaging little children, and the editors print it for the benefit of those who escape the infliction first-hand. . . .

A painstaking German student who has traced the history of humor back to its earliest foundations is of the opinion that there are eleven original jokes known to the world, or rather that there are eleven original and basic situations which have given birth to the world's jokes; and that all the pleasantries with which we are daily entertained are variations of these eleven originals, traceable directly or indirectly to the same sources. There are times when we are disposed to think eleven too generous a computation, and there are less weary moments in which the inexhaustible supply of situations still suggests fresh possibilities of laughter. . . .

Moreover, we Americans have jests of our own — poor things, for the most part, but our own. They are current from the Atlantic to the Pacific; they appear with commendable regularity in our newspapers and comic journals, and they have become endeared to us by a lifetime of intimacy. The salient characteristics of our great cities, the accepted traditions of our mining camps, the contrast between East and West, the still more familiar contrast between the torpor of Philadelphia and Brooklyn and the uneasy speed of New York — these things furnish abundant material for everyday American humor. There is, for example, the encounter between the Boston girl and the Chicago girl, who, in real life, might often be taken for each other; but who, in the American joke, are as sharply differentiated as the Eskimo and the Hottentot. And there is the little Boston boy who always wears spectacles, who is always named Waldo, and who makes some innocent remark about *Literary Ethics* or *The Conduct of Life.* We have known this little boy too long to bear a parting from him. Indeed, the mere suggestion that all Bostonians are forever immersed in Emerson is one which gives unfailing delight to the receptive American mind. It is a poor community which cannot furnish its archaic jest for the diversion of its neighbors.

The finest example of our bulldog resoluteness in holding on to a comic situation, or what we conceive to be a comic situation, may be seen every year when the twenty-second of February draws near and the shops of our great and grateful Republic break out into an irruption of little hatchets, by which curious insignia we have chosen to commemorate our first President. These toys, occasionally combined with sprigs of artificial cherries, are hailed with unflagging delight and purchased with what appears to be patriotic fervor. I have seen letter carriers and post-office clerks wearing little hatchets in their buttonholes, as though they were party buttons or temperance badges. It is our great national joke, which I presume gains point from the dignified and reticent character of General Washington and from the fact that he would have been sincerely unhappy could he have foreseen the senile character of a jest destined, through our love of absurdity, our careful cultivation of the inappropriate, to be linked forever with his name.

The easy exaggeration which is a distinctive feature of American humor, and about which so much has been said and written, has its counterpart in sober and

---

[2] *Sir Beerbohm Tree,* an English actor-manager, 1853-1917.

truth- telling England, though we are always amazed when we find it there and fall to wondering, as we never wonder at home, in what spirit it was received. There are two kinds of exaggeration — exaggeration of statement, which is a somewhat primitive form of humor, and exaggeration of phrase, which implies a dexterous misuse of language, a skillful juggling with words. . . .

Exaggeration of phrase, as well as the studied understatement which is an even more effective form of ridicule, seem natural products of American humor. They sound, wherever we hear them, familiar to our ears. It is hard to believe that an English barrister, and not a Texas ranchman, described Boston as a town where respectability stalked unchecked. Mazarin's[3] plaintive reflection, "Nothing is so disagreeable as to be obscurely hanged," carries with it an echo of Wyoming or Arizona. Gilbert's analysis of Hamlet's mental disorder —

> "Hamlet is idiotically sane,
> With lucid intervals of lunacy," —

has the pure flavor of American wit — a wit which finds its most audacious expression in burlesquing bitter things and which misfits its words with diabolic ingenuity. To match these alien jests, which sound so like our own, we have the whispered warning of an American usher (also quoted by Sir John Robinson) who opened the door to a latecomer at one of Matthew Arnold's lectures: "Will you please make as little noise as you can, sir. The audience is asleep"; and the comprehensive remark of a New England scholar and wit that he never wanted to do anything in his life, that he did not find it was expensive, unwholesome, or immoral. This last observation embraces the wisdom of the centuries. Solomon would have endorsed it, and it is supremely quotable as expressing a common experience with very uncommon felicity. . . .

The truth is that our love of a jest knows no limit and respects no law. The incongruities of an unequal civilization (we live in the land of contrasts) have accustomed us to absurdities and reconciled us to ridicule. We rather like being satirized by our own countrymen. We are very kind and a little cruel to our humorists. We crown them with praise; we hold them to our hearts; we pay them any price they ask for their wares; but we insist upon their being funny all the time. Once a humorist, always a humorist is our way of thinking; and we resent even a saving lapse into seriousness on the part of those who have had the good or the ill fortune to make us laugh. . . .

The truth is that humor as a lucrative profession is a purely modern device and one which is much to be deplored. The older humorists knew the value of light and shade. Their fun was precious in proportion to its parsimony. The essence of humor is that it should be unexpected, that it should embody an element of surprise, that it should startle us out of that reasonable gravity which, after all, must be our habitual frame of mind. But the professional humorist cannot afford to be unexpected. The exigencies of his vocation compel him to be relentlessly droll from his first page to his last, and this accumulated drollery weighs like lead. Compared to it, sermons are as thistledown, and political economy is gay.

It is hard to estimate the value of humor as a national trait. Life has its appropriate levities, its comedy side. We cannot "see it clearly and see it whole," without recognizing a great many absurdities which ought to be laughed at, a great deal of nonsense which is a fair target for ridicule. The heaviest charge brought against American humor is that it never keeps its target well in view. We laugh, but we are not purged by laughter of our follies; we jest, but our jests are apt to have a kitten's sportive irresponsibility. The lawyer offers a witticism in place of an argument; the diner-out tells an amusing story in lieu of conversation. Even the clergyman does not disdain a joke, heedless of Dr. Johnson's warning which should save him from that pitfall. Smartness furnishes sufficient excuse for the impertinence of children, and with purposeless satire the daily papers deride the highest dignitaries of the land.

Yet while always to be reckoned with in life and letters, American humor is not a powerful and consistent factor either for destruction or for reform. It lacks, for the most part, a logical basis and the dignity of a supreme aim. Molière's[4] humor amounted to a philosophy of life. He was wont to say that it was a

---

[3] *Mazarin*, a cardinal of Italian birth who was the prime minister of Louis XIV.

[4] *Molière*, a French dramatist, 1622-1673.

difficult task to make gentlefolk laugh, but he succeeded in making them laugh at that which was laughable in themselves. He aimed his shafts at the fallacies and the duplicities which his countrymen ardently cherished, and he scorned the cheaper wit which contents itself with mocking at idols already discredited. As a result, he purged society, not of the follies that consumed it, but of the illusion that these follies were noble, graceful, and wise. "We do not plough or sow for fools," says a Russian proverb; "they grow of themselves," but humor has accomplished a mighty work if it helps us to see that a fool is a fool and not a prophet in the market place. And if the man in the market place chances to be a prophet, his message is safe from assault. No laughter can silence him, no ridicule weaken his words.

Carlyle's grim humor was also drilled into efficacy. He used it in orderly fashion; he gave it force by a stern principle of repression. He had (what wise man has not?) an honest respect for dullness, knowing that a strong and free people argues best — as Bagehot puts it — "in platoons." He had some measure of mercy for folly. But against the whole complicated business of pretense, against the pious and respectable and patriotic hypocrisies of a successful civilization, he hurled his taunts with such true aim that it is not too much to say there has been less real comfort and safety in lying ever since.

These are victories worth recording, and there is a big battlefield for American humor when it finds itself ready for the fray; when it leaves off firing squibs and settles down to a compelling cannonade; when it aims less at the superficial incongruities of life and more at the deep-rooted delusions which rob us of fair fame. It has done its best work in the field of political satire, where *The Biglow Papers* hit hard in their day, where Nast's cartoons helped to overthrow the Tweed dynasty, and where the indolent and luminous genius of Mr. Dooley has widened our mental horizon. Mr. Dooley is a philosopher, but his is the philosophy of the looker-on, of that genuine unconcern which finds Saint George and the dragon to be both a trifle ridiculous. He is always undisturbed, always illuminating, and not infrequently amusing; but he anticipates the smiling indifference with which those who come after us will look back upon our enthusiasms and absurdities.

Humor, as he sees it, is that thrice-blessed quality which enables us to laugh, when otherwise we should be in danger of weeping. "We are ridiculous animals," observes Horace Walpole unsympathetically, "and if angels have any fun in their hearts, how we must divert them."

It is this clear-sighted, noncombative humor which Americans love and prize, and the absence of which they reckon a heavy loss. Nor do they always ask, "a loss to whom?" Charles Lamb said it was no misfortune for a man to have a sulky temper. It was his friends who were unfortunate. And so with the man who has no sense of humor. He gets along very well without it. He is not aware that anything is lacking. He is not mourning his lot. What loss there is, his friends and neighbors bear. A man destitute of humor is apt to be a formidable person, not subject to sudden deviations from his chosen path and incapable of frittering away his elementary forces by pottering over both sides of a question. He is often to be respected, sometimes to be feared, and always — if possible — to be avoided. His are the qualities which distance enables us to recognize and value at their worth. He fills his place in the scheme of creation; but it is for us to see that his place is not next to ours at table, where his unresponsiveness narrows the conversational area and dulls the contagious ardor of speech. He may add to the wisdom of the ages, but he lessens the gaiety of life.

VIEWING THE AUTHOR'S IDEAS

1. How do Americans regard humor? What causes our people to find laughter in their own bafflement?

2. What criticism is leveled at Americans because of their ready laughter? What does ability to laugh indicate?

3. State the characteristics of American humor. According to Miss Repplier what is our great national joke? Would you suggest another as more representative?

4. In what light do we hold humorists? Discuss what Miss Repplier says about the essence of humor. What charges are brought against American humor?

5. Compare the force of the humor of Molière and Carlyle. What should be the aim of American humor? Discuss the attitude of one who is devoid of humor.

6. In Hazlitt's whimsical statement concerning lying, what important consideration is overlooked?

1. What comparisons are used in developing the theme of this essay?

2. What does the author achieve by the use of quotations?

3. This essay contains concise statements that are worthy of remembrance. Select several pithy sentences.

4. In view of Miss Repplier's conclusion that humor should be aimed at "deep-rooted delusions and pretense," evaluate the comedy of current humorists.

5. How does the essay exhibit the author's wide background; her ability to present a truth with learning gleaned from the past?

6. Find examples of the essayist's own wit; of her use of irony.

7. Show instances of detached and restrained writing.

Mary White

William Allen White

When William Allen White wrote this tribute to his daughter the day following her funeral, he penned an editorial of permanent appeal. The article met with recognition not only because of the father's courageous and tender treatment of a poignant subject, but also because he pictured the lovable qualities of the American girl.

THE Associated Press reports carrying the news of Mary White's death declared that it came as the result of a fall from a horse. How she would have hooted at that! She never fell from a horse in her life. Horses have fallen on her and with her — "I'm always trying to hold 'em in my lap," she used to say. But she was proud of few things, and one was that she could ride anything that had four legs and hair. Her death resulted not from a fall but from a blow on the head which fractured her skull, and the blow came from the limb of an overhanging tree on the parking.[1]

The last hour of her life was typical of its happiness. She came home from a day's work at school, topped off by a hard grind with the copy on the high-school *Annual*, and felt that a ride would refresh her. She climbed into her khakis, chattering to her mother about the work she was doing, and hurried to get her horse and be out on the dirt roads for the country air and the radiant green fields of the spring. As she rode through the town on an easy gallop, she kept waving at passers-by. She knew everyone in town. For a decade the little figure with the long pigtail and the red hair ribbon had been familiar on the streets of Emporia, and she got in the way of speaking to those who nodded at her. She passed the Kerrs, walking the horse, in front of the Normal Library, and waved at them; passed another friend a few hundred feet farther on and waved at her. The horse was walking; and as she turned into North Merchant Street, she took off her cowboy hat, and the horse swung into a lope. She passed the Tripletts and waved her cowboy hat at them, still moving gaily north on Merchant Street. A *Gazette* carrier passed — a high-school boy friend — and she waved at him, but with her bridle hand; the horse veered quickly, plunged into the parking where the low-hanging limb faced her, and, while she still looked back waving, the blow came. But she did not fall from the horse; she slipped off, dazed a bit, staggered, and fell in a faint. She never quite recovered consciousness.

But she did not fall from the horse, neither was she riding fast. A year or so ago she used to go like the wind. But that habit was broken; and she used the horse to get into the open, to get fresh, hard exercise and to work off a certain surplus energy that welled up in her and needed a physical outlet. That need had been in her heart for years. It was back of the impulse that kept the dauntless, little brown-clad figure on the streets and country roads of this community and built into a strong, muscular body what had been a frail and sickly frame during the first years of her life.

[1] *parking*, a strip of turf, with trees, along a street.

But the riding gave her more than a body. It released a gay and hardy soul. She was the happiest thing in the world. And she was happy because she was enlarging her horizon. She came to know all sorts and conditions of men. Charley O'Brien, the traffic cop, was one of her best friends. W. L. Holtz, the Latin teacher, was another. Tom O'Connor, farmer politician, and Rev. J. H. J. Rice, preacher and police judge, and Frank Beach, music master, were her special friends; and all the girls, black and white, above the track and below the track, in Pepville and Stringtown, were among her acquaintances. And she brought home riotous stories of her adventures. She loved to rollick; persiflage[2] was her natural expression at home. Her humor was a continual bubble of joy. She seemed to think in hyperbole[3] and metaphor. She was mischievous without malice, as full of faults as an old shoe. No angel was Mary White, but an easy girl to live with, for she never nursed a grouch five minutes in her life.

With all her eagerness for the out-of-doors she loved books. On her table when she left her room were a book by Conrad, one by Galsworthy, *Creative Chemistry* by E. E. Slosson, and a Kipling book. She read Mark Twain, Dickens, and Kipling before she was ten — all of their writings. Wells and Arnold Bennett particularly amused and diverted her. She was entered as a student in Wellesley in 1922; was assistant editor of the high-school *Annual* this year and in line for election to the editorship of the *Annual* next year. She was a member of the executive committee of the high-school Y.W.C.A.

Within the last two years she had begun to be moved by an ambition to draw. She began as most children do by scribbling in her school books, funny pictures. She bought cartoon magazines and took a course — rather casually, naturally, for she was, after all, a child, with no strong purposes — and this year she tasted the first fruits of success by having her pictures accepted by the high-school *Annual*. But the thrill of delight she got when Mr. Ecord, of the Normal *Annual,* asked her to do the cartooning for that book this spring was too beautiful for words. She fell to her work with all her enthusiastic heart. Her drawings were accepted,

and her pride — always repressed by a lively sense of the ridiculousness of the figure she was cutting — was really a gorgeous thing to see. No successful artist ever drank a deeper draft of satisfaction than she took from the little fame her work was getting among her schoolfellows. In her glory she almost forgot her horse — but never her car.

For she used the car as a jitney bus. It was her social life. She never had a party in all her nearly seventeen years — wouldn't have one; but she never drove a block in the car in her life that she didn't begin to fill the car with pickups! Everybody rode with Mary White — white and black, old and young, rich and poor, men and women. She liked nothing better than to fill the car full of long-legged high-school boys and an occasional girl and parade the town. She never had a date, nor went to a dance, except once with her brother, Bill; and the "boy proposition" didn't interest her — yet. But young people — great, spring-breaking, varnish-cracking, fender-bending, door-sagging carloads of kids — gave her great pleasure. Her zests were keen. But the most fun she ever had in her life was acting as chairman of the committee that got up the big turkey dinner for the poor folks at the county home; scores of pies, gallons of slaw, jam, cakes, preserves, oranges, and a wilderness of turkey were loaded in the car and taken to the county home. And being of a practical turn of mind, she risked her own Christmas dinner by staying to see that the poor folks actually got it all. Not that she was a cynic; she just disliked to tempt folks. While there, she found a blind colored uncle, very old, who could do nothing but make rag rugs; and she rustled up from her school friends enough to keep him busy for a season. The last engagement she tried to make was to take the guests at the county home out for a car ride. And the last endeavor of her life was to try to get a rest room for colored girls in the high school. She found one girl reading in the toilet, because there was no better place for a colored girl to loaf; and it inflamed her sense of injustice, and she became a nagging harpy to those who she thought could remedy the evil.

The poor she had always with her and was glad of it. She hungered and thirsted for righteousness; and was the most impious creature in the world. She joined

[2] *persiflage* (pûr´sĭ-fläzh), light, bantering talk.
[3] *hyperbole* (hī-pûr´bô-lē), fanciful exaggeration.

the Congregational Church without consulting her parents; not particularly for her soul's good. She never had a thrill of piety in her life and would have hooted at a "testimony." But even as a little child she felt the church was an agency for helping people to more of life's abundance, and she wanted to help. She never wanted help for herself. Clothes meant little to her. It was a fight to get a new rig on her but eventually a harder fight to get it off. She never wore a jewel and had no ring but her high-school class ring and never asked for anything but a wrist watch. She refused to have her hair up, though she was nearly seventeen. "Mother," she protested, "you don't know how much I get by with, in my braided pigtails, that I could not with my hair up." Above every other passion of her life was her passion not to grow up, to be a child. The tomboy in her, which was big, seemed to loathe to be put away forever in skirts. She was a Peter Pan who refused to grow up.

Her funeral yesterday at the Congregational Church was as she would have wished it; no singing, no flowers save the big bunch of red roses from her brother Bill's Harvard classmen — Heavens, how proud that would have made her! and the red roses from the *Gazette* force — in vases at her head and feet. A short prayer, Paul's beautiful essay on "Love," from the thirteenth chapter of First Corinthians; some remarks about her democratic spirit by her friend John H. J. Rice, pastor and police judge, which she would have deprecated if she could; a prayer sent down for her by her friend Carl Nau; and, opening the service, the slow, poignant movement from Beethoven's[4] "Moonlight Sonata," which she loved; and closing the service a cutting from the joyously melancholy first movement of Tchaikovsky's[5] *Symphonie Pathétique,* which she liked to hear in certain moods on the phonograph; then the Lord's Prayer by her friends in the high school.

That was all.

For her pallbearers only her friends were chosen: her Latin teacher, W. L. Holtz; her high-school principal, Rice Brown; her doctor, Frank Foncannon; her friend W. W. Finney; her pal at the *Gazette* office, Walter

[4] *Beethoven,* a German composer.
[5] *Tchaikovsky,* a Russian composer.

Hughes; and her brother, Bill. It would have made her smile to know that her friend Charley O'Brien, the traffic cop, had been transferred from Sixth and Commercial to the corner near the Church to direct her friends who came to bid her good-by.

A rift in the clouds in a gray day threw a shaft of sunlight upon her coffin as her nervous, energetic little body sank to its last sleep. But the soul of her, the glowing, gorgeous, fervent soul of her, surely was flaming in eager joy upon some other dawn.

VIEWING THE AUTHOR'S IDEAS

1. According to her father what characteristics did Mary White display? Show that she was an appealing personality. Compare her with the typical eleventh-grade girl of today. How do we form our idea of the typical high-school boy or girl?

2. Discuss the list of writers that Mary White preferred. How do they compare with your favorites?

3. Mary seems to have been an admixture of simple youth and maturity. Discuss this contrast in her.

4. What are your impressions of Mary's funeral?

5. Both Mary White and Stephen Council in "Under the Lion's Paw," display attractive natural virtues. Which character influenced more people? Why? Compare their attitudes toward religion.

EVALUATING HIS MANNER OF EXPRESSION

1. Through the use of intimate detail the author achieves vividness. Select details that especially appeal to you.

2. For artists and writers, expression is often a form of relief. How may the father have relieved his soul by writing this essay? What did he achieve for his daughter? How did he provide a beautiful experience for others?

3. In this essay the writer has shown a detachment rarely achieved under such circumstances. At which points does he particularly manifest restraint and control? Which parts reveal his intense feeling? What was his purpose in stressing the fact that Mary did not *fall* from the horse?

4. Writing is often self-revealing. What shows that White is a newspaperman? How does he regard young people? What type of father and husband is he? What do you learn of the Midwestern town?

5. Choose a character from among your acquaintances, either at school or in your neighborhood, and try writing a description in which specific details produce vividness.

The Ruling Class

Finley Peter Dunne

First published in Chicago newspapers as early as 1893, the Dooley essays soon appeared in journals throughout the country. In the creation of Mr. Dooley the author produced one of the important humorous figures of our literature. This essay gives Mr. Dooley's amusing observations on reformers who are more interested in notoriety than in the improvement of social and political institutions.

"I SEE be th' pa-apers," said Mr. Dooley, "that arnychy's torch do be lifted, an' what it means I dinnaw; but this here I know, Jawn, that all arnychists is inimies iv governmint, an' all iv thim ought to be hung f'r th' first offense an' bathed f'r th' second. Who are they, annyhow, but foreigners, an' what right have they to be holdin' torchlight procissions in this land iv th' free an' home iv th' brave? Did ye iver see an American or an Irishman an arnychist? No, an' ye niver will. Whin an Irishman thinks th' way iv thim la-ads, he goes on th' polis foorce an' dhraws his eighty-three-thirty-three f'r throwin' lodgin'-house bums into th' pathrol wagon. An' there ye a-are." . . .

"What on earth's to be done about thim arnychists?" Mr. Hennessy asked. "What ails thim annyhow? What do they want?"

"Th' Lord on'y knows," said Mr. Dooley. "They don't want annything, that's what they want. They want peace on earth, an' th' way they propose to get it is be murdhrin' ivry man that don't agree with thim. They think we all shud do as they please. They're down on th' polis foorce an' in favor iv th' pop'lace, an' whin they've kilt a king they call on th' polis to save thim fr'm th' mob. An' between you an' me, Hinnissy, ivry arnychist I've knowed, an' I've met manny in me time, an' quite law-abidin' citizens they was, too, had th' makin' iv a thradeejan in him. If they was no newspapers they'd be few arnychists. They want to get their pitchers in th' pa-apers an' they can't do it be wheelin' bananas through th' sthreets or milkin' a cow, so they go out an' kill a king. I used to know a man be th' name iv Schmitt that was a cobbler be profession an' lived next

dure but wan to me. He was th' dacintist man ye iver see. He kep' a canary bur-rd, an' his devotion to his wife was th' scandal iv th' neighborhood. But bless my soul, how he hated kings. He cudden't abide Cassidy afther he heerd he was a dayscinded fr'm th' kings iv Connock, though Cassidy was what ye call a prolotoorio or a talkin' workin'man. An' th' wan king he hated above all others was th' king iv Scholizwig-Holstein, which was th' barbarous counthry he come fr'm. He cud talk fairly dacint about other kings, but this wan — Ludwig was his name an' I seen his pitcher in th' pa-apers wanst — wud throw him into a fit. He blamed ivrything that happened to Ludwig. If they was a sthrike, he charged it to Ludwig. If Schwartzmeister didn't pay him f'r half-solin' a pair iv Congress gaiters he used to wear in thim days, he tied a sthring around his finger f'r to remind him that he had to kill Ludwig. 'What have ye agin' th' king?' says I. 'He is an opprissor iv th' poor,' he says. 'So ar-re ye,' I says, 'or ye'd mend boots free.' 'He's explodin' th' prolotoorio,' he says. 'Sure,' says I, 'th' prolotoorio can explode thimsilves pretty well,' says I. 'He oughtn't to be allowed to live in luxury while others starve,' he says. 'An' wud ye be killin' a man f'r holdin' a nice job?' says I. 'What good wud it do ye?' says I. 'I'd be th' emancipator iv th' people,' says he. 'Ye'd have th' wurred on th' coffin lid,' says I. 'Why,' says he, 'think iv me, Schmitt, Owgoost Schmitt, stalkin' forth to avinge th' woes iv th' poor,' he says. 'Loodwig, th' cursed, goes by. I jumps fr'm behind a three an' society is freed fr'm th' monsther,' he says. 'Think iv th' glory iv it,' he says. 'Owgoost Schmitt, emancipator,' he says. 'I'll prove to Mary Ann that I'm a man,' he says. Mary Ann was his wife. Her maiden name was Riley. She heard him say it. 'Gus,' says she, 'if iver I hear iv ye shootin' e'er a king, I'll lave ye,' she says.

"Well, sir, I thought he was jokin', but be hivins, wan day he disappeared, an' lo an' behold, two weeks afther I picks up a pa-aper an' r-reads that me brave Schmitt was took up be th' polis f'r thryin' to cop a monarch fr'm behind a three. I sint him a copy iv a pa-aper with his pitcher in it, but I don't know if iver he got it. He's over there now an' his wife is takin' in washin'.

"It's vanity that makes arnychists, Hinnissy — vanity an' th' habits kings has nowadays iv bein' as common as life insurance agents."

"I don't like kings," said Mr. Hennessy, "but I like arnychists less. They ought to be kilt off as fast as they are caught."

"They'll be that," said Mr. Dooley. "But killin' thim is like wringin' th' neck iv a mickrobe."

VIEWING THE AUTHOR'S IDEAS

1. Does Mr. Dooley seem to understand freedom as guaranteed by the Constitution? What is his view of the right of peaceable assembly? Do you agree with him?

2. Are his views on anarchists in line with the facts? What do you think of the punishments he suggests? What rulings of the Supreme Court protecting civil liberties have a bearing on Mr. Dooley's views?

3. What is Mr. Dooley's conclusion about the causes that make men become anarchists? How does he try to prove his conclusion? Find fallacies in his argument.

4. At one time "Mr. Dooley" was a popular column in many papers. Account for this fact. Would this column be popular today?

5. What human foibles does "Mr. Dooley" satirize?

EVALUATING HIS MANNER OF EXPRESSION

1. How does Mr. Dooley avoid the monotony of unrelieved serious talk?

2. What does the dialect contribute to the effect of the essay? Compare the dialect with that in Uncle Remus.

3. Select examples of exaggeration; of understatement; of amusing definitions; of simile; of anticlimax.

4. How does brevity contribute to the effectiveness of this selection?

5. Can Dunne be compared to any popular commentator of current events today? Mention any traits he has in common with current columnists.

QUESTIONS FOR REVIEW

Read each statement carefully. Then write in your notebook only those statements that are true.

1. Although the artist may not portray life in its entirety, he aims at a complete view of life.

2. The true artist must have faith in order to portray the path by which man may come to the enjoyment of complete happiness.

3. In the study of literature it is important to learn to appraise the interpretation of the artist and measure it according to standards of truth.

4. It is as important to be able to detect what is wrong in a book as to remember what is right.

5. The purpose of literary study is to enable the student to enjoy and appraise the writings of others and aid him to worthy self-expression in his own creative endeavor.

6. The most satisfactory kind of art combines Christian idealism and realism.

7. The greatest achievement of the art of the Middle Ages, the building of the great cathedrals, was done to satisfy man's eagerness for renown.

8. Despite the fact that the honest modern realist paints truth as he knows it, his vision is frequently incomplete.

9. In story as in fact, man is fascinating to his fellow beings because he can achieve heroism against tremendous odds.

10. Realism was foreshadowed by the writings of the local-color school.

11. Naturalism preceded realism in American literature.

12. The changing social order affected the subject matter of the novelists as well as their spirit in treating it.

13. Henry James and William Dean Howells were in agreement that the novel should be definitely intellectual, with character rather than incident dominating the story.

14. The first great Catholic woman poet in America was Louise Imogen Guiney.

15. Richard Hovey and Bliss Carman are best known for their vagabondia verse, written in protest against the materialistic living of their times.

16. Maurice Francis Egan believed that although literature need never contain a forced moral, it cannot ignore the divine origin of the soul nor the operation of the moral law.

17. Most of the poems of William Vaughn Moody are reflective and deal with serious themes.

18. Henry Adams was attracted to a study of the Middle Ages because he was interested in history.

19. Through his dialect verse and his lyrics celebrating the emotions of home life, T. A. Daly has contributed to our literature.

20. The affection, pathos, whimsy of Negro family life, and the lilt of Negro music may be perceived in the verses of Paul Laurence Dunbar.

21. Garland holds a significant place in the history of American literature for his stern realism.

22. O. Henry has been unsurpassed in the technique of the surprise ending in the short story.

23. The school of naturalistic fiction began in America with the novels of Stephen Crane.

24. All of Frank Norris' novels are studies in religious and historical problems.

25. Agnes Repplier began her writing career with novels and essays.

26. Although William Allen White wrote fiction, he is best remembered as a brilliant journalist.

27. The character "Mr. Dooley" was the creation of a Chicago Journalist, Finley Peter Dunne.

28. The Civil War marked a point of change in the history of the American stage.

29. *The Great Divide,* a play by William Vaughn Moody, endeavored to present the conflict in temperament and ideals between people of the Eastern seaboard and those of the interior.

30. Reverend John Talbot Smith pioneered in the Catholic theater movement by encouraging the parish theater to stimulate American ideals.

31. Father Finn's narratives are popular stories of boy life.

32. A large number of American Catholic writers of the nineteenth century were converts.

In your notebook copy the numbers from 1 to 18. After selecting the correct choice, write the complete statement.

1. *The Portrait of a Lady* is a masterpiece among the works of (A) Howells (B) O'Reilly (C) Egan (D) James.

2. *The Rise of Silas Lapham,* a novel introducing the character of the self-made businessman to American literature, was written by (A) Howells (B) O'Reilly (C) Guiney (D) James.

3. *Moondyne Joe,* a story about an Irish prisoner in an Australian penal colony, is the work of (A) Howells (B) O'Reilly (C) Egan (D) James.

4. *Happy Ending* is the title of a book of poems by (A) O'Reilly (B) Egan (C) Hovey (D) Guiney.

5. *Songs from Vagabondia* was written by (A) O'Reilly (B) Hovey (C) Egan (D) Guiney.

6. *The Wiles of Sexton Maginnis,* witty sketches about a parish sexton, was written by (A) O'Reilly (B) Guiney (C) Egan (D) O'Malley.

7. *Mont St. Michel and Chartres,* a singularly beautiful book on the art and architecture of the Middle Ages, was written by (A) O'Reilly (B) Garland (C) Egan (D) Adams.

8. *The Four Million,* a collection of short stories, is the work of (A) Crane (B) O. Henry (C) Dunbar (D) Garland.

9. *A Son of the Middle Border,* an autobiographical work, was written by (A) Howells (B) O. Henry (C) Crane (D) Garland.

10. *The Red Badge of Courage,* a realistic story of the Civil War, was written by (A) Norris (B) London (C) Crane (D) Garland.

11. *The Pit,* a novel treating of the distribution of grain and the exchange market, was the work of (A) Norris (B) London (C) Crane (D) Bierce.

12. *The Call of the Wild,* the story of a dog in Alaska, was written by (A) Ade (B) London (C) Crane (D) Bierce.

13. *Rip Van Winkle,* a play in which the actor Joseph Jefferson achieved fame in the title role, was the work of (A) Herne (B) Fitch (C) White (D) Boucicault.

14. *Shore Acres,* a play which standardized the character of the shrewd Yankee, was written by (A) Herne (B) Belasco (C) Fitch (D) Boucicault.

15. *The Return of Peter Grimm,* written for the actor David Warfield and still popular with amateur theatrical groups, was the work of (A) John Talbot Smith (B) Clyde Fitch (C) David Belasco (D) Henry Harland.

16. *The Cardinal's Snuff Box,* a sparkling and artistic novel, was written by (A) Father Finn (B) Harland (C) Egan.

17. In Catholic fiction Tom Playfair and Percy Wynn, boy characters who take their places with Tom Sawyer and Huck Finn, were the creation of (A) Father John Talbot Smith (B) Father Finn (C) O'Reilly (D) Harland.

18. *School for Saints* was written by (A) Guiney (B) Pallen (C) Craigie (D) Harland.

QUESTIONS FOR DISCUSSION

1. What changes came with the industrial revolution in America?

2. What needs of man lead the artist to create a work of art?

3. How does the romanticist differ from the realist in writing?

4. Point out the errors in the point of view of *naturalism.* How may naturalists be classified?

5. What is meant by humanitarian fiction; by the problem novel?

6. How did Henry James influence the American novel and writers who followed him?

7. In what way did Howells contribute to the advancement of the novel in America?

8. What contribution did John Boyle O'Reilly make to the cause of Catholic culture?

9. Show that Louise Imogen Guiney lived the Christian ideal which her poetry celebrates.

10. Discuss Agnes Repplier as an essayist and a biographer.

11. Following the Civil War what forces combined to give a new impetus to acting?

12. What changes in the drama and the theater took place in the last quarter of the nineteenth century?

SUGGESTIONS FOR READING

Aldrich, Bailey, *The Story of a Bad Boy* (Houghton, Boston). Humor, surprise, and entertainment are an integral part of this story describing the pranks of a typical American boy. *A Struggle for Life* and *Marjorie Daw* by the same author are light, humorous short stories.

Allen, James Lane, *A Kentucky Cardinal* (Harper, New York). The bluegrass region of Kentucky forms the setting for a charming love story.

Bok, Edward William, *The Americanization of Edward Bok* (Scribner, New York). Biography sometimes reads like fiction. This is a fascinating story of the success of a poor boy from Holland who came to the United States and climbed to the editorship of the *Ladies' Home Journal*. His motto was: "Make the world a bit more beautiful and better because you have been in it."

Bunner, H. C., *Short Sixes* (Scribner, New York). Like Aldrich, Bunner specializes in the clever short story.

Deland, Margaret, *Old Chester Tales* (Harper, New York). This is a collection of stories treating of old seacoast towns in Maine.

Dunne, Finley Peter, *Mr. Dooley in the Hearts of His Countrymen* (Small, New York). The sayings of shrewd, witty, satirical Mr. Dooley were popular when the series first appeared. His views are still entertaining today.

Egan, Maurice Francis, *Recollections of a Happy Life* (Doubleday, New York). The book is more than a biography. It is full of entertaining and humorous anecdotes told by a writer, a diplomat, a man of winning personality. *Confessions of a Booklover,* a collection of essays on literary subjects, and *Everybody's Saint Francis,* a charming biography, are other books by the same author.

Ferber, Edna, *Cimarron* (Doubleday, New York). Prospectors rushed to Oklahoma in 1889 in search of rich oil fields. The fantastic incidents of the story are based on actual happenings.

Garland, Hamlin, *A Son of the Middle Border* (Macmillan, New York); *A Daughter of the Middle Border* (Grosset, Dunlap, New York). These books are partially autobiographical. Their keynote is struggle—the hardships of pioneer life in South Dakota—the striving for literary recognition in Boston.

Howells, William Dean, *The Sleeping Car* (Houghton, Boston). The noted American novelist and critic also wrote a number of one-act farces.

Lanier, H. W., *The Best Short Stories of Mary E. Wilkins Freeman* (Harper, New York). The stories reveal various aspects of New England Puritan life.

Lord, Daniel A., S.J., *Francis James Finn: the Story of His Life* (Benziger, New York). A fellow Jesuit tells the inside story of how Father Finn came to write his famous stories for boys.

Porter, William Sydney, *The Four Million* (Doubleday, New York). A collection of representative O. Henry stories.

Repplier, Agnes, *Under Dispute* (Houghton, New York). A representative volume of one of America's greatest essayists. *Essays in Idleness* and *In Our Convent Days* are other collections.

Roche, James J., *Life of John Boyle O'Reilly* (McVey). A study of the Catholic literary tradition of America would be incomplete without reading this stimulating biography of the great editor of the *Boston Pilot*.

Stockton, Frank, *Rudder Grange* (Scribner, New York). *Rudder Grange* is a whimsical story concerning a young married couple who begin housekeeping in a discarded ship. "The Lady or the Tiger?" is a sensational tale full of dramatic suspense.

Wallace, Lew, *Ben Hur* (Harper, New York). *Ben Hur* is a romantic novel picturing the last days of the Roman Empire and the rise of Christianity.

Lane, Rose Wilder, *Let the Hurricane Roar* (Longmans, New York). A dramatic story depicting pioneer life in Dakota in the 1870s.

Columbus Lands at San Salvador, 1492, *by Jean Gerome Ferris (1937)*

Changing Perspectives, 1914-1944

Contemporary America is a scene of extraordinary variety and complexity. No other era has ever experienced such strenuous activity nor witnessed such radical and diverse interpretations of life. Widely divergent views exist side by side; attitudes shift rapidly; a central, unifying philosophy is wholly lacking. The voluminous body of literature which records and contemplates this era is of necessity likewise varied and complex. Aside from the fact that our day is an age of multiplicity, there is another reason why a critic cannot pretend to be an unerring judge of his own era. A critic needs distance in order to gain the perspective by which things appear in their true proportion. Certain trends, however, are discernible in the mass of printed material. A study of these tendencies leaves definite impressions concerning the forces which are dominant in modern literature.

In these pages we shall limit ourselves to certain aspects of contemporary writings and a criticism of these aspects within the larger context of the Faith.

Although the history of the last three decades of our own era cannot easily be reduced to a pattern, the following divisions will prove serviceable: the period of World War I; the post-war period with its attendant cynicism and disillusionment on the one hand and its braggart optimism and counterfeit prosperity on the other; the period of the great depression, which left, temporarily, the world's wealthiest nation staggered and humiliated; the period of the Rooseveltian "New Deal," with its daring, and frequently successful, experiments with internal social and economic reform; and finally the period of World War II, which for America had its dramatic inception with the Japanese attack on Pearl Harbor on December 7, 1941.

Throughout these years, America, thanks to her technological genius, has continued to move toward a standardized way of life with amazing rapidity. The enormous growth of industry has influenced every phase of activity. Speed, wealth, and power are desired objectives. Yet, as man watches the wheels of the machine age whir faster and faster, he feels increasingly insecure, insignificant, and confused. Speed, he observes, leads to nervous exhaustion; depression sweeps wealth away; power seeks to become more powerful and wages war to achieve its end. The inventions that have made man's living more comfortable have in two world conflicts been utilized to deprive him of life. Man can use his findings to kill as well as to cure.

On the economic level, the great trusts and monopolies have continued their domination. The counter attempts to destroy them have produced an increased public awareness of social and economic issues. The contemporary era, likewise, marks the first serious attempts of the Marxists and Socialists to apply their various remedies in the cure of social ills. Schools of writers have arisen in support of rival ideologies; even the novelist and the poet feel it necessary to utilize their art in the interest of social reform.

Perhaps the most notable feature of our epoch has been the bankruptcy of those philosophies advocating unlimited freedom in politics, economics, and ethics. These ideas had long flourished in America and were especially attractive to a people for whom liberty and freedom were instinctive ideals. But Americans are beginning to discover that liberty is not an illimitable ideal. The liberty to amass wealth which is detrimental to the common good; the liberty to propagate ideas which are injurious to democratic government; the liberty to preach doctrines which are prejudicial to public and private morals — all these are too clearly a declaration of anarchy and rebellion.

So long as Americans enjoyed prosperity and peace, they did not, as a rule, resent the unfortunate union between the so-called "liberalism" and democracy. Indeed the rising standard of living, the endless multiplication of labor-saving devices, America's rank as the wealthiest among the nations, served to give eloquent support to the idea that the democratic ideal and the liberal ideal were basically the same. Although this mistaken liberalism has always had its opponents in America, it has taken two world conflicts and an enervating depression to bring about a full re-examination of the premises upon which our national life is based.

The reaction against false liberalism has been largely limited to its economic phases. But it has other aspects, equally false and equally perilous, which have received but scant attention. There is not much point in our statesmen's seeking a true standard of political and moral values when a large reading public accepts the conviction of its literary guides that nothing in life is final or absolute; that the only way we know an act is moral is when we feel good after it. Such statements make pleasurable feeling the standard of human behavior. Such authors with their amateur psychologies deprive man of all liberty and all dignity and portray him as an unmotivated mass of appetite and sensation.

It will be instructive to examine the writers introduced in this chapter not only from the viewpoint of technical skill — which is sometimes considerable — but from the viewpoint of their beliefs and attitudes. Such an examination should help you to comprehend the spiritual restlessness which frequently simmers beneath brave attitudes and sardonic poses.

POETRY

The poetry of our time has shared in the general confusion of a society in the state of transition. We have had wilful poets and traditional poets, we have had regional poets and cosmopolitan poets, and we have had bird-throated lyricists and brass-throated prophets. In the early decades, especially, American poetry strove desperately and very self-consciously to be itself. Under the obvious sway of Whitman, a whole school arose with the avowed intention of pouring the whole of the American scene — stockyards, skyscrapers, foundries, city, suburb, and slums — into the melting-pot of verse. The ugly and the sordid, these poets believed, were not alien to poetry. Poetry, like the patriarchal Whitman himself, was able to contain multitudes. The poetry produced under the impulse of this theory is hardly reassuring. At its best it has a rough lyricism not unlike that of the Camden seer; at its worst, it has a raucous sentimentalism that is the more objectionable in that it pretends to be so vigorous and masculine.

With other poets the search for originality took even more exotic forms. A little contemptuous of the English tradition to which many artists clung with an almost servile tenacity, these poets sought to establish a native tradition, not so much by exploiting the American scene, but by creating new molds or new patterns. It is of these poets that we think when we speak of the "new poetry." The "new poetry" — now, perhaps, a little faded — consisted primarily of technical innovations, of imagism and free verse, of the cinquain and the hokku. While these experiments were actually being made (and they were undertaken on a vast scale, thanks to the crusading zeal of Amy Lowell, Ezra Pound, and Harriet Monroe) it was not always easy to distinguish the charlatan from the poet. Novelty of form can disguise as well as reveal and can serve to distract us from those values which are, in the long run, more inherently poetic.

Now that the frenzy has died down we can assess these innovations with greater sanity of judgment. It is, for example, a noteworthy instance of historical irony to discover that some of the innovations were not innovations at all, but importations — from pre-Chaucer England, from medieval Provence, and even from contemporary Japan. Some of the poets sought inspiration from the French Symbolists. The French Symbolists, however, had been largely influenced by Edgar Allan Poe, and as a result we are presented with the diverting spectacle of a nineteenth-century American poet returning with Gallic accent to influence his own countrymen.

Probably the most ambitious individual movement was "Imagism." Held together in the beginning by the ideals of their "manifesto" — objectivity, precision, pattern — the poets of this group soon revealed their intense individualism by going their separate ways and by failing, or refusing, to remember the points of their manifesto. The one faithful adherent to the Imagist doctrine, Hilda Doolittle, with her exquisitely chiseled Greek figurines, has helped to keep the name of the movement alive and respectable. But Imagism, in spite of its eccentric career, has made a notable contribution to our poetry. Its discipline taught poets to be contemptuous of excess ornament; it taught them concentration and precision of metaphor; and, finally, it taught them to oppose a too fluid lyricism.

The poetic achievement of our time is not, however, entirely in the hands of the experimentalists. While it is difficult to be certain of the enduring reputation of contemporaries, two traditionalist poets, Edwin Arlington Robinson and Robert Frost, seem already to have earned a secure place in the annals of American poetry. Both of these poets are of New England and share the introspective habits of their Puritan forbears. Of the two, Robinson has the wider range but Frost the profounder lyric gift. In their best poems both have an economy of expression and a simplicity of diction which, together with new and subtle variations of rhythm, give their poems a directness and immediacy of emotional appeal unexampled in our time. Robinson's more ambitious narrative poems are, in the main, less

Edwin Arlington Robinson

successful than his shorter pieces. Here his tendency to indirection leads him into involved, roundabout conversation, and the subtlety of the content is not in proportion to the subtlety of expression. Nevertheless, Robinson, unlike Frost, had a superb gift for drama, and had he been as aware of the external world as he was of the interior world of the mind, he might have created poetic drama of a more satisfying kind than the Arthurian romances which brought him fame.

EDWIN ARLINGTON ROBINSON

A master poet of the modern era, Edwin Arlington Robinson (1869-1935) successfully blended tradition and originality. His was a new and vital spirit, but he chose to express his poetry in conventional stanza patterns such as the sonnet, the ballad, and the dramatic monologue. In brief character sketches of derelicts and misfits, Robinson examines the hidden recesses of the human mind. He gives a dramatic presentation of these "splendid failures," whose distorted lives he penetrates in turn with humor, sympathy, and irony. An individualist himself, he writes in protest against standardization in the modern world which thwarts the expression of individuality.

Robinson had been writing quietly and unheard for some twenty years before his *Man Against the Sky* (1916) won him an audience. Even after his success, he so carefully avoided publicity that when awarded the Gold Medal of the American Institute of Art and Letters, he asked to be spared a formal presentation. The few who knew him best say that he was as simple and unaffected as a child. Robinson's work three times brought him the Pulitzer Prize.

His shrewd character studies, marked by wisdom, insight and poetic competency, are Robinson's distinctive contribution to American letters. In his extensive works he has peopled a whole community with very real and human individuals. Robinson had known some of the unfortunates he depicts during his youth in Gardiner, Maine, the Tilbury Town of his poems. Others he had befriended in the days when he worked in New York as inspector of subway construction or as clerk in the Customs House. Besides the fictitious folk he has sketched, Robinson has presented in action striking historical figures such as Napoleon, Shakespeare, and Alexander Hamilton.

He has also re-interpreted the poetic material of Arthurian legend, which had appealed to the imagination of so many poets before him. His *Merlin* (1917), *Lancelot* (1920), and *Tristram* (1927) demonstrate lyric wealth and exquisite workmanship. In these poems, too, he etches character with precision and subtlety, offering the psychology of the actions which bring the Arthurian narrative to its tragic close.

Robinson has developed another type of narrative poem that might be called the psychological tale. This work paints the state of mind of a character in a dramatic situation. A powerful effect is achieved largely through the use of suggestion, which gives significant hints and allows the reader to complete the picture for himself.

The poet's shorter pieces employ a simple, colloquial diction; his longer works are written in a formal, lofty tone. Robinson's view of character is that of the detached onlooker; he writes with a reserve and restraint typical of the New Englander. Though he portrays so much of the suffering and mystery of life and shows a preoccupation with tragic character, he does not see life as futile and without purpose. In his happier moods, at least, Robinson finds in mankind some spark of a supernatural flame. When confronted with the accusation that his presentation of life was a jail house, he replied that it was a kind of spiritual kindergarten in which people tried to spell the name of God with the wrong blocks. While staying at the writers' community of MacDowell Colony in Peterborough, New Hampshire, William Thomas Walsh had the good fortune to probe beyond Robinson's reserve in religious matters. One evening Robinson read Walsh's *Thirty Pieces of Silver* in manuscript and was much attracted to Nicodemus, a minor character in the play. The New England poet wrote his own *Nicodemus* a few days later and read it to Walsh, who felt as he listened that Robinson himself "was a sort of Nicodemus, secretly attracted to Christ, venerating Him enormously, but a little afraid of his own veneration, afraid to analyze it too much."

ROBERT FROST

Within the framework of a single poem Robert Frost (1875-) captures the flavor of rural life in New England and invests the plainest subjects with universal significance. To match the simplicity of his themes, he reproduces the conversational tone of Yankee speech in the flowing rhythm of blank verse or simple rhyme. This union of subject matter with its corresponding language and rhythm marks the distinctive style of a rare artist.

When Robert Frost's father died in California, his mother brought the ten-year-old boy to his grandfather's home in Lawrence, Massachusetts. Frost entered Dartmouth at seventeen, but finding the academic atmosphere distasteful, stayed only a few months. When a long tramp through the Carolinas furnished him no work, he returned to Lawrence and a job as bobbin boy in a factory. Torn between the urge to write and the necessity of earning a living, he was in turn a cobbler, rural newspaper editor, and after his marriage, a student at Harvard for two years. He next became a teacher and a farmer until he sold the farm that his grandfather had given him and sailed to England, where he could write poetry and be poor without scandal to the family.

In England his first two volumes brought immediate acclaim, and in 1915 Frost was welcomed back to the United States as an important literary figure. He has largely given his time to cultivating his farm in New Hampshire, interesting other people in reading books, writing at intervals his own slender volumes of works, and lecturing at American University as poet in residence.

Robert Frost's background of craftsmanship and farming has helped him to gain insight into the New England character and the traditions that have shaped it. He has not only keenly observed the people "north of Boston"; he has been their neighbor and has performed the same farm duties. Because of this familiarity with his subject matter, Frost's lyrics, narratives, and dialogues seem to flow almost naturally out of the New England landscape. Following his own canon of giving uncommon expression to a common experience, his interpretations of nature contain lines of delicate beauty and strong originality. In addition to the themes of nature and familiar experience, many of Frost's poems are concerned with personality and character study. His sympathetic understanding of the rural New Englander has unlocked for him the minds of the farm people and revealed their pride, their fear, their tragedies.

Robert Frost is an artistic realist who explains his creed by saying: "There are two types of realist — the one who offers a good deal of dirt with his potato to show that it is a real one and the one who is satisfied with the potato brushed clean. . . . To me, the thing art does for life is to clean it, to strip it to form." Frost's clean lines do not treat a subject exhaustively but etch it sharply on the memory by the power of suggestion. A warm feeling surges under the meter of the New England poet, but his emotion is always disciplined to a calm, quiet strength in a style which makes no attempt to be spectacular. His message is the more impressive because he leaves much unsaid.

Robert Frost has kept to traditional verse forms in this era of experimentation. His blank verse flows with the ease of human speech, and at times his use of simple rhyme is so natural that the reader scarcely notices the pattern. His power as a poet lies in his ability to stimulate the reader's imagination and enlarge his experience. Because he touches ordinary life and common things with glory, originality, and insight, he will undoubtedly take a place as one of the major poets of our time.

Robert Frost

AMY LOWELL

Amy Lowell (1874-1925), who sought above all else permanence as a poet, fell short of her goal by a small margin and is remembered instead as the driving force of Imagism. Having captured the movement and brought it to America, she marshaled the forces of her wealth, social prestige, and indomitable will to further the interests of the new poetry. Her vigorous, eccentric leadership, which branched out into lecturing and writing in favor of the new freedom in poetry, did much to gain acceptance of Imagism as a legitimate poetic creed.

Amy Lowell's crusading habits were strangely at variance with the traditions of a family which dated back to the early seventeenth century and included, besides James Russell Lowell, a minister to England and a Harvard president. At twenty-eight she discovered poetry to be her natural mode of expression and from that moment devoted herself to study and writing. Only after eight years did she publish her first book. Her second volume, *Sword Blades and Poppy Seeds* (1914), broke with the old traditions in verse and marked the poet as one of the most individual voices of her time. This book and the ten volumes which succeeded it kept her a vital and energetic leader to the end.

A craftsman, Amy Lowell was primarily interested in form, pattern, and decoration, in sights and sounds. Her images are as definite and hard as the Imagist creed dictates; they are so perfect that life has been polished out of them. She presents a splendid spectacle but it has no apparent significance. In its exclusively intellectual quality Amy Lowell's poetry falls short of greatness, for with a few noted exceptions it lacks emotional values.

Amy Lowell's most representative poems may be found in *Selected Poems.* Her best creative work is not in her poetry at all but in her critical writing, notably *Tendencies in Modern American Poetry* (1917) and *John Keats* (1925). She proved herself as able to master the traditional verse forms as to experiment in original poetic patterns. Her best effects are in imagist poetry, free verse, and *polyphonic prose,* so called because, though printed as prose, this form makes use of such poetic devices as rhythm, alliteration, assonance, cadence, meter, and at times rhyme. Her wide range exhibits her versatility.

HILDA DOOLITTLE

Hilda Doolittle (1886-), a poet of integrity and distinction, has conformed more strictly to the Imagist principles than any other poet of the group. On vacation in England, Hilda Doolittle, a Pennsylvanian, became interested in the new literary tendencies, joined the budding Imagist group, and decided not to return to the United States. She may be said to have launched Imagism in 1913 when Ezra Pound sent three of her poems signed "H. D., Imagist" to Harriet Monroe's magazine, *Poetry.* Since the publication of her first Imagist poems, H. D., as she is known, has spent most of her life abroad, chiefly in the little Swiss town where she now lives.

In the Greek poets, H. D. recognized the clarity, simplicity, and precision which the spirit of Imagism demanded. She learned so well from these writers that the most exacting Greek scholars approve her work. The Greek sense of proportion enables her to achieve perfect form. Her precisely chiseled images are confined in exactly appropriate meter. At times she employs regular rhythms and rhyme. Her poems are usually no more than sharply-etched, richly suggestive pictures, but their perfect form and flawless expression call forth a response which Amy Lowell's poems cannot evoke. Since the appearance of *Sea Garden* (1916), her first collection, several volumes of her lyrics have been published. With skill and poetic grace Hilda Doolittle has retold in her dramas the stories of Greek myth and legend.

CARL SANDBURG

Poet of industrial America, Carl Sandburg (1878-) has devoted himself primarily to a vigorous interpretation of the machine age. The midwestern metropolis, its machinery, its common laborers, its strange contrasts of loveliness and brutality, have furnished him with poetic materials. Sandburg's ability to perceive not only the brute strength, cruelty, and unbridled energy of the city, but also its delicately beautiful aspects has resulted in the production of two diverse types of poetry: his verse of social criticism and his descriptive verse. Adapting the technique of free verse to his own individual style, he uses racy speech, slang, vigorous language, and bold imagery in his pieces on industrialism; he employs fanciful diction in his more delicate descriptive poems. "Chicago" and "Nocturne in a Deserted Brickyard" illustrate this sharp contrast in his work.

Carl Sandburg's poems reflect a wide variety of first-hand experience. The son of Swedish immigrants who settled in Galesburg, Illinois, he left school at thirteen. He drove a milk wagon, served as porter in a barber shop, operated a truck in a brickyard, shifted scenes in a theater, washed dishes in hotels in Kansas City, Omaha, and Denver, was a carpenter, painter, peddler, and a harvester in Kansas. At twenty he enlisted in the Spanish-American War. After demobilization, he attended Lombard College in Galesburg for four years, working as bellringer and janitor to pay for his tuition. Work on the college newspaper gave him an interest in writing and eventually turned him to journalism.

In spite of critics Sandburg won an audience that he has never lost. In his early poems he voiced a violent

Carl Sandburg

humanitarian protest against the suffering caused by greed and selfishness. His lines hum and rumble and roar with the rhythm of machines, factories, and construction gangs. In later works Sandburg's expression was more subdued, but one must read much that is uncouth and merely dull before coming upon lines of clearness, brightness, and significance.

Though his place as a poet may be in doubt, Sandburg has attained permanent distinction in prose by his six-volume study of Lincoln, the labor of some twenty years. Judged by critics as one of the great biographies of modern times, it brought the author the Pulitzer Prize in 1940. Sandburg's *American Songbag,* a treasury of songs and ballads gathered from all sections of the country, is an indication of his unflagging interest in the preservation of what is rich and genuine in the American tradition.

VACHEL LINDSAY

In Vachel Lindsay (1879-1931) America possessed a modern minstrel who attempted to make poetry a part of communal life, much as it had been in the days of the medieval troubadours. He was bard, evangelist, mystic, and poet, all in one. As a singing beggar he tramped over the country, chanting his poems and preaching the gospel of beauty, which stimulated men to make their own homes and neighborhood "the most democratic, the most beautiful, and the holiest in the world."

Lindsay was essentially a product of the American soil. Born in Springfield, Illinois, he received a strict religious training which cultivated in him the spirit of reform and the method of evangelical Protestantism. After three years at college he studied art in Chicago and New York. Unable to earn his living by painting or to get other work, he peddled some of his drawings at two cents apiece on the streets of New York. For a time after the publication of his early volumes, Lindsay was in great demand as a lecturer. He toured the country, reciting his poetry with all the variations his fine voice commanded. His last days were painful. Mind and body broke under the strain of trying to support his wife and two little daughters with the scanty earnings of the lecture tours which eventually lost their popularity.

Always closely in sympathy with the common people, Lindsay is a poet of the people, reflecting the panorama of America, its everyday emotional life, its history, and the deeds of its heroes. In his attempt to make poetry part of the democratic heritage, he stands in contrast with the Imagists, who wrote for a selected group. For Lindsay, every experience clothed itself in words and an appropriate meter. The jazz rhythms and exotic tones of the Negro spirituals which he heard on his wide travels resulted in an extraordinary lyric poem, "The Congo." The rousing vitality of the poems, the rich and unrestrained reaches of the poet's imagination, his overemphasized rhythms and jingling couplets, and his use of poetic tricks account for the popularity of Lindsay's performance in verse. Besides this somewhat noisy poetry Lindsay wrote lyrics in traditional forms.

In his desire to cultivate popular taste for poetry, Vachel Lindsay aimed to appeal through the ear rather than the eye. If his work is to be appreciated, it must be chanted, recited, or sung. Lindsay's own interpretations of his poetry with gestures and a chanting intonation literally made his compositions "the higher vaudeville" which he himself had named them. Truly democratic in subject matter and in spirit, a half dozen of Lindsay's best poems have made secure his place in literature.

SARA TEASDALE

While the Imagists were experimenting with the new poetry, Sara Teasdale (1884-1933) was singing in the old forms with a power that was entirely original. In the library of her home in St. Louis, Missouri, she had learned her art from the lyrics of Sappho and Christina Rossetti, from Browning and Emily Dickinson. Her delicate health and shy imaginative nature contrived to bring her into early touch with books. Before she was ten she was composing poetry and editing *The Potter's Wheel*, a monthly magazine which she wrote by hand with the aid of a friend and illustrated with photographs. Her cultural environment as well as extensive travel in this country and abroad gave her a wealth of experience out of which to write. Much of Sara Teasdale's later life was spent in New York City.

Sara Teasdale was essentially a lyric poet who voiced the primitive emotions of love, sorrow, hate, and sympathy. She had the ability to capture a mood or an emotion and mold it into memorable music in brief, direct, and simple diction. The theme of love, with beauty as its handmaid, dominates her lyrics. It was her habit to compose a poem in her mind before putting it on paper. This method caused her to avoid intricate stanzas, and she chose as her favorite the quatrain, in which four lines are linked together by simple rhyme. She depends on no striking imagery but uses a language and verse pattern that hold within themselves an overtone of the poet's own spirit. But in spite of exquisite harmony and depth of emotion, one senses the disquieting tone of a person who lacks faith.

ELINOR WYLIE

Out of personal sorrows Elinor Wylie (1885-1928) wrought distinctive poetry of highly polished workmanship and sharply individualized expression. The poet spent her childhood in Washington, D.C., where her father was Assistant Attorney General. She later lived in Paris and in London and eventually became identified with an outstanding literary group in New York. Unhappiness in early marriage gave her an attitude of proud independence, which she carried into her writing. Her poetry is deeply personal, with intense but restrained emotion.

Elinor Wylie experimented for five years before publishing *Nets to Catch the Wind,* the first volume to appear under her own name. Her rich gift of words and imaginative power exhibits itself in dazzling, if somewhat far-fetched figures of speech. She writes of a mouth "like a wing turned down"; of little puddles roofed with ice, and of silver wasp nests that hang like fruit. The same richness and artifice of diction characterizes her four novels and other prose pieces. Her interest in the seventeenth-century English poet John Donne contributed something to her emotional outlook, her method of restraint and indirection, and to her bold use of metaphor. The use of subtle speech makes the meaning of her poems elusive, something that must be carefully thought out. She seems always to be seeking escape from the problem of life, which she fails to solve, and her poems are often concerned with the meaning of death. In *Angels and Earthly Creatures*, the volume she left prepared for the printer at the time of her death, Elinor Wylie reached the full expression of her artistry.

EDGAR LEE MASTERS

Edgar Lee Masters (1869-), an Illinois lawyer and poet, was swept into fame by a single book of poems, *Spoon River Anthology*, a masterpiece of cynicism on human nature in a small town setting. Perturbing and original, with its character portrayal, love element, detective story thrills, and local color, the book immediately created a sensation and invaded the ranks of the best sellers.

From boyhood Edgar Lee Masters had wished to write. Instead, upon his father's insistence, he entered the legal profession. In Chicago he developed a successful practice of law, in the meantime producing books of verse, plays, and essays which were too ordinary to evoke praise. He was a middle aged man when his *Spoon River Anthology* met its startling success.

Nothing written by Masters before or since has attracted the attention aroused by *Spoon River*. The reading of a Greek anthology which he perused as a model of style suggested to him the idea of a collection of epitaphs on the dead of a fictitious midwestern town. The influence of realism, his own ironic philosophy of life, and the new forms in verse clinched the pattern and style of the volume. In these epitaphs the poet employed free verse, but at times managed it little better than prose. "Anne Rutledge" is one of the exceptional pieces in which music blends with dignity of theme.

Since the publication of *Spoon River,* novelists have been increasingly concerned with the psychological background of character. Masters anticipated by five years Sinclair Lewis' indictment of the complacency of middle class America.

EDNA ST. VINCENT MILLAY

The poetry of Edna St. Vincent Millay (1892-) represents the restless, faith-lacking generation of World War I. In technical skill Miss Millay stands out as one of the distinguished living lyric poets.

Edna St. Vincent Millay's literary talents as a girl caused a wealthy woman to send her from her home in Rockland, Maine, to Vassar College. Her poem, "Renascence," written when she was nineteen, startled the literary world with its lyric freshness. The piece attracted attention when it appeared in magazine form, and was used as the title poem in her first collection of poetry, published the year of her graduation from Vassar. After leaving college Miss Millay went to New York and joined the Provincetown Players, for whom she wrote several dramas. During these lean years, writing, acting, and translating earned her a poor existence. In 1923 she married Eugen Jan Boissevain, an importer, and since that time has made her home chiefly in the Berkshire Hills and in middle New York State. Numerous volumes have followed her first book of poems, one of which, *The Harp Weaver* (1923), won the Pulitzer Prize.

The poetry which made Edna St. Vincent Millay famous is intensely subjective. In its treatment of the varied aspects of love — its joy and pain — the loveliness of nature, and the solemnity of death, it is a constant revelation of the poet's breathless love of life. Taking no cognizance of class struggle or the advance of science, these early poems might well have been written by a poet of an earlier century, so absolute is their escape into the life of emotion and the senses. However, in their spirit of revolt and their display of cynicism in the face of life's problems, they strike a modern note of clever flippancy.

Edna St. Vincent Millay

Edna St. Vincent Millay's penetrating lyric voice reaches its full power and maturity in the sonnet form. Here her poetry has the ease of conversation and the flow of music. Her quick response to beauty, the spontaneity and haunting quality of her expression give strength to her work. She has never gone beyond the merit of the poems which express the transiency of beauty and human love, the sorrow and anguish of her disillusioned generation.

ARTHUR GUITERMAN

For forty years Arthur Guiterman (1871-1943) poked fun at the faults and failings of his fellows in so amiable and humorous a fashion that he became one of the most loved of American humorists. Before he turned versifier he was on the editorial staffs of several popular magazines. He wrote a great many books of light verse; he originated the "Rhymed Reviews," which first appeared in *Life*; and wrote the libretto and lyrics for Walter Damrosch's opera, *A Man Without a Country.* Joyce Kilmer called him "the most American of poets," and his place in American humor is assured as long as readers can recognize the sound philosophy beneath

Guiterman's cap and bells. To the very end he was spreading kindly wisdom; death came to him suddenly while he was on his way to deliver a lecture on Brave Laughter.

THOMAS STEARNS ELIOT

The name of Thomas Stearns Eliot (1888-) has been significant in literary circles since his *Poems* (1920) expressed the world weariness and disillusionment of the post-war generation in an unusual and learned style. Much of his poetry has continued to center round the theme of the spiritual barrenness of modern life. In *The Waste Land* (1922) he represented contemporary civilization as a desert in which there is no faith to support man's spirit and no hope of material security to encourage effort. Eliot gained a wide influence over those writers who were pleased with his wilful mingling of tragedy and triviality, of wit and dullness, of harmony and discord — discordances which reflect the confusion of the period. In *Ash Wednesday* (1930) Eliot found his way out of the wasteland into a positive religious faith, that of the Anglo-Catholic Church. In the return to the discipline of Christianity, he has seen the fulfillment of life. This seriousness also marks his recent *Four Quartets* (1943).

T. S. Eliot was born in St. Louis, Missouri, of the old and distinguished Boston Eliots. After taking two degrees at Harvard, he did graduate work at the Sorbonne and at Oxford. He settled in London, married, and in 1927 became a British citizen. Literary work has steadily engaged him. He has lectured extensively in this country and in England, has served as editor of the *Criterion*, and is at present a director of the publishing firm of Faber and Faber.

In London Eliot became associated with the Imagists, and in his own work took for granted the new freedom in poetry for which this group so militantly battled. Not only Imagism but the rhythms and ironic contrasts of the French Symbolists have been a major influence on him. He has also absorbed into his own manner of expression the traditions and technique of the seventeenth-century English poets. The poetry of T.S. Eliot is primarily intellectual rather than emotional; it is not easily understood by those who have not read widely in the literature of the past, to which he makes frequent allusion.

Murder in the Cathedral, a modern morality play, produced and published in 1935, has been the most successful of Eliot's dramas in verse. Many of the reflective passages are lyrics in themselves, and there are vigor and grandeur in the choruses which are modeled on the Greek.

Important as Eliot is as poet and dramatist, he has even more significance as a thinker and critic. Some of his appraisals undoubtedly have a lasting value in literary criticism. The ideas in *Selected Essays, 1917-1932*, his most representative critical work, are in line with the principles implied in his poetry. He has taken the lead in an effort to rid modern literature of what he calls a secularism that "simply cannot understand the meaning of the primacy of the supernatural over the natural life." In its place he has set up a definite theory of art. T. S. Eliot is in favor of forsaking realism and romanticism for the rigid standards of classicism in which individuality is submerged to order and tradition. In the revival of classicism in letters and Christianity in morals, he sees the hope of building a more harmonious literature and an improved society.

STEPHEN VINCENT BENÉT

The death in March, 1943, of Stephen Vincent Benét (1898-1943) brought warm tributes from his literary fellows — tributes to the poet and especially to the man who in the last years of his life put aside his second great epic, "Western Star," to give himself completely to the writing of radio dramas, speeches, and articles for the press in order to awaken in Americans a consciousness of the real issues of World War II.

Stephen Benét was no less a part of two earlier wars. In World War I, with three generations of American army tradition surging through his blood, he got into service in spite of his bad eyesight by memorizing an oculist's chart, but after three days his trick was discovered and he was discharged. From then on he fought that war in spirit as he did this one. As a boy his interest in the Civil War was stimulated by many quiet hours with the military records which his father, Colonel James Walker Benét, kept in his library. The dream of reinterpreting this great struggle was destined to await fulfillment for the dozen years it took him to get settled in life. During that time he took his B.A. and M.A. at Yale, studied a

Stephen Vincent Benét

year at the Sorbonne in France, met there and married Rosemary Carr, staff-writer for the Paris edition of the *Chicago Tribune,* and did five or six years of hackwriting before a Guggenheim fellowship afforded him the means to start serious work on his long narrative poem, *John Brown's Body* (1928), the publication of which gave him a following in literary circles. This poem, which some critics have called the great American epic, is a fair index of the qualities which distinguish much of Stephen Benét's work — an authentic ballad touch, a sense of drama, and a stirring patriotism. The dramatic quality first showed to advantage in a series of dramatic monologues, *Five Men and Pompey* (1915), published when he was only seventeen, and the patriotic note is strong and sure in the radio scripts, pamphlets, and speeches that he crowded into his last days of life.

Mood varies in Stephen Benét's work; his manner is at one time humorous, at another, grave. His poetic expression ranges from high to low, from well-fashioned lyric passages to mere jingle. He sometimes worked in traditional verse patterns, and sometimes experimented with new forms, one of his most striking performances in free verse being "Litany for Dictatorships." But whether the expression was high or only mediocre, his heart was always in his work to enrich it with the gold of his own sincerity.

ARCHIBALD MACLEISH

A modern poet who served his apprenticeship in the school of T. S. Eliot is the poet who became Librarian of Congress. Archibald MacLeish (1892-) was born in Glencoe, Illinois, but was educated in eastern schools — Hotchkiss, Yale, and Harvard Law School. He interrupted his law course to serve in World War I, first with a hospital unit, and then in the artillery. Discharged from the army with the rank of captain, he took his degree in law and taught a while at Harvard before beginning to practice. *Tower of Ivory*, a book of undergraduate verses, was published while he was in service, but it did not satisfy him, and during three years of law practice in Boston, he constantly felt himself drawn to literature. A trip with his wife and children to France, with short journeys as far away as Persia, gave him the leisure he needed to read and the experience he needed to write. The skillful use of light and color and brilliant visual image in his next few books shows the influence not only of T. S. Eliot, but also of Ezra Pound and the French Symbolists. But he went beyond these influences, and by experimenting with repetition, suspense, contrast, and the long sentence, achieved new effects within the traditional verse forms. His later work, written after his return to this country, bears unmistakably the mark of originality. Out of all these experiments he developed the mastery of words and of cadence so manifest in *Conquistador*, the 1932 Pulitzer Prize poem, based on Castillo's story of the conquest of Mexico by Cortez.

Since 1935 MacLeish has used current subjects with unusual ability and popular success by adapting his poetic gifts to the ballet, the drama, and the radio. It is safe to say that this use of radio to produce, through the tonal effects of poetry, feelings as intensive as those of the drama, is not the least of Archibald MacLeish's contributions to American literature.

ROBERT P. TRISTRAM COFFIN

Robert P. Tristram Coffin (1892-) draws his inspiration from the fisherfolk and farmers of his native Maine and the landscape in which they live and work. Born of a family "300 years deep in the New England soil and sea," he was early in touch with growing things on his father's farm, and with the *Arabian Nights* and the tales of Cooper and Hawthorne in his father's library. He took degrees at Bowdoin, Princeton, and Oxford, and then taught English literature at Wells College, where he introduced the Oxford idea of honors work in his department. He is now back at Bowdoin as Pierce Professor of English. The verses in *Collected Poems* (1939), selected from his other nine volumes of verse, show that he has followed faithfully his own description of poetry as "the art of putting different kinds of good things together: men and plows, boys and whistles, hounds and deer, sorrow and sympathy, life and death." The poetic framework for these "good things" ranges all the way from the ballad to the blank verse lyric. Coffin has written a prolific amount of prose; and though he publishes both prose and poetry too frequently to permit the pruning that much of his work needs, we always read it with gratitude for the philosophy of joy and good faith that he preaches in the midst of the poets of gloom who refuse to see with him

> These minute radiances that come
> And go . . .

Strange Holiness brought him the 1936 Pulitzer Prize for poetry and in the same year he was awarded the Golden Rose of the New England Poetry Society.

JESSE STUART

While Jesse Stuart (1907-) grew up in the Kentucky hills in an atmosphere of feuds, wild beauty, and hearty hillfolk, the sights and sounds and experiences of everyday seeped into his nature and made him as vigorous as they. As a very young boy he read Burns by lantern light while his dog hunted coon, barking a signal when he treed one. If poetry was pleasant, study was difficult for him; and as he struggled through high school and college, his love of his native hills compelled him to write poems and stories about them. Now he also writes, in an easy, colloquial style, stories of the high school boys and girls whom he teaches and so well understands. When he began sending his work to the magazines, manuscript after manuscript came back, until *Story* accepted one. Soon he had a contract for his whole collection of sonnets — 703 of them — which he named *The Man with a Bull-Tongue Plow*. Since then he has published his autobiography and several novels and collections of short stories.

The simplicity and natural beauty of his poems have prompted some critics to call him an American Burns. In his own words, he sees poetry in the "smell and feel of spring blossoms, . . . in the gay boys and girls of spring, alive with the blowing wind, . . . in the men and women working in their summer of life and growing their fields of grain." If he records this poetry of the Kentucky hills in a style that sometimes falters and stumbles, he is still young enough to give it something of the perfection which its warmth and sincerity merit.

JOHN GILLESPIE MAGEE, Jr.

John Gillespie Magee, Jr., (1922-1941) of the Royal Canadian Air Force, was killed in action over England on December 11, 1941, three months after he wrote his sonnet, "High Flight," on the back of an envelope and sent it to his mother. John was born in Shanghai of missionary parents, was educated in Connecticut schools and at renowned Rugby in England. He put aside a scholarship to Yale in order to join the R.C.A.F. His gallant spirit will sing, exultantly and fearlessly, in the lines of "High Flight." As we read we are reminded of Joyce Kilmer and Alan Seeger — not so young, but quite as joyous — whose voices were stilled in World War I.

ROBERT HILLYER

The reputation of Robert Hillyer (1895-) as a lyric poet has advanced steadily since 1934, when he received the Pulitzer award for his *Collected Poems*. Since then his output has not only remained steady but has attained a quality so consistently excellent that he ranks close to his friend, Robert Frost, in the estimation of qualified critics.

Hillyer's tones are quiet, yet they vibrate with controlled tension. He is a lover of tranquility, distilling his thoughts through long silences on walks far from the tumult of cities. Nobility is evident in his choice of themes and in the sagacious tenderness with which he treats of men, of places, and of the issues that must be met. It is a combination of this upward pitch, this tenderness, and this quiet pondering that runs like an obbligato through his poems, giving them cadences that strike not to the heart alone but to conviction also. He can be sardonic, too, but he reserves his scorn for the vulgar and the ignoble. Towards those zealots of the social-ferment school who would pervert art to the service of class hatred, he directs a withering hostility. At times he becomes bitter over the ruin done to human dignity, but he knows how to offer restoratives.

Hillyer's works include *The Halt in the Garden* (1925), *A Letter to Robert Frost and Others* (1937), *Pattern of a Day* (1940), and numerous earlier volumes. Hillyer was born at East Orange, New Jersey. In 1937 he was appointed Boylston Professor of Rhetoric and Oratory at Harvard. During the academic year he maintains an apartment in Cambridge, but his real home is his country house in Pomfret, Connecticut. It is there, as he puts it, that "his roots go down into the earth."

FREDERIC PROKOSCH

The meteoric rise of Frederic Prokosch (1908-), young Wisconsin poet and novelist, is one of the most remarkable phenomena of the current literary era. It is significant that Prokosch, gifted with great sensitiveness and fertile powers of self-expression, has interpreted the bewilderment and dejection—one might almost say the despair—of modern youth as it finds itself caught in the catastrophe of a world-upheaval for which it is not responsible, yet from which it cannot escape. In this dramatic role he speaks for youth defrauded of its dream, and he does it with telling effect. The very title of his books—*The Skies of Europe*, *The Conspirators*, *The Assassins*, *Death at Sea* — tell of the premonition and terror that struck young manhood everywhere as the tempest gathered and broke.

Strangely enough, Frederic Prokosch is a romanticist rather than a realist in the literary sense. Yet in his poetry as in his fiction, it is the reality behind the romance that gives his writing its sting. His style is imaginative, richly expressive, and somber. His rhythms are musical, yet full of dissonances. The imagery is exotic, at times almost voluptuous; the backgrounds dark, confused, and mysterious. Often the mood is so overpowering that it clouds the experience, yet the message is seldom lost. If the facts seem momentarily obscured, they reveal themselves in the final effect. Prokosch, for all his passionate approach to beauty, is not an escapist. Rather he hungers for that wholeness and harmony which evil forces have so tragically marred.

RIDGELY TORRENCE

The poetry of Ridgely Torrence (1875-) springs from deep sources of the American genius. In theme and in spirit it is native to our atmosphere and true to our national traditions. Torrence has technical proficiency in a high degree, but he has something more. He has soundness and honesty, a clean heart and a spacious mind. One of the great values of his poetry is the proof it gives that the mainstream of American song is still clear, melodious, and strong. He does not have to strain for an American idiom. Ridgely Torrence is a native of Ohio. The accent of our great continent is natural to him. He finds it good and speaks it without affectation. He does not find it necessary to imitate the older voices or to copy the new. His eloquence is his own. Old railroad tracks delight him, and such simple things as a tangle of orchard boughs, a cluster of children, or the sight of an American main street or battlefield will start him singing. His philosophic approach is often more Platonic than Christian, but many of his poems are braced with sturdy faith and a glad awareness of the Power that can replant glory in a world where men have trampled it down. His first book, *Hesperides*, appeared in 1925. His latest volume was published in 1941 under the simple title *Poems*. Torrence is a playwright as well as a poet.

EDWARD DAVISON

Edward Davison (1898-) is a native of Scotland and was educated at Cambridge University in England.

Coming to America shortly before the outbreak of World War II, he devoted himself to lecturing, teaching, and literary criticism. He is now professor of English literature at the University of Colorado and annually conducts a Writers' Conference at Boulder in that state. He may, therefore, be considered an American author. Intellect and emotion meet on harmonious terms in the work of this gifted poet. His verse has a river-like quality, merging music with ennobled imagination. There is a strain of melancholy in his lyrics, but never of dejection. Earth, sky, and racing waters move him to chants that are almost Druidic in spirit. But he also has a warm feeling for human fellowship. His love poems are sung with great sincerity and elevation of heart. Shadows settling upon old empires stir him deeply. His influence upon American poetry has been wholesome and invigorating. Selections from six earlier volumes were included in his *Collected Poems* (1940).

DAVID MORTON

Regarded as one of the most finished sonnet-writers in America, David Morton (1886-) has perhaps a greater following among poets than among the reading public generally. His poems are shy and unobtrusive, but they have deeper implications than are apparent at first sight. Aspects of the visible and invisible world intrigue him, as do also the subtleties of human relationship. Reticent by instinct, he has a keen sense of the value and integrity of words. He uses them sparingly but with a finality that gives them the effect of sheer thought. He transmits the poetic password precisely as it seizes and stirs him. His poems are like passages of music, so exquisitely phrased that one does not catch their full import or detect the inner harmonies upon a single hearing. But the legend and the heartlift are there for those who listen carefully. Throughout his writing there is the aroma of an essentially religious and grateful spirit. He is a devotee of St. Francis of Assisi and has an almost Catholic reverence for the Blessed Virgin Mary. David Morton is professor of English at Amherst College. Among his latest works are *All in One Breath* (1939) and *Angle of Earth and Sky* (1941).

AMOS WILDER

Amos Wilder (1895-), distinguished author of a recent critical study on *Spiritual Aspects of the New Poetry*, is a brother of Thornton Wilder. As professor of New Testament interpretation at Andover-Newton, he has devoted a great deal of research to religious forces now stirring in our literature and is one of the few modern writers who have sought to trace the relations between religion and poetry. His book *The Healing of the Waters* (1943) established him as a religious poet of fine discernment, spiritual depth, and intellectual energy. In poems of prophetic sweep he lashingly rebukes the spirit of rapacious power in high places and lays bare the cancers eating at our national culture. The book is not only one of chastening indignation. It is also one of prayer and healing.

THOMAS HORNSBY FERRIL

Thomas Hornsby Ferril (1896-) of Denver is a regional poet of strong originality. Spurred by ardent feeling for the West, where nearly all his life has been spent, he has captured its frontier spirit with a high degree of fidelity. His poems, marked by unusual word-prowess and freshness of rhythm, are pungent with place-names and replete with lore of the mining country. The importance of his work lies in the permanence it gives to the history and legends of the Rocky Mountain region, with its picturesque trading posts, Indian settlements, prospecting centers, frontier forts, and other features now fast disappearing. Ferril's first book, *Westering*, appeared in "The Yale Series of Younger Poets" in 1934. His most recent volume is *Trial by Time* (1944).

CONTEMPORARY CATHOLIC POETRY

Catholic poetry has emerged in the America of our own period as a force fully conscious of its influence and authority. No longer timid, no longer given to half-apologetic assertions of its inherent harmony with our democratic institutions, it is now speaking out in accents that compel attention. The minor voices and subdued instrumentation which marked the first soundings of Catholic song have given way to a strong choir with full orchestration.

THE CATHOLIC KILMERS

The names that come most naturally to mind in taking up a consideration of this new impetus are the Catholic Kilmers. The fame of Joyce Kilmer, journalist, magazine writer, and soldier-poet, is securely established. His heroic death in action with the "Fighting Sixty-ninth" regiment in France in 1918 endeared him to all America and to the country upon whose soil he fell. Kilmer, a native of New Jersey and an alumnus of Rutgers University, was a convert, having embraced the Faith in 1913 with a fervor that glowed to the very moment of his final sacrifice. His poetry, while not extensive, has a homely and hallowed touch. It was characteristic of his genius to find its incentive in common things and in the nobility he found along the common walks of life. Typical are his poems "Trees," "Delicatessen," "The Snowman in the Yard" and "The House with Nobody in It." Their appeal was instant and widespread. But his gifted spirit was capable of loftier excursions, as he proved by his longer poems, among which may be cited "A Blue Valentine," "Rouge Bouquet," and "The White Ships and the Red." Among his published works are *Summer of Love, Trees, and Other Poems, Main Street, Literature in the Making* and *Dreams and Images*, an anthology.

In 1908 Joyce Kilmer married Aline Murray of Norfolk, Virginia, a poet of exceptional distinction in her own right. Reticent and retiring by nature, she found expression in occasional lyrics of great penetration and skillful technique. The aloofness of her style was in marked contrast to Joyce's genial urbanity. Yet the austerity of her spirit was never without tenderness. It was always tempered with ingredients of gentleness, especially when it sought to explore the mysteries of human sorrow and separation. She sublimated life's pangs in a plaintive spirituality that deepened with her reception into the Church in 1913. Critics are agreed that Aline Kilmer will long remain in the first rank of Catholic lyric poets. She died at Stillwater in 1941,

Joyce Kilmer

leaving among her published volumes *Candles that Burn* (1919), *Vigils* (1921), and *Selected Poems* (1929).

TRANSITIONAL POETS

Before proceeding to the vigorous new growth of Catholic poets, which has stemmed, at least in a considerable degree, from the favoring public reception accorded to Joyce and Aline Kilmer, it is appropriate here to speak of a transitional phase in which the principal figures are poets belonging in part to the Tabb-Guiney-Kilmer era and in part to the post-Kilmer period. Among them are T. A. Daly, Rev. Edward F. Garesché, Francis Carlin, Rev. James J. Daly, Padraic Colum, Marie E. Blake, J. Corson Miller, Blanche Mary Kelly, Caroline Giltinan, Shaemas O'Sheel, Katherine Brégy, Rev. Hugh Francis Blunt, Rev. Charles J. Quirk, Edmund Leamy, Joseph Campbell, William Thomas Walsh, John Bunker, and Rev. Charles L. O'Donnell, C.S.C.

Father Garesché, S.J., born at St. Louis in 1876, is the author of several volumes of poetry and numerous devotional works. Known to Catholic readers for more than a generation, he still has the eager outlook of the younger poets. His latest volume, *Niagara*, is significant as a return to the stateliness of the ode, a verse-form much neglected by our modern poets. His style is, in the main, hymnal and rich in organ-tones.

Francis Carlin, after several years of silence, is once more giving his limpid songs to literature. A lonely, almost legendary spirit, he continues to isolate himself from the seeking of praise. His poetry is magical with old memories and enriched with the lore of far wanderings. His thoughts seem to hover over loved places and beloved faces that have brought him peace through fugitive years. His metrical style is always melodious, the phrasing intricate yet never obscure. Almost every stanza he writes is shot through with liturgical fragrances, as of a mind imbued with restless hungers yet tamed to the discipline of prayer. His latest poems are full of Celtic and Catholic fire. They surpass in spiritual maturity *A Cairn of Stars* and *My Ireland*, the books upon which his earlier reputation was based. Mr. Carlin is now living in retirement in New York City, but the flame of his poetry is burning brightly.

Padraic Colum is another Irish poet who may be claimed as our own, since he has become American by adoption, at least in a literary sense. Few of our Catholic poets have been so widely accepted in non-Catholic circles as he; this fact is a tribute not only to his authority as a poet but also to his charm as a person. Mr. Colum was born in Longford, Ireland, on the Feast of the Immaculate Conception, in 1881. He early won recognition by his vividly authentic poems of the Irish countryside. The strength and freshness of his poetry lie partly in its honesty and simplicity, partly in the peculiar enchantment with which he invests it. He seems to possess a sort of wizardry by which he is able to conjure before his readers the very reality of the Irish folklife, with all its lights and shadows, its native charm and flavor. The weaving of his verse-patterns is as simple, sturdy, and unembroidered as the weaving of serviceable linen, yet there is a sheen of Irish sunlight upon it. Mr. Colum came to the United States in 1914, and has been much sought after as a lecturer on Irish poetry and drama. He was one of the founders of the Irish National Theatre. His works in poetry include *Wild Earth* (1910), *Dramatic Legends and Other Poems* (1916), and *Collected Poems* (1932).

Blanche Mary Kelly and William Thomas Walsh, while occupying important teaching posts, continue to enrich Catholic letters. Dr. Kelly's *The Valley of Vision* (1916) revealed her as a poet of sterling sincerity and finished craftsmanship. Her scholarly ideals are reflected in valuable contributions to *The Catholic Encyclopedia*. Her latest work, *The Eternal Purpose*, was published in 1943.

The poetry of William Thomas Walsh, brought together in 1939 in a volume entitled *Lyric Poems*, was received enthusiastically by critics, not only for the grace and glow of the sonnets and other short lyrics, but for the cumulative impact of the longer pieces. Dr. Walsh, like Walt Whitman, has centered much of his singing upon Manhattan, and with a strain of great sweep and sonority. But, unlike the "good, gray poet," he surveys the city from a spiritual perspective. He dreads the evil done in the deep hives of the metropolis, but refuses to fall into dejection, knowing that the Holy Ghost has His sanctuaries there also. Dr. Walsh's Manhattan poems are massive in scope and often rise to majesty. As a recent critic has said, "They shatter completely the notion that modern Catholic poetry is minor and fragmentary." A native of Connecticut, Dr. Walsh has for some years been Professor of English at the College of the Sacred Heart, Manhattanville, New York City. Besides being a poet, he is a biographer, novelist, Hispanist, and historian.

From the pen of the late Rev. Charles L. O'Donnell (1884-1934) came some of the finest lyric poetry produced in America. His masterpiece, "The Dead Musician," is a winged utterance which approaches in spiritual elevation and sustained harmony the flights of Francis Thompson. A chaste and luminous quality pervades all his work, as if it were filtered through cathedral windows.

THE CATHOLIC POETRY SOCIETY

We come now to the period in which American Catholic poetry may be said to have arrived at intellectual, spiritual, and corporate maturity. Long years of patient root-spreading had given rise to a growing Catholic literary life out of which an organic unity was sure to spring. The event which marks this development was the formation in 1931 of the Catholic Poetry Society of America. Its prime mover was the Rev. Francis Talbot, S.J., then literary editor of *America*. Its first president was the last-named figure of the transitional group, the Rev. Charles L. O'Donnell. One of its more recent presidents was Katherine Brégy, another significant figure in that group.

In general the Society was dedicated to the promotion of a richer Catholic culture. More specifically its purpose was to bring Catholic poetic ideals and tendencies into coordination, encourage Catholic talent, obtain a more solid recognition of Catholic poetic achievement, afford means for constructive discussion and criticism of contemporary poetry, and establish a publication open to the work of its members.

Chartered units of the Society now exist in most of the important cities of the United States and in many of our Catholic colleges. The Society has members in every state and territorial possession of the Union. Its magazine, *Spirit*, established in 1934 and published bi-monthly, is one of the leading poetry magazines in America. Poems published in *Spirit* are syndicated to the Catholic press and are appearing with notable effect and frequency in anthologies and textbooks, as well as in the secular press.

The fifth anniversary of *Spirit* was signalized by the publication of *From the Four Winds*, a collection of selected poems from the magazine. On April 27, 1941, the tenth anniversary of the Society was celebrated at Fordham University in conjunction with the university's centenary. More recently, to mark the tenth anniversary of *Spirit*, the Society has brought out a second anthology entitled *Drink from the Rock*.

THE FATHERS FEENEY

Father Leonard Feeney, S.J. (1897-) is outstanding as a poet, wit, and philosopher. His writings in verse and prose have charmed readers of all faiths and classes. He is instinctively a poet. His prowess with words is such that even his prose has something of the prismatic and instrumental quality of poetry. His style is warm with

Thomas Feeney wrote exquisite songs to the Blessed Virgin.

tenderness and buoyant with whimsy and humor, but on occasion, as in *Song for a Listener*, he can edge his lines with chastening scorn. His books include *In Towns and Little Towns* (1927), *Riddle and Reverie* (1933), *Fish on Friday* (1934), *Boundaries* (1935), and, more recently, *The Leonard Feeney Omnibus*. His brother, Rev. Thomas Butler Feeney, S.J. (1899-), also a poet of high merit, is the author of *Ave Maria*, a sheaf of exquisite songs to the Blessed Virgin.

OUR SINGING SISTERS

Until William Stanley Braithwaite brought out in 1931 *Our Lady's Choir,* there was no sufficient public appreciation of the poetry of our Catholic Sisters. His anthology made generous amends. Today the bright roster of Sisters whose work appears in leading periodicals and on the book lists of standard publishers includes Sister Mariella, Sister M. Thérèse, Sor. D.S., Sister Mary St. Virginia, Sister Mary of the Visitation, Sister Therese, C.S.J., Sister Mary Ignatius, S.S.J., Sister Miriam, R.S.M., Sister Mary Eulalia, R.S.M., Sister Mary Jeremy,

Sister Madeleva, C.S.C.

Sister Mary Bertrand, Sister Mary Edwardine, and Sister Mary Irma. Among the Sisters who are writing poetry, Sister Madeleva, Sister Maris Stella, and Sister Miriam of the Holy Spirit (known to the world of poetry as Jessica Powers) have won outstanding distinction.

In perfection of technique and purity of style, Sister Madeleva is the peer of any poet writing in America today, and, in many judgments, superior to most. Busily preoccupied as a college president, she somehow finds time to practice her poetic gifts, much as a skilled musician must improvise as the spirit impels. The acuteness with which she perceives God's presence in the beauty of His creation leads to thrilling results. Always she sings as a lover; whether her love-songs find their inspiration in some natural bond, or in an hour of April, or in the cloister, or in the wounds of Christ, she leaves no question as to the Lover she has chosen. Her phrasing is as inevitable as the emotion which speaks through it. She is completely candid. Whatever her literary devices, she has mastered them so thoroughly that they are seldom apparent. Sister Madeleva is a member of the Congregation of the Holy Cross. She is president of St. Mary's College, Notre Dame, Indiana, and has twice been chosen as president of the Catholic Poetry Society of America. Her poetic works include *Knights Errant and Other Poems* (1928), *Penelope and Other Poems* (1927), *A Question of Lovers* (1935), *Gates and Other Poems* (1938) and *Selected Poems* (1939).

Sister Maris Stella, a native of Iowa and a member of the Sisters of St. Joseph, is a professor of English at the College of St. Catherine in St. Paul, Minnesota. She holds a master's degree from Oxford. Simple and unassuming in personality and possessing a genuine sense of humor, Sister Maris Stella takes a quiet delight in life. The calmness of her spirit gives indication of the depth from which her poetry comes. The inspiration of her teaching is evident from the achievement of her students who have won distinction for their creative writing.

Sister Maris Stella's lyrics seem to well from her spirit like water from a spring, making their own music rather than being made into music. Human and heavenly longings find eloquent release in the shy, heart-shaking series of sonnets published by this talented Minnesota Sister under the title *Here Only a Dove.*

Jessica Powers was born in Mauston, Wisconsin. Except for one year at Marquette University, her education was limited to grammar and high school grades. Through much early hardship, sustained by a special devotion to the Holy Spirit, she acquired not only self-education but a profound spirit of humility and compassion which breathes through all her poetry. Her book *The Lantern Burns* was published in 1939. Reviewing it in *Spirit,* Mary Kolars of *The Commonweal* wrote: "No singer comes to mind who sees heaven in earthly experience more confidently, or who speaks of the supernatural with a more unforcedly natural accent. This heavenly haunting is what one remembers." The tamarack trees and the whippoorwills of her native woodlands left indelible impressions upon Jessica Powers' spirit, and she often longed for them. But the mystical life, nourished by readings of St. Teresa of Avila and St. John of the Cross, kept calling her with an urgency that would not be denied. In 1941 she became a member of the Discalced Carmelites in Milwaukee.

LEADERS IN ACTION

Theodore Maynard, a convert, has made notable contributions as a poet, teacher, critic, and biographer. His carefully-patterned poetry is always concentrated, spiritually acute, and powerful in impact. He is an unsparing foe to literary pretense and superficial piety. His works include *Laughs and Whiffs of Song* (1915), *Drums of Defeat* (1916), *Carven from the Laurel Tree* (1918), *A Tankard of Ale* (1919), *The Last Knight* (1921), and *The Divine Adventure* (1921).

Daniel Sargent of South Natick, Mass., is described by Mason Wade as "a Puritan who became a Catholic, a historian, and a poet." Mr. Sargent sings with that artless spontaneity which is the truest art. He is constantly being taken by surprise at the glory of God as manifested in the visible and invisible world. It is in sensitive awareness of the Divine omnipresence that he cries out in contemplation of the hosts of guardian angels: "We are lost in God's sublime solicitude." This lifting line is from his book *God's Ambuscade*, published in 1935. Earlier works include *Our Gleaming Days* (1915) and *The Door* (1920).

An arresting voice is that of Raymond E. F. Larsson. He too is a convert, but his cry is one of prophecy and lamentation rather than of joy. There is throughout his work a spiritual panting, as of one heartsick at the sight of malice, and thirsty for peace and compassion. His verse-patterns are complex, yet full of hidden harmonies and subtle echoes. Sister Mary St. Virginia, a poet and critic of increasing authority, considers Larsson "the one successful Anglo-Saxon" among the modern poets. Mr. Larsson's *Weep and Prepare*, published in 1940, made a profound impression, as did his earlier *O Cities, Cities!* Recently he has devoted himself to a series of works on the prayers and letters of the saints.

A style of classic grace and eloquence marks the poetry of Reverend John Louis Bonn, S.J., professor of poetry and director of dramatics at Boston College before his entrance into the armed forces as chaplain. He is Grecian in his fidelity to the noblest canons of literary expression. Father Bonn was born at Waterbury, Connecticut. His *Canticle*, published in 1937, received high critical acclaim. Equally successful has been his

Fray Angelico Chavez.

work in the field of dramatics. Father Bonn has likewise contributed two books which he classifies as novel-biographies. They are *So Falls the Elm Tree* and *Down the Days*.

The increasingly-heard voice of Fray Angelico Chavez has a native validity and richness that is rayed through with mystical fervor and a glowing spirituality. A resident of Penablanca, New Mexico, he tinges much of his poetry with Western lights. In the Spanish and Indian lore of the Southwestern mission country, he finds an abundant source of literary material and ever-fresh inspiration. Fray Angelico is a member of the Order of Friars Minor. He is at present assigned to a chaplaincy with the armed forces.

In 1938 there came from the press a book of poems entitled *Mint by Night*. Its author, Reverend Alfred

Barrett, a brilliant young Jesuit, became almost overnight one of the most popular priest-poets in America. His poems sing of the early Christian martyrs and of the martyred Jesuits of North America; they sing of the priesthood and of the young woman who quits the tennis court for the cloister. Father Barrett has a way with words, making them spring into life and music. His poems are fragrant of the liturgy and of places where the Holy Ghost has stirred. He is chaplain of the Catholic Poetry Society and consulting editor of *Spirit*. His present assignment is with the Army as a chaplain overseas.

Key figures in the Catholic Poetry Society are John Gilland Brunini and Clifford J. Laube. Active as poets, editors, lecturers, and critics, they have given unflagging effort to the executive direction of the society and to the maintenance of its magazine *Spirit*. It was under their leadership, together with that of Francis X. Connolly, that the magazine was launched. An able auxiliary and a lyric poet of crystal clarity and elegance is Joseph G. E. Hopkins, until recently on the English faculty at the College of Notre Dame, Staten Island, but now serving as a lieutenant in the U. S. Maritime Service. Hopkins has been successful in satire and parody as well as in the lyric and dramatic forms.

John Brunini's poetry is subtle, compressed, and searching. His *Mysteries of the Rosary* was published in 1932 and widely distributed. He draws much of his inspiration from Scriptural sources, and finds in the claims of human friendship a theme of unfailing fascination. He has been executive director of the Catholic Poetry Society and editor of *Spirit* since their inception. He is a native of Mississippi.

Clifford J. Laube began his career as a printer's apprentice in a Colorado mining camp. He is now one of the editors of *The New York Times*. An apostle of personal craftsmanship, he brought out in 1938 his book of poems, *Crags,* setting the type by hand and printing and binding the entire edition himself. "This book," wrote Father Feeney at the time, "unquestionably would win the Pulitzer Prize if the Pulitzer Committee had any sense of sympathy or discovery." Mr. Laube is a lover of altitude and energy, both of which he infuses into his work. His poems, often evocative of his mountain boyhood, are full of wonder and eagerness. They are warmly musical, yet strictly disciplined. Christopher Morley, David Morton and others have noted his word-economy and sureness of phrasing. Lyrical in impulse and deeply felt, his poems are nevertheless intellectual in the sense that they reach for the truth as something superior to the emotion and the music. His themes range from the simple experiences of every day to the more profound recollections of a deeply religious spirit.

A Catholic pathfinder in poetry is A. M. Sullivan of St. Albans, Long Island. He is noted not only for his own poetry, of which several volumes have been published, but perhaps even more widely for conspicuous service in promoting a broader public appreciation of poetry. In the field of radio he was one of the first to gain an audience for new poets and to make the older poets better known. He has been tireless in exhorting Catholic writers to free themselves from the poetic mannerisms of the past, to look no farther than the American scene for the stuff of which poetry is made, and to express themselves in words and rhythms proper to their own time and environment. These are precepts he has put to refreshing use in his own work, of which his recent *Industrial Poems* are a striking example. Mr. Sullivan was for several years president of the Poetry Society of America.

THE NEWER VOICES

Significant new voices, such as those of Francis Maguire, John Frederick Nims, Thomas J. Merton, and John Dillon Husband are being steadily recruited to the Catholic chorus in America. Two of the most recent authors to command discriminating attention are Eleanor Slater, whose volume, *Why Hold the Hound?* (1941), brought to light a talent not unlike that of Emily Dickinson; and Reverend John W. Lynch, whose admirable if somewhat unevenly sustained narrative-poem depicting Our Lady as *A Woman Wrapped in Silence* (1942) is still the subject of spirited critical discussion. If no Dante has yet appeared, let it be remembered that American literature is still relatively young. Secular America has yet no Shakespeare. Catholic poetry has made a vital contribution to our national history. Its future is full of promise.

THE NOVEL

The novel still remains, after newspaper and periodical literature, America's primary source of literary enjoyment. Thousands upon thousands of volumes, mostly of negligible worth, issue from the presses annually, and a bemused and uncritical public consumes them with amazing avidity. It is clear that you could not "keep up" with the latest novels even if you wished to. In consequence there must be selection, and the ability to select intelligently is not easily acquired. If you are honest with yourselves, you will probably have to admit that the few novels you have read of your own choice came to your attention in one of several ways: (1) the appeal of the subject matter; (2) the recommendation of a friend; (3) popular discussion; or (4) "high-pressure" advertisements. These ways of selecting a novel are not necessarily to be condemned, but a truly educated person will want to have a set of principles on which to base selection and will want steadily to improve his tastes.

Looking back over our present century, we discover that America can boast of a fair number of arresting and competent novelists, a few craftsmen of distinguished and enduring worth, and a handful of experimentalists whose innovations are likely to affect permanently the fiction of the future. In the matter of craftsmanship alone, three women — Edith Wharton, Willa Cather, and Ellen Glasgow — have given to the history of the American novel a dignity and seriousness which had heretofore been lacking. All three of them are polished technicians.

Continuing the method of the generation before them, the majority of twentieth-century novelists have preferred to deal with the daily scene in a direct and uncompromising way. Reacting from the absurdities of ultra-romantic writers, they choose to deal with the uglier and more sordid aspects of that scene. Many of our recent novelists have likewise continued to employ their talents in the interests of social reform. The reformer-novelist employs one of two techniques, satire or drama. Sinclair Lewis is satirical; John Steinbeck is dramatic. The one seeks to reform through ridicule; the other, through a powerful portrayal of the facts as he sees them. In his latest novel Lewis has come to an impasse. In *Gideon Planish* (1943) he seeks to reform the reformers.

The historical novel maintains its privileged position in the affections of the reading public. This form of fiction, made popular two centuries ago by Sir Walter Scott, continues to solicit the talents of expert writers. The entrance of the United States into World War II has given an added fillip to its popularity, and the American past has been ransacked for material and incident. Kenneth Roberts is mentioned only as one of the more successful practitioners of this type of novel.

Finally, a word must be said in reference to the regional novel. As the name suggests, the regional novel restricts its attention to a small geographical segment having its individual cultural, geographic, and economic traits. In some instances it lends itself to a critical interpretation of historical background. Willa Cather's treatment of the Southwest classes her with the regionalists.

EDITH WHARTON

Edith Wharton (1862-1937), like Henry James, her acknowledged master, is a conscious literary artist who has clung tenaciously to her master's theory of the novel as a balanced art form. Choosing as the background for her stories aristocratic New York in the late nineteenth century, rural New England, or Parisian society, Edith Wharton employs the realistic method to portray the struggles of gifted individuals against the limitations and restraints of their social group. Mrs. Wharton's representations of New York society life during the years between the Civil War and the first World War are particularly significant. Her emphasis is always on the moral situation. She makes her characters personally responsible for the consequences of their acts and their judgments. In another period than the present one Mrs. Wharton might have produced great tragedy. Instead, she has succeeded in writing illuminating studies of American society, striking out with effective irony at men who live engrossed in purely material concerns. *The Age of Innocence* (1920), an excellent portrayal of New York society in the 1870s, shows Mrs. Wharton's splendid literary craftsmanship at its best. *Ethan Frome*

Willa Cather

(1911) best reveals Mrs. Wharton's gift for tragedy and the extent of her creative power. Edith Wharton is one of America's fine novelists.

WILLA CATHER

No other modern writer has succeeded as has Willa Cather (1875-) in making of her characters vigorous human beings, interesting primarily because of their humanity. It was by means of this ability to portray human character and the vivid impressions she retained from her early years on the Nebraska prairies that Willa Cather evolved a new type of pioneer novel in which she replaced adventure by sympathetic representation of everyday human life in a pioneer setting.

People who lived on the prairies were not the only ones Willa Cather found interesting. *The Professor's House* reveals her impatience with materialistic interpretations of life by showing that the lasting values in life are spiritual, not scientific. In her historical novels, *Death Comes for the Archbishop* (1927) and *Shadows on the Rock* (1931), Miss Cather emphasizes the civilizing and disciplinary value of the Catholic Church.

Willa Cather's novels are the creations of a writer who employs the principle of artistic selection, and her characters are free moral agents. Willa Cather's style is simple and vigorous.

SINCLAIR LEWIS

With the publication of *Main Street* (1920), Sinclair Lewis (1885-) took his place as the most important satirist of the American way of life in the present era. Finding the life of the average American insufferably standardized, circumscribed, and dull, Lewis held it up to ridicule, at the same time pointing out the desirability of a life in which man, enlightened by scientific research, has learned to satisfy his desires in an intelligent, disciplined manner. Lewis's novels, then, are didactic and satiric writings and not, primarily, realistic portrayals of twentieth-century America. In *Main Street* (1920) and *Babbitt* (1922), Lewis distorts reality for the sake of emphasis and creates characters to express his point of view. In the first of these novels he satirizes the dullness of the average American small town; the second is a satire on the greater dullness of an American city and of the typical American businessman who lives only to make money.

ERNEST HEMINGWAY

Ernest Hemingway (1898-) reduces the concept of life to its lowest possible level. Speaking for "the lost generation," the youth of the first World War period, Hemingway emphasizes the futility of all human endeavor and urges man to forget his disillusionment in pleasure. Hemingway has failed to produce work of lasting value because he has failed to realize that man does not live by bread alone. Purely physical adventure and physical enjoyment inevitably fall short of attaining the heights. Only spiritual adventures and spiritual joy can sweep man across windswept spaces into the presence of ultimate Peace.

BOOTH TARKINGTON

Booth Tarkington (1869-) earned the title of dean of middle-class letters for the interpretation of the life of average Americans in his novels and short stories. Young readers know him best for his realistic and humorous character creations such as Penrod, the comical adolescent, and more recently, little Orvie, a small boy of seven who is already considered bad. Two of Tarkington's more serious novels, *The Magnificent Ambersons* (1918) and *Alice Adams* (1921), have won the Pulitzer Prize. During his first eight years of creative work, the midwestern writer earned no more than twenty-five dollars by his pen. Only after he turned his attention to the background of his native Indiana did he achieve national success. A long series of novels on midwestern life shows his ability to individualize the numerous types of character to be found in the small town. In his amusing boy stories, Tarkington displays keen powers of observation, pointing with gentle satire to the lack of civilization in adolescent life. Maintaining an optimistic attitude in his realism, Tarkington does not offend the canons of good taste. A skilled narrator, he has remained over a long period one of the most popular and versatile writers treating life in a democracy.

HELEN C. AND OLIVE WHITE

In three distinguished novels Helen Constance White (1896-) depicts the survival of Catholic ideals in troubled epochs of history. *A Watch in the Night* (1933) projects the story of Jacopone da Todi, a worldly and self-esteeming young lawyer of thirteenth-century Italy, who is gradually led, through sorrow and repentance, to a life of atonement as a Franciscan mendicant. The pages of the book are filled with the pageantry of medieval life. A native of New England and a professor of English at the University of Wisconsin, Helen C. White has been characterized as "every inch a scholar." A long record of academic achievement has done nothing to disturb the unassuming friendly manner and quiet sense of humor that help make her classes as vitally interesting as they are illuminating. In portraying the Catholic culture of the past, Miss White has been impartial and honest, neither emphasizing the favorable factors nor suppressing the unfavorable. She weaves the romance of history into strong, brilliant prose. Because of her scholarly approach to her subject matter, she supplies

so many incidents and details that the progress of her narrative is sometimes delayed. Besides her historical novels, Helen C. White has published three studies on mysticism and devotional literature.

Olive White (1899-), the sister of Helen C. White, has exhibited scholarship and imagination in her two historical novels on sixteenth-century England, *The King's Good Servant* (1936) and *Late Harvest* (1940).

PAUL HORGAN

Because in his childhood his family moved from Buffalo, New York, to New Mexico, Paul Horgan (1903-) grew up knowing two worlds. When he began to write, he was able to portray both the East and the West, though his reputation as a writer of fiction has since come to rest on his interpretation of the New Mexico region. Horgan's skillful presentation of gripping narrative makes his books absorbing reading; his penetration of the frailties and virtues of human nature transmits life to his characters. The author's five novels have established his reputation as a writer of maturing style and emotional power. Despite their artistic value as a whole, Horgan's works cannot be recommended without reservation because of the occasional presence of vulgar passages and mature subject matter. The novelist, who is a Catholic, is now serving with the United States armed forces.

AUGUST DERLETH

August Derleth (1909-) has been called a one-man fiction factory by educators and critics, who stand amazed at the output of some thirty high-quality books by this youthful and versatile Wisconsin writer. Composing between 750,000 and a million words a year, he produces poetry, essays, novels, short stories, mystery tales, plays, biography, literary criticism, and magazine articles. "I write because I must write," he says, "because I have plots and material to keep me writing for more years than I can possibly live, and I want to put it all down . . . " Derleth's astonishing industry permits him to find time for voluminous reading and for such hobbies as swimming, fencing, collecting stamps and comic strips. He teaches a course in American regional literature at the University of Wisconsin. A Guggenheim Fellowship has enabled him to pursue work on the *Sac Prairie Saga*, a momentous undertaking which will comprise a fifty-volume prose-and-poetry interpretation of life in the area of Sauk Prairie County, Wisconsin. Eighteen books for the project have thus far been published.

JAMES BRENDAN CONNOLLY

For a period of forty years James Brendan Connolly (1868-) has been turning out fiction that gives him the distinction of being the greatest American writer of the sea. Fishing schooners and ships have taken him to the Baltic, North, and Arctic seas. He has sailed on cruisers, battleships, gunboats, destroyers, and submarines and has known intimately the men who spend their lives at sea. Connolly writes easily and naturally of the perils of the sea, of its strange influence on the lives of men. In mastery of description and power to convey atmosphere, he has often been compared to the great sea writer, Joseph Conrad. Some twenty volumes of tales of manly courage and adventure reflect Connolly's Catholic philosophy of life. *Gloucestermen* (1930) is a typical collection of dramatic stories; *Hiker Joy* (1916) and *Steel Decks* (1925) are representative of the author's full-length novels.

FRANK H. SPEARMAN

Frank H. Spearman (1859-1937), a convert author, has given Catholic literature wholesome adventure stories, novels of modern life, and a popular work of historical fiction, *The Spanish Lover* (1930). His western stories and tales of adventure run the usual course of this type of fiction, but they have a hearty refreshing quality and an occasional touch of originality. In *Marriage Verdict* (1923), a novel with modern business as a background, Spearman gives an excellent presentation of the Pauline privilege in fiction. A number of his novels have been filmed.

LUCILLE PAPIN BORDEN

As a writer of romantic fiction, Lucille Borden (1873-) describes events and characters that are more ideal than

probable. Since childhood an atmosphere of Catholic culture has surrounded the novelist. A granddaugher of Pierre Laclede, the founder of St. Louis, Lucille Papin spent part of her childhood in Rome and throughout her life has traveled widely in Europe. The thread of mysticism which may be found in her first novel, *The Gates of Olivet* (1912), runs through all her work. The *Starforth* trilogy has made Mrs. Borden known as an historical novelist. At times she is so intent on teaching a truth that the Catholic theme intrudes inartistically on the story. The merit of Lucille Borden's fiction lies chiefly in its explanation of Catholic teachings by illustrating them in life situations.

ELIZABETH JORDAN

Elizabeth Jordan (1867-) enjoys a high reputation in the field of light fiction for her successful mystery stories and romantic novels. An alumna of the Convent of Notre Dame in Milwaukee, Miss Jordan came to New York as a young woman and developed a good narrative style as a result of hard work in journalism. One of her best-selling novels is *First Port of Call* (1940), a serious study which treats the theme of transition to the next life and imaginatively transports the characters to a port beyond death. Though the plots of her novels and stories are usually slight, Elizabeth Jordan has fulfilled her high purpose of providing clean and wholesome literary entertainment, her narrative moves swiftly and its sprightly dialogue retains the reader's interest. The story of her own life, told in *Three Rousing Cheers* (1938), is more absorbing than any fabrications of the author's imagination. Elizabeth Jordan has produced plays and biography and has for many years served as a drama critic for America.

FRANCIS CLEMENT KELLEY

A strong believer in the apostolate of the pen is the Most Rev. Francis Clement Kelley (1870-), Bishop of Oklahoma City and Tulsa. Founder and first editor of *Extension Magazine*, he has written short stories, novels, essays, as well as biographical and historical works. All his writings bear the stamp of his charming personality, which manifests itself especially in his autobiography, *The Bishop Jots it Down*. The book is an historical and social document as well as an entertaining memoir. With discerning judgment and quick-moving style, Bishop Kelley recounts in *Blood-Drenched Altars* (1936) the early Spanish beginnings of Mexico in an endeavor to present the causes of modern conflict between Church and state in that country. In such novels as *Charred Wood* (1917), *When the Veil Is Rent* (1929), and *Problem Island* (1937), he shows his ability as a storyteller. A collection of his short stories recently published as *Tales from the Rectory* presents various phases of Catholic life as seen by a priest. Bishop Kelley's whimsical style and penetrating grasp of modern problems is seen to advantage in his allegorical tale, *Pack Rat* (1942).

DORAN HURLEY

In light fiction Doran Hurley's humorous tales of parish life appeal to romantic taste. Gaiety and piety mingle in the author's exposition of Catholicism as it is lived by Irish Americans. Typical of the builders of church and nation whom Hurley extols is *Herself: Mrs. Patrick Crowley* (1939), a character who appears again in *Says Mrs. Crowley, Says She* (1941). In his books the traditions of the paradoxically proud and humble Irish are preserved for this generation.

KATHLEEN NORRIS

A Catholic writer who has been inconsistent in her treatment of Christian principles is Kathleen Norris (1880-), who has been for two decades one of the most widely read American novelists. Of her seventy novels *Mother* (1911) and *Little Ships* (1925) are positive in their Catholic attitude. Some of Kathleen Norris' later books are harmless and pointless; others have a sort of negative Catholicism; some are actually erroneous.

OTHER CATHOLIC NOVELISTS

A constantly-growing company of writers has enriched the field of Catholic fiction in the past two decades. Among the authors remembered for a single outstanding contribution are Myles Connolly, editor of *Columbia*, whose sparkling satire, *Mr. Blue*, showed unusual promise; and Michael Kent, whose novel, *The Mass of Brother Michel*, appealed to a wide audience.

In a number of novels Ethel Cook Eliot, a convert, has interpreted the contemporary scene in the light of Catholic principles. E. J. Edwards, S.V.D., has drawn upon personal experience to depict the dramatic struggles of missionary life in the Orient. His three novels with tropical backgrounds are: *These Two Hands, Thy People, My People,* and *White Fire*.

THE SHORT STORY

A modern writer who suggests the morbid atmosphere and the emotional intensity of Poe is Wilbur Daniel Steele (1886-). For more than twenty years he has been considered one of our outstanding short-story writers. Born in North Carolina and educated at the University of Denver, he later moved to Nantucket, Massachusetts. Most of his stories are set in New England, especially along Cape Cod. His stories are masterpieces of unity, compression, and realistic detail. Steele has also done work in the one-act play, having dramatized some of his own stories.

Stephen Vincent Benét (1898-1943) brings to the short story a romanticism touched with patriotism. He has delved into American history and presents with dramatic force a number of national heroes, among them Paul Revere and Daniel Webster. His stories have been collected in two volumes, *Thirteen O'Clock* and *Tales Before Midnight* (1939).

Ruth Suckow (1892-), although avoiding revolting detail, is a realist in picturing ordinary people in ordinary circumstances. She finds interest in the everyday occurrences of the people in small towns in Iowa. Her sympathetic understanding of people enhances the narrative charm of her stories. Among her volumes of short stories are *Iowa Interviews* (1926) and *Children and Older People* (1931).

Brendan Gill (1914-), a promising Catholic author of short fiction, writes stories marked by a lightness of touch and a pleasing subtlety. Sometimes there is a poignancy in his revelation of truth. A quiet optimism pervades his narratives built on normal characters, themes, and situations. Brendan Gill is himself an optimist. Writing in 1941, he said, "Everybody tells me that a writer must suffer — at least a little. I'm sorry but things look better every day." Gill was born at Hartford, Connecticut, and graduated from Yale. He is married, lives in New York, and is the father of three children. He is now serving on the editorial staff of *The New Yorker.*

Leo L. Ward, C.S.C., head of the department of English at the University of Notre Dame, not only trains and inspires young writers, but finds time himself to write stories. Born near Otterbein, Indiana, he attended Notre Dame and did graduate work at Oxford. His stories are always artistic and Catholic in tone. Some of his fiction has for its setting farm life. Ward has caught the spirit of the enterprising farmer who knows how to profit by the advances and inventions at the disposal of the modern family. He has the story writer's gift for character portrayal and ability to create suspense through intense situations.

Another Notre Dame alumnus who has done artistic work in the field of the short story is Richard Sullivan (1908-). While teaching at his alma mater, he contributes stories to the *Atlantic Monthly, Scribner's Magazine,* the *New Republic, Columbia,* and *Commonweal.* Practically all his fiction is permeated with the Catholic philosophy of life. Some of his best stories center around family life. In addition to his stories Richard Sullivan has written two novels and a number of radio plays.

Born in Iowa and now living with his family at Blue Earth, Minnesota, Albert Eisele (1896-) writes stories that have the freshness and the stability of the soil. In collaboration with his wife he writes a weekly column for the *Sioux City Sunday Journal.* Since 1937 his stories showing the beauty of farm life have appeared in the *Catholic World* and *The Commonweal.*

Harry Sylvester (1908-), born in Brooklyn, New York, and a graduate of the University of Notre Dame, is a prolific writer of short stories. Bringing to his fiction the technique of the journalist and the psychologist, he has specialized for some time in the sports story, where he effectively analyzed the interior struggles of athletic heroes. Among other magazines, his stories have appeared in *Collier's, The Commonwealth,* and *Scholastic.*

THE THEATER

It is not too much to say that the commercial theater, considered in its broader aspects, is, and has been throughout the present century, in a state of indifferent health. In 1910, for example, there were 1,520 legitimate theaters in operation throughout the continent, while in 1925 there were only 634. There are many reasons for this decline in stage productions, but the most outstanding of all is the phenomenal rise of the motion picture house.

Some of our most promising playwrights, too, have sooner or later devoted their talents to Hollywood productions. The motion picture industry has, in turn, inspired interesting experiments in the mechanics and technique of the theater. Although interest in the theater throughout the country has declined, American drama has steadily improved in literary quality. It was not until the twentieth century that the country had a playwright who deserved international recognition and that America produced plays in any way comparable to Elizabethan drama.

All literature is a portrayal and an interpretation of life. Since drama is primarily action, it is one of the most forceful literary forms. While all great drama necessarily deals with soul-stirring conflicts, universal in their appeal, the dramatist is invariably influenced by the prevailing spirit of his time. Much of the twentieth-century drama reflects the disillusionment, unhappiness, bitterness, and cynicism of man in conflict with the material world of which he is a part.

A survey of the drama since World War I reveals an advance in naturalism. The interest in psychology, particularly in behaviorism, which was popular at the close of the war, found its way into the drama. According to the behaviorist, man is not responsible for his actions. New themes and a new spirit were introduced into the drama, and the conflicts were largely psychological rather than between characters. As time passed, the conflict depicted man's struggle against society. Many of the playwrights simply followed the moral conventions of the day in glorifying divorce, sex, the unscrupulous businessman, and the clever criminal. Modern drama, like much of modern literature, has failed to give a true picture of life. The abnormal, the exceptional, the outcast, have been presented as typical. Tragedy frequently makes man the helpless victim of his environment; comedy often pictures him totally irresponsible. Chesterton's honest condemnation of the modern attitude — "What pretends to be a revolt of realism is already a routine of unreality" — is applicable to the drama.

Some of the younger playwrights and producers turned their attention to theatrical technique. Following the leadership of Orson Welles, they attempted to give the theater new dimensions by placing emphasis upon stage setting and lighting effects. During the past few years, however, there has been a tendency towards simplicity — for the sake of achieving, as Richard Dana Skinner expresses it, "the maximum emotional effect with the minimum of scenic trappings." Most of the representative twentieth-century playwrights have been experimentalists in the theater.

EUGENE O'NEILL

Eugene O'Neill (1888-) is the outstanding dramatist of our day, and in the opinion of many critics the only one deserving of international consideration. Born on Broadway, New York City, the son of an actor, O'Neill grew up in close association with the stage. He spent a year at Princeton, but his restless, roaming spirit of adventure induced him to go on a prospecting expedition to Spanish Honduras. Later he sailed to Buenos Aires and South Africa. For a time he worked as a reporter in New York but soon joined his father in New London, Connecticut. Forced to take a six months' rest because of threatening tuberculosis, O'Neill decided to reveal his experiences in the form of plays. After his discharge from the sanitarium he attended Harvard and received encouragement in the art of play writing from Professor Baker. In the summer of 1916, O'Neill went to Provincetown, Massachusetts, where he became associated with the Provincetown Players, a group of artists who were interested in promoting native American drama. O'Neill's one-act plays were produced by this group and gradually established his reputation as a dramatist.

O'Neill has projected his internal odyssey upon the stage. A chronological study of his plays reveals his puzzled concern over the problems of man's destiny. With all his rich imaginative power, his poetic gifts, his Celtic insight and fondness for symbol, O'Neill is spiritually uncertain and fails to acknowledge a personal God. As with many other modern writers, many of his characters are abnormal in one way or another. While

Eugene O'Neill

the essentially human qualities of his characters are appealing, many of his plays are repellent in theme and brutally realistic. In his search for a solution for the pitiful fate of man struggling alone against overwhelming forces, O'Neill has played havoc with the accepted theatrical conventions. *Strange Interlude* (1928), for example, has nine acts, and in it O'Neill revived the use of the Elizabethan aside. O'Neill has been the recipient of several Pulitzer Prize awards and of the Nobel Prize.

MAXWELL ANDERSON

An extremely versatile dramatist, Maxwell Anderson (1888-) has a high reputation with critics. He was born in western Pennsylvania but spent his youth in North Dakota. He received his education at the state university and at Leland Stanford University in California, where he taught English. Many of his plays show an interest in the problems of society. He has attempted political satire and domestic comedy, but his best work is found in historical drama such as *Elizabeth the Queen* (1930) and *Mary of Scotland* (1933) and in his verse tragedy, *Winterset* (1935).

Robert Sherwood

ROBERT SHERWOOD

Robert Sherwood (1896-) has also contributed towards the revival of interest in the chronicle play. By centering a drama around an historical character, he reveals the human quality in this person. This he did with notable success in *Abe Lincoln in Illinois* (1938). He has also written against war, and his drama, *There Shall Be No Night* (1940), composed before our entrance into World War II, concerns the invasion of Finland.

THORNTON WILDER

Thornton Wilder (1897-), born in Wisconsin, educated at Yale, and a teacher at the University of Chicago, experimented in the theater and in the writing of one-act plays. His first full-length play, *Our Town* (1938), gave him a reputation as a dramatist. This success was followed by *The Skin of Our Teeth*. Both plays, because of their strange philosophical extravaganza, their unconventional use of plot, and skillful handling of impromptu scenic devices, have been the subject of much discussion and disagreement. Wilder has become

alarmed at the materialism of the American people and realizes that we must preserve an interest in human values to save ourselves from annihilation. *Our Town* is an endeavor to portray the human dignity of man and the nobility of life itself. At times Wilder seems to suggest personal immortality. In *The Skin of Our Teeth* he endeavors to show that much of the unhappiness and misery of man is due to his inhuman conduct and irrational outlook on life. The big problem for man is to learn how to live among his fellow men.

WILLIAM SAROYAN

Somewhat akin to Wilder as an innovator in the theater and a promoter of the doctrine of love is William Saroyan (1908-). Although his characters are drawn from lowly types of society, he is a romanticist and an idealist in treatment. He considers kindness and goodness as basic human qualities in making the world a better place in which to live. Saroyan's love of humanity sometimes degenerates into sentimentalism as in *The Beautiful People* (1941). Of late Saroyan has returned to his first love, fiction. In an endeavor to give nobility to man, Saroyan, like O'Neill and Wilder, sometimes falls into transcendentalism.

PHILIP BARRY

Philip Barry (1896-), a popular and successful writer of comedies, frequently has in his works an undertone of seriousness. Born in Rochester, New York, of Irish-Catholic parents, he was educated at Yale and was a student in the workshop of Professor Baker at Harvard. Most of his plays abound in clever dialogue revealing the seamy side of fashionable life. With a certain sophistication he shows the vanity of worldly life and laughs at the foibles of society. His characters are often frustrated and disillusioned by a loss of faith and love. His work, for the most part, is written for mature readers with an educated viewpoint. Among other writers of the comedy of manners satirizing the social life of the upper classes in swift, crisp, and brilliant dialogue are Rachel Crothers and Clara Kummer.

BOOTH TARKINGTON

Booth Tarkington and George Kelly take their places among the social satirists. Tarkington, the Indiana novelist and playwright, touches merely the surface of life. At times he humorously contrasts life in the Middle West with that of New York. *The Tweedles* (1923) is a study in universal snobbishness. Tarkington is a master of humorous situations, and predominantly romantic in treatment. His plays are wholesome and entertaining, and his romances of adolescence are still favorites with amateur groups.

GEORGE KELLY

George Kelly (1887-) has had a long career in the theater. To realism and satire in the drama, Kelly adds character study. *The Show-Off* (1924) is a study of the braggart, and *Craig's Wife* (1925) portrays the final misery of a dominating and self-centered woman. Kelly's plays are remarkable for their naturalness of dialogue and their vivid character portrayal.

PAUL GREEN AND MARC CONNELLY

Two other playwrights who in recent years have won popularity for single plays are Paul Green (1894-) and Marc Connelly (1890-). Green presents various Southern types with incisive realism. *In Abraham's Bosom* (1927), a sympathetic study of the Negro problem, is one of his best works. Quite different in tone, although centering around the Negro, is Connelly's *Green Pastures* (1930), which presents with humor, simplicity, and reverence scenes from the Old Testament.

THE RISE OF THE LITTLE THEATERS

A study of modern drama would be incomplete without some mention of the rise of the so-called little theaters. With the concentration of the commercial theater in the great metropolitan areas, vast sections of the country were left without adequate dramatic fare. New York or Chicago might boast of plays which have had successful runs for months and even years, but the great body of the nation's playgoers were not within easy access of such centers. It was to meet the needs of this neglected segment of the population that the Little Theater Movement came into being. Almost overnight there sprang up on college campuses and in summer colonies competent amateur companies, determined to present only those plays of assured artistic and dramatic excellence. While they did not succeed in bringing to light any considerable number of great writers for the stage, they did accomplish two things: first, they improved theatrical taste both in the quality of the play and of the performance; and second, they introduced to the American public the productions of celebrated Europeans such as Shaw, the Irishman; Chekhov, the Russian; and Ibsen, the Norwegian. It should not too easily be forgotten that O'Neill, Wilder, Barry, and Green found their first hospitality with a little theater group, or that actors of commanding stature, such as the Lunts, have first gone through the rigorous apprenticeship of the non-commercial theater.

Inspired, perhaps, by the success of the Little Theater groups, a small band of clerics and laymen began to envision a Catholic theater. The motives behind such a conception were not merely artistic; they were motives of art and religion. It was clear that the national stage was, as it still is, in need of a purgation. Like the English drama of the late seventeenth century, modern drama, even when it is well wrought, is frequently vulgar and sometimes vicious. In any case, the Catholic way of life received but scant attention on the American stage, and there was a clear need for a drama which would do justice to its almost infinite capacity to influence the destinies of men.

Already in 1925, Henri Ghéon and Henri Brochet had founded in France a theatrical organization under the name of the "Companions of Our Lady." As the name implies, this group was a kind of sodality which strove to give a religious impulse, not only to the writing of plays but to their production and performance as well. Their motto was:

"For the Faith, by means of the art of drama;
For the art of drama, in the spirit of the Faith."

When Father Urban Nagle, O.P., established his Blackfriars Experimental Theater in New York, he could take encouragement for his project from this successful European example. As a matter of fact, interest in a native Catholic Little Theater became so widespread throughout the States that in 1937 a number of amateur organizations banded together to form the National Catholic Theatre Conference. Besides Father Nagle, others who were instrumental in bringing into existence this national organization were Rev. Thomas F. Carey, O.P., Rev. S. G. Dineen, S. J., of the Loyola community theatre, and Emmet Lavery. A pioneer in the field of Catholic dramatic writing is Rev. Matthias Helfen, founder of the Catholic Dramatic Movement in 1922. The Conference is an association of parish, college, and community theaters whose objectives are an advancement of common standards and the development of common action. The organization is under the chairmanship of Emmet Lavery, whose play, *The First Legion*, has brought him a wide following.

Simultaneous with the organization of the National Catholic Theater Conference was the establishment of a Department of Speech and Drama at the Catholic University of America. The department has a four-fold objective: 1) to study the great drama of the past, 2) to experiment with new forms, 3) to encourage creative endeavor, 4) and to reflect and produce "a culture informed by the Catholic spirit and the Catholic tradition."

EMMET LAVERY

Emmet Lavery (1902-), born at Poughkeepsie, N. Y., and educated at Fordham, achieved remarkable success in his play, *The First Legion* (1934). This play, showing the triumph of faith over skepticism, was popular not only in America, but in Europe. *Second Spring*, a drama based on the internal struggle in the life of Cardinal Newman, was produced in 1938. For a time Emmet Lavery was connected with the Federal Theater. Although now in Hollywood writing scenarios, he still has an interest in the Catholic Theater Conference.

THE MOTION PICTURE

There was a time when it looked very much as if the motion-picture theater would make the old-fashioned playhouse a complete anachronism. Indeed, with large groups of Americans it already has, for, as we have seen, playgoers are outnumbered by moviegoers overwhelmingly. Now it is realized, however, that the stage and screen are distinct artistic media: that is, each has methods and effects of which the other is deprived. A good play may make a bad movie and a good movie may make a bad play. On the purely mechanical side, the motion picture has most of the advantages. Unlike the stage, its scope of action is not limited; it can be prodigal with time and space; and it has all the rich resources of the art of photography. Nevertheless, the screen still is less capable than the stage of projecting great character and personality. It cannot, by its very nature, allow for the inspired improvisations of great actors, and it lacks the warmth of the three-dimensional presentation. Natural color technique has so far been less than satisfactory.

In spite of extraordinary achievement on the mechanical side, the motion picture leaves much to be desired from the artistic viewpoint. By no means has this medium yet realized its tremendous potentialities for great art. The development of the motion picture has been hampered on the one side by the commercial instincts of producers and on the other by the uneducated tastes of millions of its devotees. The tawdry publicity given to screen personalities, the deliberately encouraged idolatry of Hollywood actors, "fan" mail and barbarously written screen magazines: all these devices seem devoted only to one end — the increase of box-office returns. The occasional concession to profound religious themes cannot disguise the basic irreligion of the screen's usual product.

Almost the first requisite, then, for the improvement of the motion picture is the development of artistic and ethical standards. It is true, for the most part, that producers will give the public what it asks. The problem is to have the public ask for what is good. This educational venture can begin with the high-school student if the student is willing to go through the labor of evolving critical standards. It is not the number of films which he sees, but the quality of the films, which matters.

There is one other point to be considered. The task of the Legion of Decency has, even with students, been frequently misconceived. Its purpose is not to assess the craftsmanship of the scenario or the quality of the acting. The only purpose of this organization and of its pledge is to protect morals, and this is done by calling attention to those films which, however excellent from other viewpoints, are, from the viewpoint of morals, dangerous. The intent of the Legion is not to restrict liberties but to protect souls, and the nature of its task can be called into question only by those for whom sin is an illusion and salvation a myth.

BIOGRAPHY, THE ESSAY, JOURNALISM

Besides poetry, drama, and fiction there is a vast body of miscellaneous literature to which we go in a variety of moods and for a variety of purposes. The types which we are about to study are not all, from the purely literary viewpoint, of equal eminence. The newspaper, for example, serves the excellent, though transient and prosaic, purpose of providing us with information on current affairs; while the essay, on the other hand, strives to endure beyond the present by seizing upon the universal aspects of men and things and by conserving these aspects in a style which is itself universal and permanent. Biography, the essay, the periodical, the newspaper — each has a function of its own and each can prove both enjoyable and serviceable to the reader who keeps his critical faculties alive and operative.

BIOGRAPHY

The characters who have helped to shape the destinies of men, whether in the religious, political, literary, scientific, or military field, have always exercised a fascination over the minds of men. Sometimes these elect personages write of themselves, as did Benjamin Franklin, and we have *autobiography;* sometimes they perform the deeds and leave the writing of them to others, and we have *biography* merely. The lives of the saints constitute a separate type or *genre* which we call *hagiography.*

The writing of the lives of great men is very ancient indeed. We have only to think of Plutarch's *Lives,* which Shakespeare so frequently pressed into service when composing his Roman plays. This old classic can be recommended, not only for its factual value, considerable though this is, but likewise for its literary excellence. But biography has not always had such

worthy practitioners. In the last century, biographers labored under certain conventions and restraints which interfered with the true presentation of a personality. But even with these conventions removed, the results have often been far from satisfactory. Even the most painstaking scholarship cannot summon a living personality to the printed page, and all too often the printed lives of great men have been awkward and stilted, heavy and dull. In the present century there has been a reaction away from this bad tradition, and biography deservedly ranks high among the sales of non-fiction books. Lytton Strachey in England and Gamaliel Bradford in the United States were among the first to air their grievances against the old mode and to invent a new. Their tendency was to "fictionalize" biography. By fictionalizing we mean rendering to biography the qualities of the novel as popularly understood — swiftness of movement, vitality of characterization, a sense of plot, conflict, and resolution.

Bradford called his biographical studies "psychographs," that is, "soul sketches." He wished to view his characters from the inside out rather than from the outside in. It was not, he would seem to say, the wart on Cromwell's nose which is important, but the iron in his will and in his bloodstream. The faithful biographer must examine the heart, the mind, and the mysterious realm of the subconscious.

Biographer must evade pitfalls

However attractive this ideal of biography may be, it is one very difficult of achievement. The audacious confidence with which contemporary biographers ransack the inner closets of the soul is a little breathtaking. It is a perilous business to explore the souls of the living; to do so successfully with the dead is a well-nigh impossible task. One does not psychoanalyze a corpse. Then, too, truth is sometimes sacrificed for romantic or dramatic effect, and instead of fictionalization we have fiction pure and simple. A third danger is that the biographer, no matter how fair-minded he may think himself, often allows his own prejudices and ways of thought to become mixed with his oils, and the final portrait is a kind of composite affair which may resemble the biographer more than the subject studied. If we are aware of these dangers and guard against them we may safely read the fictionalized biographies which are today so much in demand. They almost always make fascinating reading, and they are sometimes a reasonable facsimile of the interred original. Many of these popular biographies are not by native American authors. Emil Ludwig, Stefan Zweig, André Maurois are popular here in translation.

Sanctity, chiefly because it flourishes in silence, does not always provide us with the external incident which, more often than not, constitutes the major appeal of biography. Cloistered and undemonstrative, many of the saints, even the greatest, remain unknown to the average reader. St. John of the Cross is not so well known as St. John Baptist Vianney (the Curé of Ars), and this is primarily because the life of the former is almost without incident, while that of the French pastor was replete with startling, even miraculous, events. Where we have action we shall have biography, and it is the sanctity of the active life which is destined to reach the larger public. At the same time it is well to understand that the deeds of the great saints are not the cause but the flowering of their greatness. The final test of the saintly personality does not lie in the external events. These may simply be the media through which God wishes to exhibit Himself to man. The final test is in the intimacy of union with God.

Hagiography demands special skills

Hagiography, like biography, has had a bad tradition. Those who committed themselves to the task of composing the lives of the saints frequently lacked the literary and psychological skills required, and the result was that we got plaster saints who did not seem like real human beings at all. It should be seen at once, however, that literary and psychological skills are not enough to entitle a writer to delve into the mysterious realms of sanctity. The writer of the life of a saint must move with ease in the world of the supernatural. We are fortunate today in having writers who happily combine these talents in producing hagiography which is both literary and reverent. France and England have set the pace; the United States is following. Hagiography, like biography, frequently comes to us from abroad. Henri Ghéon, Evelyn Waugh, and Christopher Hollis are widely read by American Catholics. In a season which is characterized by an interest in personality and in which

men determine the worth of their fellows through the "P.Q." (personality quotient), it is well for the Catholic boy and girl to focus attention on those personalities who have best fulfilled the vocation to which we are all called. The saints are granted to us, not for admiration only, but also for imitation.

GAMALIEL BRADFORD

Gamaliel Bradford (1863-1932) was born in Boston, Massachusetts, into a family which traced its ancestry directly to Governor Bradford of the Plymouth Colony. Ill health marred his long life, cut short his study at Harvard, and sometimes limited his writing activities to five minutes a day. With remarkable perseverance, he tried all fields of composition — poetry, the drama, the essay, and the novel. Of all these, the novel pleased him most. This may explain why his biographies have so much of the flavor of fiction. In composing these studies, he determined to avoid all orderly arrangement of a man's activities, to neglect the full course of his career, and to focus his attention on one particular phase. He said that men's lives were too complex for even the biographer to chronicle.

In achieving a polished style, therefore, he was successful, but he failed to go beyond "vague approximations" to his subjects. When he wrote that Thomas Gray's life was a succession of "quiet days and quiet nights steeped in tranquillity," he achieved an interesting sentence, but he did not state a fact. When he tried to impose dialogue of his own making upon Abraham Lincoln, he created an unjust portrait of the president's simplicity of religion. The combination of picturesqueness and inaccuracy is to be found in many of his books, the most significant of which are *Lee* (1912), *Confederate Portraits* (1914), *Union Portraits* (1916), and *Damaged Souls* (1923).

JAMES C. WHITTAKER

Among the many excellent autobiographical records of World War II, Lt. James C. Whittaker's simple and moving story of the successful rescue of Captain "Eddie" Rickenbacker and his crew is outstanding for its magnificent revelation of human courage and of humble reliance on faith and earnest prayer. Lt. Whittaker was co-pilot of the plane whose crash preceded the twenty-one days of torment in an open boat. It is interesting to note that many other journals of war experiences approximate the decency and devotion to ideals of *We Thought We Heard the Angels Sing.* There have been stories of escape from concentration camps, of raft voyages in the Caribbean after the torpedoing of tankers, of the tragedy of Tarawa, of the work of chaplains on aircraft carriers. Men have become heroes, without seeking honor, and others, as in John Hersey's *Into the Valley,* have proved themselves courageous by admitting they were afraid. Coupled with this type of honest self-revelation has been the resurgence of a strong belief in religion, a note struck in the Rickenbacker account, as well as in several recent novels. The return of idealism and faith augurs well for the literature of the future.

CATHOLIC BIOGRAPHY

Of the ever-increasing volumes of Catholic biographies, a large number fall into three classifications: collective biography, memoirs and autobiography, and the lives of noted individuals whose contributions to the Church or the world have been significant.

Dr. James J. Walsh, perhaps best known for his *The Thirteenth, Greatest of Centuries,* often used the medium of the collective biography. In *These Splendid Priests* he treats of the builders of civilization from the time of St. Benedict to the nineteenth century. The most outstanding recent example of collective biography is John Farrow's *Pageant of the Popes,* which presents in the form of a continuous narrative the entire story of the papacy from Peter to the present.

Memoirs reveal search for truth

Memoirs and other records of personal experience, drawn from the stores of a rich life, enable us to share in the good things that have come to another. Some self-revelations tell a double story, the outer and the inner, as in *The Book of the High Romance,* by Michael Williams, founder and first editor of *The Commonweal,* and author of two other short but vibrant biographies, *Little Brother St. Francis* and *The Little Flower of Carmel.*

These lives of the saints would never have been written but for the events related in the earlier book, for the *High Romance* is the story of how a soul was brought through failure and pain and falseness, through beauty and longing and goodness, to the ultimate truth of Christ. Less biographical but no less personal are the books of John Moody, a businessman who puts his Father's business before Wall Street. The story of his conversion is told in *The Long Road Home,* and is followed by enlightening accounts of experiences along the way in *Fast by the Road.*

In a smaller area, but with astonishing intensity, Dorothy Day tells the story of her conversion from Communism to Catholicism in *From Union Square to Rome.* She did not lose along the way her great desire to effect social changes, for "now the creed to which I subscribe is like a battle cry engraved on my heart." The battle for God and for humanity to which it led her is told in *House of Hospitality.* Edward Doherty, Chicago journalist, shows in *Gall and Honey* how a derelict faith can be salvaged through suffering. In a more humorous — and irresistibly humorous — vein, Father Martin Doherty describes his amazing transformation from a Chicago police-reporter into a seminarian at the North American College. If he stops laughing in *The House on Humility Street,* it is only long enough to sympathize keenly or pray intently.

Less radiant than these memories is the account given in *Dark Symphony,* in which Elizabeth Adams, a young Negro woman, speaks of her search, at once happy and heart-breaking, for the Church. It ends with a simple statement of a philosophy of history which can bear the testing of any event: "I have learned that Christ lives and works through mankind on earth." Elizabeth Adams has interpreted the poignancy of one race to another. She is the first to make the portrayal with boundless Christian charity. *Dark Symphony* has done with artistry and charm what *Native Son* attempted to do with bitterness. Miss Adams, a convert, has always lived in California.

The third type of biographical writing focuses the light on one individual. At present the field explored by Catholic biographers is broad, but its most frequent subjects are those who have lived and died in our land, and expressed the Church to their fellow Americans. In the

William Thomas Walsh

Middle West we see the strong and battered form of the friend of the Red Man, facing unworthy representatives of a white government, in *Father de Smet*, by Helene Magaret. In the forests by the Northern lakes we see the intrepid Isaac Jogues, threading his way with his great-hearted companions through a panorama of heroism in *Saint Among Savages*, by Francis Talbot, S.J. *Philippine Duchesne*, by Marjorie Erskine, reveals the hard and devoted life of "the woman who prayed always," who brought the Society of the Sacred Heart to America, while *Second Sowing*, by Margaret Williams, shows the flowering of Mother Duchesne's work through the life of Mother Aloysia Hardey, who founded centers of education throughout the eastern states.

By means of careful research and lively narrative, Mabel Farnum and Mary Fabyan Windeatt have made vivid for youthful readers the lives of many zealous heroes of the Church. Mabel Farnum's novelized accounts include biographies of St. Peter Claver, Pius X, and Fray Marcos de Niza. Among Mary Fabyan Windeatt's works are *Lad of Lima* (1942), *Hero of the Hills* (1943), and *Warrior in White* (1944). Miss Windeatt is also the author of *Sing Joyfully* (1942), a volume of poems exhibiting technical skill and lyrical charm.

MAJOR BIOGRAPHICAL WRITERS

There are today four major Catholic authors who have made biographical writing a specialty.

The biographies of William Thomas Walsh are laid abroad, in the glowing past of Spain. They are full-length historical canvases of royal figures requiring great sweeps of background. There is *Isabella of Spain*, telling of a queen who molded two worlds; there is *Philip II,* which brings the figure of a great king out of the shadows of misunderstanding into the more sympathetic light of truth; there is *Characters of the Inquisition*, which does the same for a phase of Church history only too often misrepresented. Finally there is *Saint Teresa of Avila*. In this book Dr. Walsh has retranslated from the originals all passages quoted from the letters and writings of the saint, giving to them the flavor of her own vigorous speech.

Katherine Burton has developed a technique of her own, which by the skillful use of conversation makes her lives read like novels; they are fictitious fact, charmingly presented. There is *Sorrow Built a Bridge*, the uplifting story of how Rose Hawthorne went further than her father along the road to truth and to the fullest service of humanity; she became a Catholic and finally foundress of a branch of Dominican Sisters for the care of the poor suffering from incurable cancer. The life of Father Isaac Hecker, the founder of the Paulist Fathers, is told in *Celestial Homespun*. Finally, the lives of many other American converts, "seekers who found the Sought," are condensed into brilliant sketches, beautifully shaped and surprisingly complete, in the volume called *In No Strange Land*.

Theodore Maynard claims that he is a poet who stumbled into the field of biography, but he has covered a wide range in it. The story of his own life is told in *The World I Saw*, but in many lives of past saints and leaders he visits other worlds which he has seen in thought and dream. His most recent study, *Orestes Brownson*, is one of his best.

Daniel Sargent, also a poet, has written *Four Independents*, short biographies of four exceedingly individual writers, Peguy, Claudel, Hopkins, and Brownson, and also a life of Saint Thomas More. While preparing a book called *Our Land and Our Lady*, he discovered so many worthwhile men and women in American history, who all but cry out for adequate biographies, that he has turned his full attention upon them. *Catherine Tekakwitha* celebrates the Indian girl of whom divine grace, unhindered, made a mystic saint in the forests peopled with graceless Mohawks. *All the Day Long*, the life of Bishop Walsh, founder of Maryknoll, relates how America at last began to send missionaries out into pagan lands, after having so long received missionary help from abroad.

Writers on Alaska

Two Catholic authors have both stimulated and gratified the timely interest in Alaska by their books on the land of glaciers. Bernard J. Hubbard, S.J., lecturer and author, traversed the area where volcanoes are still changing the face of the north. His first book, *Mush, You Malemutes* (1932), treats of exploration in the interior of Alaska. *Cradle of the Storms* (1935) covers the Alaska Peninsula-Aleutian Island area. Alma Savage, who combines a publishing career with creative writing, also discovered Alaska as a new writing field. While in the hunting and fishing wilderness along the lower Yukon River, Miss Savage gathered material for a life of Bishop Joseph Raphael Crimont which was expanded into *Dogsled Apostles* (1942). Of the several books that have grown out of her interest in the wild life of the north, *Smoozie* (1941), the story of a reindeer fawn, has met with steady popularity.

THE ESSAY

The history of the essay has been allied, from the eighteenth century on, with the history of journalism. The alliance, however, has usually been an uneasy one, for the essay has always attempted to rise above the passing needs of time and circumstance and to lead a life of its own. Nevertheless, the informal essay, as a distinct literary form, seems well on the road to extinction. Under the pressure of modern journalism and the journalistic reading habits of society, this once leisurely and delicate mode has been so radically altered as to be beyond recognition. The columnist has supplanted the essayist. Indeed, he enjoys an influence and popularity far surpassing that of his literary forebear.

The personal or informal essay as formerly understood was leisurely, personal, and topical. It dealt with things of consequence and things trivial with an equal relish, and it aimed at distinction and beauty of style. Its purpose, insofar as it had a purpose, was the revelation of a personality and the reaction of that personality to men and things. The increased tempo of living has dealt severely with deliberate and calmly-paced modes of writing, and the essayist, where he exists at all, is usually in opposition to the hectic contemporary world. Thus, the two veteran survivors of the ancient craft, Agnes Repplier and Logan Pearsall Smith, look upon the current scene with an air superior and detached. Both are intellectually robust, and their criticism of modern habits of thought and action frequently have shrewdness and wisdom. What is more important to the student of literature, they are masters of a style unhurried and elegant, and they dwell in the aristocracy of letters by right of their quiet but secure accomplishment.

Columnist replaces essayist

In a previous paragraph we stated that the columnist has supplanted the essayist. When we speak of columnists, therefore, we enter at once into that fascinating but motley world of journalism. The columnist, however, even when he is "featured" in a newspaper, is not a mere reporter; he is also an expresser of opinion. As a matter of fact, his opinions may be at variance with the editorial policies of the newspaper, as we may learn from the prudent reminders which the publishers sometimes deem necessary to insert by way of introduction to the columnist's "squib" for the day.

From this it can be seen that the columnist enjoys a kind of literary immunity. By reason of his forceful personality and the reputation he enjoys with the reading public, he is spared the necessity of conforming to the accepted views of the paper or periodical. It is this dominance of personality, revealed in a form that is brief and flexible, that makes the columnist the legitimate heir of the essayist. But here the resemblance ceases. The columnist, aiming at an average audience, usually achieves an average style. He is held closely to a discussion of current events or current books. He is circumscribed by the national mania for brevity, and the "digest" mentality which insists on a guarantee of a minimum of "reading minutes." Above all, dealing of necessity with things of the moment, the columnist himself becomes, in a double sense, an ephemeral writer. "As dead as yesterday's newspaper" has become a truism.

Writers have varied gifts

This is not to say that all columnists are without gifts of mind or pen. In point of fact, many are highly endowed. The complaint is that such highly endowed writers are often forced to sacrifice their gifts to a literary mode which can promise money and influence but no enduring fame. Some columnists, like Walter Lippman and Anne O'Hare McCormick, have an enviable clearness and directness of style. We do not have to share their point of view to admire their absence of rhetoric or their resistance to easy conquests of public opinion. Other columnists are primarily polemicists, that is, "warriors of the pen," and there is a strong emotional fervor in their writings. Father James Gillis, in his syndicated column *Sursum Corda*, is a writer of this type, and he has championed Catholic causes with intelligence and effectiveness for many years. Heywood Broun exercised a strong influence among working-class readers. Colloquial in style and aggressive in spirit, he nevertheless championed worthy causes with courage and tenacity.

While most columnists are concerned with political and social ideas, there are others with a more limited and less serious purpose. Writers like "F.P.A." (Franklin P. Adams), familiar to all America through his association with the radio program "Information Please," and Don Marquis are best described as literary journalists. Both are men of some erudition and culture, but both make concessions to popular taste by pretending to be plain and average. "F.P.A." has a sparkling wit and a ready acquaintance with the Latin poet Horace. He, unlike so many columnists, is violently concerned with the deterioration of grammatical and syntactical standards in modern prose. His own writing more nearly approaches the ideal of the informal essay than that of most of his contemporaries.

© Brown Brothers

John Kieran

A columnist of a different sort is John Kieran, former sports writer for the *New York Times*. His name is mentioned only to remind the student that sports can be discussed in a style without jargon or clichés. Mr. Kieran writes, not only with an encyclopedic knowledge of his field, but with a broad cultural background and with an extraordinary gift of analogy and metaphor.

HEYWOOD BROUN

Heywood Broun (1888-1939) was a journalist who appeared to his contemporaries as a kind of wandering friar who gave simplicity and kindliness to the world and received affection in return. In Broun's famous column, "It Seems to Me," he waged constant war against social injustice. His death within the year of his conversion deprived the ranks of the Catholic press of a valiant recruit. The *Collected Edition of Heywood Broun*, prepared by Heywood Hale Broun after his father's death, contains the author's best work. Beneath the buoyant surface of these light essays is to be found the warmth, depth, and complete good nature of the author.

MARY ELLEN CHASE

In one sense, Mary Ellen Chase (1887-) is a regional writer. Her concern in most of her books has been with the people and with the seafaring life and background of the state of Maine, where she was born. This is evident in her novels *Mary Peters* (1934), *Silas Crockett* (1935), and *Windswept* (1941) as well as in her autobiographical recollections of her ancestors and friends, *A Goodly Heritage* (1932). In another sense, Miss Chase, who is Professor of English Literature at Smith College, is not regional at all. As a result of her wide interests in reading and in teaching, she has made studies of Thomas Hardy (1927), has recorded her enthusiasm for the home of English literature in *This England* (1936), and has edited, with incisive comments on her selections, *The Writing of Informal Essays* (1928). In this she warns that the essayist must have something to say and must not fall back on mere style; he must not only interpret his own experiences or humorous reactions or reflective observations, or emotional responses, but must also impart them clearly to the reader.

Her own excitement over all her work appears most pleasantly in *A Goodly Fellowship* (1929), in which she tells of her early years, her study at the Universities of Maine and Minnesota, and her teaching career at the latter institution, at the College of St. Catherine, and at Smith. This autobiography is one of the most stirring invitations to learning ever written.

CHRISTOPHER DARLINGTON MORLEY

Christopher Darlington Morley (1890-) has seen his name on four score and ten title-pages, books of poetry, plays and novels, lectures on Shakespeare, and reflections on the passing scene. All are marked by the love of human nature and of the written word, by mellow sentiment and wise and rich experience.

He came of a remarkable family: his English-born father was professor of mathematics at Johns Hopkins, his mother was a poet and musician, and his two brothers, Frank and Felix, have been significant in publishing, writing, and education. Three years at Oxford on a Rhodes scholarship, after his graduation

Christopher Darlington Morley

from Haverford in 1910, increased his appreciation of literature and further prepared him for the writing career on which he determined. He served a four years' apprenticeship with a publishing firm, and worked for a short period on the staffs of the *Ladies' Home Journal* and the *Philadelphia Public Ledger,* before entering two decades of column writing for the *New York Evening Post* and the *Saturday Review of Literature.*

As a familiar essayist, Christopher Morley is at his best. He is an entertaining conversationalist who pleasantly and wittily chats of people and places, books and life. He relishes all of these and wishes the reader to share his interesting experiences, his enthusiasm, and his observations. The titles of many of his collections indicate the fanciful element in his writing: *Mince Pie* (1919), *Pipefuls* (1920), *Chimneysmoke* (1921), *Streamlines* (1926). His originality of expression, his engaging whimsy and humor, and his broad interests have given his essays a wide appeal. Little and ordinary things excite him and the reader: the joy of collecting books, of talking with friends, the sounds of a city, the natural beauty of country roads, the power of a locomotive, the straining eagerness of tugboats, the adventures of commuting, the fun of mathematical puzzles, the graceful script of Poe's handwriting, and the modern significance of skywriting.

Christopher Morley carried his love of literature into the themes of two early novels, exciting and fanciful treatment of the world of bookselling, *Parnassus on Wheels* (1917) and *The Haunted Bookshop* (1919). The same gaiety is to be found in *Kathleen* (1920), in which he portrays the pleasant confusion of an American in English schools. With equal success he did the reverse in his recent novel, *Thorofare*, in which a young Englishman becomes Americanized in Baltimore. Here, as always, he is successful in his portrayal of children. He has four of his own, and has written for them in *The Goldfish Under the Ice* and about them in the "mystery" story he did with Don Marquis, *Pandora Lifts the Lid* (1924).

ROBERT MAYNARD HUTCHINS

Robert Maynard Hutchins (1899-) has been the stormy petrel of American education ever since he became President of the University of Chicago at the age of thirty. Born in Brooklyn, New York, he interrupted his brilliant career as a student to serve with the American Ambulance Corps on the Italian front from 1917 to 1919. He received his arts and law degrees from Yale and became Dean of the Law School there before assuming his duties at Chicago. In his present post he has pleaded consistently in books, lectures, and radio talks for what he calls a wider learning and what others term a too narrow one. He has opposed the national waste of leisure time; he has pleaded that Americans devote themselves to education in order that phrases such as democracy, liberty, the state, economic well being, and human good may be understood better. He has trod on many toes by insisting that the amassing of fortunes is not the principal aim of life and has questioned the value of courses which are merely practical.

These ideas appear in his *The Higher Learning in America* (1936), *No Friendly Voice* (1936), and *Speaking of Education* (1940). Of late, he has become well known for his sponsorship of the plan which recommends the teaching of world thought from a series of great books. Many have attacked the limitations of his list of such titles; others have quarreled with his definition of a life enriched by intellectual activity; some have felt that he

has not stressed sufficiently the place of theology. In the main, however, he has opposed the futile and shoddy things, which unfortunately appeal to so many, and has defended the conservative view that facts are not as important as understanding.

JAMES TRUSLOW ADAMS

From the first, the relations between English and American history and culture have attracted James Truslow Adams (1878-). They proved of interest during his prize-winning student years at Brooklyn Polytechnic Institute and at Yale, and he must have become aware of the ramifications of international finance while on the New York Stock Exchange. During World War I, he was a captain in military intelligence, gathered data for Colonel House for the Peace Conference, and attended its sessions in an official capacity. The necessity for closer understanding between nations so impressed him that he turned to a series of studies which would show the many similarities of viewpoint among English-speaking people. His first such study, *The Founding of New England* (1921), won the Pulitzer Prize and was followed by *Revolutionary New England* (1923) and *New England in the Republic* (1926). Other aspects of American thought were developed in the complementary volumes, *Hamiltonian Principles* (1928) and *Jeffersonian Principles* (1929). Perhaps as a reaction to his work on the Exchange, he wrote a brilliant attack on materialistic living in *Our Business Civilization* (1929), which was particularly prophetic in view of the subsequent depression. His most widely read study is *The Epic of America*, in which he has tried to show that the people themselves contributed to the greatness of the country and that history is not merely a record of wars and tariffs. Of late, he has been interpreting British and American unity in such works as *Empire of the Seven Seas* (1940), *Building the British Empire* (1940), and *An American Looks at the British Empire* (1941).

FULTON J. SHEEN

The oratorical and writing arts are happily allied in Monsignor Fulton J. Sheen (1895-). When at the close of his studies at Louvain his doctoral thesis, *God and*

Fulton J. Sheen

Intelligence in Modern Philosophy, was awarded the Cardinal Mercier Prize for International Philosophy, the London *Universe* called him the "new Catholic philosopher of the age." Not long after his return from Europe he accepted an appointment to the philosophy department at the Catholic University, but his activity has never been limited to the classroom. An extraordinary amount of his time goes to lectures, radio addresses, and books which interpret current issues for the average man in the light of Catholic philosophy. The style of Monsignor Sheen's early essays shows a pronounced likeness to that of Chesterton. Like the great English apologist, he saw the advantage of using a brilliant, clever style that would attract a popular audience first to itself and then to the profound truth which lay behind the words. In 1930 Monsignor Sheen gave the first series of talks on the Catholic Hour. Since then he has written most of his discourses with a view to broadcasting before publishing them in book form. The language of these later pieces is clear and precise, the imagery and paradox more reserved, the whole well suited to a voice whose great strength flows steadily beneath a quiet, restrained delivery. The collection

of addresses entitled *The Divine Romance* represents Monsignor Sheen's earlier manner; *Moral Universe,* his later. The themes of his many essays range widely through religious and moral issues.

WALTER FARRELL, O.P.

Walter Farrell, O.P. (1902-), a native of Chicago, has exercised a profound influence upon many readers. In his four-volume *Companion to the Summa* he has successfully transported into the idiom of the twentieth century the timeless truths of the philosophy of St. Thomas Aquinas. From contemporary life he draws apt illustrations of theological truths. Friends of Father Farrell characterize him as a gifted leader, industrious, methodical, and witty. Before entering the U. S. Navy as a chaplain, the priest served as Regent of Studies for the St. Joseph province of the Dominican order.

JOHN W. SIMONS

The relationship of art to morality is a topic which frequently occupies the attention of many Catholic critics today. One essayist who has elucidated the problem for high school students is Rev. John W. Simons (1910-). A literary artist and a priest, Father Simons is well qualified to discuss this significant question. Born in Philadelphia of Irish parents, Father Simons made his studies for the priesthood at St. Charles Seminary, Overbrook, and was ordained in 1937. He is now chairman of the English Department at St. Thomas More High School. The essay, "Grace Before Reading," manifests Father Simon's interest in literary criticism, philosophy, and poetry.

CARLTON JOSEPH HUNTLEY HAYES

Many American writers have been honored with diplomatic posts; Washington Irving, Nathaniel Hawthorne, Henry Adams, and Carlton Joseph Huntley Hayes (1882-) are among them. Like Irving, Professor Hayes is both historian and Ambassador to Spain. This honor is the climax to a long and successful career, long because he began to teach in 1907, while still studying at Columbia University, and successful because of the enormous output which has placed him in the front rank of Catholic historians. After serving in the first World War as a Captain of Military Intelligence, he wrote a history of that conflict in 1920.

His particular interests, however, were in the later effects of the confused thinking of the nineteenth century. In *British Social Politics* (1913) he pointed out that it was the duty of the modern democratic state to alleviate the evils set in motion by industrialism. In *Essays on Nationalism* (1926) he made the first serious modern study of the meaning of "nationalism" and "patriotism." He developed his views in *France, a Nation of Patriots* (1930), in which the greatness and weakness of the national spirit was exposed, and in *The Historical Evolution of Modern Nationalism* (1931). Here it was shown that man alone is not self-sufficient and that materialism and scientific progress will not bring about perfection upon earth. The climax of this crusade of his appears in *A Generation of Materialism, 1871-1900* (1941), which aptly develops the course of those forces that resulted in the present century of conflict.

In all his writings Professor Hayes has shown intense distaste for sham and prejudice, for Marxism and Communism and has worked devotedly to lessen religious and racial hatreds. His championing of the oppressed is but one aspect of a vital and forceful personality. His writing is marked by balance, soundness, objectivity, breadth, and deep Catholic knowledge.

LOGAN PEARSALL SMITH

Like Christopher Morley, Logan Pearsall Smith (1865-) experienced a Quaker boyhood, graduated from Haverford College, and studied at Oxford, where he obtained his M.A. degree in 1893. Unlike Morley, who returned the favor of his Rhodes scholarship by writing at length about English literature from this side of the ocean, this essayist elected to remain in England and there to write poetry and criticism, studies in literature and language, and brief sketches on that material which is on the fringe of culture, that he titled *Trivia* (1917), *More Trivia* (1921), and *All Trivia* (1933).

Robert Benchley

Critically, he is still somewhat allied to the American tradition. As a youth, he knew Whitman, as he records in his autobiography, *Unforgotten Years* (1938), and he has engaged in controversy with T. S. Eliot and Ezra Pound over the value of Milton's poetry.

His essays are pleasant bits of talk about gardens, of lilacs and bees, the breath-taking picture of an English cathedral town, companionship, vanity, Oxford hours, and the strangeness and appeal of our spoken tongue. Of his longer works, the finest is *On Reading Shakespeare* (1933), a conversation with the ordinary reader rather than a formal study.

ROBERT BENCHLEY

Few professional humorists have been able to poke fun at themselves and at the nonsense they see in the world and yet demand a dignified respect. Robert Benchley (1889-) has followed this dual course. After his graduation from Harvard in 1912, where he was editor of the *Lampoon,* he worked in advertising and in aircraft production, directed the "Books and Other Things" column in the *New York World,* and wrote dramatic criticism for the old *Life* (1920-1929) and for *The New Yorker* (1929-1940). Since 1937 he has engaged in radio work and has acted in many motion picture shorts which feature the deliberate "zany" he has made of the ordinary mortal, confused by treasurer's reports, sleeplessness, masters of ceremony, and children who ask encyclopedic questions. Many of these laughs at his own expense have appeared in such books as *Pluck and Luck* (1925), *20,000 Leagues Under the Sea, or David Copperfield* (1928), *My Ten Years in a Quandary* (1936), *Inside Benchley* (1942) and *Benchley Beside Himself* (1943).

FOUR INFLUENTIAL FIGURES

James M. Gillis, C.S.P. (1876-), distinguished essayist and radio personality, has been editor of the *Catholic World* since 1922. His chief concern as a writer is with the numerous problems which confront contemporary America. His range is wide enough to include literature, education, and sociology. He is noted for his balanced judgment and his ability to open the minds and consciences of his readers. Distinguished for rigor and clarity, his style has on occasion beauty and emotional appeal. Father Gillis' best-known books are *False Prophets* (1925), *Christianity and Civilization* (1932), and *This Our Day* (1933).

George N. Shuster (1894-), President of Hunter College, New York City, journalist, educator, and critic, was educated at Notre Dame and Columbia University. For several years he was associated with *The Commonweal*, retiring to accept a Carnegie fellowship and to study political trends in pre-Nazi Germany. His best known books are *The Catholic Spirit in Modern English Literature* (1922), *The Catholic Spirit in America* (1927), and *The Catholic Church and Current Literature* (1929). He continues to write critical articles for *The New York Times Book Review* and *The New York Herald-Tribune Weekly Book Review*. Dr. Shuster has a knowledge of several literatures, a catholic taste, and a subtle and engaging style.

Francis J. Spellman (1889-), Archbishop of New York, has become a spokesman for Catholic democratic principles in his recent books. He not only graphically

Francis J. Spellman, Archbishop of New York

presents the great conflict on the world battlefield in *Action This Day* (1943) but offers encouragement and hope in *The Risen Soldier* (1944). *The Road to Victory* is a masterly presentation of Catholic principles relating to war and peace. Archbishop Spellman's books are marked by clarity, vividness, and force. An eyewitness to many of the scenes he describes, he combines a gift for detail with precision and accuracy.

Daniel Lord's great gift is his power to inspire youth with the desire to make the world a Christo-centric sphere. Nationally known as sodality organizer and editor of *The Queen's Work*, Father Lord (1888-) has been extraordinarily productive and many-sided. He has written over a dozen books, in addition to numerous plays, pageants, musical shows, and pamphlets. His writing, skillfully adapted to the needs of youth, is colorful and animated.

ESSAYISTS AND CRITICS

James J. Daly, S.J. (1872-), has served on the staffs of *America, The Queen's Work*, and the Jesuit quarterly, *Thought*, of which he was literary editor. As an essayist he is notable for his wisdom, wit, and mellowness, no less than for the finish of his style through which radiates a gracious and persuasive personality. A fellow Jesuit, Michael Earls (1873-1937) brought together an attractive collection of essays, *Under College Towers*, and later, out of an enormous range of literary contacts, garnered the interesting chapters of *Manuscripts and Memories*. This volume of reminiscence reflects the author's genial nature and gift for friendship.

Joseph J. Reilly (1881-), educated at Holy Cross, Columbia, and Yale, has achieved a reputation here and abroad with his *Newman as a Man of Letters* (1925). In his collections of critical essays, *Dear Prue's Husband*, and *Of Books and Men* (1942), a wide range of authors comes to life. Reilly treats the works of these writers with illuminating insight and from a fresh and independent point of view.

Francis Median's critical sense has enlightened a large reading public through his book reviews in *Columbia*. Among his best-known books which illustrate his grasp of literary qualities and his stimulating style are *Religion and the Study of Literature* (1923) and *Living Upstairs* (1942).

JOURNALISM

We must now say a few words about the newspaper proper. It is the huge metropolitan daily newspaper and the popular weekly magazine which afford the literary and mental pabulum for the greater part of the literate population. Since this is so, the daily newspaper, along with the motion picture and radio, is one of the major educational agencies within the nation. The student has, as a consequence, the duty of examining the standards — journalistic, political, and ethical — of the newspapers of his community.

There are literally thousands of newspapers printed in the United States. Since the turn of the century, there has been a trend towards newspaper "chains" and a single publisher may be in control of numerous dailies throughout the nation. This makes for efficiency, but likewise for standardization. Moreover, it is doubtful whether it is healthy for the nation that individual publishers should be in control of so much power.

The efficiency of the contemporary press in gathering and disseminating news is a truly phenomenal

achievement. Correspondents stationed at strategic posts throughout the world cable "newsworthy" items with amazing promptness. The courage and persistence of the American reporter is proverbial. Foreign celebrities are in constant amazement at the stratagems of our reporters, at their sometimes ridiculous, sometimes tasteless, sometimes shrewd barrage of questions. Though there have been occasional lapses, our press has on the whole held to a difficult standard of truth and accuracy.

Yet, there is a monotonous uniformity among our city newspapers. There are the same syndicated columns, the same comic strips, and the same "features." With notable exceptions, editors feel that their papers will not be considered popular without counsels to the lovelorn, the kitchen lore, daily health article, society column, movie gossip, games and puzzles, casual gestures (in the Saturday edition) towards the "religious minded." Enterprising publishers have overlooked no one in the family as a prospective subscriber, and the interests of all are in some way appealed to. Like the motion picture, the newspaper has become the giant consultant of mass taste, and the so-called "human interest" stories are frequently of a type to interest the subhuman and morally oblique.

The student must first of all examine the editorial policy of the newspapers he is accustomed to read; he must criticize that policy in the light of his Catholic and democratic principles; and he must safeguard himself against the reading of articles which present occasion of sin. On the intellectual and cultural level he should be exacting with regard to the quality of his newspaper. He must strive to be thinking, critical, and mature. One who reads only a newspaper may boast of literacy, but he cannot pretend to be educated.

THE CATHOLIC PRESS

On the whole, the Catholic press, lacking the huge financial resources of the great dailies, must be content with less pretentious formats and a more limited coverage of the news. The journalistic standing of our diocesan newspapers is moderately high, though their outlook is sometimes a little local and provincial. In recent years the news service attached to the National Catholic Welfare Conference, with headquarters in Washington, D.C., has done much to solve the problem of the world coverage of news. Correspondents throughout the world send their reports to the central office and these reports are relayed to local and diocesan newspapers. Students should become acquainted with Catholic newspapers. They will contain news of interest not elsewhere available, and their articles will oppose and correct the judgments of the secular press.

In conclusion, some word should be said with regard to weekly and monthly magazines. They have an advantage over the newspaper in that they have some time to absorb and criticize the news of the preceding days or weeks. In the main, the more popular weeklies are merely pictorial and informational, though there is usually a real or disguised editorial policy behind the news and even behind the photographs. The two outstanding Catholic weeklies are *America* and *The Commonweal.*

Three Prominent Periodicals

America, a national Catholic weekly, was founded in 1909 by Rev. John J. Wynne, S.J., who was also the first editor. Its aim has been to interpret current events in the light of Catholic social principles, especially those enunciated in the papal encyclicals. Some particular events which have been influenced by *America's* editorial writings have been the Oregon School Bill, the recognition of the Church's plight and its amelioration in Mexico, the betterment of labor conditions in the unions, and the progress of the Legion of Decency. Among the eminent Catholic journalists who have been on the *America* staff have been Rev. Richard H. Tierney, S.J., Rev. Paul L. Blakely, S.J., Rev. Wilfrid A. Parsons, S.J., Rev. Francis X. Talbot, S.J., Rev. John La Farge, S.J. One of the noted founders of Catholic journalism in the United States, Mr. Thomas F. Meehan, labored as *America's* editorial assistant for over thirty years. The *Catholic Mind*, also founded and edited by the Jesuit staff, is the oldest reprint magazine in the United States.

The idea of a periodical which would reflect the opinion of a segment of Catholic laymen on significant political, social, and economic questions resulted, in 1924, in the foundation of a weekly, *The Commonweal.* Welcoming a diversion of opinion on topics not of faith and morals, the editors present ideas which are in accord with Catholic teaching, but which are not necessarily shared by all Catholics. Because its audience includes a large number of sympathetic non-Catholics, *The Commonweal* does not concern itself with problems of strictly internal interest to Church members. Noted figures in the early history of the magazine were Michael Williams, Thomas J. Walsh and Henry Longan Stuart. The present managing editor, Harry Lorin Binsse, before coming to *The Commonweal,* founded the *Liturgical Arts* magazine. He is a descendant of a line of Catholic leaders whose influence dates back to the beginning of the nineteenth century.

The Sign, a monthly magazine of national circulation, was founded in 1921 by the Passionist Fathers of the Province of St. Paul of the Cross, at Union City, NJ, through the initiative of Reverend Theodore Noonan, C.P. Its first editor was Reverend Harold Purcell, C.P. Its primary purpose is the promotion of intelligent Catholic reading, with emphasis upon current events in the nation and the world as seen from a Catholic point of view. Authoritative guidance is given on contemporary drama, motion pictures, and books. A secondary purpose is the support of Catholic foreign missions. The present editor is Reverend Ralph Gorman, C.P.

The Digests

Among the monthly magazines, *The Reader's Digest* leads all others in the number of its sales. Digests are a relatively new form of journalism, and they are concerned even less than most types of journalism with the refinements of style. Nevertheless, they serve a purpose, however humble, and quite obviously meet a public need. The Catholic counterpart of *The Reader's Digest*, also issued monthly, is the *Catholic Digest.* By judicious reprints from Catholic periodicals, as well as from soundly-edited secular journals, the *Catholic Digest* has won a wider acceptance for the Catholic point of view in circles where public opinion is formed. Its editor is Reverend Paul Bussard. The home office is in St. Paul, Minnesota.

Richard Cory

Edwin Arlington Robinson

Richard Cory is one of the portraits in Edwin Arlington Robinson's gallery of splendid failures. Famous as a portrayer of character, Robinson held that the nature of man does not change with the ages. For this reason both his New England studies and his characters from Arthurian times are alike. They illustrate the common theme of man beset by his own nature.

WHENEVER Richard Cory went downtown,
  We people on the pavement looked at him;
He was a gentleman from sole to crown,
  Clean-favored, and imperially slim.

And he was always quietly arrayed,   5
  And he was always human when he talked;
But still he fluttered pulses when he said,
  "Good morning," and he glittered when he walked.

And he was rich — yes, richer than a king —
  And admirably schooled in every grace;   10
In fine, we thought that he was everything
  To make us wish that we were in his place.

So on we worked, and waited for the light,
  And went without the meat, and cursed the bread;
And Richard Cory, one calm summer night,
  Went home and put a bullet through his head.   16

VIEWING THE AUTHOR'S IDEAS

1. Were you surprised at the ending? Give several possible reasons why Richard took his own life.

2. What good things of life did Richard Cory possess? Why did they not make him happy?

3. In a single sentence express the chief point which the poet is making.

EVALUATING HIS MANNER OF EXPRESSION

1. What words in the first three stanzas describe Richard Cory as a man who would command attention? What single line gives you a general impression of his character?

2. Discuss the larger meanings of the words *light*, *meat*, and *bread* in the last stanza.

3. What feeling does the poem stir in you? Give reasons for your reaction.

4. Interpret the phrase "glittered when he walked."

Miniver Cheevy

Edwin Arlington Robinson

Miniver Cheevy, the romantic dreamer, is a contrast to Richard Cory, the man who has apparently achieved material success. The poet has made the differences more pointed by giving the two characters one great likeness: a restlessness of mind and soul that keeps happiness far from each. The men in the poem are companion pieces of futility.

MINIVER Cheevy, child of scorn,
  Grew lean while he assailed the seasons;
He wept that he was ever born,
  And he had reasons.

Miniver loved the days of old   5
  When swords were bright and steeds were prancing;
The vision of a warrior bold
  Would set him dancing.

Miniver sighed for what was not,
  And dreamed, and rested from his labors;
He dreamed of Thebes[1] and Camelot,[2]   11
  And Priam's neighbors.[3]

---

[1] *Thebes*, a city of ancient Greece, famous in legend.

[2] *Camelot*, city of the Arthurian legends, where King Arthur reigned with his Knights of the Round Table.

[3] *Priam's neighbors.* Priam was the king of Troy at the time of the Trojan War, when the city was besieged and finally taken by the Greeks.

Miniver mourned the ripe renown
    That made so many a name so fragrant;
He mourned Romance, now on the town,
    And Art, a vagrant.   16

Miniver loved the Medici,[4]
    Albeit he had never seen one;
He would have sinned incessantly
    Could he have been one.   20

Miniver cursed the commonplace
    And eyed a khaki suit with loathing;
He missed the medieval grace
    Of iron clothing.

Miniver scorned the gold he sought,   25
    But sore annoyed was he without it;
Miniver thought, and thought, and thought,
    And thought about it.

Miniver Cheevy, born too late,
    Scratched his head and kept on thinking;
Miniver coughed, and called it fate,   31
    And kept on drinking.

[4] *Medici*, a well-known Florentine family, influential from the fourteenth to the sixteenth centuries.

VIEWING THE AUTHOR'S IDEAS

1. If Miniver had possessed the "gold he sought," how do you think he would have used it?

2. In the prose selections that you have read, what characters resemble Miniver? Does Robinson seem to recommend Cheevy as a type to be imitated?

EVALUATING HIS MANNER OF EXPRESSION

1. Towards which of the characters, Miniver Cheevy or Richard Cory, does Robinson seem to feel more kindly? What device does he use to give this impression? Point out certain lines and phrases in support of your answer.

2. What do the words *Thebes*, *Camelot*, and *Medici* contribute to the thought of the poem? If these words are not significant to you, learn their implication from an encyclopedia or other reference work.

3. Notice the effect produced by repeating the name as the first word of each stanza and following it by a strong verb. What impression of Miniver's character does Robinson give by word repetition in lines 27 and 28? Read the poem again as an example of skillful use of repetition.

Mending Wall

Robert Frost

This poem contrasts the man who fails to think for himself with the individual who reasons and questions his own activity. It is this difference in attitude rather than a stone wall which separates the two farmers north of Boston.

SOMETHING there is that doesn't love a wall,
That sends the frozen-ground swell under it
And spills the upper boulders in the sun;
And makes gaps even two can pass abreast.
The work of hunters is another thing: 5
I have come after them and made repair
Where they have left not one stone on a stone,
But they would have the rabbit out of hiding
To please the yelping dogs. The gaps I mean,
No one has seen them made or heard them made,   10
But at spring mending time we find them there.
I let my neighbor know beyond the hill;
And on a day we meet to walk the line.
And set the wall between us once again.
We keep the wall between us as we go.   15
To each the boulders that have fallen to each.
And some are loaves and some so nearly balls
We have to use a spell to make them balance:
"Stay where you are until our backs are turned!"
We wear our fingers rough with handling them.   20
Oh, just another kind of outdoor game,
One on a side. It comes to little more:

There where it is we do not need the wall:
He is all pine and I am apple orchard.
My apple trees will never get across   25
And eat the cones under his pines, I tell him.
He only says, "Good fences make good neighbors."
Spring is the mischief in me, and I wonder
If I could put a notion in his head:
"*Why* do they make good neighbors? Isn't it   30
Where there are cows? But here there are no cows.
Before I built a wall I'd ask to know
What I was walling in or walling out,
And to whom I was like to give offense.
Something there is that doesn't love a wall,
That wants it down." I could say "Elves" to him,   36
But it's not elves exactly, and I'd rather
He said it for himself. I see him there
Bringing a stone grasped firmly by the top
In each hand, like an old-stone savage[1] armed.   40
He moves in darkness as it seems to me,
Not of woods only and the shade of trees.

[1] *an old-stone savage*, a savage of the Old Stone Age, characterized by the use of stone implements.

He will not go behind his father's saying,
And he likes having thought of it so well
He says again, "Good fences make good neighbors." 45

VIEWING THE AUTHOR'S IDEAS

1. Which of the neighbors has the more reasonable attitude toward walls? Why? How are the two men contrasted in personality?

2. What is the "something that doesn't love a wall?" Why does the poet want his neighbor to name this "something" for himself?

3. What type of person is the writer describing in the lines beginning: "He moves in darkness . . . "?

4. Can you think of other proverbs that are sometimes unreasonably given as the causes for people's actions?

EVALUATING HIS MANNER OF EXPRESSION

1. Quote several passages which make you conscious of the New England landscape.

2. Much of the charm of this poem centers in such conversational idiom as "And on a day we meet to walk the line." Find other examples. Cite passages showing the atmosphere of friendliness between the two neighbors.

The Death of the Hired Man

Robert Frost

"The Death of the Hired Man" is a tragedy compressed into the short space of a conversation. Silas is cousin to the derelicts of Edwin Arlington Robinson. In telling the story, Frost shows much the same ability as his fellow poet in analyzing character. There is the same willingness to see beneath the tatters the man who might have been, the same trick of finding among the ruins of life the personality that has a right to recognition.

MARY sat musing on the lamp flame at the table
Waiting for Warren. When she heard his step
She ran on tiptoe down the darkened passage
To meet him in the doorway with the news
And put him on his guard. "Silas is back."
She pushed him outward with her through the door   6
And shut it after her. "Be kind," she said.

She took the market things from Warren's arms
And set them on the porch, then drew him down
To sit beside her on the wooden steps.   10

"When was I ever anything but kind to him?
But I'll not have the fellow back," he said.
"I told him so last haying, didn't I?
'If he left then,' I said, 'that ended it.'
What good is he? Who else will harbor him   15
At his age for the little he can do?
What help he is there's no depending on.
Off he goes always when I need him most.
'He thinks he ought to earn a little pay,
Enough at least to buy tobacco with,   20
So he won't have to beg and be beholden.'

'All right,' I say, 'I can't afford to pay
Any fixed wages, though I wish I could.'
'Someone else can.' 'Then someone else will have to.'
I shouldn't mind his bettering himself   25
If that was what it was. You can be certain,
When he begins like that, there's someone at him
Trying to coax him off with pocket money—
In haying time, when any help is scarce.
In winter he comes back to us. I'm done."   30

"Sh! not so loud; he'll hear you," Mary said.
"I want him to; he'll have to soon or late."

"He's worn out. He's asleep beside the stove.
When I came up from Rowe's I found him here,
Huddled against the barn door fast asleep,
A miserable sight, and frightening, too —   36
You needn't smile — I didn't recognize him —
I wasn't looking for him—and he's changed.
Wait till you see."

                    "Where did you say he'd been?"

"He didn't say. I dragged him to the house,
And gave him tea and tried to make him smoke.   41
I tried to make him talk about his travels.
Nothing would do; he just kept nodding off."

"What did he say? Did he say anything?"

"But little."

                         "Anything? Mary, confess
He said he'd come to ditch the meadow for me."   46

"Warren!"

                    "But did he? I just want to know."

"Of course he did. What would you have him say?
Surely you wouldn't grudge the poor old man
Some humble way to save his self-respect.   50
He added, if you really care to know,
He meant to clear the upper pasture, too.
That sounds like something you have heard before?
Warren, I wish you could have heard the way
He jumbled everything. I stopped to look   55
Two or three times — he made me feel so queer —
To see if he was talking in his sleep.

He ran on Harold Wilson — you remember —
The boy you had in haying four years since.
He's finished school, and teaching in his college.   60
Silas declares you'll have to get him back.
He says they two will make a team for work;
Between them they will lay this farm as smooth!
The way he mixed that in with other things.
He thinks young Wilson a likely lad, though daft   65
On education — you know how they fought
All through July under the blazing sun,
Silas up on the cart to build the load,
Harold along beside to pitch it on."

"Yes, I took care to keep well out of earshot."   70

"Well, those days trouble Silas like a dream.
You wouldn't think they would. How some things
          linger!
Harold's young college boy's assurance piqued him.
After so many years he still keeps finding
Good arguments he sees he might have used.   75
I sympathize. I know just how it feels
To think of the right thing to say too late.
Harold's associated in his mind with Latin.
He asked me what I thought of Harold's saying
He studied Latin like the violin   80
Because he liked it — that an argument!
He said he couldn't make the boy believe
He could find water with a hazel prong —
Which showed how much good school had ever done
          him,   84
He wanted to go over that. But most of all
He thinks if he could have another chance
To teach him how to build a load of hay —"
"I know, that's Silas' one accomplishment.
He bundles every forkful in its place,
And tags and numbers it for future reference,   90
So he can find and easily dislodge it
In the unloading. Silas does that well.
He takes it out in bunches like big birds' nests.
You never see him standing on the hay   94
He's trying to lift, straining to lift himself."

"He thinks if he could teach him that, he'd be
Some good perhaps to someone in the world.
He hates to see a boy the fool of books.

Poor Silas, so concerned for other folk,
And nothing to look backward to with pride,   100
And nothing to look forward to with hope,
So now and never any different."

Part of a moon was falling down the west,
Dragging the whole sky with it to the hills,
Its light poured softly in her lap. She saw
And spread her apron to it. She put out her hand   106
Among the harplike morning-glory strings,
Taut with the dew from garden bed to eaves,
As if she played unheard the tenderness
That wrought on him beside her in the night.   110
"Warren," she said, "he has come home to die;
You needn't be afraid he'll leave you this time."

"Home," he mocked gently.

                              "Yes, what else but home?
It all depends on what you mean by home.
Of course he's nothing to us, any more   115
Than was the hound that came a stranger to us
Out of the woods, worn out upon the trail."

"Home is the place where, when you have to go there,
   They have to take you in."

                              "I should have called it
Something you somehow haven't to deserve."   120

Warren leaned out and took a step or two,
Picked up a little stick, and brought it back
And broke it in his hand and tossed it by.
"Silas has better claim on us 'you think'
Than on his brother? Thirteen little miles
As the road winds would bring him to his door.   126
Silas has walked that far no doubt today.
Why didn't he go there? His brother's rich,
A somebody — director in the bank."
"He never told us that."

                              "We know it though."

"I think his brother ought to help, of course.   131
I'll see to that if there is need. He ought of right
To take him in, and might be willing to —
He may be better than appearances.

But have some pity on Silas. Do you think
If he'd had any pride in claiming kin   136
Or anything he looked for from his brother,
He'd keep so still about him all this time?"

"I wonder what's between them."

                                   "I can tell you.
Silas is what he is — we wouldn't mind him —   141
But just the kind that kinsfolk can't abide.
He never did a thing so very bad.
He don't know why he isn't quite as good
As anyone. He won't be made ashamed
To please his brother worthless though he is."   145

"*I* can't think Si ever hurt anyone."

"No, but he hurt my heart the way he lay
And rolled his old head on that sharp-edged chair
   back.
He wouldn't let me put him on the lounge.
You must go in and see what you can do.   150
I made the bed up for him there tonight.
You'll be suprised at him — how much he's broken.
His working days are done; I'm sure of it."

"I'd not be in a hurry to say that."

"I haven't been. Go, look, see for yourself.
But, Warren, please remember how it is: 156
He's come to help you ditch the meadow.
He has a plan. You mustn't laugh at him.
He may not speak of it, and then he may.
I'll sit and see if that small sailing cloud   160
Will hit or miss the moon."

                              It hit the moon.
Then there were three there, making a dim row,
The moon, the little silver cloud, and she.
Warren returned — too soon, it seemed to her,
Slipped to her side, caught up her hand and
   waited.   165

"Warren?" she questioned.

                              "Dead," was all he answered.

VIEWING THE AUTHOR'S IDEAS

1. How does the poet use natural settings to help reveal character? Who are the people in the poem? Do they appear real?

2. What contrasting standards of success are expressed in the poem?

3. Find the two definitions of home. How is each significant of the characters of Warren and Mary? What aspects in Mary's actions toward Warren throw light on human relationships?

EVALUATING HIS MANNER OF EXPRESSION

1. Find a descriptive passage that is noteworthy for the poet's choice of verbs which exactly fit the action.

2. Examine the two moonlight scenes for figurative language and for beauty of phrase.

3. Is the prevailing mood of the poem harshness or tenderness? Point out lines or passages to support your answer. Name any other emotions which the poem arouses in you and quote lines to illustrate.

4. The diction is not difficult to understand, yet the poem has great dignity. Can you give some reasons for this effect?

The Road Not Taken

Robert Frost

Frost here reflects on the results of having chosen one way rather than another at some point on life's highway. He observes that the choice made "all the difference."

Two roads diverged in a yellow wood,
And, sorry I could not travel both
And be one traveler, long I stood
And looked down one as far as I could
To where it bent in the undergrowth;

Then took the other, as just as fair,
And having perhaps the better claim,
Because it was grassy and wanted wear;
Though, as for that, the passing there
Had worn them really about the same.

And both that morning equally lay
In leaves no step had trodden black.
Oh, I kept the first for another day!
Yet knowing how way leads on to way,
I doubted if I should ever come back.

I shall be telling this with a sigh
Somewhere ages and ages hence:
Two roads diverged in a wood, and I —
I took the one less traveled by,
And that made all the difference.

VIEWING THE AUTHOR'S IDEAS

1. Why did Frost take one road in preference to the other? What unusual phrase does he use to inform us?

2. What was alike about the two roads? How were they different?

EVALUATING HIS MANNER OF EXPRESSION

1. Find two phrases that reveal the time of year.

2. Frost achieves an exceptional sound effect in the last stanza by the repetition of the letter *i*. Read the stanza aloud.

Birches

Robert Frost

Accurate description and optimistic viewpoint are merged in this poem. The birch trees on which Frost swung in his youth suggest a solution for the troubles of life. The branches help a man to get far enough away to see his difficulties in perspective. Then they bring him back to earth with an energizing bound.

WHEN I see birches bend to left and right
Across the lines of straighter darker trees,
I like to think some boy's been swinging them.
But swinging doesn't bend them down to stay.
Ice storms do that. Often you must have seen them   5
Loaded with ice a sunny winter morning
After a rain. They click upon themselves
As the breeze rises, and turn many-colored
As the stir cracks and crazes their enamel.
Soon the sun's warmth makes them shed
      crystal shells   10
Shattering and avalanching on the snow crust—
Such heaps of broken glass to sweep away
You'd think the inner dome of heaven had fallen.
They are dragged to the withered bracken[1]
      by the load,
And they seem not to break; though, once they are
      bowed   15
So low for long, they never right themselves;
You may see their trunks arching in the woods
Years afterwards, trailing their leaves on the ground
Like girls on hands and knees that throw their hair
Before them over their heads to dry in the sun.   20
But I was going to say when Truth broke in
With all her matter-of-fact about the ice storm,
I should prefer to have some boy bend them
As he went out and in to fetch the cows—
Some boy too far from town to learn baseball,   25
Whose only play was what he found himself,
Summer or winter, and could play alone.
One by one he subdued[2] his father's trees
By riding them down over and over again
Until he took the stiffness out of them,   30

And not one but hung limp, not one was left
For him to conquer. He learned all there was
To learn about not launching out too soon
And so not carrying the tree away
Clear to the ground. He always kept his poise   35
To the top branches, climbing carefully
With the same pains you use to fill a cup
Up to the brim, and even above the brim.
Then he flung outward, feet first, with a swish,
Kicking his way down through the air to
      the ground.   40
So was I once myself a swinger of birches;
And so I dream of going back to be.
It's when I'm weary of considerations,
And life is too much like a pathless wood
Where your face burns and tickles with
      the cobwebs   45
Broken across it, and one eye is weeping
From a twig's having lashed across it open.
I'd like to get away from earth awhile
And then come back to it and begin over.
May no fate willfully misunderstand me   50
And half grant what I wish and snatch me away
Not to return. Earth's the right place for love;
I don't know where it's likely to go better.
I'd like to go by climbing a birch tree,
And climb black branches up a snow-white trunk   55
Toward heaven, till the tree could bear no more,
But dipped its top and set me down again.
That would be good both going and coming back.
One could do worse than be a swinger of birches.

VIEWING THE AUTHOR'S IDEAS

1. What causes the birches to bend permanently?
2. Lines 5-13 present a description of sun upon icy branches. Find the words which describe (a) the sound of cracking ice (b) the appearance of sunlight on the ice and snow.
3. What simile in lines 17-20 describes the curves of the branches?
4. By what means are all the branches finally conquered?
5. What precautions should the swinger take?

---

[1] *bracken*, a large, coarse fern.
[2] *subdued*, conquered.

6. How does one fill a cup to the brim? Why is this figure effective in describing the boy's ascent into the tree?

7. Lines 40 and 41 describe the descending swing. How have you enjoyed something similar to this?

8. To what does the poet compare the painful and disagreeable aspects of life?

9. Why would the poet seek the birch trees when in trouble? What opinions about an afterlife are suggested?

EVALUATING HIS MANNER OF EXPRESSION

1. Select five verb forms that are especially expressive.

2. What is the significance of putting the word *toward* in italics?

3. Note the musical qualities of lines 6-16.

Stopping by Woods on a Snowy Evening

Robert Frost

Frost has infused into this brief poem his great love of the New England winter scene. The softly-drifting snow, blanketing the woodland, lures the farmer to tarry on his way home.

WHOSE woods these are I think I know.
His house is in the village though;
He will not see me stopping here
To watch his woods fill up with snow.

My little horse must think it queer
To stop without a farmhouse near
Between the woods and frozen lake
The darkest evening of the year.

He gives his harness bells a shake
To ask if there is some mistake.
The only other sound's the sweep
Of easy wind and downy flake.

The woods are lovely, dark and deep,
But I have promises to keep
And miles to go before I sleep,
And miles to go before I sleep.

VIEWING THE AUTHOR'S IDEAS

1. What prompts the poet to watch the snow in the woods? Describe the picture presented.

2. How does the poet reveal his personality in these lines?

EVALUATING HIS MANNER OF EXPRESSION

1. To what sense does the poem appeal? Cite phrases that carry this sense appeal.

2. Read the last stanza aloud and try to determine the effect of the repetition.

3. Indicate the unusual rhyme scheme. How does it contrast with the extreme simplicity of Frost's language?

The Runaway

Robert Frost

In the most ordinary experience, Frost can discover a hint of the unusual that labels it material for poetry. Here the simple act of watching a colt making its first acquaintance with snow stirs the poet's sympathy.

ONCE when the snow of the year was beginning to fall,
We stopped by a mountain pasture to say, "Whose colt?"

A little Morgan[1] had one forefoot on the wall,
The other curled at his breast. He dipped his head
And snorted at us. And then he had to bolt.
We heard the miniature thunder where he fled,
And we saw him, or thought we saw him, dim and
    gray,
Like a shadow against the curtain of falling flakes.
"I think the little fellow's afraid of the snow.
He isn't winter broken. It isn't play
With the little fellow at all. He's running away.
I doubt if even his mother could tell him,
    'Sakes,
It's only weather.' He'd think she didn't know!
Where is his mother? He can't be out alone."
And now he comes with a clatter of stone
And mounts the wall again with whited eyes
And all his tail that isn't hair up straight.

[1] *Morgan*, a celebrated American breed of horses.

He shudders his coat as if to throw off flies.
"Whoever it is that leaves him out so late,
When other creatures have gone to stall and bin,
Ought to be told to come and take him in."

VIEWING THE AUTHOR'S IDEAS

1. Does Frost's description of the little Morgan's action seem natural or exaggerated? Does Frost understand animals?

2. Follow the poet's train of reflection as he watches the colt. In what lines can you detect a subtle reference to human behavior?

EVALUATING HIS MANNER OF EXPRESSION

1. "Miniature thunder" and "winter broken" are arresting and pleasing. Find similar expressions. What is the significant word in the sentence: "And then he had to bolt"?

2. Which lines picture the colt's movements?

Night Clouds

Amy Lowell

Amy Lowell's poetry has been criticized for lack of emotion. "Night Clouds" justifies the criticism, for its lines do not stir us emotionally. Our senses of sight and of hearing, however, respond eagerly to the brilliant color and images that are like finely-cut jewels lying in a velvet case — cold and hard, since nobody is wearing them.

THE white mares of the moon rush along the sky
    Beating their golden hoofs upon the glass
        heavens;
The white mares of the moon are all standing on their
        hind legs
Pawing at the green porcelain doors of the remote
        heavens.
Fly, mares!   5
Strain your utmost,
Scatter the milky dust of stars,
Or the tiger sun will leap upon you and destroy you
With one lick of his vermilion tongue.

VIEWING THE AUTHOR'S IDEAS

1. At what time might you see this picture?

2. What are the "white mares of the moon"? Why must they "rush along the sky"?

3. Can you recall any cloud shapes that you have watched? Describe them.

EVALUATING HER MANNER OF EXPRESSION

1. The vividness of expression in this short poem results from the use of color and of striking, unusual imagery. Select lines to illustrate both characteristics.

2. Make a list of the verb forms. Do they meet the imagist requirement of accuracy of word choice? What peculiar effect do they create?

3. What two figures of speech are combined in the first four lines?

A Lady

Amy Lowell

This picture of a lady is as fragile as a cameo set in delicate gold fretwork.

YOU are beautiful and faded
  Like an old opera tune
Played upon a harpsichord;
Or like the sun-flooded silks
Of an eighteenth-century boudoir.   5
In your eyes
Smolder the fallen roses of outlived minutes,
And the perfume of your soul
Is vague and suffusing,
With the pungence of sealed spice jars.   10
Your half tones delight me,
And I grow mad with gazing
At your blent colors.
My vigor is a new-minted penny,
Which I cast at your feet.   15
Gather it up from the dust,
That its sparkle may amuse you.

VIEWING THE AUTHOR'S IDEAS

1. The term *half tones* is the key to the meaning of the poem. One of the half tones is the tempered strains of an old melody played upon a harpsichord. Be sure that you know the meaning of half tone, and then find other examples.

2. From what you know of Amy Lowell's life and activity, how appropriate are the phrases "My vigor," "new-minted penny," and "sparkle"? What qualities of the new-minted penny make the coin a good contrast to the objects mentioned in the first part of the poem?

EVALUATING HER MANNER OF EXPRESSION

1. What figures of speech run through the first ten lines of the poem? What is the figure in line 14?

2. Name the three senses to which the poem appeals. Which lines please you most? Why?

Chicago

Carl Sandburg

This is a poem that has caused much controversy. As you read, decide whether or not you like the way in which Sandburg flaunts the crude strength of a great American city. Some of Sandburg's lines bristle with the conviction that modern industrialism can be made the subject matter of poetry.

HOG Butcher for the World,
  Toolmaker, Stacker of Wheat,
Player with Railroads and the Nation's Freight Handler;
Stormy, husky, brawling,
City of the Big Shoulders: 5

They tell me you are wicked and I believe them, for I have seen your painted women under the gas lamps
   luring the farm boys.
And they tell me you are crooked and I answer: Yes, It is true I have seen the gunman kill and go free to
   kill again.
And they tell me you are brutal and my reply is: On the faces of women and children I have seen the marks
   of wanton hunger.
And having answered so I turn once more to those who sneer at this my city, and I give them back the sneer
   and say to them:
Come and show me another city with lifted head singing so proud to be alive and coarse and strong
   and cunning.   10
Flinging magnetic curses amid the toil of piling job on job, here is a tall bold slugger set vivid against the
   little soft cities;
Fierce as a dog with tongue lapping for action, cunning as a savage pitted against the wilderness,
         Bareheaded,
         Shoveling,
         Wrecking,   15
         Planning,
         Building, breaking, rebuilding.
Under the smoke, dust all over his mouth, laughing with white teeth,
Under the terrible burden of destiny laughing as a young man laughs,
Laughing even as an ignorant fighter laughs who has never lost a battle,   20
Bragging and laughing that under his wrist is the pulse, and under his ribs the heart of the people,

                          Laughing!

Laughing the stormy, husky, brawling laughter of Youth, half-naked, sweating, proud to be Hog Butcher,
   Toolmaker, Stacker of Wheat, Player with Railroads and Freight Handler to the Nation.

VIEWING THE AUTHOR'S IDEAS

1. To what industrial aspects of Chicago does the poet allude in the first five lines?

2. What qualities of the city unite to make it distinctly American?

3. In comparing the city to a human being, how does Sandburg attribute to Chicago coarse traits; vigorous action; rugged appearance?

4. Since Sandburg accepts the city as wicked, crooked, and brutal, what does he find to praise? What aspects of Chicago life does Sandburg omit? Had the poet included all phases of city life, how would the atmosphere of the poem have been changed?

EVALUATING HIS MANNER OF EXPRESSION

1. Try to read the poem as you would a piece of prose. What poetic qualities do you detect as you read?

2. Sandburg's poetry has been called coarse and brutal. Do you think the author of "Chicago" can be justified on the score that he is dealing with brutality? Would it have been possible to achieve the same effect in more refined terms? Do you consider the effect worth accomplishing?

The Hangman at Home

Carl Sandburg

Carl Sandburg can write in a rugged, burly manner about realistic themes, or he can tenderly record some subtle mood. In this poem he blends his two types of approach by treating an unusual subject with a light and sympathetic touch.

WHAT does the hangman think about
When he goes home at night from work?
When he sits down with his wife and
Children for a cup of coffee and a
Plate of ham and eggs, do they ask   5
Him if it was a good day's work
And everything went well, or do they
Stay off some topics and talk about
The weather, baseball, politics,
And the comic strips in the papers   10
And the movies. Do they look at his
Hands when he reaches for the coffee
Or the ham and eggs? If the little
Ones say, Daddy, play horse, here's
A rope — does he answer like a joke: 15
I seen enough rope for today?
Or does his face light up like a
Bonfire of joy and does he say:
It's a good and dandy world we live
In. And if a white face moon looks   20

In through the window where a baby girl
Sleeps and the moon gleams mix with
Baby ears and baby hair — the hangman —
How does he act then? It must be easy
For him. Anything is easy for a hangman,   25
I guess.

VIEWING THE AUTHOR'S IDEAS

1. Why is the hangman an unusual subject for poetry? Should a hangman's life be different from that of other men?

2. What is the poet's view about the daily existence of the hangman? State the lines which prove your view.

3. What does the hangman *really* think about?

4. What passage makes you think that Sandburg may have been thinking of one of his own little girls?

EVALUATING HIS MANNER OF EXPRESSION

1. Does Sandburg make you feel sorry for the hangman? What is the mood of the poem?

2. Except for three or four lines, the language of the poem has little to recommend it as poetry. One reason is the inartistic use of idiom. Compare this poem with Frost's "The Death of the Hired Man" and discuss the difference.

3. The last two lines are mildly ironic. Point out three other examples of irony.

Lost

Carl Sandburg

A simple description of the lake at night and the whistle of a boat telling that it is in trouble furnishes the feeling of aloneness in these lines.

DESOLATE and lone
All night long on the lake
Where fog trails and mist creeps,
The whistle of a boat
Calls and cries unendingly   5

Like some lost child
In tears and trouble
Hunting the harbor's breast
And the harbor's eyes.

VIEWING THE AUTHOR'S IDEAS

1. Does the title suit the poem? Explain why.

2. Which line gives the reason for the boat's trouble?

Abraham Lincoln Walks at Midnight

Vachel Lindsay

Born and reared within sight of the Lincoln Mausoleum at Springfield, Illinois, Lindsay from youth held the great President as his idol. In this poem he attributes to Lincoln some of the qualities of a mythical folk hero. He envisions the mourning figure of the President pacing the streets of Springfield at the outbreak of World War I, unable to rest because of the misery in the world. As contrasted with the stirring, noisy measures of "The Congo" and "The Santa Fé Trail," these lines are written in the slow, majestic movement that admirably suits the reverent mood of the poem.

IT is portentous, and a thing of state
That here at midnight, in our little town
A mourning figure walks, and will not rest,
Near the old courthouse pacing up and down.

Or by his homestead, or in shadowed yards   5
He lingers where his children used to play,
Or through the market, on well-worn stones
He stalks until the dawn stars burn away.

A bronzed, lank man! His suit of ancient black,
A famous high top hat and plain worn shawl   10
Make him the quaint great figure that men love,
The prairie lawyer, master of us all.

He cannot sleep upon his hillside now.
He is among us: — as in times before!
And we who toss and lie awake for long   15
Breathe deep, and start, to see him pass the door.

His head is bowed. He thinks on men and kings.
Yea, when the sick world cries, how can he sleep?

Too many peasants fight, they know not why,   19
Too many homesteads in black terror weep.

The sins of all war lords burn his heart.
He sees the dreadnoughts scouring every main.
He carries on his shawl-wrapped shoulders now
The bitterness, the folly, and the pain.

He cannot rest until a spirit dawn   25
Shall come; — the shining hope of Europe free:
The league of sober folk, the workers' earth,
Bringing long peace to Cornland, Alp, and Sea.

It breaks his heart that kings must murder still,
That all his hours of travail here for men   30
Seem yet in vain. And who will bring white peace
That he may sleep upon his hill again?

VIEWING THE AUTHOR'S IDEAS

1. Which lines allude to World War I? Choose phrases that might apply to the war that followed.

2. What specific reasons does the poet give for the restlessness of Lincoln's spirit? What places does the President's spirit visit? State the significance of these places.

3. In a single sentence express the leading idea of this poem.

EVALUATING HIS MANNER OF EXPRESSION

1. What emotion dominates the poem? Select lines to illustrate.

2. Why is the ending effective?

3. Choose two lines which you consider good poetic expression. Explain the meaning of "white peace."

Franciscan Aspiration

Vachel Lindsay

Many of Lindsay's poems must be read with the ear in order to appreciate the remarkable sound effects, but "Franciscan Aspiration" should be read with the heart. It expresses accurately the poet's religious feeling and his great admiration for the Franciscan spirit of poverty.

WOULD I might wake Saint Francis in you all,
    Brother of birds and trees, God's Troubadour,
Blinded with weeping for the sad and poor;
Our wealth undone, all strict Franciscan men,
Come, let us chant the canticle again   5
Of mother earth and the enduring sun.
God make each soul the lowly leper's slave;
God make us saints, and brave.

VIEWING THE AUTHOR'S IDEAS

1. Is "God's Troubadour" a suitable title for St. Francis? Why? Why does Lindsay call him "Brother of birds and trees"? Explain the reference to the canticle of "mother earth and the enduring sun."

2. Judging from the sentiment of this short poem, what qualities does Lindsay think make a saint? Do you agree with his conception of sainthood?

EVALUATING HIS MANNER OF EXPRESSION

1. Is the poem noteworthy for thought or for expression?

2. What emotional reaction do you feel while reading the poem?

Arcturus in Autumn

Sara Teasdale

Looking upon the bright star Arcturus in the October twilight, Sara Teasdale suddenly became conscious that her youth had passed. In a note to an editor describing this experience, she observed that she had never seen Arcturus more beautiful:

"Watching it sink and vanish, I found myself saying the first lines of this poem; and the others followed easily and naturally."

WHEN, in the October dusk,
    I saw you near to setting,
  Arcturus, bringer of spring,
Lord of the summer nights, leaving us now in autumn,
  Having no pity on our withering;
Oh, then I knew at last that my own autumn was
      upon me,
  I felt it in my blood,
Restless as dwindling streams that still remember
  The music of their flood.

There in the thickening dark a windbent tree above me
  Loosed its last leaves in flight —
I saw you sink and vanish, pitiless Arcturus,
  You will not stay to share our lengthening night.

VIEWING THE AUTHOR'S IDEAS

1. With what autumnal signs does the poet identify the closing years of life?

2. What awareness comes to the poet? Substitute literal terms for the figurative phrase "music of their flood."

3. Which of the following emotions are reflected in this poem: (a) despair (b) bitterness (c) regret (d) loneliness? Explain your choice.

EVALUATING HER MANNER OF EXPRESSION

In how many different ways does the poet refer to the star?

The Net

Sara Teasdale

Occasionally everyone realizes the inadequacy of words to express his emotion. The poet here uses her magical word power to depict this experience.

I MADE you many and many a song,
  Yet never told you all you are —
It was as though a net of words
   Were flung to catch a star;

It was as though I curved my hand
   And dipped sea water eagerly,
Only to find it lost the blue,
   Dark splendor of the sea.

VIEWING THE AUTHOR'S IDEAS

1. To what two things does the poet compare the person? What admirable human qualities are implied in these comparisons?
2. Show the inadequacy of the "net of words" and the handful of sea water for the purpose desired.
3. Describe the personality of one to whom these words might apply.

EVALUATING HER MANNER OF EXPRESSION

1. To what senses do the last six lines appeal?
2. What colors do you find in the poem?

Let It Be Forgotten

Sara Teasdale

In these two quatrains the poet gives us a gay melody and stirs our curiosity as to what should be forgotten.

L ET it be forgotten as a flower is forgotten,
   Forgotten as a fire that once was singing gold;
Let it be forgotten forever and forever;
   Time is a kind friend; he will make us old.

If anyone asks, say it was forgotten
   Long and long ago,
As a flower, as a fire, as a hushed footfall
   In a long forgotten snow.

VIEWING THE AUTHOR'S IDEAS

1. Sara Teasdale generally treats the love theme in one of its variations: joy, grief, ecstasy, or suffering. In which mood are these lines written?
2. Explain the last two lines of the poem.

EVALUATING HER MANNER OF EXPRESSION

1. How is the effect of stillness achieved?
2. The poet uses the word *forgotten* many times within these lines, yet the repetition is not dull. What other words are repeated without dullness?
3. What lines bring images to your mind? Analyze the phrase "singing gold."

Silence

Edgar Lee Masters

This poem reflects the dignity and splendor of the human being. So penetrating are the observations it offers that there is little to discuss after reading the poem. One wishes merely to acknowledge its truth.

I HAVE known the silence of the stars and of the sea,
And the silence of the city when it pauses,
And the silence of a man and a maid,
And the silence for which music alone finds the word,
And the silence of the woods before the winds of
    spring begin,   5
And the silence of the sick
When their eyes roam about the room.
And I ask: For the depths
Of what use is language?
A beast of the field moans a few times   10
When death takes its young.
And we are voiceless in the presence of realities —
We cannot speak.

A curious boy asks an old soldier
Sitting in front of the grocery store,   15
"How did you lose your leg?"
And the old soldier is struck with silence,
Or his mind flies away
Because he cannot concentrate it on Gettysburg.
It comes back jocosely,   20
And he says, "A bear bit it off."
And the boy wonders, while the old soldier
Dumbly, feebly lives over
The flashes of guns, the thunder of cannon,
The shrieks of the slain,   25
And himself lying on the ground,
And the hospital surgeons, the knives,
And the long days in bed.
But if he could describe it all,
He would be an artist.   30
But if he were an artist, there would be deeper wounds
Which he could not describe.

There is the silence of a great hatred,
And the silence of a great love,
And the silence of a deep peace of mind,   35
And the silence of an embittered friendship.
There is the silence of a spiritual crisis,
Through which your soul, exquisitely tortured,
Comes with visions not to be uttered
Into a realm of higher life,   40
And the silence of the gods who understand each other
    without speech.
There is the silence of defeat.
There is the silence of those unjustly punished;
And the silence of the dying whose hand
Suddenly grips yours.   45
There is the silence between father and son,
When the father cannot explain his life,
Even though he be misunderstood for it.

There is the silence that comes between husband and
    wife;
There is the silence of those who have failed;   50
And the vast silence that covers
Broken nations and vanquished leaders.
There is the silence of Lincoln,
Thinking of the poverty of his youth.
And the silence of Napoleon   55
After Waterloo.
And the silence of Jeanne d'Arc
Saying amid the flames, "Blessed Jesus" —
Revealing in two words all sorrow, all hope.
And there is the silence of age,   60
Too full of wisdom for the tongue to utter it
In words intelligible to those who have not lived
The great range of life.
And there is the silence of the dead.
If we who are in life cannot speak   65
Of profound experiences,
Why do you marvel that the dead
Do not tell you of death?
Their silence shall be interpreted
As we approach them.   70

1. What is the poet's attitude toward spoken language? Why are we "voiceless in the presence of realities"?

2. Explain why the soldier did not attempt to describe his war experience. To what "deeper wounds" does the poet refer in line 31?

3. Give the thought of the lines which constitute the climax.

4. What power does the literary artist possess which enables him to break the silence of a profound experience?

1. In what ways would a more rigid verse form have altered the poet's manner of expression?

2. Critics rank this poem as one of Masters' best. What literary qualities does it possess?

Lucinda Matlock

Edgar Lee Masters

Edgar Lee Masters published a book in 1915 which became instantly popular, Spoon River Anthology. *The work was a series of epitaphs for residents in an imaginary Illinois town. In each poem the dead person tells the real story of his life. Masters took the plan of the book from a collection of ancient epigrams, the* Greek Anthology; *but in spirit and in form the verses exemplify the new freedom in poetry. In the free verse of the period and under the guise of the ghosts of Spoon River, Masters parades before his readers all sorts of vice with only a meager sprinkling of virtue. "Lucinda Matlock" is one of the bright figures in this procession of human misery.*

I WENT to the dances at Chandlerville
And played snap-out at Winchester.
One time we changed partners,
Driving home in the moonlight of middle June,
And then I found Davis.   5
We were married and lived together for seventy years,
Enjoying, working, raising the twelve children,
Eight of whom we lost
Ere I had reached the age of sixty.
I spun, I wove, I kept the house, I nursed the sick   10
I made the garden, and for holiday
Rambled over the fields where sang the larks,
And by Spoon River gathering many a shell,
And many a flower and medicinal weed —
Shouting to the wooded hills, singing to the green
   valleys.   15

At ninety-six I had lived enough, that is all —
And passed to a sweet repose.
What is this I hear of sorrow and weariness,
Anger, discontent, and drooping hopes?
Degenerate sons and daughters,   20
Life is too strong for you —
It takes life to love Life.

1. How would you describe the life of Lucinda Matlock?

2. Choose three adjectives from the following list which best describe her character: courageous, practical, joyous, sad, industrious, forlorn, optimistic, moody, self-centered, energetic. Give reasons for your choice.

3. What sorrows did Lucinda have? What is your impression of her as mother of a family? List the kinds of activity that occupied her life. Why does she regard the sons and daughters as degenerate?

4. Write in your own words the meaning of the last two lines. Show that Lucinda's explanation of the source of human strength is not complete.

1. Select the two lines that you think are most poetically expressed.

2. Where does the mood of the poem change?

Anne Rutledge

Edgar Lee Masters

"Anne Rutledge," another of the character sketches from Spoon River Anthology, *is a tender tribute to the sweetheart of Lincoln's youth. The daughter of Lincoln's landlord at New Salem, Illinois, Anne died in her youth from malaria fever, causing her lover great grief. The poem suggests the inspiration which her memory gave to Lincoln throughout life.*

O UT of me unworthy and unknown
The vibrations of deathless music;
"With malice toward none, with charity for all."
Out of me the forgiveness of millions toward millions,
And the beneficent face of a nation   5
Shining with justice and truth.
I am Anne Rutledge who sleep beneath these weeds,
Beloved in life of Abraham Lincoln,

Wedded to him, not through union,
But through separation,   10
Bloom forever, O Republic,
From the dust of my bosom!

VIEWING THE AUTHOR'S IDEAS

1. According to this poem, in what way did Anne Rutledge influence American events?
2. From which of Lincoln's addresses is the third line quoted?
3. To what historical facts do lines 4-6 refer?

EVALUATING HIS MANNER OF EXPRESSION

1. Explain the paradox in lines 9-10.
2. What figure of speech do you find in the last two lines?

Prayer of a Soldier in France

Joyce Kilmer

Like all soldiers in the line of battle, Kilmer learned the meaning of pain, but in suffering he found union with God.

M Y shoulders ache beneath my pack
(Lie easier, Cross, upon His back)

I march with feet that burn and smart
(Tread, Holy Feet, upon my heart.)

Men shout at me who may not speak
(They scourged Thy back and smote Thy cheek)

I may not lift a hand to clear
My eyes of salty drops that sear.

(Then shall my fickle soul forget
Thy agony of Bloody Sweat)

My rifle hand is stiff and numb
(From Thy pierced palm red rivers come)

Lord, Thou didst suffer more for me
Than all the hosts of land and sea.

So, let me render back again
This millionth of Thy gift. Amen.

VIEWING THE AUTHOR'S IDEAS

1. How does the poet transform suffering and privation into prayer?
2. Which lines summarize the idea of the poem? What is the purpose of the parentheses?
3. What is the Catholic view concerning the endurance of suffering?

Experience

Aline Kilmer

A mother as well as a poet, Aline Kilmer here lyrically observes her little daughter's first consciousness of self.

DEBORAH danced, when she was two,
As buttercups and daffodils do;
Spirited, frail, naïvely bold,
Her hair a ruffled crest of gold,
And whenever she spoke, her voice went singing
Like water up from a fountain springing.

But now her step is quiet and slow;
She walks the way primroses go;
Her hair is yellow instead of gilt;
Her voice is losing its lovely lilt,
And in place of her wild, delightful ways
A quaint precision rules her days.

For Deborah now is three, and oh,
She knows so much that she did not know.

VIEWING THE AUTHOR'S IDEAS

1. Contrast the two pictures of Deborah. In what respect is she compared to certain flowers; to gold; to a fountain?
2. Have you observed changes in children similar to those recorded by the poet?

EVALUATING HER MANNER OF EXPRESSION

Show how accurate details have been given a poetic interpretation in this poem.

I Shall Not Be Afraid

Aline Kilmer

With her husband's departure for war, the poet finds herself no longer fearful when making the house safe for the night. A deeper emotion has supplanted fear — that of sorrow.

I SHALL not be afraid any more,
Either by night or day;
What would it profit me to be afraid
With you away?
Now I am brave. In the dark night alone,
All through the house I go,
Locking the doors and making windows fast
When sharp winds blow.

For there is only sorrow in my heart,
There is no room for fear.

But how I wish I were afraid again,
My dear, my dear!

VIEWING THE AUTHOR'S IDEAS

1. Why would it be useless for the wife to be afraid during her husband's absence? What is implied concerning the husband's power to dispel fear?
2. In what household task is the wife's bravery shown? Why is there no room for fear in her heart?

EVALUATING HER MANNER OF EXPRESSION

1. What unexpected idea does the last stanza contain? How does her emotion justify her altered view?

Heat

(From *Garden*)
Hilda Doolittle

In this apostrophe to the wind the poet asks for help against the assaults of the heat. She achieves the peculiar effect of a stifling heat by following carefully three principles of the imagists: direct treatment, economy of words, and sequence of musical phrase.

O WIND, rend open the heat,
cut apart the heat,
rend it to tatters.

Fruit cannot drop
through this thick air —   5
fruit cannot fall into heat
that presses up and blunts
the points of pears
and rounds the grapes.

Cut the heat —   10
plough through it,
turning it on either side
of your path.

VIEWING THE AUTHOR'S IDEAS

Several clauses of parallel construction carry the thought of the poem; "rend open the heat" is one of them. Find several others.

EVALUATING HER MANNER OF EXPRESSION

1. Observe that every word in the poem contributes to the meaning and that few are longer than one syllable. Select three phrases as examples of accurate expression.

2. What images come to you as you read? Choose the one which pleases you most and comment on it.

Quivira

Arthur Guiterman

In his long wanderings, Cabeza de Vaca had heard rumors of Indians who dwelt in seven golden towns called the Cities of Cibola. Before sending Coronado to seek this wealth, the Spanish viceroy of Mexico dispatched Fray Marcos de Niza in 1539 to discover the truth of the report. Taking with him the Moor, Estevanico, who had been one of Cabeza de Vaca's companions, Fray Marcos walked until he came to the pueblos of the Zuñi Indians. Narrowly escaping the death that Estevanico met from the natives, the friar approached close enough to observe the pueblos—terraced houses of adobe—cliffs, mesas, colorful rock formations, and blue sky. Here indeed, thought Fray Marcos, were cities of advanced civilization. Less interested in gold than in souls, he named the cities The New Kingdom of St. Francis and returned to Mexico. His reports of his discoveries have been the topic of great discussion. Whatever opinion one may adopt concerning them, these reports became the basis for fabulous accounts of newly-discovered wealth. Small wonder, then, that when the friar retraced his steps to guide the expedition of Coronado, the soldiers were disappointed. When Coronado reached the Tiguex pueblos in New Mexico, the Indians raised his hopes by telling him of the golden city of Quivira in the far north. In the spring of 1541 he pushed as far northward as the Indians had directed him to go. The place where he terminated his march has been the matter of much dispute. Sites have been suggested in Kansas, Nebraska, and Texas. Wherever it was, Coronado found not glittering streets but the beaten paths of the buffalo. Only one man was not disappointed. A Franciscan priest, Fray Juan de Padilla, wished so much to work among the Indians of the plains that after he left Quivira with Coronado's men, he returned to labor among the newly-found tribes in 1542. Attacked by a hostile group of natives, Fray Juan knelt down on the broad plains to receive the arrows which made him the first martyr of the United States.

F RANCISCO CORONADO rode forth with all his train,
     Eight hundred savage bowmen, three hundred spears of Spain,
   To seek the rumored glory that pathless deserts hold —
   The City of Quivira[1] whose walls are rich with gold.

Oh, gay they rode with plume on crest and gilded spur at heel;   5
With gonfalon[2] of Aragon and banner of Castile;[3]
While High Emprise[4] and Joyous Youth, twin marshals[5] of the throng,
Awoke Sonora's[6] mountain peaks with trumpet note and song,

   Beside that brilliant army, beloved by serf and lord,
   There walked as brave a soldier as ever smote with sword,   10
   Though nought of knightly harness his russet gown revealed —
   The cross he bore as weapon; the missal was his shield.

But rugged oaths were changed to prayers, and angry hearts grew tame,
And fainting spirits waxed in faith where Fray Padilla came;
And brawny spearmen bowed their heads to kiss the helpful hand   15
Of him who spake the simple truth that brave men understand.

   What pen may paint this daring — those doughty cavaliers!
   The cities of the Zuñi[7] were humbled by their spears;
   And Arizona's barrens grew pallid in the glow
   Of swords that won Granada[8] and conquered Mexico.   20

They fared by lofty Acoma; their rally call was blown
Where Colorado rushes down through God-hewn walls of stone;
Still, North and East, where deserts spread and treeless prairies rolled,
A Fairy City lured them on with pinnacles of gold.

   Through all their weary marches, in all their pain and dole,   25
   They turned to Fray Padilla for aid of heart and soul.
   He bound the wounds that lance-thrust and flinty arrow made;
   He cheered the sick and failing; above the dead he prayed.

Two thousand miles of war and woe behind their banners lay;
And sadly fever, drought, and toil had lessened their array,   30
When came a message fraught with hope for all the steadfast band:
"Good tidings from the northward, friends! Quivira lies at hand!"

   How joyously they spurred them! How sadly drew the rein!
   Here gleamed no golden palace; there blazed no jeweled fane;
   Rude tents of hide of bison, dog guarded, met their view —   35
   A squalid Indian village, the lodges of the Sioux.[9]

---

[1] *Quivira* (kē̆-vē'rä).

[2] *gonfalon*, a standard used by meieval princes.

[3] *Aragon … Castile*, former kingdoms of Spain.

[4] *emprise*, adventure; endeavor.

[5] *marshals*, those who direct processions or military operations.

[6] *Sonora*, a state in northern Mexico.

[7] *Zuñi*, the pueblo Indians of western New Mexico.

[8] *Granada*, a province of Spain.

[9] *Sioux*, a warlike Indian tribe of the Northwest.

Then Coronado bowed his head; he spake unto his men:
"Our quest is vain, true hearts of Spain; now turn we home again.
And would to God that I could give that phantom city's pride
In ransom for the gallant souls that here have sunk and died!" 40

Back, back to Compostela[10] the wayworn handful bore;
But sturdy Fray Padilla took up the quest once more.
His soul still longed for conquest, though not by lance and sword;
He burned to show the heathen the pathway to the Lord.

Again he trudged the flinty hills and parching desert sands; 45
And few were they that walked with him, and weaponless their hands —
But faithfully the man-at-arms, Decampo, rode him near,
Like Greatheart[11] warding Christian's way through wastes of Doubt and Fear.

Where still in silken harvests the prairie lilies toss,
Among the red Quiviras, Padilla reared his cross. 50
Within its sacred shadows the warriors of the Kaw[12]
In wonder heard the gospel of love and peace and law.

They gloried in their brown-robed priest; and oft in twilight's gold
The tribesmen grouped, a silent ring, to hear the tale he told;
While round the kindly man-at-arms their lithe-limbed children played 55
And shot their arrows at his shield and rode his guarded blade.

When thrice the silver crescent had filled its curving shell,
The friar rose at dawning and bade his flock farewell:
" — And if your brothers northward be cruel, as ye say,
My Master bids me seek them — and dare I answer, 'Nay'?" 60

But where, unfaltering, he trod the path of thorns once more,
A savage cohort swept the plain in paint and plume of war.
Then Fray Padilla spake to them whose hearts were most his own:
"My children, bear the tidings home; let me die here alone."

He knelt upon the prairie, begirt by yelling Sioux — 65
"Forgive them, O my Father, they know not what they do!"
The twanging bowstrings answered. Before his eyes unrolled
The City of Quivira whose streets are paved with gold.

---

10 *Compostela*, a city in New Galicia, a former province of western Mexico.

11 *Greatheart*, in Bunyan's *Pilgrim's Progress*, the guide of Christian's wife and children upon their journey to the Celestial City.

12 *Kaw*, the Kansa, a western Indian tribe occupying the territory of Kansas.

VIEWING THE AUTHOR'S IDEAS

1. Describe Coronado's expedition as it sets forth; as it returned. How did Fray Padilla differ from the others in dress, in motive? By what means does the author represent him as a very good man?

2. How far did the explorers travel? What places did they visit? What success had they; what failure? Instead of Quivira, the city of gold, what did they find? Did any of them reach Quivira? Explain the last two lines of the poem.

3. Name two Indian tribes which appear in the story. What had Fray Padilla to do with each? Who was his companion? What English classic is referred to in stanza 12?

1. Observe the expressions "rode him near," line 47, and "spake his flock farewell," line 58. Is this kind of language suitable to the old tale the author is telling? Would it be the proper style for a more recent incident?

2. Explain the following terms: *gonfalon, doughty, fane, guarded blade, crescent.*

3. What emotional effects do you find? Quote lines or stanzas to illustrate them.

4. Mention the figure of speach in stanzas 2, 5, 6, 16.

Daniel Boone

Arthur Guiterman

The early days of America saw scouts and trappers pushing into the wilderness. Stories of their feats were so extraordinary that these pioneers now loom up as legendary figures. They were, in reality, simple-hearted men with a love of freedom and adventure. One such eminent scout was Daniel Boone.

DANIEL BOONE at twenty-one
Came with his tomahawk, knife, and gun
Home from the French and Indian War
To North Carolina and the Yadkin[1] shore.
He married his maid with a golden band,   5
Builded his house and cleared his land;
But the deep woods claimed their son again,
And he turned his face from the homes of men.
Over the Blue Ridge, dark and lone,
The Mountains of Iron, the Hills of Stone,   10
Braving the Shawnee's[2] jealous wrath,
He made his way on the Warrior's Path.
Alone he trod the shadowed trails;
But he was the lord of a thousand vales
As he roved Kentucky, far and near,   15
Hunting the buffalo, elk, and deer.
What joy to see, what joy to win
So fair a land for his kith and kin,
Of streams unstained and woods unhewn!
"Elbowroom!" laughed Daniel Boone.   20

On the Wilderness Road that his axmen made,
The settlers flocked to the first stockade;
The deerskin shirts and the coonskin caps
Filed through the glens and the mountain gaps;
And hearts were high in the fateful spring   25
When the land said, "Nay!" to the stubborn king.

While the men of the East of farm and town
Strove with the troops of the British Crown,
Daniel Boone, from a surge of hate,
Guarded a nation's westward gate.   30
Down on the fort in a wave of flame
The Shawnee horde and the Mingo came,
And the stout logs shook in a storm of lead;
But Boone stood firm, and the savage fled.
Peace! And the settlers flocked anew;   35
The farm lands spread; the townlands grew;
But Daniel Boone was ill at ease
When he saw the smoke in the forest trees.
"There'll be no game in the country soon.
Elbowroom!" cried Daniel Boone.   40

Straight as a pine at sixty-five —
Time enough for a man to thrive —
He launched his bateau[3] on Ohio's breast,
And his heart was glad as he oared it west;
There was kindly folk and his own true blood   45
Where great Missouri rolls his flood;
New woods, new streams, and room to spare,
And Daniel Boone found comfort there.
Yet far he ranged toward the sunset still
Where the Kansas runs and the Smoky Hill,   50
And the prairies toss, by the south wind blown;
And he killed his bear on the Yellowstone.
But ever he dreamed of new domains
With vaster woods and wider plains;
Ever he dreamed of a world-to-be   55
Where there are no bounds and the soul is free.
At four-score-five, still stout and hale,
He heard a call to a farther trail;

---

[1] *Yadkin,* a river in the Carolinas.
[2] *Shawnee,* an Indian tribe from Tennessee.

[3] *bateau,* a boat.

So he turned his face where the stars are strewn.
"Elbowroom!" sighed Daniel Boone. 60

Down the Milky Way in its banks of blue
Far he has paddled his white canoe
To the splendid quest of the tameless soul —
He has reached the goal where there is no goal.
Now he rides and rides an endless trail 65
On the Hippograff[4] of the flaming tail,
Or the Horse of the Stars with the golden mane,
As he rode the first of the bluegrass strain.
The joy that lies in the Search he seeks
On breathless hills with crystal peaks; 70
He makes his camp on heights untrod,
The steps of the shrine, alone with God.
Through the woods of the vast, on the plains of Space
He hunts the pride of the Mammoth race,
And the Dinosaur[5] of the triple horn, 75
The Manticore, and the Unicorn,[6]
As once by the broad Missouri's flow
He followed the elk and the buffalo,
East of the Sun and west of the Moon,

"Elbowroom!" laughs Daniel Boone. 80

VIEWING THE AUTHOR'S IDEAS

1. What made Boone move westward?

2. Describe the appearance of Boone in old age. What is your impression of this hero of the West? What contribution did he make to the development of our country?

3. Who wore deerskin shirts and coonskin caps? When did the land say "Nay" to the stubborn king?

4. Explain the nature of Boone's search.

EVALUATING HIS MANNER OF EXPRESSION

1. What is meant by "elbowroom"? Show that each time Boone says the word the meaning varies. Is elbowroom the central idea of the poem?

2. In more simple language express the following statement: ". . . the stout logs shook in a storm of lead."

3. Which stanza is the most imaginative? Explain. Find an example of each of the following figures: (a) metaphor (b) simile (c) hyperbole (d) personification.

4. Where is the goal where there is "no goal"? Find lines that contain allusions to (a) the horses of Kentucky (b) the happy hunting grounds (c) Boone's defense of the land against the Indians.

[4] *Hippograff*, a fabulous animal.
[5] *Dinosaur*, a large extinct reptile.
[6] *Unicorn*, a fabulous animal having one horn in the middle of the forehead.

O Light Invisible, We Praise Thee

(From *Choruses from "The Rock"*)
T. S. Eliot

T. S. Eliot's poetry is difficult for readers who cannot readily pass from a poet's symbol to the idea he wishes to convey. This hymn of praise, however, is clear to anyone who has learned to follow liturgical forms of prayer.

This selection is taken from The Rock, *a pageant in which Eliot expresses his religious beliefs as an Anglo-Catholic. In these lines all the little lights of earth, God-given and man-made, cause the poet to be grateful to God, the Light Invisible, upon whose brightness his earthly eyes could not yet look.*

O LIGHT Invisible, we praise Thee!
Too bright for mortal vision.
O Greater Light, we praise Thee for the less;
The eastern light our spires touch at morning,
The light that slants upon our western doors at
  evening, 5
The twilight over stagnant pools at bat flight,
Moonlight and starlight, owl and moth light,
Glowworm glow light on a grass-blade,
Light Invisible, we worship Thee!

We thank Thee for the lights that we have kindled,   10
The light of altar and of sanctuary;
Small lights of those who meditate at midnight
And lights directed through the colored panes of windows
And light reflected from the polished stone,
The gilded carven wood, the colored fresco.   15
Our gaze is submarine, our eyes look upward
And see the light that fractures[1] through unquiet water.
And see the light but see not whence it comes.
O Light Invisible, we glorify Thee!

In our rhythm of earthly life we tire of light. We are glad when the day ends, when the play ends;
    and ecstasy is too much pain.   20
We are children quickly tired; children who are up in the night and fall asleep as the rocket is fired;
    and the day is long for work or play
We tire of distraction or concentration, we sleep and are glad to sleep,
Controlled by the rhythm of blood and the day and the night and the seasons.
And we must extinguish the candle, put out the light and relight it;
Forever must quench, forever relight the flame.   25
Therefore we thank Thee for our little light, that is dappled with shadow.
We thank Thee who hast moved us to building, to finding, to forming at the ends of our fingers
    and beams of our eyes.
And when we have built an altar to the Invisible Light, we may set thereon the little lights
    for which our bodily vision is made.
And we thank Thee that darkness reminds us of light.
O Light Invisible, we give Thee thanks for Thy great glory!   30

---

[1] *fractures*, refracts, i.e., deflects from a straight path.

VIEWING THE AUTHOR'S IDEAS

1. What are the lesser lights sent by Providence? Name some of the lights that are kindled by mankind. What does *light* signify to human beings?

2. Why does darkness help us to appreciate light?

3. In the third stanza, for what things is the poet grateful?

EVALUATING HIS MANNER OF EXPRESSION

1. What devices has the poet used to produce melody in lines 1-9?

2. Why is the phrase "our spires touch at morning" more vivid than would be the wording "the morning light shines on our spire"?

3. Describe the pictures suggested by the following phrases: "dappled with shadow"; "at bat flight."

Those Two Boys

Franklin P. Adams

In this poem Franklin P. Adams concludes with his usual surprise, a single artless line tossed off with an impish grin after he has led one to expect some momentous conclusions.

WHEN Bill was a lad, he was terribly bad.
  He worried his parents a lot;
He'd lie and he'd swear and pull little girls' hair;
  His boyhood was naught but a blot.

At play and in school he would fracture each rule —
  In mischief from autumn to spring;
And the villagers knew when to manhood he grew,
  He would never amount to a thing.

When Jim was a child, he was not very wild;
  He was known as a good little boy;
He was honest and bright and the teachers' delight —
  To his father and mother a joy.

All the neighbors were sure that his virtue'd endure,
  That his life would be free of a spot;
They were certain that Jim had a great head on him
  And that Jim would amount to a lot.

And Jim grew to manhood and honor and fame
  And bears a good name;
While Bill is shut up in a dark prison cell —
  You never can tell.

VIEWING THE AUTHOR'S IDEAS

1. What end does Adams lead you to expect for each boy? Explain how he leads you to expect a different conclusion.

2. Do you think that the author may be more serious than he pretends? Why is it reasonable to expect that the two boys would have ended as they did?

EVALUATING HIS MANNER OF EXPRESSION

1. These stanzas have the pleasant jingle which characterizes much light verse. Does it help or hinder the humorous effect? Mention earlier writers who have written humorous verse.

2. Compare the technique of this poem with any humorous verses by Hilaire Belloc.

To Be an American

Archibald MacLeish

These brief stanzas contrast the unchanging customs of the European village with the wide sweep of American life — as expansive as the wind or the sea gull.

IT IS a strange thing — to be an American.
Neither an old house it is with the air
Tasting of hung herbs and the sun returning
Year after year to the same door and the churn
Making the same sound in the cool of the kitchen   5
Mother to son's wife, and the place to sit
Marked in the dusk by the worn stone at
  the Wellhead —
That — nor the eyes like each other's eyes and the
  skull
Shaped to the same fault and the hands' sameness.   10
Neither a place it is nor a blood name.
America is West and the wind blowing.
America is a great word and the snow,
A way, a white bird, the rain falling,
A shining thing in the mind and the gull's call.
America is neither a land nor a people,   15
A word's shape it is, a wind's sweep —
America is alone: many together,
Many of one mouth, of one breath,
Dressed as one — and none brothers among them:
Only the taught speech and the aped tongue.   20
America is alone and the gulls calling.

VIEWING THE AUTHOR'S IDEAS

1. Why is it a "strange thing" to be an American?

2. What does the poet say in the first stanza that America *is not?* What *is* America? In your own words tell what it means to be an American.

3. How are Americans brothers? Explain the poet's meaning in the line "Dressed as one — and none brothers among them."

4. What is the meaning of "the taught speech and the aped tongue"?

EVALUATING HIS MANNER OF EXPRESSION

1. What lines imply that the theory of race superiority is un-American?

2. Show that the poet conveys the impression of scope and vastness in the apparently unrelated ideas contained in the following expressions: (a) "West and the wind blowing" (b) "a great word and the snow" (c) "a shining thing in the mind and the gull's call" (d) "a word's shape it is, a wind's sweep."

The Secret Heart

Robert P. Tristram Coffin

Writing of the incident which led him to compose this poem, Robert P. Tristram Coffin says: "The best sudden poem that ever came to me came as a light in my father's hands. I was nine, and I was desperately ill, in a high fever, and lying on my bed in the dead of night, half awake, half asleep. My father came in to see how I was, and he struck a match and stood at the foot of my bed, looking down. His face, lit up by the sudden fire in his hands, was one of the most beautiful sights I ever saw. My father did not know that I was looking at him from under my eyelids, or he would never have looked at me that way. Again, though I was a boy, I knew a poem when I saw one at the foot of my bed. I thought I would always remember that poem. But I didn't. The memory faded from my mind. I should never have recalled that poem if it hadn't been that a few years ago I found myself in the same situation, when my own small son lay ill in his room, in the dead of the night, in a fever, too; and I went in to see how he did. I went in the gloom and struck a match. In the spurt of the flame the old poem of my father's face came back to me, and all I had to do was write it down."

Across the years he could recall
His father one way best of all.

In the stillest hour of night
The boy awakened to a light.

Half in dreams, he saw his sire
With his great hands full of fire.

The man had struck a match to see
If his son slept peacefully.

He held his palms each side the spark
His love had kindled in the dark.

His two hands were curved apart
In the semblance of a heart.

He wore, it seemed to his small son,
A bare heart on his hidden one,

A heart that gave out such a glow
No son awake could bear to know.

It showed a look upon a face
Too tender for the day to trace.

One instant, it lit all about,
And then the secret heart went out.

But it shone long enough for one
To know that hands held up the sun.

VIEWING THE AUTHOR'S IDEAS

1. In your own words describe what the boy saw when he awoke at night. Why was he not afraid?

2. Select the words indicating that the little boy was only half awake.

3. Is the title appropriate? Which lines first make the title clear? What is the secret heart?

4. What evidence is there that the boy is the poet himself? Is it expressed or implied?

High Flight

John Gillespie Magee, Jr.

In Magee's tumbling about in the clouds, modern Americans find an expression of the high courage of thousands of airmen. This sonnet sent to his mother three months before his death reveals the boy's daring and bravery in the defense of freedom.

OH, I have slipped the surly bonds of earth,
    And danced the skies on laughter-silvered wings;
Sunward I've climbed and joined the tumbling mirth
Of sun-split clouds — and done a hundred things
You have not dreamed of — wheeled and soared and
    swung
High in the sunlit silence. Hov'ring there,
I've chased the shouting wind along and flung
My eager craft through footless halls of air.

Up, up the long delirious, burning blue
I've topped the wind-swept heights with easy grace,
Where never lark, or even eagle flew;
And, while with silent, lifting mind I've trod
The high, untrespassed sanctity of space,
Put out my hand, and touched the face of God.

VIEWING THE AUTHOR'S IDEAS

1. After reading the sonnet, give your idea of the personality of the author.

2. What serious thoughts come to the aviator? Is there any indication that he prayed while flying?

3. Why do you think the British authorities made "High Flight" the official poem of the Empire's flying forces?

EVALUATING HIS MANNER OF EXPRESSION

1. How do the words of the poem make you aware of the freedom of the skies; of the movement of the plane?

2. What emotion did the author experience while flying? Do you share the emotion as you read?

3. Quote lines in which he describes extraordinary height. Why does he mention the lark and the eagle? Choose an unusual expression describing a vast stretch of space.

Lily of Light

Edward F. Garesché, S.J.

The whitest objects in nature furnish imagery for the poet as he seeks some earthly comparison for Mary's purity.

LILY of Light.
    Bloomed from the dark and fester[1] of our night.

Your radiance far is borne,
Like the white splendors of the Star of Morn.
Lily of Light,   5
Mary most pure, guide all our thoughts aright.

Summit of Snow.
Lifted in glory where the dawnings glow.

[1] *fester*, a sore containing pus; used figuratively to denote the ills resulting from man's fall.

On whose clear crest the loving sunbeams cling.
Half earth's, half Heaven's; to the world below   10
Beacon and promise of eternal Spring.
Summit of Snow,
Virgin and Mother, help our crowded woes.

Moon of the Deep.[2]
Flower of our midnight's purple-shadowed sleep.   15
Your silver-pointed ray
Shatters the dusk, and makes our darkness day.
Moon of the Deep,
Mirror of God, enlighten us, who weep.

VIEWING THE AUTHOR'S IDEAS

1. What does the lily usually symbolize? To which of the following does "our night" seem to refer: (a) darkness (b) sin (c) unhappiness? In what sense does Mary's radiance resemble the morning star?

[2] *the Deep*, the ocean.

2. Why does the poet apply the metaphor "Summit of Snow" to the Blessed Virgin? When the imagery in lines 8-9 is added to this title, what picture do you obtain? In what way is Mary "half earth's, half Heaven's"? From her high place how does Our Lady aid those below?

3. What has the third title in common with the first two? What flower might the moon's reflection in water resemble? Of what is "purple-shadowed sleep" the symbol?

4. According to the poet, what power has the light of the moon? In what event of her life did Mary "make darkness day"? Why is "Mirror of God" an appropriate title for Mary?

EVALUATING HIS MANNER OF EXPRESSION

1. In your opinion which of the metaphors is most fitting? Why? To which of Our Lady's prerogatives do they refer?

2. Find in each stanza the references to the following qualities: (a) light (b) purity (c) power. Show that by changing three metaphors which suggest these qualities the writer has achieved unity in his poem.

Silentium Altum[1]

Blanche Mary Kelly

Sometimes in the silence of a majestic height one comes close to the supernatural. This spiritual awareness is so real that the poet can only compare it to the vision of Heaven granted to St. Monica and St. Augustine.

I KNOW a windswept hill where all day long
Comes never footfall nor the sound of word,
Only by swallow's wing or woodlark's song
Is that immense and brooding stillness stirred.

I sat awhile in that lost, listening place,
And felt the pulse of Time beat slow, beat slow
Watching, upon the mountain sides of space,
The bright feet of God's heralds come and go.

On pinions of that silence was I raised,
With awe pervaded and pierced utterly,

Like theirs that from an Ostian window[2] gazed
Beyond the bastions[3] of eternity.

VIEWING THE AUTHOR'S IDEAS

1. Why was the windswept hill an ideal place for meditation? What sounds disturbed the stillness?

2. In what way did the silence make the poet conscious of the passing of time? Who were the heralds seen in far space?

3. Name three effects of the silence on the poet. To what does she compare the experience?

EVALUATING HER MANNER OF EXPRESSION

1. List the adjectives in the poem which have the greatest poetic value.

2. What is the central idea of the poem? To what senses does the lyric appeal?

[2] *Like theirs . . . Ostian window.* Once as St. Augustine and his mother, St. Monica, stood at a window of their house in Ostia, conversing upon the nature of eternal life, they were granted an ecstatic vision of the joys of heaven.

[3] *bastions*, fortified outposts.

[1] *Silentium Altum*, High Silence.

Song for a Listener

Leonard Feeney, S.J.

These lines present the climax of Father Feeney's poem in which he interweaves a tribute to Our Lady with caustic comments on present-day modes of thinking. If possible, secure a copy of the poem and read the earlier stanzas. Among other things, you will learn that two women helped the young Leonard Feeney to understand Our Lady. The first of these women was his mother. In her he beheld the beauty of maternity. The second was his teacher, a nun, who "had the Holy Ghost for Spouse." With this background of motherly love and virginal purity, the small boy was able to contemplate Mary at the Nativity of Our Lord.

21

WHEN toys were trunked and school begun,
    I was, among a many, one
Entrusted to a wimpled nun:

A virgin vestaled with three vows
Who had the Holy Ghost for spouse,   5
And tried devoutly to arouse

An aptitude for long divisions
Involving cerebral collisions
With theological precisions.

22

This gentle girl in cape and coif   10
With softest silver in her laugh,
Prepared me for my epitaph:

"Here lies a lad whose sins were sins,
Not streptococcic orange skins;
Nor were his virtues vitamins.   15

He learned the rules and knew the game;
If Hell or Heaven hold the same,—
Himself, not spinach, was to blame."

27

The barn was ready and the straw;
I saw what nudging angels saw,   20
And shepherds open-mouthed with awe.

I found what hitherto had been
The fragments of the feminine
Welded at last, without, within.

My happy Heaven had begun: 25
I knew the nursery and the nun,
The convent and the crib in one.

28

When once the heart has been uphurled
And glimpsed this Glory in the world,
Whatever's ringleted or curled   30

Takes on a newer, nobler guise,
Usurps the function of surprise,
Asserts a symbol in the eyes

Which one is soon intrigued to trace
In the most worn and wrinkled face,   35
In the most mean, improper place.

29

Because of Her who flowered so fair
The poor old apple-wench will wear
A sprig of roses in her hair;

The strumpet strolling on the quay   40
Who puts in pawn her purity
Will sue for sailors' chivalry;

The lily garbaged in a brawl
Out of her refuse-heap will crawl
Back to her trellis on the wall.   45

30

Because this Beacon blanched our shore
Our daughters dazzle us once more,
Our mothers mellow as of yore.

And through this sentiment I sing
Is fraught with an old-fashioned ring,   50
"In case you like that sort of thing"—

In case I don't, I hope it's true
A good old-fashioned brimstone brew
Someday in Hell will coax me to.

31

The crown and crest of creaturehood   55
Has not been seen so great, so good
As in our race, as in our brood.

The Cherubim and Seraphim
Have been o'er-vaulted and made dim
By something slender, something slim   60

Assembled on our satellite
To move as any maiden might
Familiar to our common sight.

32

Truth to attraction one must tether;
Reason and rapture rolled together   65
Will settle whether not or whether

The philosophic proof must pass
Inspection near the looking-glass
To learn the logic of a lass

And find if in mythology   70
What sense there is, if sense there be,
Was not a need for such as She.

33

A girl did God, I do believe,—
Created, courted by,—conceive;
And would that every word I weave   75

Her Sire, her Spouse, her Son might please
In this frail ditty darned in threes
With threads of triple harmonies.

One riddle and my rhyme is through:
A bull will butt at red, but you,   80
Beelzebub, will butt at blue!

VIEWING THE AUTHOR'S IDEAS

1. What experience is recounted in the first eighteen lines?

2. Explain how the next nine lines describe the poet's youthful realization that Our Lady is both virgin and mother. What effect did this truth have upon him?

3. What is meant by the "Glory" that gives added loveliness to all earthly beauty? What lines tell you that for a person who loves Mary, all women can become a symbol of Our Lady?

4. How did devotion to Mary help to raise the status of womanhood during the era when Europe was being christianized? Discuss the place of Mary in the medieval code of chivalry. What relation has this historic background to the flower in the hair of the old apple-vender? How does it help a woman who has lost her virtue to regain grace and her standing in society?

5. What glory is added to women in their homes because of Mary? For those who consider the poet's view sentimental, what disagreeable fact may teach proper appreciation of Our Lady in God's plan of redemption?

6. In describing Mary as the crowning act of creation, the poet keeps her before our sight as a young girl. What aspects of youthful beauty help us to picture the woman who surpasses the Cherubim and Seraphim?

7. The loveliness of Our Lady appeals to our hearts. How does our reason also help us to increase our devotion to Mary?

8. To what promise does the poet refer in the last three lines? How does Mary continuously arouse the ineffectual anger of the devil?

EVALUATING HIS MANNER OF EXPRESSION

1. Reread the poem to notice the effect of the "triple harmonies" in the rhyme scheme. How does the facility in rhyme contribute to the movement of the poem?

2. Contrast the line "The crown and crest of creaturehood" with the line "A good old-fashioned brimstone brew." What qualities do you see in each? In what other lines of the poem do you find such diverse modes of expression? Upon which note does the poem close? What is the effect of the last word?

Charity

Theodore Maynard

Lest you think that kindness implies weakness, the poet convincingly asserts that charity is strong with the strength of God.

WHO think of charity as milky-eyed
   Know not of God's great handmaid's terrible
      name,
Who comes in garments by the rainbow dyed
   And crowned and winged and charioted with flame.

For Truth and Justice ride abroad with her   5
   And Honor's trumpets peal before her face;
The high archangels stand and minister
   When she doth sit within her holy place.

None knoweth in the depth nor in the height
   What meaneth Charity, God's secret word   10
But kiss her feet, and veil their burning sight
   Before her naked heart, her naked sword.

VIEWING THE AUTHOR'S IDEAS

1. What wrong ideas do people sometimes entertain about charity? How does the poet depict its beauty and strength?

2. What conditions result from the practice of charity? Why should the archangels show respect for the virtue?

3. What is the source of charity? How does its origin account for man's inability fully to understand its value?

4. In the last two lines the poet suggests the attitude with which men should undertake the practice of charity. What other virtue does he recommend as an aid in acquiring charity?

EVALUATING HIS MANNER OF EXPRESSION

1. Show how the energy and force of these lines support the author's idea that charity is a virtue of great might.

2. Point out instances of personification in the poem.

3. What pictures are conveyed by the poet's description of Charity in action? How do these pictures suggest the pageantry of medieval civilization?

Hidden

Daniel Sargent

With modern emphasis upon success, publicity, and practical values, it is necessary that a poet remind us occasionally that the best things in life are hidden.

ALL THE best things are hidden, that is why
   Children are always whispering in your ear.
That's why the best friends in the graveyard lie
Hiding their face to make their face more dear.
That's why the kindness which brought tears to the eye
Came from the rag-hid beggar; why the sheer
Glory of angels never left the sky;
Why the sweet laughter lay in ambush near.
That's why the Maker of the sun and moon
Beautified both with miracle of cloud.
That's why the summer wood thrush takes her tune
Deep in the hush to hermitage green-boughed.

That's why the wise go desert-ward once more.
That's why the Carmelites have shut their door.

VIEWING THE AUTHOR'S IDEAS

1. How do the two things mentioned in the first four lines differ? What qualities of the beggar might be hidden under his ragged appearance?

2. Name other good things hidden throughout life or sometimes concealed. What is the "best thing" sought by those who go desert-ward; by the Carmelites in their cloister?

EVALUATING HIS MANNER OF EXPRESSION

This poem implies an appreciation of the contemplative life.

A Question of Lovers

Sister Madeleva, C.S.C.

No earthly lover can be so profuse with gifts as the Lover of Souls. The poet is here pursuing a favorite method of making divine love better understood by describing it in the language of human affection.

THERE be lovers who bring me roses, the velvet of buds upcurled;
But only one lover gives me the blossoms of all the world.

There be those who have pearls, have rubies; but much as I care for these,
This night will my true love bring me the moon and the Pleiades.

I have tokens, if gifts could buy me, till love and its quest be done.
Who will catch me a cloud's white splendor; who will fetch me the dying sun?

Or who, on the wings of the morning, will hasten, when dawn is sweet,
To meet and possess me solely? One only, with pierced feet.

And who, for he loves me truly, will give me as token this,
This poignance of love unspoken, two wounds in his hands to kiss?

VIEWING THE AUTHOR'S IDEAS

1. Contrast the gifts offered by the two lovers. How are the Divine qualities of the Infinite Lover suggested?

2. What kind of love is indicated by the clause "If gifts could buy me"? Which is more important in the development of love, the giving of gifts or the unselfish sharing of one's personality?

3. What spiritual gift is referred to in the last two stanzas?

EVALUATING HER MANNER OF EXPRESSION

1. Observe that the gifts are arranged in the order of climax. How is each offering more significant than the one preceding?

2. Parallel structure combined with antithesis, or contrasting ideas, has proved an effective poetic device since the days of David. Point out places where balance and parallelism are used. Is the hint of the lover's identity more poetic than the mention of His Name would have been?

Te Deum at Matins

Sister Mary St. Virginia, B.V.M.

Read a translation of the great hymn of the Church, the Te Deum. Then you will understand why the poet, with the majestic phrases still in her mind, hears Earth giving response to Heaven's praise. The conclusion of this sonnet contains a reference to Christ's words to St. Peter. When many people had different ideas about the identity of the Son of Man, Our Lord looked to the chief apostle. It was then that the great saint uttered the words, "Thou art the Christ, the Son of the Living God."

Now is the earth made vocal with Thy glory,
Now does frail man give back antistrophe[1]
Unto angelic choirs telling the story
Of Him Who was, Who is, and Who will be.
Now do Thy prophets and Thy pristine[2] heroes
Lend us their voices and Thy name confess,

---

[1] *antistrophe* (ăn-tĭs trŏ-fĕ), in the Greek choral dance and song a portion answering a previous part.

[2] *pristine*, primary, earliest.

Now white-robed victims of the hate of Neroes
Crowd all about us as our God we bless.
O Christ, the answer to the ancient dreaming —
O Christ, the dream that wise men dream again —
O Christ, turning to Peter from men's scheming:
But Who do you say I am? — Christ! listen when
Peter still bids his cleaving tongue be loose:
Tu Patris sempiternus es Filius.[3]

VIEWING THE AUTHOR'S IDEAS

1. How can the earth become vocal with God's glory? Discuss the dignity and excellence of the liturgy as the official prayer of the Church.

[3] *Tu . . . es Filius,* Thou art the eternal Son of the Father.

2. What knowledge does man have of God which enables him to contribute an antistrophe to the angels' song?

3. Refer to the *Te Deum* to determine who were the pristine heroes of the Church; who were the victims of Nero?

4. To what ancient dream is Christ the answer? How is He the dream "which wise men dream again"?

5. What did Christ ask the apostles? State Peter's answer. In the *Te Deum* how does the whole Church re-echo Peter's words?

EVALUATING HER MANNER OF EXPRESSION

1. How do the stressed syllables at the beginning of the lines give emphasis to the poet's ideas? How frequently do these initial strong syllables occur?

2. Show that elevated emotion rising from a great thought is the basis for this poem.

Riddles

Sister Maris Stella

Have you ever had the discouraging experience of trying innumerable keys in a lock? Do you recall your tremendous relief when you found the right one? Modern civilization has become so confusing that we seem to have lost our key, our path, our basic directions. This poem shows man's need for a single solution to the problems of existence.

OUT OF this tangle of threads to find the thread
    that will untangle the threads. Out of the maze
to find the amazing path and so be led
back to the beginning by incredible ways.
Out of the confusion of keys to find the key
that fits each keyhole, unlocks every lock.
Among a multitude of suns to see
only the sun. To find the moveless rock
under the shifting stones, under the sand,
the rock no shifting sands can ever shake,
nor great wind crying out over a shaking land,
nor lightning blast, nor breaking water break.
To find in multiplicity but one
end, beginning, thread, path, key, rock, sun . . .

VIEWING THE AUTHOR'S IDEAS

1. How may life be compared to a tangle of threads? Under what circumstances is the comparison to a maze fitting?

2. What aspects of life sometimes appear as a locked door? To what mental experience would the phrase "confusion of keys" correspond?

3. Explain the meaning of "sun" in lines 7-8.

4. Show that the poet expects the answer to the riddles to be a defense against doubt, change, and time.

5. State some aspects of twentieth-century life that contribute to man's confusion. Is a solution for man's problems in this poem? What is your answer to these riddles? How does the poem parallel the statement of St. Augustine: "Thou madest us for Thyself, and our heart is restless until it repose in Thee"?

EVALUATING HER MANNER OF EXPRESSION

1. Reread the poem to observe the sweeping cadences which greatly contribute to its subtle music. In how many verses does the poet terminate the sentence at the end of the line? What would the poem have lost had the author in every case concluded the idea with the rhyming word?

2. What does alliteration and repetition of words add to the musical quality of the lines? Find instances in which repetition gives emphasis to the ideas.

Flight

Sister Maris Stella

This sonnet presents a rare and penetrating analysis of the swiftness with which the soul at death speeds toward God.

THIS indescribable thing will one day burst
its sheath and into lucid daylight fly
with wings that strongly beat even at the first,
though unaccustomed to the air they try.
Here is no drowsy moth awakening:
within the woven fabric of the brain
strains even now the unsubstantial wing
once taking flight will never come again.
Without a cry of warning, without a word,
without the whiz of arrow leaving the bow,
suddenly shooting, swifter than any bird,
on indescribable wings will surely go
straight to the mark of an invisible star
this terrible joy unsheathed, darting afar
. . .

1. Observe that the poet implies a comparison in the first four lines without stating it directly. What two things does she compare?

2. How does she prove that the soul is no drowsy moth awakening?

3. Will the soul ever return to the body under the same conditions that existed during life on earth?

4. How many quilities of the soul's flight can you infer from the poet's description? Account for the direct aims and swift motion of the flight.

EVALUATING HER MANNER OF EXPRESSION

In which lines does the rythm of the poem correspond with the idea of impetuous flight?

The Spy

Sister Mariella

With a flash of spiritual insight, men sometimes see in natural beauty a reflection of God's splendor and power. It is this momentary awareness of God's Being, this split second of contemplation, that the author calls spying.

I AM a spy, and I have seen . . .
But first I must tell you
About the chinks and the keyholes
Where you may be certain of spying.
You know some of them yourself if you   5
Have ever lain on summer grass
To watch the smooth white daylight pass,
And seen the night come down the sky
Pouring gray wonder silkily
Through apple boughs that straightway bloom   10
With little stars and a full-blown moon.

But the stars
And the filigree[1] of apple boughs
Against a satin sky
Are not the things on which you spy.   15
They are the signs
That the time and the place are as right for peeking
As down in the pasture by the granite rock
Where cool, damp, earthy smells come stealing
Out of the tamarack[2] swamp when day goes by.   20
What was it I saw in the orchard and down
  by the swamp?
It was . . .
I ought to be able to tell you
Because
I ran all the way back from the pasture   25

[1] *filigree*, ornamental openwork of delicate design.
[2] *tamarack*, any of the several American larches.

With my eyes shut
So that I could remember.
But I cannot tell you anything.

That is why it is safe, I think,
For every keyhole and every chink   30
To be unstuffed and unguarded.
A daisy poising perilously
Is a keyhole open for those who see.
But you can never remember
What it was that you saw.   35
That is why Lazarus never told anything when he
    came
Back from the grave,
Nor Jairus' daughter,
Nor the son of the widow of Naim.

Some day   40
I shall go over into the strange land
That I've been spying on,
But then
I can never come back
And finish the first line of this poem.   45

VIEWING THE AUTHOR'S IDEAS

1. What train of thought is interrupted in the first line? Why does the poet stop abruptly?

2. What information does she give about "the chinks and keyholes"? State her clues that the time is ripe for spying.

3. Can you guess the information which the poet almost gave? Why had she hoped to be able to tell what she saw down by the swamp? What does she conclude from her inability to remember?

4. In what sense might a daisy be a keyhole? What did the three persons in the Biblical allusions have in common? Why was their experience a magnificent one? Where is the land upon which the poet had been spying?

EVALUATING HER MANNER OF EXPRESSION

1. How does the final stanza give unity to the lyric?

2. Describe the most vivid pictures in the poem. What details make the imagery notable?

In Avila

Sister M. Thérèse, Sor. D.S.

Teresa of Avila, the great Carmelite saint of the sixteenth century, attained through prayer the highest degree of mystical life. Because of her spiritual insight into heavenly things, she has been called a Doctor of the Church. Thousands of souls were converted through her influence and prayers. Longing for God is said to have been the cause of her death. Artists have tried to express St. Teresa's great love of God. She is often represented with a fiery dart piercing her heart. Notice how the poet expresses the intensity of her love in prayer.

THE matin chant she scarcely heard;
    There was a light about each word
And in her heart a singing bird.

There was no letter she could say;
Nor could she turn her soul away;
And yet by night and yet by day

The very air that wrapped her round
Was wet with coolnesses of sound
Like crystal rivers underground.

There was no place that she could hide—
As easy push the stars aside
As hush the singing in her side.

Song that was sound she could not hear;
Song that was touch she could not fear;
A presence piercing like a spear.

What is this bird that can subdue
The heart, the mind, the spirit too,
Then in a sudden light she knew

Love is the lock and love the key
That opens wide this mystery
Of swift invasion by the Three.

VIEWING THE AUTHOR'S IDEAS

1. What is meant by the singing bird in the first stanza? Why was the saint unable to hear the matin chant?

2. In contemplation, a high degree of prayer, the soul is so concentrated upon God that it forgets everything else. What evidences are there that St. Teresa's prayer was one of contemplation?

3. What is the significance of the line "A presence piercing like a spear"?

4. Express in your own words the meaning of the last two stanzas.

EVALUATING HER MANNER OF EXPRESSION

1. Is there anything significant about the triple line and the triple rhyme of the poem?

2. Point out examples of alliteration. Notice the variety of effects the poet produces by the frequent use of *s* sounds.

3. Comment upon the emotional intensity and the imaginative force of the phrase "as easy push the stars aside."

4. Explain the symbolism of the bird and the spear.

Our Lady of the Weather

Alfred Barrett, S.J.

Realizing how numerous are the inglorious days when the soul wavers in its high purposes, the poet invokes Our Lady under a new title. In response to his prayer, Mary speaks with her accustomed graciousness.

SNOW-MAIDEN, Rainbow-virgin, Sun-gowned
 Queen —
So might I hail you were the skies serene
My every morning. Yet on days of storm
I need you near as on the sunniest day,
And how in winter find your flowery form
If you were only Our Lady of the May,
How through the sultry months companioned go
Were you alone Our Lady of the Snow.

Our Lady of the Weather, through my soul
Four winds revolving blow, four seasons roll
The weather of my own inconstancy.
I am not marble, Mother!
   "Nor yet dust;
But rather is my Son a growing tree,

Filius accrescens,[1] that with every gust
Will bend resilient[2] and return to me."

VIEWING THE AUTHOR'S IDEAS

1. Why must Mary be more than merely Our Lady of the May and Our Lady of the Snow?

2. What title does the poet suggest to indicate Mary's place in our turbulent lives? How does he carry out the comparison of the spiritual life to the four seasons? What trials are symbolized by stormy weather?

3. State the answer of Our Lady to the poet's plea that he is not marble.

EVALUATING HIS MANNER OF EXPRESSION

Explain why the three compounds in the first line are appropriate. What other words or phrases suggest imagery from the four seasons?

---

[1] *Filius accrescens,* growing son.
[2] *resilient,* rebounding; returning to the original position or shape.

To a Baffled Idealist

J. G. E. Hopkins

Seeking perfection in man, the idealist is sometimes baffled when he beholds human foibles. On the other hand, a person who remembers man's fallen nature is not discouraged when confronted with weakness. Rather he rejoices in glimpsing flashes of hidden or unexpected virtue.

BECAUSE the upper and the nether stones[1]
Of things that are, ground close and slew
That dreamer who was you;
Because the flowers your heart set in your mind,
So aptly ordered and so beautiful,
Were withered within the wind
That life sends hot and blighting over those
Who must dispose
A grand and God-like spirit in their kind;
You have turned inward-seeking and have cried
Out of your simple pride,
"See, Lord, how men are bitter and unsouled:
There is none just save me."
While we
Expecting little, happen on the gold,
Seamy and tough of assay[2] that runs through
The coarse ore of the mine-run[3] that is Man,

Often enough to make our hearts grow glad
Out of humility,
Remembering that in Man are many men
Who live and die and hope for heaven, too.

[1] *upper and nether stones*, the two circular millstones used for grinding grain.

[2] *assay*, analysis.

[3] *mine-run*, unassorted product of a mine.

VIEWING THE AUTHOR'S IDEAS

1. To whom are the words of the poem addressed? How does the writer represent the effect of the harsh realities of life upon the dreamer?

2. Why is the idealist disappointed? How does he react?

3. According to the poet, what service do those with lofty aspiration render mankind?

4. What do those find who expect less of man? How do they regard the gold they discover?

EVALUATING HIS MANNER OF EXPRESSION

1. To what does the poet compare the "things that are"? Find other metaphors.

2. Express the central idea of the poem in a single sentence. Does thought or feeling predominate?

3. What is the effect of the varying length of the lines? Indicate the rhyme scheme.

Southwestern Night

Fray Angelico Chavez

This poem captures the spell of the New Mexican starlight. The men who merge so harmoniously into the night scene are of that blended race which combines the dignity of Old Spain with the endurance of the native Indian. In their isolation from modern activity the shepherds reveal something of the culture which came with the padres.

THE night had pitched her tar dark tent
Which leaked with starlight everywhere,
When by the road on which I went
I came upon the firelit shapes
Of shepherds, lean and bent.

There was no wind to shake the flame
To which they drew me civilly,
Much less their voices when I came,
(My coming did not cut their words
To even ask my name.)

Their talk was unaware of wars
And innocent of rapes or polls;
Each phrase fell in Gregorian bars,
And while their cadence skimmed the soil
They seemed to touch the stars.

Up to the ceiling's taut, dark crown
They flowed as one, the strand of smoke,
Their thread of thought; and as my own
Turned heavenward to follow them,
The dew of stars dripped down.

VIEWING THE AUTHOR'S IDEAS

1. To what is the sky likened? What caused the figures of the shepherds to appear in silhouette?

2. How do you know that the shepherds took for granted the presence of the stranger? How does the poet describe the topics of conversation; the voices of the shepherds?

3. What is the subject of *they* in line 17? Why would the shepherds' thread of thought seem to ascend to heaven? How was there an intermingling of heaven and earth in the scene?

EVALUATING HIS MANNER OF EXPRESSION

Quote phrases which suggest the effects of light and shadow; the isolation of the shepherds.

To Fear

Clifford Laube

Rarely have poets praised the fear of God. Seldom, too, have readers looked upon it as a gift aiding them to merit heaven. In these lines the poet sees fear of the Lord as an angel of restraint.

BY THIS body's lonely ark,
Through the daylight and the dark
You have kept your vigil well,
Archangelic sentinel.

Long ago in secret moods
Of my boyhood solitudes
Dimly I could feel the care
Of your hand upon my hair.

Limbs that ventured, rashly brisk,
Out upon the roads of risk,
Tamed their truant enterprise
To the caution in your eyes.

When these senses five caught fire
At the dawnrise of desire,
Touches of your frosty wing
Cooled their sudden smoldering.

Dark companion of my path,
Whisper still some hint of wrath
Lest these rebel fervors slip
Reins of grace and guardianship.

When this strength, less proudly nerved,
Droops, the dread subpoena served,
Stand beside me at my bier,
Bodyguard of holy fear.

VIEWING THE AUTHOR'S IDEAS

1. Why may the body be aptly compared to an ark? How does the holy sentinel make its presence known? Why was this presence felt only lightly at first?

2. In the third stanza what was the effect of fear of God when the temptations of youth arose?

3. Why is fear needed throughout life? What is the connection between original sin and the "rebel fervors" of man?

EVALUATING HIS MANNER OF EXPRESSION

1. The lines of the poem are clean-cut and carefully chiseled. How does the frequent use of stressed syllables contribute to this effect?

2. Show that the metaphor is sustained throughout the poem.

Fool's Martyrdom

William Thomas Walsh

Daringly the poet questions whether Christians today are worthy of martyrdom. Is it because they are so ill-prepared that they must die slowly — by inches?

RATHER than waste in bed, or undergo
The long disintegration of a cheese,
I would be cradled early on the knees
Of an outrageous death. If I could know
The joy that cheered Saint Thomas More, brought low
For conscience, jesting in his hair chemise,
Greeting the headsman with those pleasantries
About his beard;[1] if I could touch the glow
That warmed Saint Paul's great heart under the pain
Of mortal dread and loneliness that day
He bared his shaggy neck to Caesar's sword —
Then, like those nuns who sang[2] till they were slain,
I'd cheaply hold the veil, which, shorn away,
Would leave me face to face with Christ Our Lord.
But such high gifts may not be hoped for — not
By men like me. That gorgeous blossoming
Of spirit from the calyx[3] of a thing
So perishable as flesh was never bought
Without much cost of seed, much digging fraught[4]
With sweaty tears. Did ever bird on wing
Leap in the face of the joyous sun to sing

Without first limping, flopping, being taught?
And so did Paul prepare for splendid death
By God knows what small daily crosses borne
In the Arab desert, alone, And so did More,
By prayer, and many a human foible torn
From youth. The Carmelites' expiring breath
Was sweet from fast and scant rest on bare floor.

Then let romantic sluggards hold their peace,
And those who have no stomach for the gall
And vinegar of penance never call
For living wine from that Christ-cup whose lees
Have cleansed with blood the whole world's calvaries.
For how can fools who hardly speak at all
Without offense, aspire to die with Paul?
Can they bear swords who dread sharp words,
        draughts, fleas?
Oh, God, is it because great stuff is lacking
In our complacent[5] souls that You ordain
That we must die by inches, year by year,
Like heavy ships against Your mercy tacking,[6]
Stealing the wind they dare not face, to gain
Calm shores at last, beyond this dearth[7] and fear?

---

[1] *headsman . . . beard.* As he lay his head upon the block, St. Thomas More asked the executioner to wait until he moved aside his beard, saying that it had never committed any treason.

[2] *nuns who sang,* sixteen Carmelite nuns of Compiègne, who sang as they met death at the guillotine during the French Revolution.

[3] *calyx,* the outer leaves of a flower.

[4] *fraught,* filled or burdened.

[5] *complacent,* satisfied.

[6] *tacking,* steering a zigzag course.

[7] *dearth,* want.

VIEWING THE AUTHOR'S IDEAS

1. What is the "outrageous death" which the poet prefers? What type of death is suggested by "waste in bed"; "the long disintegration of a cheese"?

2. How did St. Thomas More meet martyrdom? Recalling other biographical facts about More, relate the jest he made about his beard during his last moments. In what sense was he brought to death "for conscience"? Tell the manner of St. Paul's death? How would the poet desire to imitate Paul? What gift of More's does he wish to share? Who are the nuns to whom the poet refers?

3. Express in your own words the meaning of "I'd cheaply hold the veil." What is to be seen when the veil is "shorn away"? How is martyrdom compared to a flower? Why is the seed costly? Is the flower easily cultivated? Explain how preparation for martyrdom is similar to a bird's learning to fly. State the preparation for martyrdom made by St. Paul; by St. Thomas More; by the Carmelites.

4. What does the poet call persons who talk about martyrdom but do not sincerely wish it? Why must one learn to swallow the bitter drink of penance before he is ready for the living wine of martyrdom?

5. Explain the wrong done by those "who hardly speak at all without offense"? What does the poet imply concerning those who cannot bear small sufferings? Does the poet seem to consider the ordinary Christian worthy of martyrdom? Why?

EVALUATING HIS MANNER OF EXPRESSION

1. Find and explain the metaphors referring (a) to life (b) to martyrdom. How does the writer carry out the simile which compares the soul to a ship?

2. After reading the poem, what do you consider to be the "fool's martyrdom"?

The Uninvited

Jessica Powers

This is a picture of a land without boundaries — the city of the poor. Jessica Powers shows gentle compassion for the excluded guests at Fortune's banquet. She understands their resignation because she knows the aloofness with which they would be treated.

THERE is a city that through time shall lie
   In a fixed darkness of the earth and sky;
  And many dwell therein this very hour.
  It is a city without seed or flower,
Estranged from every bird and butterfly.

Who walk these streets of night? I know them well.
Those who come out of life's sequestered places
   The lonely, the unloved, the weak and shy;
   The broken-winged who piteously would fly;
The poor with bleak submission in their faces.

They are the outcast ones, the last, the least,
Whom earth has not invited to her feast,
   And who, were they invited in the end,
   Finding their wedding clothes too frayed to mend,
Would not attend.

VIEWING THE AUTHOR'S IDEAS

1. Why does the poet call the city of the poor dark? What kinds of darkness frequently surround those who are poverty-stricken?

2. According to the poet, what things of beauty do the poor lack?

3. What states of mind does the poet find among the destitute?

4. Name some enjoyments of the feast to which the poor are not invited.

5. Why would the poor decline even if they did receive an invitation?

EVALUATING HER MANNER OF EXPRESSION

1. In what mood does the poem seem to have been written? Cite phrases to support your opinion.

2. Does the poem merely state a problem or does it suggest a solution?

3. Explain the significance of "a city without seed or flower"; "the broken-winged"; "bleak submission in their faces."

4. In your opinion what atmosphere does the poem convey?

5. Quote the two lines which seem most musical.

Project

Mary Fabyan Windeatt

What shelter can the soul find in a storm-tossed world?
The poet suggests that we should plan for our protection
by building a fortress within ourselves.

Now it is well
That we should start
Planning a fortress
In the heart;

Building with things
Which will endure
Longer than Sorrow's
Signature.

(Take away stone,
Take away wood;
Faith is ten thousand
Times as good!

Take away steel,
Take away lead;
Charity, hope, will
Do instead!)

Thus when the years
Pile up the pain,
We can go seeking
Peace again;

Back of the walls
Heaven designed
Just for the hurts of
Humankind.

VIEWING THE AUTHOR'S IDEAS

1. State precautions taken by the poet in the construction of the fortress. What material does she reject? What does she substitute?

2. Explain the unusual defense given by this fortress. Why could it ensure such protection?

EVALUATING HER MANNER OF EXPRESSION

1. What significance do you find in the title of the poem? Why does the poet use italics? What is the effect of the short line?

2. Observe the direct and compressed method of expression in this lyric. How many adjectives can be found? Are there any words which could have been omitted without loss to the poem? How many sentences have been used to express the idea of the lyric?

3. Show how the thought of the poem is, in a spiritual sense, parallel to the idea of defense in modern civilization.

4. What effect has the use of the imperative voice in stanzas three and four?

5. Explain the significance of "Sorrow's Signature."

Photograph

James J. Galvin, C.SS.R.

The little magic box which strollers carry on fine days
is not wholly mechanical. When it captures a beautiful
moment, it gives the permanence of art.

Click, click! like an elfin musket
A camera flickered . . . and puff!

The clock was halted forever
With a pinch of enchanted stuff;
And the fields surrendered to magic,
And the surf hushed under the bluff.

And a charm was cast over Mother
Between the sea and the sky
Sitting apron-deep in daisies
And watching the clouds go by;
For now she shall never grow older a breath
And the daisies shall never die.

VIEWING THE AUTHOR'S IDEAS

1. In what ways can the camera be compared to an elfin musket?

2. Describe three magic happenings recorded in lines 3-6.

3. What was the setting for the picture; the result achieved in the snapshot?

EVALUATING HIS MANNER OF EXPRESSION

Which do you believe would be of greater value: the photograph described in the poem or this poetic account of the picture?

Bridewater's Half Dollar

Booth Tarkington

Tarkington has remarked that he wishes this story to portray the misery caused by a fixed state of mind. Obsessed with the idea that the economic system has been unfair to him and deluded by fantastic schemes for the redistribution of wealth, Bridewater rages against those he considers more fortunate than he. In a fool's paradise of vain expectation he lulls his mind to sleep. His manner of spending half a dollar indicates his fitness to dispose of the wealth he covets.

GEORGE Bridewater looked upon a certain bench in Garfield Square as his own. The Square, a smoky green parklet in the shabby oldest part of the city, had a small central space of gravel about which were twelve benches, three on a side; and it was the middle bench on the north side, facing the sun, that Mr. Bridewater looked upon as his. The seven or eight other habitués[1] respected his feeling; and if a stranger loitered near, Bridewater yawned and extended both arms along the top of the bench, kept them there until the intruder either passed on or made another selection. He performed this maneuver a little after five o'clock one afternoon of last May to discourage an unknown saunterer whose appearance was that of a young workman out of a job; but, though he thus significantly stretched himself, Bridewater was interested in the conversation he was having with acquaintances upon other benches and didn't interrupt it.

"I'm fifty-four, Mr. Schleeman," he said, speaking loudly because he was addressing the seedy fat man who sat upon a bench across the graveled central space. "I'm fifty-four and I ain't never yet let no foreman work me to death. 'Who do you think I am?' I'd say. 'Don't get talky with me,' I'd say, 'or I'll put the heat on you! Give me my time and I'll go,' I'd say, 'but don't get talky!' I says just that the last job I had. It was in nineteen twenty-seven; and if they think they can take advantage of me now on account of the depression, make me work for nothin', and get talky with me, too, I'll show 'em!"

The loitering young workman sat down upon an unoccupied bench and addressed Mr. Bridewater. "I wouldn't," he said. "I wouldn't care how talky they got if they'd give me a job. Guess me and my family might all died if we hadn't got on Relief; but I sure am sick of bein' on it!"

Mr. Bridewater, Mr. Schleeman, and the four other regulars present all looked at him coldly. They didn't mind listeners but disliked a talking stranger. This was the year 1935, and of course great public themes absorbed them; they were in accord upon the new politics, and, as views in opposition upset their nerves, they naturally didn't wish to hear any. An articulate[2] stranger, therefore, was open to the suspicion of being a propagandist until he proved, by agreeing with them, that he wasn't.

---

[1] *habitués*, those who frequent certain places.

[2] *articulate*, able to express one's self.

"Listen!" Bridewater said. "You take Relief as long as you can get it. It's only the guvment givin' a man what's already his by rights. In this guvment one man's supposed to be as good as another, ain't he? Then its logic he's entitled to as much as any other man is, ain't it? How do you get around that?"

"You can't!" Mr. Schleeman called across the open space. "One man's got the rights to the same as any other man; and it's a good thing for them politicians they're commencin' to see it, or we'd kick 'em all to hell out." He frowned. "What I don't like about this two-hundred-dollar-a-month plan, though, it's the sixty year clause. I don't begrudge anybody sixty years old from gettin' their money; but it ought to be widened at the base. Lots of people sixty years old's got better constitutions than some only fifty and fifty-five. It's too much regimentation,[3] making it exactly sixty years old."

The other habitués looked at Mr. Schleeman respectfully; they admired him for language like "widened at the base" and "regimentation." Bridewater, however, ventured to take an argumentative tone. "No, no, Mr. Schleeman; that's a good plan. I only got six years to wait myself till I begin to draw the money; but to get right down to brass tacks, it's the other plan I favor the most. Five thousand dollars redistabution of wealth to everybody, paid down. Cold cash. That's what I say." He appealed to the others. "Five thousand dollars flat. Ain't that what you favor, gentlemen?"

On the next bench a gloomy man with a blade of grass waggling from his mouth shook his head, not in disagreement but in perplexity. "I ain't got the straight o' that yet, Mr. Bridewater. Are we all supposed to be going to get five thousand dollars — or is it three thousand?"

"Five."

"Well, then, is it five thousand dollars flat or five thousand dollars a year?"

"A year!" Bridewater exclaimed with emphasis. "They proved they can do it; proved it in cold figures over the radio."

"Who?" The young workman was skeptical. "Who proved that they can give everybody five thousand dollars a year?"

"Who?" Mr. Bridewater gave him another cold look. "Don't you never listen to the radio? Ain't you

never read any litter-chewer? The biggest men in this country's goin' to do it."

"How? How they goin' to do it?"

"How!" Bridewater exclaimed. "Why, by redistabution of the wealth. All the guvment's got to do's put on taxes and take it away from everybody that's got over five thousand dollars a year and hand it to the rest of us that's got under that much. The guvment'll take all them stocks and bonds and high-priced cars and show-off jewelry from the wealthy and — "

"And pass 'em around?" the young man asked. "F'r instance, hand me a couple diamonds and part of a used limousine and some stock of a railroad that's in the red and — "

"No sir!" Bridewater was irritated. "Any child knows the guvment can't do that and make a fair redistabution. What they'll do, they'll simply take all them things and sell 'em and then divide up the money fair and square, so that everybody all alike gets just exackly five — "

"Hold up!" the young man said. "Who they goin' to sell all them things to?"

"What?"

The disturber laughed harshly. "Who's goin' to buy 'em?"

Mr. Bridewater hadn't thought of this. Baffled, he stared in helpless annoyance at the young man; but Mr. Schleeman came to the rescue with a smile of pity for the questioner's ignorance. "Who's goin' to buy 'em? Why, Uncle Sam. The United States Guvment's goin' to buy 'em, that's who!"

"What with?" the young man asked derisively. "If the guvment's got the money to buy 'em, then it can already hand us out five thousand dollars a year right now without buyin' anything."

"What?"

"Why, certainly!" The intruder, once started, became disagreeably voluble. "On the other hand, if the guvment ain't got the money, why, it'd haf to buy all that stuff with paper currency. So if the paper currency's worth anything they could just as well hand it over to us, instead. So that proves this paper currency wouldn't be worth anything at all or else they'd do it. Besides, if the guvment could pay the rich for all their stocks and bonds and limousines and diamonds, then the rich'd have the money and be just as rich as they was before. How you goin' to get around that?"

3 *regimentation*, the process of reducing to uniformity.

"How?" Bridewater, flushed and frowning, made oratorical gestures. "Listen to me! Uncle Sam can do anything he wants to. He can take the shirt right off your back if he wants to. He could lock you up in jail this minute if he took the notion to. Uncle Sam'll simply take all that wealth and —"

"Will he? Well s'pose Uncle Sam does, what'll he *do* with it? He can't sell it because there'd be nobody to buy it, and he can't just hand around five thousand dollars a year for everybody because he can't split diamonds and stocks and limousines up even; and they wouldn't be worth anything much if they *got* split up. So listen here! If any you guys got a good five-cent cigar on you to trade, I'll sign over my five thousand dollars a year to you right now, and I'll throw in the two hundred dollars a month I'm goin' to get when I'm sixty, just for extra; and then laugh in your face! Any takers?"

Pleased with himself, the talkative young workman burst into loud laughter in which his hearers did not join. The gloomy man on the bench next to Mr. Bridewater began to murmur plaintively.

"I can't make nothin' of it," he said. "Sometimes it looks like a man's goin' to get his rights in this world and then right away again it don't. Take me now. I'm makin', say, an average of four to seven dollars a week for cuttin' grass, weedin', and so on. I got a second cousin, Joe Entringer, never done a day's work in his life — nothin' but a souse[4] since the day he was weaned and got such a paunch on him now he couldn't work if he wanted to. Yet he's foreman, settin' all day on a stump with a bun on[5] and smokin' cigars where they're raisin' the levee up at Mill Creek. Eighty dollars a month! Does that look right, with me only makin' twenty-eight, best I can do?"

"There's plenty worse off'n you," the man who shared the bench with him responded. "On the other hand, look at the nice jobs floatin' around if a man was only fixed to land one of 'em. Why, f'r instance, I know a colored mulatto girl that gets twenty-five dollars a week, guvment money — yes, sir, a cool hundred a month — just for handin' out Relief. She's a high educated colored girl; but they'd ought to hired some man with a family, instead. You know her, too, Mr. Bridewater

— Ellamora Thompson that lives right across the street from your house and always moves so kind of slow. Ain't it like I say?"

Mr. Bridewater did not reply. He was staring distastefully at the young workman and not listening. His mind was confused, and he hadn't understood the interloper's argument; but he felt resentfully that here was an ominous force hostile to himself personally— somebody who wanted to deprive him of radiant prospects lately opened before him. "Listen here you!" he said, frowning heavily. "You sound like you're tryin' to argue in behalfs of them intanational Wall Street schemers. Their day's about over, let me tell you! My own dead father used to say over and over in his old age he hoped his chuldern'd never haf to work as hard as he had, and I never forgot it. What's the use a man's workin' himself to death and Wall Street gettin' all the money? The time's come for a turnover; we're goin' to get our rights, and any man that comes around here arguin' against it —"

"Me?" The young man laughed ruefully. "I only wish them fairy stories was true!"

"Fairy stories!" Bridewater's voice was husky with anger. He rose and shook a lank forefinger at the young workman. "Listen here! You're the kind that wants to upset their own country just when it's gettin' straightened out the way it ought to be! Talkin' about fairy stories! You're the kind that wants to take the bread out of the mouths of the poor! I bet you're paid for it! I bet you're hired by the banks to come around here and —"

"Paid? Hell, don't I wish I was, though!"

"I don't want no more truck with you!" Bridewater made a furiously obliterative[6] gesture with his extended hand, turned abruptly, and strode down a graveled path that led to Dellavan Avenue, the dismal west boundary of Garfield Square.

His shabby figure moved gauntly against the soiled gilt light of a sun edging its way downward into the western smoke of the sprawling city; and he muttered aloud as he walked. The mutterings were fragmentary; he conceived himself to be addressing the too talkative young workman. In more ways than one he called this creature a dog; he labeled him rodent also, and defied him. "Man to man now, just you try it! I been waitin'

---

[4] *souse* (slang), a drunkard.
[5] *with a bun on* (slang), under the influence of an intoxicating liquor.

[6] *obliterative*, effacing.

all my life for it, and now I got it and it's mine. Just you try to get it away from me, you rat, you!"

Naturally George Bridewater was in a state of rage. His always brittle temper, combined with his reverence for the hope so often expressed by his aged father, deceased, had led to long periods of moody idleness throughout his life. Now, at last virtual possessor of five thousand dollars a year, with two hundred dollars a month in prospect, all to be assured to him by Uncle Sam himself, he found upspringing dastards in his path, casting doubts that infuriated him because they frightened him. Talking about "fairy stories" and sneering at that bright income — when all the time millions and millions of people were going to help him get it, because they couldn't get theirs without seeing that he got his! Bridewater didn't care whether they got theirs or not, just so he got his.

"Sock in the jaw's what you need!" he said, as he crossed Dellavan Avenue. "Big Mouth!"

The house at the corner of Dellavan Avenue and Fourth Street added to his anger; he had always hated it without ever knowing anybody who lived in it. Opulently of the Seventies when the town was young, its whole stone facade, its tall plate-glass windows, and its inside shutters of black walnut had been the front of high fortune and of "family"; but the twentieth century had long ago made the imposing house into an uncherished relic. Ill kept, dinged with years of soot, neighbored by lifeless used-car salesrooms, and a dead restaurant, it was now as apologetic as an old dress coat in a secondhand dealer's window. George Bridewater, annoyed in his youth by its early splendors, remained woodenly unaware of its slow, complete change; his resentful mood still associated it with millionaires. Sheerly out of long habit he saw this pathetic house still enveloped in its same old air of bondholding superiority and exploiters' arrogance.

Therefore the lady who came forth from its front double doors of carved black walnut appeared arrogant to Bridewater as he crossed the street. She was delicate-looking, pale, slender, and elderly; but her little black hat, her brown shoes, her well-brushed tweed skirt and neat old brown cloth coat seemed to him offensively fashionable. What was worse and gave him a sense of being personally affronted, there capered and barked beside her, as she came down the stone steps, a

long-haired little white dog obviously exclusive, high-toned, and ill disposed toward the common people. George Bridewater hated all dogs; but what he felt about this one can't respectably be even suggested. Horrid silver gleams came from its little collar; the preservation of its detested life was secured by a leather leash looped about the gloved wrist of its mistress.

Moreover, Bridewater knew this dog, both by sight and hearing, especially by hearing. His daughter's house, where he lived, faced upon Ackley Street, which was the next thoroughfare to Dellavan Avenue, but unlike the Avenue had never been fashionable. The back yard of the hated mansion on Dellavan Avenue was separated by only a narrow alley from his daughter's back yard, and more than once George Bridewater's Sunday morning slumbers had been ruined by the egoistic barking of this little white dog, let out for air in the back yard of the pompous house.

The neat elderly lady and her noisy little pet, bound for a short airing in Garfield Square, came face to face with Bridewater at the corner of the crossing. "No, Rocket!" she said affectionately, as the dog made a short oblique dash toward Mr. Bridewater's left leg. Rocket, restrained by the leash, barked importantly at this moving leg; and his owner and the owner of the threatened limb exchanged a glance in passing — the briefest momentary gaze, but fateful.

Bridewater's eye was hard with old prejudice and with the new wrong being done him. This was not the first time he'd encountered the lady or been snapped at by Rocket. In them both he saw representatives of wealth, living in a wealthy house, luxurious aristocrats able to despise him because they had despoiled him. They'd better look out; he'd have his rights back from them before long!

The elderly lady's glance was a metallic one, too; she'd often noticed Bridewater about the neighborhood and disapproved of him, thinking him a surly loafer. She was a Miss Pency, a retired schoolteacher. She'd worked hard until she had passed sixty-five; and Bridewater was right in thinking her a bondholder — invested savings brought her forty-two dollars a month. She and Rocket lived pretty sparsely in the struggling boarding house that the grandiose mansion had long ago become.

Miss Pency lived there more sparsely than Rocket did. She had no relatives; her old friends, too, were all dead now, and except for him she was alone in the world. She made every sacrifice for him and kept him happy. Failing sight no longer permitted her to read, and he was really more than the great thing in her life. She lived for him; and he, in return, though he was self-centered and conceited, loved only her — something no one else had ever done.

Rocket despised everybody in the world except Miss Pency and himself. As Bridewater, having given Miss Pency the one look, passed on his way, the little dog made plain in a final dart and snarl what he thought about that shabby leg. He believed he'd frightened off a marauder, and barking with insufferable vanity, and looking all the way up to his mistress' face to reassure her of his protection, went on with her to the Square.

Bridewater, walking along dingy Fourth Street toward Ackley Street, tasted gall. The unprovoked attack upon him by a high-living, costly, dangerous pet of the haughty rich woman who looked at him as if he were dirt burned in his heart with that other live coal, the young workman's argufying. Rocket's now distant, joyous barking epitomized[7] into a sound all the forces that Bridewater had felt working against him throughout his life. "*You! You!*" that barking seemed to say. "*You* won't get it! Never! Not *you!*"

"I'd ought to kicked the liver out of him!" Bridewater said, pausing at the corner of Ackley and Fourth Streets; and mentally conjoining Rocket and the young workman in the single pronoun, delivered the kick retrospectively to this hybrid. Then he saw upon the other side of the street a person with whom he wished to talk. He crossed over, dodging homeward-bound sedans, and approached her.

She was a comely young colored woman, sprightly in dress, and much more expensively of the fashion than was Miss Pency, for instance. She sat, chewing gum absent-mindedly, upon the rather tumble-down front veranda of a small wooden house; and the veranda was so close to the street that Bridewater, halting upon the sidewalk before the house, could speak to her intimately and without raising his voice.

"Listen here, Ellamora," he said, "I been a good while tryin' to get ahold of you for another little talk."

"That so?" Chewing her gum slowly, though at times allowing it to be visible, she seemed to feel a faint preoccupied interest in the passing sedans; none at all in Bridewater.

"Just like I told you the other day, Ellamora," he said, "you're gettin' a great big salary administrating Relief, and I been a good family neighbor of yours a couple years now. Well, there must be some big money pass through your hands that the guvment's turning over to the people, so why oughtn't some it to come my way just the same as it does to any other man that ain't got a job?" His voice, more than friendly, became insinuating. "You always been a nice, good-lookin' girl, Ellamora. How about it?"

Ellamora turned her head to call into an open window behind her chair. "Gran'ma! You're allowing that skillet to remain exposed to the heated coals too long again. It causes the odor of scorching. Step on it, Gran'ma!" She looked forward again, over Bridewater's head, and seemed drowsily absorbed in her chewing gum; but finally took cognizance of his question. "Well, no, Mr. Bridewater. I'm unable to see my way clear towards accommodating you like you been requesting me."

"Why not?" he asked urgently. "That guvment money all belongs to the people, and ain't I — "

"No," she said. "We don't favor the policies of handing out cash for the present time, Mr. Bridewater. I provide food and fuel exclusive only, and I'm already engaged with the total sum of one hundred and eleven families. I couldn't admit you inside this quota because I've made a ruling cases like you don't come under it."

"Why don't I?" She maddened him; but he contained himself, hoping to placate her. "Big Sam Lesloe told me yesterday him and his whole family been livin' on the guvment eight months now, and if you let Sam and his family in — "

"No, I couldn't do it," Ellamora informed him languidly. "Mr. Lesloe and his family don't possess any property or any employment, so they come under the case; whereas you live with your daughter in a house owned in her name with an income from roomers. You're complete outside all our rulings and under the class of property owners."

"Listen!" Bridewater's voice was husky with his struggle to control it and still speak persuasively. "Them damn roomers owe their rent; they don't pay it. That house is mortgaged up to every cent it's worth, and we ain't paid last October's taxes and don't never expect to.

---

[7] *epitomized*, summarized.

Big Sam Lesloe told me himself he turned down two jobs only last week because if he'd took them he'd had to get off guvment money. Listen here, Ellamora; if you let the Lesloes stay in and go on keepin' me out, ain't somebody liable to say it's because Lesloes is cousins of yours and I ain't? Big Sam's your cousin, ain't he?"

All he achieved was a further distention of his spleen. Ellamora looked at him sleepily, rose, yawned, and turned toward the open doorway of the house. "I desire to lay down awhile before supper, Gran'ma!" she called as she went in. "Fix the sofa cushions for me. Step on it, Gran'ma!"

George Bridewater, in strong agitation upon the sidewalk, stared at the vacant veranda and uttered three words, two of them irreverent and the other hot with racial superiority.

It seemed to him that insult and outrage stalked him; that he was being used as a doormat by colored people, by rich women's dogs, and by pseudo-workmen hired by the banks. He repeated the three words twice; then he turned and strode across the street to his own home, a wooden house somewhat larger than Ellamora Thompson's grandma's but in greater disrepair. Half way across the street he encountered drifts of the smell of hot cabbage; the odor solidified as he penetrated farther into it; and when he opened his front door, it filled his lungs, the orifices[8] of his head, and all the air spaces within his clothes.

His daughter, Effie Bridewater, met him in the narrow front hall. "I saw you across the street, Papa," she said in an affectionate, tired voice. "Junior's home and I was just coming to call you. I got supper all ready now, and I got a nice surprise for you, Papa."

"Surprise? Cabbage? You call that a —"

"No, we got cabbage soup; but you wait and see what else!" She took his hand and gazed up at him with a tender fondness. She was thirty but looked a driven and dried-up forty. "Come on, Papa. Junior's waiting for his supper."

She retained her father's hand until they had reached the hot little kitchen and sat down at the oilcloth-covered table, where her brother, Junior, had already helped himself to a plate of cabbage soup. Junior, a thin boy of twenty-two with an unfortunate complexion, said nothing to either of them. He was always quiet

at home, had no trade or profession but sometimes seemed to have a little money, which a girl in the next block always got away from him — something his father and sister had long ago learned they needn't hope to do. Once or twice a plain-clothes man had come to the house inquiring about Junior when he was away; and sometimes Junior disappeared from home for as much as a month but was stonily uncommunicative on his return.

He didn't get along well with his father; and, though he declined to argue with him, sometimes jeered at him a little. Junior was a Communist, and Bridewater hated all radicals, believed they were trying to ruin the country and might upset the great new plans for redistributing the wealth of the wealthy.

Effie didn't really care for Junior, either, though she supported him. All her life, for reasons lost in some fathomlessly obscure predilection of her infancy, her whole power to love was concentrated upon her father. To Effie her father was all that little Rocket was to Miss Pency; and though Bridewater lacked Rocket's reciprocal intense devotion, the deepest feeling he had, except one, was for Effie.

"No, I ain't," he replied gruffly to an anxious question of hers, as he finished his soup. "I certainly ain't feelin' any too good this evening."

"You didn't eat anything disagreed with you this afternoon, Papa? A sangwich or anything?"

"How could I ate any sangwich without even a nickel on me?"

"Then what's the trouble, Papa?"

"Never you mind; I got enough! Where's this surprise you was talkin' so much about?"

"You'll see!" She removed the soup, brought fresh plates; then brightly set the surprise upon the table. "It's a steak, Papa! Just what you love the most. I thought for once we'd just splurge. Ain't it a dindy?"

His lowering brow lightened a little, and he said he hoped so; but, when about half the steak had been placed upon his plate and he tested its quality, he made plain his disappointment. "Wha'd you pay for this steak?"

"Oh, my!" Effie cried, stricken. "They told me it was a tender one. Ain't it all right for your teeth, Papa?"

Bridewater clenched his fingers round the handle of his fork, stabbed the prongs heavily into the steak.

[8] *orifices*, openings.

"Might be all right for dog's teeth," he said; and the thought of a dog made him sorer. "Leather!" He gave his slyly smiling son a hard glance. "Might be all right for them Russians' teeth, too. I hear they'll eat anything you care to give 'em."

Junior's eye showed a gleam of malicious mirth. "Say! You'd last about five minutes in Russia. Everybody's got to work there."

He put only a slight emphasis upon the word *got;* but the effect upon Bridewater was sufficient. "You shut your mouth!" he said. "I been all my life hopin' my chuldren wouldn't haf to work as hard as I have; but I never thought I'd bring a loafer into the world that'd try to upset the United States Guvment!"

"So it was you who brought me into the world, was it?" Junior uttered a single harsh sound of laughter. "Glad I know who I got to thank for it. Done a lot for me since, too, haven't you?"

An impulse to violence swelled Bridewater's reddening neck. He seemed about to swing his long arm across the table; but Effie interposed hurriedly. "Here's fried potatoes, Papa. You always do love fried potatoes, dearie; and I got a dish of awful nice applesauce for dessert, besides. I feel awful bad about the steak, Papa; but you can eat all the fried potatoes because Junior and I can chew the steak all right and that's plenty for us. Won't you try to enjoy the fried potatoes and applesauce, please, Papa?"

Bridewater, morose, made no vocal response; but ate all of the fried potatoes, almost all of the applesauce and also drank two cups of brownly transparent fluid Effie called coffee. Junior, rising, gave his father a brief, unbearable glance of amusement and departed; was heard ascending the creaky stairway in the hall, on his way to his own quarters in the attic. Effie washed the dishes, glancing now and then placatively at her father. He remained broodingly in his chair at the table, and sometimes his thoughts caused him to breathe so heavily that she heard the sound. When this happened, she sighed deeply with a loving compassion; and when she had finished the dishes, she sat down beside him and looked at him entreatingly.

"Papa, I got a feeling something's gone awful wrong with you today. Couldn't you tell me about it, dearie?"

"On top of everything else," he said, "think of my havin' a son like that! Sometimes I get so sick of — " He paused and looked toward the open window through which there came from the dusk beyond a repeated sharp little sound that seemed to sting him. "A man can't hear himself talk in his own house!"

"It's only that little white dog in the yard behind our alley," Effie said soothingly. "They always let him out now for a few minutes and again about ten o'clock; but just for a little while. There; he's stopped. They've took him in the house again. Go on, Papa, tell me what you was goin' to. Won't you, dearie?"

"I'm sick of this life!" he said. "I ain't goin' to put up with it no longer. If it ain't goin' to change right from now on, I'm through!"

The desperation in his voice and in his face alarmed her. "Oh, Papa, don't say that! You don't mean you'd — you'd — "

"I mean just what I say, I can tell you! If things don't look like gettin' better right from now on, what I got to live for? I ain't goin' to put up with it, gettin' balked and flouted and high-hatted and bit at and walked on and treated like I ain't got a word to say in this world. I'm ready to quit, I tell you!"

"No, no, dearie; don't talk like this!" Effie implored him. "It's my fault. I'd ought to made sure that steak was going to be tender; I'd ought to paid a few cents more and got a better cut. I can't stand for you to feel so bad. I'd give you anything in the world, Papa, if I had it. I'd give my life's blood to have you feel happier. You know I would, don't you, dearie?"

"Would you?" He looked at her penetratingly. "You honest mean you would, Effie?"

"Of course I would. A thousand times!"

At that, his mood seemed to lighten a little; his frown relaxed, and he gave her a kind look. "Listen, honey. For a good while back I been thinkin' over ways to make things better, and it's just begun to look to me like I've worked out a plan to where I could swing it. All I need's a little ready money. Less'n three hundred dollars would do it."

She looked frightened. "Would do what, Papa?"

"Would give me something to go on," he explained. "Money to live on. Honey, I'm so sick and tired of goin' around without a cent in my pocket — not a single solitary red penny! — I just can't stand it no longer, Effie. I don't ask much — just a few dollars in my pants, enough to feel like a human bein', anyhow, and get my shoes patched and buy a cigar or a sangwich if I wanted to and take a bus ride somewheres maybe. A man can't go forever without even a nickel on him, honey!"

Her fright increased as she stared at him. "Papa, you don't mean the house, do you? You ain't talking about that again?"

"Yes, I am," he said; and now his tone became earnestly persuasive. "Honey, I got it all figured out, prackly to the dot. We ain't got long to wait for that redistabution of the wealth to be worked out. It'll be six years before I get my two hundred dollars a month; but the biggest men in the country are workin' every minute right now, fixin' to give everybody five thousand dollars a year; and it's just like wildfire. Nine-tenths of everybody you talk to's for it, and anybody in Congress or anywheres else that stands against it's goin' to get what's comin' to 'em! All I want's a little to go on while we're waitin' for the big money to begin comin' in. That's all I'm askin' you to do, Effie — just enough to tide me over till then."

"Oh, Papa, if I only had it! If I only — "

"But you have!" he urged. "Anyways you could lay hands on it inside of a few days. I was down at them real estate men's, Smith and Angel's, this morning again; and they says yes, they still got this client that's buyin' up depression property, and they're still willin' to take over the mortgage and on top of it pay you cash down two hundred and eighty-five dollars for your equity in this house."

"Papa!" she gasped. "I can't!"

"Yes, you can." He was increasingly urgent. "Wait till you see the beauty of it! The minute we don't own the house no longer, we go on Relief and get all our food and fuel. Ellamora Thompson as good as told me this evening she couldn't keep us off Relief if we didn't own the house. And we'd rent the house from Smith and Angel and go on livin' here just the same, but not pay only just part of the first month's rent, and after that, under this new law, Smith and Angel couldn't evict us out for over a year anyways. And all the time we'd have close on three hundred dollars to be spendin' any way we please, pure velvet! And by that time the redistabution plan'll be workin', and we'll be livin' a life *worth* livin' and — "

"Oh, Papa dear!" Effie cried pleadingly, in sharpest distress. "I can't! Don't ask me that. You know I told

Mamma before she died I'd always try to hold on to the house and keep our little family together. I haven't told you; but the roomers been payin' a little better lately. I'm keepin' up the mortgage interest all right, and only this afternoon I was down at the Treasurer's Office and paid off the taxes."

"What!" Bridewater shouted, and, electrified by a sudden anguish, sprang to his feet. "The taxes? You paid 'em? You didn't!"

"Yes, I did."

Bridewater called loudly upon his Creator and began to pace the floor. "Threw it away when you knew I was walkin' the streets without a nickel to my name! Yes, and just when we're goin' to sell the house and them real estate men would had to pay the taxes and we needn't ever thought about 'em again! Threw it away just when we could had that much more money to spend as we please and — "

"But I *can't* sell the house!" Effie cried. "I can't! I can't! I just can't!"

"Why not?"

Effie began to cry. "Papa, it was mostly for you I worked so hard to buy it. Eight years workin' in that laundry to save the money and always thinkin' I'd have a nice place for you and me to live anyhow, no matter what else happened! Anyways, we got a roof over our heads and we *mustn't* give it up, Papa. Don't push me to sell it, Papa; please don't! Suppose this redistribution got stopped some way and didn't come about and — "

"Quit that talk!" he bellowed at her. "I had enough of that this afternoon from a smart-aleck in Garfield Square, and I won't hear not another damn word against the United States Guvment doin' what it's goin' to do, and got to do, and *better* do — else it'll get a revolution and be *made* to do it! All I want to know now is just this. Are you goin' to do like I say or aren't you?"

"Wait!" Effie ran into her small pantry, whence there issued, a moment later, a thin sound of tinkling. She came out extending toward her father eagerly but with trembling fingers a silver half dollar. "Take it, Papa. I know it's awful mean for you to go around without anything at all on you. I been too close with you, I know; but I been so terrible scared over the taxes and interest. It's fifty cents, Papa; won't you take it?"

"Half a dollar!" With bitterest irony Bridewater faced his tragedy — denied close on three hundred dollars and offered fifty cents! His passionate open palm struck the coin from Effie's shaking fingers; it rolled upon the floor. "Half a dollar! Now I *am* through! Said you'd give your life's blood for me, and then go and fiddle me out half a dollar! Half a dollar!"

Effie began to sob aloud. "I would — I would give you my life's blood. You know I would!" She sank down in the chair he'd left vacant, put her arms upon the table and her head, face downward, upon her arms. "I can't let the house go, Papa! It seems like I hear Mamma always whispering me to keep it for you. I can't! I can't! I can't!"

"I'm through, I tell you!" Bridewater shouted. "I don't haf to stand such a life and I won't! I'll do something! I'll go crazy if I don't do something now!"

Effie, shaking all over and sobbing, could only protest babblingly, not lifting her head. To these incoherent sounds there came no other response than a brief scuffling of Bridewater's shoes upon the wooden floor. Then, while she still moaned to him entreatingly, the flimsy house felt the shock of the front door's being hurled shut with a crash. Bridewater had gone, but his daughter continued to sob upon her desolate arms.

After awhile, still sniffling, she rose, took a dishcloth from a nail upon the wall and wiped the oilcloth of the table where her tears had trickled. "Oh, Papa, dearie!" she moaned, and moaning, looked wetly about, searching the floor for the fallen half dollar. She couldn't find it; and when she understood that he must have retrieved it and taken it with him, she was a little cheered for a time but later had a thought that disquieted her. Once in her mind, that thought grew, did more than disquiet her, slowly became sinister.

At nine o'clock she went up to the attic, where her brother, still dressed, lay stretched upon his bed reading a pamphlet. She stood at the foot of the bed, trembling, her fingers twitching and her eyes staring.

"Junior, I'm scared about Papa!"

Junior looked at her amusedly over the top of his pamphlet. "What for? Is he goin' to commit suicide some more?"

"Junior, I'm scared! Will you help me go look for him?"

He didn't move. "Will you buy me a pack of cigarettes if I do?"

"Yes, I will, Junior. I'm scared."

"O.K." He smiled with one side of his mouth, congratulating himself on an easy bargain, and rolled himself lazily off the bed. "Bet you a quarter he's down at Abe Trissel's Place on First Street watchin' a pool game."

Effie didn't take the bet, though not because she knew she wouldn't be paid if she won it; she only asked him to hurry. On the street Junior objected to the pace she set. "What's the use breakin' your neck? He ain't goin' to do anything to himself, not that guy! What you pantin' like that for? He'll be settin' there all right; you'll see."

Junior was mistaken. Bridewater wasn't at Abe Trissel's Place and hadn't been there; nor was he at Johnny March's Cafe or at Frank's Bar, Junior's other suggestions. "Quit that pantin', can't you?" he said as they came out of Frank's Bar. "There's one other place he hangs around sometimes; so that's where he's got to be. It's Horling's out on West Eighth, quite a ways unless you want to get bighearted and give us a trolley ride."

"No, no," she said. "We can walk it just as easy, and you say he's sure to be there anyways, Junior, so —"

He laughed bleakly. "O. K. Come on, then, if we got to hoof it."

Neither Bridewater nor any news of him at Horling's; and, when they came out to the street, Effie was weeping as well as panting. Junior again complained of her emotion.

"But that's all the places he ever goes; you told me so!" she explained, defending herself. "You don't *know* the state he was in, Junior; you didn't hear him when he went out. You didn't —"

"Say, listen! I know the kind that do that; he ain't built that way."

"Maybe not most the time, Junior," she whimpered; "but he's different tonight. You didn't hear his voice when he said he was through and was goin' crazy if he didn't do something. You didn't —"

"Say! Listen, I'm tired. How's he goin' to do it, suppose even he tries to? He hasn't got a gun, and if he went over to the river he couldn't let himself stop swimmin', even if he did take a notion to jump in and wet himself. He hasn't got any money, so he couldn't go to a drug store and —"

"Oh, but he has!" Effie cried. He's got money. I gave him fifty cents."

"Went haywire, did you?" Junior asked, sardonic.[9] "Just throwin' your money around! Short life but a merry one, what? Tell me next time you get that way, will you? Come on; we got to hoof it all the way back home."

"No, no! I want to — I want to ask at the drug store if he — if he bought anything like that. Let's go to Hait's drug store."

"Hait's? Nopy," Junior said. "He can't go there because he talked 'em into givin' him credit last January. If he wanted to buy carbolic to drink his own health in, they prob'ly wouldn't sell it to him except some place where they know him, and Hait's is the only place they do."

"No, it isn't. Mr. Kleever, that used to have the bedroom over the kitchen, clerks at Brown's Cash Drug Store, corner Ackley and Sixth, and he knows Papa. We got to go there, Junior."

Junior consented. "It's on the way home anyhow," he said; and presently was again objecting to the speed at which she kept him scurrying through the long, darkling streets. But when finally they reached the place they sought, she faltered outside the lighted doorway and with twisting fingers clutched her brother's sleeve.

"You ask Mr. Kleever. I'm — I'm too scared to. You just ask him if Papa's been there; and, if he has, you — you ask Mr. Kleever if he bought anything. I'm scared. I'll wait here, Junior."

Junior grinned at her. "Goofy, huh? O.K., I'll ask him." He slouched into the drug store; but Effie didn't watch him through either the doorway or the broad bright window beside it. Instead, she stood with her back to these areas of light, faced the melancholy street, and twisted her fingers. When Junior came out, he was smoking another of the cigarettes she'd bought for him at Abe Trissel's. "Come on," he said, taking her arm. "No place else to go; me for home. It's only a couple blocks. Come on."

She came with him slowly, and her voice was weak when she contrived to use it. "Junior, you — you never took ahold of my arm before. Did — did they say —"

"Walk on," he said. "I told you he wouldn't do it, and they haven't got me believin' so yet."

"Yet? Then they — then they did —"

"Don't get so excited!" Junior's voice was a little unsteady. "If he was goin' to do it, why wouldn't he done it soon's he got outside the store? Had the stuff in his hand, so why not?"

Effie uttered a gulping outcry. "Then he did —"

"Yep. Kleever says he come in the drug store about half past nine. Told Kleever he wanted strychnine pills for his heart, and Kleever sold 'em to him. I give a laugh and asked if they'd do him any harm; and Kleever says no, not unless he took about half of 'em all at once. Says then it might be pretty bad; but says the old man knew all about that himself. Here! What you —"

Effie cried out again. "*Papa!*" and began to run.

Junior ran with her. Side by side they reached the gate in the picket fence that was the decrepit barrier between their home and the public sidewalk. "Look in the yard," Junior said, panting now himself. "Look in the yard. If I was goin' to do anything like that, I'd do it in the yard, not in the house — most likely the back yard. He *might* be out here — somewheres."

The yard was small, mangily patched with grass here and there, and without trees. The light from street lamps showed no form extended upon the forepart of this limited, unlovely expanse; and the brother and sister passed round the house to the thicker darkness that was in the rear. Effie, convulsive all over, clutched at her throat and shoulders, shut her eyes, and ceased to go forward.

"You'll — you'll haf to do the looking," she sobbed. "But you tell me if —"

She could say no more, stood praying within herself; then she heard a sickish laugh from Junior.

"Come here," he said; and, when she stumblingly had come beside him, he pointed to the unshuttered kitchen window. "Look a-yonder!"

The saving Effie had turned out the electric bulb in the kitchen before she left the house, but the warm little room was lighted now. In the sufficient illumination from above his head, Bridewater sat tilted back in a chair and had his shoeless feet on the table. He smoked a five-cent cigar and read a magazine of Hollywood full of alluring pictures of ladies. His expression was placid. After all the arguments and insults and barkings he'd had to bear this hard day, he seemed at peace.

Outside in the darkness Effie clung feebly to Junior. "Poor Papa!" she said, sobbing no longer but weeping gently in thankfulness. "He never told me his heart give him any trouble. I won't be so close with him after this. I got to find ways to make him happier."

George Bridewater had already found one way to make himself happier. That is to say, he just now felt comparatively satisfied and, in a measure, avenged upon the wealthy — at least temporarily. He had saved his reason by doing that something he had declared he must do or go crazy.

Effie's ninety-nine-cent clock on the wall behind him showed the time to be about twenty minutes of eleven; and at ten o'clock there had been the usual sprightly barking in the yard beyond the alley. The sound had stopped abruptly when the scampering Rocket came upon a bit of toughish steak near the alley fence. Thence onward he was quiet. Nevermore would that gay spirit disturb honest neighbors at bedtime or break the peace of a Sabbath morning.

Now, through the darkness of the yard of the pompous Dellavan Avenue mansion there groped a brokenhearted old schoolteacher, stifling her faint outcries to whisper bits of loving baby talk. She walked stoopingly, holding her dead little white dog close to her under a shawl. Miss Pency hoped to evade the landlady and to get up to her own meager room unseen, so that she could have this one last night with Rocket.

VIEWING THE AUTHOR'S IDEAS

1. What does Bridewater reveal of his past life? What opinion do you form of him very early in the story? Discuss his views about a citizen's rights. What lack does he manifest in his words and manner?

2. Summarize the plan for old-age security described by Bridewater. How did the young man regard these plans? How did he look upon the plans for government relief? Account for his attitudes.

3. What seems to be the cause for the unemployment of Bridewater and his group? Why was Bridewater irritated by Miss Pency; by the interview with Ellamora Thompson?

4. How is Bridewater contrasted with his son; with his daughter?

5. What distress does Bridewater cause with his half dollar? Why? Discuss the causes of the other evils revealed by this story.

EVALUATING HIS MANNER OF EXPRESSION

1. What period of time does the story cover? Where does the action really begin? How do the opening scenes lead up to the complications arising from Bridewater's half dollar? Was the ending a complete surprise?

2. How is the story a satire upon paternalism in government? Point out instances of humor, irony, and pathos.

3. Account for the effectiveness of the phrase "dodging homeward-bound sedans." Find examples of similar diction. Describe Tarkington's style.

4. How does the dialogue contribute to the delineation of character and to the development of the action of the story? What effect did education have upon Ellamora Thompson?

The Sculptor's Funeral

Willa Cather

This story is a vigorous condemnation of persons who are so absorbed in material pursuits that they have no appreciation of the finer things of mind and spirit. Into her account of the sculptor's funeral the author skillfully weaves the tragedy of a sensitive artist reared in the sordid atmosphere of a small Western town. At the cost of pain and misunderstanding the sculptor achieves high fame, which finds little recognition among his relatives and neighbors.

A GROUP of the townspeople stood on the station siding of a little Kansas town, awaiting the coming of the night train, which was already twenty minutes overdue. The snow had fallen thick over everything; in the pale starlight the line of bluffs across the wide, white meadows south of the town made soft, smoke-colored curves against the clear sky. The men on the siding stood first on one foot and then on the other, their hands thrust deep into their trousers pockets, their overcoats open, their shoulders screwed up with the cold; and they glanced from time to time toward the southeast, where the railroad track wound along the river shore. They conversed in low tones and moved about restlessly, seeming uncertain as to what was expected of them. There was but one of the company who looked as if he knew exactly why he was there; and he kept conspicuously apart, walking to the far end of the platform, returning to the station door, then pacing up the track again, his chin sunk in the high collar of his overcoat, his burly shoulders drooping forward, his gait heavy and dogged. Presently he was approached by a tall, spare, grizzled man clad in a faded Grand Army suit,[1] who shuffled out from the group and advanced with a certain deference, craning his neck forward until his back made the angle of a jackknife three-quarters open.

"I reckon she's agoin' to be pretty late agin tonight, Jim," he remarked in a squeaky falsetto.[2] "S'pose it's the snow?"

"I don't know," responded the other man with a shade of annoyance, speaking from out an astonishing cataract of red beard that grew fiercely and thickly in all directions.

The spare man shifted the quill toothpick he was chewing to the other side of his mouth. "It ain't likely that anybody from the East will come with the corpse, I s'pose," he went on reflectively.

"I don't know," responded the other more curtly than before.

"It's too bad he didn't belong to some lodge or other. I like an order funeral myself. They seem more appropriate for people of some repytation," the spare man continued with an ingratiating concession in his shrill voice as he carefully placed his toothpick in his vest pocket. He always carried the flag at the G. A. R. funerals.

The heavy man turned on his heel without replying and walked up the siding. The spare man joined the uneasy group. "Jim's ez full ez a tick, ez ushel," he commented commiseratingly.

Just then a distant whistle sounded, and there was a shuffling of feet on the platform. A number of lanky boys, of all ages, appeared as suddenly and slimily as eels wakened by the crack of thunder; some came from the waiting-room, where they had been warming themselves by the red stove or half asleep on the slat benches; others uncoiled themselves from baggage trucks or slid out of express wagons. Two clambered down from the driver's seat of a hearse that stood backed up against the siding. They straightened their stooping shoulders and lifted their heads, and a flash of momentary animation kindled their dull eyes at that cold, vibrant scream, the world-wide call for men. It stirred them like the note of a trumpet, just as it had often stirred the man who was coming home tonight, in his boyhood.

The night express shot, red as a rocket, from out the eastward marshlands and wound along the river shore under the long lines of shivering poplars that sentineled the meadows, the escaping steam hanging in gray masses against the pale sky and blotting out the Milky Way. In a moment the red glare from the headlight streamed up the snow-covered track before the siding and glittered on the wet, black rails. The burly man with the disheveled red beard walked swiftly up the platform toward the approaching train, uncovering his head as he went. The group of men behind him hesitated, glanced questioningly at one another, and awkwardly followed his example. The train stopped; and the crowd shuffled up to the express car just as the door was thrown open, the man in the G. A. R. suit thrusting his head forward with curiosity. The express messenger appeared in the doorway, accompanied by a young man in a long ulster and traveling cap.

"Are Mr. Merrick's friends here?" inquired the young man.

The group on the platform swayed uneasily. Philip Phelps, the banker, responded with dignity: "We have come to take charge of the body. Mr. Merrick's father is very feeble and can't be about."

"Send the agent out here," growled the express messenger, "and tell the operator to lend a hand."

The coffin was got out of its rough box and down on the snowy platform. The townspeople drew back enough to make room for it and then formed a close semicircle about it, looking curiously at the palm leaf which lay across the black cover. No one said anything.

---

[1] *Grand Army suit*, uniform of the G.A.R. (Grand Army of the Republic), an organization composed of those who served in the Union army during the Civil War.

[2] *falsetto*, a false or artificial voice.

The baggageman stood by his truck, waiting to get at the trunks. The engine panted heavily, and the fireman dodged in and out among the wheels with his yellow torch and long oilcan, snapping the spindle boxes. The young Bostonian, one of the dead sculptor's pupils who had come with the body, looked about him helplessly. He turned to the banker, the only one of that black, uneasy, stoop-shouldered group who seemed enough of an individual to be addressed.

"None of Mr. Merrick's brothers are here?" he asked uncertainly.

The man with the red beard for the first time stepped up and joined the others. "No, they have not come yet; the family is scattered. The body will be taken directly to the house." He stooped and took hold of one of the handles of the coffin.

"Take the long hill road up, Thompson, it will be easier on the horses," called the liveryman as the undertaker snapped the door of the hearse and prepared to mount to the driver's seat.

Laird, the red-bearded lawyer, turned again to the stranger: "We didn't know whether there would be anyone with him or not," he explained. "It's a long walk; so you'd better go up in the hack." He pointed to a single battered conveyance, but the young man replied stiffly: "Thank you, but I think I will go up with the hearse. If you don't object," turning to the undertaker, "I'll ride with you."

They clambered up over the wheels and drove off in the starlight up the long, white hill toward the town. The lamps in the still village were shining from under the low, snow-burdened roofs; and beyond on every side the plains reached out into emptiness, peaceful and wide as the soft sky itself and wrapped in a tangible, white silence.

When the hearse backed up to a wooden sidewalk before a naked, weather-beaten frame house, the same composite, ill-defined group that had stood upon the station siding was huddled about the gate. The front yard was an icy swamp; and a couple of warped planks, extending from the sidewalk to the door, made a sort of rickety foot-bridge. The gate hung on one hinge and was opened wide with difficulty. Steavens, the young stranger, noticed that something black was tied to the knob of the front door.

The grating sound made by the casket as it was drawn from the hearse was answered by a scream from the house; the front door was wrenched open, and a tall, corpulent woman rushed out bareheaded into the snow and flung herself upon the coffin, shrieking: "My boy, my boy! And this is how you've come home to me!"

As Steavens turned away and closed his eyes with a shudder of unutterable repulsion, another woman, also tall but flat and angular, dressed entirely in black, darted out of the house and caught Mrs. Merrick by the shoulders, crying sharply: "Come, come, Mother, you mustn't go on like this!" Her tone changed to one of obsequious[3] solemnity as she turned to the banker: "The parlor is ready, Mr. Phelps."

The bearers carried the coffin along the narrow boards, while the undertaker ran ahead with the coffin rests. They bore it into a large, unheated room that smelled of dampness and disuse and furniture polish and set it down under a hanging lamp ornamented with jingling glass prisms and before a Rogers group[4] of John Alden and Priscilla, wreathed with smilax. Henry Steavens stared about him with the sickening conviction that there had been a mistake and that he had somehow arrived at the wrong destination. He looked at the clover-green Brussels, the fat plush upholstery, among the handpainted china plaques and panels and vases for some mark of identification — for something that might once conceivably have belonged to Harvey Merrick. It was not until he recognized his friend in the crayon portrait of a little boy in kilts and curls, hanging above the piano, that he felt willing to let any of these people approach the coffin.

"Take the lid off, Mr. Thompson; let me see my boy's face," wailed the elder woman between her sobs. This time Steavens looked fearfully, almost beseechingly into her face, red and swollen under its masses of strong, black, shiny hair. He flushed, dropped his eyes, and then, almost incredulously, looked again. There was a kind of power about her face — a kind of brutal handsomeness, even; but it was scarred and furrowed by violence and so colored and coarsened by fiercer passions that grief seemed never to have laid a gentle finger there. The long nose was distended and knobbed at the end, and there were deep lines on either side of it;

---

[3] *obsequious*, servilely attentive.

[4] *Rogers group*, small figures by the American sculptor John Rogers. They were extensively reproduced.

her heavy, black brows almost met across her forehead, her teeth were large and square, and set far apart — teeth that could tear. She filled the room; the men were obliterated, seemed tossed about like twigs in an angry water, and even Steavens felt himself being drawn into the whirlpool.

The daughter — the tall, rawboned woman in crepe, with a mourning comb in her hair which curiously lengthened her long face — sat stiffly upon the sofa, her hands, conspicuous for their large knuckles, folded in her lap, her mouth and eyes drawn down, solemnly awaiting the opening of the coffin. Near the door stood a mulatto woman, evidently a servant in the house, with a timid bearing and an emaciated face pitifully sad and gentle. She was weeping silently, the corner of her calico apron lifted to her eyes, occasionally suppressing a long, quivering sob. Steavens walked over and stood beside her.

Feeble steps were heard on the stairs, and an old man, tall and frail, odorous of pipe smoke, with shaggy, unkempt gray hair and a dingy beard, tobacco-stained about the mouth, entered uncertainly. He went slowly up to the coffin and stood rolling a blue cotton handkerchief between his hands, seeming so pained and embarrassed by his wife's orgy of grief that he had no consciousness of anything else.

"There, there, Annie, dear, don't take on so," he quavered timidly, putting out a shaking hand and awkwardly patting her elbow. She turned and sank upon his shoulder with such violence that he tottered a little. He did not even glance toward the coffin but continued to look at her with a dull, frightened, appealing expression, as a spaniel looks at the whip. His sunken cheeks slowly reddened and burned with miserable shame. When his wife rushed from the room, her daughter strode after her with set lips. The servant stole up to the coffin, bent over it for a moment, and then slipped away to the kitchen, leaving Steavens, the lawyer, and the father to themselves. The old man stood looking down at his dead son's face. The sculptor's splendid head seemed even more noble in its rigid stillness than in life. The dark hair had crept down the wide forehead; the face seemed strangely long, but in it there was not the repose we expect to find in the faces of the dead. The brows were so drawn that there were two deep lines above the beaked nose, and the chin was

thrust forward defiantly. It was as though the strain of life had been so sharp and bitter that death could not at once relax the tension and smooth the countenance into perfect peace — as though he were still guarding something precious, which might even yet be wrested from him.

The old man's lips were working under his stained beard. He turned to the lawyer with timid deference: "Phelps and the rest are comin' back to set up with Harve, ain't they?" he asked. "Thank 'ee, Jim, thank 'ee." He brushed the hair back gently from his son's forehead. "He was a good boy, Jim, always a good boy. He was ez gentle ez a child and the kindest of 'em all — only we didn't none of us ever onderstand him."

The tears trickled slowly down his beard and dropped upon the sculptor's coat.

"Martin, Martin! Oh, Martin! come here," his wife wailed from the top of the stairs. The old man started timorously: "Yes, Annie, I'm coming." He turned away, hesitated, stood for a moment in miserable indecision; then reached back and patted the dead man's hair softly and stumbled from the room.

"Poor old man, I didn't think he had any tears left. Seems as if his eyes would have gone dry long ago. At his age nothing cuts very deep," remarked the lawyer.

Something in his tone made Steavens glance up. While the mother had been in the room, the young man had scarcely seen anyone else; but now from the moment he first glanced into Jim Laird's florid face and bloodshot eyes, he knew that he had found what he had been heartsick at not finding before — the feeling, the understanding, that must exist in someone, even here.

The man was red as his beard with features swollen and blurred by dissipation and a hot, blazing blue eye. His face was strained — that of a man who is controlling himself with difficulty — and he kept plucking at his beard with a sort of fierce resentment. Steavens, sitting by the window, watched him turn down the glaring lamp, still its jangling pendants with an angry gesture, and then stand with his hands locked behind him staring down into the master's face. He could not help wondering what link there had been between the porcelain vessel and so sooty a lump of potter's clay.

From the kitchen an uproar was sounding; when the dining-room door opened, the import of it was clear. The mother was abusing the maid for having forgotten to make the dressing for the chicken salad which had been prepared for the watchers. Steavens had never heard anything in the least like it; it was injured, emotional, dramatic abuse, unique and masterly in its excruciating cruelty, as violent and unrestrained as had been her grief of twenty minutes before. With a shudder of disgust the lawyer went into the dining room and closed the door into the kitchen.

"Poor Roxy's getting it now," he remarked when he came back. "The Merricks took her out of the poorhouse years ago; and if her loyalty would let her, I guess the poor old thing could tell tales that would curdle your blood. She's the mulatto woman who was standing in here a while ago, with her apron to her eyes. The old woman is a fury; there never was anybody like her. She made Harvey's life a hell for him when he lived at home; he was so sick ashamed of it. I never could see how he kept himself sweet."

"He was wonderful," said Steavens slowly, "wonderful; but until tonight I have never known how wonderful."

"That is the eternal wonder of it, anyway; that anyone can come *even* from such a dung heap as this," the lawyer cried with a sweeping gesture which seemed to indicate much more than the four walls within which they stood.

"I think I'll see whether I can get a little air. The room is so close I am beginning to feel rather faint," murmured Steavens, struggling with one of the windows. The sash was stuck, however, and would not yield; so he sat down dejectedly and began pulling at his collar. The lawyer came over, loosened the sash with one blow of his red fist, and sent the window up a few inches. Steavens thanked him, but the nausea which had been gradually climbing into his throat for the last half hour left him with but one desire—a desperate feeling that he must get away from this place with what was left of Harvey Merrick. Oh, he comprehended well enough now the quiet bitterness of the smile that he had seen so often on his master's lips!

Once when Merrick returned from a visit home, he brought with him a singularly feeling and suggestive bas-relief[5] of a thin, faded old woman, sitting and sewing something pinned to her knee; while a full-lipped, full-blooded little urchin, his trousers held up by a single gallows, stood beside her, impatiently

twitching her gown to call attention to a butterfly he had caught. Steavens, impressed by the tender and delicate modeling of the thin, tired face, had asked him if it were his mother. He remembered the dull flush that had burned up in the sculptor's face.

The lawyer was sitting in a rocking chair beside the coffin, his head thrown back and his eyes closed. Steavens looked at him earnestly, puzzled at the line of the chin, and wondering why a man should conceal a feature of such distinction under that disfiguring shock of beard. Suddenly, as though he felt the young sculptor's keen glance, Jim Laird opened his eyes.

"Was he always a good deal of an oyster?" he asked abruptly. "He was terribly shy as a boy."

"Yes, he was an oyster, since you put it so," rejoined Steavens. "Although he could be very fond of people, he always gave one the impression of being detached. He disliked violent emotion; he was reflective and rather distrustful of himself — except, of course, as regarded his work. He was sure enough there. He distrusted men pretty thoroughly and women even more, yet somehow without believing ill of them. He was determined, indeed, to believe the best; but he seemed afraid to investigate."

"A burnt dog dreads the fire," said the lawyer grimly and closed his eyes.

Steavens went on and on, reconstructing that whole miserable boyhood. All this raw, biting ugliness had been the portion of the man whose mind was to become an exhaustless gallery of beautiful impressions — so sensitive that the mere shadow of a poplar leaf flickering against a sunny wall would be etched and held there forever. Surely, if ever a man had the magic word in his finger tips, it was Merrick. Whatever he touched, he revealed its holiest secret, liberated it from enchantment, and restored it to its pristine loveliness. Upon whatever he had come in contact with, he had left a beautiful record of the experience — a sort of ethereal signature, a scent, a sound, a color that was his own.

Steavens understood now the real tragedy of his master's life — neither love nor wine, as many had conjectured, but a blow which had fallen earlier and cut deeper than anything else could have done — a shame not his, and yet so unescapably his to hide in his heart from his very boyhood. And without — the frontier warfare; the yearning of a boy cast ashore upon a desert

---

[5] *bas-relief* (bä-rĕ-lēf), sculpture in low relief.

of newness and ugliness and sordidness for all that is chastened and old and noble with traditions.

At eleven o'clock the tall, flat woman in black announced that the watchers were arriving and asked them to "step into the dining room." As Steavens rose, the lawyer said dryly: "You go on — it'll be a good experience for you. I'm not equal to that crowd tonight; I've had twenty years of them."

As Steavens closed the door after him, he glanced back at the lawyer, sitting by the coffin in the dim light, with his chin resting on his hand.

The same misty group that had stood before the door of the express car shuffled into the dining room. In the light of the kerosene lamp they separated and became individuals. The minister, a pale, feeble-looking man with white hair and blond chin whiskers, took his seat beside a small side table and placed his Bible upon it. The Grand Army man sat down behind the stove and tilted his chair back comfortably against the wall, fishing his quill toothpick from his waistcoat pocket. The two bankers, Phelps and Elder, sat off in a corner behind the dinner table, where they could finish their discussion of the new usury law and its effect on chattel security loans.[6] The real-state agent, an old man with a smiling, hypocritical face, soon joined them. The coal-and-lumber dealer and the cattle shipper sat on opposite sides of the hard coal burner, their feet on the nickel work. Steavens took a book from his pocket and began to read. The talk around him ranged through various topics of local interest while the house was quieting down. When it was clear that the members of the family were in bed, the Grand Army man hitched his shoulders and, untangling his long legs, caught his heels on the rounds of his chair.

"S'pose there'll be a will, Phelps?" he queried in his weak falsetto.

The banker laughed disagreeably and began trimming his nails with a pearl-handled pocketknife.

"There'll scarcely be any need for one, will there?" he queried in his turn.

The restless Grand Army man shifted his position again, getting his knees still nearer his chin. "Why, the ole man says Harve's done right well lately," he chirped.

The other banker spoke up. "I reckon he means by that Harve ain't asked him to mortgage any more farms lately, so as he could go on with his education."

"Seems like my mind don't reach back to a time when Harve wasn't bein' edycated," tittered the Grand Army man.

There was a general chuckle. The minister took out his handkerchief and blew his nose sonorously. Banker Phelps closed his knife with a snap. "It's too bad the old man's sons didn't turn out better," he remarked with reflective authority. "They never hung together. He spent money enough on Harve to stock a dozen cattle farms, and he might as well have poured it into Sand Creek. If Harve had stayed at home and helped nurse what little they had and gone into stock on the old man's bottom farm, they might all have been well fixed. But the old man had to trust everything to tenants and was cheated right and left."

"Harve never could have handled stock none," interposed the cattleman. "He hadn't it in him to be sharp. Do you remember when he bought Sander's mules for eight-year olds, when everybody in town knew that Sander's father-in-law give 'em to his wife for a wedding present eighteen years before, an' they was full-grown mules then?"

The company laughed discreetly, and the Grand Army man rubbed his knees with a spasm of childish delight.

"Harve never was much account for anything practical, and he shore was never fond of work," began the coal-and-lumber dealer. "I mind the last time he was home; the day he left, when the old man was out to the barn helpin' his hand hitch up to take Harve to the train, and Cal Moots was patchin' up the fence; Harve, he come out on the step and sings out in his ladylike voice: 'Cal Moots, Cal Moots! please come cord my trunk.'"

"That's Harve for you," approved the Grand Army man. "I kin hear him howlin' yet when he was a big feller in long pants, and his mother used to whale him with a rawhide in the barn for lettin' the cows git foundered[7] in the cornfield when he was drivin' 'em home from pasture. He killed a cow of mine that-a-way onct — a pure Jersey and the best milker I had, an' the ole man had to put up for her. Harve, he was watchin' the sun set acrost the marshes when the animile got away."

"Where the old man made his mistake was in sending the boy East to school," said Phelps, stroking his goatee

---

[6] *chattel security loans*, loans made on personal property as security.

[7] *foundered*, caused to become lame.

and speaking in a deliberate, judicial tone. "There was where he got his head full of nonsense. What Harve needed, of all people, was a course in some first-class Kansas City business college."

The letters were swimming before Steavens's eyes. Was it possible that these men did not understand, that the palm on the coffin meant nothing to them? The very name of their town would have remained forever buried in the postal guide had it not been now and again mentioned in the world in connection with Harvey Merrick's. He remembered what his master had said to him on the day of his death, after the congestion of both lungs had shut off any probability of recovery, and the sculptor had asked his pupil to send his body home. "It's not a pleasant place to be lying while the world is moving and doing and bettering," he had said with a feeble smile, "but it rather seems as though we ought to go back to the place we came from, in the end. The townspeople will come in for a look at me; and after they have had their say, I shan't have much to fear from the judgment of God!"

The cattleman took up the comment. "Forty's young for a Merrick to cash in; they usually hang on pretty well. Probably he helped it along with whisky."

"His mother's people were not long-lived, and Harvey never had a robust constitution," said the minister mildly. He would have liked to say more. He had been the boy's Sunday-school teacher and had been fond of him, but he felt that he was not in a position to speak. His own sons had turned out badly, and it was not a year since one of them had made his last trip home in the express car, shot in a gambling house in the Black Hills.

"Nevertheless, there is no disputin' that Harve frequently looked upon the wine when it was red, also variegated, and it shore made an oncommon fool of him," moralized the cattleman.

Just then the door leading into the parlor rattled loudly, and everyone started involuntarily, looking relieved when only Jim Laird came out. The Grand Army man ducked his head when he saw the spark in his blue, bloodshot eye. They were all afraid of Jim; he was a drunkard, but he could twist the law to suit his client's needs as no other man in all western Kansas could do; and there were many who tried. The lawyer closed the door behind him, leaned back against it, and

folded his arms, cocking his head a little to one side. When he assumed this attitude in the courtroom, ears were always pricked up as it usually foretold a flood of withering sarcasm.

"I've been with you gentlemen before," he began in a dry, even tone, "when you've sat by the coffins of boys born and raised in this town; and, if I remember rightly, you were never any too well satisfied when you checked them up. What's the matter, anyhow? Why is it that reputable young men are as scarce as millionaires in Sand City? It might almost seem to a stranger that there was in some way something the matter with your progressive town. Why did Ruben Sayer, the brightest young lawyer you ever turned out, after he had come home from the university as straight as a die, take to drinking and forge a check and shoot himself? Why did Bill Merrit's son die of the shakes in a saloon in Omaha? Why was Mr. Thomas's son, here, shot in a gambling house? Why did young Adams burn his mill to beat the insurance companies and go to the pen?"

The lawyer paused and unfolded his arms, laying one clenched fist quietly on the table. "I'll tell you why. Because you drummed nothing but money and knavery into their ears from the time they wore knickerbockers; because you carped away at them as you've been carping here tonight, holding our friends Phelps and Elder up to them for their models, as our grandfathers held up George Washington and John Adams. But the boys were young and raw at the business you put them to, and how could they match coppers with such artists as Phelps and Elder? You wanted them to be successful rascals; they were only unsuccessful ones — that's all the difference. There was only one boy ever raised in this borderland between ruffianism and civilization who didn't come to grief, and you hated Harvey Merrick more for winning out than you hated all the other boys who got under the wheels. Lord, Lord, how you did hate him! Phelps, here, is fond of saying that he could buy and sell us all out any time he's a mind to; but he knew Harve wouldn't have given a tinker's damn[8] for his bank and all his cattle farms put together; and a lack of appreciation, that way, goes hard with Phelps.

"Old Nimrod thinks Harve drank too much; and this from such as Nimrod and me!

_____
[8] _tinker's damn_, something absolutely worthless.

"Brother Elder says Harve was too free with the old man's money — fell short in filial consideration, maybe. Well, we can all remember the very tone in which Brother Elder swore his own father was a liar, in the county court; and we all know that the old man came out of that partnership with his son as bare as a sheared lamb. But maybe I'm getting personal, and I'd better be driving ahead at what I want to say."

The lawyer paused a moment, squared his heavy shoulders, and went on: "Harvey Merrick and I went to school together back East. We were dead in earnest, and we wanted you all to be proud of us some day. We meant to be great men. Even I, and I haven't lost my sense of humor, gentlemen, I meant to be a great man. I came back here to practice, and I found you didn't in the least want me to be a great man. You wanted me to be a shrewd lawyer — oh, yes! Our veteran here wanted me to get him an increase of pension because he had dyspepsia; Phelps wanted a new county survey that would put the widow Wilson's little bottom farm inside his south line; Elder wanted to lend money at five per cent a month and get it collected; and Stark here wanted to wheedle old women up in Vermont into investing their annuities[9] in real-estate mortgages that are not worth the paper they are written on. Oh, you needed me hard enough, and you'll go on needing me!

"Well, I came back here and became the damned shyster[10] you wanted me to be. You pretend to have some sort of respect for me; and yet you'll stand up and throw mud at Harvey Merrick, whose soul you couldn't dirty and whose hands you couldn't tie. Oh, you're a discriminating lot of Christians! There have been times when the sight of Harvey's name in some Eastern paper has made me hang my head like a whipped dog; and, again, times when I liked to think of him off there in the world, away from all this hog wallow, climbing the big, clean upgrade he'd set for himself.

"And we? Now that we've fought and lied and sweated and stolen and hated as only the disappointed strugglers in a bitter, dead little Western town know how to do, what have we got to show for it? Harvey Merrick wouldn't have given one sunset over your marshes for all you've got put together, and you know it. It's not for me to say why, in the inscrutable wisdom of God, a genius should ever have been called from this place of hatred and bitter waters; but *I* want this Boston man to know that the drivel he's been hearing here tonight is the only tribute any truly great man could have from such a lot of sick, sidetracked, burnt-dog, land-poor sharks as the here-present financiers of Sand City — upon which town may God have mercy!"

The lawyer thrust out his hand to Steavens as he passed him, caught up his overcoat in the hall, and had left the house before the Grand Army man had had time to lift his ducked head and crane his long neck about at his fellows.

Next day Jim Laird was drunk and unable to attend the funeral services. Steavens called twice at his office but was compelled to start East without seeing him. He had a presentiment that he would hear from him again and left his address on the lawyer's table; but if Laird found it, he never acknowledged it. The thing in him that Harvey Merrick had loved must have gone under ground with Harvey Merrick's coffin; for it never spoke again, and Jim got the cold he died of driving across the Colorado mountains to defend one of Phelps's sons who had got into trouble out there by cutting government timber.

VIEWING THE AUTHOR'S IDEAS

1. Reconstruct the past life of the sculptor as revealed in the reflections of Steavens and in the conversation of the other characters. How is Merrick's fame suggested? Why does the author describe the funeral from Steavens' point of view? Show the changes that would have to be made in the story if it were told from the viewpoint of another character.

2. From suggestions in the story, sketch the life of Jim Laird. What is the attitude of the other townspeople toward the sculptor? Why do relatives and neighbors often fail to appreciate men of genius?

3. What picture of life in Sand City is painted in Jim Laird's scathing denouncement of the watchers? List details which show the "newness and ugliness and sordidness" of life in the frontier town. Mention ways in which a manner of life "chastened and old and noble with traditions" would differ from that in Sand City.

4. How does the story show the evil effects of materialism? Is the materialistic view of life prevalent only in small towns? What makes it less crude in centers of culture?

5. Describe the atmosphere of the funeral? How do the characters show their lack of a supernatural viewpoint?

[9] *annuities*, amounts of money payable yearly.

[10] *shyster*, a lawyer who does business in a petty or tricky way.

1. What period of time does the story cover? Why is the arrival of the corpse an effective starting point? Where is suspense greatest?

2. Is the emphasis in this story upon incident or character? What is the author's purpose? Find the sentence in which this purpose is best expressed.

3. How is the character of the mother revealed; of the father; of the sister; of the servant? Why does the author emphasize only sordid aspects of Sand City? Did she purposely omit much good that doubtless existed?

4. Select passages of vivid description. Find an example of pathos.

5. How are the following statements related to the central idea of the story:

(a) "He could not help wondering what link there had been between the porcelain vessel and so sooty a lump of potter's clay"

(b) "That is the eternal wonder of it anyway; that it can come *even* from such a dung heap as this"

(c) "All this raw, biting ugliness had been the portion of a man whose mind was to become an exhaustless gallery of beautiful impressions"?

The Bishop's Beggar

Stephen Vincent Benét

When you begin this story, you may think Benét intends to depict a worldly-minded prelate interested only in his own comfort and ambitious for future power. As you proceed, however, you begin to see the bishop in another light. Despite the fact that his intentions in taking Holy Orders were not the highest, he nevertheless shows a great regard for duty. It is evident that his early neglect of the poor resulted from a lack of knowledge of social conditions. The bishop ends by illustrating the time-honored axiom that an individual can bring about reform only in proportion to his own spiritual perfection.

IT SEEMS that in the old days there was a bishop of Remo, and he was a heedless and proud young man, though of good intentions. Now, that was possible in those days, when the fire and light of the new learning had spread through Italy and men drank, as if intoxicated, at a new spring. There were bishops who cared less for the Word of God than for their own splendor, and cardinals who were rather men of the world — and of no good world — than sons of the Church. I do not say that our bishop was as idle and self-seeking as some of these; I do say that he was a child of his time. He would have liked to be a lord, but his eldest brother was the lord; he would have liked to be a soldier, but his second brother was the soldier. So he went into the Church, for there, too, a man who bore a great name could rise. He was clever; he was ambitious; he had great connections. Now and then, to be sure, he asked a disquieting question; but the Baldis had always been original. The path that is rugged for many was made smooth for him from the first. When he was made bishop of Remo at an early age, the fact did not surprise him. Since he was to be neither lord nor soldier, he found that pleasant enough.

All went well for him at first. They were glad to have a young and handsome bishop at Remo, for the bishop before him had been old and ill-favored. It was a pleasure to no one to kiss his ring, and he frightened the children with his peering eyes. With the coming of our bishop, all this was changed. There was a great to-do and refurbishing of the bishop's palace; the smells of good cooking drifted again from the bishop's kitchens; when the bishop drove through the city, men threw their caps in the air. There were fine new frescoes in the cathedral, a new way of chanting in the choir. As for sin and suffering — well they are always with us. The people of Remo liked to sin pleasantly and be reminded of it as little as possible.

Nevertheless, at times a grayness would come over our bishop's spirit. He could not understand why it came. His life was both full and busy. He was a friend to art, a host to the gay and the learned, a ruler of men. He did not meddle in things which did not concern him; he felt in his heart that there was no prize in the Church which might not be within his grasp. And yet at times there was a grayness within him. It was singular.

He could not show that grayness before the world; he could not show it to his secretary or the witty company that gathered at his table. He could wrestle with it in prayer; and so he did. But he found it no easy task. Had the Devil appeared before him with horns and a tail, he would have known what to do. But a grayness of spirit — a cool little voice in the mind which said to him now and then, "What do you in these robes at this place, Gianfrancesco Baldi?" — that was another matter.

He came to find by experience that motion in the open air helped him as much as anything. When the grayness oppressed him too severely, he would summon his coach and drive about the countryside. So one day as he drove through a small country village in the hills beyond Remo, it happened. It was nobody's fault, the bishop's least of all. He saw to it that he had a skillful coachman and good horses as he saw to all such matters. But when a tall, gangling boy darts across the street right under the nose of the horses, the most skillful coachman cannot always save him. There was a cry and a scream and a soft jar. Then where the coach had passed, the boy lay writhing in the street.

The bishop always showed at his best in emergency. When he got out of the coach, the angry shouts of the crowd died away to a respectful murmur. He lifted the boy into the coach with his strong arms and drove back with him to Remo. On the way he talked to him soothingly, though the boy was in too much pain to pay much attention to this graciousness. When they got to Remo, he had the boy carried to a servant's room in the palace and doctors summoned for him. Later on he gave instructions about cleaning the coach.

At dinner his secretary recounted the little incident, and all men praised the kindliness of the bishop. The bishop passed it off pleasantly, but at heart he felt a trifle irritated. He had not felt particularly drawn toward the boy; on the other hand, he could not have left him lying in the road.

By the next day, as such things do, the story had gone all over Remo; and there were unusual demonstrations of good will as the bishop passed to the cathedral. The bishop received them with dignity, but his irritation remained. He disliked ostentatious shows of virtue and distrusted the fickleness of crowds. Nevertheless, it was his duty to see the boy, and he did so.

Washed, combed, and rid of his vermin, the boy looked ordinary enough, though somewhat older than the bishop had thought him. His body was slight and emaciated, but he had a well-shaped head and large liquid eyes. These stared at the bishop with some intensity; indeed with such intensity that the bishop wondered at first if the boy might not be an idiot. But a little conversation proved him sound of mind, though rustic in speech.

His name was Luigi, and he was an orphan living as best he could. In the summer he tended goats; in the winter he lived with his uncle and aunt, the tavern keepers, who fed him and beat him. His age was about nineteen. He had made his Easter duty as a Christian. He would never walk again.

Such were the facts of the case, and the bishop thought them over clearheadedly. He wondered what to do with the boy.

"Luigi," he said, "would you like to go back to your village?"

"Oh, no," said the boy. "It is a very good village; but now that I can no longer herd goats, there is no place in it for me. Besides, one eats better in Remo — I have had white cheese twice already." And he smacked his lips. His voice was remarkably strong and cheerful, the bishop noticed with surprise.

"Very well," said the bishop patiently. "You need not go back if you do not choose. You are now in some sense a ward of the Church, and the wings of the Church are sheltering." He looked at the boy's legs, lying limp and motionless under the covers, and felt, though against his will, the natural distaste of the hale man for the maimed. "You might learn some useful trade," he said thoughtfully. "There are many trades where the hands do all — a cobbler's, a tailor's, a basket weaver's."

The boy shook his head joyfully. "Oh, no, your lordship," he said. "Trades take so long to learn, and I am very stupid. It would not be worth the expense; your lordship would be embarrassed."

"My lordship perhaps is the best judge of that," said the bishop a trifle grimly. He kept thinking of the boy's remark about white cheese; it must be a spare life indeed where white cheese was such a treat. "But we are reasonable," he said. "Come, what would you be?"

"A beggar!" said the boy, and his dark eyes shone with delight.

"A beggar?" said the bishop, astonished and somewhat revolted.

"Why, yes," said the boy as if it were the most natural thing in the world. "For ten years my father begged on the cathedral steps. That was before your lordship's time, but he was an excellent beggar and a master of his craft. True, he was subject to continual persecutions and jealousies from the honorable corporation of the beggars of Remo, coming as he did from outside the city. It was that which caused the ruin of our fortunes; for in the end when he had begun to fail, they threw him down a well, where he caught a bad cold and died of it. But in his good days he could outbeg any two of them. If your lordship would care to have me demonstrate his celebrated fainting fit, when his eyeballs rolled backward in his head —"

"I can think of nothing I should like less," said the bishop, shocked and disgusted, for it seemed to him an unworthy thing that a sturdy young man, though a cripple, should think of nothing better than beggary. "Besides," he said, "these other beggars you speak of — if they persecuted your father, no doubt they would persecute you."

"Me?" said the boy and laughed. "Oh, once they understood, they would not dare touch me — not even Giuseppe the Hook. I would be your lordship's beggar — the bishop's beggar!" And a light of great peace and contentment spread over his countenance.

The bishop stared at him for a long time in silence. "That is what you wish?" he said, and his voice was dry.

"That is what I wish, your lordship," said the boy, nodding his head.

"So be it," said the bishop with a sigh, and left him. But when his coachman came to him the next morning for orders, it was all he could do to keep from reviling the man.

The bishop was not the sort of man who liked beggars. Indeed, were it not for custom and Christian charity, he would long since have cleared them from the steps of his cathedral. He could not very well do that; he knew what an impression such a move would make. Nevertheless, when he passed among them, as he must

at times, he saw to it that his almoner[1] made a suitable distribution of small coins, but he himself did his best to see and smell them as little as possible. Their whines and their supplications, their simulated[2] sores and their noisome[3] rags — these were a fret and a burden to him.

Now, it seemed he was to have a beggar of his own. He would have taken it as a suitable humiliation for pride, but he did not feel himself to be a proud man. Nor could he think of the accident as anything but an accident. Had he deliberately trodden the lad beneath the hoofs of his horses — but he had not. He was well liked, able, decisive, a rising son of the Church. Nevertheless, he was to have a beggar — every day he must see his beggar on the steps of the cathedral, a living reproach, a living lesson in idleness and heedlessness. It was a small thing to be sure, but it darkened his dinner and made him sore at heart.

Therefore, being the man he was, he put a mask upon his face. He meant to speak of the thing, so it should be known — at least that might ward off ridicule. He spoke of it to his secretary; the secretary agreed that it was a very seemly and Christian idea of his lordship's, while the bishop wondered if the man laughed at him in his sleeve. He spoke of it to others; there were compliments, of course. Each time he spoke of it, it turned a small knife in his breast. But that did not keep him from speaking of it nor from seeing that every care was given Luigi.

Nevertheless, he dreaded the day when Luigi would take up his post on the steps of the cathedral. He dreaded and yearned for it, both. For then at last the thing would be done. After that like many things it would become a custom, and in time Luigi himself would fade into the mass of whining beggary that haunted the steps of the cathedral. But things were not to be quite that way.

He admired, while he detested, the thoroughness with which Luigi prepared himself for his profession. He heard the whine ring out from the servants' quarters — "ten scudi[4] for Luigi!" — he saw the little cart and the crutches Luigi had made for himself. Now and then

---

[1] *almoner*, one who dispenses alms for another.

[2] *simulated*, pretended.

[3] *noisome*, offensive to the smell or other senses.

[4] *scudi*, silver and gold coins used in Italy several centuries ago.

he heard his own servants laugh at the beggar's stories. This was hard enough to bear. But at last the day of parting came.

To his disgust the bishop found the boy neither clean nor well clad, as he had been since his accident, but dirty and dressed in tatters. He opened his mouth to reprove the boy; then he shut it again, for it seemed pitifully true that a beggar must dress his part. Nevertheless, the bishop did not like it. He asked Luigi coolly how he meant to live.

"Oh, your lordship's secretary has found me a very suitable chamber," said Luigi eagerly. "It is on the ground floor of a rookery[5] by the river, and it has room for my crutches, my gear, and my cart. He will move me there tonight. Tomorrow I will be at my post on the steps of the cathedral." And he smiled gratefully at the bishop. "That will be a great day," he said.

"So," said the bishop, who could not trust himself to say anything further.

"Yet before I go," said Luigi, "I must thank your lordship for his kindness and ask your lordship's blessing on my work. That is only suitable."

The bishop stiffened. "I may bless you, Luigi," he said, "but your work I cannot bless. I cannot give the blessing of the Church to the work of a man who lives by beggary when he might live otherwise."

"Well, then I must go unblessed," said Luigi cheerfully. "After all, your lordship has already done so much for me! The bishop's beggar! How my uncle and aunt will stare!"

Now of all the vainglorious, self-seeking, worthless, rascally sons of iniquity — and to think that I stand your sponsor, said the bishop; but fortunately he did not say it aloud. Silently he extended his ring, and Luigi kissed it with such innocent reverence that the bishop was sorely moved to give him his blessing after all. But he summoned up his principles and departed in silence.

The bishop slept ill that night, tormented by dreams of Luigi. He dreamed that for his sins he must carry Luigi on his back all the way up the steps of the cathedral. And as he mounted each step, the weight upon his back became more crushing till at last he awoke, unrefreshed.

The next day he went to the cathedral in great state, though it was an ordinary Sunday. Yet he felt the state to be in some measure a protection. When he passed by the steps of the cathedral, the beggars set up their usual supplications. He sent his almoner among them; it was over quicker than he thought. He did not look for Luigi, and yet he felt Luigi's eyes upon him as he stood there for a moment, splendid in robe and miter. Then the thing was finished.

In the cathedral that same day, he preached passionately against the sins of idleness and heedlessness. Seldom had he been so moving — he could feel that from his congregation. When Mass was over, he retired to his palace, exhausted. Yet it was pleasant for him to walk about the palace and know that Luigi was not there.

It was just after vespers when his secretary came to him and told him that a man called Giuseppe, self-styled provost[6] of the company of the beggars of Remo, requested an audience. The bishop sighed wearily and ordered the man brought before him. He was a squat fellow of great strength and an evil cast of countenance, for one side of his face had been so burned in a fire that it was as if he had two faces, one of them inhuman. Also, his left arm terminated in an iron hook.

"This is Giuseppe, the beggar, your lordship," said the secretary with repugnance.

"Giuseppe, called Double-Face, also called the Hook, provost of the honorable company of the beggars of Remo," said Giuseppe in a rusty voice and plumped on his knees.

The bishop raised him and asked his business.

"Well, your lordship, it's this new fellow, Luigi Lamelegs," said Giuseppe. "I've got nothing against him personal — I wouldn't hurt a fly myself in a personal way," and he grinned horribly — "but there he is in a good place on the steps, and your lordship's servants put him there. Well, now if he's your lordship's beggar, that's one thing — though, even so, there's fees and vails[7] to be paid, for that's the custom. But if he isn't your lordship's beggar — and your lordship paid him no attention this morning —"

[5] *rookery,* a dilapidated building with many rooms and occupants.

[6] *provost,* a presiding officer.
[7] *vails,* tips.

"Stop!" said the bishop with anger. "Do you mean to tell me that the very steps of the cathedral are bartered and sold among you? Why, this is simony[8] — this is the sin of simony!"

"Your lordship can call it hard words," said Giuseppe stolidly, "but that's been the way it's been done ever since there were beggars in Remo. I paid twenty crowns for my own place and fought old Marco too. But that's beside the point. Your lordship has a right to a beggar if your lordship wants one — we're all agreed on that. But the question is: Is this man your lordship's beggar or isn't he?"

"And supposing I said he was not my beggar?" said the bishop, trembling.

"Well, that's all we'd want to know," said Giuseppe. "And thank your lordship kindly. I had my own suspicions of the man from the first. But we've got him down by the river now — Carlo and Benito and old blind Marta; she's a tough one, old blind Marta — and once we're through with him, he'll trouble your lordship no more." And sketching a clumsy salute, the man turned to go.

"Stop!" said the bishop again. "Would you have the guilt of murder upon your conscience?"

"Oh, your lordship takes it too hard," said Giuseppe, shuffling his feet. "What's one beggar more or less? We're not rich folk or learned folk to bother a mind like your lordship's. We breed and we die, and there's an end. And even at the best it's no bed of roses on the steps of the cathedral."

The bishop wished to say many things, but he could think of only one.

"I declare to you that this man is my beggar," he said. "I stretch my hand over him."

"Well, that's very nicely spoken of your lordship," said Giuseppe in a grumbling voice, "and I dare say we can make room for him. But if the man's to keep a whole skin, your lordship had best come with me — old Marta was talking of ear slitting when I left her."

So they found Luigi, bound but cheerful, in his first-floor chamber by the river, guarded by the persons Giuseppe had described — a hunchback, a dwarf, and a blind woman. The window which gave upon the river was open, and a large sack weighted with stones lay in one corner of the room. The bishop's arrival produced a certain consternation on the part of all but Luigi, who seemed to take it as a matter of course. After the boy had been unbound, the bishop addressed the beggars with some vivacity, declared that Luigi was his beggar, and gave him a piece of silver before them all in token. This seemed to satisfy the company, who then crept away in silence.

"And yet have I done right? Have I done right?" said the bishop, striding up and down the chamber. "I greatly fear I have condoned the sin of simony! I have spent Mother Church's substance among the unworthy! And yet, even so, your blood may be upon my head!" and he looked at Luigi doubtfully.

"Oh, your lordship need not take it so hard," said Luigi, rubbing his arms. "All is safe enough now. I arranged about the dues and vails with Giuseppe while your lordship was discussing her state of grace with Marta. He's an honest fellow enough, and his point is reasonable. One should not take a good place without money to keep it up. Had your lordship given me alms with your own hand this morning, our little difficulty would never have arisen. That was my fault — I assumed that your lordship knew."

"Knew?" said the bishop. "What should I know of such things? And yet, God forgive me, I am a priest and I should have knowledge of evil."

"It is merely a difference in knowledge," said Luigi gently. "Now, your lordship, doubtless, has never been in a room quite like this before."

The bishop stared at the damp walls and the mean chamber. He smelled the smell that cannot be aired from a room, the smell of poverty itself. He had never doubted his own experience before — when he had been first made a priest, he had gone on certain works of charity. Now it seemed to him that those works must have been rather carefully selected.

"No," he said, "I have never been in a room just like this one."

"And yet there are many of us who live in such rooms — and not all beggars," said Luigi. He changed his tone. "That was a fine rousing sermon your lordship gave us on idleness and heedlessness this morning," he said. "Hey, it brought the scudi forth from the good folks' pockets! An admirable sermon!"

[8] *simony*, traffic in sacred things.

"I am grateful for your encomiums,"[9] said the bishop bitterly. He glanced around the room again. "Is there nought else I can do?" he said unwillingly.

"No, thank your lordship," said Luigi, and his eyes were smiling. "I have a woman to cook my dinner — it is true she is a thief, but she will not steal from a cripple — and soon with your lordship's patronage I shall be able to afford a charcoal brazier.[10] Moreover, my friends seem to have left me a sack. So after dinner I shall say my prayers and go to bed to refresh myself for tomorrow's labor."

I shall say mine too, for I need them, said the bishop, though he did not say it to Luigi.

So that was how it began. Soon enough the bishop's beggar was a familiar figure on the steps of the cathedral — one of the admitted curiosities of the town. He was well liked in his trade, for he always had a merry word or a sharp one for his clients — and it passed around until "Luigi says" became a byword. The bishop became used to him as one becomes used to a touch of rheumatism. Other men had their difficulties; he had his beggar. Now and then it seemed odd to the bishop that he had ever thought of the beggars on the steps as a vague and indistinguishable heap of misery and rags. He knew them all by now — blind Marta and Carlo, the dwarf, Giuseppe Double-Face and Benito, the hunchback. He knew their ways and their thoughts. He knew the hovels where they lived and the bread they ate. For every week or so he would slip from his palace to visit Luigi's chamber.

It was necessary for him to do so, for to him Luigi represented the gravest problem of the soul that he had yet encountered. Was the man even a Christian? The bishop was not sure. He professed religion; he followed the rites of the Church. Yet sometimes when he confessed him, the bishop was appalled. Every sin that could ravage the human heart was there — if not in act then in desire — and all told so gaily! Sometimes the bishop angrily would tax him with willful exaggeration, and Luigi with a smile would admit the charge and ask for still another penance. This left the bishop confused.

Yet through the years there grew up between the two men a singular bond. The bishop may have been heedless; he was not stupid. Very soon he began to realize that there was another Remo than the city he had come to first — a city not of lords and scholars and tradesmen and pious ladies but a city of the poor and the ignorant, the maimed and the oppressed. For, as Luigi said, when one lay all day on the steps of the cathedral, one heard stories; and anyone will talk to a beggar. Some of the stories struck the bishop to the heart. He could hardly believe them at first; yet when he investigated them, they were true. When he was convinced they were true, he set himself stubbornly to remedy them. He was not always successful — pleasant sinners like the Church to keep its own place. Now and then he discussed his efforts with Luigi, who listened, it seemed to the bishop, with an air of perfect cynicism. His attitude seemed to be that it was all very well for a man like the bishop to concern himself about these things, but he was the bishop's beggar; and if other folk starved and died, it was none of his concern. This irritated the bishop inordinately and made him more determined than ever.

Gradually he noticed the composition of his table changed. There were fewer courtiers and scholars; there were more priests from the country, smelling of poverty and chestnut bread. They came in their tattered cassocks with their big red wrists; at first they were strange and ill at ease at his table. But the bishop was able to talk to them. After all, were they not like the old parish priest that Luigi talked of so often? When the ceremony of his table disturbed them, he saw to it that there was less ceremony. Luigi mocked him for this and told him bluntly what his richer clients were saying. The bishop rebuked him for impertinence to his spiritual director and persisted.

It is strange how time flies when the heart is occupied. In no time at all it seemed to the bishop he was a middle-aged man with gray at his temples, and Luigi a man in his thirties. That seemed odd to the bishop; he did not know where the time had gone. He thought of it one morning with a sense of loss. He had meant to do many things — he was still ambitious. Now when night came, he was often too tired to think. The troubles of many people weighed upon his heart — the troubles of the peasants in the hills, who lived from hand to mouth; the troubles of Domenico, the shoemaker, who

---

[9] *encomiums,* high praises.

[10] *brazier,* a pan for holding burning coals.

had too pretty a daughter; the troubles of Tessa, the flower seller, whose son was a thief. When he had first come to Remo, he had not had all these troubles. He picked up a letter on his desk — a letter that had lain there for days — and, having read it, sat staring.

The dreams of his youth came back to him, doubly hot, doubly dear. While he idled his life away in Remo, his brother and his friends had been busy. They had not forgotten him, after all. Cardinal Malaverni, the great sage statesman whose hand was ever upon the strings of policy, meant to pass by Remo on his way to Rome. The bishop knew the cardinal — once, long ago, he had been one of the cardinal's promising young men. There was a letter also from the bishop's brother, the lord — a letter that hinted of grave and important matters. The bishop almost sobbed when he thought how long both letters had lain unanswered. He summoned his secretary and set himself about an unaccustomed bustle of preparation.

It often occurred to him sorrowfully within the next few days how foolish it was to leave one's letters unopened. The preparations went forward for the cardinal's visit; yet it seemed to him that they went forward ill, though he could not put his finger upon the cause. Somehow he had got out of the way of the world where such things go forward smoothly; he was more used to his country priests than to entertaining distinguished visitors. Nevertheless, he botched together a few Latin verses, saw to it that the hangings in the guest chambers were cleaned and mended, drove his choirmaster nearly frantic, and got in the way of his servants. He noticed that these were no longer afraid of him but treated him with tolerant patience, more like a friend than a master; and this irked him oddly. What irked him even more perhaps was Luigi's shameless undisguised self-interest in the whole affair.

"Ah, your lordship, we've waited a long time for this," he said, "but it's come at last. And everyone knows that a great man like Cardinal Malaverni doesn't come to a place like Remo for nothing. So all we have to do is to play our cards well; and then when we move on, as we doubtless shall — well, I for one, won't be sorry."

"Move on?" said the bishop, astonished.

The beggar yawned.

"But how else?" he said. "I have been the bishop's beggar. When your lordship is made a cardinal, I will be the cardinal's beggar. The post will entail new responsibilities, no doubt; but I have confidence in my abilities. Perhaps I shall even employ an assistant for my actual begging — after all, it is often drafty on the steps of the cathedral."

The bishop turned and left him without a word. Yet what Luigi had said caused trouble and disquiet in his heart, for he knew that Luigi often had news of things to come before even the count of Remo had an inkling of them.

At last the great day of the cardinal's visit came.

Like all such days, it passed as a dream passes, with heat and ceremony and worry about small things. The Latin verses of welcome were unexpectedly well read; on the other hand, the choristers were nervous and did not sing their best. Two gentlemen of the cardinal's suite had to be lodged over the stables, much to the bishop's distress, and the crayfish for dinner had been served without sauce.

The bishop hoped that all had gone well, but he did not know. As he sat at last alone with his old friend in his study that overlooked the garden, he felt at once wrought up and drowsy.

This should be the real pleasure of the day, to sit with his old friend in the cool of the evening and renew contact with the great world. But the bishop was used to country hours by now, and the feast had broken up late. He should be listening to the cardinal with the greatest attention, and yet those accursed crayfish kept coming into his mind.

"Well, Gianfrancesco," said the cardinal, sipping delicately at his wine, "you have given your old tutor a most charming welcome. Your wine, your people, your guests — it reminds me somehow of one of those fine Virgilian eclogues we used to parse together. '*Tityre, tu patulae recubans* — ' "[11]

"The choir," said the bishop — "the choir usually is — "

"Why, they sang very well!" said the cardinal. "And what good, honest, plainspoken priests you have in

---

[11] *Virgilian eclogues . . . "Tityre . . . recubans,"* the first of the eclogues, or pastoral poems, of the Roman poet Virgil, beginning, "You, Tityrus, lying under the cover of a spreading beach."

your charge!" He shook his head sadly. "I fear that we do not always get their like in Rome. And yet each man to his task."

"They have a hard charge in these hills," said the bishop wearily. "It was a great honor for them to see Your Eminence."

"Oh, honor!" said the cardinal. "To see an old man with the gout — yes, I have the gout these days, Gianfrancesco — I fear we both are not so young as we were." He leaned forward and regarded the bishop attentively. "You too have altered, my old friend," he said softly.

"Your Eminence means that I have rusticated,"[12] said the bishop a trifle bitterly. "Well, it is true."

"Oh, not rusticated," said the cardinal with a charming gesture. "Not at all. But there has been a change — a perceptible one — from the Gianfrancesco I knew." He took a walnut and began to crack it. "That Gianfrancesco was a charming and able young man," he said. "Yet I doubt if he would have made the count of his city do penance in his shirt for his sins before the doors of his cathedral."

"I can explain about that," said the bishop hurriedly. "The shirt was a silk one and the weather by no means inclement. Moreover, the count's new tax would have ruined my poor. It is true we have not always seen eye to eye since then; yet I think he respects me more than he did before."

"That is just what I said to your brother Piero," said the cardinal comfortably. "I said, 'You are wrong to be perturbed about this, Piero; it will have a good effect.' Yes, even as regards the beggar."

"My beggar?" said the bishop and sighed.

"Oh, you know how small things get about," said the cardinal. "Some small thing is seized upon; it even travels to Rome. The bishop's beggar — the beggars' bishop — the bishop who humbles his soul to protect the poor."

"But it was not like that at all," said the bishop. "I — "

The cardinal waved him aside. "Do not hide your good works beneath a bushel, Gianfrancesco," he said. "The Church herself has need of them. These are troubled times we live in. The French king may march

any day. There is heresy and dissension abroad. You have no idea what difficult days may lie ahead." He watched the bishop intently. "Our Holy Father leans much upon my unworthy shoulder," he said, "and our Holy Father is beginning to age."

"That is sore news for us all," said the bishop.

"Sore indeed," said the cardinal. "And yet one must face realities. Should our Holy Father die, it will be necessary for those of us who truly love the Church to stand together — more especially in the college of cardinals." He paused and with a silver nutpick extracted the last meat from the walnut. "I believe that our Holy Father is disposed to reward your own labors with the see of Albano," he said.

"The see of Albano?" said the bishop as if in a dream; for, as all men knew, Albano was an old and famous diocese outside the walls of Rome, and he who was bishop of Albano wore a cardinal's hat.

"It might have a most excellent effect," said the cardinal. "I myself think it might. We have clever and able men who are sons of the Church. Indeed. And yet just at this moment with both the French and the German parties so active — well, there is perhaps need for another sort of man — at least as regards the people." He smiled delightfully. "You would be very close to me as cardinal-bishop of Albano — very close to us all," he said. "I should lean upon you, Gianfrancesco."

"There is nought that would please me more!" cried the bishop like a boy. He thought for a moment of the power and the glory of the great, crowded streets of Rome and the Church that humbles kings. "I would have to leave Remo?" he said.

"Well, yes, naturally it would mean your having to leave Remo," said the cardinal. "Your new duties would demand it."

"That would be hard," said the bishop. "I would have to leave Luigi and all my people." He thought of them suddenly — the lame, the halt, the oppressed.

"Your people perhaps," said the cardinal, "but certainly not Luigi. He should come with you by all means as a living example."

"Oh, no, no, that would never do," said the bishop. "Your Eminence does not understand. Luigi is difficult enough as a bishop's beggar. As a cardinal's beggar he would be overweening.[13] You have no idea how overweening he would be."

The cardinal regarded him with a puzzled stare.

"Am I dreaming, Gianfrancesco?" he said. "Or are you declining the see of Albano and a cardinal's hat for no more reason than that you are attached to a beggar?"

"Oh, no, no, no!" cried the bishop in an agony. "I am not in the least attached to him — he is my cross and my thorn. But you see, it would be so bad for him if I were to be made a cardinal. I tremble to think what would happen to his soul. And then there are all his companions — Giuseppe the Hook is dead, but there is still blind Marta, and Benito, the hunchback, and the new ones. No, I must stay in Remo."

The cardinal smiled — a smile of exasperation. "I think you have forgotten something, Gianfrancesco," he said. "I think you have forgotten that obedience is the first law of the Church."

"I am five times obedient," said the bishop. "Let our Holy Father do with me as he wills. Let him send me as a missionary to savages; let him strip me of my bishopric and set me to work in the hills. I shall be content. But while I have been given Remo, I have work to do in Remo. I did not expect it to be so when I first came here," he said in a low voice, "and yet somehow I find that it is so."

The cardinal said nothing at all for a long time.

Then at last he rose, and, pressing the bishop's hand, he retired to his own quarters. The bishop hoped that he was comfortable in them, though it occurred to him in the uneasy sleep before dawn that the chimney smoked.

Next morning the cardinal departed on his journey toward Rome without speaking of these matters further. The bishop felt sorry to see him go and yet relieved. He had been very glad to see his old friend again — he told himself that. Yet from the moment of the cardinal's arrival there had been an unfamiliar grayness upon his spirit, and now that grayness was gone. Nevertheless, he knew that he must face Luigi — and that thought was hard for him.

Yet it went well enough, on the whole.

The bishop explained to him, as one explains to a child, that it did not seem as if God had intended him to be a cardinal, only bishop of Remo, and with that Luigi

had to be content. He grumbled about it frequently and remarked that if he had known all this in the first place, he might never have accepted the position of bishop's beggar. But he was not any more overweening than before, and with that the bishop had to be satisfied.

Then came the war with the French, and that was hard upon the bishop. He did not like wars; he did not like the thought of his people being killed. Yet when the count of Remo fled with most of his soldiery and the mayor locked himself in his house and stayed there shaking, there was no one to take over the rule of the town but the bishop. The very beggars in the streets cried out for him; he could not escape the task.

He took it with a heavy heart under the mocking eyes of Luigi. With Luigi in his cart he inspected the walls and defenses.

"Well, your lordship has a very pretty problem," said Luigi. "Half a dozen good cannon shot and the city will be taken by storm."

"I thought so, I feared so," said the bishop, sighing. "And yet my people are my people."

"Your lordship might easily compromise with the enemy," said Luigi. "They are angry with the count, it is true — they thought they had him bought over. Yet it would mean but two score hangings or so and a tribute properly assessed."

"I cannot permit my flock to be harried and persecuted," said the bishop.

"Well, if your lordship must die, I will die with your lordship," said Luigi. "Meanwhile, we might set the townsfolk to work on the walls — at least it will give them something to do. And yet there may be another way."

So it was done, and the bishop worked day and night enheartening and encouraging his people. For once, all Remo was one, and the spirit and will that burned within it were the bishop's. Yet it seemed no time at all before the French sat down before Remo.

They sent a trumpet and a flag to demand the surrender of the city. The bishop received the young officer who came with the trumpet — a dark-faced man he was with a humorous twist to his mouth. The bishop even took him on a tour of the walls, which seemed to surprise him a little.

"You are well defended," said the Frenchman politely.

[13] *overweening*, unduly confident or arrogant.

"Oh, no, we are very ill defended," said the bishop. "My good children have been trying to strengthen the wall with sandbags, but, as you perceive, it is rotten and needs rebuilding. Moreover, the count was badly cheated on his powder. I must speak to him of it sometime, for hardly a gun we have is fit to fire."

"I do not wish to doubt your lordship's word," he said, "but if those things are so, how does your lordship propose to defend Remo?"

"By the will of God," said the bishop very simply. "I do not wish my poor people killed; neither do I wish them oppressed. If needs must, I shall die in their stead, but they shall go scatheless.[14] Ere you hang one man of Remo, I shall take the noose from around his neck and put it around my own."

"Your lordship makes things very difficult," said the Frenchman thoughtfully. "My king has no desire to attack the Church — and indeed the walls of Remo seem stronger than your lordship reckons."

Then he was conscious of a plucking at his sleeve. It was Luigi, the beggar, in his little cart, who by signs and grimaces seemed to wish the Frenchman to follow him.

"What is it, Luigi?" said the bishop wearily. "Ah, yes, you wish to show our friend the room where we store the powder. Very well. Then he may see how little we have."

When the Frenchman rejoined the bishop, he was wiping sweat from his forehead and his face was white. The bishop pressed him to stay for a glass of wine, but he said he must return to his camp and departed, muttering something incoherent about it being indeed the will of God that defended Remo.

When he had gone, the bishop looked severely upon Luigi. "Luigi," he said sternly, "I fear you have been up to some of your tricks."

"How your lordship mistakes me," said the beggar. "It is true I showed him three of my fellow beggars — and they did not seem to him in the best of health. But I did not say they had plague; I let him draw his own conclusions. It took me four days to school them in their parts, but that I did not tell him either."

"That was hardly honest, Luigi," said the bishop. "We know there is no plague in the town."

"We know also that our walls are rotten," said Luigi, "but the French will not believe that either. Men of war are extremely suspicious — it is their weakness. We shall wait and see."

They waited and saw, for that night a council of war was held in the French camp and the officer who had come with the trumpet reported (a) that Remo was held in great force and strongly defended; (b) that its bishop was resolved to die in the breach; and (c) that there was a plague in the city. Taking all these factors into account, the French wisely decided after some forty-eight hours' delay to strike camp and fall back on their main army — which they did just in time to take part in the historic defeat of the whole French invasion a week later. This defeat sealed for all time the heroic defense of Remo; for had the part of the French army occupied before Remo rejoined their main body before, the historic defeat might have been as historic a victory for the French. As it was, all Italy rang with the name of the bishop of Remo.

But of all this the bishop knew nothing, for his beggar, Luigi, was dying.

As the French moved away, they had loosed off a few cannon shot, more in irritation than for any real military purpose. However, one of the cannon shot, heedlessly aimed, struck the steps of the cathedral; and you may still see the scars. It also struck the cart wherein Luigi lay directing his beggars at one task of defense or another. When the bishop first heard that his beggar was hurt, he went to him at once. But there was little that man could do but wait, and the waiting was long. It was not until seven weeks later that Luigi passed from this earth. He endured indeed till the messengers came from Rome.

After they had talked with the bishop, the bishop went alone to his cathedral and prayed. Then he went to see Luigi.

"Well?" said the dying man earnestly, staring at him eagerly with limpid eyes.

"His Holiness has been graciously pleased to make of me the first archbishop of Remo, placing under my staff, as well, the dioceses of Ugri and Soneto," said the bishop slowly. "But I have the news from Cardinal Malaverni, and I may remain here till I die." He stared at Luigi. "I do not understand," he said.

---

[14] *scatheless*, unharmed.

"It is well done. You have stood by the poor in their poverty and the wretched in their hour of trial," said Luigi, and for once there was no trace of mockery in his voice.

"I do not understand. I do not understand at all," said the bishop again. "And yet I think you deserve recompense rather than I, Luigi."

"No," said Luigi, "that I do not."

The bishop passed his hand across his brow. "I am not a fool," he said. "It was well done, to humble my spirit. And yet why did you do so, Luigi?"

"Why, that was my great sin," said Luigi. "I have confessed many vain and imaginary sins but never the real one till now." He paused as if the words hurt him. "When your lordship's coach rolled over my legs, I was very bitter," he said. "A poor man has little. To lose that little — to lose the air on the hills and the springing step, to lie like a log forever because a bishop's coachman was careless — that made me very bitter. I had rather your lordship had driven over me again than taken me back to your palace and treated me with kindness. I hated your lordship for your indifferent kindness — I hated you for everything."

"Did you so, Luigi?" said the bishop.

"Yes," said Luigi. "And I could see that your lordship hated me — or, if not hated, loathed, like a crippled dog that one must be kind to without liking. So I set myself out to tease and torment your lordship — at first by being your beggar, then in other ways. I could not believe in goodness; I could not believe there would not come a moment when your lordship would turn upon me and drive me forth."

He paused a moment and wiped his mouth with a cloth.

"Yes, I could not believe that at all," he said. "But you were not to be broken, Gianfrancesco, my brother. The evil I showed you daily was like a knife in your heart and a burden on your back, but you bore the knife and the burden. I took delight in showing you how ill things went in your city — how below the fair surface there was misery and pain. And had you once turned aside from that misery and pain, I would have been satisfied;

for then, bishop or no bishop, you would have lost your soul. Was that evil of me, Gianfrancesco?"

"Very evil in intent," said the bishop steadily, "for while it is permitted to be tempted, it is evil to tempt. And yet proceed."

"Well," said Luigi, with a sudden and childlike stare, "it did not work. The more I tried to make you a bad man, the better man you became. You would not do what was ill; you would not depart from your poor, once you had known them — not even for a red hat or a count's favor. You would not do ill at all. So now we have defended Remo, the two of us, and I am dying." He stirred uneasily in his bed. "It is just as well," he said with a trace of his old mockery. "I told my uncle I would live to be a cardinal's beggar, but I am not sure that I would have liked it. I have been the bishop's beggar so long. And yet from the first I have loved you also, Gianfrancesco. Will you give me your blessing now, on me and my work — the blessing you denied me once?"

The bishop's face was wrung. Yet he lifted his hand and absolved and blessed Luigi. He blessed Luigi and his work in the name of the Father and of the Son and of the Holy Ghost. When that had been done, a smile appeared on Luigi's face.

"A very fine blessing," he said. "I must tell that to the Hook when I see him; he will be envious. I wonder is it drafty on the steps of heaven? A very fine blessing, your lordship . . . ten . . . scudi . . . for . . . Luigi." And with that his jaw dropped and it was over. But the bishop knelt beside the bed with streaming eyes.

And all that, to be sure, was a long time ago. But they still tell the story in Remo when they show the bishop's tomb. He lies upon it fairly carven in marble. But carved all around the tomb are a multitude of beggars, lame, halt, and misshapen, yet all praising God. And there are words in Latin which say, "It is not enough to have knowledge — these also are my sheep." Of the tomb of Luigi, the beggar — that no man knows. They say it was beside the bishop's, but in one war or another it was destroyed and there is no trace of it now.

Yet Luigi was an arrogant spirit; perhaps he would have liked that best.

VIEWING THE AUTHOR'S IDEAS

1. Show that the bishop was a sincere religious and reflective man when he arrived in Remo. Account for his having become an ecclesiastic.

2. What was the nature of the bishop's grayness of spirit? How did this oppression disappear? Why did the bishop treat the injured boy so soothingly?

3. What did the intensity in Luigi's eyes indicate? Trace the gradual way in which the boy becomes the bishop's beggar. How did he hide his own evil designs and rascality? Of what sins was he guilty? How does the bishop remonstrate with him about his sins?

4. As a result of his contact with the beggar, how was the bishop influenced intellectually; socially; religiously?

5. How are the cardinal and the bishop contrasted? Why did the bishop's grayness of spirit return at this time?

6. What was the ruse that helped to defeat the French? Was Luigi justified in his deception? Did the bishop condone his action? To what causes can you ascribe Luigi's attitude towards the bishop: his mockery, deception, and evil intentions? Was he finally forgiven?

7. What truths regarding the improvement of social evils does the story suggest?

EVALUATING HIS MANNER OF EXPRESSION

1. Explain how the following sentence is a hinge on which the narrative turns: "The bishop always showed at his best in an emergency."

2. Luigi's discussion of begging is done with veiled mockery. Find two other examples of this ironical deceit. Why is not Giuseppe's talk a display of mockery? Account for the cynical attitude toward loss of life that Giuseppe displays.

3. Why is the style of the narrative leisurely; moving; gripping? What might be the result had the writer increased the tempo of the story?

4. Which one of the following words characterizes the author's treatment of the characters and theme: (a) antagonistic (b) indifferent (c) enthusiastic (d) sympathetic? Support by referring to specific sentences or passages.

5. In a well-knit sentence, express the theme of this story.

A Little Rain

Brendan Gill

This Christmas story, artfully told, touches a warmly human note.

FATHER Carroll opened the window of the parish house. He blew drifts of coal dust from the sill, then set his palms against it and leaned into the night. The air was hot. Rain was falling noisily on the tin roof, silently on the nearly invisible statue of Mary crowning the chapel. Between the house and the chapel, a bank of red Carolina clay had been cut to frothing gullies. The first day of the downpour, Father Carroll had said to Buck, his colored altar boy, "Now the heat is bound to break. Now winter's coming at last." But Buck had said, "Hit don't make no difference about the rain, sir. Rain'll just gobble up the air."

That was what the rain had done. Father Carroll felt as if he had been drowning minute after minute for five days. He could hardly breathe. From his narrow window, he looked across the town. Hundreds of dancing oblongs of light fell from the windows on the opposite hillside, where the white people lived. Here, about the new Franciscan chapel, and the school for colored children, a handful of yellow lamps swam in the dark. Father Carroll shivered. How was he to learn what lay beyond the lamps? With the roads growing impassable, school had been dismissed. One by one, the children had been drawn back into their crowded, unpainted, inscrutable shacks. Buck, Father Carroll's first convert, had missed Mass this morning. Unless the rain stopped soon, it was plain to Father Carroll that his year's work down here might go for nothing.

Buck was sixteen, two years beyond the age limit for school, so Father Carroll had trained him as an altar boy. That had turned out to be such excellent strategy that Father Carroll suffered occasional twinges of conscience. The younger boys were eager to worship what Buck worshiped. Buck would whisper to them after Mass, "Look at 'em candles, boy! Look at 'em shine! And do you smell what I smell? Do you smell that ol' incense burnin'? Ain't that some smell?"

The younger boys would roll their eyes. "And you can light 'em candles, Buck?" one of them would say. "And swing that goldy-lookin' thing?"

"Sure I can. Anybody can that gets this here rollin' Catholicism," Buck would answer.

"What's 'em words, Buck?"

"Why, if you want to know — why, I reckon Father Carroll's the man you want to see. I just reckon he's the one."

In less than a year Father Carroll had raised the school's enrollment from twenty-five to over seventy colored boys and girls. Three extra nuns had been sent down from the mother house in Alleghany, New York, to take charge of the overflow. Plans had been drawn for an addition to the chapel. But lately, after summer passed and the burning sun held on through autumn, Father Carroll felt less certain of himself. Perhaps the job had seemed too simple. Perhaps those grinning, unfathomable kids would slip away from him as easily as they had come. Watching the rain, trying to draw a breath in the still night air, Father Carroll saw that he held no proof of his success. He stood alone in an empty house, beside an empty chapel, on Christmas Eve. The world that lay about him was not his world.

He tightened his grip on the sill. In the North tonight the snow would be lying deep in the yards or piled high beside the roads by the big ploughs. The air would be cold and sharp, the sky crammed with stars. Candles would be lighted in the windows of houses. Through the windows you would see — as last year, walking about the city where he had been living, Father Carroll had seen — trees covered with tinsel and ornaments, trees glittering with tiny bulbs. In one yard he had caught sight of a spruce, taller than the house behind it, glowing with blue lights. In another yard someone had fashioned out of snow Mary and the Child, the moonlight falling ice-blue, like satin, on Mary's head and cradled arms.

Up there, Father Carroll had seen Christmas in the faces passing him on the street. He had heard it in voices speaking while doors were opened and closed against the cold: "Come in. How good of you to come!" "I can't stay. But I had to tell you merry Christmas." He had been shaken by it, standing under the brassy amplifiers in the city park: "Oh, little town of Bethlehem, how still we see thee lie!" And later, in his room in that other parish house, Father Carroll had arranged last year his private Christmas. He had set a shoe box on its side on the table beyond his cot. He had covered it with pine twigs broken from shrubs around the house. He had placed inside the shoe box a plaster Jesus and Mary from the five-and-ten, a prayerful Joseph, and two placid cows. When he went shopping that morning, he had had money enough to buy either a set of shepherds or a set of Wise Men. He had weighed the decision carefully, while the girl behind the counter tapped with her painted nails on a hill of sparkling snow. Father Carroll had chosen the shepherds. They had seemed closer to him than the Wise Men, with their proud names and gorgeous clothes. That night he had propped the shepherds upright by the Infant Jesus. Then he had knelt in front of the shoe box to say his rosary.

For a moment now the rain seemed to slacken. Father Carroll heard water foaming in the gullies and circling the open foundations of the house. He heard a report that might have been a shot fired at a rat in a nearby shanty or a car backfiring. Somewhere down the slope a tethered donkey began to bray. Then the rain came down once more through its sieve of heat, on the slick banks and the sodden road. Father Carroll turned from the window to study the room behind him. No crèche stood on the flat pine table. Somehow, hundreds of miles from home, Father Carroll had lacked the will to make one. Coming among these people, he had promised himself to follow their customs. Apparently they had no customs. The room was bare.

He heard a second report, followed by a sound of voices. Beyond the roofs of the house and chapel, a faint glow colored the sky. It looked to Father Carroll like a fire. Nearly every week a faulty stove set ablaze one of the shanties surrounding the chapel. Father Carroll leaned out of the window but saw nothing. The glow faded and returned, closer to the chapel. Father Carroll heard a series of reports behind the curtain of rain. A bright-yellow explosion lighted the road in front of the house. He saw that the road was filled with boys, and he shouted, "What's happened? What's the matter? Do you need help?"

The crowd surged under his window, ankle-deep in mud. Father Carroll saw that Buck was leading them, his kinky hair glittering with raindrops, a pine torch in his right hand. The crowd shouted, "Merry Christmas, Father!" A dozen firecrackers exploded over his head. He said sharply, "Buck, what's the meaning of this? Firecrackers on Christmas Eve!"

Buck's eyes gleamed. He lighted a fuse with his torch, then he sent the firecracker looping beyond the crowd. In cheerful contempt he said, "Don't you celebrate Christmas up North?"

"Of course we celebrate Christmas," Father Carroll said, "but we celebrate it as it ought to be —-" He bit his lip. After a moment he said, "Can I light one, too?"

The crowd grinned up at him. Buck pulled a six-inch salute from his pocket and said, "We bought this little old baby just for you." He handed the salute to Father Carroll, then he lifted his pine torch to the sill. Father Carroll held the fuse against the torch's flame. "Watch this little old baby fly!" he shouted, and with all his strength he hurled the salute toward the chapel roof. It climbed through the streaming dark, its fuse faintly spiralling; then it burst in a white flame over Mary's head.

To the bare room, Father Carroll whispered, "Now, that's what I call a regular Christmas firecracker." He crossed himself. It would take him only a minute to put on his hat and rubbers and join the boys. A little rain never hurt anybody.

VIEWING THE AUTHOR'S IDEAS

1. What discouraging facts did Father Carroll face at Christmas Eve? How had the weather undermined nearly a year's progress in his missionary work? In general how may climate affect the problems of missionary labors?

2. What qualities are exhibited by Buck?

3. Explain the effect gained by contrasting the priest's last Christmas in the North with his first one in the Southern community.

4. How does Father Carroll show adaptability? Point out indications that it was not perfectly easy for him to adjust himself to the manner in which his parishioners celebrated. Why is adaptability an important trait to be cultivated? How does it aid the missionary?

5. Account for the priest's happiness at the close of the story.

EVALUATING HIS MANNER OF EXPRESSION

1. How does the author show economy of description in presenting the setting of the story? Which words indicate the community industry?

2. What insight into Father Carroll's character is gained by relating the incident of the shoe-box crib; by telling of his choice of the shepherds?

3. Point out artistry in the description of Christmas in the North.

4. Show how conversation is used to convey the atmosphere of heat; to indicate the warm spirit of the Northern Christmas. Why is the use of conversation here effective?

The Husking Contest

Albert Eisele

Since Hamlin Garland wrote his protest against the farmers' economic struggles, social legislation and labor-saving devices have changed many aspects of rural life. Today, a new interest in the land indicates that many people prefer the freedom and vigor of the farm to compact city life.

IT HAD been somewhat of a struggle for George to consent to take a day off for the state husking contest. The husking season was at its height; George still had twenty acres left, and it seemed downright absurd to drive fifty miles to watch other fellows husk corn when he himself had corn to husk. On the other hand, the contest came this year to Moville, and it would probably never come any nearer. And Esther wished to go. Esther had been cooped up rather close of late. The children, too, were eager for the outing, and as a matter of fact George himself deserved a day off.

They left toward midday, and had a basket of fried chicken along, to be eaten when they got there. In the back seat were the children. It was a lovely October day, with the hazes of Indian summer heavy in the distances.

"Well, there's one fellow," said George, nodding towards a field, "who isn't going to the contest. He's plowing."

"Is he hurting the ground, daddy?" asked Junior.

"No, he's not hurting the ground, and I want you children to behave yourselves back there. Don't make me nervous when I'm driving, and Junior, don't wave those husking gloves about. What do you want to take them along for?"

"He thinks we're going to husk corn, and that's why he picked up a pair of your husking gloves," said Esther. "He's been gloating over them all morning."

They came at length upon signs that read "Husking Contest" and had arrows pointing. "Daddy!" called Willie, "I and you we shot arrows with my bow, didn't we? Up! in the sky! and you shot one far'er than I did — so high that we wonder what the birds think!"

"Be quiet now!" said George sternly, "we're getting into the traffic!" The contest was being held on a farm several miles from town, and the road was now gravel, over which the dust from many cars hung thick. "I wonder if we'll find a place to park?" asked Esther.

"Sure! They've got a whole forty acre pasture for parking purposes . . . Hello! here we are!" From the crest of a hill they saw, below and before them a vast area of parked cars that glistened and sparkled under the sun. "Look at the cars!" exclaimed George, "like a big farm sale! New cars, too. Who says the country's broke!"

"They expect forty thousand people here today," said Esther. Parking officials waved them along with canes, and they drew up presently at the end of a parking line.

"Forty thousand people!" said George. "And do you know, a lot of people living close aren't even coming. All the way over here I saw husking wagons tied up for dinner, with the fellows going out husking again this afternoon. By tonight, I'll be two loads short. But there's no use having regrets. I've taken the day off, and I'm going to feel free about it. First, let's eat the chicken; the contest starts at one, you know."

They spread a blanket on the close-pastured white clover beside the car and unpacked the basket. The cold chicken was excellent.

"That's four wishbones you children have wished on already," said Esther, nodding towards Willie and Mary; "there were only two chickens."

"They must have been wishing on the necks," said George.

"Take the spoon out of your cup, daddy!" sang Mary.

"See my big stomach!" said Willie, rising and thrusting his midriff forward.

"See mine!" cried Mary.

"Now Mary, is that like a lady?" admonished the mother.

"They all got bigger pieces of cake than me!" bawled Junior.

"There's plenty of cake," said George. "Here, I'm going now . . . I don't want to miss the start! I'll see you all later."

George hurried away between the long files of cars. "Where's the husking field?" he asked of an official with a cane. "You're a mile from the field yet," said the man. "When does the husking start?" "Pretty soon," said the man. George hurried on.

On a small rise near the farmplace, which itself was perhaps a mile away, stood a machinery exhibit, together with various other tents and booths, and it was while George was approaching this mushroom growth that he heard, borne through the hazy air, the sound of ears striking the bangboards. The contest had started! He paused — it was the old familiar sound of corn being husked — and suddenly he found himself isolated from all thought of athletics, or pageantry, or milling crowds, and he was again alone and at work. But he was late . . . he was late to the field in the morning: The sun was up, and the neighbors were all far down in the fields with their husking wagons. They already had bushels of corn, and they were throwing in additional bushels to the accompaniment of that unmistakable sound of ears striking bangboards, that sound which he had heard each autumn ever since he was old enough to remember. Ah, yes, here again he was, in overalls and husking gloves: he could hear the rattling of the stalks as he worked, and the foraging of his horses; he could feel the rough caress of a broken tassel against his cheek, or the more tender caress of a stray cornsilk; he could smell the whiskey-like odor of ears that had blown off and were rotting on the ground; he could see himself working through the day and on into the dusk, when the inner and unspotted husks that had been loosened by his work lay behind him, between the rows, like white papers strewn. He could see . . . But what foolishness was this?

There were about twenty contestants, all moving abreast up a long field. Lanes had been cut out in between, leaving only four rows of corn for each husker, two to husk up on, and two back. The husking wagons were all new, with high bangboards of bright new lumber, and drawn by new tractors. Close behind the huskers the people swarmed in dense galleries.

George had never been to a state contest before. He had been to county contests, which were pretty much the same, except that today everything was on a grander scale. The husking equipment was all new and more showy, the huskers all a little swifter, and the crowds larger. It was difficult for George to get near enough to each husker to get a good view, or to get some idea of the husking technique employed. That's what George was interested in, the manner in which each husker worked. George had husked corn for twenty-five years, ever since he was twelve years old. He had husked thousands of bushels of corn, and he was interested in knowing how the top-notchers did the trick.

The huskers moved swiftly, and were halfway up the long field almost before one was aware of it. The galleries had thinned out a little: many had fallen behind: mothers with children; people renewing acquaintances; boys and girls bantering; elderly farmers discussing, not huskers but corn, ears of which they held in their hands. "Now that," said one farmer as he held an ear of corn before him, "is no ear!"

George walked to one side of the field, where he followed the first husker for a rod or two, then moved on to the second. In this way he went from one to the other, and was able to have a close view of each husker. Some were tall, some were short. Most of them were young, but one or two had gray hair. One of the older wore a patched work shirt and overalls faded from many a family wash. Some of the younger were stripped to the waist. "Now is that a way to husk corn?" some

farmer asked indignantly. "Why don't they dress like cornhuskers and not like prize fighters? He can husk stripped to the waist for eighty minutes, but I'd like to see him husk like that all day. He'd think he'd been run through a dozen barbed-wire fences!"

At several wagons the wife or sweetheart of the husker followed near at hand, carrying his coat and hat. Some of the huskers jumped about nervously, making "hard work" of it, while others were more graceful. The day was warm, and the sweated faces of the men were becoming dark with dust.

The steady banging of the ears, the droning of the tractors, the crackling of the cornstalks and the chatter of the galleries made a subdued but exciting uproar. The galleries pushed and surged, and occasionally there was a whiskey smell that was not due to decaying corn. Farmers craned their necks over the rear end of the wagon box, to see how much corn there was. Remarks like "Gee, but he's throwing corn!" or "Ain't he agoing it?" filled the air. Here and there spectators with watches in hand were timing the ears per minute.

George reached the opposite side of the field, where the last husker had just gained the crest of a slight hill and from where all the other nineteen contestants were visible, most of them bunched, but with a few far ahead and a few far behind, the bright new bangboards gleaming in the sun like the sails of some flotilla of ships. He left the race to itself then and started back across the large field in the hope of finding his wife and children. "Henry Wallace did a fine thing when he invented the corn-husking contest!" said a farmer loudly. "When I was a young fellow, father once hired a big redheaded Swede. The Swede challenged me to husk faster than he could. So he went on ahead with his wagon, and I followed. I chased him all day. The next morning he said, 'Now you go ahead!' So I went ahead, and he chased me all day. This went on for day after day. First, I'd chase him and then he'd chase me. In the end we were both half-dead and nothing was settled. The cornhusking contest used to last three weeks. Now it lasts only eighty minutes, and Henry Wallace never gave us any finer form of farm relief!"

George walked among the straggling crowds but was unable to find his family. In the meantime the huskers had turned at the far end of the field and were husking back. The eighty-minute period was nearing its close. George walked to the nearest wagon, and in a short time a distant bomb went off. The contest was over. A dozen spectators swarmed upon the load of corn for a ride to the weighing place, a half-mile away. "Get off!" roared one of the officials. "Make room for the husker!"

"Oh never mind!" said the husker, "I'll walk up. I'm hot." He drew on a large red sweater and set off walking, surrounded by friends. George followed. The husker's face was black with dust, and his hands and arms were scratched and bleeding, and this, together with the large red sweater and the admirers clustered about him, gave him a heroic air. And he was a hero, George conceded.

Up at the weighing place he found his family. Together they waited until the results were tabulated and chalked up on a large scoreboard.

They set out for home. It had taken them a long time to get out of the jammed traffic, and the sun was low. Soon there was a many-hued sunset. Along the roadway, inside the fences, farmers with huge loads of corn had reached the end of the fields and were preparing to go home. For them it was the afternoon load, husked from midday till dusk. Some of them stood beside their wagons removing their husking gear; others were leveling off the corn that was piled high; still others were putting on sweaters and coats.

George drove ten, twenty, thirty miles. Night was falling, but still there were huskers drawn up at the end of fields with huge loads of corn. Forty thousand people had attended the husking contest. But not everybody had attended. These men along the road, with their afternoon loads — they had ignored the contest. And George saw that they, too, were heroes. Along the road the cornfields were becoming dim in the darkness, but even then could be seen sweatered and weary figures climbing upon high loads of corn.

VIEWING THE AUTHOR'S IDEAS

1. How does the story suggest the simplicity of rural life; the wholesomeness of life on the farm?
2. What details show the normal, well-adjusted family life of George and Esther and their children?
3. What dominant impression or idea does the author wish to leave on the mind of the reader?

We Made This Thing—This Dream

(From *Listen to the People*)
Stephen Vincent Benét

With courage, with pride, even with tenderness, Stephen Vincent Benét contemplates the crisis which the second World War brought to our country. Benét is confident that the people will defend their freedom.

Listen to the People *made its first appearance as an experiment in a new technique for dramatic radio presentation. The speaking voices were supported by an original musical score for a forty-piece orchestra.*

IT'S A long way out of the past and a long way forward.
It's a tough way, too, and there's plenty of trouble in it.
It's a black storm crowding the sky and a cold wind blowing,
Blowing upon us all.
See it and face it. That's the way it is. 5
That's the way it'll be for a time and a time.
Even the easy may have little ease.
Even the meek may suffer in their meekness.
But we've ridden out storms before, and we'll ride out this one,
Ride it out and get it through. 10
It won't be done by the greedy and go-easies.
The stuffed shirts, the "yes but — " men, and the handsome phonies,
The men who want to live in their fathers' pockets,
The folks who barely believe and the bitter few,

It'll be done by the river of the people, 15
The mountain of the people, the great plain
Grown to the wheat of the people,
Plowed by their suffering, harrowed by their hope,
Tall with their endless future.
It'll be done by the proud walker, Democracy, 20
The walker in proud shoes.
Get on your feet, Americans, and say it!
Forget your grievances, wherever you are,
The little yesterday's hates and the last year's discord,
This is your land, this is your independence, 25
This is the people's cause, the people's might.
Say it loud and speak it loud, United, free . . .

What do the people say?
Well, you've just heard some questions and
   some answers,
Not all, of course. No man can say that's all. 30
A man's a humbug if he says that's all.
But look in your own minds and memories,
And find out what you find and what you'd keep.
It's time we did that, and it won't be earlier.
I don't know what each one of you will find, 35
What memory, what token, what tradition;
It may be only half a dozen words
Carved on a stone, carved deeper in the heart.
It might be all a life, but look and find it —
Sun on Key West, snow on New Hampshire hills, 40
Warm rain on Georgia, and the Texas wind
Blowing across an empire, and all part,
All one, all indivisible and one —
Find it and keep it and hold on to it;
For there's a buried thing in all of us, 45
Deeper than all the noise of the parade,
The thing the haters never understand
And never will, the habit of the free.

Out of the flesh, out of the minds and hearts
Of thousand upon thousand common men, 50
Cranks, martyrs, starry-eyed enthusiasts
Slow-spoken neighbors, hard to push around,
Women whose hands were gentle with their kids,
And men with a cold passion for mere justice.
We made this thing, this dream. 55

This land unsatisfied by little ways,
Open to every man who brought good will,
This peaceless vision, groping for the stars,
Not as a huge devouring machine
Rolling and clanking with remorseless force 60
Over submitted bodies and the dead,
But as live earth where anything could grow.
Your crankiness, my notions, and his dream,
Grow and be looked at, grow and live or die.
But get their chance of growing and the sun. 65
We made it and we make it and it's ours.
We shall maintain it. It shall be sustained.

VIEWING THE AUTHOR'S IDEAS

1. To what does the poet compare World War II? How would he have the American people regard the crisis? What type of people will not defend freedom? By whom will the cause be won?

2. What plea for union does the poet make? Mention some discords and grievances that have divided America in recent years.

3. What things in America are worth fighting for? Cite memories and traditions of the past that are worth keeping. Do Americans have any traits and habits that should be abandoned?

4. What features show the greatness of our country? What can the enemies of democracy never understand about the American way of life?

5. By what kinds of people has the dream of democracy been realized? Name other groups the poet might have mentioned. How does he contrast the freedom of America with the tyranny in antidemocratic countries? What resolution concludes the poem?

EVALUATING HIS MANNER OF EXPRESSION

1. To what emotions does the poet appeal? Which passages have the greatest emotional force?

2. How does the poem express the mood of the people? Make a list of the phrases in which the poet uses everyday speech of the people. Why are these phrases appropriate?

3. Which lines have greatest poetic beauty? Comment upon the figures of speech in lines 3-4; 9; 15-19; 59-61. Is the poetic speech sustained? What does the rhythm of the lines contribute to the effect?

The Quest

(From *Dark Symphony*)
Elizabeth Laura Adams

When the young Negro Elizabeth Laura Adams set out to find the true religion, she encountered unusual difficulties. This chapter from her autobiography shows the courage and perseverance with which she faced her struggle.

I BEGAN to consider religion seriously. Memories of the one Good Friday service that I had witnessed at the Old Mission still lingered with me. I knew I wanted to be a Catholic. But as Mother was grief-stricken, I would not burden her by mentioning that which Father and I had disagreed upon.

I tried to content myself by finding another church as a substitute and eventually found one similar to the Catholic, a quiet edifice with candle-lighted altar and stained-glass windows.

Though I had always been identified with a colored congregation, this one being white did not make me self-conscious, as my thoughts were not centered upon its members but upon the religious service. I never spoke to anybody. However, the clergyman noticed that every Sunday morning at seven o'clock a dark lamb knelt in the midst of his fleecy white flock. One morning as I was leaving he addressed me.

"You come alone to church every Sunday, child; have you no parents?"

I had never talked much to ministers, not even those of my own race. I told him that I liked the quietude of the church. He smiled kindly and offered to give me two books to read which I accepted; one a book of prayers — the other entitled *The Holy Eucharist.*

I read both books from cover to cover, then asked Mother's permission to join the new church. I became a member of it and succeeded in interesting Mother to do likewise. Dogmas meant nothing to me, and I never gave any thought as to who founded a church or why. I only wanted a quiet place in which to pray, believing the serenity would assuage our grief.

Shortly afterwards we moved to another town, located a church of the same denomination, and presented our letters from the former pastor.

Determined to be steadfast in the faith, I faithfully observed Sunday worship. In his sermons the clergyman often pictured Jesus Christ hanging on the Cross.

"Jesus died to save all mankind!" he preached zealously.

He laid stress upon the terrible sin of missing Sunday worship unless hindered by serious causes, and his sermons convinced me that I had committed grievous wrong by not wanting to attend church in the past. I even decided that I had something to repent over and often closed my eyes, prayed, and told God that I was sorry that I had not loved Him sufficiently to go to church some mornings instead of staying at home to read the funny papers. And when I heard the clergyman tell the congregation that it was wrong to visit other churches, I decided to believe that too. No human being ever tried to be more sincere in adhering to church rules than I.

Mother and I never attended any social affairs at the church or had any desire to, because the group was white. If there had been a colored church of this particular denomination, we would have worshiped there. In order to have social contact with our own race, Mother suggested that we visit the colored Methodist church gatherings on Sunday evenings. Conflict tortured my soul. How could we be faithful members if we wandered from the fold? The clergyman had said that God disapproved of such infidelity. Believing this, I felt that the only solution of the problem was to abandon the idea.

One Sunday morning, the sun's rays blazed against the stained-glass windows, the organ played soft music, white candles burned on the altar, and Mother and I knelt at the altar rail to receive Holy Communion. As I looked up to gaze at the cross and thank God for the gift of Communion, I beheld a strange sight. The clergyman was wiping the chalice where my lips had touched it, briskly polishing it as though it were tarnished. Then turning the chalice round he served the white communicant kneeling beside me.

Thoughts are like birds; they can wing their way speedily. The thought came to my mind like a newspaper headline: "Race Prejudice at the Altar!" Then I became terrified; how could I think such a thought at such a holy time and in such a holy place? I begged God to forgive me. I spent the following week asking forgiveness.

Next Sunday the same thing happened. In serving Communion from white to colored the chalice was not wiped, but from colored to white the minister paused, polished it briskly as before that all might see, and then proceeded.

I did not say anything to Mother. She did not say anything to me. But during the next week the white clergyman called to see us. He stated his mission, tears filling his eyes and streaming down his cheeks. He informed us that white communicants did not wish to kneel at the altar with Negroes . . . he regretted having to tell us . . . he hoped that we would not hate him . . . but he had to make a living. . . . White people contributed so much to the church . . . he had more white parishioners than colored.

Mother told him she was sorry that our presence had caused disturbance and assured him that we would not attend the church again and reassured him that we would not hate him.

After delivering his message, he went his way.

In a meditative fashion Mother said: "We must not think unkindly of the minister — or of the congregation." She next added that since the incident had occurred, so far as she was concerned, I could use my own judgment in selecting a spiritual path.

I wondered: What about God — dogmas and creeds? What about the theory that God was displeased if a member of one denomination visited another church? What about the theory of regular church attendance? There were no colored churches of that denomination in the town. What then was a colored person supposed to do? What sort of a God would lay down a lot of rules and then not make a way for them to be observed?

Lost in a maze of retrospection, I recalled that some of the colored students who were neither Methodist nor Baptist had, from time to time, told me stories of race discrimination that I had refused to believe. One girl had said that she joined a church, and the white parishioners refused to recognize her as a member and asked her to leave. Another girl had said that she knew some colored people who had had a similar experience. Both girls had laughed about the incidents. But I had responded angrily: "You are misjudging white people. They do not do such things." And the girls had sneered: "Go on taking up for white people. Some day they'll show you what's really in their hearts."

Now that I had experienced being turned out of the house of God, I had reason to believe there could be truth in the girls' stories.

Doubts crept in from the blind confusion of my thoughts. I doubted God's justice; I doubted His love for the colored race.

I can remember shrugging my shoulders, thinking: Oh, well, I never liked church anyway — guess I made a mistake bothering about religion.

I never set foot in the church again. I passed by though, on two Sunday mornings, and heard the congregation singing, singing hymns of praise to the Almighty.

Mother had planned to spend fall and winter in Santa Monica, a beach town; and as fall was almost upon us, my trend of thought was infused with the joyousness of registering in Santa Monica High School.

For a long time I tried to avoid thinking of religion or mentioning it. But I found this an impossibility. . . .

As I was a stranger in the community the colored students invited me to their churches. And, believe it or not, so did some of the white.

Never once did I refer to the race discrimination endured in the past. Whenever anyone made inquiry about my church affiliation, I casually remarked: "I do not belong to any church." But I soon stopped this because some of the students tried to convert me. I listened patiently to their impromptu lectures. I never argued. Because I had nothing to say, they thought me a "stubborn, rebellious sinner."

One white girl told me that I could never expect a blessing, never expect any good to come to me until I "repented and believed" and went faithfully to church, adding that without going to church no one could be saved.

Where, I asked myself, had I heard that before?

Realizing that the colored students would consider me unfriendly unless I accepted their invitations to go into a house of worship, I had to visit their churches. This of course brought on the ordeal of living through older people's telling me to "get salvation."

After a while I grew weary of going to some church just to be "in vogue spiritually."

I made up my mind to find out everything I wanted to know about God if it took me the rest of my life. I was dissatisfied with the opinion I had formed of God. I certainly considered Him a God for the white race — and decided that unless I could be convinced that His Son's death for the redemption of all people included the colored, I could put my time to better use than praying to One Who heard only the fair of skin. If God was just and did love the colored race — then by not trying to solve the problem of how to serve Him I would miss the benefit of His help.

While looking up some reference data at the public library, I found some books written by a priest named Father Finn. They were children's stories, but one in particular attracted me because it bore the title, *By Thy Love and Thy Grace*. Reading it revived the thought that the only church I had ever really wanted to join was the Catholic. It gave me information about something I knew nothing of, the confessional.

A confessional, I learned, was built like a little closet. It had three sections. A priest sat in the center and penitents knelt on either side. Partitions with small, curtained gratings separated the three sections. A priest could hear those who confessed but could not see them.

What an ideal place, I thought, to ask some questions about God. I could not be seen; therefore no one would ever know that I was colored. No — I would never ring a doorbell and face a white clergyman. I was afraid the door would be closed in my face. But the confessional was dark . . . and I was dark. No one could see me.

Since the majority of colored ministers were Methodist and Baptist, I did not think they could be of help in solving my particular problem. The confessional idea seemed the best course to take, but I lacked courage. Only God knows the fear in a Negro's heart.

One day I met two nuns in the library. One of them smiled, and as she stood near me looked at the author's name on the book in my hand and then asked if I were a Catholic. I told her no. She did not turn away but continued the conversation. Her pleasing smile and sweet personality made me wish to know her better. By the time I left the library, I had an invitation to call at the convent to see her.

Obtaining Mother's permission, I called.

The moment I crossed the convent threshhold I was impressed by the tranquillity of the interior. Religious paintings, exquisitely carved statuary, and fragrant flowers adorned the parlor wherein I waited. Sister Mary Mercedes greeted me with true friendliness. We talked of books and school.

I had no knowledge of religious orders. She explained that the community to which she belonged was made up of Sisters who taught school and was known as the Holy Names Order.

When I was ready to go, she showed me the chapel. Pausing before a statue, she lowered her voice so as not to break the silence rudely: "This is a statue of Our Blessed Mother," she whispered. "She is your heavenly mother, Elizabeth, and loves you. She will always help you."

I noticed that in the center of the altar there was something shaped like a miniature house — a tiny house without windows but two closed doors. This she explained was called a tabernacle.

"Our Lord is present in the Blessed Sacrament," Sister whispered. "If you are ever in doubt, in trouble, beset by worries, go to a Catholic church, kneel before the Tabernacle, and He will hear your prayers."

For days I dreamed of the visit to the convent. But one thought kept revolving in my mind, Don't be foolish. Remember white Christians told you about God once before. Don't run the risk of being turned out again.

In meeting more young people of my race, I discovered that not just a few of them had been subjected to segregation in churches. One young man, boasting of several baptisms in different denominations, said:

"There's nothing to religion. Every time I tried to find the Light, white Christians threw me right back into the pit of darkness. Now I don't believe in anything."

Another told me: "White people want the whole world and God too. Let them keep God — but get your share of the worldly goods before they beat you to it."

After hearing these things, I withdrew from the young people. I withdrew from the elderly. I withdrew from white people. I withdrew from colored people. I withdrew from Protestants. I withdrew from Catholics. . . .

I went to the Religious Reading Room of the Santa Monica Public Library. There I secluded myself after school hours. There I sought to find the Christ.

And I came upon a book written by a man named Henry Van Dyke. And in the book were many poems. But one he had written for souls like myself and called it "The Toiling of Felix." It began:

"Brother-men who look for Jesus, long to see Him close and clear,
Hearken to the tale of Felix, how he found the Master near.
Born in Egypt, 'neath the shadow of the crumbling gods of night,
He forsook the ancient darkness, turned his young heart toward the Light.
Seeking Christ, in vain he waited for the vision of the Lord;
Vainly pondered many volumes where the creeds of men were stored;
Vainly shut himself in silence, keeping vigil night and day;
Vainly haunted shrines and churches where the Christians came to pray."

And reading on, I learned that Felix sought the Christ everywhere; but not until he had labored among the common folk and helped his fellow men did he find and see Him as:

"Through the dimness of the temple slowly dawned a mystic light;
There the Master stood in glory, manifest to mortal sight."

In preference to wasting time listening to people broadcast scandals about Protestant clergymen or evangelists or Catholic priests or nuns, I selected the companionship of good books and walked in the company of the valiant. . . .

I read the life of Rose Hawthorne Lathrop (younger daughter of the great writer, Nathaniel Hawthorne), a convert to the Catholic faith who, inspired by Christ, opened an impromptu hospital for cancer patients too ill and destitute to support themselves; who later forsook the world, became a Religious, and was known as Mother Alphonsa, foundress of the refuge for the cancer poor, Rosary Hill Home.

I read the life of the Anglican nurse, Florence Nightingale, who had followed the Son of God forth to war, and in thought walked beside her at the Crimea and at Scutari. And a spark from the bright flame burning in her lamp of dauntless courage kindled the smouldering coals of hope struggling within my own soul.

In spirit I sailed on a vessel twice to the dread isle of Molokai, where crippled, mutilated, and sore-infected lepers were isolated.

On the first trip I saw a young follower of Christ taking census of eight hundred of the outcasts — he who had exiled himself to work among them as priest, physician, and teacher — Father Damien DeVeuster.

And on the second trip in spirit, I saw him, years hence, a weary soul, beginning a sermon to the outcasts with the words: "We lepers" — knowing that he would die in the service of Christ, a victim of the plague.

And so I found consolation and gained courage, as all do who walk in the company of the valiant.

Sister Mary Mercedes' advice did not go unheeded. I found a Catholic Church and prayed at the altar when the church was empty. But the scorching brand of race discrimination had left its mark; and at times I doubted that the prayer would be answered because of my color. Always I could hear a thought-voice reminding: "Remember what happened the last time you sought God."

Hoping to find out how the Negro ranked in the Catholic church, I obtained a copy of a Negro magazine that listed all the religious denominations that had exhibited racial prejudice. My heart sank when I read, "The Roman Catholic Church of America owes the American Negro an apology."

That meant that somewhere, at some time, either in schools or churches, some among my people had suffered humiliation because of segregation.

Well, I reasoned, if some members of the Church that claimed to be the one true Church treated Negroes unkindly — why belong to it?

The book *Wonder Works of Lourdes* stood out among books in the public library. I read it. Who can read this book and doubt the presence of Christ in the Blessed Sacrament? It described the thousands of pilgrims who prayed annually at this famous shrine. All were not Catholic, all were not white. Here the blind waited for the Light. The crippled and diseased hoped to be cured. Priests chanted prayers: "Hosanna to the Son of David! Blessed is He that cometh in the Name of the Lord!" A procession of the Blessed Sacrament wended its way through the crowds. All were not healed in body — some only in spirit. But faith was a living thing at Lourdes!

There in the public library with the *Wonder Works of Lourdes* and the Negro magazine I made the final decision; I would continue the quest.

Saturday afternoon found me in the Catholic church. I went into a confessional and knelt down. I did not know what to say — but at least I had the satisfaction of knowing that I was making a brave effort to find a church home.

The inner shutter slid back. I heard a voice asking: "How long since your last confession?"

As I had never made a confession, I merely replied: "Father — I am not a Catholic."

Evidently the priest thought his hearing had failed him. He asked me to repeat the statement. I repeated it.

"You *are not* a Catholic?" he questioned.

My voice grew a little weaker, but I had one consolation. He did not know that I was colored. I would not be asked out because my skin was black.

He offered to pray for me, but explained that absolution could be granted only to a Catholic.

I thanked him and went my way, somewhat disappointed though, as I had anticipated hearing him quote a passage from a spiritual book.

Determined to find a spiritual guide, I returned to church on a Christmas eve — one of the busiest times of the year. Long lines of penitents waited. I, too waited — looking as somber as the rest of them.

In the confessional I announced my presence as before. The priest, a zealous-sounding man, suggested I join the convert class.

Remembering that I was colored — I muttered something about being very busy — too busy to study.

"I cannot give you absolution," he said. "But I can give you a blessing."

I wondered if I dared to state my problem — to say that I was colored.

When he stepped outside the confessional, I asked him to bless a rosary. He did not appear very courteous. After the blessing of the rosary, I journeyed on.

At times I decided to give up the quest. And I know that I would have done so had it not been for one who gave me courage — one to whom I turned in desperation. When I told her my story, revealing how the effects of race discrimination in the religious world had caused me to doubt God and human beings, she spoke to me in the eloquent language of silence. Intuitively I knew that she understood my problem — Mary the Mother of the Crucified Christ.

And I know that it was the "Mother Invisible" who guided my footsteps to a confessional where a very saintly priest told me that though non-Catholics were supposed to study in the convert class, if I had a reason for not wishing to attend one at the present, he would gladly advise me spiritually in the confessional.

Gradually, my confidence in God and in human beings was restored.

VIEWING THE AUTHOR'S IDEAS

1. What first attracted Elizabeth Adams to religion? How do the art and the sacramentals of the Church speak to the soul?

2. Compare the reactions of the mother and daughter to the first experience of race discrimination recorded in this selection. Why was the author dissatisfied with the churches she attended at Santa Monica? What details show her confusion and sense of frustration?

3. By what books was Elizabeth Adams' interest in the Church revived? How did she learn about the confessional? What does the nun's sympathy and interest reveal concerning the correct attitude toward racism? Why did the girl's visit to the convent not bring immediate results?

4. Trace the steps by which Elizabeth Adams' confidence in God and in human beings was gradually restored. List the books which gave her courage and consolation. What virtue did she learn from the silence of the Blessed Mother?

5. What is the attitude of the Church towards racism? Do individual members always act in accordance with this attitude?

EVALUATING HER MANNER OF EXPRESSION

1. How does the unadorned style of this narrative reveal the author's sincerity and desire to report her experiences truthfully? What would a writer of fiction do with the same

material? How would a psychological novelist treat the mental and spiritual struggle of Elizabeth Adams?

2. Make a list of books you would recommend for the religious reading room of a public library. What steps might you take to have such books placed in the public library of your community?

3. Select what you consider the most picturesque passages in the autobiography. Give reasons for your choice.

4. Read all of *Dark Symphony* if you wish to learn more about Elizabeth Adams and the problems of the Negro.

Hard-Boiled Parish

Stephen V. Feeley

Leadership and co-operation help to make democracy function. When this leadership is found in the spiritual father of a large section of people, the benefits of democracy are more readily achieved. It was fortunate for the citizens of Buffalo that Father Gartska was made pastor of one of their churches. A journalist here reviews the priest's achievement for his flock.

IN 1910 the district surrounding St. John Kanty's Church in East Side Buffalo was known widely as the "Bloody Eighth Precinct." It had blocks of drab houses, occupied almost exclusively by poor immigrants and their American-born children. About twenty years before, Buffalo had received more than 100,000 of the same race; but those settled around St. John Kanty's were conceded to differ from the rest. Stanchly they clung to old-country language and customs and fiercely and literally fought the rest of the city.

There were fifteen gangs of railroad-car burglars in the area, who fought each other for supremacy; but often they collaborated in gun battles with railroad detectives and city police. The district had the reputation of sending more men to the electric chair than any other sector of New York State. So many of its boys were sent to Elmira State Reformatory that local wags dubbed the institution "East Buffalo Prep School."

Policemen walked the side streets in pairs, because so many lone policemen had been mobbed. One citizen, who dared join the hated police department, had to be rescued from angry neighbors who hanged him from a railroad bridge in an effort to express their attitude toward such an evidence of civic mindedness and personal ambition on the part of one in their midst.

The gang leaders were undisputed neighborhood heroes and held court in the numerous saloons. The saloons were the only recreation centers in the area and had poolrooms for young men and dance halls for young women. There was one large field in the congested precinct; but it was owned by a railroad, and its no-trespass signs were rudely enforced.

Shootings and brawls were common in the saloons on Saturday nights, when a special riot squad waited in the Eighth Precinct House. But if no call came for the squad, it raided one of the taverns anyway to avenge the recent beating of a patrolman or "just to beat a little law into 'em."

At least ninety per cent of the people were Catholics, but only about a third practiced their religion. Several pastors, appalled by conditions in the parish, fled as soon as they could. After one had stayed two months, the Reverend Andrew S. Gartska was sent there. Immediately he was nicknamed "Shorty" by the corner loungers, who insulted him as he passed. Although the church had a debt of $150,000, his first Sunday collections amounted to just $7.30.

To meet his parishioners he gave a lawn fete. This was a great social success, but St. John Kanty's parish profited nothing, because willing workers stole every cent that came into their hands.

Father Gartska came as a surprise to the few faithful parishioners. He never ascended his pulpit to complain or scold, but one Sunday he preached a sermon in which he sounded harsh because he was telling plain facts. He said he knew what was wrong with his erring flock and said he intended to do something about it.

The most valuable asset the parish had was a large school building with a hall in the basement. He began dances in the hall on Saturday evenings, with a nominal admission fee. The dances were permitted to last just as long as the dancers' endurance, which usually was early Sunday morning. Some elements professed to be scandalized by these early Sabbath soirees, but they had another shock coming. Father Gartska learned that some of the poorest girls preferred to go to the dimly-lit saloon dance halls, where their old and unfashionable clothes would not be as noticeable as in the parish hall.

Without more ado, he hired a dressmaker-hairdresser to give free lessons in the parochial school. Young and old women flocked to the classes, and Buffalo's first free beauty-culture school was established.

Early in 1911 Father Gartska broke down the hostility between the people and railroads enough to get permission to use the railroad lot as a playground. Then he organized a baseball team, deliberately selecting nine young men who were considered the toughest in a district which gloried in being the toughest in Buffalo. Six of the original nine had spent time either in Elmira State Reformatory or Auburn State Prison. To equip them, he sold statues out of his church to newer parishes.

This team was what the French might term "a success foolish." Fortified by a frenzied neighborhood loyalty, it won consistently and by the end of its first season was well on its way to the championship of the Buffalo Municipal Baseball League. As Father Gartska hoped, this quickly ousted the gang leaders as heroes for the boys and young men. At their pleading, he formed ten other teams and coached them all.

Adroitly he called team meetings on Saturday evenings in the school. After the meetings the young men naturally joined the young women for the usual dance. Few except the saloonkeepers suspected that an ingenious Saint George was giving to the saloon-dragon some blows. A few came to complain and were met by a sympathetic businessman, who had financial problems of his own and sincerely asked them for advice. Soon the St. John Kanty's Businessmen's Committee, named with tactful euphony, was in existence. This committee not only gave Father Gartska sterling advice, but even took some from him, for in a steady, unspectacular way

members dropped the more nefarious attractions which had thrived in their saloons.

It didn't take the hard-bitten and hard-pressed people of the parish long to discover that Father Gartska's rectory was the place to take their troubles. Wives thought nothing of calling him out of bed early in the morning to bring a tardy husband home from a saloon, because he always went. Women came to cry over meals ruined by the inept operation of the new-fangled gadgets which came into the neighborhood with gas and electricity; so he set up model kitchens in the school at the expense of the utility companies, who also supplied lecturers on cooking.

Classes in English, American history, and civics were begun after men complained that their poor English or lack of American citizenship held them to menial jobs. Teachers came willingly or were worn down by Father Gartska's persistence. Parents could not afford higher education for their boys; but Father Gartska decided that some, with specialized study, might qualify for civil service posts, and men in important government positions in Buffalo gladly came to guide the studies. Good craftsmen and tradesmen in the parish were flattered by being asked to teach their vocations.

By 1915 St. John Kanty's parochial school building literally trembled with activity every night in the week and all day Sunday. The spirit of self-improvement was infectious; in time, hardly a man, woman, or child in the parish but found some business to take him to the parish school several times a week.

Church attendance began a steady rise when the baseball players came to Mass on Sunday mornings to pray for victory on the diamonds that afternoon. More women began to approach the altar for communion after the grateful sewing class began to make vestments and altar linens. The first books they bought explaining church history and liturgy to guide their sewing, have since grown into a four-thousand-volume library.

St. John Kanty's Church and its kindly pastor had become such a necessity to the parishioners that support of them was a pleasure; Sunday collections by 1915 had increased to about $300.

The police were the last to appreciate what Father Gartska had accomplished in the Eighth Precinct, although records of decreasing arrests lay under their noses and they could patrol the streets singly. When a resolute Father Gartska appeared beside one of his parishioners in court any time they were arrested, police stopped exaggerating trivial offenses into great crimes before the judge. The judges sensed the great social vision of the earnest priest, and before long they had made him something of a one-man probation department.

A common boyish peculation was the raiding of farmers' stalls in the Broadway Market. This stopped when Father Gartska showed mothers that their heavy, monotonous meals were driving their children to theft in order to vary them; and the cooking classes got new pupils. Shoplifting was common among young women, but this stopped when Father Gartska sent them to the sewing classes to make their own pretty clothes. Juvenile delinquency was vanishing in Father Gartska's district — until automobiles became common, and then it rose sharply. Police were the first to say "We told you they were born crooks." But Father Gartska bought some old automobiles, put them in the school yard, and urged the boys to tinker to their hearts' content. The auto thefts dropped, and from then on police were on Father Gartska's side. More often delinquents were rushed to his rectory rather than to the precinct house.

From 1920 to 1930 Buffalo had more crime than at any time in its history, and East Buffalo had one of the city's most vicious bootlegger gangs; but crime continued to decrease where Father Gartska was an influence. He kept his people too busy to be bad. During the decade the old school building became too small to contain the parish social program.

Despite the growing economic depression the parishioners demanded a new building. With some misgivings St. John Kanty's Lyceum was built at a cost of $400,000 and was opened in September, 1931. Built to accommodate the forty parish societies and organizations, the building is a city block long and four stories high, including the basement. When the WPA, New York State, and Buffalo began their adult educational program, they could find no better model than St. John Kanty's parish. The agencies started twenty-seven classes in the building, and at times more than eight thousand persons were working or playing in the Lyceum at one time.

The debt on the building is still large, but nobody is worried about it. The building could not be duplicated today for $500,000, architects say. At the request of Buffalo authorities, St. John Kanty's gave its educational and recreational services to persons outside the parish free for two years, but four years ago the city appropriated $150 a month for the parish's services. This is a mere pittance compared to what parishioners donate and earn from their own program. One spectacular pageant given by parish talent brought in $15,000. Rentals of the halls, bowling alleys, cafeteria, gymnasium, classrooms, and art studio amount to about $8000 a year. Dramas and social affairs given by the parish also bring in a steady income. The Holy Name Society, one of the largest now in Buffalo, donates $1000 every year. Recently the sewing class turned over its treasury of $400 to be used by Father Gartska to combat juvenile delinquency.

The Lyceum is closed only from 3 to 8 a.m. — every day of the week. Rules for its use are sensible and enforced. Only one person has been excluded from the building for misconduct in nine years.

Police Commissioner Austin J. Roche was one of the policemen who used to patrol in pairs in the old "Bloody Eighth Precinct." "The entire Buffalo police department could not have accomplished what Father Gartska did there," Commissioner Roche says. "The precinct is now one of the most law-abiding in Buffalo. If we had more Father Gartskas, we might not need a Crime Prevention Bureau."

On September 25, 1935, the late Pope Pius XI made Father Gartska a monsignor. Pope Pius cited him as "a priest imbued with the best spirit of religion, who exercised his parochial duties to the great benefit of needy youth and souls."

Father Gartska is the despair of reporters who attempt to interview him. Instead of talking about himself or his work, he tries to inveigle the newspaper people into starting journalism classes for his young people.

VIEWING THE AUTHOR'S IDEAS

1. What were the undesirable conditions that obtained when Father Gartska became pastor of St. John Kanty's Church?

2. What obligations did Father Gartska assume when he commenced his duties? Why?

3. How did he show zeal; initiative; knowledge of human nature? Discuss his other characteristics.

4. The improvements at St. John Kanty's show the results of capable leadership. In what manner did Father Gartska manifest his ingenuity?

5. What did the response of the people and of the authorities indicate? How has Father Gartska been honored? In what manner does this essay reveal democracy in action? How may the success of a small democratic group influence larger groups?

EVALUATING HIS MANNER OF EXPRESSION

1. By what device does the author stress the improvements made in the Parish?

2. What qualities do specific details contribute to the narrative?

3. How can the reader discover the author's fairness; his enthusiasm?

4. This selection was first printed as a feature article in *The Commonweal*. What qualities give it popular journalistic appeal?

The Tournament at Ravallo

(From *A Watch in the Night*)
Helen C. White

A Watch in the Night *is an historical novel based upon the life of the saintly Franciscan poet, Jacopone da Todi. The tragic death of Jacopone's wife actually occurred at Todi in 1268 as described in this selection. A lawyer of noble birth and brilliant capacities, Jacopone gave up the world at the height of the successful career which he had so much enjoyed. He first became a wandering preacher and then a Franciscan friar. His story as a friar epitomizes the struggles in the second generation of the Franciscans. Many of the ablest members of the community questioned the practicability of realizing literally the founder's hopes and purposes.*

The novel opens with the return from Rome of the distinguished lawyer (called Jacomo in the narrative). He is making final preparations for the tourney which his father-in-law, the Lord of Ravallo, is giving to celebrate the first marriage anniversary of his beautiful daughter Vanna to Jacomo. The young lawyer is very much in love with his wife, but he is quite aware that the shy, convent-bred girl has had to make an effort to adapt her ways to those of her worldly and splendor-loving husband. He is reminded of this afresh when he finds his wife talking to her confessor, Father Filippo, this proud morning. He feels ill at ease when he overhears the priest, answering Vanna's question, tell her that it is right for her to do penance for her husband's sins but that she must not think of them as Jacomo's faults and not hers. But the fact that she is wearing the gold dress which he had provided for the occasion reassures him of her desire to please him, and he sets out with confidence for what he expects to be the happiest day of his life.

FATHER FILIPPO had left them with a murmured excuse of some priest's business which Jacomo did not trouble to hear. So they rode alone to the bridge over the chasm, pointing out to each other as they rode the gorgeous details of the scene in the meadows beneath them. The lists were completed now, the freshly-cut wood gleaming white against the greensward, and the stands draped and hung with banners of every conceivable shade; great folds of purple and scarlet and, stretching out on the soft blue air, the gold and silver bars and chevrons and beasts of heraldry, all the splendor of ancient lineage in their glowing fantasies. And across the green between the shining barriers moved a great crowd of equally brilliant figures on horseback and afoot, slender curves and angles of flashing color on the gleaming browns and whites of the horses' bodies, firmer curves and angles still more shining on the armor of the knights as they rode from tent to tent. There was a low sound, not more loud nor more articulate than the summer grumble of the mountain stream beneath them, impersonal, hardly human, as if, like the colors and the forms of the men and women below, it had been washed in the sunshine. It was all so incredibly neat and brilliant, the discrepancies and roughnesses of ordinary life refined in the distance, that Jacomo and Vanna reined in their horses and stood looking over the stone parapet of the bridge at the scene below them, as if fascinated.

"It is as beautiful as a dream, isn't it?" said Vanna, with the light sigh of a girl. Jacomo smiled at her.

"Oh, much more beautiful, because this is real. And dreams —" he raised his eyebrows. Vanna smiled a little at the banter in his voice, and again her eyes fell on the scene below. And then she looked up at him again, with a slight pursing of her upper lip, that had just a tinge of mischief in it.

"You know, I sometimes wonder if the angels do not find the world a lovely place after all when they look down upon it. It is always so much prettier when you look upon it from a high place." Jacomo could tell from the way she looked at him that she was a little frightened at her audacity. He reined in his horse a little closer to hers and shook his head.

"But it is so much nicer to be down there. To feel the life of the crowd, to be one of the picture."

But this time it was she who demurred. "It is nicer to look down from up here. We will lose some of the beauty when we go down."

Jacomo was a little surprised at the positive tone in her gentle voice, a little surprised and a little amused. "But isn't it pleasanter to sit at a feast than to look at it?" And then with the air of a man who rouses himself to the business of the world, he turned his horse to the road ahead. But even as he caught her smile of obedience, he noticed also that inward look on her mouth, as of one who yields the point but keeps her counsel. She must have caught, however, the momentary shadow in his eyes, for she smiled up at him so frankly and so yieldingly, as if she held up the whole cup of her spirit to him to drink from, that his heart leaped up again. What a perfect day!

He had without thinking let the rein slip on his horse's neck, and now he had to pull him up sharply, for at the turn of the road someone was standing out from the bushes at the side, holding up his hands. A dirty, wretched-looking old man it was, in a ragged brown smock, stiff with mud and filth. Jacomo held his horse from trampling him, but the old man did not draw back. He gazed up at the face glaring down at him and lifted up both skinny arms above his head.

"Remember, man," he cried in a high, shrill voice, "that thou art dust, and to dust returnest." For a moment Jacomo looked at him in amazement, and

then as the red-rimmed, small beady eyes remained fixed on his eyes without blinking, a great heat of anger surged up in him, and he swung his whip with a flash of light and a sharp hiss in the man's face. The latter made no effort to avoid it, and when the blood started in the white edges of the cut on his cheek, he paid no heed but still looked at Jacomo. Again Jacomo raised his whip, but Vanna laid her hand on his. He turned upon her, but there was something sick in her white face. When he looked for the old man again, the road was empty. There was a slight moving in the tall grass, as if an animal had just slipped through.

"Toad!" For a moment he glared at Vanna, but she seemed unaware of his presence, with a still, white look on her face, as if she were preoccupied with her own thoughts.

"Gaetani is right. Something must be done with these beggars. Coffin worms soiling the clean sunshine of God!" He was angry at having the edge taken off his delight, angrier still at having Vanna's pleasure smirched. The color had come back to her face, and she looked up at him and smiled sympathetically.

And at that look all the annoyance went out of him, and he was aware again that the birds were singing in the trees about their road. God had made the world beautiful for men to enjoy. Incongruously he remembered what he had heard from the pulpit ever since he was a child — the vale of tears, the misery of man's life, the glory to come. To the resurgent energy of Jacomo it had always seemed unreal. Now it seemed fantastic. He could not conceive of any happiness greater than this, riding along the road to the field of his triumph, with his wife riding at his side, fair and golden like an angel.

There was a shout, and in a moment he was in the midst of the crowd that had come out to meet them. As they pressed about Jacomo, the warmth of their welcome and their applause flowed through his whole being like the warmth of wine. But his instinctive lawyer's caution knew that he must take care not to get intoxicated. There was the same flush in Vanna's clear cheeks, but her eyes sought his in the crowd, and then a group of women bore her off with them. The Lord of Ravallo had already come by a shorter, steeper way, and the tourney was ready to begin.

Like the other men of his age and a little older, too old to care about shivering a lance for the crown in Vanna's hands and too young to sit contentedly on the cushions about the Lord of Ravallo, Jacomo stayed on his horse by the barrier below, watching the swordplay and the horsemanship with the keen attention of a connoisseur and, between the combats, discussing both with the other nobles at his side.

In an hour the clean turf of the lists was beaten to mud, and where Jacomo stood by the barriers, the warm air was heavy with the acrid smell of the horses and, when occasionally it freshened on a lazy breeze, with the lighter salt of men's sweat. Here in the dust of the onset the colors of the pennons and the cloaks and the tents looked flatter, heavier than they had an hour ago from the hillside. The lust for battle had stirred in the game, and everywhere men were leaning forward so as not to miss a flying splinter from the blue steel of the swords and the lances. Only the pavilion where the women sat looked as fresh and bright as when the tourney began.

In a moment's lull on the field Jacomo turned and looked more closely at those packed galleries, and there in the center of the pressed colors he found the fresh yellow gold of Vanna's dress and the heavy shine where the sun caught the crown in her hands. She was sitting tall and slim, with her golden hair about her pale face, looking strangely cool and remote there, with the serried ranks of color billowing behind her. For a moment it seemed to Jacomo that everything about him, the whole brilliant and stirring scene, melted and fell back until it was nothing but a background for that figure in gold. And then a yell from the men about him recalled his attention to the field.

"It is that young Colonna from Palestrina," explained one of the men by the barrier. The cloud of dust in the middle of the field lifted slowly, and Jacomo saw again the young horseman who had fascinated him a half hour ago. Now his helmet was off, and his dark hair fell over his gold-chased steel gorget, about a keen brown face. But it was not the face with its terrific concentration that held the attention of the onlookers. It was rather the extraordinary suppleness and grace of the youth's body that moved with the body of the horse as if horse and rider had but one being. It was a magnificent

black Arabian, smaller than the horse of the knight with whom the young Colonna was at that moment contending, but incredibly swift, and seemingly as responsive to every impulse of his rider's will as the man's own right hand. Jacomo watched with delight how the horse reared and the body of the rider for a moment flew against the sky, only to double slightly just as the tips of his toes rose in the stirrups and then, with an exquisitely beautiful arc, curve forward for the plunge.

But as horse and rider fell lightly to the ground just out of reach of their assailant, Jacomo's eyes shifted to the other warrior. Obviously, he was the older, perhaps thirty to the young Colonna's eighteen, and equally clearly he was accustomed to relying on his tremendous strength to overpower any adversary. Again he charged with what seemed irresistible power, and again the young Colonna waited until the charge was upon him. Then he swerved again to one side. But not quickly enough, for the lance held level along the giant's arm just grazed his arm. Apparently, the young Colonna had turned just in time for the blunted point of the lance to stir the air above his sleeve, but in a second it was clear that he had not, for the arm shook for a moment and then steadied. But in that moment the rein slackened on the neck of his horse. Apparently, the strain of those lightning maneuvers had overwrought the high-spirited animal, for he suddenly seemed to go wild as he dashed to the side of the lists. The judges wheeled out of his way, and a couple of men-at-arms put spurs into their horses and started after him. With his left hand the young Colonna strove frantically to check the black Arabian, but it was clear that the frightened animal was beyond all control. With his jaws foaming at the silver bit, the maddened beast came tearing into the barriers.

They were new wood, unseasoned, mere willow withes in the path of the crazed Arabian, and they broke like hempen cords. A terrific yell went up from all over the field, but it served only further to infuriate the horse, for he flung his helpless rider to the ground and flew forward on his maniacal way, his torn jaws dripping with blood-flecked foam.

Jacomo had been among the first of those who had rushed toward the broken barrier. He had reached it but a moment after the black Arabian, for his own Bella was the swiftest horse in Todi. And then as so often chances in a crisis, something happened to his eyes. Where but a moment before all was lightning motion with his horse and himself the quickest of all, everything had suddenly frozen, including himself. It seemed as if he saw the black Arabian slowly lift one foreleg, then the other, with perhaps the length of a horse's body still between the raised foreleg and the tapestry-hung gallery where the women sat. He saw the massed colors in the long ranks sheer back the way a wave draws back before it breaks into foam. And in the middle of them he saw a thin line of gold. Palsied, he yet strove to jab his spurs into the steaming flanks of Bella, but his knees had gone to water. He leaned forward on his horse's neck, but his movement was so slow and leaden-heavy that he scarcely felt the horse stir under him. He tried to shout, but the sound gurgled impotently at the back of his throat. And then the spell broke. There was a terrific crash, followed by a moment's silence, then a ghastly melee of women's screams and wrenches of tearing wood and crack of falling beams.

By the time he reached the fallen gallery, the huddle of men and horses and broken planks and shredded tapestry was piled so high that he literally had to tear his way through. The whole central section of the pavilion had fallen into an instantaneously-created pit of destruction. Already limp and broken bundles of silk and satin were being picked out of the broken timbers, the bright colors torn and dripping with an even brighter color.

"Vanna!" shrieked Jacoma, tearing his way through the wreck, without stopping to look at the obstacles in his path. "Vanna!" But in the screams that rose all about him he heard no answer, and as he clawed desperately at the entangled planks and beams and struggled through piles of tapestry and rugs, he saw nothing of either gold hair or gold dress. Quite unseeing, he lifted several women with bruised or broken limbs from the debris and all but flung them to the men behind him. His breath came in thick pants, and his head swam; but still he fought on, lifting a beam which three men had vainly tugged at for the last five minutes, scooping up an armful of rugs and cushions and hurling them into the faces of the rescuers behind, covering the whole scene with incredible speed while inside his throbbing head

the slow hours seemed to creep away. All about him vague shapes were moving as in a fog, shapes that took things from his hands, that took hold of timbers with him, but now and then made a low rumble of sound; but he neither saw nor heard anything distinctly.

"Vanna!" the cry sobbed in his throat. Then he felt a sudden rush of air. Strong arms gripped his arms, and all at once he was without power or energy. Slowly he turned and looked up into the eyes of Father Filippo. They were looking into his steadily and pityingly.

"She is over here in a tent," the young priest said reassuringly and took a firmer hold on Jacomo's right arm.

"Is she — ?" Jacomo stammered for the word. The priest looked at him with the same steadiness as if his look could help to support him and answered very calmly, "She is all right. She is in God's hands." Jacomo broke from his hold and ran toward the tent which Filippo had pointed out.

The flap was up, and the sunshine was streaming into the dark interior. On the ground lay Vanna, her gold dress and her gold hair shimmering mockingly in the bright sunshine. Her face was perfectly composed, with a blush still fading in the cheeks.

Jacomo cried aloud, "Vanna!" For a moment her eyelids fluttered, and she looked up at him with her clear violet eyes. Then she smiled and drew her breath with a contented little sigh. Jacomo bent over her, frenzied with relief, and kissed her. But even as his lips touched hers, he felt them cool. With a wild cry he raised his head. The priest was holding a tiny crucifix and murmuring, " — in pace." And then Jacomo looked back at that still face, with the smile yet lingering on the rosy lips.

For the first time he became aware that the hand which he laid on her breast was wet. The gold dress was drenched in scarlet, the scarlet deepening about a rent in the bodice. Frantically he tore at the brocade until his desperate fingers clutched at the blood-stained linen beneath. It gave under his hands, and he wrenched it from her breast. Why had they not stanched her wound? And then he stopped, for as he tore the linen away, his hands fell not on the fair flesh of his bride, but on a rough, thick mat, blood-soaked. It was a hair shirt. Choking a cry of amazement and agony, he tore at this, and it gave way, showing the delicate white flesh blue where the hair had scratched it. He fell back, and when Father Filippo caught him, he made no resistance, for the darkness rising about him had engulfed him completely.

VIEWING THE AUTHOR'S IDEAS

1. How does the author prepare the reader for the tragic outcome of the story? Are there any definite hints of tragedy? What is the purpose of the incident in which the mendicant reminds the happy pair of death?

2. When the reader learns that Vanna wore a hair shirt, what new significance is given to the references to her hair, dress, and gay but pensive mood? Why did she look strangely remote and cool as she sat among the women in the pavilion?

3. Does the author present enough details to enable the reader to picture the tournament? How does she suggest the strenuousness of the early part of the contest? What incident does she emphasize?

4. How did Jacomo react to the crashing of the pavilion? What did the priest mean when he said of Vanna, "She is all right. She is in God's hands"? You may wish to read the entire novel to see how Vanna's death was the turning point in the life of her husband.

5. Into what mood of her husband did Vanna not enter? What indication do you find that Jacomo had any sins for which his wife might do penance?

6. How does this story reveal the Catholic culture of the Middle Ages?

EVALUATING HER MANNER OF EXPRESSION

1. How does the author indicate the time and place of the narrative?

2. Show that the action in this chapter of the novel is complete in itself; that is, that it has beginning, development, and climax.

3. By what remarks and actions is the character of Jacomo depicted? What are Vanna's outstanding traits?

4. Select passages of effective description.

5. Quote examples of the author's use of long flowing sentences and picturesque phrases.

The Joyous Season

Philip Barry

It is Christmas Eve on Beacon Hill in Boston — by tradition the joyous season. But not everything is joyous for the Farleys. An unpretentious Irish family before the death of their parents, the grown children have moved into a fashionable residential district, increased their financial prosperity, and attained social prestige while discarding their Catholic heritage. Materialistic and selfish, they lead restless, discontented lives, unaware of their great loss. Three of the brothers are unmarried: JOHN, *the eldest, a complacent banker, who has undertaken the task of holding the family together;* ROSS, *who is disillusioned with Communism, and* HUGH, *a young college student. Another brother,* MARTIN, *has brought the family into social prominence by marrying* EDITH CHOATE. *The Farleys are living in the former home of the Choate family and are attempting to measure up to the social standards of their predecessors.* TERESA FARLEY, *married to* FRANCIS BATTLE, *a young law professor, does not understand her husband and has lost faith in marriage.* MONICA, *the youngest Farley, not only sympathizes with her brother-in-law but is secretly in love with him. Into* this disturbing atmosphere comes CHRISTINA, *the eldest daughter, now a young Superior in a teaching order. You will be interested in watching what happens during the twenty-four hours which the wise and happy nun spends at home.*

CHARACTERS

JOHN FARLEY

MARTIN FARLEY

ROSS FARLEY

HUGH FARLEY

CHRISTINA FARLEY

TERESA FARLEY BATTLE

MONICA FARLEY

EDITH CHOATE FARLEY

FRANCIS BATTLE

SISTER ALOYSIUS

PATRICK

NORA

ACTION AND SCENE

The action of the play takes place in the living room of the Farleys' house on Beacon Street, Boston.

ACT I

Christmas Eve.

ACT II

Christmas Morning.

ACT III

Christmas Afternoon.

Act One

The old Choate House on Beacon Hill has been the Farleys' for a scant two years. It retains, however, all of the original and slightly pompous dignity of a past age. This is because the Farleys have manners of their own and, except in the case of one or two of them, a real and abounding reverence for the qualities for which this venerable Boston Mansion has so long stood.

Tonight is Christmas Eve of last year, past eleven o'clock, cold and snowy. The living room is long and spacious, characteristically furnished and decorated: little has been changed. There is an entrance from the hall, at back, and another into the library, at right. At left in the windows which face out upon Beacon Street, Christmas wreaths have been hung and lighted candles set. The occasional panes of lavender glass are unnoticeable at night but will be remarked in the morning. A fire of cannel-coal burns in the fireplace, and here and there about the room lamps are lighted.

Teresa Farley Battle, in a simple evening dress, sits near the fire, smoking and gazing with a fierce intent into it. She is twenty-eight, slim, straight, fine. Francis Battle comes in from the library at right. He is a year younger, likable looking, somewhat scholarly in appearance. He is taking off spectacles which he puts into his pocket.

For a moment he looks at Terry without speaking. Then:

Francis: Terry — (He waits for a reply, which does not come.) — Of course if you want to act like a child — (She stretches her legs and settles deeper into her chair.) Terry, John's waiting for you.

Terry: Let him.

Francis: They all are.

Terry: Let them.

Francis: I don't know what you hope to prove.

Terry: I'm not trying to prove things. I just don't like conferences.

Francis: Oh come on, please, dear.

Terry: Be a good husband and go in my place, Francis.

Francis: It's the family John wants — something to do with your sister apparently.

Terry: I wouldn't doubt it for a minute. Who went to meet the boat?

Francis: Edith.

Terry: I thought so! — Martin too?

Francis: No. Edith said that only a woman should meet her.

Terry: The true Boston spirit. I hope she took something to dump into the harbor.

Francis: — Anyhow, John asked me to tell you that he wants to talk to us all about an important matter.

Terry: Well, you can tell John for me to go to — which is precisely what I'd like to tell her when she comes.

(He smiles.)

Francis: You must; it would be so very sisterly and considerate.

Terry: What consideration did she ever show us — show Mother? Religious vocation, my eye. I don't like deserters. I grant you life's a mess, but I like people who can stand and take it. (She rises and throws away her cigarette.) I think I'll go to bed.

Francis: I should think that if Martin and Edith could put off their trip west, put off seeing their children on Christmas, you might strain a point and —

Terry (*contemptuously*): — "Christmas!" I'll bet she deliberately timed it to land Christmas Eve in order to make the homecoming all the more sweet and pious.

(Martin Farley comes in. He is forty-three, keen-looking, altogether prepossessing.)

Francis: I can't budge her. You might try.

Martin: Teresa, would you mind telling me why you want to make difficulties?

(The telephone rings.)

TERRY: — Forego the formality, Martin. Just call me Mrs. Battle. (*To the telephone.*) Hello? — who — ? (*She gives the telephone to* MARTIN.)

MARTIN (*sharply now*): It is extremely important to the entire family that we hear what John has to say before she gets here.

(PATRICK, a thin, merry-looking Irish manservant, about sixty-five, enters from the hall.)

PATRICK: Mr. Martin, it's Mrs. Farley at the dock. She — ah, you've got it.

MARTIN (to the telephone): Hello? (*To* TERRY.) — So he particularly asks that we all meet at once in the library, and — (*To the telephone.*) Hello! Hello, Edith — where are you? — What? — I told you one of us should have gone with you. — What?

TERRY: — There's no need for you and Nora to wait up, Patrick.

MARTIN: Quiet, please. I can't hear. (*To the telephone.*) Yes? Yes, I can hear —

PATRICK: Oh, we wouldn't think of going to bed before greeting Miss — before greeting *her*, Miss.

MARTIN: Will you please be quiet? (PATRICK *goes out.* MARTIN *continues to the telephone.*) Well, ask for Joe Riordan, the chief inspector. If he isn't there, call me back. — "R-i-o-r-d-a-n." — Say I'll consider it a particular favor. — Better not tell Christina. Right! (*He replaces the telephone.*)

FRANCIS: Trouble?

MARTIN: Riordan will fix it. — Come on now, both of you, or they'll be in on top of us. (*He goes out into the library.*)

FRANCIS: Well, Terry? (*She does not move.*) Well, in my opinion, which, if you'll allow me to say so, is based upon a fairly intimate knowledge of the Farley family —

TERRY: Please don't be professorial with me, Francis. Save it for your freshman classes.

FRANCIS: Ah! Now we're getting down to it —

TERRY: Are we? I wasn't sure that we ever could again.

FRANCIS: What *is* it all about, Terry?

TERRY: I wish I knew.

FRANCIS: So do I.

TERRY: Let's get out of here on our own. Will you?

FRANCIS: It was your idea, living with the family, wasn't it?

TERRY: Maybe I was wrong. (*He laughs shortly.*)

FRANCIS: You? — Oh no, Terry! (*A moment. Then:*) — I was dead against it at first, if you'll remember. But things are different since then. — So for the time being, I think we're very well off as and where we are. It's a big house.

TERRY: Then it never occurs to you how essentially ridiculous it is.

FRANCIS: What is?

TERRY: — For a simple Irish family to huddle together in a Back Bay[1] mansion.

(FRANCIS *laughs.*)

FRANCIS: Is that what we're doing? It makes a pretty picture.

TERRY: — From a farm up the Merrimac to a mansion on Beacon Hill — a long, tough climb, but we made it, eh? — Trust a bunch of true micks for persistence, anyhow. — I suppose there's only one town in the world harder for an Irish family to arrive in — Dublin.

(HUGH *comes in from the library. He is twenty-three, in evening clothes, very much a man of the world.*)

HUGH: Terry? Francis? — We're waiting! get a move on you!

(*And goes out again.*)

FRANCIS: — Nobody's done any climbing that I know of, Terry. John's a genius at banking, and Martin's almost as good. They've worked hard for the place they've made here. Even my little job at the Law School I can honestly say I earned.

TERRY: — But a teacher! — When you and I married two years ago, you were going to do such wonders in the Law as had never been heard of. You had the most beautiful violence about it.

FRANCIS: I also had some money then.

TERRY: You're a strange case, Francis Battle; about as strange as they come. You've been softened by the loss of it.

FRANCIS: "Softened" — because I may find myself more interested in teaching law than in practicing it? — Didn't John teach for years?

TERRY: Yes and John should have stayed at it! You're not John. You've simply got the gift of the gab. I've seen with my own eyes the way your stream of fine energy has turned into a stream of talk — heard it, rather.

---

[1] *Back Bay*, a fashionable residential section of Boston.

FRANCIS: Thanks, Terry.

TERRY: The way you sit in your room for hours at a time, playing the phonograph to yourself. — You're beginning to like the soft life, and you know it — the nice little easy esteem — and at your age! — Is that why you spend so much time in Cambridge — do you get more esteem there? — From whom?

FRANCIS: Honestly, Terry —

TERRY: Oh, I hate the way we're living! — Let's get out — now — at once!

FRANCIS: What?

TERRY: Let's get out — away!

FRANCIS: At the moment I think it would be senseless to.

(A moment. Then:)

TERRY: — You wouldn't be too surprised, would you, Francis?

FRANCIS: At what?

TERRY: — If suddenly I should call it a day — call *us* a day.

(He stares at her, speechless. ROSS comes in from the library. He is about thirty, dark, slight, sensitive.)

ROSS: Terry? *(She looks at him.)* What's the point, anyhow?

(He gazes at her for a moment, then shrugs and goes out. TERRY turns again to FRANCIS.)

TERRY: Well? — And if I should —

FRANCIS: Terry, what are you talking about?

TERRY: Oh, don't think it's a new idea. It's been around quite awhile now.

FRANCIS: I don't see how you can say it even.

TERRY: But it seems I can. Yes, at last it seems I can. *(She looks at him.)* — You think I never would.

FRANCIS: I know you wouldn't. You've no reason to, that I know of.

TERRY: I don't need any. — What about our agreement?

FRANCIS: Agreements are easy enough *before* marriage.

TERRY: — But what's really to prevent? Am I too good a Catholic?

FRANCIS: That's one thing I've never thought of any of you.

TERRY: No? How so? Why not? — Because we don't run to church the entire time like new-born Edith? Maybe you'd better turn convert as she did — and soon, very soon, be more Catholic than the Pope!

FRANCIS: Now you *are* being Irish.

TERRY: — Anyhow, maybe you're right: maybe I'm not one. There! I've said that as well! I'm not one. I'm nothing. — Let the rest of them keep on pretending, if they like. Not me. — Church about once a month — when we get around to it. *(FRANCIS looks at her. There is a silence. Suddenly, violently, she exclaims.)* Look here, do you love me? Do you love me any more?

FRANCIS: What do you think.

TERRY: Then why don't you say something?

FRANCIS: In my opinion when the necessity arises for putting a question of that sort —

TERRY: Professor! — May I go out? I think I'm going to be sick, Professor.

(FRANCIS stiffens, and confronts her.)

FRANCIS: Terry, there's more to this than meets the eye. It's more than a question of where or how we live, whether I teach law or practice it. You've got something on your mind and have had for months. Why not out with it?

TERRY: Well, then — I don't love you! — You hear me, Professor? Professors get no love of me. It's the doers this girl loves!

(ROSS comes in again from the library.)

ROSS: Terry, John says — *(He stops and looks at them.)* What's the row? *(FRANCIS turns away with an exclamation.)* Can I get in on it? *(They are silent.)* Then come on in the other room. John's got a piece to speak.

TERRY: Ross, is it or is it not ridiculous for a simple Irish family to live in — *(She looks about her. Then, with a gesture:)* Oh, well —

ROSS: Sure it is — but so's everything else under The System. The one good thing about the capitalist class in this country is the way its membership keeps changing.

TERRY: I hate it here.

ROSS: Our hard-won symbol of security? Why, Terry! — But maybe it's less permanent than we thought, eh?

FRANCIS: How do you mean?

ROSS: Or so I've gathered from John. I don't know what else would make him so jumpy. — Unless we've lost all our precious dough or been asked not to walk in the Public Garden.

TERRY: Francis thinks it's got something to do with — I can't say her name — with *her* visit.

ROSS: Christina's? Maybe. You know, I'm a little vague on her, it was so long ago. What do you really suppose made her do that? What was she anyhow? — Another one of those people with an exaggerated sense of their own unimportance?

TERRY: Probably. — Into a convent at twenty — safe and snug for the rest of your life — what bliss!

ROSS: I seem to remember her as always being a jump or two ahead of the rest of us. Christina always knew what went on, all right — got it out of the air, from a pricking in her thumbs or something.

TERRY: Are you going to call her Christina?

ROSS: Why not?

TERRY: *I* intend using the full title — and serve her right.

ROSS: We oughtn't to be too rough on her, you know.

TERRY: Except that I think we should.

ROSS: You will keep driving through the lights, won't you, Terry?

TERRY: Will I?

(FRANCIS *laughs.*)

FRANCIS: She will!

(HUGH *and* MONICA *have come in.* MONICA *is not yet twenty, pretty as a picture in a pretty party dress.*)

HUGH: Listen, Terry. Monique and I left the Ferrises right after dinner.

MONICA: The music hadn't arrived even.

TERRY: Why, you poor little martyrs, you.

MONICA: Hello, Francis.

FRANCIS: Hello, Monique.

MONICA: Why wouldn't you and Terry come back with us afterwards? Mrs. Ferris particularly said for you to. They're going to have the Friedenberg String Quartet during supper.

FRANCIS: What do you think, Terry?

TERRY: No, thanks. You go if you like.

FRANCIS: I just might.

TERRY: Do, by all means.

MONICA: They're — they're especially good this year, they say.

FRANCIS: I'll see later.

(*A moment. Then:*)

HUGH: John says will you kindly step into the office without further delay.

MONICA: He's quite red in the face. Edith's due back any minute.

TERRY: I hear that she's planning to give a dance for you at the Copley.

MONICA: Isn't it divine of her?

TERRY: Too, too. What will you wear, dear?

MONICA: I hadn't decided. It's to be a very smart party. (*Her A is very short.*)

ROSS: Lowells will tramp over Cabots[2] to get to it.

TERRY: — Flat heels to match the flat "A's," I'd suggest.

MONICA: Would you? — And would you also go to hell?

TERRY: "Why should I travel?" asked the Young Lady from Boston, "when I am already there?"

MONICA: What is it, Fran? Is she in one of her moods?

FRANCIS: It sounds like it, doesn't it?

MONICA: Very. (*She goes to the piano, where she sits upon the bench reading a music score to herself.*)

HUGH (*to* ROSS): What are you staring at?

ROSS: Your best bib and tucker. You look so unformed in it.

HUGH: Listen, you great, big Man of the People, you Red, you Bolshevik, you —

ROSS: You're beginning to speak with a lisp, did you know it?

(JOHN *and* MARTIN *come in from the library.* JOHN *is forty-five, the oldest. Square, set, brief, determined, the acting head of the family.*)

JOHN: So we prefer this to the library, do we? All right! (*No one replies.*) I wouldn't for the world have you disturb yourself, Terry.

TERRY: Oh, I haven't in the least.

JOHN: You'll be able to stay through tomorrow, won't you, Ross?

ROSS: Longer. Eighty per cent are laid off now. I'll have to come home to live for awhile.

JOHN: You know where you're welcome, old boy.

ROSS: Thanks, John. — I'm really cleaned out this time.

---

[2] *Lowells . . . Cabots*, prominent New England families.

HUGH: Who got it? Your friends of the proletariat?

JOHN: Never mind that, Hugh. (*A moment.*) Are we ready now? (*A silence.*) I want to put what I have to say as briefly as I can. To begin with, I hope you realize that my main concern, now and as always, has been to keep this family together and to guard its fortunes as well as I am able.

(*Unnoticed by anyone but* FRANCIS, TERRY *takes a deep breath, rises, and goes out.*)

I've felt that responsibility very keenly ever since Father died — particularly keenly since Mother so quickly and unexpectedly followed him.

ROSS: I don't think any of us would question it, John.

JOHN: Years ago when Christina did what she did, naturally none of us approved of it. But that's past history now; and during her stay with us tonight and tomorrow, I should like us all to be most kind to and considerate of her.

MARTIN: It shouldn't be difficult. I'm sure she's a very charming woman. She always was.

(MONICA *looks up from her music score.*)

MONICA: I scarcely remember her, and I'm petrified at the thought of her.

(*And returns to it.*)

JOHN: I asked His Eminence to radio merely that she was to spend the night en route. So she doesn't know yet why she is stopping over.

ROSS: We wouldn't mind knowing ourselves, John.

(*A moment. Then:*)

JOHN: You may have wondered at Martin's and my delay in settling Mother's estate. As I told you originally, she left equal shares to all of us — that is, to all but Christina.

HUGH: Well, I should hope.

MONICA: Francis — (*He turns to her.*) The symphony this afternoon was heavenly. You should have heard it.

FRANCIS: I wish I might have.

JOHN: Will you kindly pay attention to what I am saying? Due to the — er — peculiar circumstances of Christina's life and knowing that the rest of us had definitely given up Good Ground as a place to live —

HUGH: How'd they ever happen to call that farm "Good Ground"?

JOHN: Because it was and is! Please don't interrupt me. — Mother wanted Christina to have it. — The trouble's with the way she worded the request. "Any piece of real property that may be in my possession at the time of my death," she said.

MARTIN: The farm won't rent or sell, and the taxes have been jumped to a point now where — anyhow, what's a burden to us will probably be a windfall for *them.*

JOHN: In fact, for some time they've been trying to get a location nearby — Ned Ellis tells me that twice they've made offers for the Lefferts' place up the river from us. Christina might have suggested that to them.

MARTIN: Almost certainly did.

HUGH: All right! Good Ground, good riddance.

JOHN: I quite agree — but unfortunately that isn't the whole story. Now, Terry, perhaps you'll realize the importance of this — where is she?

(*No one replies. A moment, then* ROSS *laughs.*)

ROSS: All right, John. We're with you, anyway. So quit pulling your punches, and let's have it, will you?

(*A moment. Then:*)

JOHN: When Father bought this house, the business outlook was at its worst. So, as a precaution — a safeguard in unsettled times —

(*He stops, as* EDITH CHOATE FARLEY *enters from the hall. She is in her late thirties, bright, capable, trim-looking in her coat and hat.*)

MARTIN: Edith! Already?

JOHN: Oh, Lord —

EDITH: She stopped downstairs to say a word to Nora and Mrs. Carey. (*She looks at them.*) What's the matter?

MARTIN: I'll explain later. How — does she seem?

EDITH: Splendid. Quite young and gay, in fact. I must see to a room for the other one. (*She goes out again.*)

HUGH: Other one? What other one?

ROSS: They always travel in pairs.

MONICA: A nun — "gay"! How ghastly—

(*She replaces the score on the piano and begins to powder her nose.*)

Ross: She'll find changes, all right, won't she? From a lovely, wild lot of shouting, laughing Irish to a stiff, self-conscious group of almost-true-Bostonians.

Martin: Stop that, Monique. (Monica *looks up blankly.*) Stand up, Hugh.

Hugh: I think I know how to conduct myself.

John: What makes you think that? — Get up — get up at once!

(Hugh *rises.*)

Monica: Me too?

John: All of you.

(Monica *rises.* Ross *and* Francis *are already upon their feet.*)

Monica: But what can one say to her? How do you speak to them?

Ross: I imagine she understands English, Monique. (Martin *moves toward the hall.*) All right, John — "precaution," "safeguard" — against what?

John: It may very well happen that Christina will take this house from us.

Hugh: What?

Ross: Oh, my!

Monica: How could she?

John: You'll find out soon enough. All I ask for the moment, is that you remember who she is and what she is.

Martin: Yes — whether you respect it or not. (*He stops in the hall doorway.*) Ah! Here you are!

(*Into the hall doorway come* Christina Farley *and her traveling companion,* Sister Aloysius. Christina's *dress, the habit of a religious, is gray with a black veil, a white linen bonnet tied beneath her chin, a band across her brow, a white bertha across her bosom.* Sister Aloysius *is dressed as she is. In the crook of one arm she carries quite a large package, done up in brown paper. Both nuns wear heavy gray capes of a slightly darker shade than their habits.* Christina *slips off her cape and hands it to* Nora, *a fine, burly Irishwoman, who, with* Patrick *stands behind her in the hallway, each with a small black bag in her hand.*)

Christina: Thank you, Nora. (*We have not yet seen her face.*) — And perhaps you and Patrick would like to come with us. Could you be ready in time?

Nora: Ah, indeed we could, Miss Christina! There'd be no greater pleasure in all the — (Suddenly appalled, she claps her hand to her mouth.) — "Miss Christina" — there! I've done it! I knew I would. Patrick — didn't I tell you, man?

(*Christina laughs merrily.*)

Christina: Don't mind, my dear. I'm sure no one else does. Now run and show Sister where she's to sleep.

Nora (*turning*): Ah yes, yes —

Christina: One moment — (*She places her hand upon* Sister Aloysius's *arm and bends toward her.*) I must make you acquainted with my family, dear. (*Now she turns, and we see her face for the first time — a lovely face, a memorable face, a face eternally youthful, lit from within — merry eyes, fine nose, sensitive, sympathetic, humorous mouth. For a moment she gazes silently, eyes shining, upon all of them. She murmurs softly, with love:*) My family. (*Then briskly, the practical, matter-of-fact woman.*) This is Sister Aloysius, who travels with me here and there and is a comfort to me always. (*There is a murmur of "How-do-you-do's" from the family. Without raising her eyes, without removing her hands from her sleeves,* Sister Aloysius *bows solemnly to them,* Christina *pats her arm.*) Poor thing — such weather we had. There, now, go and take a bit of rest, you need it. Here — let me have this. — I'll see that you're called in time. (*She takes the package from her arms, places it upon a table and turns to* Patrick.) Perhaps a glass of wine for her, Patrick, and a biscuit or two?

(Sister Aloysius *shakes her head.*)

Patrick: Oh, yes, Miss — yes, yes, straight off, your Reverence — (*He goes quickly from view.* Christina *calls after him laughing.*)

Christina: — My what?

(Sister Aloysius *goes out down the hall, following* Nora. Christina *advances into the room.*)

John: Well! At last!

Christina: Oh, my dears, my dears! — How good, how good to see you! The boys first — (*She turns to* John, *who is nearest her, and kisses him on either cheek, the convent kiss.*) John —

JOHN: You do look fine, you know.

CHRISTINA: And you, John — and all of you! — Martin — (*She kisses him as she has* JOHN. *Then as she moves past* MARTIN *toward* ROSS.) What a handsome lot you are! I've always said the dear Lord took his own time when he made the Farley boys.

(*Suddenly she stops and looks around her.*)

Where is Terry?

FRANCIS: She'll be right down.

CHRISTINA: Is she sweet? Is she the darling she always was? Of course, of course! If I have a favorite among you, Terry — (*Her face clouds.*) And which is it you are? Hugh, maybe?

HUGH: I'm Hugh.

(*She goes to him, takes his face in her hands and kisses him.*)

CHRISTINA: Little Hughie — to be sure! (*She kisses him.*) My, how manly you look! Is it your first dress suit?

HUGH (*embarrassed*): No, not quite.

(ROSS *laughs.* HUGH *scowls at him. She turns to* ROSS.)

CHRISTINA: Ross —

(*He laughs again.*)

ROSS: Right, this time!

(*She kisses him.*)

CHRISTINA: Did you ever find the watch, Ross?

ROSS: The — what watch was that, Christina?

CHRISTINA: Why, the one you lost in the orchard the day I left.

(*He fingers his unlighted pipe uncertainly.*)

ROSS: Do you know, I'm afraid I've entirely forgotten —

CHRISTINA: But it was the silver watch that Mother gave you for your birthday!

ROSS: Oh, of course! No, it — er — it never turned up.

(*She looks at him keenly.*)

CHRISTINA: Yes. It's true. It was a long time ago. For me, you see, time — (*She bows her head, looks at her hands a moment. Then again, brightly:*) Ah, well!

FRANCIS: I'm Terry's husband. Francis Battle, my name is.

CHRISTINA: Terry's — ? So Terry has married — and without a word to me. Ah, you've treated me shamefully, all of you! — Only the sad news of Father and Mother. — Could you not save her, John? She wasn't old.

(*He shakes his head.*)

JOHN: Not possibly.

CHRISTINA: They wanted her. There is sometimes an impatience about Them. (*Then to* MONICA.) Monica — come here, my darling — (MONICA *moves uncertainly toward her outstretched hands.* CHRISTINA *laughs and kisses her.*) You were all pink and white when last I saw you, with a yellow head, like a Baroque angel.[3]

MONICA: Really?

CHRISTINA: Yes, really. Darling, how pretty you are. What a pretty dress.

MONICA: Why, thank you.

(EDITH *re-enters without her hat and coat.*)

EDITH: She's been to a party.

CHRISTINA: I thought as much! — Turn around, dear — (*Obediently, a little awkwardly,* MONICA *turns.* CHRISTINA *regards the dress.*) So pretty. — Not just a little low in the back, maybe?

MONICA: That's the style now.

CHRISTINA: To be sure! — Aren't American women lovely, Martin? — In all my travels up and down the world and to and fro in it, I've never seen their equal. — Look at your wife —

MARTIN: Bow, Edith!

EDITH: Thank you! You make me feel quite worldly.

(CHRISTINA *is still regarding* MONICA'S *dress, to* MONICA'S *discomfort.*)

CHRISTINA: And a convert, too, she tells me.

EDITH: Since last year. I've never been so happy. (*She laughs her rather affected laugh.*) It caused quite a stir, you know — a Bostonian and all that —

---

[3] *baroque angel,* an angel figure used in the highly decorative style of architecture of the 16th, 17th, and 18th centuries.

CHRISTINA: Of course it takes a little time. It's not like being born one. (*To* MONICA.) You could put a handkerchief across it.

MONICA: A — ? But — . Why yes, yes — I suppose I could.

CHRISTINA: Or a scarf — a bright scarf. Yes, I think that's just what it needs. (*To* EDITH.) Don't you agree?

EDITH: Perhaps a lace insertion. I have some lovely old point d'esprit of my grandmother's.

CHRISTINA: No. — Gayer. It should be gay for a party dress. — How are your children, Martin?

MARTIN: Fine. We were to have spent Christmas with them, but —

EDITH: They're at school in Arizona. They both had such colds all last winter — that is, Winthrop did — and I was afraid little Choate would develop the same tendency.

CHRISTINA: "Winthrop" and "Choate" — ?

EDITH: Yes. Family names, you know.

CHRISTINA: I see. (*A moment, then:*) Have you had their throats blessed? (*She turns to* ROSS *who is still playing with his pipe.*) Do light it, Ross. I would, if I were you.

ROSS: Thank you. (*He lights the pipe.* HUGH *offers a cigarette to* MONICA.)

HUGH: Cigarette, Monique?

(*She extends her hand, but* JOHN's *forbidding glance arrests her.*)

MONICA: No, thank you.

(FRANCIS *is at the house telephone.*)

FRANCIS: Terry? — Come down, will you, Terry? (*A moment.*) Yes. Several minutes ago. (*Another moment.*) I think you're wrong. (*He replaces the receiver, stands staring at it, frowning.*)

CHRISTINA: "Francis Battle" you said it was?

(*He turns to her.*)

FRANCIS: That's right.

CHRISTINA: It's a fine name, a fine, strong name.

MONICA: It really is, isn't it?

CHRISTINA: "Francis X" would it be?

(*He laughs.*)

FRANCIS: No. I'm a rank outsider.

CHRISTINA: Oh, we'll catch you yet, — won't we? — if you're worth catching!

JOHN: It's really so nice having you home, Christina —

CHRISTINA: Home? — But whose house is it, John?

JOHN: Why — er —

MARTIN: Ours, now. We'll have been here two years in March.

CHRISTINA: All of you?

MARTIN: All of us! (*He laughs.*) Still the same strong family feeling, you see!

(CHRISTINA *looks about her at the room.*)

CHRISTINA: Of course, it does take a little time to make a place your own. We often find that when we open a new house.

(EDITH *smiles brightly.*)

EDITH: But it was *my* family's for many, many years, you see.

CHRISTINA: I see. — And did the famous people come here who used to visit at Good Ground?

EDITH: Well — that is to say — there *were* some rather celebrated guests in Father's and Grandfather's time.

CHRISTINA: Yeats came to us and his father before him. And George Russell and once Michael Collins — will you ever forget that day, John? — And then there was that red-bearded Stephens,[4] who fought so with Father over — oh, I do miss Father — I miss them both so much.

JOHN: We all do.

CHRISTINA: Mother was a saint — I'm sure she went straight to heaven. I wasn't so certain about Father, he was such a proud man. I said to the other nuns: "Get to work now and work hard! We must slip him in somehow! —" (*She goes to the table upon which the package rests.*) I brought something for the chapel at Good Ground. It's a Holy Child — so sweet and such a dress! — But we musn't open it until tomorrow. It's by way of being a Christmas present.

EDITH: — And a lovely one.

MARTIN: But how thoughtful of you.

---

[4] *Yeats* (yats). . . *Stephens*, Irish authors.

JOHN (*simultaneously*): Why, thank you, Christina.

CHRISTINA: Some fellow on the dock who didn't know his business was for holding it there to charge me duty on it. He said it looked new. New! Imagine!

EDITH: He was really rude at first.

MARTIN: I'm so sorry you had trouble.

CHRISTINA: I just stood and looked at him, though it was all I could do not to tell him a thing or two. I was very, very angry. But I'm glad I didn't give way to it, for I thought of exactly the right thing to do: I said a little prayer to St. Joseph. — Do you know, it wasn't two minutes before he was called away — and came back all smiles and apologies with a — a — Mr. Riordan.

JOHN: Amazing.

MARTIN: Really extraordinary.

CHRISTINA: Not at all. — I must teach you that prayer. It is infallible. (*A silence. Then:*)

JOHN: Do you remember Ned Ellis, Christina?

CHRISTINA: Indeed I do! And why should I not? — Such a nice boy. What became of him?

JOHN: He's the Cardinal's right-hand man now. He entered the priesthood.

CHRISTINA: No! But how fine that is! I always knew there was adventure in Ned Ellis.

JOHN: I suppose you were surprised to get the Cardinal's message.

CHRISTINA: Very much. Has he left word for me? It must be important. Would you believe it? — I almost forgot in the sheer joy of seeing you.

JOHN: It — er — no, it was not exactly an official matter.

CHRISTINA: But I don't understand. We intended, of course, to proceed at once to New Orleans.

JOHN: They've been advised to expect you on Tuesday. You have special permission to travel on Christmas. I've made reservations for you on the four-forty tomorrow.

CHRISTINA: What is it, John? — I should never have been allowed to stop for personal reasons. That would have been pleasant, but highly irregular, in fact quite impossible. I was sure it had to do with — with — well —

MARTIN: With what, Christina? — Perhaps it has.

CHRISTINA (*after a moment, in a sudden rush*): Well, you see, it's — it's something of a secret, and of course you mustn't let it go any further — but for some time now we've — the Community — we've been negotiating for a place in this diocese for a boarding school. It was

I who convinced Mother Provincial last year that we needed representation near Boston, particularly in view of the fact that another teaching Order — you know which, as well as I do — has a City House here, and for years they've been enjoying a practical monopoly. *Our* methods are quite as advanced as theirs, if not more so; and there's no reason I can see why Boston girls shouldn't have the benefit of them. The country around Good Ground seemed to me quite ideal, so I suggested the Lefferts' place. But the devil was in old Lefferts, and he wouldn't accept our offers and he *wouldn't* accept them. Apparently the depression hadn't touched him. Then, just before I left Rome, suddenly I knew how to manage it — (*She stops, breathless.*)

JOHN: Really? How was that?

(*She nods her head rapidly, swallows, and proceeds.*)

CHRISTINA: I got permission and arranged to have every community in the Order make a special novena to St. Jude. Jude is the patron of desperate cases, you know. — And when I got His Eminence's message on the boat I was sure, I was *sure* that our request had been graciously received and that old Lefferts had been brought around at last, the stubborn old rascal, I didn't much care how. I just felt in my bones that — (*Suddenly she stops herself. A moment, then:*) — I'm talking too much. Yes, I am certainly talking too much. (*She laughs lightly.*) — But you see, traveling in Advent, I thought we ought to make a little retreat. Also, it seemed the only possible way to escape an old Dominican Father on board, who grew more tiresome by the minute. So for the last five days we practiced silence. This is — an accumulation.

(JOHN *has gone to the telephone.*)

JOHN: I want you to come down here immediately. John, yes. That doesn't matter. Please come at once. (*He replaces the receiver.* CHRISTINA *turns to him.*)

CHRISTINA: Terry? — But perhaps she —

JOHN: She's coming. — The Cardinal wirelessed you at my request, Christina, because he thought your visit might be of considerable importance both to your Order and to the diocese.

CHRISTINA: I know I may have business with the Cardinal, but —

JOHN: Indeed you may. We all may.

(He waits, portentously. She gazes at him, puzzled.)

Ross: Oh, why all the mystery, John? Why not out with it?

(She looks from one to the other blankly. Then:)

John: You see, Mother left the farm on the Merrimac to you.

Christina: She — ?! To *us*? We're to have Good Ground? — Oh, you don't mean it! (John *and* Martin *nod solemnly.*) Oh, God bless her dear heart, God bless her —

Ross (*to* John): But I thought you said that wasn't the whole story?

John: I was about to —

Christina: Wait! Don't speak for a minute. (*They are still for a moment. At last* Christina *looks up again, her face shining.*) — She was inspired to do it. She must have been. — I shall tell you another secret; if we had got the Lefferts place, I was to have organized the new House there. — And now it will be *I* who — !

(Suddenly she stops and frowns. Then:)

Oh no, it's too good! It wouldn't do at all. It would be too like coming home again — or never having left it. (*Then in confusion:*) It isn't too good, I mean — it's too worldly. When one elects to leave the world — but I mustn't talk like this. This is between me and Mother Provincial. (*She straightens to her full height.*) — I shall particularly ask to be relieved of the post.

John: What the clause actually said was "Any piece of real property in my possession." — That's been construed to mean any one particular piece and to give you the right of choice.

Christina: Choice?

Edith: I don't understand, John.

John: Well, as a mere formality — a kind of protection in unsettled times —

Christina: — The farm would be a godsend to us — a perfect godsend. — You'll remember that when I entered it was without the dowry that most nuns bring with them. — So I have a double duty to my Order — though I'm sure I should never be told I had. Sometimes I think mine is the only good business head in it. (*Suddenly her face clouds. She cries:*) Oh, but you —! You, poor dears — where will you live?

John: Oh — we'll manage.

Martin: The fact is we use the farm very little any more.

Hugh: Hardly at all, in fact.

Ross (*sharply*): In fact, *not* at all.

Christina: But the springs — the summers — the lovely autumns there —

John: For the last few years we've been renting a place on the North Shore, near Nahant.

Hugh: Probably buy it eventually, won't we?

Edith: You see, the other country is hardly suitable for living now.

Christina: It has changed in some way?

Martin: No — *it* hasn't precisely.

Ross (*again sharply*): But, you see, *we* have.

Christina: How is that, Ross?

Ross: Don't you remember? Some sections fashionable — some sections not?

Hugh: Oh, for heaven's sake, Ross —

Christina: — And so that's the change —

Monica: Really, I think it's in the worst possible taste to talk about whether or not one's family is — is —

Christina: Is the word difficult, Monica?

(Monica smiles her sweetest smile.)

Monica: Would you mind terribly calling me *Monique*?

Christina: Yes, I should mind that.

Monica: It's only that everyone does. It doesn't really matter.

Christina: So the Farleys have become "fashionable," and should live on the North Shore.

Ross: Are becoming — and therefore must.

Edith: Ross — how absurd you are.

Christina: Strange — strange — (*Then to* John:) What is it to be fashionable, John? What constitutes it? What special virtue is there in it?

(John laughs, offhand.)

John: They're all talking the blankest nonsense. We've simply "got on," as the saying goes, and somewhat different things are expected of us.

Christina: But got on how? You mean in worldly ways?

John: Why yes, I suppose I do.

(She shakes her head.)

CHRISTINA: John, John — I thought you were too intelligent. I did really.

(*Unnoticed by her,* TERRY *comes in from the hall in pajamas and a short wrapper, a small glass in her hand.*)

JOHN: When one elects to *live* in the world, Christina —

CHRISTINA: Of course — up to a point. But haven't you passed that long since?

JOHN: Times have changed. There's no security for anyone anymore.

CHRISTINA: I doubt if there ever has been.

TERRY (*cooly, quietly*): Unless possibly in a life like yours.

(CHRISTINA *turns and goes to her swiftly.*)

CHRISTINA: Terry! Ah, my dear —

(TERRY *extends a cool hand, avoiding the impending kiss.*)

TERRY: How do you do, Reverend Mother? We're so glad you were able to come for Christmas. (*To the others.*) Anyone care for a brandy against the cold? This is my third. I think the house is freezing. (*She takes a sip from the glass.*)

CHRISTINA: Terry —

TERRY: Yes, Reverend Mother?

CHRISTINA: I — (*But she cannot go on.*) No — no matter —

(TERRY *takes another sip from her glass.*)

EDITH: Terry, isn't it some years since you have seen your sister?

TERRY: Twelve or fourteen, I should say. — You've kept well, I hope?

CHRISTINA: Very well, thank you.

TERRY: No rush, no worries — it must be like heaven.

(CHRISTINA *smiles.*)

CHRISTINA: A few worries now and then. And quite a little rush at times.

HUGH: I don't imagine being a *Mother Superior* is any snap exactly.

MARTIN (*with pride*): And she's the youngest in the order! — Isn't that true, Christina?

(*She looks away from him, not replying.*)

EDITH: It's really extraordinary. Only last week we were speaking of it.

FRANCIS: Well, I've always said it was a brilliant family we married into.

JOHN: Yes, Christina, it must be just as much of a satisfaction to you at your age to have — er — shall we say — risen to such prominence — such —

CHRISTINA: — No, let's not, John. (*Then:*) It seems to me that in a great cause it matters very little whether one is general or private. With us *Mother Superior* means only — well, in my case, that I am strong and able to stand traveling. It — I am sorry, I should not have thought it necessary to explain.

(*A silence which* TERRY *breaks.*)

TERRY: But how interesting.

(CHRISTINA *gazes at her for a moment, then extends her hand toward her glass which she is again raising to her lips.*)

CHRISTINA: Please — may I have a sip? — Just a small one. Suddenly I feel so cold myself. (TERRY *extends the glass to her. She takes the smallest of sips and returns it.*) Thank you.

TERRY: Not at all.

(FRANCIS *rises abruptly.*)

FRANCIS: — Hard — hard as nails.

(TERRY *smiles and raises the glass to him.*)

TERRY: Your good health, Professor.

(*He turns from her and goes out. From now on* CHRISTINA *never takes her eyes from* TERRY. JOHN *clears his throat and speaks:*)

JOHN: Terry, I've been explaining to your sister the terms of a bequest Mother made her.

TERRY: Yes?

JOHN (*to* CHRISTINA): I hadn't finished. I was about to tell you that in addition to Mother's ownership of the farm — are you listening, Christina?

CHRISTINA: Yes, John.

(*And so, suddenly are all the rest of them.*)

JOHN: Father, as a mere formality to protect the family interest, had also temporarily put this house in Mother's name.

(EDITH *starts in alarm.*)

EDITH: But certainly the intention could not have been — ! Martin, you never told me that he —

(*He gestures her to silence, watching* CHRISTINA.)

CHRISTINA: You are white, Terry. Your face is drawn. You have no color.

TERRY: Sorry. My make-up's off for the night.

JOHN: Did you hear me, Christina?

CHRISTINA: This house — yes?

JOHN: So — well, at least according to the letter of the law — you're entitled to make your choice between them.

(Ross *laughs.*)

ROSS: The symbol — the precious symbol —

(CHRISTINA *smiles faintly.*)

CHRISTINA: I don't think it will be difficult, John.

(HUGH *sinks back again, relieved. The alarm fades from* EDITH's *eyes.* JOHN *and* MARTIN *exchange glances.*)

JOHN: We — er — we rather anticipated your preference in the matter and had a deed prepared. — Shall we go into the library?

CHRISTINA: Let's let it wait until morning, shall we?

JOHN: Why certainly, if you wish.

MARTIN: And of course if you want anyone else to examine it —

CHRISTINA (*still watching* TERRY): I don't believe that will be necessary.

(*A moment. Then:*)

ROSS: It seems to me Christina ought to be advised that so far as actual value goes, this house is worth more than the farm.

CHRISTINA: "Actual value" has always seemed to me a most variable thing. It depends, I should think, a great deal on "to whom."

EDITH: Exactly.

CHRISTINA: Were you not all fond of it there — the land we roamed, the house that we grew up in?

MARTIN: It — er — why, yes — of course it has many tender associations for us, many —

JOHN: Yes — and a fine year-around place — no better, really. The house is in excellent condition. I've checked that. They built well in those days.

CHRISTINA: Terry — do you not love the farm?

TERRY: It's so long since I've been out there.

(*A moment. Then* CHRISTINA *throws out her hands and lifts her face in sudden exaltation.*)

CHRISTINA: Well — *I* love Good Ground! I think Heaven's blessing is upon it. I think there was never land I have ever known so lovely!

MARTIN: We're happy it's to be yours, Christina.

(*She sends darting, questioning looks from one to the other, then draws herself erect and speaks with great dignity.*)

CHRISTINA: I find all of you much changed — very sedate, most solemn, most unlike the brothers and sisters I had expected — and in this, the Church's most joyous season, when always we were so gay. I cannot imagine what has done it. It's as if a light had been let die out, a light that I thought would always — (*Her voice catches. For a moment there is silence. At length she recovers herself and laughs a laugh from which all merriment has gone.*) Well — Time is a villain sometimes, isn't he? I have small use for Time, sometimes — (*She searches in the depths of her pocket for her watch, which she draws forth.*) But we must see to it that he doesn't escape us now, musn't we? See, Ross — *I* have a silver watch. It is not mine, precisely, but I have the use of it. (*She glances at it and returns it to her pocket.*) Yes — it's after half-past. It will be crowded, if I remember rightly. — I hope you have a warm coat, Monica.

MONICA: For what —

CHRISTINA: We'd best get ready, don't you think, John?

JOHN: Er — why — er — why, yes. That's right.

HUGH: Are we going somewhere?

(CHRISTINA *looks from one to the other, again uncertain, again bewildered.*)

CHRISTINA: But aren't we? Aren't we, Martin? I thought of course — Christmas Eve — the way we always — *aren't* we, John?

(JOHN *moves to the telephone.*)

JOHN: Why, yes — yes. Certainly.

ROSS: Midnight Mass? You bet your hat we are!

HUGH: But listen; Monique and Francis and I —

CHRISTINA: Don't you remember? Oh, surely you remember! We always came into town for it — then spent the night at the Parker House — and drove back to the country in time for Christmas dinner. Such an event it was! — Once, I remember, it had been snowing hard, and Father ordered the sleighs out — that was a time! Poor Terry — you had a cold — oh, such a cold — and couldn't go —

TERRY: I hope I was brave about it.

CHRISTINA: I felt I should have stayed with you, but Father said no, one was enough. — Yes, you were brave. You had always such a gallantry about you, Terry.

TERRY (*murmuring*): Gone, too.

CHRISTINA: My dear?

TERRY: Nothing.

(*Again the light fades from* CHRISTINA's *face as she looks from one to the other, sees them stiff, solemn, unsmiling.*)

CHRISTINA: But perhaps you had all planned otherwise. Perhaps you prefer waiting for morning Mass. I don't want to interfere.

MONICA: As a matter of fact, Hugh and Francis and I —

ROSS: If you can go at twelve, you can go at one.

CHRISTINA (*suddenly*): I dislike immensely to interfere, but I think there are special graces that attach to Midnight Mass, so I intend to! (*Her voice falters again.*) Please be so kind —

JOHN: Get your coat, Monique.

EDITH: And a hat, don't forget! (*To* CHRISTINA.) I think it is the most lovely spectacle of all, and the music really charming.

JOHN (*at the telephone*): Patrick? Order two — no, three — taxis right away, will you? We're going to church. Yes, all of us.

CHRISTINA: Nora and him, I asked as well.

JOHN: You and Nora are to come too, if you like. That's right. (*He replaces the telephone and turns to them, rubbing his hands, heartiness itself.*) Well, now — this is going to be fine! Come along, now — Hugh — Monique — Terry — (*He digs* MARTIN *playfully in the ribs.*) Get going, old boy. Don't stand there! (*He goes out into the hall.*) Coats — hats — mufflers — cold and still snowing! Come along, you lazy lot of good-for-nothings —

(HUGH, MONICA, *and* MARTIN *follow him to the doorway. Again* CHRISTINA *is silently watching* TERRY, *who does not move.*)

CHRISTINA: And will someone tell Sister Aloysius, please? She may have fallen asleep, she was so tired.

EDITH: I shall. — Come, Terry.

(*She goes out, followed by* HUGH, MONICA, *and* MARTIN.)

ROSS: May I bring your cape, Christina?

CHRISTINA: Will you, Ross?

(*He goes out.* CHRISTINA *turns to* TERRY.)

TERRY: I'm not going. I don't qualify. (*A silence.*) And I detest hypocrisy. So please excuse me. (*For a moment she meets* CHRISTINA's *silent, searching gaze, then moves to the table where she takes a cigarette from a box, standing with her back to* CHRISTINA. *The silence continues,* CHRISTINA's *eyes still upon her.* TERRY's *shoulders come together. She turns suddenly, and demands:*) Well? — What if I am? (CHRISTINA *raises her brows questioningly.* TERRY *laughs shortly.*) Say it! "changed"! (CHRISTINA *says nothing. A moment. Then:*) Well, you looked as if you thought it.

CHRISTINA: Did I, Terry?

TERRY: Well, even if it's so, I don't see that there's much to be done about it, do you?

CHRISTINA: I don't know.

TERRY: *I* do. — So do you mind if I go up now?

CHRISTINA: I think I should mind very much.

TERRY: Sorry, but I must. I've had rather a hard day. (*She moves toward the doorway.*) Good night. (*Near the doorway she stops. Again her shoulders come together. She turns.*) Well, Reverend Mother?

(CHRISTINA *smiles faintly.*)

CHRISTINA: Well, Terry? (TERRY *returns a few steps toward her.*)

TERRY: I suppose you find me quite a little changed. (CHRISTINA *nods. A moment.*) Yes — I suppose it's contact with the world that's done it. But you see, I believe in it. I don't believe in dodging.

CHRISTINA: — Dodging.

TERRY: Mother was ill. She'd been ill a long time. If you didn't care about having a home of your own, you should have stayed on to look after her.

(CHRISTINA *nods.*)

CHRISTINA: — A life, a career you might have respected more than the one I chose.

TERRY: I think I should have respected it a very great deal.

CHRISTINA: I could not have been a good companion so much longer. There was — constantly something drawing me away. — You see, one time the Lord sat down with me for a moment, then rose, and left me to follow Him. However much I loved you all, there was nothing to do but gather up my life and go.

TERRY: — And that doesn't seem to you selfish.

CHRISTINA: Of course. But I assure you that when it happens there's nothing else to do. Why, life wouldn't be worth living! (*A moment.*) I should not have said that because it never is not.

TERRY: You don't think so?

CHRISTINA: I am sure of it.

TERRY: Well, if I could save mine by moving from here to there, I should stay where I am.

(*A moment. Then:*)

CHRISTINA: And I had always thought that life would be so good to you.

TERRY: You — you were mistaken.

CHRISTINA: But that you should lose your faith in it — you, Terry, who were life itself!

TERRY: I guess it went with my faith in Francis.

CHRISTINA: That too?

(TERRY'*s head sinks.*)

TERRY: Everything. (*And she raises it again, sharply.*) But I'm not asking anyone to be sorry for me, thanks!

CHRISTINA: Not you.

TERRY: I guess I expected too much of marriage.

CHRISTINA: It would be difficult to. It would be easier not to expect enough. That sometimes happens among *us*, and when it does, it's very sad.

TERRY: Well, anyhow, I don't believe my husband loves me — how's that, for instance?

CHRISTINA: It is sad.

TERRY: And maybe I don't love him anymore — how's that?

CHRISTINA: That is sadder.

TERRY: Oh, not so, maybe. *He's* not the man I married — he's nothing like him. Why should I care? (*There is a moment's pause, then she continues:*) I don't know what it is, but the air's full of something. — Maybe there's someone else for him — I don't know. All I know is that there's something awful hanging over us. I do know that. — I feel it! *I* get some things out of the air myself — *my* thumbs prick too. (*Another moment. Then:*) I wish I could die. I want to die. (*She laughs, brokenly.*) How's that, for instance? (*Then suddenly, blindly she reaches for* CHRISTINA'*s hand, grasps it, bends her head over it.*) Oh, Christina — everything's so awful —

(CHRISTINA *strokes her bowed head.*)

CHRISTINA: I know — I know, dear. — We'll find something to do.

TERRY: Oh yes, we must! We must, or I'll go crazy! (*She presses her face hard against* CHRISTINA'*s hand, and sobs.*) — Crazy. — I hate living — Why can't I die?

CHRISTINA: What was your word? — "Dodging"? (*She shakes her head decisively.*) Not you. Not any Farley.

TERRY: I think all of us are, in one way or another. I thought you were the first to.

CHRISTINA: — Something will come to us, dear. (*She raises her up and kisses her on both cheeks.*) We must wait.

TERRY: Wait! — That's all I've been doing —

CHRISTINA: And still we must wait.

(Ross *comes whistling "Holy Night" down the hall.* TERRY *goes to the windows and stands there rigid, her back to the doorway in which* Ross *appears,* CHRISTINA'*s cape over his arm.*)

Ross: The others have gone down — (*He holds out the cape.*) I hope you'll be warm enough. It looks like a blizzard. (*A moment.* CHRISTINA *looks at him without moving.*) Terry — get dressed! (*There is no reply. He turns again to* Christina.) We're late already.

Christina: Hurry. — I shall wait until morning Mass.

Ross: But —

Christina: Terry has another cold.

(*A moment. Then* Ross *nods, lays her cape on the chair, and goes out, whistling.* Christina *turns to* Terry. *The clock in the hall begins to strike the hour.*)

CURTAIN

Act Two

It is about eleven o'clock the following morning. The candles have been removed, and a bright, cold winter sun shines through the windows, with their occasional panes of lavender glass. Vases of flowers stand here and there, and somehow the room seems less somber.

Edith, *in a tweed suit, is giving the finishing touches to the flowers.* Nora *stands near by, a pile of empty boxes in her arms.* John *sits deep in an easy chair near the table, head upon chest, thinking heavily.* Martin *stands at the windows looking out, also deep in thought. He wears a short morning coat,* John *one with tails.* Edith *flutters at the flowers.*

Edith: There! Much brighter — much more Christmassy. (There is a disinterested grunt from Martin and no reply from John.) — That's all, I think, Nora.

(Nora *turns and moves toward the doorway.*)

Nora: Very good, Ma'am.

(Edith *flashes a brief smile after her.*)

Edith: "Madam."

Nora: "Madam." (She goes out.)

Edith: — We must telephone the boys at their lunch time. That will be — let's see — about four o'clock here. Choate will be thrilled, I'm sure. Of course Winthrop's so grown up and dignified, that — (*Silence. She looks from one to the other.*) — Really, you're both being so absurd. (John *changes his position in his chair.* Martin *does not stir*). Don't you realize how impossible it is that she should do anything of the sort?

(John *looks up.*)

John: You heard what she said: "A little longer to think about it."

Martin: Mass must have been out half an hour ago. She and Terry must be driving all over town — I don't blame John for worrying. I'm worried myself. Lord knows what the two of them talked about till all hours.

Edith: But this house belongs to me — to *us*!

John: Only if she says it does.

Edith: I don't see how she can say anything else.

John: It's unlikely, but it's possible. (*He ponders a moment. Then:*) — Edith, I wish you'd arrange for Patrick and Nora and Mrs. Carey, the cook, to — . No, wait a minute — (*He ponders further, then rises decisively.*) Yes! Tell them to be prepared on a few minutes' notice to load everything necessary for dinner into the small car, to be taken out to the farm.

(Edith's *eyes enlarge.*)

Edith: — To the — ? But why, John?

Martin: Yes — what's the point of that?

John (*to* Martin): — And I wish you'd telephone Maloney to open up — light fires, and all that. The furnace must be going full blast as it is. Lord knows I paid a coal bill on Wednesday that would heat the Ritz.

Edith: — All the way out there, in such weather?

John: I presume you'd like to keep this house in the family —

Edith: I see very little danger that we shan't.

John: "Little" is enough. Once she makes up her mind there'll be little time for argument which, incidentally, would come with very little grace from us. She leaves at four-forty, and the decision's hers.

Edith: Oh, you are so ridiculous! It's a country house they want for a convent. She dislikes the city — she as much as said she did!

John: I don't expect to have to go. I simply want to be ready in case there's any further indication of an unwise decision on her part. She may need to refresh her memory about the place.

Martin: — Now I begin to see what you're driving at.

Edith: Well, I don't. *I* think it's an utterly unnecessary, elaborate, farfetched precaution against something that can't possibly happen. — And I can't tell you how I hate dinner at midday.

John: All my precautions have always been unnecessary, farfetched and elaborate. That's why a number of Boston families, including this one, have been able to keep their heads above water for the past few years.

EDITH: I only meant —

MARTIN: Shall I tell the household, or will you, Edith?

EDITH: I'll tell them.

JOHN: Say I'll let them know definitely within the half hour.

(EDITH *sees* CHRISTINA *and* TERRY *coming in from the hall.*)

EDITH: Ah! You're back.

CHRISTINA: Merry Christmas!

JOHN and MARTIN (*together*): Merry Christmas.

TERRY: Who's seen Francis?

MARTIN: He went out before you did.

TERRY: I know, but —

MARTIN: He said he had to run out to Cambridge about something.

TERRY: To? — oh — (*She falls silent.*)

EDITH: Church must have been lovely. Did the Cardinal preach?

CHRISTINA: Guess who it was. (EDITH *looks puzzled.*) — It was Ned Ellis — actually! Oh, it was fine! He speaks with so much joy, such fine delight! He didn't — you know — preach —

JOHN: I might have asked him to take Christmas dinner with us.

CHRISTINA: It would be pleasant to have him, if you think he could come.

JOHN: He might. He's still — what did you always call him? — "unexpected" —

CHRISTINA: — He never said or did an indifferent thing.

JOHN: I'll give him time to get his breakfast.

CHRISTINA: — Which brings mine suddenly to mind.

EDITH: It's coming. I told Nora.

CHRISTINA: — It *is* a joyful religion, you know — it is, truly. I think that for some little time now — for the past few centuries at least — there's been too much emphasis placed upon suffering, too little upon —

EDITH: — You actually criticize the Church? But how astonishing!

CHRISTINA: Not at all. It's always provided for reform from within. — And I don't criticize. I — make comment among friends.

EDITH: I'm afraid I simply accept everything.

CHRISTINA: You converts always go to such extremes. For us — do you remember Father, boys? — He used to look around the table and say, "Well! now that we're all Catholics, we can talk about the Pope." (*She laughs.*) — Not that we ever did, to be sure — or that there was ever anything to say against the holy man. (NORA *comes in with a breakfast tray.*) — God bless you, Nora! — Is it for me?

NORA: It's for nobody else at all. (*She places the tray upon a table before her.*)

NORA: Just take what ye want, dear, and leave the rest for Miss Manners.

(CHRISTINA *touches the single flower in its small vase upon the tray.*)

CHRISTINA: — And a flower!

NORA: — Be way of decoration.

CHRISTINA: You were always for spoiling me, Nora.

NORA (*angrily to the others*): Do ye hear her? Her, that was forever — ? — Agh — go along with ye! (*She goes out, scolding.* CHRISTINA *takes a deep breath.*)

CHRISTINA: My, how good the coffee smells — (*She pours a cup.*)

TERRY: You must be famished.

CHRISTINA: — We have the most abominable coffee. I've never got used to it. (*And takes a swallow.*)

EDITH: This is a special blend I get from S. S. Pierce's.

CHRISTINA: It is delicious. (*She opens the lid of the pot, peers into it apprehensively, then smiles her satisfaction and snaps it shut.*) It's Christmas. I shall have a second cup. (*She opens the jam pot, and murmurs:*) — And marmalade. Oh, heaven forgive me. (*With infinite care she spreads some upon a piece of toast.*)

TERRY (*at the window*): Kids are coasting on the hill.

EDITH: But it's so dangerous.

CHRISTINA: Oh, they don't mind a spill or two. — You know, it really is a lovely city under snow. All the way home this morning I kept thinking I'd never done it justice.

MARTIN: Ah?

CHRISTINA: The common was a field of white. They had already cleared the pond in the Fenway. Children were skating there, all in bright caps.

(JOHN *clears his throat.*)

JOHN: It must be beautiful in the country now.

CHRISTINA: — *I* used to skate quite well.

— Remember my figure eights, Terry?

TERRY: They were marvels.

CHRISTINA: If my girls at St. Mary's Wood knew the capers I used to cut! (*She laughs merrily.*) Oh dear! Dear, dear, dear — (*As suddenly she becomes serious again, thrusts her feet out before her, peers down at them, and quickly retires them.*) — But I am really astonished at the beauty of this city. Why should I have remembered it as grim and forbidding?

MARTIN (*to* JOHN): I — er — I suppose the Merrimac's frozen over. What do you think?

JOHN: Yes, I'm sure it must be.

CHRISTINA: — And the Public Library and the Art Museum, Martin. They are excellent, aren't they?

MARTIN: Why — er — yes. Yes — supposed to be.

(CHRISTINA *puts down her coffee cup and gazes thoughtfully into space.*)

CHRISTINA: So many facilities for instruction — for recreation — and all so close at hand.

JOHN: Edith — would you mind doing what I asked about — er — Nora — the cook — ?

(EDITH *moves toward the hall.*)

EDITH: I'm so sorry —

JOHN: Tell them I'll let them know definitely within the half-hour.

(EDITH *goes out.*)

MARTIN: I'll call Father Ellis. (*He moves toward the library.* JOHN *follows.*)

JOHN: Let me speak to him.

(*They go out.* CHRISTINA *and* TERRY *are left alone. A silence. Then:*)

TERRY: Well — I'd better go and write thank-you notes, I expect.

CHRISTINA: I thought something would come to me during Mass this morning. (*She shakes her head.*) — I don't know what's the matter with Them up there.

TERRY: Please don't worry anymore. I'll manage.

(CHRISTINA *looks about her at the room.*)

CHRISTINA: — I don't know anything here. Even the walls are against me.

TERRY (*to herself*): Straight out to Cambridge — bright and early Christmas morning —

CHRISTINA: That needn't mean anything.

TERRY: I was horrible to him when he came in last night. He tried to tell me good night and I wouldn't speak to him. He just turned without another word and walked out of the room. — Maybe there *is* someone else for him — the way he looks at me, speaks to me — his oversolicitous manner with me —

CHRISTINA: — And maybe the lack's in yourself, Terry.

TERRY: Lack? What lack?

CHRISTINA: Oh, believe in him, my dear! Why can't you believe in him?

TERRY: I just can't. We've grown too many miles apart.

CHRISTINA: Did you ever — completely?

(TERRY *shrugs.*)

TERRY: What's that got to do with it now?

CHRISTINA: A great deal, I think.

TERRY: Other things are important now.

CHRISTINA: That is first, always.

TERRY: I don't see it.

CHRISTINA: — Something will make you see! Something must!

TERRY: I don't know what.

(CHRISTINA *averts her head.*)

CHRISTINA: Nor I — nor I. —

(JOHN *comes in from the library, a legal document in hand.*)

JOHN: Father Ellis will come with pleasure.

CHRISTINA: I am glad.

(JOHN *turns to* CHRISTINA *with the document.*)

JOHN: — I thought you might like to look this over.

CHRISTINA: I should rather look at you, John. (*She indicates a chair facing her. He smiles and seats himself. She gazes at him a moment, then touches her brow, between her eyes.*) This line — it's become so much deeper.

JOHN: — Your "typical American businessman," I expect.

CHRISTINA: Do you like it?

JOHN: I'd better! I am it. (*He leans toward her.*) — But don't think it's just for myself I've been working. It's not. It's for the family. Father made the name Farley mean something here. I've worked that it might keep on meaning it.

(TERRY *looks at him, sighs, and goes out into the hall.*)

CHRISTINA: Did he know he was going to die, John?
JOHN: Why do you ask that?
CHRISTINA: I just wondered.

(JOHN *nods.*)

JOHN: — But after the first attack he never mentioned it again. That time he said, "I'll pull out of it, Johnny — but the mark's on me now; this tree must come down."
CHRISTINA: That was like him.
JOHN: It was his purpose that was really fine, you know: To found a family in a new land. You can't see that in a man and not want to carry on with it.
CHRISTINA: There are a lot of you.
JOHN (*with satisfaction*): Eight now, with Francis and Edith.
CHRISTINA: Not too many flowers in one flowerpot?
JOHN: Don't you believe it! There'd be room and to spare for you, if you'd come back.

(CHRISTINA *laughs.*)

CHRISTINA: No thank you!
JOHN: Renegade —
CHRISTINA: — The wonder to me is that all packed together this way something really dreadful hasn't happened.
JOHN: A murder or two, maybe?

(*She laughs.*)

CHRISTINA: — Something! (*And is serious again.*) We were always a family of strong individuals, John. It may be that you should separate. It may be that each should be following his star.
JOHN: The star is the family, and united we stand — always have, except for you.
CHRISTINA: But don't people stand together sometimes for being afraid to stand alone? — At Good Ground when we sang about the wraggle-taggle gypsies, I always used to think of us as very close to being them.
JOHN: What kind of gypsies?

CHRISTINA: Don't you remember it?
JOHN: Oh — er — yes. That is — yes —
CHRISTINA: It's a long time since we thumped our spoons on the table and sang it. I'm not even sure I know the words myself now. (*She closes her eyes tight. A moment. Then:*) — Even the tune's gone. Oh — that's too bad. (*She looks at her hands. Another moment, then:*) I suppose I mustn't think that just because *I* left —
JOHN: No, you must not, Christina.
CHRISTINA: A strong, united family *is* something to be preserved, maybe.
JOHN: To me it is. — Two days ago the New York Clearing House invited me to come down and thaw out a couple of their frozen banks. It was the chance of a lifetime, but it would have meant living there. (*He laughs.*) — I guess I've got to face the fact that being a Bostonian is a full-time job at half pay.
CHRISTINA: — But banking — somehow it seems cold for you.
JOHN: — Banking cold?
CHRISTINA: Yes.
JOHN: You mean you really think banking is cold?
CHRISTINA: — For you, John. — Yes, I'm afraid I do.
JOHN: Why, my dear girl, it can be one of the most romantic jobs on this earth! — Making capital work for the growth of your country? — Financing the growing crops — moving them to market? — Building railroads, airplanes, fleets of merchantmen, cities! — Making great and impossible dreams come true overnight! Why, it's the —
CHRISTINA: — Irishman.

(*A silence. Then:*)

JOHN: "Can" be, I said.
CHRISTINA: Then why not?
JOHN: Well, you see, I had the bad luck to turn into what they call a "custodian of funds."
CHRISTINA: What an expression: It sounds like a watchman.
JOHN: It is. — Instead of opening the highways of the world, *I* open vaults — and close them — and stand with my back against them. — "Honest John Farley" — and their careful, calm, contented four per cent.
CHRISTINA: Theirs? Whose, John?
JOHN: — Your true Bostonians, of course. Security's all they ask — sweet security!

CHRISTINA: — Just what you think Father wanted for us.

JOHN: — But a quite different kind of it. What he chiefly wanted was to know that even without him we'd still hang together. I grew quite close to the old gentleman in his last years. Finally I was able to see through to that as the last real desire left in him — through all his manner and elegance, I mean. — They were there till the end.

CHRISTINA: I loved his manner. I loved his elegance. (MARTIN *comes in from the library on his way to the hall.*) — Here they are again in Martin.

JOHN: He never forgave you, you know.

CHRISTINA: Heaven help me, I even loved that in him. (*A moment.* MARTIN *pauses at the table to find a cigarette and light it.*) — And yet I had a letter from him once.

MARTIN: From Father?

(CHRISTINA *nods.*)

CHRISTINA: It was written a month before he died. It followed me to England and back again — so I never could ask what he meant by it. It was a strange letter.

MARTIN: What did it say?

(CHRISTINA *closes her eyes.*)

CHRISTINA: "Dear Daughter: Your Mother and I may surprise you some day. But don't be too surprised. Just remember the Irish need trouble."

JOHN: Trouble?

MARTIN: — Trouble.

JOHN: — I've had plenty since Mother died, just keeping the home fires burning. — It seems it's when the mother goes that the family's most apt to scatter.

CHRISTINA: Yes, I suppose.

JOHN: — Fortunately we'd just moved into this house. That helped enormously: it was like new cement in the cracks. — Of course, Terry's always a handful, and Martin still gets a bit restless now and then, but on the whole —

MARTIN: Restless? Me? — Why I'm like a cat before the fire.

CHRISTINA: — And Ross, of course —

JOHN: Ross is the least of my worries. He always comes back. I envy Ross; he's doing what he likes. He's

got his cause, and his cause keeps him happy. — Of course, at times it's a little embarrassing to the rest of us —

MARTIN: — Go on! — The best thing in the world for a banking family is a good, sound radical right in its midst. (*A moment. He looks thoughtfully at the fire. He murmurs:*) Yes — just like a cat. (*And goes out.* JOHN *gazes after him.*)

JOHN: There's an odd one. You can't get at him. I never know what he really thinks. He just says what you want to hear.

CHRISTINA: I expected great things of Martin — he was to have been "The Statesman."

JOHN: He gave up politics when he married Edith. — A pity, too, in a way. He has plenty of friends in Washington, now — or would have had.

CHRISTINA: She didn't approve?

(JOHN *laughs.*)

JOHN: She strongly disapproved.

CHRISTINA: But ministers of state must learn their trade somehow!

JOHN: Try persuading her of that.

(CHRISTINA *shivers at the prospect.*)

CHRISTINA: Oh — I'm sure I couldn't.

JOHN: — A first-rate woman, though.

CHRISTINA: Oh, I'm sure!

JOHN: A fine mother to those boys.

(*A moment.*)

CHRISTINA: — And wife to Martin?

JOHN: Well — (*He hesitates. Then, heartily:*) Yes. That's right. Fine!

CHRISTINA: Sometimes I don't quite understand her expression.

(JOHN *glances about him, places his hand upon* CHRISTINA'*s arm, moves his head close to hers, and whispers with great relish and considerable venom:*)

JOHN: "Fish face" —

(CHRISTINA *gestures him away.*)

CHRISTINA: John — what are you saying?

(JOHN shouts:)

JOHN: Fish face! Fish face!

CHRISTINA: Hush, John. *(But she cannot help laughing.)*

JOHN: — For years I've wanted to call her it: Fish face!

(CHRISTINA finally controls her laughter.)

CHRISTINA: But you musn't. You must not.

(JOHN wipes his eyes.)

JOHN: What a blessed relief —

CHRISTINA: I expect you need one occasionally.

JOHN: I don't often get it. *(She gazes at him, searchingly. He smiles.)* — Well — what is it you see?

CHRISTINA: A man who should have married and had a family of his own.

JOHN: Well — maybe there's still time, eh?

CHRISTINA: — I think you might find some woman sweet-tempered enough to stand you.

JOHN: Do you? I don't know —

CHRISTINA: Then there's no one now —

(His astonishment seems almost genuine.)

JOHN: For me? — Oh, no — oh, dear, no. I'm too busy. Probably not the marrying type anyhow, you know —

CHRISTINA: But is there no one you can talk to? No one to — unbend a little with? Must you be always such a tower of strength — so noble? *(JOHN looks at her, is about to reply, but thinks better of it.)* — I mean it. Your laugh used to be one of the loveliest things of my childhood.

(He is silent. Then:)

JOHN: I — I'm sorry our day is going to be so full. There's — there *is* someone I should like to have had you meet. — Not possible now, I'm afraid. *(He laughs embarrassedly.)* Oh, well — another time! Very nice young lady — very — er — understanding — sweet — exceedingly good business head — very — er — amusing, too, you know. I think you would have liked her.

CHRISTINA: I'm sure I should have.

(Another pause. Then, suddenly:)

JOHN: Listen to me, Christina: I'm not such a terribly old fellow. Perhaps sometime, if I can get this family of ours really settled — *(But he stops as suddenly.)*

CHRISTINA: Well, John — ?

(But he deliberately breaks the mood, rises, brings out his watch, and glances at it.)

JOHN: — Where is everyone? What's happened to them? — I can see I'll have to shake up that lazy pair of youngsters. Those two could sleep the clock around. (ROSS *comes in from the hall in a shabby suit.)* Ah — good morning, Ross!

ROSS: Hello, John.

(CHRISTINA is gazing intently at JOHN. He moves toward the library. Suddenly CHRISTINA speaks:)

CHRISTINA: John — *(He turns inquiringly. A moment. Then:)* — In the garden at St. Mary's Wood there is a sundial. It says, "It is later than you think." *(A moment. Then he gestures helplessly, and goes out.)* Ross — *(He turns to her.)* — Who is John's secretary?

ROSS: A Miss Evans — Mary Evans, her name is. Why?

CHRISTINA: Is she — is she nice?

ROSS: Extremely. — In fact, a darling. *(He sees the question in her eyes and laughs briefly.)* — No, Christina. — Boston wouldn't approve.

CHRISTINA: He has a better reason than that!

ROSS: Of course he has! — Don't mind me. I've just come from seeing a few ghosts, that's all.

CHRISTINA: — And I'm just seeing them.

ROSS: — I took a turn around the soup kitchens of a bright Christmas morning. It was quite a treat.

CHRISTINA: You'd expect to find misery there. Somehow you'd be better prepared for it.

ROSS: I remember what Father used to say: "The worst misfortune that can befall a man is to become poor. Poverty drains the spirit of all desire but the desire to escape it." *(He laughs shortly.)* The trouble with me is I used to believe I knew the way to fix it. It was something, just believing that. — But you see, I don't anymore. — It'd be too bad if I ended on the side of the so-called "Superior People," wouldn't it?

CHRISTINA: Not if their superiority had nothing to do with their birth or their pocketbooks.

Ross: — But you see for a long time I believed with my whole heart in — well — in the practicability of communism. — And I wasn't just one of the theory boys, either. I gave it everything I had. I really worked at it.

Christina: I'm sure you did. I'm sure you would.

Ross: — But the rotten part of it now is, I no longer think it is the way. Not here. Maybe I'm wrong again. But I no longer believe in it. — And it was so much a part of me for so long. It makes me feel very empty — you know — not having it — you know; having lost it.

Christina: Indeed I do know! Something of the sort almost happened to me once. You'll get it back again.

Ross: No, it's hopeless now. I'm completely stumped.

(She smiles.)

Christina: — Try St. Jude.

Ross: I thought it was Anthony who ran the Lost and Found Department.

Christina: Jude's a partner to all of them. — I'm glad Ned Ellis is coming. I only wish he were Thomas Aquinas.

Ross: You're stumped about something yourself, are you?

(She smiles.)

Christina: I'm very close to being.

Ross: — But how? By what?

Christina: "Which house?" (*He frowns, puzzled. She explains:*) I live in a communistic society, you know, a pure one. We're nearly five thousand — it's a little world. — You see, I have two families. — And I so dearly love them both and feel to each so strong a duty. — So which house? — Which, Ross?

(A moment. Then:)

Ross: No. I've too much respect for you to try to influence you.

Christina: — But a poor nun really at the end of her wits?

Ross: I don't believe for a minute that you are.

Christina: — I do feel sure that the farm is right for my new family. At least practically sure. — Oh, but what about my old? Good Ground seemed so right; you belonged to it, it to you. Here you seem to lean on each other — you who used never to lean. Tell me; don't you think all of you — secretly maybe — maybe without even knowing it — don't you think all of you long for Good Ground again?

Ross: I don't believe it's as simple as that.

(She looks at him intently.)

Christina: — You have a second family too, you know: humanity.

(He laughs shortly.)

Ross: I don't seem to have been able to do much for it yet.

Christina: No. — Perhaps you and I have the same weakness, Ross.

Ross: I'd be honored! What?

(Hugh and Monica come in from the hall. Hugh wears a sweater, his shirt open at the neck. Monica has a book in her hand, her finger marking the place.)

Christina: — Our love for our first one — our love of the Farleys.

(He stares at her a moment. Then:)

Ross: By heaven, I believe there's something in it.

(She laughs lightly.)

Christina: — I think Jude is our man.

Hugh: Hi, Ross. (*Goes to sofa and sits.*)

Ross: Hello, Hugh.

(He sits silent, thoughtful, staring at his feet.)

Monica (*extending a timid hand to* Christina): Happy Christmas.

Christina: Thank you very much.

Hugh: Yes. Same from me.

(Christina releases Monica's hand.)

Christina: Thank you very much.

(Hugh sinks into a chair. Monica does likewise. She opens her book and begins to read. He gazes sleepily at Monica.)

Hugh: What's that you've got, Monique?

Monica: A book.

Hugh: Really?

MONICA: — From Francis for Christmas.

HUGH: I drew a necktie. (*He glances at* CHRISTINA *and brings himself to his feet again.*) I beg your pardon.

CHRISTINA: Oh, no — please! I like to be on my feet.

(*A moment. He passes his hand over his brow.*)

HUGH: Lord! that party. — I can't drink the way I used to.

ROSS: You never could. (*A moment. Then:*) Monique — (*She glances up at him.*) — You oughtn't to take that stuff, you know.

MONICA: What stuff?

ROSS: That I saw on your dressing table last night.

(*She returns to her reading.*)

MONICA: It's only to make me sleep, when I can't sleep.

(CHRISTINA *goes to her, takes her chin in her hands, raises her face and searches it.*)

CHRISTINA: How old are you, child?

MONICA: I'm not a child at all! I'm — I'll be twenty in September.

CHRISTINA: — And cannot sleep?

(JOHN *re-enters from the library.*)

JOHN: Hello, children.

(HUGH *gestures without change of expression.*)

MONICA: Thanks terribly for the presents, everyone. I meant to get you all something, but the shops had people in them.

HUGH: You got one for Francis.

MONICA (*turning on him with sudden violence*): Why shouldn't I? What affair's that of yours?

HUGH: Hey! Wait a minute —

MONICA: I — I happen to know what Francis likes, that's all. He — Fran's easy to choose for.

HUGH: Who said he wasn't?

(*A silence.* CHRISTINA *turns from* MONICA *to the window.*)

CHRISTINA: The sun is really lovely here. It does pour in. (*She moves to the library.*) — This is the library — ?

JOHN: That's right.

(CHRISTINA *stands at the library door, looking in.*)

MARTIN (*from within*): Something you wanted, Christina?

(*He comes into the living room.* CHRISTINA *is now very businesslike. She moves to the hallway, looks both ways into it and up and down the stairs.*)

CHRISTINA: No thank you. — It's quite a large house.

MARTIN: Fairly, yes. (*He and* JOHN *exchange glances.*)

JOHN: — Of course nothing to compare to Good Ground.

(*Again* CHRISTINA *turns toward the window.*)

CHRISTINA: — And a really pleasant street.

MARTIN: Er — yes. Yes, we find it so.

HUGH: Not what it was, they say.

(EDITH *re-enters.*)

CHRISTINA: — What they call "a good neighborhood."

ROSS: They certainly do.

CHRISTINA: I like the outlook. I like a place on a hill. (*Again she moves toward the hall.*) — I should like to see the kitchen. (*To* EDITH.) You won't mind?

EDITH: Why — not at all. Shall I — ?

CHRISTINA: No. Please don't disturb yourself. Nora will show me.

(*She goes out. There is an appalled silence.* MONICA *turns a page of her book and reads on, oblivious.* JOHN's *and* MARTIN's *faces are a study.* ROSS *chuckles.*)

ROSS: "God rest you, Merry Gentlemen. Let nothing you dismay."

(JOHN *goes to the house telephone.*)

JOHN: — All right, Ross.

EDITH: But what is it? What did she mean by that?

JOHN (*to the telephone*): Nora? — Let me speak to Patrick.

EDITH: I simply can't believe she'd think of taking our home from us.

HUGH: What's come over her anyway? — She seemed meek enough at first.

ROSS: That was before she felt the lot of us working on her.

JOHN: Working on her! What do you mean? Who's been — (*To the telephone.*) Patrick? Yes. It's settled; we're going out. — That's all right. I've arranged everything at that end. — That's it. — And not a word to Miss Christina, do you hear? Yes, I know she is. Tell Nora to show her around. But not a word, understand? — Right! (*He replaces the telephone and stares thoughtfully at it.*)

HUGH: — Out where?

JOHN: Good Ground, for Christmas dinner.

HUGH: What!

MONICA: What?

MARTIN: If you aren't ready, get ready. — Monique — (*She appears not to hear him.*)

HUGH: — But that hole — on Christmas.

JOHN: — And you will kindly not refer to it as a hole. It is not a hole.

MARTIN: Good Ground's an unusually beautiful spot, and always has been. Get that in your heads, both of you. (*He goes out into the library,* EDITH *after him.*)

JOHN: — And you might change your clothes, Ross.

(*Ross looks down at his shabby suit.*)

ROSS: I might, at that. (JOHN *follows* MARTIN *into the library.*) — Come on, Hugh — let's make ourselves decent. (*He and* HUGH *go out into the hall.* MONICA *rises to follow them, moving slowly toward the doorway, reading as she goes.*)

MONICA: Lovely — lovely — (FRANCIS *comes in. She stops.*) Oh —

FRANCIS: Where's Terry? I —

MONICA (*simultaneously*): Happy Christmas, Fran —

FRANCIS: — And to you. It's a pretty one, isn't it? — Thanks for the Stravinsky records. They look fine. (*Obviously he is preoccupied.* PATRICK *comes in, picks up* CHRISTINA'S *breakfast tray and goes out with it.*)

MONICA: It's an awfully good recording, I thought you might like them.

FRANCIS: They look fine.

MONICA: Fran — (*He turns to her. She raises the book in her limp hand and lets it fall again.*) I love this. You were sweet.

FRANCIS: Oh — that —

MONICA: I love it. (*A moment.*) I wonder if — (*She stops.*)

FRANCIS: — If what, Monique?

MONICA (*in a rush*): I wonder if you'd write in it for me?

FRANCIS: Why, of course. (*He takes a fountain pen from his pocket. She holds out the book to him. He opens it and writes in it.*) — This book was awfully important to me once. I used to love it.

MONICA: Don't you still?

FRANCIS: Of course. But when I was about your age —

MONICA: I'm not — so hopelessly young, Fran.

FRANCIS: I know you're not. (*He gives her back the book. She reads the inscription, breathes upon the page to dry it.*) I just meant — oh, well.

MONICA: "With love for Christmas." Oh, thank you.

FRANCIS: Thank you.

MONICA: I — I've found my favorite among them already. You know which?

FRANCIS: No. Which?

(*She reads. He stands against the table, listening:*)

MONICA:
"I fled Him, down the nights and down the days;[5]
  I fled Him, down the arches of the years;
I fled Him, down the labyrinthine ways
  Of my own mind; and in the mist of tears
I hid from Him, and under running laughter.
    Up vistaed hopes I sped;
    And shot, precipitated,
Adown Titanic glooms of chasmed fears,
From those strong Feet that followed, followed after."

(*Her voice grows more intense. Now she is speaking to him.*)

"But with unhurrying chase,
And unperturbéd pace,
Deliberate speed, majestic instancy,
    They beat — and a Voice beat
    More instant than the Feet —
'All things betray thee, who betrayest Me.' "

(*Unnoticed by them,* CHRISTINA *has come through the hall.* MONICA *stops. Her head bends lower over the book. Silence. Finally* CHRISTINA *speaks:*)

---

5 *"I fled Him . . . down the days,"* the opening line of "The Hound of Heaven" by Francis Thompson.

CHRISTINA: It's lovely. Go on, dear.

(MONICA *starts at the sound of her voice.*)

MONICA: Oh!
CHRISTINA: Do go on —
MONICA: I—I thought it was so — so musical —
CHRISTINA: It is. Go on, dear —

(*With growing difficulty* MONICA *continues:*)

MONICA:
" — I pleaded, outlaw-wise
By many a hearted casement, curtained red,
    Trellised with intertwining charities;
For, though I knew His love Who followèd,
    Yet was I sore adread
Lest, having Him, I must have naught beside.
    I said — I said — "

(*She stops, overcome. A moment, then* CHRISTINA *closes her eyes and continues it:*)

CHRISTINA:
— "I said to Dawn: Be sudden; — to Eve:
        Be soon —
    With thy young skyey blossoms heap me over
    From this tremendous Lover —
Float thy vague veil about me, lest He see!
    I tempted all His servitors, but to find
My own betrayal in their constancy,
In faith to Him their fickleness to me,
Their traitorous trueness, and their loyal deceit."

(*She stops. A silence. Then:*)

MONICA: How — how did you know?
CHRISTINA: It has a deep religious significance.
MONICA: A — ?
CHRISTINA: A profound one.

(*A moment.* MONICA *glances at* FRANCIS, *her face distracted.*)

MONICA: I — I must get ready —

(*Swiftly she goes through the hall and out.* CHRISTINA *gazes after her for an instant, then at* FRANCIS. *She murmurs:*)

CHRISTINA:
"My freshness spent its wavering showed i' the dust;
And now my heart is as a broken fount — "
(*Another moment. Then:*) Francis —

(*He turns to her.*)

FRANCIS: Yes?

(*She indicates something down the hall.*)

CHRISTINA: That door — it leads to the back stairs?
FRANCIS: — And sewing room. That's right.

(*She goes down the hall and out of view. For a moment he is alone. His head sinks lower. He stares in front of him, deep in thought.* TERRY *comes in from the hall. She stops at the sight of him.*)

TERRY: — I thought I heard your step. Happy Christmas.
FRANCIS: Very.
TERRY (*offhand*): Where've you been?
FRANCIS: I ran out to Cambridge to say hello to Claudia Perkins.
TERRY: "Claudia Perkins — ?" — I don't believe I know her.
FRANCIS: No. I don't believe you do.
TERRY: It's a preposterous name, all right.
FRANCIS: Do you think so?
TERRY: Is her father's name "Claude"?
FRANCIS: I couldn't say.
TERRY: — That might be some justification.
FRANCIS: I don't consider it needs any. She happens to be a good friend of mine.
TERRY: How nice. We must meet sometime. — She lives in Cambridge?
FRANCIS: — For the time being. She's studying law.
TERRY: — A lady lawyer — oh, my sainted aunt!
FRANCIS: That's an ignorant remark, Terry.
TERRY: I beg your pardon?
FRANCIS: — Every day you get harder-shelled about things you don't understand.
TERRY: You seem to be in quite a mood.
FRANCIS: I am. I'm in a beauty.

(CHRISTINA *comes in from the hall.*)

TERRY: Do you mind if I don't take any?

FRANCIS: I'd so infinitely prefer it.

(TERRY picks up a magazine.)

TERRY: — And a very happy New Year.

(She leans against the table, glancing through the magazine. Then FRANCIS turns to CHRISTINA:)

FRANCIS: I'm sorry — I'm afraid at times we're not very good about marriage.

(CHRISTINA smiles faintly.)

CHRISTINA: If it's only "at times" you may improve.

TERRY: — But it isn't.

(A silence. Then FRANCIS speaks slowly.)

FRANCIS: — You see, when a person devotes every waking moment to making another feel mean and little, after a while he's likely to get — almost enough of it.

TERRY: You're not referring to yourself, by any chance —

FRANCIS *(to CHRISTINA)*: It's hard to believe, isn't it — that in Terry's eyes the sun just about used to rise and set on me. — It was great while it lasted, I can tell you! It made me feel I could do anything. — Only it was too good to last, of course. It probably shouldn't have, anyway: I didn't rate it. — But she needn't suddenly have turned into — into quite such a —

TERRY: What is it you want me to be? All sweetness and light?

FRANCIS: No. — But even such a great lover of action as you might try to keep an open mind about a life in which it comes second.

TERRY: — To what?

FRANCIS: Thought, for instance. *(TERRY takes a deep breath and turns away. FRANCIS turns to CHRISTINA.)* — She doesn't know what I mean. I imagine you do.

(CHRISTINA nods. TERRY wheels about abruptly.)

TERRY: — I think that those who can, do — and those who can't, teach!

FRANCIS: — And I think that's a shallow statement, full of a great many holes.

(Again she turns away.)

TERRY: All right; have it your own way.

FRANCIS: — So snap the mind goes shut again. *(To CHRISTINA:)* I suppose you heard Terry's side of it last night, and I — I like you so much I'd like to say a word for the Defense, weak as his case may be —

TERRY: Oh, pray do —

FRANCIS *(to CHRISTINA)*: My father was a man of action, and left me a good deal of money. A year ago most of it went. My first instinct was to buckle under and get it back, however long it took. But I got to thinking of him and how little satisfaction he had from life — and of myself and how I felt so light and free all of a sudden. — So I made up my mind to go after other things.

CHRISTINA: I see.

FRANCIS: — Regardless of what Terry thinks of it, I believe what I'm doing now may be of real value sometime. I respect the profession of the law, and at present the law's a mess. A few of us are trying to replace the mess with sense. It seems to me a matter of getting back to first principles — to divine law and natural law, if you like — and — and of getting them pulling together again for the decent good government of good and bad human beings.

TERRY: — All right! — Then why not *do* something about it?

FRANCIS: I am in the best way I know: I'm helping to turn out new lawyers with a new light on the law. I'd rather be a small gun in a great cause than a big gun in a little one.

TERRY: So you've made up your mind to go on teaching, have you?

FRANCIS: I've made up my mind.

TERRY: I don't believe in your reasons, Francis.

FRANCIS: I hardly hoped that you would, Terry.

TERRY: — So that's that, eh?

FRANCIS: Yes, I suppose it is.

TERRY: — And we're back where we started.

FRANCIS: No, I think we're past that now. *(A moment. Then:)* — I've got to admit I'm licked, Terry. I woke in the night and knew it. I agree now with what you said yesterday: it's just about all up for us. *(She throws down her magazine.)*

TERRY: Well — we allowed for that before we started, didn't we?

FRANCIS: Yes.

TERRY (*to* CHRISTINA): — So you see.

CHRISTINA: No, I'm afraid I don't.

FRANCIS: It was Terry's idea — and we were both so very modern: we made a solemn agreement that if marriage didn't work for us, we'd part, and no hard feelings.

CHRISTINA (*to* TERRY): Was that what you called "expecting too much" of it?

TERRY: I didn't want us ever to feel caught, that's all.

(A moment.)

CHRISTINA: It's very interesting, very. (*She regards them intently. Then:*) — When I was in Rome the last time, there was an almost identical case before the Rota. The Rota's our supreme court, you know. — It decided the case in remarkably short order. The marriage was annulled — their way of saying it never existed. — Rather a roundabout way, perhaps — but the only one for a Church so stubbornly idealistic about marriage.

TERRY: — And you think they'd decide the same for us —

CHRISTINA: I think there's little doubt of it. — You appear to have neither thought nor instinct in common. You're completely without faith in each other or in marriage. You were so skeptical about it you agreed to part at the first sign of trouble. No! It won't do. It won't do at all. It's too thoughtful — too considered — too — (*She rises.*) — too cowardly.

TERRY (*surprised*): You're angry, aren't you?

CHRISTINA: A little. You see, I believe faith to be of first importance. I believe it is the soul's adventure out of sight of land. It seems to me that in this house you all of you hug the shore.

FRANCIS (*reflectively*): — It'd be very strange to think that we aren't really married — never were — never have been.

TERRY: Don't be foolish, Francis.

FRANCIS: I don't think it is. I think it explains a great many things: suspicions — distrusts — misunderstandings — everything! (*A moment. Then, abruptly.*) All right! Not married!

TERRY: — If you want to quit, quit. Why go such a long way round?

FRANCIS: — Possibly because I've been "stubbornly idealistic" too.

TERRY: Very well. As you like.

FRANCIS (*to* CHRISTINA): — Of course, it's nothing at all to her that we've lived together for two years — that back in the beginning we were as much in love as any two people ever —

TERRY: I swear it is, Francis.

FRANCIS: — No, Terry — suddenly I've got it straight; we've turned out to be a bad assortment of people. If we stay together, we'll destroy each other. We've begun to already. — And with or without love that seems to me pretty senseless.

TERRY: Now, Francis — really —

(He shakes his head.)

FRANCIS: — No, my dear. — I get things slowly, but once I have them, they stick. I think your sister's right; it's lack of faith that's done it. We've hugged the shore so close we've foundered on it.

TERRY: You're actually serious?

FRANCIS: Yes. I am. (*He turns to* CHRISTINA, *bows slightly, then moves toward the library.*) Where are — where are John and Martin? (*He goes out.* TERRY *stands speechless, gazing after him.*)

CHRISTINA: I didn't think the Defense was so weak.

TERRY: — His reluctance to leave me was touching, wasn't it? Reno or Mexico couldn't beat that.

CHRISTINA: I thought him very sad.

TERRY: Did you, Christina? Not me. All that fine talk only makes me the surer.

CHRISTINA: Shame!

TERRY: He saw a way out and he took it.

CHRISTINA: Shame on you, Terry.

TERRY: Why?

CHRISTINA: — All you heard was no more than another attempt to deceive you —

TERRY: — And himself, maybe — yes!

(A moment. Then:)

CHRISTINA (*quietly*): Then I think you deserve to lose him. I think you are better apart than together.

(HUGH and ROSS *come in.)*

HUGH: — A punch-drunk champion of a lost cause: that's what you are.

ROSS: — Sweet Hughie — so young and such a mischief.

(MONICA *comes in, goes to* TERRY.)

MONICA: Is it too much to ask for my gray coat back again?

TERRY: Gladly, darling. It must keep itself warm —

(JOHN *and* MARTIN *come in from the library.* JOHN *is spluttering:*)

JOHN: — in all my born days!

MARTIN (*to* TERRY): What is all this stuff, anyhow?

TERRY: Why? Didn't Francis make it clear?

JOHN: No. He did not.

ROSS: — Now what?

TERRY: Oh, it just seems that Francis and I aren't married, that's all.

JOHN: Nonsensical nonsense —

(ROSS *laughs.* MONICA *stops abruptly where she is.*)

ROSS: No?

HUGH: — You don't tell me!

JOHN: Nonsense — nonsense —

TERRY: — In fact, never have been.

HUGH: Funny, how well I remember the wedding. (*To* MONICA.) You wore pink, didn't you?

JOHN: Nonsense —

(MONICA *does not reply. She is gazing wide eyed at* TERRY.)

ROSS: The crowd is muttering.

(FRANCIS *enters.*)

EDITH: It seems we don't see the joke, Terry.

TERRY: — You might ask Christina about it. It was she who discovered it. Francis is convinced, all right. (*A moment.*) — Aren't you, Francis?

FRANCIS: Yes. I expect I am.

MONICA (*suddenly*): What are you going to do?

HUGH: — You don't seriously believe that they —

MONICA: What are you going to do?

TERRY: Well, I think Francis intended to leave right away — but it being Christmas, and all that, perhaps we might persuade him to wait till after lunch. (*To* FRANCIS.) What do you think?

FRANCIS: Of course.

ROSS: Francis — (FRANCIS *turns to him.*) — just in words of one syllable — would you mind?

FRANCIS: — Before we married we agreed that if it didn't work out, we'd separate.

EDITH: You — ? Oh, how dreadful!

FRANCIS: — And according to your Church, in that case there's no marriage.

EDITH: That's perfectly true, perfectly.

MARTIN: Oh, for heaven's sake, forget it.

(EDITH'S *eyes enlarge.*)

EDITH: — Forget it! — But I distinctly remember Father Andrews at the Spring Retreat last May explaining — (*To* TERRY *and* FRANCIS.) — Oh, how could you have been so stupid?

TERRY: — As it turns out, maybe it wasn't so.

MONICA: What are you going to *do*?!

TERRY: I'm afraid we haven't had time to plan, darling.

EDITH: — Do? They'll be remarried at once, of course — and properly this time!

ROSS: — Let them eat wedding cake.

MARTIN: What perfect foolishness, Edith.

JOHN: Well, I should think so! — They can simply cancel the agreement — abrogate it.

CHRISTINA: I thought you understood your religion better than that, John.

JOHN: How so?

CHRISTINA: For a sacrament to be valid one must receive it with a whole heart, a whole soul, and in its intended spirit.

JOHN: I know, Christina — that's all very well — er — spiritually and religiously and quite understandable on those grounds. — But practically, legally, let's say —

FRANCIS: — Pretty good law, too, John; the prior contract invalidates the second.

(JOHN *turns on him.*)

JOHN: Who said anything about the law?

ROSS: — Terry's a pretty good girl, too, Francis.

HUGH (*darkly*): Yes! — Who started this?

TERRY: Thank you, dears. You're sweet. But never mind.

EDITH: — Obviously it must be arranged for at once — just a simple, quiet ceremony. They can settle their difficulties afterward.

MONICA: But what if they don't want to?

EDITH: Of course they want to! (*Then — a sudden idea:*) I know! — Father Ellis — and the chapel in the house out there! This afternoon — this very day! (*She clasps her hands fervently.*) — A wedding on Christmas — in the old family chapel — oh, won't it be sweet? (*Suddenly to* FRANCIS.) Don't think only of yourselves — think of all of us — of Reverend Mother! How it would please *her* — oh, *wouldn't* it, Reverend Mother?

(*A silence. Then:*)

CHRISTINA: No, I'm afraid not. No, not in the least. (*To* FRANCIS *and* TERRY.) You are not at all fitted to marry, and I'm sure both of you realize it.

TERRY: I know, Christina. But if later on we —

CHRISTINA: — Possibly at some time in the future. That remains to be seen. For now, it is not a sacrament to be received or rejected at one's convenience. —

EDITH: Oh, but surely —

CHRISTINA (*to* EDITH): — And in the meantime, I think we embarrass them by discussing it.

EDITH: Still, if — (*She stops as* PATRICK *comes in with a decanter of sherry and glasses on a tray.*)

PATRICK: Sherry?

MONICA: For me, please.

CHRISTINA: John, the sight of Patrick reminds me of something outrageous I've done —

(PATRICK *smiles broadly and continues to pass the sherry.* CHRISTINA *refuses. He passes on.*)

JOHN: What else, my dear?

CHRISTINA: — You remember the way I used to manage everything —

JOHN: Yes?

CHRISTINA: Well — the kitchen must have gone to my head. (*She smiles at him.*) — Everything was laid out so neatly in rows. I had a sudden inspiration: "Pack it all up," I said, "we shall have Christmas at Good Ground."

JOHN: You — ?

(*But he cannot speak.*)

CHRISTINA: Suddenly it seemed we should.

(ROSS *laughs.*)

ROSS: Now I know what inspiration is: thought transference.

MARTIN: What do you think, Patrick? Can it be managed?

PATRICK (*filling his glass*): 'Twas a heavy cat, Sir, but we swung it over the fence.

MARTIN: Which means it can and has been.

JOHN: And a fine idea it is, too! — I wonder I didn't think of it myself.

CHRISTINA (*a little primly*): — Of course, there's a — a kind of obligation upon me to — inspect the property, you know.

(*Again* ROSS *laughs.*)

ROSS: Christina, you fraud, you —

CHRISTINA: There is! — Though I remember every tree and stone! Every corner in every room!

(NORA *comes in with a plate of small biscuits which she passes around.*)

EDITH: It ought to be lovely out there today.

JOHN: A fine idea — it should have occurred to me — should have occurred to me.

CHRISTINA: Oh — to see it again! Really to be there! (*She fishes for her watch.*) What time is it now? Oughtn't we start? (*She examines it and returns it to her pocket, as* SISTER ALOYSIUS *enters, hands in sleeves as usual.*) Gracious — nearly twelve o'clock. (SISTER ALOYSIUS *turns, as if this was a reproach directed at her.* CHRISTINA *shakes her finger at her.*) Sister, Sister —

SISTER ALOYSIUS: — But no one called me, Reverend Mother. (CHRISTINA *shakes her head severely.* SISTER ALOYSIUS *defends herself stoutly:*) — The bed was so soft. First I couldn't sleep. Then I could. It could have happened to anyone.

(CHRISTINA *laughs and throws out her hands.*)

CHRISTINA: My dear, my dear — it's Christmas — Christmas!

(PATRICK *presses a glass of sherry upon* SISTER ALOYSIUS. *She shakes her head.*)

PATRICK: Ah, come on, Sister! 'Twill do ye little harm.

CHRISTINA: — Take it, dear, for good appetite.

(*But* SISTER ALOYSIUS *has not yet forgiven her for her joke.*)

SISTER ALOYSIUS: — I shall take it to wake me up.

(CHRISTINA *laughs.* SISTER ALOYSIUS *accepts it, sips it.* PATRICK *leaves the wine on the table.*)

MARTIN: Father loved this wine. Remember what he used to say? (*He speaks in a thin musical voice, with a faint but noticeable brogue:*) " — And do you know what happens to you if you drink too much? — Your arteries harden. — And do you know what happens if you don't? Your arteries harden."

JOHN (*an attempt at the same voice*): "They tell me I've got a heart as big as a house and that the pressure of me blood would blow the average man's head off. — But I've never been an average man."

CHRISTINA (*better than either of them*): " — My father married your grandmother on Easter Day in Belfast, a town black with Protestants and herself one at the time by the name of Ross. 'Twas a hard and fast rule: no marrying on a feast day. But he had a pull with the parish priest; he kept him in pigs."

(*NORA's feet have begun to jig.*)

NORA: "Ah, Nora, woman, the spring's gone out of me. I'm no longer a lad of seventy." (*She dances out into the hall. They all laugh.*)

CHRISTINA: Oh, the dear man —

(*JOHN raises his glass.*)

JOHN: Here's to him!

(*CHRISTINA raises her hand, as if with a glass.*)

CHRISTINA: — And to Mother. (*They drink.*) — John and I were trying to remember the "Wraggle-taggle Gypsies" song and couldn't.

TERRY: *I* ought to remember that.

SISTER ALOYSIUS: I like it here. I think it's nice.

HUGH: — Look at the step I do in the Hasty-Pudding show. (*He executes a labored shuffle.*)

ROSS: Get your shoulders into it.

JOHN: Not a ray of talent.

MARTIN: — None.

CHRISTINA: — Hughie, Hughie — at least you'll never be an actor!

HUGH: You don't think — ?

TERRY: I knew that song backwards —

CHRISTINA: — But if Mart had wanted to — Mart, do you remember Gillette in *Sherlock Holmes?*

(*MARTIN stretches a bored arm along the mantel-piece and speaks in a voice utterly spent and world-weary:*)

MARTIN: " — You're a very interestin' woman, Mrs. Larabee, and a thorough musician. Your knowledge of Brahms and Beethoven is truly astonishin'. — Which makes it all the more remarkable that the piano has not been touched in two days. — Good evening."

EDITH: Martin — you ninny.

(*CHRISTINA laughs and claps her hands together.*)

CHRISTINA: Oh, fine, Martin! I hope Father heard you.

JOHN (*in his father's voice*): "Now, now — what's this, what's this? What brand of a barrel of monkeys did I beget, anyhow? Is this a man's family?"

CHRISTINA: It is! — And a lovely one! (*She turns and regards them all.*) — I think you're the loveliest family anyone ever had.

(*There is a silence. Then:*)

TERRY: Christina — (*CHRISTINA turns to her.*) — We love you.

(*CHRISTINA, her hands in her sleeves for the first time, bows, very much as SISTER ALOYSIUS would.*)

CHRISTINA: Thank you.

(*NORA re-enters from the hall.*)

NORA: His Reverence has arrived and Patrick is helping his coat off. Shall I stop him? — The autos is here.

(*MARTIN moves toward the doorway.*)

MARTIN: — Come on, everyone — time to go! Hugh — bring down a glass for him.

(*EDITH moves into the hallway.*)

EDITH: Father Ellis?

(*A hearty voice replies from below:*)

VOICE: Hello!

EDITH: Wait — we're coming down! (*She goes out, followed by MARTIN and NORA. CHRISTINA moves to the doorway, and calls:*)

CHRISTINA: Merry Christmas, Reverend Father!

VOICE: Merry Christmas, Reverend Mother!

CHRISTINA: Ned Ellis! How are you?

VOICE: Christina! — And you? What do you look like?

CHRISTINA: — A nun, of course! A nun in a gray habit —

VOICE: Is it becoming?

CHRISTINA: That's not its intention! — You've got a surprise in store for you, my fine fellow!

VOICE: Have I? How's that?

CHRISTINA: Oh, Ned — wait till you hear! We're going out to Good Ground.

VOICE: Magnificent!

(CHRISTINA *beckons to them.*)

CHRISTINA: Hugh — Monica — Francis — Terry, go on; I'll take the child. (*She takes the package from the table and tucks it into the crook of her arm.* HUGH *goes out. Suddenly* TERRY *exclaims:*)

TERRY: — I've got it! (*She sings.*) "O what care I for my new-wedded lord — " (*She throws a kiss to* FRANCIS.) "And my shoes of Spanish leather-O?"

(MONICA *stares at her with set face, narrowing eyes.*)

CHRISTINA: Yes — ah, yes! That's it!

TERRY:
"Tonight I shall sleep in a cold, open field,
Along with the wraggle-taggle gypsies-O."

(*Suddenly* MONICA *bursts out with unexpected venom:*)

MONICA: — You haven't a note of music in your whole body! (TERRY *turns and looks at her.* CHRISTINA's *smile vanishes. A moment, then* MONICA *falters:*) I'm sorry — I only meant —

TERRY: — It's all right.

(*She goes out.* CHRISTINA *motions to* FRANCIS *and* ROSS *to follow her. They do so.* CHRISTINA *turns and regards* MONICA *fixedly. For a moment she meets her gaze, then goes out.* JOHN *holds his arm out to* CHRISTINA. *She takes it, still following* MONICA *with her eyes.* JOHN *and* CHRISTINA *move toward the hallway.* SISTER ALOYSIUS *has gone.* CHRISTINA *glances back apprehensively over her shoulder at the room.* JOHN *begins to sing:*)

JOHN:
"O, what care I for a goose-feather bed
With sheet turned down so bravely-O?"

(CHRISTINA, *in a somewhat uncertain voice, picks up the refrain as they go out.*)

JOHN and CHRISTINA (*together*):
" — Tonight I shall sleep in a cold, open field,
Along with the wraggle-taggle gypsies-O."

(*Then:*)

CHRISTINA: — Only it is not so cold. It need not be cold —

CURTAIN

Act Three

It is about four o'clock, Christmas afternoon. The room is dimly lighted by the last rays of the winter sun.

MARTIN *comes in from the hall. He pulls a woolen muffler from around his neck and throws it on a chair, then blows on his hands to warm them. He stares in front of him, frowning, and hums a measure of "The Wraggle-taggle Gypsies." He moves to the table, seats himself, suddenly seizes the telephone, but thinks better of it and puts it down. He taps his fingers upon the table, this time whistling the song lowly. Again he seizes the telephone, waits a moment, jigs the receiver up and down, and demands:*

MARTIN: Long Distance, please.

(EDITH's *voice is heard from the hall.*)

EDITH: Martin?

MARTIN (*to the telephone*): Never mind.

(*He replaces the telephone.* EDITH *comes in, still in hat and coat. She has a sheaf of Christmas cards in her hand, some opened, some still in their envelopes.*)

EDITH: Aunt Grace sends you her love.

MARTIN: Good.

EDITH: — And asks for a contribution for The Charitable Eye and Ear Infirmary.

MARTIN: Tell her for me that in all my years in Boston I have never encountered a charitable eye or ear.

(EDITH *laughs, tears open an envelope and examines the card, in sudden dismay.*)

EDITH: Oh, dear! Look — (*She gives it to him.*) — And we never sent them one. What can we do? (MARTIN *tears the card into small pieces and tosses them into the air.*) Martin, stop it! Pick them up this instant!

MARTIN: No.

(She bends to pick up the pieces.)

EDITH: Then I —
MARTIN: No! *(She looks up in surprise.)* Leave them —
EDITH: But what on — ?
MARTIN: I like them there.
EDITH: Martin, what on earth —
MARTIN: Just leave them, please —
EDITH: You've lost your mind — all of you have.
MARTIN: Possibly.
EDITH: I'm really worried sick about Monica.
MARTIN: Yes?
EDITH: Could she have had a glass too much wine, do you suppose?
MARTIN: I don't believe so. What makes you think that?
EDITH: The way she laughed and carried on, of course.
MARTIN: She was simply enjoying herself. We all were.

(CHRISTINA enters from the hallway.)

EDITH: I hope she's not going to turn into one of those loud, giggling girls. — And Francis and Terry. — I'm very unhappy about them, Reverend Mother. Father Ellis quite agreed with us, you know.
CHRISTINA: I know.
EDITH: I can't understand Francis' attitude.
MARTIN: Francis is absolutely first-rate — He's as good as they come, I trust his judgment implicitly. — The trouble's with Terry. She treats him abominably. If I were Francis, I'd look for peace somewhere else.
EDITH: You'd do nothing of the sort.
MARTIN: No?
EDITH: We must do something about them, we really must.
CHRISTINA: I'm afraid whatever's to be done, they must do.
EDITH: I think what they need most is real spiritual guidance. What they lack above all is true religious feeling.
MARTIN: — Of which Edith is compact, of course.
EDITH: Not at all.
MARTIN: Even to the exclusion of any humor in regard to it — aren't you, dear?
CHRISTINA: Give her time, Martin! It's only the old hands who can joke about it!

EDITH *(to* CHRISTINA): You know, you've made me feel that something's amiss in my attitude toward my Faith.
CHRISTINA *(sincerely)*: Oh, I beg your pardon. I do indeed.
EDITH: But won't you tell me what?
CHRISTINA: — If I were you, I should try to take it whole, my dear, instead of — instead of piecemeal.
EDITH: I see.
CHRISTINA: Forgive me —

(SISTER ALOYSIUS, PATRICK and NORA come in. PATRICK carries CHRISTINA's cape, NORA her overshoes. EDITH gathers up more Christmas cards from the table.)

EDITH: We'll all be here for supper, Patrick.
PATRICK: Very good, Madam.

(EDITH moves toward the library.)

EDITH: Martin, I do wish you'd help me with these. *(She goes out. He moves after her.* PATRICK *bends to pick up the pieces of the Christmas card.)*
MARTIN: Leave them, Patrick.
PATRICK: Sir?
MARTIN: I want them there. *(He goes out.)*
PATRICK: Isn't he the caution, though? *(He sighs in deep satisfaction.)* — Well — 'twas the best celebration we've had since we tucked the Old Gentleman up for his last sleep.
NORA: It was the best. It was surely.
PATRICK: — For all her complaints on the state of the stove, Mrs. Carey outdid herself.
NORA: Mrs. Carey now lies flat on her back with a satisfied smile set deep in her features.
CHRISTINA: Thank her for me. Thank you all.

(SISTER ALOYSIUS holds out her hand for the overshoes.)

SISTER ALOYSIUS: I'll take those.
NORA: Let me dry them and wrap them first. *(She chuckles.)* — Such goings on at table. Wasn't Mr. Martin fine as the Irish Ambassador?
PATRICK: It was Reverend Mother put him up to it, wasn't it, Reverend Mother? — And then he wouldn't drop it. It's full of the Old Nick he is today.
NORA: — And Miss Monica, now — I've never heard the like of her laughing.

CHRISTINA: No. Nor I.

NORA: Once, there, I thought she was headed straight for the hysterics.

CHRISTINA: — With whom did she come back?

PATRICK: All alone by herself.

NORA: She runs that little car of hers too fast entirely. Once I was in a bus on my way to my sister's in Brookline —

CHRISTINA: Let me know when she arrives. (*A moment.*) What time is my train? Exactly four-forty?

PATRICK: I have not a timetable by me, but's it's me passionate conviction that that is the hour.

NORA: Toolin's at the door now.

CHRISTINA: I'm not much on good-bys, you know.

NORA: I remember that well. When you went the first time, it came like the blast of a horn to me.

CHRISTINA: God bless you both. Say a prayer for me now and then.

PATRICK: And maybe you'd be so kind as to do likewise for us?

CHRISTINA: Indeed I shall, my dears.

(*A moment. They are reluctant to go.*)

PATRICK: Shall I light up a bit for you?

CHRISTINA: Not yet.

(NORA *holds the overshoes up and peers at them.*)

NORA: — The size of 'em! (*She laughs.*) They're no bigger than a mouse would wear. They're no bigger than —

(*She is overcome with laughter in which there is more than a suspicion of tears. She goes out into the hall,* PATRICK *after her whispering:*)

PATRICK: Quiet, woman! Control yourself.

CHRISTINA: — The moment Miss Monica arrives.

PATRICK: I'll tell her, Miss.

(*They are gone.* CHRISTINA *passes her hand over her eyes. Suddenly she shudders, closes her eyes sharply, grasps the arm of her chair.*)

SISTER ALOYSIUS: — But what is it?

CHRISTINA: Oh, Sister — suddenly I have such fear for her! Say a prayer — quick — quick! (*A moment. Then she rises.*) There — there — (*She turns about once or twice and reseats herself. Then:*) Well, what did you think of it out there?

SISTER ALOYSIUS: I thought it was lovely.

CHRISTINA: You can see what a fine place it will make for us.

SISTER ALOYSIUS: Indeed I can.

CHRISTINA: You should see it in spring, when the fruit trees are out. There are days when if you stand under the big plum at the back door, I defy you to hear yourself think for the bees in it.

SISTER ALOYSIUS: — And the house — for such a big one, it — it felt like friends.

CHRISTINA: It has been said at last.

SISTER ALOYSIUS: — The way you all sang at table — it sounded so sweet.

CHRISTINA: You didn't think there was a — kind of false ring to it?

SISTER ALOYSIUS: Oh, no!

CHRISTINA: You're a great comfort to me, dear. — Say it again.

SISTER ALOYSIUS: No, Reverend Mother. (*A moment. Then:*) — I thought Father Ellis had such a fine voice.

CHRISTINA: Yes — he meant it all right.

SISTER ALOYSIUS: He's just like one of the family, isn't he?

CHRISTINA: Just. — Oh, I can't believe that all that gaiety, all that comradeship was put on for my benefit! They — (*She stops. A moment. Then:*) — And the land itself's as good as any in New England. Today my brother Ross drove a spade through the snow and turned up a brown clump of it that smelled, he said, of all the good things that the earth brings forth. (*Another moment.*) — Yes — he is more romantic than he thinks, is Ross. — And I'm a little inclined that way myself — (*She rises and shakes herself.*) Well — from now on I shall be — I shall be the iron woman. (*She pauses thoughtfully.*) — I told myself that last year. (*Then:*) Strange — strange — the place was the same — (*Then, iron:*) — Mind you don't let me forget my galoshes.

(SISTER ALOYSIUS *turns to the doorway:*)

SISTER ALOYSIUS: No, Reverend Mother.

CHRISTINA: I wish Monica would come.

(MARTIN *enters from the library.*)

SISTER ALOYSIUS: Yes, Reverend Mother.

CHRISTINA: — We'll give the three rosaries to Patrick, Nora and Mrs. Carey.

(SISTER ALOYSIUS *stops and turns.*)

SISTER ALOYSIUS: — The ones you had the Holy Father bless for Monsignor Mack?

CHRISTINA: Did I?

SISTER ALOYSIUS: You certainly did. You know you did.

CHRISTINA: Well, he can whistle for them.

SISTER ALOYSIUS: Yes, Reverend Mother.

(*She goes out into the hall.*)

MARTIN: — Cold out there, wasn't it?

CHRISTINA: Did you think so?

(*He shivers and blows upon his fingers.*)

MARTIN: M-m-m — raw! — That's the trouble with being on a river.

CHRISTINA: I thought it looked beautiful.

MARTIN: Oh, it looks all right. (*A moment.*) You've decided between the houses, have you?

CHRISTINA: I think so.

MARTIN: Good Ground —

CHRISTINA: I think so.

(*He sighs.*)

MARTIN: Yes — of course.

CHRISTINA: It seems not to please you.

MARTIN: Well, I didn't see much chance of it, but I did hope something would swing you over to — (*He rises, looks at the library door, bends close to* CHRISTINA, *and touches her arm, speaking lowly, almost slyly:*) Why don't you take this house, Christina? — I mean it. Why don't you take this one?

CHRISTINA: — Take advantage of a mistake Father made — do you think I could?

MARTIN: Father didn't make mistakes. Not of that sort. — He was as foresighted a man as lived in this world. He must have known the terms of Mother's bequest to you. He knew he wouldn't be here to see how the house worked out for us. He'd let us talk him into it, but he wasn't convinced. He kept saying it looked too set, too final. "When the Irish arrive, they turn British," he said.

CHRISTINA: — And his note to me: "Your Mother and I may surprise you someday — "

MARTIN: Exactly — done with deliberate intent.

CHRISTINA: It can't be! I won't have it.

MARTIN: He left it for you to decide — and I think he had more thought for us than for you when he did it —

(CHRISTINA *looks about her.*)

CHRISTINA: But Edith — she speaks of it as hers — I think it is hers.

MARTIN: — The best thing that ever happened to Edith was when she married away from all this and stood on her own. She was a happy woman for a few years then. But she gravitated back and drew us with her. Now she's only a content one.

CHRISTINA: You're a surprising man, Martin.

(*He looks wryly at the ceiling.*)

MARTIN: I just don't want to die in that room upstairs.

(*She beats her hands in her lap.*)

CHRISTINA: But it's Good Ground I love! It's Good Ground I want for us!

(MARTIN *nods, with a resigned sigh.*)

MARTIN: Of course, of course. — I only thought you — you ought to have the whole picture, you know.

TERRY (*comes in from the hall*): Back again —

MARTIN: Good! — Now I've a chance to tell you —

TERRY: What — ?

MARTIN: — That I think you're in luck, my girl, and should be thanking your stars.

TERRY: Luck about what?

MARTIN: — Francis, of course. You're well out of it. I've always distrusted the fellow. — Anyone who tries to cover up a natural laziness with a lot of big talk about "the contemplative life" and —

(TERRY *bridles.*)

TERRY: — I don't think I've ever heard him use the term.

MARTIN: — He would at the drop of a hat. — And teaching — and all those elaborate theories about the law — and drugging himself with music and art and all that —

TERRY: — I think you'd do well to be a little less critical of things you don't understand. Quite a number of the great men of this world have *been* rather than *done*. (MARTIN *turns, aggrieved, and looks at* CHRISTINA. TERRY'S *voice rises:*) — And in addition to that who do you of all people, think you are to — (FRANCIS *comes in. She stops.*) Oh. Here you are. A pleasant trip home?

FRANCIS: Very, thanks.

(MARTIN *holds his hand out to* CHRISTINA *and speaks in an elaborate undertone:*)

MARTIN: Come, Christina. I can't be in the same room with the fellow.

(*He leads* CHRISTINA *out into the library. The sunlight is fading fast now, and a somberness gradually settles upon the room.* FRANCIS *goes to the table and takes a cigarette from the box there.*)

FRANCIS: — One for you?

TERRY: No thanks. (*He lights his.*) — It's good to be out of that howling mob for a moment. (*He does not reply. A moment. Then:*) Why is it that when I count the people in a room, I always count myself as two people?

FRANCIS: There are more of you than that.

TERRY: And you don't care for any of them —

FRANCIS: A few.

TERRY: I might kill off the others. (*He laughs shortly. Embarrassed, she looks down at her feet, murmurs:*) — I have quite pretty feet, for feet. (*Another moment.*) — They've got me almost persuaded now — that we aren't married I mean. It's a funny feeling, isn't it?

FRANCIS: Extremely.

TERRY: I'm not sure but what I like it.

FRANCIS: Yes?

TERRY: Quite a lot. — I have a pleasant sense of meeting a terribly nice man for the first time. (*Again his short laugh.*) — You do look so awfully sweet standing there.

FRANCIS: You look all right yourself.

TERRY: I expect it's because the room is so dark.

FRANCIS: Do you, Terry?

(*A pause. Then:*)

TERRY: — All that that you said about your work — I didn't know there was anything you so definitely believed in. You might have let a fellow in on it, don't you think?

FRANCIS: What would have been the good? It's nothing to argue over.

TERRY: Have we, over everything?

FRANCIS: Pretty much.

TERRY: — A little gun-shy now.

FRANCIS: Possibly.

(*A silence.*)

TERRY: Maybe I don't know you at all the way I thought I did.

FRANCIS: Maybe neither of us does.

TERRY: — Just no go, eh, Francis?

FRANCIS: Let's not fool ourselves again, my dear.

(*A silence. Then:*)

TERRY: — Who is she?

FRANCIS: Oh, Terry —

(*Another silence.*)

TERRY: Very well, Fran.

(*She moves toward the library as* MONICA *comes in from the hall.*)

MONICA: Terry? Is that you?

TERRY: Hello.

MONICA: I missed a truck by two inches. Where's — where's Christina?

TERRY: — In here, I think.

(*She goes out.*)

MONICA: — Such a glare on the snow — I can't see a — (*She sees Francis, catches her breath.*) Oh —

FRANCIS: It's all right — it's only me.

MONICA: — Only you.

FRANCIS: That's right. (*He moves from the table.*) Dark, isn't it? I'll light up.

MONICA: Wait! (*He turns to her questioningly. She falters:*) — Wait a moment.

FRANCIS: But what is it, Monique?

MONICA: Francis —

FRANCIS: Yes?

MONICA : Francis —

FRANCIS: But what, darling? — Anything wrong? What can I do?

MONICA: Don't call me "darling."

(He laughs.)

FRANCIS: — I'll call you anything I like! Darling — dear — goldilocks!

MONICA: Oh, please don't —

FRANCIS: It's been a pretty tough day all around, I expect.

MONICA: — It's been horrible.

FRANCIS: But is something really the matter?

MONICA: Everything's the matter. Don't you realize that?

(Again his short laugh.)

FRANCIS: Well, I'll admit that if I were in charge, there are a few small changes I'd make.

MONICA: You don't give — that for me, do you?

FRANCIS: What?

MONICA: I said — *(She turns away.)* — You heard what I said.

FRANCIS: Why, my dear child, I've always been extremely fond of you, you know that.

MONICA: — Just what I thought.

FRANCIS: But —

MONICA: It's all right. I know.

FRANCIS: I must be even stupider than I —

MONICA: It's all right. I'm used to it. — But I'd like — very much — to tell you something —

FRANCIS: Please do, by all means —

(She comes to him, confronts him.)

MONICA: — It's only that I'd — like you to know that — that I believe with my whole heart in everything you do — and are — and will be.

FRANCIS: Why thanks, Monique. Thanks very much. That's good to know. *(He pats her hand lightly and turns away, but she catches his hand to her lips, kisses it, holds it.)*

MONICA: Oh, Fran —

FRANCIS: Listen, child —

MONICA: Not "child" — not "child"!

(A moment. Then:)

FRANCIS: — But I don't know what to say to you, at all.

MONICA: Never mind! — Just remember what I told you.

FRANCIS: I shall, you know. I always shall.

MONICA: Francis —

FRANCIS: Yes?

(She moves nearer him, her face averted. She murmurs:)

MONICA: — Put your arms around me — once — just once — so I may have something real to keep of you.

FRANCIS: No, Monique. There's just nothing in it, I assure you.

MONICA: You won't — . *(He shakes his head.)* Then I —

(She comes against him, puts her arms about him, her head upon his breast, FRANCIS remonstrating:)

FRANCIS: Monique — Monique — *(But she only tightens her arms about him. For a moment they stand so. TERRY comes in from the library. Another moment, then, suddenly the street light outside the window is lit.)* — There's the street light — it's late — I'll light up.

(Slowly MONICA's arms fall to her side. He moves swiftly to the hall doorway, presses a button, and the lamps in the room are lighted all at once. MONICA turns and sees TERRY.)

MONICA: Oh! *(She stands, a pitiable little figure, huddling herself in her arms. CHRISTINA comes in from the library, glances from one to the other. A moment. Then:)* — Excuse me. Please excuse me.

(CHRISTINA holds her hand out to her.)

CHRISTINA: Monica — *(TERRY gazes steadily at MONICA, then at FRANCIS who returns from the doorway. CHRISTINA repeats:)* Monica —

(MONICA is drawn to her.)

TERRY: It's this, then — this I've been feeling.

(MONICA turns upon her.)

MONICA: Don't think it was his fault! It wasn't!

(A moment, FRANCIS meets TERRY's level gaze. Then:)

TERRY: Of course it wasn't. No — nor yours. If it was anyone's it was —

MONICA *(a cry)*: Why are you so cruel to him? Why — why?

CHRISTINA: Come, child, come —

(*She draws* MONICA *toward the library.*)

TERRY: No — wait! Wait, please — (*Then:*) Why am I, Fran? Why? — When I love you so —

FRANCIS: Terry —

TERRY: Oh, I think you're fine, Fran. — And me — fighting you every inch of the way —

FRANCIS: Never mind that. I've been wrong a thousand times.

TERRY: Is Christina right? Is it faith in life I lack?

(FRANCIS *turns and regards* CHRISTINA.)

FRANCIS: I envy her hers. I'd give my eyes for what she's got.

TERRY: We must find something like it.

FRANCIS: — If we can.

TERRY: Can? Don't you believe we can?

FRANCIS: I don't know where to look.

TERRY: Anywhere but here — if we spend our lives looking! (*A moment. She averts her head, sings falteringly:*) "Oh, what care I for a goose-feather bed —" (*And stops.*) You were right, Monique; there's no music in my body. (*She goes out. A moment. Then* FRANCIS *follows her.*)

MONICA: Oh — I'm so ashamed —

CHRISTINA: No, no!

MONICA: — For months and months I've kept it to myself, fighting it the whole time. (*She clenches her fists, beats them up and down.*) — I can't sleep! I can't sleep!

CHRISTINA: That's past —

MONICA: He never even — he's always treated me like a child.

CHRISTINA: That is past too.

MONICA: Of course, I'd made up my mind I could never possibly have him; he was Terry's. But today —

CHRISTINA: He is Terry's.

(*A moment. Then* MONICA *speaks lowly:*)

MONICA: The worst of it was I was getting to hate her — and I love Terry! — Oh, why did this have to happen to me?

CHRISTINA: I believe you've been used as an instrument, Monica. It's not easy to be. (MONICA *clings to her suddenly, her head on her shoulder.*)

MONICA: Oh, take me with you, won't you?

(CHRISTINA *smiles and shakes her head.*) — But I'll do whatever I'm told, truly I will! I won't mind any kind of hardship, truly I won't. I had the same father and mother as you — if you could be one, why can't I?

CHRISTINA: — For a broken heart? — No, my dear. Sometimes one slips in among us unawares. But they never stay long. Our work requires a whole heart.

MONICA: But I haven't any work! (*She reads* CHRISTINA's *eyes.*) — Except — just living maybe.

CHRISTINA: Do it, Monica! Do it well! It's worth it.

MONICA: And you believe I can?

(CHRISTINA *nods her head.*)

CHRISTINA: — But not by running from it.

MONICA: Excuse me — but that's what I always thought you'd done.

(CHRISTINA *laughs.*)

CHRISTINA: Oh, when will people realize what life is! — My dear — we run *at* it — yes and more often than not bump our heads on it! — But it seems not to matter — (*She touches her bonnet, smiling.*) This — this helmet helps. (*She takes* MONICA's *head in her hands.*) You have a helmet too, darling — it has only one dent in it — it will have many more. — But, you know, I think heaven is full of dented helmets. What else can they make crowns of?

(*She kisses her tenderly.* HUGH, ROSS, *and* JOHN *come in from the hall.* MONICA *goes to the window.* JOHN *takes an envelope from his pocket and gives it to* CHRISTINA.)

JOHN: — Your tickets, Christina. I might forget at the station.

CHRISTINA: Thank you, John. (*She looks at her watch.*) — It's later than I thought.

ROSS: It doesn't take more than ten minutes from here.

JOHN (*heartily*): Well — it's been a great day, hasn't it? — Regular Fishman's Friday. (*He moves toward the library.*) Where is everyone? (*And calls into it:*) Oh, Martin! You and Edith —

HUGH: How'd you bend your fender, Monique?

MONICA: Is it bent?

(MARTIN *and* EDITH *come in from the library.*)

EDITH: Oh, here you are at last, John! — Miss Evans called.

JOHN: Yes, any message?

EDITH: No. She just said she wanted to wish you a happy Christmas.

JOHN: That's a message. (CHRISTINA *gazes in front of her. There is a silence, which* JOHN *breaks:)* — Certainly a pleasant day all around.

HUGH: More and bigger Christmases, say I. — How about it, Monique?

MONICA: Perfect.

JOHN: — Warm, happy old sort of place, out there.

EDITH: — The little chapel — and those lovely woods! How you must have loved to wander in those woods as children.

(Still CHRISTINA *is silent.)*

HUGH: — I've knocked around a good deal — seen most of the best country places in the East, I suppose. — But what struck me out there today was the wonderful sense of space — of — er — you know — spiritual peace. (*He catches* JOHN's *glowering eye and concludes lamely:)* — I thought it was simply swell. I'd like to spend a lot of time there.

ROSS: I'm sure it would like to have you.

CHRISTINA: — You say nothing of it, Ross.

ROSS: I say nothing.

CHRISTINA: — But loving it as you all do, perhaps it should be yours.

HUGH: I didn't mean exactly that.

JOHN (*suddenly*): — To be perfectly honest, Christina —

CHRISTINA: At last! Thank heaven, at last!

JOHN: — The fact is we aren't as well off as we were. The fact is it's more of a burden than anything.

CHRISTINA: But you mustn't be too well off, must you? — That way lies security — such a shabby ideal, John — not even a glitter to it!

JOHN: We — we like it pretty well here, you know.

CHRISTINA: Are you sure?

JOHN: Well — er — that is, it never occurred to me not to be.

EDITH: But how foolish! Of course we do!

JOHN: I like to decide these things for myself, Edith.

MARTIN: — *I* never cared for it after we got it.

EDITH: Martin!

CHRISTINA: Oh believe me, all of you, nothing fails like success!

JOHN: Then you've made up your mind —

CHRISTINA: No. It's too full of other things.

MARTIN: But Christina —

CHRISTINA: "Which house" is a small problem now, Martin.

*(*JOHN *passes his hand over his eyes.)*

JOHN: Yes — I know — I know —

(She turns to him quickly.)

CHRISTINA: Do you, John?

(He looks up at her.)

JOHN: — But — but — I suppose we'd better get it settled, eh?

(A moment. Then:)

CHRISTINA: I shall leave you to settle it.

JOHN: Oh no! No, no, no. Don't do that!

CHRISTINA: What are brothers for?

JOHN: — I wish I knew. — I wish I knew something —

ROSS: It's Good Ground you wanted first, Christina. — Remember what you said: "Good Ground, where — where a person can — "?

CHRISTINA: Yes — where it's open and free! Where you can throw up the windows and call out to each other! Indeed I did, Ross — oh, indeed I did!

MARTIN: Then take it, my dear, take it.

CHRISTINA: No. You shall decide. — And whichever way, I shall abide by it gratefully, knowing that it's a small matter at best.

*(*TERRY *and* FRANCIS *come into the doorway.* TERRY *in hat and coat.)*

JOHN: There was a time when it loomed very large. (*He looks about him.)*

CHRISTINA: — And to me too!

JOHN: — When was that?

CHRISTINA: — Oh, why do we, in this world, cling so? — The plum tree in the back yard — *it* must come down as well — every tree must come down, however deep its roots. The only doubt is how long — yet we cling, we do cling —

JOHN: — Don't we just?

(A moment. She looks away.)

CHRISTINA: — Even to things we don't want. — You, to this house — and no one is happy here. — Your wagons hitched to what? — and the sky full of stars! — There is a look in the eye of those who follow their stars. I think they are the happy ones of this world and the next. They hold their heads high — there is great joy in them.

MARTIN: Well — I don't know what's to become of us.

(A moment.)

CHRISTINA: — Nor I. All I know is that when the Good Lord made the Farleys, he had a better life in mind for them than one without adventure, side by side in a safe haven.

(TERRY turns to FRANCIS.)

TERRY. Yes.

CHRISTINA: My good hope for all of you is that each will find his start and follow it.

ROSS: Yes!

CHRISTINA: I think I came here to you half expecting it would be a return to my childhood. I've found that it's not possible to return there and that it's well that it is not. Ahead is the only way — ahead but with a difference! *(Then softly to herself.)* Who are you? What are you? Where are you bound for? — What do you want of life? Who are your heroes? — Do you know anymore? You must — you must find out again! And there's so little time — no time but for the best. *(She looks at her watch.)* Time! Time! — John please tell Miss Evans that I am sorry not to have known her and trust that some day I shall. (JOHN *stares at her, wide-eyed. How on earth did she know that?* CHRISTINA *continues:)* Now I must get my bag. (TERRY *goes to her.)* No, I must get it — then it will be time to go.

(TERRY holds out her hand to FRANCIS.)

TERRY: It's time for us already. — Good-by, everyone — Francis and I are off by ourselves.

EDITH: But you can't — you aren't marr —

TERRY: Do you think we should marry, Christina?

(CHRISTINA kisses her.)

CHRISTINA: I think you have[6] *(She turns to the others, hands out.)* Oh, my dear ones — I love you dearly and always shall. — And I have great faith in you! *(She goes out into the hall. There is a moment's silence. Then:)*

JOHN: What do you think we could get for this house, Mart?

MARTIN: Is that important?

JOHN: No. Not in the least. *(He goes to telephone.)* Commonwealth one-six-one-four.

TERRY *(to* FRANCIS): I packed us. The bags are downstairs. *(To* MONICA.) Good-by, darling —

(MONICA goes to her and embraces her.)

MONICA: Good-by, Terry. *(And turns to* FRANCIS.) Good-by, Francis.

FRANCIS: Good-by, Monique. Keep working at the music.

MONICA: Indeed I shall!

(Smiling, TERRY holds out her hand to FRANCIS.)

TERRY: Come on, Professor —

(And out they go.)

JOHN *(at the telephone)*: Hello. — Mary? — Take a telegram, will you? — Prichard, in New York. That's right. "Reconsidering. Will telephone tomorrow." That's it. — Will you be there for awhile? Good. I'll come around. Something — er — very important. — What? *(He laughs.)* You foolish girl! Yes. In twenty minutes. *(He replaces the telephone and stands beaming.)*

MARTIN: Give me that telephone —

(He goes to it.)

JOHN: — All father's hopes for his family, eh? *(It amuses him so that he begins to shake with laughter.)*

MARTIN: Long distance, please.

(CHRISTINA comes along the hallway with SISTER ALOYSIUS. Each now wears her cape and carries her little black traveling bag. CHRISTINA puts her finger to her lips, glances into the room, sees they are not

---

[6] *I think you have.* It should be noted that if the marriage were invalid in the first instance, as suggested by Christina's reference to the Rota decision (Cf. page 530), no subsequent consent of the parties would have sufficed unless expressed according to the regular Catholic form, in the presence of a duly authorized priest and two witnesses.

observed, holds out her arms to her family, folds their images to her for a moment, then goes out with SISTER ALOYSIUS.)

EDITH (*to* MARTIN): The children?

MARTIN: Something else first.

EDITH: But what? — Martin, what is it? — I shan't stir from Boston, you know!

HUGH (*rises*): Nor I. Hanged if I'm going to be stampeded by any — by any nun, for instance.

(JOHN *glances at his watch.*)

JOHN: What's keeping Christina? Those trains run on the dot.

HUGH: — I like it here, and I'm going to stay. All I ask now is a good steady income.

ROSS: — Fat.

HUGH: You think?

ROSS: I know.

EDITH: I mean it, Martin! I shan't stir!

(MARTIN *smiles aggravatingly.*)

MARTIN: — You will do as I say.

(*She turns away with an exclamation.* ROSS *has gone to window and stands gazing out.* MONICA *is at the piano.*)

HUGH: Well, she's certainly balled things up — I'll say that for her.

JOHN: It was fine having had her.

MARTIN (*to the telephone*): — No, there's no hurry. This has waited for years.

(ROSS *leans closer to the window.*)

HUGH: — And you let her get away with it — Honestly, you're all so childish. — She's fooled the lot of you. — But she hasn't me, you bet!

(*Suddenly* ROSS *flings up the window, leans out, and shouts:*)

ROSS: Good luck, Christina! (*He waits a moment. There is no sound. He closes the window and turns to the others, wonder upon his face.*) — She was crying.

(*The clock in the hall strikes the half-hour.*)

CURTAIN

ACT I

VIEWING THE AUTHOR'S IDEAS

1. As the play opens and progresses, what clashes in ideas and temperament do you recognize? What two events are anticipated?

2. What seems to be Terry's grievance? Why do not she and Francis move away from the others? How did the loss of money change Francis' outlook? What do Francis and Monica have in common? What impression do you get of the character of Terry? How do Terry and Ross inform us of the importance of their city home? How does Terry react to Christina's love and solicitude?

3. What do we learn of the family? How do the Farleys show indifference to their faith? Point to indications that they have become social climbers. What seems to be John's main purpose in life?

4. How much do you know of Christina before she appears? When do you learn of the reason for Christina's visit; of the family's attitude toward Good Ground; of the terms of the will? What problem does the will present to Christina? How do her loyalties to her family and community make it difficult to make a decision? Of what is Good Ground a symbol to her? What impression does the family make on Christina? How do they regard her?

5. What words of Christina show the dramatist's regard for the vocation of the priesthood? Does Barry hold the vocation in esteem? Explain. What seem to be the writer's views on the teaching profession? Keep in mind your answer at this point, and compare it with your views at the end of the play.

6. In what manner does Christina account for her vocation? Which one of the family is first won to Christina's way of looking at life? How do the other Farleys regard Ross? How is he contrasted with his brothers and sisters? Account for his sympathetic attitude toward Christina.

EVALUATING HIS MANNER OF EXPRESSION

1. Point out allusions to the following: (a) the Boston Tea Party (b) the social register in New England (c) the power of political connections.

2. How does the drama get its name? In what way does Terry's attitude help to create the conflict? How does the dramatist inform the audience as to the one who was speaking to Martin on the phone?

3. How is Boston satirized in regard to (a) speech (b) feeling of superiority (c) social climbing?

4. What is the progress of the action at the end of Act I? What outcome are you led to expect? What is happening to the characters? Which character has the best lines in Act I?

Recall some of the wittiest comments.

5. What is the purpose of delaying Christina's entrance? How is the delay achieved? What would be their reaction at the point where Christina turns to face the audience?

6. Point out humorous irony in the following instances: (a) Christina's account of the customs officer who tried to collect *duty* on the *statue* (b) the names Winthrop, Choate, and Monique Farley (c) Edith's reminding Monica to wear a hat to Mass.

ACT II

VIEWING THE AUTHOR'S IDEAS

1. As the scene opens, why are John and Martin silent? What is John's decision? State changes in mannerism and speech which Terry manifests in this scene.

2. How does Christina show her interest in John? What kind of a life does she wish for her eldest brother? What are John's reasons for all his labors and solicitude?

3. According to the remarks made by the characters, what kind of man was the father of the Farleys? With what feelings do the sons and daughters remember him?

4. When does Christina show her interest in Martin? What does John think about Martin?

5. How does Christina learn of Ross's disappointment in his cause? What is Christina's own problem? Why does Monica show concern for Francis? How does she manifest her great interest in Terry's marriage? Why does she make such a biting comment about Terry's lack of music? To what does Christina refer when she says " . . . it is not so cold. It need not be so cold."

6. When in the course of the discussion the word *law* is used, why does John become disturbed? How do the other brothers come to Terry's defense?

EVALUATING HIS MANNER OF EXPRESSION

1. Are the clever lines in Act II given to one character, or are they evenly distributed? Which characters impress you with their conversation?

2. How is Ned Ellis praised when Christina says of him: "He never said or did an indifferent thing"?

3. Select the dialogue between John and Christina in which there is an allusion to blarney and the blarney stone. Explain the allusion in Ross's comment: "Let them eat wedding cake."

4. Point out the irony and wit in Ross's words to John and Martin: "God rest you, Merry Gentlemen. Let nothing you dismay."

5. Comment on Ross's remark to Francis: "Just in words of one syllable — would you mind?" Do these words imply that Ross is stupid; that Francis is a professor and has a command of language; or that the nature of the topic of dicussion is simple and the words should be in keeping with the topic?

6. In what way have the action and the plot of the story advanced?

ACT III

VIEWING THE AUTHOR'S IDEAS

1. Christina remarks that Martin is a surprising man. What actions, words, or silences of Martin confirm Christina's statement?

2. What was Christina trying to discover when she and Sister Aloysius discuss the singing at the Christmas dinner? What considerations incline Christina to decide on the Beacon Hill mansion?

3. What was the nature of Monica's struggle? How did the restraint and maturity of Francis help Monica? Why did Christina refuse to take Monica with her? What advice did Christina give her younger sister?

4. Which members of the family were influenced happily by the twenty-four hour visit of Christina? How was the situation of the family as a whole improved? How do the new circumstances remove from Christina the necessity of choosing between the two houses? Why would it have been unfortunate had she been obliged to make a decision?

5. Explain why Christina was right when she said, "'Which house?' is a small problem now, Martin." Which members of the family seem unmoved by Christina's good sense and spirituality? Why was Christina weeping when leaving the house?

EVALUATING HIS MANNER OF EXPRESSION

1. The wit of a dramatist is seen through the dialogue of the characters. What is especially clever in the words, "Heaven is full of dented helmets"? Find other pithy statements.

2. Explain the irony of John's moving the family to Good Ground for Christmas dinner in order that Christina might choose her old home for her community. Which characters show enthusiasm for the place? How does this emotion influence the plot?

3. How does the song "The Wraggle-taggle Gypsies" symbolize the former carefree existence of the Farleys?

4. Does Christina achieve a solution of the family problems, or does she give her brothers and sisters something with which they can solve their own difficulties?

The Easter Story

Heywood Broun

Heywood Broun is best remembered as a newspaper columnist. This Easter editorial appeared in the New York World Telegram. *In the women of the Gospel narrative, Broun sees the spirit which will always conquer in the struggle between hope and despair.*

"AND they said among themselves, 'Who shall roll us away the stone from the door of the sepulcher?'" To me the most vivid account of the Easter morning is the sixteenth chapter of St. Mark. It contains as lovely a verse as any in the Bible.

"And very early in the morning, the first day of the week, they came unto the sepulcher at the rising of the sun." I am not thinking of the strictly theological significance of the Gospel account but of other connotations. The Easter story is the story of the fundamental fight between life and death, between hope and despair. I think it is fair to note that those who came to the rising of the sun did not come in the spirit of surrender. They knew the stone was very great, but the query, "Who shall roll us away the stone?" was no mere rhetorical question. It was in the minds of these devoted believers that the task could be accomplished.

They sought a means and a method, "and when they looked they saw that the stone was rolled away." That faith which can move a mountain is sufficient to roll away a mighty rock. But I like to think if the Angel of the Lord had not intervened, the women themselves would have set their hands against the stone which barred their way. The idea of defeat or frustration never entered their minds. They came very early in the morning not to celebrate a lost cause but to perform a practical task. Indeed, they had "brought sweet spices that they might come and anoint Him."

Of course, they knew that the tomb was sealed, but their faith was lively that a way could be found to break through that wall of death. They talked it over among themselves. Their very normal instinct was to co-operate in solving the problem. As far as a precedent and tradition went, they may well have seemed visionaries.

Mark names those who came to the tomb at the rising of the sun as "Mary Magdalen, and Mary the mother of James, and Salome." It might have seemed utterly impractical for three women to bear spices to a tomb which was guarded by a huge and heavy stone. And probably there were those among the disciples who turned their love of the crucified leader into nothing more than loud lamentations. All they could contribute was grief and despair. They may even have told the three women that their mission was a fruitless one and that all hope lay buried behind a rock too mighty to be moved.

But the Easter story has been repeated again and again in the history of the world. Those who follow the course of the sun have found that every morning may mark a miracle in the life of man. Life is greater than death. And the true realist is not the person who is content to look at the stone and sigh. There are those who look about the world today and declare that civilization is done. Men who profess to be of good intent say that war is inevitable. In our own land the headshakers and the naysayers are always with us. They even condemn as cynical and destructive people who suggest that peace can be won and the woes of the world solved by taking thought and action and quitting the dead modes of the past.

To some, history itself is a sort of hard rock. What has been, must forever endure. If man has always turned to battle, so it must be until the end of time. Poverty has been set as the lasting lot of humankind. There were days in America when we had pioneers. They were not crippled by precedent. They went out and created it. It is true that we no longer possess unlimited forests to be cut down or rich land to be taken over by the hardy and the adventurous. We must pioneer along new lines of endeavor. We must make the adjustment between man and the machine. A world more great and gay awaits us when the problem of distribution is solved.

To pioneer is to experiment. Let us leave by the roadside those who simply sit and say, "Isn't everything terrible?"; and here and now at the rising of the sun it is for us to answer it.

VIEWING THE AUTHOR'S IDEAS

1. What is the theological significance of the Easter account? List the additional meanings which the story has for the author.

2. In what spirit did the women come to the sepulcher? How would they have solved the problem of the stone if the angel had not intervened? Why might they be called visionaries? How did their actions differ from those of the disciples?

3. How has the Easter story been repeated in the history of the world? Who are the "naysayers" in our own land? What do those who follow the course of the sun find?

4. In what sense is history a sort of hard rock? Explain "pioneers are not crippled by precedent." How may Americans still be pioneers?

5. What two lines of pioneering endeavor does the author suggest? Can you think of other modern problems that need to be explored? Show that the problem of fair distribution involves questions of justice and charity as well as economics. Will fair distribution remove all the evils of the world? Is it necessarily included in our program for a just and lasting peace?

EVALUATING HIS MANNER OF EXPRESSION

1. Studies have shown the great literary influence of the Bible on the theme and language of American newspaper columns. Why did the author choose his text from the Gospel of St. Mark? Discuss the appeal of this selection as an editorial for the Easter season.

2. Why has this selection been classified as a parable? What truth does the author draw from the Easter story?

3. Show that the final sentence is a summary of the main ideas of the editorial.

On Kitchens and Cloisters

Mary Ellen Chase

In this informal essay the author meditates upon the essential unity of the temporal and the spiritual in man's life. She finds this union best exemplified in cloisters like the ancient Abbey of Gloucester and the modern convent of St. Hilda. There reflection and prayer are united with concern for such common but equally necessary things as bread and meat, cheese and ale, milk and spice cake. Thus the cloister walk joining the kitchen and the chapel becomes a symbol of the chain that links the human with the divine.

THE cloister[1] at Saint Hilda's Convent at once separates and unites the convent kitchen and the chapel of Our Lady of Victory. The two verbs would seem to be at variance; in fact, one is likely through force of temperament alone to take his choice between them. As for me, I am inclined irrevocably toward the latter. Recalling those common gifts of the faithful to the early Church, the offertory of fresh bread loaves, of ears of corn and clusters of grapes, of cakes of finest flour, I see little reason for the idea of separation. Saint Monica, the mother of the great Augustine, rose early, one remembers, to bake her own loaves, which she thereafter distributed in person to the village churches.

Doubtless she carried to Mass, concealed in the folds of her gown, some such delectable and aromatic odors as I have more than once enjoyed, kneeling by Sister Ambrosine, the mistress of Saint Hilda's kitchen, and noting in what a sweet and seemly manner they are wont to ascend with the incense above the white altar.

I should banish forever the notion that a kitchen is separated from a chapel. Once in a high Swiss hamlet on a clear summer morning I attended an early Mass in a tiny, rose-covered church. The priest was frail and old; the congregation consisted of a handful of peasants, a kind and attentive dog, and me; but our responses were immeasurably strengthened and swelled by the loud and cheerful tones of the priest's housekeeper, who, in his cottage adjoining the church, attended at once to her own devotions and his breakfast. Through the open windows came her lively voice fervently praising the Lord; her pots and pans were the tabors and the cymbals adjured by the psalmist;[2] and mingling with the fragrance of the high, thin air came the warm, comfortable smell of her ham and coffee. Well did Saint Francis de Sales extol the similar household devotions

---

[1] *cloister*, an enclosed walk or passage in a monastery or convent.

[2] *tabors . . . psalmist*, an allusion to Psalm 150, which is an exhortation to praise God upon various musical instruments.

of Saint Anne and Saint Martha; and Saint Teresa, in *The Way of Perfection*, it will be remembered, warns her young nuns against irreverence for sculleries[3] and kitchens.

In Gloucester[4] — loveliest of cloisters! — the hawkers' door[5] leading to the kitchen immediately adjoined the cloister walk. What cries and scents and colloquies may well have drifted in those lancet windows,[6] echoing through those arched and shadowy recesses and dying away among the soaring, fanlike tracery of that lofty roof! At their desks in the carols of the scriptorium,[7] intent on their illumination of psalters and books of hours[8] with gold leaf and blue dyes, more than one Benedictine Brother of Saint Peter must have felt a twitching of the nostrils at the cry of fresh salmon from the Severn or of early strawberries from the valley of the Wye. Who knows indeed what delicate golden spiral completing an initial letter, what depths and shades of blue in flowery borders, what eager-faced ox or ass may have owed a better being to the simple proximity of that monastery kitchen? And if to some more contemplative Brother, sitting in his carol between the fluted columns, there appeared from the high palaces of heaven a singing company of saints to chant their litanies in the cloister close, there came no less into the thoughts and the hands of those Gloucester masons, from good Gloucester bread and cheese and ale, the exquisite, unearthly traceries of those beautiful aerial arches.

The south walk of the Gloucester cloisters, claiming and receiving all possible rays of that niggardly English sunshine, utilized them to the full by throwing upon the broad stone floor latticed and leaf-strewn shadows from its high windows. Saint Hilda's south walk is recompensed in its endowment of sunlight for its lack of age and mellowed beauty. Rare indeed are those summer mornings which withhold the sun from its gray arches and columns, from its lancet, trefoiled windows, which Sister Ambrosine on her way to Mass

has swung wide upon their hinges. Shadows, too, has Saint Hilda's from a great grapevine that, covering the western wall with its riotous life, sends, each in its own season, the sunlit counterparts of bare tendrils of leaves and of fruit clusters to dance upon the walls and to rest uneasily upon the stone floor. And as for the prospect from the westward-facing windows of that south walk, Gloucester itself assuredly has nothing to show more fair.

Pacing the cloister in silence on their way from Mass to breakfast, the Sisters glimpse through the narrow openings the high chapel porch with its sculptured saints. Below, the land falls to a tiny lake, rises again to wooded knolls, and slopes once more to the great river.[9] Sandstone bluffs on its farther side are purple in the morning light and tease the gaze yet higher to blue, tumbling hills and a wide, clear expanse of blue and silver sky. And although the nuns, fretting not "at their narrow convent room"[10] and bathed in a deeper, surer knowledge, do not need the information, one who has known both places will see in the quiet sloping of the land and the rising of the hills a likeness between those Gloucestershire valleys loved by Wordsworth and this sunnier newer country.

Rain, too, at Saint Hilda's can never be that intrusive, wetter rain of southern England. On soggy mornings in that chill cloister how welcome to the shivering monks of Gloucester must have been the rich, warm odor of roast beef, browning slowly on the kitchen spits. What comfort in even the lowly smell of well-smoked herring as it fought for supremacy with the fog and the mist! Saint Hilda's cloister enjoys rain that is less tenacious, less personal in nature. The skies that pour down their crystal and silver are beneficent rather than willful of face, meditative rather than sullen. Having, in fact, watched a summer rain through the open windows of the cloister, one is not infrequently driven to wish — curious as it sounds — for less sunlight.

On such a midafternoon the gray walls take on a purple tinge, like Massachusetts hills on a dull November day. The rain falls upon the roof in a subdued, rhythmic undertone, strikes with a sharp spatter the wide leaves of the grapevine, and drips from under the eaves into widening pools with clear musical

---

[3] *sculleries*, rooms for washing dishes and kitchen utensils.

[4] *Gloucester*. The Benedictine Abbey of St. Peter was founded in 681. The cathedral, completed in 1104, is one of the most beautiful examples of Gothic architecture in England. The cloister is noted for the fan tracery of the roof.

[5] *hawkers' door*, the door at which food was delivered to the kitchen. The hawker was one who sold his wares by crying them in the street or at the doors of dwellings.

[6] *lancet windows*, the narrow, pointed windows of Gothic architecture.

[7] *carols of the scriptorium*, alcoves in the room set apart in a monastery for those who copied or decorated manuscripts.

[8] *illumination . . . hours*. During the Middle Ages books containing the Divine Office and the Little Office of the Blessed Virgin were adorned with elaborate designs and brilliant colors.

[9] *the great river*, the Mississippi.

[10] *fretting not . . . convent room*, a partial quotation of the first line of one of Wordsworth's sonnets.

tones like the running notes of the clavichord.[11] The poplars on the slopes increase their silver; the stalks of larkspur over the distant garden hedge are wisps of blue smoke.

At this hour of the afternoon the nuns are at prayer, at work, asleep. I am alone in the cloister except for one Sister who stands at the dim turn of the south into the chapel walk, tells her beads, and looks out upon the rain. She is a Dominican, sojourning for a season among her black-robed friends. The deep cream color of her habit against the gray walls on this day is like the color of a pale daffodil against a mass of purple. Watching her quiet figure, hearing in the brooding stillness the click of her rosary beads as she lifts and drops them, I think of Pater saying: "All life should be conceived as a kind of listening" and of Saint Teresa: "The kingdom of heaven is won by a wise passiveness."

At the sound of the benediction bell she goes into the chapel. The Sisters pass me silently, the echo of their beads the undertones for the thin, clear notes of raindrops on the pools below. The flushed cheeks and fragrant skirts of Sister Ambrosine assure me there is fresh spice cake for supper. Soon the organ throbs through the soft, muted air, and voices singing the *Sancta Maria, Mater Dei* echo and re-echo through the uniting cloisters. They reach the kitchen and add their consecrating power to milk and bread, meat and spice

[11] *clavichord*, a keyboard instrument used before the invention of the piano.

cake, objects of poetic and spiritual significance surely could we but break through the veil of our familiarity with them, fit symbols of life, *gratia plena*, indeed!

VIEWING THE AUTHOR'S IDEAS

1. How does the author show that a kitchen and a chapel should be united rather than separated? When is work equivalent to prayer?

2. What comparisons does the author make between the ancient Abbey of St. Peter at Gloucester and the modern convent of St. Hilda? How do these comparisons illustrate the continuity of Catholic culture from the Middle Ages to our own times?

3. List details which show the author's admiration of conventual life. What aspects of that life does she find most attractive?

4. How does the essay show that the writer has traveled extensively; that she has read widely?

EVALUATING HER MANNER OF EXPRESSION

1. In *A Goodly Fellowship* the author says, "Words began to fascinate me, their choice and combination, their sound and color, their height and depth, the possibilities within them of rhythm and movement." Select passages which show the author's artistry in the use of words. Make a list of unusual words.

2. Can you find any partial quotation so wrought into the texture of the sentences as to be scarcely recognizable? What is the effect of these echoes from great writers?

3. Select four beautiful descriptive passages from the essay.

On Unanswering Letters

Christopher Morley

If you have ever written a letter in which you have had to apologize for a delayed answer, you will enjoy this essay. Underneath apparent nonsense is genial satire on man's tendency to postpone matters that are not urgent.

THERE are a great many people who really believe in answering letters the day they are received, just as there are people who go to the movies at nine o'clock in the morning; but these people are stunted and queer.

It is a great mistake. Such crass and breathless promptness takes away a great deal of the pleasure of correspondence.

The psychological didoes involved in receiving letters and making up one's mind to answer them are very complex. If the tangled process could be clearly analyzed and its component involutions isolated for inspection, we might reach a clearer comprehension of that curious bag of tricks, the efficient Masculine Mind.

Take Bill F., for instance, a man so delightful that even to contemplate his existence puts us in good humor and makes us think well of a world that can exhibit an individual equally comely in mind, body, and estate. Every now and then we get a letter from Bill, and immediately we pass into a kind of trance, in which our mind rapidly enunciates the ideas, thoughts, surmises, and contradictions that we would like to write to him in reply. We think what fun it would be to sit right down and churn the inkwell, spreading speculation and cynicism over a number of sheets of foolscap to be wafted Billward.

Sternly we repress the impulse, for we know that the shock to Bill of getting so immediate a retort would surely unhinge the well-fitted panels of his intellect.

We add his letter to the large delta of unanswered mail on our desk, taking occasion to turn the mass over once or twice and run through it in a brisk, smiling mood, thinking of all the jolly letters we shall write some day.

After Bill's letter has lain on the pile for a fortnight or so, it has been gently silted over by about twenty other pleasantly postponed manuscripts. Coming upon it by chance, we reflect that any specific problems raised by Bill in that manifesto will by this time have settled themselves. And his random speculations upon household management and human destiny will probably have taken a new slant by now, so that to answer his letter in its own tune will not be congruent with his present fevers. We had better bide a wee until we really have something of circumstance to impart.

We wait a week.

By this time a certain sense of shame has begun to invade the privacy of our brain. We feel that to answer that letter now would be an indelicacy. Better to pretend that we never got it. By and by Bill will write again, and then we will answer promptly. We put the letter back in the middle of the heap and think what a fine chap Bill is. But he knows we love him; so it doesn't really matter whether we write or not.

Another week passes by, and no further communication from Bill. We wonder whether he does love us as much as we thought. Still — we are too proud to write and ask.

A few days later a new thought strikes us. Perhaps Bill thinks we have died, and he is annoyed because he wasn't invited to the funeral. Ought we to wire him? No, because after all we are not dead; and even if he thinks we are, his subsequent relief at hearing the good news of our survival will outweigh his bitterness during the interval. One of these days we will write him a letter that will really express our heart, filled with all the grindings and gear work of our mind, rich in affection and fallacy. But we had better let it ripen and mellow for a while. Letters, like wines, accumulate bright fumes and bubblings if kept under cork.

Presently we turn over that pile of letters again. We find in the lees of the heap two or three that have gone for six months and can safely be destroyed. Bill is still on our mind but in a pleasant, dreamy kind of way. He does not ache or twinge us as he did a month ago. It is fine to have old friends like that and keep in touch with them. We wonder how he is and whether he has two children or three. Splendid old Bill!

By this time we have written Bill several letters in imagination and enjoyed doing so, but the matter of sending him an actual letter has begun to pall. The thought no longer has the savor and vivid sparkle it had once. When one feels like that, it is unwise to write. Letters should be spontaneous outpourings; they should never be undertaken merely from a sense of duty. We know that Bill wouldn't want to get a letter that was dictated by a feeling of obligation.

Another fortnight or so elapsing, it occurs to us that we have entirely forgotten what Bill said to us in that letter. We take it out and con it over. Delightful fellow! It is full of his own felicitous kinks of whim, though some of it sounds a little old-fashioned by now. It seems a bit stale, has lost some of its freshness and surprise. Better not answer it just yet, for Christmas will soon be here and we shall have to write then anyway. We wonder can Bill hold out until Christmas without a letter?

We have been rereading some of those imaginary letters to Bill that have been dancing in our head. They are full of all sorts of fine stuff. If Bill ever gets them, he will know how we love him. To use O. Henry's immortal joke, we have days of Damon and Knights of Pythias[1] writing those uninked letters to Bill. A curious thought comes to us. Perhaps it would be better if we

---

[1] *Damon . . . Pythias.* Damon and Pythias were famous friends in ancient Syracuse. The Knights of Pythias are a secret society founded at Washington in 1864.

never saw Bill again. It is very difficult to talk to a man when you like him so much. It is much easier to write in the sweet, fantastic strain. We are so inarticulate when face to face. If Bill comes to town, we will leave word that we have gone away. Good old Bill! He will always be a precious memory.

A few days later a sudden frenzy sweeps over us, and though we have many pressing matters on hand, we mobilize pen and paper and literary shock troops and prepare to hurl several battalions at Bill. But, strangely enough, our utterance seems stilted and stiff. We have nothing to say. "My dear Bill," we begin, "it seems a long time since we heard from you. Why don't you write? We still love you in spite of all your shortcomings."

That doesn't seem very cordial. We muse over the pen and nothing comes. Bursting with affection, we are unable to say a word.

Just then the phone rings. "Hello?" we say.

It is Bill, come to town unexpectedly.

"Good old fish!" we cry, ecstatic. "Meet you at the corner of Tenth and Chestnut in five minutes."

We tear up the unfinished letter. Bill will never know how much we love him. Perhaps it is just as well. It is very embarrassing to have your friends know how you feel about them. When we meet him, we will be a little bit on our guard. It would not be well to be betrayed into any extravagance of cordiality.

And perhaps a not altogether false little story could be written about a man who never visited those most dear to him because it panged him so to say good-by when he had to leave.

VIEWING THE AUTHOR'S IDEAS

1. By what startling statement in the opening sentences does the author arouse interest? What subject for a similar essay does he suggest in conclusion?
2. How does the writer show that Bill's letter was challenging and interesting? State the nature of its contents?
3. List the seriocomic excuses which the author advances for not answering Bill's letter? Compute the time which elapses between his receiving the letter and the telephone call.
4. What does the greeting, "Good old fish!" tell of the relationship between the two friends? In what ways have the telephone, telegraph, and radio affected letter writing?
5. How does the essay illustrate the habit of procrastination?

EVALUATING HIS MANNER OF EXPRESSION

1. Is the essay an apology for not answering letters promptly; a whimsical treatment of an idea; a satire on man's tendency to postpone doing things?

Education for Freedom

Robert Maynard Hutchins

Education is a much-discussed topic today. With how many of Hutchins' ideas do you agree?

WE DO not seem to get very far by talking about democracy. We know that Germany is not one. She says so. We know that Russia is not one, though Stalin says she is one. We are not sure about some elements in the government of England and France. We are not altogether sure about this country. The reason is, of course, that we do not know what a democracy is or grasp the fundamental notions on which it rests. We set out in the last war to make the world safe for democracy. We had, I think, no very definite idea of what we meant. We seemed then to favor a parliamentary system.[1] No matter what the system concealed, if the system was there, it was democracy; and we were for it. Though Hitler is infinitely worse than the Kaiser, though the danger to the kind of government we think we believe in is infinitely greater than in 1917, we have less real, defensible conviction about democracy now than we had then. Too many so-called democracies have perished under the onslaught of an invader whose technical and organizing ability commands the

[1] *parliamentary system,* a system of government in which the legislature is given complete control over the making and administration of the law; a government by an assembly that proceeds by discussion and examination.

admiration of a people brought up to admire technical and organizing skill. With our vague feeling that democracy is just a way of life, a way of living pleasantly in comparative peace with the world and one another, we may soon begin to wonder whether it can stand the strain of modern times, which, as our prophets never tire of telling us, are much more complicated than any other times whatever.

Is democracy a good form of government? Is the United States a democracy? If we are to prepare to defend democracy, we must be able to answer these questions. I repeat that our ability to answer them is much more important than the quantity or quality of airplanes, bombs, tanks, flame throwers, and miscellaneous munitions that we can hurl at the enemy. . . .

Now democracy is not merely a good form of government; it is the best. Though the democratic ideal has long been cherished in this country, it has never been attained. Nevertheless, it can be attained if we have the intelligence to understand it and the will to achieve it. We must achieve it if we would defend democracy. J. Middleton Murry, an Englishman, said of England a year ago, "This country, as it is, is incapable of winning a Christian victory because it simply is not Christian." Without passing on the specific application of this general principle, we can at least agree that the principle is sound and that no country can win a democratic victory unless it is democratic.

The reasons why democracy is the best form of government are absurdly simple. It is the only form of government that can combine three characteristics: law, equality, and justice. A totalitarian[2] state has none of these; and hence, if it is a state at all, it is the worst of all possible states.

Men have reason, but they do not always use it. They are swayed by emotions and desires that must be held in check. Law is an expression of their collective rationality,[3] by which they hope to educate and control themselves. Law is law only if it is an ordinance of reason directed to the good of the community. It is not law if it is an expression of passion or designed for the benefit of pressure groups.[4]

We have a government of men and not of laws when the cause of legislative enactments is anything but reason and its object anything but the common good.

The equality of all men in the political organization results inexorably[5] from the eminent dignity of every individual. Every man is an end; no man is a means. No man can be deprived of his participation in the political society. He cannot be exploited or slaughtered to serve the ends of others. We have no compunctions about refusing animals the ballot. We have few about exploiting or slaughtering them in our own interest. But the human animal is bound to recognize the human quality of every other human animal. Since human beings, to achieve their fullest humanity, require political organization and participation therein, other human beings cannot deny them those political rights which human nature inevitably carries with it.

These same considerations help us to understand that the state is not an end in itself, as the Nazis think, or a mere referee, as the Liberty Leaguers used to say. Political organization is a means to the good of the community. And the common good itself is a means to the happiness and well-being of the citizens. The common good is peace, order, and justice, justice in all political, social, and economic relations. Justice is the good of the community. But what is the community? It is certainly something more than an aggregation of people living in the same area. A community implies that people are working together, and people cannot work together unless they have common principles and purposes. If half a crew of men are tearing down a house as the other half are building it, we do not say they are working together. If half a group of people are engaged in robbing, cheating, oppressing, and killing the other half, we should not say the group is a community. Common principles and purposes create a community; justice, by which we mean a fair allocation[6] of functions, rewards, and punishments, in terms of the rights of man and the principles and purposes of the community, holds it together.

The state, then, is not merely conventional, representing a compromise of warring interests who have finally decided that mutual sacrifices by

[2] *totalitarian*, pertaining to a highly centralized government under the control of a political group which does not recognize any other political party.

[3] *rationality*, reasonableness; power to reason.

[4] *pressure groups*, minority groups that bring pressure to bear upon legislators through nonofficial or unavowed channels to force or defeat legislation or change public policy.

[5] *inexorably*, immovably.

[6] *allocation*, an apportionment.

subordination to a central authority are preferable to mutual extermination. The state is necessary to achieve justice in the community. And a just society is necessary to achieve the terrestrial ends of human life.

We see, then, that we are back where we started. We began with the importance of principles in defense. We must now add that without principles and common principles clearly understood and deeply felt there can be no political community at all. There can be only a conglomeration of individuals wrestling with one another in the same geographical region.

Let us inquire into what is needed if we are to understand clearly and feel deeply the principles on which democracy rests. What is the basis of these principles of law, equality, and justice? In the first place, in order to believe in these principles at all, we must believe that there is such a thing as truth and that in these matters we can discover it. We are generally ready to concede that there is truth, at least of a provisional variety, in the natural sciences. But there can be no experimental verification of the proposition that law, equality, and justice are the essentials of a good state. If there is nothing true unless experiment makes it so, then what I have been saying is not true, for I have not relied on any experimental evidence. But principles which are not true are certainly not worth fighting for. We must then agree that truth worth fighting for can be found outside the laboratory.

Now truth is of two kinds, theoretical and practical. Theoretical truth tells us what is the case; practical truth tells us what should be done. The test of theoretical truth is conformity to reality. A statement about the nature of man, for example, is true if it describes man as he actually is. The test of practical truth is the goodness of the end in view. The first principle in the practical order is that men should do good and avoid evil. The statement, for example, that men should lay down their lives in a just war is true, if the war is just. The statement that they should wage war to gain power or wealth or to display their virility[7] is false.

In order to believe in democracy, then, we must believe that there is a difference between truth and falsity, good and bad, right and wrong, and that truth, goodness, and right are objective standards even though they cannot be experimentally verified. They are not whims, prejudices, rationalizations,[8] or Sunday school tags. We must believe that man can discover truth, goodness, and right by the exercise of his reason, and that he may do so even as to those problems which, in the nature of the case, science can never solve.

It follows, of course, that in order to believe these things we must believe that man has reason, that he does not act from instinct alone, and that all his conduct cannot be explained in terms of his visceral reactions[9] or his emotional inheritance. As Gilbert Murray once put it, not all human activities are the efflorescence[10] of man's despair at finding that by the law of his religion he may not marry his grandmother. But in order to believe in democracy, we must believe something more. We must see that the moral and intellectual powers of men are the powers which make them men and that their end on earth is the fullest development of these powers. This involves the assumption, once again, that there is a difference between good and bad and that man is a rational animal. There is no use talking about moral powers if there is no such thing as morals, and none in talking about intellectual powers if men do not possess them.

Our great preoccupation today is freedom. When we talk about freedom, we usually mean freedom from something. Freedom of the press is freedom from censorship. Academic freedom is freedom from presidents, trustees, and the public. Freedom of thought is freedom from thinking. Freedom of worship is freedom from religion. So too civil liberty, the disappearance of which throughout the world we watch with anxious eyes, is generally regarded as freedom from the state. This notion goes back to Rousseau. He located the natural man in a world of anarchy. The natural man had no political organization, and Rousseau strongly hinted that this was the most delightful aspect of his condition. The political state was a compromise, no less unfortunate because it was necessary. This view has been popular ever since. It is reflected every day in the attitude of those who look upon the activities of government as an evil. Though they admit that society must suffer certain necessary evils, they naturally have no wish to multiply them. Hence the attraction and

---

[7] *virility*, manly vigor and power.

[8] *rationalizations*, acts of making up reasons to explain behavior for which the real motives are different and not easily seen.

[9] *visceral reactions*, the heightened activities of one's internal organs.

[10] *efflorescence*, a pouring out or gushing forth in an unrestrained way.

power of the slogan: that government is best which governs least.

This notion of government and its role is based on a myth, on a misconception of the nature of man and the nature of the state. It is not surprising that a doctrine absurdly grounded and workable only in countries of vast and untapped resources should contain in itself the seeds of an opposing doctrine, the doctrine that the state is all, that men are nothing but members of it, and that they achieve their ultimate fulfillment, not through freedom from the state, but through complete surrender to it. This is fascism. It ascribes to the political organization qualities that can belong only to God. It denies the eminent dignity of the person. It deprives man of the characteristic that raises him above the beasts, his reason. It sacrifices all that is specifically human, that is, moral, intellectual, spiritual development, and glorifies a specifically sub-human attribute, namely force.

These are the consequences of thinking of freedom as freedom from something. Freedom is not an end in itself. We do not want to be free merely to be free. We want to be free for the sake of being or doing something that we cannot be or do unless we are free. We want to be free to obtain the things we want.

Now the things we want are good things. First, we want our private and individual good, our economic well-being. We want food, clothing, and shelter, and a chance for our children. Second, we want the common good: peace, order, and justice. But most of all we want a third order of good, our personal or human good. We want, that is, to achieve the limit of our moral, intellectual, and spiritual powers. This personal, human good is the highest of all the goods we seek. As the private good, which is our individual economic interest, is subordinate to the common good, which is the interest of the community, so the common good is subordinate to our personal and human good and must be ordered to it. Any state in which the common good is sacrificed to private interests, or in which the moral, intellectual, and spiritual good of the citizens is sacrificed to the political organization is not a state. It is a fraud subsisting by force.

We in the universities are concerned with free minds. How can we get them? We must remember that it is not freedom from something that we are seeking. We want

minds that are free because they understand the order of goods and can achieve them in their order. The proper task of education is the production of such minds. But we can now see that we are not likely to produce them by following the recommendations of the more extreme of those called progressives in education. Freedom from discipline, freedom to do nothing more than pursue the interests that the accident of birth or station has supplied may result in locking up the growing mind in its own whims and difficulties.

The identification of freedom with lack of discipline is, in the somewhat lurid[11] language of Mr. Butler of Columbia, the "rabbit theory" of education, according to which, he says, "any infant is encouraged to roam about an enclosed field, nibbling here and there at whatever root of flower or weed may, for the moment, attract his attention or tempt his appetite." Mr. Butler adds, varying the figure slightly, "Those who call this type of school work progressive reveal themselves as afloat on a sea of inexperience without chart or compass or even rudder." Obviously we should not look to rudderless rabbits to lead us through the mazes of the modern world.

If we cannot produce free minds by adopting the suggestions of the more undisciplined progressives, we cannot hope for much better luck by continuing the almost universal practice of regarding education as a tour of the current events in the various fields of knowledge. . . .

It is doubtful, too, whether we can achieve free minds by concentrating our efforts on making our pupils economically independent. We want free minds which will seek the goods in their order. Those who seek primarily their private economic interests may become enslaved to them and try to enslave the rest of us as well.

When we say we want free minds, we mean that we want minds able to operate well. The glory and the weakness of the human mind is that it is not determinate[12] to certain things. It may range at will over the good and the bad. To be free to operate well, therefore, the mind requires habits that fix it on the good. So St. Augustine remarked that virtue, or good habits, is the right use of our freedom. What is needed for free

---

[11] *lurid*, harshly vivid.

[12] *determinate*, limited; fixed.

minds is discipline, discipline which forms the habits which enable the mind to operate well. Nothing better can be said on this subject than the concise statement of John Dewey. "The discipline," he said, "that is identical with trained power is also identical with *freedom*." The free mind is first of all the disciplined mind. The first step in education is to give the mind good habits.

The next step in the education of free minds is the understanding of what is good. The mind cannot be free if it is a slave to what is bad. It is free if it is enslaved to what is good. To determine the good and the order of goods is the prime object of all moral and political education. We cannot hope that one who has never confronted these issues can be either a good citizen or a good man. Yet today it is perfectly possible to attain to the highest reaches of the university without ever facing these questions. An educational system which does not make these questions the center of its attention is not an educational system at all. It is large-scale housing venture. It may be effective in keeping young people out of worse places until they can go to work. It cannot contribute to the growth of free minds. It cannot help the rising generation solve the great problem of our time.

The great problem of our time is moral, intellectual, and spiritual. With a superfluity[13] of goods we are sinking into poverty. With a multitude of gadgets we are no happier than we were before. With a declining death rate, we have yet to discover what to do with our lives. . . . With a love of liberty we see much of the world in chains.

How can these things be? They can be because we have directed our lives and our education to means instead of ends. We have been concerned with the transitory and superficial instead of the enduring and basic problems of life and of society.

Since the freedom of autonomy[14] is the end of human life, everything else in life should be a means to it and should be subordinate to it as means must be to ends. This is true of material goods, which are means, and a very necessary one, but not an end. It is true of the state, which is an indispensable means, but not an end. It is true of all human activities and all human desires;

they are all ordered to, and must be judged by, the end of moral and intellectual development.

The political organization must be tested by its conformity to these ideals. Its basis is moral. Its end is the good for man. Only democracy has this basis. Only democracy has this end. If we do not believe in this basis or this end, we do not believe in democracy. These are the principles which we must defend if we are to defend democracy.

VIEWING THE AUTHOR'S IDEAS

1. What aspects of democracy tend to confuse us? Which two questions about democracy are most important? Why is democracy the best form of government? Contrast the totalitarian with the democratic state.

2. Why do men have laws? What is the purpose of law? Explain why men are equal before the law. State the purpose of organized government. From whence do human beings get the right of participation in government?

3. Discuss what is meant by the common good of the community. Define community. What holds a community together? Why is government necessary in a community? Why must men have a just society? What is needed that a political community may function?

4. What is the basis of the principles of law, equality, and justice? Does all truth have to be verified by experiment in a laboratory? Why are principles that are true worth fighting for?

5. Discuss the kinds of truth. What is the test of theoretical truth; of practical truth? What is the first principle of practical truth? Why is it wrong to wage war for wealth, power, or display? How may man discover truth, goodness, and right? How does the development of man's moral and intellectual powers help democracy?

6. When people speak of freedom, what do they usually mean? What does civil liberty mean; what does it imply? How does Hutchins regard the idea that the least governed state is the best? What is fascism? Point out the errors in this system of government.

7. Why does man wish to be free? Enumerate the good things which man desires. What is the order in importance of these goods? How do we judge the merits of a government?

8. Why should institutions of learning be concerned with freedom? How do these institutions help men to be free? What is the task of education? What types of education are inadequate for man's needs?

9. According to the author what is the glory and the weakness of the human mind? How can the mind be made free? Why is a mind in error or a soul in sin not free? What is the first step in education?

---

[13] *superfluity*, something in excess.

[14] *autonomy*, the power or right to govern oneself.

10. Discuss the objectives of moral and political education. What is lacking in a system of education that does not train students to recognize good things and the order of these things? What problems do the present times present? How should citizens regard means and ends to a successful life? How do we test a system of government? In what way does democracy meet this test?

EVALUATING HIS MANNER OF EXPRESSION

1. Directness and clarity contribute to the force of this selection. What other elements of the author's style are important? Select a paragraph or passage that you consider forceful; comment on the reasons for the power in the passage.

2. How does Hutchins allude indirectly to the Catholic system of education? What seems to be his attitude toward the work of Catholic schools?

3. Is the tone of this essay challenging, bitter, despairing, or dispassionate? Explain.

4. Compare Hutchins' viewpoint on democracy and government with that of some well-known journalist, magazine writer, or radio commentator. What is unusual about the viewpoint and argument of Hutchins?

5. In what way do quotations strengthen the author's argument? In a discussion how important are references to an authority?

The City That Never Was

(From *The Book of the High Romance*)
Michael Williams

In 1906 Michael Williams was city editor of the San Francisco Daily News. *At two o'clock on the morning of April 18, he shut his desk and walked homeward through the sleeping city. What would be the result, he thought, should all those thousands of sleepers awaken bereft of egoism. What if they should employ in unity and for unity the energies they were now deriving together from the secret springs of sleep and silence? In this narrative the author tells how his question was answered when the great earthquake wrecked the city a few hours later.*

I HAD reached my home; I let myself in and got noiselessly to bed.

I suppose it was nearly four o'clock when at last my excited brain ceased its working, and sleep came.

And almost at once I came awake again — vaguely wondering what was the matter.

The big bed in which I lay was trying its best to imitate a bucking bronco and to throw me out of the window toward which it was lurching. The air itself seemed to be pulling at me with invisible fingers clutching from all directions at once, but unevenly; the plaster was falling in big chunks, and there was a vast crescendic roaring noise, incomprehensible, a vast sea of sound.

There was the commingling of the crash of falling walls, the tumbling of millions of bricks, the rending and cracking and splintering of wood, the shattering of window glass by the hundreds of thousands of sheets and panes, and myriads of other sounds. All these were based, as it were, on another, unwordable sound, which was the roaring of the earthquake — the groaning of the very earth itself.

What a racket!

It was like — well, it was like — let me see now, it was like — Oh, heavens above, *I don't know what it was like!* Nobody knows. Fancy a billion big drays loaded with iron rails passing along over rough cobblestones with the rails clangorously falling and the windows of all the houses being shattered by the concussions, and then fancy — but no, you can't! Neither can I. That noise is not to be conjured up by fancy; it can only be remembered.

Yet that terrible noise was nothing at all, a mere trifle, a trivial incident, a bagatelle, compared to the impression of the earthquake *as earthquake*, if I may so express myself.

But how can I tell you? I really cannot tell you!

For there was something about that shock that struck deeper than any sound could penetrate into the substance of your soul. You know how it is when we try to suggest some tremendous emotion or altogether unusual sense of calamity; we say, "It was as if the earth moved under our feet," or "It was as if the earth trembled."

So what can we say — what is there left to say — when the earth in fact *does* move under our feet, when actually the earth does tremble?

For we are so accustomed to the earth being — well, reliable, trustworthy, safe, sane, and conservative, so to speak. We are so used to being its boss, to using it as we please, ploughing and digging it, sowing and reaping it, building our cities with its own stuff, brick and stone and wood, without a murmur from it, without any tricks being played with us, such as the untamable sea and the mysterious air and that dangerous character, fire, take pleasure in perpetrating. We're up against trouble all the time in our dealings with water, and fire, and air; but we consider the earth a straight, clear-cut proposition.

So when *it* cuts loose . . . Oh, I give it up! There aren't any words for what you feel in an earthquake shock.

Here's a bit of a hint. Suppose you were on a ship at sea on a long, long voyage, so that the motion, the fluidity, the freedom of movement were part of your very being — you are saturated with motion; and suddenly the water becomes a solid substance, and the air becomes rigid, and the ship stops and is held without a quiver, like a toy ship frozen inside a block of ice. Well, the solid earth that morning in San Francisco was behaving like the unstable sea . . .

My little daughter was in the crib by the bed. Her mother gathered her up quickly in her arms; and I arched myself above them both to ward off the plaster or the universe I didn't know which. Our baby boy was in the adjoining room in a crib by the bedside of a friend who lived with us, a lady who appeared a second or two after the start of the trouble in her nightdress in the doorway. She was a maiden lady from New England; so you see how unconventional this occasion must have been. She it was who gave a name to it.

"Earthquake!" she said.

I had vaguely thought of an explosion; of a sudden and awful storm approaching, or a flood, a tidal wave; but sure enough, now I understood that it was an earthquake. When you come back from sleep after only an hour, you are not as bright-minded as you'd like to be able to say you were.

"The baby!" cried the lady in her doorway.

Then as neither the plaster nor the universe had crushed us so far, I ceased my imitation of a cat with its back arched and ran into the outer room.

The force of the shock had been much greater there. All the furniture was crowding into the middle of the room and trying to play a clumsy game of leapfrog. It was bright daylight of a perfect April day outside, but the blinds were drawn in the room and the light was dim, mild, and milky. And through this placid, opalescent light I saw the wide untroubled eyes of the baby boy, who was perfectly calm, looking at me. He was like a philosopher from some other planet nonchalantly observing a queer human being in pajamas scrambling over a mountain of furniture in a room which was apparently trying to turn itself inside out. I have often wondered what can go on in the mind of a child in such a moment.

The earthquake came a little after five. It lasted eighteen seconds. According to the scientific gentlemen it appears that the coast-range mountains along a line of some three hundred miles shrugged their shoulders or made a slight gesture, as it were, and cities and towns and villages along that line behaved very much as a child's building blocks behave when he pulls the tablecloth on which they are stacked. Mount Tamalpais,[1] a mass of how many billions of tons only science can tell you, shifted its position. Redwood trees three or four thousand years old were split wide open. Torrents and springs of water or sand leaped from the broken and tortured earth. Landslides streamed down the hills. Trees were overthrown. All this, outside the city. As for the city — Well, let me return to my own adventures; it is hopeless to attempt the description of the city's fate, just yet.

The house I lived in was an old wooden structure, solidly and honestly made. Like all such it swayed and shook; plaster fell, shelves were emptied, but there was no serious damage. Honestly made steel buildings also stood the racket.

Before the shock had finished its course by more than a few seconds, we were in the street, part of the fantastic multitude disgorging out of doorways up and down all the streets of the city. Some, but these were the few, were dressed, housewives or servants or workers

---

[1] *Mount Tamalpais* (tăm-ăl-pīs´), a mountain near San Francisco.

early astir; but the most of us were in all the stages of extraordinary dishabille.[2] There was a vacant lot not far from the house, and to this we ran; and soon the place was crowded with fat men in nighties, women with children in their arms, blankets about some of them, others merely in their nightgowns, and all sorts and conditions of men, women, and children.

There was a brief pause, as it were, a scant breathing spell; and then very suddenly my heart tried to jump out of my mouth and then seemed to fall back, fluttering like a wounded creature.

Another earthquake had begun . . . again the earth and the air and all that was upon the earth and in the air was throbbing, was swaying, was quivering, was palpitating enormously. It was frightful! But thank God, it didn't last so long, nor was it nearly so severe as the first one. Nevertheless, it shook down walls that had been weakened by the other shock; and bricks and chimneys came raining down, and people who had ventured back into their houses came rushing out in fresh dismay. Some of them didn't come out again, falling walls or beams pinning them down, killed or badly injured; caught in some places like animals in pits or deadfall traps.[3]

There came a fresh wave of people rushing through the streets, but we remained in the open space.

And up in the middle of the street a little bit later there walked two well-dressed men, Orientals or mulattoes, looking as if they had been up all night waiting for this moment. They were proclaiming the end of the world. It was Judgment Day they cried; the Book was open, the Book of Life and Death, and they bade us fall upon our knees and pray. And really you know — we weren't sure they were not right. Truly, it was like the end of things mortal. Somebody looking at the wall of fire marching toward us later on — that strangely silent, quietly busy advance of a wall of flame — said, "Yes, it surely must be Judgment Day." Somebody else replied, "And this must be the gates of hell."

It ought to have been a perfectly tremendous moment, I suppose . . . but it wasn't.

The trouble was that we couldn't believe our prophet. Daylight, I expect, is not congenial to belief in prophets, even when the daylight is one of a day of disaster. There

seems to be something in us, something that belongs to our very life — perhaps it is the force of life itself — that utterly refuses to believe in death until death itself says, "Here I am." Even if April 18, 1906, really had been doomsday, you couldn't have got us to believe it out there in San Francisco, not if a regiment of black prophets had been on the job.

I saw a few troubled faces here and there amid the crowd, but the trouble was more what you might feel when somebody acts indecorously than anything deeper.

"That mutt must be crazy," I heard a fat man wheezing near me.

"Somebody ought to make him shut up — or knock his block off," answered the man the fat chap spoke to. "Say, even if he is right, what business has he to try to scare folks?"

Personally I felt quite indifferent. Maybe the prophet was right. Quite likely he was. But if this was the end of the world — Oh, very well, it was the end of the world — but we might just as well carry on, without any fuss.

And that, you might say, was the common, the general feeling, not only there in Geary Street, but throughout all the terrible days that followed. It was not that we were indifferent to fears and horrors and disasters; not at all; nor was it that we were endowed with heroic courage to overcome all things. No, that was not the case. We were full of fears all the time. I think there was hardly one of us who didn't keep in mind the dark horror of a tidal wave. Others, I know from what they told me, felt that at any moment the earth might open and swallow them. The menace of shaky walls loomed always over us. In the first few days there came more than forty minor shocks, and each shock sent many nervously disordered persons temporarily insane. The sand hills toward the sea were full of wandering, harmless, mad folk, talking and muttering to themselves, or sitting on the ground staring at the smoke and crimson reflections of the fire in the sky. And we knew the fear of plague, pestilence, starvation, and sudden death. And always there were circulating the most dreadful rumors. We believed them too, more or less. Why not? Anything at all. Nothing was impossible. We heard that Los Angeles had been wiped out completely. Mount Rainier was in eruption; torrents of lava were covering the north country with burning lakes. Chicago had

---

[2] *dishabille* (dĭs-à-bēl′), state of being dressed carelessly.
[3] *deadfall traps*, traps for wild animals consisting of a heavy log or weighted board which falls upon and crushes the prey.

been swallowed by Lake Michigan. The catastrophe was countrywide; maybe it was universal, for London had been smitten, so we heard. There were no telegraph wires working for days, of course, but only a few of us were aware of this. Anyhow, rumors, as we all know, whether false or true, do not need telegraph wires in order to travel about; they seem to use the all-pervading ether, like the waves of the wireless. Or else they spread through telepathy.[4]

But, all the same, we did not get badly excited. We were bewildered; some of us were bedazed; we were all nerve-shaken and we all had our own particular fears to face — but taking us altogether, by and large, taking us as a crowd of human beings, as a mob, if you like, as a multitude — we stood everything mighty well. There was a calmness; there was a grave, yet kindly, almost smiling kind of acceptance of the situation on the part of the people as a whole, the memory of which remains with me like the memory of noble and harmonic music. For after all, you see, there was something in San Francisco which the quake could not overthrow, nor even agitate seriously; and this thing was the intangible something which is the spirit of human nature, the spirit of human life, which shows itself in human nature's unbreakable habit of keeping busy at the business of living on in this world just as long as there is any shred of world left in which to live. What is that inner something? That inmost assurance? Mere instinct? Self-preservation? The will-to-live? Or is it Faith?

Anyhow, we do, we will carry on. Some day we'll know why . . .

Save for those whom death had struck with loss and pain, through taking away loved ones, the vast majority of San Franciscans were not merely stoical; they were gallantly brave, romantically chivalrous, superbly generous. In my goings about through the worst of the stricken districts, I saw many instances of loss and disaster; but my memory of those days is not stained with a single incident of cowardice or of meanness.

The obvious thing to say is that social conventions and distinctions were laid aside. Well, so they were, but that only expresses a small part of the truth. After all, the only place where men are truly, quite literally equal, is in their souls. God made us all; and when the red

ruin was raging from the waterfront on towards Van Ness Avenue, a line of fire ten miles wide, at times; and later when amid the shards and dust and smoke of the vanished city, men and women no longer felt that doomsday was upon them, they acted toward each other as fellow creatures, as human beings, not merely as employer and employee, rich man, poor man, beggarman, thief.

Will Irwin wrote an excellent description of Old San Francisco, which he called "The City-That-Was." Well, the glimpses of Paradise, or of Utopia, which came to me while San Francisco, riven and shattered, was being bound, as it were, upon the monstrous pyre of its burning, was a vision of the City-That-Never-Was, the city of the world-wide dream, the city which John of Patmos saw descending out of heaven to earth[5], out of aspiration into accomplishment, out of the ideal into reality, the city of peace and of brotherly love, of the kingdom of God upon earth. The City that never was, that never, never was, yet which surely is to be, which surely is to be.

Perhaps I saw everything magnified by my own mood, colored by my own desire; nevertheless, it is true that for several marvelous days in San Francisco we lived as people might live if they but willed it so — we lived a life of goodwill. Nearly all the artificial barriers and distinctions with which we isolate class from class and person from person were thrown down more effectually than the 'quake threw down the walls of houses — the walls of evil houses and the walls of churches together. For days there was no use for money; there was nothing to buy or sell. Rich and poor were no longer either rich or poor. The bread line was no respecter of persons. The women of the Tenderloin were cared for by virtuous women. Food was in common. He who had not, asked and he who had, gave. Your neighbor was as yourself. You did not see the mote in his eye, for there was no distorting beam in yours. Generosity, kindness, pity, mercy, tenderness — all the brave and beautiful angels of the heart of man walked in the streets of the shattered city. Oh, yes, there were exceptions, no doubt. I've heard of them; but I did not myself see them; but it is God's own truth I'm telling you when I say that the great disaster which for several

---

[4] *telepathy*, apparent communication from one mind to another.

[5] *John of Patmos . . . earth.* St. John on the Island of Patmos had a vision of the new Jerusalem, which he describes in *The Apocalypse*, Chapter XXI.

days shut off San Francisco from the world that still went on in the ordinary way, brought out what is best, and what is strongest, and what will finally prevail in mankind — that which is good. Those three or four days, despite all the dreadful things that happened, were days of the Golden Age returned again; and to me their memories remain, as prophecies of the time to come when we shall all together so live without change or shadow of turning.

Indeed, it almost seemed as if Goethe's dream[6] was realized, and that San Francisco had been shocked out of its egoism and had found in the midst of this apocryphal[7] overthrowal the poet's spring of goodness and had become quite literally the City of Brotherly Love, the City of Peace — the City-that-Never-Has-Been. . . .

VIEWING THE AUTHOR'S IDEAS

1. What were the author's first impressions of the earthquake? How did the scientists explain the phenomenon? What feature of the disaster most impressed the author?

2. List details which show the fear and bewilderment of the people. How does the author account for the spread of

wild rumors? What reasons does he suggest for the calm acceptance of the situation on the part of the people as a whole?

3. Quote the passage in which the author explains the title of the selection. Why does he think of San Francisco in its disaster as "the City That Never Was"? How did the people manifest the spirit of Christian democracy and brotherhood?

4. What benefits of a practical nature may have resulted from the earthquake in San Francisco? Where does the author suggest that many of the structures were not honestly built? Do you know of any laws that have been passed to safeguard life in case of an earthquake?

5. What do the concluding words suggest concerning the conduct of the people when the disaster was forgotten?

EVALUATING HIS MANNER OF EXPRESSION

1. Is this selection chiefly narrative, descriptive, or expository? Select a passage of forceful narrative; of vivid description; of reflective comment.

2. Discuss the artistic value of the concrete illustrations which the author uses to describe his impressions of the earthquake. Why is the broken, ejaculatory style effective in these passages?

3. What features of the selection show that the author was a journalist? How does this portion of the autobiography reveal his personality?

4. Read the entire autobiography to see how the author found high romance in other experiences of life.

---

[6] *Goethe's dream*, a reference to a passage from Goethe quoted earlier in the narrative: "There is in man a force—a spring of goodness—which counterbalances egoism; and if by a miracle it could for a moment suddenly be active in all men, the earth would be at once free from evil."

[7] *apocryphal*, fabulous.

Mary and the Modern Ideal

(From *A Companion to the Summa, Volume IV, The Way of Life*)
Walter Farrell, O.P.

Mary Immaculate, patroness of the United States, has received many tributes from Catholic authors. In this essay, Father Farrell takes the practical viewpoint in which he sees the imitation of Our Lady's virtues as a solution for the ills of modern life.

THE housewife bustling about her kitchen, the tired shopgirl smilingly meeting the discourtesy of customers, the product of a finishing school stepping into a world that is always glamorous to youth, these

may all seem far removed from the abstract philosophies of life which mold the thought and action of an age. Actually, the status of woman, any woman in any age, is a concrete expression of the philosophy of life on which the citizens of that age proceed in the living of life. This statement does not demand mental gymnastics for its comprehension, nor does it ask philosophy to work the modern miracle of standing erect in a careening streetcar serenely powdering its nose. It merely demands a consideration of the solid fact that the life of woman is one of the most vivid and accurate of all the norms[1] of judgment of an age and its philosophy.

A moment's examination of our age, or any age, will bring out unmistakably the only three bases for human life: the animal, the human, and the divine. The life of every age is physical, human, or divine; built up on the basis, that is, of strength, justice, or charity. It is true, of course, that some men of every age have acted like animals; it is also true that in the most debased ages there were some men who were uprightly human, even some who were saints. The question here is not of the exception but of the rule, of the ideal to which an age looks and the things that it condemns or mocks. Considered in that general light, there is nothing in an age that so sharply mirrors its philosophy as the lives of its women.

Perhaps this fact can be brought out most briefly by a short comparison. A seaplane can stagger through pounding seas for awhile, for it has something in common with the sea, some bond of unity; but in a very short time it is pounded to pieces. When it soars above the sea into the air, its flight is swift, accurate, though often enough, quite rough; the air is its proper medium; that is where it belongs. If it is equipped with superchargers, variable-pitch propellers, and a sealed cabin, it can get above the level of ordinary air to travel in the stratosphere;[2] there its flight is of such speed and grace as to stagger the imagination.

Woman has something in common with the animal level of life, some bond of union with it; but if she is forced to live on that level very long, she must break up. Physically she is no match for a man; in an age whose philosophy is based on strength, she becomes a toy, an instrument of pleasure, an inferior creature, for the principle of such an age is that might makes right. She was made to live on a human level; on that plane she is the equal of the mightiest and the wisest. Yet, because on the purely human plane, strength so often usurps the place of justice, the course of her life may often be very rough. On the supernatural, the divine plane, where she can expect not merely justice but also

charity, she reaches her highest perfection; there her life is one of smooth grace, for there, above all other planes, is where she belongs.

Every age has had a practical opinion of woman, because every age has had a philosophy of life whose expression has thundered ceaselessly on the shores of woman's life. Strangely enough, in the ages most unkind to women it is women themselves who are often the most aggressive champions of the debased philosophy by which those ages live. It may be that such women have actually become convinced of the philosophy of that age; it may be that they have been tricked by the specious[3] promises such an age always holds out to its victims; or it may be that woman's championship of such a philosophy is merely another expression of that subtle, feminine practicality which knows so well how to listen and to say the things that men most willingly hear.

The repercussions[4] of a philosophy of life upon women have been so clearly seen that the attempt to dodge them has produced queer results in the history of humanity. In some ages, the nineteenth century for example, the result was an hypocrisy that approached the comic. Apparently the nineteenth century was a romantic age; actually, its romantic glorification of women was fatalism that tried to hold to the Christian respect for women. It found itself helpless to do so except by glorifying the only weapons its philosophy had left for women in a world of brute strength and mechanical inevitability,[5] namely, youth and beauty. Women, trying to live up to the demands of their age, lived in a nightmare of absurdity that found a feeble reflection in the very clothes they wore. Still other ages attempted to hold to an animal abuse of women in an age of a human philosophy of life by maintaining that woman was something less than a human being.

More frequently, however, there has been a frank application of a definite philosophy of life to the women of that particular age. In an age based on animal philosophy, woman is a toy, a domestic instrument, or a necessary nuisance; in any case, she is to be used and discarded. In a rational age she will be an equal who

---

[1] *norms*, rules or standards.
[2] *stratosphere*, the upper portion of the atmosphere where there are no clouds and practically no movement.

[3] *specious*, deceptively beautiful; superficially just or correct.
[4] *repercussions*, impacts or blows given in return; hence, reciprocal actions or effects.
[5] *inevitability*, having consequences that cannot be avoided.

could yet be taken advantage of when the need arose. In a divine or supernatural age she is the daughter of the mother of God, a member of the mystical body of Christ, coming directly from God and going to Him, redeemed by His blood, and co-operating in one of His greatest works, the generation of human beings.

To discover the status of woman, it is not necessary to carry on extensive researches into the philosophy by which an age lives. No more is necessary than the application to woman's life of the basic tests of human and divine life for a woman. We need only ask a few questions. What value does she (and her contemporaries) place on sanctity; i.e., has the divine any place in her life? What is her estimate of virginity? What is the attitude of her contemporaries and herself to marriage? What part has the consecration of love and the stability of justice in the living of her life? What is a child; what is the evaluation of infant life? In a word, has reason any place in her life?

More concretely, it can be said positively that an age which mocks sanctity, considers virginity a matter of taste or lack of opportunity, declares marriage a legal convenience for the satisfaction of passion, and strips the child of rights, giving it consideration only in accord with parental convenience — such an age is based on an animal philosophy of life. Its norm of living is purely physical; its yardstick is brute strength.

Ultimately, of course, the difference between an animal age and a rational age boils down to the difference between the denial and the admission of the spiritual nature of the soul of man. If the vote of an age goes against the spiritual character of man's soul, then the only basis of judgment is the material; the weaker must, of course, suffer. And the weaker are always the women and children. It may seem fairly safe to deny a child's rights, since the child is, after all, quite helpless; so the thing is promptly done by abortion and its cousins. But once the lie has started, it is hard to stop. If the child presents an opportunity for the expression, in a particularly cowardly way, of materialism's social principle that might is right, why should the principle stop there? It does not stop there. We talk half laughingly today of the battle of the sexes; but it is not a very good joke. There was never such a thing except in a materialistic age; even then, the war

has never lasted very long. In such a war, on such a basis, woman always loses.

All this is on the negative side. The positive side can be seen, clear-cut and decisive, by even a hurried glance at womanhood's model, Mary, the Mother of God. There we can see not only what woman can be, but what she is. This is woman's place and her titles to it.

The perfection of Mary's womanhood stands out most sharply in the supreme moments of her life: in her divine maternity and her preparation for it. To put the same thing in the words we have been using up to this point, Mary's perfection is brought out from the confused detail of her age by the application of these basic tests of any woman's life: sanctity, virginity, marriage, the evaluation of the infant. Mary, seen from the vantage point of these basic tests, leaves no room for doubt of the basis upon which woman's life is lived to its fullest. It must, of course, be remembered that Mary is a model in the order of nature as well as in the order of grace. Grace does not destroy but rather perfects nature. Mary, then, is the exemplar for women, not only in so far as she is the holiest of women, but also as the most womanly of women, the most free, winning the highest possible place in the hearts and minds of men.

Mary's preparation for her divine maternity began in the first instant of her life in the womb of her mother by that singular privilege which is called the Immaculate Conception. It is necessary to stop here for a moment and remark on a world-wide instance of that obtuseness[6] which is the despair of teachers. An explanation is given, made very clear, repeated again and again; and every student agrees that he understands perfectly; then a recitation is called for and the students not only have the matter backwards, they give it that way. It has been explained again and again that the Immaculate Conception has nothing to do with Mary's conception of Christ; that it refers to Mary's conception by St. Ann, and it has nothing to do with a virgin birth. Yet year after year, it is taken as a statement of the virgin birth of Christ. The Immaculate Conception is not a statement of a miraculous conception; but of a miraculous preservation from sin in the entirely natural conception of Mary by her mother. . . .

[6] *obtuseness*, dullness or stupidity.

Mary's proximity to her child and its effects is brought out beautifully in Corregio's "Holy Night" which, I believe, hung in Dresden before night fell in Germany. In it Mary is bending over the Child Who, however, does not appear in the picture; over Mary's shoulder Joseph can be seen standing in the shadow. The Virgin's whole face and body is alight with a brilliant, soft splendor as though she had just put her arms around the sun. The moving beauty of the picture has solid foundation in the profound truth of the effects on Mary of her divine Son. The farther we take her away from Christ, the less we know about Mary herself; the closer we bring Mary to Christ, the better we understand her. It is this proximity to the source of all grace that makes it so easy for us to understand something of the fullness of the grace of Mary. He was the fountain-head; she was the closest of all men and women to this source of living water.

Perhaps we can get a still further insight into the perfection of Mary's grace through a homely example. An oaken log, lying in the damp underbrush, is only a potential source of the comfort of fire. When it is first exposed to the flames, it undergoes a period of disposition, of drying out. When that is over, the form of the fire invades the log; and we see miniature flames, dancing like elves, catching tentatively at its huge sides with finger tips that slip again and again; as they grow bolder and stronger, the flames seem to rush at the log in solid ranks, are repulsed, to try again and again. Finally, the whole log entirely aflame is a holocaust worthy of the dignity of an oak. In the perfection of Mary's grace we can distinguish three somewhat similar stages. The first, the stage of disposition, makes her worthy to be the Mother of God and is called the Immaculate Conception. The form of perfection really took full hold on her soul in the conception of Christ and her constant life with Him. Finally, in the glory of heaven she is a blazing holocaust of grace, one with God in the beatific vision.

Mary's preparation of soul was perfect. She was sinless in her conception, spotless through all the days of her life. Others had been sanctified in their mother's womb, Jeremias and John the Baptist for instance, but only she was immaculately conceived. Others all through their lives have avoided mortal sin; she alone passed through the course of human life without the slightest stain of even venial sin. . . .

The Annunciation was an instance in which the human heart most closely imitated the enduring embrace of angelic love. It was right that Mary be told of the mystery beforehand. It was right that she receive the Son of God in her mind and her heart before receiving Him in her body; certainly that faith in Him would bring her more joy and more merit than the mere physical bringing of Him into the world. It was right that she who was to be the principal witness of the mystery should, above all others, be certain; and how could she be certain except by divine instruction?

Mary, it must be understood, was not an ignorant peasant girl pushed into divine things unwittingly. This was the Queen of heaven in her youth. Her offer of herself to God was a willing surrender of youth and beauty made with eyes wide open and heart unwavering; her gesture was regal, majestic, marking one of the heights achieved by human nature, for her acceptance was an "I will" of human nature to a spiritual matrimony with God. The Annunciation was a hushed moment in the history of the universe when the fate of the world hung on the response of the Virgin Mary.

The longer we study the scene of the Annunciation, the deeper it digs into our heart with that quietly mysterious penetration we notice in loving regard of the strange familiarity of a loved face. How thoughtful of God to send an angel! It was in complete accord with His general order of providence which makes angels the leaders of men to divine things as it makes all higher things the leaders of the lower; but it was more than that. It was a gesture of apology from angelic nature for the original betrayal by an angel of that nature through a woman. What a pair they make, the Virgin and the angel! How close they approach one another; if St. Jerome was right in maintaining that to live in the flesh but not according to the flesh is not an earthly but a heavenly life, never did human nature approach closer to the angelic. . . .

The material of this chapter might well be summed up in a comparison of Mary with the woman of the modern world, if it be soundly understood that the modern part of that comparison does not signify this or that woman, or group of women, but the modern ideal. What is said of modern woman, then, is by no means a wholesale condemnation of the women of the twentieth century; rather, it is an exposition of the position of woman today in the light of the things approved or disapproved, applauded or mocked by the philosophy by which our age directs its life. With this caution well in mind, we may ask what is the result of the application of the fundamental tests of woman's life to Mary's and the Christian woman's life as against the woman of the pagan world.

We have seen something of Mary's sublime sanctity, her absolute virginity; something of her regard for marriage; and her justice to herself, her Child, to Joseph, and to society. We have seen her response to the high call of love. What of the modern woman?

What chance has she to strive for sanctity when the very existence of the soul is denied, the freedom of the will rejected, and the moral code scoffed at as a mere convention? Virginity? A personal matter of fastidiousness or of social fitness, when it is not something to be tossed away quickly in the name of development of personality. Is marriage thought of in terms of justice to the child, to the husband, to society; or rather in terms of physical beauty and social convenience? . . .

We have looked at Mary's life as a preparation for divine maternity, a preparation of soul through sanctity, of body through virginity; as enveloping the lives of men in relation to marriage, and as reaching to the heights of the angels in the Annunciation. What would be the preparation of the woman of our time if she were to follow the ideals of her age? Surely not sanctity. Hardly virginity. For marriage there would be some physical, financial, emotional, and social reasons considered; but that would pretty well sum it all up. A shorter summary could be made by simply listing the considerations of self.

The fruits of such lives are fruits worthy of the sowing. Mary was blessed among women. In her lifetime she won unselfish love, the joy of caring for her Son, the triumph of Calvary, the sorrows of earth, and the glories of heaven. Just such fruits have come to the Christian mother ever since. The pagan earns the scorn of men for her cowardice, her shallowness, her selfishness, her lust,

or her weakness, though it was at the behest of men that these things were cultivated. She wins indifference from her child, who returns what he has received. There is none of the triumph or exquisite joy of sacrifice, for there is no sacrifice. The shallow pleasures of earth will not drown earth's sorrows. In eternity, at least, there will be many questions to answer.

After all, a woman was not made to live in a world whose philosophy of life is on an animal basis, where strength alone counts, where might is right. In such a world it is the weak who suffer, the women and children; in such a world woman has but two strong points, her youth and her beauty. Who shall blame her for clutching so desperately at them; who shall blame her for not exposing others to such a burden, for refusing to weaken her own precarious[7] position by the burden and dependence of children? Certainly not one who embraces the philosophy by which she is asked to live; yet, in the end, it is precisely such as these that give her the bitterest scorn.

Her life was meant to be lived at least on a human basis of justice. In the divine life of charity she attains her fullest development, her fullest happiness; for here justice and love rule, not strength. On such a basis she has open to her a life of fullest perfection, the kind of life portrayed by the model of women, Mary, the Virgin and Mother. In these two alone a woman can find happiness; she must be either the mother or the virgin, with virginity maintained or, by the bitter path Magdalene walked, regained.

VIEWING THE AUTHOR'S IDEAS

1. According to the author, what are the three bases of human living? By what comparison does he illustrate woman's life on the three levels? On what plane does woman reach her greatest perfection?

2. How was woman regarded in the nineteenth century? What is the status of woman in an age of materialism; an age of rationalism; an age where the supernatural is the ideal? What questions does the author suggest for determining the status of woman in any age?

3. By what four basic tests is Mary the model for all women? Show the difference between the Immaculate Conception and the virgin birth of Christ. What examples does the author use to show the perfection of grace in Mary?

[7] *precarious*, insecure.

4. Summarize the author's reflections on the Annunciation. How was Mary the Queen of Heaven even in her youth?

5. In what respects does the woman of the modern world fail to achieve the ideal exemplified by Mary? Compare the fruits of Mary's life with those of the pagan way of life. How does the author account for the failure of woman in an animal age? In what two paths can woman find greatest happiness?

EVALUATING HIS MANNER OF EXPRESSION

1. Express in your own words the central thought of the selection.

2. From the style of the author is it possible to know that he is a teacher, a magazine writer, an orator, or a person solely engaged in creative literary work? Explain the reasons for your choice.

3. Where is the paradox in the fact that in ages that are most unkind to women, it is women themselves who are often the most aggressive champions of the debased philosophy by which those ages live?

4. Point to the allusion that there have been ages when woman was not considered a free, thinking, and responsible personality. Do you know of ages or times in which woman was considered less than a human being?

5. Outline the argument against the error that *might is right*.

6. Point out three striking analogies; find effective figures of speech. What is the advantage of using nouns, verbs, and adjectives in threes? Note the author's first sentence. Are there other examples of this use of a trilogy of words or phrases?

7. *The Companion to the Summa* is a popular presentation of the teachings of St. Thomas. What features of this selection would appeal to modern readers?

Grace Before Reading

John W. Simons
"On bokes for to rede I me delyte": Chaucer

I

IN THE following essay we are going to discuss an art, the art of reading. Moreover, we are going to discuss it from a specialized viewpoint, that of morality. For reading, like all human activity which is performed with freedom and deliberation, is a moral act. Reading, therefore, has a bearing on the formation of character and influences the direction of our souls. It is well to read, but it is better to read well; and in order to read well we must have a trained, efficient, Catholic conscience. We simply cannot read promiscuously. To do so is to risk the loss of values,—values which are final, supernatural, and eternal.

So far you ought to find it easy to agree. And yet the fact that books are instruments of both good and evil, of light and darkness, is not always admitted by "advanced" thinkers. They feel that any "taboo" on reading frustrates the flowering of the personality; they feel that free men should be allowed to browse the fields of literature with bovine abandon. And this sort of recklessness is made to seem more attractive than repugnant, more a virtue than a vice, when it is recommended in the name of "academic freedom."

Still, however it may be argued, this truth must remain clear: the printed word is power for both good and evil in human affairs. Not long ago a group of American publicists, thinkers, and writers published a symposium entitled *Books That Have Changed Our Minds*. Among noteworthy writers whose influences were reverently acknowledged were Karl Marx, Henry Adams, Charles Darwin, and John Dewey. Authors, of course, are aware of and frequently revel in the authority they exercise over the minds and emotions of men. Both Dickens and Hugo allowed themselves to become intoxicated with this dictatorship of the pen, and in the end came to have a certain contempt for the public, unthinking and tractable, whose suffrages had brought them distinction and wealth.

We start, then, with this axiom: the morally responsible man must be discriminating in his choice of books. The practical application of this axiom is, however, fraught with difficulties. There are two extremes which must be avoided. For convenience we shall call them the ultra-liberal solution (which is not a solution at all, but a flat denial that reading can be a moral problem) and the ultra-conservative solution. The ultra-liberal solution we have already seen, and it may be stated thus: read what you will according to taste and inclination. If there are standards in reading they are intellectual and aesthetic, not moral.

And now for the ultra-conservative solution. Those of you who are familiar with the Puritan backgrounds of American literature know that the reading of books was looked upon with something akin to horror. With the exception of a very few books,— such as the *Bible*, *Pilgrim's Progress*, and *Paradise Lost*,—our forefathers of the New England theocracy eschewed reading as a profane and even satanic preoccupation. It is only fair to add, however, that the few books they did read were studied assiduously and that the strength of these books became part of the Puritan marrow.

All things considered, it remains true that for the Puritan a book was a kind of passport to perdition. We can, perhaps, restate the Puritan solution to reading as a moral problem in the following manner: Almost all books are possible occasions of sin; all possible occasions of sin must be avoided; therefore, almost all books are to be avoided. Now, it is possible to save one's soul in this way, and the price would not be too great if it were the only solution. But it is not the only solution. It is faulty, partial, and narrow. It is altogether too contemptuous of the dignity of our human nature.

The ultra-conservative solution, like the ultra-liberal, has one important advantage. It is exceedingly simple. The Catholic solution is much more complex, but it will be truer to the conditions of human nature, and to that extent will prove more balanced and liberal. This solution will employ a multiplicity of distinctions, but true distinctions are the *magna carta*[1] of a free and active mind and the recognition of them should enlist our best efforts. In the next paragraph we shall enumerate some of the distinctions required by the Catholic solution.

With most of them you will already be familiar. The others you should analyze for yourselves.

We must distinguish between causes and occasions of sin. Occasions of sin may be possible or actual, and actual occasions may be either proximate or remote. Since almost anything *could* be an occasion of sin, we are not obliged to avoid merely possible occasions. We are, of course, obliged to avoid proximate or near occasions. We are not obliged to avoid remote occasions; neither are we expected to court or encourage them. We must also distinguish among the types of consciences. There is the lax conscience which is almost totally indifferent to sin, the scrupulous conscience which creates sin *ex nihilo*[2], the callous conscience which is insensitive to sin, and the tender conscience which has a healthy awareness of sin. A conscience which is in conformity with God's law is a true conscience; a conscience which deviates from God's law is a false conscience.

You will have observed that these distinctions apply, not only to the reading of books, but to all human acts, that is, to all acts involving deliberation and choice. But insofar as the reading of books is, in one of its aspects, a moral act, these distinctions have an eminently practical bearing. And while you may find these distinctions disappointing in that they are familiar and even trite, it is only fair that you ask yourselves whether or not you have put them into practice in your actual reading experience. A sincere Catholic will try to cultivate a true and tender conscience. He will constantly check his conscience against the norm established by his Faith. He will, from the moral viewpoint, read well: neither in panic nor bravado, but with a sane consciousness of the possibilities of evil and an invincible confidence in the soundness of his ethical principles and in the overreaching power of grace.

II

In the second part of our essay we shall speak of the mature as against the immature reader. There are many ways in which a person may be said to mature. He may mature physically, spiritually, intellectually, and — the word will be explained later — aesthetically. In a truly balanced personality there is some kind of

---

[1] *magna carta*, as here used, guarantee of rights.

[2] *ex nihilo*, out of nothing.

co-ordination among these various types of growth. If there is development in one direction and very little or none in others we have an unbalanced personality. At the same time it must be recognized that not all these ways of maturing are of equal importance. Since man's final purpose in life is a spiritual one, spiritual growth is the growth of chief moment. On the other hand, if we make bodily development our almost exclusive concern, as though man's ultimate goal were to wrestle with dinosaurs, we shall have something very like a monster. Swift may call him a Yahoo; Arnold may call him a barbarian or, in another sense, a philistine. In any case, we all recognize the gargantuan impostor.

As one grows spiritually the reading of books becomes less and less a problem. At first sight this may seem strange. Nevertheless it is true, and for two reasons. First of all, a saint need not worry about occasions of sin as much as the rest of us. It was St. Augustine who said *"Ama, et fac quod vis,"* "Love, and you may do what you will." As we grow to love God more, the more detestation we shall have of sin; and the more detestation we have of it, the less likely we are to succumb to its coquetry. Secondly, as we grow in the love of God there will be fewer books that we shall want to read. Indeed, some of the great saints abandoned reading altogether, not because they had no love for beauty or truth, but because, being in intimate contact with Supreme Beauty and Supreme Truth, all lesser manifestations of these attributes were without savor. (You will note how removed this attitude is from that of the Puritan. Love is the arbiter here, not fear.) It is not likely, however, that most of us will be able to approach the problem of reading from this high altitude. Still, in proportion to our becoming spiritually mature, the problem should become less and less.

So far as intellectual growth is concerned we are still "in process." Anyone who has made an effort to disengage a central idea from the clinging folds of language knows that thinking is not play, but arduous and exacting labor. Our minds are true but imperfect instruments for probing into the opacity[3] of things. Yet the mind is our noblest faculty and is worthy of careful development. In order, however, to use the mind efficiently we must be sure just how trustworthy

an instrument it is. Although the object of the mind is truth, there are truths above and beyond its search. Certain of the revealed truths, such as the Trinity or the Incarnation, could not be known had not God taken the world into His confidence. And even those truths which are within the scope and power of human intelligence oftentimes elude us, not because these truths are in themselves incomprehensible, but because all minds are not equally astute[4] and because emotion and prejudice have a way of hampering their free activity.

What has all this to do with reading? Many of the books which you will read, and many others which you ought to read, are of their very nature a challenge to your aptitude for deep thought. Since they traffic in ideas, they must be read actively if they are to yield their full cultural value. To read well we must think well. Reading and thinking are related activities, and to mature in thought is to mature in reading ability. (Incidentally, if you wish to examine this relationship in greater detail and at the same time improve your efficiency as a reader, you can hardly do better than to study Mortimer Adler's book, *How to Read a Book*.) We usually enjoy the reading we deserve to enjoy. If your reading ability does not progressively increase after you leave school, and usually it does not, it is quite likely that as a thinker you have reached a cul de sac[5]. Intellectually you will be immature.

An intelligent reader will be, at the same time, a docile reader. Knowing as he does the limitations of the human mind, he will sense the fact that certain ideas are in some subtle way false, and, unable to cope with these ideas, will look for guidance to his intellectual superiors. The Catholic reader has an infallible guide to warn him off from ideas which militate against the Eternal Truths of which Christ has made her the custodian. The Church is not an obscurantist[6], and she seldom directly condemns books, but when she does so it is a danger signal that we must in conscience obey. Perhaps we can illustrate by example.

A philosopher sets out to discover the nature of language. It seems an innocent enough occupation and would certainly seem to have very little to do with the

---

[3] *opacity*, the quality of being obscure.

[4] *astute*, keen.

[5] *cul de sac*, a passage having only one outlet.

[6] *obscurantist*, one who strives to prevent progress or the spread of knowledge.

problem of eternal salvation. But in the course of his inquiry he comes to some startling conclusions. He says that words stand for something in the mind, but that this something in the mind has no real relationship with things outside the mind. He finally decides that we are shut up in ourselves as in a prison, that there is no way of breaking through this prison, that when we talk to one another we are exchanging mere words, and that no real knowledge results from this communication, and so on. Now, the Church has no theory of language of her own. A theory of language is not, in and of itself, a question of Faith or morals. But the Church does teach, and claims Divine sanction for so teaching, that man can arrive at a knowledge of God from created things. Obviously, if, as our philosopher contends, we cannot know created things, then neither can we, through their mediation, come to a knowledge of God. I cannot reach Times Square by means of a bus if I cannot reach a bus. The Church, therefore, may condemn such a book because of its danger to faith. She does not say that its arguments are unanswerable, but she does maintain that the average nonphilosophic mind is unable to see through their speciousness[7], and this is a fact of experience. If you think you are a philosopher, you may receive permission to read such a book, but you cannot give that permission to yourself.

III

Besides intellectual and spiritual maturity there is aesthetic maturity. By reading aesthetically we mean reading with a prompt and sensitive response to beauty. In literature and in the fine arts generally — painting, music, sculpture — we discover the material which of its nature claims both to incite and alleviate our nostalgia for the beautiful. In literature it is poetry, more exclusively than the other verbal arts, which bears the burden of beauty.

Now it is an extraordinary fact that while "beauty" is one of the most commonly employed words of our language it is one of the most difficult to analyze. This is because the concept of beauty is what philosophers call a transcendental, and one of the things that this means is that beauty is a concept which eludes definition. St.

Augustine defines beauty as *"splendor ordinis,"* "the radiance of order"; St. Thomas Aquinas defines it as "the splendor of form shining on the proportioned parts of matter." But definitions like these, though arrived at only by the long and labored scrutiny of the philosophic mind, are not very helpful to the ordinary reader. It was Plato who reminded us centuries ago that "the beautiful is difficult." It is indeed; and the only reason we have dealt with the notion at all is in the hope that it will make you more wary in its use. If we insist on making "beautiful" a synonym for "pretty" or "handsome" or "elegant," we have thoroughly debased the word and at the same time revealed the poverty of our aesthetic experience.

It is true that many high school students have a prejudice against poetry. As a matter of fact, a dislike for a certain type of over-excited and sentimental verse is a sign of health rather than disease. But there cannot be a reasoned objection to poetry unless there is dislike of beauty, and all of us, at however rudimentary a stage, are lovers of beautiful things. It is not the business of this essay to tell you how to educate this rudimentary sense of the beautiful, but a few hints will scarcely be out of order. First of all, those who are prejudiced against poetry must make an honest effort to rectify their attitude. Ordinarily, this cannot be done without help, and the best help will come from one who at an earlier time shared your prejudices. This is imperative, for if you have decided in advance that all poetry is "silly" or "sissy," you have already insulated yourselves against whatever magic it may possess.

Second, you must experiment with that vast body of literature which has long been accepted as containing in an eminent way the quality we designate as beautiful. This experimentation must be done with skill and deliberation. Patience is as much a requirement for the apprehension of the beautiful as it is for the apprehension of the true. As you progress in your appreciations you will begin to isolate the quality of experience which we term aesthetic. You will discover that this quality of experience is something unique, something infinitely superior to earlier and more mechanical perceptions. You will begin to become impatient with too ready and too obvious emotional stimulants and you will begin to reject earlier aesthetic experiences as in some way trivial or crude. In short, you will have begun to grow critical.

[7] *speciousness*, the quality which makes a thing actually erroneous appear to be correct.

It is of the nature of beauty that the joy which it solicits is of a kind which overflows the mind and inundates the senses. That is to say, the aesthetic experience is not only intellectual, but affective and emotional. Now all emotional states are not of the same quality or value. We all know that there are unworthy emotions and that the indulgence in certain types of emotion can be sinful. It is possible that a truly beautiful poem may stimulate, though secondarily and accidentally, the lower passions. It is not this fact which constitutes the beauty of the poem, for the aesthetic response is not an erotic response, and it would be very wrong to condemn the poem as a *poem* on purely moral grounds. The converse[8] is likewise a danger. We cannot toy with all kinds of poetry merely on the plea of devotion to the beautiful. An occasion of sin is, according to its immediacy, to be shunned, and one is saved, not through art, but through grace. Finally, it is to be remembered that the emotional life of individuals is variously constituted and that there are degrees of sensitivity to emotional stimuli. The *poem* which constitutes an occasion of sin for one does not necessarily do so for another. "Watch ye and pray, that ye enter not into temptation."

IV

Our final paragraphs will treat of the novel, since this is by far and away the most popular of literary forms. We may say that, in general, the novel is of two types, romantic and realistic. The romantic novel deals with life, not as it is, but either as it might be, or ought to be, or is imagined to have been in some remote time or place. It is basically an escape from life as we know it; it is a retreat from actuality. The realistic novel, on the other hand, pretends to evoke life as it is actually lived; it dwells by preference in the here and now and is immensely concerned with the why's and wherefore's of human behavior.

Now in our own day it is the realistic novel which has captured the imagination of the reading public. The reason for this is, in part, the perennial interest of mankind in man. There are, however, other factors which must be taken into consideration; particularly the advent of new sciences or pseudosciences, such as sociology and psychology, with their innumerable subalterns.[9] Still, and this is most important, a novel remains fiction whether it is romantic or realistic. This is only to say that it is the product of an artist. It is he who creates the characters and the situations which provide their milieu, and this remains true no matter to what extent he may depend upon his observation of actual life. It is the author who gives form and movement to the novel as a work of art, and it is he who is responsible for the impact it makes upon the minds of his readers.

It should be clear from this that the novelist himself, rightly or wrongly, becomes an important factor in the selection of a novel. We must know from what vantage point he views reality, what preconceptions he has of the nature and function of man, what meaning, if any, he gives to life. If, for example, a novelist disbelieves in original sin and its consequences, his projection of character will be unfocused and unreal. The misbehavior of man must be accounted for, and, in the absence of the Christian concept of sin, other concepts must be substituted. It is not unusual, therefore, to find a novelist who accounts for man's less desirable antics by placing the full burden on factors extrinsic to himself—on environment, for example, or heredity, or over-active glands. Where the burden is not placed on factors extrinsic to the personality, as in the case of certain of the Freudian novelists, the human personality is treated as a case study in pathology, and sin becomes a disease to be cured rather than a wrong to be repented. Now all these things, external or internal, do condition man's behavior and the novelist is right in taking them into account. On the other hand, they by no means account for the whole of man's activity, and they leave him untouched at that central point where good and evil struggle for possession under the auspices of grace and free will.

Sin is, unfortunately, an all too obvious fact of human experience, and we cannot expect our novelists to ignore it. What is important is the attitude from which they view it and the skill and delicacy with which they portray it. Sigrid Undset, to take an instance, is, from the Catholic viewpoint, a very sound analyst of human behavior, and she depicts characters who are often hopelessly caught in the toils of sin. Since she is

---

8 *converse*, the reverse in order.

9 *subalterns*, subordinates.

a powerful and dramatic writer, the episodes dealing with sin are highly evocative. Sin, after all, is attractive; else we should not commit it. This is the artist's justification. But the problem is not nearly so simple as that, for it is quite possible that in portraying sin the novelist unwittingly incites to sin. A truly conscientious novelist recognizes the gravity of this problem and is tortured by it. Francois Mauriac, sensitively Catholic, has dealt with it understandingly in his essay "God and Mammon."

Writing in behalf of the Catholic novelist, Maritain tells us that the essential question is not whether the writer can legitimately portray any given aspect of moral evil. What is of primary importance is *from what altitude* he depicts it "and whether his art and mind are pure enough and strong enough to depict it without connivance."[10] And he goes on to quote Bernanos: "Take the characters of Dostoievsky, those whom he himself called *The Possessed*. We know the diagnosis of the great Russian in regard to them. But what would have been the diagnosis of a Curé d'Ars, for instance? What would he have seen in those obscure souls?"

What is true of the writer is also true of the reader. All depends on the integrity of the mind and will, on the purity and simplicity of the heart. At the same time the adolescent reader is confronted with particular problems, and he must not complicate or jeopardize their solution. The average high school student is busy integrating his life into a new and more complex pattern. He is, as a rule, being confronted for the first time with an emotional world which has a tendency to be intractable and unruly, and he has the task to legislate for that world and reduce it to order. He cannot afford at this time, more than at any other, to expose himself rashly to a realm of fiction in which sin has a dominant place. St. Teresa calls the imagination "the clown of the house." It is the faculty which, by the pictures it offers and suggests, disturbs the peace of our interior selves. We must be wise porters, and repulse from the threshold of our souls all that may disturb or corrupt, all that may sear or destroy.

In summary, the good Catholic reader must develop himself along three lines—the spiritual, the intellectual, and the aesthetic. He must have a firm grasp of moral

principles and a deep and active love for God if he is to submit himself to that world of art where moral evil plays a legitimate and integral role. He will honestly recognize the peculiar difficulties attendant upon his adolescent state and will be more than usually wary at this critical stage. He will be a docile reader, and he will heed alike the danger signals broadcast from his own conscience and from the watch tower of his Mother, the Church. And, as a colophon: he will read frequently God's own word in the New Testament; he will read the great devotional classics; he will read of the splendid spiritual adventures of the Saints. In brief, he will frequently read as an act of prayer, so as to develop a mind and heart at ease in the climate of the supernatural. We do not live to read; we read to live, and to live in the most exalted sense. "Every moment," says St. Francis de Sales, "comes to us pregnant with a command from God, only to pass on and plunge into eternity, there to remain forever what we have made of it." Wake up and live!

VIEWING THE AUTHOR'S IDEAS

1. What makes reading a moral act?

2. Within the paragraphs of the essay find three statements which explain the influence of books and other reading material.

3. How are so-called advanced thinkers erroneous in believing that men may read indiscriminately without risk?

4. Explain the ultra-liberal solution to the moral problem involved in reading. What was the ultra-conservative solution advocated by the Puritans? Show the weakness of each of these viewpoints.

5. What distinction does the Catholic teaching make concerning the possibility of exposing the reader to occasions of sin? Show what bearing these distinctions have on one's reading.

6. Name the types of development which are required for the cultivation of a balanced personality. In what does undue emphasis on the physical development of man result?

7. Show how sanctity solves the moral problem involved in reading.

8. Why is it necessary to read well if one is to think well? What guide has the Catholic when he senses a false philosophy in a book?

9. Point out the falsehood in the theory of language here presented as an example of erroneous thought.

---

[10] *connivance*, passive consent.

10. What is meant by reading aesthetically? Give the definition of beauty offered by St. Augustine; by St. Thomas Aquinas. Why is it debasing to make the meaning of the word beauty synonymous with such words as *pretty* and *elegant?*

EVALUATING HIS MANNER OF EXPRESSION

1. Show instances in which the author's style reveals its simplicity, directness, and grace.

2. The author does not make statements without strongly reinforcing them. He first states a fact and then proves its truth. Point out several paragraphs in which you find the statement of a significant thought followed by a logical development of the idea.

3. Point out examples of vocabulary in which the words are particularly well suited to the thought.

Pontificate of Leo XIII

(From *A Generation of Materialism*)
Carlton J. H. Hayes

The author here presents Pope Leo XIII as the great champion of Christian principles in the last quarter of the nineteenth century. The spirit of the times — a devotion to material concerns and a disregard for spiritual and eternal values — was directly opposed to the ethical standards promulgated by the Supreme Pontiff. In this generation of materialism Professor Hayes sees the seedtime of contemporary disillusionment and conflicts.

WHEN Pius IX died on February 7, 1878, after the longest and one of the stormiest pontificates in Christian history, the Catholic Church seemed to be at losing a feud with the whole modern world, intellectually, politically, and morally. Its influence on the life and thought of the fashioners of public opinion — leading men of letters, journalists, educators, and scholars — was fast disappearing; and its hold was gone on a large fraction of the bourgeoisie[1] and on the bulk of the urban proletariat.[2] It appeared impotent to dike anywhere the flood tide of "science," liberalism, Marxism,[3] anti-clericalism, and secularization. Its foes had mastered Italy and despoiled the church of its age-old capital city and of a vast deal of popular prestige. They were dominant in Austria and Switzerland and were waging in Germany a bitter

Kulturkampf[4] against it. They had recently assailed it with revolutionary ardor in Spain, and in Belgium they were just returning to power and battle. Likewise in France, "the eldest daughter of the church," foes of Catholicism in the guise of Radical Republicans were besting its friends, the Monarchists. And in England the "second spring" which the Oxford movement once promised had proved disappointingly backward. The definition of papal infallibility at the Vatican Council in 1870 seemed a Pyrrhic victory[5] for the papacy; if it closed the Catholic ranks, it also depleted them and aggravated enemy attacks.

With fear and trembling, sixty-four elderly cardinals entered the conclave in the Vatican to choose Pius' successor. To forestall possible external interference, they acted quickly; and on the third scrutiny,[6] on February 20, they chose Cardinal Pecci, the scion[7] of an impoverished noble family, who took the title of Leo XIII. He was already close to sixty-eight years of age and had been archbishop of Perugia for thirty-two years. He was almost unknown outside Italy, except by the few who recalled him as papal nuncio to Belgium back in the 1840's. His election was a makeshift. He was frail and not expected to live long.

---

[1] *bourgeoisie* (bŏŏ-zhwä-zē'), a social order dominated by the middle classes.

[2] *urban proletariat*, laboring classes in cities.

[3] *Marxism*, the socialist theories of Karl Marx.

[4] *Kulturkampf,* the nineteenth-century struggle between the Church and the German government over educational and ecclesiastical appointments.

[5] *Pyrrhic victory*, a success gained at too great cost.

[6] *scrutiny*, an ecclesiastical method of election by secret written ballot, as in a conclave.

[7] *scion* (sī'-ŭn), a descendant.

Yet Leo XIII lived on a quarter century to the age of ninety-three, acquiring fame comparable with any medieval pope's. This unexpected outcome was a product of his personal qualities and of changing circumstances of his pontificate. Leo might be frail of physique, but within his emaciated body resided a brilliant mind and an iron will. He was, too, a humanist, at once artist and scholar and cultured man of the world. A facile writer of Latin verse and Ciceronian prose, he also had sympathetic understanding of the intellectual problems of the modern age and a singular practicality in dealing with them. He was as determined as any of his predecessors to combat materialism, agnosticism, and indifferentism; but he was not content simply to repeat the anathemas[8] of Pius IX. He must constructively expound Christian alternatives.

In almost the first of his long series of encyclicals — the *Æterni Patris* of 1879 — Leo pointed to the medieval scholastic philosophy of St. Thomas Aquinas, with its reconciling of faith and reason, of theology and "science," as the fundamental corrective of the vagaries of modern philosophy, and urged its revival and extension. To this end he founded and endowed at Rome an academy bearing the great schoolman's name, directed the preparation and publication of a new edition of the *Summa,*[9] and patronized centers for neo-Thomistic[10] study at Louvain, Paris, Fribourg, and Salzburg, and also at the Catholic University of America, which he personally chartered in 1889. Similarly, he encouraged the study of church history, opening the Vatican archives and library to historical research in 1883 and honoring such scholars as Newman and Hergenröther (whom he made cardinals in 1879), Denifle, Grisar, Pastor, Gasquet, Mancini, Ulysse Chevalier, Luchaire, Duchesne, and Baudrillart. He also fostered Christian archaeology[11] and biblical studies; and to demonstrate his respect for natural science, he procured an eminent staff of physicists and the most up-to-date instruments for the astronomical observatory at the Vatican.

Of the political principles of Pius IX, Leo XIII professed not to change an iota. He insisted that the Catholic Church is a perfect society in itself whose authority in its own spiritual realm is, by divine institution, independent of and superior to the authority of any temporal state or sovereignty; and hence that it should occupy a privileged position in the state. Yet he was never a "reactionary" in the earlier sense. He contended, especially in the encyclicals *Immortale Dei* (1885) and *Libertas* (1888), that democracy is as compatible with Catholic philosophy and tradition as any other modes of civil government; and that real personal liberty, as distinct from sectarian liberalism,[12] has its firmest base and surest prop in Catholic Christianity. He would Christianize democracy and liberty.

Church support of the current trend toward democracy, Leo perceived, might be serviceable to the church. It would show the masses that they could expect the fulfillment of their political aspirations under Catholic as well as non-Catholic auspices, and it might thus bring them back to the faithful practice of their religion. A like policy, looking toward the same end, Leo pursued in respect of popular demands for social reform. He would Christianize modern industrial society; and for such a Catholic social movement his most famous encyclical, *Rerum novarum* (1891), supplied chart and inspiration. Against Marxian socialism this document defended private property as a natural right, emphasized the key importance of the family, protested against the exalting of the state, condemned the doctrines of economic materialism and determinism,[13] and declared that "class is not naturally hostile to class." On the other hand, against economic liberalism,[14] it held that "labor is not a commodity"; that "it is shameful to treat men like chattels to make money by"; that the state has both right and duty to prevent the exploitation[15]

---

[8] *anathemas*, denunciations, excommunications.

[9] *Summa*, the *Summa Theologica*, a comprehensive work on theology by St. Thomas Aquinas.

[10] *neo-Thomistic*, pertaining to the revival of Scholasticism, or the teachings of St. Thomas.

[11] *archaeology*, the scientific study of the remains of past human life and activity.

[12] *sectarian liberalism*, a term applied to the principles of the nineteenth-century liberal parties which promoted the interests of industrial and professional groups. This liberalism was characterized by its devotion to personal liberty, wealth, and material comforts, science, secular education, and free enterprise. It was hostile to the restraints of religion and morality and persecuted the Church as its chief opponent.

[13] *economic materialism and determinism*, the view that social betterment is the result of material prosperity.

[14] *economic liberalism*, the theory that business and industry should be left free to develop without any restrictions.

[15] *exploitation*, the base use of persons or things for selfish gain or profit.

of labor, to encourage collective bargaining,[16] and to enact social legislation. Specifically the encyclical urged a wider distribution of private property, a fostering of industrial trade-unions and agricultural co-operative undertakings, a restriction of the hours of employment, especially of women and children, and the assurance of a "living family wage." It stressed the dignity of labor and stated that "everyone has the right to procure what is required to live." It dwelt upon the part which religion in general and Christianity in particular should perform in bringing about a better social order; and it besought the co-operation of Catholics everywhere.

The response to this as to other pleas of Leo XIII was not altogether gratifying. Many Catholic employers paid little attention to it, and it did not stop the spread of Marxian socialism among workingmen, just as the Pope's democratic counsels went unheeded by numerous Catholic aristocrats and snobs; or just as, in the general intellectual life of Europe, there was no marked abatement of materialism and positivism. Yet the response was considerable. In Germany, Belgium, Austria-Hungary, Switzerland, and Holland well-knit Catholic parties subscribed to Leo's platform of Christian democracy and Christian liberty and gained large popular followings. In these countries, moreover, and also in France and elsewhere, the Leonine social movement gradually developed with attendant Catholic trade-unions and Catholic propaganda among urban and rural workers. Thereby, new energy was infused into Catholic ranks, and the drift away from the Church was checked among the masses as among the classes. "We must not have any illusions on this score," said a prominent French Marxist in 1898; "the only redoubtable adversary which confronts revolutionary socialism is organized Catholicism, which now has a social conscience and is a party of concessions."

---

[16] *collective bargaining*, the process for settlement of wages and hours of work by agreement between employers and organized groups of workers.

The organizing of Catholics on the religious, intellectual, social, and political *terrains* was an outstanding achievement of the pontificate of Leo XIII. Its climax was the series of Eucharistic Congress, inaugurated in 1881, which, by bringing together in one city after another throughout Christendom ever vaster multitudes of worshipers, periodically testified in most impressive manner to the hold which their religion had upon them.

VIEWING THE AUTHOR'S IDEAS

1. What conditions existed in the Church at the time of Pius IX's death? Why does the author call the definition of papal infallibility a Pyrrhic victory?

2. Describe the election of Leo XIII. What positions had the new Pope held previously? How does the author account for Leo XIII's fame?

3. By what means did Leo XIII foster Catholic learning? How did he uphold democracy? What did he hope to achieve for the Church by supporting the democratic movement?

4. What social and economic reforms are charted in the famous encyclical of Leo XIII, *Rerum novarum?* Why was the response to the document not entirely gratifying? Show that the encyclical did not correct all abuses.

5. What was the outstanding achievement of the pontificate of Leo XIII? Find out when and where the Eucharistic Congress has been held in the United States.

EVALUATING HIS MANNER OF EXPRESSION

1. What makes this selection a good example of historical exposition?

2. Why is the following sentence forceful: "It appeared impotent to dike anywhere the flood tide of 'science'?" Find other examples of forceful phraseology.

3. What is the purpose of the quotation from "a prominent French Marxist in 1898"? Does the quotation achieve its purpose?

4. By consulting an encyclopedia or the *Dictionary of Catholic Facts*, show the relationship between the encyclicals *Quadragesimo anno* and *Rerum novarum*.

Letter to Jackie

Commander John J. Shea, U.S.N.

In November, 1942, the aircraft carrier Wasp *was sunk in the Battle of the Solomons. Commander John J. Shea went down to his death with his ship. Five months before, he had written the following letter to his son Jackie. His letter stands today a memorial to his patriotism and Catholicity.*

June 29, 1942

Dear Jackie:

This is the first letter I have written directly to my little son. I am thrilled to know you can read it all by yourself. If you miss some of the words, Mother will help you, I am sure.

I was certainly glad to hear your voice on the long-distance telephone. It sounded as if I were right in the living room with you. You sounded as if you missed Daddy very much. I miss you, too, more than anyone will ever know. It is too bad this war could not have been delayed a few years, so that I could grow up again with you and do all the things I planned, when you were older.

How nice it would have been to come home early in the afternoon and play ball and go mountain climbing and see the trees and brooks, to learn all about woodcraft, hunting, fishing, swimming, and other things like that. I suppose we must be brave and put these things off now for awhile.

When you are a little bigger, you will know why Daddy is not home so much any more. We have a big country, with ideals as to how people should live and enjoy its riches, how each is born with equal rights to life, freedom, and pursuit of happiness. Unfortunately, there are countries in the world where they don't have these ideals; where a boy can't grow up to what he wants to be — such as a great priest, a statesman, a doctor, a soldier, or a businessman.

Because of these countries who want to change our nation, its ideals, its form of government and way of life, we must leave our homes and families to fight. Defending our country, ideals, homes, and honor is a duty which Daddy must do before he can come home to you and Mother. When it is done, he is coming home to be with you always and forever. So wait just a little while longer. I'm afraid it will be more than the two weeks you told me on the phone.

Meanwhile, take good care of Mother, be a good boy, and grow up to be a good young man. Study hard at school. Be a leader in everything good in life. Be a good Catholic, and you can't help being a good American. Play fair always. Strive to win; but if you lose, lose like a gentleman and a good sportsman. Don't ever be a quitter, either in sports or in your work when you grow up. Get all the education you can. Stay close to Mother and follow her advice. Obey her in everything, no matter how you may at times disagree. She knows what is best and will never let you down or lead you away from the right and honorable things of life.

If I don't get back, you'll have to be Mother's protector because you will be the only one she has. You must grow up to take my place as well as your own in her life and heart. Love Grandmother and Grandad as long as they live. They, too, will never let you down. Love your aunts and see them often. Last of all, don't ever forget Daddy, pray for him to come back; and if it is God's will that he does not, be the kind of boy and man Daddy wants you to be. Kiss Mother for me every night. Goodby for now. With all my love and devotion for Mother and you.

Your Daddy.

1. What prompted Commander Shea to write this letter? How would such a letter be likely to influence the development of a son's character?

2. Which passages do you consider the most important; the most touching?

3. How does the letter reveal Commander Shea's character? Why is he a representative American?

4. Discuss the statement, "Be a good Catholic, and you can't help being a good American."

5. What reasons are stated for going to war? Is Commander Shea's participation the result of conviction or expediency? Support your view by citing phrases and sentences.

EVALUATING HIS MANNER OF EXPRESSION

1. Did Commander Shea write for publication? Explain your view. In one word suggest the oustanding characteristic of the content of this letter.

2. What are the qualities of a good letter? To what extent are these qualities present in the letter to Jackie?

Adrift on the Pacific

(From We Thought We Heard the Angels Sing)
Lieutenant James Whittaker

In October, 1942, the Flying Fortress carrying Captain Eddie Rickenbacker and his seven companions crashed in the South Pacific. Adrift on small rubber rafts, the men fought hunger, thirst, sharks, and death for twenty-one days. Lieutenant Whittaker tells how the experience led him from agnosticism to faith in God. In this selection, narrating the happenings of the eleventh to the thirteenth day, he gives an account of an answer to prayer.

Throughout the late watches of the chilling night I sat sleeplessly thinking over our condition and the state of my own soul. It was not a pleasant line of thought.

I had been an agnostic;[1] an atheist, if you will. I am not sure I am using either term correctly. I imagined that I doubted the existence of any such being as God. I reasoned further when religion was mentioned that God never had done much for me in my life; so why should I go through the motions of worshiping Him? The most I could salvage for myself from these gloomy thoughts was that I at least had never been a hypocrite.

I pondered that night on an expression I had heard somewhere out in the Southwest Pacific: "There are no atheists in the foxholes of Guadalcanal." I can tell you now that there can be no atheists in rubber rafts amid whitecaps and sharks in the equatorial Pacific. I was finding my God in those watery wastes, and we were meeting as strangers. I don't deny that there was still a reluctance somewhere deep within me. After forty years and more of indifference and selfishness, it would have been strange indeed if I hadn't felt something of the sort.

We might have remained strangers had it not been for Him. He soon was to send two divine miracles that twice more were to save my life and change the way of it, about as completely as a life can be changed.

My thoughts now shifted to the physical state of our little band. It seemed years since we had eaten Bill Cherry's baby shark.[2] But somehow that didn't matter. I wasn't hungry any more. The thing I felt I must have before another day had passed was water — and lots of it. I prayed. I began to believe we would have the water. He would send it.

But I had a feeling also of apprehension. In more than ten days of helpless drifting with thirst, hunger, and heat, and the ever-present shadow of death as my companions, I seemed to have become strangely psychic.[3] We had endured the first three. Now Death was ready at last to strike at our little band.

The sun rose behind a bank of threatening clouds on that eleventh morning. As it grew brighter, we could see rain squalls dotting the ocean. The clouds drifting low in the distance would open up without warning, and

---

[1] *agnostic*, one who believes that neither the existence nor the nature of God is known or knowable.

[2] *Bill Cherry's baby shark*, Captain Bill Cherry, the pilot, had killed a baby shark which had served as food.

[3] *psychic*, sensitive to nonphysical forces.

that deep blue curtain we had so often prayed for would descend to the sea.

While we watched, a heavy black cloud floated over us, and the bottom seemed to fall out of it. The rain flooded down on our rafts.

We were wise this time and used every facility available for catching and storing water. I have spoken before of the rubber seats that we inflated by hand, separately from the raft itself. We now cut one of these out of our boat and used it as a rain catcher, storing the water in Bill Cherry's Mae West.[4] We slaked our thirst. And again the sheets of cleansing and cooling water washed our bodies free of the caked salt. This was a grand relief for the men who were suffering from saltwater ulcers.

We had put away four quarts of rain water when a squall hit our area, and we were kept busy bailing the rafts and keeping them from going over. The two bigger ones weathered the blow. The wind was too much, however, for the doughnut[5] in which De Angelis and Alex Kaczmarczyk were riding. Just as the rain was ending, the little raft went over.

We soon saw that Alex was unable to get back in alone. De Angelis was trying to help him. De Angelis was weak also, and it was too much for him. We all helped, and after a struggle got Alex back into his place. It was obvious that he was in a bad way.

Thirst, hunger, exposure, and exhaustion had dissipated the little store of strength he had mustered after his discharge from the hospital at Honolulu. De Angelis now told us that Alex had been drinking salt water during moments of delirium.

Alex was delirious now. He didn't recognize us. His head felt very hot. Every now and then he would call out some meaningless remark. Rickenbacker spoke to him sharply, trying to snap him out of it. Then realizing the Sergeant's true condition, Rick ordered that he be put into the larger raft. Johnny Bartek was sent over to ride the doughnut boat with De Angelis.

During the day Alex was given regular doles[6] of water. If there had only been nourishing food to give him! All that night Rickenbacker held the boy in his arms to protect him from the spray and to keep him warm. He appeared improved at dawn of the twelfth day, but it was the last dawn he was ever to see.

Alex remained rational during the morning, becoming delirious only after the sun had driven the clouds away in the early afternoon. He rallied again when it got cooler, and just at dark he said he felt well enough to spend the night in his own raft. We all were greatly relieved. If he could only hold out just a little longer!

De Angelis now moved into Rickenbacker's boat, and Bartek remained in the little raft with Alex, who was able to whisper his part in the saying of the Lord's Prayer at our service. The rafts strung out again in line, and for a time all was quiet except for the slap and slosh of the ocean.

Alex's delirium returned late in the night. The things he said and talked about I haven't the heart to repeat. They concerned his mother and a girl. Sometime after midnight his voice dropped to a mumble. At two a.m. Bartek called to us:

"Hey, you fellows, I'm afraid Alex is dead."

We hauled the small raft up so that it lay between the two larger ones. Rickenbacker examined him and asked that Cherry and I do the same. It was true. Rickenbacker said we could do nothing until daylight. The rafts were allowed to string out again.

When our thirteenth dawn came up, I saw that Johnny Bartek had been holding his little Testament in his hands, although it was too dark to read. The east flamed up in spectacular shafts of red, purple, and gold. The sun seemed to leap out of the sea into the sky.

With the fleet reassembled we said the Lord's Prayer. Then Lieutenant De Angelis recited as much as he could remember of the moving Roman Catholic burial service.[7] Both he and Alex were of that faith. I remember a little here and there:

"O God, great and omnipotent Judge of the living and dead! before Whom we are all to appear after this short life; let our hearts be moved at this sight of death; and as we consign the body to the sea, let us be mindful of our own frailty and mortality . . . Eternal rest grant to him, O Lord, and may eternal light shine upon him."

Johnny Bartek fastened the zippers of Alex's flying suit. We said the Lord's Prayer again and put him into

---

[4] *Mae West*, a life preserver that is inflated before use.

[5] *doughnut*, an inflated rubber raft.

[6] *doles*, portions.

· [7] *burial service*, this is one of the prayers of the burial service recited in many places after Mass or at the grave. Whittaker reproduces the prayer exactly with the exception of a few phrases.

the water. I could see him for a long time. Nothing bothered him.

We held our usual morning-prayer service; then we were quiet for a long time. Alex had been a good boy. It was maddening to think we lacked the food and medicines that would have saved him. We had done all we could.

The burial service took our minds off ourselves for a time. The blazing heat was not long, however, in bringing back our thirst and intensifying the agonies of the six afflicted with salt-water ulcers. I think I was more depressed than at any other time. It was hard to keep from seeing in Alex's fate the precursor of my own.

I couldn't know, of course, that the first of the two miracles was almost upon us. The thing that happened was miraculous then, and it grows in proportion as I think of it now.

This thirteenth day adrift had burst upon us as a scorcher. Just after ten o'clock a rain squall blotted out the sun. Our hopes rose. The familiar blue curtain of rain moved toward us across the sea. We prayed aloud for it to reach us. It was less than a quarter of a mile off when a perverse wind shunted it away.

Somehow my faith did not die. For the first time I found myself leading the rest in prayer. Like many of the others I didn't know how to address God properly. I talked to Him, therefore, as I would have to a parent or a friend.

"God," I prayed, "You know what that water means to us. The wind has blown it away. It is in Your power, God, to send back that rain. It's nothing to You, but it means life to us."

Some of the others had given up. Someone said in disgust that the bloody wind would blow in that direction another forty years. I took my cue from this and continued:

"God, the wind is Yours. You own it. Order it to blow back that rain to us, who will die without it."

There are some things that can't be explained by natural law. The wind did not change, but the receding curtain of rain stopped where it was. Then ever so slowly it started back toward us — against the wind!

Maybe a meteorologist[8] can explain that to your satisfaction. One tried it with me; something about

crosscurrents buffeting the squall back. I tell you that there was no buffeting. It moved back with majestic deliberation. It was as if a great and omnipotent hand was guiding it to us across the water. And for my money that's exactly what happened.

We caught a great store of water and luxuriated as the cool deluge flooded down our bodies. Many of the men had shed skin three or four times by now. There were raw spots where they had chafed against the walls of the narrow rafts. In addition, the ulcers were growing worse hourly.

Those men will know until the end of their days what it means to have salt in a wound. The cool rain that came from the skies was their only relief.

The rain that came that day was a Godsend. I use the capital *G* intentionally. Without this relief I don't know how we would have got through the four days of doldrums[9] that were just ahead and which were to be the most terrible part of our ordeal.

VIEWING THE AUTHOR'S IDEAS

1. What thoughts filled the mind of Lieutenant Whittaker after ten days of drifting on the Pacific? Describe the condition of the men. What characteristics are shown in their care and consideration of their sick companion? Why was Sergeant Kaczmarczyk unable to survive the ordeal?

2. List the most impressive aspects of the burial at sea. How can you account for the fact that Lieutenant De Angelis remembered so much of the Catholic service? What significance did the circumstances give to the lines quoted by Lieutenant Whittaker?

3. How does the author suggest the thoughts of the men after the burial? What help did Johnny Bartek find in his khaki-covered New Testament?

4. Describe the happening that gave the men water. Why did Lieutenant Whittaker refuse to believe the explanation of the meteorologist? What qualities did his prayer have?

EVALUATING HIS MANNER OF EXPRESSION

1. Why may Lieutenant Whittaker's narrative be called "the odyssey of a man's faith in God"?

2. This account was first published in the *Chicago Tribune*. What characteristics of the newspaper article are evident in the selection? What gives such great pathos to the account of Sergeant Kaczmarczyk's death?

---

[8] *meteorologist*, one who makes a study of the variations of heat, moisture, winds, and pressures of the atmosphere.

[9] *doldrums*, the depressing calms that mariners often experience in equatorial waters.

QUESTIONS FOR REVIEW

In your notebook copy the numbers from 1 to 10. After selecting the correct choice, write the complete statement.

1. The "new poetry" consisted primarily of (A) the return to ancient poetic forms (B) the use of new subjects (C) technical innovations.

2. Three leading crusaders for the "new poetry" were (A) T. S. Eliot, Hilda Doolittle, and Elinor Wylie (B) Edna St. Vincent Millay, Amy Lowell, and Edward Arlington Robinson (C) Amy Lowell, Ezra Pound, and Harriet Monroe.

3. The poetry of Robinson (A) treats only of world heroes and historical figures (B) often gives a dramatic presentation of men who are "splendid failures" (C) pictures the dead of a Midwestern village.

4. Amy Lowell's poetry is generally lacking in (A) clear, polished images (B) emotional values (C) intellectual qualities.

5. In his poems Robert Frost has (A) conformed carefully to the Imagist principles (B) captured the flavor of New England life (C) exalted industrial America.

6. The poet who has most perfectly adhered to Imagist principles is (A) Robert Frost (B) Amy Lowell (C) Hilda Doolittle.

7. Carl Sandburg has found much poetic material in (A) the loveliness and brute strength of the midwestern metropolis (B) rural New England life (C) the disillusionment of modern youth.

8. Sara Teasdale's reputation rests on her (A) long narrative poems (B) brief lyric poems (C) blank-verse dramas.

9. A poet who writes frequently about the spiritual barrenness of modern life is (A) Arthur Guiterman (B) Robert Frost (C) T. S. Eliot.

10. An author who is well-known for his realistic and humorous stories of adolescents is (A) Ernest Hemingway (B) Booth Tarkington (C) Sinclair Lewis.

Read each statement carefully. Then write in your notebook only those statements which are true.

1. Contemporary America is a land in which a single philosophy dominates.

2. The most ambitious individual movement in the "new poetry" was Imagism.

3. The poet Carl Sandburg is remembered for his tramping tours on which he recited his poetry and preached the gospel of beauty.

4. Some of Edna St. Vincent Millay's best poems express the transiency of beauty and human love, the sorrow and anguish of a disillusioned generation.

5. Edith Wharton has evolved a new type of pioneer novel.

6. In novels and short stories Booth Tarkington has interpreted the lives of average Americans.

7. Such national heroes as Paul Revere and Daniel Webster have been brought into fiction with dramatic force by Stephen Vincent Benét.

8. Although interest in American drama has steadily improved, the literary quality of American plays has declined in recent years.

9. In modern literature the columnist has supplanted the essayist.

10. It is impossible for the student to examine the editorial policy of newspapers in the light of Catholic and democratic principles.

Copy the following statements in your notebook and supply the word or words that make each statement complete.

1. Sympathetic representation of everyday human life in a pioneer setting is characteristic of a number of novels by _____.

2. A masterpiece of cynicism in a small-town setting is _____.

3. *John Brown's Body*, a long narrative poem, is one of the works of _____.

4. The _____ still remains, after newspaper and periodical literature, America's primary source of literary enjoyment.

5. An author who depicts the survival of Catholic ideals in troubled epochs of literary history is _____.

6. Most of the plays of _____ abound in clever dialogue, revealing the seamy side of fashionable life.

7. _____ by Thornton Wilder is an endeavor to portray the dignity of man and the nobility of life itself.

8. In the opinion of many critics the only American dramatist deserving international recognition is _____.

9. A prominent Catholic poet noted for perfection of technique and purity of style is _____.

10. The style of _____, Catholic poet, wit, and philosopher, is warm with tenderness and buoyant with whimsy and humor.

QUESTIONS FOR DISCUSSION

1. Why is it difficult to judge the literature of our own age? Explain briefly how contemporary America has been influenced by the growth of industry; by modern economic developments; by false philosophies advocating unlimited freedom in politics, economics, and ethics.

2. How does twentieth-century drama reflect the spirit of our own era?

3. What two contributions have been made by the Little Theater?

4. Contrast briefly the possibilities of the motion picture and the stage. How has the development of the motion picture been hampered?

5. What is the purpose of the Legion of Decency?

6. How does the purpose of the newspaper differ essentially from that of the essay? In what way does the columnist differ from the mere reporter?

7. What is meant by fictionalized biography?

8. What three risks are involved in the new biography which examines the heart, the mind, and the subconscious?

9. What requirements are necessary for the writer of hagiography?

10. What is the present status of Catholic poetry? State the purpose of the Catholic Poetry Society of America.

SUGGESTIONS FOR READING

Borden, Lucille, *Silver Trumpets Calling* (Macmillan, New York). The Bolshevik persecution in Russia forms the background for a thrilling and inspirational story of love and sacrifice.

Cather, Willa, *Death Comes for the Archbishop* (Houghton, Boston). The main interest in this story centers around two French missionaries in their endeavor to organize the dioceses of New Mexico and Colorado. *My Antonia* (Houghton, Boston). This romantic novel pictures immigrant life on the Nebraska plains.

Chase, Mary Ellen, *Mary Christmas* (Little, Brown, Boston). An American peddler whose life is dominated by love and spiritual idealism brings joy to the inhabitants of the Maine villages where she visits.

Connolly, Myles, *Mr. Blue* (Macmillan, New York). The story of a skyscraper saint who is totally detached from material goods.

Day, Clarence, *Life With Mother* and *Life With Father* (Knopf, New York). The inimitable wit of Clarence Day is seen in these stories describing the Victorian traditions of his family.

Farnum, Mabel, *Street of the Half Moon* (Bruce, Milwaukee). This biography gives insight into the heroic work of Saint Peter Claver, who spent his life rescuing galley slaves.

Feeney, Leonard, S.J., *An American Woman* (America Press, New York). Sanctity in America and in the midst of a busy life is possible, as Father Feeney convincingly shows in his life of Elizabeth Seton.

Feeney, Leonard, S.J., *Survival Till Seventeen* (Sheed and Ward, New York). The delightful escapades and spiritual adventures of Father Feeney are related in this autobiography.

Gillis, James M., C.S.P., *This, Our Day.* A collection of Father Gillis' most enduring editorials.

Kelley, Most Reverend Francis Clement, *Blood-Drenched Altars* (Bruce, Milwaukee). Although this book is concerned mainly with the persecutions in Mexico, certain chapters furnish background for a better understanding of the Spanish influence in North America.

Jordan, Elizabeth, *Three Rousing Cheers* (Appleton, New York). The autobiography of an outstanding American Catholic journalist.

Lavery, Emmet, *Theatre for Tomorrow* (Longmans, New York). The book contains three inspirational plays centering around Father Damien, Savonarola, and Father Campion.

MacNutt, Francis Augustus, *A Papal Chamberlain* (Longmans, New York). The author records his personal experiences as a reporter to the Vatican during the pontificates of Leo XIII and Pius X.

Maynard, Theodore, *The Odyssey of Francis Xavier* (Longmans, New York). The famous story of the adventures of the great Jesuit missionary who traveled from Europe to India, China, and Japan in his quest for souls.

McAllister, Anna Shannon, *In Winter We Flourish* (Longmans, New York). Mrs. Sarah Peter, virile and cultured, queenly in her social grace, far-visioned in her vast charitable enterprises, forms a link between pioneer days and modern culture.

Sandburg, Carl, *Abraham Lincoln: The Prairie Years* (Harcourt, New York). The poet-biographer "makes one feel the poetry at the heart" of pioneer life as he sketches the life of Abraham Lincoln. *Abraham Lincoln, the War Years*, pictures Lincoln as the Great Emancipator.

White, Olive B., *Late Harvest* (Macmillan, New York). A story of martyrdom during the days of Queen Elizabeth.

Wise, Evelyn, *The Long Tomorrow* (Appleton, New York). The prairies of Minnesota form a background for this charming story of love and sacrifice.

Index